Lecture Notes of the Institute for Computer Sciences, Social Informatics and Telecommunications Engineering 704

The LNICST series publishes ICST's conferences, symposia and workshops.

LNICST reports state-of-the-art results in areas related to the scope of the Institute.

The type of material published includes

- Proceedings (published in time for the respective event)
- Other edited monographs (such as project reports or invited volumes)

LNICST topics span the following areas:

- General Computer Science
- E-Economy
- E-Medicine
- Knowledge Management
- Multimedia
- Operations, Management and Policy
- Social Informatics
- Systems

Yinzhi Cao · Bo Luo · Weizhi Meng
Editors

Security and Privacy in Communication Networks

22nd EAI International Conference, SecureComm 2026
Lancaster, UK, July 21–24, 2026
Proceedings, Part I

Springer

Editors
Yinzhi Cao
Johns Hopkins University
Baltimore, MD, USA

Bo Luo
The University of Kansas
Lawrence, KS, USA

Weizhi Meng
Lancaster University
Lancaster, UK

ISSN 1867-8211 ISSN 1867-822X (electronic)
Lecture Notes of the Institute for Computer Sciences, Social Informatics and Telecommunications Engineering
ISBN 978-3-032-32763-5 ISBN 978-3-032-32764-2 (eBook)
https://doi.org/10.1007/978-3-032-32764-2

This Springer imprint is published by the registered company Springer Nature Switzerland AG
The registered company address is: Gewerbestrasse 11, 6330 Cham, Switzerland

Preface

We are delighted to introduce the proceedings of 22nd EAI International Conference on Security and Privacy in Communication Networks (SecureComm 2026). Hosted in Lancaster UK, the conference was held from July 21–24, 2026. This conference brought together researchers, developers, and practitioners around the world to discuss cyber security and privacy issues.

The technical program of SecureComm 2026 consisted of 45 research track papers, one demo, and five papers in the track of Work-in-Progress and Emerging Results. The research track received 143 submissions across two cycles, resulting in an acceptance rate of 31.4%. The reviewing process for each cycle comprised two rounds: each paper in the first round received two reviews, and papers with non-positive scores were early rejected. Papers that advanced to the second round received additional reviews. The two PC Chairs had extensive discussions based on all the reviews to decide the final program.

We would like to thank the general chairs, Weizhi Meng, Daniel Prince, and Xiaojiang Du, for organizing and hosting the conference. We sincerely appreciate their constant support and guidance. It was also a great pleasure to work with Veronika Kissova throughout the process. We are grateful for all her help with the Confy+ system and the website.

We strongly believe that the SecureComm conference provides a good forum for all researchers, developers and practitioners to discuss all security and privacy aspects that are relevant to computing and communication networks. We also expect that the future SecureComm conferences will continue to be as successful and stimulating, as indicated by the contributions presented in this volume.

Bo Luo
Yinzhi Cao
Weizhi Meng

Organization

Steering Committee

Peng Liu	Pennsylvania State University, USA
Sencun Zhu	Pennsylvania State University, USA
Xiapu Luo	Hong Kong Polytechnic University, China

Organizing Committee

General Chair

Weizhi Meng	Lancaster University, UK

General Co-chairs

Daniel Prince	Lancaster University, UK
Xiaojiang Du	Stevens Institute of Technology, USA

TPC Chairs and Co-chairs

Bo Luo	University of Kansas, USA
Yinzhi Cao	Johns Hopkins University, USA

Sponsorship and Exhibit Chairs

Chunhua Su	University of Aizu, Japan
Xiaozhen Lu	Nanjing University of Aeronautics and Astronautics, China

Local Chairs

Mark Bellwood	Lancaster University, UK
Grace Wang	Lancaster University, UK

Workshops Chair

Taeho Jung	University of Notre Dame, USA

Publicity and Social Media Chairs

Zhengxin Yu	Lancaster University, UK
Yang Lu	Lancaster University, UK
Kuan-Ching Li	Providence University, Taiwan

Publications Chair

Wenjuan Li	Education University of Hong Kong, China

Web Chair

Wei-Yang Chiu	National Yang Ming Chiao Tung University, Taiwan

Posters and PhD Track Chair

Yuan Lu	Institute of Software, Chinese Academy of Sciences, China

Panels Chair

Ashley Fraser	Lancaster University, UK

Demos Chair

Wenjuan Yu	Lancaster University, UK

Tutorials Chairs

Ling-Huey Li	University of Salerno, Italy
Guhan Zheng	Shanghai University, China

Technical Program Committee

Ali Padyab	University of Skövde, Sweden
Anna Grocholewska-Czurylo	Poznań University of Technology, Poland
Antreas Dionysiou	Delft University of Technology, Netherlands
Arcangelo Castiglione	University of Salerno, Italy
Bo Chen	Michigan Technological University, USA
Carlton Shepherd	Durham University, UK
Christos Chrysoulas	Heriot-Watt University, UK
Cong Zuo	Beijing Institute of Technology, China
Ding Wang	Nankai University, China
Dongseong Kim	University of Queensland, Australia
Ehab Al-Shaer	Carnegie Mellon University, USA
Elias Bou-Harb	Louisiana State University, USA
Erik Rye	Johns Hopkins University, USA
Bo Luo	University of Kansas, USA
Fei Zuo	University of Central Oklahoma, USA
Furkan Alaca	Queen's University, Canada
Guillaume Hiet	CentraleSupélec, France
Haibing Lu	Santa Clara University, USA
Haibo Wang	University of Kentucky, USA
Hailun Yan	University of Chinese Academy of Sciences, China
Hongsheng Hu	University of Newcastle, Australia
Hongxin Hu	University at Buffalo, USA
Irdin Pekaric	University of Liechtenstein, Liechtenstein
Jacques Traore	Orange Innovation, France
Javaria Ahmad	University of Central Missouri, USA
Jiaojiao Jiang	University of New South Wales, Australia
Jinjin Liang	Qi An Xin Group, China
Jinpeng Wei	University of North Carolina at Charlotte, USA
Jun Dai	Worcester Polytechnic Institute, USA
Jun Shao	Zhejiang Gongshang University, China
Kehuan Zhang	Chinese University of Hong Kong, China
Lei Xue	Sun Yat-sen University, China
Leo Zhang	Griffith University, Australia
Liang Zhao	Sichuan University, China
Lu Zhou	Nanjing University of Aeronautics and Astronautics, China
Marko Hölbl	University of Maribor, Slovenia
Meng Yu	Governors State University, USA
Michalis Pavlidis	University of Brighton, UK

Mujeeb Ahmed	Newcastle University, UK
Nan Wang	CSIRO's Data61, Australia
Nicola Zannone	Eindhoven University of Technology, Netherlands
Nikolaos Pitropakis	American College of Greece, Greece
Ning Zhang	Washington University in St. Louis, USA
Ningyu He	Peking University, China
Nishant Vishwamitra	University of Texas at San Antonio, USA
Ntantogian Christoforos	Ionian University, Greece
Omar Abed Alkarim Darwish	Eastern Michigan University, USA
Paria Shirani	University of Ottawa, Canada
Qingchuan Zhao	City University of Hong Kong, China
Qinhong Jiang	Hong Kong Polytechnic University, China
Rodrigo Roman	University of Málaga, Spain
Rupeng Yang	University of Wollongong, Australia
Savio Sciancalepore	Eindhoven University of Technology, Netherlands
Sergio Esposito	University of Catania, Spain
Shashidhar Reddy Polepalli	Fortinet, USA
Shuai Hao	Old Dominion University, USA
Shujie Cui	Monash University, Australia
Srinivasa Ravi Teja Peri	Microsoft Corporation, USA
Stefano Cirillo	University of Salerno, Italy
Thangavel Murugan	United Arab Emirates University, UAE
Tsz Hon Yuen	Monash University, Australia
Wang Huanting	University of Leeds, UK
Wanlun Ma	Swinburne University of Technology, Australia
Wanpeng Li	University of Aberdeen, UK
Wei Tang	Xi'an Jiaotong University, China
Wojciech Mazurczyk	Warsaw University of Technology, Poland
Wufei Wu	Nanchang University, China
Wun-She Yap	Universiti Tunku Abdul Rahman, Malaysia
Wenjuan Li	Education University of Hong Kong, China
Xiang Li	Nankai University, China
Xiaogang Zhu	Adelaide University, Australia
Xiaokuan Zhang	George Mason University, USA
Xiaoyan Sun	Worcester Polytechnic Institute, USA
Xiapu Luo	Hong Kong Polytechnic University, China
Yang Yu	Tsinghua University, China
Yangguang Tian	University of Surrey, UK
Ye Guixing	Northwest University, China
Yingjiu Li	University of Oregon, USA
Yinzhi Cao	John Hopkins University, USA
Youngjoo Shin	Korea University, South Korea

Yuan Lu	A*STAR, Singapore
Yuguo Liu	Chinese Academy of Sciences, China
Yuchen Yang	Penn State University, USA
Zhanyong Tang	Northwest University, China
Zhen Ling	Southeast University, China
Zhenkai Liang	National University of Singapore, Singapore
Zhiyuan Tan	Edinburgh Napier University, Scotland
Zongyang Zhang	Beihang University, China
Zuobin Ying	City University of Macau, China

Contents

Authentication, Biometrics and Human Factors

SAFE: Secret Algebraic Fusion of Embeddings for Private Multi-modal Biometric Authentication

Yatish Dubasi and Qinghua Li(✉)

University of Arkansas, Fayetteville, AR 72701, USA
{yrdubasi,qinghual}@uark.edu

Abstract. Multi-modal biometric systems provide stricter access control but introduce significant privacy risks, as storing multiple biometric templates on a server increases the attack surface. These templates are vulnerable to inversion attacks that can reconstruct a user's irreplaceable biometric data. To address this challenge, we introduce SAFE: Secret Algebraic Fusion of Embeddings, a novel framework for privacy-preserving multi-modal authentication. SAFE generates a non-invertible and cancellable template by fusing feature vectors from multiple modalities using a user-specific Fusion Secret composed of algebraic operations. This process creates a single, unified SAFE embedding that protects the underlying biometric information. We conduct a comprehensive evaluation of SAFE, comparing its performance against common fusion techniques and single-modality systems. Our results demonstrate that SAFE achieves high authentication accuracy, with an F1 score of up to 97.06%, while providing robust privacy. Importantly, the server-side authentication matching is highly efficient, requiring just 1.33 µs, making the framework suitable for scalable, low-latency applications. SAFE provides a practical pathway for deploying high-security multi-modal biometric systems that protect user privacy.

Keywords: multi-modal biometrics · cancellable biometrics · authentication · privacy

1 Introduction

Biometric authentication, the use of unique physiological or behavioral traits for identity verification, has become a cornerstone of modern security systems. While single-modality systems are widely used, they can be susceptible to challenges such as noisy data, non-universality of traits, and spoofing attacks. To overcome these limitations, the field has increasingly shifted towards multi-modal biometric systems, which combine information from multiple sources to enhance security, accuracy, and robustness [1,2]. These systems leverage fusion techniques at various levels—such as feature, score, or decision—to build a more comprehensive and reliable biometric profile [3,4].

Y. Cao et al. (Eds.): SecureComm 2026, LNICST 704, pp. 3–22, 2027.
https://doi.org/10.1007/978-3-032-32764-2_1

However, the deployment of multi-modal systems in server-based architectures introduces a significant privacy challenge [5]. The server must store biometric reference data, known as *templates*, to perform authentication. This centralized storage creates a high-value target for adversaries. A data breach could lead to an irreversible compromise of a user's most private information, their biometric identity. Unlike a password, a fingerprint or an iris pattern cannot be revoked or reissued. This threat is exacerbated by the proven risk of template inversion attacks, where adversaries can reconstruct a realistic image of a user's biometric trait from the stored template [6], completely nullifying user privacy. While many multi-modal schemes focus on improving accuracy [7,8], the critical need for robust, privacy-preserving template protection is often inadequately addressed.

To address these pressing privacy challenges, this paper introduces Secret Algebraic Fusion of Embeddings (SAFE), a novel fusion method that provides strong template protection for multi-modal biometric authentication. Figure 1 illustrates the proposed SAFE method, which generates a single, non-invertible, and cancellable embedding by fusing feature vectors from multiple biometric modalities according to a user-specific Fusion Secret. This secret, composed of a unique sequence of algebraic operations and feature indices, acts as a key that transforms the raw templates into a secure, unified representation. If compromised, the entire SAFE embedding can be revoked, and a new one can be generated with a new Fusion Secret.

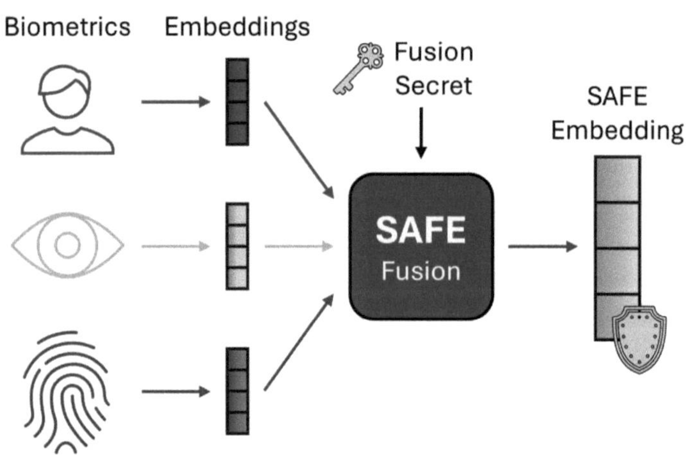

Fig. 1. SAFE Framework.

The key contributions of this work are as follows:

1. We propose SAFE, a novel feature-level fusion transform that uses a user-specific secret to generate a single, secure, and cancellable biometric embedding from multiple modalities.

2. We provide a thorough security analysis, including a formal proof demonstrating the non-invertibility of the SAFE transform.
3. We design a general, end-to-end multi-modal authentication protocol built around the SAFE transform, detailing the enrollment and authentication processes.
4. We conduct a comprehensive performance evaluation of SAFE using face, iris, and fingerprint modalities, comparing its accuracy and computational efficiency against baseline single-modality and traditional multi-modal fusion approaches.
5. We make our code and compiled dataset publicly available to ensure reproducibility and encourage further research in the community [9].

The remainder of this paper is organized as follows. We review related work and research gaps in Sect. 2. Section 3 outlines our system and threat model. We detail the proposed SAFE transform with its security analysis in Sect. 4 and the full authentication protocol in Sect. 5. Finally, we present our experimental evaluation in Sect. 6 and conclude in Sect. 7.

2 The State of the Art and Our Novelty

In this section, we review the two primary domains that inform our work: multi-modal fusion strategies and biometric template protection schemes. We also identify the research gap that SAFE aims to bridge.

2.1 Multi-modal Fusion Strategies

The fusion of information in multi-modal biometric systems can occur at various stages, a topic extensively covered in surveys by Garg et al. [3] and others [1,2]. The primary levels of fusion are decision-level, score-level, and feature-level.

Decision-level fusion combines the final authentication decisions from individual biometric systems, often using boolean operators like AND/OR. While simple to implement, it utilizes the least amount of information and is generally less effective.

Score-level fusion, the most common approach, combines the matching scores generated by different biometric matchers [10]. This method offers a good balance between ease of implementation and performance, as scores are relatively easy to normalize and fuse.

Feature-level fusion operates by concatenating or combining the raw feature vectors extracted from different modalities before the matching stage [4,11,12]. This level is considered to have the highest potential for improving accuracy, as the fused feature vector can contain richer and more discriminative information than the individual templates. However, it is also the most challenging due to the potential incompatibility of feature sets and the high dimensionality of the resulting vector. Our proposed SAFE method operates at the feature level, uniquely integrating a privacy-preserving transform directly into the fusion process itself.

2.2 Biometric Template Protection Schemes

The need to protect biometric templates stored on servers has led to the development of various template protection schemes, which can be broadly categorized into two main groups: cryptographic approaches and cancellable biometrics [13].

Cryptographic approaches leverage cryptographic primitives to secure biometric templates. Homomorphic encryption (HE) is a promising technique that allows computations to be performed directly on encrypted data without decryption. This enables biometric matching in the encrypted domain, theoretically eliminating the need to expose the raw template on the server [14]. While HE offers strong privacy guarantees, its practical deployment in biometric systems is often hindered by high computational overhead and latency, making it unsuitable for real-time authentication in many scenarios.

Cancellable biometrics, the category under which SAFE falls, focuses on applying an intentional, repeatable, and non-invertible transformation to the biometric template [15]. The goal is to create a secure template that meets two primary criteria: non-invertibility, meaning the original template cannot be recovered from the transformed one, and revocability, meaning a new template can be reissued if the current one is compromised. Common approaches include salting, non-invertible transforms based on random projections, and other user-specific transformations [16]. SAFE introduces a new type of cancellable transform that is intrinsically tied to the multi-modal fusion process itself.

2.3 Gap Analysis and Our Novelty

The existing literature reveals a significant gap between the domains of multi-modal fusion and template protection. On one hand, a large body of research on multi-modal biometrics focuses on enhancing authentication accuracy through novel fusion algorithms, but often treats templates as plaintext and overlooks robust privacy protection [7,8]. On the other hand, most template protection schemes, including cancellable biometrics, have been predominantly designed and evaluated for single-modality systems [17].

Few systems have attempted to deeply integrate these two domains. The common approach is to apply a known privacy transform to each modality's template individually before fusion, or to a concatenated feature vector after fusion (i.e., the fusion method is simply concatenation of features). This separation fails to leverage the fusion process itself as a mechanism for privacy enhancement.

The SAFE framework is designed to fill this critical gap. It does not simply apply a privacy layer on top of a fusion method; instead, it defines a novel approach where the fusion and the privacy-preserving transformation are a single, inseparable algebraic step. By using a user-specific secret to dictate how features from different modalities are algebraically combined, SAFE creates a unified and secure embedding that is both highly discriminative and inherently non-invertible. Furthermore, SAFE offers the practical benefit of revocability, allowing for the generation of a new SAFE embedding if the previous one is compromised. This unique combination of enhanced security, privacy, and cancellability distinguishes SAFE from prior work in multi-modal biometric authentication.

3 System Overview

This section details the architectural components of the SAFE framework, the specific biometric modalities utilized, and a formal definition of the threat model assumed in our privacy analysis.

3.1 System Architecture

The SAFE framework operates on a client-server architecture, designed to facilitate secure and privacy-preserving multi-modal biometric authentication. This architecture comprises two primary entities: the client and the server, interacting during both enrollment and authentication phases.

Client components are responsible for biometric data acquisition, feature extraction, and the generation of the privacy-preserving SAFE embedding. It consists of:

- User Identity Module (e.g., ID Card or Secure Element): This component securely stores the user's identity and their unique Fusion Secret (S). The S is a crucial element for generating the cancellable SAFE embedding. This module facilitates the transfer of the user's identity and S to the biometric capture devices for on-device processing.
- Biometric Capture Devices: These devices are equipped with sensors capable of capturing raw biometric data for various modalities (e.g., cameras for face and iris, fingerprint scanners).
- Local Processing Unit: Integrated within or connected to the biometric capture device, this unit performs the tasks of extracting biometric feature embeddings from the raw captured data and then applying the SAFE transform using the user's S to generate the final SAFE embedding.

During an access request, the client's Local Processing Unit generates a fresh SAFE embedding. This embedding, along with the user's identity, is then transmitted to the server.

Server acts as the central authority for storing enrolled SAFE embeddings and performing authentication matching. It comprises:

- Central Database: This database securely stores the registered SAFE embeddings for enrolled users.
- Authentication Engine: The authentication engine receives access requests from clients. Upon receiving a user's identity and their freshly generated SAFE embedding, it retrieves the corresponding stored SAFE embedding from the database. It then computes a similarity or distance metric between the two SAFE embeddings and compares this value against a predefined threshold. Based on this comparison, the server makes an authentication decision (grant or deny).

The server's role is strictly limited to comparison of the SAFE embeddings, ensuring it never has access to the original, sensitive biometric data.

3.2 Biometric Modalities

Our framework utilizes a multi-modal approach, integrating embeddings from three distinct biometric modalities. The selection of these modalities—face, iris, and fingerprint—is based on their widespread adoption, distinct physiological characteristics, and complementary strengths.

Face recognition is a widely adopted biometric modality due to its non-intrusive nature and ease of capture. In our system, face embeddings are extracted using a pre-trained deep learning model, specifically VGG-Face [18], chosen for its robustness in generating discriminative representations. The Deep-Face Python module [19,20] is employed for this purpose, and the extracted embeddings are normalized to a $[0, 1]$ range.

Iris recognition is known for its high accuracy and uniqueness, making it a highly reliable biometric. The IRIS module [21] is utilized to extract iris codes from grayscale eye images. These binary iris codes are then converted into a numerical representation, mapping the boolean values to normalized floating-point numbers within $[0, 1]$.

Fingerprints are another highly unique and stable biometric trait. For fingerprint feature extraction, we leverage the flx module [22], which combines texture and minutiae embeddings for a comprehensive fixed-length representation. The raw fingerprint images undergo enhancement using the fingerprint_enhancer module [23] and binarization before being fed into the extraction model. The resulting texture and minutiae embeddings are concatenated and normalized to a $[0, 1]$ range.

3.3 Threat Model

We assume an "honest-but-curious" threat model, specifically targeting the server-side operations. This is a common and practical assumption in privacy-preserving biometric systems.

An honest-but-curious server-side attacker is assumed to have the following capabilities and goals:

- Honest: The server faithfully executes the specified protocol and does not deviate from its prescribed operations. It performs the authentication matching correctly as per the protocol.
- Curious: Despite being honest in execution, the server is curious and attempts to learn sensitive information. Its primary capability is having full access to the stored SAFE embeddings in the central database. The attacker also has access to the authentication logic and any publicly available information about the system design.

- Attacker's Goal: The attacker's ultimate goal is to reconstruct or infer the original biometric data (face, iris, or fingerprint) from the SAFE embeddings. This reconstruction would directly compromise user privacy. The attacker may also attempt to determine the individual feature vectors of each modality or the user's Fusion Secret, as these could potentially aid in the reconstruction of raw biometrics.

By focusing on the honest-but-curious server, we aim to demonstrate that SAFE effectively protects user privacy by preventing the reconstruction of sensitive biometric data.

The client, which directly processes the user's fusion secret and raw biometric data, is assumed to be trusted. Hence, attacks involving the compromise of the client device to extract such information are outside the scope of this paper.

4 Secret Algebraic Fusion of Embeddings (SAFE)

This section details the core methodology of our proposed framework. We begin by defining the notations used throughout our formulation. We then describe the two central components of SAFE: the generation of a user-specific Fusion Secret and the SAFE transform function that uses this secret to create a secure embedding. Finally, we provide a thorough security analysis of the SAFE transform, proving its properties of revocability, non-invertibility, and privacy.

The key notations used in the formulation of SAFE are summarized in Table 1.

Table 1. Main Notations

M	Set of biometric modalities, e.g. {face, iris, fingerprint}
V_m	Feature vector for modality m, where $m \in M$
L_m	Length/dimensionality of the feature vector V_m $L_{face} = 4096, L_{iris} = 8192, L_{fingerprint} = 512$
L_{SAFE}	Length of the final SAFE embedding $L_{SAFE} = \max(L_m) = L_{iris} = 8192$
$\mathcal{O}$	Set of allowed algebraic operations, e.g. $\{+, -, \times\}$
S	User-specific Fusion Secret
S_k	k-th instruction within the Fusion Secret S
E_{SAFE}	SAFE embedding
τ	Authentication threshold

4.1 Fusion Secret Generation

A user's unique Fusion Secret, S, is a structured instruction set that dictates the entire fusion process. It is generated once per user (or per re-enrollment) and stored securely in the User Identity Module. The generation process is detailed in Algorithm 1.

For each of the L_{SAFE} elements, the algorithm constructs an instruction S_k by randomly selecting:

1. A permutation of the three biometric modalities, M
2. A feature index from each of the three modality vectors $(V_{face}, V_{iris}, V_{fingerprint})$
3. Two algebraic operations from the set $\mathcal{O}$ (repetitions allowed)

Since the input vectors have different lengths, the algorithm employs a structured sampling method to ensure that indices from the shorter vectors (V_{face} and $V_{fingerprint}$) are reused to fill the L_{SAFE}-length secret. This ensures that all features from all modalities have the potential to contribute to the final embedding, while maintaining the unpredictability of the Fusion Secret.

4.2 SAFE Fusion

The SAFE transform applies the instructions defined in the Fusion Secret S to a user's biometric feature vectors to compute the final SAFE embedding, E_{SAFE}. This transformation is executed entirely on the client-side, ensuring that the raw biometric data never leaves the Local Processing Unit.

Formally, for each element k (where $k \in [0, L_{SAFE} - 1]$), the corresponding value in the SAFE embedding, $E_{SAFE}[k]$, is computed as follows:

$$E_{SAFE}[k] = (V_{m_1}[i_1] \ op_1 \ V_{m_2}[i_2]) \ op_2 \ V_{m_3}[i_3]$$

where the modality permutation (m_1, m_2, m_3), the feature indices (i_1, i_2, i_3), and the operations (op_1, op_2) are all specified by the instruction $S_k \in S$. The complete process is formalized in Algorithm 2.

4.3 Security Analysis

The security of the SAFE framework hinges on the properties of its fusion transform. Our analysis, guided by the threat model in Sect. 3, demonstrates that the SAFE transform is revocable and non-invertible, providing robust privacy protection.

Revocability and Cancellability. A critical feature of SAFE is its ability to be revoked and reissued, a core principle of cancellable biometrics. If a user's SAFE embedding (E_{SAFE}) is ever compromised (e.g., through a server data breach), the user's raw biometric data remains secure. The user can simply re-enroll with a new Fusion Secret, S'. Applying the SAFE transform with S' to the user's biometric vectors will produce a completely new and independent SAFE embedding, E'_{SAFE}. The compromised embedding is rendered useless for future authentication, effectively addressing the challenge of using irreplaceable raw biometric data in multi-modal authentication systems.

Algorithm 1. Fusion Secret Generation

```
function FUSION_SECRET_GENERATION
    L = [L_face, L_iris, L_fingerprint]
    m_count = len(L)
    reps_allowed = [⌈L_SAFE/x⌉ for x in L]
    available_idxs = [range(x) for x in L]
    idx_usage_counts = [[0] * x for x in L]

    S = []
    for k in L_SAFE do
        chosen_m_order = random.sample(
    *3range(m_count), m_count)
        chosen_ops = random.choices(O, m_count − 1)
        chosen_idxs = []
        for m_i, idx_list in enumerate(available_idxs) do
            c_idx = random.choice(idx_list)
            chosen_idxs.append(c_idx)
            usage = idx_usage_counts[m_i][c_idx] + 1
            idx_usage_counts[m_i][c_idx] = usage
            if usage ≥ reps_allowed[m_i] then
                available_idxs.remove(c_idx)
            end if
        end for
        m_idx_pairs = []
        for m in chosen_m_order do
            m_idx_pairs.append([m, chosen_idxs[m]])
        end for
        S_k = [m_idx_pairs, chosen_ops]
        S.append(S_k)
    end for
    return S
end function
```

Privacy and Non-invertibility. The non-invertibility of the SAFE transform is established through the following propositions, which demonstrate the infeasibility of reconstructing the original biometric vectors $(V_{face}, V_{iris}, V_{fingerprint})$ from a given SAFE embedding (E_{SAFE}). The analysis assumes the attacker knows the SAFE algorithm but not the user's Fusion Secret (S), per the threat model defined in Sect. 3.

Proposition 1. *Recovering the Fusion Secret S is infeasible.*

Proof. The Fusion Secret S is composed of $L_{SAFE} = 8192$ independent instructions, $[S_0, S_1, \cdots, S_{8191}]$. For any given instruction S_k, an adversary must correctly guess:

- The permutation of three modalities, which has $3! = 6$ possibilities.
- The indices of biometric vectors, which has $4096 \times 8192 \times 512 \approx 1.7 \times 10^{10}$ possibilities.

Algorithm 2. SAFE Fusion

```
function SAFE_FUSION(S, V)
    ▷ V ← [V_face, V_iris, V_fingerprint]
    E_SAFE = []
    for m_idx_pairs, ops in S do
        fused_str = ""
        for i, (m, idx) in enumerate(m_idx_pairs) do
            if i == 0 then
                fused_str += "({})".format(V[m][idx])
            else
                fused_str += "{}({})".format(
*5ops[i − 1], V[m][idx])
            end if
            fused_str = "({})".format(eval(fused_str))
        end for
        E_SAFE.append(eval(fused_str))
    end for
    return E_SAFE
end function
```

- The two algebraic operations from the set $\mathcal{O}$, which has $|\mathcal{O}|^2 = 3^2 = 9$ possibilities.

The total number of possible structures for a single instruction S_k is therefore $6 \times 1.7 \times 10^{10} \times 9 \approx 10^{12}$. An adversary would need to guess this structure correctly for all 8192 instructions, leading to a search space of ${10^{12}}^{8192} = 10^{98304} \approx 2^{326558}$ possibilities. Additionally, the attacker has no means to verify the correctness of a hypothesized Fusion Secret, as they do not possess a raw biometrics and SAFE embedding pair. The attacker only has access to the SAFE embedding E_{SAFE}. Therefore, this renders any attempt to determine the Fusion Secret S practically impossible.

Proposition 2. *The problem of uniquely determining the complete set of original feature values $\{V_{face}, V_{iris}, V_{fingerprint}\}$ from the SAFE embedding E_{SAFE} is mathematically ill-posed.*

Proof. An attacker's attempt to reverse the SAFE transform can be modeled as solving a system of equations. The attacker has access to $L_{SAFE} = 8192$ known values, which constitute 8192 individual equations of the form $E_{SAFE}[k] = f_k(v_1, v_2, v_3)$.

The total number of unknown variables the attacker seeks to find is the sum of the lengths of the biometric feature vectors:

$$\begin{aligned} N_{unknowns} &= L_{face} + L_{iris} + L_{fingerprint} \\ &= 4096 + 8192 + 512 \\ &= 12800 \end{aligned}$$

Since the number of unknowns (12800) is greater than the number of independent equations (8192), the system is mathematically underdetermined. An underdetermined system of equations does not have a unique solution. Therefore, an infinite number of distinct input vector combinations $\{V_{face}, V_{iris}, V_{fingerprint}\}$ could produce the exact same SAFE embedding E_{SAFE}, making it impossible to identify the true, original set. Furthermore, the problem is harder than just solving an underdetermined system. The structure of each equation (which variables are used and how they are combined) is itself part of the Fusion Secret.

Proposition 3. *For any given element $E_{SAFE}[k]$, a unique triplet of feature values (v_1, v_2, v_3) cannot be recovered, even if the corresponding instruction S_k (i.e., modality order, feature indices, and operations) was known.*

Proof. Assuming an attacker learns the exact instruction S_k for a single element $E_{SAFE}[k]$, the problem reduces to solving one equation with three unknown variables: $E_{SAFE}[k] = f_k(v_1, v_2, v_3)$, where the solution space is constrained to the unit cube, $(v_1, v_2, v_3) \in [0, 1]^3$. We prove the non-uniqueness/ambiguity of the solution by construction.

Let us assume a valid solution $\mathrm{v}_0 = (v_{1_0}, v_{2_0}, v_{3_0})$ exists where each value is in the interior of the range $(0, 1)$. We can construct a new, distinct solution v' by introducing a small, non-zero perturbation δ to one variable and compensating with another.

Case A: Linear Operations (e.g., Addition/Subtraction)
Consider a function of the form $f(\mathrm{v}) = (v_1 + v_2) - v_3$. We define a new value $v_1' = v_{1_0} + \delta$. To maintain the equality, we can introduce an opposing perturbation to v_2, such that $v_2' = v_{2_0} - \delta$, while keeping $v_3' = v_{3_0}$. The new solution vector $\mathrm{v}' = (v_{1_0} + \delta, v_{2_0} - \delta, v_{3_0})$ satisfies the original equation:

$$\begin{aligned} f(\mathrm{v}') &= ((v_{1_0} + \delta) + (v_{2_0} - \delta)) - v_{3_0} \\ &= (v_{1_0} + v_{2_0}) - v_{3_0} \\ &= f(\mathrm{v}_0) \\ &= E_{SAFE}[k] \end{aligned}$$

Since v_0 is in the interior of the unit cube, a sufficiently small δ can always be chosen such that v' is also a valid and distinct solution within the cube.

Case B: Non-Linear Operations (e.g., Multiplication)
Consider a function of the form $f(\mathrm{v}) = (v_1 \times v_2) + v_3$. Again, we perturb v_1 to get $v_1' = v_{1_0} + \delta$ and keep $v_3' = v_{3_0}$. To maintain the equality, the product $v_1' \times v_2'$ must equal the original product, $v_{1_0} \times v_{2_0}$. The new value for v_2 can be computed as follows:

$$\begin{aligned} v_1' \times v_2' &= v_{1_0} \times v_{2_0} \\ (v_{1_0} + \delta) \times v_2' &= v_{1_0} \times v_{2_0} \\ v_2' &= \frac{v_{1_0} \times v_{2_0}}{v_{1_0} + \delta} \end{aligned}$$

For a sufficiently small δ, this new solution $v' = (v_{1_0} + \delta, \frac{v_{1_0} \times v_{2_0}}{v_{1_0} + \delta}, v_{3_0})$ is distinct and remains within the valid solution space.

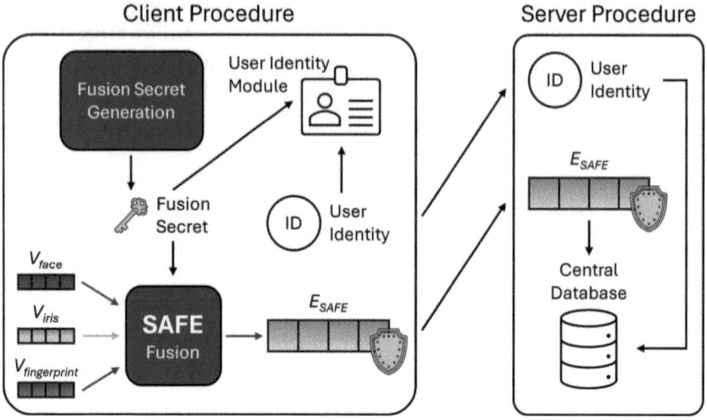

Fig. 2. SAFE Enrollment.

These constructive cases demonstrate that for any given solution, it is possible to find another distinct solution in its immediate vicinity. Geometrically, a single equation with three variables defines a 2D surface in a 3D space. The set of all valid solutions is the subsection of this surface within the unit cube. This subsection is a continuous curve or surface patch, which contains an infinite number of points. Therefore, an attacker cannot resolve this inherent mathematical ambiguity to isolate the single, true set of feature values.

Collectively, these propositions establish that the SAFE transform is non-invertible by demonstrating mathematical infeasibility at the Fusion Secret level (Proposition 1), the system level (Proposition 2), and the individual element level (Proposition 3), thus ensuring the privacy of the user's raw biometric data.

5 SAFE Authentication Protocol

The SAFE transform, detailed in Sect. 4, serves as the core primitive within a complete multi-modal authentication framework. This section describes the two fundamental protocols that govern the system's operation: the *Enrollment Protocol* for user registration and the *Authentication Protocol* for identity verification.

5.1 Enrollment Protocol

The Enrollment Protocol is performed by a new user to register their biometric identity with the access control system. The primary goal is to generate a secure, privacy-preserving SAFE embedding and store it on the server without ever exposing the user's raw biometric data or their Fusion Secret. The process, illustrated in Fig. 2, involves the following steps:

1. Fusion Secret Generation: The client-side Local Processing Unit generates a unique Fusion Secret (S) using the procedure detailed in Algorithm 1. This secret is immediately stored in the User Identity Module (e.g., ID Card or Secure Element).
2. Biometric Capture: The user presents their face, iris, and fingerprint to the respective sensors on the Biometric Capture Devices.
3. Feature Extraction: The Local Processing Unit extracts the feature vectors $V_{face}, V_{iris}, V_{fingerprint}$ from the captured raw data.
4. SAFE Fusion: The Local Processing Unit applies the SAFE transform, Algorithm 2, using the newly generated secret S and the extracted feature vectors to compute the user's enrollment SAFE embedding, E_{SAFE}.
5. Registration: The client transmits the user's identity (ID) and the enrollment embedding E_{SAFE} to the server. Crucially, the Fusion Secret S and the raw feature vectors never leave the client's secure environment.
6. Server-Side Storage: The server receives the (ID, E_{SAFE}) pair and stores it in its Central Database, linking the embedding to the user's identity.

At the conclusion of this protocol, the user is successfully enrolled in the access control system. The complete enrollment process is formalized in Algorithm 3.

5.2 Authentication Protocol

The Authentication Protocol is executed each time an enrolled user seeks to verify their identity to gain access. This protocol leverages the user's stored Fusion Secret to generate a fresh SAFE embedding for comparison against the enrollment embedding. The steps, shown in Fig. 3, are as follows:

1. Initiation: The user initiates an authentication attempt by presenting their User Identity Module to the client's Local Processing Unit.
2. Secret Retrieval: The Local Processing Unit securely retrieves the user's identity (ID) and Fusion Secret S from the module.

Algorithm 3. SAFE Enrollment

▷ Client procedure
$u \leftarrow$ user identity (ID)
$S =$ fusion_secret_generation()
User Identity Module stores u, S
$V \leftarrow [V_{face}, V_{iris}, V_{fingerprint}]$
$E_{SAFE} =$ SAFE_fusion(S, V)
Client transmits u, E_{SAFE} to server

▷ Server procedure
Server stores u, E_{SAFE} in Central Database

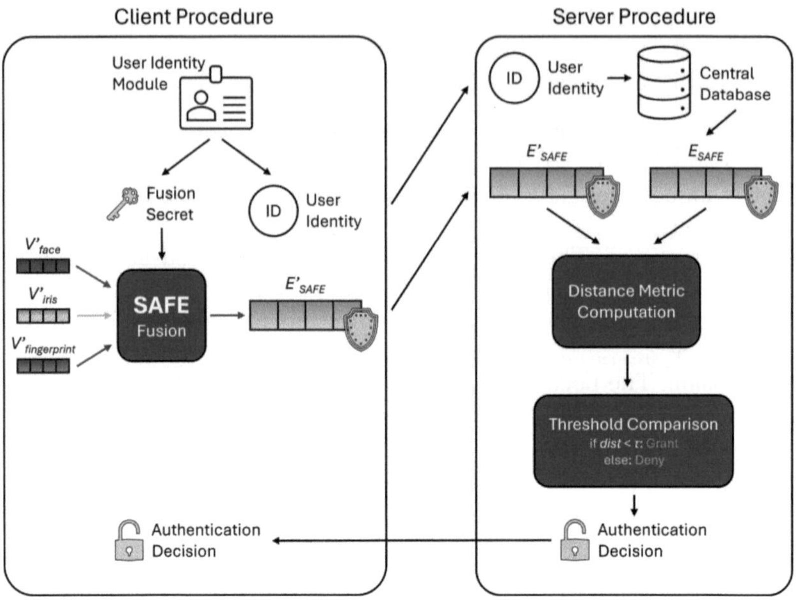

Fig. 3. SAFE Authentication.

3. Biometric Capture: The user presents their face, iris, and fingerprint to the respective sensors on the Biometric Capture Devices.
4. Feature Extraction: The Local Processing Unit extracts a fresh set of feature vectors $V'_{face}, V'_{iris}, V'_{fingerprint}$.
5. SAFE Fusion: The client applies the SAFE transform using the retrieved secret S and the fresh feature vectors (V') to compute an authentication SAFE embedding, E'_{SAFE}.
6. Transmission: The client sends the user's ID and the authentication embedding E'_{SAFE} to the server.
7. Matching and Decision: Upon receiving the request, the server's Authentication Engine performs the final matching steps:
   (a) It uses the user's ID to retrieve the stored enrollment embedding, E_{SAFE}, from its Central Database.
   (b) It computes a distance metric, *dist*, between the stored embedding E_{SAFE} and the received embedding E'_{SAFE}.
   (c) This distance is compared against a predefined authentication threshold, τ. If $dist < \tau$, the authentication is successful and access is granted. Otherwise, the authentication fails.

The server's role is confined to this final comparison, ensuring it only ever processes the privacy-preserving SAFE embeddings. The complete authentication process is formalized in Algorithm 4.

Algorithm 4. SAFE Authentication

▷ Client procedure
u, S retrieved from User Identity Module
$V' \leftarrow [V'_{face}, V'_{iris}, V'_{fingerprint}]$
$E'_{SAFE} = \text{SAFE\_fusion}(S, V')$
Client transmits u, E'_{SAFE} to server

▷ Server procedure
E_{SAFE} retrieved from Central Database using u
$dist = \text{dist\_metric}(E_{SAFE}, E'_{SAFE})$
if $dist < \tau$ **then**
    Grant access
else
    Deny access
end if

6 Evaluation

This section details the experimental evaluation of the SAFE framework. We describe the datasets and implementation of our method and baseline schemes, followed by a detailed analysis of the computational cost and biometric performance. The full source code, compiled multi-modal dataset, and all experimental scripts are publicly available to ensure reproducibility [9].

All experiments were conducted on a desktop computer equipped with an AMD Ryzen™ 5 3600 6-Core Processor (3.6 GHz) and 16 GB of RAM, running Windows 11 Pro (version 24H2).

6.1 Dataset and Implementation

To construct our multi-modal dataset, we aggregated data from several public sources. Face images were sourced from the Labeled Faces in the Wild (LFW) dataset [24,25], iris scans from the MULB dataset [26], and fingerprints from a combination of the Neurotechnology U.are.U dataset [27] and two Fingerprint Verification System (FVS) datasets [28]. From these sources, we compiled a multi-modal dataset of 102 users. Each user is represented by a unique face, iris, and fingerprint, with two images per modality: one for enrollment and one for authentication testing.

We implemented the proposed SAFE Authentication Protocol and several baseline methods for comparison, as denoted in Table 2. For multi-modal baselines, we included a Concatenation method, which fuses feature vectors by appending them, and a Summation method, which performs feature-wise addition with zero-padding for vectors of unequal length. We also evaluated the performance of each single-modality system (Face, Iris, Fingerprint) independently. Among these baselines, Summation has some privacy protection, since it mix multi-modal features via the addition operation, but the other four schemes do not have privacy protection.

Table 2. Method Denotations for Evaluation

SAFE	SAFE Multi-Modal Authentication Protocol
Concatenation	Concatenation-based Multi-Modal Authentication
Summation	Summation-based Multi-Modal Authentication
Face	Face-based Authentication
Iris	Iris-based Authentication
Fingerprint	Fingerprint-based Authentication

Table 3. Accuracies with Cosine Distance Metric in Comparison with Five Baselines

Methods	Threshold τ	Accuracies (%)		
		Precision	Recall	F1 Score
SAFE	0.225	96.94	93.14	95.00
Concatenation	0.340	95.79	89.22	92.39
Summation	0.310	92.93	90.20	91.54
Face	0.680	96.81	89.22	92.86
Iris[a]	0.430	98.95	92.16	95.43
Fingerprint	0.230	100.00	90.20	94.85

[a]Iris method uses Hamming distance metric

6.2 Biometric Performance

We evaluated the biometric performance of each method using precision, recall, and F1 score. Impersonation attempts were simulated by matching one user's authentication biometrics against a different user's enrolled template. For SAFE, this simulates a powerful adversary who has stolen the victim's User Identity Module and thus has access to their Fusion Secret.

Tables 3 and 4 show the performance results for all methods using the Cosine and Euclidean distance metrics, respectively. With the Euclidean metric, SAFE achieves an F1 score of 95.52%, outperforming both the Concatenation (90.20%) and Summation (91.54%) baselines. Its performance is also competitive with the best-performing single-modality systems (Fingerprint at 95.96% and Iris at 95.43%), demonstrating that SAFE effectively preserves the discriminative power of the biometric traits while protecting the biometric traits' privacy.

To analyze the impact of the algebraic operations $\mathcal{O}$ on performance, we tested several variants of SAFE using the Cosine distance metric, with results shown in Table 5. The best performance was achieved by the variant using the operation set $\{+, \wedge\}$, with a 97.06% F1 score. This result is noteworthy, as it surpasses not only the baseline fusion methods but also all of the single-modality systems, highlighting SAFE's ability to create a highly discriminative embedding. The default set of $\{+, -, \times\}$ also yields a strong F1 score of 95.00%. These findings indicate that the set of operations $\mathcal{O}$ can be tuned as a hyperparameter to optimize authentication accuracy.

Table 4. Accuracies with Euclidean Distance Metric in Comparison with Five Baselines

Methods	Threshold τ	Accuracies (%)		
		Precision	Recall	F1 Score
SAFE	37.00	96.97	94.12	95.52
Concatenation	47.00	90.20	90.20	90.20
Summation	47.00	92.93	90.20	91.54
Face	1.17	100.00	90.20	94.85
Iris[a]	0.43	98.95	92.16	95.43
Fingerprint	1.00	98.96	93.14	95.96

[a]Iris method uses Hamming distance metric

Table 5. Accuracies of SAFE Variants

Set of Algebraic Operations $\mathcal{O}$	Threshold τ	Accuracies (%)		
		Precision	Recall	F1 Score
$\{+, -, \times\}$	0.225	96.94	93.14	95.00
$\{+, \wedge, \times\}$	0.105	96.97	94.12	95.52
$\{+, \wedge\}$	0.105	97.06	97.06	97.06
$\{-, \times\}$	0.300	96.00	94.12	95.05
$\{\wedge, \times\}$	0.097	95.92	92.16	94.00
$\{+, -\}$	0.220	97.87	90.20	93.88
$\{+, \times\}$	0.150	94.90	91.18	93.00
$\{\wedge\}$	0.095	96.04	95.10	95.57
$\{-\}$	0.300	98.94	91.18	94.90
$\{\times\}$	0.800	95.92	92.16	94.00
$\{+\}$	0.120	95.79	89.22	92.39

6.3 Computational Cost Analysis

We analyzed the computational overhead of each method by measuring the average time required for the client and server to perform enrollment and authentication. The results are presented in Table 6.

The client-side times for all multi-modal methods (SAFE, Concatenation, Summation) is approximately the sum of the individual modality processing times, as all features must be extracted. SAFE's client-side enrollment time is slightly higher than the baselines due to the additional overhead of generating the Fusion Secret and applying the SAFE transform. However, this one-time cost during enrollment is minimal.

Critically, the server-side authentication time for SAFE is 1.33 µs (μs), which is competitive with the other methods. This demonstrates that the enhanced privacy and security of SAFE do not introduce significant latency at the server,

Table 6. Timing Results in Comparison with Five Baselines

Methods	Average Time Per User			
	Enrollment		Authentication	
	Client (s)	Server (μs)	Client (s)	Server (μs)
SAFE	3.74	0.99	3.41	1.33
Concatenation	3.18	0.97	3.30	1.02
Summation	3.28	1.23	3.18	1.18
Face	0.19	1.15	0.19	0.96
Iris	1.21	0.95	1.21	0.86
Fingerprint	1.72	1.83	1.71	1.17

making it well-suited for scalable, real-time authentication systems where low latency is paramount.

7 Conclusion

This paper addressed the critical privacy risks inherent in server-based multi-modal biometric authentication systems. While combining modalities enhances access security, the storage of multiple irreplaceable biometric templates exposes users to template inversion attacks and data breaches. To solve this, we proposed SAFE, a novel framework that integrates privacy protection directly into the feature-level fusion process. By using a user-specific Fusion Secret to guide the algebraic combination of features, SAFE generates a single, non-invertible, and cancellable template. Our comprehensive evaluation demonstrated that SAFE provides robust privacy guarantees while achieving superior authentication accuracy (up to a 97.06% F1 score) compared to standard fusion baselines, and maintaining highly efficient server-side matching times. SAFE successfully bridges the gap between high access security and user privacy, offering a practical and effective solution for deploying next-generation multi-modal biometric authentication systems.

Looking forward, this work opens several exciting avenues for future research:

- Exploring New Modalities: The SAFE framework is modality-agnostic by design. Future work could involve applying SAFE to other biometric traits, such as hand geometry, gait, voice patterns, or physiological signals like electrocardiograms (ECG), to evaluate its generalizability and performance in different contexts.
- Machine Learning Integration: SAFE embeddings are fixed-length, privacy-preserving representations of a user's multi-modal identity. These secure embeddings could be used to train machine learning models for continuous authentication.

Acknowledgment. This work is supported in part by the National Science Foundation under Cooperative Agreement OIA-1946391.

References

1. Pahuja, S., Goel, N.: Multimodal biometric authentication: a review. AI Commun. **37**(4), 525–547 (2024)
2. Bala, N., Gupta, R., Kumar, A.: Multimodal biometric system based on fusion techniques: a review. Inf. Secur. J. Glob. Perspect. **31**(3), 289–337 (2022)
3. Garg, S.N., Vig, R., Gupta, S.: A survey on different levels of fusion in multimodal biometrics. Indian J. Sci. Technol. **10**(44) (2017)
4. Vekariya, V., Joshi, M., Dikshit, S., et al.: Multi-biometric fusion for enhanced human authentication in information security. Meas. Sens. **31**, 100973 (2024)
5. Sarier, N.D.: Multimodal biometric authentication for mobile edge computing. Inf. Sci. **573**, 82–99 (2021)
6. Vendrow, E., Vendrow, J.: Realistic face reconstruction from deep embeddings. In: NeurIPS 2021 Workshop Privacy in Machine Learning (2021)
7. Rajasekar, V., et al.: Enhanced multimodal biometric recognition approach for smart cities based on an optimized fuzzy genetic algorithm. Sci. Rep. **12**(1), 622 (2022)
8. Vatchala, S., et al.: Multi-modal biometric authentication: leveraging shared layer architectures for enhanced security. IEEE Access (2025)
9. A. Name: Safe code and compiled dataset. GitHub Repository (2025). https://anonymous.4open.science/r/SAFE
10. Ammour, N., Bazi, Y., Alajlan, N.: Multimodal approach for enhancing biometric authentication. J. Imaging **9**(9), 168 (2023)
11. Yang, H., Sun, E., Cheng, C., Ding, A.H.: Multi-modal biometrics based on data fusion. In: Journal of Physics: Conference Series, vol. 1684, no. 1, p. 012023. IOP Publishing (2020)
12. Jagadiswary, D., Saraswady, D.: Biometric authentication using fused multimodal biometric. Procedia Comput. Sci. **85**, 109–116 (2016)
13. Sarkar, A., Singh, B.K.: A review on performance, security and various biometric template protection schemes for biometric authentication systems. Multimedia Tools Appl. **79**(37), 27 721–27 776 (2020)
14. Dubasi, Y., Burroughs, W., Li, Q.: POP-FA: Paillier and order-preserving encryption-based facial authentication. In: 2024 IEEE Conference on Communications and Network Security (CNS), pp. 1–9. IEEE (2024)
15. Maurya, S., Bharti, J., Roy, B.: A survey on cancellable biometrics techniques. In: 2024 IEEE International Students' Conference on Electrical, Electronics and Computer Science (SCEECS), pp. 1–7. IEEE (2024)
16. Dubasi, Y., Li, Q., Luu, K.: Pop-hit: partially order-preserving hash-induced transformation for privacy protection in face recognition access control. In: International Conference on Security and Privacy in Communication Systems, pp. 80–98. Springer (2023)
17. Yang, W., Wang, S., Hu, J., Tao, X., Li, Y.: Feature extraction and learning approaches for cancellable biometrics: a survey. CAAI Trans. Intell. Technol. **9**(1), 4–25 (2024)

18. Parkhi, O., Vedaldi, A., Zisserman, A.: Deep face recognition. In: BMVC 2015-Proceedings of the British Machine Vision Conference 2015. British Machine Vision Association (2015)
19. Serengil, S.I., Ozpinar, A.: A benchmark of facial recognition pipelines and co-usability performances of modules. Bilisim Teknolojileri Dergisi **17**(2), 95–107 (2024). https://dergipark.org.tr/en/pub/gazibtd/issue/84331/1399077
20. Serengil, S.I., Ozpinar, A.: LightFace: a hybrid deep face recognition framework. In: 2020 Innovations in Intelligent Systems and Applications Conference (ASYU), pp. 23–27. IEEE (2020). https://ieeexplore.ieee.org/document/9259802
21. AI, W.: Iris: Iris recognition inference system of the worldcoin project (2023). https://github.com/worldcoin/open-iris
22. Rohwedder, T., Osorio-Roig, D., Rathgeb, C., Busch, C.: Benchmarking fixed-length fingerprint representations across different embedding sizes and sensor types. In: Intl. Conf. of the Biometrics Special Interest Group (BIOSIG). IEEE (2023)
23. Deshmukh, U.: Fingerprint-enhancement-python. GitHub Repository (2024). https://github.com/Utkarsh-Deshmukh/Fingerprint-Enhancement-Python
24. Huang, G.B., Ramesh, M., Berg, T., Learned-Miller, E.: Labeled faces in the wild: a database for studying face recognition in unconstrained environments, University of Massachusetts, Amherst. Technical report 07–49 (2007)
25. Huang, G.B., Learned-Miller, E.: Labeled faces in the wild: updates and new reporting procedures, University of Massachusetts, Amherst, Technical report. UM-CS-2014-003 (2014)
26. Kadhim, O.N., Abdulameer, M.H.: A multimodal biometric database and case study for face recognition based deep learning. Bull. Electr. Eng. Inform. **13**(1), 677–685 (2024)
27. Neurotechnology: U.are.u fingerprint dataset (2007). https://www.neurotechnology.com/download.html#databases
28. Patel, S.: Fingerprint verification system (FVS) datasets (2002). https://fvs.sourceforge.net/download.html

How Enforcement Shapes 2FA Usability and Perceived Workload: A Comparative Study Across Populations

Zhiyu He[1], Francisco Vega[2], and Yuan Cheng[1](✉)

[1] University of Nottingham Ningbo China, Ningbo, China
{scxzh2,yuan.cheng}@nottingham.edu.cn
[2] River Islands High School, Lathrop, CA 95330, USA
fvega@riacademies.net

Abstract. Two-factor authentication (2FA) is widely used to enhance online security, yet its impact on users' perceived workload in everyday use is not well understood. We compare 2FA experiences among college students and Amazon Mechanical Turk workers based on 212 survey responses, using NASA-TLX workload ratings and open-ended questions. The results show that users who have previously experienced 2FA-related access loss report significantly higher workload across all dimensions of NASA-TLX, suggesting that poor user experience is a major factor contributing to the perceived burden of using 2FA. Additionally, users who are required to use 2FA report higher levels of time pressure, effort, and frustration than those who adopt 2FA voluntarily or through incentives. In contrast, the frequency with which users pay attention to security cues, such as IP addresses, devices, and locations, shows little effect on their subjective workload, indicating that security prompts themselves are not a major source of burden. Open-ended responses also highlight issues such as time pressure from CAPTCHA countdowns, delays caused by multi-step authentication processes, missed events due to login friction, and anxiety during account recovery. Overall, this study suggests that improving 2FA should focus on enhancing user experience, particularly through clearer guidance and more reliable account recovery processes, rather than reducing security cues or relying solely on stricter verification.

Keywords: Two-factor authentication · Usability · User workload

1 Introduction

With the rising number of password breaches and sophisticated phishing attacks, protecting user account security has become a major challenge for cybersecurity. Over the years, organizations have tried to combat account compromises by enforcing various password policies, such as requiring complex password requirements and mandatory periodic changes. However, despite these efforts, such

Y. Cao et al. (Eds.): SecureComm 2026, LNICST 704, pp. 23–47, 2027.
https://doi.org/10.1007/978-3-032-32764-2_2

policies have not been fully effective in preventing account breaches [25]. Moreover, users tend to reuse the same or similar passwords across multiple services, which exacerbates the consequences of password breaches by enabling credential stuffing and other advanced password guessing attacks [8,15,19].

To overcome the limitations of password-based authentication, many organizations now use two-factor authentication (2FA) as an additional security measure. 2FA requires users to provide another form of authentication, such as a one-time verification code, a biometric, or a hardware security key, in addition to a password. This extra step can make it considerably harder for attackers to gain unauthorized access. However, each method of 2FA comes with its own usability and security challenges. Inconsistent implementation across organizations further complicates the user experience, often leading to confusion and frustration. As a result, despite its clear security benefits, many users remain hesitant or skeptical about adopting 2FA. An early study reported that only 6.4% of sampled Google users used 2FA [21]. While adoption has grown substantially since then, rising to roughly 89% of consumers who report having at least one account that requires 2FA as of 2023 [7], there is still a lack of research focusing on the factors that influence users' decisions to adopt or reject 2FA technology. Understanding these factors can help promote 2FA adoption from the users' perspective.

Universities provide a useful setting for studying these questions because many institutions have recently deployed 2FA, often with mandatory enrollment. Prior work has leveraged campus rollouts to examine user opinions about 2FA use and adoption [1,6,23]. For example, Abbott et al. conducted a series of surveys at a university during its phased 2FA rollout, comparing perceptions between mandatory users and voluntary users [1]. Their findings revealed that mandatory policies led to decreased user satisfaction. Prior work has primarily focused on acceptance and satisfaction during campus rollouts (e.g., [1,6]). Less is known about how enforcement shapes multidimensional workload, whether these patterns generalize beyond a single institutional context, and whether specific user experiences, such as 2FA-related account access loss and attention to contextual security cues, explain perceived burden.

Building on this line of work, we conduct a comparative usability analysis of 2FA across adoption models and user populations. We address the following research questions:

- **RQ1:** How does the adoption context (mandatory, voluntary, or incentivized) affect users' perceived workload and attitudes toward the usability of 2FA?
- **RQ2:** In what ways do university users differ from general Internet users in their perceptions of workload and usability when controlling for adoption mode and other factors?
- **RQ3:** To what extent do users report noticing or consulting contextual security information (e.g., IP address, device, location, and time) during authentication?

We collected data through two online surveys administered to two distinct cohorts: Amazon Mechanical Turk (MTurk) workers and students recruited from a Computer Science major at a U.S. public university. The university survey was conducted approximately one year after 2FA became mandatory for campus accounts. The MTurk survey included a screening question to exclude participants without any 2FA-enabled accounts. After removing invalid or low-quality responses, the final analytic sample comprised 212 participants. Using responses from both cohorts and analyzing NASA-TLX workload measures, we report the following main findings:

- **Adoption Mode (RQ1):** Users subject to mandatory 2FA report significantly higher levels of time pressure, effort, and frustration than those who adopted 2FA voluntarily. Users who adopted 2FA through incentives fell between these two groups.
- **User Group (RQ2):** After accounting for age, adoption mode, and prior 2FA-related account access loss, we find only marginal differences in overall workload between university users and general Internet users.
- **Security Attention (RQ3):** Users who pay closer attention to contextual security information (e.g., device, location, login alerts) do not report increased workload, indicating that security awareness does not inherently add cognitive burden.

These findings indicate that 2FA burden mainly comes from mandatory enforcement and negative user experiences (particularly account access loss), rather than from security cues themselves. Accordingly, we recommend that developers and policy makers prioritize usability improvements that reduce 2FA-related account access loss risk, make recovery processes more convenient, and provide clearer interface guidance, rather than focusing solely on stricter verification.

The rest of this paper is organized as follows. Section 2 reviews related work on the usability and adoption of 2FA. Section 3 describes the survey design, measures, participant recruitment, and analysis procedures. Section 4 reports the quantitative results (NASA-TLX workload comparisons and regression analyses) and summarizes themes from open-ended responses. Section 5 discusses implications for 2FA design and deployment, as well as limitations and directions for future work. Section 6 concludes the paper.

2 Related Work

2FA Adoption and User Attitudes

Previous research has examined how users adopt and respond to 2FA, with many studies focusing on academic settings where institutions have increasingly enforced its use.

Colnago et al. [6] conducted a longitudinal study during the rollout of Duo 2FA at Carnegie Mellon University, where 2FA was mandatory for employees and voluntary for students. They found that although users initially expressed concerns about burden, their actual experiences were more positive than expected.

Over time, the perceived hassle diminished, and learning costs were relatively low. Similarly, Abbott and Patil [1] studied the phased 2FA deployment at Indiana University using both user surveys and system logs. They observed that while users mandated to adopt 2FA were slightly less satisfied than voluntary adopters, the difference was smaller than anticipated. Overall, the transition to mandatory 2FA did not significantly reduce user acceptance, and users generally found Duo to be annoying but manageable and secure. These findings align with insights from Golla et al. [14] and the Cybercrime Support Network (CSN) [7], which concluded that user motivation and perceived time pressure strongly influence 2FA acceptance.

Attitudes toward 2FA varied among different roles within the university context. At Brigham Young University, Dutson et al. [11] found that students and faculty generally report more negative attitudes toward Duo compared to staff, with nearly half of respondents reporting account access loss due to 2FA. Many users indicated that they would opt out of 2FA if given the choice. However, other studies consistently show that while mandatory policies may spur some user resistance, they do not necessarily worsen users' actual usability ratings [1,6].

User education and familiarity play crucial roles in mitigating perceived burdens associated with 2FA. Effective training can reduce user resistance, and as users become accustomed to the process, their subjective burden diminishes, allowing them to gradually adopt 2FA as a habit. Weidman and Grossklags [26] noted the role of habit formation in fostering long-term acceptance of authentication mechanisms. Arnold et al. [5] studied the emotional reactions of college students to mandatory MFA and reported strong negative feelings such as frustration and stress. Over half of the participants reported that MFA caused them to miss deadlines, and only 40% thought it was worth the inconvenience. Their work is particularly relevant to our investigation into user perceptions of subjective load and responses to safety cues.

Usability of 2FA Mechanisms

Marky et al. [17] conducted interviews with participants from diverse backgrounds to explore the usability of various 2FA methods. Their findings indicate that users prefer solutions that seamlessly integrate into their daily lives rather than those focused solely on enhancing technical security. Many existing 2FA methods fail to meet user satisfaction. Das et al. [10] analyzed over 12,500 user reviews and found that most users were resistant to 2FA because of the complexity of setup, poor cross-device support, and unclear recovery processes. Consequently, SMS-based codes remain the most popular method despite their weaker security, while professional authentication apps and hardware tokens continue to suffer from low adoption. Issues related to account recovery and a lack of guidance were also major sources of frustration. Other studies [12,18,20,24] revealed that when 2FA mechanisms become inconvenient or poorly integrated into users' daily life, resistance increases.

Security Notifications, Recovery, and Advanced 2FA Schemes

Security notifications are an important yet often overlooked aspect of the 2FA experience. Markert et al. [16] found that users typically rely on device and location information to determine the legitimacy of login notifications. However, confusing or ambiguous information can lead to misunderstanding, and frequent alerts may cause alarm fatigue. Only 22% of users in their study responded appropriately after receiving a suspicious notification. To mitigate such burden, Wiefling et al. [27] proposed risk-based authentication, which prompts additional verification only when anomalies are detected, striking a balance between security and convenience.

Furthermore, inconsistencies in 2FA interaction design across different platforms contribute to cognitive burden. Lyastani et al. [13] found that a lack of unified design patterns can lead to user confusion, increased cognitive burden, and elevated security risks. These inconsistencies, along with unclear instructions and complex recovery processes, contribute significantly to user frustration.

3 Methodology

This section describes the survey design, participant recruitment, data collection and pre-processing procedures, and the key variables used in our analysis. Our study aims to investigate user perceptions of 2FA, with a focus on usability, perceived workload, and attention to security cues.

3.1 Survey Design

We designed two online surveys and distributed them separately to two participant cohorts: (1) general Internet users recruited via Amazon Mechanical Turk (MTurk) and (2) university students from a U.S. public university. Both surveys shared a common structure, with minor adaptations for the campus context. In particular, the university survey included four additional questions about the campus rollout of Duo 2FA, which had been mandatory for approximately one year before data collection. The MTurk version contained 23 questions, while the university version contained 27 questions. Participants were allowed up to one hour to complete the survey; MTurk participants completed it in 23 min on average.

The survey comprised four parts:

1. **Demographics and 2FA background (Q1–Q9):** Participants provided information on age, gender, education, tech-savviness, the number of accounts with 2FA enabled, reasons for adopting 2FA (including adoption mode), and usage frequency and duration.
2. **2FA context and methods (Q10–Q11):** Participants indicated where they use 2FA (e.g., school, work, personal) and which authentication methods they employed (e.g., SMS, push notification, authenticator apps, security keys).
3. **Usability and workload (Q12–Q17):** Based on the NASA-TLX framework, six Likert-scale statements (1 = strongly disagree to 5 = strongly agree) assessed users' mental and physical demand, time pressure, effort, annoyance, and perceived difficulty during 2FA login. Follow-up prompts collected brief explanations when applicable.

4. **Security attention and recovery (Q18–Q27):** Participants were asked about their attention to security cues (e.g., device, IP address, location, and time information presented during authentication), their experience with 2FA-related access loss, and what they disliked about their current 2FA systems.

3.2 Data Collection and Demographics

We initially received 133 MTurk submissions and 119 university survey responses from participants based in the United States. MTurk participants were required to have a HIT approval rating of at least 98% and a minimum of 10,000 approved HITs. A screening question excluded participants without any 2FA-enabled accounts. Each MTurk participant received $1.00 in compensation. University participants were recruited through Computer Science courses and were required to be at least 18 years old. All procedures were approved by the institution's Institutional Review Board.

To ensure data quality, survey questions were mandatory where appropriate, and open-ended responses were manually reviewed. We removed responses with missing key fields or clearly irrelevant or nonsensical text. After cleaning, the final dataset included 212 valid responses (129 MTurk and 83 university), corresponding to the exclusion of 40 submissions (15.9%).

Table 1 summarizes the sample demographics (N = 212). Gender information was provided by 199 respondents (6.1% missing): 144 identified as male (72.4% of valid responses), 53 as female (26.6%), and 1 as non-binary/third gender and 1 preferred not to say (both 0.5%). Age information was provided by 197 respondents (7.1% missing), ranging from 19 to 71 years, with a mean age of 33.6, a median of 31, and an interquartile range of 24–39.

Table 1. Demographic summary of survey participants (N = 212)

Characteristic	Category	n (%)
User group	MTurk	129 (60.8%)
	Sac State	83 (39.2%)
Gender	Male	144 (67.9%)
	Female	53 (25.0%)
	Non-binary/third gender	1 (0.5%)
	Prefer not to say	1 (0.5%)
	Missing	13 (6.1%)
Age		19–71 (M = 33.6, SD = 11.1; n = 197)

3.3 Measures

To examine how enforcement context and user characteristics relate to perceived workload and usability of 2FA, we define a set of key variables for analyzing survey responses.

Adoption Mode and User Group. The primary independent variables in our comparative analysis are:

- Adoption Mode: Participants reported how they initially enabled 2FA, categorized as *Mandated*, *Incentivized*, and *Voluntary*. Our comparisons mainly focus on the *Mandated* and *Voluntary* groups to assess how enforcement impacts usability perceptions.
- User Group: A binary variable distinguishing between university users and general Internet users (i.e., MTurk participants).

NASA-TLX Workload. We adopted the NASA Task Load Index (NASA-TLX) to assess the subjective workload of users during the use of 2FA. It is a widely used instrument in human-computer interaction and usability studies. Originally developed by NASA to assess operator workload, the NASA-TLX captures subjective workload across six dimensions: psychological demand, physical demand, time pressure, operational effort, frustration, and task performance. Unlike single satisfaction or ease of use score, it can reveal the source of usability problems in more detail. In addition, the scale results are easy to be compared across groups and statistically analyzed, which can be used as a quantitative basis for usability differences between different adoption patterns and user groups. Each response is converted into a numerical score for analysis.

Security-Attention Variables. During 2FA login, many services display contextual security information (e.g., IP address, device type, and location). A key goal of this study is to understand whether users notice and leverage these cues. To measure users' attention to contextual security information based on their responses, the survey included four questions. Questions Q18_1 to Q18_3 asked participants about their engagement with IP- and device-related information in authentication contexts, while Q20 asked how often they pay attention to displayed contextual details such as IP address, time, or location.

All four items used a five-point frequency scale (*Never*, *Rarely*, *Sometimes*, *Often*, *Always*). For quantitative analysis, we mapped these responses to numerical values from 1 to 5, respectively. In the analyses reported below, Q20 is used to capture how often participants attended to contextual details displayed during authentication, such as IP address, time, or location, while the Q18 items are used for descriptive summaries and correlation analysis.

3.4 Data Preparation

Our dataset includes responses from two cohorts: university users and general Internet users. During data cleaning, we retained only completed responses and removed submissions with missing key fields or clearly invalid/irrelevant open-ended answers.

For analysis, five-point Likert-scale items were mapped from 1 (*strongly disagree/never*) to 5 (*strongly agree/always*). Technical proficiency (Q6), 2FA usage duration (Q7), and login frequency (Q9) were recoded into ordered numeric scales (Table 2). For workload measures, each NASA-TLX item was coded on a 1–5 scale for the six dimensions (mental demand, physical demand, temporal demand, effort, frustration, and perceived difficulty). We also computed an overall workload index, `TLX_total`, as the mean of the six subscales.

Table 2. Recoding of key ordinal variables used in the analysis

Question	Coding scheme
Technical proficiency (Q6)	"Somewhat", "Moderately", "Very", "Extremely" → 1–4
2FA usage time (Q7)	"Less than a year", "1–2 years", "More than 2 years" → 1–3
Login frequency (Q9)	"A few times a year", "A few times per month", "A few times per week", "1 or more times a day" → 1–4

3.5 Analytical Strategy

Quantitative Analysis. Our quantitative analysis consists of three steps. First, we computed descriptive statistics to summarize the sample and to identify potential differences between two cohorts (e.g., age, gender, education level, 2FA methods, and the distribution of compulsory and voluntary adoption). Second, we conducted cross-sectional group comparisons of perceived workload and usability results. We compared TLX total and subscale scores (e.g., perceived difficulty and frustration) across adoption modes (mandatory vs. voluntary) and across user groups (university vs. MTurk). We selected statistical tests based on the scale and distribution of each variable. Third, we used regression models to estimate the association between adoption mode and workload while adjusting for potential confounders. For continuous results, we used linear regression with adoption mode and user group as primary predictors, included their interaction, and controlled for covariates such as technical proficiency, years of use, login frequency, age, gender, and 2FA type. For binary results, we used logistic regression with the same set of predictors and controls. These models allow us to isolate the effect of mandatory adoption beyond simple mean comparisons and to test whether mandate effects differ by population.

Qualitative Analysis. To perform a qualitative analysis, we analyzed open-ended survey responses to capture users' authentic experiences with 2FA. The questions asked participants to elaborate on why they found 2FA demanding (mentally or physically), why they felt rushed, what difficulties they encountered during login, why they did not enable 2FA on all accounts, and any additional comments about 2FA. After removing incomplete or clearly irrelevant responses, we preprocessed the remaining answers by lowercasing the text, removing punctuation, and filtering stopwords. We then performed manual coding by assigning descriptive labels and consolidating them into higher-level themes. Finally, we used the resulting themes to interpret the quantitative findings. For example, topics related to countdown timers and session timeouts helped explain higher temporal demand scores, while topics related to lost equipment and missing codes shed light on frustration scores.

3.6 Ethical Considerations

All participants were informed of the study's purpose, the nature of the questionnaire, the intended use of the data, and their rights as participants prior to data collection. Participation was voluntary, and informed consent was obtained before respondents proceeded with the survey. Participants were free to withdraw at any time without penalty, and only individuals aged 18 or older were eligible to participate. The study posed minimal risk to participants and collected no personally identifiable information. Data were limited to self-reported two-factor authentication (2FA) usage experiences, subjective workload measures (NASA-TLX), and relevant background variables. All responses were anonymized and associated only with randomly assigned identifiers. Ethics approval was obtained for both the original data collection and the secondary analysis at the respective institutions. All data were used exclusively for academic research purposes.

4 Results

This section reports the results of our analysis. We first summarize the overall distribution of NASA-TLX workload scores for 2FA use. We then compare perceived workload across adoption modes and user subgroups. Next, we examine how negative experiences relate to perceived workload. Finally, we perform correlation analyses among different variables.

4.1 Overall Workload Distribution

Figure 1 shows that the overall 2FA workload in our sample is low to moderate. Most TLX total scores fall between approximately 2.3 and 3.1, with a median slightly below 2.7. While 2FA is not perceived as highly burdensome by most respondents, the presence of outliers indicates substantial variation across individuals.

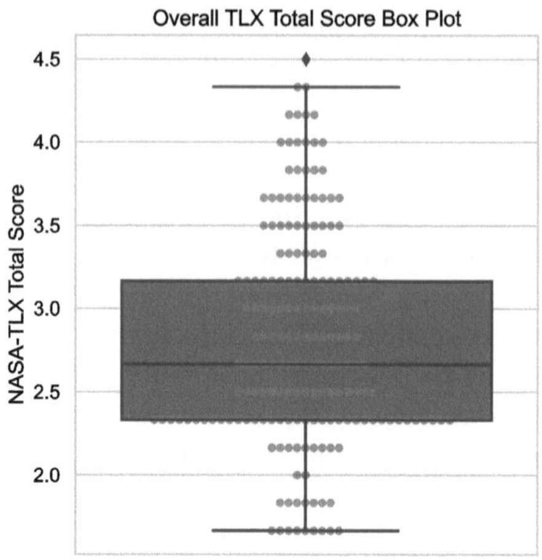

Fig. 1. TLX total score distribution.

4.2 Group Comparisons

We compared perceived workload across three grouping types: adoption mode (voluntary, incentivized, mandatory), user group (university vs. MTurk), and gender.

Figure 2 summarizes average NASA-TLX subscale scores by adoption mode. Mandated users report higher *temporal demand*, *frustration* and *subjective effort* than voluntary users, suggesting that enforcement is associated with feeling more "rushed" and "troubled" during authentication. The incentivized group generally falls between the mandated and voluntary groups.

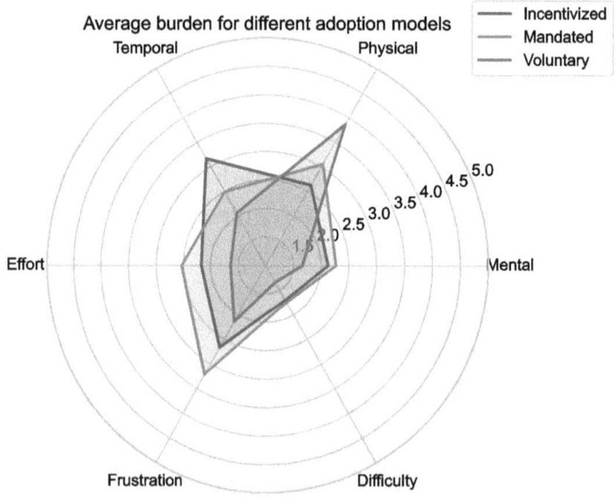

Fig. 2. Average burden for different adoption models.

Figure 3 shows the distribution of total TLX scores across adoption modes. The mandated group has a higher median and a wider interquartile range than the voluntary and incentivized groups, indicating both higher typical workload and greater variability under mandatory enforcement. In contrast, the voluntary group is more tightly clustered around lower TLX scores, suggesting a generally lighter perceived burden.

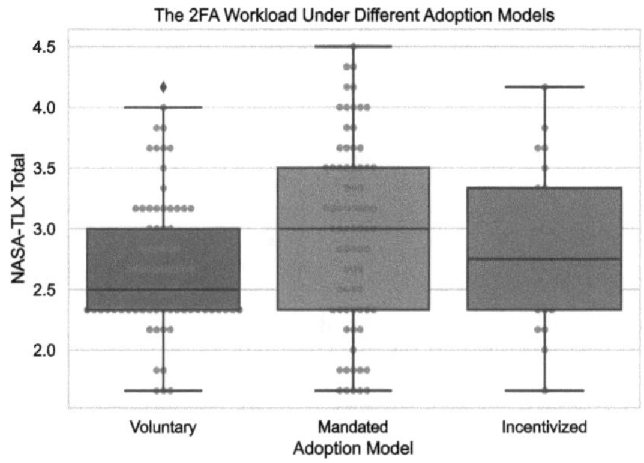

Fig. 3. The 2FA workload under different adoption models.

We next compared university and MTurk respondents. As shown in Fig. 4, TLX total scores are broadly similar across the two cohorts, although the student group shows a slightly higher median and a wider spread. In contrast, the MTurk group's scores are more tightly clustered, with fewer extreme high or low values, indicating a more consistent overall experience without particularly severe or unusally easy cases.

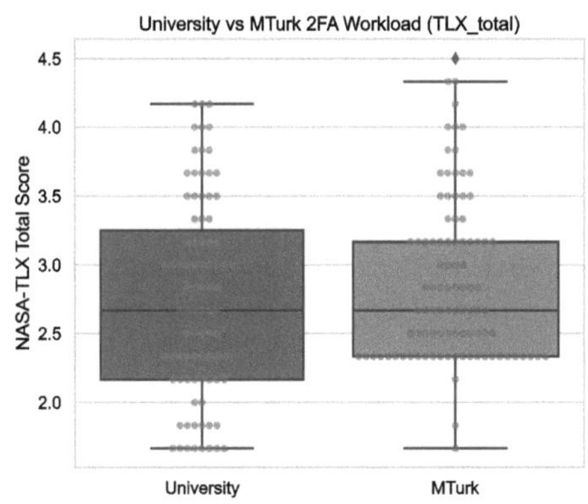

Fig. 4. Workload for students vs non-students (TLX_total).

Figure 5 further compares average scores across the six NASA-TLX dimensions. University students report higher average *mental demand*, *temporal pressure*, *effort*, *frustration* and *difficulty*, whereas the MTurk group reports higher *physical demand*, indicating that their burden was more often associated with physical actions, such as switching devices or retrieving authentication hardware.

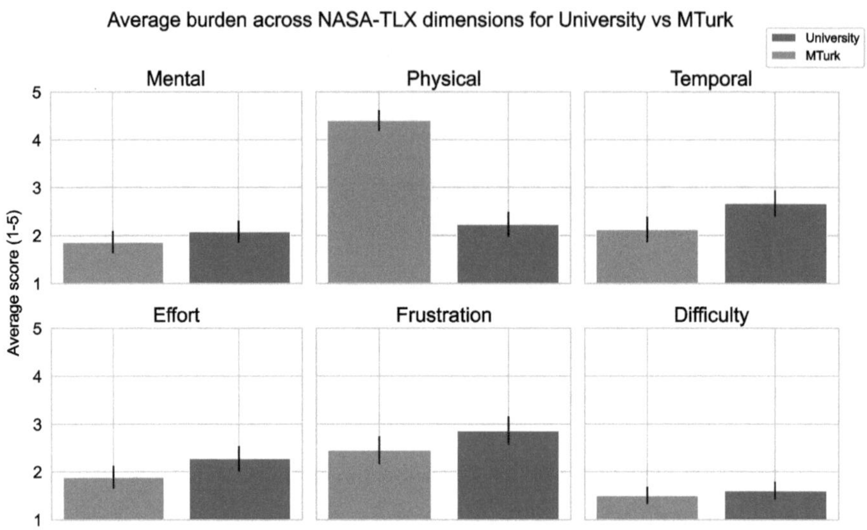

Fig. 5. Average burden across NASA-TLX dimensions for students vs non-students.

4.3 Impact of 2FA-Related Access Loss Experiences

We next examined whether negative experiences with 2FA are associated with greater perceived workload. Figure 6 compares TLX total scores between respondents who reported access loss experience due to 2FA and those who had not. The "Yes" group has a noticeably higher median and a wider score distribution, indicating both elevated perceived workload and greater variability in individual experiences. In contrast, users in the "No" group has lower and more tightly clustered TLX scores, suggesting that without prior 2FA-related access loss incidents, 2FA tends to be perceived as only a light to moderate burden. This finding underscores the lasting impact of negative security experiences on user sentiment.

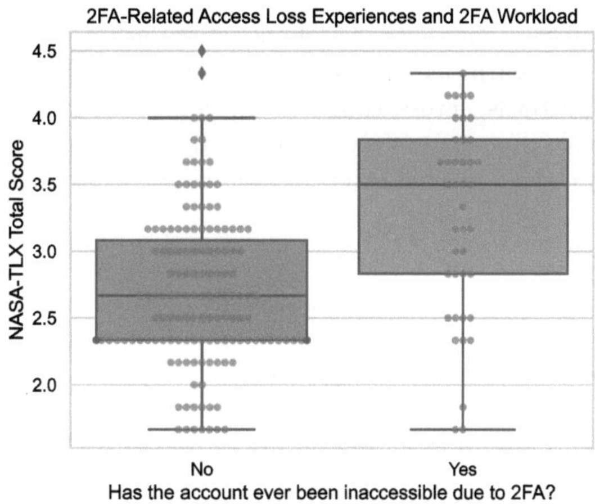

Fig. 6. 2FA-related access loss experiences and 2FA workload.

4.4 Correlation Analysis

Understanding the relationships between user attributes and perceived workload is a critical part of our analysis. Since variables such as age, technical proficiency, 2FA usage duration, 2FA usage frequency, and the NASATLX scores are ordinal or approximately ordinal in nature, we used Spearman's rank correlation to examine their associations.

Figure 7 presents the correlation matrix between these user characteristics and the six TLX dimensions, as well as the overall TLX total score. As expected, all six TLX subscales are positively and significantly correlated with each other and with `TLX_total`. Among them, *effort*, *frustration* and *temporal* exhibit the strongest correlations with the total score (coefficients ranging from 0.64 to 0.76), suggesting that these factors are the primary drivers of perceived workload during 2FA. *Mental demand* also shows a strong correlation with the total score, while *physical demand* and *task difficulty* are slightly less influential.

Regarding background variables, age shows a moderate positive correlation with physical demand (approximately 0.51), indicating that older users were more likely to perceive physical inconvenience when using 2FA. At the same time, age is negatively correlated with the frequency of 2FA usage (`frequency_2fa`) (approximately −0.44), indicating that young users engage in 2FA-required logins more frequently. Notably, usage frequency itself is negatively correlated with physical demand (approximately −0.43), implying that more frequent users may experience less physical burden. This is likely due to increased familiarity and operational fluency. By contrast, both `tech_level` and `duration_2fa` have weak or negligible correlations with TLX scores, indicating a limited effect on perceived workload in our sample.

We also examined whether responses to contextual security information is associated with workload. Figure 8 shows correlations between `TLX_total` and four survey-based attention measures capturing how often participants attend to security cues in different contexts. The four attention measures are moderately to strongly correlated with one another (approximately 0.5 to 0.75), suggesting similar response patterns across contexts. In contrast, their correlations with `TLX_total` are weak (approximately −0.11 to 0.03), indicating no meaningful association between self-reported attention to security cues and overall workload in our sample.

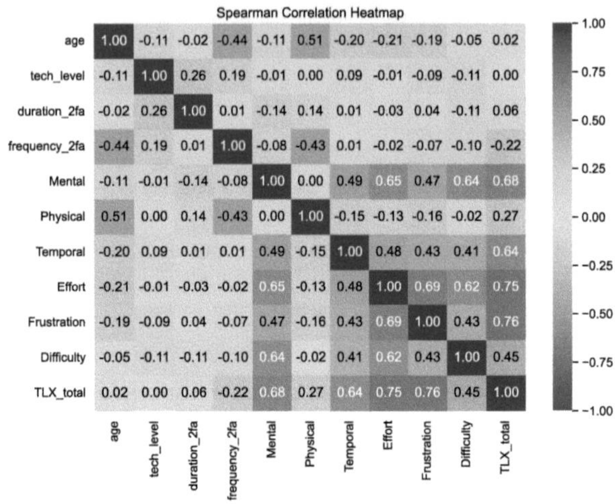

Fig. 7. Spearman correlation heatmap among ordinal variables and TLX scores.

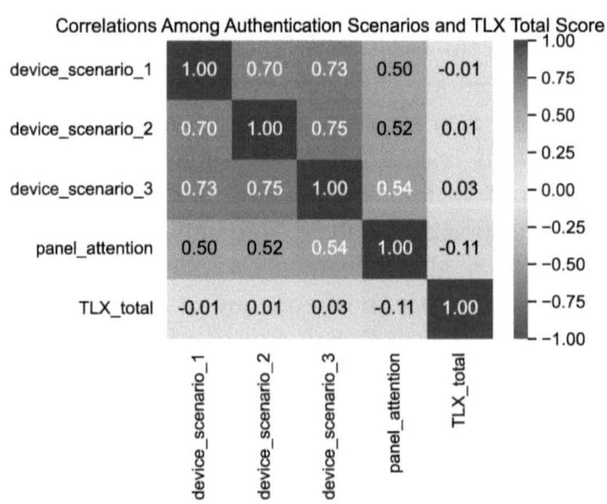

Fig. 8. Correlations Among Authentication Scenarios and TLX Total Score.

4.5 Effect of Notification Attention Levels

We examined whether users who more frequently inspect security details in 2FA push notifications report higher perceived workload. As shown in Fig. 9, participants were divided into a lower-attention group ($\leq$ *Rarely*) and a higher-attention group ($\geq$ *Sometimes*) based on how often they viewed the notification details panel. The resulting TLX total score distributions largely overlap in median and interquartile range, with both groups concentrated in the low-to-moderate workload range. This pattern is consistent with the correlation analysis above, which shows weak associations between security push notification attention measures and `TLX_total`.

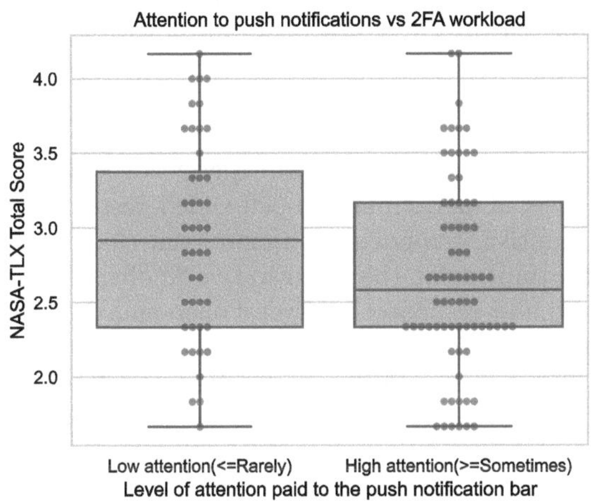

Fig. 9. Attention to push notifications vs 2FA workload.

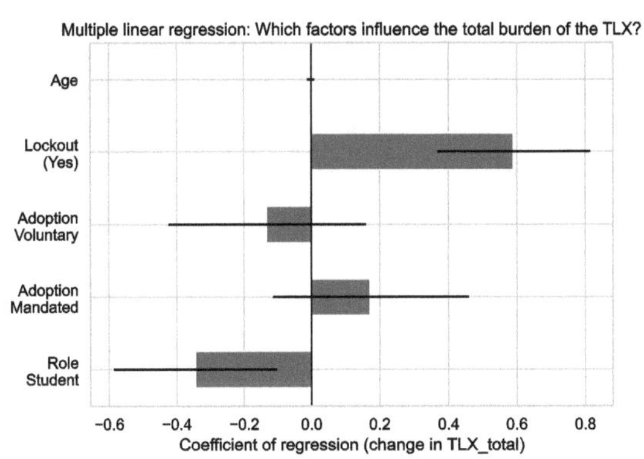

Fig. 10. Multiple linear regression results.

4.6 Regression Analysis

We fit a multiple linear regression model with `TLX_total` as the dependent variable to estimate the association between key predictors and overall perceived 2FA workload while controlling for other factors (Fig. 10). Prior 2FA-related access loss is the strongest predictor. Respondents who reported a access loss have substantially higher TLX scores, even when other factors are held constant. Adoption mode is the next most influential factor. Mandatory 2FA use is associated with higher perceived workload than voluntary or incentivized adoption. This supports our earlier findings that enforced usage introduces more friction and user burden. In contrast, the coefficient for `Student` is negative, indicating that after controlling for age, adoption mode, and access loss experience, students report slightly lower overall workload than non-students. Age has a near-zero coefficient, suggesting limited association with workload in this model.

4.7 Qualitative Analysis of Open-Ended Responses

To gain deeper insight into users' actual experiences with 2FA, we conducted a qualitative analysis of participants' open-ended responses. These responses illuminated the cognitive, temporal, and emotional challenges users face while using 2FA, which complement the quantitative findings from the NASA-TLX survey. We analyzed user responses to several open-ended prompts related to (1) mental and temporal workload, (2) sources of effort and frustration, (3) reasons for not enabling 2FA on all accounts, and (4) general feedback or suggestions. We applied TF-IDF and word frequency techniques to extract key terms, and then grouped them semantically similar responses into distinct themes.

Table 3 summarizes the most frequent keywords from each question. For example, participants frequently mentioned *time pressure*, *countdown*, and *slow or unstable network* in relation to mental and temporal workload (Q10, Q12), particularly in high-pressure situations such as exams or assignments. Responses regarding effort and frustration (Q14, Q16) often cited concerns about the *multi-step login process* and the inconvenience of *switching back and forth between different devices*. Reasons for not enabling 2FA on all accounts (Q24) included *inconvenience*, *complexity*, and *unclear instructions*. In responses to the open comment question (Q25), many users expressed a desire for *clearer guidance*, *better recovery options*, and *fewer access loss risks*.

From this analysis, we identified five recurring themes, summarized in Table 4. These themes help interpret the common sources of user burden:

1. **Time Pressure and Countdown Pressure**. Users often felt rushed due to short expiration windows and session timeouts, especially during high-stakes tasks like tests or assignments. Some expressed anxiety that authentication would "expire before I even finished typing."
2. **Process Complexity and Multi-step Friction**. Participants described the 2FA process as unnecessarily complicated, citing repeated steps, app-switching, and juggling between devices, which was particularly frustrating when repeated multiple times a day.

Table 3. Top keywords extracted from open-ended responses

Question	Top Keywords (TF-IDF / frequency)
Q10: Mental demand	time pressure, countdown, stressful, switching devices
Q12: Temporal demand	timeout, code expires, rush, delay, slow network
Q14: Effortfulness	multiple steps, switching apps, typing code, verification loop
Q16: Frustration sources	lost device, wrong code, waiting, repeated attempts
Q24: Why not enable 2FA	inconvenience, too many steps, confusing setup, device dependency
Q25: Additional comments	improve recovery, clearer instructions, reduce access loss

3. **Access loss and Recovery Anxiety**. Users who has access loss experience expressed fear and anxiety about using 2FA again. Many found the account recovery process to be slow, unclear, or overly restrictive.
4. **Device Dependency and Portability Issues**. Many respondents noted that 2FA becomes a major obstacle when a trusted device is unavailable, dead, or replaced, effectively locking them out of important accounts and services.
5. **Need for Clearer Guidance and More Forgiving Design**. Participants expressed frustration with technical jargon in security prompts and called for more intuitive guidance and flexible fallback mechanisms.

5 Discussion

5.1 Comparison with Prior 2FA Rollout Studies

Our analyses suggest that the overall perceived workload of 2FA, as measured by NASA-TLX, falls within a low to moderate range for most users. This is broadly consistent with prior 2FA rollout studies, which generally report that 2FA is perceived as manageable after initial adoption. For example, Colnago et al. [6] found that although CMU users initially anticipated 2FA to be burdensome, their actual experiences were often more positive than expected, with perceived burden decreasing over time. Similarly, Abbott and Patil [1] observed that while mandatory users were somewhat less satisfied than voluntary adopters, the transition to mandatory 2FA did not substantially reduce overall user acceptance. These findings and ours suggest that 2FA is often experienced as manageable rather than overwhelmingly burdensome.

At the same time, our results extend this literature in several important ways. First, rather than focusing primarily on satisfaction or acceptance, we examine 2FA through the lens of multidimensional workload. This reveals that the burden associated with mandatory adoption is concentrated in specific dimensions, particularly temporal demand, effort, and frustration, rather than being uniformly distributed across all aspects of the user experience. Second, our findings show that negative experiences are not driven by enforcement alone. Many users described 2FA as merely an "extra step" or "a bit of a hassle" unless they

Table 4. Themes identified from qualitative coding of open-ended responses

Theme	Description	Example quote
Time pressure and countdown stress	Users describe feeling rushed by expiring codes, session timeouts, and strict time limits during critical tasks (e.g., tests, exams, deadlines).	"The code times out so fast that I feel rushed every time I log in."
Process complexity and multi-step friction	Burden caused by multi-step flows, switching between apps or devices, and repeating the same verification steps many times a day.	"There are too many steps just to log in, especially when I have to do it several times a day."
Access loss and recovery anxiety	Negative experiences of access loss, fear of losing access again, and frustration with slow or confusing recovery procedures.	"I was locked out once, and now I get anxious every time I see a 2FA prompt."
Device dependence and portability issues	Difficulties when the trusted device is not at hand, broken, or replaced, leading to disruption in everyday activities.	"If I forget my phone or it dies, I basically can't do anything that needs 2FA."
Need for clearer guidance and more forgiving design	Users ask for clearer instructions, less technical wording, and more forgiving mechanisms (e.g., easier fallback or recovery).	"The security messages are too technical; I just want clear steps telling me what to do next."

had experienced 2FA-related access loss or recovery failure. Once such incidents occurred, however, the perceived burden increased substantially. Some respondents reported severe consequences, including missed exams and extended periods of inaccessibility. These perspectives help refine prior interpretation of 2FA rollout studies. While earlier work emphasizes the role of mandatory adoption in shaping user attitudes, our results indicate that the interaction between enforcement and failure scenarios is critical. Mandatory 2FA becomes particularly burdensome when combined with punitive or poorly supported recovery processes.

Our findings are broadly consistent with prior campus-based studies but provide additional explanatory details. Like Abbott and Patil [1], we observe that mandatory adoption is associated with more negative user experience than voluntary adoption. However, our data further shows that a stronger indicator of elevated workload is prior 2FA-related access loss rather than enforcement status alone. This complements the findings of Dutson et al. [11], who reported frequent access loss and more negative attitudes among students and faculty than staff, and Arnold et al. [5], who documented frustration, stress, and missed deadlines among university students under mandatory MFA. In our study, students reported slightly higher TLX scores than general Internet users, but qualitative responses suggest that this difference is largely driven by situational factors. In particular, students often encountered 2FA in high-pressure situations such as deadlines and exams, which amplified perceived burden. In summary, our main contribution is to show that 2FA workload is best understood not as a simple consequence of mandatory adoption, but as the result of interactions among enforcement context, recovery mechanisms, and situational factors.

5.2 Design Implications for 2FA Deployment

Rather than modeling 2FA adoption as a binary question of whether it should be mandatory, our findings emphasize the complex influence of multiple factors. Mandatory 2FA policies do increase users' perceived time pressure, effort, and frustration, but not every mandated user experiences a high burden. Thus, the more important design question is not simply whether 2FA should be required, but how enforcement policies can be implemented in a way that is fair, supportive, and user-friendly.

Based on users' self-reported behavior, our results show that attention to security-related notifications is not associated with higher perceived workload. This challenges the common assumption that increasing the visibility of security information inevitably disrupts the user experience. Instead, users' attention to contextual security information may reflect habitual vigilance rather than additional cognitive burden. While excessive or frequent prompts can still lead to notification fatigue, as noted in previous studies [2,3,14,22], our findings imply that designers can incorporate clearer and more informative contextual cues without necessarily increase user burden.

At the same time, the top themes derived from the qualitative analysis, which are countdown pressure, multi-step verification, device dependency, and complex recovery procedures, suggest that future efforts should prioritize creating more forgiving authentication systems. Prior work has likewise emphasized the importance of recovery support, clearer guidance, and reducing friction in multi-factor authentication [4,9,13,17]. Instead of focusing solely on strengthening defenses, designers should also consider how to reduce friction, make recovery easier, and support users through challenging scenarios. In particular, reducing avoidable access loss and providing clearer fallback paths may do more to improve long-term acceptance than simply adding more factors or more frequent prompts.

In summary, our study reveals that the perceived burden of 2FA not only from its enforcement but also from how it is implemented and experienced. Well-designed interfaces, intuitive guidance, and robust recovery mechanisms may do more to improve long-term acceptance than simply adding more factors or controls. It is entirely possible that 2FA can evolve into an effective, reliable, and unobtrusive protection method rather than a punitive mechanism users are forced to endure.

5.3 Limitations

This study has several limitations. First, it is based on cross-sectional, self-reported survey data. Thus, the results capture perceived workload and reported experiences rather than directly observed behavior, and do not support causal claims. Second, our sample is limited to two populations: MTurk workers and students from a single U.S. public university, which may limit generalizability to other user groups. Third, our measures of attention to contextual security cues should be interpreted with caution. Not all 2FA systems expose the same information (e.g., IP address, location, or device details), so lower reported attention may reflect limited cue availability rather than reduced user vigilance. Finally, while we applied response-quality screening and manually reviewed open-ended responses, low-effort or inattentive responding cannot be entirely ruled out.

6 Conclusion and Future Work

Our analysis of survey data from 212 participants reveals that 2FA-related access loss are the strongest contributor to increased workload, while mandatory 2FA adoption is associated with higher time pressure, effort, and frustration compared to voluntary or incentivized adoption. Differences between university users and general Internet users are relatively small after controlling for relevant factors, and attention to security cues does not meaningfully increase perceived workload. Overall, the findings indicate that 2FA burden stems primarily from enforcement policies and negative usage experiences rather than from security prompts themselves, suggesting that improving recovery processes, reducing access loss, and providing clearer verification guidance are more effective ways to improving usability.

In future work, we plan to move beyond self-reported survey data by examining real-world 2FA usage logs within a large organization. In particular, we aim to analyze behavioral indicators such as authentication completion time, repeated login attempts, device switching, recovery requests, and unsuccessful access episodes, enabling a more direct assessment of the relationship between perceived workload and actual authentication behavior. We also plan to conduct a longitudinal study to track how users' workload, attitudes, and coping strategies evolve over time, especially before and after mandatory 2FA deployment and after negative experiences such as 2FA-related access loss or recovery failure. Finally, building on our qualitative findings, we will design and evaluate targeted improvements to lockout and recovery user experience, including clearer fallback guidance, more transparent recovery workflows, and less disruptive authentication prompts. We will assess whether these changes can reduce frustration, effort, and time pressure during authentication.

A Survey Questionnaire

The questionnaire items used in the analysis are listed below.

Q1. How many accounts have you enabled 2FA for?
- 1
- 2
- 3
- 4 or more

Q2. What is your age?

Q3. What is your gender?
- Male
- Female
- Non-binary/third gender
- Prefer not to say

Q4. What is your highest level of education?
- Some high school
- High school graduate
- Some college, no degree
- Associate's degree
- Bachelor's degree
- Master's degree
- Doctorate degree

Q5. Are you a:
- College student
- College faculty
- College staff
- None of the above

Q6. How tech-savvy are you?
- Not at all
- Somewhat
- Moderately
- Very
- Extremely

Q7. How long have you been using Two-Factor Authentication (2FA)?
- Less than 1 year
- 1–2 years
- More than 2 years

Q8. When you first enabled 2FA, why did you enable it?
- Mandated
- Incentivized
- Voluntary

Q9. How frequently do you log in with your 2FA authenticator?
- 1 or more times a day
- A few times per week
- A few times per month
- A few times per year

Q10.(1–3) Which accounts have you enabled 2FA for?

	Enabled	Not enabled	N/A
School account	☐	☐	☐
Workplace account	☐	☐	☐
Personal account	☐	☐	☐

Q11.(1–3) When you initially enabled 2FA, which two-factor authenticator(s) did you enable?

	Text message	Push	Phone Call	App Code	Security Key	N/A
School account	☐	☐	☐	☐	☐	☐
Workplace account	☐	☐	☐	☐	☐	☐
Personal account	☐	☐	☐	☐	☐	☐

Q12.(1–6) Do you agree or disagree with the following statements?

(a) Using my 2FA authenticator to login is mentally demanding (e.g. thinking, searching, deciding)

SD SWD N SWA SA
[] [] [] [] []

(b) Using my 2FA authenticator to login is physically demanding

SD SWD N SWA SA
[] [] [] [] []

(c) I feel rushed when having to use my 2FA authenticator to log in

SD SWD N SWA SA
[] [] [] [] []

(d) Using my 2FA authenticator to login to my account requires too much effort

SD SWD N SWA SA
[] [] [] [] []

(e) I feel annoyed when having to use my 2FA authenticator

SD SWD N SWA SA
[] [] [] [] []

(f) I have difficulty using my authenticator to log into my account

SD SWD N SWA SA
[] [] [] [] []

SD = Strongly disagree; SWD = Somewhat disagree; N = Neither agree nor disagree; SWA = Somewhat agree; SA = Strongly agree.

Q13. Why is using your 2FA authenticator to login mentally demanding?
Q14. Why is using your 2FA authenticator to log in physically demanding?
Q15. Why do you feel rushed when using your 2FA authenticator?

- Having to input the code before the countdown timer expires
- Other ________________

Q16. Why do you feel that having to use your 2FA authenticator to login requires too much effort?
Q17. What difficulty did you have with using your 2FA authenticator to log in?
Q18.(1–3) Can you recognize the IP address from the device you logged in from memory?

	Never	Rarely	Sometimes	Often	Always	N/A
Personal computer	☐	☐	☐	☐	☐	☐
Workplace computer	☐	☐	☐	☐	☐	☐
Personal Phone	☐	☐	☐	☐	☐	☐

Q19. Have you used the push authenticator?
- No
- Yes

Q20. Did you ever pay attention to the IP address, time, or location that is displayed?
- Never
- Rarely
- Sometimes
- Often
- Always

Q21. Have you ever been unable to access your account because of 2FA?
- No
- Yes

Q22. Why were you unable to access your account because of 2FA?
Q23. Have you ever canceled an authentication request?
- No
- Yes

Q24. Why did you cancel the authentication request?
- Did not have 2FA authenticator
- Mistake
- Other ________________

Q25. Have you ever not responded to an authentication request?
- No
- Yes

Q26. Why did you not respond to the authentication request?
- Did not have 2FA authenticator
- Other ________________

Q27. What do you dislike about 2FA?

References

1. Abbott, J., Patil, S.: How mandatory second factor affects the authentication user experience. In: Proceedings of the 2020 CHI Conference on Human Factors in Computing Systems, pp. 1–13 (2020)
2. Akanda, M.M.R.R., Lacy, A., Saxena, N.: SoK: inaccessible & insecure: an exposition of authentication challenges faced by blind and visually impaired users in state-of-the-art academic proposals. In: 34th USENIX Security Symposium (USENIX Security 2025), pp. 1393–1413 (2025)
3. Akanda, M.M.R.R., Mahdad, A.T., Saxena, N.: Broken access: on the challenges of screen reader assisted two-factor and passwordless authentication. In: Proceedings of the ACM on Web Conference 2025, pp. 1116–1128 (2025)
4. Amft, S., Ali, M., Preuveneers, D., Albayram, Y., Volkamer, M., Acar, Y.: "We've Disabled MFA for You": an evaluation of the security and usability of multi-factor authentication recovery deployments. In: Proceedings of the 2023 ACM SIGSAC Conference on Computer and Communications Security (CCS 2023), Copenhagen, Denmark, pp. 1380–1394. ACM (2023)
5. Arnold, D., et al.: The emotional impact of multi-factor authentication for university students. In: CHI Conference on Human Factors in Computing Systems Extended Abstracts, pp. 1–4 (2022)
6. Colnago, J., et al.: "It's not actually that horrible" exploring adoption of two-factor authentication at a university. In: Proceedings of the 2018 CHI Conference on Human Factors in Computing Systems, pp. 1–11 (2018)
7. Cybercrime Support Network: MFA Consumer Sentiment Report (2023). https://fightcybercrime.org/mfa-consumer-sentiment-report/. Accessed 19 Apr 2026
8. Das, A., Bonneau, J., Caesar, M., Borisov, N., Wang, X.: The tangled web of password reuse. In: NDSS. vol. 14, pp. 23–26 (2014)
9. Das, S., Kim, A., Jelen, B., Huber, L., Camp, L.J.: Non-inclusive online security: Older adults' experience with two-factor authentication. In: Proceedings of the 54th Hawaii International Conference on System Sciences (HICSS), pp. 5392–5401 (2021)
10. Das, S., Wang, B., Tingle, Z., Camp, L.J.: Evaluating user perception of multi-factor authentication: a systematic review. In: Proceedings of the Thirteenth International Symposium on Human Aspects of Information Security & Assurance (HAISA 2019) (2019)
11. Dutson, J., Allen, D., Eggett, D., Seamons, K.: Don't punish all of us: measuring user attitudes about two-factor authentication. In: 2019 IEEE European Symposium on Security and Privacy Workshops (EuroS&PW), pp. 119–128. IEEE (2019)
12. Farke, F.M., Lorenz, L., Schnitzler, T., Markert, P., Dürmuth, M.: "You still use the password after all"–exploring FIDO2 security keys in a small company. In: Sixteenth Symposium on Usable Privacy and Security (SOUPS 2020), pp. 19–35 (2020)
13. Ghorbani Lyastani, S., Bugiel, S., Backes, M.: A systematic study of the consistency of two-factor authentication user journeys on top-ranked websites. In: Network and Distributed System Security (NDSS) Symposium, p. 2023 (2023)
14. Golla, M., Ho, G., Lohmus, M., Pulluri, M., Redmiles, E.M.: Driving 2FA adoption at scale: Optimizing two-factor authentication notification design patterns. In: 30th USENIX Security Symposium (USENIX Security 2021), pp. 109–126 (2021)
15. Han, W., Li, Z., Ni, M., Gu, G., Xu, W.: Shadow attacks based on password reuses: a quantitative empirical analysis. IEEE Trans. Dependable Secure Comput. **15**(2), 309–320 (2016)

16. Markert, P., Lassak, L., Golla, M., Dürmuth, M.: Understanding users' interaction with login notifications. In: Proceedings of the 2024 CHI Conference on Human Factors in Computing Systems, pp. 1–17 (2024)
17. Marky, K., et al.: "Nah, it's just annoying!" a deep dive into user perceptions of two-factor authentication. ACM Trans. Comput.-Hum. Interact. **29**(5), 1–32 (2022)
18. Nanda, A., Jeong, J.J., Shah, S.W.A., Nosouhi, M., Doss, R.: Examining usable security features and user perceptions of physical authentication devices. Comput. Secur. **139**, 103664 (2024)
19. Nosenko, A., Cheng, Y., Chen, H.: Password and passphrase guessing with recurrent neural networks. Inf. Syst. Front. **25**(2), 549–565 (2023)
20. Owens, K., Anise, O., Krauss, A., Ur, B.: User perceptions of the usability and security of smartphones as FIDO2 roaming authenticators. In: Seventeenth Symposium on Usable Privacy and Security (SOUPS 2021), pp. 57–76 (2021)
21. Petsas, T., Tsirantonakis, G., Athanasopoulos, E., Ioannidis, S.: Two-factor authentication: is the world ready? Quantifying 2FA adoption. In: Proceedings of the Eighth European Workshop on System Security, pp. 1–7 (2015)
22. Stanton, B., Theofanos, M.F., Prettyman, S.S., Furman, S.: Security fatigue. IT Prof. **18**(5), 26–32 (2016)
23. Tetlay, A., Treharne, H., Ascroft, T., Moschoyiannis, S.: Lessons learnt from a 2FA roll out within a higher education organisation, arXiv preprint arXiv:2011.02901 (2020)
24. Turner, M., Schmitz, M., Bierey, M.M., Khamis, M., Marky, K.: Tangible 2FA-an in-the-wild investigation of user-defined tangibles for two-factor authentication. In: Nineteenth Symposium on Usable Privacy and Security (SOUPS 2023), pp. 245–261 (2023)
25. Zezschwitz, V., De Luca, E., Hussmann, A., H.: Survival of the shortest: a retrospective analysis of influencing factors on password composition. In: IFIP Conference on Human-Computer Interaction, pp. 460–467. Springer (2013)
26. Weidman, J., Grossklags, J.: I like it, but i hate it: employee perceptions towards an institutional transition to BYOD second-factor authentication. In: Proceedings of the 33rd Annual Computer Security Applications Conference, pp. 212–224 (2017)
27. Wiefling, S., Dürmuth, M., Lo Iacono, L.: More than just good passwords? A study on usability and security perceptions of risk-based authentication. In: Proceedings of the 36th Annual Computer Security Applications Conference, pp. 203–218 (2020)

Full-Stack Model Extraction: Evaluating System-Wide Stealing Attacks

William Hackett[1,2(✉)], Stefan Trawicki[1,2], Zhengxin Yu[1], Neeraj Suri[1], and Peter Garraghan[1,2]

[1] Lancaster University, Lancaster, UK
william.hackett@mindgard.ai
[2] Mindgard, London, UK

Abstract. Model extraction attacks are an insidious threat against Deep Learning (DL) models, enabling adversaries to steal the architecture, parameters, and hyper-parameters. Existing literature observes varying attack success, but the underlying causes for model susceptibility remain unclear due to analysis difficulty. In this paper, we provide a comprehensive empirical study of state-of-the-art extraction attacks using SWIPE, an AI security assessment framework. Through large-scale experimentation across a plethora of DL models and attack scenarios, our work establishes a new fundamental understanding of extraction attacks, drawing parallels to API and low-level side-channel attacks, exploring transferability, extraction equivalency, and staging. Our findings: (1) elucidate key extraction characteristics showing strong resilience in particular configurations, (2) demonstrate that even partial extraction success enables further attack staging, (3) show equivalent stolen models, despite expressive power differences, exhibit similar captured knowledge, and (4) identify model compilers as a sufficient defense technique.

Keywords: AI security · Model Extraction · Model Inversion

1 Introduction

Deep Learning (DL) is proliferating as a critical technology to support a growing diversity of applications. However, the successful deployment and execution of DL is threatened by cyber attacks within systems [2,14,22,42], compromising DL model integrity, privacy, and confidentiality [48]. A particularly damaging threat against DL models are *extraction attacks*. Extraction attacks occur when an adversary attempts to extract fundamental characteristics of a target DL model (architecture, parameters, hyper-parameters) [47,53] to reconstruct an identical or highly similar DL model [24]. Such attacks result in information leakage, IP theft, and enable further DL model attacks to be staged [22,46,53].

Extensive studies of extraction attacks have been conducted to understand and mitigate their impact [5,48]. However these studies have predominately been performed with isolated attacks, each leveraging distinctive threat models and deployment scenarios with different DL model types, datasets, and hardware

Y. Cao et al. (Eds.): SecureComm 2026, LNICST 704, pp. 48–75, 2027.
https://doi.org/10.1007/978-3-032-32764-2_3

platforms. Given that extraction attacks yield varying degrees of success when exposed to different model architectures and datasets [22,42,47,52], it is necessary to study extraction attacks across a multitude of deployment scenarios to determine whether there exist common associations between extraction attack success, DL model characteristics and platform hardware properties.

Attaining such knowledge is constrained by the high technical effort and time required to understand, implement and evaluate the large number of distinctive combinations of extraction attacks, platforms and DL model architectures in existence [23,28,35]. This is because current studies are bespokely designed to operate for a targeted or small sub-set of deployment scenarios (e.g. a single hardware platform or DL model architecture) [21,22,42]. Whilst this approach is effective to demonstrate extraction attack feasibility, it is not possible to study attack effectiveness and generalizability without extensive re-designing and engineering of attacks to operate within different operational scenarios [25,29,45].

In this paper, we explore extraction attacks across three distinct attack surfaces: Inference API, GPU side-channel, and CPU side-channel. Our work contributes fundamental new knowledge to the understanding of these attacks by establishing parallels to API and low-level side-channel attacks, by rigorously exploring attack transferability, extraction equivalency, and further attack staging. To achieve this, we present *SWIPE*: an adversarial threat assessment framework designed for the generalizable deployment of a large number of DL models, diverse attacks, and varied deployment environments. SWIPE's utility stems from three core capabilities: (1) Dynamic framework-independent model loading and training via transfer learning and curated AI deployment repositories; (2) Configuration of attacks, encapsulated as attack scenarios; and (3) Experiment automation for reliable recording and reporting.

We utilize our proposed framework to undergo an empirical analysis and evaluation of a large set of extraction scenarios across different state-of-the-art extraction attack types [21,22,36] exposed to various DL model architecture types and configurations. Furthermore, we demonstrate how rapid adversarial threat assessment can enable deeper understanding of extraction attacks, measuring extraction similarity, conducting further privacy-concerning model inversion attacks, and evaluate a state-of-the-art defense technique for deployed DL models [43]. Our research makes the following contributions:

- **SWIPE**: An end-to-end automated attack framework capable of executing extraction attack scenarios and detailed evaluation across a variety of model families, architectures, datasets, and hardware platforms (Sect. 5).
- **Key extraction characteristics**: Through extensive experimentation, we identify various key extraction attack characteristics that affect success spanning model architecture, dataset complexity, and hardware (Sect. 7).
- **Stolen model equivalency**: We identified that stolen models can achieve equivalent target performance and knowledge capture while retaining uniquely different DL characteristics (Sect. 8.2).

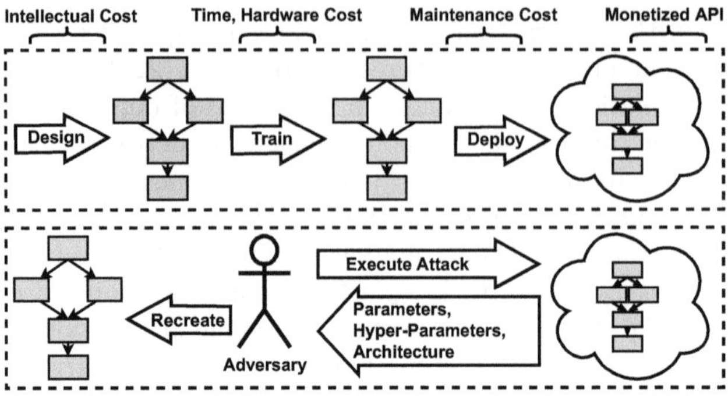

Fig. 1. Overview of extraction attack process.

- **Compilation-as-a-Defense**: We demonstrate the viability of using model compilers as a novel defense technique against side-channel attacks targeting model architecture characteristics (Sect. 8.3).

2 Background

2.1 Model Extraction

Model extraction, also known as *model stealing*, are a set of attacks that extract fundamental *characteristics* of a DL model: its architecture, parameters and hyper-parameters (Fig. 1). A *stolen model* is created using extraction techniques to collect information leakage (model characteristics) via access to a target DL model or its underlying DL system, and *recreating* a copy of the *target model* [22,47,53]. A stolen model can be used for further attacks [42] or designing a replica model with similar performance [42,53].

Extraction Techniques. DL models can be stolen across a wide range of attack surfaces. For instance, an adversary can perform inference API attacks by obtaining predictions on input feature vectors to train a local substitute model [42,51,52], or a side-channel attack by extracting information leakage from Peripheral Component Interconnect Express (PCIe) traffic. Many works have demonstrated that system operation (*i.e.*, timing, computation, cache) can be exploited to infer DL model operators to perform model extraction [21,22,47]. Based on *MITRE ATLAS*, attacks have different numbers of intermediate stages depending on their *tactics* and their enabling *techniques* [10]. (1) *Initial Access*, adversary prepares the environment such as deploying spy kernels and monitoring code [22,53]. (2) *Attack Staging*, preliminary attacks are launched to gather DL system and model information [22]. (3) *Exfiltration* of the information collected from the attack staging. [34,47,53].

Model Recreation. Recreation focuses on training a model, either uninitialized or pre-trained, that provides an architecture and weights [22,51] with the intention of replicating a target model by leveraging collected information leakage of DL model characteristics. Extracted target model characteristics can be acquired using a number of attacks, such as a training set created from synthetic or ground truth inputs paired with confidence values or labels gained from a prediction API attack [42,51,53]. It is feasible for sophisticated approaches using side-channels to observe DL system traffic to infer DL model characteristics [22,47,53]. Using gathered metrics, GPU kernels mappings and inference inputs and outputs enable the creation of a dataflow graph representing model architecture layout. Model recreation complexity varies due to the possible combinations of ML frameworks, compute libraries, model architectures, among other variables partially and unknown to an adversary when attacking a DL system.

Consequence. Failure to defend against extraction attacks can compromise the integrity, privacy and confidentiality of the DL system. System integrity can be compromised during attack preparation and execution, with potential backdoors created for future access [40]. Data privacy is degraded via stolen model characteristics being exploited to stage further attacks that extract training data information [18,42]. DL model confidentiality is compromised since adversaries have access to model characteristics, and can reverse engineer and steal confidential data, such as the training dataset.

2.2 Challenges in Model Extraction Research

In model extraction literature, studies have demonstrated the feasibility and practicality of extraction attacks against DL models [36,42,53]. However these studies are predominately performed with isolated attacks targeting one DL model characteristic, leveraging distinctive threat models, and bespoke deployment scenarios with different DL types [22,42,47,52]. This is problematic given the evolving DL landscape of extraction scenarios whereby current extraction attack implementations are obsolete when paired with state-of-the-art DL types [29,45], and DL systems [8,25].

From extraction attack literature, it is observable that extraction attacks yield varying degrees of success when exposed to different DL model types and datasets [42,53]. However, current extraction attacks lack the generalizability required to execute attacks across different extraction scenarios making exploring common associations challenging due to the technical effort required across heterogeneous software and hardware systems. Understanding the associations attributed to DL types, datasets, and deployment scenarios can greatly benefit the fundamental understanding towards varying extraction success observed in literature [22,42,47,52]. Therefore, given the vast amount of deployment scenarios, it is necessary to alleviate the limitations and systematically study the common associations in extraction attacks across a multitude of deployment scenarios, DL types, and datasets.

SWIPE targets the capability of an efficient and automated extraction attack framework able to deploy and evaluate DL model security across heterogeneous DL systems and extraction attack scenarios with design goals of: (1) *Generalizability*, providing a unified platform for the hardware and software used in DL system deployments, and for the attacks that target them. (2) *Configuration & Automation*, providing a machine independent system to define an attack scenario and deploy it for repeatable experimentation at scale.

3 Threat Model

The objective of a DL model is to map an input to a provided classification. Given an input, the model propagates through its operators to output a vector of probabilities denoting the confidence of classification associated to the input. The threat models underpinning extraction attacks within this paper are categorized into three aspects: *Model knowledge*, *DL System Environment knowledge* and access to the *Auxiliary dataset* [28].

Model Knowledge. We define two access types: *observed* (M_o) and *hidden* (M_h). With *observed* knowledge, the adversary has sufficient[1] access to the target architecture and parameters. In *hidden* knowledge, access is limited to API calls (queries and outputs), with attacks [17] often assuming the model architecture is known to build a shadow model. *Hidden* knowledge typically involves API-based access, common in Machine Learning as a Service (MLaaS), while *observed* knowledge includes leakage from gradients, bus snooping or side-channel attacks.

DL System Knowledge. Knowledge pertaining the DL system environment is used to infer target characteristics. Three types of knowledge are considered for the DL environment: *full* (S_f), *partial* (S_p), and *none* (S_n). Types denote the adversaries knowledge associated with the DL environment the target model is executing upon. This includes knowledge regarding the DL framework, GPU, and CPU devices. *Partial* knowledge of the environment enables an adversary to have direct or indirect knowledge about the DL environment, for example, knowing the type of CPU (Intel, AMD), or GPU (Nvidia, AMD). *None* states the adversary has no information regarding the DL environment, and encompasses scenarios whereby an adversary has no knowledge about the DL system.

Auxiliary Dataset. To construct an auxiliary dataset an adversary may require knowledge across dataset characteristics; Domain, heterogeneity, and dimensionality [3]. We consider three scenarios in decreasing order of adversarial "strength": (1) *Full* (D_f) where the attack has full knowledge of the target dataset. (2) *Partial* (D_p) - an adversary has some knowledge of target dataset and therefore can obtain or construct a similar dataset used by the target (e.g. via public knowledge, or staging previous attacks). (3) *None* (D_n) whereby the adversary has no information regarding the dataset. We assume the attacker has access to open source datasets commonly provided by DL libraries or online repositories for inference upon the target [11,30,49].

Considering the knowledge of the model, system environment, and auxiliary dataset, a total of 18 distinctive threat models are possible. We focus on two

[1] We use the term "sufficient", as some attacks only need partial model information to succeed [36].

scenarios in our paper: (M_h, S_n, D_p), and (M_o, S_p, D_n) which represent realistic settings with varying levels of attacker access [44].

4 Model Extraction Attacks

Our empirical study focuses on three critical areas of the system stack: Inference API, GPU Side-Channel, and CPU Side-Channel. This approach allows us to demonstrate the capabilities of SWIPE across these distinctly different layers and explore the interactions between high-level API and low-level system attack surfaces. Furthermore, we highlight the effectiveness of attack staging and the transferability of extracted models using a model inversion attack.

4.1 Inference API

In the context of Inference API, we examine KnockOff Nets (KON) [36], an extraction attack whereby an adversary queries a target model with data randomly sampled from the *auxiliary dataset* to steal the underlying model characteristics and recreate a stolen model. All predictions made by the target model are combined into a new *stolen dataset*, containing the previously queried samples and confidence values or label pairs. The stolen dataset is then used to reconstruct a stolen model via a training recreation technique, in which an untrained model of a similar architecture as the target is fine-tuned using the stolen dataset. The adversary's intention is for the stolen model to be equivalent when compared to the target model within the targets task achieving the desired similarity.

KnockOff Nets relies on the assumptions (M_h, S_n, D_p). The adversary has hidden knowledge of the target model and unrestricted access to the API, assuming no rate limiting or inference countermeasures. As the attack targets the model's API, the underlying DL system is abstracted away, requiring no knowledge of the system itself. Finally, the adversary is assumed to have partial auxiliary dataset knowledge regarding the target model's architecture and training dataset, which is used to establish the required datasets for the attack.

4.2 GPU Side-Channel

To study extraction attacks in GPU Side-Channel we select DeepSniffer (DS), an architectural extraction attack utilizing leaky information from the GPU to infer target model architecture [22]. This attack captures 4 kernel metrics during operator execution; *execution duration* (Exe_{Lat}), *read volume* (R_V), *write volume* (W_V), *and I/O output volume* (I_V/O_V), to understand the relationship between operators and variance of metrics. From this relationship, DeepSniffer can infer one of seven operators within a target model architecture; *Conv, ReLU, BN, Pool, Concat, Add, and FC kernels* via a pre-trained DL model trained upon previous examples leaked by the GPU, called the *DeepSniffer model.* There are two attack stages: (1) *Attack Staging*: Whereby DeepSniffer gathers required GPU metrics during target model execution. (2) *Exfiltration:* Using gathered data to undergo architecture prediction via a previously trained DeepSniffer model.

We make the following assumptions (M_o, S_p, D_n). The adversary is assumed to have partial knowledge of the DL system and the capability to access low-level system functionality. This includes capturing streams of memory and PCI metrics for CPU/GPU communication to infer kernel metrics via profiling tools like NVPROF [12]. Knowledge of the target model's ML framework is also required for attack staging. While the adversary must be capable of performing inferences, auxiliary dataset knowledge is not required because the focus of the attack is activating network operators, not the model's prediction.

4.3 CPU Side-Channel

DeepRecon (DR) [21] is a CPU side-channel extraction attack that gathers target model architecture information by using information leakage from a device's CPU L3 cache. DeepRecon extracts eight DL operators (*Conv, MatMul, Softmax, Relu, MaxPool, AveragePool, Merge & Bias*) by associating them with symbols from the target model framework binary and identify their execution by starting a co-located programme to monitor L3 cache. In the case of a CPU attack, Flush+Reload [50] is used to flush the CPUs L3 cache to observe which symbols repopulate the cache on the assumption that frequently occurring symbols belong to a target executing DL process. Dimensional reduction techniques, such as Principle Component Analysis (PCA), can then be used to cluster symbols during a model execution, enabling an adversary to infer the architecture of a model by comparing reduced dimensions to that of other known models.

DeepRecon leverages the assumptions (M_o, S_p, D_n). The adversary has observed model and partial DL system knowledge whereby it is known that targeted systems are vulnerable to Flush+Reload. Similarly to DS, auxiliary dataset knowledge is not required. It is assumed that: (1) An adversary is capable of launching co-located user-level processes on the target system. (2) The target and attacking processes use the same DL framework, to associate symbols with DL operators. (3) The adversary knows which CPU architecture is in use.

4.4 Further Attack Staging

To explore attack transferability, we study further attack staging upon extracted models by implementing MiFace, a model inversion attack by Fredrikson et al. [16]. Model inversion is a privacy-violating technique whereby an adversary seeks to reconstruct a representative input for each class, potentially leaking images associated with trained classes. The attack is performed via back-propagation over the stolen model's parameters for each class, optimising the input sample until the corresponding class output exceeds an established threshold.

MiFace leverages the assumptions (M_o, S_n, D_p). The adversary requires observed knowledge of the target model and the capability to perform prediction queries on specific feature vectors. No DL system environment knowledge is required, as MiFace only requires access to the model for inference. Furthermore, partial knowledge of model classes is necessary (e.g. knowing a facial recognition model responds to faces) to create an auxiliary dataset for input initialization values and attack execution.

5 Framework Design

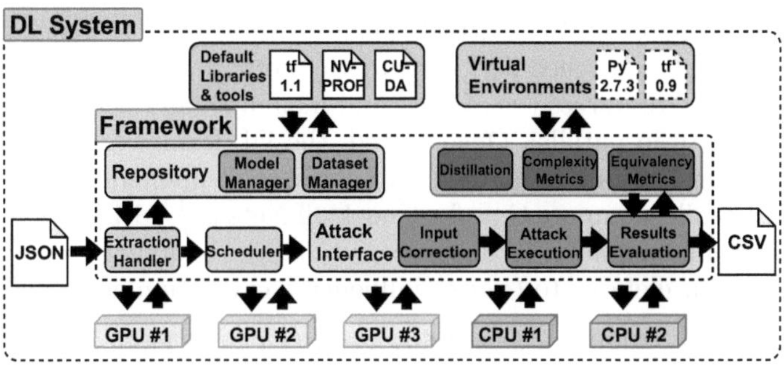

Fig. 2. Extraction framework system model.

The objective of SWIPE is to simplify and generalize the process of executing extraction attacks, facilitating the exploration of associations between attacks, DL model characteristics, and DL systems. The framework accomplishes this by generalizing model inputs, datasets and software environments, providing compatibility for the execution of attacks enabling readily reproducible configuration and automation of attack scenarios. Figure 2 depicts SWIPE and its four key components: *Extraction Handler*, *Repositories*, *Scheduler*, and *Attack Interface*.

Extraction Handler. We implement the pipeline software design pattern [4] by instantiating components required for an attack scenario and having unidirectional data flow, with the *extraction handler* being the pipeline orchestrator. Given large datasets and models are I/O and memory intensive to load and unload, the extraction handler requests the dataset and model managers to begin loading resources from disk immediately when executed to reduce pipeline latency. Additionally, software environments (libraries, frameworks, interpreters) are preemptively created for a given attack to execute within, either referencing software installed on the DL system, or through the use of virtual environments. Alternative Python library versions are created and accessed using *venv* [31], creating lightweight site directories isolated from the default system packages. Attacks with more complex dependencies and build processes, such as DeepRecon, are assigned and run in a containerized environment via docker.

Repositories. The repositories contain two managers. (1) *Dataset manager*, which handles the loading and standardization of datasets from both local and online repositories [15,30], processes essential metadata (e.g., number of classes, input dimensions), and ensures compatibility for efficient querying and preprocessing. (2) *Model manager*, which facilitates model loading and querying for target inference [7,15,30]. The model manager maintains a repository of pretrained DL models, standardizes inputs and outputs for attack processing, and supports model deployment as a server with automatic transfer learning [54] for adapting architectures or fine-tuning class subsets.

Scheduler. We enable multiple attack scenarios to be executed concurrently on a DL system through a scheduler. A heuristic method assesses the attacks, the currently available resources (*e.g.* GPUs and memory), and decides whether the attacks can be ran in parallel. Once agreed, the DL frameworks are configured to use the assigned resources and attack interfaces components instantiated for each attack. Parallel compute time for KnockOff Nets is $\frac{1}{n}$ with n GPUs installed in the DL system, compared to linear execution. Side-channel snooping attacks are not run in parallel due to (*noise*) influencing extraction accuracy.

Attack Interface. The *attack interface* creates a valid input configuration for executing a given attack scenario. As mentioned in Sect. 2.2, successful attack execution is highly dependent on input data being syntactically correct. The attack interface implements stub methods that manipulate the attack input from intermediate representations to the standard compatible for the attack depending on scenario. The interface wraps the attack execution calls, recording queries and responses or predicted architectures. The recorded results then enable results evaluation, analyzing and quantifying the effectiveness of the performed extraction attacks, such as calculating the extraction success and any similarity methods to provide a rigorous assessment of the attack outcome [32].

6 Experimental Setup

All experiments are defined as attack scenarios, characterized by their target model, system, dataset, and extraction attack, which are then processed and executed by the SWIPE (See Sect. 5).

6.1 Datasets

Experiments leveraged four datasets selected based on their complexity (class size, image size, number of channels) [28]: MNIST (60k/10k greyscale, 28×28, 10 classes [27]); CIFAR100 (50k/10k color, 32×32, 100 classes [26]); CelebA (200k greyscale faces, 218×178, 10,177 identities [49])—with a subset used for advanced attack staging (Sect. 7.4); and an ImageNet subset (80k/20k color, 224×224, 1000 classes [11]). Two types of datasets were used for evaluation: the *Query dataset* (inputs used to extract stolen labels, defining the query limit) and the *Testing dataset* (used to evaluate the final extraction fidelity).

6.2 Extraction Attacks

KnockOff Nets (KON). MNIST, CIFAR100, and ImageNet are used as query datasets. Stolen models were trained with an lr of 0.01 and batch size of 10 for 10, 20, and 100 epochs respectively. All inputs were resized to 224×224. To explore complexity, the impact of class size was tested using smaller dataset subsets across all architectures. Query dataset sizes for CIFAR and ImageNet were their maximum dataset size, while MNIST used a max of 10k queries.

DeepSniffer (DS). Kernel metrics were collected using NVPROF [12] during a single inference per model, which was repeated 25 times across the GTX 970, GTX 1080, and Tesla V100 GPUs, yielding 750 total results.

DeepRecon (DR). Target models were deployed in containerized environments using TensorFlow 1.10, or 2.10. Each model performed 10 inferences repeated 100 times, totaling 8,000 inferences per machine. Symbols were extracted using default threshold of 200. PCA was then used to fingerprint models via a trained KNN-classifier to predict depth, architecture, and family.

6.3 Target Systems and Model Configuration

Experiments were conducted on multiple hardware platforms to test both hardware independent and hardware dependent attacks. KON, being hardware independent, was evaluated on a Nvidia TESLA V100 and an Intel Xeon Gold 5218. Side-channel attacks (DS, DR) were extensively studied across three Nvidia GPUs (V100, GTX 1080, GTX 970, covering Maxwell, Pascal, and Tesla architectures) and four Intel CPUs (i5-3470, i7-3770k, i7-4770, i7-6850k—spanning 3rd to 6th Gen and 6MB to 15MB cache sizes). All systems ran Ubuntu 20.04.2 with CUDA 11.3, utilizing PyTorch 1.11.0 and TensorFlow 1.10.0/2.10.0.

We target 21 diverse DL model architectures trained across three datasets (Sect. 6.1), with a CelebA target dedicated to studying advanced attack staging (see Appendix Table 2). The selected architectures ensure diversity in parameter size, model family, and usage in image classification literature, covering models from convolutional to transformer architectures [13,29,38]. Target models were acquired either from online repositories (TorchVision for KON/DS [30], Keras for DR [7]) using pre-trained ImageNet weights, or locally trained. MNIST and CIFAR target models were created via a transfer learning where pre-trained ImageNet models were fine-tuned. Training was done using a v100 GPU [8] with a batch size of 10, cross-entropy loss, and a learning rate (lr) of 0.01. Following established literature [26,27], models were trained for 3 epochs (MNIST) and 40 epochs (CIFAR).

6.4 Evaluation Metrics

Extraction success is primarily measured by extraction *fidelity* [36,42], which compares the characteristics of the stolen and original models (e.g., Top-1 accuracy for KON, or architecture prediction for DS/DR). Additional metrics captured include query amount (KON), GPU kernel metrics (DS), and L2 cache

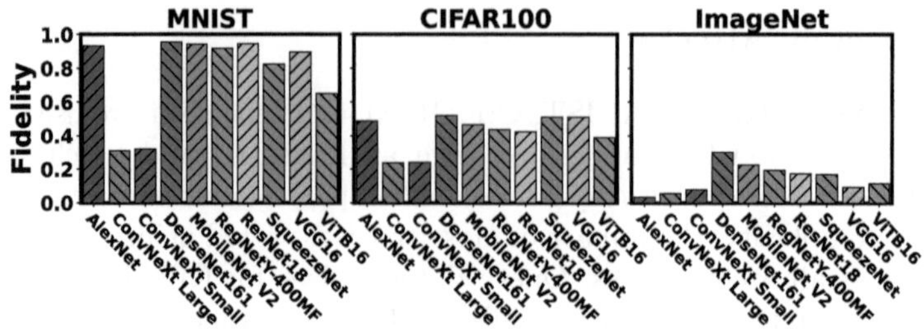

Fig. 3. KnockOff Nets extraction results. Extraction success across architectures and datasets. CSG: MNIST (7.54), CIFAR100 (79.67), ImageNet (648.99).

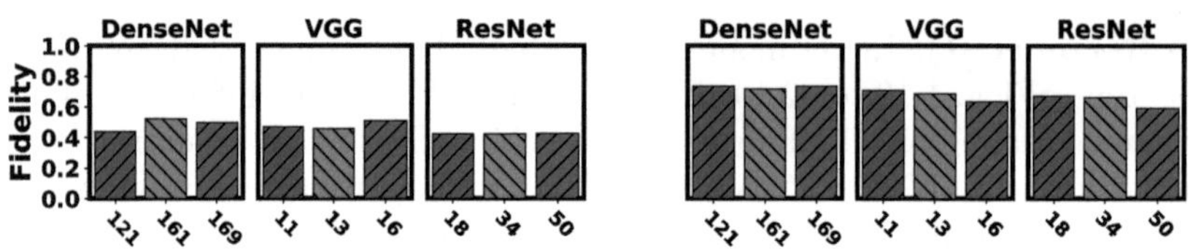

(a) KnockOff Nets

(b) DeepSniffer

Fig. 4. Architecture family depth comparison. Fidelity variance with models of different depths/parameters using same model architecture family.

hits (DR). Complexity was quantified using two methods: Dataset complexity was measured by the Cumulative Spectral Gradient (CSG) method [3], which projects extracted features into lower dimensions to calculate class overlap via a Monte Carlo approach (higher CSG indicating greater complexity).[2] Architecture complexity was computed using the Multiply-Add (MAdd) method [41], which calculates the total number of multiplication operations by evaluating the sizes of operator feature maps within the deep learning model.

7 Empirical Evaluation

7.1 Inference API

KnockOff Nets exhibited varying success across different target model and dataset combinations as shown in Fig. 3, with DenseNet161 achieving highest overall success in MNIST (0.95), CIFAR100 (0.52) and ImageNet (0.29).

Model Architecture. We observed that target models (AlexNet, DenseNet161, VGG16) leveraging more conventional CNN architecture achieved higher success. In contrast, state-of-the-art target model architectures (ConvNeXt Small,

[2] We note that CSG does not scale well to datasets with varying class sizes and draw parallels to this in our evaluation.

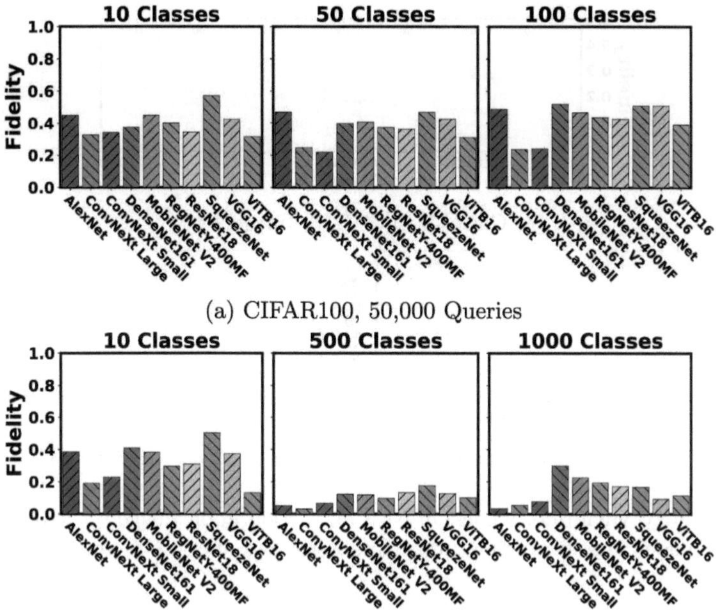

(a) CIFAR100, 50,000 Queries

(b) ImageNet, 80,000 Queries

Fig. 5. KnockOff Nets fidelity impact with varying target class sizes. CIFAR100, and ImageNet targets reduced to various class sizes.

ViTB16, RegNetY-400MF) reported lower overall success, with the ConvNeXt family of models exhibiting the lowest fidelity (0.08–0.36). As shown in Fig. 4a, we determined that the number of architecture layers for target model family had minor impact, with minimal variation in extraction fidelity across families. Such architectures exhibit exceedingly complex high amount of trainable parameters and MAdd (see Appendix Table 2). Therefore, successfully extracting target models via attacks requiring exact architecture knowledge (such as KON) are increasingly difficult for models with large training requirements (queries and time). Such findings indicate that using complex architectures can intrinsically hinder adversary success without considerable effort, similarly to security methods that attempt to exceed adversary effort as a deterrent [48].

Dataset Complexity. Dataset complexity emerged as a strong determinant of attack success. Target models using MNIST (CSG of 7.54), the least complex dataset, exhibited the highest attack success, with multiple architectures reporting fidelity over 0.9. ImageNet (CSG of 648.99) indicated the lowest success, ranging between 0.03 and 0.29 (Fig. 3), supporting findings that increased complexity hinders class generalization and leads to overfitting, reducing extraction success [28,33]. While the CSG measurement is sensitive to varying class sizes, we observed the impact of class sizes on effectiveness (Fig. 5): reducing the class size of a DenseNet161 model trained on ImageNet from 1,000 to 10 resulted

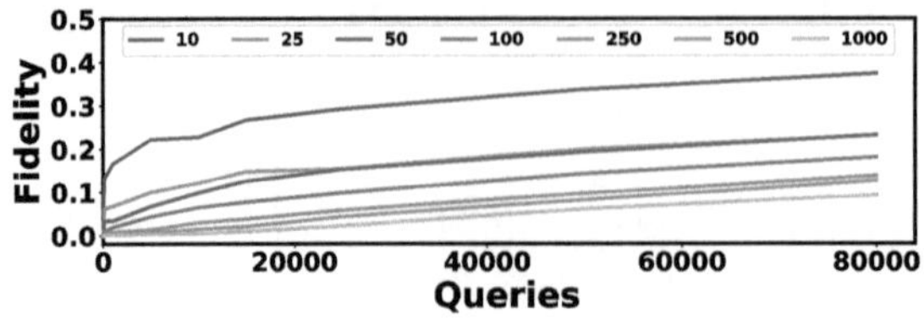

(a) Class size (VGG16, ImageNet)

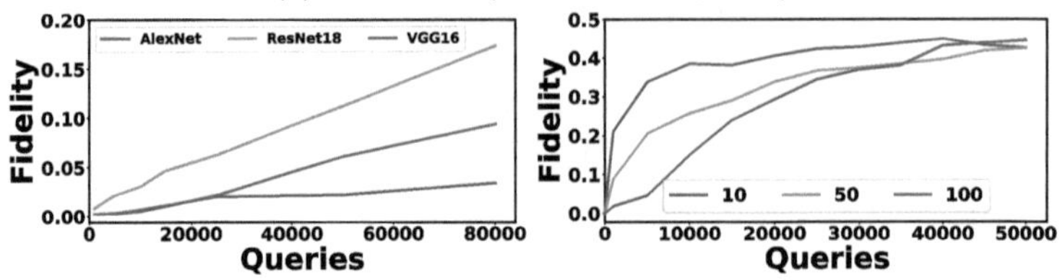

(b) Models (1000 classes) (c) Class size (VGG16, CIFAR100)

Fig. 6. Fidelity variance. KnockOff Nets extraction upon ImageNet and CIFAR100 across DL model various architectures, class sizes, and query amounts.

in increased extraction success from 0.29 to 0.41. Furthermore, Figs. 6a and 6c highlight that smaller class sizes produce higher fidelity with fewer queries and that our CIFAR100 fidelity converged.

Query Amount. As provided in Fig. 3, we found across all target models, the number of queries launched [10,000, 50,000, 80,000] for MNIST, CIFAR100, and ImageNet, respectively exhibited the highest impact on attack success whereby datasets of less complexity are stolen quicker. Given the training recreation technique used within KON, whereby more training data would lead (in moderation) to higher success due to greater learning generalization and diversity of data as shown in Fig. 6b, also reported in [28]. Architectures and datasets of higher complexities, such as ConvNeXt upon ImageNet, require larger amount of queries for adequate extraction success.

7.2 GPU Side-Channel

DeepSniffer also exhibited varying attack success across all evaluated architectures but also DL environments, with ResNet18 achieving the highest success for GTX 970 (0.68) and GTX 1080 (0.69), and SqueezeNet within Tesla V100 (0.76). We determined that extraction attack success was influenced by three main factors; model architecture, ML framework, and GPU architecture.

Model Architecture. Model architecture significantly influenced attack success (Fig. 7). While DeepSniffer (DS) achieved high fidelity against conventional CNNs (ResNet, VGG), it was ineffective when applied to newer models like ConvNeXt and ViTB16. These architectures implement novel components such as Gaussian Error Linear Units (GELU) [19] (replacing ReLU) and Transformer operators [45] therefore introduce operators and network designs [13,29] that

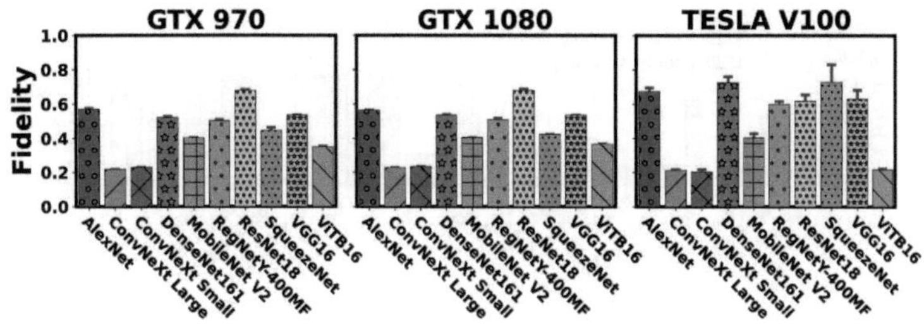

Fig. 7. DeepSniffer Extraction Success. Fidelity across various GPU devices and ImageNet targets.

cannot be correctly transformed into the dimensions recognized by DeepSniffer, which is inherently limited to CNN operators [22]. Conversely, RegNet, despite its new design paradigm [38], uses only traditional operators and achieves better success. Moreover, Fig. 4b demonstrates that models with more layers (depth) within the VGG and ResNet families consistently resulted in reduced fidelity due to the increased number of operators and higher likelihood of layer misclassification and more noise.

ML Framework. DS was ineffective when targeting models using TensorFlow (TF), regardless of the target architecture. Analysis of profiled data between PyTorch and TF revealed that TF generated a higher number of captured operations and distinct kernel calls. This unexpected increase in profiled operations introduced noise, causing the DeepSniffer (DS) classifier to predict architectures of incorrect length. This noise can be attributed to low-level framework optimizations during kernel execution in TF compared to PyTorch. This demonstrates that DeepSniffer is framework-specific indicating that extraction requires distinct training datasets for different frameworks to generalize the attack, thereby necessitating refinement of the threat model to incorporate adversary knowledge of the system framework (See Appendix Table 5).

GPU Architecture. GPU architecture significantly impacts attack success, as evidenced by the substantive variance observed across devices (Fig. 7). While the GTX 970 and GTX 1080 exhibited similar trends with only slight variation, all tested GPUs demonstrated a clear extraction ineffectiveness when targeting modern architectures like ConvNeXt and ViTB16. Specifically, ConvNeXt Small and ConvNeXt Large consistently showed low attack success (0.21–0.23) across all devices. This indicates that architectural susceptibility to the attack is strongly dependent on the GPU device. These hardware differences directly affect the information leakage gathered by NVPROF, as low-level optimizations and floating-point precision vary between GPUs, causing substantial changes in recorded kernel metrics (e.g., execution duration, read/write volume).

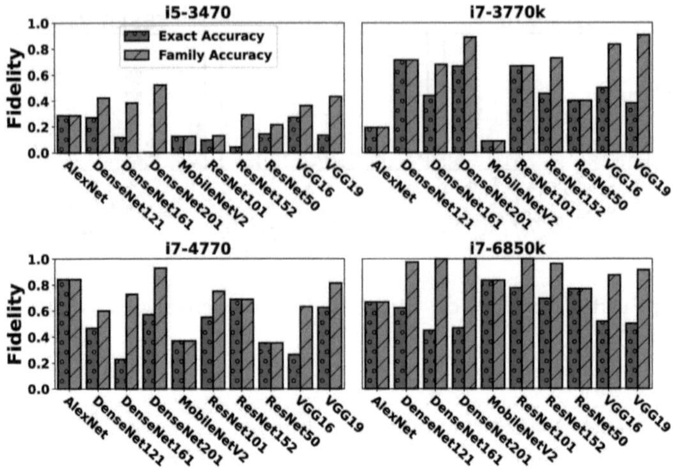

Fig. 8. **DeepRecon Model Family and Architecture Prediction Success.**

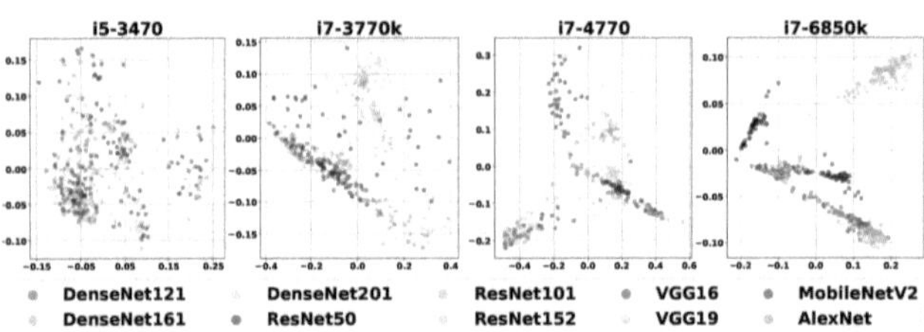

(a) TensorFlow 1.10

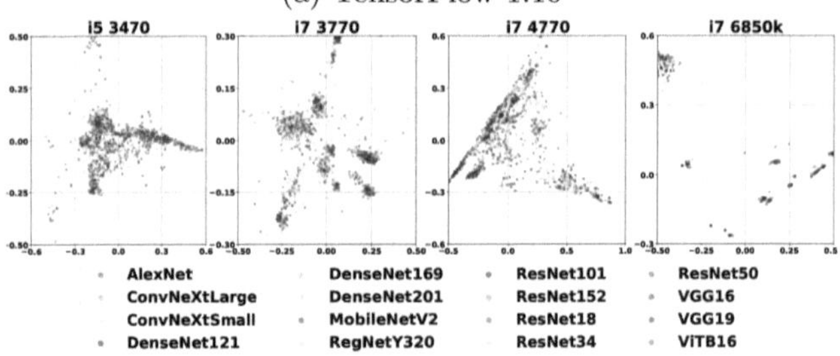

(b) TensorFlow 2.10

Fig. 9. **DeepRecon PCA Clustering of Cached Operators.** PCA for 26,000 DeepRecon inferences (16 models, 4 CPUs, 2 TF releases). Clustering denotes models with similar proportions of cached operators (reduced from 8 symbols to 2 dimensions). Clearer clustering indicates similar caching behavior.

7.3 CPU-Side Channel

DeepRecon (DR) demonstrated varying success across the hardware platforms evaluated (Fig. 8). We highlight three areas which influenced extraction attack success; CPU architecture, model architecture, and TensorFlow framework.

CPU Architecture. We observed that higher performance CPUs were more vulnerable to DR, with i7-6850k achieving the highest average family classification accuracy (0.836), and i5-3470 lowest (0.316). We attribute this to cache policies and older CPUs being less responsive to timings of Flush+Reload– e.g. i5-3470 generating large but disparate symbol logs leading to a disturbed PCA result (Fig. 9a). Figure 8 highlights that higher performance CPUs (i7-3770k, i7-4770, i7-6850k) reported a higher effectiveness in exact and family fingerprinting compared to i5-3470. Finally, findings show cache size does not influence results, as Hong *et al.* [21] evaluated with a Gen4. 4MB CPU successfully, smaller than all our tested CPU caches (See Sect. 6.3).

Model Architecture & Family. As shown in Fig. 9, target models within families possessing distinct operator traits (e.g. residual operators in ResNet, dense blocks in DenseNet) were successfully fingerprinted, but often misclassified individually while showing high success within their family. Across all machines, DenseNet exact classification never exceeded 0.518 for any depth (121: 0.518, 161: 0.307, 201: 0.426), yet family classification averaged 0.835, with similar results seen in VGG (see Appendix Table 4). This indicates that families with homogeneous operators build strong, identifiable fingerprints, but using this to train classifiers for specific depths is insufficient.

TensorFlow (TF) Framework. TF 2.10 displayed a general decrease in exact and family classification compared to TF 1.10 (See Appendix Fig. 13). Fidelity decreased across i5-3470, i7-4770 & i7-6850k systems while i7-3770k performed unexpectedly well with high fidelity on ConvNeXt Small/Large, RegNetY320, and ViTB16. We attribute this to the missing MatMul operator decreasing the reducible dimensions for component analysis.

7.4 Further Attack Staging

Extraction attacks have been identified as a means to stage further attacks [22, 46, 53], therefore, we conduct a case study to explore attack transferability using a stolen model to stage a privacy concerning model inversion attack.

Setup. To explore attack transferability scenario two target models—a 3-layer architecture for MNIST and a 4-layer architecture for CelebA are first stolen by the KON attack. The resulting stolen model is then exposed to the MiFace model inversion attack [16] to generate images representative of the target model's classes. The MiFace attack is executed on the stolen model across various query amounts (100 to 10,000 for MNIST; 1,000 to 35,000 for CelebA) to measure inversion success variance. Consistent with the threat model (Sect. 3), the adversary leverages an auxiliary dataset and partial knowledge to use representative images (written numbers for MNIST, random faces for CelebA) for image initialization [16, 18]. Inversion success is evaluated by comparing images generated from the stolen model against those generated by the target model.

Inversion Success. Figure 10 highlights that even with partial extraction success (0.83 and 0.95), MiFace generated features comparable to the target model.

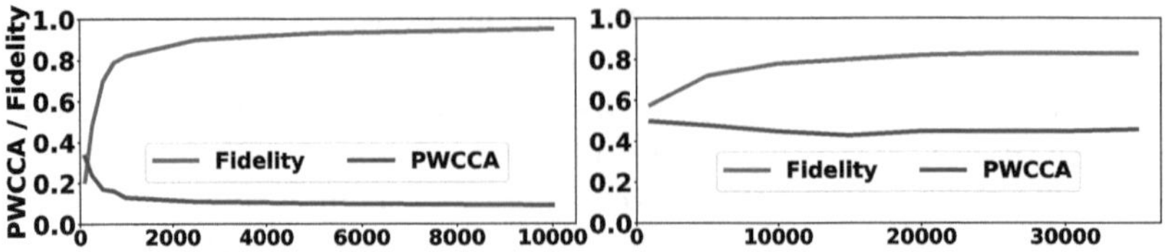

(a) MNIST PWCCA vs Fidelity (b) CelebA PWCCA vs Fidelity

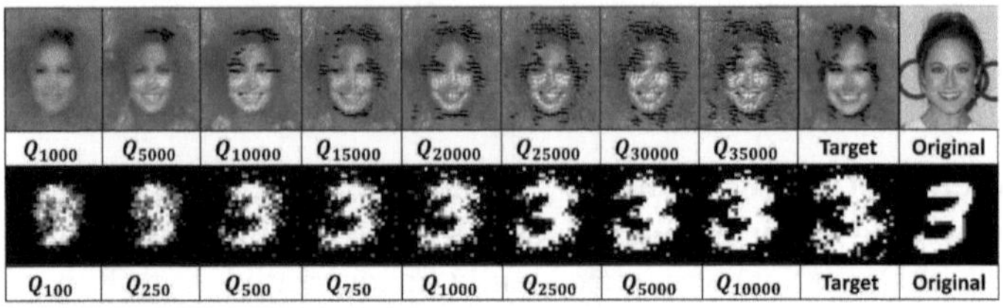

(c) Model Inversion Results, CelebA (Top), MNIST (Bottom)

Fig. 10. Model inversion upon stolen models. Stolen models across varying KON query amounts (Q_n) evaluated against target model, and original image.

Specifically, class features such as shape are captured with a high degree of accuracy. For example, the CelebA inversion successfully captured dataset-specific features—including face shape, eye, and mouth positioning—which align with the actual class image (Fig. 10). These captured features provide the adversary with additional knowledge, which can be leveraged to further augment the model inversion attack or tune the subsequent extraction queries. Predictably, dataset complexity affects inversion success: a less complex dataset like MNIST yields highly similar images, whereas CelebA introduces more noise due to its granular greyscale features and greater internal distinctiveness [27,49].

Extraction Sensitivity. MiFace demonstrates that successful model inversion is achieved with low query amounts, though fidelity varies by dataset complexity (Fig. 10c). We found a high contrast in query needs: MNIST established clear class features at 500 queries, while CelebA required 10,000 queries for similar progress. Interestingly, the CelebA stolen model displayed fidelity convergence beyond 25,000 queries, yet continued to produce visibly different model inversion results without a corresponding fidelity increase.

Architecture Similarity. To measure the similarity between target and stolen models, we applied Projection Weighted Canonical Correlation Analysis (PWCCA) [32] that calculates the distance between the activation layers of two models during inference (Figs. 10a and 10b). We observed increased queries for MNIST resulted in higher fidelity and PWCCA distance to decrease, denoting high similarity. CelebA also follows this trend until 15,000 queries where the PWCCA distance was lowest, however additional queries increase PWCCA distance despite increased fidelity. We suspect this is due to training being a high dimensional optimization problem, with high numbers of *Local Optimum*, causing large parameter space, achieving similar fidelity and accuracy due to similar outputs but exhibiting high PWCCA distance [1].

8 Discussion

8.1 Key Extraction Characteristics

We identified multiple characteristics influencing extraction success (Sect. 7), each exhibiting a particular affinity for certain techniques (e.g., dataset complexity for KON, hardware for DS/DR). Crucially, differences in model architecture directly altered the success of all evaluated attacks. It is therefore apparent that DL models exhibit varying degrees of architectural resistance against specific extraction attacks. We suspect this phenomenon extends to other types of DL model attacks. Further study of this architectural resistance would enable researchers to more effectively explain commonalities between attacks in complex networked systems, and allow practitioners to focus engineering efforts (validation, countermeasures, design) on securing DL models against attacks with the highest likelihood of success based on their target architecture.

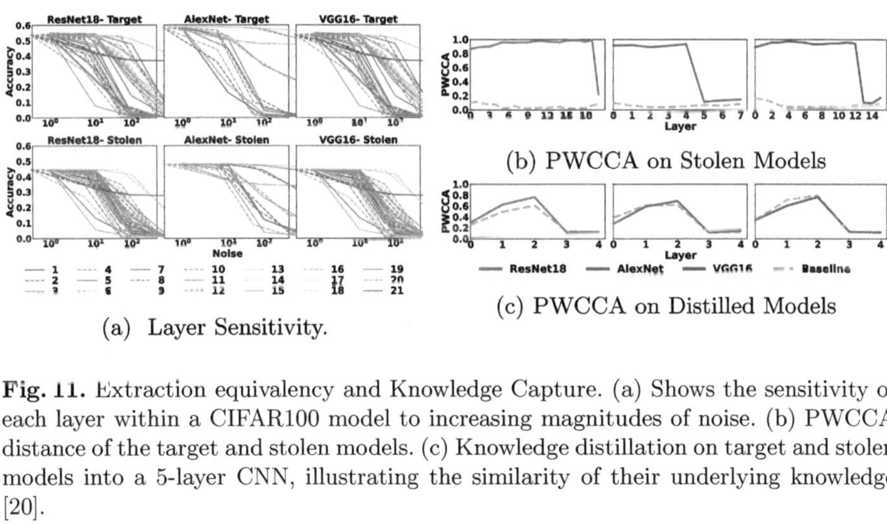

(a) Layer Sensitivity.

(b) PWCCA on Stolen Models

(c) PWCCA on Distilled Models

Fig. 11. Extraction equivalency and Knowledge Capture. (a) Shows the sensitivity of each layer within a CIFAR100 model to increasing magnitudes of noise. (b) PWCCA distance of the target and stolen models. (c) Knowledge distillation on target and stolen models into a 5-layer CNN, illustrating the similarity of their underlying knowledge [20].

8.2 Extraction Equivalency

Further Attack Staging & Metric Divergence. Experiments in Sect. 7.4 demonstrated strong attack transferability within stolen models, showing that even partially successful extraction can be leveraged to stage further attacks, such as model inversion, to attain reasonable success (0.7+ fidelity). While less complex datasets like MNIST yield clear features, the inversion attack successfully extracted privacy-sensitive features like face shape and gender from complex datasets like CelebA (Fig. 10). The ability to extract such features is highly concerning for facial recognition models, as it allows an adversary to reverse engineer classes to expose images associated with real-world people [16,18]. This success occurs despite high-dimensional optimization causing Fidelity and PWCCA to diverge (See Sect. 7.4). Stolen models can achieve equivalent performance and knowledge capture while retaining uniquely different DL characteristics. This divergence indicates the need for new similarity measurements to better understand attack success and inform the creation of countermeasures.

Expressive Power of Models. We analyzed the expressiveness of both the target and stolen models by comparing their accuracy degradation against increasing magnitudes of noise [39] (See Fig. 11a). Consistent with existing methods, stolen models demonstrated greater sensitivity in their lower (initial) layer weights. However, the target and stolen models exhibited different sensitivity patterns across the majority of the network layers, highlighting how fundamentally the models have learned and structured knowledge differently. Further understanding these differences in expressiveness would provide crucial foresight for developing adversarial defenses and securing DL models by illustrating how stolen models adapt target knowledge into their own unique expressive structure.

Knowledge Capture. The extent of knowledge capture between the target and stolen models was explored by utilizing Knowledge Distillation (KD) [20] to transfer their extracted knowledge into smaller distilled models, whose representation similarities were then measured using the PWCCA distance. Experimental results indicate a significant similarity in captured knowledge: after distilling the target and stolen models of three DNNs into smaller 5-layer CNNs (Appendix A), the PWCCA distance of the distilled models (Fig. 11c) is drastically lower compared to the original models (Fig. 11b). This result strongly suggests that stolen models are capable of capturing essential knowledge contained within a target model, even though their expressive structures may differ (Fig. 11a).

8.3 Model Compilation as a Defense

Throughout the paper we identify model architecture as a key characteristic influencing extraction success (Sect. 8.1). Therefore, to confirm this, we use *Compilation as a Defense*, which uses model compilers (nvFuser [9], TorchInductor [37], and TVM [6]) to alter the underlying model architecture, therefore limiting extraction success [43]. Fundamentally, these compilers employ optimization techniques, such as graph-level optimization, operator fusing, and convolution combination, which directly impact model architecture and execution on hardware [6,9,37]. We evaluate the effectiveness of this defense by empirically testing DeepSniffer against 7 model architectures across 3 different compilers, measuring extraction success relative to the original (non-optimized) PyTorch model.

Defense Effectiveness. Figure 12 demonstrates that model compilers successfully limited DS extraction success in the majority of scenarios. TVM exhibited

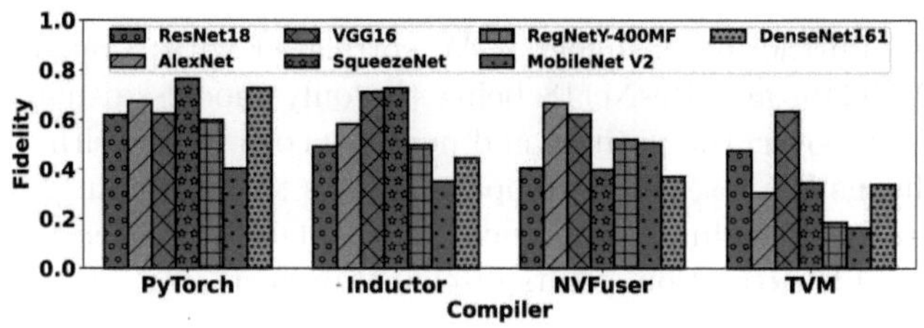

Fig. 12. Compilation-as-a-Defense. DeepSniffer fidelity across architectures and compilers vs. baseline PyTorch model.

Table 1. Correlation of DeepSniffer Kernel Metrics & Compiler Defense Effectiveness. Correlation matrix for kernel metrics (R/W derived from read/write), alongside the most effective Compiler as a Defense.

Architecture	Samples	Reads	Writes	Duration	R/W	Best Compiler	
						Name	Reduction
ResNet18	0.754	-0.082	0.378	0.570	-0.393	nvFuser	34.8%
Alexnet	-0.997	0.976	-0.985	0.976	0.976	TVM	54.8%
VGG16	0.328	-0.319	0.476	-0.138	-0.505	nvFuser	0.01%
SqueezeNet	-0.118	0.644	0.565	0.634	0.602	TVM	54.9%
RegNetY-400MF	-0.939	0.998	-0.998	0.989	0.998	TVM	69.0%
MobileNetV2	-0.998	-0.712	-0.587	0.280	0.630	TVM	59.4%
DenseNet161	-0.430	-0.676	-0.823	0.751	0.777	TVM	53.5%

the highest effectiveness, lowering extraction fidelity on average by 44.75%, followed by nvFuser 17.30% and TorchInductor 13.38%. Notably, VGG16 showed no reduction in success, and TorchInductor made this target more susceptible. The variance in effectiveness is directly due to compilers altering the DL model's execution characteristics, specifically the number of kernel samples, reads, writes, and duration (See Appendix Table 7). Changes in graph-level optimizations, kernel-level read/write counts, and execution duration all directly alter the effectiveness of the DS attack. The overall success of these compilers corroborates the feasibility of defending against side-channel extraction attacks by leveraging different compiler optimization techniques. However, it is important to note that future extraction attacks may transition beyond targeting a single type of fundamental DL model characteristic.

Kernel Metric Correlation. We observed that defense success was dependent on the selected model architecture and compiler pairing, therefore to attain a better understanding we compute the correlation coefficient in relation to defense success. We observe in Table 1 that increased kernel duration leads to higher defense success across 6 out of 7 architectures, VGG16 was the only model not to have significant duration increase, and interestingly, ResNet18 exhibited higher duration upon nvFuser thus achieving better defense success paired with that compiler. Furthermore, higher R/W correlated with 5 out of 7 architectures, with VGG16, and ResNet18 being the only models displaying negative correlations. Moreover, the positive and negative correlation within the number of samples affirms DS is sensitive to optimizations that alter the amount of kernel operators executed during inference, and explains why TensorFlow models produced unusable extraction results discussed in Sect. 7.2.

9 Conclusion

In this paper we have conducted an empirical study of extraction attacks against DL models. Utilizing SWIPE to rapidly design, deploy, and analyze a large number of extraction attack scenarios, we have conducted an analysis of extraction effectiveness against different DL systems. We identify key insights into the extraction attacks: We have (1) uncovered extraction characteristics whereby specific model configurations exhibit strong resilience to different attacks; (2) stolen models exhibit equivalent functionality with fundamentally different model characteristics and expressive power; (3) demonstrated even partial extraction success enables staging of further privacy attacks; and (4) highlighted the viability of model compilers as a defense to defend against low level side-channel extraction attacks. We hope that these findings will aid researchers and practitioners within the AI/ML security communities to better understand the nature of extraction attacks, as well the creation of future defenses.

A Appendix

(See Tables 3 and 6)

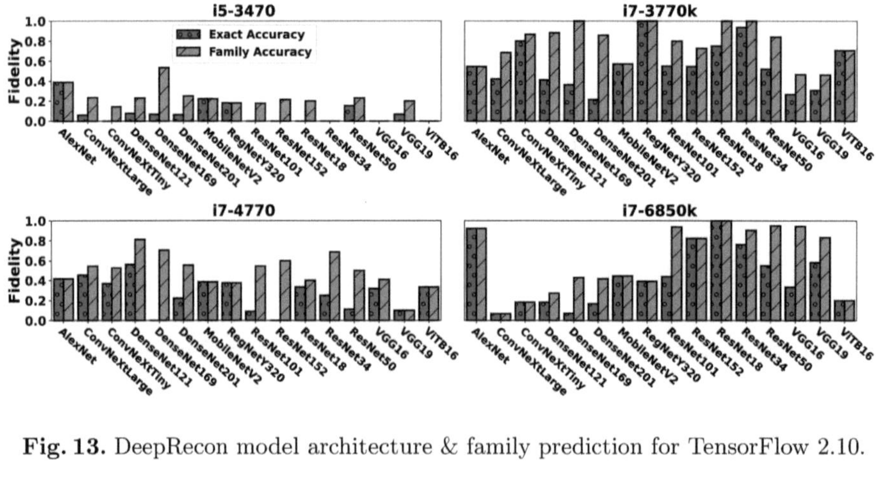

Fig. 13. DeepRecon model architecture & family prediction for TensorFlow 2.10.

Table 2. Evaluated model architectures. (KON = KnockOff Nets, DS = DeepSniffer, DR = DeepRecon).

Name	Family	Parameters	GMAdd	KON	DS	DR
Alexnet	-	61.10 m	0.72	Y	Y	Y
ConvNeXt_Small	ConvNeXt	50.21 m	8.70	Y	Y	Y
ConvNeXt_Large		197.74 m	34.40	Y	Y	Y
DenseNet121	DenseNet	7.99 m	2.88	Y	Y	Y
DenseNet161		28.68 m	7.82	Y	Y	Y
DenseNet169		14.14 m	3.42	Y	Y	N
DenseNet201		20.01 m	4.37	N	N	Y
ResNet18	ResNet	11.68 m	1.82	Y	Y	N
ResNet34		21.79 m	3.68	Y	Y	N
ResNet50		25.55 m	4.12	Y	Y	N
ResNet101		44.55 m	7.85	N	N	Y
ResNet152		60.19 m	11.58	N	N	Y
VGG11	VGG	132.86 m	7.63	Y	Y	N
VGG13		133.04 m	11.34	Y	Y	N
VGG16		138.358 m	15.50	Y	Y	Y
VGG19		143.67 m	19.67	N	N	Y
RegNetY-400MF	-	4.344 m	0.41	Y	Y	N
SqueezeNet	-	1.248 m	0.83	Y	Y	N
ViTB16	-	86.568 m	11.28	Y	Y	Y
MobileNetV2	-	3.50 m	0.32	Y	Y	Y
InceptionV3	-	27.161 m	2.85	N	N	Y

Table 3. Hardware platforms evaluated against the DeepRecon side-channel attack, and PCA feature prevalence. Well-fingerprinted systems i7-4770 and i7-6850k closely align on the most prevalent features (*Conv*, *Merge*, *ReLU*).

System	Cache (MB)		Feature Prevalence								Simplified
			convs	fcs	softms	**relus**	mpool	apool	merge	bias	
i5-3470	4	X	0.0003	−0.1643	−0.0583	0.6807	−0.6021	0.3475	−0.069	−0.1340	relus>mpool>apool
		Y	−0.0004	−0.4484	0.3590	−0.4292	−0.0839	0.5101	0.373	−0.2805	apool>relus>fcs
i7-4770	8	X	−0.8412	0.0808	0.0776	0.0119	0.0625	0.1082	0.5136	−0.0136	convs>merge>apool
		Y	0.3603	−0.0684	−0.0680	−0.6455	−0.0605	−0.0983	0.6524	−0.0718	merge>relus>convs
i7-6850k	15	X	−0.7878	−0.0029	−0.0038	0.5642	−0.0054	0.0044	0.2462	−0.0148	convs>relus>merge
		Y	−0.1529	0.0051	0.0001	−0.5671	−0.0118	−0.0081	0.8060	−0.0712	merge>relus>convs

Table 4. DeepRecon Average Results Across Models. Includes results collected across all runs and hardware.

Model	Average Exact Accuracy Across All Hardware (1 d.p.)	Family	Average Family Accuracy Across All Hardware (1 d.p.)	Hardware Average Family Accuracy (1 d.p.)			
				i5-3470	i7-3770k	i7-4770	i7-6850k
AlexNet	0.50	AlexNet	0.50	0.29	0.19	**0.84**	0.67
DenseNet121	0.52	DenseNet	0.84	0.52	0.89	0.93	**1.0**
DenseNet161	0.31						
DenseNet201	0.43						
MobileNetV2	0.35	MobileNet	0.35	0.13	0.09	0.37	**0.83**
ResNet50	0.42	ResNet	0.43	0.21	0.40	0.35	**0.77**
ResNet101	0.52						
ResNet152	0.47						
VGG16	0.39	VGG	0.77	0.43	0.91	0.81	**0.91**
VGG19	0.41						

Table 5. DeepSniffer Framework Comparison PyTorch vs TensorFlow. Recorded fidelity between actual and predicted architecture from PyTorch and TensorFlow frameworks. TensorFlow returns unusable results.

Name	PyTorch	TensorFlow
VGG16	0.62	−28.76
MobileNet_V2	0.40	−3.76
ResNet50	0.57	−6.96
Inception_V3	0.13	−10.56

Table 6. Distillation Accuracy Results. Accuracy scores based on CIFAR100 test set upon original, distilled target and stolen models.

Name	Target	Stolen	Distilled Target	Distilled Stolen
ResNet18	0.54	0.45	0.35	0.36
AlexNet	0.59	0.48	0.36	0.35
VGG16	0.61	0.44	0.36	0.35

Table 7. DeepSniffer Collected Metrics Averaged Across 25 Experiments and Three Model Compilers. Four recorded metrics; Number Kernel Samples, Reads, Writes, and Total Model Duration across three compilers; TorchInductor (shortened to Inductor), nvFuser and TVM compared against baseline model using standard PyTorch inference. Δ is calculated on recorded baseline values.

Total Number of Kernel Samples							
Model	Baseline	Inductor	Δ	nvFuser	Δ	TVM	Δ
ResNet18	99	94	**-5.05%**	134	**35.35%**	50	**-49.49%**
Alexnet	31	26	**-16.13%**	32	**3.23%**	12	**-61.29%**
VGG16	65	52	**-20.00%**	65	**0.00%**	46	**-29.23%**
SqueezeNet	104	71	**-31.73%**	104	**0.00%**	39	**-62.50%**
RegNetY	395	338	**-14.43%**	473	**19.75%**	136	**-65.57%**
MobileNetV2	165	188	**13.94%**	277	**67.88%**	55	**-66.67%**
DenseNet161	826	825	**-0.12%**	1148	**38.98%**	249	**-69.85%**
Total Number of Kernel Reads							
Model	**Baseline**	**Inductor**	Δ	**nvFuser**	Δ	**TVM**	Δ
ResNet18	9052505	8847740	**-2.26%**	8716430	**-3.71%**	8540755	**-5.65%**
Alexnet	10091852	10019043	**-0.72%**	10096129	**0.04%**	140668624	**1293.88%**
VGG16	67091273	65513949	**-2.35%**	67159065	**0.10%**	47160107	**-29.71%**
SqueezeNet	5416071	4485851	**-17.18%**	5395375	**-0.38%**	20917108	**286.20%**
RegNet	5390036	4920333	**-8.71%**	4903637	**-9.02%**	20454922	**279.50%**
MobileNetV2	4792820	4536924	**-5.34%**	4042138	**-15.66%**	2913147	**-39.22%**
DenseNet161	77817397	71891919	**-7.61%**	73998158	**-4.91%**	45168738	**-41.96%**
Total Number of Kernel Writes							
Model	**Baseline**	**Inductor**	Δ	**nvFuser**	Δ	**TVM**	Δ
ResNet18	3670091	3358808	**-8.48%**	3398412	**-7.40%**	2179268	**-40.62%**
Alexnet	907951	878750	**-3.22%**	908513	**0.06%**	354989	**-60.90%**
VGG16	9468851	8332400	**-12.00%**	9449538	**-0.20%**	18773515	**98.27%**
SqueezeNet	2706038	2345904	**-13.31%**	2868360	**6.00%**	2457337	**-9.19%**
RegNetY	2517000	2030176	**-19.34%**	2030931	**-19.31%**	1787738	**-28.97%**
MobileNetV2	3140373	3089387	**-1.62%**	2296828	**-26.86%**	1330149	**-57.64%**
DenseNet161	30674810	31677864	**3.27%**	27371573	**-10.77%**	6413888	**-79.09%**
Total Kernel Duration (ms)							
Model	**Baseline**	**Inductor**	Δ	**nvFuser**	Δ	**TVM**	Δ
ResNet18	1.651907	1.693572	**2.52%**	1.960894	**18.70%**	0.914028	**-44.67%**
Alexnet	0.813266	0.83358	**2.50%**	0.822659	**1.15%**	4.57945	**463.09%**
VGG16	3.33617	3.16576	**-5.11%**	3.34707	**0.33%**	2.666236	**-20.08%**
SqueezeNet	0.794223	0.646071	**-18.65%**	0.805306	**1.40%**	4.48165	**464.28%**
RegNetY	2.580169	2.463748	**-4.51%**	3.343017	**29.57%**	11.14547	**331.97%**
MobileNetV2	1.077561	1.236549	**14.75%**	1.793075	**66.40%**	1.973429	**83.14%**
DenseNet161	9.465594	9.193542	**-2.87%**	11.427964	**20.73%**	55.954332	**491.13%**

References

1. Allen-Zhu, Z.: Natasha 2: Faster non-convex optimization than sgd. In: Advances in neural information processing systems, p. 31 (2018)
2. Biggio, B., Roli, F.: Wild patterns: Ten years after the rise of adversarial machine learning. Pattern Recogn. **84**, 317–331 (2018). https://doi.org/10.1016/j.patcog.2018.07.023
3. Branchaud-Charron, F., Achkar, A., Jodoin, P.M.: IEEE/CVF Conference on Computer Vision and Pattern Recognition (CVPR) (2019). Spectral metric for dataset complexity assessment
4. Buschmann, F., Meunier, R., Rohnert, H., Sommerlad, P., Stal, M., Sommerlad, P., Stal, M.: Pattern-Oriented Software Architecture, A System of Patterns, vol. 1. John Wiley & Sons New York (1996)
5. Chandrasekaran, V., Chaudhuri, K., Giacomelli, I., Jha, S., Yan, S.: Exploring connections between active learning and model extraction. In: USENIX Security Symposium, pp. 1309–1326. USENIX Association (2020)
6. Chen, T., et al.: TVM: an automated End-to-End optimizing compiler for deep learning. In: 13th USENIX Symposium on Operating Systems Design and Implementation (OSDI 18), pp. 578–594. USENIX Association, Carlsbad, CA, October 2018. https://www.usenix.org/conference/osdi18/presentation/chen
7. Chollet, F.: Keras: The python deep learning library. Astrophysics source code library pp. ascl–1806 (2018)
8. Corporation, N.: Nvidia v100, December 2017. https://www.nvidia.com/en-gb/data-center/tesla-v100/. Accessed 15 Jan 2026
9. Corporation, N.: nvFuser (2026). https://github.com/NVIDIA/Fuser. Accessed 15 Jan 2026
10. Corporation, T.M.: MITRE ATLAS Adversarial Attack Knowledge Base (2024). https://atlas.mitre.org/. Accessed 15 Jan 2026
11. Deng, J., Dong, W., Socher, R., Li, L.J., Li, K., Fei-Fei, L.: Imagenet: a large-scale hierarchical image database. In: IEEE Conference on Computer Vision and Pattern Recognition (CVPR), pp. 248–255. IEEE (2009)
12. Documentation, N.D.: Cuda toolkit profiler documentation, May 2024. https://docs.nvidia.com/cuda/profiler-users-guide/index.html. Accessed 15 Jan 2026
13. Dosovitskiy, A., et al.: An image is worth 16x16 words: Transformers for image recognition at scale (2020). arXiv:2010.11929 arXiv preprint
14. Duddu, V., Samanta, D., Rao, D.V., Balas, V.E.: Stealing neural networks via timing side channels (2018). arXiv:1812.11720 arXiv preprint
15. Face, H.: Hugging face: State-of-the-art natural language processing. https://huggingface.co (2026). Accessed 15 Jan 2026
16. Fredrikson, M., Jha, S., Ristenpart, T.: Model inversion attacks that exploit confidence information and basic countermeasures. In: ACM SIGSAC Conference on Computer and Communications Security (CCS), pp. 1322–1333 (2015)
17. Ganju, K., Wang, Q., Yang, W., Gunter, C.A., Borisov, N.: Property inference attacks on fully connected neural networks using permutation invariant representations. In: ACM SIGSAC conference on computer and communications security (CCS), pp. 619–633 (2018)
18. He, Z., Zhang, T., Lee, R.B.: Model inversion attacks against collaborative inference. In: Annual Computer Security Applications Conference (ACSAC), pp. 148–162. Association for Computing Machinery (2019). https://doi.org/10.1145/3359789.3359824

19. Hendrycks, D., Gimpel, K.: Gaussian error linear units (gelus) (2016). https://doi.org/10.48550/ARXIV.1606.08415, https://arxiv.org/abs/1606.08415
20. Hinton, G., Vinyals, O., Dean, J., et al.: Distilling the knowledge in a neural network. arXiv preprint arXiv:1503.02531 **2**(7) (2015)
21. Hong, S., et al.: Security analysis of deep neural networks operating in the presence of cache side-channel attacks. arXiv preprint arXiv:1810.03487 (2018). https://doi.org/10.48550/ARXIV.1810.03487, https://arxiv.org/abs/1810.03487
22. Hu, X., et al.: Deepsniffer: A dnn model extraction framework based on learning architectural hints. In: Conference on Architectural Support for Programming Languages and Operating Systems (ASPLOS), pp. 385–399 (2020). https://doi.org/10.1145/3373376.3378460
23. Hussain, S., Wang, P., Miller, J.: Privacyraven: Comprehensive privacy testing for deep learning (2020). https://github.com/trailofbits/PrivacyRaven
24. Jagielski, M., Carlini, N., Berthelot, D., Kurakin, A., Papernot, N.: High accuracy and high fidelity extraction of neural networks. In: USENIX Security Symposium, pp. 1345–1362 (2020)
25. Keller, B., et al.: Deep learning inference accelerator with per-vector scaled 4-bit quantization for transformers in 5nm. In: IEEE Symposium on VLSI Technology and Circuits (VLSI Technology and Circuits), pp. 16–17 (2022). https://doi.org/10.1109/VLSITechnologyandCir46769.2022.9830277
26. Krizhevsky, A., Hinton, G.: Learning multiple layers of features from tiny images, pp. 32–33 (2009). https://www.cs.toronto.edu/~kriz/learning-features-2009-TR.pdf
27. Lecun, Y., Bottou, L., Bengio, Y., Haffner, P.: Gradient-based learning applied to document recognition. Proc. IEEE **86**(11), 2278–2324 (1998). https://doi.org/10.1109/5.726791
28. Liu, Y., Wen, R., He, X., Salem, A., Zhang, Z., Backes, M.: ML-Doctor: Holistic risk assessment of inference attacks against machine learning models. In: USENIX Security Symposium (2022). https://www.usenix.org/conference/usenixsecurity22/presentation/liu-yugeng
29. Liu, Z., Mao, H., Wu, C.Y., Feichtenhofer, C., Darrell, T., Xie, S.: A convnet for the 2020s. In: IEEE/CVF Conference on Computer Vision and Pattern Recognition (CVPR), pp. 11976–11986 (2022)
30. Marcel, S., Rodriguez, Y.: Torchvision the machine-vision package of torch. In: ACM International Conference on Multimedia (MM), pp. 1485–1488. Association for Computing Machinery (2010). https://doi.org/10.1145/1873951.1874254
31. Meyer, C.: Python Enhancement Proposal 405 – Python Virtual Environments (2011). https://peps.python.org/pep-0405/. Accessed 15 Jan 2026
32. Morcos, A., Raghu, M., Bengio, S.: Insights on representational similarity in neural networks with canonical correlation. Adv. Neural. Inf. Process. Syst. 31, (2018)
33. Morcos, A.S., Raghu, M., Bengio, S.: Insights on representational similarity in neural networks with canonical correlation (2018). https://doi.org/10.48550/ARXIV.1806.05759, https://arxiv.org/abs/1806.05759
34. Naghibijouybari, H., Neupane, A., Qian, Z., Abu-Ghazaleh, N.: Rendered insecure: Gpu side channel attacks are practical. In: ACM SIGSAC conference on computer and communications security (CCS), pp. 2139–2153 (2018)
35. Nicolae, M.I., et al.: (2018). arXiv:1807.01069 Adversarial robustness toolbox v1.0.0. arXiv preprint
36. Orekondy, T., Schiele, B., Fritz, M.: Knockoff nets: Stealing functionality of black-box models. In: IEEE/CVF Conference on Computer Vision and Pattern Recognition (CVPR), pp. 4954–4963 (2019)

37. PyTorch: TorchInductor (2022). Accessed 15 Jan 2026
38. Radosavovic, I., Kosaraju, R.P., Girshick, R., He, K., Dollár, P.: Designing network design spaces. In: IEEE/CVF conference on computer vision and pattern recognition (CVPR), pp. 10428–10436 (2020)
39. Raghu, M., Poole, B., Kleinberg, J., Ganguli, S., Sohl-Dickstein, J.: On the expressive power of deep neural networks. In: International Conference on Machine Learning (ICML), pp. 2847–2854 (2017) PMLR
40. Salem, A., Wen, R., Backes, M., Ma, S., Zhang, Y.: Dynamic backdoor attacks against machine learning models. In: IEEE European Symposium on Security and Privacy (EuroS&P), pp. 703–718. IEEE (2022)
41. Sandler, M., Howard, A., Zhu, M., Zhmoginov, A., Chen, L.C.: Mobilenetv 2: inverted residuals and linear bottlenecks. In: IEEE/CVF Conference on Computer Vision and Pattern Recognition (CVPR), pp. 4510–4520. (2018)
42. Tramèr, F., Zhang, F., Juels, A., Reiter, M.K., Ristenpart, T.: Stealing machine learning models via prediction apis. In: USENIX Conference on Security Symposium, pp. 601–618. USENIX Association (2016)
43. Trawicki, S., Hackett, W., Birch, L., Suri, N., Garraghan, P.: Compilation as a defense: Enhancing dl model attack robustness via tensor optimization. In: "Conference on Applied Machine Learning for Information Security, CAMLIS; Conference date: 19-10-2023 Through 20-10-2023 (Oct 2023). https://www.camlis.org/
44. Truong, J.B., Maini, P., Walls, R.J., Papernot, N.: Data-free model extraction. In: Proceedings of the IEEE/CVF Conference on Computer Vision and Pattern Recognition (CVPR) (2021)
45. Vaswani, A., et al.: Attention is all you need. Advances in neural information processing systems **30** (2017)
46. Wang, X., Li, J., Kuang, X., an Tan, Y., Li, J.: The security of machine learning in an adversarial setting: a survey. J. Parallel Distribut. Comput. **130**, 12–23 (2019). https://doi.org/10.1016/j.jpdc.2019.03.003, https://www.sciencedirect.com/science/article/pii/S0743731518309183
47. Wei, J., Zhang, Y., Zhou, Z., Li, Z., Al Faruque, M.A.: Leaky dnn: stealing deep-learning model secret with gpu context-switching side-channel. In: IEEE/IFIP International Conference on Dependable Systems and Networks (DSN), pp. 125–137 (2020). https://doi.org/10.1109/DSN48063.2020.00031
48. Xue, M., Yuan, C., Wu, H., Zhang, Y., Liu, W.: Machine learning security: threats, countermeasures, and evaluations. IEEE Access **8**, 74720–74742 (2020). https://doi.org/10.1109/ACCESS.2020.2987435
49. Yang, S., Luo, P., Loy, C.C., Tang, X.: From facial parts responses to face detection: a deep learning approach. In: IEEE International Conference on Computer Vision (ICCV), pp. 3676–3684 (2015). https://doi.org/10.1109/ICCV.2015.419
50. Yarom, Y., Falkner, K.: Flush+reload: a high resolution, low noise, l3 cache side-channel attack. In: USENIX Conference on Security Symposium, pp. 719–732. USENIX Association (2014)
51. Yu, H., Yang, K., Zhang, T., Tsai, Y.Y., Ho, T.Y., Jin, Y.: Cloudleak: large-scale deep learning models stealing through adversarial examples. In: Network and Distributed Systems Security Symposium (NDSS) (2020)
52. Yuan, X., Ding, L., Zhang, L., Li, X., Wu, D.: Es attack: model stealing against deep neural networks without data hurdles (2020). https://doi.org/10.48550/ARXIV.2009.09560

53. Zhu, Y., Cheng, Y., Zhou, H., Lu, Y.: Hermes attack: Steal {DNN} models with lossless inference accuracy. In: USENIX Security Symposium) (2021)
54. Zhuang, F., Qi, Z., Duan, K., Xi, D., Zhu, Y., Zhu, H., Xiong, H., He, Q.: A comprehensive survey on transfer learning. Proc. IEEE **109**(1), 43–76 (2021). https://doi.org/10.1109/JPROC.2020.3004555

Mobile/Network Security and Measurement

Beyond Local Views: Static-Guided Exploration for Deep-State Android Security Auditing

Jinghang Wen[1], Yuliang Zhang[1], Yongliang Chen[1], Ruoqin Tang[1], Xichen Yu[2], Guowen Xu[3], and Qingchuan Zhao[1(✉)]

[1] City University of Hong Kong, Hong Kong SAR, China
{jh.wen,yzhang5785-c,r.tang}@my.cityu.edu.hk,
{cs.ylchen,qizhao}@cityu.edu.hk
[2] Shandong University, Jinan, China
xcyu@mail.sdu.edu.cn
[3] University of Electronic Science and Technology of China, Chengdu, China
guowen.xu@uestc.edu.cn

Abstract. Automated dynamic analysis is pivotal for mobile security auditing; however, its efficacy is inherently constrained by coverage limitations. Despite the advent of Large Language Models (LLMs), existing agents suffer from a "local perspective" limitation—relying solely on real-time visual feedback—which often traps them in shallow UI states while critical deep-state functionalities remain difficult to reach. To bridge this gap, we propose NAVIGATOR, a hybrid framework that integrates offline static analysis with online LLM-driven exploration. Unlike reactive explorers, NAVIGATOR constructs a global "attack surface map" from decompiled bytecode to proactively guide the agent through complex logic barriers. Our evaluation on 20 real-world apps shows that NAVIGATOR improves deep-state reachability over existing tools, outperforming the state-of-the-art LLM-Explorer by discovering 6.4% more unique activities. Moreover, NAVIGATOR matches the average human baseline in activity coverage (67.55% vs. 66.60%) while operating at low cost ($0.056/app), suggesting a scalable complement to manual auditing.

Keywords: Mobile security · Automated auditing · Large language models · Static analysis · Deep-state exploration

1 Introduction

Mobile applications have become the primary interface for sensitive digital interactions, managing critical assets ranging from health records [6,27] to financial credentials [13,23]. Given their access to high-value data, ensuring the security and privacy compliance of these apps is paramount. While static analysis offers code-level insights, it suffers from inherent limitations such as obfuscation and the inability to resolve dynamic behaviors (e.g., reflection, dynamic loading).

Y. Cao et al. (Eds.): SecureComm 2026, LNICST 704, pp. 79–102, 2027.
https://doi.org/10.1007/978-3-032-32764-2_4

Consequently, dynamic analysis—monitoring apps during runtime execution—has become the de facto standard for identifying privacy leaks [1,20,26,30] and logic vulnerabilities [18,19].

The foundational premise of effective dynamic security auditing is *code coverage*. A dynamic analysis tool can only identify a vulnerability (*e.g.*, a PII leak triggered by a specific button) if it can successfully navigate the user interface (UI) to trigger the corresponding code path. However, modern apps feature increasingly complex user interfaces (UIs) and intricate business logic, creating a significant barrier for automated explorers. Deeply nested functionalities often contain critical security checks or sensitive operations, but are guarded by complex interaction sequences. For instance, a sequence like "Register → Login → Settings → Enable Dev Mode" represents a semantic barrier that traditional tools often fail to traverse. Traditional automated explorers, such as pseudo-random event generators (*e.g.*, Monkey [7]) or reinforcement learning agents [17,21,22], struggle to traverse these semantic barriers, resulting in shallow exploration and significant security blind spots.

Recently, Large Language Models (LLMs) have shown promise in mimicking human interaction for app exploration [15,19,34]. By interpreting UI semantics, LLM-based agents can navigate login screens and forms better than traditional explorers. However, we observe that existing LLM explorers inevitably hit a "semantic plateau." Relying solely on real-time visual feedback (a local perspective), they lack the strategic foresight to navigate complex, multi-step dependency chains—such as creating a prerequisite database entry before accessing a management dashboard. From a security auditing perspective, this is analogous to navigating a maze with a flashlight but no map: The agent efficiently explores its immediate surroundings but remains blind to deep-state targets where critical business logic and vulnerabilities often reside. This limitation results in redundant interactions with low-value screens (e.g., endlessly toggling settings), while high-risk targets hidden deep within the app remain untouched.

To bridge the gap between shallow crawling and deep-state auditing, we propose that dynamic exploration agents must be guided by a global map of the attack surface. We observe that while static analysis cannot perfectly resolve runtime control flows, it can reconstruct a high-fidelity catalog of the application's UI layouts from decompiled code [3,4]. By leveraging this static "inventory of targets," we can shift the paradigm of automated auditing from aimless wandering to directed auditing.

In this paper, we present NAVIGATOR, a task-oriented hybrid framework designed to maximize deep-state reachability for mobile security auditing. NAVIGATOR operates in two distinct phases to ensure comprehensive coverage. First, it performs an offline static analysis to reconstruct all defined UI layouts from the codebase. Crucially, this step exposes the complete theoretical attack surface—including screens that are hard to reach dynamically—providing a global roadmap for the auditor. An LLM then analyzes these static layouts to discover distinct functionalities and generates a prioritized sequence of "auditing tasks." Second, during the online phase, an LLM-powered agent executes these tasks to drive the application into the targeted deep states. Unlike traditional tools that rely on rigid transition graphs [4,14,16], NAVIGATOR leverages the LLM's semantic intelligence to dynamically infer navigation paths required to reach the target screens. To support this, we introduce a Dual-Memory System—comprising Short-Term Task Memory for immediate context and a Long-Term Knowledge Base for app-wide shortcuts—enabling the agent to handle complex logic loops and dependency chains efficiently.

We evaluate NAVIGATOR on a benchmark of 20 diverse real-world apps. The results demonstrate that NAVIGATOR substantially improves deep-state reachability over existing LLM explorers. It outperforms the state-of-the-art baseline, LLM-Explorer [34], by discovering 6.4% more unique activities, thereby expanding the visible attack surface. Moreover, NAVIGATOR matches the average human baseline in activity coverage (67.55% vs. 66.60%), although the union-of-human total activity count remains slightly higher. While manual auditing still offers advantages on the most complex apps, NAVIGATOR achieves comparable deep-state penetration at negligible computational cost (approx. $0.056 per app), making scalable, low-cost security auditing more practical.

In summary, we make the following three contributions to automated mobile security:

- **Hybrid Proactive Framework:** We propose NAVIGATOR that shifts auditing from reactive exploration to proactive navigation. It constructs a global attack surface map via static analysis to guide LLM agents in penetrating complex logic barriers that remain invisible to dynamic-only tools.
- **Context-Aware Navigation:** We design a robust online execution system featuring a Dual-Memory mechanism, enabling the agent to maintain context across complex interaction sequences and mitigate navigation loops common in automated dynamic explorers.
- **Near-Human Reachability:** We demonstrate that NAVIGATOR achieves the strongest automated coverage in our evaluation and matches the average human baseline in activity coverage (slightly higher), substantially narrowing the gap between automated and manual deep-state exploration while reducing the operational cost to mere cents per app.

2 Background And Motivation

2.1 UI Layouts as Static Attack Surface

In the context of Android security, the User Interface (UI) serves as the primary gateway for user inputs and, consequently, constitutes a critical attack surface. While the runtime UI is rendered as a hierarchical view tree of objects, a significant portion of this structure can be recovered statically from the application package (APK) without execution.

Static Layout Definition. Android developers predominantly define UI structures using declarative XML files, which act as blueprints for the app's visual states. Crucially, these static layouts provide an "inventory" of potential interaction targets, such as input fields and buttons. This characteristic aligns with our core insight: Static analysis can reconstruct a "global map" of the application. Although some UI elements are instantiated dynamically via Java/Kotlin code to handle runtime data, the static XML resources typically represent the skeleton of the app's logic flow and business boundaries. Even if the underlying bytecode is heavily obfuscated, these files typically remain unencrypted to ensure efficient parsing by the Android resource manager.

UI Nodes as Auditing Targets. From an auditing perspective, UI nodes are not merely visual components but entry points for security analysis. *Widget nodes* (*e.g.*, `EditText`, `Button`) often serve as sources for sensitive data entry or triggers for critical transactions. *Container nodes* (*e.g.*, `LinearLayout`) define the structural relationship between these elements. By analyzing them, a security tool can identify high-value targets—such as password fields or banking transaction forms—before the dynamic agent even launches the app. This static knowledge is essential for guiding agents toward deep-state functionalities that purely dynamic explorers might overlook due to their restricted local view.

2.2 Reachability in Dynamic Security Auditing

Dynamic analysis has become the de facto standard for detecting runtime vulnerabilities, such as privacy leaks and permission misuse, and logic flaws. However, the efficacy of any dynamic security tool is strictly bound by its ability to reach vulnerable code paths.

The Reachability Challenge. To audit a specific security-sensitive operation, the analysis agent must simulate a precise sequence of user interactions (*e.g.*, click, input, scroll) to navigate from the launch screen to the target state. We define this as the *Reachability* problem in security auditing. Formal verification or static taint analysis often fails to resolve these paths due to the event-driven nature of Android. Therefore, automated explorers are employed to drive the app execution. The success of a security audit is thus directly correlated with *Activity Coverage*, which measures the ratio of unique screens (activities) visited by the agent. Low coverage implies that significant portions of the app's logic remain unexecuted and unaudited, leaving potential vulnerabilities in "deep states" undiscovered.

2.3 Motivation: The Semantic Gap in Auditing

Current automated explorers lack the semantic understanding required to navigate complex business logic, creating blind spots in security audits. We refer to this limitation as the *Semantic Gap*.

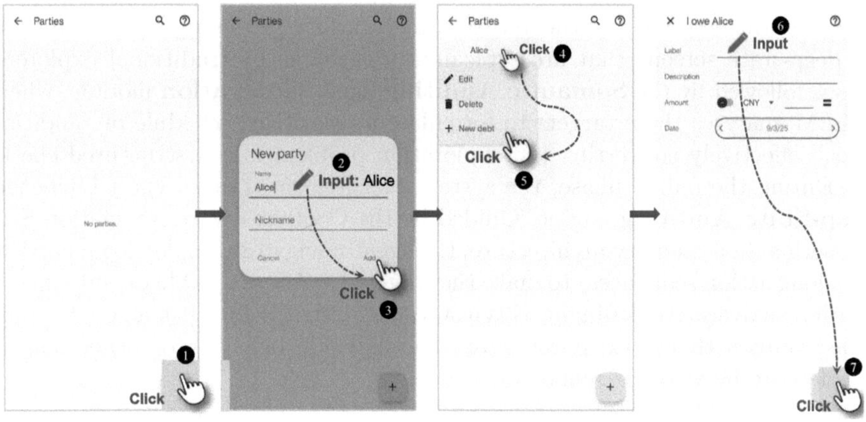

Fig. 1. An illustration of a logic dependency in the "My Expenses" app, acting as a barrier to security auditing. The critical functionality "Add a new debt" (Step 5) is unreachable unless the agent logically deduces the prerequisite of creating a "Party" (Steps 2 and 3) and creates a counterparty.

Consider the scenario in Fig. 1, which depicts the "My Expenses" app. Suppose a security analyst needs to audit the "Add a new debt" functionality for potential data leakage or input validation vulnerabilities. This target state (Step 5) is guarded by a logical dependency: A debt cannot exist without a counterparty. Consequently, the "New debt" button remains hidden until the user explicitly creates a "Party" (Steps 2 and 3). A traditional automated explorer acts as a "blind" auditor in this scenario. Lacking the semantic insight that a "Party" is a prerequisite for a "Debt," it will likely loop endlessly in the initial empty state. More critically, even a standard LLM agent might fail here. If the agent relies solely on real-time visual feedback (the local view), it may never see the "New debt" button and thus never formulate the plan to reveal it. To bridge this gap, an intelligent agent requires global awareness: It must know that the "Debt" layout exists in the static map to proactively deduce the prerequisite steps required to reach it.

3 Our Approach: NAVIGATOR

3.1 Overview

We present NAVIGATOR, a task-oriented hybrid framework designed to maximize deep-state reachability for mobile security auditing. Unlike traditional dynamic analysis tools that rely on aimless exploration, NAVIGATOR operates on the premise that effective auditing requires a global map of the attack surface. As illustrated in Fig. 2, our architecture consists of two distinct phases.

In the offline phase, the **Static Attack Surface Mapping** module reconstructs a comprehensive catalog of UI layouts from the decompiled codebase.

Crucially, this exposes the theoretical attack surface of the application, including deep-state screens that are typically unreachable by traditional explorers. This is followed by the **Semantic Auditing Task Generation** module, where an LLM analyzes these targets to formulate a prioritized schedule of "auditing tasks," effectively converting the exploration problem into a structured checklist. During the online phase, the system executes these tasks via a **Directed Deep-State Auditing** engine. Guided by the Context-Aware Navigation System with a dual-memory architecture, the agent navigates complex logic barriers (e.g., long action sequences) to make the targeted states reachable for subsequent security analysis. Accordingly, NAVIGATOR is designed for UI-triggered attack paths; threats that arise purely from backend-side behavior or other non-UI channels are beyond our scope.

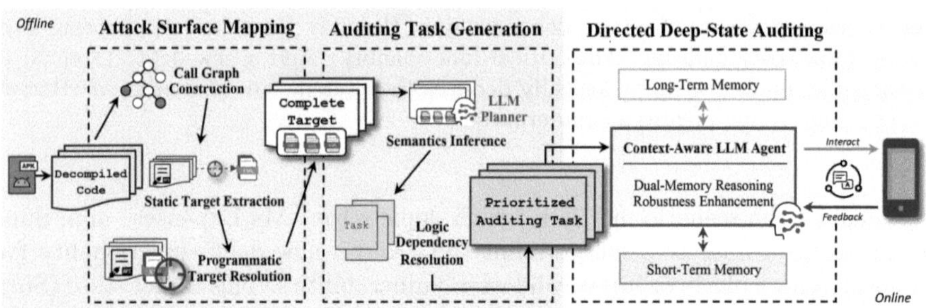

Fig. 2. The workflow of NAVIGATOR. The system leverages static analysis to build a global map, guiding the LLM agent to penetrate deep states.

3.2 Static Attack Surface Mapping

This module is responsible for reconstructing the application's global UI map without execution. While previous agents [15, 34] rely on runtime observations—often missing code paths hidden behind complex logic—our approach statically extracts the complete inventory of interaction targets from the APK.

Call Graph Construction. NAVIGATOR begins by decompiling the APK to build a call graph from lifecycle methods (*e.g.*, `onCreate()`) of all activities. A critical design choice here is our resilience to code obfuscation (e.g., ProGuard/R8). While obfuscation can rename user-defined classes and methods (e.g., changing `PaymentActivity` to `a.b.c`), it cannot alter Android Framework APIs without breaking the application's interaction with the OS.

Therefore, we anchor our analysis on identifying *Sink APIs*—immutable system methods responsible for UI mutation (e.g., `inflate`). Specifically, we target layout configuration APIs (e.g., `setContentView`), resource binding APIs (*e.g.*, `setImageResource`), and content configuration APIs (*e.g.*, `setText`). Since the signatures of these framework methods are preserved, our call graph construction remains robust even in heavily obfuscated bytecode, allowing us to reliably trace data flows from the app entry points to these critical UI sinks.

Static Target Extraction. We employ static taint analysis to recover the XML layout definitions associated with each activity. This step is resistant to the semantic loss caused by identifier renaming. Even if an activity class is obfuscated to a meaningless string, the structure of its interface is defined in XML resources, which typically remain unencrypted to allow the Android resource manager to parse them efficiently. By performing backward slicing from the identified Sink APIs (e.g., `setContentView(int id)`), we resolve the integer resource IDs passed as arguments. These IDs map directly to the layout files (e.g., `res/layout/login.xml`), which contain the semantic richness required for auditing—such as text attributes (e.g., "Password"), widget types (e.g., `EditText`), and hierarchy. Consequently, NAVIGATOR reconstructs a high-fidelity *Simulated View Tree* that preserves the business logic semantics required for LLM reasoning, irrespective of the underlying bytecode obfuscation. For clarity, a simulated view tree is serialized as a simplified XML-like hierarchy that preserves widget types, key text/hint attributes, and parent-child structure, e.g., `<LinearLayout><TextView text="Login"/><EditText hint="Email"/> <EditText hint="Password"/><Button text="Sign in"/></LinearLayout>`. It is not intended to be pixel-identical to the runtime view tree; rather, it serves as a semantic abstraction for downstream LLM reasoning.

Programmatic Target Resolution. Static XML definitions often fail to capture elements loaded programmatically at runtime—a common blind spot. To bridge this gap, we perform a secondary analysis to *resolve* these dynamic targets (e.g., code-generated input fields or logic containers). We categorize them into three types based on their initialization logic:

- *Widget Nodes (Input Vectors):* Atomic components like `Button` or `EditText` represent direct interaction points. We resolve their attributes by tracing calls to configuration APIs (*e.g.*, `setText`) in the code, updating the simulated view tree to reflect their likely runtime state.
- *Container Nodes (Structural Logic):* Complex containers like `Fragment` or `RecyclerView` often load their content dynamically. For fragments, we analyze transactions (*e.g.*, `FragmentTransaction.add()`) to link the host activity to the fragment's layout file. For adapters, where exact content is data-dependent, we extract static descriptors or placeholder IDs to provide the agent with semantic hints about the node's purpose.
- *Custom Nodes (Proprietary Components):* Developer-defined views often encapsulate complex logic. We trace their initialization back to the constructor and identify associated layout files via `inflate()` calls. Furthermore, we simulate the resolution of custom attributes (*e.g.*, defined in `attrs.xml`) by tracking `TypedArray` usage, allowing us to reconstruct the proprietary properties of these non-standard components.

3.3 Semantic Auditing Task Generation

Mere knowledge of UI layouts is insufficient for security auditing; the agent must understand the *semantics* of these layouts to navigate effectively. In this phase, we leverage an LLM to interpret the static map and generate a strategic plan for deep-state penetration.

Semantics Inference. For each reconstructed layout, NAVIGATOR tasks the LLM with inferring its business logic and potential interaction capabilities. We construct a prompt containing the activity's class name (*e.g.*, "MoneyTransfer-Activity") and its simplified UI hierarchy. The LLM acts as a security auditor, analyzing these inputs to deduce the screen's purpose. The output is a structured JSON object containing: (i) a *State Summary*, describing the screen's role in the app (e.g., "Financial Transaction Interface"); (ii) a set of *Auditing Tasks*, distinguishing between main tasks and sub-tasks; and (iii) *Navigation Keywords*, which are semantic markers used to locate this screen during dynamic exploration (as detailed in Sect. 3.5).

For instance, when presented with the "DebtOverview" activity and its layout, the LLM correctly infers its role in managing financial debts. It generates main tasks like "View debt overview" and "Manage debts," breaks them down into sub-tasks such as "Add new debt" and "Edit existing debt," and extracts keywords like "debt," "overview," and "manage."

Logic Dependency Resolution. A critical barrier to deep-state reachability is the logical dependency between tasks (e.g., a "Transfer" cannot occur before "Adding a Card"). To prevent attempting tasks out of order, we employ a heuristic-based prioritization scheme to resolve these dependencies:

- *Prerequisite Satisfaction:* We prioritize foundational states such as "Login," "Register," or "Setup," which is fully automated through heuristics. These states act as gateways to the rest of the attack surface in the app.
- *Constructive Logic First:* Actions that create state (*e.g.*, "Add Item") are ranked higher than those that modify or delete state. This ensures the agent populates the app with necessary data objects before attempting to manipulate them.
- *Core Business Targeting:* We prioritize activities identified as central hubs (*e.g.*, "Dashboard") or high-value targets (*e.g.*, "Payment"), as they typically contain the densest concentration of business logic.

This prioritization process transforms a disordered set of potential actions into a directed "Auditing Plan," steering the agent through the app's logic in a valid execution order.

3.4 Context-Aware Navigation System

To navigate the complex state machines of modern apps, the agent requires a robust context management system. We introduce a **Dual-Memory Archi-**

tecture to mitigate the statelessness of standard LLMs, enabling the agent to handle long interaction sequences without losing focus.

Short-Term Context (Task Scope). This memory module maintains the immediate context for the current auditing task. It is reset upon task completion and consists of:

- *Execution Trace:* A rolling window of the last few atomic actions (*e.g.*, clicked on the "Help" button) and their outcomes (`success`, `failure`, `ineffective`). This allows the system to programmatically detect local navigation loops, such as repeatedly clicking a button that yields no UI change (*i.e.*, the outcome is `ineffective`) or toggling between two UIs.
- *Semantic State Summary:* An LLM-generated summary of current progress, elevating the raw action entry into strategic insights (e.g., "Explored the main screen and the navigator drawer, but found no tag preferences. Key Insight: The target function is likely within the app's internal settings.").
- *Tactical Plan:* A distinct instruction for the immediate next step, which aligns with the insights from the summary and prevents the model from drifting into irrelevant interactions (e.g., "Return to main screen and enter settings in 'More Options' menu").

Long-Term Knowledge Base (App Scope). This persistent module accumulates a global map of the visited screens and their transitions across all auditing tasks for a given app. To efficiently index visited states, we introduce the Abstract User Interface (AUI)—a structural hash of the view tree that is invariant to dynamic content changes (e.g., varying timestamps in a `TextView`). When the agent successfully reaches a new AUI, it is indexed in the Knowledge Base along with the discovered layout and transition. This creates a system of "Semantic Shortcuts": If a future task requires returning to a specific screen, the agent can query the Knowledge Base to retrieve the precise navigation path (as detailed in Sect. 3.5), bypassing redundant exploration.

3.5 Directed Deep-State Auditing

In the online stage, NAVIGATOR executes the prioritized auditing tasks. The LLM-driven agent operates in a closed-loop cycle for auditing, specifically tuned for robustness against the unpredictability of dynamic execution.

The Auditing Cycle. Algorithm 1 outlines the systematic process of the directed deep-state auditing. For each prioritized task, the system first queries the *Long-Term Memory* (LTM) Knowledge Base (K_{lt}) to check for existing paths to the target state. Specifically, it attempts to match the Navigation Keywords of the current task (as identified in Sect. 3.3) in the Knowledge Base, identifying relevant screens that have been previously visited. The Knowledge Base is initially *seeded* with the theoretical map reconstructed during the Static Attack Surface Mapping phase. If a relevant screen is found, the agent is initialized with a "Semantic Shortcut" plan to jump-start navigation; otherwise, it begins exploration from the app's root activity.

Once initiated, the engine operates in a closed loop to drive the application toward the target state. In each iteration, the agent captures the view hierarchy and converts it into a simplified XML format, filtering non-essential attributes (e.g., purely decorative ones) through deterministic rules to reduce token consumption. The system constructs a context-aware prompt that fuses three information sources: (1) the current *Auditing Task*, (2) the perceived UI layout, and (3) the *Short-Term Memory* (STM), including the Semantic State Summary, Execution Trace, and Tactical Plan. Based on this context, the LLM analyzes

Algorithm 1. Directed Deep-State Auditing.

Input: *App*, prioritized tasks T, knowledge base K_{lt}
Output: Updated knowledge base K_{lt} and execution logs
function AUDIT(*App*, T, K_{lt})
    for each task t in T **do**
        $STM \leftarrow \emptyset$ ▷ Init Short-Term Context
        rel_screen ← FINDRELEVANTSCREEN(K_{lt}, t.keywords)
        if *rel_screen* ≠ null **then**
            STM.plan ← GENNAVPLAN(*rel_screen*) ▷ Apply Semantic Shortcut
        end if
        while ¬ISTASKFINISHED(t, STM) **do**
            $s_i \leftarrow$ Observe GUI state of the *App*
            if ISDEADEND(STM, s_i) **then** ▷ Robustness: Dead-End Pruning
                break ▷ Abandon task to preserve resources
            end if
            if ISLOOPING(STM, s_i) **then** ▷ Robustness: Loop Breaking
                if ISLOOPPERSIST(STM, s_i) **then**
                    $s'_i \leftarrow$ MASKELE(s_i, STM.history) ▷ Mask problematic elements
                    prompt ← GENPROMPT(t, s'_i, STM)
                else
                    prompt ← GENPROMPT(t, s_i, STM, Warning)
                end if
            else
                prompt ← GENPROMPT(t, s_i, STM)
            end if
            a_i, *summ*, *plan* ← INVOKELLM(*prompt*)
            EXECUTEACTION(a_i)
            $s_{i+1} \leftarrow$ Observe GUI state of the *App*
            result ← GETACTIONRESULT(s_i, s_{i+1}, a_i)
            $STM \leftarrow$ UPDATESTM(STM, a_i, *result*, *summ*, *plan*)
            $K_{\text{lt}} \leftarrow$ UPDATEKNOWLEDGE(K_{lt}, s_{i+1})
        end while
    end for
end function

You are now analyzing an app named "My Expenses," the current UI shows following elements:

<button id=0 alt='Navigate up' bound_box=0,91,158,249></button>
<p id=1 bound_box=169,135,468,204>New budget</p>
<p id=3 bound_box=45,260,327,401>Title</p>
<input id=4 bound_box=327,270,1035,391>Q3 Budget</input>
...
<button id=24 description='Save'></button>

Semantic State Summary: The agent has discovered that the "Budgeting" feature is behind a paywall. It is now creating a new budget to see if management options will appear. It has already filled in the details for a new budget.
Tactical Plan: Confirm whether creating a new budget leads to the management screen.
Execution Trace:
1. On the MyExpenses screen, clicked 'More options' -> success
2. On the MyExpenses screen, clicked 'Budgeting' -> success
3. On the ContribInfoDialogActivity screen, clicked 'Try' -> success
4. On the ManageBudgets screen, clicked 'New budget' -> success
5. On the BudgetEdit screen, filled input fields: filled input 4: Q3 Budget; filled input 6: Budget for Q3 marketing campaigns including social media and PPC; filled input 9: 5000 -> success

Task: Your task is to generate the next action to Manage Budgets in BudgetActivity. Respond in JSON format. ```json {...} ```

```
{
    "action_type": "click",
    "element_id": 24,
    "input_text": "",
    "rationale": "Save the new budget and check if it leads to the budget management screen.",
    "task_context": {
      "summary": "Navigated through 'More options' > 'Budgeting' and is now creating a new budget.",
      "tactical_plan": "Verify that after saving, the app returns to a management screen where the new
      budget can be seen and managed."
    }
}
```

Fig. 3. An example of the Directed Deep-State Auditing. The prompt includes system instructions, the simplified UI state, task context, and the specific auditing task.

the current state and infers the most effective *operation* (*e.g.*, clicking a button, scrolling, or inputting text) to advance the task, together with a rationale and an updated tactical plan. The system then executes the command on the device and programmatically validates the outcome. The execution result—whether the interface transitioned to a new state or remained static—is recorded in the STM to inform decision-making in the next cycle.

Following execution, if a unique screen (identified by a new AUI) is encountered, it is indexed into the Knowledge Base to aid future tasks. This cycle repeats until the task is successfully completed or the Dead-End Pruning mechanism (Algorithm 1, Line 12) determines that the target logic is unreachable, at which point the STM is reset for the next task. Figure 3 illustrates an example of this prompt engineering and reasoning process.

Robustness Enhancement Mechanisms. We implement two safeguards to maintain continuous auditing. (i) **Loop Breaking Strategy:** Automated agents often get trapped in infinite loops (*e.g.*, toggling a switch repeatedly). NAVIGATOR detects these patterns via the Execution Trace. It first warns the LLM to alter its strategy. If the loop persists, the system masks the problematic UI element from the agent's view. This is crucial because LLMs can sometimes lack the creativity [11] to break a failing pattern; this intervention compels them to explore alternative paths. (ii) **Dead-End Pruning:** If a task fails to progress after a threshold, the LLM performs a feasibility assessment based on the entire execution history for that task. If the agent concludes the functionality is likely a "hallucination" of the static analysis or effectively unreachable, the task is abandoned to preserve resources for other high-value targets.

4 Evaluation

We implemented a prototype of NAVIGATOR using Soot [24] and FlowDroid [2] for static analysis, DroidBot [16] for device orchestration, and DeepSeek-V3 [5] as the LLM reasoning engine. To validate its efficacy as a security auditing tool, we conducted extensive experiments to demonstrate its superiority over state-of-the-art tools. Our evaluation specifically examines its ability to expand the visible attack surface and efficiency for automated auditing pipelines.

4.1 Experimental Setup

Benchmark Apps. We utilized the benchmark dataset established by LLM-Explorer [34], consisting of 20 diverse real-world applications sourced from F-Droid [9] and Google Play. This dataset comprises apps with a wide range of logic complexity, spanning from simple tools (8 activities) to complex financial and communication applications (64 activities). Crucially, this benchmark includes a *Human Baseline*, derived from the union of unique screens discovered by six human testers. We treat this as the "Gold Standard" for the theoretical maximum reachable attack surface under manual auditing conditions.

Hardware. The experiments were conducted on a Linux server running Ubuntu 24.04 equipped with two Intel Xeon Platinum 8383C CPUs, with 80 cores in total, alongside 1 TB of memory and 32 TB of storage. The Android device we used was a OnePlus A6000 running Android 11, equipped with eight 2.8 GHz ARM-based cores (Snapdragon 845 CPU) and an Adreno 630 GPU.

Baselines. We benchmark NAVIGATOR against two baselines:

- *LLM-Explorer* [34]: The current state-of-the-art (SOTA) in automated exploration. It is LLM-driven and employs a local-view merging strategy. Comparing against LLM-Explorer allows us to quantify the advantage of our "Global Map" approach over purely dynamic "Local View" agents.

- *Human Baseline:* Derived from a user study involving six experienced participants as detailed in [34], this baseline represents the union of unique activities visited during manual exploration. To ensure reliability, each app underwent at least two independent exploration sessions, with each session lasting a minimum of 10 min. It serves as a practical upper bound for semantic reachability. It is important to note that this baseline typically does not reach 100% coverage, as many apps contain "orphan" activities that lack developer-defined navigation logic or remain as residual dead code, making them theoretically unreachable even for humans.

We do not directly re-evaluate random/learning-based tools (e.g., Monkey [7], DroidBot [16], and Humanoid [17]) or earlier LLM-driven agents (e.g., DroidAgent [32], GPTDroid [19]), because prior work [34] has already reported that LLM-Explorer substantially outperforms them on the same benchmark. Given our goal of isolating the benefit of NAVIGATOR's global-map guidance against the strongest prior baseline under a matched benchmark setting, we therefore focus our empirical comparison on LLM-Explorer and the human baseline. To ensure a rigorous and controlled comparison with [34], we configured LLM-Explorer using its original implementation, except that we replaced its original LLM backend (i.e., GPT) with the same LLM backend (i.e., DeepSeek) used by NAVIGATOR. This modification was made to control for model effects and isolate the benefit of the exploration strategy itself. We otherwise followed the evaluation protocol of [34], including the 2-hour audit window per app.

Metric: Activity Coverage. Following established practices [34], we adopt *Activity Coverage* (together with *Activity Count*) as our primary evaluation metric, defined as the ratio of unique Android activities visited by the agent (A_{visited}) to the total activities declared in the `AndroidManifest.xml` file (A_{total}). While Activity Coverage is a standard metric in automated testing, in the context of UI-driven security auditing, it serves as a practical proxy for *attack-surface reachability* rather than a direct measure of vulnerability discovery. Since activities typically encapsulate distinct functional modules or business boundaries, reaching a deeply nested activity implies that the agent has successfully bypassed antecedent logic guards (*e.g.*, authentication or prerequisite setups), thereby making the associated functionality reachable for subsequent security analysis.

4.2 Effectiveness in Surface Expansion

We define effectiveness as the system's ability to maximize the reachability of app states within a constrained audit window (defaulting to 2 h).

Improvement over the SOTA Baseline. As detailed in Table 1, NAVIGATOR demonstrates the ability to penetrate logic barriers. Cumulatively, NAVIGATOR successfully navigated to 216 unique activities, outperforming the SOTA baseline LLM-Explorer (203 activities). This represents a 6.4% expansion of the visible attack surface. Although the numerical margin is moderate, these additional activities often correspond to the "tail end" of deep-state logic (e.g., hidden finance panels), which are guarded by complex dependencies and are difficult for dynamic agents to reach. This result suggests that static guidance helps local-view agents reach deeper functionalities that would otherwise remain difficult to access.

Table 1. The activity coverage achieved by NAVIGATOR and baselines.

App Name	Activity Count(#)	Complexity	NAVIGATOR		LLM-Explorer		Human	
			#	%	#	%	#	%
Activity Diary	11	Medium	**10**	**90.91%**	**10**	**90.91%**	11	100.00%
App Launcher	8	Low	**7**	**87.50%**	**7**	**87.50%**	7	87.50%
Calculator	12	Medium	**10**	**83.33%**	**10**	**83.33%**	10	83.33%
Calendar	18	Medium	**12**	**66.67%**	11	61.11%	11	61.11%
Camera	8	Low	**7**	**87.50%**	**7**	**87.50%**	7	87.50%
Clock	14	Medium	**8**	**57.14%**	**8**	**57.14%**	8	57.14%
Contacts	12	Medium	**9**	**75.00%**	**9**	**75.00%**	10	83.33%
Draw	8	Low	**6**	**75.00%**	5	62.50%	6	75.00%
File Manager	15	Medium	**11**	**73.33%**	**11**	**73.33%**	8	53.33%
Gallery	23	High	**14**	**60.87%**	12	52.17%	13	56.52%
Google Mail	64	High	**16**	**25.00%**	**16**	**25.00%**	18	28.13%
Keyboard	10	Low	**7**	**70.00%**	**7**	**70.00%**	7	70.00%
Markor	11	Medium	**6**	**54.55%**	**6**	**54.55%**	6	54.55%
Music Player	16	Medium	**13**	**81.25%**	10	62.50%	12	75.00%
My Expenses	53	High	**19**	**35.85%**	13	24.53%	28	52.83%
Notes	10	Low	**8**	**80.00%**	**8**	**80.00%**	8	80.00%
Open Tracks	24	High	**16**	**66.67%**	**16**	**66.67%**	12	50.00%
SMS Messenger	16	Medium	**14**	**87.50%**	13	81.25%	12	75.00%
Voice Recorder	12	Medium	**8**	**66.67%**	**8**	**66.67%**	8	66.67%
Wikipedia	57	High	15	26.32%	**16**	**28.07%**	20	35.09%
Average	–	–	–	**67.55%**	–	64.49%	–	66.60%
Total	402	–	**216**	–	203	–	222	–

Note: The Human data are based on a revised dataset obtained through correspondence with the authors of [34], rather than the figures originally reported in that paper

Matching the Average Human Baseline. In terms of average activity coverage, NAVIGATOR (67.55%) matches the Human Baseline (66.60%). At the same time, the total number of unique activities discovered by human auditors remains slightly higher (222 vs. 216), indicating that human auditors still retain an advantage on the most complex apps. Nevertheless, NAVIGATOR reaches 97.3% of the total human-discovered activities at a fraction of the cost (approx. $0.056 per app, as detailed in Table 3). These results suggest that our *Static Attack Surface Mapping* (Sect. 3.2) substantially narrows the gap between machine efficiency and human intuition, converting "hidden" code into a more testable surface without requiring human intervention.

Table 2. Activity coverage after 2 and 4 h of exploration by NAVIGATOR for selected high-complexity apps.

App Name	2H Exp.		4H Exp.		Human	
	#	%	#	%	#	%
Google Mail	16	25.00%	21	32.81%	18	28.13%
My Expenses	19	35.85%	26	49.06%	28	52.83%
Wikipedia	15	26.32%	21	36.84%	20	35.09%
Overall (20 Apps)	216	67.55%	**234**	**69.13%**	222	66.60%

Persistence in Deep Auditing. Security audits often require sustained interaction to bypass complex dependency chains. To evaluate persistence, we extended the audit window for NAVIGATOR to 4 h, excluding the baseline LLM-Explorer because its coverage trajectory plateaus early within the standard timeframe (detailed in Sect. 4.3). In contrast, NAVIGATOR sustains a robust upward trajectory. Table 2 confirms that NAVIGATOR continues to unlock critical deep-state screens (*e.g.*, in "Google Mail" and "Wikipedia") beyond the standard 2-hour audit window. Although extending the duration increases the temporal cost, this trade-off is acceptable for a fully automated system when deeper unattended exploration is desired.

4.3 Efficiency of Auditing

Time-to-Coverage Analysis. Figure 4 illustrates the progressive activity coverage over time. While LLM-Explorer exhibits a steep initial climb by capturing shallow states, its discovery rate declines significantly after the initial phase. In contrast, NAVIGATOR exhibits a sustained discovery rate. This validates our "Directed Auditing" paradigm: NAVIGATOR leverages its static roadmap and dual-memory context to methodically penetrate deeper states, whereas local-view agents hit a "semantic wall" once the shallow surface is exhausted.

Step Efficiency Analysis. Figure 5 plots coverage against the number of interaction steps. From an auditing perspective, efficiency is measured by the number

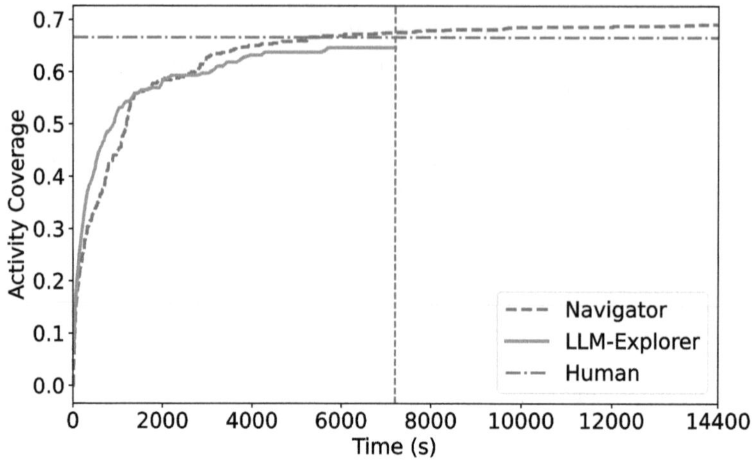

Fig. 4. Progressive activity coverage over time. NAVIGATOR demonstrates sustained penetration capability, continuing to uncover new activities where the baseline plateaus. The gray dashed line (vertical) represents 7200 s (2 h). (Color figure online)

of meaningful interactions. Our analysis reveals that NAVIGATOR achieves deep-state reachability with significantly fewer redundant steps than the baseline. By avoiding local loops via the Short-Term Memory and utilizing shortcuts from the Long-Term Memory, NAVIGATOR ensures that a higher proportion of generated actions contribute to legitimate state transitions.

Table 3. The average number of tokens consumed and estimated cost by NAVIGATOR and LLM-Explorer when exploring an app. We report the cost for NAVIGATOR under both standard (2 h) and extended (4 h) audit windows.

Method	Input	Output	Total	Cost($)
NAVIGATOR (4h)	269,443	22,765	292,208	0.103
NAVIGATOR (2h)	139,723	13,620	153,343	0.056
LLM-Explorer (2h)	81,576	18,312	99,888	0.044

Cost-Benefit Analysis. Table 3 compares the token consumption. We acknowledge that NAVIGATOR incurs a higher token cost due to the maintenance of the Dual-Memory context (approx. \$0.056 per app vs. \$0.044 for the baseline). However, we argue that this trade-off is highly favorable for security auditing. The cost of missing a single deep-state vulnerability far outweighs the marginal computational expense. Furthermore, the ability to automate what was previously only achievable by human auditors represents a significant reduction in total operational costs.

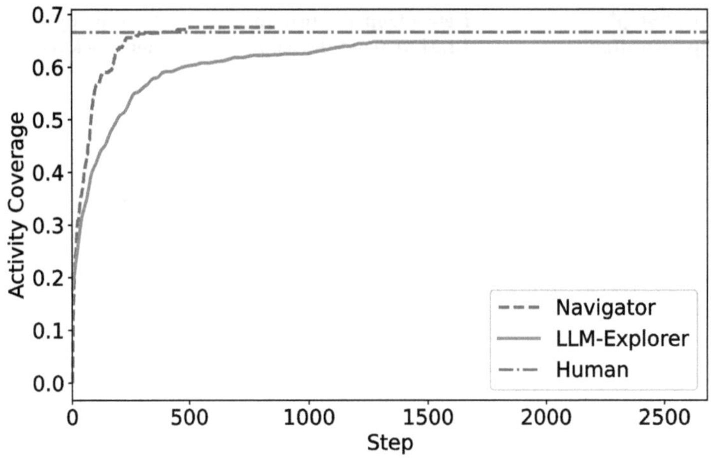

Fig. 5. Progressive activity coverage over steps. NAVIGATOR achieves deep-state reachability with fewer actions, minimizing interaction overhead in auditing.

4.4 Qualitative Analysis: Overcoming Logic Barriers

We analyze three distinct scenarios to qualitatively illustrate how NAVIGATOR resolves common logic barriers in automated dynamic auditing, effectively validating our design choices.

Case 1: Breaking Semantic Loops via STM. Automated agents often become trapped in "Semantic Loops" where an action appears logically correct to the LLM but remains ineffective at runtime. A prime example occurred in the "Open Tracks" app (refer to Fig. 6), where the agent repeatedly clicked a "Stop" button to end a recording. The action failed because the app required a *long-click*, a nuance hinted at only by a transient Toast message invisible to the agent. NAVIGATOR's Robustness Enhancement module detected this repetitive pattern via the execution trace in the *Short-Term Memory* and identified that the button can be long-clicked. Consequently, it prompted the agent to try this alternative action, successfully breaking the loop. Another example is in the "Activity Diary" app, where the agent repeatedly clicked a non-interactive "Statistics" label. Crucially, the module detected this loop and intervened by forcefully masking the problematic element from the agent's view, compelling it to explore alternative actions. This capability to recover from dead ends is typically absent in standard reinforcement learning agents.

Case 2: Accelerated Navigation via LTM Shortcuts. Deep-state functionalities are often guarded by lengthy navigation sequences. In the "My Expenses" app (refer to Fig. 7), when tasked with "Add a new tag," a memory-less agent would inefficiently restart exploration from the root activity. In contrast, NAVIGATOR queried its *Long-Term Knowledge Base*. It recognized that the target

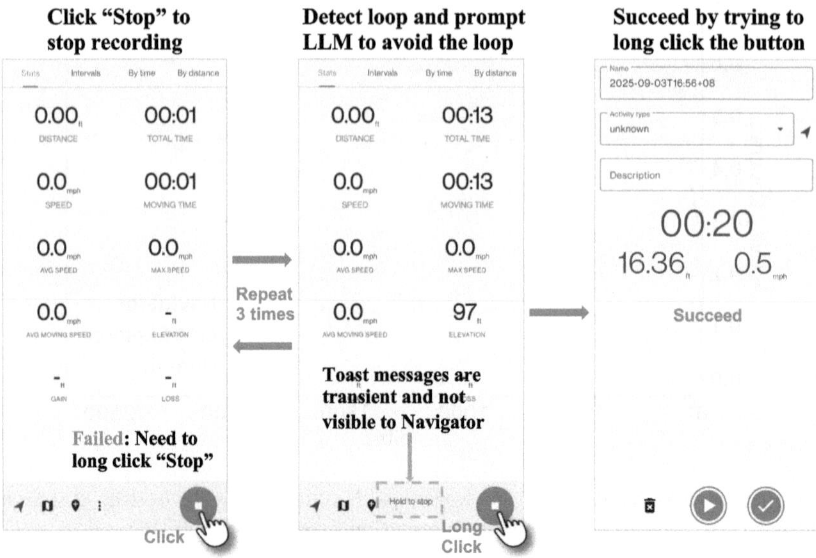

Fig. 6. Logic Trap Mitigation: The system detected the loop and prompted the agent to try an alternative action (i.e., long click) in the action space.

UI resided within the "Data" screen, which had been indexed during a previous task. Leveraging this global persistence, the agent executed a "Shortcut," instantly navigating to the relevant state without re-exploring the path. This mechanism mimics the behavior of a skilled human auditor who remembers navigation paths, significantly reducing the overhead of deep penetration.

Case 3: Bridging the Semantic Gap with Static Maps. The core advantage of our hybrid framework is its ability to find targets that are invisible to dynamic-only tools. In the "My Expenses" app (refer to Fig. 8), the entry points for the "ManageTags" and "BudgetEdit" screens were not intuitively obvious in the visual hierarchy. However, during the offline phase, the *Static Attack Surface Mapping* module successfully reconstructed these screens (into the XML format) from the decompiled bytecode. The LLM planner analyzed the static XML artifacts—identifying specific input fields like "Title" and "Description"—and formulated precise tasks such as "Create a new budget." This prior knowledge allowed the online agent to actively hunt for the path to these specific targets, rather than waiting to stumble upon them by chance. This advantage is also reflected quantitatively in Table 1: Under the same 2-hour budget, NAVIGATOR reached 19 activities in "My Expenses," whereas LLM-Explorer reached 13. The additional states were first surfaced by the offline map and then pursued during online execution.

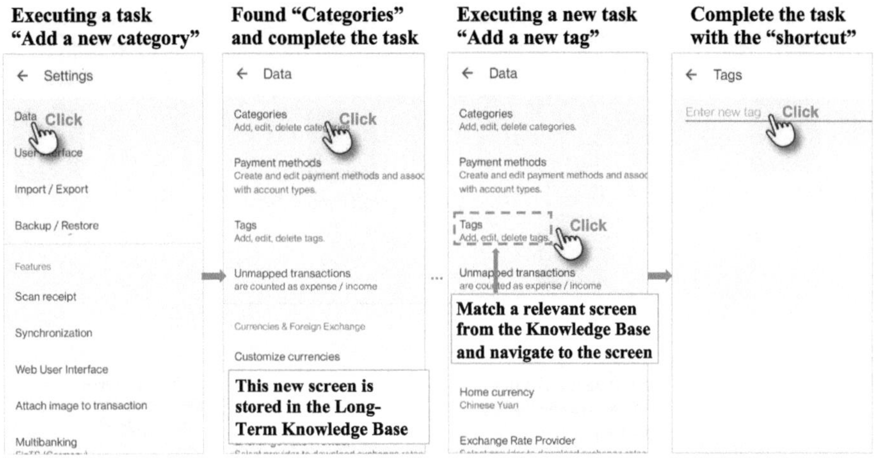

Fig. 7. Shortcuts Leverage: The system reuses a previously indexed state to accelerate deep penetration.

5 Related Work

5.1 Activity Transition Graph Construction

In mobile security auditing, the application's attack surface is typically modeled as an *Activity Transition Graph* (ATG), where nodes represent UI states (Activities), and edges denote user interactions. The completeness of this ATG serves as a proxy for the coverage of the attack surface: Any vulnerability residing in a node (screen) not included in the ATG remains unreachable and undetectable. Existing approaches to construct or traverse this graph generally fall into two categories: *static modeling* and *dynamic exploration.*

Static Modeling. Static approaches [4,14,31,33] aim to reconstruct the ATG by analyzing the codebase without execution. Tools like Gator [31] and Goal-Explorer [14] perform control-flow analysis on callbacks and API usages to statically infer screen transitions. While these methods may provide a global view of the app's structure, they suffer from inherent limitations in resolving modern Android complexities. Specifically, static analyzers often fail to handle obfuscated code, reflection, and dynamic UI loading (e.g., Fragment transactions). This results in an ATG that is either over-approximated (containing infeasible paths) or fragmented (missing critical links to deep-state targets).

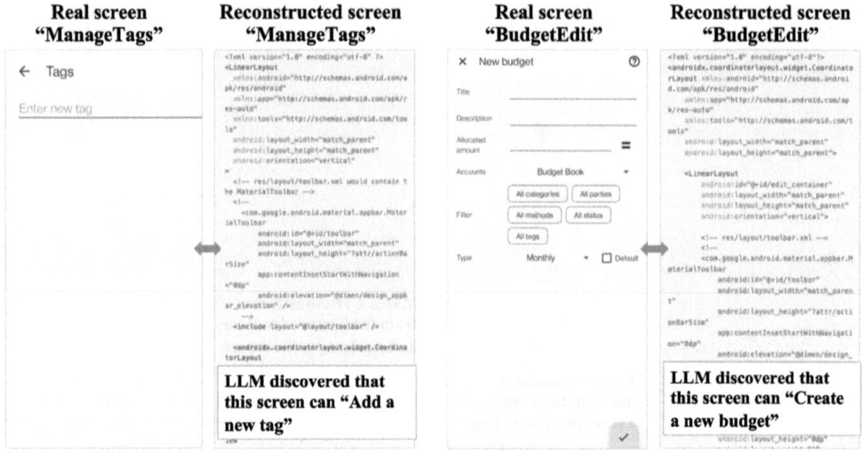

Fig. 8. Static Map Guidance: Offline static analysis exposes hidden targets that dynamic-only agents might overlook.

Dynamic Exploration. To overcome the inaccuracies of static modeling, dynamic analysis tools [8,12,16,17] attempt to discover the ATG by interacting with the running application. Traditional automated explorers, represented by random-based (e.g., Monkey [7]) and model-based testing tools (e.g., Stoat [25]), act as heuristic crawlers to traverse the graph. More advanced tools like DroidBot [16] and Humanoid [17] employ learning-based strategies to improve node coverage. However, these tools generally lack semantic understanding [34] and a global view of the app's structure. They effectively explore the "shallow" portion of the ATG but frequently fail to bypass semantic guards (e.g., login forms or complex setup wizards), leaving the "deep" nodes of the graph—and their associated attack surface—unexposed. Unlike these distinct approaches, NAVIGATOR utilizes the static inventory to provide a semantic map that guides the LLM-based dynamic agent to proactively expand the reachable states.

5.2 LLM-Driven Mobile App Automation

The emergence of Large Language Models (LLMs) has introduced new possibilities for semantic-aware mobile app automation. LLMs possess the cognitive capability to interpret UI contexts, making them suitable for navigating complex logic that traditional automated explorers struggle to comprehend.

Recent works have applied LLMs to various mobile tasks, including bug replay [10], GUI testing [18,19], and user task automation [15,28,29]. In the specific domain of automated exploration, tools like MobileGPT [15] and LLM-Explorer [34] leverage LLMs for local decision-making, while DroidAgent [32] introduces an intent-driven planner for strategic exploration. However, these existing agents remain bound by a reactive paradigm. They derive next steps solely from real-time visual observations without a complete view of the app, a limitation we refer to as the "local perspective." This hinders the discovery of deep-state functionalities guarded by complex prerequisites.

In contrast, NAVIGATOR bridges this gap by leveraging static analysis to build a *prior* knowledge base of the app's theoretical attack surface. This allows our agent to proactively "hunt" for screens that are statically known to exist but dynamically elusive, effectively guiding the LLM to penetrate logic barriers that runtime-only agents might overlook.

6 Discussion and Limitations

Despite NAVIGATOR's improvements in deep-state reachability, this work still has several limitations. First, our static analysis operates on decompiled bytecode. Although it is generally robust to standard obfuscation because it relies on stable framework API invocations, it can still be affected by more aggressive protections (e.g., string encryption). Second, the current reconstruction pipeline is tailored to native Android views, which may reduce its effectiveness on apps built with cross-platform frameworks (e.g., Flutter) or those heavily relying on opaque *WebViews*. Third, our text-based UI abstraction improves token efficiency, but omits visual cues such as image-only widgets. Incorporating Multimodal LLMs may therefore further improve reasoning over spatial and visual semantics. Fourth, our evaluation focuses on UI reachability rather than end-to-end vulnerability yield. We therefore treat activity coverage as an enabling proxy for exposing deeper states to downstream security analyses, rather than as a direct measure of confirmed vulnerabilities. Fifth, we adopt the public 20-app benchmark from LLM-Explorer to support controlled comparison, but this benchmark may underrepresent heavily protected commercial apps. Finally, we evaluate NAVIGATOR using a single reasoning backend and do not include a dedicated STM/LTM ablation in the current version. Cross-model sensitivity, component-isolation analyses, and broader validation on more diverse app sets remain important directions for future work.

7 Conclusion

In this work, we addressed the critical reachability challenge in automated mobile security auditing. Current dynamic explorers often fail to penetrate complex logic barriers due to a lack of semantic understanding and global awareness, leaving significant portions of the attack surface unaudited. To bridge this gap, we proposed NAVIGATOR, a hybrid framework that synergizes the global foresight of static analysis with the semantic adaptability of LLMs. By statically reconstructing a global map of targets and employing a dual-memory agent for navigation, NAVIGATOR transforms the auditing process from aimless to strategic. Our extensive evaluation demonstrates that NAVIGATOR expands reachable activities by 6.4% compared to the state-of-the-art agent and matches the average human baseline in activity coverage, while remaining slightly below the total number of unique activities discovered by human auditors. These results validate the efficacy of using static artifacts to guide generative agents and suggest a practical paradigm for exposing deeper app states to subsequent security analyses.

Acknowledgements. We sincerely appreciate all anonymous reviewers for their constructive feedback and invaluable comments. This work was fully supported by the Hong Kong Research Grants Council (RGC) under Grants CityU 21219223 and C1029-22G. Any opinions, findings, and conclusions in this paper are those of the authors and are not necessarily those of the supported organizations.

References

1. Andow, B., et al.: Actions speak louder than words: entity-Sensitive privacy policy and data flow analysis with PoliCheck. In: 29th USENIX Security Symposium (USENIX Security 20), pp. 985–1002 (2020)
2. Arzt, S., et al.: FlowDroid: precise context, flow, field, object-sensitive and lifecycle-aware taint analysis for android apps. ACM SIGPLAN Not. **49**(6), 259–269 (2014)
3. Chen, S., Fan, L., Chen, C., Liu, Y.: Automatically distilling storyboard with rich features for android apps. IEEE Trans. Software Eng. **49**(2), 667–683 (2022)
4. Chen, S., et al.: StoryDroid: automated generation of storyboard for android apps. In: 2019 IEEE/ACM 41st International Conference on Software Engineering (ICSE), pp. 596–607. IEEE (2019)
5. DeepSeek: DeepSeek-V3. https://github.com/deepseek-ai/DeepSeek-V3 (2025)
6. Deniz-Garcia, A., et al.: Quality, usability, and effectiveness of mHealth apps and the role of artificial intelligence: current scenario and challenges. J. Med. Internet Res. **25**, e44030 (2023)
7. Developers, A.: Ui/application exerciser monkey. https://developer.android.com/studio/test/other-testing-tools/monkey (2024)
8. Dong, Z., Böhme, M., Cojocaru, L., Roychoudhury, A.: Time-travel testing of android apps. In: Proceedings of the ACM/IEEE 42nd International Conference on Software Engineering, pp. 481–492 (2020)
9. F-Droid: F-droid - free and open source android app repository. https://f-droid.org/tutorials/ (2025)
10. Feng, S., Chen, C.: Prompting is all you need: automated android bug replay with large language models. In: Proceedings of the 46th IEEE/ACM International Conference on Software Engineering, pp. 1–13 (2024)
11. Franceschelli, G., Musolesi, M.: On the creativity of large language models. AI Soc. 1–11 (2024)
12. Gu, T., et al.: Practical GUI testing of android applications via model abstraction and refinement. In: 2019 IEEE/ACM 41st International Conference on Software Engineering (ICSE), pp. 269–280. IEEE (2019)
13. Kajol, K., Singh, R., Paul, J.: Adoption of digital financial transactions: a review of literature and future research agenda. Technol. Forecast. Soc. Chang. **184**, 121991 (2022)
14. Lai, D., Rubin, J.: Goal-driven exploration for android applications. In: 34th IEEE/ACM International Conference on Automated Software Engineering (ASE), pp. 115–127. IEEE (2019)

15. Lee, S., et al.: MobileGPT: augmenting LLM with human-like app memory for mobile task automation. In: Proceedings of the 30th Annual International Conference on Mobile Computing and Networking, pp. 1119–1133 (2024)
16. Li, Y., Yang, Z., Guo, Y., Chen, X.: DroidBot: a lightweight UI-guided test input generator for android. In: 2017 IEEE/ACM 39th International Conference on Software Engineering Companion (ICSE-C), pp. 23–26. IEEE (2017)
17. Li, Y., Yang, Z., Guo, Y., Chen, X.: Humanoid: a deep learning-based approach to automated black-box android app testing. In: 34th IEEE/ACM International Conference on Automated Software Engineering (ASE), pp. 1070–1073. IEEE (2019)
18. Liu, Z., et al.: Fill in the blank: context-aware automated text input generation for mobile GUI testing. In: 2023 IEEE/ACM 45th International Conference on Software Engineering (ICSE), pp. 1355–1367. IEEE (2023)
19. Liu, Z., et al.: Make LLM a testing expert: bringing human-like interaction to mobile GUI testing via functionality-aware decisions. In: Proceedings of the IEEE/ACM 46th International Conference on Software Engineering, pp. 1–13 (2024)
20. Nguyen, T.T., Backes, M., Marnau, N., Stock, B.: Share first, ask later (or never?) studying violations of GDPR's explicit consent in android apps. In: 30th USENIX Security Symposium (USENIX Security 21), pp. 3667–3684 (2021)
21. Pan, M., Huang, A., Wang, G., Zhang, T., Li, X.: Reinforcement learning based curiosity-driven testing of android applications. In: Proceedings of the 29th ACM SIGSOFT International Symposium on Software Testing and Analysis, pp. 153–164 (2020)
22. Romdhana, A., Merlo, A., Ceccato, M., Tonella, P.: Deep reinforcement learning for black-box testing of android apps. ACM Trans. Softw. Eng. Methodol. (TOSEM) **31**(4), 1–29 (2022)
23. Sharma, A., Singh, S.K., Kumar, S., Chhabra, A., Gupta, S.: Security of android banking mobile apps: challenges and opportunities. In: International conference on cyber security, privacy and networking, pp. 406–416. Springer (2021)
24. Soot: Soot: a framework for analyzing and transforming java and android applications. http://soot-oss.github.io/soot (2023)
25. Su, T., et al.: Guided, stochastic model-based GUI testing of android apps. In: Proceedings of the 2017 11th Joint Meeting on Foundations of Software Engineering, pp. 245–256 (2017)
26. Trimananda, R., Le, H., Cui, H., Ho, J.T., Shuba, A., Markopoulou, A.: OVRseen: Auditing network traffic and privacy policies in oculus VR. In: 31st USENIX Security Symposium (USENIX security 22), pp. 3789–3806 (2022)
27. Ventola, C.L.: Mobile devices and apps for health care professionals: uses and benefits. Pharm. Ther. **39**(5), 356 (2014)
28. Wang, B., Li, G., Li, Y.: Enabling conversational interaction with mobile UI using large language models. In: Proceedings of the 2023 CHI Conference on Human Factors in Computing Systems, pp. 1–17 (2023)
29. Wen, H., et al.: AutoDroid: LLM-powered task automation in android. In: Proceedings of the 30th Annual International Conference on Mobile Computing and Networking, pp. 543–557 (2024)
30. Xiao, Y., et al.: Lalaine: measuring and characterizing Non-Compliance of apple privacy labels. In: 32nd USENIX Security Symposium (USENIX Security 23), pp. 1091–1108 (2023)
31. Yang, S., et al.: Static window transition graphs for android. Autom. Softw. Eng. **25**, 833–873 (2018)

32. Yoon, J., Feldt, R., Yoo, S.: Intent-driven mobile GUI testing with autonomous large language model agents. In: 2024 IEEE Conference on Software Testing, Verification and Validation (ICST), pp. 129–139. IEEE (2024)
33. Zhang, X., Fan, L., Chen, S., Su, Y., Li, B.: Scene-driven exploration and GUI modeling for android apps. In: 38th IEEE/ACM International Conference on Automated Software Engineering (ASE), pp. 1251–1262. IEEE (2023)
34. Zhao, S., et al.: LLM-explorer: towards efficient and affordable LLM-based exploration for mobile apps. In: Proceedings of the 31st Annual International Conference on Mobile Computing and Networking, pp. 589–603 (2025)

Fingerprinting and Biasing Bandwidth Measurements

Vahab Pournaghshband(✉) and Lawrence Ng

University of San Francisco, San Francisco, CA 94117, USA
{vahab.p,lsng}@usfca.edu

Abstract. Bandwidth measurement tools play a central role in shaping user trust, regulatory oversight, and competition among Internet Service Providers (ISPs). These tools are commonly assumed to provide neutral, end-hostbased measurements that reflect true network performance. However, this assumption critically depends on the network behaving in a benign manner. In this paper, we show that this assumption is fragile in adversarial settings. We introduce a threat model in which a moderately capable on-path ISP identifies bandwidth measurement traffic and selectively manipulates it to inflate reported performance while leaving ordinary user traffic unaffected. Our aim is to reveal a previously underexplored vulnerability in existing bandwidth measurement tools and to highlight the need for adversary-aware measurement design.

We demonstrate that simple and lightweight static fingerprints are sufficient to reliably identify popular bandwidth measurement tools in practice. By implementing an emulated ISP with such static fingerprinting capabilities, we show that selectively boosting identified measurement flows systematically inflates reported throughput across multiple tools. We further outline a design space of behavioral fingerprints based on traffic dynamics, such as throughput ramp-up patterns, concurrent sessions, and packet size distributions, that could strengthen such attacks even as protocol metadata becomes less visible.

Keywords: Bandwidth Measurement · Traffic Fingerprinting · Traffic Classification

1 Introduction

Bandwidth measurement tools such as Speedtest.net and Fast.com play a central role in shaping user trust, regulatory oversight, and competition among Internet Service Providers (ISPs). Consumers rely on these tools to assess the quality of their service, regulators use them to inform policy and enforcement, and providers themselves cite them in performance claims and marketing. These tools are commonly assumed to provide neutral, end-hostdriven measurements that reflect true network performance, and to operate in environments where the network does not behave adversarially with respect to measurement traffic.

Y. Cao et al. (Eds.): SecureComm 2026, LNICST 704, pp. 103–112, 2027.
https://doi.org/10.1007/978-3-032-32764-2_5

In practice, however, ISPs possess both the technical capability and the economic incentives to treat different classes of traffic differently [7,17]. Modern networks already implement traffic classification and differentiation mechanisms for purposes ranging from congestion management to application optimization [8,9,13,16,18]. This raises a natural question: can bandwidth measurement traffic itself be recognized and selectively manipulated? If so, reported performance could be inflated without affecting normal user traffic, thereby undermining the integrity of bandwidth measurement results.

While prior work has studied methodological biases [15], environmental variability [10], and contextual limitations [19] of bandwidth measurement tools, the security implications of strategic, adversarial network behavior in this context have received little attention.

This paper takes an adversarial perspective on bandwidth measurement. We consider a threat model in which a moderately capable on-path ISP seeks to identify and selectively manipulate measurement traffic while remaining indistinguishable from a benign network to users and external observers. Our goal is not to quantify the prevalence of such behavior in the wild, but rather to expose a structural vulnerability and thus to motivate the design of more robust, adversary-aware bandwidth measurement tools.
Our contributions are as follows:

1. We formalize an adversarial threat model for bandwidth measurement in which an on-path network adversary attempts to recognize and selectively manipulate measurement traffic without disrupting normal application traffic or triggering user-visible anomalies.
2. We demonstrate the feasibility of fast and lightweight detection of measurement traffic using only static metadata and validate this approach experimentally in a controlled testbed. The results show that current measurement tools are already vulnerable to simple classification mechanisms that can be implemented at line rate with minimal overhead.
3. We outline behavioral fingerprints such as throughput ramp-up dynamics that could enable or strengthen such attacks even as encryption mechanisms evolve. Although these behavioral features are not experimentally evaluated, they are presented to highlight the structural fingerprintability of existing measurement tools and to motivate adversary-aware measurement design.

The remainder of the paper is organized as follows. Section 2 presents related work, followed by the methodology in Sect. 3. Evaluation and Discussion are presented in Sects. 4 and 5, respectively. Section 6 concludes the paper.

2 Related Work

Prior work has demonstrated that measurement configurations (e.g., thread counts, test duration, and server selection) can systematically bias speed test results across tools [14,15]. These studies show that reported performance can be influenced by non-adversarial factors such as access technology (WiFi vs.

wired), device limitations, background cross-traffic, server placement, and subscription tier.

Environmental variability, such as demographic, geographic, and temporal sampling bias, also significantly affects the interpretation of crowdsourced speed test data [10]. Other work further demonstrates that measured performance varies with network context (e.g., latency, geographic distribution of tests, and peering relationships), revealing limitations in interpreting raw speed test results without additional contextual awareness [19].

Complementary work [20] focuses on characterizing the internal behavior of web-based speed tests, including the complexity introduced by browser execution models, CDN selection, and proprietary testing strategies. This line of research emphasizes that speed tests can be opaque systems whose internal algorithms and server choices significantly affect measured throughput, even when ISPs behave benignly.

In contrast to existing work, which primarily treats ISPs as non-adversarial and focuses on methodological bias, variability, and tool design limitations, this work studies a strategic ISP adversary that actively attempts to (i) detect measurement traffic using static and behavioral fingerprints, and (ii) bias outcomes by selectively prioritizing suspected measurement flows.

3 Methodology

3.1 Threat Model

We consider a moderately capable commercial ISP that seeks to identify bandwidth measurement traffic and bias measurement outcomes in its favor (e.g., by inflating reported throughput). The ISP's objective is not to disrupt connectivity or compromise end hosts, but rather to selectively prioritize suspected measurement traffic or bypass shaping policies during tests, while keeping such manipulation difficult to detect by end users.

Adversary Capabilities. The ISP is on-path (e.g., at the access or aggregation layer) and can:

- Observe network and transport metadata for all packets, including IP addresses, ports, protocols, TCP flags, flow durations, and TLS handshake metadata that is typically visible in practice (e.g., Server Name Indication (SNI) when not protected by encrypted ClientHello).
- Track flow-level behavioral features using lightweight per-flow state, including connection concurrency, ramp-up dynamics, burstiness, throughput evolution, and inter-arrival timing.
- Enforce traffic management policies that differentially affect flows, such as shaping, prioritization, or queue selection, enabling selective performance boosts for suspected measurement traffic.

Adversary Limitations. We assume the ISP:

- Cannot decrypt application payloads for TLS-protected traffic.
- Does not deploy computationally expensive per-flow analysis at line rate (e.g., deep learning classifiers), and instead relies on efficient heuristics feasible in operational networks.
- Cannot arbitrarily influence routing outside its administrative domain.

Assumptions about Measurement Tools. We assume that popular bandwidth measurement tools:

- Use encrypted transport (e.g., TLS), exposing only limited protocol and flow metadata.
- Are not explicitly designed to evade fingerprinting through obfuscation, padding, or traffic morphing.

3.2 Selection of Bandwidth Measurement Tools

In this paper, we examined five bandwidth measurement tools: Speedtest.net [6], Fast.com [1], SpeedOf.Me [5], Speedcheck.org [4], and iPerf3 [2]. These tools were chosen to represent a diverse cross-section of most popular bandwidth measurement platforms, spanning commercial and research tools, web-based and native implementations, proprietary and open-source systems, and differing testing architectures. This diversity ensures that our results reflect general properties of bandwidth measurement tools.

3.3 System Overview

Our system consists of three stages: traffic observation, fingerprinting engine, and policy engine (Fig. 1).

The observation layer monitors packet headers and flow-level metadata available to an on-path ISP, such as IP addresses, ports, protocol identifiers, TLS handshake fields, packet sizes, timing, and flow concurrency.

The fingerprinting engine classifies observed flows as either bandwidth measurement traffic or regular traffic. We consider two classes of fingerprints. Static fingerprints rely on protocol metadata, such as TLS SNI fields and known server address ranges; these fingerprints are fast, lightweight, and are implemented and evaluated in this work. Behavioral fingerprints rely on traffic dynamics, such as ramp-up behavior, connection concurrency, packet size distributions, and temporal rate patterns; these are more robust to evasion but are computationally more complex.

Following classification, flows identified as measurement traffic are routed to an unthrottled queue or given higher priority, while all other traffic remains subject to the ISP's baseline shaping or throttling policies. This selective treatment enables the ISP to inflate reported performance during measurement tests while leaving ordinary user traffic unaffected.

Figure 1 illustrates the adversarial ISP pipeline from metadata observation to selective traffic manipulation

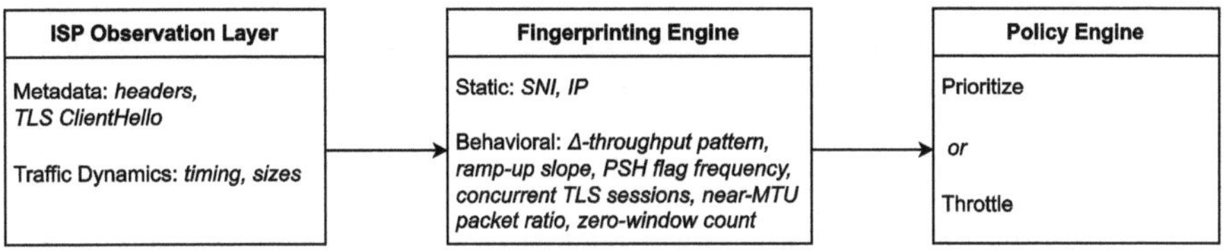

Fig. 1. Adversarial ISP pipeline. An on-path ISP observes encrypted traffic metadata and flow-level dynamics, applies static and behavioral fingerprinting to classify bandwidth measurement traffic, and selectively manipulates identified flows (e.g., by prioritizing or bypassing shaping) to inflate reported performance while leaving other traffic unchanged.

3.4 Static Fingerprinting

We implement static identification using TLS SNI fields and destination IP address matching. For each observed TLS ClientHello message, we extract the SNI field to create a list of known bandwidth measurement server domains.

In practice, we observe that the SNI values used by most tools are few in number and stable over time, making them a reliable and lightweight basis for static fingerprinting. Table 1 summarizes the server names extracted from TLS connections for the evaluated tools.

The exception is iPerf3, which does not use TLS and instead connects directly to publicly available iPerf3 servers. For iPerf3, we construct static fingerprints using the IP addresses of known iPerf3 servers obtained from a public directory [3]. This approach is inherently less robust, as server IP addresses may change over time and therefore require periodic updates. We were unable to find publicly available information on how frequently these server addresses change.

Overall, among the static indicators we considered, SNI proved to be the most consistent and reliable feature for identifying bandwidth measurement traffic.

3.5 Behavioral Fingerprinting

After analyzing the traffic generated by bandwidth measurement tools and running experiments multiple times, several behavioral features are proposed that could further improve identification in adversarial settings where static metadata becomes unavailable or server names and IP addresses change. The following features capture common behavioral themes across tools and can be used jointly to improve classification:

Table 1. Bandwidth measurement tools and associated server names observed in TLS connections.

fast.com	speedof.me	speedcheck.org	speedtest.net
`fast.com`	`speedof.me`	`www.speedcheck.org`	`www.speedtest.net`
`api.fast.com`	`cdn.speedof.me`	`cdn.speedcheck.org`	`b.cdnst.net`
`ichaea-web.netflix.com`		`api.speedspot.org`	`cdn.ziffstatic.com`
`*.oca.nflxvideo.net`	`b1.etrality.com`		

1. *Δ-Throughput Pattern.* Behavioral signatures can be encoded as symbolic sequences derived from per-second changes in throughput. Traffic is divided into 1-second windows, and each window is assigned a symbol based on the change relative to the previous window: 2 indicates an increase in throughput, 1 indicates approximately constant throughput, and 0 indicates a decrease. This produces a symbolic time series that captures the control dynamics of each tool rather than its absolute sending rate.
   Applying this encoding to a small subset of tools—specifically iPerf3, Fast.com, and Speedtest.net—reveals that each exhibits a distinct and repeatable signature. Table 2 shows representative examples. iPerf3 typically produces fast ramp-up sequences followed by extended plateaus, while Fast.com exhibits more oscillatory patterns due to its multi-server probing behavior. Speedtest.net shows a characteristic ramp-up followed by alternating increases and plateaus as it shifts traffic across multiple CDN endpoints.
   As an illustration, the longest patterns observed for each tool are summarized in Table 2. Such long signatures are highly specific and unlikely to occur by chance in non-measurement traffic. However, matching long sequences requires observing many seconds of traffic, which delays detection and thus manipulation. On the other hand, using shorter prefixes enables earlier classification but increases the risk of false positives.
2. *Flow Concurrency.* The number of overlapping TLS sessions inferred from distinct TLS handshakes and 5-tuples can be used as a feature, as speed tests typically open several concurrent connections to saturate available bandwidth.
3. *TCP Zero-Window Frequency.* The frequency of TCP zero-window advertisements can be recorded, as these indicate receiver-side backpressure under aggressive transfers.
4. *PSH Flag Frequency.* The frequency of TCP packets with the PSH flag set reflects application-level intent to push data to the receiver promptly rather than allowing additional buffering. Bandwidth measurement tools often set PSH on a large fraction of packets in order to tightly control transfer timing and reduce buffering during tests. As a result, a high PSH frequency can serve as a behavioral indicator of measurement traffic.
5. *Throughput Ramp-Up Spikes.* To capture the rapid startup behavior characteristic of bandwidth measurement tools, throughput ramp-up spikes can be

computed by measuring the maximum positive change in throughput over consecutive windows.

6. *Near-MTU Packet Ratio.* The near-MTU packet ratio, defined as the fraction of packets with payload sizes close to the MTU (≈1400 bytes), reflects sustained bulk transfer behavior.

Table 2. Example symbolic behavioral patterns observed for different bandwidth measurement tools.

Tool	Δ-Throughput Pattern
iPerf3	20111111111001
	2111111111111110
Fast.com	22212121002121121
Speedtest.net	21011000121111110
	2101100012111111
	2111112000111
	20001100120110
	2021112111011100
	20111211210210011111111110

Individually, these behavioral features are not unique to bandwidth measurement traffic; however, when combined, they can form a more robust fingerprint.

4 Evaluation

4.1 Testbed Setup

We conducted our experiments in a controlled environment consisting of the bandwidth measurement tool servers and two machines: one acting as the client and one emulating an on-path ISP. The ISP behavior was implemented using the Click Modular Router [11], with the fingerprinting engine implemented inside Click's `Classifier` element.

We configured the emulated ISP to enforce a bandwidth cap of 10 Mbps for all traffic using Click's `Shaper` element, which implements traffic shaping policies. Flows identified as belonging to bandwidth measurement tools were instead routed to an unthrottled path. This configuration enables us to directly observe whether measurement tools are selectively boosted relative to the true capacity in the presence of an active biased ISP.

We evaluated five tools: SpeedOfMe, Speedcheck, Fast.com, Speedtest.net, and iPerf3. Each tool was executed 24 times, once per hour over a 24-hour period, for both upload and download directions, yielding a total of 48 measurements per tool.

4.2 Results

Figure 2 shows the distribution of measured bandwidth across tools and directions under the adversarial ISP configuration.

For all tools and directions, the measured bandwidth significantly exceeds the throttled baseline, indicating that the static fingerprint—based on TLS SNI and known server address ranges—successfully identifies measurement traffic and routes it to the unthrottled path. All tools tested consistently report both download and upload speeds well above 10 Mbps (see Fig. 2).

These results demonstrate that simple and lightweight metadata-based fingerprints are sufficient to selectively manipulate the reported performance of multiple popular bandwidth measurement tools.

We also observe occasional outliers, defined as measurements outside 1.5 × IQR. These correspond to instances where measured bandwidth is lower than expected even for identified measurement traffic and are primarily attributable to transient background cross-traffic during the measurement period. We further acknowledge that our results may be partly affected by known performance limitations and processing overhead introduced by the Click framework [12].

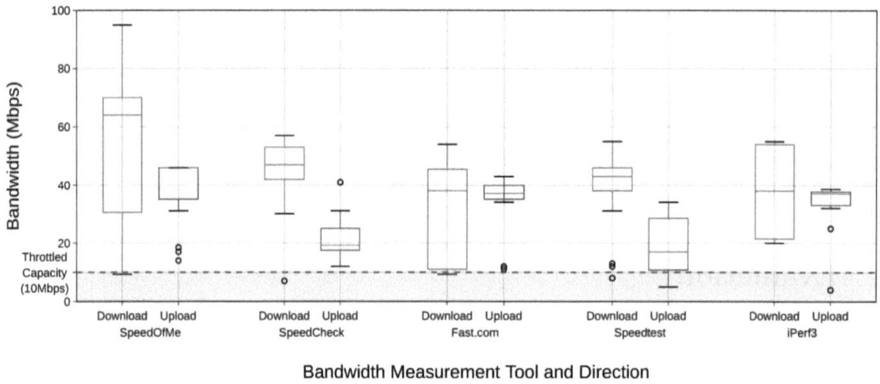

Fig. 2. Distribution of measured bandwidth across tools and directions under an adversarial ISP configuration. The dashed line and shaded region indicate the throttled capacity (≤10 Mbps). Each boxplot summarizes 24 runs (one per hour). Outliers (shown as circles) are defined as observations outside 1.5 × IQR.

5 Discussion

Static fingerprinting represents a best-case scenario for the adversary in terms of impact. Because static fingerprints can be extracted from the very first packets of a flow (e.g., the TLS ClientHello), detection occurs with minimal latency. This allows the ISP to apply preferential treatment from the start of a measurement, maximizing the fraction of the test that is boosted and thus maximizing the inflation of reported performance. In this sense, static fingerprinting provides an upper bound on how much an on-path adversary can bias measurement results.

At the same time, static fingerprinting relies only on lightweight and widely available metadata that is readily accessible to an on-path ISP. Therefore, it represents a conservative baseline on adversarial capability, establishing a lower bound on the sophistication required to identify and manipulate measurement traffic. Together, these properties make static fingerprinting a useful reference point for evaluating both stronger attacks and potential defenses.

Fingerprinting also introduces an abuse vector: a user could deliberately generate traffic that mimics bandwidth measurement flows in order to trigger the fingerprinting mechanism and obtain preferential treatment for non-measurement traffic. For example, a user could prepend or interleave ordinary application traffic with measurement-like traffic to induce classification as a speed test and thereby tunnel arbitrary traffic through the unthrottled path. To mitigate this risk, preferential treatment can be restricted to a short time window following detection. In our implementation, the unthrottled path is enabled only for a limited duration after fingerprint detection. This window was empirically set to 8 s, as most evaluated bandwidth measurement tools complete or nearly complete their tests within this timeframe. This limits the feasibility of effective tunneling while still allowing measurement tools to complete their tests.

6 Concluding Remarks

In this paper, we showed that popular bandwidth measurement tools can be identified and selectively manipulated by an on-path ISP using simple static fingerprints, exposing a structural vulnerability in existing bandwidth measurement tools. We also outlined behavioral fingerprints that could further strengthen such attacks even as protocol metadata becomes less visible.

Several directions remain for future work. First, extending the implementation to include behavioral fingerprints would allow evaluation of their robustness and detection latency in practice. Second, developing secure bandwidth measurement tools that are resilient to adversarial ISP traffic manipulation remains an open problem.

Acknowledgments. The authors would like to thank James Ambat, Jayanarayanan Jayaganesh, Ashutosh Malla, and Maxwell Weidmer for their technical contributions to the design, implementation, and evaluation of the system.

References

1. Fast.com: Internet Speed Test by Netflix. https://fast.com/
2. iPerf: The TCP, UDP and SCTP Network Bandwidth Measurement Tool. https://iperf.fr/
3. Public iPerf3 servers. https://iperf.fr/iperf-servers.php

4. Speedcheck.org: Internet Speed Test. https://speedcheck.org/
5. SpeedOf.Me: HTML5 Internet Speed Test. https://speedof.me/
6. Speedtest.net: Internet Speed Test. https://www.speedtest.net/
7. Fierce-Network: Confirmed: T-Mobile Exempting Speed-Testing Data from Monthly Data Allotments (2014). https://www.fierce-network.com/wireless/confirmed-t-mobile-exempting-speed-testing-data-from-monthly-data-allotments
8. Flach, T., et al.: An internet-wide analysis of traffic policing. In: Proceedings of the 2016 ACM SIGCOMM Conference, pp. 468–482. SIGCOMM '16, ACM (2016)
9. Garrett, T., Setenareski, L.E., Peres, L.M., Bona, L.C., Duarte, E.P.: Monitoring network neutrality: a survey on traffic differentiation detection. IEEE Commun. Surv. Tutorials (2018)
10. Han, J., Lyu, M., Sivaraman, V.: On the validity of internet speed test tools and broadband measurement programs. In: Proceedings of the 17th Asian Internet Engineering Conference, pp. 1–9. AINTEC '22, Association for Computing Machinery, New York, NY, USA (2022)
11. Kohler, E., Morris, R., Chen, B., Jannotti, J., Kaashoek, M.F.: The click modular router. ACM Trans. Comput. Syst. (TOCS) **18**(3), 263–297 (2000)
12. Kohler, E.: Programming language optimizations for modular router configurations. In: Proceedings of the 2002 ACM SIGPLAN Symposium on Principles and Practice of Parallel Programming, pp. 174–181 (2002)
13. Li, F., Niaki, A.A., Choffnes, D., Gill, P., Mislove, A.: A large-scale analysis of deployed traffic differentiation practices. In: Proceedings of the ACM Special Interest Group on Data Communication, pp. 130–144. SIGCOMM '19, Association for Computing Machinery (2019)
14. MacMillan, K., Mangla, T., Saxon, J., Marwell, N.P., Feamster, N.: A comparative analysis of Ookla Speedtest and measurement labs network diagnostic test (NDT7). Proc. ACM Meas. Anal. Comput. Syst. **7**(1) (2023)
15. Paul, U., Liu, J., Gu, M., Gupta, A., Belding, E.: The importance of contextualization of crowdsourced active speed test measurements. In: Proceedings of the 22nd ACM Internet Measurement Conference, pp. 274–289. IMC '22, ACM, New York, NY, USA (2022)
16. Pournaghshband, V.: Identifying Traffic Prioritization on the Internet. In: Proceedings of IEEE International Conference on Metaverse Computing, Networking and Applications, pp. 23. IEEE MetaCom (2023)
17. Pournaghshband, V., Pournaghshband, H., Vance, E.: Middlebox detection: Evasion and effectiveness. In: 2024 IEEE International Black Sea Conference on Communications and Networking (BlackSeaCom), pp. 328–331. Tbilisi, Georgia (2024). https://doi.org/10.1109/BlackSeaCom61746.2024.10646300
18. Pournaghshband, V., Reiher, P.L.: End-to-end detection of middlebox interference. In: IEEE/IFIP Network Operations and Management Symposium. NOMS '24, IEEE (2024)
19. Sharma, T., Schmitt, P., Bronzino, F., Feamster, N., Marwell, N.P.: Beyond data points: regionalizing crowdsourced latency measurements. Proc. ACM Meas. Anal. Comput. Syst **8**(3) (2024)
20. Yang, R., Mok, R.K.P., Wu, S., Luo, X., Zou, H., Li, W.: Design and implementation of web-based speed test analysis tool kit. In: Proceedings of Passive and Active Measurement: 23rd International Conference (PAM), pp. 83–96. Springer-Verlag, Berlin, Heidelberg (2022)

Imperceptible Key Generation with Delay Side-Channel and Multi-path Routing over Wide-Area Networks

Yaohui Guo[1], Aiqun Hu[1,2](✉), Dongbin He[1], Jiangtao Wang[1], and Wenjie Ma[1]

[1] National Mobile Communications Research Laboratory, Southeast University, Nanjing, China
{aqhu,dbhe,jetau,wjma}@seu.edu.cn

[2] Frontiers Science Center for Mobile Information Communication and Security, Southeast University, Nanjing, China

Abstract. With the rapid advancement of Internet technology, secure key distribution serves as a cornerstone of network communication. Traditional solutions often suffer from issues such as distinguishable traffic patterns, high computational complexity, or excessive cost. To address these challenges, this paper proposes a scheme for imperceptible key generation over the wide-area Internet—a transparent process to third parties. The scheme leverages round-trip time (RTT) as a side-channel entropy source to extract inherent Internet randomness, coupled with clock synchronization, implicitly establishing reciprocal signals during normal data interactions for sustained, long-range, and low-overhead key generation. To further enhance security and signal randomness, the scheme incorporates a multi-path parallel measurement mechanism that employs controlled active packet loss and random delay injection. On this basis, the key generation is finalized through equal-probability quantization, polar code-based forward error correction, and privacy amplification. Experimental results demonstrate that in both static and mobile scenarios, the initial key disagreement rate ranges between 10% and 20%, which is reduced to zero after polar code error correction. The sustained key generation rates for static and mobile scenarios reach 7.01 bit/s and 3.78 bit/s, respectively. Moreover, the generated keys successfully pass 10 core NIST randomness tests. Finally, a probabilistic model shows that the scheme exhibits strong resilience against both eavesdropping and collusion attacks.

Keywords: Key Generation · Network Delay · Side-Channel · Network Measurement

1 Introduction

With the deep integration of the Internet of Things and mobile Internet, information has become a critical asset for societal operation. The security of its transmission and storage forms the bedrock for the proper functioning of society.

Y. Cao et al. (Eds.): SecureComm 2026, LNICST 704, pp. 113–133, 2027.
https://doi.org/10.1007/978-3-032-32764-2_6

In this context, symmetric encryption techniques have emerged as a cornerstone for protecting data security due to their simplicity and computational efficiency. However, these techniques require communicating parties to possess an identical shared secret key. Consequently, how to achieve secure and efficient key sharing between parties over an open, wide-area network remains a fundamental and critical challenge in the field of network security.

Traditional cryptographic key distribution schemes represent the most widely deployed method for key sharing, whose security is founded upon the computational intractability of specific mathematical problems. Needham and Schroeder first introduced the concept of a Key Distribution Center (KDC) [12]. Diffie and Hellman introduced the Diffie-Hellman key exchange protocol [4], based on the discrete logarithm problem, enabling two communicating parties to collaboratively establish a shared secret by exchanging public information over an open channel. The RSA algorithm [13] and elliptic curve cryptography [7], coupled with the digital certificate infrastructure [11], have laid the foundation for secure key transmission and asymmetric cryptosystems. However, with the advancement of quantum computing, algorithms such as Shor's algorithm have been proven capable of solving these underlying mathematical problems in polynomial time [15], theoretically undermining the long-term security of traditional public-key cryptosystems. Additionally, these schemes face challenges including high computational complexity, distinguishable traffic patterns, and dependence on Public Key Infrastructure (PKI).

Physical layer security-based key generation schemes leverage the randomness and spatiotemporal variation characteristics of wireless channels to generate shared secret keys. Wyner pioneered the wiretap channel model [18], inspiring extensive research into utilizing channel state information for secure communications. Ahlswede, Maurer, and other scholars subsequently laid the theoretical groundwork from an information-theoretic perspective [1,10], proving its information-theoretic security under ideal conditions. Ye et al. validated wireless channel propagation properties, realizing Maurer's theoretical framework in practice [20]. Currently, commonly utilized channel characteristics encompass the received signal strength (RSS) [9,14], channel impulse response (CIR) [16], and channel frequency response (CFR) [19]. Wang et al. [17] conducted in-depth research on network delay; however, their approach relies on the deployment of random forwarding networks. Such schemes typically rely on short-range, highly dynamic wireless environments, making them difficult to deploy directly in wide-area Internet scenarios.

Quantum mechanics-based key distribution schemes leverage the quantum no-cloning theorem and the measurement collapse effect to achieve theoretically unconditional secure key distribution. The BB84 protocol, proposed by Bennett and Brassard, realized the first quantum key distribution (QKD) system through the preparation and measurement of single photons [3]. Ekert proposed the use of photon entanglement for encoding and decoding [5]. Grosshans et al. further proposed Continuous-Variable QKD (CV-QKD) [6], enhancing the system's encoding and transmission efficiency. However, a significant limitation of such schemes is their reliance on specialized hardware, including quantum light sources and single-photon detectors, which entail substantial deployment and maintenance costs and hinder efficient integration with the conventional TCP/IP Internet architecture.

To address the limitations of the aforementioned key sharing schemes, this paper proposes an imperceptible key generation scheme tailored for wide-area Internet environments. The core of this scheme lies in leveraging the delay as a side-channel, enabling the continuous and transparent generation of cryptographic keys by extracting inherent Internet randomness without disrupting normal communication. This approach features low computational overhead, broad applicability, and imperceptible traffic characteristics. The main contributions of this work are manifested at the following three levels:

1. Proposed a continuous and imperceptible reciprocal signal extraction mechanism based on the delay side-channel. By continuously measuring the RTT between communicating parties, coupled with clock synchronization and authentication, this mechanism transforms the inherent attribute of network delay into a secure key entropy source, enabling the continuous, covert, and transparent extraction of reciprocal signals during normal data interactions.
2. Designed a multi-level security enhancement mechanism. To address challenges such as single-path eavesdropping and insufficient entropy sources in stable channels, this scheme innovatively integrates multi-path parallel measurement, controlled active packet loss, and artificial random delay injection. These techniques significantly enhance robustness against eavesdropping and traffic analysis while improving key generation rate and randomness.
3. Constructed a comprehensive post-processing and key reconciliation framework. The raw signals are efficiently encoded using equal-probability quantization and Gray code to generate initial key bits. Furthermore, a polar code-based forward error correction scheme is designed to achieve low-overhead information reconciliation with sufficient flexibility, ultimately ensuring that both communicating parties obtain consistent and secure shared keys.

2 Background

This chapter establishes the theoretical foundation for network delay measurement. It first analyzes the composition of network delay and identifies its key influencing factors, then examines short-term delay stability to support subsequent reciprocal signal extraction. Together, these elements form the technical basis for the key generation scheme.

2.1 Network Delay Composition

Network delay is defined as the time interval required for a data packet to traverse from one network endpoint to another, typically measured in milliseconds (ms). In computer networks, delay is generally composed of four primary components: transmission delay, propagation delay, processing delay, and queuing delay [8].

Transmission Delay (t_{trans}): Transmission delay is defined as the duration between the first bit and the last bit of a packet entering the transmission medium. It represents the time required to push the entire packet onto the link. Its value depends on the packet length L (in bits) and the link bandwidth R (in bits per second).

Propagation Delay (t_{prop}): This represents the time required for an electromagnetic signal to propagate from the sender to the receiver through the physical medium. This delay depends on the propagation speed of the signal in the medium v and the physical length of the link d.

Processing Delay (t_{proc}): This refers to the time consumed by a network node (e.g., a router or switch) in processing the data packet, including operations such as parsing the header, looking up the routing table, and performing error detection. This delay is primarily influenced by the hardware performance and processing capability of the node.

Queuing Delay (t_{queue}): When a data packet arrives at a network node that is busy processing other data, the current packet must wait in a buffer. The resulting waiting time is the queuing delay. This delay is closely related to the node's processing capacity and the current network load; if the buffer is full, packet loss may occur, potentially triggering retransmission.

In delay measurement practice, it is often further categorized into one-way delay and round-trip time. One-way delay refers to the time required for a packet to travel unidirectionally from the source to the destination. Round-trip time (RTT), also referred to as bidirectional delay, is defined as the time interval from the transmission of a data packet until the receipt of its corresponding acknowledgment signal. This paper primarily focuses on the measurement and study of RTT.

2.2 Short-Term Delay Stability

In the Internet, end-to-end data communication relies on the hop-by-hop forwarding of packets across multiple network nodes. To ensure communication efficiency, the core principle of data forwarding typically follows "shortest path first." Based on this principle, the industry has developed various routing protocols. Categorized by their hierarchical structure, these protocols can be primarily divided into Interior Gateway Protocols and Exterior Gateway Protocols.

Interior Gateway Protocols operate within an Autonomous System (AS) and are responsible for routing decisions inside the AS. Typical representatives include the Routing Information Protocol (RIP) and the Open Shortest Path First (OSPF) protocol. Exterior Gateway Protocols are used for exchanging routing information between different Autonomous Systems, with the Border Gateway Protocol (BGP) being the commonly used protocol. Regarding routing algorithms, RIP calculates paths based on the distance-vector algorithm (specifically, the Bellman-Ford algorithm); OSPF, as a link-state protocol, uses Dijkstra's algorithm to compute the shortest path; and BGP is a path-vector protocol that makes decisions based on path attributes rather than mere distance metrics. Although their mechanisms differ, these protocols are all designed to follow or approximate some form of the shortest path first principle.

Based on the aforementioned routing mechanisms, it is reasonable to assume that the forwarding path of data packets is typically the global optimal or near-optimal solution under the current network topology. Therefore, under the premise of a relatively stable network environment, one can reasonably hypothesize that the forwarding route of packets remains essentially fixed in the short term. Furthermore, as modern network protocols commonly incorporate load balancing mechanisms, when local congestion occurs in the network, traffic can be dynamically scheduled to several alternative paths with similar costs. Provided the network state does not undergo drastic changes, integrating the relative stability of routes with the path consistency inherent in load balancing leads to the inference that the end-to-end network delay remains relatively stable in the short term.

3 Reciprocal Signal Extraction Based on Network Delay

This chapter aims to construct a complete framework for reciprocal signal extraction. It begins by introducing a RTT model to demonstrate signal reciprocity. Building on this, multi-path measurement is introduced to enhance both the key generation rate and eavesdropping resistance. Furthermore, a randomness enhancement mechanism is established to improve the randomness of reciprocal signals, thereby laying the foundation for key generation.

3.1 Round-Trip Time Measurement

In key generation schemes, selecting a stable and reciprocal signal source is fundamental to system design. This paper adopts network Round-Trip Time (RTT) as the key entropy source, due to its ease of measurement in engineering practice and the high correlation observed between RTT sequences independently measured by communicating parties under relatively stable network conditions, making it suitable as a shared random source.

The reciprocal signal extraction method employed in this study is based on the classical RTT model [17]. This model derives reciprocal signal sequences from the transmission and reception timestamps recorded by both parties through multiple rounds of RTT measurements, as illustrated in Fig. 2. However, in actual network environments, clock offset and skew between communicating parties can affect measurement accuracy. To address this, we introduce PTP-based clock synchronization at time t_0 on the basis of the original model, calibrating the clocks of Alice and Bob prior to measurement to eliminate the impact of clock offset and skew, thereby obtaining more accurate RTT measurements, which improves the correlation of the reciprocal signals, providing a higher-quality entropy source for subsequent key generation (Fig. 1).

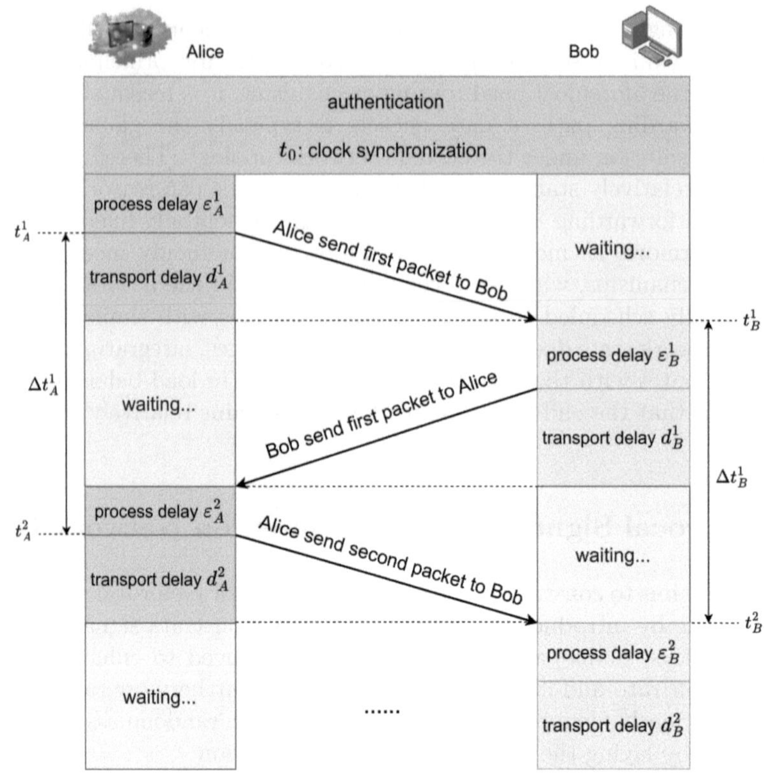

Fig. 1. Bidirectional Delay Model.

Based on the assumption of short-term stability of network delay ($d_A^n \approx d_A^{n+1}$), by comparing the time interval between two consecutive transmissions observed at Alice's side $\Delta t_A^n = d_A^n + \epsilon_B^n + d_B^n + \epsilon_A^{n+1}$ with the time interval between two consecutive receptions observed at Bob's side $\Delta t_B^n = d_A^{n+1} + \epsilon_B^n + d_B^n + \epsilon_A^{n+1}$ for the n-th round of interaction, it can be deduced that $\Delta t_A^n \approx \Delta t_B^n$. This verifies the reciprocity of the delay signals observed by both parties [17].

Upon completing N rounds of interaction, reciprocal signal sequences can be extracted from the measurement data of Alice and Bob respectively, where each reciprocal signal Δt is composed of the bidirectional propagation delay d and the processing delays ε from both parties. Further analysis of the composition of the reciprocal signal ΔT reveals:

1. Non-reciprocal differences between ΔT_A and ΔT_B are introduced only when the unidirectional propagation delay d_A^n from Alice to Bob fluctuates between two consecutive measurements.
2. Fluctuations in the unidirectional propagation delay d_B^n from Bob to Alice, as well as variations in the processing delays ε_A^n and ε_B^n of both parties, do not compromise the reciprocity of the signal. Instead, they enhance the

overall randomness of the signal, providing the necessary entropy source for subsequent quantized key generation and thereby ensuring the security of the key.

3.2 Multi-path RTT Measurement

In the scheme described in Sect. 3.1, if eavesdropping nodes exist along the data transmission path, they could potentially acquire partial delay information through traffic analysis. Furthermore, gateways directly connected to the communicating hosts, being in critical positions for data forwarding, can typically obtain strongly correlated delay data. To enhance system security, this section builds upon Sect. 3.1 by proposing a delay measurement and key generation scheme based on multiple paths.

Currently, mainstream computing devices are typically equipped with multiple independent network interfaces, such as native Ethernet controllers and wireless network adapters, with some mobile devices further supporting internet access through integrated cellular modems. Beyond these integrated solutions, computers can additionally expand physical port availability through hardware expansion methods. Unlike software-based port multiplexing, each physical network interface possesses independent packet transmission and reception capabilities at the hardware level, enabling data packets to be transmitted through different routing paths. Using the traceroute command to perform route tracing on two network interfaces, the results (as shown in Fig. 2) verify the routing independence between different physical network interfaces.

```
Tracing route to 8.8.8.8 over a maximum of 30 hops

  1     1 ms     2 ms     1 ms  121.248.48.1
  2     2 ms     2 ms     2 ms  10.255.254.26
  3     1 ms     1 ms     1 ms  10.80.3.10
  4     2 ms     2 ms     2 ms  153.3.60.1
  5     5 ms     *        *     122.96.66.73
  6     *        *        *     Request timed out.
  7    24 ms     *        *     219.158.15.133
  8    27 ms     *       27 ms  219.158.3.18
  9    39 ms     *       24 ms  219.158.3.162
 10    29 ms    29 ms    29 ms  219.158.3.190
 11     *        *        *     Request timed out.
 12     *        *        *     Request timed out.
 13   107 ms   106 ms   109 ms  203.131.241.220
 14   180 ms   180 ms   181 ms  203.131.250.82
 15   198 ms   197 ms   198 ms  108.170.231.19
 16   188 ms   187 ms   187 ms  142.250.208.147
 17   181 ms   181 ms   181 ms  8.8.8.8
```

(a) First path

```
Tracing route to 8.8.8.8 over a maximum of 30 hops

  1    11 ms     4 ms    62 ms  192.168.35.137
  2     *        *        *     Request timed out.
  3    39 ms    36 ms    38 ms  172.21.1.1
  4     *        *        *     Request timed out.
  5    68 ms     *        *     10.136.232.41
  6     *        *        *     Request timed out.
  7     *        *        *     Request timed out.
  8    57 ms    51 ms    49 ms  221.183.89.17
  9    54 ms    54 ms    50 ms  221.183.89.34
 10     *       39 ms     *     221.183.89.169
 11     *        *        *     Request timed out.
 12     *        *        *     Request timed out.
 13    85 ms    78 ms    86 ms  223.119.17.154
 14    84 ms    79 ms    77 ms  209.85.244.25
 15    78 ms    77 ms    74 ms  142.251.244.223
 16    75 ms    79 ms    78 ms  8.8.8.8
```

(b) Second path

Fig. 2. Routing paths from PC to 8.8.8.8.

Leveraging this routing independence, our scheme extends the measurement methodology outlined in Sect. 3.1 by performing RTT measurements concurrently across multiple network interfaces. The delay signals acquired from each path are subsequently integrated to construct a unified composite signal, as illustrated in Fig. 3. Within this architecture, even if a node on a specific transmission path is malicious, it can only eavesdrop on the partial delay information from that single path. Simultaneously monitoring all independent paths presents significant difficulty, thereby preventing the adversary from obtaining measurement data from other routes. This design not only enhances key security but also effectively increases the key generation rate through parallel measurement.

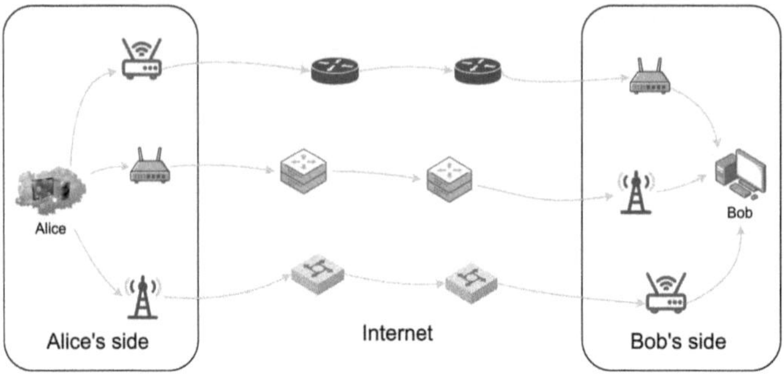

Fig. 3. Schematic Diagram of the Multi-Path Scheme.

3.3 Key Randomness Enhancement

According to the derivation in Sect. 3.1, the reciprocal signals ultimately extracted by the communicating parties are jointly constituted by the bidirectional propagation delay d and the processing delays ε from both parties. However, under highly stable network conditions (e.g., both communication parties are connected via wired networks or high-quality Wi-Fi), the fluctuation range of the bidirectional propagation delay d is limited, making it difficult to provide sufficient randomness required for key generation. Therefore, it is necessary to artificially introduce additional random perturbations. This scheme primarily addresses this issue from two aspects: enhancing the randomness of processing delays and actively perturbing channel transmission stability.

The processing delay ε mainly comprises components such as interrupt response latency, process scheduling latency, and code execution latency. Among these, interrupt handling and process scheduling are primarily managed by the operating system kernel, with their randomness stemming from underlying system behaviors. Code execution latency can be intervened programmatically, for instance, by invoking sleep functions like `sleep()` to artificially inject controllable delays.

After introducing artificial delays, the processing delay ε for each communicating party can be modeled as:

$$\varepsilon = \varepsilon_1 + \varepsilon_2 \tag{1}$$

Here, ε_1 represents the inherent natural processing delay of the system, which can typically be modeled as following a certain random distribution (e.g., normal distribution). ε_2 denotes the artificially injected random delay via sleep functions, which can be configured to follow a uniform distribution within a specific interval. The exact range of this distribution can be adjusted according to the actual network environment. By artificially introducing ε_2, the overall randomness of the processing delay ε is effectively enhanced, thereby improving the security of the generated key.

On the other hand, to introduce random fluctuations in the propagation delay within stable networks, tools such as Traffic Control (tc) can be employed on communication nodes to actively configure a controlled sporadic packet loss strategy. The core of this strategy is to ensure that packet loss events do not occur consecutively: specifically, after triggering a single packet loss, several subsequent data packets are guaranteed not to be dropped. This approach can induce the TCP protocol to initiate its fast retransmission mechanism (as opposed to the more time-consuming timeout-based retransmission). Consequently, while maintaining connection continuity, the bidirectional propagation delay d exhibits randomized fluctuations, further enhancing the randomness of the key signal.

4 Key Generation

This chapter establishes the complete key generation pipeline. Key quantization first converts signals into bit streams, information reconciliation then eliminates key discrepancies, and privacy amplification finally enhances security, collectively ensuring key consistency and confidentiality.

4.1 Key Quantization

Key quantization refers to the process of mapping continuous raw reciprocal signal values to discrete quantization levels, i.e., replacing the original value with the nearest quantization step value, thereby generating a binary bit stream. This process not only accomplishes analog-to-digital conversion but also effectively mitigates the non-reciprocal components present in the raw signals of the communicating parties, thus enhancing the consistency of the final generated key.

The strategy for selecting quantization steps directly depends on the adopted quantization algorithm. This paper employs the equal-probability quantization algorithm, a type of non-uniform quantization, to process the reciprocal signals. The core principle of the equal-probability quantization algorithm is to determine quantization intervals according to the statistical ranking of the sample sequence. Its design objective is to ensure equal occurrence probability for each quantization level, thereby fundamentally preventing the potential imbalance between '0' and '1' bits that may occur with uniform quantization. As a result, the bit sequences generated through equal-probability quantization demonstrate a well-balanced 0-1 distribution, yielding superior randomness.

When encoding the quantization levels into binary bit strings, this scheme adopts Gray code. The characteristic of Gray code lies in the fact that the binary code words corresponding to any two adjacent quantization levels differ by only one bit. This property ensures that if the quantization results of the same signal from the two communicating parties fall into adjacent levels due to imperfect signal reciprocity, the generated key sequences will differ by only one bit. This reduces the bit errors caused by quantization boundary discrepancies, thereby effectively lowering the key disagreement rate between the communicating parties.

4.2 Information Reconciliation

After equal-probability quantization, the communicating parties obtain initial key bit streams with relatively high consistency. However, due to non-reciprocal factors such as one-way delay fluctuations, the key bits between the legitimate parties (Alice and Bob) may still exhibit a disagreement rate of approximately 10% to 20%. To ensure final key consistency, an information reconciliation scheme is required to correct these errors. To this end, this paper proposes a forward error correction scheme based on polar codes.

Polar codes, introduced by Turkish scholar Erdal Arikan in 2007, represent the first class of codes rigorously proven to achieve the Shannon limit, possessing exceptional error correction performance [2]. Moreover, both encoding and decoding complexities are $O(N \log N)$, ensuring high implementation efficiency. Additionally, polar codes offer strong flexibility, allowing for adaptation of code length and code rate according to different network environments to meet varying scenario requirements.

The information reconciliation process is initiated by Alice, with the core objective of utilizing error-correcting codes to rectify the erroneous bits in Bob's key, thereby achieving complete consistency between both parties' keys. The specific steps are as follows (as illustrated in Fig. 4):

At Alice's Side:

1. Encoding: Generate an auxiliary random sequence X for reconciliation, and encode it using a polar code encoder to obtain the polar codeword $Polar(X)$.
2. Perform a bitwise XOR operation between the polar codeword $Polar(X)$ and the local quantized key Key_A (padding with zeros if the key length and codeword length mismatch), resulting in the encrypted sequence $Polar(X) \oplus Key_A$.
3. Transmit this encrypted sequence to Bob over the public channel.

At Bob's Side:

1. Decryption: Upon receiving the encrypted sequence, Bob decrypts it using his local quantized key Key_B, obtaining $Polar(X) \oplus Key_A \oplus Key_B$. Since Key_A and Key_B have some discrepancies, this decryption result is equivalent to introducing errors into the original codeword $Polar(X)$, where the error

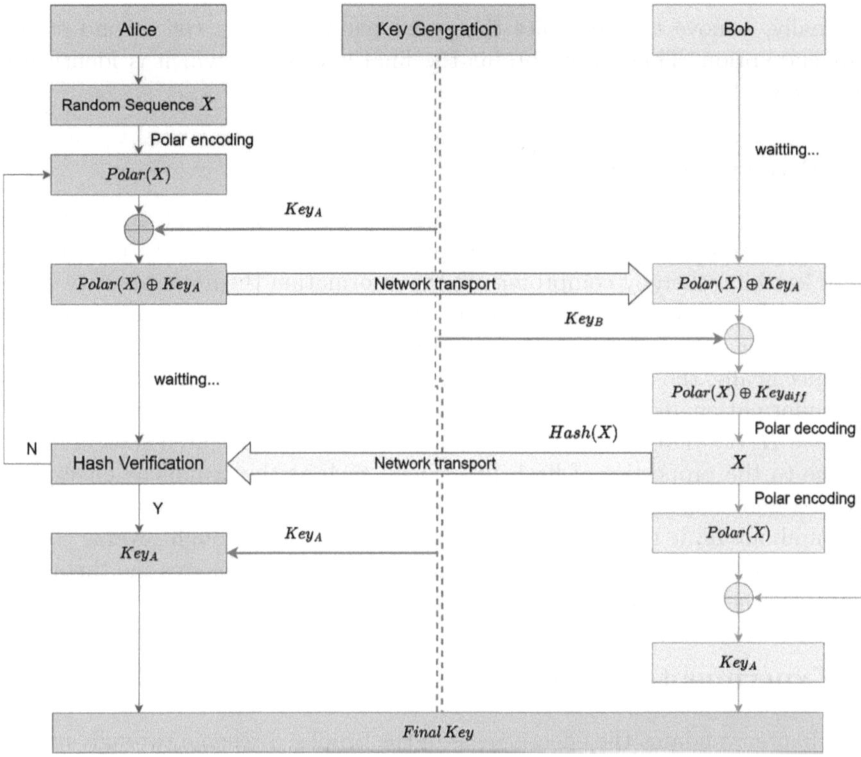

Fig. 4. Information Reconciliation Scheme.

positions correspond to the bit positions where the two keys disagree, denoted by Key_{diff}.

$$\begin{aligned} &Polar(X) \oplus Key_A \oplus Key_B \\ =&Polar(X) \oplus Key_{diff} \end{aligned} \tag{2}$$

2. Error Correction: Decode the sequence $Polar(X) \oplus Key_{diff}$, which contains errors, using the polar code decoder. Given an appropriate code length and channel conditions, the decoder can successfully correct all errors and recover the error-free auxiliary random sequence X.
3. Verification: Perform a hash verification on the recovered sequence X over the public channel. If the verification succeeds, the error correction process is confirmed as complete. If it fails, both parties negotiate to increase the polar code length and retransmit.
4. Key Recovery: Bob re-encodes the recovered error-free sequence X using the polar code encoder to obtain $Polar(X)$, and performs another XOR operation with the encrypted sequence originally received from Alice:

$$Polar(X) \oplus Key_A \oplus Polar(X) = Key_A \tag{3}$$

Finally, remove the zero bits that were padded during the second step of XOR encryption. Thus, Bob obtains the final key Key_A, which is identical to Alice's key.

4.3 Privacy Amplification

During the information reconciliation process described in Sect. 4.2, the auxiliary information transmitted over the public channel may lead to partial leakage of key bits, thereby compromising the information-theoretic security of the final key. To address this, our scheme employs privacy amplification technology, utilizing a hash function (e.g., SHA-256), to post-process the reconciled key. Specifically, the communicating parties take the consistent key K, obtained after information reconciliation, as input and jointly compute its hash value $K_{final} = H(K)$. This hash value is then used as the final shared session key.

Due to the properties of hash functions—such as the avalanche effect, one-wayness, and collision resistance—even if an eavesdropper obtains partial information about K, it remains infeasible to derive K_{final} through reverse computation. This eliminates potential information leakage and ensures the theoretical security of the key and the confidentiality of communications.

5 Experimental Design and Results Analysis

This chapter validates the effectiveness of the proposed scheme through systematic experiments. It begins by constructing typical testing scenarios to evaluate the scheme's performance, followed by a quantitative analysis from three dimensions: key consistency, generation efficiency, and randomness, thereby providing empirical support for the scheme's practicality.

5.1 Experimental Scenario

To validate the proposed key generation scheme, we set up two test hosts in Nanjing, China, using an Alibaba Cloud server in Hong Kong with FRP to enable public network communication. The cloud server acts only as a controllable relay, and data traverses the mainland China–Hong Kong Internet backbone, exhibiting clear WAN characteristics. We evaluate the scheme's practical performance under two scenarios: static and medium-speed mobile.

In the static scenario, the two hosts reside in different local area networks. Each host is equipped with two independent network interfaces to establish two concurrent physical transmission links.

1. Static link 1 (Wi-Fi Link): Both ends were connected to the Internet via routers supporting the Wi-Fi 6 standard, with a 3% random packet loss rate and an artificial delay uniformly distributed between 0 and 0.1 s configured on this link.
2. Static link 2 (Cellular Network Link): Both ends access the Internet via 5G mobile cellular networks by connecting to mobile phone portable hotspots.

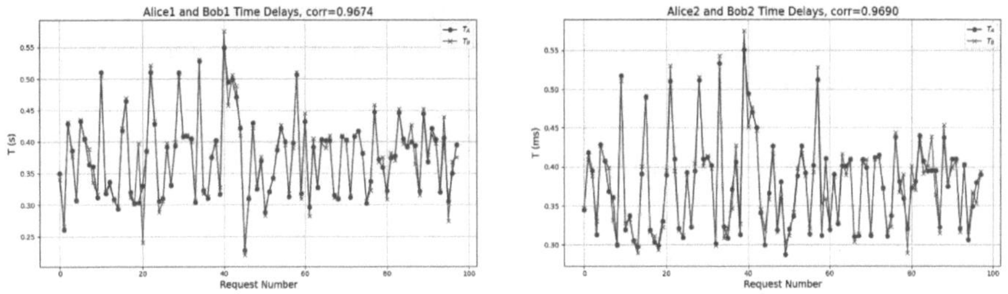

(a) Static link 1 (Wi-Fi Link) (b) Static link 2 (Cellular Network Link)

Fig. 5. Link Delay.

In each test round, the communicating parties completed 100 interaction measurements, with a total of 20 rounds conducted. The most representative data from these tests was selected, and the RTT sequences measured on the two links are shown in the Fig. 5 The correlation coefficients (corr) for the two links are 0.9674 and 0.9690, respectively.

In the mobile scenario, the two hosts were secured within a vehicle, moving clockwise at a constant speed of 30 km/h through an urban road environment around buildings. The test scenario is illustrated in Fig. 6:

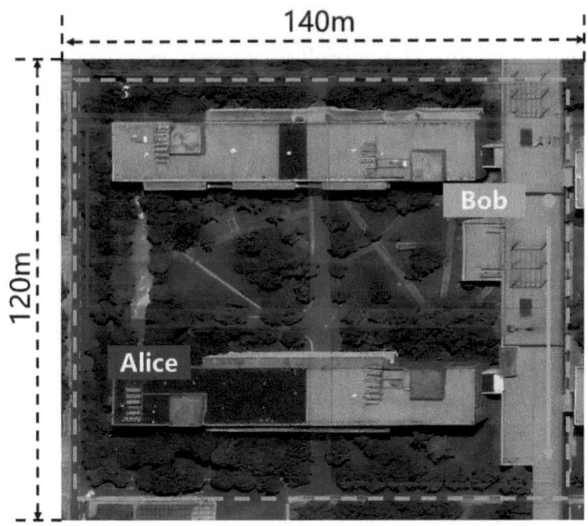

Fig. 6. Schematic Diagram of the Test Scenario.

Both ends accessed the Internet via mobile phone hotspots and 5G cellular networks. Given the inherent significant volatility of channel conditions in mobile environments, no additional artificial delays or packet loss were introduced in this scenario. The two parties performed 100 consecutive interactions, and the measured RTT sequences are shown in Fig. 7. The correlation coefficients for the two links are 0.9519.

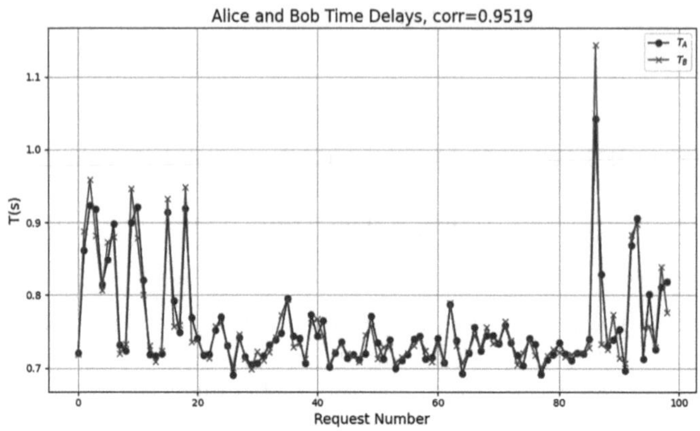

Fig. 7. Mobile Link.

5.2 Experimental Results and Analysis

To comprehensively evaluate the overall performance of the proposed key generation scheme, this section analyzes the experimental data using three common evaluation metrics in the field of key generation: key consistency, generation efficiency, and randomness [21]. The following discussion provides a detailed analysis of the test results from the three experimental scenarios described in Sect. 5.1, under the condition of eight-level equal-probability quantization and a polar code rate of 0.25.

Key Disagreement Rate: Key Disagreement Rate (KDR) is a crucial metric for evaluating the initial performance of a key generation system. It is defined as the proportion of inconsistent bits in the initial key sequences generated by the communicating parties after the quantization step. The KDR is primarily influenced by the network environment and the number of quantization levels. Increased network fluctuations reduce the reciprocity of the measured delay signals between the parties, leading to a higher KDR. Conversely, increasing the number of quantization levels amplifies the inherent non-reciprocal noise in the signals, which also causes the KDR to rise.

To evaluate the performance of our scheme, we analyzed the data collected from the three experimental scenarios described in Sect. 5.1. The results are presented in Table 1:

Table 1. Key Disagreement Rate Across Different Scenarios

	Static Link 1	Static Link 2	Mobile Link
Key Disagreement Bits	34	50	58
Key Disagreement Rate	12%	17%	20%
Error Correction Success	Yes	Yes	Yes

The experimental results indicate that the initial KDR of our scheme ranges between 10% and 20% across different scenarios. After applying polar codes with a 0.25 code rate for forward error correction, key reconciliation was successfully achieved in all scenarios, validating the effectiveness of the error correction mechanism. Further analysis reveals that the KDR of the mobile link is higher than that of the static links, primarily due to reduced network stability in mobile environments, which diminishes signal reciprocity. In static scenarios, the KDR of the Wi-Fi link (Link 1) is lower than that of the cellular network link (Link 2), indicating inherent differences in delay stability among different access technologies.

Key Generation Rate: In a key generation system, the key generation rate serves as a critical performance metric for evaluating system efficiency. This metric is defined as the number of shared key bits successfully generated by the communicating parties per unit time, measured in bits per second (bit/s). In the proposed scheme, the key generation rate is similarly influenced by two factors: the network environment and the number of quantization levels. When network delay increases or the packet loss rate rises, the time required to complete a single interaction round increases, leading to a decrease in the key generation rate. Conversely, increasing the number of quantization levels allows more bits to be extracted per measurement, thereby enhancing the key generation rate.

To evaluate the key generation rate of the proposed scheme, measurements were conducted under the three experimental scenarios described in Sect. 5.1, using 8-level equal-probability quantization. The resulting key generation rates are presented in Table 2.

Table 2. Key Generation Rate Across Different Scenarios

	Static Link 1	Static Link 2	Mobile Link
Valid Data Count	99	99	99
Average RTT(ms)	366	378	757
Key Generation Rate	7.01	6.82	3.78

Experimental results demonstrate significant differences in key generation rates across different network environments. This variation is primarily attributed to the notably increased network delay and persistent fluctuations in channel conditions within the mobile scenario, which prolong the duration of each interaction round and consequently reduce key generation efficiency. Overall, the proposed scheme exhibits favorable key generation efficiency in static network environments, capable of meeting real-time requirements in specific application scenarios. Compared to the establishment time of traditional asymmetric key agreement protocols, our scheme enables the establishment of a continuously generated key stream, demonstrating its efficiency advantage in long-term communication.

Key Randomness: The NIST Statistical Test Suite is a standard developed by the National Institute of Standards and Technology (NIST) for evaluating the statistical randomness of binary sequences. This suite comprises 15 independent tests, each computing a p-value to measure the conformity between the test sequence and a truly random sequence. Typically, if the p-value exceeds the significance level of 0.01, the sequence is considered to have passed that particular test.

To assess the randomness of the keys generated by our scheme, this section selects 10 core tests from the NIST suite. Using the NistRng package in a Python environment, we tested the key sequences generated under the three experimental scenarios described in Sect. 5.1. The test results are presented in Table 3.

Table 3. NIST Test Results

	Static Link 1	Static Link 2	Mobile Link
Frequency	0.907	0.907	0.954
Frequency Within Block	0.079	0.057	0.558
Runs	0.641	0.484	0.954
Longest Run Ones in a Block	0.129	0.031	0.048
Discrete Fourier Transform	0.470	0.156	0.831
Serial	0.929	0.991	0.272
Approximate Entropy	0.887	0.855	0.492
Cumulative Sums	0.361	0.361	0.977
Random Excursions	0.459	0.057	0.270
Random Excursion Variant	0.644	0.315	0.581

As shown in the table, under all three test scenarios, the p-values of the 10 NIST test items for the key sequences are greater than 0.01, passing all randomness tests. This result indicates that the key sequences generated by our scheme exhibit sound statistical randomness across different network environments, meeting the standards for cryptographic applications.

6 Security Analysis

To ensure the security of the proposed scheme in network environments, this section provides a quantitative analysis of its resilience against collusion attacks from a theoretical perspective. We construct a security model based on probability theory to evaluate the difficulty for an adversary to obtain all delay information in a multi-path environment. Consider the following threat scenario:

1. The network contains a total of N nodes, among which M are eavesdropping nodes capable of colluding.
2. Eavesdropping nodes are randomly distributed and can acquire the delay information of all data packets passing through them.
3. The communicating parties establish k independent routes (with no intersecting nodes), and each route passes through an average of n nodes.
4. A successful attack is defined as the scenario where the M eavesdropping nodes can obtain the delay information from all k routes.
5. The security probability P is defined as the probability of a failed attack, i.e., at least one route remains uncovered by any eavesdropping node.

When $M < k$: The number of eavesdropping nodes is insufficient to cover all routes, hence:

$$P = 1 \tag{4}$$

When $M \geq k$: Let A_i denote the event that "the i-th route contains no eavesdropping nodes". Then:

$$P = P(\bigcup_{i=1}^{k} A_i) \tag{5}$$

Applying the inclusion-exclusion principle:

$$\begin{aligned} P = & \sum P(A_i) - \sum P(A_i \cap A_j) + \sum P(A_i \cap A_j \cap A_p) \\ & \ldots + (-1)^{k+1} P\left(\bigcap_{i=1}^{k} A_i\right) \end{aligned} \tag{6}$$

The probability of a single event A_i is calculated using the hypergeometric distribution:

$$P(A_i) = \frac{\binom{N-M}{n}}{\binom{N}{n}} \tag{7}$$

Since the routes are independent and share no common nodes, for any i distinct routes we have:

$$P(A_1 \cap A_2 \cap \ldots \cap A_i) = \frac{\binom{N-M}{i \cdot n}}{\binom{N}{i \cdot n}} \tag{8}$$

Substituting into the equation:

$$P = \sum_{i=1}^{\min\left(k, \left\lfloor \frac{N-M}{n} \right\rfloor\right)} (-1)^{i+1} \cdot \binom{k}{i} \cdot \frac{\binom{N-M}{i \cdot n}}{\binom{N}{i \cdot n}} \tag{9}$$

The constraint $i \leq \min\left(k, \left\lfloor \frac{N-M}{n} \right\rfloor\right)$ ensures there are enough trustworthy nodes to form the routes.

To validate the accuracy of the theoretical model and conduct an in-depth analysis of the system security, we performed systematic simulation experiments. The simulation environment was built on the Python platform, with the number of eavesdropping nodes and their proportion serving as independent variables on the horizontal axis, and the security probability as the dependent variable on the vertical axis. Simulations were conducted under different numbers of routes, with each data point calculated over 10,000 simulation runs. The parameter ranges were set as follows:

- Total number of nodes (N): 10,000
- Number of nodes per route (n): 10
- Number of eavesdropping nodes (M): 0–1,000 (covering 0%–10% eavesdropping ratio)
- Number of routes (k): 1–8

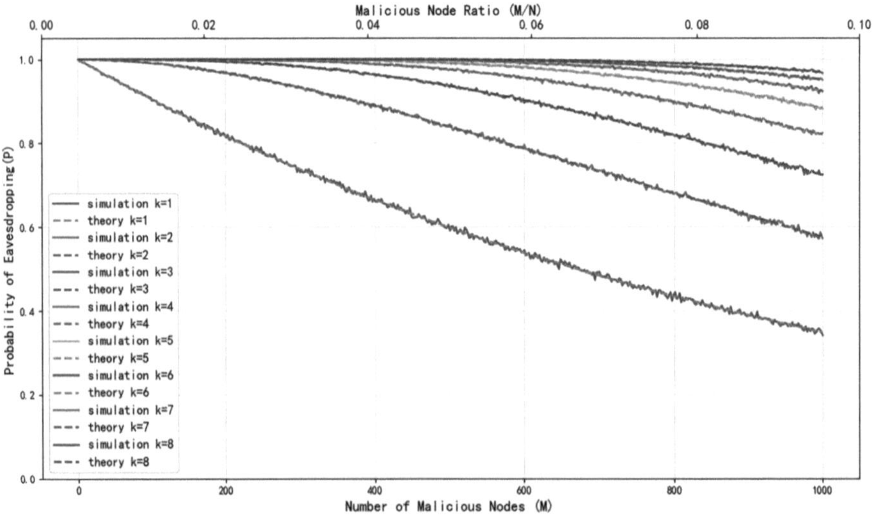

Fig. 8. Simulation for Security Analysis.

Figure 8 illustrates the variation trend of the security probability P with the increase in the number of eavesdropping nodes M when the number of routes k ranges from 1 to 8. The dashed lines represent the theoretically calculated security probabilities, while the solid lines represent the security probabilities computed after simulating each data point 10,000 times. It can be observed that the theoretical and simulation results exhibit close agreement. The simulation results indicate that:

1. Multi-Path Gain: With the number of eavesdropping nodes fixed at $M = 1000$, the security probability increases from 0.37 to 0.96 as the number of paths k grows from 1 to 8, thereby conclusively demonstrating the effectiveness of the multi-path strategy. Consequently, increasing the number of paths should be prioritized over relying on the security of a single route.
2. Security Probability Analysis: When the eavesdropping node ratio $\frac{M}{N} < \%5$, configuring more than $k = 4$ routes can ensure a security probability exceeding 95%. As the eavesdropping node ratio increases, P shows a non-linear decreasing trend. Even when the eavesdropping node ratio $\frac{M}{N}$ reaches 10% (a realistically challenging scenario), maintaining more than $k = 4$ routes still guarantees a security probability above 80%.
3. Marginal Benefit: When the number of routes $k > 6$, the magnitude of improvement in security probability gradually diminishes, indicating the presence of a diminishing marginal benefit. For practical systems, it is recommended to deploy 4 to 6 routes based on the specific network environment, thereby achieving a balance between security and system overhead.

Through systematic model simulation, we have not only verified the theoretical security of the multi-path key generation scheme but also provided a quantitative basis for parameter configuration and operational maintenance of practical systems. This ensures the feasibility and effectiveness of the scheme in real-world network environments.

7 Summary

To overcome the drawbacks of traditional key distribution schemes—such as high computational complexity and distinguishable traffic patterns—this paper proposes a lightweight key generation scheme based on multi-path RTT measurement. The proposed scheme enables covert key negotiation during normal data exchanges, achieving continuous key generation with low overhead. Experimental results demonstrate that the scheme effectively generates keys with strong randomness and high consistency on commercial hardware, offering a practical solution for lightweight secure communication.

Future work will focus on enhancing eavesdropping resistance, including security analysis under active attacks and the development of corresponding enhancement mechanisms. Additionally, we will investigate the use of routing information to construct path fingerprints for authenticating communicating parties, thereby improving system security.

Acknowledgements. This work was supported by the Fundamental Research Funds for the Central Universities 2242022k60005.

References

1. Ahlswede, R., Csiszár, I.: Common randomness in information theory and cryptography. I. Secret sharing. IEEE Trans. Inf. Theor. **39**(4), 1121–1132 (2002)
2. Arikan, E.: Channel polarization: a method for constructing capacity-achieving codes for symmetric binary-input memoryless channels. IEEE Trans. Inf. Theor. **55**(7), 3051–3073 (2009). https://doi.org/10.1109/TIT.2009.2021379
3. Bennett, C.H., Brassard, G.: Quantum cryptography: public key distribution and coin tossing. Theoret. Comput. Sci. **560**, 7–11 (2014)
4. Diffie, W., Hellman, M.E.: New Directions in Cryptography, 1st edn., pp. 365–390. Association for Computing Machinery, New York, NY, USA (2022). https://doi.org/10.1145/3549993.3550007
5. Ekert, A.K.: Quantum cryptography based on Bell's theorem. Phys. Rev. Lett. **67**(6), 661 (1991)
6. Grosshans, F., Van Assche, G., Wenger, J., Brouri, R., Cerf, N.J., Grangier, P.: Quantum key distribution using Gaussian-modulated coherent states. Nature **421**(6920), 238–241 (2003)
7. Koblitz, N.: Elliptic curve cryptosystems. Math. Comput. **48**(177), 203–209 (1987)
8. Kurose, J.F., Ross, K.W.: Computer Networking: A Top-Down Approach, 7th edn. Pearson Education, Boston (2017)
9. Liu, H., Yang, J., Wang, Y., Chen, Y.: Collaborative secret key extraction leveraging received signal strength in mobile wireless networks. In: Proceedings IEEE Infocom, pp. 927–935. IEEE (2012)
10. Maurer, U.M.: Secret key agreement by public discussion from common information. IEEE Trans. Inf. Theor. **39**(3), 733–742 (2002)
11. Miller, V.S.: Use of elliptic curves in cryptography. In: Williams, H.C. (ed.) CRYPTO 1985. LNCS, vol. 218, pp. 417–426. Springer, Heidelberg (1986). https://doi.org/10.1007/3-540-39799-X_31
12. Needham, R.M., Schroeder, M.D.: Using encryption for authentication in large networks of computers. Commun. ACM **21**(12), 993–999 (1978)
13. Rivest, R.L., Shamir, A., Adleman, L.: A method for obtaining digital signatures and public-key cryptosystems. Commun. ACM **21**(2), 120–126 (1978)
14. Rottenberg, F., Nguyen, T.H., Dricot, J.M., Horlin, F., Louveaux, J.: CSI-based versus RSS-based secret-key generation under correlated eavesdropping. IEEE Trans. Commun. **69**(3), 1868–1881 (2020)
15. Shor, P.W.: Algorithms for quantum computation: discrete logarithms and factoring. In: Proceedings 35th Annual Symposium on Foundations of Computer Science, pp. 124–134. IEEE (1994)
16. Wang, J., Hu, A., Chen, Y., Dong, B., Sun, S.: FineLorKey: an efficient lora physical-layer key generation scheme utilizing fine-grained channel impulse response. IEEE Internet Things J. **13**(5), 10035–10054 (2026). https://doi.org/10.1109/JIOT.2025.3648010
17. Wang, X., Huang, J., Qi, C., Peng, Y., Zhang, S.: An anti-collusion attack defense method for physical layer key generation scheme based on transmission delay. PeerJ Comput. Sci. **9**, e1349 (2023)

18. Wyner, A.D.: The wire-tap channel. Bell Syst. Tech. J. **54**(8), 1355–1387 (1975). https://doi.org/10.1002/j.1538-7305.1975.tb02040.x
19. Xi, W., et al.: KEEP: fast secret key extraction protocol for D2D communication. In: 2014 IEEE 22nd International Symposium of Quality of Service (IWQoS), pp. 350–359. IEEE (2014)
20. Ye, C., Mathur, S., Reznik, A., Shah, Y., Trappe, W., Mandayam, N.B.: Information-theoretically secret key generation for fading wireless channels. IEEE Trans. Inf. Forensics Secur. **5**(2), 240–254 (2010)
21. Zhang, J., Duong, T.Q., Marshall, A., Woods, R.: Key generation from wireless channels: a review. IEEE Access **4**, 614–626 (2016)

CRChecker: LLM-Based Semi-automated Compliance Checking of 5G Core Implementations Against 3GPP Change Requests

Jiazhang Wang[1], Taous Madi[2], and Lianying Zhao[1](✉)

[1] Carleton University, Ottawa, ON, Canada
maywang3@cmail.carleton.ca, lianying.zhao@carleton.ca
[2] Ericsson Security Research, Montreal, QC, Canada
taous.madi@ericsson.com

Abstract. 5G networks are gradually becoming the backbone of modern society. Therefore, their security and resilience are of growing importance. The Third Generation Partnership Project (3GPP) specifies the functional and security requirements for mobile networks, and uses a Change Request (CR) procedure to manage revisions: approved CRs are incorporated into subsequent specification releases. However, technical implementations do not always follow every recommendation in approved CRs. When CRs carrying security updates (i.e., security-relevant CRs) are overlooked by implementations, non-compliance situations may arise leading to vulnerabilities and security breaches. However, the semantic gap between CRs (written in natural language) and the large code-base for 5G network implementations, on one side, and the complex task of identifying security-relevant CRs on the other side, make security compliance checking challenging. To address these challenges, this work-in-progress aims to eventually achieve a semi-automated compliance-checking pipeline that verifies whether CRs have been implemented in a given implementation. The proof-of-concept, CRChecker, combines Uncertainty-Aware Self-Training (UST), Large Language Models (LLMs), and Retrieval-Augmented Generation (RAG) to perform classification tasks and to extract indicators that help to map CRs to code locations. CRChecker then applies static analysis with CodeQL to pinpoint code regions corresponding to the requested changes.

Keywords: 3GPP Change Requests · 5G Core · Compliance Verification · Static Analysis

1 Introduction

Telecommunication networks have recently been recognized by governments as national critical infrastructures [4,11]. From society to business and mission critical, many vital services rely on the resilience and robustness of Fifth Generation

Y. Cao et al. (Eds.): SecureComm 2026, LNICST 704, pp. 134–154, 2027.
https://doi.org/10.1007/978-3-032-32764-2_7

(5G) networks to operate safely and reliably. In this context, checking the compliance of those infrastructures with regulations and standards is of paramount importance. The 3rd Generation Partnership Project (3GPP) [2] is a standardization body that plays a pivotal role in specifying and securing telecommunication networks, ensuring global compatibility and reliability. 3GPP uses Change Requests (CRs) as a central mechanism in the specification maintenance process [3]. CRs identify issues in the specification documents and recommend necessary modifications to address those issues. Once CRs are approved, they lead to new versions of the specifications. The 5G network implementations (e.g., core Network Functions) are expected to adhere to those specifications and reflect all the changes introduced by the CRs. However, implementations may not fully reflect the approved CRs [8]. Those non-compliance situations are particularly concerning [8] when security-relevant CRs are not enforced, leading to potential vulnerabilities and breaches. Therefore, it is crucial to verify the compliance of 5G implementations with the claimed 3GPP specification versions as to whether security-relevant CRs have been properly implemented.

However, checking mobile network implementations for compliance with security-relevant CRs is a difficult task. This mainly stems from the fact that CRs are written in natural language, which limits the effectiveness of conventional Machine Learning (ML) approaches for identifying those that carry security implications. From another perspective, even if relevant CRs can be identified, mapping them to the corresponding locations in a large code-base (e.g., free5GC[1] has over 163,450 lines of source code across all file types) requires domain expertise and remains labor-intensive. Both challanges are worsened when labeled ground truth is missing. Although an initial investigation has been conducted in [8] to analyze the security implications of CRs, compliance checking with minimal manual effort remains unexplored.

In this work, we set out to design a semi-automated pipeline for checking the compliance of 5G core implementations (e.g., free5GC) against security-relevant CRs. To this end, our pipeline, namely CRChecker, comprises two main tasks. In the first task, we leverage cutting edge ML/Artificial Intelligence (AI) technologies to filter/classify the CRs so that only relevant ones are retained for subsequent verification, i.e., security-relevant and implementation-involved CRs. Using technologies such as Large Language Models (LLMs) allows to minimize the need for domain experts and for a labeled ground-truth. The second task involves mapping the requested changes to potential locations in the 5G core implementation and checking for compliance. In this task, static analysis techniques are used to partially automate the code-lookup process.

CRChecker first performs a coarse-grained analysis of the entire CR documents. It employs the Uncertainty-Aware Self-Training (UST) algorithm [19] to categorize CRs as either implementation-involved (code changes) or editorial-only (text changes). Afterwards, CRChecker leverages a reasoning LLM integrated with a Retrieval Augmented Generation (RAG) system to perform a finer-grained, item-by-item analysis of the CR's "summary of change". The RAG

[1] free5GC is an Open Source Core network implementation. https://free5gc.org/.

system utilizes a vector database containing 3GPP specifications for the classification of security-relevant CRs. The LLM model also classifies security-relevant CRs that involve implementation changes into several behavior types (e.g., *Entity Addition*, *Entity Removal*, *Behavior Change*). Furthermore, the model extracts structured metadata, such as data types and Application Programming Interface (API) operations, into a strictly formatted JSON output. In the subsequent phase of the pipeline, CRChecker uses the extracted metadata as input to CodeQL [6] along with the 5G core implementation to perform static analysis to 1) produce binary answers whenever possible (e.g., presence or absence of an attribute) in order to *automatically* validate or refute compliance, or 2) reduce the manual effort by identifying candidate locations in the code reflecting where changes are expected in the case of behavior changes.

The contributions of this work-in-progress are summarized as follows: We devise and develop CRChecker, a semi-automated pipeline to check the compliance of a given 5G core implementation with respect to 3GPP security-relevant CRs. CRChecker not only overcomes the crucial challenge of efficiently and accurately comprehending CR documents, but also alleviates the complexity of specifications and the absence of a direct one-to-one mapping between natural language CRs and implementations.

2 Background and Related Work

In this section, we explain several concepts necessary for understanding subsequent discussions and several existing works similar or related to ours.

3GPP CRs and Classification. A 3GPP change request is a document that proposes amendments by a member organization of 3GPP to a particular version of its specification. The CR document captures essential management information related to a proposed change. It includes fields such as the target specification and version, the source of the CR, the rationale for the change and its potential consequences if not approved, the category of the change, and any relevant cross-phase compatibility considerations. Some fields contain free-form natural language content, e.g., *title*, *reason for change*, and *summary of change*. Occasionally the summary of change field includes multiple action items. Others use predefined values, such as *category*, *release*, and *CR number*. CRs are organized into five categories: F (corrections), A (changes aligned with a previous release), B (feature additions), C (functional modifications), and D (editorial modifications) [1]. For detecting security-relevant CRs (SR-CRs), The CREEK pipeline [8] presents an automated approach, utilizing BERT-based embeddings and ML to classify SR-CRs from over 400,000 3GPP CRs. More recently, the SPEC5G dataset [16] was curated as the first-ever public 5G dataset specifically for NLP research, containing millions of sentences from specifications and online sources. This work also discusses the application of large-scale pre-trained language models and the creation of expert-annotated datasets for tasks like security-related text classification and summarization. These approaches do not aim to check for compliance and are limited by the scarcity of labeled data.

OpenAPI Specification (OAS). The OpenAPI Specification (OAS) serves as a foundational standard for open APIs. OAS defines a machine-readable API specification format that supports a wide range of applications, including interactive API documentation, static document generation, and the generation of client SDKs or server stubs by external tools. Listing 1.2 in Sect. A.1 is an example snippet and illustrates how the specification captures endpoint definitions and other API details.

The *OpenAPI Generator* [9] accepts an OAS as input and produces code scaffolding, including client libraries in multiple programming languages, server stubs that implement the described API interface, configuration files, and documentation. The 3GPP specifications after release 15 also adopts the OpenAPI format, allowing developers to use conversion tools like OpenAPI Generator to generate parts of the project's code. Open-source implementations such as free5GC [12] and SD-Core [21] rely on the OpenAPI Generator tool, which derives function names from the `operationId` field in an OAS [24]. The generator also applies the specifications's data type, attribute name, and enumeration value identifiers directly within the generated source code.

Self-training. Self-training is an effective semi-supervised learning approach used to mitigate the high cost and difficulty associated with acquiring the vast amount of labeled data typically required for fine-tuning pre-trained language models [5]. It involves a Teacher model, initialized using a small labeled dataset (D_l), which generates pseudo-labels for selected instances from a large unlabeled pool (D_u). This augmented data is subsequently used to train a Student model, with the process iterating until convergence.

RAG for 3GPP. Retrieval Augmented Generation (RAG) augments an LLM with an external information retrieval system that supplies relevant domain-specific or up-to-date data at generation time, thus addressing limitations of solely relying on the model's internal parameters [17]. Nikbakht et al. introduce TSpec-LLM [20], a comprehensive open-source dataset of all 3GPP specifications, and demonstrate the effectiveness of a naive RAG framework for enhancing LLM performance by retrieving relevant documents from the dataset. Chat3GPP [15] is an open-source RAG framework specifically tailored to overcome the complexity and scale challenges of 3GPP telecom documents, employing specialized chunking strategies to achieve superior performance in answering complex queries without costly domain-specific model fine-tuning. While these systems advance linking text to responses in the telecom domain, they focus primarily on document retrieval and answering questions rather than explicit code-mapping from specification artifacts to implementation changes.

CodeQL. CodeQL [6] is a static analysis framework developed by GitHub that treats code as data and enables queries for detecting vulnerabilities. A CodeQL database contains multiple intermediate representations of code. These representations include abstract syntax tree, control flow graph, and data flow graph.

3 Motivation and Assumptions

In this section, we start by showing the necessity of CR compliance verification with a representative example (among potentially many), and the challenges therein. Then, we discuss our assumptions under which CRChecker functions.

3.1 Motivating Example

C4-213583 was initially proposed in TS 29.518 version 17.1.0, approved and adopted in version 17.2.0. The "summary of change" section lists two action items: 1) adding a new enumeration value for the 200 response code, 2) amending paragraph wording and referencing. The first change item involves an implementation change, as it adds a new enumeration value and new message sending logic, and the second change item involves an editorial change, addressing the behavior change described in the first action item.

free5GC is an open-source 5GC implementation, and in free5GC version 4.0.0 [13], it claims the SBI server/consumer implementations are upgraded for all of NFs (except for NEF) to 3GPP R17 standards. Therefore, this version is expected to have *C4-213583* implemented. Upon manual inspection of the source code, we noticed that the newly added enumeration value "`N2_MSG_NOT_TRANSFERRED`" was never used or referenced by "`N1N2MessageTransferRspData`".

Apparently, if this verification process were to be conducted by a 5G practitioner, a thorough high-level understanding (if not all the details) of the codebase and significant manual effort would already be a roadblock. Even if we want to automate it, the following major challenges still remain: 1) Complexity and large quantity of 3GPP specifications. This is worsened by the fact that CRs propose modifications to existing/past specifications which can chain up numerous versions. 2) Mapping from natural language description to large-scale implementation code. As an example, the free5GC project has over 150,000 lines of code. 3) Lack of a ground truth. Unlike software patch verification [25] relying on a clear benchmark version against which fixes are verified, 3GPP CRs address specification-based security concerns and guide implementation without prescribing exact code-level details. Therefore, no single reference function or artifact exists across various implementations, and validation requires interpretation rather than a direct comparison.

3.2 Assumptions

Honest Developers. If an implementation fails to apply certain CRs, we consider it to be either a benign mistake or a lack of proper maintenance (e.g., delays). The developer of the implementation in question would by no means try to craft the code to evade detection by CRChecker or introduce vulnerabilities intentionally into the code. Otherwise, the implementation would already lose security due to dishonest developers, not to mention compliance with CRs.

Correctness vs. Presence. Based on the honest developer assumption above, we currently consider compliance to be syntactical presence in the code, as opposed to security correctness (i.e., properly implemented), which will be our next-step work.

Minimal Manual Effort. CRChecker's goal is to automate the compliance verification process on a best-effort basis. This is because sometimes a request change can be blended with various other modifications or involve scattered changes in multiple locations, the handling of which might involve significant computational power but more importantly, the confirmation of any non-compliance needs to involve manual examination anyways. Therefore, in the best-case scenario, CRChecker will be able to output a binary result (compliant/non-compliant), while in the worst-case scenario, CRChecker will point the user to several potential locations in the code to check, which still saves the effort to read and understand the lengthy specification and huge code base.

OpenAPI-Generator Codebase. CRChecker assumes that the 5G core implementation to be checked was generated by OpenAPI Generator, as opposed to manually written, to facilitate locating entities with the CodeQL queries. This assumption is reasonable as current 5G cores (e.g., free5GC, SD-Core and OAI [24]) are more and more OpenAPI Generator-generated. We leave the support for other cases as future work.

4 Multi-stage Pipeline Architecture

In this section, we introduce our pipeline, CRChecker, as shown in Fig. 1. CRChecker is a semi automated analysis pipeline with three sequential engines

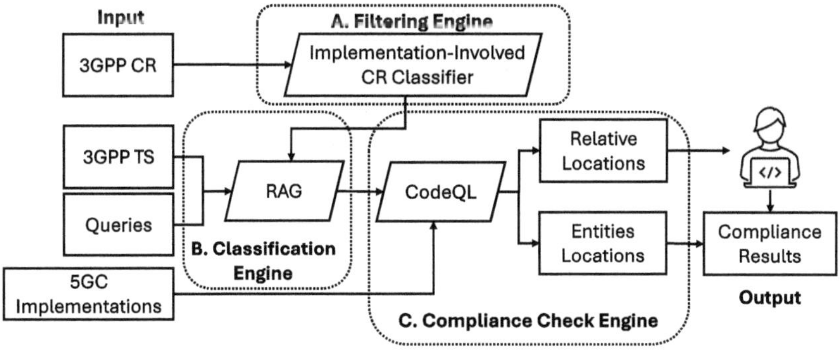

Fig. 1. Workflow of CRChecker. Module A analyzes CRs and retains only those involving implementation changes. Module B uses the RAG system for fine-grained analysis, categorizing CRs into security-relevant and behavior types, and extracting structured metadata. Module C uses structured metadata to run static code analysis via CodeQL.

that map natural language CRs to code modifications in large 5GC implementations: the Filtering Engine (A), the Classification Engine (B), and the Compliance-Check Engine (C). Together, these stages allow CRChecker to pinpoint potential locations of approved CRs in 5GC implementations.

4.1 Filtering Engine

The Filtering Engine in CRChecker provides a first-pass classification of all CRs. It assigns each CR to one of two categories: implementation-involved (requests involving code changes) or editorial-only (modifying only the text documents). More detailed explanation can be found in Sect. A.1. Only implementation-involved CRs continue to the verification stage.

The category field in the CR document can already distinguish such two categories to some extent. One of these categories is category D, which represents editorial modifications. According to TR21.900 [1], category D refers to "*editorial modifications shall have no impact on an implementation*". Category C corresponds to the functional modification of a feature. However, despite the two dedicated categories, the large quantity of CRs in other categories may still be editorial-only or involve implementation changes. As such, the primary goal of this step is to efficiently filter out editorial-only CRs from a large number of CRs. Still, the absence of an available open-source, large labeled dataset on 3GPP CRs poses a challenge for traditional ML classification training. As a result, any effective ML solution must rely on a small set of ground-truth data.

The UST algorithm [19] is an effective solution for few-shot text classification. This technique is designed to overcome the annotation bottleneck by leveraging a small amount of labeled data, typically 20 to 30 instances per class for training and validation, alongside a large pool of unlabeled data. Notably, the method achieves performance comparable to fully supervised models fine-tuned on thousands of labels. In CRChecker, UST is used to train and validate a two-class CR dataset in the Filtering Engine, which classifies CRs (not already in category D or category C) as either implementation-involved or editorial-only. The process begins with fine-tuning a base teacher model on a small labeled dataset. Next, the teacher model computes uncertainty estimates over a large pool of unlabeled CRs by adopting Monte Carlo (MC) Dropout [14]. Based on these estimates, the algorithm selects pseudo-labeled samples from the unlabeled pool for self-training, with a bias toward choosing easier samples for retraining. This strategy is employed because, within the self-training framework, hard examples often contribute noisy pseudo-labels.

4.2 Classification Engine

After the initial coarse-grained filtering of implementation-involved CRs in Sect. 4.1, a finer analysis prepares them for verification. The core problem addressed here is that developers require clear, structured information regarding *which entity or service is impacted* and *what specific type of implementation behavior applies* (e.g., entity addition or removal) to ensure compliance.

The Classification Engine in CRChecker performs this fine-grain analysis of implementation-involved CRs.

This level of detailed classification is essential because CRs are initially presented in natural language free text, creating a semantic and lexical gap between the specification changes and the corresponding source code. More importantly, before mapping the changes to code, we need to ensure to focus only on those with security implications (otherwise it will be simply a version difference/choice about functionality). Therefore, the Classification Engine, augmented by a RAG system, executes two core classification tasks in sequence: Security Classification and Behavior Classification.

CR Breakdown by Action Items. The "summary of change" field in the CR normally lists the required changes. However, a single CR occasionally includes multiple action items, as exemplified by *C4-186511* in Appendix A.1. To address multi-item CRs, specific breakdown steps are required. In most cases, the CR explicitly lists the action items either as a numbered list, bullet points, or as entries in distinct paragraphs. To begin the preprocessing phase for the Classification Engine, CRChecker first converts CR files originally supplied in `.doc` or `.docx` format into XML, by using LibreOffice [23] as a conversion tool, leveraging the Open XML structure of the documents. It then parses each XML file to identify structural elements such as paragraphs `<w:p>`, runs `<w:r>`, and text segments `<w:t>` [18], to locate the "summary of change" field. By querying paragraph styles, numbering properties, indentation settings and revision markers, the pipeline separates discrete action items when they appear as lists or distinct paragraphs within a CR document. If the text appears as multiple paragraphs or a numbered list, CRChecker classifies the summary as containing multiple action items and extracts each item individually. The scenario in which a single sentence contains multiple action items remains part of future work.

RAG Workflow. This process is guided by prompt engineering. When a user prompt containing CR data is received, the engine initiates retrieval, ranking, and generation stages. This process constructs a high-quality, non-redundant context set that supplies robust evidence for subsequent tasks. During retrieval, the module obtains candidate chunks from the vector store using dense similarity search. The system scores and filters these segments based on relevance, thereby reducing low-quality or irrelevant chunks and enhancing retrieval efficiency. The ranking module further refines the segments using Maximum Marginal Relevance (MMR) [7], which balances relevance and redundancy by selecting segments that meet both criteria. Subsequently, the module applies Reciprocal Rank Fusion (RRF) [10] across multiple retrieval paths. RRF combines ranked lists by summing the reciprocal rank from each list, resulting in a unified ordering of evidence chunks. The combined MMR and RRF approach produces the retrieved text chunks necessary for downstream tasks. The Classification Engine incorporates these chunks and the CR data into a unified prompt template. This template defines all relevant categories and entities, including CR categories for security and behavior. The template then executes the security and behavior classification tasks in sequence. After these tasks conclude, the system reuses the same template for the metadata extraction task and guides the LLM to generate structured metadata in a strictly formatted JSON output.

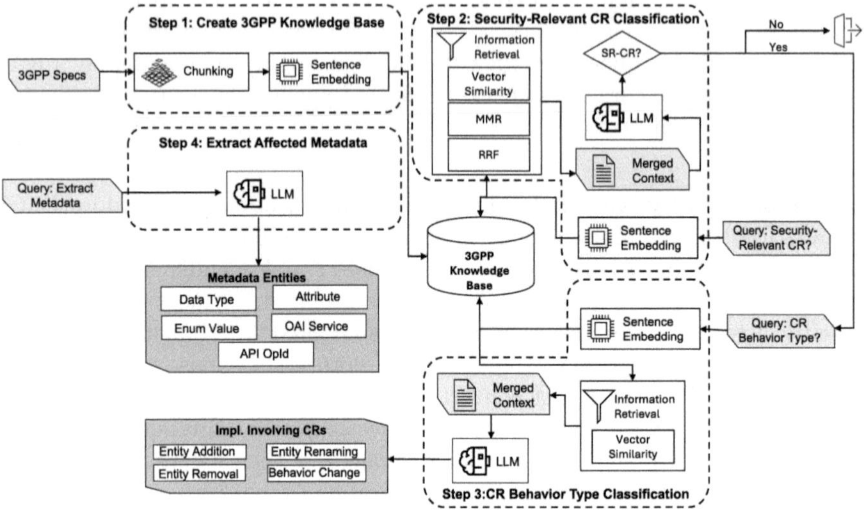

Fig. 2. Classification Engine workflow.

1. 3GPP Knowledge Base Creation. As shown in Fig. 2 step 1, the Classification Engine first applies chunking and embedding to prepare the knowledge base for retrieval. The 3GPP documents are split into manageable chunks that respect model input limits and preserve semantic coherence, ensuring that no chunk exceeds the embedding model's context window and that each chunk still captures a meaningful piece of information. Each chunk is then transformed into an embedding vector using a pretrained sentence embedding model. Finally, the embedding vectors, along with their associated metadata, are stored in a vector database that supports similarity-based searches. Constructing the data this way enables the Classification Engine to quickly and effectively retrieve relevant chunks in response to a query.

2. Security Classification. As shown in Fig. 2, step 2, the security classification involves prompting with the security-relevant CR definition and key CR fields (see Listing 1.3 in the Appendix), followed by the retrieval of evidence chunks from the 3GPP RAG knowledge base. A CR is security-relevant if it could lead to vulnerabilities, if not implemented, affecting system integrity, confidentiality, or availability. This approach reduces reliance on expert judgment.

Since missing a true security issue is significantly higher cost than producing a false alarm, the Classification Engine prioritizes high recall. The security classification stage begins with query expansion via LLM-generated paraphrases to address vocabulary mismatch caused by heterogeneous, vendor-specific phrases in security text (see Appendix Listing 1.4). Next, MMR [7] selects relevant, non-redundant passages to increase coverage of distinct security-related cues. Finally, RRF [10] merges the ranked lists from multiple expanded queries into a unified ranking, prioritizing documents that achieve high rankings across various query formulations, thereby further improving recall.

3. Behavior Classification. Next, the RAG system classifies action items into specific behavioral categories (as shown in Fig. 2 step 3). This classification is essential because the resulting classification dictates the type-specific outputs provided by CRChecker, such as binary compliance results for straightforward changes or potential code locations for behavior changes. The classification system comprises five predefined behavior categories, denoted by Γ: *Entity Addition*: A new entity, such as a data type, attribute, or enumeration value, is introduced, leading to a check of whether a corresponding datatype or attribute already exists. *Entity Removal*: An existing entity is being removed from the implementation. *Entity Renaming*: The name of an existing entity is being changed, without changing the functionality or behavior of the code. *Behavior Change*: The logic or operational behavior of existing code is being changed. For instance, *C4-205537* specifies the condition under which the AMF sends a Reachability Report event. In this Behavior Change, no new enumeration value is proposed; instead, several new conditions are specified. One such condition states that if the Mobile Reachable Timer expires, the AMF shall send a Reachability Report with `UNREACHABLE` state. *Editorial Change*: This is the same as the editorial-only CRs but as one action item after the breakdown of its parent CR, which is classified as implementation-involved due to its other action items.

The Classification Engine employs a structured prompt template that integrates the behavior category definitions and key CR fields to query the 3GPP knowledge base, retrieving relevant passages through vector similarity search. Using this prompt (see Appendix Listing 1.5), the LLM synthesizes the retrieved context, category definitions, and CR information to determine the appropriate behavior category for each action item.

4. Metadata Extraction. The final task of the Classification Engine is to extract structured metadata (Fig. 2 step 4), after excluding editorial-only action items from behavior classification . This extraction step employs a prompt template incorporating entity definitions and few-shot examples (see Appendix Listing 1.6), enabling the LLM to extract CR-impacted entities. CodeQL within the Compliance-Check Engine then leverages the extracted metadata to conduct compliance analysis based on the identified set of data type, $\mathcal{D}$, attributes, $\mathcal{A}$, Enumeration values, $\mathcal{E}$, API operation IDs, $\mathcal{O}$, and API services, $\mathcal{S}$.

4.3 Compliance-Check Engine

The goal of the CRChecker Compliance-Check Engine is to use metadata extracted by the Classification Engine to locate entities in implementation code.

Definition (Routing Condition). The set of all routing conditions $\mathcal{C}$ is a set of tuples. Let $\mathcal{M} = (\mathcal{D}, \mathcal{A}, \mathcal{E}, \mathcal{O}, \mathcal{S})$ be the metadata bundle and let $\gamma \in \Gamma$ be a CR category. Define availability indicators $\mathcal{M}_{\text{full}}, \mathcal{M}_{\text{partial}} \in \{0, 1\}$ by $\mathcal{M}_{\text{full}} = 1$ when $\mathcal{D} \neq \emptyset$, $\mathcal{A} \neq \emptyset$, $\mathcal{E} \neq \emptyset$, $\mathcal{O} \neq \emptyset$, and $\mathcal{S} \neq \emptyset$, and otherwise $\mathcal{M}_{\text{full}} = 0$; and $\mathcal{M}_{\text{partial}} = 1$ when $\mathcal{D} \neq \emptyset$ and $\mathcal{O} \neq \emptyset$, and otherwise $\mathcal{M}_{\text{partial}} = 0$. A routing condition $C \in \mathcal{C}$ is the tuple $C = ((\mathcal{M}_{\text{full}}, \mathcal{M}_{\text{partial}}), \gamma, \mathcal{O})$ obtained from metadata extraction and CR classification.

Routing Decision and Outputs. The dispatcher takes a routing condition C and chooses between two analysis paths (see Algorithm 1). When metadata is available (either full or partial), and the CR category is one of "Entity Addition," "Entity Removal," or "Entity Renaming," the dispatcher invokes `locateDatatype`, which produces the locations of the relevant entities; based on the category, this step outputs a binary compliance result. Otherwise, when operation IDs are present, and the CR category is not "Editorial Change," the dispatcher invokes `CallGraph`, which identifies the affected service locations at the function level in the implementation and outputs the function locations for subsequent manual review by a user.

Algorithm 1: Dispatch by routing condition.

Input: $C = ((\mathcal{M}_{\text{full}}, \mathcal{M}_{\text{partial}}), \gamma, \mathcal{O})$
if $(\mathcal{M}_{full} = 1 \vee \mathcal{M}_{partial} = 1) \wedge (\gamma \in \{$ *"Entity Addition"*, *"Entity Removal"*, *"Entity Renaming"* $\})$ **then**
  `locateDatatype`$(\mathcal{M}, \gamma)$;
end
else if $(\mathcal{O} \neq \emptyset) \wedge \gamma \neq$ *"Editorial Change"* **then**
  `CallGraph`$(\mathcal{M})$;
end

After the dispatcher makes the decision based on the condition, a CodeQL database is built for the 5GC implementation code so that each source file, type declaration, AST node, field reference and file-path metadata appears in relational form. Within this database, code artifacts (types, fields, files and their relationships) appear as tuples in a relational schema.

The remainder of this section describes two analysis paths at different levels of granularity. One path locates affected entities at the entity level and the other identifies impacted services at the function level.

Datatype Query. The goal of this analysis is to determine the presence or absence of a specific data structure or field in the codebase. We implement a query that leverages entity metadata extracted by the Classification Engine to identify the presence of the datatype, as shown in Algorithm 2. The CodeQL query begins by defining a predicate that matches a type-name whose target entity name equals a specified identifier. The query then locates occurrences of a structural type expression within files containing a specific NF, ensuring that the structural type expression and a type declaration for the target entity reside in the same file. It further ensures that the structural type's field includes a child node whose string value matches a given attribute pattern. The query outputs structural information for each match, including declared type, struct expression, field-child name and source file path. This information enables assessment of whether the targeted schema modification (for example, a CR for attribute addition) appears in the implementation or remains absent and may require migration.

Algorithm 2: Algorithm to locate the relevant entities.

Input : Target Datatype Name $\mathcal{D}$; Network Function $\mathcal{NF}$; Target Attribute Name $\mathcal{A}$.

Output: Type of the struct definition, AST node, Field's identifier (name) or its type expression, Source file location.

```
foreach TypeName n do
    if n.getTarget().getName() = D then
        t ← n.getTarget();
        f ← t.getDeclaration().getFile();
        if matches(f.getRelativePath(), "%NF%") then
            foreach StructTypeExpr s with s.getFile() = f do
                if ∃c ∈ s.getAField().getAChild() :
                 matches(toLowerCase(c.toString()), "%A%") then
                    emit;
                    (t.getDeclaration().getType(), s, c.toString(),
                     f.getRelativePath());
                end
            end
        end
    end
end
```

Call Graph Query. By leveraging entity metadata extracted through RAG system from last step, the CodeQL query implements a static analysis. This analysis builds a partial call graph rooted at a specific service operation within files associated with a particular network function component. First, the query identifies the function definition whose name matches the target operation in a case-insensitive manner and whose file path includes the target substring. Subsequently, using a predicate that describes call graph edges, the analysis traverses outward from the root function to find all functions directly invoked by it, as shown in Listing 1.1. For each call site, the query extracts metadata, including the calling function's name, the source file location, and the call's arguments. This process produces a map of "who calls what," starting from the operation of interest, and supports an understanding of the behavior propagation related to that service throughout the codebase.

```
predicate callGraphEdge(CallGraphNode pred, CallGraphNode succ) {
    // Go from a call to the called function.
    pred.(CallExpr) = succ.(FuncDef).getACall().asExpr()
    or
    // Go from a function to an enclosed call.
    pred = succ.(CallExpr).getEnclosingFunction()
}

src.getName().matches("callGraphEdge(src,␣sink)
␣␣␣␣
```

Listing 1.1. Lowe-level CodeQL call graph query

5 Preliminary Evaluation

In this work-in-progress, we present a preliminary evaluation of the effectiveness of the proposed pipeline, with planned next-steps explained in Sect. 5.1.

5.1 Next Steps

We plan to continue and improve this work in the directions including, but not limited to, the following items (ordered by priority): 1) Conduct an end-to-end evaluation to show the actual performance of CRChecker (which involves the creation of the corresponding end-to-end ground truth). 2) Improve the current CodeQL stage or/and further replace it with a better alternative static analysis tool, to reflect security implications, e.g., buggy/incorrect implementation. 3) Explore options to see how the current approach can generalize to none-CR contexts or at least code based not generated with the OpenAPI-Generator.

5.2 Revisiting the Motivating Example

We first apply CRChecker to *C4-213583*, an implementation-involved CR, to demonstrate the pipeline's end-to-end functionality. After initial preprocessing of the `.docx` input, the text snippet describing the required change (title, reason for change, summary of change, consequences if not approved) is first fed into the Filtering Engine, which correctly determines that implementation is involved. It is then passed to the Classification Engine for security classification, which confirms that this CR is security-relevant. Although the Classification Engine initially misclassifies the first action item as a Behavior Change rather than the correct Entity Addition, the Classification Engine subsequently executes the Metadata Extraction task successfully. The Extraction task correctly identifies the affected data type (`N1N2MessageTransferCause`), enumeration value (`N2_MSG_NOT_TRANSFERRED`), API service (`Namf_Communication`), and service operation ID (`N1N2MessageTransfer`). After running the CodeQL query on the call graph, it outputs the expected locations that need modifications to satisfy the CR as shown in Table 1 in the Appendix.

5.3 Datasets

Due to the lack of existing labeled ground truth for each stage, we involved different datasets (readily labeled) for evaluating individual stages/purposes.

Datasets for the Filtering Engine. To train the UST algorithm for few-shot classification (distinguishing implementation-involved and editorial-only), 30 samples randomly picked from CRs after Release 15 up to April 2025 were manually labeled (by one of the authors) for each class. This quantity is used because training with this sample size demonstrates the highest accuracy for the base teacher model [19]. These training CRs were selected from categories A, B, or F. To further evaluate the trained Filtering Engine, any Category C and Category D CRs are used, as they are naturally (by definition, (see Sect. 2)) implementation-involved and editorial-only, respectively. We chose those of Releases 15 and later from the CT and SA working groups.

Datasets for the Classification Engine. For security classification, the manually labeled dataset provided by CREEK [8,22] is employed, considering their peer-reviewed nature. For behavior classification, approved CRs derived from TS29.518 (Technical Specification) Release 17 and discussed at Technical Specification Group (TSG) meeting numbers 90-e and 91-e serve are selected.

3GPP Knowledge Base. CRChecker adopts the TSpec-LLM dataset [20], which processes and converts the specification files into markdown format and makes them ready for use.

5.4 Results

Implementation Classification. The precision, recall, and F1-score for the two classes (Implementation-involved, Editorial-only) are 83.4%/77.5%, 84.6%/75.9%, and 84.0%/76.7%, respectively. The overall accuracy is approximately 81%.

Security Relevance Filtering. Noe that this evaluation uses the manually labeled dataset provided by CREEK [8] for better comparison. The Classification Engine incorrectly predicts 3 CRs that should fall under security-relevant (SR) as non-security relevant (NSR), and 1 NSR as SR. CRChecker achieves a precision of 95.7% at this stage, which exceeds CREEK's reported performance (91.6%).

Behavior Classification The classification is based on three classes: Entity Modification (addition or removal), Behavior Change, and Editorial-only. Editorial-only achieves the highest accuracy (precision:95.0%/recall:90.5%/F1:92.7 %), while Behavior Change ends up the lowest (precision:72.7%/recall:61.5%/F1: 66.7%) compared to the other classification types. Such misclassification has only a minor effect on the final outcome as long as the correct relevant code locations that require modifications are identified (as opposed to Editorial-only).

CodeQL Compliance Verification. If a CR involves adding a new entity and metadata explicitly references that entity, the query reports compliance when static analysis via CodeQL locates that entity in the source code. In such cases, the presence and reference of the entity would satisfy compliance criteria. There are 16 action items from the 91-e dataset above classified as Entity Addition and using verified metadata, all requested added entities are found to exist via the datatype CodeQL query. For example, *C4-211699* requires the addition of a "Home Network Public Key identifier" to `UeContext`. The CodeQL datatype query identifies an attribute named `hNwPubKeyId` under type `UeContext` in file `model_ue_context.go`.

6 Conclusion

Given the importance of applying approved 3GPP CRs and the inherent difficulty in directly mapping specification changes to code, manually verifying 5GC implementation compliance remains infeasible. To overcome this, we proposed a semi-automated analysis pipeline, CRChecker, which integrates NLP, LLMs, and RAG to classify CRs and extract crucial structured metadata. Such metadata drives the compliance check, by performing static analysis using CodeQL and specialized queries. CRChecker pinpoints specific code locations for user inspection, substantially reducing manual effort.

A Appendix

A.1 Additional Examples

```yaml
openapi: 3.0.0
info:
  version: 1.2.0-alpha.1
  title: Namf_Communication
  description:
    ...
servers:
  - url: '{apiRoot}/namf-comm/v1'
  ...
paths:
  /ue-contexts/{ueContextId}:
    put:
      summary: Namf_Communication CreateUEContext service Operation
      tags:
        - Individual ueContext (Document)
      operationId: CreateUEContext
      parameters:
        - name: ueContextId
      ...
```

Listing 1.2. A snippet of Namf_Communication Service OAS

CRs Containing Multiple Items. *C4-186511* comprises three action items as shown in Fig. 3. The first action item defines new enumeration values in the datatype `NgapIeType`. The second action item changes the datatype of the attribute `ngapIeType`. The third action item modifies the OAS accordingly based on the preceding two action items.

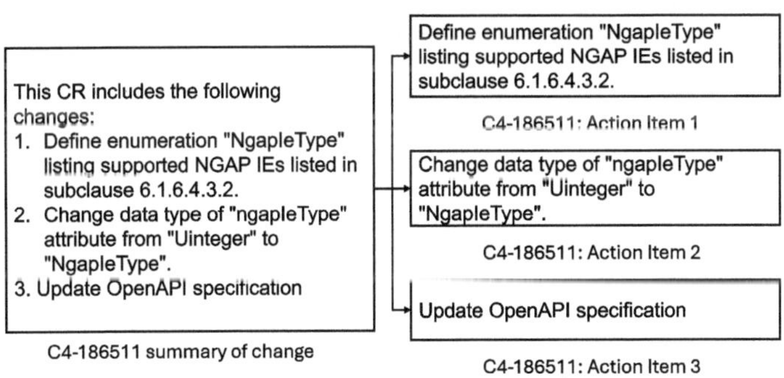

Fig. 3. An example CR containing multiple items (C4-186511).

Editorial-Only CRs The 3GPP CR document specifies detailed modifications to a specification. However, not all approved CRs affect the system behavior. Some CRs fall into the editorial-only category, indicating the proposed change involves only textual revisions and does not modify system behavior. For instance, *C3-216512*[2] increases the API version number from '1.0.0-alpha.2' to '1.0.0-alpha.3' and updates the TS version in the externalDocs field from '17.1.0' to '17.3.0'. Other CRs require developers to implement functional modifications.

Categories C and D already correspond to implementation-involved and editorial-only, respectively, leaving only CRs in categories A, B, and F to be classified by the UST algorithm, as shown in Fig. 4.

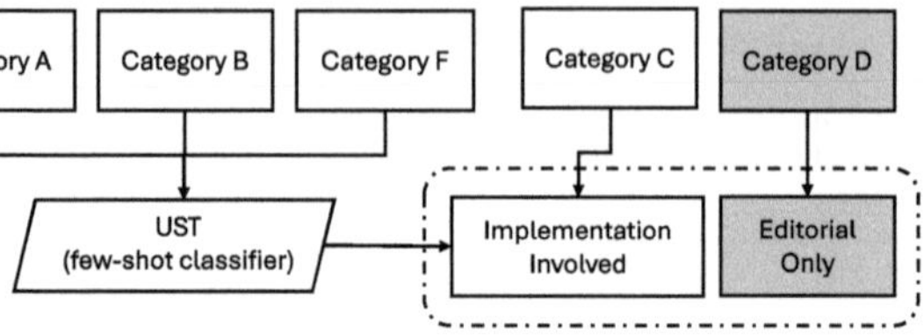

Fig. 4. CR classification.

Identified Code Locations in the Motivating Example. Table 1 shows the outcome from processing the CR *C4-213583*. In function `N1N2MessageTransferProcedure`, the code defines a set of switch cases on possible values for the `cause` information element within the `N1N2MessageTransferRspData` data type. However, the code does not include a case in which the cause is set to `N2_MSG_NOT_TRANSFERRED`, even though that value is specified in the approved CR *C4-213583*.

Table 1. C4-213583: CodeQL-identified relevant code locations in free5GC v4.

Function Name	File Path
`HTTPN1N2MessageTransferStatus`	`NFs/amf/internal/sbi/api_communication.go`
`HTTPN1N2MessageTransfer`	`NFs/amf/internal/sbi/api_communication.go`
`N1N2MessageTransferStatusProcedure`	`NFs/amf/internal/sbi/processor/n1n2message.go`
`HandleN1N2MessageTransferStatusRequest`	`NFs/amf/internal/sbi/processor/n1n2message.go`
`N1N2MessageTransferProcedure`	`NFs/amf/internal/sbi/processor/n1n2message.go`
`HandleN1N2MessageTransferRequest`	`NFs/amf/internal/sbi/processor/n1n2message.go`
`N1N2MessageTransfer`	`openapi/amf/Communication/api_n1_n2_message_collection_collection.go`

[2] C3-216512, update of OpenAPI version and TS version in externalDocs field. https://www.3gpp.org/ftp/tsg_ct/WG3_interworking_ex-CN3/TSGC3_119e/Inbox/Draft/OpenAPI-version-updates/C3-216512_r1.zip.

A.2 Prompt Templates

```
You are tasked with reviewing a given change request and classify it into
 exactly one of these two categories:
1. Security Related
2. Non Security Related

For a CR is considered to be security-relevant: If the proposed change
request fix is not applied, it will introduce weaknesses or
vulnerabilities in the implementation, potentially compromising the
system's integrity, confidentiality, or availability.
{CR Information}
```

Listing 1.3. Security classification prompt

```
You are a helpful assistant that generates multiple search queries based
on a single input query. Generate exactly 3 relevant search queries
related to: "{question}". Provide your output with only the queries,
formatted one per line, without any additional text or explanation.

Use the following format to answer:
1.
2.
3.
```

Listing 1.4. Query expansion prompt

```
You'll receive a Change Request (CR) and must classify it **into exactly
one** of the following categories:

1. Entity Addition - Adding a new component (information element(IE),
entity, parameter, attribute, function, or operation).
2. Entity Removal - Removing an existing component (information element(
IE), entity, parameter, attribute, function, or operation).
3. Renaming Changes - Renaming elements such as variables, identifiers,
or API operation names **while leaving behavior unchanged**.
4. Behavior Change - Altering logic or functionality.
5. Editorial Change - Non-functional edits including:
    - Documentation-only changes
    - Corrections, formatting, reference or cross-reference updates
    - Structural label or heading changes
    - Style adjustments
    - Clause/section reference changes (e.g., 'amended to refer to clause
    5.2.2.3.1.2')
    - Any change with no effect on actual system behavior or API surface

**Important Guideline:**
- If the CR contains only a correction (such as fixing a typo, reference
ID, or version string) and there is **no name rename**, **no logic
alteration**, and **no API or behavior change**, then it must be
classified as an **Editorial Change**, regardless of wording.
- **Important:** A CR classified as an **Entity Addition**, **Entity
Removal**, or **Renaming Change** should not also be classified as a **
Behavior Change**, even if the change could affect behavior.

**Choose exactly one category** based on these definitions.

Your final response MUST be a JSON object matching this format exactly:
{{
  "impl_indicator": "Entity Addition" or "Entity Removal" or "Renaming
  Change" or "Behavior Change" or "Editorial Change"
}}
```

Listing 1.5. Behavior classification prompt

```
Task: Analyze the provided Change Request (CR) and extract the required fields.

You MUST follow this procedure:

Step A - Candidate extraction (short lists, no reasoning):
- Collect every token from the CR that looks like a potential change target:
    - Type or data-structure names (e.g., CamelCase like N1N2MessageTransferRspData)
    - Field/parameter/attribute names (e.g., SubscriptionId)
    - Enum/constant values (SCREAMING_SNAKE_CASE like N2_MSG_NOT_TRANSFERRED)
    - Literal protocol/status codes (3-digit HTTP codes like 200)
    - Operation IDs and service names exactly as written
- Include items only if the CR states or unambiguously implies they are affected.
- If a CR includes a table (e.g., TS spec tables), extract only the values under the ‘‘Attribute name’’ and ‘‘Data type’’ columns.

Step B - Filter to what is actually modified:
- From Step A, keep only the low-level entities that require modification based on the CR

Decision rule for requires_data_type_change:
- Answer true if the CR adds/removes/modifies any data type or enum value (e.g., adding N2_MSG_NOT_TRANSFERRED to an existing enum).
- Otherwise false.

1. Affected Data Types: list the names of data types or structures (types, classes, records, schemas) that are added, removed, or modified.
2. Affected Attributes: list the names of attributes/fields/parameters whose definitions change (e.g. their data type, name, presence), excluding attributes that are part of a data type change already captured if you want to avoid duplication.
3. Affected Enum Values: list the names of enum / constant values that are added, removed, or modified.
4. Affected OpenAPI Services: Specify the OpenAPI services impacted by the change.
5. Affected Service Operation IDs: List the operation IDs of the services affected by the change.

If any required element cannot be determined, put ‘‘I don’t know’’ for that element.

Additional enforcement rules:
- When listing **Affected OpenAPI Services**, strip any ‘‘API’’ suffix. For example, ‘‘Namf_EventExposure API’’ must be listed as ‘‘Namf_EventExposure’’.
- Do NOT include any entity name that is not a single-token (CamelCase, snake_case, or CONSTANT_CASE).
- Do NOT include any additional explanation or commentary. Only return the JSON structure exactly as shown.

Return ONLY this JSON (no extra text):
{
  ‘‘affected_data_types’’: [strings],
  ‘‘affected_attributes’’: [strings],
  ‘‘affected_enum_values’’: [strings],
  ‘‘affected_api_services’’: [strings],
  ‘‘affected_operation_ids’’: [strings]
}
```

Listing 1.6. Metadata extraction prompt

References

1. 3GPP: 3rd generation partnership project; technical specification group working methods; working methods of TSGS WGS and support team. Technical Report (TR) 21.900. Tech. rep., 3rd Generation Partnership Project (3GPP) (2016). https://portal.3gpp.org/desktopmodules/Specifications/SpecificationDetails.aspx?specificationId=555
2. 3GPP: 3GPP specifications (2025). https://www.3gpp.org/
3. 3rd Generation Partnership Project (3GPP): Digital cellular telecommunications system (Phase 2+); Universal Mobile Telecommunications System (UMTS); Technical Specification Group working methods (3GPP TR 21.900 version 11.0.1 Release 11)
4. America's Cyber Defense Agency: Introduction to the communications sector risk management agency (2021). https://www.cisa.gov/sites/default/files/publications/Communications
5. Amini, M.R., Feofanov, V., Pauletto, L., Hadjadj, L., Devijver, E., Maximov, Y.: Self-training: a survey. Neurocomputing **616**, 128904 (2025)
6. Avgustinov, P., De Moor, O., Jones, M.P., Schäfer, M.: QL: object-oriented queries on relational data. In: 30th European Conference on Object-Oriented Programming (ECOOP 2016), pp. 2–1. Schloss Dagstuhl–Leibniz-Zentrum für Informatik (2016)
7. Carbonell, J., Goldstein, J.: The use of MMR, diversity-based reranking for reordering documents and producing summaries. In: Proceedings of the 21st Annual International ACM SIGIR Conference on Research and Development in Information Retrieval, pp. 335–336 (1998)
8. Chen, Y., et al.: Seeing the forest for the trees: understanding security hazards in the {3GPP} ecosystem through intelligent analysis on change requests. In: 31st USENIX Security Symposium (USENIX Security 22), pp. 17–34 (2022)
9. Cheng, W., Schubert, J., Bornet, C., Bresson, J., sunn: Hello from OpenAPI generator (2025), https://openapi-generator.tech/
10. Cormack, G.V., Clarke, C.L., Buettcher, S.: Reciprocal rank fusion outperforms condorcet and individual rank learning methods. In: Proceedings of the 32nd International ACM SIGIR Conference on Research and Development in Information Retrieval, pp. 758–759 (2009)
11. Ericsson: Evolving the security posture for critical infrastructure (2025). https://www.ericsson.com/en/blog/north-america/2025/evolving-the-security-posture-for-critical-infrastructure
12. free5GC: free5GC: An Open-Source 5G Core Network (2025). https://free5gc.org/ (2025). Accessed 17 Nov 2025
13. free5GC Project: History (2025). https://free5gc.org/history/. Accessed 30 Apr 2025
14. Gal, Y., Ghahramani, Z.: Dropout as a Bayesian approximation: representing model uncertainty in deep learning. In: International Conference on Machine Learning, pp. 1050–1059. PMLR (2016)
15. Huang, L., Zhao, M., Xiao, L., Zhang, X., Hu, J.: Chat3GPP: an open-source retrieval-augmented generation framework for 3GPP documents. arXiv preprint arXiv:2501.13954 (2025)
16. Karim, I., Mubasshir, K.S., Rahman, M.M., Bertino, E.: SPEC5G: a dataset for 5G cellular network protocol analysis. arXiv preprint arXiv:2301.09201 (2023)
17. Lewis, P., et al.: Retrieval-augmented generation for knowledge-intensive NLP tasks. Adv. Neural. Inf. Process. Syst. **33**, 9459–9474 (2020)

18. Microsoft Corporation: Structure of a wordprocessingml document (2024). https://learn.microsoft.com/en-us/office/open-xml/word/structure-of-a-wordprocessingml-document?tabs=cs. Accessed 08 Nov 2025
19. Mukherjee, S., Awadallah, A.: Uncertainty-aware self-training for few-shot text classification. Adv. Neural. Inf. Process. Syst. **33**, 21199–21212 (2020)
20. Nikbakht, R., Benzaghta, M., Geraci, G.: TSpec-LLM:: an open-source dataset for LLM understanding of 3GPP specifications. arXiv preprint arXiv:2406.01768 (2024)
21. Open Networking Foundation (ONF): SD-Core: A Cloud Native 4G/5G Disaggregated Mobile Core (2025). https://opennetworking.org/sd-core/. Accessed 17 Nov 2025
22. Project, C.: Evaluation on manual labeled testing set (2022). https://sites.google.com/view/3gpp-creek/homepage/evaluation-manual-testing-set. Accessed 08 Nov 2025
23. The Document Foundation: LibreOffice (2025). https://www.libreoffice.org/, free and open-source office suite
24. Thorn, S., English, K.V., Butler, K.R., Enck, W.: 5GAC-analyzer: identifying over-privilege between 5G core network functions. In: Proceedings of the 17th ACM Conference on Security and Privacy in Wireless and Mobile Networks, pp. 66–77 (2024)
25. Wu, H., Wu, J., Wu, R., Sharma, A., Machiry, A., Bianchi, A.: VeriBin: adaptive verification of patches at the binary level. In: Network and Distributed System Security Symposium (NDSS), San Diego, CA, USA (2025)

Cryptanalysis, Post-quantum and Smart-Contract Incentives

Strengthening Practical Non-profiling Side-Channel Attacks via Kalman Filter-Based Power–EM Fusion on AES-128 Devices

Xiaoyong Kou, Wei Yang, Gongxuan Zhang(✉), and Jiabei Wang

School of Computer Science and Engineering, Nanjing University of Science and Technology, Nanjing, China
{kouxy,generalyzy,gongxuan}@njust.edu.cn

Abstract. Side-channel analysis (SCA) remains a major threat to embedded/IoT devices, yet under high noise the efficiency of single-source measurements (power-only or EM-only) degrades sharply. Lightweight denoising (e.g., moving average, wavelet filtering) is largely single-channel and cannot exploit complementarity between power and EM leakage; moreover, large trace budgets are impractical under drift, aging, or dynamic keys, where a few byte-dependent hard cases dominate full-key failure. We present a non-profiling dual-observation fusion framework based on a Kalman filter (KF). After alignment and normalization, power and EM traces are modeled as two noisy observations of a shared latent leakage state. Assuming approximately uncorrelated modality noise, KF yields the optimal LMMSE estimate and outputs one fused trace per encryption, compatible with standard correlation power analysis (CPA). On paired AES-128 measurements from an Artix-7 FPGA and an Atmel ATSAM3U2C MCU, KF fusion improves SNR and accelerates key recovery. On FPGA, conservative TTS@95% (min N for 95% full key success) improves from 4000 traces (EM-only) to 2000 (KF), while power-only does not reach 95% within 5000; KF also outperforms inverse-variance weighted averaging (2500). On MCU, KF reduces conservative full-key TTS@95% from 200 to 160 traces (20%) and mitigates hard-byte tail risk.

Keywords: Side-channel analysis · correlation power analysis · power · electromagnetic leakage · Kalman filter · multi-modal fusion · AES-128

1 Introduction

Secure communication in IoT and embedded systems depends on the correct deployment of cryptographic primitives on resource-constrained hardware. In practice, security is often limited not by the cryptographic algorithm but by *physical leakage* observable to an on-device adversary.

Y. Cao et al. (Eds.): SecureComm 2026, LNICST 704, pp. 157–172, 2027.
https://doi.org/10.1007/978-3-032-32764-2_8

Side-channel analysis (SCA) exploits physical leakage such as power consumption and electromagnetic (EM) radiation to recover secrets from cryptographic implementations [3,4]. Despite extensive progress in profiling attacks, non-profiling attacks—particularly correlation power analysis (CPA)—remain central in practical security evaluation, red-teaming, and countermeasure verification due to their minimal training requirements and transparent statistical interpretation [5,6,9]. However, the practical success of CPA hinges on measurement constraints and on modality-specific artifacts: the best-performing sensor in one setup can underperform in another due to coupling changes, environmental noise, time misalignment, and byte-dependent leakage strength.

A recurring issue in real measurements is the mismatch between *average* byte recovery and *end-to-end* key recovery. Byte-wise CPA often recovers most AES key bytes at modest trace budgets, but full-key recovery (16/16 correct) can remain unreliable if one or two bytes are systematically harder (e.g., due to weaker leakage, stronger noise, or poorer temporal alignment). This produces a pronounced *tail-risk* phenomenon: byte-level metrics appear strong, yet full-key success remains low for the same budget. We observe this pattern clearly on EM-only measurements, where byte-level success can exceed 95% while full-key success remains far below 95% in the same budget range.

This paper investigates a pragmatic strengthening approach: if an attacker (or evaluator) can measure *paired* power and EM traces for the same encryptions, can simple fusion reduce noise and stabilize the hardest bytes enough to materially reduce the trace budget needed for reliable full-key CPA? We answer positively using a Kalman filter (KF) formulation. KF fusion is attractive for a practical full-paper contribution because it is (i) lightweight and attack-side, (ii) requires no profiling data, (iii) has linear time overhead in trace length, and (iv) integrates into existing CPA pipelines as a drop-in preprocessing step.

Contributions.

1. **Power–EM two-observation state-space modeling.** We model time-aligned power and EM samples as two independent observations of a shared latent leakage state and fuse them with a scalar Kalman filter, yielding a single fused trace per encryption that can be processed by any standard CPA implementation without modification.
2. **Optimal fusion under an uncorrelated-noise assumption.** We formalize the key assumption that the dominant power and EM noise terms are weakly correlated and show that the resulting Kalman update implements an inverse-variance optimal linear combination, with the process noise providing temporal regularization across samples.
3. **Cross-platform empirical validation and hard-byte mitigation.** On paired measurements from AES-128 implementations on an MCU and an FPGA, we demonstrate improved sample efficiency and reduced tail risk in full-key recovery, and we report "hardest-byte success" as an explicit mechanism-level metric.

1.1 Threat Model and Attack Goal

We assume a standard physical attacker who can observe multiple encryptions under a fixed secret key and record side-channel traces. The attacker knows the plaintext corresponding to each trace (known-plaintext) and performs offline processing and statistics. We do not assume device manipulation, fault injection, or ability to alter internal randomness. Our attack goal is to recover the AES-128 key using CPA. We consider three observation modalities: Power-only, EM-only, and paired Power+EM fused offline.

Leakage and Synchronization Assumptions. For both targets, we approximate the instantaneous leakage in each modality by a Hamming-weight (HW) model of an AES intermediate value (e.g., the SubBytes output). Power and EM traces are acquired *synchronously* using a shared trigger, so each encryption operation yields a strictly paired $(y_p[\cdot], y_e[\cdot])$ record with consistent indexing across modalities. We further assume the dominant measurement noises in the power path (e.g., supply/ground switching, global activity) and in the EM path (e.g., probe positioning jitter, local field coupling) are sufficiently decorrelated to justify a diagonal measurement-noise covariance; Sect. 3.2 discusses the straightforward extension when residual correlation is present.

1.2 Related Work

CPA and Non-profiling SCA. CPA and related differential attacks correlate a leakage model (e.g., Hamming weight) with measured traces to identify key-dependent intermediate values [1,3,4]. Their relevance persists because they require neither templates nor training data and thus align with practical attacker and evaluation assumptions.

Multi-modal Measurements. Power and EM leakages are complementary: power captures global activity through supply networks, whereas EM probes can localize emission sources [10]. Multi-modal acquisitions can improve signal availability but introduce challenges: different noise spectra, coupling instabilities, and alignment differences. A key open question for practical evaluation is whether multi-modal processing improves *full-key* recovery under realistic budgets, rather than merely improving the easiest bytes.

Multi-channel Fusion Attacks and Interpretability. Yang *et al.* proposed *multi-channel fusion attacks* and showed that principled fusion metrics (including correlation-based formulations) can strengthen key recovery when multiple leakage channels are available [11]. While that line of work emphasizes statistical fusion across channels and points of interest, recent SecureComm work by Shen *et al.* highlights a complementary perspective: *visual interpretability* of deep learning-based multi-channel attacks to diagnose channel contributions and failure cases [7]. These studies motivate our focus on a lightweight, transparent fusion mechanism whose gains can be analyzed at the level of byte-wise and hardest-byte success.

Filtering and Fusion. Filtering methods are routinely applied as preprocessing in SCA (e.g., smoothing, bandpass filtering, dimensionality reduction) [8]. Kalman filtering provides an interpretable, parameterized approach for fusing noisy observations under a linear Gaussian model [2]. In contrast to heavy learning-based fusion, KF offers a transparent mechanism with limited hyperparameters and predictable complexity, making it suitable for attack-side enhancement studies.

2 Preliminaries

2.1 Target and Leakage Model

We target AES-128 implementations and apply first-round CPA independently on each byte. Let $P_{t,i}$ denote the i-th plaintext byte of trace t, and k_i denote the secret key byte. For key hypothesis $k \in \{0, \ldots, 255\}$, the attacked intermediate is:

$$V_{t,i}(k) = \text{SBox}(P_{t,i} \oplus k), \tag{1}$$

and we use a Hamming-weight model:

$$H_{t,i}(k) = \text{HW}(V_{t,i}(k)) \in \{0, \ldots, 8\}. \tag{2}$$

2.2 CPA Score and Key Decision

For a trace modality X (Power, EM, or fused), let $X_t[\ell] \in \mathbb{R}$ denote sample index $\ell \in \{1, \ldots, L\}$ of trace $t \in \{1, \ldots, N\}$. For each byte position $i \in \{0, \ldots, 15\}$ and key hypothesis $k \in \{0, \ldots, 255\}$, we compute the hypothetical leakage under a standard HW model as

$$H_{t,i}(k) \triangleq \text{HW}(S(P_{t,i} \oplus k)), \tag{3}$$

where $P_{t,i}$ is plaintext byte i of trace t, $S(\cdot)$ is the AES S-box, and $\text{HW}(\cdot)$ is the Hamming weight. CPA evaluates the Pearson correlation between $H_{t,i}(k)$ and the measured samples $X_t[\ell]$ across traces:

$$\rho_i(k, \ell) \triangleq \frac{\sum_{t=1}^{N} \left(H_{t,i}(k) - \overline{H}_i(k)\right) \left(X_t[\ell] - \overline{X}[\ell]\right)}{\sqrt{\sum_{t=1}^{N} \left(H_{t,i}(k) - \overline{H}_i(k)\right)^2} \sqrt{\sum_{t=1}^{N} \left(X_t[\ell] - \overline{X}[\ell]\right)^2}}, \tag{4}$$

with $\overline{H}_i(k) \triangleq \frac{1}{N} \sum_{t=1}^{N} H_{t,i}(k)$ and $\overline{X}[\ell] \triangleq \frac{1}{N} \sum_{t=1}^{N} X_t[\ell]$. The score of hypothesis k at byte i is defined by the standard maximum-correlation rule

$$s_i(k) \triangleq \max_{\ell \in \{1, \ldots, L\}} |\rho_i(k, \ell)|, \tag{5}$$

and the recovered key byte is

$$\hat{k}_i \triangleq \arg \max_{k \in \{0, \ldots, 255\}} s_i(k). \tag{6}$$

Model-Based Interpretation. Under the common linear leakage model $X_t[\ell] = \alpha_\ell H_{t,i}(k^\star) + \eta_t[\ell]$ for the correct key $k^\star$, maximizing $|\rho_i(k,\ell)|$ over ℓ searches for the sample(s) with the strongest signal-to-noise ratio, while incorrect hypotheses behave approximately like noise with near-zero correlation. Throughout the paper we keep the CPA scorer and decision rule fixed as in Eqs. (5)–(6) to isolate the performance gain attributable to fusion rather than to changes in the distinguisher.

2.3 Metrics: Full-Key vs. Byte-Level Success

To characterize both average-case performance and tail risk across the 16 AES key bytes, we report the following metrics over repeated trials:

- **Byte-level success rate** ($\mathrm{SR}_{\mathrm{byte}}$): for each trial, we compute the fraction of correctly recovered key bytes (out of 16), and then report the mean over trials (in %).
- **Full-key success rate** ($\mathrm{SR}_{\mathrm{full}}$): the fraction of trials in which all 16 key bytes are recovered correctly, i.e., exact full-key recovery.
- **Hardest-byte success rate** ($\mathrm{SR}_{\mathrm{hard}}$): for each trace budget N and modality, we identify the byte index with the lowest per-byte success and report that worst-byte success rate (in %). This metric directly quantifies the bottleneck that governs full-key recovery.
- **Time-to-success at 95% (TTS@95%)**: the smallest trace budget N for which the corresponding success rate reaches 95%. We report both point estimates and conservative criteria (e.g., a lower confidence bound or an empirical lower bound across runs, depending on the platform and evaluation protocol).

2.4 Kalman Filtering Basics

Kalman filtering provides a minimum mean-squared error (MMSE) estimator for linear systems under Gaussian noise. In its standard form, a latent state $x[\ell]$ evolves according to a state equation

$$x[\ell] = Ax[\ell-1] + w[\ell], \qquad w[\ell] \sim \mathcal{N}(0, Q), \tag{7}$$

and measurements are generated by an observation equation

$$z[\ell] = Hx[\ell] + v[\ell], \qquad v[\ell] \sim \mathcal{N}(0, R). \tag{8}$$

Given a prior estimate $(\hat{x}[\ell-1], P[\ell-1])$, the filter performs a *predict* step

$$\hat{x}^-[\ell] = A\hat{x}[\ell-1], \tag{9}$$

$$P^-[\ell] = AP[\ell-1]A^\top + Q, \tag{10}$$

followed by an *update* with Kalman gain

$$K[\ell] = P^{-}[\ell]H^{\top}\left(HP^{-}[\ell]H^{\top} + R\right)^{-1}, \tag{11}$$

$$\hat{x}[\ell] = \hat{x}^{-}[\ell] + K[\ell]\left(z[\ell] - H\hat{x}^{-}[\ell]\right), \tag{12}$$

$$P[\ell] = (I - K[\ell]H)P^{-}[\ell]. \tag{13}$$

For scalar fusion with multiple sensors at the same time index, one can apply sequential measurement updates (one update per sensor) using each sensor's (H, R); this is equivalent to a single multi-sensor update under the usual conditional independence assumption.

3 Proposed Methodology

CPA is sensitive to noise and sample variance: even if the expected leakage is correlated with the model, finite-sample noise can cause incorrect hypotheses to win, especially for hard bytes whose true correlation peak is weaker or less stable. A fusion method is useful if it reduces effective noise variance while preserving the timing and structure of the key-dependent component. Kalman filtering [2] provides a principled estimator for combining noisy observations and naturally handles different noise levels across modalities via its R parameters.

3.1 Alignment and Pre-processing

Fusion requires that power and EM traces correspond to the *same* encryption operations and are aligned in time so that sample index ℓ refers to the same micro-architectural activity in both modalities. In our pipeline, we (i) ensure one-to-one plaintext indexing across modalities, (ii) apply time alignment using standard SCA alignment techniques (e.g., correlation-based alignment or elastic alignment), and (iii) normalize amplitudes so that the two sensors are comparable in scale. Unless otherwise stated, we apply per-trace mean removal and ℓ_2 normalization before fusion and CPA to reduce trace-to-trace baseline drift and to prevent a small number of high-energy traces from dominating correlation estimates.

3.2 State-Space Model Construction

We consider a pair of aligned measurements at sample index ℓ from a single encryption: the power sample $p[\ell]$ and the EM sample $e[\ell]$. Let $x[\ell]$ denote the latent *useful leakage* (i.e., the noise-reduced component that is informative for CPA) at index ℓ. We adopt a standard linear-Gaussian state-space model.

State Equation. To regularize the estimation across adjacent samples, we use a random-walk (or nearly-static) prior:

$$x[\ell] = Fx[\ell-1] + w[\ell], \qquad w[\ell] \sim \mathcal{N}(0, Q), \tag{14}$$

where F is the state transition (typically $F = 1$) and Q is the process-noise variance. This dynamic is not intended to be a circuit-accurate model; it is a lightweight smoothness prior that stabilizes point-wise fusion on high-dimensional traces.

Observation Equation. We stack the two modalities into a 2-D observation vector $\mathbf{z}[\ell] = [\,p[\ell]\; e[\ell]\,]^T$:

$$\mathbf{z}[\ell] = \mathbf{H}\,x[\ell] + \mathbf{v}[\ell], \qquad \mathbf{H} = \begin{bmatrix} h_p \\ h_e \end{bmatrix}, \tag{15}$$

where h_p and h_e capture the (possibly different) linear scaling between the latent leakage and each sensor. In the simplest normalized setting we set $h_p = h_e = 1$; alternatively, (h_p, h_e) can be estimated via a short calibration step (e.g., matching variances in a profiling-free manner).

The measurement noise is modeled as zero-mean Gaussian: $\mathbf{v}[\ell] \sim \mathcal{N}(\mathbf{0}, \mathbf{R})$, with

$$\mathbf{R} = \begin{bmatrix} R_p & 0 \\ 0 & R_e \end{bmatrix}. \tag{16}$$

Key Assumption. The dominant noise sources of power acquisition (e.g., global switching noise, ground bounce, thermal noise) and EM acquisition (e.g., spatial radiation, probe coupling and positioning jitter) are often weakly correlated. Accordingly, we assume $\mathrm{Cov}(n^{(p)}, n^{(e)}) \approx 0$, which motivates the diagonal form in Eq. (16). If cross-correlation is non-negligible in a particular setup, the framework naturally generalizes by using a full $\mathbf{R}$.

3.3 Fusion Algorithm

Given aligned and normalized traces $\{p[\ell]\}_{\ell=1}^{L}$ and $\{e[\ell]\}_{\ell=1}^{L}$ for each encryption, we perform *sample-wise* fusion to obtain a single fused trace $\hat{x}[1{:}L]$ that can be directly consumed by standard CPA. At each sample index ℓ, the latent leakage $x[\ell]$ is predicted by the state equation in Eq. (14) and updated using the two-sensor observation model in Eq. (15).

Joint (Stacked) Update. With stacked observation $\mathbf{z}[\ell] = [\,p[\ell]\; e[\ell]\,]^T$, the Kalman update for a scalar state and a 2-D observation takes the standard form:

$$\hat{x}^-[\ell] = A\,\hat{x}[\ell{-}1], \qquad P^-[\ell] = A\,P[\ell{-}1]A^T + Q, \tag{17}$$

$$\mathbf{y}[\ell] = \mathbf{z}[\ell] - \mathbf{H}\hat{x}^-[\ell], \qquad \mathbf{S}[\ell] = \mathbf{H}P^-[\ell]\mathbf{H}^T + \mathbf{R}, \tag{18}$$

$$\mathbf{K}[\ell] = P^-[\ell]\mathbf{H}^T\mathbf{S}[\ell]^{-1}, \qquad \hat{x}[\ell] = \hat{x}^-[\ell] + \mathbf{K}[\ell]\mathbf{y}[\ell], \tag{19}$$

$$P[\ell] = (1 - \mathbf{K}[\ell]\mathbf{H})P^-[\ell]. \tag{20}$$

Algorithm 1. Scalar Kalman fusion of paired power and EM traces (per trace).

Require: Power trace $p[1{:}L]$, EM trace $e[1{:}L]$, parameters Q, R_p, R_e
Ensure: Fused trace $\hat{x}[1{:}L]$
1: Initialize $\hat{x} \leftarrow 0$, $P \leftarrow P_0$ ▷ P_0 large after normalization (e.g., P_0=1)
2: **for** $\ell = 1$ to L **do**
3: **Predict:** $\hat{x}^- \leftarrow \hat{x}, \quad P^- \leftarrow P + Q$
4: **Update (power):** $K_p \leftarrow P^-/(P^- + R_p)$
5: $\hat{x} \leftarrow \hat{x}^- + K_p(p[\ell] - \hat{x}^-); \quad P \leftarrow (1 - K_p)P^-$
6: **Update (EM):** $K_e \leftarrow P/(P + R_e)$
7: $\hat{x} \leftarrow \hat{x} + K_e(e[\ell] - \hat{x}); \quad P \leftarrow (1 - K_e)P$
8: $\hat{x}[\ell] \leftarrow \hat{x}$
9: **end for**

Here, $\mathbf{K}[\ell] \in \mathbb{R}^{1\times 2}$ acts as a *data-driven, time-varying* weighting of the two modalities: when the EM channel is noisier (larger R_e), the corresponding gain component decreases, and the estimator relies more on the power channel, and vice versa.

Efficient Sequential Update. When the cross-channel noise correlation is negligible, $\mathbf{R} = \mathrm{diag}(R_p, R_e)$ (Sect. 3), the stacked update above is equivalent to applying two scalar measurement updates at the same ℓ (e.g., power first, then EM). We implement this sequential form to avoid explicit 2×2 matrix inversion while preserving the optimality guarantee under the uncorrelated-noise assumption. Algorithm 1 summarizes the per-trace fusion procedure.

3.4 Weighted-Average Baseline

To disentangle the benefit of *dual-modality fusion* from the benefit of *temporal regularization*, we include a parameter-light baseline that fuses each sample independently by inverse-variance weighting. Assuming the normalized observations satisfy $p = x + n_p$ and $e = x + n_e$ with independent zero-mean Gaussian noise variances R_p and R_e, the minimum-variance unbiased estimator for a *single* sample is:

$$\hat{x}_{\mathrm{WA}} = w_p\, p + w_e\, e, \quad w_p = \frac{1/R_p}{1/R_p + 1/R_e} = \frac{R_e}{R_p + R_e}, \quad w_e = \frac{R_p}{R_p + R_e}. \tag{21}$$

WA is attractive due to its simplicity and its clear interpretation as modality-level SNR balancing. However, WA cannot exploit the strong temporal structure of side-channel leakage (e.g., concentration around round operations) and is sensitive to local noise bursts because it does not propagate uncertainty across time. Kalman fusion generalizes WA by coupling samples through the process model (via Q and the evolving $P[\ell]$), yielding adaptive gains and temporal smoothing while still respecting relative modality noise levels.

3.5 Parameter Selection and Implementation Details

Normalization and Initialization. After alignment, we normalize each modality to comparable scale (z-score per sample index or per trace, depending on the dataset characteristics). We initialize $\hat{x}[0] = 0$ and P_0 to a relatively large value (e.g., $P_0 = 1$ under z-score normalization) so that early updates are driven by measurements rather than the prior.

Estimating R_p and R_e. We set R_p and R_e proportional to empirical noise power of each modality. In practice, this can be obtained (i) from a "quiet" region outside the encryption window, (ii) from repeated-encryption variance at each sample index, or (iii) from robust residual statistics after a light smoothing prefilter. We use global scalars per modality to keep the method lightweight and avoid overfitting to a specific operation window.

Choosing Q. The process-noise variance Q controls smoothness: smaller Q increases temporal regularization, while larger Q tracks fast leakage variations more closely. Across our platforms, a small constant Q (relative to normalized measurement variances) provides stable behavior; we report the chosen Q in the experimental setup for reproducibility.

Computational Cost and Compatibility with CPA. Fusion is performed trace-by-trace in $\mathcal{O}(L)$ time and $\mathcal{O}(1)$ extra memory, producing a fused dataset $\{\hat{x}_t[1{:}L]\}_{t=1}^{N}$. The fused traces are attacked with the *same* CPA pipeline (same leakage model, same POI/ROI strategy) as the raw modalities, ensuring that improvements reflect enhanced leakage quality rather than changes to the attacker.

4 Experimental Sctup

4.1 Targets and Measurement Setup

We evaluate the proposed fusion framework on two representative AES-128 hardware targets: (i) an 8-bit MCU implementation on Atmel ATSAM3U2C and (ii) a parallel AES-128 implementation on Xilinx Artix-7. For each platform, we capture *paired* power and EM traces from the *same* encryption operations under a fixed secret key. Both modalities are triggered by the *same* hardware trigger signal, ensuring synchronous acquisition at the trace level. Across both platforms, the observed leakage in power and EM can be well-approximated by a *Hamming-weight (HW)* leakage model, which motivates the CPA evaluation in Sect. 4.4. We record $N_{\text{all}} = 5000$ encryptions with known plaintexts; each raw trace contains $L = 100000$ samples (before any optional ROI cropping).

Acquisition Instrumentation. Power is acquired using a dedicated probe on the device supply path (e.g., shunt-based measurement or a power probe), while EM is acquired using a **10 mm-diameter near-field H-field probe** positioned above the cryptographic core region. Both channels are captured simultaneously on the same digital oscilloscope and share a common hardware trigger, yielding strictly synchronized power/EM trace pairs.

Paired Indexing. To ensure a correct plaintext-to-trace mapping, power and EM are captured for the *same* encryption indices. In all experiments, we reuse identical trial indices across modalities (Power, EM, KF, and WA) so that any performance difference is attributable to the trace quality rather than to sampling variance.

4.2 Alignment and Pre-processing

Fusion requires the two modalities to be time-aligned. We align power and EM traces in the time domain using correlation-based synchronization (and, where necessary, elastic alignment for residual clock drift). After alignment, we apply per-trace mean removal and scale normalization (e.g., ℓ_2 normalization or z-score standardization) to reduce amplitude mismatch across traces and modalities. KF fusion is then applied point-wise along the trace index and outputs a fused trace of the same length.

Optional ROI Cropping. When a coarse leakage location is available (e.g., from TVLA or by inspecting preliminary correlation peaks), we crop each trace to a fixed region of interest (ROI) to reduce computation and suppress non-AES activity. All results reported in this paper use a single, platform-specific ROI window that is kept constant across methods to ensure a fair comparison; we report ROI settings as integer sample indices, `[start:end]`, where `start` and `end` denote the first and last retained samples (inclusive) in each trace after alignment and normalization. All methods on the same platform share exactly the same ROI to ensure fair comparisons; when needed, the corresponding time span can be obtained as $\left[start/f_s,\ end/f_s\right]$ using the sampling rate f_s.

4.3 CPA Configuration and Leakage Model

We use standard correlation power analysis (CPA) targeting the first-round AES S-box output. For each byte index $i \in \{0,\ldots,15\}$ and key hypothesis $k \in \{0,\ldots,255\}$, we compute the intermediate value

$$v_{i,k} = \mathrm{Sbox}(p_i \oplus k)\,, \tag{22}$$

and use the Hamming-weight (HW) leakage model

$$\ell_{i,k} = \mathrm{HW}(v_{i,k})\,. \tag{23}$$

For each hypothesis we compute the Pearson correlation between $\ell_{i,k}$ and each sample index of the trace, taking the maximum absolute correlation over time as the score. The recovered key byte is the hypothesis with the highest score.

4.4 Evaluation Protocol and Metrics

Monte-Carlo Resampling Over Trace Budgets. To characterize key recovery under varying measurement budgets, we perform Monte-Carlo sub-sampling. For each trace budget N, we randomly select N paired traces without replacement and run CPA. We repeat this procedure for T trials (MCU: $T = 70$; FPGA: repeated runs and/or trials as detailed below), always reusing the same indices across modalities for fair comparison.

Success Rate Metrics. We report both byte-level and full-key success:

$$\mathrm{SR_{byte}}(N) = \frac{1}{16T} \sum_{t=1}^{T} \sum_{i=1}^{16} \mathbb{I}\left[\hat{k}_{t,i} = k_i^\star\right], \tag{24}$$

$$\mathrm{SR_{full}}(N) = \frac{1}{T} \sum_{t=1}^{T} \mathbb{I}\left[\forall i : \hat{k}_{t,i} = k_i^\star\right], \tag{25}$$

where $k_i^\star$ is the ground-truth key byte and $\hat{k}_{t,i}$ is the recovered byte in trial t. To capture *tail risk* in full-key recovery, we additionally compute the *hard-byte* index and its success rate:

$$i_{\mathrm{hard}}(N) = \arg\min_i \ \mathrm{SR}_i(N), \qquad \mathrm{SR_{hard}}(N) = \min_i \ \mathrm{SR}_i(N). \tag{26}$$

Guessing Entropy (GE). For completeness, we also report guessing entropy as the average rank of the true key hypothesis, either per byte or averaged over bytes. (When GE curves are included, we use the same resampling protocol as above.)

Trace-to-Success (TTS@95%). We define TTS@95% as the smallest budget N such that a target success metric reaches 95%. We report both point estimates and conservative criteria: on MCU we use Wilson 95% lower bounds across trials for $\mathrm{SR_{full}}$; on FPGA we additionally report a conservative *run-wise minimum* across repeated runs.

4.5 Baselines and Runtime Accounting

We compare four modalities: Power-only, EM-only, KF fusion, and a lightweight weighted-average (WA) fusion baseline (Sect. 3). For runtime accounting, we measure (i) fusion time and (ii) CPA time separately. In practice, CPA dominates: fusion is $O(NL)$ with small constants, whereas CPA scales as $O(16 \cdot 256 \cdot NL)$ due to key-hypothesis scoring. We therefore report fusion timing as an engineering overhead and focus performance claims on sample efficiency and success metrics.

5 Results and Analysis

5.1 MCU: Small-Budget Regime and Full-Key Tail Risk

Figure 1(a) and (b) report $\mathrm{SR_{full}}$ and $\mathrm{SR_{byte}}$ for budgets up to $N \leq 400$. Across this small-budget regime, KF fusion consistently *left-shifts* both curves, indicating higher sample efficiency and improved stability across trials.

A central phenomenon here is *full-key tail risk*: even when the *average* byte-level success is already high, full-key recovery can remain substantially lower because one or two bytes converge much more slowly than the others. Equivalently, full-key success is governed by the bottleneck byte(s), so a small tail of hard cases can dominate the failure probability.

At $N = 400$ (70 trials), EM-only attains $SR_{byte} = 97.32\%$ (Wilson 95%: [96.10, 98.09]) but only $SR_{full} = 62.86\%$ (Wilson 95%: [51.15, 73.23]). In contrast, Power-only and KF-fused traces reach $SR_{full} \approx 100\%$ at the same budget, with conservative lower bounds of 94.80%. Table 1 summarizes the time-to-success metric (TTS@95%) under both point and conservative criteria.

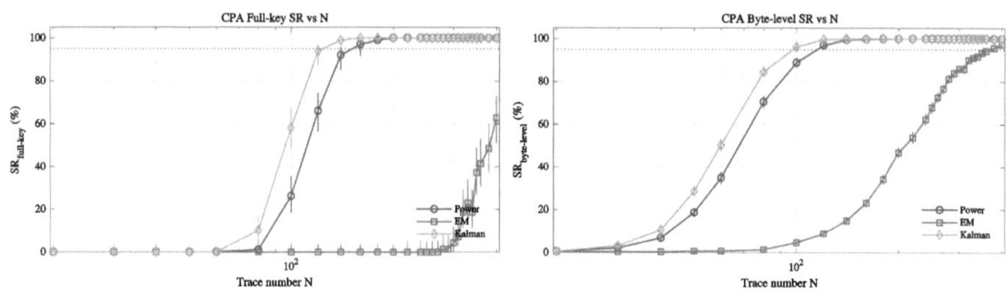

(a) Full-key success rate $SR_{full}(N)$. **(b)** Byte-level success rate $SR_{byte}(N)$.

Fig. 1. MCU (Atmel ATSAM3U2C): CPA success rates versus trace budget N for Power-only, EM-only, and KF-fused traces.

Table 1. MCU: TTS@95% (point estimate / conservative lower bound).

Method	Full-key (point)	Full-key (LB)	Byte-level (point)	Byte-level (LB)
Power	160	200	120	120
EM	∞	∞	380	400
Kalman	140	160	100	100

5.2 FPGA: Large-Budget Regime and Saturation Behavior

We next evaluate the FPGA platform for budgets up to $N \leq 5000$. Table 2 reports SR_{full} as mean±std and the min–max range over repeated runs. KF fusion exceeds 99% mean full-key success by $N = 2000$ (mean 99.1%, min 97%), whereas EM-only requires substantially larger budgets and Power-only does not reach 95% success within 5000 traces.

Using the TTS@95% definition in Sect. 4.4, KF achieves TTS@95% at $N = 2000$ under both the mean and conservative criteria. EM-only reaches

TTS@95% at $N = 4000$ (mean) and $N = 5000$ (conservative). As a lightweight ablation, inverse-variance weighted-average (WA) fusion reaches TTS@95% at $N = 2500$ (mean), placing it between EM-only and KF and highlighting the value of uncertainty propagation and adaptive gains in KF.

5.3 Hard-Byte Analysis: Why Min-Over-Bytes Predicts Full-Key Recovery

Full-key recovery requires all 16 bytes to be correct. Therefore,

$$\mathrm{SR_{full}}(N) \leq \min_i \mathrm{SR}_i(N) = \mathrm{SR_{hard}}(N), \tag{27}$$

Table 2. FPGA: full-key success summary $\mathrm{SR_{full}}$ (%) at selected budgets. We report mean, standard deviation, and the min–max range over repeated runs.

N	Power				EM				Kalman			
	mean	std	min	max	mean	std	min	max	mean	std	min	max
500	0.0	0.0	0	0	0.0	0.0	0	0	0.0	0.0	0	0
1000	0.0	0.0	0	0	0.0	0.0	0	0	29.5	6.5	20	40
1500	0.0	0.0	0	0	0.0	0.0	0	0	89.7	4.2	82	96
2000	0.4	0.8	0	2	5.5	1.4	3	7	99.1	1.0	97	100
2500	3.6	1.7	1	7	34.3	3.7	28	38	100.0	0.0	100	100
3000	16.3	2.8	11	20	71.2	4.9	65	79	100.0	0.0	100	100
4000	64.5	3.4	59	70	96.7	1.8	94	100	100.0	0.0	100	100
5000	90.4	1.8	88	93	99.8	0.4	99	100	100.0	0.0	100	100

Table 3. FPGA: hardest-byte identification and success rate $\mathrm{SR_{hard}}$ (%). "hardByte" is the byte index with the lowest per-byte success at the given N.

N	Power		EM		Kalman	
	hardByte	$\mathrm{SR_{hard}}$	hardByte	$\mathrm{SR_{hard}}$	hardByte	$\mathrm{SR_{hard}}$
500	5	4.5	4	5.5	5	35.1
1000	2	12.5	13	21.3	5	85.0
1500	5	25.9	3	44.9	13	97.2
2000	5	44.2	13	64.0	13	99.7
2500	5	57.9	13	79.0	1	100.0
3000	5	69.6	13	92.9	1	100.0
4000	5	88.7	13	98.7	1	100.0
5000	5	97.2	4	99.9	1	100.0

i.e., the minimum per-byte success rate is an *upper bound* on full-key success and reveals the bottleneck byte. Figure 2 visualizes this bottleneck via the *min-over-bytes* curve, and Table 3 reports the corresponding hard-byte identity and its success rate.

Cross-Platform Interpretability. Although the MCU target (8-bit, iterative AES) and the FPGA target (parallel AES) exhibit different micro-architectural timing structures, the byte-wise CPA evaluation and hard-byte diagnostic remain comparable because (i) both implementations compute the same SubBytes-based intermediates per byte, and (ii) both power and EM leakages are well-approximated by the HW model. Consequently, improvements in trace quality due to fusion (higher effective SNR and reduced tail risk) translate into faster convergence of $\mathrm{SR}_i(N)$ and, crucially, of the bottleneck $\mathrm{SR}_{\mathrm{hard}}(N)$ that governs full-key recovery.

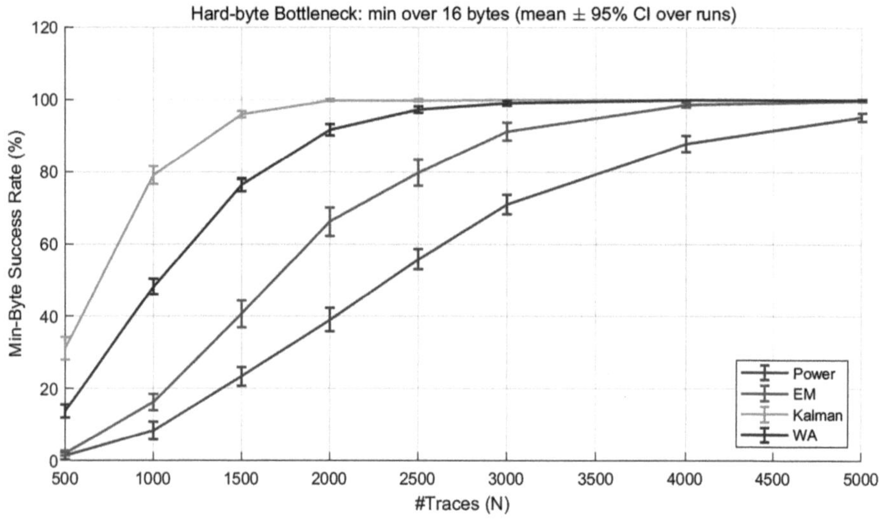

Fig. 2. FPGA: hard-byte bottleneck analysis via $\mathrm{SR}_{\mathrm{hard}}(N) = \min_i \mathrm{SR}_i(N)$. The min-over-bytes curve highlights the hardest byte that dominates full-key recovery.

Table 4. Cross-platform comparison of trace budgets required to reach 95% success (TTS@95%). For full-key, "LB" denotes a conservative criterion (MCU: Wilson 95% lower bound; FPGA: run-wise minimum across runs). ">5000" indicates the threshold is not reached within the available traces.

Platform (budget)	Metric	Power	EM	WA	Kalman
MCU ($N \leq 400$)	Full-key TTS@95% (LB)	200	∞	–	160
	Byte-level TTS@95% (LB)	120	400	–	100
FPGA ($N \leq 5000$)	Full-key TTS@95% (mean)	>5000	4000	2500	2000
	Full-key TTS@95% (conservative)	>5000	5000	2500	2000

5.4 Cross-Platform Summary and TTS@95%

Table 4 aggregates the trace budgets required to reach 95% success. Across both platforms, KF fusion reduces the traces required for full-key recovery and accelerates the stabilization of the hardest byte. WA provides a meaningful reference point: it improves over EM-only but remains consistently weaker than KF, supporting the benefit of KF's uncertainty propagation and adaptive, sample-wise weighting.

5.5 Complexity and Practical Overhead

Let N be the number of traces and L the (ROI) length. Scalar KF fusion costs $O(NL)$ with small constants and $O(L)$ memory. By comparison, byte-wise CPA dominates runtime because it evaluates 256 hypotheses for each of 16 bytes, yielding $O(16{\cdot}256{\cdot}NL)$ operations. In our implementation, the online KF update-only overhead is on the order of 1.6×10^{-2} s at $N = 2000$ and 3.2×10^{-2} s at $N = 4000$ (mean over repeated runs), confirming that fusion overhead is negligible relative to CPA in typical experimental settings.

6 Conclusion

We presented a lightweight Kalman filter fusion method to combine paired power and EM traces and strengthen non-profiling CPA attacks. Across MCU and FPGA platforms, KF fusion improves sample efficiency and mitigates hard-byte driven tail risk, enabling earlier and more reliable full-key recovery. Our full-paper evaluation includes both byte-level and full-key success curves, conservative TTS@95% criteria, and explicit hardest-byte analysis to support mechanism-level claims.

Acknowledgments. This research was supported by the National Natural Science Foundation of China under Grant Nos. 62272232 and 62172224, and the Fundamental Research Funds for the Central Universities under Grant No.2025201015, and Henan Key Laboratory of Network Cryptography Technology under Grant LNCT2022-A22.

References

1. Brier, E., Clavier, C., Olivier, F.: Correlation power analysis with a leakage model. In: Joye, M., Quisquater, J.-J. (eds.) CHES 2004. LNCS, vol. 3156, pp. 16–29. Springer, Heidelberg (2004). https://doi.org/10.1007/978-3-540-28632-5_2
2. Kalman, R.E.: A new approach to linear filtering and prediction problems. J. Basic Eng. **82**(1), 35–45 (1960). https://doi.org/10.1115/1.3662552
3. Kocher, P., Jaffe, J., Jun, B.: Differential power analysis. In: Wiener, M. (ed.) CRYPTO 1999. LNCS, vol. 1666, pp. 388–397. Springer, Heidelberg (1999). https://doi.org/10.1007/3-540-48405-1_25
4. Mangard, S., Oswald, E., Popp, T.: Power Analysis Attacks: Revealing the Secrets of Smart Cards. Springer, New York (2007). https://doi.org/10.1007/978-0-387-38162-6
5. Masure, L., Dumas, C., Prouff, E.: A comprehensive study of deep learning for side-channel analysis. IACR Trans. Cryptogr. Hardw. Embed. Syst. **2020**(1), 348–375 (2020). https://doi.org/10.13154/tches.v2020.i1.348-375
6. Prouff, E., Strullu, R., Benadjila, R., Cagli, E., Dumas, C.: Study of deep learning techniques for side-channel analysis and introduction to ASCAD database. IACR Cryptology ePrint Archive, Report 2018/053 (2018)
7. Shen, Z., Gao, Y., Cheng, W., Wang, J., Zhou, Y.: Improving interpretability: visual analysis of deep learning-based multi-channel attacks. In: Security and Privacy in Communication Networks (SecureComm 2024). Lecture Notes of the Institute for Computer Sciences, Social Informatics and Telecommunications Engineering, vol. 627. Springer, Cham (2026). https://doi.org/10.1007/978-3-031-94445-1_16
8. Souissi, Y., Flament, O., Danger, J.: Novel applications of wavelet transforms in the side-channel context. In: NIST Non-Invasive Attack Testing Workshop (2011)
9. Standaert, F.-X., Malkin, T.G., Yung, M.: A unified framework for the analysis of side-channel key recovery attacks. In: Joux, A. (ed.) EUROCRYPT 2009. LNCS, vol. 5479, pp. 443–461. Springer, Heidelberg (2009). https://doi.org/10.1007/978-3-642-01001-9_26
10. van Woudenberg, J.G.J., Witteman, M.F., Bakker, B.: Improving differential power analysis by elastic alignment. In: Kiayias, A. (ed.) CT-RSA 2011. LNCS, vol. 6558, pp. 104–119. Springer, Heidelberg (2011). https://doi.org/10.1007/978-3-642-19074-2_8
11. Yang, W., Zhou, Y., Cao, Y., Zhang, H., Zhang, Q., Wang, H.: Multi-channel fusion attacks. IEEE Trans. Inf. Forensics Secur. **12**(8), 1757–1771 (2017). https://doi.org/10.1109/TIFS.2017.2672521

Fine-Grained Residual Interval Screening Enhanced Least Square for the Secret Key Recovery of Dilithium

Kailong Shi[1,3], Hailong Zhang[2(✉)], Donddai Lin[1,3], and Zichen Wang[4]

[1] Key Laboratory of Cyberspace Security Defense, Institute of Information Engineering, Chinese Academy of Sciences, Beijing, China

[2] School of Control and Computer Engineering, North China Electric Power University, Beijing, China
zhanghailong@ncepu.edu.cn

[3] School of Cyber Security, University of Chinese Academy of Sciences, Beijing, China

[4] Department of Electrical and Computer Engineering, School of Engineering and Applied Science, George Washington University, Washington, DC, USA

Abstract. In practice, the amount of side channel leakage related to the random polynomial generation of Dilithium can be limited. In this case, the coefficients of the random polynomial may not be recovered accurately, which then makes the secret key recovery with least square a difficult problem. Therefore, how to recover the secret key used by Dilithium with noisy equations becomes a meaningful concern. In light of this, the fine-grained residual interval screening is proposed to enhance the ability of least square to recover the secret key used by Dilithium. The core idea is to estimate the distributions of the residuals related to both correct and erroneous equations computed with the least square recovered candidate secret key in a profiling scenario. Then, according to the distribution difference of the residuals related to two types of equations, an interval can be screened. Note that a majority of erroneous equations are out of the screened interval while a majority of correct equations are in the screened interval. Therefore, least square can be used to recover a more accurate candidate secret key polynomial with equations in the screened interval. By iterating the process several times, the secret key polynomial can be successfully recovered. The efficiency of the proposed technique is verified with power traces measured from the Dilithium reference implementation running on a Cortex-M4 processor. The evaluation results show that only several hundreds of power traces are enough to recover the secret key used by Dilithium.

Keywords: Post-Quantum Cryptography · Dilithium · Side-Channel Resistance · Secret Key Recovery · Residual Interval Screening

Y. Cao et al. (Eds.): SecureComm 2026, LNICST 704, pp. 173–196, 2027.
https://doi.org/10.1007/978-3-032-32764-2_9

1 Introduction

In the scenario of quantum computing, the mathematical problems (e.g., the large integer factorization [20] and the discrete logarithm solving [11]) that the security of traditional public-key algorithms based on may not be hard to solve anymore. The reason is that the algorithm proposed by Shor [21] can solve these problems in polynomial time on a quantum computer. Therefore, traditionally deployed public-key algorithms may not be secure anymore, and it is necessary to design public-key algorithms that are secure in the quantum computing scenario. In light of this, the National Institute of Standards and Technology (NIST) has initiated the standardization process for Post-Quantum Cryptography (PQC) in 2017. In 2022, NIST announced three PQC digital signature algorithms, i.e., Dilithium [9], Falcon [22], and SPHINCS+ [3]. In fact, according to the PQC standardization status report released in July 2022 [1], Dilithium can be a good choice in terms of efficiency, implementation cost, and security. Therefore, NIST decided to prioritize the standardization of Dilithium under the name Module Lattice-Based Digital Signature Algorithm (ML-DSA) [16]. Note that Dilithium follows the Lyubashevsky–Peikert–Regev (LPR) design paradigm [14]. Besides, its security relies on the Module Learning With Errors (MLWE) problem [15].

In practice, Dilithium can be implemented into a chip to achieve the goal of information security. When a chip is in operation, different types of side-channel leakage can be measured and exploited to recover the secret key used by Dilithium, posing a serious threat to the practical security of Dilithium. In light of this, it is necessary to investigate the side-channel resistance of Dilithium in practice. In fact, since Dilithium was proposed at TCHES 2018 [9], researchers in the cryptographic engineering community have fully realized the importance of analyzing its side-channel resistance. Consequently, different types of side-channel attacks have been proposed to recover the secret key used by Dilithium, and representatives of them are summarized as follows.

- First, NTT-based polynomial multiplication can be chosen as the target. Here, NTT is the abbreviation of number theory transform, which is fast Fourier transform in the finite field. In detail, Chen et al. at ICCD 2021 [7] as well as Tosun and Savas at IEEE TIFS 2024 [25] exploited the leakage of $\hat{\mathbf{c}}\hat{\mathbf{s}}_1$ to recover the private key $\mathbf{s}_1$ of Dilithium reference implementation running on a Cortex-M4 processor using correlation power analysis (CPA). Recently, Fan et al. at IEEE TIFS 2025 [12] exploited both the leakage of $\hat{\mathbf{c}}\hat{\mathbf{s}}_1$ and $\hat{\mathbf{A}}\hat{\mathbf{y}}_1$ to recover $\mathbf{s}_1$ of Dilithium reference implementation on Cortex-M4 with the so called Multivariate Template Attack (MTA).
- Second, secret key unpacking can be chosen as the target. In detal, Wang et al. [28] used deep learning assisted power analysis to recover the secret keys $\mathbf{s}_1$ and $\mathbf{s}_2$ of a fast Dilithium implementation on Cortex-M4 by exploiting the side-channel leakage related to the unpacking of $\mathbf{s}_1$ and $\mathbf{s}_2$. Recently, Wang et al. [27] showed that with the side-channel leakage related to the unpacking of $\mathbf{t}_0$, deep-learning based profiling power analysis can be used to partially recover the least significant bit of $\mathbf{t}_0$. Then, the number of signatures

required for the reconstruction of $\mathbf{t}_0$ is reduced by roughly half, and the new $\mathbf{t}_0$ reconstruction method enhances the efficiency of recovering $\mathbf{s}_1$.
- Third, the computation of the low-order bits of $\mathbf{w}_0$ can be chosen as the target. In detail, at TCHES 2023, Berzati et al. [4] used the side-channel leakage related to the computation of $\mathbf{w}_0$ to recover $\mathbf{w}_0$ with template attack (TA). Then, the value of $\mathbf{w}_0$ can be used to build linear equations related to $\mathbf{s}_1$, and the solving of which can recover $\mathbf{s}_1$ used by the Dilithium reference implementation running on a Cortex-M4 processor.
- Fourth, the random polynomial generation can be chosen as the target. In detail, Marzougui et al. at SAC 2022 [26], Qiao et al. at IEEE TIFS 2023 [18], and Fan et al. at IEEE TIFS 2024 [13] used the side-channel leakage related to the random polynomial generation to recover coefficients of the random polynomial with profiling attacks. Then, coefficients of the random polynomial can be used to build linear equations related to $\mathbf{s}_1$, and the solving of which with least square or linear programming can recover $\mathbf{s}_1$.
- Fifth, NTT can be chosen as the target of side-channel attacks. In detail, at CHES 2017, Primas et al. [17] used the side-channel leakage related to NTT to recover the secret key of an ring learning with errors encryption scheme on an ARM Cortex-M4F processor with the soft analytic side-channel attacks. Then, at PQCRYPTO 2023, Steffen et al. [24] used the side-channel leakage related to NTT to recover $\mathbf{s}_1$ and $\mathbf{s}_2$ used by an FPGA implementation of Dilithium.

It can be seen that existing works chose to recover $\mathbf{s}_1$ used by Dilithium. The reason is that according to [19] and [6], the knowledge of $\mathbf{s}_1$ is adequate to forge a valid signature for an arbitrary message with a high probability. Besides, it can be noticed that the generation of the random polynomial is a main target of side-channel attacks. However, when the generation of the random polynomial is chosen as the target, the amount of side-channel leakage available is limited. The reason is that the polynomial is randomly generated. In this case, one can only use the side-channel leakage contained in one power trace to recover coefficients of the random polynomial. Because the amount of side-channel leakage available in one power trace is limited, coefficients of the random polynomial may not be correctly recovered. In this case, linear equations related to $\mathbf{s}_1$ may be noisy, and $\mathbf{s}_1$ may not be correctly recovered with least square or linear programming. Therefore, how to recover $\mathbf{s}_1$ with noisy equations becomes a meaningful concern. In light of this, the fine-grained residual interval screening technique is proposed to enhance the ability of least square to recover $\mathbf{s}_1$. In detail, the contributions of this work are summarized as follows.

- We empirically estimate the distributions of the residuals related to both correct and erroneous equations computed with the least square recovered candidate secret key polynomial in a profiling scenario. Note that whether or not coefficients of the random polynomial are correctly recovered can be known in a profiling scenario. If the coefficients related to an equation are correctly recovered, the equation is referred to as a correct equation; else, it is referred to as an erroneous equation. Then, according to the distribution difference of the residuals related to two types of equations, an interval can be screened. In detail, a majority of erroneous equations are out of the screened interval while a majority of correct equations are in the screened interval. In this case, least square can be used to recover a more accurate candidate with equations in the screened interval. By iterating the process several times, the secret key polynomial can be successfully recovered.

- The effectiveness of the fine-grained residual interval screening technique to enhance the efficiency of least square to recover $\mathbf{s}_1$ of Dilithium is verified in the real scenario. In detail, power traces related to the generation of the random polynomial of Dilithium reference implementation on Cortex M4 are used. The evaluation results show that MTA proposed by Fan et al. [13] can recover coefficients of the random polynomial with the accuracy of 7.08% for Dilithium 2 and the accuracy of 4.15% for Dilithium 3. In this case, screening least square technique (SLST) proposed by Fan et al. [13] cannot recover $\mathbf{s}_1$ used by Dilithium, while fine-grained residual interval screening enhanced least square can recover $\mathbf{s}_1$ used by Dilithium 2 with 270 power traces and $\mathbf{s}_1$ used by Dilithium 3 with 400 power traces. Therefore, the evaluation results show that fine-grained residual interval screening enhanced least square can be used to more accurately evaluate the practical security of Dilithium.

The rest of this paper is organized as follows. The notation, the signature algorithm of Dilithium, and the least square used to recover $\mathbf{s}_1$ of Dilithium are introduced in Sect. 2. Section 3 provides a detailed description of the proposed fine-grained residual interval screening technique. In Sect. 4, the effectiveness of the fine-grained residual interval screening technique to enhance the efficiency of least square to recover $\mathbf{s}_1$ of Dilithium is verified in the real scenario. Finally, Sect. 5 concludes the paper.

2 Preliminary

First, notations used in this work are introduced. Second, details about the signature algorithm of Dilithium are introduced. Third, the least square used to recover $\mathbf{s}_1$ of Dilithium is introduced.

2.1 Notations

Let $\mathbb{Z}_q$ denote the ring of integers modulo q. Then, $\mathbb{Z}_q[x]$ denotes the set of polynomials with coefficients in $\mathbb{Z}_q$. We can define $R_q = \mathbb{Z}_q[x]/(x^n + 1)$ as the polynomial ring modulo $x^n + 1$. In Dilithium q is set to $2^{23} - 2^{13} + 1$ and n is set to 256. $\mathbf{A}$ denotes a matrix with k rows and l columns, and each element in $\mathbf{A}$ is a polynomial in R_q. The value of (k, l) varies with the version of Dilithium. In detail, for Dilithium 2, $(k, l) = (4, 4)$; for Dilithium 3, $(k, l) = (6, 5)$; and for Dilithium 5, $(k, l) = (8, 7)$. $\mathbf{y}$ is a random polynomial vector with l elements, and each element in $\mathbf{y}$ is a polynomial in R_q. The coefficients of an element in $\mathbf{y}$

are in the range of $[-\gamma_1, \gamma_1]$, and γ_1 can be set to 2^{17}, 2^{19}, and 2^{19} in Dilithium 2, 3, and 5, respectively. $\mathbf{c} \in R_q$ is the challenge polynomial, which has exactly τ coefficients equal to ± 1 and the rest coefficients of $\mathbf{c}$ are equal to 0. In Dilithium 2, 3, and 5, τ can be set to 39, 49, and 60, respectively. The secret key $\mathbf{s}_1$ is a vector with l elements while the secret key $\mathbf{s}_2$ is a vector with k elements, and each element in $\mathbf{s}_1$ and $\mathbf{s}_2$ is a polynomial in R_q. The coefficients of elements in $\mathbf{s}_1$ and $\mathbf{s}_2$ are in the range of $[-\eta, \eta]$. In Dilithium 2, 3, and 5, η can be set to 2, 4, and 2, respectively. $\hat{\mathbf{w}}$, $\hat{\mathbf{A}}$, $\hat{\mathbf{y}}$, $\hat{\mathbf{c}}$, and $\hat{\mathbf{s}}_1$ denote $\mathbf{w}$, $\mathbf{A}$, $\mathbf{y}$, $\mathbf{c}$, and $\mathbf{s}_1$ in the NTT domain, respectively. Besides, $\hat{\mathbf{w}}$, $\hat{\mathbf{A}}$, $\hat{\mathbf{y}}$, $\hat{\mathbf{c}}$, and $\hat{\mathbf{s}}_1$ can be obtained from $\mathbf{w}$, $\mathbf{A}$, $\mathbf{y}$, $\mathbf{c}$, and $\mathbf{s}_1$ through the *NTT* function, respectively. $\|\mathbf{z}\|_\infty$ is the ∞-norm of $\mathbf{z}$, whose value equals to the largest absolute value of coefficients of $\mathbf{z}$.

2.2 The Signature Algorithm of Dilithium

Dilithium is consisted of three algorithms, i.e. the key generation algorithm, the signing algorithm and the verification algorithm. In this work, the side-channel leakage related to the random polynomial generation is used to recover $\mathbf{s}_1$ used by Dilithium. Here, the random polynomial generation is a step in the signing algorithm of Dilithium. Therefore, only the signing algorithm of Dilithium is introduced, which is shown in Algorithm 1.

According to Algorithm 1, in order to sign a message M using the secret key sk, one should compute $\hat{\mathbf{w}} = \hat{\mathbf{A}}\hat{\mathbf{y}}$. Then, $\mathbf{w}$ can be obtained by applying the inverse *NTT* function. The challenge polynomial $\mathbf{c}$ can be derived from the high-order bits $\mathbf{w}_1$ of $\mathbf{w}$. Then, a part of the signature, i.e. $\mathbf{z}$, can be computed as $\mathbf{z} = \mathbf{y} + \mathbf{c}\mathbf{s}_1$. Finally, in order to ensure that the signature does not leak information about the private key and for correctness purposes, several boundary checks are performed. If one check fails, a new signature candidate should be generated; otherwise, $\mathbf{z}$ and $\tilde{\mathbf{c}}$, together with the hint information $\mathbf{h}$, are output as the signature.

2.3 Least Square

For a noisy linear system $\mathbf{C}\mathbf{s}_1 \approx \mathbf{b}$ (hereafter abbreviated as $(\mathbf{C}, \mathbf{b})$), the solution of $\mathbf{s}_1$ can be obtained using least square. Here, least square aims to find a solution $\mathbf{s}_1^*$ that minimizes the ℓ_2 (Euclidean) norm of the residual $\mathbf{e} = \mathbf{C}\mathbf{s}_1 - \mathbf{b}$ [5]. In fact, according to line 14 of Algorithm 1, one has $\mathbf{z} = \mathbf{y} + \mathbf{c}\mathbf{s}_1$, where $\mathbf{z}$ and $\mathbf{c}$ are known while $\mathbf{y}$ and $\mathbf{s}_1$ are unknown. With the side-channel leakage contained in one power trace related to the generation of $\mathbf{y}$, coefficients of $\mathbf{y}$ may not be correctly recovered. If $\mathbf{y}^*$ is used to denote the random polynomial recovered with side-channel attacks, we have $\mathbf{z} \approx \mathbf{y}^* + \mathbf{c}\mathbf{s}_1$, which can be seen as a noisy linear system. In detail, in order to compute $\mathbf{c}\mathbf{s}_1$, $\mathbf{c}$ can be expressed as a matrix $\mathbf{C}$ composed of coefficients of $\mathbf{c}$. In detail, we have

$$\mathbf{C} = \begin{bmatrix} c_0 & -c_{255} & -c_{254} & \cdots & -c_1 \\ c_1 & c_0 & -c_{255} & \cdots & -c_2 \\ \vdots & \vdots & \vdots & \ddots & \vdots \\ c_{255} & c_{254} & c_{253} & \cdots & c_0 \end{bmatrix},$$

Algorithm 1. Sign(sk, M)

Require: $sk = (\rho, K, tr, \mathbf{s}_1, \mathbf{s}_2, \mathbf{t}_0), M$
Ensure: $sig = (\mathbf{z}, \mathbf{h}, \tilde{\mathbf{c}})$
$\hat{\mathbf{A}} \in R_q^{k\times l} \leftarrow \text{ExpandA}(\rho)$
$\mu \in \{0,1\}^{512} \leftarrow H(tr \parallel M)$
$k \leftarrow 0, (\mathbf{z}, \mathbf{h}) \leftarrow \perp$
$\rho' \in \{0,1\}^{512} \leftarrow H(K \parallel \mu)$ $\quad\triangleright$ or $\rho' \leftarrow \{0,1\}^{512}$ for randomized signing
while $(\mathbf{z}, \mathbf{h}) = \perp$ **do**
  $\mathbf{y} \in S_{\gamma_1}^{l} \leftarrow \text{ExpandMask}(\rho', k)$
  $\hat{\mathbf{y}} \leftarrow \text{NTT}(\mathbf{y}), \hat{\mathbf{w}} \leftarrow \hat{\mathbf{A}}\hat{\mathbf{y}}$
  $\mathbf{w} \leftarrow \text{NTT}^{-1}(\hat{\mathbf{w}})$
  $\mathbf{w}_1 \leftarrow \text{HighBits}_q(\mathbf{w}, 2\gamma_2)$
  $\tilde{\mathbf{c}} \in \{0,1\}^{256} \leftarrow H(\mu \parallel \mathbf{w}_1)$
  $\mathbf{c} \leftarrow \text{SampleInBall}(\tilde{\mathbf{c}})$
  $\hat{\mathbf{c}} \leftarrow \text{NTT}(\mathbf{c})$, $\hat{\mathbf{s}}_1 \leftarrow \text{NTT}(\mathbf{s}_1)$
  $\hat{\mathbf{u}} \leftarrow \hat{\mathbf{c}}\hat{\mathbf{s}}_1$
  $\mathbf{z} \leftarrow \mathbf{y} + \text{NTT}^{-1}(\hat{\mathbf{u}})$
  $\mathbf{r}_0 \leftarrow \text{LowBits}_q(\mathbf{w} - \mathbf{c}\mathbf{s}_2, 2\gamma_2)$
  if $\|\mathbf{z}\|_\infty \geq \gamma_1 - \beta$ **or** $\|\mathbf{r}_0\|_\infty \geq \gamma_2 - \beta$ **then**
    $(\mathbf{z}, \mathbf{h}) \leftarrow \perp$
  else
    $\mathbf{h} \leftarrow \text{MakeHint}_q(-\mathbf{c}\mathbf{t}_0, \mathbf{w} - \mathbf{c}\mathbf{s}_2 + \mathbf{c}\mathbf{t}_0, 2\gamma_2)$
    if $\|\mathbf{c}\mathbf{t}_0\|_\infty \geq \gamma_2$ **or** the # of 1's in $\mathbf{h}$ is greater than ω **then**
      $(\mathbf{z}, \mathbf{h}) \leftarrow \perp$
    end if
  end if
  $k \leftarrow k + l$
end while
return $sig = (\mathbf{z}, \mathbf{h}, \tilde{\mathbf{c}})$

where c_i are i^{th} coefficient of $\mathbf{c}$. Besides, we have $\mathbf{b} = \mathbf{z} - \mathbf{y}^*$. Then, least square can be used to recover $\mathbf{s}_1$. Note that the probability of least square to recover $\mathbf{s}_1$ depends on the accuracy of $\mathbf{y}^*$ and the number of equations contained in the noisy linear system. On one hand, the lower the accuracy of $\mathbf{y}^*$, the lower the probability of least square to recover $\mathbf{s}_1$; on the other hand, the larger the number of equations contained in the noisy linear system, the higher the probability of least square to recover $\mathbf{s}_1$.

3 Fine-Grained Residual Interval Screening Enhanced Least Square

At IEEE TIFS 2024, Fan et al. [13] proposed the SLST technique, which can be used to recover $\mathbf{s}_1$ with noisy linear system $\mathbf{C}\mathbf{s}_1 \approx \mathbf{b}$. In this technique, a candidate of $\mathbf{s}_1$ should be recovered with ($\mathbf{C}$,$\mathbf{b}$), which can be denoted as $\mathbf{s}_1^*$. Then, the absolute value of the residual $\mathbf{e}$, i.e., $|\mathbf{e}| = |\mathbf{C}\mathbf{s}_1^* - \mathbf{b}|$ is computed. If the average of elements in $|\mathbf{e}|$ is denoted as $m_{|\mathbf{e}|}$, equations with absolute values of residuals in the interval $[0, m_{|\mathbf{e}|}]$ are screened. In this case, $(\mathbf{C}, \mathbf{b})$ is updated for the next iteration. After repeating this iteration several times, $\mathbf{s}_1$ can be recovered from $\mathbf{s}_1^*$ by using the *Round*() function. Here, the function of *Round*() is to round a value to its nearest integer. The idea of SLST is to choose equations with small residuals to make it easier to recover $\mathbf{s}_1$. However, according to the evaluation result, it can be infeasible to recover $\mathbf{s}_1$ used by the Dilithium reference implementation running on a Cortex-M4 processor with SLST.

In order to find out the reason for the failure of SLST, the distributions of the residuals of correct and erroneous equations are estimated in the simulated scenario. Note that in the simulated scenario values of different parameters are under full control. In this case, the distributions of the residuals of two types of equations can be accurately estimated. In detail, power traces related to the random polynomial generation of the Dilithium 2 reference implementation on Cortex-M4 are simulated with Python. Here, the simulated power traces contain side-channel leakages related to the processing of $\mathbf{y}$, the unsigned number vector $\mathbf{x}$, and the random byte vector $\mathbf{a}$, where $\mathbf{x}$ and $\mathbf{a}$ are two vectors closely related to $\mathbf{y}$. For more details about $\mathbf{x}$ and $\mathbf{a}$, please refer to [13]. For each coefficient of $\mathbf{y}$, $\mathbf{x}$ and $\mathbf{a}$, the number of interesting points is set to 10 empirically to make MTA perform well. Here, interesting points are samples in power traces related to the processing of the target intermediate value. The leakage at each interesting point is composed of two parts, i.e., the signal part which depends on the processed value and the noise part which can be irrelevant to the processed value. Because the leakage of a value on Cortex-M4 follows the Hamming weight model [13], the signal part is simulated under the Hamming weight model. Comparatively, the noise part should be simulated under the multivariate normal distribution assumption. Besides, the correlation coefficient of the noise part at different interesting points is empirically set to 0.2 to simulate the cross correlation of the noise part at different interesting points. Finally, the signal-to-noise ratio (SNR) of the simulated leakage is set to 5, 0.35, and 0.15 to approximate the SNR of the leakage related to the processing of $\mathbf{y}$, $\mathbf{x}$, and $\mathbf{a}$ on Cortex-M4.

Subsequently, MTA proposed by Fan et al. [13] is used to recover $\mathbf{y}$. Here, under the assumption that high bits of $\mathbf{y}$ are equal to high bits of $\mathbf{z}$ with a high probability, only low bits of $\mathbf{y}$ need to be recovered with MTA. In detail, low 5, 6, and 7 bits of $\mathbf{y}$ can be recovered with MTA. Then, together with high bits of $\mathbf{z}$, $\mathbf{y}$ can be recovered. In detail, in order to recover low bits of $\mathbf{y}$, 50000 power traces are used in the profiling phase to characterize the leakage properties related to the processing of $\mathbf{y}$, $\mathbf{x}$ and $\mathbf{a}$. Then, one trace can be used in the attack phase of MTA to recover low bits of $\mathbf{y}$. Together with high bits of $\mathbf{z}$, $\mathbf{y}$ can be recovered. By repeating the attack phase 2000 times with 2000 randomly generated power traces, the accuracy to recover $\mathbf{y}$ can be estimated. In detail, the accuracy to recover $\mathbf{y}$ in three cases can be 7.84%, 4.63% and 2.33%, respectively.

With the value of $\mathbf{y}^*$, the linear system $(\mathbf{C}, \mathbf{b})$ can be built. Note that one value of $\mathbf{y}^*$ is related to a linear system of 256 linear equations. If multiple values of $\mathbf{y}^*$ are available, the number of linear equations in the linear system can be multiples of 256. In our case, in order to estimate the distributions of the residuals of correct and erroneous equations, 180 power traces are used, and MTA is used to recover low 5 bits of $\mathbf{y}$. Then, with 180 values of $\mathbf{z}$, 180 values of $\mathbf{y}^*$ can be obtained. In theory, the linear system is composed of 180*256=46080 linear equations. With the linear system built, a candidate $\mathbf{s}_1^*$ of $\mathbf{s}_1$ can be recovered with least square. Then, one can compute the absolute value of the residual $\mathbf{e}$, i.e. $|\mathbf{e}| = |\mathbf{C}\mathbf{s}_1^* - \mathbf{b}|$. Note that in a profiling scenario, 180 values of $\mathbf{y}$ are known. In this case, 46080 equations in the linear system can be divided into two groups, one containing equations whose values in $\mathbf{b}$ are correct, while the other containing equations whose values in $\mathbf{b}$ are erroneous. Finally, the distributions of the residuals of correct and erroneous equations can be estimated.

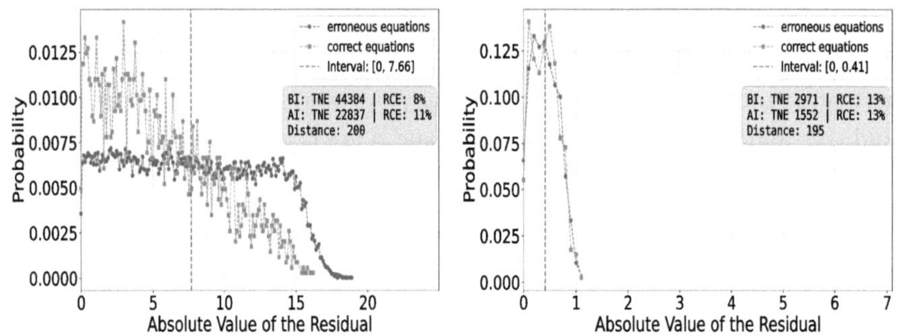

(a) Result after the 1st iteration (b) Result after the 5th iteration

Fig. 1. Performances of SLST after the 1st iteration and the 5th iteration.

In Fig. 1, BI is the abbreviation of before iteration, AI is the abbreviation of after iteration, TNE is the abbreviation of total number of equations, RCE is the abbreviation of rate of correct equations, Distance denote the number of coefficients of $Round(\mathbf{s}_1^*)$ that are not equal to coefficients of $\mathbf{s}_1$. Figure 1a shows the distributions of the residuals of correct and erroneous equations after the 1st iteration, while Fig. 1b shows the distributions of the residuals of correct and erroneous equations after the 5th iteration. By observing Fig. 1a, the difference between the distributions of the residuals of correct and erroneous equations can be significant. In this case, by choosing equations with residuals in the interval $[0,m_{\mathbf{e}}]$, RCE increases from 8% to 11%. However, according to Fig. 1b, the difference between the distributions of the residuals of correct and erroneous equations can be minor. In this case, by choosing equations with residuals in the interval $[0,m_{\mathbf{e}}]$, RCE does not increase anymore. Therefore, the Distance between $Round(\mathbf{s}_1^*)$ and $\mathbf{s}_1$ can still be large, and it is infeasible to recover $\mathbf{s}_1$ with SLST. Finally, note that for some Hamming weights that occur with a small probability, the related templates are not built. Then, coefficients of $\mathbf{y}$ related to these Hamming weights are not recovered. Therefore, the total number of equations shown in Fig. 1 is 44384 rather than 46080.

Overall, the reason for the failure of SLST is that the number of correct equations in the chosen interval is small and the rate of correct equations is low. In light of this, we decide to enlarge the interval to increase the number of correct equations while maintaining the rate of correct equations. According to Fig. 1a, we empirically choose equations whose residuals are in the interval of $[0, m_e + 3]$. Then, the performances of least square after the 1st iteration, the 4th iteration, the 8th iteration and the 12th iteration can be evaluated.

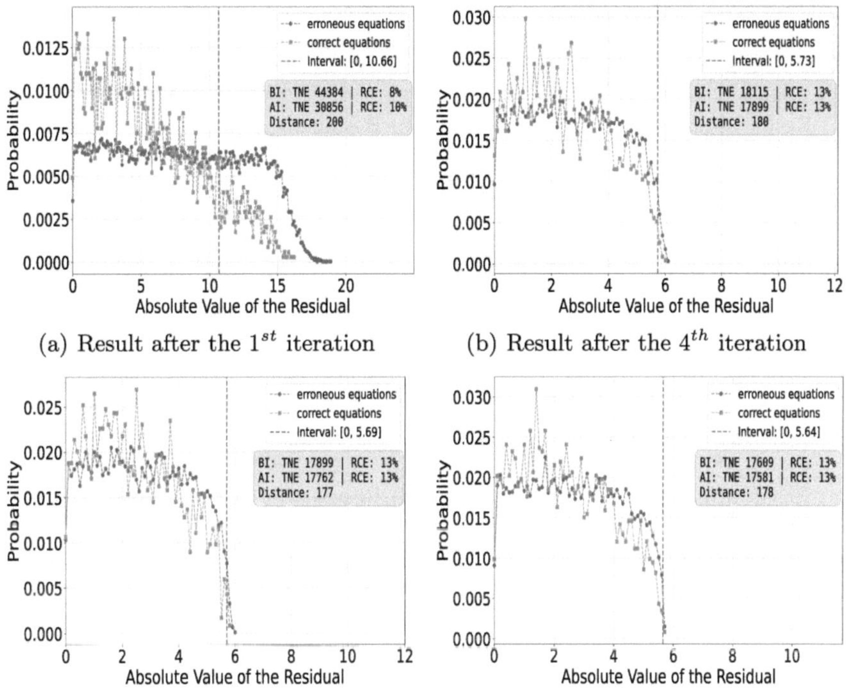

(a) Result after the 1st iteration

(b) Result after the 4th iteration

(c) Result after the 8th iteration

(d) Result after the 12th iteration

Fig. 2. Performances of least square after different times of iteration with equations whose residuals are in the interval of $[0, m_e + 3]$.

According to Fig. 2a, the number of correct equations is increased and the rate of correct equations is maintained. Therefore, after the 4th iteration, the distance between $Round(\mathbf{s}_1^*)$ and $\mathbf{s}_1$ can be decreased to 180. However, further repeating the iteration does not help to decrease the distance between $Round(\mathbf{s}_1^*)$ and $\mathbf{s}_1$. According to Fig. 2b

Then, considering that after the 4th iteration the distance between $Round(\mathbf{s}_1^*)$ and $\mathbf{s}_1$ is reduced to 180, we come up with the idea of using $\mathbf{s}_1^*$ as the new candidate of $\mathbf{s}_1$ to repeat the above iteration. Here, we refer to the above four times iteration as a Type-I global iteration. We believe that with this more accurate candidate of $\mathbf{s}_1$, the distance between $Round(\mathbf{s}_1^*)$ and $\mathbf{s}_1$ can be further reduced by repeating the global iteration. The evaluation results after different times of Type-I global iteration are shown as follows.

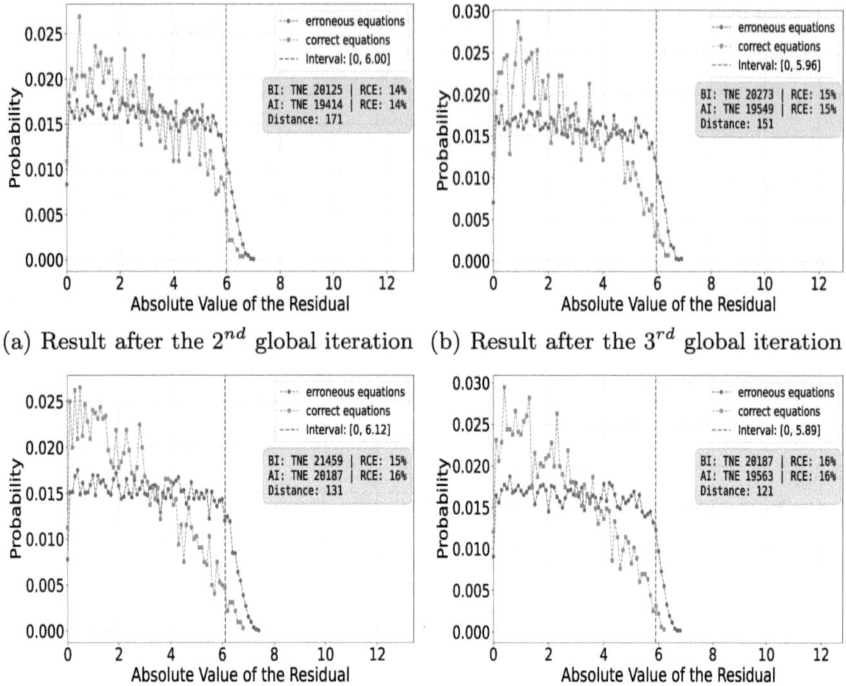

(a) Result after the 2nd global iteration (b) Result after the 3rd global iteration

(c) Result after the 4th global iteration (d) Result after the 5th global iteration

Fig. 3. Performances of least square after different times of Type-I global iteration with equations whose residuals are in the interval of $[0, m_\mathbf{e} + 3]$.

According to Fig. 3, by repeating Type-I global iteration three times, the distance between $Round(\mathbf{s}_1^*)$ and $\mathbf{s}_1$ is reduced further. However, after the 4th Type-I global iteration, the decrease of the distance between $Round(\mathbf{s}_1^*)$ and $\mathbf{s}_1$ is not obvious. Therefore, it seems that for equations with residuals in the interval of $[0, m_\mathbf{e} + 3]$, the number of Type-I global iteration should be set to 4.

It can be seen from Fig. 3 that after several times of Type-I global iteration, the residuals of correct equations are distributed in a more compact interval. In light of this, we shrink the screening interval from $[0, m_\mathbf{e} + 3]$ to $[0, m_\mathbf{e} + 2]$ and repeat Type-I global iteration several times with more accurate candidates of $\mathbf{s}_1$, and the evaluation results can be seen in Fig. 9 shown in Appendix A. It can be seen that after four times of Type-I global iteration, the distance between $Round(\mathbf{s}_1^*)$ and $\mathbf{s}_1$ is reduced to 103, and further repeating Type-I global iteration does not help to reduce the distance between $Round(\mathbf{s}_1^*)$ and $\mathbf{s}_1$. Therefore, the number of Type-I global iteration should be set to 4. Still, because the residuals of correct equations after four times of Type-I global iteration are distributed in a more compact interval, we shrink the screening interval from $[0, m_\mathbf{e} + 2]$ to $[0, m_\mathbf{e} + 1]$ and repeat Type-I global iteration several times with more accurate candidates of $\mathbf{s}_1$. Figure 10 in Appendix A shows that by performing Type-I global iteration four times with more accurate candidates of $\mathbf{s}_1$, the distance between $Round(\mathbf{s}_1^*)$ and $\mathbf{s}_1$ is reduced to 90, and further repeating Type-I global iteration does not help to reduce the distance between $Round(\mathbf{s}_1^*)$ and $\mathbf{s}_1$. Therefore, the number of Type-I global iteration is set to 4. Following the similar observation, we shrink the screening interval from $[0, m_\mathbf{e} + 1]$ to $[0, m_\mathbf{e}]$ and repeat Type-I global iteration several times with more accurate candidates of $\mathbf{s}_1$. Figure 11 shows that after four times of Type-I global iteration, the distance between $Round(\mathbf{s}_1^*)$ and $\mathbf{s}_1$ is only reduced from 90 to 85, which can be not obvious. Therefore, it is not advisable to follow this residual interval screening routine further.

In light of this, we use the more accurate candidate of $\mathbf{s}_1$ recovered after four times of Type-I global iteration with equations whose residuals are in the interval of $[0, m_\mathbf{e}]$ to estimate the distributions of the residuals of correct and erroneous equations, and the evaluation result is shown in Fig. 4.

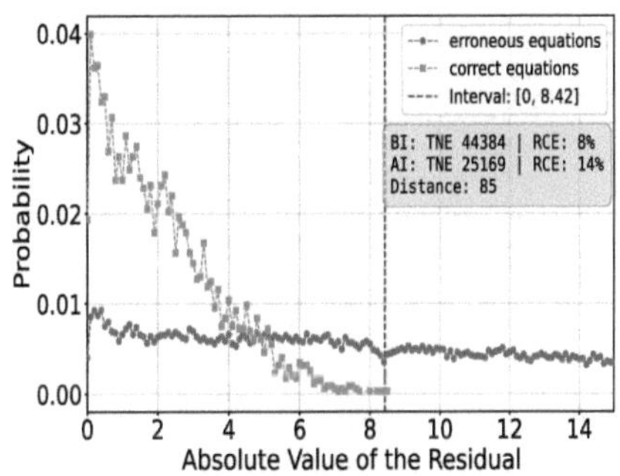

Fig. 4. Distributions of the residuals of correct equations and erroneous equations with the more accurate candidate of $\mathbf{s}_1$.

It can be seen that in this case the residuals of correct equations are mainly in the interval of $[0, 5]$. In light of this, the screening interval should be set to $[0, 5]$. Then, using equations with residuals in the interval of $[0, 5]$, least square can be repeatedly used 6 times to recover a more accurate candidate of $\mathbf{s}_1$. The reason for repeating least square 6 times with equations whose residuals are in the interval of $[0, 5]$ is that further repeating least square in this case does not help to reduce the distance between $Round(\mathbf{s}_1^*)$ and $\mathbf{s}_1$. As can be seen from Fig. 5a, the distance between $Round(\mathbf{s}_1^*)$ and $\mathbf{s}_1$ in this case is reduced to 77. Then, because the residuals of most correct equations are in the interval of $[0, 3.5]$, least square can be repeatedly used 6 times to recover a more accurate candidate of $\mathbf{s}_1$ with equations whose residuals are in this interval. Still, the reason for repeating least square 6 times is that further repeating least square in this case does not help to reduce the distance between $Round(\mathbf{s}_1^*)$ and $\mathbf{s}_1$. According to Fig. 5b, although the distance between $Round(\mathbf{s}_1^*)$ and $\mathbf{s}_1$ is not reduced in this case, the value of RCE is increased. Similarly, least square can be repeatedly used 6 times with equations whose residuals are in the intervals of

[0, 2] and [0, 0.5] in order to further reduce the distance between $Round(\mathbf{s}_1^*)$ and $\mathbf{s}_1$. According to Fig. 5c and Fig. 5d , the distance between $Round(\mathbf{s}_1^*)$ and $\mathbf{s}_1$ after 18 and 24 times of iteration is reduced from 75 to 72 and RCE is increased from 26% to 29%.

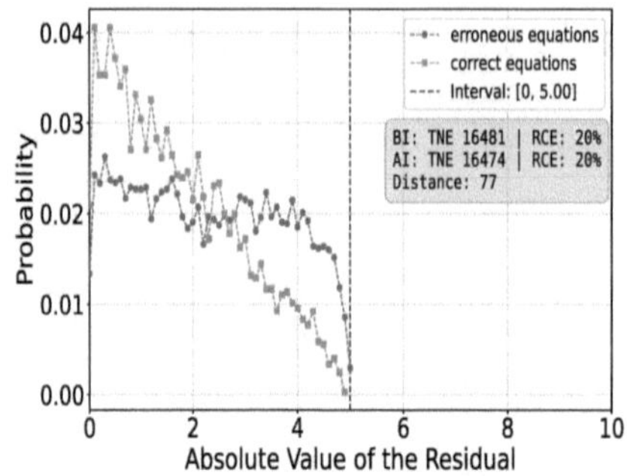

(a) Result of the 6th iteration

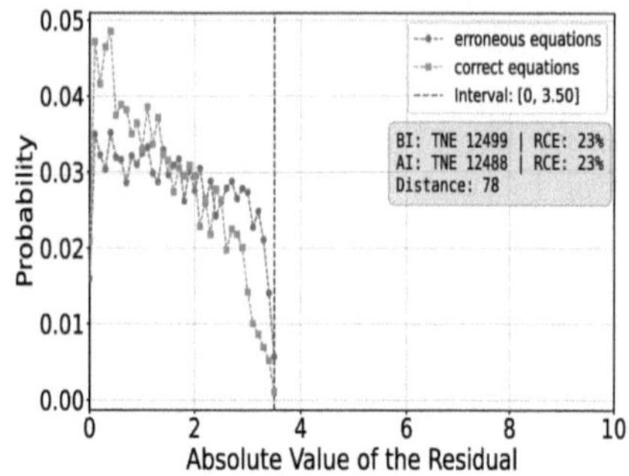

(b) Result of the 12th iteration

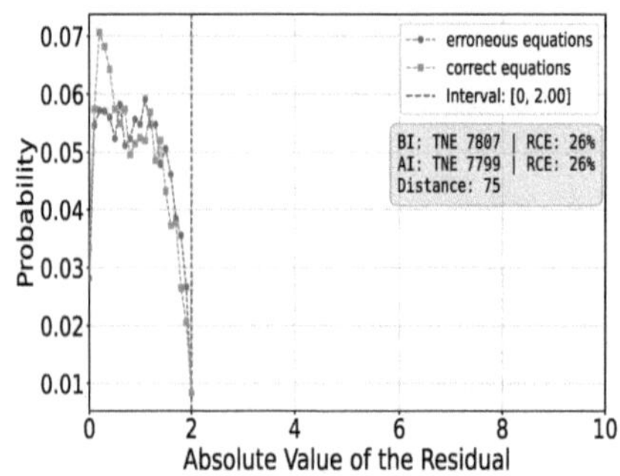

(c) Result of the 18th iteration

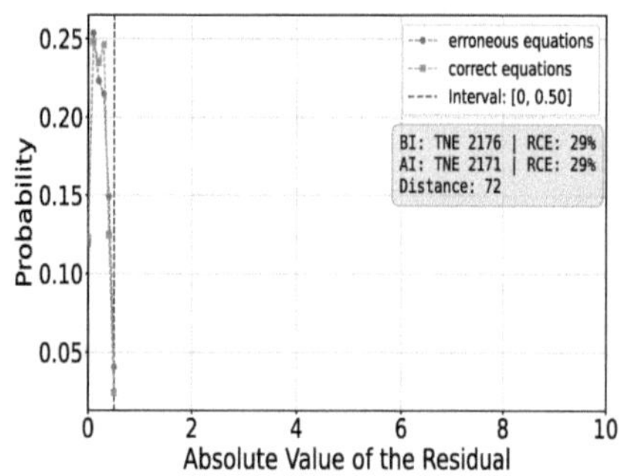

(d) Result of the 24th iteration

Fig. 5. Performances of least square after different times of iteration with equations whose residuals are in the intervals of [0, 5], [0, 3.5], [0, 2] and [0, 0.5].

If the above 24 times of iteration are referred to as Type-II global iteration, the distance between $Round(\mathbf{s}_1^*)$ and $\mathbf{s}_1$ is expected to be reduced by iterating Type-II global iteration several times with more accurate candidates of $\mathbf{s}_1$.

Table 1. Distance between $Round(\mathbf{s}_1^*)$ and $\mathbf{s}_1$ after 15 times of Type-II global iteration.

Time	1	2	3	4	5	6	7	8	9	10	11	12	13	14	15
Distance	72	61	50	40	28	16	14	10	8	8	7	7	6	6	6

Indeed, Table 1 shows that it is very effective to reduce the distance between $Round(\mathbf{s}_1^*)$ and $\mathbf{s}_1$ by repeating Type-II global iteration several times. However,

$\mathbf{s}_1$ can still be not recovered even if Type-II global iteration is repeated further. In light of this, the distributions of the residuals of correct and erroneous equations are estimated with the candidate of $\mathbf{s}_1$ recovered after the 15th global iteration, and the estimation result is shown in Fig. 6.

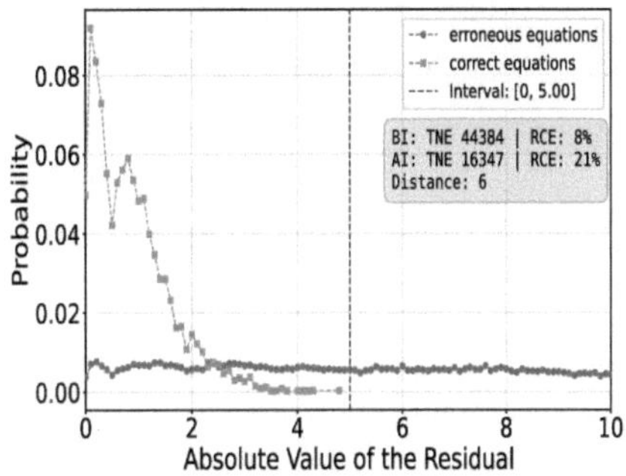

Fig. 6. Distributions of the residuals of correct equations and erroneous equations with the candidate of $\mathbf{s}_1$ recovered after the 15th Type-II global iteration.

It can be seen that after the 15th Type-II global iteration, the residuals of correct equations are mainly in the interval of $[0, 2]$. In light of this, equations with residuals in the interval of $[0, 2]$ should be used to recover a more accurate candidate of $\mathbf{s}_1$. In detail, least square should be repeatedly used 6 times with equations whose residuals are in the interval of $[0, 2]$ to recover a more accurate candidate of $\mathbf{s}_1$. Here, the reason to repeat least square 6 times with equations whose residuals are in the interval of $[0, 2]$ is that it does not help to reduce the distance between $Round(\mathbf{s}_1^*)$ and $\mathbf{s}_1$ anymore if further iterations are performed. According to Fig. 12a shown in Appendix A, after the 6th iteration, RCE increases to 38%. Then, it seems that the residuals of most correct equations are in the interval of $[0, 1.5]$. In light of this, least square is repeatedly used 6 times with equations whose residuals are in the interval of $[0, 1.5]$. Still, the reason to repeat least square 6 times here is that it does not help to reduce the distance between $Round(\mathbf{s}_1^*)$ and $\mathbf{s}_1$ anymore if further iterations are performed. According to Fig. 12b shown in Appendix A, after the 12th iteration, RCE increases to 43%. Similarly, least square is repeatedly used 6 times with equations whose residuals are in the intervals of $[0, 1]$ and $[0, 0.5]$. According to Fig. 12c and Fig. 12d shown in Appendix A, RCE increases to 49% after the 18th iteration, while RCE increases to 54% after the 24th iteration. Besides, after the 24th iteration, the distance between $Round(\mathbf{s}_1^*)$ and $\mathbf{s}_1$ is reduced to 2.

Still, if the above 24 times of iteration together are referred to as Type-III global iteration, Fig. 12 in Appendix A shows that after a Type-III global iteration $\mathbf{s}_1$ can still be not recovered. In light of this, Type-III global iteration can be repeated several times with more accurate candidates of $\mathbf{s}_1$ to recover $\mathbf{s}_1$. In fact, the distance between $Round(\mathbf{s}_1^*)$ and $\mathbf{s}_1$ after different times of Type-III global iteration is evaluated, and the evaluation result is shown in Table 2. It can be seen that $\mathbf{s}_1$ can be recovered after only 2 times of Type-III global iteration.

Table 2. Secret key $\mathbf{s}_1$ recovery result after 20 times of Type-III global iteration.

Time	1	2	3	4	5	6	7	8	9	10	11	12	13	14	15	16	17	18	19	20
Distance	2	0	0	0	0	0	0	0	0	0	0	0	0	0	0	0	0	0	0	0

Overall, the fine-grained residual interval screening enhanced least square is composed of three phases. In phase 1, 4 times of Type-I global iteration should be performed. During each Type-I global iteration, 4 times of iteration whose residuals are in the intervals of $[0, m_\mathbf{e} + 3]$, $[0, m_\mathbf{e} + 2]$, $[0, m_\mathbf{e} + 1]$, and $[0, m_\mathbf{e}]$ should be performed in order. Then, 15 times of Type-II global iteration should be performed in phase 2. During each Type-II global iteration, 6 times of iteration with equations whose residuals are in the intervals of $[0, 5]$, $[0, 3.5]$, $[0, 2]$, and $[0, 0.5]$ should be performed in order. Finally, 20 times of Type-III global iteration should be performed in phase 3. During each global iteration, 6 times of iteration with equations whose residuals are in the intervals of $[0, 2]$, $[0, 1.5]$, $[0, 1]$, and $[0, 0.5]$ should be performed in order. Therefore, the overall procedure can be summarized in Algorithm 2.

Note that the intervals shown in Algorithm 2 are screened with the samples of $\mathbf{y}^*$ obtained by performing MTA on the low 5 bits of $\mathbf{y}$ used in Dilithium 2. In fact, under the same style, the intervals screened with the samples of $\mathbf{y}^*$ obtained by performing MTA on the low 6 or 7 bits of $\mathbf{y}$ used in Dilithium 2 can be obtained. The results show that in three cases the screened intervals can be about the same. Besides, the intervals screened with the samples of $\mathbf{y}^*$ obtained by performing MTA on the low 5, 6, and 7 bits of $\mathbf{y}$ used in Dilithium 3 and 5 can also be obtained. In detail, the intervals screened with the samples of $\mathbf{y}^*$ obtained by performing MTA on the low 5, 6, and 7 bits of $\mathbf{y}$ used in Dilithium 3 can be about the same, while the intervals screened with the samples of $\mathbf{y}^*$ obtained by performing MTA on the low 5, 6, and 7 bits of $\mathbf{y}$ used in Dilithium 5 can be about the same. However, when $\mathbf{s}_1$ of Dilithium 3 is targeted, the value of V in phase 2 of Algorithm 2 should be started from 8.5 and ended to 0.5 with the step of -1, while the value of V in phase 3 of Algorithm 2 should be started from 3.5 and ended to 0.5 with the step of -0.5. Besides, when $\mathbf{s}_1$ of Dilithium 5 is targeted, the value of V in phase 2 of Algorithm 2 should be started from 6.5 and ended to 0.5 with the step of -1.5, while the value of V in phase 3 of Algorithm 2 should be started from 3 and ended to 0.5 with the step of -0.5. Then, $\mathbf{s}_1$ used by Dilithium 3 and 5 can be recovered with Algorithm 2. Note that according to the running result, on a PC with AMD Ryzent 9 7845HX CPU (2.5GHz), 16G memory and NVIDIA GeForce RTX 4060 GPU graphics card, less than 3 min can be enough to recover $\mathbf{s}_1$ with Algorithm 2.

Algorithm 2. fined-grained residual interval screening enhanced least square

Define $\text{LeastSquares}(\mathbf{C}, \mathbf{b})$ as solving $\mathbf{s}_1$ from $\mathbf{C}\mathbf{s}_1 \approx \mathbf{b}$ with least square.
Define $\text{Screen}(\mathbf{C}', \mathbf{b}', \mathbf{s}_1^*, T)$ as screening equations in $(\mathbf{C}', \mathbf{b}')$ whose residuals are smaller than T and obtaining the updated linear system $(\mathbf{C}', \mathbf{b}')$.

Require: $(\mathbf{C}, \mathbf{b})$
Ensure: $\mathbf{s}_1$

```
s_1^* ← LeastSquares(C, b)                          ▷ Obtain the candidate of s_1
                                                    ▷ phase 1
for V ← 3 down to 0 step −1 do
    for i ← 0 to 3 do
        C′ = C, b′ = b
        e ← |C′s_1^* − b′|,  T ← m_e + V            ▷ T = m_e + V
        (C′, b′) ← Screen(C′, b′, s_1^*, T)
        for j ← 0 to 3 do
            s_1^* ← LeastSquares(C′, b′)
            e ← |C′s_1^* − b′|,  T ← m_e + V
            (C′, b′) ← Screen(C′, b′, s_1^*, T)     ▷ T = m_e + V
        end for
    end for
end for
                                                    ▷ phase 2
for i ← 0 to 14 do
    C′ = C, b′ = b
    (C′, b′) ← Screen(C′, b′, s_1^*, 5)             ▷ T = 5
    for V ← 5 down to 0.5 step −1.5 do
        for j ← 0 to 5 do
            s_1^* ← LeastSquares(C′, b′)
            (C′, b′) ← Screen(C′, b′, s_1^*, V)     ▷ T = V
        end for
    end for
end for
                                                    ▷ phase 3
for i ← 0 to 19 do
    C′ = C, b′ = b
    (C′, b′) ← Screen(C′, b′, s_1^*, 2)             ▷ T = 2
    for V ← 2 down to 0.5 step −0.5 do
        for j ← 0 to 5 do
            s_1^* ← LeastSquares(C′, b′)
            (C′, b′) ← Screen(C′, b′, s_1^*, V)     ▷ T = V
        end for
    end for
end for

s_1 ← round(s_1^*)
return s_1
```

4 Efficiency Evaluation in the Real Scenario

In the real scenario, power traces are measured during the random polynomial generation of the Dilithium reference implementation on a Cortex-M4 processor. In detail, the target device is ChipWhisperer CW308 STM32F415 running at a clock frequency of 7.38 MHz. The oscilloscope used is a Pico 5244D operating in the 12-bit mode with the time base set to 10, which corresponds to a sampling rate of approximately 8.93 MHz. During the measurement, the low-pass filter is used to decrease the noise level, with the parameter of DC–5MHz 50ohm. The amplifier is not used during the measurement.

First, in order to recover $\mathbf{s}_1$ used by Dilithium 2, MTA [13] should be used to recover the coefficients of $\mathbf{y}$. Here, ρ-test proposed at EUROCRYPT 2016 [10] is used to choose the interesting points related to the processing of a coefficient of $\mathbf{y}$, $\mathbf{x}$, and $\mathbf{a}$ with 50000 power traces. The results are shown from Fig. 7a to Fig. 7c. It can be seen that the leakages related to the processing of $\mathbf{y}$, $\mathbf{x}$, and $\mathbf{a}$ are clearly visible. Then, 20, 20 and 10 interesting points related to the processing of a coefficient of $\mathbf{y}$, $\mathbf{x}$, and $\mathbf{a}$ are chosen, and the leakages at interesting points are used in MTA to recover the coefficients of $\mathbf{y}$.

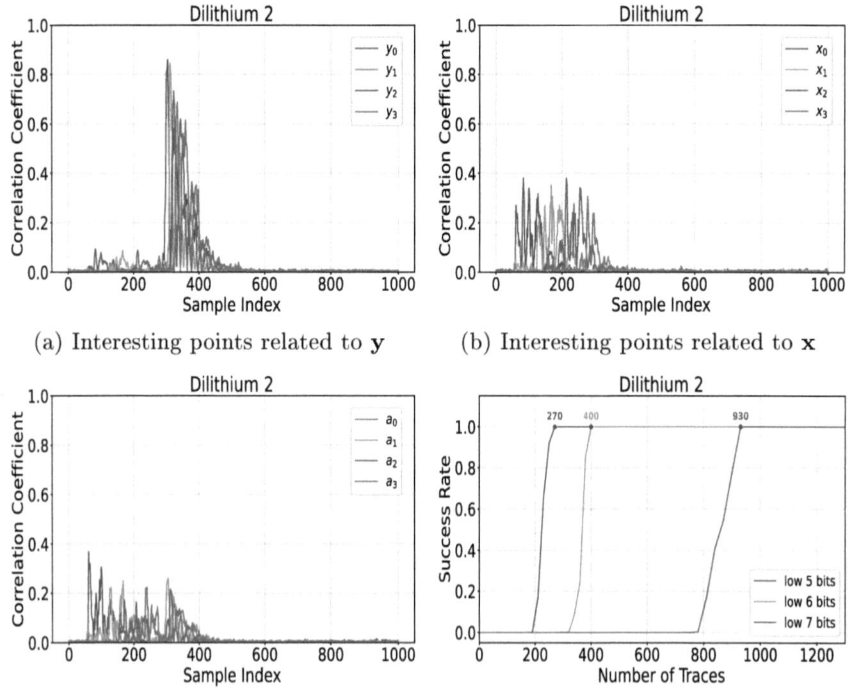

(a) Interesting points related to $\mathbf{y}$

(b) Interesting points related to $\mathbf{x}$

(c) Interesting points related to $\mathbf{a}$

(d) Success rate to recover $\mathbf{s}_1$

Fig. 7. Using the side-channel leakages related to the processing of $\mathbf{y}$, $\mathbf{x}$, and $\mathbf{a}$ to recover $\mathbf{s}_1$ used by Dilithium 2.

During the profiling phase, 50,000 power traces are used to characterize the leakage property related to the generation of $\mathbf{y}$. In the attack phase, using the leakage contained in one power trace, low 5, 6, and 7 bits of a coefficient of $\mathbf{y}$ can be recovered with MTA. Together with the high bits of a coefficient of $\mathbf{z}$, a coefficient of $\mathbf{y}$ can be recovered. The accuracy to recover a coefficient of $\mathbf{y}$ with MTA is evaluated by repeating the attack phase of MTA 2000 times. According to the evaluation results, the accuracy to recover a coefficient of $\mathbf{y}$ can be 7.08%, 4.09%, and 2.14%, respectively. Then, with noisy samples of $\mathbf{y}$, Algorithm 2 can be used to recover $\mathbf{s}_1$ used by Dilithium 2, and the evaluation result is shown in Fig. 7d. Here, the success rate metric [23] is used to evaluate the efficiency to recover $\mathbf{s}_1$. It can be seen that in the best case only 270 power traces can be enough to recover $\mathbf{s}_1$ used by Dilithium 2.

Second, in order to recover $\mathbf{s}_1$ used by Dilithium 3, the leakages related to the processing of $\mathbf{y}$ are used to recover the coefficients of $\mathbf{y}$. In detail, ρ-test is used to choose the interesting points related to the processing of $\mathbf{y}$, $\mathbf{x}$, and $\mathbf{a}$ with 55000 power traces. The results are shown in Fig. 8a to Fig. 8c. Then, 20, 20 and 10 interesting points related to the processing of a coefficient of $\mathbf{y}$, $\mathbf{x}$, and

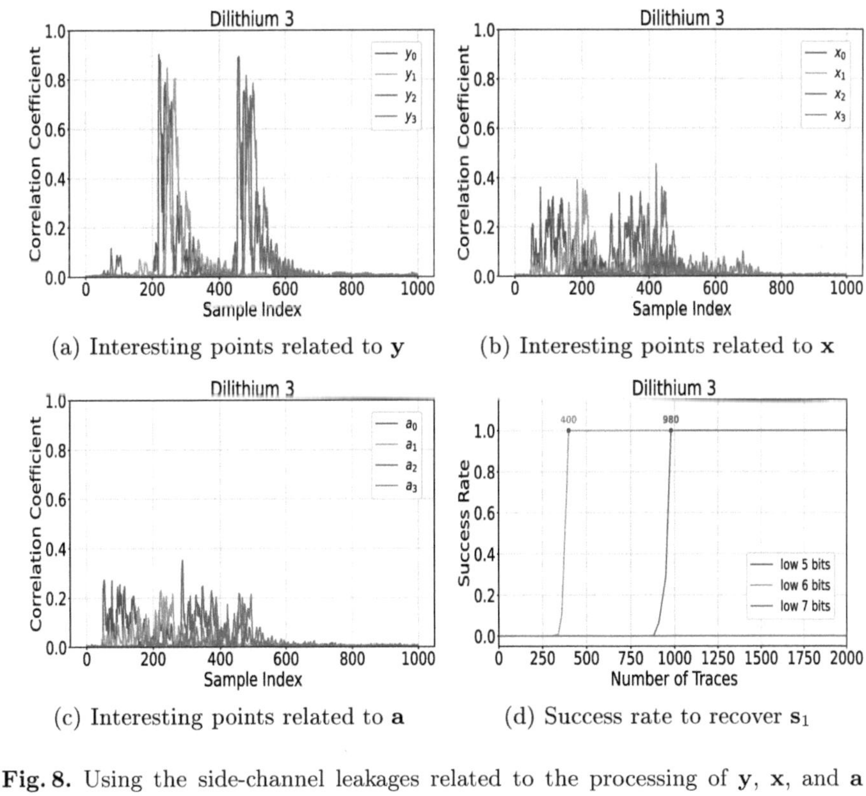

Fig. 8. Using the side-channel leakages related to the processing of $\mathbf{y}$, $\mathbf{x}$, and $\mathbf{a}$ to recover $\mathbf{s}_1$ used by Dilithium 3.

$\mathbf{a}$ are chosen, and the leakages at interesting points are used in MTA to recover $\mathbf{y}$.

In detail, 55000 power traces are used in the profiling phase of MTA to characterize the leakage properties related to the processing of $\mathbf{y}$, $\mathbf{x}$, and $\mathbf{a}$. Then, the leakages contained in one power trace can be used in the attack phase of MTA to recover the coefficients of $\mathbf{y}$. Still, we evaluate the accuracy to recover a coefficient of $\mathbf{y}$ when low 5, 6, and 7 bits of a coefficient of $\mathbf{y}$ are targeted in MTA, and the evaluation results show that the accuracy can be 5.27%, 4.15%, and 2.35% in three cases. Then, with noisy samples of $\mathbf{y}$, Algorithm 2 is used to recover $\mathbf{s}_1$ used by Dilithium 3. According to Fig. 8d, only 400 power traces can be enough to recover $\mathbf{s}_1$ used by Dilithium 3 in the best case. However, if the samples of $\mathbf{y}^*$ are obtained by recovering the low 5 bits of $\mathbf{y}$ with MTA, $\mathbf{s}_1$ used by Dilithium 3 cannot be recovered. The reason is that the distributions of the residuals of correct and erroneous equations in this case can be about the same. In this case, erroneous equations cannot be screened out to recover $\mathbf{s}_1$ used by Dilithium 3.

Finally, the performance of fine-grained residual interval screening enhanced least square is compared with its counterparts. Note that Marzougui et al. at SAC 2022 [26], Qiao et al. at IEEE TIFS 2023 [18] and Fan et al. at IEEE TIFS 2024 [13] all used the leakage related to the generation of $\mathbf{y}$ to recover $\mathbf{s}_1$ used by Dilithium. First, Marzougui et al. at SAC 2022 [26] used 780000 power traces to recover $\mathbf{s}_1$ used by Dilithium 2. Second, Qiao et al. at IEEE TIFS 2023 [18] used 10000, 35000, and 18000 power traces respectively to recover $\mathbf{s}_1$ used by Dilithium 2, 3, and 5. Third, Fan et al. at IEEE TIFS 2024 [13] claimed that 38, 40, 39 power traces can be enough to recover $\mathbf{s}_1$ used by Dilithium 2, 3, and 5. However, in our attack scenario, $\mathbf{s}_1$ used by Dilithium 2 and 3 cannot be recovered with even 1000 power traces. Comparatively, this work shows that $\mathbf{s}_1$ used by Dilithium 2 and 3 can be recovered with only 270 and 400 power traces. In light of this, fine-grained residual interval screening enhanced least square can be quite effective to recover $\mathbf{s}_1$ used by the Dilithium reference implementation on a Cortex-M4 processor with the leakage related to the generation of $\mathbf{y}$.

5 Conclusions

In this work, fine-grained residual interval screening is proposed to enhance the ability of least square to recover $\mathbf{s}_1$ used by Dilithium. In this technique, by observing the difference between the distributions of residuals of correct and erroneous equations, a residual interval can be chosen. Because most of the correct equations are in the chosen interval while most of the erroneous equations are not in the chosen interval, by using equations with residuals in the chosen interval, a more accurate candidate of $\mathbf{s}_1$ can be recovered. By iterating the above process several times, $\mathbf{s}_1$ can be recovered. The effectiveness of the technique is verified in the real scenario. Note that when a masked Dilithium implementation (e.g., [2] or [8]) is targeted, MTA can be used to recover each share of $\mathbf{y}$. Then, $\mathbf{y}$ can be recovered by combing each share of $\mathbf{y}$. However, in this case, the accuracy to recover $\mathbf{y}$ may be even lower. In light of this, the usability of this technique to recover $\mathbf{s}_1$ used by a masked Dilithium implementation is left as a future work.

Acknowledgements. This work is supported in part by the National Natural Science Foundation of China 62272451, the Beijing Natural Science Foundation L234079.

Appendix A

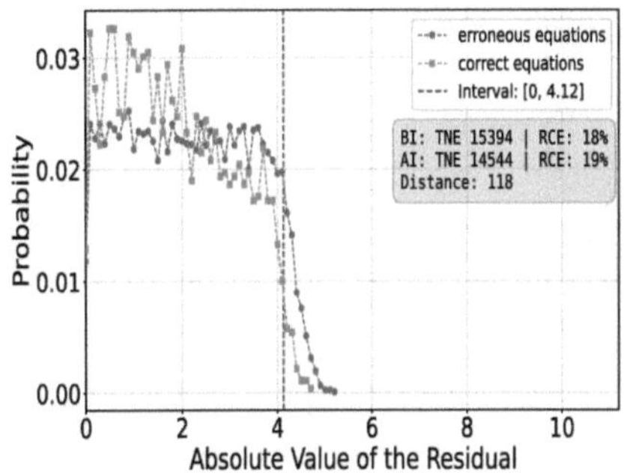

(a) Result after the 1st global iteration

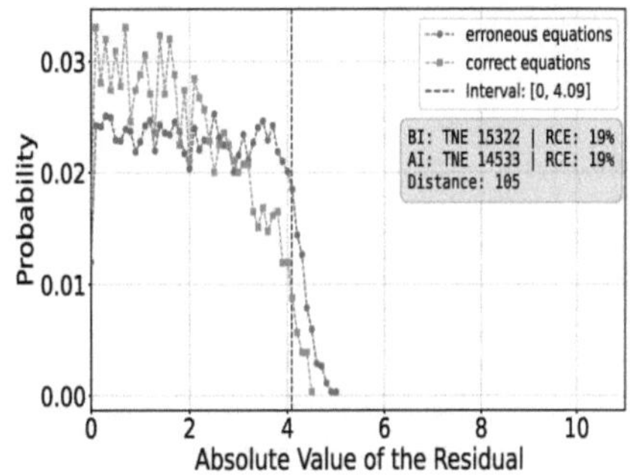

(b) Result after the 2nd global iteration

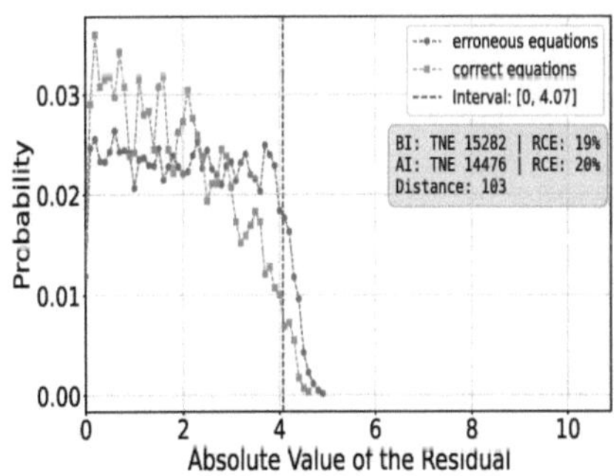

(c) Result after the 3rd global iteration

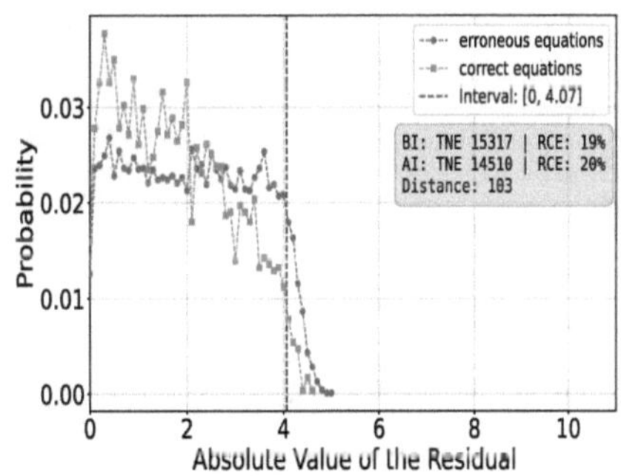

(d) Result after the 4th global iteration

Fig. 9. Performances of least square after different times of Type-I global iteration with equations whose residuals are in the interval of $[0, m_{\text{e}} + 2]$.

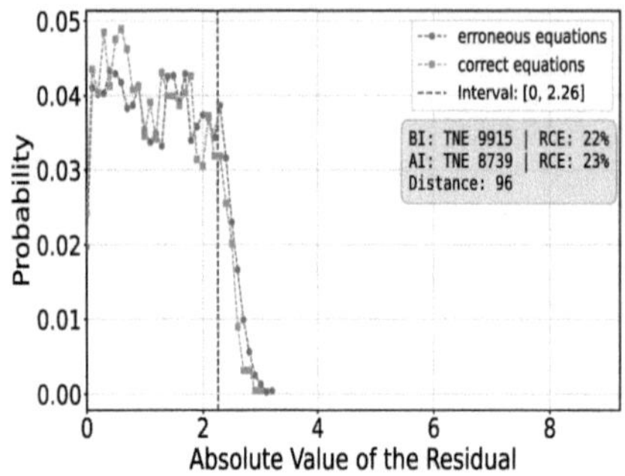

(a) Result after the 1st global iteration

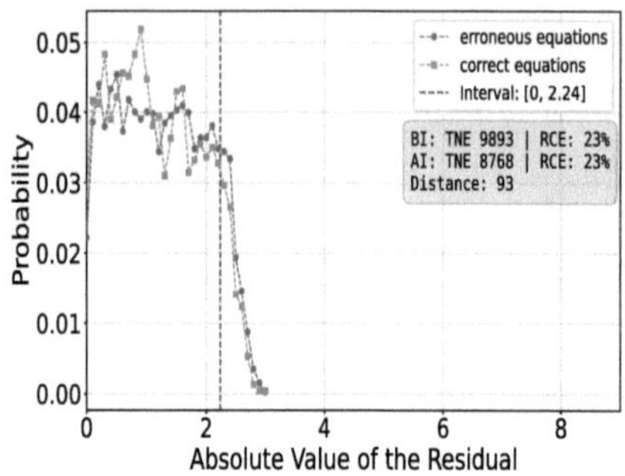

(b) Result after the 2nd global iteration

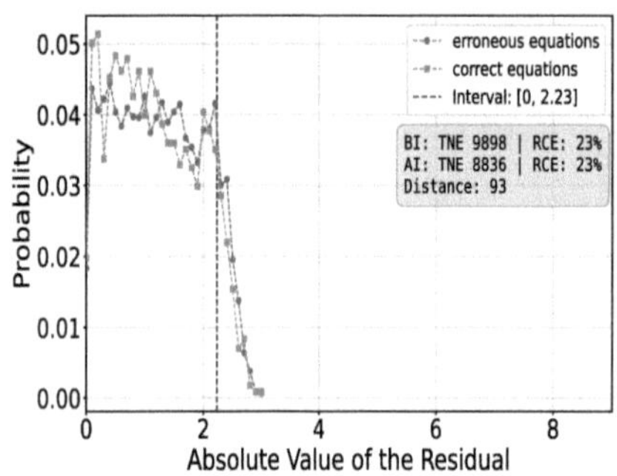

(c) Result after the 3rd global iteration

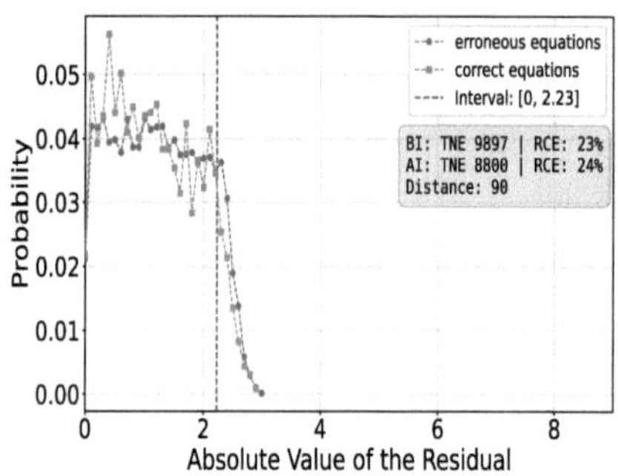

(d) Result after the 4th global iteration

Fig. 10. Performances of least square after different times of Type-I global iteration with equations whose residuals are in the interval of $[0, m_e + 1]$.

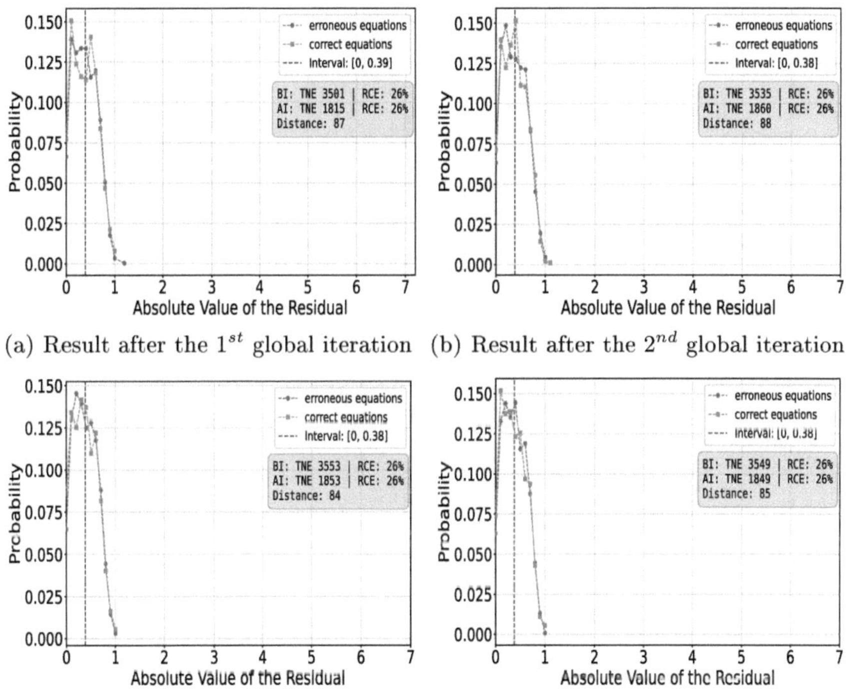

(a) Result after the 1st global iteration (b) Result after the 2nd global iteration

(c) Result after the 3rd global iteration (d) Result after the 4th global iteration

Fig. 11. Performances of least square after different times of Type-I global iteration with equations whose residuals are in the interval of $[0, m_{\mathbf{e}}]$.

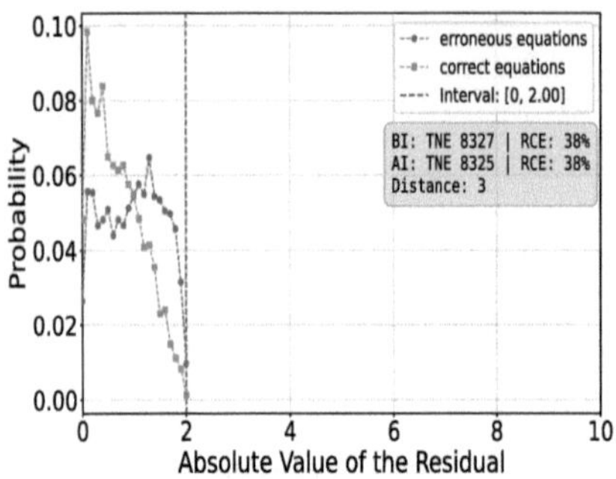

(a) Result of the 6th iteration

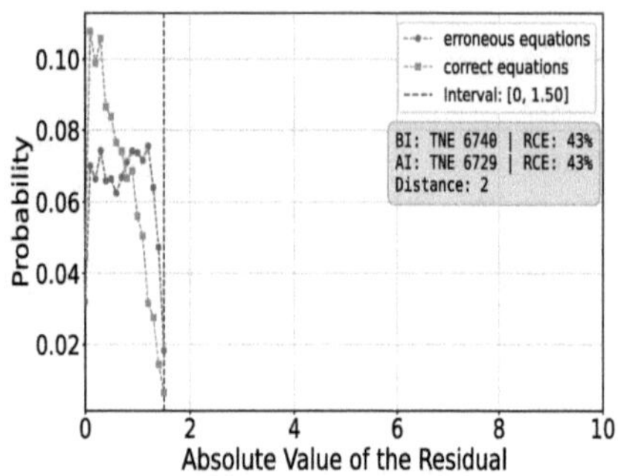

(b) Result of the 12th iteration

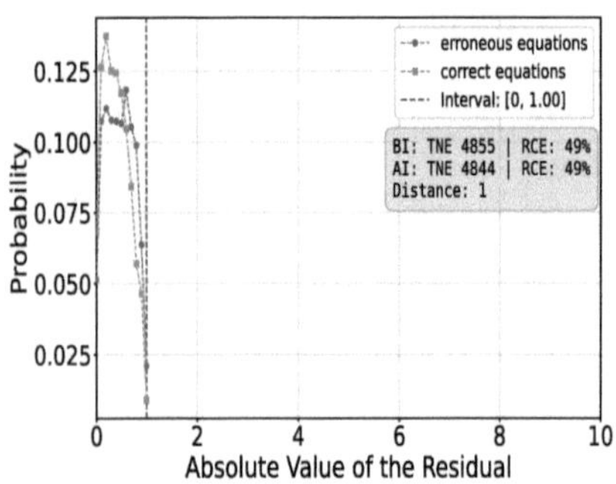

(c) Result of the 18th iteration

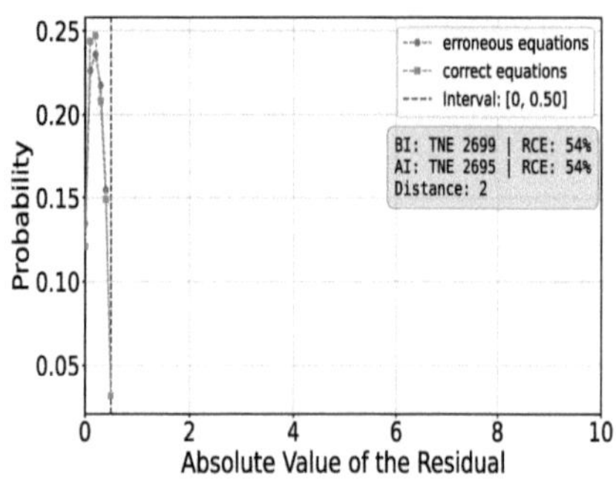

(d) Result of the 24th iteration

Fig. 12. Performances of least square after different times of iteration with equations whose residuals are in the intervals of $[0, 2]$, $[0, 1.5]$, $[0, 1]$ and $[0, 0.5]$.

References

1. Alagic, G., et al.: Status report on the third round of the NIST post-quantum cryptography standardization process. Tech. rep, National Institute of Standards and Technology (2022)
2. Azouaoui, M., et al.: Protecting Dilithium against leakage: revisited sensitivity analysis and improved implementations. IACR Trans. Cryptogr. Hardw. Embed. Syst. **2023**(4), 58–79 (2023)
3. Bernstein, D.J., Hülsing, A., Kölbl, S., Niederhagen, R., Rijneveld, J., Schwabe, P.: The SPHINCS+ signature framework. In: ACM SIGSAC Conference on Computer and Communications Security, CCS 2019, pp. 2129–2146 (2019)
4. Berzati, A., Calle Viera, A., Chartouny, M., Madec, S., Vergnaud, D., Vigilant, D.: Exploiting intermediate value leakage in Dilithium: a template based approach. IACR Trans. Cryptograph. Hardw. Embed. Syst. **2023**(4), 188–210 (2023)
5. Björck, Å.: Least squares methods. Handb. Numer. Anal. **1**, 465–652 (1990)
6. Bruinderink, L.G., Pessl, P.: Differential fault attacks on deterministic lattice signatures. IACR Trans. Crypt. Hardw. Embed. Syst. **2018**(3), 21–43 (2018)
7. Chen, Z., Karabulut, E., Aysu, A., Ma, Y., Jing, J.: An efficient non-profiled side-channel attack on the crystals-Dilithium post-quantum signature. In: International Conference on Computer Design - ICCD 2021, pp. 583–590 (2021)
8. Coron, J.S., Gérard, F., Trannoy, M., Zeitoun, R.: Improved gadgets for the high-order masking of Dilithium. IACR Trans. Cryptogr. Hardw. Embed. Syst. **2023**(4), 110–145 (2023)
9. Ducas, L.: Crystals-Dilithium: a lattice-based digital signature scheme. IACR Trans. Cryptogr. Hardw. Embed. Syst. **2018**(1), 238–268 (2018)
10. Durvaux, F., Standaert, F.-X.: From improved leakage detection to the detection of points of interests in leakage traces. In: Fischlin, M., Coron, J.-S. (eds.) EUROCRYPT 2016. LNCS, vol. 9665, pp. 240–262. Springer, Heidelberg (2016). https://doi.org/10.1007/978-3-662-49890-3_10
11. ElGamal, T.: A public key cryptosystem and a signature scheme based on discrete logarithms. IEEE Trans. Inf. Theor. **31**(4), 469–472 (1985)
12. Fan, H., Zhang, H., Wang, Y., Wang, W., Zhang, H., Yuan, Q.: Multivariate template attack against NTT-based polynomial multiplication of Dilithium. IEEE Trans. Inf. Forensics Secur. **20**, 8570–8582 (2025)
13. Fan, H., et al.: Screening least square technique assisted multivariate template attack against the random polynomial generation of Dilithium. IEEE Trans. Inf. Forensics Secur. **19**, 7118–7132 (2024)
14. Lyubashevsky, V., Peikert, C., Regev, O.: On ideal lattices and learning with errors over rings. In: Gilbert, H. (ed.) EUROCRYPT 2010. LNCS, vol. 6110, pp. 1–23. Springer, Heidelberg (2010). https://doi.org/10.1007/978-3-642-13190-5_1
15. Micciancio, D., Peikert, C.: Trapdoors for lattices: simpler, tighter, faster, smaller. In: Pointcheval, D., Johansson, T. (eds.) EUROCRYPT 2012. LNCS, vol. 7237, pp. 700–718. Springer, Heidelberg (2012). https://doi.org/10.1007/978-3-642-29011-4_41
16. National Institute of Standards and Technology (NIST): Module-Lattice-Based Digital Signature Standard (ML-DSA), FIPS 204 (2024)
17. Primas, R., Pessl, P., Mangard, S.: Single-trace side-channel attacks on masked lattice-based encryption. In: Fischer, W., Homma, N. (eds.) CHES 2017. LNCS, vol. 10529, pp. 513–533. Springer, Cham (2017). https://doi.org/10.1007/978-3-319-66787-4_25

18. Qiao, Z., Liu, Y., Zhou, Y., Ming, J., Jin, C., Li, H.: Practical public template attacks on crystals-Dilithium with randomness leakages. IEEE Trans. Inf. Forensics Secur. **18**, 1–14 (2023)
19. Ravi, P.V., Jhanwar, M.P., Howe, J., Chattopadhyay, A., Bhasin, S.: Side-channel assisted existential forgery attack on Dilithium - a NIST PQC candidate. IACR Cryptology ePrint Arch. **2018**(821), 1–21 (2018)
20. Rivest, R.L., Shamir, A., Adleman, L.: A method for obtaining digital signatures and public-key cryptosystems. Commun. ACM **26**(1), 96–99 (1983)
21. Shor, P.W.: Polynomial-time algorithms for prime factorization and discrete logarithms on a quantum computer. SIAM Rev. **41**(2), 303–332 (1999)
22. Soni, D., Basu, K., Nabeel, M., Aaraj, N., Manzano, M., Karri, R.: Falcon. In: Hardware Architectures for Post – Quantum Digital Signature Schemes, pp. 31–41 (2021)
23. Standaert, F.-X., Malkin, T.G., Yung, M.: A unified framework for the analysis of side-channel key recovery attacks. In: Joux, A. (ed.) EUROCRYPT 2009. LNCS, vol. 5479, pp. 443–461. Springer, Heidelberg (2009). https://doi.org/10.1007/978-3-642-01001-9_26
24. Steffen, H., Land, G., Kogelheide, L., Güneysu, T.: Breaking and protecting the crystal: side channel analysis of Dilithium in hardware. In: Johansson, T., Smith-Tone, D. (eds.) Post Quantum Cryptography — PQCrypto 2023. LNCS, vol. 14154, pp. 688–711. Springer, Cham (2023). https://doi.org/10.1007/978-3-031-40003-2_25
25. Tosun, T., Savas, E.: Zero-value filtering for accelerating non-profiled side-channel attack on incomplete NTT-based implementations of lattice-based cryptography. IEEE Trans. Inf. Forensics Secur. **19**, 3353–3365 (2024)
26. Ulitzsch, V.Q., Marzougui, S., Tibouchi, M., Seifert, J.P.: Profiling side-channel attacks on Dilithium: a small bit-fiddling leak breaks it all. In: Selected Areas in Cryptography, SAC 2022. LNCS, vol. 13742, pp. 3–32 (2022). https://doi.org/10.1007/978-3-031-58411-4_1
27. Wang, R., Gärtner, J., Dubrova, E.: Decompressing Dilithium's public key with fewer signatures using side channel analysis. In: International Symposium on Multiple-Valued Logic - ISMVL 2025, pp. 135–140 (2025)
28. Wang, R., Ngo, K., Gärtner, J., Dubrova, E.: Unpacking needs protection: a single-trace secret key recovery attack on Dilithium. IACR Commun. Cryptol. **1**(3), 1–26 (2024)

Delegate: Coalition Proof Incentivized Outsourced Computation with Smart Contracts

Osman Biçer[1] and Alptekin Küpçü[2(✉)]

[1] University of Basel, Basel, Switzerland
osman.bicer@unibas.ch
[2] Koç University, Istanbul, Turkey
akupcu@ku.edu.tr

Abstract. In incentivized outsourced computation, an outsourcer hands a computation to multiple contractors, and in return expects the same computation output from each. The state-of-the-art proposals succeed in incentivizing all contractors for honest computation by setting this behavior as the unique Nash equilibrium of the system. Yet, they are either limited to the two-contractor case or the multi-contractor case without security proof against fully collaborating coalitions. Further, employing a smart contract for managing submissions from the contractors has been a non-trivial task due to the copy attack. In this work, we target this issue and propose a smart contract based multi-contractor incentivized outsourced computation protocol `Delegate`, which is provably secure against coalitions. We further mitigate the copy attack by a universally composable response submission protocol based on commitments, in contrast to previous solutions which only disincentivize it.

Keywords: outsourced computation · smart contract · game theory

1 Introduction

A client can improve its computation capability and memory capacity by outsourcing computation to cloud providers or to volunteer nodes. To securely and dependably outsource a heavy computation to third parties, there has been a long line of approaches ranging from the ones based on cryptography [24,25,34,37,41] to those based on game theory [2,4,18,19,26,30,31]. Among the latter, game-theory based *incentivized outsourced computation*, where the same computational task is outsourced to more than one contractor, is an interesting arising subject studied in the two-party [2,4,31] and multi-party [5,30] settings. In this approach, a **boss** plans to outsource a computation on an input (while neither the computation nor the input being necessarily private), and is interested in receiving the **correct computation result**. If the boss runs the computation from

We acknowledge the support of TÜBİTAK (the Scientific and Technological Research Council of Türkiye) projects 119E088 and 123E462.

Y. Cao et al. (Eds.): SecureComm 2026, LNICST 704, pp. 197–217, 2027.
https://doi.org/10.1007/978-3-032-32764-2_10

scratch to verify the correctness of the computation, outsourcing it would not result in targeted efficiency improvement. Although specifically for NP problems there exist polynomial-time verification algorithms, we are interested in practical efficiency, which may not be achieved by high degree polynomial verification.

Regarding the multiple contractor setting, the probability of all the contractors being maliciously driven is lowered. The previous work [30] and its extension [5] provide a mechanism where the *honest* **contractors** help the outsourcer catch and punish *lazy contractors*. The former achieves all contractors diligently executing the computation as the Nash equilibrium, while the latter fine-tunes the mechanism for ensuring security against a coalition with up to all involved contractors except one. However, none of these works analyze the full collaboration of contractors for sharing the computation load.

A recent approach in incentivized outsourced computation has been using *smart contracts* [2,18,19,26,31]. Each party deposits some amount to the smart contract at the beginning of the protocol execution. The smart contract collects the results on behalf of the boss and returns to each party the corresponding outcome of the protocol, e.g., the computation result to the boss and a **reward** or a **fine** to each contractor. This way, the use of smart contracts allows a higher efficiency for the resource-restrained boss and protects a diligent contractor from the boss's potential malicious actions, i.e., not paying the reward. However, none of these protocols are in the multi-contractor setting or provide any security guarantee against Sybils or coalitions.

Avizheh et al. proposed the *copy attack* in the smart contract setting [2]. As the contractors need to send the computation result publicly to the smart contract for verification, a copy attacker can copy a response previously submitted instead of executing the computation herself. Although [31] provides a "Match Check" protocol in the two-party setting to resolve this problem, there still exists a need for analyzing complicated outcomes that combine the copy attack with various other strategies and resolving it in the multi-party setting.

Overview of Our Techniques: In this work, we target to resolve the above-mentioned issues with incentivized outsourced computation. The setting that we consider is a combination of those of [30,31] such that a boss outsources the computation to $n > 1$ contractors and delegates the work of checking the final result to a smart contract. We model each contractor as a *bounded rational* adversary (inspired by [36]), which is rational by having the main interest to maximize its utility and is bounded to execute only a probabilistic polynomial time (PPT) interactive Turing machine (ITM).

At the start of the execution, the boss deposits to the smart contract (SC) a sufficient amount of currency for rewarding all the contractors. Each contractor deposits to the SC a sufficient amount of currency for the fine. Then, the contractors are given a deadline τ_{SC} for executing the computation and submitting their commitments to the computation results and the Merkle hash tree root of the computation steps. After τ_{SC}, they have another deadline τ_F to submit the openings of their commitments. We create a response submission protocol that is universally composable (UC) [10] based on non-interactive reusable-CRS (common reference string) commitments.

At τ_F, the SC gets activated and checks whether there exists a consensus in the submitted results from the contractors. If this is the case, then SC returns the result to the boss, gives back the deposit of fines to the contractors, and distributes the rewards to the contractors. Otherwise, it runs the MismatchCheck protocol of [30] to determine the final result. Each MismatchCheck execution takes place among two contractors and SC, and assigns one of the contractors as the winner and the other one as the loser (never both are assigned as the winner or the loser). It is designed in a way that it will always assign a diligent contractor as the winner, and incentivizes participation.

To involve the used cryptographic protocols in the game theoretical analysis, regarding the Merkle hash tree, the bounded rational adversary may take any malicious action with negligible probability. Let the utility from this attack be a polynomial $poly_a(\lambda)$ of the security parameter λ if this attack is successful. Then, the expected utility due to this attack action is a negligible utility computed as $poly_a(\lambda) \cdot \epsilon$, where ϵ is the negligible probability of success.

Regarding the involvement of the UC-secure response submission protocol, we consider that each participant in the protocol is controlled by a player and the possible messages by the environment to that participant are essentially actions of each player. Although we do not assume the existence of the ideal functionality, any distinguishable outcome results in a breach for UC-security, therefore can only succeed with negligible probability, resulting in negligible utility.

We highlight that the equilibrium and coalition-proofness concepts in our game theoretical analysis are computational versions of the generic definitions. They allow a deviation to receive a higher utility only by a negligible function, compatible with bounded rational adversaries [27]. **Our Contributions are:**

- In Sect. 2, we provide a UC-secure [10] response submission protocol for smart-contract-assisted multi-party incentivized outsourced computation based on UC commitments [11,15,21–23]. Our protocol prevents the copy attack of [2], and eliminates the need for further analysis of strategies involving this attack, as long as the submitter of a response does not choose to leak it on purpose, which can be considered as forming a coalition. Being UC-secure, our proposal has strong security in scenarios where multiple protocols run concurrently, such as a blockchain-based distributed system.
- In Sect. 3, we propose our smart-contract-assisted n-party incentivized outsourced computation mechanism: `Delegate`. Compared to previous n-party protocols [5,30], our proposed protocol incentivizes each contractor not only to execute the computation diligently but also to submit the correct computation output as soon as he can, and to help catch the cheating contractors. Further, our proposed n-party mechanism achieves a low fine-to-reward ratio f/r, which, according to [4], should be kept low for incentivization of contractors to join the system. This becomes a particularly important issue in a smart-contract-managed system, as each contractor is expected to deposit a fine at the beginning of the execution. More concretely, we achieve a fine-to-

Table 1. Detailed comparison of our incentivized outsourced computation scheme with the state-of-the-art in terms of our goals listed in Sect. 4. We highlight that the lower the ratio f/r is the more servers are incentivized to join as constructors [4]. Coalitions in [5] were not considered as collaborating for computation.

IOC scheme	Number n of Contractors	Smart Contract	Ratio f/r	Fast Submission	Cheater Hunt	Coalition/Sybil Proofness
[4]	2	N/A	~ 0	No incentive	N/A	N/A
[30]	≥ 2	N/A	$\sim (n-1)$	No incentive	Volunteered	Arrangeable as [5]
[31]	2	Yes	~ 0	No incentive	Forced	N/A
[5]	≥ 2	N/A	$\sim (n-1)$	No incentive	Volunteered	$n-1$, non-collaborating
`Delegate`	≥ 2	Yes	$\sim 1/(n-1)$	Incentivized	Incentivized	$n-1$, collaborating

Table 2. Comparison of the copy attack countermeasures: our response submission protocol π_{RS} with the Match Check protocol of [31]. The costs are provided per contractor.

Scheme	Effectiveness	Offline Cost	Online Cost	Cost to SC
[31]	disincentivizes attack	no cost	Merkle tree proofs	Merkle tree verifications
π_{RS}	prevents attack	commitment	no cost	commitment verification

reward ratio of $\frac{f}{r} \approx \frac{1}{n-1}$ that is much lower than that of [5,30], which was $1 \leq \frac{f}{r} \leq n-1$.

- In Sect. 4, we analyze our mechanism in the setting where contractors are allowed to form coalitions and to collaborate for sharing the computation load and the payment of fines and rewards. We show that in this setting, our mechanism is $n-1$-repellent according to the ℓ-repellence definition of [5]. This shows that as long as all contractors in the system do not establish a coalition (i.e., there exists a separate party outside the coalition), the boss is guaranteed to receive the correct output since rational contractors will compute the task diligently.

Related Work. For the sake of space, we discuss only the most related work.

Incentivized Outsourced Computation. The previous incentivized outsourced computation works that have the closest settings and goals to ours can be listed as [4,18,19,26,30,31,38]. Our setting differs from them as follows:

- [18,26] are in a single-contractor setting, while [4,19,31] are in a two-contractor setting. Our work essentially differs from these works by outsourcing to *multiple* contractors.

- [5,30] are in a multi-contractor setting as our work. They also outsource the same computation to multiple contractors and incentivize them to submit the correct responses. [5] further achieves security against coalitions. Yet, our proposal further incentivizes submitting the correct and early computation output and helping catch cheaters, and we are in a smart-contract setting.

We compare our proposal with the existing mechanisms in Table 1. We acknowledge that these previous works do not target our listed goals, and it may be possible to further improve them to achieve some of the given features (e.g., it may be possible to improve [5,30] by allowing the boss to employ a smart contract and to use our response submission protocol).

According to [4] a lower f/r ratio is better for incentivization of a server to join the system as a contractor. Therefore, it is considered as desirable. Although the ratios are not strictly enforced by any of the given protocols, we consider minimum possible ratios for each of them. It can be seen that the only limiting factors for the number of contractors in our mechanism are the number of available servers and the value of the reward $r > \mathsf{cost}(d)$ as $n \cdot r$ plus gas costs needs to be higher than the value of the computation to the boss. Another line of work uses trusted execution environments [13,42].

Copy Attack. Proposed by Avizheh et al., the copy attack exploits the vulnerability on smart contract based incentivized outsourced computation schemes [2], as the involved contractors can just copy the first submitted response and obtain consensus of the results without actually executing the computation steps. Then, obtaining the correct result relies solely on the diligence of the first submitter. [31] disincentivizes the attack at the cost of a Match Check protocol by the contractors and the smart contract that takes place at the end of the computation. On the other hand, our UC secure response submission protocol π_{RS} prevents this attack completely without the need of any protocol at the end. We highlight that π_{RS} only takes as input the computation results (y, z), whereas an execution of Match Check is also dependent on the function f that is computed. Therefore, the costs from π_{RS} is constant no matter what the number of the computation steps of f is. This contrasts with the costs from [31], which are asymptotically logarithmic with the number of the computation steps of f. Nevertheless, in cases of an implementation with the state-of-the art primitives, the Match Check may be less costly then π_{RS}, due to the availability of lighter weight hash algorithms compared to the public key operations required by UC-secure commitment schemes (see Table 2).

Simultaneously with our work, Avizheh et al. [3] created another smart contract based solution similarly in the universal composability (UC) model. Their main solution works for two contractors, and then they use $\binom{n}{2}$ instances of their two-contractor solution to achieve a multi-contractor solution. While techniques used (UC commitments) are similar, our analysis additionally includes collaborating coalition based game theoretic models (see Sect. 5). Another recent work specializes on Federated Learning [39].

2 Preliminaries and Subprotocols

Negligible Function. A function $\mathsf{n}(\cdot) : \mathbb{N} \rightarrow \mathbb{R}$ is *negligible*, if for each positive polynomial $poly(\cdot)$ there exists an integer $N > 0$ such that for all $\lambda > N$ we have $|\mathsf{n}(\lambda)| < \frac{1}{poly(\lambda)}$. If a negligible function takes as input the security parameter to output a probability or a utility, we may call it negligible probability or negligible utility, respectively.

Smart Contract. A smart contract (SC) is utilized for establishing binding contracts in cryptocurrencies (e.g., Ethereum [8]). SC is publicly executed by the underlying consensus protocol. It collects the submitted transactions and appends them to the blockchain. We assume SC as a trusted party just as in other smart contract based protocols [1,2,29,31]. It can get activated at a set time by a trustless service such as Ethereum Alarm Clock.[1]

We define an n-player game by a set of players $N = (P_1, \ldots, P_n)$, the m_i possible actions $\mathcal{A}_{P_i} = (a_{P_i,1}, \ldots, a_{P_i,m_i})$ of each player $P_i \in N$, and a utility function $u_{P_i}(\cdot)$ of each player $P_i \in N$ that assigns a real value for each possible action profile. Each player targets to maximize her own utility. A strategy s_{P_i} of player P_i is a probability distribution over the possible actions of the player P_i. When we call an action a as a strategy a, we mean the strategy that assigns probability 1 to action a. Also, we denote by $s = (s_{P_1}, \ldots, s_{P_n})$ a strategy profile composed of the strategies of all players. Further, we denote by $s_{-P_i} = s - \{s_{P_i}\}$ the strategy profile of all players excluding the player P_i. Given a strategy profile s, we denote by $u_i(s)$ the expected utility of the player P_i. We utilize the notion of *computational Nash equilibrium* defined as follows:

Definition 1 (Computational Nash equilibrium). *A strategy set $s = (s_{P_1}, \ldots, s_{P_n})$ is a computational Nash equilibrium if $\forall P_i \in N$ $\forall s'_{P_i} \neq s_{P_i}$ $u_{P_i}(s_N) \geq u_{P_i}(s'_i \cup s_{-i}) - \mathsf{n}(\lambda)$ where $\mathsf{n}(\cdot)$ is a negligible function and λ is the security parameter.*

Transferable Utility. In many cooperative games, one can assume that players can simply and freely sign binding agreements for sharing the game outcome. The conventional name of this assumption is the transferable utility assumption [35]. This simplifies the analysis by defining a single total utility per coalition. More concretely, the utility of a coalition is defined as follows:

Definition 2 (Coalition Utility). *Let s be a strategy set for a game Π played by n players. Then, the utility $u_G(s)$ of a coalition G is defined as $u_G = \sum_{P_i \in C} u_{P_i}(s)$.*

This assumption is also useful in cases where a rational party joins a protocol with multiple identities, e.g., as in Sybil attack in peer-to-peer systems [20].

Definition 3 (Computationally Dominant Strategy). *A strategy s_{P_i} of a player P_i is its computationally dominant strategy if for all strategies $s'_{P_i} \neq s_{P_i}$ of*

[1] https://github.com/ethereum-alarm-clock/ethereum-alarm-clock.

P_i and for all strategy profiles s'_{-i} of players other than P_i, $u_i(s_{P_i} \cup s'_{-P_i}) + \mathsf{n}(\lambda) > u_i(s'_{P_i} \cup s'_{-P_i})$ where $\mathsf{n}(\cdot)$ is a negligible function and λ is the security parameter.

ℓ-Repellence [5]. [5] provides transferable utility based threshold security definitions that are useful for disincentivizing coalitions up to certain sizes. We provide below the computational version of ℓ-repellence.

Definition 4 (Computational ℓ-Repellent Mechanism). *A joint strategy s_N is a computational ℓ-repellent equilibrium, if $\forall G \subseteq N$ with $|G| \leq \ell$ and for all strategies s'_G played by G, there exist a negligible function $\mathsf{n}(\cdot)$ s.t. $u_G(s_N) + \mathsf{n}(\lambda) > U_G(s'_C \cup s_{-C})$ where $s_N = s_C \cup s_{-C}$. For some functionality F, (Π, s_N) is a computationally ℓ-repellent mechanism for F, if s_N is a computational ℓ-repellent equilibrium of Π and the outcome of (Π, s_N) satisfies F.*

Merkle Hash Tree. A Merkle hash tree is a binary tree generated by hashing a set of data elements $E = (e_1, \ldots, e_s)$. Each leaf with index i of the tree is constructed as $H(e_i)$ where $H : \{0,1\}^* \rightarrow R$ is a collision resistant hash function, and R is a set whose each element can be encoded as a bit string and whose number of elements is $O(poly(\lambda))$. Each other node of the tree is constructed by $H(i,j)$ where i and j are the children of that node. The root hash is denoted by $z = MHRoot(E)$. We denote the Merkle proof of element e_i as $p_i = MHproof(E, e_i)$. This proof is composed of the hash values of the sibling nodes along the path between $H(e_i)$ and the root, and is used for proving the inclusion of an element in z with one minus negligible probability. $VerifyMHProof(z, i, e_i, p_i)$ is the verification algorithm that runs on input the root hash z, an index i, and the indexed element e_i and its proof p_i. This algorithm can be computed in complexity $O(\log s)$ to obtain an output *Success* or *Failure* depending on the success of the verification.

Computation Trace. The computation is represented by a Turing machine $TM()$ with an input tape initially storing the input string. The reduced configuration rc_j of the computation state at the step j is assigned as $(s_j, h_j, v_j, MHRoot(t_j))$, where s_j , h_j, v_j, and t_j are the state, the head position, the tape at the given head, and the tape of the related TM configuration [12]. We let the set $RC = (rc_1, \ldots, rc_s)$ and the hash root of the computation $z = MHRoot(RC)$ as in [31].

MismatchCheck Protocol. Proposed for use in two-party incentivized outsourced computation [31], this protocol is run among a checker (the smart contract in our setting) and two contractors C_i and C_j who are assigned to execute the same computation TM on some input x. The aim is to catch the cheater (set to lose) if only one of C_i and C_j is diligent (set to win) and the other one is lazy. This protocol always makes at least one contractor lose if their inputs are different (i.e., mismatching). Before the protocol is run, the checker receives the responses (y_i, z_i) and (y_j, z_j) from the contractors. The execution flow of *MismatchCheck* is given in [31]. The protocol has $O(\log s)$ complexity where s is the number of computation steps. In our proposal, we use multiple executions

Functionality $\mathcal{F}_{\text{MCOM}}$

Running with parties $P_1, \ldots, P_n$ and an adversary $\mathcal{S}$, $\mathcal{F}_{\text{MCOM}}$ proceeds as follows.

1. On receiving a message $(\mathsf{Commit}, sid, cid, P_i, P_j, s)$ from P_i, record the tuple (cid, P_i, P_j, s) and send the message $(Receipt, sid, cid, P_i, P_j)$ to P_j and $\mathcal{S}$, where sid is the session id, cid is the commitment id, and $s \in \{0,1\}^*$ is the committed string. Ignore subsequent $(\mathsf{Commit}, sid, cid, \cdot)$ messages.
2. On receiving a message $(\mathsf{Open}, sid, cid, P_i, P_j)$ from P_i, proceed as follows: If there exists a record for the tuple (cid, P_i, P_j, s), then send the message $(Open, sid, cid, P_i, P_j, s)$ to P_j and $\mathcal{S}$. Otherwise, do nothing.

Protocol 1.1. The ideal functionality for multiple UC commitments

Functionality $\mathcal{F}_{\mathsf{CRS}}$

Parameterized by a distribution D, $\mathcal{F}_{\mathsf{CRS}}$ proceeds as follows.

1. When activated for the first time on input $(value, sid)$, choose a value $d \leftarrow_R D$ and send d back to the activating party. In each other activation, return d to the activating party.

Protocol 1.2. The ideal functionality for the common reference string

of this protocol to obtain the final result in case of the absence of consensus in the submitted responses by the contractors. This protocol does not catch deviant strategies, where the player runs the diligent algorithm and then maliciously alters some of the reduced steps. This is because it is assumed that once the player goes with incorrect step all the steps afterwards will be spoiled as playing lazy.

Non-Interactive and Reusable-CRS Commitment Schemes: Commitment schemes (Commit, Open) are useful cryptographic primitives that enable Alice to commit to a value for Bob via Commit operation, and later open it via Open operation. The two traditional requirements for commitment schemes are being hiding (i.e., Commit does not reveal the committed value without Open) and binding (i.e., once Commit takes place, Alice cannot execute Open for different values). A commitment scheme is non-interactive if both Commit and Open costs one round, i.e., for each of them, one string is sent to Bob. The way that we utilize the commitment scheme in Sect. 3 requires commitments from multiple parties, and possibly many similar protocols may run concurrently. We stress that commitment schemes in the standard model are not secure by default in this setting as other users' commitments and their openings can be utilized for copying or generating different commitments. Instead, we expect the commitment scheme to satisfy the ideal functionality given in Protocol 1.1, i.e., the string commitment version of the multiple bit commitment ideal functionality given in [11]. Unlike the ones in standard model, $\mathcal{F}_{\text{MCOM}}$ ensures each commitment is generated as a completely blinded envelop and is bound to its generator.

UC-secure commitments are shown to be non-existent without a common reference string CRS (see ideal functionality in Protocol 1.2) by [11]. Therefore the ideal functionality given in Protocol 1.1 is the one with reusable-CRS for efficiency. Any non-interactive commitment scheme realizing $\mathcal{F}_{\text{MCOM}}$, e.g. [11,15, 21–23], can be used for realizing our protocol. Concurrent commitment schemes

Functionality $\mathcal{F}_{\text{RS}}$

Running with contractors $P_1, \ldots, P_n$, the smart contract SC, and an adversary $\mathcal{S}$, $\mathcal{F}_{\text{RS}}$ proceeds as follows.

1. When the current time $\tau_C < \tau_{SC}$, on receiving a message $(\mathsf{Response}, sid, P_i, (y, z))$ from P_i for the first time, record the tuple $(P_i, sid, (y, z))$. Send the message $(Receipt, sid, P_i)$ to $\mathcal{S}$. Ignore other $(\mathsf{Response}, sid, P_i, \cdot)$ tuples. On receiving a message $(\mathsf{Leak}, sid, P_i)$ from P_i, if there exists a record $(P_i, sid, (y, z))$, send $(Leak, sid, P_i, (y, z))$ to $\mathcal{S}$. Otherwise do nothing.
2. When $\tau_{SC} = \tau_C$, send each recorded $(P_i, sid, (y, z))$ tuple to $\mathcal{S}$.
3. When $\tau_C = \tau_F$, send each recorded $(P_i, sid, (y, z))$ tuple to SC.

Protocol 1.3. The ideal functionality for response submission of contractors

are also shown to UC-secure by [33], therefore, the non-interactive ones [6,28, 32] are also eligible. However, stand-alone non-malleable commitments [16,17] should be shown to realize $\mathcal{F}_{\text{MCOM}}$ before their use.

3 Our Response Submission Protocol

The Ideal Functionality $\mathcal{F}_{\text{RS}}$. Protocol 1.3 provides the ideal functionality $\mathcal{F}_{\text{RS}}$ for the response submissions of the contractors. Response messages from the contractors to $\mathcal{F}_{\text{RS}}$ need to be sent before τ_{SC}. A contractor may send Leak messages to $\mathcal{F}_{\text{RS}}$, to model the action of leaking the response to another contractor. Once the response is submitted, it cannot be altered or re-submitted.

Protocol π_{RS}. Protocol 1.4 provides our proposed protocol π_{RS} to realize $\mathcal{F}_{\text{RS}}$ in the $\mathcal{F}_{\text{MCOM}}$-hybrid model. π_{RS} runs with a single copy of $\mathcal{F}_{\text{MCOM}}$. Until the current time $\tau_C = \tau_F$, SC just records the obtained messages and then gets activated to run the algorithm for the output. We highlight that in the implementation of this protocol the value CRS will be required for the realization of the functionality $\mathcal{F}_{\text{MCOM}}$, which needs to be submitted to SC by the boss before the start of the protocol execution as part of the auxiliary information aux. We assume that commitments are tied to the unique identities of the participants and therefore cannot be copied without being noticed. Proof is in the full version [7].

4 Our Incentivized Outsourced Computation Proposal

System Model: Essentially, the setting that we are interested in is a multi-party version of the two-party incentivized outsourced computation setting [4,31] and the inclusion of smart contracts and rational coalitions on top of [30], as we describe in what follows.

There exist three types of entities: (i) a *boss*, who is interested in outsourcing the computation of a deterministic polynomial time[2] Turing machine $TM()$ on

[2] If it is a randomized algorithm, it should be converted to a deterministic one by providing the randomization script (e.g., pseudorandom seed) as part of the input.

The Response Submission Protocol π_{RS}

Running with contractors $C_1, \ldots, C_n$, the smart contract SC, and an adversary $\mathcal{H}$, π_{RS} proceeds as follows in the presence of one copy of $\mathcal{F}_{\text{MCOM}}$ functionality with session id sid_{MCOM} running with parties $P_1, \ldots, P_n$, and SC.

1. When the current time $\tau_C < \tau_{SC}$, an honest P_i and an honest SC proceed as follows. Upon the first input $(\mathsf{Response}, sid, P_i, (y, z))$, P_i picks a unique cid and sends the message $(\mathsf{Commit}, sid_{\text{MCOM}}, cid, P_i, \text{SC}, (y, z))$ to $\mathcal{F}_{\text{MCOM}}$. Then, $\mathcal{F}_{\text{MCOM}}$ sends $(\mathsf{Commit}, sid_{\text{MCOM}}, cid, P_i, \text{SC})$ to SC. P_i ignores other $(\mathsf{Response}, *)$ inputs. Upon the input $(\mathsf{Leak}, sid, P_i)$, P_i sends the message $(\mathsf{Open}, sid_{\text{MCOM}}, cid, P_i, \text{SC})$ to $\mathcal{F}_{\text{MCOM}}$, which in turn sends $(Open, sid_{\text{MCOM}}, cid, P_i, \text{SC}, (y, z))$ to SC. SC just keeps appending all the messages coming from $\mathcal{F}_{\text{MCOM}}$ to its database.
2. When $\tau_{SC} \leq \tau_C < \tau_F$, an honest P_i and SC proceed as follows. P_i sends the message $(\mathsf{Open}, sid_{\text{MCOM}}, cid, P_i, \text{SC})$ to $\mathcal{F}_{\text{MCOM}}$. If there is a related record, $\mathcal{F}_{\text{MCOM}}$ sends $(\mathsf{Open}, sid_{\text{MCOM}}, cid, P_i, \text{SC}, (y, z))$ to SC. Again, SC just passively keeps appending all the messages coming from $\mathcal{F}_{\text{MCOM}}$ to its database.
3. When $\tau_C = \tau_F$, on its database, SC deduces each P_i's first $(\mathsf{Commit}, sid_{\text{MCOM}}, cid, P_i, \text{SC})$ message among the ones sent before τ_{SC} on its database. These messages are combined to obtain a table T with up to n entries. Then, SC generates another table T' with entries $(P_i, sid, (y, z))$ obtained from the corresponding $(\mathsf{Open}, sid_{\text{MCOM}}, cid, P_i, \text{SC}, (y, z))$ entries sent in the interval (τ_{SC}, τ_F) for each $(P_i, sid_{\text{MCOM}}, cid)$ on T. For the ones that are found, SC outputs each entry of T'.

Protocol 1.4. The $\mathcal{F}_{\text{MCOM}}$-hybrid protocol for response submission

an input tape x, (ii) a set N of n *contractors* that execute the computation to obtain the reward, and (iii) a *Smart Contract (SC)* that rules the system interactions between the parties on behalf of the boss, and handles the transactions. We can consider the boss as an honest designer of the mechanism rather than a player involved in it, as in [4,30,31]. She outsources the computation to the contractors and generates SC at the beginning of the game. Her goal is to obtain the correct computation result from the contractors at the end of the protocol, and she is willing to pay a total reward R for this goal.

We model a contractor as a rational party whose main interest is to maximize its utility. We bound each contractor to execute only a probabilistic polynomial time (PPT) interactive Turing machine (ITM).

Non-Collaborating and Collaborating Coalitions. The contractors may establish coalitions; thus the boss is naturally advised to pick the contractors in a manner that lowers the probability of coalitions. For simplicity, as usual [4,30,31], we assume the contractors are picked randomly from a pool. We identify two types of possible coalitions among the contractors: (i) the *non-collaborative setting*, where the members of a coalition together decide the strategy that each of them individually plays, among the available strategies, and (ii) the *collaborative setting*, where the members of a coalition can go beyond the individual strategies. In particular, they can simply decide that only one of them performs the computation (honestly or not), and then all of them submit the same result. We note that the previous work [5] only analyzes the non-collaborative setting. Following the transferable utility assumption, we assume a single total utility for the coalition. This allows our setting to address Sybil contractors in the sense that all Sybils can form a coalition and our theorems address this issue directly (except when all contractors picked for a particular job turn out to be Sybils).

Threat Model. The network is asynchronous, i.e., under adversarial control. Further, the communication can be eavesdropped by the adversary but cannot be modified (i.e., they are authenticated). Each party has a unique identity. The adversary can actively and adaptively corrupt any number of parties. SC is an ITM that is trusted for running the program that it has been given, but its computation and storage are public, so it cannot protect any private values. The communication with SC is over authenticated public channels. **Goals:**

1. With high probability, the boss receives the correct computation result (considered by [4,5,30,31]).
2. The contractors are not discouraged by setting a high fine to reward ratio (considered by [4]).
3. There is an incentive for contractors to act honestly, i.e., an honestly acting contractor gets rewarded (considered by [4,5,30,31]).
4. There is an incentive for contractors to submit the response early (not considered before).
5. Contractors playing the honest strategy are incentivized to help catch deviating contractors.
6. The mechanism is safe against collaborating contractors, i.e., the workload of computation can be shared within the coalition (only non-collaborating coalitions are considered by [5]).
7. The workload to SC in case of mismatching submissions is kept low for the budget of the boss (considered by [31]).

4.1 Our `Delegate` Protocol

To prepare for outsourcing, the boss specifies SC for the involved contractors, the computation $TM()$ to be executed, and the input x. SC collects deposits from the boss and the contractors. In accordance with the protocol π_{RS} (see Protocol 1.4), until a predetermined time τ_{SC}, SC passively collects computation results from the contractors. The computation results are submitted as Commit to (y_i, z_i) by each contractor P_i, where y_i is the computation result and z_i is the Merkle hash root of all computation steps (see Sect. 2). Then, until another predetermined time τ_F, the contractors send Open of their submitted responses to SC. After τ_F, SC checks all the submissions, determines the result of the computation, and delivers fines and rewards. It also returns the boss's residual deposit if there is any remaining. Finally, it sends the computation result to the boss. Protocol 1.5 shows the high-level flow of `Delegate`.

Notation (extended from [31]) TM is the function to be computed, picked by the boss. x is its input. aux is the auxiliary information submitted to SC at the beginning of the protocol by the boss. y is the computation result and z is the Merkle root of the computation steps, submitted by a contractor. r is reward, f is fine, τ_{SC} is the deadline for committing to the response (y, z). τ_F is the deadline for opening the committed response. τ_C is the current time.

Algorithm 1 shows the algorithm of SC throughout the protocol. The algorithm activates at τ_F and collects fine deposits and responses submitted by the contractors. If no consensus in the submitted responses exists, SC executes the for loop in the mismatch resolution part. At each round of the for loop, the algorithm sets two of the submitted responses to compete by $MismatchCheck$ executions (see Sect. 2). In each of these executions, submitters of the two responses are involved. When a submitter of a response loses, the algorithm continues by the next submitter of that response, until all submitters of a response are set to lose. Then that response gets eliminated. This way we make sure a submitted response can only get eliminated after all of its submitters are involved in $MismatchCheck$ executions as a submitter of a response can be part of a hidden separate coalition and can lose $MismatchCheck$ on purpose. After one response gets eliminated the for loop continues to the next round by picking another response to compete with the winner of the previous round.

Unlike the previous works [5,30,31], the fine deposits by cheaters will be delivered to the diligent contractors that get actively involved in catching the cheaters in $MismatchCheck$ executions. The number of executions that a diligent contractor gets involved in is less than or equal to the number of fine gains that he will receive. We consider this as a further incentivization to get involved and to stay online, as long as f is greater than the $MismatchCheck$ execution cost for the diligent contractor. Further, the algorithm takes into account the response submission order in assigning $MismatchCheck$ executions, as an incentivization of early submission by the diligent contractors. If a diligent contractor submits earliest, stays online, and joins each $MismatchCheck$ asked by SC, he gets all the fines of the cheaters. An honest contractor algorithm is provided as Algorithm 2.

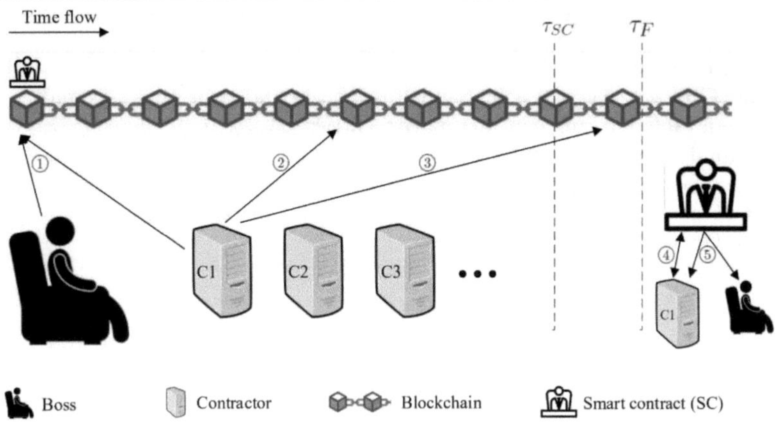

(1) The boss generates SC. She also submits $TM()$, x, aux, reward r, fine f, deadlines τ_{SC} and τ_F to SC. The boss also deposits the amount $n{\cdot}r$ as her commitment to paying the rewards. Each contractor deposits the amount f.

(2) Each contractor C_i submits Commit to his response (y_i, z_i) until the deadline τ_{SC} to SC.

(3) Each contractor C_i submits Open of its committed response until the deadline τ_F to SC.

(4) SC gets activated. SC collects the submitted responses by the contractors. SC verifies commitment openings. SC then checks whether there exists a consensus (y, z) in the submitted responses. If no consensus is reached, SC runs the *MismatchCheck* protocol with the contractors until obtaining a single result (y, z) (see Algorithm 1).

(5) SC returns to the boss the computation result y. If there exists a consensus in the submitted responses, SC transfers the reward r to the balance of each contractor. It also returns each deposit f to its depositor. Otherwise, SC publishes the diligent contractors and the cheaters and transfers the reward r to the balance of each diligent contractor. It also returns the deposit f to each diligent contractor. Further, it distributes the collected fines from cheaters to the diligent contractors (see Algorithm 1 for details of the distribution) and sends the remaining reward deposit to the boss.

Protocol (1.5) Our Delegate protocol flow

5 Game Theoretical Analysis of Delegate

Strategies of Contractors Outside Coalition: We define the strategy set in the setting without any coalition based on the strategies given in [4,30,31]. The available actions for each contractor are briefly as follows.

Algorithm 1: Complete algorithm of SC

Activate at τ_F
Initial Check: Check the sent blinded responses and their openings and prepare a table for each contractor with entries $(P_i, (y_i, z_i))$ where (y_i, z_i) is the first submitted commitment by P_i.
for *each contractor* P_i **do**
    if P_i *did not submit a commitment or its opening* **then**
        $Cheaters.add(P_i)$
    else
        $Response(y_i, z_i).add(P_i)$

if $\forall i, j\ (y_i, z_i) = (y_j, z_j)$ **then**
    $ResultingResponse \leftarrow Response(y, z)$
    Go to **Delivery**

Mismatch resolution:
Initialize *ResultingResponse* as the most common $Response(y, z)$
$ResultingResponse[0].count \leftarrow Cheaters.size$
for *each* $Response(y, z)$ **do**
    $i \leftarrow 0, j \leftarrow 0$
    Execute *MismatchCheck* with $ResultingResponse[i]$ and $Response(y, z)[j]$, during execution:
        if $ResultingResponse[i]$ *fails to comply* **or** *loses MismatchCheck* **then**
            if $i < ResultingResponse.size$ **then**
                $i \leftarrow i + 1$, restart *MismatchCheck*
            else
                $Cheaters.add(ResultingResponse)$
                $Response(y, z)[j].count \leftarrow Cheaters.size$
                $ResultingResponse \leftarrow Response(y, z)$
        else if $Response(y, z)(j)$ *fails to comply* **or** *loses MismatchCheck* **then**
            if $j < Response(y, z).size$ **then**
                $j \leftarrow j + 1$, restart *MismatchCheck*
            else
                $ResultingResponse[j].count+ = Response(y, z).size$,
                $Cheaters.add(Response(y, z))$

Delivery: Publish *ResultingResponse*, *Cheaters*, *Quitters*
Deliver $(n - ResultingResponse.size) \cdot r$ to the boss
Deliver $r + f + j.count \cdot f$ to each $j \in ResultingResponse$

Algorithm 2: Algorithm of Honest Contractor

Activate at the protocol start: Deposit f to SC and learn $TM()$ and x. Compute $TM(x)$ diligently to obtain (y, z). Submit Commit to the response (y, z).
Activate at τ_{SC}**:** Submit Open of the commitment.
Activate at τ_F**:** Comply with each *MismatchCheck* request from SC.

- Regarding computation of the task:
  1. *Diligent computation.* This is the preferred action by the boss. The contractor runs the correct computation honestly and submits the result in the given time. The cost of the computation is denoted as $\mathsf{cost}(d)$.
  2. *Lazy algorithm computation.* This action corresponds to choosing a lazy algorithm from the set $L = (l_1, \ldots, l_m)$ where $m \in O(poly(\lambda))$. In a lazy strategy with the algorithm l_i, the contractor runs l_i whose cost is defined as $\mathsf{cost}(l_i) < \mathsf{cost}(d)$. In presence of a single diligent contractor in the system, the probability of the lazy algorithm l_i producing a successful result is defined as $q_i < \mathsf{n}(\lambda)$ for some negligible function $\mathsf{n}(\cdot)$, thanks to the $MismatchCheck$ protocols executed by SC. We highlight that this is a generalization of the previous "lazy q-algorithm" of [5,30,31] and "Guess" strategy by [31]. We also highlight that, unlike the previous works, we do not limit the contractors to play a single lazy algorithm. Note that the algorithms with $\mathsf{cost}(l_i) \geq \mathsf{cost}(d)$ are simply dominated by the diligent algorithm and excluded from the consideration.
- Regarding response submission (based on actions in $\mathcal{F}_{RS}$):
  1. *Honest submission.* This corresponds to submitting the output of the computation algorithm (can be a lazy one).
  2. *Leaking.* This is a deviant submission action. The submitter of a response deliberately leaks the submitted response. We disincentivize leaking.
  3. *Copy strategies.* The copy attack [2] is that the contractor waits for some response from the other contractors on the SC, then copies and submits that response, as if it is the contractor's own result. [31] describes combined strategies including copy attack and diligent and lazy strategies. In this work, we proposed a UC-secure response submission protocol that allows any PPT contractor to conduct this attack with at most a negligible probability, as long as the original submitter does not leak it.
- Regarding $Mismatch$ protocol executions:
  1. *Not complying.* This includes trying to cheat during a $Mismatch$ execution or failing to send messages in time.
  2. *Complying.* Honestly preparing and sending the messages in time per the protocol requirements.

Analysis of Leaking and $MismatchCheck$ Actions: Table 3 shows the utility matrix of a diligent contractor based on the leaking decision. Not leaking is computationally dominant, as it can be better if there exist non-diligent contractors. In such a case, the contractor can obtain an extra reward by cheater hunting. In this case, leaking results in utility $r - \mathsf{cost}(d)$ due to copiers.

Analysis Without Coalitions: Now we allow each contractor to choose only Diligent and Lazy as strategies (i.e., honest submission and complying is ensured), and disallow any group of contractors from forming coalitions. Therefore, this setting is also interesting if there is no SC and the boss is managing the verification, as in [4,5,30]. We start by showing that by adjusting the parameters, one can ensure all-diligent is the unique computational Nash equilibrium

Table 3. Utility matrix of a diligent contractor based on leaking.

Others ╲ This	Do not leak	Leak
All Diligent and Honest Submission	$r - \mathsf{cost}(d)$	$r - \mathsf{cost}(d)$
Some Lazies and Copiers	$\geq r - \mathsf{cost}(d)$	$r - \mathsf{cost}(d)$

in this setting. Table 4 provides the utility matrix of the contractor. All proofs are in the Appendix. In all the theorems below, we obviously assume that the rewards, fines, and extra rewards are all noticeable (not negligible).

Table 4. Utility matrix of a contractor if no coalition exists, only honest submission and complying is allowed. k should satisfy $0 < k < n - 1$.

Others ╲ This	Diligent	Lazy l_i
All Diligent	$r - \mathsf{cost}(d)$	$r \cdot q_i - f(1 - q_i) - \mathsf{cost}(l_i)$
k Diligent	$\geq r - \mathsf{cost}(d)$	$\leq r \cdot q_i - f(1 - q_i) - \mathsf{cost}(l_i)$
All Lazy L'	$r + f \sum_{l_j \in L'}(1 - q_j) - \mathsf{cost}(d)$	*depends on l_i and L'

Theorem 1. *If the hash function utilized in Merkle hash tree is collision resistant and the boss sets the fine and reward as* $f > \frac{r}{(n-1)\left(1-\mathsf{n}(\lambda)\right)}$ *for all negligible functions* $\mathsf{n}(\cdot)$ *where* λ *is a security parameter, then in the setting described in this subsection, the strategy with diligent computation, honest submission, and complying during MismatchCheck for each player is the unique computational Nash equilibrium.*

We show that all diligent computation is still a computational Nash equilibrium and that there does not exist any Nash equilibrium where no contractor is honest. Note that a simple setting would be $f = r/(n-1)$ satisfying the requirement. We allow ourselves by not requiring all diligent computation and honest submission without leaking strategy as the unique computational Nash equilibrium anymore. This is forced as leaking does not decrease the utility of any diligent player. Thus, the unique equilibrium above does not take into account leaking behavior. Hence, it is OK to leak as long as the result is honest. Yet the boss obtains the correct output (guaranteed by the Theorems 2 and 3).

Theorem 2. *If the hash function utilized in Merkle hash is collision resistant, and the response submission protocol* π_{RS} *given in Protocol 1.4 securely emulates the ideal functionality* $\mathcal{F}_{RS}$ *given in Protocol 1.3; then in the setting described in this subsection, each player following diligent computation, honest submission, and complying without leaking is a computational Nash equilibrium.*

Theorem 3. *If the hash function utilized in Merkle hash is collision resistant, and the response submission protocol* π_{RS} *given in Protocol 1.4 securely emulates the ideal functionality* $\mathcal{F}_{RS}$ *given in Protocol 1.3, and the boss sets the fine and reward as* $f > \frac{r}{(n-1)\left(1-\mathsf{n}(\lambda)\right)}$ *for all negligible functions* $\mathsf{n}(\cdot)$ *where* λ *is a security parameter; then in the setting described in this subsection, there exists no computational Nash equilibrium where at least one player does not follow the diligent computation and honest submission with or without leaking strategies.*

Analysis with Non-Collaborating Coalitions: By using the computational ℓ-repellence definition, we show that our mechanism is secure against coalitions with up to $n-1$ contractors.

Definition 5 (non-collaborating diligent strategy). *Non-collaborating diligent strategy is defined as a non-collaborating coalition strategy where the diligent algorithm is executed by each player in the coalition, the output is submitted honestly, and during* $MismatchCheck$ *the first submitter of the response complies.*

Theorem 4. *If the hash function utilized in Merkle hash is collision resistant, and the response submission protocol* π_{RS} *securely emulates the ideal functionality* $\mathcal{F}_{RS}$*, then in the setting provided in this subsection, all non-collaborating diligent strategy is computationally* $(n-1)$*-repellent.*

Analysis with Collaborating Coalitions: A coalition may benefit from reducing computation costs by parallelizing the task (or letting only one player handle it), resulting in a total cost of $\mathsf{cost}(d)$ for a coalition of size k, instead of $k \cdot \mathsf{cost}(d)$, to play the all diligent strategy. Assuming the boss is only interested in obtaining the correct result (not necessarily in every player executing the computation), we obtain an equilibrium.

Definition 6 (collaborating diligent strategy). *Collaborating diligent strategy is defined as a collaborating coalition strategy where the diligent algorithm is executed once in the coalition, the output is submitted honestly by all players in the coalition without leaking, and during* $MismatchCheck$ *the first submitter of the response complies.*

We acknowledge that this is a slight abuse of the previous computational ℓ-repellence definition, where the desired coalition strategy was expected to be the collection of the desired strategies of each contractor inside it. Yet, it is justified due to the following reasons: (1) cost cancellations due to interactions of coalitional partners are inevitable as the same computation is outsourced, (2) the boss only cares about the outcome, i.e., obtaining the correct result.

Theorem 5. *If the hash function utilized in Merkle hash is collision resistant, and the response submission protocol* π_{RS} *securely emulates the ideal functionality* $\mathcal{F}_{RS}$*, then in the setting provided in this subsection, all collaborating diligent strategy is computationally* $(n-1)$*-repellent.*

Proofs of all the theorems are in the full version [7].

6 Implementation and Results

Implementation and Test Environment. We have a proof-of-concept implementation of our protocol using Python and web3.py. Also, we implement the algorithms for SC with Solidity on Remix IDE. For simplicity, we model the given function f as a random access computer as in [14] instead of Turing machines. We highlight that the contractors still execute the computation step-by-step and the Merkle hash tree is computed from these steps. Regarding the function f, we pick finding the x-th Fibonacci number by brute force, where x is given as input to f. The implementation of *MismatchCheck* use SHA-3 (256 bits) for constructing the Merkle hash tree. Also, the UC commitment scheme used for π_{RS} is [11], which uses SHA-2 and SHA-3 (256 bits) for clawfree trapdoor permutations (for simplicity) and the Cramer-Shoup encryption scheme [9] as CCA-secure public key encryption. The tests for the contractor implementation are executed on Apple M1 CPU 16 GB RAM. The tests for SC implementation are conducted on Truffle Ganache environment. For tests of the *MismatchCheck* protocol, we take two contractors one diligent and the other one lazy deviating at a step picked uniformly at random. Our tests our repeated 5 times averaged.

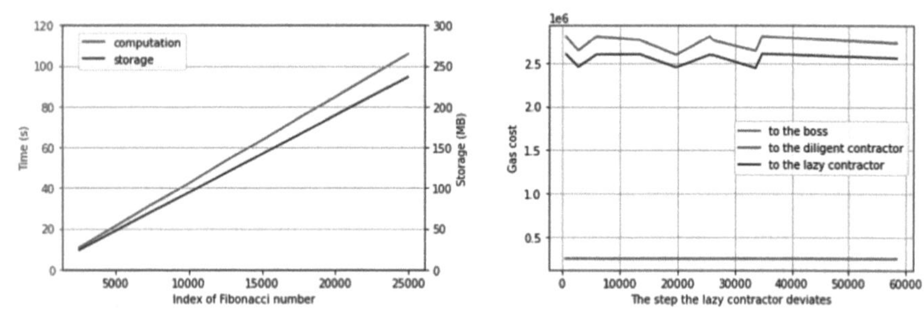

(a) Offline computation and storage costs to a contractor

(b) Gas costs to the boss and the diligent and the lazy contractors

Fig. 1. The costs of our protocol (excluding the response submission protocol). The costs in 1a are w.r.t. index of the Fibonacci number to be computed. The costs in 1b are w.r.t the deviating step of the lazy contractor.

Our results include the cost of computation of a function f (we exemplify as $f(x) := [x^{th}$ Fibonacci number found by brute force]) together with the construction of the Merkle tree hash z and executing *MismatchCheck* protocol. These costs include the offline computation cost of a contractor, and, *only in the case of existence of a lazy contractor*, the online gas costs to a diligent contractor, a lazy contractor, and the SC (i.e., the boss). We stress that online gas costs will be only incurred if there exists a lazy contractor, who will be the payer of those costs as a fine (but if all participants are rational, they will all be diligent anyways). Figure 1 shows our results. Our costs do not include the costs of the

UC response submission protocol, which is highly dependent on the commitment scheme used.

Limitations: We acknowledge that our performance evaluation is simplistic, and a full implementation including UC commitments with a more realistic workload would strengthen the contribution. Such further experiments should also highlight the impact of irrational contractors in the system, which is currently outside our system model. Secondly, while our solution addresses Sybils since they can be thought as a form of a coalition, it does not take into account the case where all contractors picked for a particular job consist of Sybils. Finally, [40] released a tool for automatically analyzing ℓ-repellence. We leave its usage as potential future work.

References

1. Afanasev, M.Y., Fedosov, Y.V., Krylova, A.A., Shorokhov, S.A.: An application of blockchain and smart contracts for machine-to-machine communications in cyber-physical production systems. In: IEEE ICPS (2018)
2. Avizheh, S., Nabi, M., Safavi-Naini, R., Venkateswarlu, K., M.: Verifiable computation using smart contracts. In: ACM CCSW (2019)
3. Avizheh, S., Nabi, M., Safavi-Naini, R.: Refereed delegation of computation using smart contracts. In: IEEE TDSC (2024)
4. Belenkiy, M., Chase, M., Erway, C.C., Jannotti, J., Küpçü, A., Lysyanskaya, A.: Incentivizing outsourced computation. In: NetEcon (2008)
5. Biçer, O., Yıldız, B., Küpçü, A.: m-stability: Threshold security meets transferable utility. In: ACM CCSW (2021)
6. Bitansky, N., Lin, H.: One-message zero knowledge and non-malleable commitments. In: TCC. (2018)
7. Biçer, O., Küpçü, A.: Delegate: Coalition Proof Incentivized Outsourced Computation with Smart Contracts. IACR Cryptol. ePrint Archive **2026/658** (2026)
8. Buterin, V.: Ethereum white paper: A next-generation smart contract and decentralized application platform (2013)
9. Camenisch, J., Stadler, M.: Efficient group signature schemes for large groups. CRYPTO (1997)
10. Canetti, R.: Universally composable security: A new paradigm for cryptographic protocols. In: IEEE FOCS (2001)
11. Canetti, R., Fischlin, M.: Universally composable commitments. CRYPTO. (2001)
12. Canetti, R., Riva, B., Rothblum, G.N.: Practical delegation of computation using multiple servers. In: ACM CCS (2011)
13. Cheng, R., et al.: Ekiden: A platform for confidentiality-preserving, trustworthy, and performant smart contracts. In: EuroS&P (2019)
14. Cook, S.A., Reckhow, R.A.: Time bounded random access machines. J. Comput. Syst. Sci. **7**(4), 354–375 (1973)
15. Damgård, I., Groth, J.: Non-interactive and reusable non-malleable commitment schemes. In: ACM STOC (2003)
16. Crescenzo, D., Ishai, G., Ostrovsky, Y., R.: Non-interactive and non-malleable commitment. In: ACM STOC (1998)
17. Dolev, D., Dwork, C., Naor, M.: Non-malleable cryptography. In: ACM STOC (1991)

18. Dong, B., Wang, H., Monreale, A., Pedreschi, D., Giannotti, F., Guo, W.: Authenticated outlier mining for outsourced databases. IEEE TDSC **17**(2), 222–235 (2020)
19. Dong, C., Wang, Y., Aldweesh, A., McCorry, P., van Moorsel, A.: Betrayal, distrust, and rationality: Smart counter-collusion contracts for verifiable cloud computing. In: ACM CCS (2017)
20. Douceur, J.R.: The sybil attack. IPTPS (2002)
21. Fischlin, M., Libert, B., Manulis, M.: Non-interactive and Re-usable Universally Composable String Commitments with Adaptive Security. In: Lee, D.H., Wang, X. (eds.) ASIACRYPT 2011. LNCS, vol. 7073, pp. 468–485. Springer, Heidelberg (2011). https://doi.org/10.1007/978-3-642-25385-0_25
22. Fujisaki, E.: All-But-Many Encryption. In: Sarkar, P., Iwata, T. (eds.) ASIACRYPT 2014. LNCS, vol. 8874, pp. 426–447. Springer, Heidelberg (2014). https://doi.org/10.1007/978-3-662-45608-8_23
23. Fujisaki, E.: Improving practical uc-secure commitments based on the ddh assumption. SCN (2016)
24. Gennaro, R., Gentry, C., Parno, B.: Non-interactive Verifiable Computing: Outsourcing Computation to Untrusted Workers. In: Rabin, T. (ed.) CRYPTO 2010. LNCS, vol. 6223, pp. 465–482. Springer, Heidelberg (2010). https://doi.org/10.1007/978-3-642-14623-7_25
25. Goldwasser, S., Kalai, Y.T., Rothblum, G.N.: Delegating computation: Interactive proofs for muggles. J. ACM **62**(4) (2015)
26. Jiang, X., Tian, Y.: How to construct rational protocols with nash equilibrium consistency in the uc framework. Cryptology ePrint Archive, Report 2019/1398 (2019)
27. Kamara, S., Küpçü, A.: DogFish: Decentralized Optimistic Game-theoretic FIle SHaring. In: Preneel, B., Vercauteren, F. (eds.) ACNS 2018. LNCS, vol. 10892, pp. 696–714. Springer, Cham (2018). https://doi.org/10.1007/978-3-319-93387-0_36
28. Khurana, D., Sahai, A.: How to achieve non-malleability in one or two rounds. In: IEEE FOCS (2017)
29. Kothapalli, A., Miller, A., Borisov, N.: Smartcast: An incentive compatible consensus protocol using smart contracts. FC (2017)
30. Küpçü, A.: Incentivized outsourced computation resistant to malicious contractors. IEEE TDSC **14**(6) (2017)
31. Küpçü, A., Safavi-Naini, R.: Smart contracts for incentivized outsourcing of computation. In: ESORICS CBT (2021)
32. Lin, H., Pass, R., Soni, P.: Two-round and non-interactive concurrent non-malleable commitments from time-lock puzzles. In: IEEE FOCS (2017)
33. Lin, H., Pass, R., Venkitasubramaniam, M.: A unified framework for concurrent security: Universal composability from stand-alone non-malleability. In: ACM STOC (2009)
34. Parno, B., Raykova, M., Vaikuntanathan, V.: How to delegate and verify in public: Verifiable computation from attribute-based encryption. TCC (2012)
35. Peters, H.: Cooperative games with transferable utility. In: Game Theory: A Multi-Leveled Approach. Springer, Cham (2008). https://doi.org/10.1007/978-3-540-69291-1_6
36. Premnath, S.N., Haas, Z.J.: Security and privacy in the internet-of-things under time-and-budget-limited adversary model. IEEE Wireless Commun. Lett. **4**(3) (2015)
37. Sadeghi, A.R., Schneider, T., Winandy, M.: Token-based cloud computing. TRUST (2010)

38. Susilo, W., Guo, F., Zhao, Z., Jiang, Y., Ge, C.: Secure replication-based outsourced computation using smart contracts. IEEE Trans. Serv. Comput. **16**(05), 3711–3722 (2023)
39. Tang, W., et al.: Game-theoretic incentive mechanism for blockchain-based federated learning. IEEE Trans. Mob. Comput. (2025)
40. Taweel, A., Yıldız, B., Küpçü, A.: Gamu blue: A practical tool for game theory security equilibria. In: IEEE/IFIP NOMS Mini Conference (2024)
41. Thaler, J., Roberts, M., Mitzenmacher, M., Pfister, H.: Verifiable computation with massively parallel interactive proofs. In: USENIX HotCloud (2012)
42. Xiao, Y., Zhang, N., Li, J., Lou, W., Hou, Y.T.: Privacyguard: Enforcing private data usage control with blockchain and attested off-chain contract execution. In: ESORICS (2020)

Secure and Privacy-Preserving Federated Learning

DOOR: Dynamic Orthogonal Obfuscation for Secure and Collusion-Resistant Federated Learning Aggregation

Cangming Liang[1,2], Yinchuan Cong[3(✉)], Yuxiang Chen[1,2], Kan Yang[4], Sisi Zhou[1,2], Zulong Diao[1,2], Wei Liang[5], Kuanching Li[1,2(✉)], Francesco Palmieri[6], and Tianxiong Liu[7(✉)]

[1] School of Computer Science and Engineering, Hunan University of Science and Technology, Xiangtan, Hunan 411201, China
{cmliang,sisizhou}@mail.hnust.edu.cn, {chenyuxiang,diaozulong,aliric}@hnust.edu.cn

[2] Hunan Engineering Research Center of Software Design and Services of Intelligent Connected Vehicles, Xiangtan 411201, China

[3] College of Computer Science and Electronic Engineering, Hunan University, Changsha 410082, China
congyinchuan2020@hnu.edu.cn

[4] Aerospace Information Research Institute, Chinese Academy of Sciences, Beijing 100094, China
yangkan@aircas.ac.cn

[5] School of Computing/Software, University of South China, Hengyang 421001, China
2025001208@usc.edu.cn

[6] Dipartimento di Informatica, Università degli Studi di Salerno, Salerno, Italy
fpalmieri@unisa.it

[7] Research and teaching department, Hunan Aerospace Hospital, The Affiliated Aerospace Hospital of Hunan Normal University, Changsha, China
liutianxiong@gt.cn

Abstract. Federated Learning (FL) enables collaborative model training without centralizing data, yet shared model updates remain vulnerable to privacy attacks, particularly white-box membership inference. This risk escalates when malicious servers collude with compromised clients. Existing defenses—such as differential privacy or cryptographic techniques—often incur prohibitive utility loss or computational overhead, while lighter-weight methods typically fail against colluding adversaries. This work introduces DOOR, a lightweight, client-side obfuscation framework that protects model updates via dynamic orthogonal transformations. Each client applies a unique, round-specific orthogonal matrix to its local update before uploading, rendering the update indecipherable to external observers while preserving the mathematical structure required for effective aggregation. We prove theoretically that DOOR maintains FedAvg convergence and provides strong privacy guarantees against both individual and colluding attackers. Implemented on the Plato FL platform, DOOR reduces membership inference success rates

Y. Cao et al. (Eds.): SecureComm 2026, LNICST 704, pp. 221–238, 2027.
https://doi.org/10.1007/978-3-032-32764-2_11

to near-random levels—even under strong collusion—with no significant drop in accuracy relative to vanilla FedAvg. Experiments on standard benchmarks confirm that DOOR introduces minimal computational and communication overhead, offering a practical and deployable solution for privacy-preserving federated learning.

Keywords: Federated Learning · Membership Privacy · Orthogonal Obfuscation · Collusion Resistance

1 Introduction

Federated Learning (FL) enables collaborative model training across distributed clients without centralizing raw data, thereby aligning with privacy-by-design principles [1,2]. However, the shared model updates remain vulnerable to privacy attacks. In particular, white-box adversaries—such as a curious server or compromised clients—can exploit these updates to infer sensitive information about participants' training data through membership inference attacks (MIAs) [3].

This threat is especially pronounced in realistic FL deployments where the server may be semi-trusted or even adversarial, and multiple clients can collude to reconstruct a victim's update [4]. While some defenses assume the presence of a non-colluding privacy guardian, such assumptions rarely hold in open or cross-organizational settings. Moreover, in practical systems used by large-scale platforms, raw gradients are often not exposed due to optimizer state encapsulation [5]. This limits the feasibility of gradient-based reconstruction attacks but also renders many existing defenses ineffective.

Current approaches to mitigate these risks fall into three main categories. Differential privacy (DP) [6] provides rigorous theoretical guarantees but typically incurs significant utility loss, especially under tight privacy budgets or non-IID data distributions. Cryptographic techniques, including homomorphic encryption and secure multi-party computation, offer strong security yet introduce prohibitive computational and communication overhead, hindering scalability in cloud-edge scenarios [7]. Lightweight alternatives, such as GPVO-FL [8], rely on trusted components that contradict the zero-trust assumption inherent in open federations.

Generalization-based methods, such as MemberShield [9], mitigate overfitting by employing self-distillation and soft labeling, thereby reducing the impact of MIAs. However, they assume non-colluding adversaries and offer limited protection when the server coordinates with malicious clients. Similarly, frameworks such as SAEV-FL [10] improve efficiency in edge environments but remain vulnerable under collusion.

To address these limitations, we propose a Dynamic Orthogonal Obfuscation framework for secure and collusion-resistant FL aggregation, namely DOOR, by applying client-specific, round-dependent orthogonal transformations to local model updates before transmission. This obfuscation preserves the mathematical structure required for effective FedAvg aggregation while rendering individual updates indistinguishable to external observers. Our key contributions are:

- To propose a client-side obfuscation mechanism that protects against white-box MIAs and collusion without requiring trusted third parties or modifying server logic. It adds only a small seed to the communication per round.
- To provide theoretical analysis showing that DOOR maintains FedAvg convergence due to the norm-preserving nature of orthogonal transformations, and establish formal privacy guarantees against both individual and colluding adversaries.
- To implement DOOR on the Plato FL platform and evaluate it on standard benchmarks. Results show near-random MIA success rates—even under strong collusion—with negligible accuracy degradation and minimal overhead compared to vanilla FedAvg.

2 Related Work

Federated learning has gained widespread attention for enabling collaborative training without data centralization. Nevertheless, model updates exchanged during training can leak sensitive information about participants' private datasets. Membership inference attacks (MIAs) represent one of the most practical threats, allowing an adversary to determine whether a specific sample was used in training by analyzing model behavior [11]. The adversary typically trains shadow models that mimic the target's architecture and data distribution, then learns to distinguish members from non-members based on output properties such as confidence, loss, or entropy [12]. In FL, such attacks become more effective when the server is semi-trusted or when multiple clients collude to jointly infer a target client's update [4]. A global adversary, such as the FL server, can perform client-level membership inference by determining both whether a sample was used in training and which client contributed it. This capability renders global adversaries strictly stronger than those limited to attacking the aggregated global model [13].

Differential Privacy (DP) is a widely adopted defense that bounds individual influence by adding calibrated noise to updates [6]. Although DP offers strong theoretical guarantees, it often leads to substantial utility degradation, particularly in cross-silo settings with few participants or under non-IID data distributions [14]. Moreover, practical DP deployments often use relaxed privacy budgets (*e.g.*, $\epsilon > 2$) to maintain utility. However, such settings provide only weak protection against MIAs, as shown by empirical evaluations across multiple benchmarks [15].

Cryptographic approaches, such as secure aggregation (SecAgg) [16], homomorphic encryption, and secure multi-party computation, aim to hide individual contributions during aggregation. While these methods prevent the server from observing raw updates, they do not inherently protect against MIAs on the aggregated model. Furthermore, their computational and communication costs scale poorly with model size and client count, limiting applicability in large-scale or resource-constrained environments [7].

Another line of research focuses on improving model generalization to reduce overfitting—the primary enabler of MIAs. Techniques such as label smoothing, early stopping, and self-distillation have been shown to mitigate membership leakage without introducing noise [17]. For instance, MemberShield [9] uses knowledge distillation and soft labels to produce less informative updates. However, these methods assume non-colluding adversaries and offer limited resilience when the server collaborates with compromised clients—a common scenario in open federations. Importantly, minimizing the generalization gap alone is insufficient for privacy: while early work linked membership advantage directly to overfitting [18], subsequent studies showed that models with low generalization error can still leak membership information through subtle statistical differences in their outputs. While Song and Mittal *et al.* [19] first established that low generalization error does not guarantee privacy in centralized learning, subsequent work has confirmed this vulnerability persists in federated settings: well-generalizing global models remain susceptible to client-level membership inference.

Knowledge transferbased defenses attempt to decouple private training from public model sharing by leveraging auxiliary public data [15]. Yet, high-quality public data is often unavailable or distributionally mismatched in sensitive domains, such as healthcare or finance, which restricts its practicality. Their FL adaptations suffer from underfitting when client datasets are small and heterogeneous.

Recent efforts have started to explicitly address collusion. CaPC [4] introduces a semi-honest third party to mediate aggregation, but this reliance on trusted intermediaries conflicts with the decentralized ethos of FL. Other works evaluate privacy under multi-client attacks but focus on gradient reconstruction rather than membership inference in realistic settings where only model deltas—not raw gradients—are shared [5]. To date, no lightweight method has simultaneously achieved strong privacy against colluding adversaries, preserved model utility, and avoided the need for trusted infrastructure.

In contrast, DOOR resolves these challenges through dynamic orthogonal obfuscation. It operates entirely on the client side, incurs no utility loss from added noise, introduces negligible overhead, and remains effective even when the server colludes with multiple clients. By preserving the norm and inner-product structure of updates, DOOR ensures compatibility with standard FedAvg while rendering individual contributions indistinguishable. This design directly addresses the privacyutilityefficiency trilemma that plagues prior approaches.

3 Methodology

3.1 System Model and Problem Formulation

We consider a federated learning (FL) system consisting of a central server $\mathcal{S}$ and K distributed clients $\{\mathcal{C}_1, \mathcal{C}_2, \dots, \mathcal{C}_K\}$. Each client $\mathcal{C}_k$ holds a private dataset $\mathcal{D}_k = \{(x_i, y_i)\}_{i=1}^{n_k}$ with $n_k = |\mathcal{D}_k|$ samples. The global objective is to learn model parameters $\omega \in \mathbb{R}^d$ that minimize:

$$\min_{\omega} F(\omega) = \sum_{k=1}^{K} \frac{n_k}{N} F_k(\omega) \tag{1}$$

where $N = \sum_{k=1}^{K} n_k$ is the total sample count, and $F_k(\omega)$ is the local objective with loss function $\ell(\cdot)$.

The standard FedAvg algorithm operates iteratively. In each round t:

1. Server $\mathcal{S}$ broadcasts global model ω^t to selected clients.
2. Each client $\mathcal{C}_k$ computes local update $\Delta\omega_k^t$ via Stochastic Gradient Descent (SGD).
3. Server aggregates updates: $\omega^{t+1} = \omega^t + \eta \sum_{k=1}^{K} \frac{n_k}{N} \Delta\omega_k^t$.

Despite the "data never leaves its source" principle, model updates $\Delta\omega_k^t$ leak information about training data. We consider two adversary models:

- **Honest-but-curious server** $\mathcal{A}_s$: Follows protocol but attempts to infer private information from received updates, including membership inference attacks.
- **Colluding clients** $\mathcal{A}_c$: Malicious clients collaborate to breach target clients' privacy by pooling observations.

Membership inference attacks exploit statistical differences in model behavior between training and non-training samples. In FL, adversaries can observe multiple update rounds, thereby enhancing the effectiveness of their attacks. Non-IID data distributions further amplify privacy risks by increasing the distinguishability of individual contributions.

Existing defenses face critical limitations: differential privacy severely degrades utility, cryptographic methods incur prohibitive overhead, knowledge distillation requires external datasets, and adversarial regularization lacks generalization.

This reveals the fundamental privacy-utility-efficiency trilemma. We aim to design a transformation mechanism $\mathcal{T}$ that converts raw updates $\Delta\omega_k^t$ to protected versions $\widehat{\Delta\omega_k^t}$ satisfying the following four criteria:

1. **Privacy**: The obfuscated update should prevent successful membership inference, i.e.,

$$\left| \Pr[\mathcal{A}(\widehat{\Delta\omega_k^t}) = \text{Member}] - \frac{1}{2} \right| \leq \epsilon_{\text{priv}}, \tag{2}$$

where $\mathcal{A}$ denotes an adversary, and ϵ_{priv} is a small privacy budget that quantifies the maximum allowable advantage over random guessing.

2. **Utility**: The global model accuracy should be preserved, i.e.,

$$|\text{Acc}_{\text{raw}} - \text{Acc}_{\text{prot}}| \leq \epsilon_{\text{util}}, \tag{3}$$

where Acc_{raw} and Acc_{prot} represent the test accuracies of the global models trained with raw (unprotected) and protected updates, respectively, and ϵ_{util} is a small utility tolerance.

3. **Efficiency**: The computational or communication overhead should scale sublinearly with respect to the base method, i.e.,

$$\frac{O_{\text{prot}}}{O_{\text{base}}} \leq 1 + \delta, \tag{4}$$

where O_{prot} and O_{base} denote the overhead (e.g., time or bandwidth) of the protected (DOOR) and base (vanilla FedAvg) methods, respectively, and δ is a small positive constant.
4. **Convergence**: The framework must preserve the convergence guarantees of the standard FedAvg algorithm.

This formulation captures the core challenges in privacy-preserving FL and establishes evaluation criteria for our solution.

3.2 Overview of the DOOR Framework

The DOOR framework introduces a novel approach to privacy-preserving federated learning through dynamic orthogonal obfuscation of model updates. Unlike traditional methods that add noise or employ heavy cryptography, DOOR leverages carefully constructed orthogonal transformations that preserve the mathematical properties needed for effective model aggregation while rendering individual updates indecipherable to adversaries.

DOOR operates as a lightweight middleware seamlessly integrated into standard FL workflows. As shown in Algorithm 1 and Fig. 1, each training round proceeds as follows: First, the server generates a fresh random seed s^t and broadcasts it along with the current global model ω^t to participating clients. This seed ensures synchronization while providing the necessary entropy for generating deterministic yet unpredictable transformations. Each client then performs local training and obtains weight updates $\Delta\omega_k^t$. Before transmission, clients apply client-specific orthogonal transformations to their updates using the DOOR-OBFUSCATE procedure, which generates unique orthogonal matrices based on the client ID k, round t, and server seed s^t. The server aggregates these obfuscated updates directly without any decryption, as the transformations preserve the linear relationships essential for federated averaging.

The framework's security is based on three synergistic design principles. First, *deterministic yet unpredictable matrix generation* ensures each client produces consistent orthogonal transformations using only lightweight cryptographic hashing, eliminating the need to transmit bulky matrix data. Second, *architecture-aware selective obfuscation* applies transformations only to fully-connected and convolutional layers—parameters most revealing of training data characteristics—minimizing computational overhead. Third, *mathematically sound secure aggregation* exploits the group properties of orthogonal matrices, ensuring that aggregation of transformed updates yields meaningful global improvements while individual contributions remain protected.

DOOR's practical advantages are substantial. It introduces minimal communication overhead (only 32-byte seeds per round), requires no changes to core

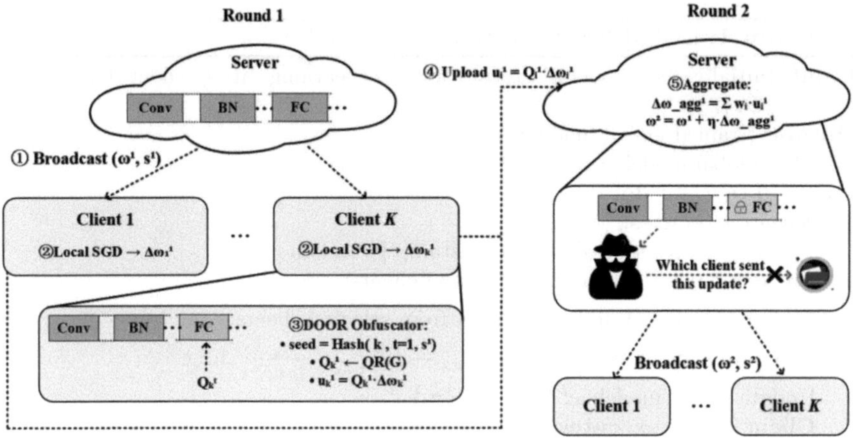

Fig. 1. The DOOR framework.

optimization algorithms, and maintains compatibility with existing FL infrastructures. The client-side obfuscation adds a fixed computational cost independent of dataset size, making it suitable for resource-constrained edge devices. These characteristics position DOOR as a viable solution for real-world deployment where privacy, utility, and efficiency must be balanced.

3.3 Dynamic Orthogonal Obfuscation

The dynamic orthogonal obfuscation mechanism forms the mathematical core of the DOOR framework, providing strong privacy guarantees while preserving the convergence properties of federated learning. This approach leverages the geometric properties of orthogonal transformations to protect individual model updates without disrupting the global aggregation process.

We refer to this orthogonal transformation as orthogonal obfuscation. Unlike noise-based perturbations (e.g., Gaussian noise), which distort update magnitudes and directions, orthogonal obfuscation preserves the geometric structure of updates—including norms and inner products—while effectively hiding sensitive information through random rotation.

Mathematical Foundation and Security Analysis. An orthogonal matrix $\mathbf{Q} \in \mathbb{R}^{d\times d}$ satisfies the fundamental property $\mathbf{Q}^\top\mathbf{Q} = \mathbf{Q}\mathbf{Q}^\top = \mathbf{I}_d$, where $\mathbf{I}_d$ denotes the $d \times d$ identity matrix. This orthogonality condition ensures two crucial properties for federated learning: (1) preservation of Euclidean norms $\|\mathbf{Q}\mathbf{v}\|_2 = \|\mathbf{v}\|_2$, and (2) preservation of inner products $\langle \mathbf{Q}\mathbf{v}, \mathbf{Q}\mathbf{w}\rangle = \langle \mathbf{v}, \mathbf{w}\rangle$. These properties allow DOOR to maintain gradient directions while altering coordinate representations in a mathematically controlled manner.

Algorithm 1: DOOR Federated Learning Workflow

Input: Initial global model ω^0, total rounds T, learning rate η, client datasets $\{\mathcal{D}_k\}_{k=1}^K$
Output: Trained global model ω^T
Initialize global model ω^0;
for $t \leftarrow 0$ **to** $T-1$ **do**
  Server executes:;
  Generate server seed $s^t \leftarrow \mathcal{H}(\text{timestamp} \,\|\, \text{random} \,\|\, t)$;
  Broadcast (ω^t, s^t) to all participating clients;
  Collect obfuscated updates $\{\widehat{\Delta\omega}_k^t\}$ from selected clients;
  Compute aggregated update: $\Delta\omega_{\text{agg}}^t \leftarrow \sum_{k\in S_t} \frac{n_k}{\sum_{j\in S_t} n_j} \widehat{\Delta\omega}_k^t$;
  Update global model: $\omega^{t+1} \leftarrow \omega^t + \eta\Delta\omega_{\text{agg}}^t$;
  Client $k \in S_t$ **executes:**;
  Receive (ω^t, s^t) from server;
  Compute local update via SGD: $\Delta\omega_k^t \leftarrow \text{SGD}(\omega^t, \mathcal{D}_k)$;
  Apply DOOR obfuscation: $\widehat{\Delta\omega}_k^t \leftarrow \text{DOOR-Obfuscate}(\Delta\omega_k^t, k, t, s^t)$;
  Send $\widehat{\Delta\omega}_k^t$ to server;
return ω^T;

Consider client k's model update $\Delta\omega_k^t \in \mathbb{R}^d$. DOOR applies an orthogonal transformation to produce the obfuscated update:

$$\widehat{\Delta\omega}_k^t = \mathbf{Q}_k^t \Delta\omega_k^t \tag{5}$$

The security of this approach stems from the rotational invariance of orthogonal transformations. To any observer without knowledge of $\mathbf{Q}_k^t$, the transformed vector $\widehat{\Delta\omega}_k^t$ appears as a random rotation in the high-dimensional parameter space, making it statistically indistinguishable from other random vectors with the same norm. This obfuscation provides strong privacy protection against membership inference attacks, as the original update direction—which encodes information about the training data—is completely hidden by the random rotation.

Crucially, when multiple clients' transformed updates are aggregated via federated averaging, the orthogonality ensures mathematical coherence. Let $\mathbf{Q}_k^t$ denote the orthogonal matrix for client k at round t, and let $\Delta\omega_k^t$ be the true local update. The server receives $\widehat{\Delta\omega}_k^t = \mathbf{Q}_k^t \Delta\omega_k^t$ and computes the weighted average over participating clients S_t:

$$\overline{\widehat{\Delta\omega}}^t = \sum_{k\in S_t} \frac{n_k}{\sum_{j\in S_t} n_j} \widehat{\Delta\omega}_k^t = \sum_{k\in S_t} \frac{n_k}{\sum_{j\in S_t} n_j} \mathbf{Q}_k^t \Delta\omega_k^t \tag{6}$$

Under the assumption that $\mathbf{Q}_k^t$ are drawn uniformly from the orthogonal group $\mathcal{O}(d)$, the expected value of the aggregated update is zero, indicating complete directional obfuscation:

$$\mathbb{E}_{\mathbf{Q}_k^t \sim \mathcal{O}(d)} \left[\widehat{\Delta\omega}^t \right] = \mathbf{0} \tag{7}$$

However, the norm relationships essential for gradient descent are preserved:

$$\mathbb{E}_{\mathbf{Q}_k^t \sim \mathcal{O}(d)} \left[\|\widehat{\Delta\omega}^t\|^2 \right] = \sum_{k \in S_t} \left(\frac{n_k}{\sum_{j \in S_t} n_j} \right)^2 \|\Delta\omega_k^t\|^2 \tag{8}$$

This delicate balance between obfuscation and preservation forms the mathematical foundation of DOOR's privacy guarantees. The security properties can be formally stated: for any polynomial-time adversary $\mathcal{A}$ attempting to distinguish $\widehat{\Delta\omega}_k^t$ from a random vector with the same norm, the distinguishing advantage is negligible in the security parameter, assuming the underlying cryptographic hash function is secure, and the server seed contains sufficient entropy. The client-specific nature of matrices prevents colluding parties from establishing correlations between updates, while the dynamic rotation per round thwarts temporal analysis attacks.

Deterministic Orthogonal Matrix Generation. The practical implementation of orthogonal obfuscation necessitates a method for generating high-dimensional orthogonal matrices that are both deterministic (for reproducibility) and unpredictable (for security). DOOR achieves this through a cryptographically secure pipeline that transforms minimal shared information into full-rank orthogonal transformations.

The generation process begins by constructing a unique identifier for each client, round, and layer combination. This identifier is formed by concatenating the client ID k, current round number t, the server-provided seed s^t, and a layer identifier ℓ. The resulting string $\text{input}_k^{t,\ell}$ serves as input to a cryptographic hash function (SHA-256 in our implementation). The hash output $\text{digest}_k^{t,\ell}$ provides a uniformly distributed 256-bit value, ensuring unpredictability.

From this hash digest, we extract the first 32 bits and convert them to an integer $\text{seed}_k^{t,\ell}$, which seeds a deterministic pseudo-random number generator. Using this seeded generator, we produce a $d \times d$ matrix $\mathbf{G}$ filled with independent standard normal random variables, where d corresponds to the output dimension of neural network layer ℓ.

The matrix $\mathbf{G}$ is then orthogonalized through QR decomposition, which factors it into the product of an orthogonal matrix $\mathbf{Q}$ and an upper triangular matrix $\mathbf{R}$. However, standard QR decomposition suffers from sign ambiguity: multiplying any column of $\mathbf{Q}$ by -1 and the corresponding row of $\mathbf{R}$ by -1 yields another valid decomposition. To ensure deterministic generation, we extract the sign pattern from the diagonal entries of $\mathbf{R}$ and construct a diagonal sign correction matrix $\mathbf{D}$. The final deterministic orthogonal matrix is computed as $\mathbf{Q}_k^{t,\ell} = \mathbf{QD}$.

This generation process ensures three key properties. First, given the same inputs, any client generates identical matrices, ensuring consistency in the obfuscation and de-obfuscation processes. Second, different inputs produce matrices that are statistically indistinguishable from random orthogonal matrices uniformly distributed over $\mathcal{O}(d)$. Third, the computational cost is dominated by the $O(d^3)$ QR decomposition, which is performed once per layer per round and amortized over the entire training process. For typical neural network layers with dimensions in the hundreds to low thousands, this overhead constitutes less than 5% of total training time.

Practical Implementation and Efficiency Considerations. The practical deployment of orthogonal matrix generation addresses several implementation concerns to ensure efficiency and scalability. For fully-connected layers with weight matrix $\mathbf{W} \in \mathbb{R}^{d_{\text{out}} \times d_{\text{in}}}$, the transformation is applied as $\widehat{\mathbf{W}} = \mathbf{QW}$, where $\mathbf{Q} \in \mathbb{R}^{d_{\text{out}} \times d_{\text{out}}}$ is generated as described. For convolutional layers with weight tensor $\mathcal{W} \in \mathbb{R}^{c_{\text{out}} \times c_{\text{in}} \times h \times w}$, the transformation is applied along the output channel dimension by reshaping the tensor into a matrix of dimensions $c_{\text{out}} \times (c_{\text{in}} \times h \times w)$, applying the orthogonal transformation, and then reshaping back to the original dimensions. Parameters such as biases and batch normalization statistics remain unchanged, as they are of much lower dimensionality and exhibit weaker correlation with individual input samples, making them significantly less sensitive to membership inference attacks; meanwhile, preserving them is essential for stable model convergence.

Memory efficiency is maintained through on-demand generation of orthogonal matrices. Rather than storing matrices for all layers across all rounds, clients regenerate them as needed from the compact seed information. This approach trades modest recomputation for significant memory savings, which is particularly important for edge devices with limited storage capacity. The matrices can be cached during each round to avoid redundant computation when applying transformations to multiple layers with the same dimensions.

Communication overhead is minimal, limited to the 32-byte server seed broadcast each round. This represents negligible additional bandwidth compared to transmitting model updates, which typically range from megabytes to gigabytes depending on model size. The selective application of transformations to fully-connected and convolutional layers—which contain the majority of parameters and are most vulnerable to privacy attacks—further optimizes performance without compromising security.

Numerical stability is ensured through the use of established linear algebra libraries. Our implementation leverages highly optimized LAPACK routines available through NumPy and PyTorch, which employ Householder reflections or Givens rotations for stable QR decomposition even for large matrices. The orthogonal matrices maintain their properties up to machine precision, ensuring that the mathematical guarantees hold in practical implementations.

These efficiency characteristics make DOOR suitable for real-world federated learning deployments with diverse resource constraints. The framework introduces minimal overhead while providing strong privacy guarantees, striking an effective balance between security and performance that addresses the fundamental privacy-utility-efficiency trilemma in federated learning.

4 Experimental Results

This section presents a comprehensive evaluation of DOOR's effectiveness in protecting federated learning against privacy attacks while maintaining model utility and efficiency. We address three key research questions: (1) How well does DOOR protect against membership inference and attribute inference attacks compared to state-of-the-art defenses? (2) What impact does DOOR have on global model accuracy? (3) What is the memory overhead introduced by DOOR's orthogonal transformation mechanism?

4.1 Experimental Setup

Datasets and Models. We evaluate DOOR on four standard image classification datasets: MNIST, Fashion-MNIST, CIFAR-10, and CIFAR-100. For the MNIST and Fashion-MNIST datasets, we utilize the LeNet-5 architecture. For CIFAR-10 and CIFAR-100, we use ResNet-18. All models are trained using cross-entropy loss with an SGD optimizer.

Federated Learning Configuration. We simulate a cross device FL environment with 100 clients, randomly selecting 10 participants per communication round. To emulate realistic non-IID data distributions, we partition each dataset using a Dirichlet distribution $\mathrm{Dir}(\alpha)$ with concentration parameter $\alpha = 0.3$. Each client trains locally with a batch size of 128. We conduct different numbers of communication rounds for different datasets: 50 rounds for MNIST and Fashion-MNIST, 150 rounds for CIFAR-10, and 200 rounds for CIFAR-100. The final results are averaged over 5 independent runs with different random seeds.

Baseline Methods. We compare DOOR against five representative defense approaches. *FedAvg* serves as the utility baseline, implementing standard federated averaging without any privacy protection. *Gaussian-Noise* adds i.i.d. Gaussian noise $\mathcal{N}(0, 0.01^2)$ to local model updates before transmission. *GC (Gradient Clipping)* [20] clips the norm of gradients to a threshold of 1.5. *DP-FedAvg* [6] implements differential privacy via the Gaussian mechanism with gradient clipping norm 1.0, noise multiplier 0.01, and approximate privacy budget $\epsilon \approx 2.0$. Finally, *MemberShield* [9] is a generalization-based defense that leverages self-distillation and soft labeling to reduce membership leakage.

Attack Methods. We evaluate privacy under two white-box threat models. First, we implement a *Membership Inference Attack (MIA)* following the shadow-model framework of Nasr *et al.* [3], where an adversary trains shadow models and binary classifiers to distinguish member from non-member samples. Second, we consider an *Attribute Inference Attack*, in which the adversary trains multi-class classifiers to infer sensitive attributes from model updates. For CIFAR-10 and CIFAR-100, these attributes correspond to semantic super-categories derived from class similarity.

Evaluation Metrics. We assess each method using four metrics: (1) *Global Model Accuracy*, measured as the test accuracy of the final aggregated model; (2) *Attack Accuracy*, defined as the success rate of the membership inference attack (lower is better); (3) *Attribute Inference Accuracy*, the success rate of attribute inference (lower is better); and (4) *Average Memory Usage*, reported in megabytes (MB) as the average per-client memory consumption during local training and obfuscation.

Implementation Details. All experiments are implemented using the Plato federated learning framework (v1.5) with PyTorch 2.5.0+cu124 and Torchvision 0.20.0+cu124, running on a server with Intel Xeon Gold 6330 CPU, 128 GB RAM, and NVIDIA RTX 4090 GPU. Memory usage is measured using Python's 'tracemalloc' module.

4.2 Comparison with State-of-the-Art Methods

Global Model Accuracy. Table 1 presents the global model accuracy across four datasets. DOOR maintains near-optimal model utility, with accuracy within 0.4–1.2% of unprotected FedAvg. This minimal utility loss is notably smaller than that of DP-FedAvg, which suffers a degradation of 3.0–6.7% due to noise addition. GC-FedAvg exhibits a more uniform but significant drop in accuracy across all datasets (3.3–7.6%). Gaussian-Noise shows moderate and consistent utility loss (0.9–3.2%), while MemberShield achieves competitive accuracy (within 0.7–2.1% of FedAvg) but offers weaker privacy protection, as discussed below.

Table 1. Global model accuracy comparison (higher is better). Values are percentages with 95% confidence intervals.

Method	MNIST	Fashion-MNIST	CIFAR-10	CIFAR-100
FedAvg	99.1 ± 0.1	88.5 ± 0.3	82.9 ± 0.3	55.3 ± 0.5
Gaussian-Noise	98.5 ± 0.2	87.2 ± 0.4	80.3 ± 0.4	52.1 ± 0.6
GC-FedAvg	95.8 ± 0.2	80.9 ± 0.3	81.7 ± 0.3	53.8 ± 0.5
DP-FedAvg	97.3 ± 0.3	85.4 ± 0.5	76.4 ± 0.5	48.6 ± 0.7
MemberShield	98.6 ± 0.2	87.8 ± 0.3	81.2 ± 0.4	53.2 ± 0.6
DOOR (Ours)	98.7 ± 0.1	88.2 ± 0.2	82.1 ± 0.3	54.9 ± 0.5

Membership Inference Attack Protection. Table 2 shows the success rates of membership inference attacks. DOOR reduces attack accuracy to near-random guessing levels (52.3–53.6%) across all datasets, representing substantial absolute reductions of 22.0–26.6% compared to the vulnerable FedAvg baseline. In contrast, DP-FedAvg provides moderate protection (61.5–65.2% attack accuracy) at a significant utility cost. MemberShield offers better protection than DP-FedAvg but still allows 58.1–61.7% attack accuracy, which is 5.8–8.4% higher than DOOR's results.

Table 2. Membership inference attack accuracy comparison (lower is better). Values are percentages with 95% confidence intervals.

Method	MNIST	Fashion-MNIST	CIFAR-10	CIFAR-100
FedAvg	83.4 ± 1.2	80.1 ± 1.4	76.8 ± 1.5	75.2 ± 1.6
Gaussian-Noise	72.6 ± 1.4	70.3 ± 1.5	70.1 ± 1.7	68.4 ± 1.7
GC-FedAvg	69.8 ± 1.3	67.5 ± 1.4	67.4 ± 1.6	65.9 ± 1.6
DP-FedAvg	65.2 ± 1.5	63.8 ± 1.6	62.9 ± 1.8	61.5 ± 1.8
MemberShield	61.7 ± 1.4	60.2 ± 1.5	59.3 ± 1.7	58.1 ± 1.7
DOOR (Ours)	52.3 ± 0.8	51.8 ± 0.9	53.6 ± 0.9	52.9 ± 1.0

Attribute Inference Attack Protection. Table 3 presents the results of attribute inference attacks on CIFAR-10 and CIFAR-100. DOOR achieves the lowest attack accuracy, with 50.9% on CIFAR-10 and 50.2% on CIFAR-100 (close to random guessing). This demonstrates DOOR's effectiveness in protecting sensitive attributes embedded in model updates. MemberShield also demonstrates strong performance on this metric; however, as shown in the MIA results, it is less effective against membership inference.

Table 3. Attribute inference attack accuracy comparison (lower is better). Values are percentages with 95% confidence intervals.

Method	CIFAR-10	CIFAR-100
FedAvg	68.3 ± 2.1	$65.4 \pm\pm 2.0$
Gaussian-Noise	62.5 ± 2.3	59.8 ± 2.2
GC-FedAvg	59.8 ± 2.2	57.2 ± 2.1
DP-FedAvg	55.7 ± 2.4	53.1 ± 2.3
MemberShield	52.6 ± 2.3	50.8 ± 2.2
DOOR (Ours)	50.9 ± 1.3	50.2 ± 1.2

Memory Overhead Analysis. Figure 2 provides a detailed comparison of the client peak memory usage across methods and datasets. As the baseline, FedAvg consumes between 85.3 MB (MNIST) and 100.1 MB (CIFAR-100). DOOR introduces minimal memory overhead, with usage ranging from 87.0 MB (MNIST) to 102.4 MB (CIFAR-10), representing an increase of only 1.9–2.3% over FedAvg. This efficiency stems from DOOR's lightweight on-demand matrix generation. In contrast, MemberShield exhibits the highest memory consumption across all datasets (168.7–205.5 MB), which is 97.8–105.2% higher than FedAvg, due to its additional buffers for self-distillation and soft labeling processes. DP-FedAvg also exhibits noticeable overhead (94.2–111.1 MB, 10.4–10.9% increase) due to the generation of noise buffers.

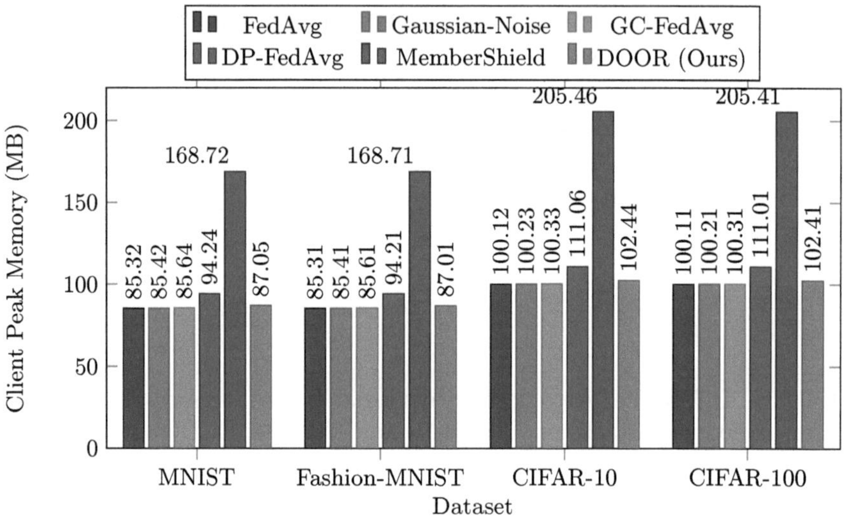

Fig. 2. Client peak memory usage (MB) of different methods across datasets.

Statistical Significance. The performance improvements of DOOR over baseline methods are clearly demonstrated in the experimental results. As shown in Tables 1, 2, and 3, DOOR consistently achieves the best privacy protection with minimal utility loss. The reported 95% confidence intervals provide a measure of statistical certainty for these results, and the non-overlapping intervals between DOOR and other methods indicate significant performance differences.

4.3 Ablation Study

We conduct comprehensive ablation studies to analyze the impact of DOOR's design choices across multiple datasets. Table 4 presents global accuracy results for four transformation strategies, while Table 5 shows membership inference attack accuracy, and Table 6 presents attribute inference attack accuracy.

Table 4. Ablation study: Global accuracy comparison across transformation strategies (higher is better). Values are percentages with 95% confidence intervals.

Variant	MNIST	Fashion-MNIST	CIFAR-10	CIFAR-100
Static (FC only)	98.9 ± 0.1	87.8 ± 0.3	81.8 ± 0.3	54.1 ± 0.5
Static (FC + Conv)	98.7 ± 0.2	87.5 ± 0.4	81.5 ± 0.4	53.8 ± 0.6
Dynamic (FC only)	98.7 ± 0.1	88.2 ± 0.2	82.1 ± 0.3	54.9 ± 0.5
Dynamic (FC + Conv)	98.5 ± 0.2	87.9 ± 0.3	81.9 ± 0.4	54.3 ± 0.6

Table 5. Ablation study: Membership inference attack accuracy comparison across transformation strategies (lower is better). Values are percentages with 95% confidence intervals.

Variant	MNIST	Fashion-MNIST	CIFAR-10	CIFAR-100
Static (FC only)	58.7 ± 1.1	57.3 ± 1.2	58.3 ± 1.1	57.9 ± 1.2
Static (FC + Conv)	56.9 ± 1.2	55.8 ± 1.3	56.7 ± 1.2	56.2 ± 1.3
Dynamic (FC only)	52.3 ± 0.8	51.8 ± 0.9	53.6 ± 0.9	52.9 ± 1.0
Dynamic (FC + Conv)	51.9 ± 0.9	51.4 ± 1.0	52.8 ± 0.8	52.3 ± 1.1

Dynamic vs Static Transformations. The ablation results clearly demonstrate the superiority of dynamic transformations. As shown in Tables 5 and 6, dynamic transformations consistently achieve lower attack accuracy across all datasets. For instance, on CIFAR-10, dynamic transformations reduce membership inference attack accuracy by 4.7–5.5% points and attribute inference accuracy by 3.9–4.3 percentage points compared to their static counterparts. This significant improvement underscores the effectiveness of round-specific transformations in preventing adversaries from learning patterns across multiple communication rounds.

Transformation Granularity. The comparison between applying transformations to fully connected (FC) layers only versus both FC and convolutional (Conv) layers reveals a trade-off. While the 'FC + Conv' variants consistently

Table 6. Ablation study: Attribute inference attack accuracy comparison across transformation strategies (lower is better). Values are percentages with 95% confidence intervals.

Variant	CIFAR-10	CIFAR-100
Static (FC only)	55.2 ± 1.3	54.1 ± 1.4
Static (FC + Conv)	53.8 ± 1.4	52.9 ± 1.5
Dynamic (FC only)	51.3 ± 1.2	50.7 ± 1.3
Dynamic (FC + Conv)	50.7 ± 1.1	50.3 ± 1.2

show marginally better privacy protection (lower attack accuracy in Tables 5 and 6), this comes with a slight, consistent drop in global model utility, as seen in Table 4. The 'FC only' configuration, particularly in its dynamic form, achieves an excellent balance, offering strong privacy guarantees (e.g., 53.6% MIA accuracy on CIFAR-10) while maintaining model accuracy very close to the unprotected baseline.

Consistency Across Datasets. The observed trends are remarkably consistent across the four datasets of varying complexity. Dynamic transformations outperform static ones in both privacy and utility metrics. The 'Dynamic (FC only)' configuration emerges as a robust and efficient choice, delivering reliable protection without compromising the primary task performance of the federated learning model.

Practical Implications. Based on the ablation study, the 'Dynamic (FC only)' configuration is recommended as the default setting for DOOR. It provides a compelling combination of strong privacy defense, minimal impact on model utility, and lower implementation complexity compared to transforming all layers. The consistent near-random guessing-level attack accuracy achieved by this configuration highlights its effectiveness as a practical privacy-preserving solution for federated learning.

5 Concluding Remarks and Future Work

In this work, we propose DOOR, a lightweight client-side obfuscation framework that leverages dynamic orthogonal transformations to protect model updates in federated learning. This effectively thwarts white-box membership and attribute inference attacks—even under strong collusion between the server and malicious clients—while preserving model utility and FedAvg convergence. Experimental results across multiple benchmarks demonstrate that DOOR reduces attack success rates to near-random levels with negligible accuracy loss and minimal computational and communication overhead.

The exploitation and deployment of the DOOR on resource-constrained edge platforms, where an extremely lightweight design is essential, have been successful, yielding notable achievements. While this direction remains in its early stages, analysis suggests that DOOR's on-demand matrix generation and selective layer obfuscation make it a promising candidate for such scenarios. As future work, we focus on further optimizing DOOR's runtime and memory footprint to meet the stringent requirements of real-time UAV-based federated learning systems.

We note that our privacy guarantee relies on the assumption that clients independently generate and securely retain their orthogonal matrices (derived from cryptographic seeds); a complete compromise of all client-side secrets would invalidate the obfuscation and expose raw updates.

Acknowledgement. This work is supported by the Joint Key Project of National Natural Science Foundation of China under Grant U2468205, the National Natural Science Foundation of China under Grants 62202156 and 62472168, the Hunan Provincial Key Research and Development Program under Grant 2024AQ2028, and the Natural Science Foundation of Hunan Province under Grants 2024JJ6220, 2025JJ50399, and 2025JJ90176, and the Major Project of Xiangjiang Laboratory under Grant 25XJ01002, and Postgraduate Scientific Research Innovation Project of Hunan Province under Grants CX20251545.

References

1. Zhou, S., Li, K., Chen, Y., Yang, C., Liang, W., Zomaya, A.Y.: TrustBCFL: mitigating data bias in IoT through blockchain-enabled federated learning. IEEE Internet Things J. **11**(15), 25648–25662 (2024). https://doi.org/10.1109/JIOT.2024.3379363
2. Xie, R., et al.: StarCPFL: star-centric personalized federated learning with layer-wised clustering. Fut. Gener. Comput. Syst **175**, 108037 (2025). https://doi.org/10.1016/j.future.2025.108037
3. Zhu, G., Li, D., Gu, H., Yao, Y., Fan, L., Han, Y.: FedMIA: an effective membership inference attack exploiting "all for one" principle in federated learning. In: Proceedings of the IEEE/CVF Conference on Computer Vision and Pattern Recognition (CVPR), pp. 20643–20653 (2025)
4. Choquette-Choo, C.A., et al.: CaPC Learning: confidential and private collaborative learning. arXiv preprint arXiv:2102.05188 (2021). https://arxiv.org/abs/2102.05188
5. Wang, F., Hugh, E., Li, B.: More than enough is too much: adaptive defenses against gradient leakage in production federated learning. IEEE/ACM Trans. Netw **32**(4), 3061–3075 (2024). https://doi.org/10.1109/TNET.2024.3377655
6. Geyer, R.C., Klein, T., Nabi, M.: Differentially private federated learning: a client level perspective. arXiv preprint arXiv:1712.07557 (2017). https://arxiv.org/abs/1712.07557
7. Zhang, S., Zhang, W., Liang, W., Li, K., Dobre, C.: Blockchain-based secure and verifiable storage scheme for IPFS-assisted IoT with homomorphic encryption. Computing **107**(7), 148 (2025). https://doi.org/10.1007/s00607-025-0148-y
8. Zhang, S., Ren, F., Liang, W., Li, K., Ling, N.: GPVO-FL: grouped privacy-preserving and verification-outsourced federated learning in cloud-edge collaborative environment. IEEE Trans. Netw. Serv. Manage. **22**(5), 4175–4191 (2025). https://doi.org/10.1109/TNSM.2025.11096921
9. Ahmed, F., Sanchez, D., Haddi, Z., Domingo-Ferrer, J.: MemberShield: a framework for federated learning with membership privacy. Neural Netw. **181**, 106768 (2025). https://doi.org/10.1016/j.neunet.2024.106768
10. Zhang, S., Ren, F., Liang, W., Li, K., Ling, N.: SAEV-FL: lightweight secure aggregation and efficient verification scheme for federated learning in cloud-edge collaborative environment. IEEE Trans. Intell. Veh. **1**(1), 1–17 (2025). https://doi.org/10.1109/TIV.2025.3599909
11. Bai, L., Hu, H., Ye, Q., Li, H., Wang, L., Xu, J.: Membership inference attacks and defenses in federated learning: a survey. ACM Comput. Surv. **57**(4), 1–35 (2024)

12. Carlini, N., Chien, S., Nasr, M., Song, S., Terzis, A., Tramer, F.: Membership inference attacks from first principles. In: 2022 IEEE Symposium on Security and Privacy (SP), pp. 1897–1914. IEEE (2022)
13. Shen, M., Meng, J., Xu, K., Yu, S., Zhu, L.: MemDefense: defending against membership inference attacks in IoT-based federated learning via pruning perturbations. IEEE Trans. Big Data **11**(5), 2135–2147 (2025). https://doi.org/10.1109/TBDATA.2024.3403388
14. Yuan, X., Ni, W., Ding, M., Wei, K., Li, J., Poor, H.V.: Amplitude-varying perturbation for balancing privacy and utility in federated learning. IEEE Trans. Inf. Forensics Secur. **18**, 1884–1897 (2023)
15. Gad, G., Gad, E., Fadlullah, Z.M., Fouda, M.M., Kato, N.: Communication-efficient and privacy-preserving federated learning via joint knowledge distillation and differential privacy in bandwidth-constrained networks. IEEE Trans. Veh. Technol. **73**(11), 17586–17601 (2024). https://doi.org/10.1109/TVT.2024.3423718
16. Buyukates, B., So, J., Mahdavifar, H., Avestimehr, S.: LightVeriFL: a lightweight and verifiable secure aggregation for federated learning. IEEE J. Sel. Areas Inf. Theor. **5**, 285–301 (2024)
17. Liu, G., Zhang, W., Wang, X., King, S., Yu, S.: A membership inference and adversarial attack defense framework for network traffic classifiers. IEEE Trans. Artif. Intell. **6**(2), 317–332 (2024)
18. Yeom, S., Giacomelli, I., Fredrikson, M., Jha, S.: Privacy risk in machine learning: analyzing the connection to overfitting. In: IEEE 31st Computer Security Foundations Symposium (CSF), pp. 268–282. IEEE (2018)
19. Song, L., Mittal, P.: Systematic evaluation of privacy risks of machine learning models. In: 30th USENIX Security Symposium (USENIX Security 21), pp. 2615–2632 (2021)
20. Xue, Y., Su, L., Lau, V.K.N.: FedOComp: two-timescale online gradient compression for over-the-air federated learning. IEEE Internet Things J. **9**(19), 19330–19345 (2022)

GroHFL: A Group Aggregation Method for Hierarchical Federated Learning Based on Data Distribution and Training Efficiency

Sisi Zhou[1], Xuanya Wang[1], Jiahong Xiao[1(✉)], Yuxiang Chen[1(✉)], Kan Yang[2], Cangming Liang[1], Wei Liang[3], Kuanching Li[1], Joanna Kołodziej[4], and Tianxiong Liu[5(✉)]

[1] The School of Computer Science and Engineering, Hunan University of Science and Technology, Xiangtan 411201, China
{sisizhou,wangxuanya,xiaoiaong,cmliang}@mail.hnust.edu.cn, {chenyuxiang,aliric}@hnust.edu.cn

[2] Aerospace Information Research Institute, Chinese Academy of Sciences, Beijing 100094, China
yangkan@aircas.ac.cn

[3] The School of Computer Science, University of South China, Hengyang 421001, China
2025001208@usc.edu.cn

[4] NASK Warsaw and Cracow University of Technology, Warsaw, Poland

[5] Research and Teaching Department, Hunan Aerospace Hospital, Changsha 410205, China
liutianxiong@gt.cn

Abstract. Hierarchical Federated Learning (HFL) effectively alleviates communication pressure on the central server, enhancing resource utilization and making it ideal for intelligent transportation and vehicular networks. In these networks, vehicles and traffic devices transmit large volumes of data; however, the distribution of this data across working nodes is often uneven, resulting in significant variability in computational capabilities and training efficiency. Potential bottlenecks can negatively affect the overall efficiency of model training. To address these challenges, this work introduces GroHFL, a group aggregation method for HFL based on data distribution and training efficiency. This method groups working nodes based on their data distribution and devices' training efficiency.

This work is supported by the Joint Key Project of National Natural Science Foundation of China under Grant U2468205, the National Natural Science Foundation of China under Grants 62202156 and 62472168, the Hunan Provincial Key Research and Development Program under Grant 2024AQ2028, the Natural Science Foundation of Hunan Province under Grants 2024JJ6220, 2025JJ50399, 2025JJ90176 and 2026JJ90204, the Major Project of Xiangjiang Laboratory under Grant 25XJ01002, the Guangdong Provincial Ordinary University Characteristic Innovation Project under Grant 2023WTSCX135, and the Postgraduate Scientific Research Innovation Project of Hunan Province under Grant CX20251515.

Y. Cao et al. (Eds.): SecureComm 2026, LNICST 704, pp. 239–254, 2027.
https://doi.org/10.1007/978-3-032-32764-2_12

Specifically, it clusters nodes with lower data distribution similarity and similar training efficiency, ensuring diversity and synchronization within each group. This strategy enhances training efficiency and effectively reduces delays caused by bottleneck nodes. Additionally, we employ synchronous aggregation within groups and asynchronous aggregation between groups, which helps mitigate overall training delays from slower groups. Experimental results indicate that our method effectively alleviates communication pressure, accelerates convergence, and improves model accuracy. Compared to existing classical federated learning methods, our approach improves model accuracy by 1.95% and 2.11% in the independent and identically distributed (IID) and non-independent and identically distributed (Non-IID) experimental groups, respectively. Additionally, the training time required to achieve the same level of accuracy is reduced by 62.48% and 64.48% in the IID and Non-IID experimental groups, respectively.

Keywords: Hierarchical Federated Learning · Group Aggregation · Synchronous Aggregation · Asynchronous Aggregation

1 Introduction

Federated Learning (FL) enables decentralized data storage and processing while preserving privacy through a distributed machine learning framework. It facilitates data sharing and collaboration among multiple parties, finding applications in privacy-sensitive fields such as intelligent healthcare [1], intelligent transportation [2], and mobile Internet of Things [3,4]. Personalized recommendation systems [5]. However, traditional federated learning relies on a centralized architecture that tasks a central server with generating or updating global model parameters. This creates significant communication pressure on the central node, resulting in performance bottlenecks and making it vulnerable to privacy breaches and attacks. Consequently, enhancing this architecture to mitigate these issues has become a key research focus.

To reduce communication overhead on the central server, Wu *et al.* [6] proposed incorporating edge computing into federated learning to create a hierarchical framework that alleviates communication pressure. Chen *et al.* [7]noted that this framework can flexibly adapt to diverse cross-domain collaborative scenarios. Nevertheless, Yang *et al.* [8] identified security risks associated with increased single points of failure in edge services and proposed a dual-layer filtering mechanism to enhance security. Despite this, challenges such as uneven data distribution across nodes and variable device training capabilities persist within the hierarchical framework. The challenges of hierarchical federated learning (HFL) are illustrated in Fig. 1.

To address the issue of uneven data distribution, a standard solution is to improve local training for clients [9], though this does not enhance the averaging effect of FL models. Another approach involves modifying the model aggregation methods on the server, such as using tensor filling for heterogeneous features [10],

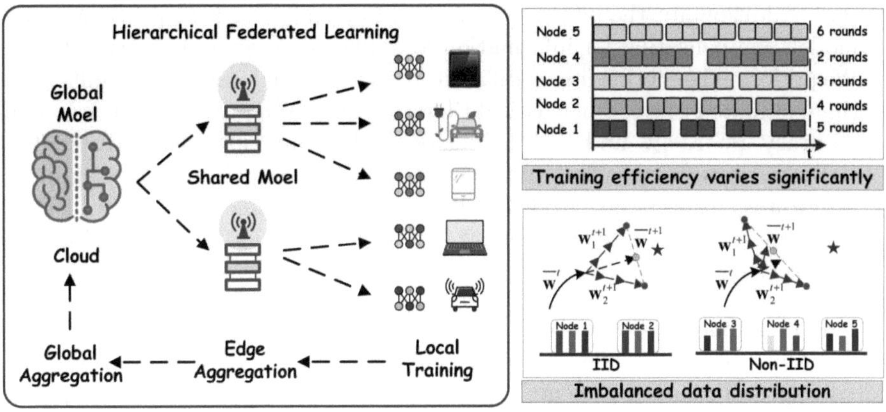

Fig. 1. The challenges of hierarchical federated learning.

normalizing local model updates [11], or introducing adaptive momentum [12]. However, these methods lack universality. Additionally, some approaches utilize diffusion models in conjunction with blockchain technology. While diffusion models effectively share local datasets to mitigate data distribution issues [13], they compromise the privacy protection feature of FL. On the other hand, blockchain-based methods [14] focus on the security and trustworthiness of the training process [15,16] but do not address communication efficiency and overhead [3,17,18]. Therefore, resolving the uneven data distribution among FL clients remains a critical research direction.

Moreover, most of the solutions mentioned above rely on synchronous FL, requiring all clients to complete local model training before updating the global model. Bottleneck clients can hinder the training efficiency of FL. Although existing studies [19,20] have proposed asynchronous FL to alleviate this issue, these solutions often rely on outdated models, which can negatively affect convergence. Therefore, improving model training efficiency, reducing communication overhead, and protecting data privacy are critical for the sustainable development of HFL.

Thus, this work focuses on the issues of uneven data distribution among working nodes and varied device training capabilities. We propose a grouping aggregation method for HFL based on data distribution and training efficiency. The main contributions of this work are as follows:

- To propose a grouping aggregation method based on local data distribution and device training efficiency, which enabled each group to learn more comprehensive features while reducing the broadcast of local data across the network.
- To design an aggregation approach that combined synchronous methods within groups and asynchronous methods between groups, effectively mitigating the impact of bottleneck clients on model convergence speed and accu-

racy. Additionally, the inter-group aggregation considered the previous global model, compensating for information loss due to uneven data distribution.
- We performed experiments on different models and datasets. The results show that compared to existing classical FL methods, our approach improves model accuracy by 1.95% and 2.11% in independent and identically distributed (IID) and non-independent and identically distributed (Non-IID) experimental groups, respectively. Additionally, the training time required to achieve the same accuracy is reduced by 62.48% and 64.48% in the IID and Non-IID groups, respectively.

The remainder of this work is organized as follows: Sect. 2 discusses related work, Sect. 3 introduces relevant background information, Sect. 4 details the proposed approach, Sect. 5 presents experimental results and analysis, and finally, concluding remarks and prospects for future research are presented in Sect. 6.

2 Related Work

2.1 Hierarchical Federated Learning

Hierarchical model aggregation can effectively alleviate communication pressure on the central server in FL, enhancing its flexibility. Liu *et al.* [21] proposed a client-edge-cloud HFL system, but they did not address the issue of uneven data distribution among distributed nodes. Luo *et al.* [22] introduced a HFL system with edge association; however, it primarily considered network bandwidth without accounting for the performance of the devices themselves. Liu *et al.* [23] optimized the distance of data distribution but focused mainly on resource allocation. To address data distribution imbalance, Duan *et al.* [24] proposed rearranging node training via intermediary nodes to balance the data skew of mobile nodes. Mhaisen *et al.* [25] suggested minimizing the distribution distance between edge nodes to mitigate accuracy degradation in FL caused by imbalanced data. However, research on HFL remains insufficient, particularly regarding studies that comprehensively consider both data distribution and device performance.

2.2 Communication Strategies in FL

Existing FL typically uses a synchronous aggregation method, where bottleneck nodes, such as those with slower processing speeds or lower computational capabilities, can lead to delays in the model synchronization process, causing other nodes to wait and resulting in a decrease in the overall throughput of the system. Additionally, when numerous clients upload gradient parameters simultaneously, it can cause communication bottlenecks. To ensure successful collaborative training despite partial node failures, Zheng *et al.* [26] proposed asynchronous communication using asynchronous gradient descent; however, delayed gradients can impact model accuracy. Jang *et al.* [27] incorporated pruning strategies into FL to effectively reduce communication overhead, but this affected model precision. Lu *et al.* [28] introduced an adaptive gradient compression algorithm to minimize privacy leakage risks, yet client training status remains unbalanced. Chen *et al.* [29] and Lu *et al.* [30] integrated blockchain technology to construct a decentralized asynchronous FL framework; however, the global model updates still rely on synchronous methods. Thus, research on asynchronous FL remains insufficient.

3 Preliminaries

FL training typically includes the following three steps:

1. local training,
2. model aggregation, and
3. global updating.

Assuming there are K worker nodes participating in the FL task, let the local dataset of the $k-th$ worker node be D_k with $n_k = |D_k|$ samples. Denote the local model of the $k-th$ worker node in the $t-th$ round as $\mathbf{w}_k^{(t)}$ and the global model as $\overline{\mathbf{w}}^{(t)}$. Then, the local objective function for the $k-th$ worker node is represented as:

$$F_k(\mathbf{w}) = \frac{1}{n_k^{(t)}} \sum_{\xi \in D_k^{(t)}} f\left(\mathbf{w}_k^{(t)}, \xi_k^{(t)}\right) \tag{1}$$

where, $f\left(\mathbf{w}_k^{(t)}, \xi_k^{(t)}\right)$ represents the loss function for a single sample $\xi_k^{(t)}$ and the local model $\mathbf{w}_k^{(t)}$. Typically, model training employs the gradient descent algorithm, and the update for the local model is given by:

$$\mathbf{w}_k^{(t)} = \mathbf{w}_k^{(t-1)} - \eta_k^{(t)} \frac{1}{\left|D_k^{(t)}\right|} \sum_{\xi \in D_k^{(t)}} \nabla f\left(\mathbf{w}_k^{(t)}, \xi_k^{(t)}\right), \tag{2}$$

where $\eta_k^{(t)}$ represents the learning rate for the local model iteration in the $t-th$ round. When using weighted averaging, the global model is given by:

$$\overline{\mathbf{w}}^{(t)} = \overline{\mathbf{w}}^{(t-1)} - \eta^{(t)} \sum \frac{1}{K} \mathbf{g}_k^{(t)} \left(\mathbf{w}_k^{(t)}, D_k^{(t)}\right), \tag{3}$$

where $g_k^{(t)}\left(\mathbf{w}_k^{(t)}, D_k^{(t)}\right)$ represents the local gradient for the $k-th$ worker node. $\eta^{(t)}$ represents the global learning rate.

Hierarchical model aggregation extends from single-layer federated learning. GroHFL considers grouping worker nodes for training and group aggregation to accelerate the training process. It primarily includes grouping worker nodes, local model training, intra-group aggregation, and inter-group aggregation. Assuming there are K worker nodes in the HFL and E edge servers, they are divided into G edge server groups. The K worker nodes are categorized into G groups based on data distribution and training efficiency, with each group corresponding to an edge server group.

In the proposed GroHFL method, our goal can be articulated as maximizing the diversity of data distribution associated with edge nodes while alleviating the impact of bottleneck worker nodes on overall training.

4 Proposed Method

This paper proposes an HFL grouping and aggregation method based on data distribution and training efficiency, which is primarily divided into two components: clustering worker nodes and a combination of synchronous and asynchronous aggregation. The clustering of worker nodes groups them based on data distribution and training efficiency, clustering nodes with low data distribution similarity and high training efficiency similarity to ensure diversity within the data samples of each group.

The hierarchical aggregation method, which combines synchronous and asynchronous approaches, executes synchronous aggregation within groups to ensure data sample diversity and minimize data loss, while performing asynchronous updates between groups to maintain training efficiency. The overall process is illustrated in Fig. 2, with the specific steps outlined as follows:

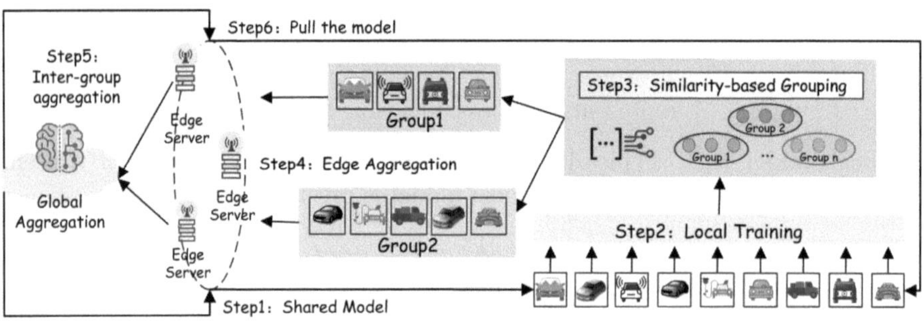

Fig. 2. The Framework of GroHFL.

- Step 1: Each device retrieves the global model.
- Step 2: Each device conducts local training and submits its training efficiency along with the locally updated model.
- Step 3: Based on a comprehensive metric formed from local data distribution and device training efficiency, devices are grouped.
- Step 4: The aggregation edge servers for each group complete synchronous aggregation.
- Step 5: Between groups, asynchronous aggregation is performed by using the models submitted by each group and the most recent historical global model to produce the global model for the current round.
- Step 6: The groups that submitted updates pull the aggregated global model and commence the next round of local training within their groups.

Steps 2 through 6 are repeated until the model reaches the specified number of training rounds, at which point training is halted.

Overall, this approach integrates considerations of both the similarity of data distributions across worker nodes and the similarity of computational capabilities, allowing as much data as possible to be learned from each device and addressing data imbalance across worker nodes. Additionally, grouping reduces communication overhead and avoids unnecessary broadcasting of local information across the network. Moreover, by employing synchronous aggregation within groups and asynchronous aggregation between groups, the method enhances training efficiency while ensuring model performance.

4.1 Work Nodes Grouping

GroHFL groups the working nodes according to their data distribution and training efficiency.

Similarity of Computing Capabilities of Working Nodes. For the computing capability measurement of each working node, we adopt the device CPU cycle count measurement method used by Zheng *et al.* [31] to measure and upload the CPU cycle frequency f_k of the device. Vector $\mathbf{F}_{cpu}$ representation of f_k. Let c_k denote the number of CPU cycles required for device k to execute a single data sample. Then, the number of CPU cycles required for device k to run one local iteration is $c_k |D_k|$. Combined with the number of groups G, we sort the K devices in ascending order of CPU cycle frequency f_k and divide them into G groups. The computing capability similarity between device k and device j is defined as:

$$sim_{train}(k, j) = \begin{cases} 0, k \in G_i, \text{and } j \notin G_i \\ 1, k \in G_i, \text{and } j \in G_i \end{cases} \tag{4}$$

Similarity of Data Distribution among Working Nodes. Drawing on the idea of PFA [32], this paper leverages the sparsity of neural networks to reflect the data distribution of working nodes. In each local training round, we define that working node k trains a local model $\mathbf{w}_k$ using its local dataset $D_k = \{\xi_k(x_k^i, y_k^i)\}$. Feature maps are extracted from the ReLU layers of $\mathbf{w}_k$. Working node k extracts a feature matrix matrix$F_h(x_k^i)$ from the output of the c_h channel for a given input x_k^i, and the c_h channel feature of x_k^i is calculated as follows:

$$fea_h(x_k^i) = \frac{zero(\text{matrix}F_h(x_k^i))}{H \times W}, \tag{5}$$

where $zero(\bullet)$ is a function that counts the number of zeros in a matrix, and H and W denote the height and width of the feature matrix, respectively. By averaging the features of all samples, the c_h channel feature on dataset D_k is calculated as:

$$fea_h(D_k) = \frac{1}{n_k}\sum_{i=1}^{n_k} fea_h(x_k^i) \tag{6}$$

Working node k generates a feature vector during local training. The feature vector is calculated as follows:

$$Fea_k = (fea_1(D_k), fea_2(D_k), ..., fea_n(D_k)) \tag{7}$$

Each working node generates a feature vector that reflects the distribution of its local data. At the top layer, cosine similarity is used as a metric to measure vector similarity. Given the feature vectors Fea_k and Fea_j of working nodes k and j, their distribution similarity is calculated as follows:

$$sim_{\text{data}}(k, j) = \frac{Fea_k Fea_j}{\|Fea_k\| \times \|Fea_j\|} \tag{8}$$

To ensure the efficiency of federated learning, the feature Fea_z of the $z - th$ working node is randomly selected, and then its feature similarity with other working nodes is calculated to generate a final similarity vector:

$$\mathbf{Sim}_{data} = \left(sim_{data}(z, k_1), sim_{data}(z, k_2), ..., sim_{data}(z, k_K)\right) \tag{9}$$

Working nodes with high similarity values are selected and aggregated into a single group. Although we group working nodes with similar efficiency into the same cluster, the aggregation process within the cluster remains synchronous. Therefore, a timeout mechanism is set to avoid continuous waiting for stragglers.

4.2 The Combination of Synchronous and Asynchronous

This paper combines the advantages of synchronous and asynchronous aggregation, adopting a strategy that utilizes synchronous aggregation within groups and asynchronous aggregation between groups.

After the working nodes are grouped, they submit model updates to the edge server for intra-group aggregation, where synchronous aggregation is performed to reduce sample loss. To improve training efficiency, asynchronous aggregation is used across groups to complete global model aggregation. Meanwhile, given the impact of unbalanced data distribution on the international model, historical global models are used to compensate for the information loss in individual group models. The global model aggregation is implemented by iterating over historical models, and the formula for global model aggregation is given as follows:

$$\overline{\mathbf{w}}^{(t)} = \alpha\overline{\mathbf{w}}_{G_s}^{(t)} + (1-\alpha)\overline{\mathbf{w}}^{(t-1)} \tag{10}$$

where α is the aggregation weight.

The pseudocode for the complete process of GroHFL is presented in Algorithm 1.

Algorithm 1. GroHFL Training

Input: K (Number of training clients), D_k (Local Dataset), $\mathbf{w}^{(0)}$ (Initialized global model), T_{Cloud} (Maximum global training rounds),G (Number of groups)
Output: Global model $\overline{\mathbf{w}}^{(T)}$
// Initialize global model
$t \leftarrow 0$, $\overline{\mathbf{w}}^{(t)} \leftarrow \mathbf{w}^{(0)}$
// Training Loop
while $t \leq T_{Cloud}$ **do**
  for each $k \in K$ **do**
    k Do Local Training $g_k^{(t)}(\mathbf{w}_k^{(t)}, D_k^{(t)})$ via Eq. 2
    k Upload Local Model $\mathbf{w}_k$ and CPU clock frequency f_k
  end for
  // Grouping
  $Fea_z \leftarrow$ randomly selected $z-th$ worker node as criterion
  Sim_{data} via Eq. 9
  $Groups \leftarrow$ Clusters(Sim_{data},$\mathbf{F}_{cpu}$,G)
  // Aggregation
  for each $G_s \in Groups$ **do**
    Do Edge Aggregation via Eq. 3
    if $\overline{\mathbf{w}}_{G_s}^{(t)}$ **then**
      $\overline{\mathbf{w}}^{(t)} \leftarrow$ Eq. 10
      $t \leftarrow t+1$
    end if
  end for
end while
Return global model $\overline{\mathbf{w}}^{(T)}$

5 Experimental Evaluation and Discussion

5.1 Experimental Environment

In this subsection, we describe the experimental environment

Hardware Specifications. CPU: 16 vCPUs (Intel(R) Xeon(R) Platinum 8481C); GPU: NVIDIA GeForce RTX 4090 (24 GB). The operating system is Ubuntu 22.04. The software environment primarily consists of Python 3.11, PyTorch 2.5.1, CUDA 12.5, and other relevant libraries/tools.

Model and Dataset. The experiments in this study use ResNet18 and GoogLeNet models, and evaluate their performance on the CIFAR-10 and FashionMNIST (FMNIST) datasets. Two distribution scenarios are considered: IID and Non-IID. In the IID scenario, the working nodes are randomly assigned datasets of equal size. For the Non-IID scenario, we use the Dirichlet distribution [33] to simulate the Non-IID distribution of data across the working nodes. In the experiments, the parameter for the Dirichlet probability distribution in the Non-IID setting is set to 0.5.

Baseline. This paper selects FedAvg [34], FedProx [35], MOON [36], and FedAsync [37] for comparative evaluation and analysis.

Key Parameter Settings. In this study, we set up 25 work nodes and performed 200 rounds of global communication. The early stopping condition is defined as no improvement in the validation set performance for 50 consecutive rounds. The learning rate is set to 0.05, and we employ the SGD optimizer, with a batch size of 32.

5.2 Experimental Results and Analysis

The method's performance in this paper is excellent. The model's best accuracy is presented in Table 1, and its test accuracy is illustrated in Fig. 3.

Table 1. The Best Test Accuracy of Global Model.

Methods	ResNet18 - CIFAR-10		FMNIST - GoogLeNet	
	IID	Non-IID(0.5)	IID	Non-IID(0.5)
FedAvg	0.8731	0.7791	0.8942	0.8422
FedProx	0.8792	0.7876	0.9089	0.8519
MOON	0.8927	0.7881	**0.9109**	0.8532
FedAsync	0.8615	0.7527	0.8797	0.8371
Ours	**0.9167**	**0.8126**	0.9071	**0.8631**

Compared to other methods, the proposed method achieves an average accuracy improvement of 3.21% over the baseline methods in the ResNet18 model training on CIFAR-10 dataset experimental group, and an average improvement of 0.70% in the GoogLeNet model training on FMNIST dataset experimental group. In the Non-IID (0.5) scenario, the proposed method shows an average accuracy improvement of 2.86% in the ResNet18 model training on the CIFAR-10 dataset, and 1.36% in the GoogLeNet model training on the FMNIST dataset.

The accuracy improvement is more pronounced in the ResNet18 model trained on the CIFAR-10 dataset than in the GoogLeNet model trained on the FMNIST dataset, which is related to the models' performance. Additionally, in the Non-IID settings, all methods experience a decline in accuracy, indicating that data distribution has a significant impact on performance. However, the proposed method demonstrates better adaptability in Non-IID environments.

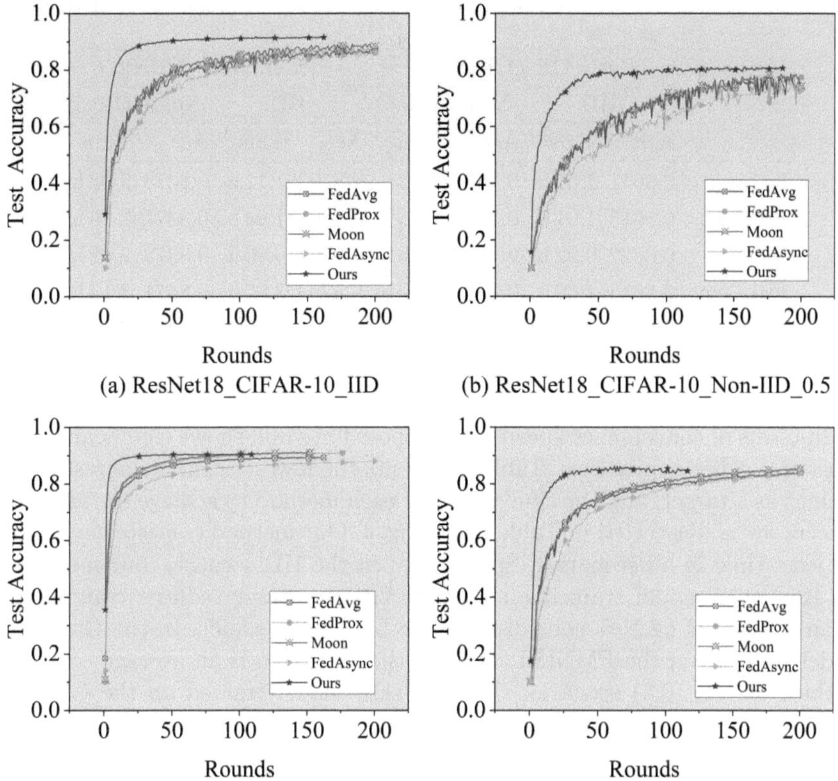

(a) ResNet18_CIFAR-10_IID (b) ResNet18_CIFAR-10_Non-IID_0.5

(c) GoogleNet_FMNIST_IID (d) GoogleNet_FMNIST_Non-IID_0.5

Fig. 3. The Test Accuracy of Global Model.

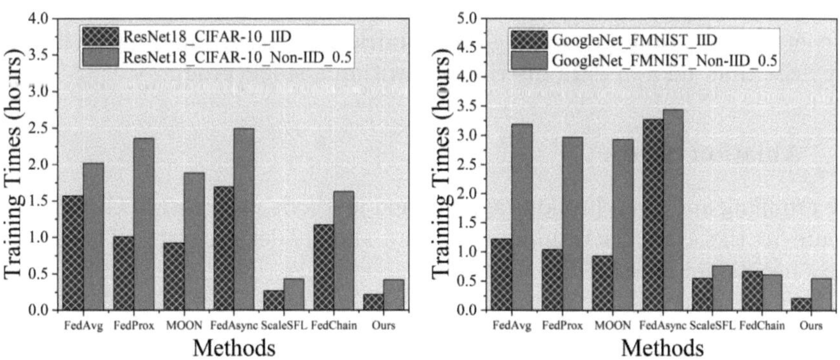

(a) ResNet18_CIFAR-10 (b) GoogleNet_FMNIST

Fig. 4. The Training Times.

Table 2. The Time Taken by Each Method to Achieve the Same Level of Accuracy.

Methods	ResNet18 - CIFAR-10				GoogLeNet - FMNIST			
	IID		Non-IID(0.5)		IID		Non-IID(0.5)	
	Acc	Time	Acc	Time	Acc	Time	Acc	Time
FedAvg	0.8611	1.57 h	0.7521	2.02 h	0.8793	1.17 h	0.8374	3.08 h
FedProx	0.8615	1.01 h	0.7528	2.36 h	0.8791	1.04 h	0.8377	2.85 h
MOON	0.8622	0.92 h	0.7523	1.88 h	0.8797	0.86 h	0.8372	2.82 h
FedAsync	0.8615	1.69 h	0.7527	2.49 h	0.8793	3.07 h	0.8371	3.13 h
Ours	0.8623	**0.27 h**	0.7524	**0.43 h**	0.8801	**0.26 h**	0.8374	**0.56 h**

In terms of convergence speed, the proposed method shows significant advantages over other approaches. Table 1 presents the lowest accuracy across various settings as a target, and the time taken by each method to achieve the same level of accuracy is illustrated in Table 2 and Fig. 4. Our method consistently requires the least time in all scenarios. Specifically, in the IID scenario, our method for the ResNet18 model trained on the CIFAR-10 dataset reduces training time by an average of 62.15% compared to the baseline methods. In the GoogLeNet model training on the FMNIST dataset, the reduction is an average of 62.82%. In the Non-IID (0.5) scenario, the ResNet18 model trained on the CIFAR-10 dataset shows a 64.07% decrease in training time with our method compared to the baseline. In contrast, the GoogLeNet model training on the FMNIST dataset group shows a 64.88% reduction.

The faster convergence of our method is a significant factor in reducing training time. Additionally, GroHFL groups nodes with dissimilar data characteristics and similar computational capabilities together, enabling asynchronous aggregation across multiple groups and enhancing training efficiency. It also accounts for contributions from historical global models, mitigating information loss that may arise from uneven data distribution within a single group.

5.3 Ablation Study

The grouping and asynchronous aggregation methods proposed in GroHFL contribute to the system's training efficiency and model accuracy. The ablation study results are presented in Table 3.

Table 3. Ablation Study: Average Training Time per Epoch and Test Best Accuracy of Global Model

Methods	ResNet18 - CIFAR-10				GoogLeNet - FMNIST			
	IID		Non-IID(0.5)		IID		Non-IID(0.5)	
	Acc	Time	Acc	Time	Acc	Time	Acc	Time
GroHFL	0.9053	45.77 s	0.8105	44.46 s	0.9036	60.12 s	0.8618	58.38 s
w/o Grouping	0.9022	46.58 s	0.7672	46.24 s	0.8886	61.05 s	0.8580	60.21 s
w/o Asynchronous	0.9034	57.63 s	0.7326	56.75 s	0.8959	73.14 s	0.8495	74.21 s

In the IID data distribution, removing grouping resulted in an average accuracy reduction of 0.48%, while the average training time per epoch increased by 23.78%. In the case of Non-IID (0.5) distribution, the average accuracy decreased by 4.51% with an average training time increase of 27.38%.

In the IID data distribution, removing asynchronous aggregation resulted in a 1.39% drop in average accuracy, with average training time per epoch increasing by 25.44%. For the Non-IID (0.5) distribution, the model accuracy decreased by 6.87% on average, and the training time increased by 30.95%.

The grouping method has a greater effect on improving model accuracy, while asynchronous aggregation reduces training time more effectively. This is primarily because grouping enhances the representativeness of samples within each group, preventing the loss of minority-feature samples. Meanwhile, asynchronous aggregation alleviates the impact of bottleneck nodes on the system while ensuring accuracy.

6 Concluding Remarks

This paper presents a hierarchical federated learning grouping and aggregation method designed to address uneven data distribution and varying computational capabilities among worker nodes. The objective of GroHFL is to maximize the diversity of data distribution across edge nodes while reducing the impact of bottleneck nodes on training.

Grouping is achieved through a model sparsification feature matrix extraction method that links distributed nodes with different data distributions to the same edge aggregator, thereby promoting a more balanced data distribution. The approach utilizes synchronous aggregation within groups and asynchronous aggregation between groups, mitigating the short-board effect and ensuring training efficiency. Additionally, inter-group aggregation considers historical global models, compensating for information loss due to uneven data distribution to enhance model convergence speed and accuracy.

Extensive experiments demonstrate that our method outperforms others in terms of model accuracy and training time. Specifically, it improves model accuracy by 1.95% and 2.11% in the IID and Non-IID experimental groups, respectively, while reducing training time by 62.48% and 64.48%. As future work, we will focus on enhancing security measures, implementing defenses against poisoning and inference attacks, and implementing lightweight privacy protection solutions for data.

References

1. Khan, S., Perumal, K., Alsolai, H., Aljohani, A.: FedTinyMed: federated learning enabled tiny multi task machine learning model for smart healthcare monitoring for IoMT. Comput. Electr. Eng. **128**, 110761 (2025)
2. Zhang, S., Ren, F., Liang, W., Li, K., Ling, N.: SAEV-FL: lightweight secure aggregation and efficient verification scheme for federated learning in cloud-edge collaborative environment. IEEE Trans. Intell. Veh. **5**, 88 (2025)
3. Zhou, S., Li, K., Chen, Y., Yang, C., Liang, W., Zomaya, A.Y.: TrustBCFL: mitigating data bias in IoT through blockchain-enabled federated learning. IEEE IoT J. **11**(15), 25 648–25 662 (2024)
4. Zhou, S., Chen, Y., Li, K., Liang, W., Meng, W.: TrustHFL: an efficient aggregation method for trustworthy hierarchical federated learning. IEEE IoT J. (2026)
5. Liang, W.: TMHD: twin-bridge scheduling of multi-heterogeneous dependent tasks for edge computing. Futur. Gener. Comput. Syst. **158**, 60–72 (2024)
6. Wu, J., Dong, F., Leung, H., Zhu, Z., Zhou, J., Drew, S.: Topology-aware federated learning in edge computing: a comprehensive survey. ACM Comput. Surv. **56**(10), 1–41 (2024)
7. Chen, X., Xu, G., Xu, X., Jiang, H., Tian, Z., Ma, T.: Multicenter hierarchical federated learning with fault-tolerance mechanisms for resilient edge computing networks. IEEE Trans. Neural Netw. Learn. Syst. **36**(1), 47–61 (2024)
8. Yang, C.: Robust hierarchical federated learning with dual-layer filtering mechanism. Int. J. Adv. Rob. Syst. **22**(2), 17298806251322260 (2025)
9. Li, Z., Lin, Z., Shao, J., Mao, Y., Zhang, J.: FedCiR: client-invariant representation learning for federated non-IID features. IEEE Trans. Mob. Comput. **23**(11), 10 509–10 522 (2024)
10. Liang, C., Liang, W., Chen, Y., Li, K., Zomaya, A.Y.: FedTCTF: tensor completion-based federated learning for device heterogeneity. IEEE Trans. Sustain. Comput. **5**, 55 (2025)
11. Zhang, L., Luo, Y., Bai, Y., Du, B., Duan, L.-Y.: Federated learning for non-IID data via unified feature learning and optimization objective alignment. In: Proceedings of the IEEE/CVF International Conference on Computer Vision, pp. 4420–4428 (2021)
12. Jin, J., Ren, J., Zhou, Y., Lyu, L., Liu, J., Dou, D.: Accelerated federated learning with decoupled adaptive optimization. In: International Conference on Machine Learning, PMLR 2022, pp. 10 298–10 322 (2022)
13. Yang, M., Su, S., Li, B., Xue, X.: Exploring one-shot semi-supervised federated learning with pre-trained diffusion models. In: Proceedings of the AAAI Conference on Artificial Intelligence, vol. 38, no. 15, pp. 16 325–16 333 (2024)
14. Feng, L., Yang, Z., Guo, S., Qiu, X., Li, W., Yu, P.: Two-layered blockchain architecture for federated learning over the mobile edge network. IEEE Netw. **36**(1), 45–51 (2021)
15. Liang, W., Xie, S., Li, K.-C., Li, X., Kui, X., Zomaya, A.Y.: MC-DSC: a dynamic secure resource configuration scheme based on medical consortium blockchain. IEEE Trans. Inf. Forensics Secur. **19**, 3525–3538 (2024)

16. Liang, W., Liu, Y., Yang, C., Xie, S., Li, K., Susilo, W.: On identity, transaction, and smart contract privacy on permissioned and permissionless blockchain: a comprehensive survey. ACM Comput. Surv. **56**(12), 1–35 (2024)
17. Peng, Z., et al.: VFChain: enabling verifiable and auditable federated learning via blockchain systems. IEEE Trans. Netw. Sci. Eng. **9**(1), 173–186 (2021)
18. Ji, S., Zhang, J., Zhang, Y., Han, Z., Ma, C.: LAFED: a lightweight authentication mechanism for blockchain-enabled federated learning system. Futur. Gener. Comput. Syst. **145**, 56–67 (2023)
19. Fraboni, Y., Vidal, R., Kameni, L., Lorenzi, M.: A general theory for federated optimization with asynchronous and heterogeneous clients updates. J. Mach. Learn. Res. **24**(110), 1–43 (2023)
20. Xu, C., Qu, Y., Xiang, Y., Gao, L.: Asynchronous federated learning on heterogeneous devices: a survey. Comput. Sci. Rev. **50**, 100595 (2023)
21. Liu, L., Zhang, J., Song, S., Letaief, K.B.: Client-edge-cloud hierarchical federated learning. In: 2020 IEEE International Conference on Communications (ICC), ICC 2020, pp. 1–6. IEEE (2020)
22. Luo, S., Chen, X., Wu, Q., Zhou, Z., Yu, S.: HFEL: joint edge association and resource allocation for cost-efficient hierarchical federated edge learning. IEEE Trans. Wirel. Commun. **19**(10), 6535–6548 (2020)
23. Liu, S., Yu, G., Chen, X., Bennis, M.: Joint user association and resource allocation for wireless hierarchical federated learning with IID and non-IID data. IEEE Trans. Wirel. Commun. **21**(10), 7852–7866 (2022)
24. Duan, M., Liu, D., Chen, X., Liu, R., Tan, Y., Liang, L.: Self-balancing federated learning with global imbalanced data in mobile systems. IEEE Trans. Parallel Distrib. Syst. **32**(1), 59–71 (2020)
25. Mhaisen, N., Abdellatif, A.A., Mohamed, A., Erbad, A., Guizani, M.: Optimal user-edge assignment in hierarchical federated learning based on statistical properties and network topology constraints. IEEE Trans. Netw. Sci. Eng. **9**(1), 55–66 (2021)
26. Zheng, S., et al.: Asynchronous stochastic gradient descent with delay compensation. In: International Conference on Machine Learning. PMLR, pp. 4120–4129 (2017)
27. Jiang, Y., et al.: Model pruning enables efficient federated learning on edge devices. IEEE Trans. Neural Netw. Learn. Syst. **34**(12), 10 374–10 386 (2022)
28. Lu, X., Liao, Y., Lio, P., Hui, P.: Privacy-preserving asynchronous federated learning mechanism for edge network computing. IEEE Access **8**, 48 970–48 981 (2020)
29. Chen, X., Wang, X., Yang, K.: Asynchronous blockchain-based privacy-preserving training framework for disease diagnosis. In: 2019 IEEE International Conference on Big Data (Big Data), pp. 5469–5473. IEEE (2019)
30. Lu, Y., Huang, X., Zhang, K., Maharjan, S., Zhang, Y.: Blockchain empowered asynchronous federated learning for secure data sharing in internet of vehicles. IEEE Trans. Veh. Technol. **69**(4), 4298–4311 (2020)
31. Zheng, G., Ni, Q., Navaie, K., Pervaiz, H.: Semantic communication in satellite-borne edge cloud network for computation offloading. IEEE J. Sel. Areas Commun. **42**(5), 1145–1158 (2024)
32. Liu, B., Guo, Y., Chen, X.: PFA: privacy-preserving federated adaptation for effective model personalization. Proc. Web Conf. **2021**, 923–934 (2021)
33. Hsu, T.-M.H., Qi, H., Brown, M.: Measuring the effects of non-identical data distribution for federated visual classification. arXiv preprint arXiv:1909.06335 (2019)
34. McMahan, B., Moore, E., Ramage, D., Hampson, S., y Arcas, B.A.: Communication-efficient learning of deep networks from decentralized data. In: Artificial Intelligence and Statistics. PMLR, pp. 1273–1282 (2017)

35. Yuan, X., Li, P.: On convergence of FedProx: local dissimilarity invariant bounds, non-smoothness and beyond. In: Advances in Neural Information Processing Systems, vol. 35, pp. 10 752–10 765 (2022)
36. Li, Q., He, B., Song, D.: Model-contrastive federated learning. In: Proceedings of the IEEE/CVF Conference on Computer Vision and Pattern Recognition, pp. 10 713–10 722 (2021)
37. Xie, C., Koyejo, S., Gupta, I.: Asynchronous federated optimization. arXiv preprint arXiv:1903.03934 (2019)

Lightweight Privacy-First Federated Learning for Medical AI

Al Amin[1(✉)], Kamrul Hasan[2], Liang Hong[2], Sergei Chuprov[3], Rohan Thompson[1], Azubike D. Okpalaeze[1], Primo Abena[1], Tariqul Islam[5], and Imtiaz Ahmed[4]

[1] Huston–Tillotson University, Austin, TX, USA
{aamin,rrthompson,adokpalaeze,acprimo}@htu.edu
[2] Tennessee State University, Nashville, TN, USA
{mhasan1,lhong}@tnstate.edu
[3] The University of Texas Rio Grande Valley, Edinburg, TX, USA
sergei.chuprov@utrgv.edu
[4] Howard University, Washington, D.C., USA
imtiaz.ahmed@howard.edu
[5] Syracuse University, Syracuse, NY, USA
mtislam@syr.edu

Abstract. Medical AI systems require large, diverse datasets from multiple institutions to achieve clinical-grade diagnostic accuracy. However, aggregating patient data into centralized repositories violates privacy regulations. To solve this, researchers developed federated learning (FL) that lets hospitals keep their data private while still training AI together, but they still transmit weights/gradients to the central server, which introduces new privacy attack surfaces and computational overhead. These challenges intensify when inputs are privacy-transformed (e.g., block-wise permutations or sign flips), where conventional convolutional networks (CNNs) lose critical spatial structure. To address these issues, this study proposes a lightweight, privacy-first federated framework that shares only compact [CLS] embeddings from client-side Vision Transformers (ViTs), never transmitting weights, gradients, or pixels. ViTs' global self-attention still captures key patterns even when images are patched or shuffled, maintaining accuracy on obfuscated inputs. Adding Gaussian DP noise to the shared embeddings further reduces inference and inversion risks with minimal accuracy loss. On colon histopathology data, our method achieves 96% validation accuracy while cutting communication by about 20 times compared to gradient sharing, making it practical for real-world medical AI with strong privacy and low bandwidth needs.

Keywords: Federated learning · medical imaging · Vision Transformer · [CLS] embedding · differential privacy · privacy-preserving AI

Y. Cao et al. (Eds.): SecureComm 2026, LNICST 704, pp. 255–268, 2027.
https://doi.org/10.1007/978-3-032-32764-2_13

1 Introduction

Medical AI systems require large amounts of data to achieve clinical-grade performance [2,5,27]. However, privacy regulations and institutional policies such as HIPAA (U.S.) and the GDPR (EU) prevent hospitals from sharing patient data directly [14,23,29,44]. Federated learning (FL) offers a solution by training models collaboratively without centralizing data [20,38], but existing approaches face significant challenges in healthcare. They exchange model weights or gradients between participants, creating two major problems. First, this requires substantial communication bandwidth [3,6,21,37,41]. Second, recent studies show that shared gradients can leak sensitive patient information [3,4,9,11,28,33,39], undermining privacy protection. These limitations make deployment difficult in real healthcare environments, where bandwidth is limited and privacy is paramount.

An additional challenge arises when applying privacy-preserving techniques to medical images. Existing methods often use CNNs on encrypted or obfuscated images, but CNNs rely on spatial relationships between neighboring pixels. When images are transformed for privacy protection through block-wise permutation and pixel shuffling, these relationships break down, and model performance degrades significantly [8,12,15,16,25].

To solve this, this study introduces a lightweight FL framework as shown in Fig. 1 using [CLS] embedding aggregation with optimized vision transformers [32]. The client-side shares only compact [CLS] embeddings from locally trained ViTs instead of model weights or gradients. ViTs self-attention mechanisms capture global patch relationships despite spatial disruption from privacy transforms, making them ideal for obfuscated medical images. We integrate differential privacy (DP) into embedding aggregation and validate on brain tumor MRI and colon cancer histopathology, achieving competitive accuracy with reduced communication overhead and stronger privacy. **The key contributions of this work are summarized as follows:**

- **Lightweight FL with [CLS]**: Clients keep their ViTs local and share only compact, encrypted [CLS] embeddings no weights, no gradients.
- **Built-in privacy**: We add Gaussian DP noise to embeddings, cutting membership/inversion leakage with a small accuracy cost.
- **Low bandwidth, real data**: Fixed-size embeddings reduce communication by $\sim 20\times$ and work well on brain tumor MRI and colon histopathology (up to 96% val. accuracy).

The remainder of this paper is organized as follows. Section 2 reviews related work. Section 3 presents our methodology including the FL setup, lightweight efficiency analysis, custom Vision Transformer architecture, and DP integration, while Sect. 4 provides experimental results and baseline comparison, followed by conclusions in Sect. 5.

2 Related Work

2.1 Federated Learning with Model Updates

Classical federated learning like parallel FL (PFL) and sequential FL (SFL) trains a shared model by exchanging model weights or gradients between a server and many clients [18,30,40,42]. This reduces centralized data collection but introduces substantial communication cost and privacy issues [18,19,24]. In contrast, the proposed approach does not transmit weights or gradients: clients keep their encoders local and share only fixed-size, encrypted [CLS] embeddings, providing a lightweight, low-bandwidth alternative.

2.2 Practical Privacy in Representation Sharing

Gradients and intermediate features can leak sensitive details [33,35,36], motivating defenses such as clipping and Gaussian noise under DP [7]. Split learning reduces raw gradient exposure by splitting the model between client and server, yet the transmitted intermediate activations still carry exploitable feature-level information and incur variable communication cost tied to cut-layer size. In contrast, our framework avoids sharing weights, gradients, or intermediate activations entirely; clients communicate only fixed-size [CLS] embeddings, reducing the attack surface to a compact, low-dimensional representation. To further harden against membership and inversion attacks, Gaussian DP noise is added to embeddings before aggregation, and when formal DP guarantees are required, each embedding is clipped and noise is calibrated to report (ε, δ) via a standard accountant.

2.3 Learning on Encrypted Images: CNN Limitations and Transformer Advantages

Recent work explores training deep models directly on privacy-preserving or obfuscated images, with many studies adopting CNN backbones in these settings [17,34]. However, the architectural choice significantly impacts model performance when images undergo privacy-preserving transformations.

CNNs rely fundamentally on local spatial relationships between neighboring pixels. Convolutional kernels operate on small receptive fields, extracting features by assuming that adjacent pixels are semantically related. When images are transformed through block-wise permutation or pixel shuffling for privacy protection, this critical assumption breaks down. The local pixel adjacency that CNNs depend upon is destroyed, causing convolutional filters to extract weak or noisy patterns from unrelated neighboring pixels. As a result, both training and testing accuracy drop significantly [13,16,31].

In contrast, Vision Transformers offer inherent resilience to such spatial disruptions. Transformers treat an image as a sequence of patches rather than a spatially-coherent grid. Their multi-head self-attention mechanism compares every patch with every other patch globally, independent of spatial proximity [10,26]. Even when nearby pixels are shuffled out of their original positions,

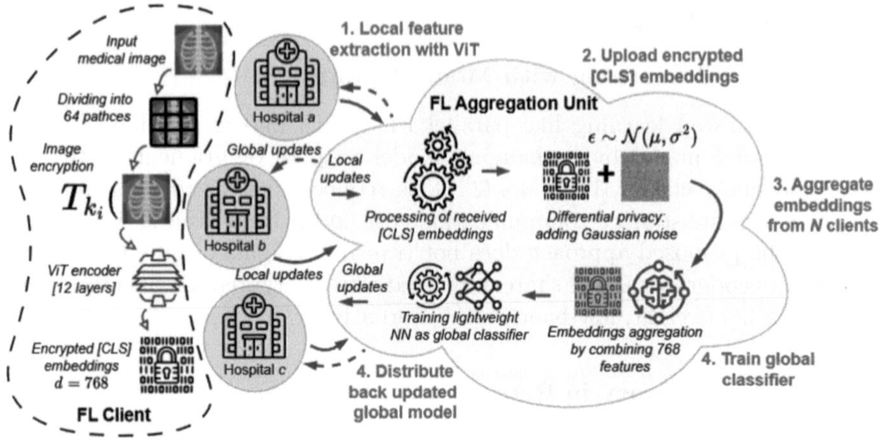

Fig. 1. [CLS]-Embedding FL. Clients encrypt images, extract a d=768 [CLS] vector via a 12-layer ViT (optionally DP-noised), and upload it to the server, which trains a lightweight global classifier.

the model can identify and link distant but semantically-related patches through attention mechanisms, thereby forming meaningful global representations.

In our framework, client-specific keyed patch transforms ensure that raw data remains obfuscated while the ViT learns cross-patch dependencies. The attention layers and positional encodings adapt to the key-conditioned layout, preserving meaningful features for effective learning. This architectural choice makes Vision Transformers particularly well-suited for privacy-preserving federated learning in medical imaging, where maintaining both data utility and privacy is paramount.

3 Methodology

3.1 Scope and Roadmap

This section presents a lightweight, privacy-preserving FL framework for eHealth as shown in Fig. 1. We establish the problem setting and threat model in Sect. 3.2, quantify communication reduction to demonstrate the lightweight property in Sect. 3.3, detail the proposed custom ViT architecture optimized for encrypted images in Sect. 3.4, and describe DP integration with the complete training protocol.

3.2 Federated Learning Setup and Privacy Assumptions

The framework assumes M participating clinical institutions, each with a private dataset

$$\mathcal{D}_i = \{(x_{ij}, y_{ij})\}_{j=1}^{N_i}, \quad x_{ij} \in \mathbb{R}^{H \times W \times C}, \;\; y_{ij} \in \{1, \ldots, K\}, \tag{1}$$

where x_{ij} is a medical image and y_{ij} its diagnostic label. Dataset sizes N_i may differ across sites, reflecting the typical non-IID nature of medical data.

Before training, each image is first divided into patches, which are then obfuscated using a client-specific transform $T_{k_i}(\cdot)$ parameterized by a secret key k_i. The transform permutes these patches and applies random sign flips:

$$\tilde{x}_{ij} = T_{k_i}(x_{ij}). \tag{2}$$

This destroys local spatial adjacency while preserving global statistics, producing images that are visually unintelligible yet still suitable for representation learning as shown in Fig. 1.

Each client then trains a custom ViT encoder f_{θ_i} on the encrypted images. Instead of transmitting full model updates, only the fixed-size [CLS] embedding is extracted:

$$h_{ij} = f_{\theta_i}(\tilde{x}_{ij}) \in \mathbb{R}^d, \qquad d = 768. \tag{3}$$

This compact vector summarizes the encrypted image and ensures uniform, low-cost communication.

On the server-side, embeddings and labels are aggregated to train a lightweight classifier $g_\phi : \mathbb{R}^d \to \Delta^{K-1}$. No raw pixels, model parameters, or gradients are exchanged, removing bandwidth and gradient-leakage risks. The threat model assumes an honest-but-curious server. Although the server receives only compact [CLS] embeddings rather than raw pixels or gradients, the client-specific transform T_{k_i} remains necessary as a defense-in-depth measure: it protects raw images against insider threats or breached clients before any embedding is produced, operating independently of what the server observes. Privacy is protected at two levels: (i) client-side transforms T_{k_i} guarantee raw data never leaves local sites; and (ii) embeddings may be perturbed with Gaussian DP noise before aggregation, details are given in Sect. 3.5.

3.3 Lightweight Efficiency in FL

A central contribution of the proposed framework is its ability to reduce communication and computation overhead compared to conventional FL.

Communication Footprint. In classical FL, each client transmits a full-precision model update of size

$$\text{Comm}_{\text{weights}} = 4P \quad \text{bytes per client per round}, \tag{4}$$

where P is the total number of trainable parameters. By contrast, the proposed framework requires client i to send only N_i embeddings, each of length d:

$$\text{Comm}_{\text{CLS}}(i) = 4\,d\,N_i \quad \text{bytes}. \tag{5}$$

The reduction factor relative to weight sharing is therefore

$$\mathcal{R}_i = \frac{\text{Comm}_{\text{CLS}}(i)}{\text{Comm}_{\text{weights}}} = \frac{d\,N_i}{P}. \tag{6}$$

For ViT-Base with $P \approx 86 \times 10^6$ parameters, embedding dimension $d = 768$, and $N_i = 5{,}000$ images, the communication per client is

$$\mathrm{Comm}_{\mathrm{CLS}}(i) \approx 15 \text{ MB} \quad \text{vs.} \quad \mathrm{Comm}_{\text{weights}} \approx 344 \text{ MB}, \tag{7}$$

a reduction of more than 20× per round. On a per-sample basis, transmitting one embedding costs only $4d = 3{,}072$ bytes (≈ 3 KB), which is negligible compared to model updates or raw image transmission.

Per-image Cost, Computation, and Summary. A 200×200 RGB image occupies ≈0.46 MB as `float32`, whereas a single [CLS] embedding (d=768) requires only 3,072 bytes (≈0.003 MB), i.e., ∼150× smaller, independent of model size. Client cost is dominated by local ViT training (the transform T_{k_i} is negligible), and server-side MLP fitting on $\mathbb{R}^d$ remains efficient at scale. Fixed-size embedding sharing thus delivers large communication savings with modest compute, making the framework practical in bandwidth-constrained healthcare deployments.

3.4 Custom ViT for Encrypted Images

The encoder must remain effective even when local spatial order is disrupted by client-keyed transforms Eq. (2). To achieve this, a compact ViT is employed, whose global self-attention captures long-range dependencies and produces a single fixed-size `[CLS]` embedding for federation Fig. 1.

Patch Embeddings and Initialization. An encrypted image $\tilde{x} \in \mathbb{R}^{H \times W \times C}$ is partitioned into P non-overlapping patches. Each patch is flattened and linearly projected into a d-dimensional token:

$$z_p = W_e \operatorname{vec}\big(\tilde{x}^{(p)}\big) + b_e \in \mathbb{R}^d, \quad p = 1, \ldots, P, \tag{8}$$

with projection matrix $W_e \in \mathbb{R}^{d \times (p^2 C)}$. A learnable class token z_{cls} is prepended, and positional parameters E_{pos} are added to encode the (permuted) order:

$$\hat{Z}_0 = \big[\, z_{\text{cls}}; z_1; \ldots; z_P \,\big] + E_{\text{pos}}. \tag{9}$$

Transformer Encoding and `[CLS]` Readout. For each layer $\ell = 1, \ldots, L$, multi-head self-attention is applied:

$$\mathrm{MHA}(\hat{Z}_{\ell-1}) = \bigoplus_{h=1}^{H} \operatorname{softmax}\Big(\tfrac{Q_h K_h^\top}{\sqrt{d_k}}\Big) V_h W_O, \tag{10}$$

where Q, K, V are linear projections of $\hat{Z}_{\ell-1}$, and $\oplus$ denotes concatenation over heads. Residual connections and feed-forward MLP updates give

$$U_\ell = \mathrm{LayerNorm}\big(\hat{Z}_{\ell-1} + \mathrm{MHA}(\hat{Z}_{\ell-1})\big), \tag{11}$$

$$\hat{Z}_\ell = \mathrm{LayerNorm}\big(U_\ell + \mathrm{MLP}(U_\ell)\big). \tag{12}$$

After L=12 layers, the class token is exported as the embedding:

$$h = \hat{Z}_L^{(0)} \in \mathbb{R}^d, \qquad d = 768. \tag{13}$$

Limitations of CNN Locality and the Advantage of Self-attention. Convolutions assume that nearby pixels are related and therefore aggregate only a small spatial neighborhood. A $k \times k$ filter at location (u, v) computes

$$y_{u,v} = \sum_{m=1}^{k} \sum_{n=1}^{k} w_{m,n} \, \tilde{x}_{u+m,v+n}, \tag{14}$$

which mixes the values in a $k \times k$ window around (u, v). This locality prior works for natural images, where adjacent pixels typically belong to the same structure. Under client-keyed block-wise permutations, discussed in Sect. 3.2, adjacency is destroyed: two neighbors can originate from unrelated regions. Equation (14) then aggregates mismatched content, producing weak or noisy features and causing CNN performance to deteriorate.

Transformers do not rely on strict locality. Self-attention compares *all* patches and weights them by content similarity. The attention from patch p to patch q is

$$\alpha_{pq} = \frac{\exp\left((z_p W_Q)(z_q W_K)^\top / \sqrt{d_k}\right)}{\sum_{r=1}^{P} \exp\left((z_p W_Q)(z_r W_K)^\top / \sqrt{d_k}\right)}, \tag{15}$$

where z_p and z_q are patch embeddings and W_Q, W_K are learnable projections. Each patch attends to any other based on feature similarity, regardless of physical distance, allowing the model to re-link semantically related regions even when spatial order is scrambled. By learning positional embeddings E_{pos} conditioned on each client's permutation, the [CLS] token remains consistent across encrypted views of the same class, keeping the model discriminative where CNNs degrade.

3.5 Federated Aggregation with DP

After local training, clients transmit only their [CLS] embeddings and may add DP noise to lower leakage risk.

DP-perturbed Embeddings. For client i, each embedding is randomized before upload:

$$\tilde{h}_{ij} = h_{ij} + z_{ij}, \qquad z_{ij} \sim \mathcal{N}(0, \sigma^2 I_d), \tag{16}$$

where the noise scale σ sets the privacyutility trade-off. We consider two operating modes. In a *practical DP* setting, a fraction r of embeddings is perturbed to balance robustness and accuracy. In a *formal DP* setting, each embedding is first clipped to radius C and Gaussian noise is added to *all* samples with

$$\sigma = \frac{\sqrt{2 \ln(1.25/\delta)} \cdot \Delta_2}{\varepsilon}, \qquad \Delta_2 = 2C, \tag{17}$$

while tracking (ε, δ) via a Rényi DP accountant.

Algorithm 1: Lightweight Privacy-Preserving Federated CLS Aggregation

Input: Clients i=1:M with data $\mathcal{D}_i$; keys k_i; encoders f_{θ_i}; noise σ; server classifier g_ϕ.

Output: Trained global classifier $\phi^\star$.

1 **forall the** *clients i in parallel* **do**
2   **Encrypt:** $\tilde{x}_{ij} \leftarrow T_{k_i}(x_{ij})$ for all (x_{ij}, y_{ij});
3   **Local train:** update θ_i on encrypted data with the custom ViT Figure 1;
4   **Embed/noise:** $h_{ij} \leftarrow f_{\theta_i}(\tilde{x}_{ij})$; optionally $\tilde{h}_{ij} = h_{ij} + z_{ij}$;
5   **Upload:** send $(\tilde{h}_{ij}, y_{ij})$ to the server;
6 **Aggregate:** $\mathcal{H} \leftarrow \bigcup_i \{(\tilde{h}_{ij}, y_{ij})\}$;
7 **Train** g_ϕ**:** minimize (19) on $\mathcal{H}$ to obtain $\phi^\star$;
8 **return** $\phi^\star$;

Server-Side Pooling and Llightweight Training. The server pools the perturbed embeddings and labels

$$\mathcal{H} = \bigcup_{i=1}^{M} \{(\tilde{h}_{ij}, y_{ij})\}_{j=1}^{N_i}, \tag{18}$$

and fits a compact classifier $g_\phi : \mathbb{R}^d \rightarrow \Delta^{K-1}$ by minimizing

$$\mathcal{L}(\phi) = -\frac{1}{|\mathcal{H}|} \sum_{(\tilde{h}, y) \in \mathcal{H}} \log g_\phi(\tilde{h})[y]. \tag{19}$$

A two-layer MLP (256128 units, dropout 0.3) converges quickly on this low-dimensional input.

Accuracy Under Moderate Noise and Protocol Summary. For a Lipschitz classifier g_ϕ and $\tilde{h} = h + z$,

$$\|g_\phi(h) - g_\phi(\tilde{h})\|_2 \leq L\|z\|_2, \tag{20}$$

and

$$\mathbb{E}\|z\|_2 = \sigma\sqrt{2}\frac{\Gamma\left(\frac{d+1}{2}\right)}{\Gamma\left(\frac{d}{2}\right)} \approx \sigma\sqrt{d}. \tag{21}$$

Moderate noise (e.g., $\sigma \leq 0.2$) preserves accuracy while hardening against membership and inversion attacks; the class margins of ViT embeddings Sect. 3.4 further stabilize performance. End-to-end: clients encrypt images, train local ViTs, extract (and optionally perturb) [CLS] vectors, and upload them with labels; the server aggregates $\mathcal{H}$ and trains a lightweight global classifier. Algorithm 1 demonstrates the full workflow of the framework.

Information-Theoretic Justification. Sharing compact [CLS] vectors reveals less than sharing gradients or weights. Let X be raw images, G gradients, and H [CLS] embeddings. Then

$$I(X; H) \leq I(X; G), \tag{22}$$

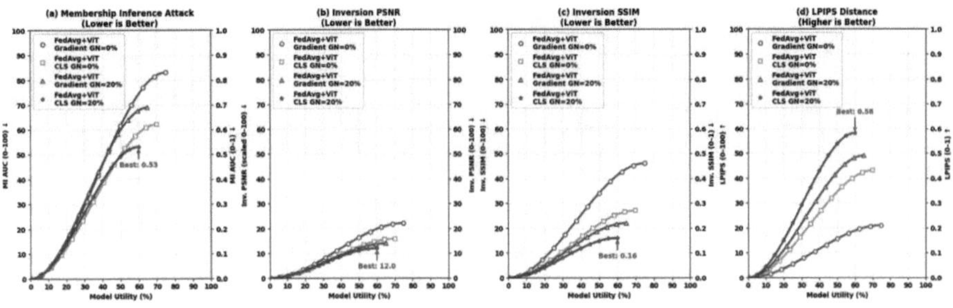

Fig. 2. Privacy–utility trade-offs for four FedAvg+ViT variants (Gradient vs. [CLS], GN=0%/20%). Curves show (a) MI AUC, (b) inversion PSNR, (c) inversion SSIM (all ↓), and (d) LPIPS (↑). **[CLS]+20% GN** achieves the strongest privacy at comparable utility.

since H is a low-dimensional projection, whereas G encodes high-dimensional sensitivities to X. Empirical gradient inversion [43] shows inputs can be reconstructed from G; fixed-size [CLS] vectors discard pixel-level detail, and DP noise further reduces leakage.

4 Results and Experimental Analysis

4.1 Experimental Configuration

This study evaluated on two medical imaging datasets [1,22]: brain tumor MRI (5,712 images; 1,311 test) and lung–colon histopathology (2,980 images; 311 test). Experiments ran in Google Colab Pro+ (Python 3) on a single NVIDIA A100 GPU; when A100s were unavailable, L4/T4 served as fallbacks with consistent trends across hardware. For reproducibility, we used mixed-precision training, fixed random seeds, and identical data pipelines and hyperparameters across methods. The server-side classifier was trained in the same environment with negligible overhead. Following the practical DP setting in Sect. 3.5, Gaussian noise was injected into [CLS] embeddings at σ=0.1 (10%) and σ=0.2 (20%) to evaluate the privacy–utility trade-off; formal (ε, δ) guarantees can be derived via a Rényi DP accountant applied to these noise levels.

4.2 Quantitative Performance

The results clearly demonstrate the advantages of the proposed framework. As shown in Fig. 3, conventional CNN-based FL degrades severely when encrypted gradients are shared for example, VGG19 validation accuracy drops from 93% to 62%. In addition, the computational burden in the encrypted domain increases drastically, with per-epoch training times up to 21×–25× higher than in the non-encrypted setting Fig. 3. In contrast, the ViT-based approach remains robust under federation. Figure 4 shows that sharing only compact `[CLS]` embeddings

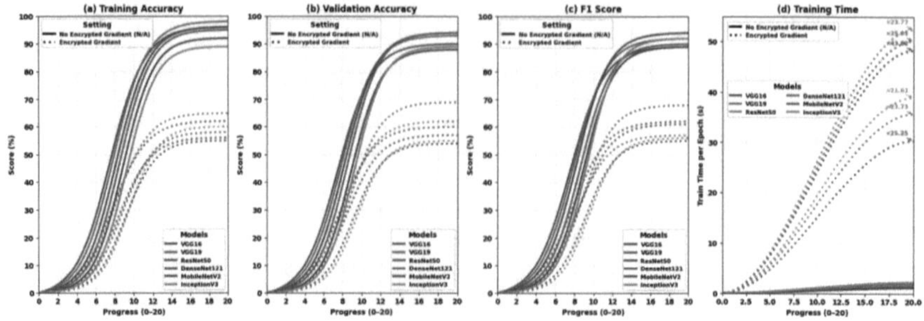

Fig. 3. Federated CNN baselines under encryption. Metrics: (a) train accuracy, (b) validation accuracy, (c) F1, (d) time/epoch for VGG16/19, ResNet50, DenseNet121, MobileNetV2, and InceptionV3. Solid = no encryption; dotted = encrypted gradients. Panel (d) shows slow-down factors (×).

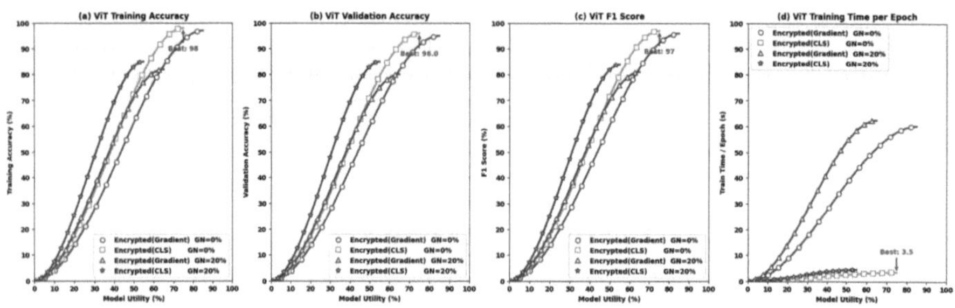

Fig. 4. ViT federated variants under encrypted sharing (Gradient vs. CLS; GN = 0% and 20%): (a) training accuracy (↑), (b) validation accuracy (↑), (c) F1 score (↑), and (d) training time per epoch (↓) versus model utility.

sustains high validation accuracy (95–96%) while dramatically reducing per-epoch training time (3.5 s vs. 60.2 s). Finally, adding 20% Gaussian DP noise introduces only a modest accuracy reduction (to 85%), yet still outperforms CLS-based FL in both accuracy and efficiency as shown in Fig. 4. Together, these findings provide strong empirical evidence that `[CLS]` embedding aggregation offers a practical balance of accuracy, privacy, and efficiency proving it as a viable solution for secure, real-world medical FL.

4.3 Privacy Evaluation

Figure 2 reports four standard privacy tests, each capturing a different attack surface, and together showing that `[CLS]` aggregation especially with DP noise offers the best privacy–utility trade-off (Tables 1 and 2).

- **Membership Inference Attack AUC (lower is better):** measures the ability of an attacker to determine whether a specific patient image was part of the training set; the `[CLS]`+DP curve (best ≈ 0.53) indicates much lower leakage risk than gradient sharing (up to ≈ 0.83) as shown in Fig. 2(a).

Table 1. Comparison between Efficiency: [CLS] vs. gradient sharing.

Sharing Method	Train Acc (%)	Val Acc (%)	Time per Epoch (s)	Efficiency Gain
CLS Embeddings	**98**	**96**	**3.5**	**20× faster**
Gradient Sharing	97	95	60.2	Baseline

Table 2. Privacy protection across multiple attack vectors

Attack Type	Gradient Sharing	[CLS] Only	[CLS] +20% DP
Membership Inference AUC ↓	0.83	0.62	**0.53**
Reconstruction PSNR ↓	22.1 dB	15.8 dB	**12.0 dB**
Reconstruction SSIM ↓	0.46	0.27	**0.16**
LPIPS Distance ↑	0.21	0.43	**0.58**

- **Inversion Peak Signal-to-Noise Ratio (PSNR, lower is better):** quantifies pixel-level reconstruction quality of private images; lower PSNR for `[CLS]`+DP (best ≈ 12.0) means reconstructed images are much less faithful than with gradients (up to ≈ 22.1) as shown in Fig. 2(b).
- **Inversion Structural Similarity Index Measure (SSIM, lower is better):** captures the preservation of anatomical structure; `[CLS]`+DP (best ≈ 0.16) produces reconstructions with weaker structural similarity compared to gradient sharing (up to ≈ 0.46) as shown in Fig. 2(c).
- **Learned Perceptual Image Patch Similarity (LPIPS, higher is better):** evaluates perceptual dissimilarity from real images; `[CLS]`+DP achieves the most dissimilar results (best ≈ 0.58), making inversions less clinically recognizable than gradient-based sharing (as low as ≈ 0.21) as shown in Fig. 2(d).

5 Conclusion

This study introduced a lightweight FL pipeline that shares only compact CLS embeddings from client-side ViTs instead of gradients or weights. This design cuts communication by over 20×, sustains high diagnostic performance (up to 96%), and when adding modest Gaussian DP noise substantially reduces leakage with limited accuracy cost. The result is a practical balance of accuracy, privacy, and bandwidth for real eHealth deployments.

Acknowledgment. This work was supported by Houston-Tillotson University, College of Business and Technology, Department of Computer Science. It was partially supported through mentorship at Tennessee State University under the U.S. Department of Energy (DOE) Award No. DE-NA0004189 and the National Science Foundation (NSF) Award No. 2409093.

References

1. Lung and colon cancer histopathological images. https://www.kaggle.com/datasets/andrewmvd/lung-and-colon-cancer-histopathological-images (2019)
2. Aliferis, C., Simon, G.: The development process and lifecycle of clinical grade and other safety and performance-sensitive ai/ml models. In: Artificial Intelligence and Machine Learning in Health Care and Medical Sciences: Best Practices and Pitfalls, pp. 289–340 (2024)
3. Amin, A., Hasan, K., Hong, L., Ullah, S.: Privacy-preserving federated vision transformer learning leveraging lightweight homomorphic encryption in medical AI (2025). arXiv:2511.20983 arXiv preprint
4. Amin, A., Hasan, K., Ullah, S., Hong, L.: Ai-driven secure data sharing: a trustworthy and privacy-preserving approach. In: 2025 International Conference on Computing, Networking and Communications (ICNC), pp. 174–179 (2025). https://doi.org/10.1109/ICNC64010.2025.10993885
5. Chai, Z., Luo, L., Lin, H., Heng, P.A., Chen, H.: Deep omni-supervised learning for rib fracture detection from chest radiology images. IEEE Trans. Med. Imaging **43**(5), 1972–1982 (2024). https://doi.org/10.1109/TMI.2024.3353248
6. Che, H., Jin, H., Guo, Z., Lin, Y., Jin, C., Chen, H.: LLM-driven medical report generation via communication-efficient heterogeneous federated learning. IEEE Trans. Med. Imaging **45**(1), 28–39 (2026). https://doi.org/10.1109/TMI.2025.3591185
7. El Ouadrhiri, A., Abdelhadi, A.: Differential privacy for deep and federated learning: a survey. IEEE access **10**, 22359–22380 (2022)
8. Feng, Q., et al.: Evit: privacy-preserving image retrieval via encrypted vision transformer in cloud computing. IEEE Trans. Circuits Syst. Video Technol. **34**(8), 7467–7483 (2024). https://doi.org/10.1109/TCSVT.2024.3370668
9. Guan, F., Zhu, T., Tong, H., Zhou, W.: Attention-based membership inference attacks on graph neural network through topological features. IEEE Trans. Dependable Secure Comput. **22**(6), 6469–6486 (2025). https://doi.org/10.1109/TDSC.2025.3586251
10. Han, K., et al.: A survey on vision transformer. IEEE Trans. Pattern Anal. Mach. Intell. **45**(1), 87–110 (2023). https://doi.org/10.1109/TPAMI.2022.3152247
11. Hatamizadeh, A., et al.: Do gradient inversion attacks make federated learning unsafe? IEEE Trans. Med. Imaging **42**(7), 2044–2056 (2023). https://doi.org/10.1109/TMI.2023.3239391
12. Hirose, M., Imaizumi, S., Kiya, H.: Learnable image encryption without key management for privacy-preserving vision transformer. IEEE Access **13**, 201351–201362 (2025). https://doi.org/10.1109/ACCESS.2025.3635235
13. Huang, Q.X., Yap, W.L., Chiu, M.Y., Sun, H.M.: Privacy-preserving deep learning with learnable image encryption on medical images. IEEE Access **10**, 66345–66355 (2022). https://doi.org/10.1109/ACCESS.2022.3185206
14. Huang, Y., Huang, C.Y., Li, X., Li, K.: A dataset auditing method for collaboratively trained machine learning models. IEEE Trans. Med. Imaging **42**(7), 2081–2090 (2023). https://doi.org/10.1109/TMI.2022.3220706
15. Ito, H., AprilPyone, M., Kiya, H.: Access control using spatially invariant permutation of feature maps for semantic segmentation models. In: 2021 Asia-Pacific Signal and Information Processing Association Annual Summit and Conference (APSIPA ASC), pp. 1833–1838 (2021)

16. Ito, H., Kinoshita, Y., Kiya, H.: Image transformation network for privacy-preserving deep neural networks and its security evaluation. In: 2020 IEEE 9th Global Conference on Consumer Electronics (GCCE), pp. 822–825. IEEE (2020)
17. Jiang, S., et al.: Dpfedsam-meas: Comparison of differential privacy federated learning in medical image classification. In: GLOBECOM 2024-2024 IEEE Global Communications Conference, pp. 1233–1238. IEEE (2024)
18. Jiang, Z., Xu, Y., Xu, H., Wang, Z., Qian, C.: Heterogeneity-aware federated learning with adaptive client selection and gradient compression. In: Proceedings of IEEE INFOCOM 2023. New York, NY, USA (2023)
19. Lee, J., Seif, M., Cho, J., Poor, H.V.: Exploring the privacy-energy consumption tradeoff for split federated learning. IEEE Network **38**(6), 388–395 (2024). https://doi.org/10.1109/MNET.2024.3395904
20. Lin, L.: Fedlppa: learning personalized prompt and aggregation for federated weakly-supervised medical image segmentation. IEEE Trans. Med. Imaging **44**(3), 1127–1139 (2025). https://doi.org/10.1109/TMI.2024.3483221
21. Malan, E., Peluso, V., Calimera, A., Macii, E., Montuschi, P.: Automatic layer freezing for communication efficiency in cross-device federated learning. IEEE Internet Things J. **11**(4), 6072–6083 (2024). https://doi.org/10.1109/JIOT.2023.3309691
22. Nickparvar, M.: Brain tumor MRI dataset (2021). https://doi.org/10.34740/KAGGLE/DSV/2645886, https://www.kaggle.com/dsv/2645886
23. Nikolovski, S.: Evaluating gdpr and hipaa in the integration. In: Applied Artificial Intelligence 4: Medicine, Biology, Chemistry, Financial, Games, Engineering: The Third Serbian International Conference on Applied Artificial Intelligence (SICAAI), vol. 1446, p. 289. Springer Nature (2025)
24. Oh, S.: Mix2sfl: two-way mixup for scalable, accurate, and communication-efficient split federated learning. IEEE Trans. Big Data **10**(3), 238–248 (2024). https://doi.org/10.1109/TBDATA.2023.3328424
25. Perez, F., Lopez, J., Arguello, H.: Privacy-preserving deep learning using deformable operators for secure task learning. In: ICASSP 2024 - 2024 IEEE International Conference on Acoustics, Speech and Signal Processing (ICASSP), pp. 5980–5984 (2024) https://doi.org/10.1109/ICASSP48485.2024.10446218
26. Raghu, M., Unterthiner, T., Kornblith, S., Zhang, C., Dosovitskiy, A.: Do vision transformers see like convolutional neural networks? Adv. Neural. Inf. Process. Syst. **34**, 12116–12128 (2021)
27. Rajpurkar, P., Chen, E., Banerjee, O., Topol, E.J.: Ai in health and medicine. Nat. Med. **28**(1), 31–38 (2022)
28. Shahid, S.S., Salman, T., Baza, M.: Mitigating gradient inversion attacks in energy theft using hierarchical federated learning. In: 2025 1st International Conference on Secure IoT, Assured and Trusted Computing (SATC), pp. 1–5. (2025). https://doi.org/10.1109/SATC65530.2025.11136999
29. Shi, Y., Xia, W., Niu, C., Wiedeman, C., Wang, G.: Privacy-preserving latent diffusion-based synthetic medical image generation. IEEE Trans. Med. Imag. (2025) https://doi.org/10.1109/TMI.2025.3618511
30. Tan, A.Z., Yu, H., Cui, L., Yang, Q.: Towards personalized federated learning. IEEE Trans. Neural Netw. Learn. Syst. **34**(12), 9587–9603 (2023). https://doi.org/10.1109/TNNLS.2022.3160699
31. Thang, D.D., Matsui, T.: Image transformation can make neural networks more robust against adversarial examples (2019). arXiv:1901.03037 arXiv preprint
32. Vaswani, A., et al.: Attention is all you need. In: Advances in Neural Information Processing Systems, vol. 30 (2017)

33. Wang, J., Guo, S., Xie, X., Qi, H.: Protect privacy from gradient leakage attack in federated learning. In: IEEE INFOCOM 2022-IEEE Conference on Computer Communications, pp. 580–589. IEEE (2022). https://doi.org/10.1109/INFOCOM48880.2022.9796841
34. Wang, Z., et al.: Hybrid makes better: Privacy-preserving medical image classification based on federated learning. In: GLOBECOM 2024 - 2024 IEEE Global Communications Conference, pp. 2816–2821 (2024) https://doi.org/10.1109/GLOBECOM52923.2024.10901764
35. Wang, Z., Chang, Z., Hu, J., Pang, X., Du, J., Chen, Y., Ren, K.: Breaking secure aggregation: label leakage from aggregated gradients in federated learning. In: Proceedings of IEEE INFOCOM 2024,, Vancouver, Canada (2024)
36. Wei, W., Liu, L.: Gradient leakage attack resilient deep learning. IEEE Trans. Inf. Forensics Secur. **17**, 303–316 (2022). https://doi.org/10.1109/TIFS.2021.3139777
37. Wen, J., Zhang, Z., Lan, Y., Cui, Z., Cai, J., Zhang, W.: A survey on federated learning: challenges and applications. Int. J. Mach. Learn. Cybern. **14**(2), 513–535 (2023)
38. Wu, R., Li, C., Zou, J., Liu, X., Zheng, H., Wang, S.: Generalizable reconstruction for accelerating mr imaging via federated learning with neural architecture search. IEEE Trans. Med. Imaging **44**(1), 106–117 (2025). https://doi.org/10.1109/TMI.2024.3432388
39. Xavier, D., Leite, L., Riker, A., Tsilopoulou, E.E.: Federated learning attack: Fast image leakage from gradients. In: 2025 IEEE 30th International Workshop on Computer Aided Modeling and Design of Communication Links and Networks (CAMAD), pp. 1–6. (2025). https://doi.org/10.1109/CAMAD67323.2025.11229909
40. Yan, X.: Sequential federated learning in hierarchical architecture on non-iid datasets. IEEE Trans. Mob. Comput. **24**(10), 11110–11124 (2025). https://doi.org/10.1109/TMC.2025.3573928
41. Zhang, P., Xu, L., Mei, L., Xu, C.: Sketch-based adaptive communication optimization in federated learning. IEEE Trans. Comput. **74**(1), 170–184 (2025). https://doi.org/10.1109/TC.2024.3475578
42. Zhou, J., Zhao, Y., Xu, Y., Xiao, M., Wu, J., Zhang, S.: PSFL: Parallel-sequential federated learning with convergence guarantees. In: IEEE INFOCOM 2025 - IEEE Conference on Computer Communications, pp. 1–10 (2025).https://doi.org/10.1109/INFOCOM55648.2025.11044534
43. Zhu, L., Liu, Z., Han, S.: Deep leakage from gradients. Adv. Neural. Inf. Process. Syst. **32**, (2019)
44. Zhu, M., Mao, A., Liu, J., Yuan, Y.: Deer: deviation eliminating and noise regulating for privacy-preserving federated low-rank adaptation. IEEE Trans. Med. Imaging **44**(4), 1783–1795 (2025). https://doi.org/10.1109/TMI.2024.3518539

TEE-Aided Asynchronous Trust Verification for Federated Learning via Functional Encryption

Nengjie Hua[1], Yufeng Li[1], Jiangtao Li[1(✉)], Yongqiu Wang[2], and Dandan Xiao[2]

[1] Shanghai University, Shanghai, China
{nengjiehua,liyufeng_shu,lijiangtao}@shu.edu.cn
[2] Yutong Bus Co., Ltd., Zhengzhou, China
{wyq,xiaodd}@yutong.com

Abstract. Federated Learning (FL) enables collaborative training for Internet of Vehicles (IoV) while protecting data privacy. However, encrypting shared gradients creates a "blind spot" that malicious nodes exploit to launch stealthy poisoning and Sybil attacks. To resolve this privacy-integrity paradox, we propose a TEE-aided asynchronous trust verification framework leveraging Function-Hiding Inner Product Encryption (FH-IPE) and Trusted Execution Environments (TEEs). Our framework enables the aggregator to verify the geometric consistency of updates directly in the encrypted domain. We introduce three core mechanisms: 1) hardware-enforced identity binding to prevent node spoofing; 2) TEE-enforced secure random projection to capture malicious deviations in high-dimensional data; and 3) a cryptographic dual-payload binding mechanism for integrity. This design supports non-blocking asynchronous execution, optimizing system throughput. Experimental results with 100 clients show that the framework reduces critical path latency by 12% by exploiting data homogeneity. Furthermore, it accurately detects stealthy poisoning attacks (AUC > 0.99) and deterministically prevents Sybil attacks, ensuring both privacy and safety for autonomous fleets.

Keywords: Federated Learning · Trust Verification · Function-Hiding Inner Product Encryption · TEE · Internet of Vehicles

1 Introduction

Federated Learning (FL) has emerged as a powerful paradigm for collaborative intelligence. It allows multiple parties to train a shared model without ever exchanging their raw private data. This approach is particularly valuable for safety-critical applications like the Internet of Vehicles (IoV). For example, a fleet of autonomous vehicles can collaboratively refine a trajectory prediction model using real-world driving datasets, such as NGSIM [1]. By sharing only

Y. Cao et al. (Eds.): SecureComm 2026, LNICST 704, pp. 269–289, 2027.
https://doi.org/10.1007/978-3-032-32764-2_14

local model updates rather than sensitive sensor logs, the system gains collective intelligence while protecting user privacy.

In this framework, protecting the gradients shared by vehicles is essential. Research has shown that raw gradients can leak sensitive information about the underlying training data, such as specific driving trajectories or locations, through "gradient leakage attacks" [25]. To prevent this, gradients are often encrypted or masked using techniques like Secure Multi-Party Computation or Homomorphic Encryption [4].

However, this layer of protection introduces a significant security dilemma: the lack of transparency. Because the gradients are encrypted to ensure privacy, the central server cannot inspect their individual contents to verify their honesty. Malicious vehicles can exploit this "blind spot" to launch stealthy poisoning attacks [26]. Specifically, attackers can inject carefully engineered gradients that manipulate scaling factors or directions to bypass traditional anomaly filters while remaining hidden within the encrypted pool. They may also employ "cloning attacks," where multiple malicious nodes upload identical forged updates to artificially increase their influence on the global model. Over time, these malicious updates cumulatively degrade the model's accuracy, ultimately compromising the safety and reliability of the entire autonomous fleet [16].

Establishing trust in this context, however, faces a fundamental conflict between *verification efficiency* and *privacy compliance*. First, the high mobility and unstable connectivity of vehicles make *strict synchronous* verification risky; waiting for global consensus binds the system's speed to the *slowest node (straggler)*, rendering the training pipeline vulnerable to network instability. Second, privacy regulations mandate the use of Secure Aggregation (e.g., SMPC [2]), which creates a "blind aggregator" dilemma: the server must filter malicious updates without accessing the underlying plaintext.

Existing defenses fail to resolve this dichotomy simultaneously. Privacy-centric methods (e.g., TEE-based aggregation [16,17]) often assume client honesty and lack mechanisms to detect internal poisoning. Conversely, trust-aware defenses [18,24] typically rely on plaintext inspection, violating privacy guarantees. While Zero-Knowledge Proofs (ZKPs) [15,22] and recent neighbor-based checks like Secure-FLOATING [10] attempt to bridge this gap, they exhibit distinct limitations. ZKPs primarily verify local syntactic constraints rather than semantic consistency. Secure-FLOATING, while computationally efficient, relies on *blocking synchronous execution*. This dependency limits its scalability and resilience in large-scale IoV networks, where network jitter is unavoidable.

To address these limitations, we propose a TEE-aided asynchronous trust verification framework. We leverage Function-Hiding Inner Product Encryption (FH-IPE) [11] to enable semantic consistency checks entirely in the encrypted domain. To tackle the blocking bottleneck, we introduce a dual-payload mechanism that decouples verification from aggregation. Our main contributions are:

1. **Encrypted Semantic Verification:** Leveraging the statistical homogeneity of honest updates, we utilize FH-IPE with TEE-enforced secure projection to verify the geometric consistency of encrypted updates. This mechanism

resolves the'blind aggregator' dilemma by detecting poisoning behaviors without leaking raw gradients.
2. **Asynchronous Architecture:** We propose a cryptographically bound dual-payload protocol. This allows the aggregator to broadcast the global model immediately while verification proceeds in the background, eliminating blocking latency caused by synchronous checks.
3. **Efficiency & Robustness:** Extensive experiments in high-dimensional settings ($N = 100$) demonstrate that our framework reduces end-to-end latency by approximately 12% compared to synchronous variant while maintaining high detection accuracy (AUC > 0.99) against stealthy poisoning attacks.

1.1 Related Work

Existing solutions for trustworthy FL typically face a tension between strict privacy and robust verification.

Privacy-Preserving Aggregation. Privacy-preserving federated learning methods aim to prevent the server from inspecting individual client updates. Representative approaches include SMPC-based secure aggregation protocols [2, 27] and differential privacy mechanisms [7]. In particular, differential privacy (DP), in both central and local variants, provides formal protection against gradient leakage and inference attacks by perturbing model updates. However, these techniques primarily address privacy risks rather than malicious update detection. Recent hardware-assisted systems (e.g., OLIVE [9], PPFL [16], and Flatee [17]) further improve efficiency by offloading aggregation to Trusted Execution Environments (TEEs). Despite these advances, most approaches assume client honesty and still suffer from the "blind aggregator" dilemma: while confidentiality is preserved, the server cannot verify the semantic consistency of updates against poisoning attacks. Our framework addresses this limitation by enabling trust verification under encrypted aggregation. Unlike DP-based approaches, which mainly mitigate inference risks, our method focuses on detecting malicious behavior without revealing underlying gradients. As a result, the two approaches are complementary and can be naturally combined in practice.

Robustness and Trust Assessment. Defense mechanisms for malicious client detection—such as reputation scores [24], reinforcement learning strategies [21], and geometric clustering (e.g., FLTrust [3] and FLAME [18])—typically rely on plaintext updates or observable statistical distributions, making them incompatible with strict secure aggregation. SafeFL [6] detects malicious clients using a synthetic dataset derived from early training trajectories, but still requires direct server-side access to model parameters or gradients. Secure-FLOATING [10] moves closer to privacy-preserving verification via neighbor-prediction consistency, yet it relies on synchronous execution and partially exposes geometric distances, introducing blocking latency without achieving strict function hiding.

Verifiable and Encrypted FL. To ensure integrity without revealing data, Zero-Knowledge Proof (ZKP) frameworks such as RoFL [15] and EIFFeL [22] allow clients to prove local constraints (e.g., norm bounds). However, they generally verify local syntactic correctness rather than inter-client semantic consistency, and often incur high overhead. By contrast, our framework combines Function-Hiding Inner Product Encryption (FH-IPE) [11] with TEE-based secure preprocessing to enable semantic consistency verification directly in the encrypted domain, while uniquely decoupling verification from the aggregation critical path through an asynchronous architecture.

Organization. Section 2 outlines the cryptographic and hardware preliminaries. Section 3 details the system architecture, threat model, and the proposed asynchronous verification protocol. Section 4 provides a comprehensive security analysis. Section 5 presents the experimental evaluation and efficiency analysis. Finally, Sect. 6 concludes the paper.

2 Preliminaries

2.1 Function-Hiding Inner-product Private-Key Functional Encryption

We recall the private-key Function-Hiding Inner Product Encryption (FH-IPE) scheme proposed by Kim et al. [11]. FH-IPE allows for the computation of the inner product $\langle \mathbf{x}, \mathbf{y} \rangle$ without revealing any additional information about the vectors $\mathbf{x}$ and $\mathbf{y}$.

Definition 1. *An FH-IPE scheme defined over the message space* $\mathbb{Z}_q^d$ *consists of the following polynomial-time algorithms:*

- $\mathsf{Setup}(1^\lambda, 1^d) \to \{\mathsf{pp}, \mathsf{msk}\}$: Given a security parameter λ and a dimension d, outputs public parameters pp and a master secret key msk associated with dimension d.
- $\mathsf{KeyGen}(\mathsf{msk}, \mathbf{y}) \to \mathsf{SK}_\mathbf{y}$: Given the master secret key msk and a vector $y \in \mathbb{Z}_q^d$, outputs the corresponding functional secret key $\mathsf{SK}_\mathbf{y}$.
- $\mathsf{Enc}(\mathsf{msk}, \mathbf{x}) \to \mathsf{CT}_\mathbf{x}$: Given the master secret key msk and a vector $x \in \mathbb{Z}_q^d$, outputs a ciphertext $\mathsf{CT}_\mathbf{x}$.
- $\mathsf{Dec}(\mathsf{pp}, \mathsf{SK}_\mathbf{y}, \mathsf{CT}_\mathbf{x}) \to Y$: Outputs the group element $Y = g^{\langle \mathbf{x}, \mathbf{y} \rangle}$. Subsequently, the scalar inner product $z = \langle \mathbf{x}, \mathbf{y} \rangle$ is recovered by solving the Discrete Logarithm Problem (DLP). *Note*: Decryption is only effective when the inner product result z lies within a polynomial range due to the computational hardness of the DLP.

Correctness. An FH-IPE scheme satisfies correctness if for all non-zero vectors $\mathbf{x}, \mathbf{y} \in \mathbb{Z}_q^d$ generated as above,

$$\Pr\left[\mathsf{Dec}(\mathsf{pp}, \mathsf{SK}_\mathbf{y}, \mathsf{CT}_\mathbf{x}) = \langle \mathbf{y}, \mathbf{x} \rangle\right] = 1 - \text{negl}(\lambda).$$

Function-Hiding Property. The security requirement of FH-IPE states that:

$$(\mathsf{SK}_{\mathbf{y}}, \mathsf{CT}_{\mathbf{x}}) \text{ reveals no information about } \mathbf{x}, \mathbf{y} \text{ beyond } \langle \mathbf{y}, \mathbf{x} \rangle.$$

In particular, even an adversary who holds both objects cannot distinguish between vectors with the same inner product.

2.2 Trusted Execution Environment (TEE)

Trusted Execution Environments (TEEs), such as Intel SGX [5] or ARM TrustZone [20], provide a hardware-enforced isolated execution context known as an *enclave*. TEEs guarantee the confidentiality and integrity of the code and data loaded within them, even when the underlying operating system (OS) or hypervisor is compromised. We focus on two fundamental capabilities relevant to secure computation frameworks:

- **Isolated Execution.** The memory regions allocated to an enclave are hardware-encrypted and access-controlled. This mechanism ensures that the internal execution state (including registers, stack, and heap) remains opaque to any external processes, including privileged system software. Consequently, sensitive data processed within the enclave is strictly protected from inspection or tampering by a malicious host.
- **Remote Attestation.** TEEs provide a cryptographic mechanism to prove the identity of the software running inside the enclave to a remote party. During attestation, the TEE hardware generates a digitally signed report containing a measurement (e.g., a hash) of the enclave's initial code and data layout. A remote verifier can validate this report to establish trust that they are communicating with a specific, unmodified algorithm running on genuine hardware, prior to provisioning any secrets or trusting its outputs.

3 Asynchronous Trust Verification Framework

3.1 System and Threat Model

As illustrated in Fig. 1, our framework operates within a standard Federated Learning architecture enhanced by Trusted Execution Environments (TEEs). The system comprises **Clients** (C_i) equipped with TEE (e.g., Intel SGX [5]) to securely execute sensitive projection operations, a semi-honest **Aggregator** ($\mathcal{A}$) that coordinates training, and a TEE-protected **Verifier** ($\mathcal{V}$) responsible for computing trust scores. Clients interact via a logical neighbor graph $G = (V, E)$, generating encrypted predictions to validate their peers.

Threat Model. We consider a robust threat landscape where a subset of clients may be fully malicious, launching data or model poisoning attacks [16], or attempting large-scale Sybil attacks by spawning multiple logical identities to subvert the consensus mechanism. While these adversaries may collude, we assume they cannot compromise the physical TEE hardware or break standard cryptographic primitives. Side-channel attacks (e.g., access patterns or timing leaks) are considered orthogonal threats that can be mitigated by complementary oblivious execution techniques [19]. The Aggregator is modeled as semi-honest; it follows the aggregation protocol but attempts to infer private information from transcripts. **Crucially, we assume $\mathcal{A}$ controls the network channel**, granting it the capability to drop, delay, or replay messages to manipulate verification outcomes.

To ensure protocol validity, we rely on three key assumptions: (1) hardware integrity of the TEE (isolation and attestation); (2) non-collusion between $\mathcal{A}$ and $\mathcal{V}$; and (3) a majority of honest neighbors for any benign client, ensuring that consensus-based trust scores are not dominated by attackers. These assumptions reflect a common operating regime in collaborative federated learning deployments where secure aggregation is combined with logically separated verification services. In this setting, the separation between the Aggregator and Verifier enforces practical role isolation, while a local honest majority ensures coarse geometric alignment among benign updates. Similar assumptions are widely adopted in robust FL literature. Extending the framework to more adversarial environments (e.g., fully colluding servers or highly heterogeneous client populations) would require additional mechanisms such as verifier replication, MPC-based verification, or personalized trust policies, which are beyond the scope of this work. Under this model, our goal is to achieve strict **Confidentiality** of gradients, **Integrity** of verification artifacts against forgery, and **Robustness** against poisoning attacks.

3.2 Security Enforcement Mechanisms

To ensure the integrity of the asynchronous verification process, our framework incorporates three cryptographic binding mechanisms designed to defend against interface abuse, replay attacks, and data inconsistency.

TEE Access Control via Tokens. A critical risk in TEE-aided systems is the "interface misuse" attack, where adversaries invoke the KeyGen function on arbitrary vectors to harvest information. To mitigate this, we introduce a **TEE Access Token** (token_i) that serves as a mandatory "gatekeeper" [5]. This token is cryptographically bound to the client's identity ID_i and the measurement of the authorized enclave code. It ensures that sensitive TEE functions can only be triggered by legitimate hardware running unmodified software, effectively preventing unauthorized key generation or cross-device key misuse. Beyond preventing function misuse, this binding mechanism implicitly fortifies the system against large-scale identity spoofing (Sybil attacks). During token issuance, the Key Generation Center (KGC) validates the unique hardware identifiers (e.g., PPID) in the remote attestation report. By rejecting registration requests from duplicate hardware signatures, we ensure that each logical identity is anchored to a distinct physical TEE. This imposes a prohibitive hardware cost on adversaries attempting to spawn mass malicious clients, thereby safeguarding the honest majority assumption required for effective verification.

Context and Version Binding. To defeat cross-round replay attacks—where a network adversary ($\mathcal{A}$) intercepts a legitimate update from round r and replays it in round $r+1$—we enforce strict **Context Binding**. Each client constructs a tag $tag_i = H(ID_i||r||\rho_r||w_{global}^{(r-1)})$ inside the TEE. By including the hash of the previous global model $w_{global}^{(r-1)}$, this tag explicitly binds the current update to the specific model version it was trained on. This allows the Verifier to detect and reject stale updates even if they carry valid signatures from previous rounds.

Dual-Payload Cryptographic Linkage. A unique challenge in our decoupled architecture is the "bait-and-switch" attack, where a malicious client might generate legitimate verification artifacts $\{SK_i, CT_i\}$ to pass the consistency check while simultaneously submitting a poisoned payload $C_{agg,i}$ for aggregation. We address this via **Dual-Payload Linkage**. The TEE treats the training update and verification artifacts as an atomic unit, generating a unified signature:

$$\sigma_{\text{TEE}} = \mathsf{Sign}_{\text{TEE}}(ID_i \,\|\, \mathsf{ctx}_i \,\|\, \mathsf{tag}_i \,\|\, H(C_{\text{agg},i}) \,\|\, H(SK_i) \,\|\, H(CT_i)) \qquad (1)$$

This signature mathematically locks the high-dimensional training payload to the low-dimensional verification keys. Any inconsistency between the two (e.g., substituting $C_{agg,i}$) invalidates σ_{TEE}, ensuring that the Verifier accepts only updates that are consistent with their trust scores.

3.3 Protocol Description

In the proposed framework, trust verification is implemented as an *implicit prediction mechanism* enabled by FH-IPE. Specifically, for a directed edge (i, j) in the neighbor graph, the Verifier utilizes the functional secret key SK_i—derived from client C_i's local update $\bar{w}_i$—to decrypt the ciphertext CT_j submitted by neighbor C_j. While the cryptographic operation mathematically computes the inner product $\langle \bar{w}_i, \bar{w}_j \rangle$, semantically this process represents client C_i using its own local update as a **reference prediction** to validate the behavior of client C_j. By enforcing a high similarity threshold, the protocol verifies that the neighbor's update is geometrically consistent with the local consensus derived from C_i, thereby effectively "predicting" the legitimacy of C_j entirely within the encrypted domain. However, to simultaneously thwart Sybil attacks, the Verifier also filters out updates exhibiting mathematically anomalous hyper-similarity (e.g., $s \approx 1$, as in Algorithm 1, Line 26), thereby ensuring that trust is grounded in genuine behavioral correlation rather than synthetic duplication.

To ensure the computational feasibility of FH-IPE on high-dimensional model updates and to enable efficient decryption (solving the discrete logarithm), we first introduce two TEE-enforced preprocessing functions utilized within the protocol:

- **Random Projection** (Map)**:** Let $\mathbf{R} \in \mathbb{Z}^{d' \times d}$ be a public random projection matrix, where $d' \ll d$ (e.g., $d' = 256$). Based on the Johnson-Lindenstrauss lemma [8], we define the projection of a vector $\mathbf{x} \in \mathbb{R}^d$ as:

$$\mathbf{v} = \mathsf{Map}(\mathbf{x}) = \mathbf{R} \cdot \mathbf{x}$$

This mapping preserves the cosine similarity of gradient updates in the lower-dimensional subspace with high probability.

- **Quantization (Q):** To bound the inner product for the discrete logarithm solver(e.g., BSGS [23]), we quantize the projected vector $\mathbf{v}$ into a finite integer ring $\mathbb{Z}_p$:

$$\bar{\mathbf{v}} = Q(\mathbf{v}) = \text{clip}(\lfloor \mathbf{v} \cdot \Delta \rceil, -B, B)$$

where Δ is a scaling factor and B is the quantization bound.

Algorithm 1: Async Trust Verification via TEE-Aided FH-IPE

Require: Clients i, Round r, Global Model $w_{global}^{(r-1)}$, Clone Tolerance δ, Thresholds θ, γ

Phase 1: Client-Side TEE Execution (Parallel)
for each client C_i **do**
  Input: Update w_i, Nonce ρ_r, Identity ID_i, Token token_i
  Assert: Verify token_i authorizes execution for ID_i.
  Construct Context: $ctx_i \leftarrow (ID_i, r, \rho_r)$
  Compute Tag: $tag_i \leftarrow H(ctx_i || w_{global}^{(r-1)})$
  Derive Matrix & Process: $R^{(r)} \leftarrow \text{PRNG}(seed_{pub} || \rho_r)$, $\bar{w}_i \leftarrow Q(R^{(r)} \cdot w_i)$
  Generate Artifacts: $SK_i \leftarrow \text{KeyGen}(\bar{w}_i)$, $CT_i \leftarrow \text{Enc}(\bar{w}_i)$
  Encrypt Payload: $C_{agg,i} \leftarrow \text{Enc}_{SA}(w_i)$
  Sign: $\sigma_i \leftarrow \text{Sign}_{\mathsf{TEE}}(ID_i || ctx_i || tag_i || H(C_{agg,i}) || H(SK_i) || H(CT_i))$
  Upload: $(C_{agg,i}, SK_i, CT_i, ID_i, ctx_i, tag_i, \sigma_i)$
end for
Phase 2: Authenticated Aggregation (Critical Path)
if Verify(σ_i) is valid for all i **then**
  Global Aggregation: $W_{enc}^{(r)} \leftarrow \text{SecureAgg}(\{C_{agg,i}\})$
  Broadcast $W_{enc}^{(r)}$ immediately. *// Non-blocking*
  Forward $\{SK_i, CT_i, ID_i, ctx_i, tag_i, \sigma_i\}$ to Verifier $\mathcal{V}$.
end if
Phase 3: Encrypted-Domain Verification (Asynchronous)
for each client i **do**
  Verify ctx_i, tag_i, σ_i. *// Check freshness & integrity*
  Initialize support count $cnt_i \leftarrow 0$.
  for each neighbor $j \in \mathcal{N}(i)$ **do**
    Compute Similarity: $z \leftarrow \text{FHIPE.Dec}(SK_j, CT_i)$
    Recover Scalar: $s_{j \to i} \leftarrow \text{BSGS}(z)$
    if $s_{j \to i} > 1 - \delta$ **then**
      // Clone Check: Reject anomaly
      $cnt_i \leftarrow cnt_i$ *// Skip counting (Potential Sybil)*
    else if $s_{j \to i} \geq \theta$ **then**
      $cnt_i \leftarrow cnt_i + 1$
    end if
  end for
  Compute Trust Score: $\tau_i^{(r)} \leftarrow cnt_i / |\mathcal{N}(i)|$
  if $\tau_i^{(r)} \geq \gamma$ **then**
    Add i to Trusted Set $\mathcal{T}^{(r)}$.
  end if
end for

We now describe the full verification protocol executed in each FL round.

Setup (Phase 0). Prior to training, the Key Generation Center (KGC) generates public parameters pp and master secret key msk. The msk is securely provisioned into each client's TEE. Crucially, the KGC also issues a cryptographically bound access token token_i to each client C_i, which serves as a mandatory authorization credential. Finally, a global seed $seed_{pub}$ is published to root the dynamic projection. **Following this one-time initialization, the per-round asynchronous verification protocol executes as detailed in Algorithm 1.**

Protocol Workflow Fig 1 summarizes the end-to-end message flow among clients, the Aggregator, and the Verifier in the proposed TEE-supported FH-IPE verification protocol.

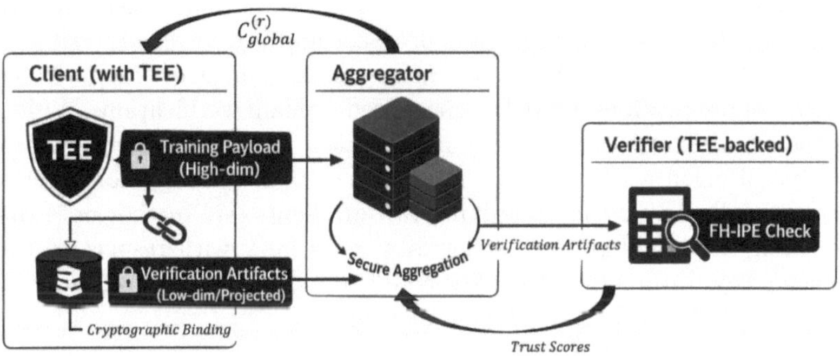

Fig. 1. System architecture and workflow of the TEE-aided FH-IPE trust verification framework. The Client's TEE generates cryptographically bound dual payloads to enable asynchronous trust verification decoupled from secure aggregation.

4 Security Analysis

We analyze the security of the proposed framework under the threat model defined in Sect. 3.1, focusing on three critical properties: confidentiality, integrity, and robustness.

4.1 Confidentiality and Function Hiding

The confidentiality of client gradients relies on the semantic security of the underlying cryptographic primitives and the isolation guarantees of the TEE. **Data Confidentiality.** Raw gradients w_i are processed exclusively within the client's TEE. Following the standard TEE threat model [5], assuming the hardware enforces memory isolation, the adversary (including the OS and the semi-honest Aggregator) observes only the encrypted payload $C_{agg,i}$ and the verification artifacts $\{SK_i, CT_i\}$. The confidentiality of $C_{agg,i}$ is guaranteed by the semantic security of the Secure Aggregation protocol. **Function Privacy.** For the verification artifacts, our reliance on FH-IPE ensures that the functional secret key SK_i and the ciphertext CT_j reveal nothing beyond the scalar inner product $z = \langle \bar{w}_i, \bar{w}_j \rangle$. As proven by Kim et al. [11], the FH-IPE scheme is SIM-security secure against chosen-plaintext attacks. Consequently, even if the Aggregator colludes with other clients, it cannot recover the underlying projected vectors $\bar{w}_i$ from the verification tokens, ensuring that the verification process reveals no information about the raw gradients beyond the scalar similarity score. **On KGC Compromise.** We clarify the confidentiality implications of a potential compromise of the Key Generation Center (KGC). In our framework, the KGC is responsible for generating the FH-IPE master secret key and provisioning it, together with enclave-bound access credentials, only to remotely attested client TEEs during initialization. Importantly, a compromise of the KGC does not directly expose the original high-dimensional gradients, since these updates are protected by the Secure Aggregation protocol and are never accessible to the KGC. The KGC only participates in the key management of the projected and quantized representations used for encrypted-domain verification. While leakage of the FH-IPE master secret key may weaken the confidentiality guarantees of these verification artifacts and enable misuse of the verification interface, it does not trivially reveal the underlying raw gradients. We further note that the current design does not provide strict forward secrecy with respect to the FH-IPE master key; in practice, this risk could be mitigated through periodic key rotation or distributed key-generation mechanisms.

4.2 Integrity Against Bait-and-Switch

A central threat in our decoupled architecture is the "bait-and-switch" attack. We prove the integrity of the dual-payload mechanism via reduction to the unforgeability of the TEE's signature scheme (EUF-CMA).

Proof Sketch. Let $\mathcal{A}$ be an adversary attempting to pass verification with an honest key SK_{honest} while injecting a poisoned payload C_{mal}. To succeed, $\mathcal{A}$ must produce a valid signature σ^* such that $\text{Verify}(\sigma^*, ID, \ldots, H(C_{mal}), H(SK_{honest})) = 1$. However, the legitimate signature σ_{TEE} is generated inside the enclave only after hashing the specific inputs provided by the trusted code path. Since the private signing key sk_{TEE} is hardware-bound and never leaves the enclave, any successful forgery of σ^* without executing the honest binding code reduces to breaking the EUF-CMA security of the underlying signature scheme (e.g., ECDSA). Therefore, the probability of such an attack is negligible.

4.3 Robustness Analysis

Finally, we address the resilience of the system against adversaries attempting to subvert the consensus via mass identity forgery (Sybil attacks), malicious update engineering (Collision attacks), or key probing (Adaptive attacks). **Resistance to Manipulation.** While the TEE-enforced hardware binding (Sect. 3.2) inherently rules out large-scale Sybil attacks by imposing prohibitive physical costs, a sophisticated adversary may still attempt to engineer malicious updates or probe the key using a single compromised device. **Dynamic Hardness.** The resistance against collision attacks relies on the unpredictability of the round-specific random projection matrix $R^{(r)}$. Since $R^{(r)}$ is derived from a fresh nonce ρ_r broadcast only at the start of each round, the adversary cannot anticipate the exact projection in advance and must operate under a strictly time-bounded setting. Constructing a poisoned vector w_{mal} such that $Q(R^{(r)} \cdot w_{mal}) \approx Q(R^{(r)} \cdot w_{benign})$, while still preserving a harmful deviation in the original parameter space, therefore reduces to a time-constrained high-dimensional constrained optimization problem. Intuitively, under the Johnson–Lindenstrauss property of random projections, maintaining such adversarial alignment after an unknown random mapping becomes increasingly unstable as the projected dimension d' grows. As a result, although not impossible in principle, such online evasion attempts become significantly more difficult in practice. **Restricted Interface.** To prevent adaptive chosen-ciphertext attacks where $\mathcal{A}$ probes SK_i with crafted vectors, our TEE-enforced protocol imposes a restricted interaction model. The Verifier accepts ciphertexts only if they carry a valid TEE attestation proving they were generated via the authorized projection code. This effectively limits the adversary to "honest-but-potentially-poisoned" inputs, preventing mathematical cryptanalysis of the FH-IPE keys.

5 Experimental Evaluation and Performance Analysis

5.1 Experimental Setup and Metrics

Implementation Environment. All experiments were conducted on a MacBook Pro (Apple M1, 8-core CPU, 16 GB RAM) running macOS 14.3. The core cryptographic primitives were implemented in **Rust** (v1.78) using the `fhipe` library to ensure realistic timing for elliptic-curve operations, and exposed to Python (v3.10) via `maturin`.

Topology and Assumptions. Unless otherwise specified, scalability experiments were conducted with varying numbers of Clients ($N \in \{20, 30, 50, 70, 100\}$) connected through synthetic neighbor graphs with controlled average degree.

For the general FL experiments (e.g., MNIST [13] and CIFAR 10 [12]), the neighbor graph is constructed based on logical participant association. In this setting, the trust verification mechanism relies on the **Homogeneity Assumption**: we postulate that in a benign training environment, honest clients contributing to the same global task will produce statistically similar gradient update directions. Consequently, when the Verifier applies C_i's key (SK_i) to C_j's ciphertext (CT_j), it is effectively verifying whether C_j's gradient vector falls within the reasonable subspace "predicted" by C_i's local observation. The FH-IPE protocol allows this pairwise consistency check to be performed without revealing the underlying gradient values, relying on the inner-product magnitude as a proxy for semantic alignment.

In the vehicular case study utilizing the NGSIM [1] dataset (Sect. 5.5), the verification logic is grounded in physical reality. First, the neighbor topology is dynamically constructed based on **real spatial proximity** within a synchronized time window. Once the physical neighbor graph is established, trust verification operates as a **cooperative consistency check**. Since vehicles in close spatiotemporal proximity typically exhibit highly correlated driving behaviors (e.g., consistent velocity flows or lane trajectories), a vehicle's local trajectory update serves as a robust **reference prediction** for its neighbors. The system employs FH-IPE to compute the similarity between these encrypted trajectory vectors, thereby identifying malicious clients that exhibit motion patterns deviating significantly from the local group trend.

Dimensionality and Quantization Settings. Consistent with the design rationale in Sect. 3, we acknowledge that applying FH-IPE directly to high-dimensional vectors (e.g., $d \approx 10^6$) is impractical. Therefore, unless otherwise stated, our experiments employ a **secure random projection** protocol, which can be deployed inside a TEE or other trusted execution environments. Local updates are mapped to a feature subspace of dimension $d' = 256$. This choice is not an ad hoc tuning decision, but is supported by the **sensitivity analysis** in Sect. 5.4, which shows that $d' = 256$ reaches a practical saturation point for detection accuracy ($AUC > 0.99$) while incurring only modest computational overhead. Subsequently, we apply scalar quantization to the projected vectors so that the resulting inner products remain within the tractable range of the Baby-step Giant-step (BSGS [23]) discrete logarithm solver. We emphasize that the practicality of FH-IPE in our framework relies on this controlled dimensionality reduction and bounded quantization strategy, which is an explicit part of the system design rather than a post-hoc parameter adjustment.

Evaluation Metrics. We primarily evaluated the proposed scheme from a system-level perspective, focusing on computational latency and verification behavior. In particular, we measured the *aggregator blocking time*, which captures the additional latency introduced on the aggregation Aggregator's critical path by the verification process. For synchronous schemes, this metric includes the full verification cost, whereas for asynchronous schemes it only accounts for task submission and in-memory aggregation overhead, as measured by `t_round_main` in our prototype. In addition, we assess verification throughput by examining how the system's processing capacity scales with the number of participating clients N and the underlying graph density.

5.2 Latency and Scalability Results

End-to-End Round Latency. Table 1 compares the critical-path latency across different schemes. While Secure-FLOATING (Baseline-1) achieves the lowest latency due to lightweight additive secret sharing, it lacks the function-hiding guarantees provided by FH-IPE. Among the encrypted verification schemes, **Ours-Async** demonstrates significant scalability advantages. As shown in Table 1, for $N = 100$, the asynchronous design reduces the critical-path latency by approximately **12%** (428.12 ms vs. 485.53 ms) compared to the synchronous variant (**Ours-Sync**). This improvement stems from our dual-payload architecture, which effectively offloads the computationally intensive FH-IPE verification and strict consistency checks to the background. Unlike the synchronous approach where verification blocks aggregation, our design limits critical-path overhead to deterministic TEE signature checks, ensuring high throughput as illustrated in Fig. 2.

Table 1. Round critical-path latency (ms) vs. Clients N (Density = 10). We compare against **Baseline-0** (SecAgg [2]) and **Baseline-1** (Secure-FLOATING [9]). Note that for **Ours-Async**, verification is offloaded to the background and thus excluded from critical-path latency. Configuration: MNIST ($d \approx 10^5 \rightarrow d' = 256$).

N	Baseline-0 [2]	Baseline-1 [10]	Ours-Sync	Ours-Async
20	27.34 ms	50.57 ms	105.67 ms	87.17 ms
30	36.06 ms	71.43 ms	143.52 ms	134.58 ms
50	61.20 ms	117.41 ms	246.43 ms	212.19 ms
70	88.97 ms	160.80 ms	371.57 ms	338.48 ms
100	118.37 ms	228.12 ms	485.53 ms	428.12 ms

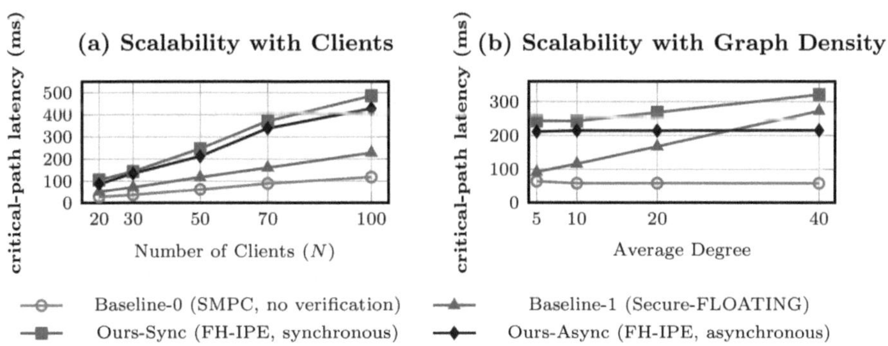

Fig. 2. Critical-path latency scalability. (a) Impact of participant count N; (b) Impact of graph density. Note that for *Ours-Async*, plotted latency excludes non-blocking background verification, demonstrating the efficiency of the asynchronous design.

Latency and Cost Analysis. To evaluate the practical efficiency of the proposed verification protocol, we conducted a system-level latency analysis using a real FH-IPE implementation with bounded discrete logarithm recovery (BSGS). All cryptographic operations are executed on an ARM64 platform, and the reported time reflects measured wall-clock latency.

Figure 3 provides a detailed cost breakdown based on our real-world FH-IPE implementation. While projection and quantization dominate the computational cost (Fig. 3(b)), our asynchronous architecture removes these operations from the critical path (Fig. 3(c)). Consequently, although the total verification effort remains comparable to the synchronous case, it no longer affects round completion time. This structural separation enables the system to maintain linear scalability (Fig. 3(a)) even with increasing client populations.

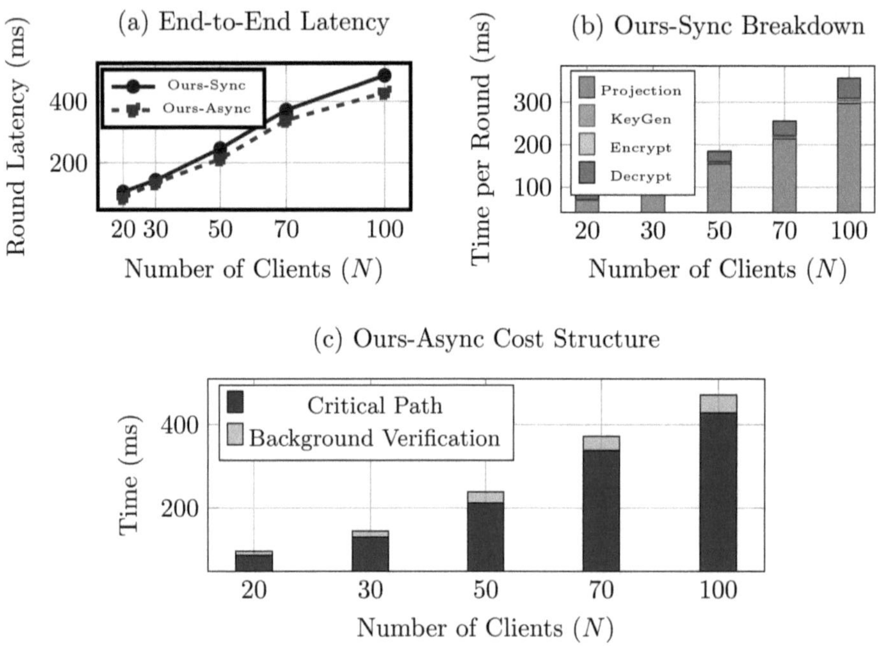

Fig. 3. Latency and cost analysis. (a) End-to-end comparison; (b) Synchronous cost breakdown; (c) Asynchronous cost structure (verification decoupled from critical path).

Estimation on Real TEE Hardware. While our prototype evaluation relies on the ARM64 architecture (Apple M1) to verify algorithmic feasibility, we estimate the performance latency on real TEE hardware (e.g., ARM TrustZone or Intel SGX) by referencing state-of-the-art benchmarks. According to the extensive evaluation in PPFL [16], the system overhead introduced by executing neural network layers inside TEE is approximately **15% for CPU execution time** and **18% for memory usage** compared to native REE execution.

Based on our sensitivity analysis in Sect. 5.4, the average client-side preprocessing latency (random projection and quantization) on the simulation platform is measured at $T_{sim} \approx 259.8$ ms. Applying the conservative TEE overhead factor ($\alpha \approx 1.15$) derived from PPFL, the estimated latency on real TEE hardware would be:

$$T_{\mathsf{TEE}} \approx T_{sim} \times (1 + 15\%) \approx 298.8\,\text{ms}.$$

This estimation indicates that even with hardware-enforced isolation, the verification overhead remains in the sub-second range. Crucially, since our framework employs an *asynchronous* architecture, this computation is offloaded from the critical aggregation path. Therefore, these results suggest that the additional context-switching costs of real TEE environments are unlikely to negate the low-latency advantages reported in Table 1. Nevertheless, a full enclave-native deployment and end-to-end evaluation on commodity SGX or TrustZone platforms remain important directions for future work.

5.3 Robustness of Malicious Client Detection Under Dimensionality Reduction

Attack Model (Stealthy Model Poisoning). We note that large-scale Sybil attacks are deterministically prevented by the hardware-binding mechanism at the registration phase (Sect. 3.2) and thus do not require probabilistic experimental validation. Consequently, under the threat model defined in Sect. 3, our evaluation focuses on the more challenging *stealthy model poisoning attack* launched by legally registered compromised clients. In this attack, malicious clients generate perturbed updates by linearly distorting benign updates and injecting structured noise:

$$\tilde{\mathbf{u}} = \alpha \mathbf{u} + \boldsymbol{\epsilon},$$

where $\alpha < 0$ controls the directional distortion and $\boldsymbol{\epsilon}$ denotes zero-mean Gaussian noise with variance proportional to the update scale. This attack preserves coarse statistical similarity with benign updates, making it difficult for naive distance- or norm-based detectors. Unless otherwise stated, all experiments in Sect. 5 adopt this attack instantiation.

We evaluate robustness under varying adversarial intensities by increasing the fraction of malicious clients from 0% to 40%. The key question is whether the proposed **secure projection** ($d' = 256 \ll d$) preserves sufficient discriminative information to reliably separate malicious updates from benign ones after dimensionality reduction.

Impact of Similarity Threshold. Figure 4 presents the detection performance across varying thresholds θ. Results indicate that $\theta \approx 0.2$ serves as the optimal operating point (Fig. 4(c)). At this threshold, the framework maintains near-perfect recall (>0.92) even when malicious clients constitute 30% of the population (Fig. 4(a)), while keeping the False Positive Rate (FPR) negligibly low

(Fig. 4(b)). Although the FPR naturally rises under extreme adversarial ratios (40%) due to stricter consistency enforcement, the system successfully prioritizes the exclusion of poisoners over benign inclusion, ensuring global model safety.

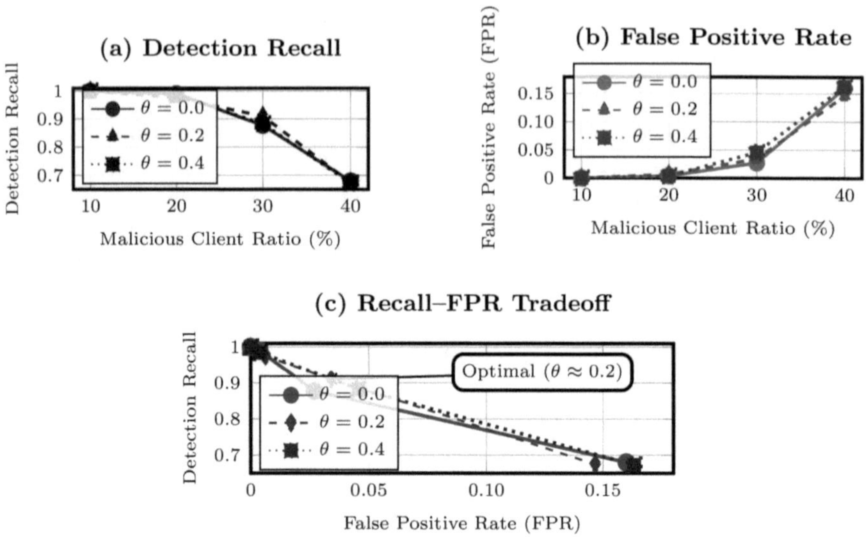

Fig. 4. Performance analysis and threshold selection. (a)-(c) Comparison of detection metrics under varying similarity thresholds θ. The results indicate that $\theta \approx 0.2$ (triangle markers) achieves the optimal trade-off, maintaining high recall (>0.92) even under 30% malicious ratios while keeping FPR low.

5.4 Sensitivity Analysis: Dimensionality vs. Security Trade-Off

While the previous experiments demonstrate that malicious clients can be reliably detected after secure projection with a fixed configuration ($d' = 256$), a natural question arises: *how should the projection dimension be chosen in practice?* In this subsection, we conducted a sensitivity analysis to quantify the trade-off between detection robustness and client-side computational overhead under different projected dimensions.

To determine the optimal projection dimension d', we evaluate the trade-off between detection robustness (AUC) and client-side overhead on CIFAR-10 ($d \approx 10^6$) using an ARM64 platform. Figure 5 illustrates this dynamic. At low dimensions ($d' = 64$), the projection loss obscures the malicious signal ($AUC \approx 0.88$). However, detection performance saturates rapidly at $d' = 256$, achieving near-perfect accuracy ($\mathbf{AUC} > 0.99$) with negligible marginal gains at higher dimensions (e.g., $d' = 1024$). Crucially, at this dimension, the TEE pre-processing overhead (projection + quantization) is merely ~259.8 ms per round.

Considering typical local training times (seconds to minutes), this overhead represents a minor fraction (<10%) of the total round latency. These results identify $d' = 256$ as the definitive **"sweet spot"**, balancing rigorous security guarantees with edge-device feasibility.

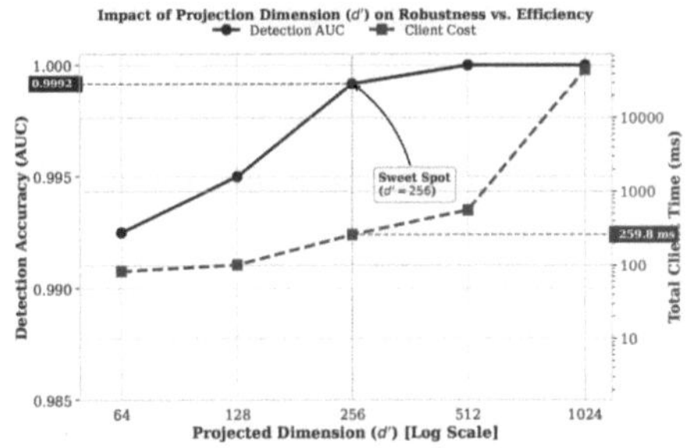

Fig. 5. Security (AUC) vs. Efficiency (Client Time) across dimensions d'. Results identify $d' = 256$ as the optimal "sweet spot," achieving near-perfect detection (AUC > 0.99) with minimal millisecond-level overhead.

5.5 Case Study: Vehicular FL Update Trust Verification with Real-World Trajectories

While the previous experiments on CIFAR-10 demonstrated the framework's robustness for high-dimensional neural networks, it is equally important to validate its performance in realistic edge scenarios with distinct data characteristics. Therefore, to validate the framework in a realistic cyber-physical setting, we evaluate it using real-world vehicle trajectories from the NGSIM dataset [1]. Unlike high-dimensional neural updates, trajectory vectors are compact, rendering projection overhead negligible (< 1 ms). Table 2 reports the performance metrics. While the synchronous approach achieves slightly better instantaneous precision (AUC $= 0.96$), it incurs higher blocking latency. In contrast, **Ours-Async** drastically reduces the critical-path latency (**5.53 ms** vs. 27.16 ms). Although the decoupled verification introduces a minor temporal lag (resulting in a slightly higher False Positive Rate of 0.075), the detection performance effectively converges over time as trust scores accumulate. This confirms that the framework can support real-time vehicular requirements without compromising long-term safety.

5.6 Discussion

Based on the experimental results, we further analyze the system's asymptotic efficiency, theoretical foundations, and limitations.

Table 2. Vehicular trust verification on NGSIM trajectories ($N = 50$, malicious ratio $= 20\%$).

Mode	Latency (ms)	Recall	FPR	AUC	Verification	Critical Path
Secure-FLOATING [10]	16.22	1.00	0.05	0.96	Secure-FLOATING	Yes
Ours-Sync	27.16	1.00	0.05	0.95	FH-IPE + DLP	Yes
Ours-Async	5.53	1.00	0.075	0.93	FH-IPE + DLP	No

Efficiency Analysis: Computation vs. Communication. A core advantage of our framework is the strategic shift from communication-bound MPC paradigms to a computation-bound yet optimized TEE model. While traditional MPC methods (e.g., Secure-FLOATING) suffer from bandwidth overheads scaling with graph density, our approach maintains a constant communication footprint (≈ 16 KB overhead for $d' = 256$), making it superior for bandwidth-constrained edge scenarios (e.g., IoV). Furthermore, the "curse of dimensionality" in FH-IPE is effectively neutralized by our TEE-enforced projection, reducing the complexity from $O(d)$ to $O(d')$, ensuring that cryptographic verification remains feasible even for high-dimensional models.

Dimensionality Sufficiency. Regarding whether $d' = 256$ is sufficient, studies on the intrinsic dimensionality of objective landscapes [14] suggest that gradients often reside in low-dimensional subspaces. Our results confirm that malicious updates aiming to diverge from the consensus direction exhibit significant angular deviations even in this projected space, validating the effectiveness of our compressed verification.

Limitations. Our framework relies on TEE hardware integrity and assumes a semi-honest Aggregator to enforce the exclusion of detected adversaries. This introduces a centralized trust point for revocation, which could be mitigated by decentralized accountability mechanisms (e.g., immutable public ledgers) to provide transparent audit trails and rollback support for asynchronous leakage. Because verification is decoupled from aggregation, a poisoned update may still exert a transient influence on the current round before its trust score is finalized. Although this effect is temporally bounded by subsequent exclusion, practical deployments may further reduce such exposure through staged model release, delayed activation, or rollback-assisted recovery. Regarding threat coverage, adaptive attacks exploiting TEE side-channels [19] remain out of scope. Another limitation arises in highly heterogeneous or strongly non-IID settings, where benign clients may naturally produce divergent updates, weakening the geometric alignment assumption behind similarity-based verification. In such cases, normal statistical heterogeneity may be difficult to distinguish from malicious manipulation, potentially increasing false positives under fixed trust thresholds. Addressing this issue would require scenario-aware threshold calibration, personalized trust policies, or other heterogeneity-aware extensions. Similarly, rare but legitimate updates caused by black-swan or out-of-distribution events may deviate from the dominant geometric trend and require adaptive trust policies to avoid over-filtering benign participants. Finally, our current evaluation validates algorithmic feasibility and system-level cost trends through a prototype implementation and benchmark-based TEE estimation. A full enclave-native deployment on commodity SGX or TrustZone platforms remains future work.

6 Conclusion

This work resolves the "blind aggregator" dilemma in Federated Learning by integrating TEE with Function-Hiding Inner Product Encryption (FH-IPE). We bridge the gap between cryptographic theory and system practicality through two key mechanisms: a TEE-enforced secure random projection that neutralizes the "curse of dimensionality," and a dual-payload cryptographic binding that enables fully asynchronous verification. Experimental results confirm that this design effectively decouples verification from the critical path, reducing end-to-end latency by approximately **12%** in high-dimensional settings while maintaining robust detection accuracy (**AUC** > 0.99) against stealthy poisoning. Future work will explore non-linear similarity metrics (e.g., approximated L_2 distance) and integration with decentralized ledgers, establishing a scalable foundation for accountable and real-time Federated Learning.

Acknowledgement. The work is supported by Major Science and Technology Special Projects in Henan Province (No. 241100240300); National Science Foundation of China (No. 62402305, 62476164).

References

1. Alexiadis, V., Colyar, J., Halkias, J., Hranac, R., McHale, G.: The next generation simulation program. Inst. Transp. Eng. (ITE) J. **74**(8), 22 (2004)
2. Bonawitz, K., et al.: Practical secure aggregation for privacy-preserving machine learning. In: Proceedings of the 2017 ACM SIGSAC Conference on Computer and Communications Security, pp. 1175–1191 (2017)
3. Cao, X., Fang, M., Liu, J., Gong, N.Z.: FLTrust: Byzantine-robust federated learning via trust bootstrapping. arXiv preprint arXiv:2012.13995 (2020)
4. Collins, E., Wang, M.: Federated learning: a survey on privacy-preserving collaborative intelligence. arXiv preprint arXiv:2504.17703 (2025)
5. Costan, V., Devadas, S.: Intel SGX explained. IACR Cryptology ePrint Archive **2016**, 086 (2016). https://eprint.iacr.org/2016/086
6. Dou, Z., Wang, J., Sun, W., Liu, Z., Fang, M.: Toward malicious clients detection in federated learning. In: Proceedings of the 20th ACM Asia Conference on Computer and Communications Security, pp. 456–472 (2025)
7. Dwork, C., McSherry, F., Nissim, K., Smith, A.: Calibrating noise to sensitivity in private data analysis. In: Halevi, S., Rabin, T. (eds.) TCC 2006. LNCS, vol. 3876, pp. 265–284. Springer, Heidelberg (2006). https://doi.org/10.1007/11681878_14
8. Johnson, W.B., Lindenstrauss, J.: Extensions of Lipschitz mappings into a Hilbert space. In: Conference in Modern Analysis and Probability, vol. 26, pp. 189–206. American Mathematical Society, Providence, RI (1984)

9. Kato, F., Cao, Y., Yoshikawa, M.: OLIVE: oblivious federated learning on trusted execution environment against the risk of sparsification. arXiv preprint arXiv:2202.07165 (2022)
10. Khan, J.A., Ozbay, K.: Secure-floating: scalable federated learning framework for real-time trust in mobility data using secure multi-party computation and blockchain. In: Proceedings of the 3rd USENIX Symposium on Vehicle Security and Privacy (VehicleSec '25), pp. 133–141. USENIX (2025). https://www.usenix.org/system/files/vehiclesec25-khan.pdf
11. Kim, S., Lewi, K., Mandal, A., Montgomery, H., Roy, A., Wu, D.J.: Function-hiding inner product encryption is practical. In: Catalano, D., De Prisco, R. (eds.) SCN 2018. LNCS, vol. 11035, pp. 544–562. Springer, Cham (2018). https://doi.org/10.1007/978-3-319-98113-0_29
12. Krizhevsky, A., Hinton, G.: Learning Multiple Layers of Features from Tiny Images (2009)
13. LeCun, Y., Bottou, L., Bengio, Y., Haffner, P.: Gradient-based learning applied to document recognition. Proc. IEEE **86**(11), 2278–2324 (2002)
14. Li, C., Farkhoor, H., Liu, R., Yosinski, J.: Measuring the intrinsic dimension of objective landscapes. In: International Conference on Learning Representations (ICLR) (2018). https://arxiv.org/abs/1804.08838
15. Lycklama, H., Burkhalter, L., Viand, A., Küchler, N., Hithnawi, A.: RoFL: robustness of secure federated learning. In: 2023 IEEE Symposium on Security and Privacy (SP), pp. 453–476. IEEE (2023)
16. Mo, F., Haddadi, H., Katevas, K., Marin, E., Perino, D., Kourtellis, N.: Ppfl: privacy-preserving federated learning with trusted execution environments. In: Proceedings of the 19th Annual International Conference on Mobile Systems, Applications, and Services (MobiSys), pp. 94–108. ACM (2021). https://doi.org/10.1145/3458864.3466628
17. Mondal, A., More, Y., Rooparaghunath, R.H., Gupta, D.: Poster: FLATEE: federated learning across trusted execution environments. In: 2021 IEEE European Symposium on Security and Privacy (EuroS&P), pp. 707–709. IEEE (2021)
18. Nguyen, T.D., et al.: {FLAME}: Taming backdoors in federated learning. In: 31st USENIX Security Symposium (USENIX Security 22), pp. 1415–1432 (2022)
19. Ohrimenko, O., et al.: Oblivious {Multi-Party} machine learning on trusted processors. In: 25th USENIX Security Symposium (USENIX Security 16), pp. 619–636 (2016)
20. Pinto, S., Santos, N.: Demystifying arm TrustZone: a comprehensive survey. ACM Comput. Surv. (CSUR) **51**(6), 1–36 (2019). https://doi.org/10.1145/3291047
21. Rjoub, G., Wahab, O.A., Bentahar, J., Cohen, R., Bataineh, A.S.: Trust-augmented deep reinforcement learning for federated learning client selection. Inf. Syst. Front. **26**, 1261–1278 (2024). https://doi.org/10.1007/s10796-022-10313-7
22. Roy Chowdhury, A., Guo, C., Jha, S., van der Maaten, L.: Eiffel: ensuring integrity for federated learning. In: Proceedings of the 2022 ACM SIGSAC Conference on Computer and Communications Security, pp. 2535–2549 (2022)
23. Shanks, D.: Class number, a theory of factorization, and genera. In: Proceedings of Symposia in Pure Mathematics, vol. 20, pp. 415–440. American Mathematical Society, Providence, RI (1971)
24. Tan, X., Ng, W.C., Lim, W.Y.B., Xiong, Z., Niyato, D., Yu, H.: Reputation-aware federated learning client selection based on stochastic integer programming. IEEE Trans. Big Data **10**(6), 953–964 (2022)
25. Wei, W., et al.: A framework for evaluating gradient leakage attacks in federated learning. arXiv arXiv:2004.10397 (2020)

26. Wu, J., Luo, F., Sun, T., Wang, H., Zhang, W.: Privacy-preserving federated learning scheme with mitigating model poisoning attacks: vulnerabilities and countermeasures. arXiv preprint arXiv:2506.23622 (2025)
27. Xu, R., Baracaldo, N., Zhou, Y., Anwar, A., Ludwig, H.: HybridAlpha: an efficient approach for privacy-preserving federated learning. In: Proceedings of the 12th ACM Workshop on Artificial Intelligence and Security (AISec), pp. 13–23. ACM (2019). https://doi.org/10.1145/3338501.3357371

Blockchain Protocols, Mining and Cross-Chain Systems

Ontology-Driven Authorization Semantics for Cross-Chain Bridges

Ylvie Khoo(✉), Leonardo Aniello, and Vladimiro Sassone

University of Southampton, Southampton, UK
{y.khoo,L.Aniello,vsassone}@soton.ac.uk

Abstract. Cross-chain bridges have become critical infrastructure for today's blockchain ecosystem, routinely carrying assets worth hundreds of millions of dollars across heterogeneous chains. Yet many of the most damaging bridge failures do not stem from broken cryptography, but from mismatches between what a proof or message is assumed to guarantee and what the destination contract actually verifies. These authorization-time assumptions are usually implicit, scattered across code, configuration, and informal documentation, and are therefore hard to audit, compare, or reason about systematically.

We argue that secure cross-chain communication requires an explicit, long-lived, machine-readable semantic interface at the authorization boundary. We present an ontology-driven interface that models messages, evidence, routes, headers, runtime policy, and context as first-class concepts, organized into reusable semantic anchors for domain binding, finality, ordering, uniqueness, and context compatibility. On top of this ontology, we build a SHACL-based diagnostic layer that classifies, for each evidence package, whether each anchor is evidenced, contradicted, or not established.

Using (i) a controlled mutation regression suite that targets each semantic anchor family and (ii) incident-aligned interface snapshots for three widely documented bridge incidents (Nomad, Wormhole, and Poly Network), we show that the resulting "assumption graphs" can localize semantic failures such as misconfigured trust roots, out-of-policy context, and route/domain misbinding—often without inspecting contract code. From these controlled and incident-aligned reconstructions, we derive a reusable interface template: a minimal set of fields and invariants that make authorization-time assumptions explicit, auditable, and comparable across bridge designs. Our results suggest that many catastrophic bridge failures could have been diagnosed earlier, had their authorization semantics been made visible at the interface level.

Keywords: Cross-chain bridges · Authorization boundary · Ontology · SHACL · Security diagnostics

Y. Cao et al. (Eds.): SecureComm 2026, LNICST 704, pp. 293–329, 2027.
https://doi.org/10.1007/978-3-032-32764-2_15

1 Introduction

1.1 Cross-Chain Security Needs a Semantic Interface

Cross-chain bridges and interoperability protocols have become critical infrastructure in today's blockchain ecosystem: they move assets and state across heterogeneous chains and increasingly sit on the main path of DeFi activity. Systematization work and surveys already give a detailed picture of bridge architectures, attack surfaces, and interoperability patterns [4,11,14,18,22]. They highlight recurring attack families—forged light-client proofs, compromised relayers and committees, misconfigured oracles, and cross-chain replay—and show that many catastrophic losses stem from subtle design flaws rather than low-level cryptographic breaks.

A growing subset of these incidents are not simple "code bugs", but failures of implicit assumptions at the *authorization boundary* on the destination side: what exactly is the destination contract assuming about the origin domain, the evidence, and the intended semantics of an incoming message? Recent bridge-hack reviews and incident analyses [4,14,22] repeatedly surface themes such as missing domain separation, ambiguous finality guarantees, replay of old messages across forks or chains, and misinterpretation of what a proof or signature actually attests to.

What is missing, however, is a *structured, machine-readable interface* that lives exactly at the authorization-time boundary and forces these assumptions to be spelled out and checked systematically. Destination contracts often treat a message as "valid" if its proof or signature passes verification, without any separate representation of what that proof is *supposed* to guarantee (e.g., that it is bound to a specific domain, that the underlying state is final and not subject to reorgs, that the message has not been consumed before, or that it was evaluated under a compatible security profile).

1.2 From Utopian Threat Lists to Semantic Anchors

A natural reaction to bridge failures has been to draw up increasingly rich "utopian" lists of things a secure cross-chain protocol should guarantee. Existing work often lists such desiderata, but rarely turns them into a concrete, reusable interface for running systems.

A natural next step after identifying these desiderata is to enforce them at the authorization boundary via concrete checks on messages, evidence, and runtime state. This paper takes a more foundational view: we ask how to *structure the assumptions themselves* into an explicit, machine-readable interface. Rather than starting from a specific bridge design and writing bespoke checks, we synthesize reusable *semantic anchors* that capture what must be true at authorization time and can later be mapped to enforcement mechanisms.

Concretely, we introduce the notion of *semantic anchors*: compact, reusable semantic units that describe "what must be true" about a cross-chain message or its evidence at the moment the destination authorizes an action. Examples include an anchor for *domain linkage* (what origin domain is this message intended to come from, and how is that bound to the evidence?), *finality and ordering* (what guarantees do we require about the block that produced this message?), *uniqueness and replay protection*, and *context compatibility* (e.g., key version, security profile, or validation scheme). Each anchor is designed to be:

- **Threat-aligned:** it is motivated directly by classes of failures documented in SoKs and empirical studies (e.g., cross-chain replay, ambiguous finality, misrouting, or stale context) [14,22];
- **Implementation-agnostic:** it does not commit to a specific bridge architecture or verification mechanism, but can be instantiated for different families (committee-based, optimistic, light-client-based, etc.);
- **Executably checkable:** it is designed so that the anchors can, in principle, be mapped to concrete checks over messages, proofs, and contract state by an implementation.

This paper is about how to *name*, *relate*, and *diagnose* these anchors in a principled way, not about how to implement low-level checks. We argue that an ontology-based representation of authorization-time semantics gives a suitable abstraction barrier: expressive enough for nuanced cross-chain assumptions, yet structured enough to support automated diagnostics and coverage analysis. Executable enforcement and deployment-scale audit measurement are therefore explicitly outside the scope of the present paper: here we focus on making authorization-time assumptions visible, structured, and diagnostically checkable at the interface level.

1.3 Ontology-Driven Semantic Interface and Contributions

Ontologies and constraint languages such as RDF(S), OWL 2, and SHACL are widely used to model rich domains with explicit concepts, relations, and machine-checkable constraints. Their use in security is more limited, and mostly focused on access-control policies or threat catalogues. In the cross-chain setting, we argue that an ontology-based approach is particularly attractive because:

- it allows us to treat authorization-time semantics as a *shared conceptual space* between protocol designers and enforcement engines, rather than as opaque code-level details;
- it provides native mechanisms to express consistency constraints and coverage properties, which we can leverage to detect missing or contradictory assumptions before they manifest as exploits;
- it decouples the evolution of semantic requirements (e.g., adding a new notion of "security profile") from the evolution of individual bridge implementations.

Building on these observations, we make the following contributions:

- We extract, from existing SoKs, surveys, and incident analyses on cross-chain bridges and replay vulnerabilities [11,14,18,22], a compact set of recurring authorization-time concerns (domain linkage, finality and ordering, uniqueness and replay protection, and context compatibility).

- We design a *semantic interface* for cross-chain authorization based on an RDF/OWL ontology whose primary building blocks are *semantic anchors*. Each anchor is modeled as a small, composable pattern of entities and relations, with associated integrity constraints expressed in SHACL. This interface is intentionally independent of any specific executable engine or bridge protocol.
- We define a family of diagnostic queries and SHACL constraint sets that operate over annotated cross-chain message schemas. These diagnostics are engineered to detect three classes of problems: (i) *missing anchors* (assumptions that are relevant to a given threat model but never made explicit), (ii) *internal inconsistencies* (anchors whose constraints cannot be jointly satisfied), and (iii) *mismatches between anchors and protocol families* (e.g., requesting strong finality properties from a protocol that only provides probabilistic finality). We instantiate our ontology on several representative bridge designs from the literature and from documented incidents, and we empirically show that the resulting diagnostics surface precisely the kinds of semantic gaps that have led to real-world exploits, while remaining robust across different architectural families.
- We evaluate semantic discriminability and diagnosability in two complementary settings: (i) a controlled mutation regression suite that targets each anchor family and exhibits anchor-level orthogonality (only the targeted family flips to *Contradicted*), and (ii) incident-aligned *interface-limited* vs. *augmented* snapshots for Nomad, Wormhole, and Poly Network that quantify diagnosability gaps (*NotEstablished*) and show how additional post-mortem evidence can turn them into explicit contradictions.
- Finally, we discuss how the ontology composes with a separate enforcement layer and why separating semantics from implementation details matters.

Scope and Relation to Subsequent Work. This paper focuses on the *representation and diagnosis layer* of cross-chain authorization semantics. Its primary contributions are the ontology, the SHACL-based diagnostic layer, the assumption-graph methodology, and the resulting interface template. It does *not* formalize executable authorization predicates under partial evidence, nor does it provide deployment-scale measurement of predicate decidability across live bridges. Those directions are developed in subsequent companion studies that build on the semantic abstractions introduced here, but address distinct theoretical and empirical questions. Accordingly, the present paper should be read as the semantic foundation of that broader research line, with distinct scope and novelty at the representation/diagnosis level.

This work addresses secure interpretation of cross-domain evidence and authorization-time semantics, aligning with SecureComm's focus on secure communication, distributed systems security, and Web3 infrastructures.

2 Background and Motivation

Cross-chain systems extend the security boundary of a blockchain beyond a single consensus domain: assets and state are locked, represented, or reflected across heterogeneous ledgers (source and destination chains plus intermediary systems such as oracles or committee chains). Existing surveys describe this ecosystem as both diverse and fragile [4,11,18]. Robinson provides an early taxonomy of cross-chain communication protocols and already notes subtle security assumptions around message delivery and replay [18]. Han et al. systematize cross-chain technologies more broadly and argue that interoperability mechanisms must treat trust, latency, and privacy assumptions as first-class rather than informal background conditions [11]. Bridge-focused SoK work catalogues dozens of high-impact bridge hacks and links them to recurring design flaws in how cross-chain evidence is interpreted on the destination side [14].

2.1 Cross-Chain Security Assumptions

Across SoKs and incident reports, a recurring pattern emerges: bridge designs implicitly rely on a small set of security-relevant assumption families: (i) *domain binding*, i.e., that an event or asset truly belongs to the expected source domain; (ii) *finality*, i.e., that the exported event will not be reverted or equivocated on the source chain; (iii) *ordering and temporal validity*, e.g., that a right or asset is claimed within a specific time window or after certain prerequisites; and (iv) *uniqueness and non-replay*, i.e., that the same source event cannot be used to claim value multiple times across destinations.

Bridge SoKs show how violations of these assumptions lead to large losses [14,22]. Recent reports document cases where destination contracts accept messages signed by a compromised validator set without binding those signatures to a specific source chain, fork-choice rule, or epoch [14]. Empirical analyses of signature replay in smart contracts make a similar point in a single-chain context: a cryptographic signature can be re-used across logically distinct transaction contexts if the contract does not explicitly encode the intended domain and purpose [5]. In cross-chain settings, replay risks are amplified by heterogeneous address formats, replayable signatures across chains, and intermediary systems that normalize or re-encode messages [7].

We refer to such intended meanings as *semantic anchors*: small, composable authorization-time statements that can be compared and checked against boundary-visible evidence.

2.2 Ontologies and SHACL in Security

Ontologies and constraint languages such as RDF(S), OWL 2, and SHACL are widely used to capture domain concepts and validate data in a machine-readable way [20,21]. Security research has adopted them mainly for modeling assets, threats, and controls, and for supporting compliance and risk analysis [9,12,15,19]. The closest prior security ontologies focus on generic access-control or compliance concepts—for example, subject/object/policy vocabularies in OSNAC [15], broader information-security concept hierarchies [12], or control/compliance mappings [9,19]. They are valuable, but they do not model cross-chain boundary artefacts such as message/evidence linkage, route binding, trusted headers and roots, replay state, or bridge-specific context as first-class concepts. Existing ontologies therefore rarely address low-level authorization semantics across chains, such as how a relayed message is bound to a specific source domain, finality policy, or uniqueness guarantee. This gap motivates our focus on an ontology tailored to cross-chain authorization-time assumptions, coupled with a SHACL-based constraint layer that can expose omissions and inconsistencies in how bridges encode these assumptions.

3 Semantic Interface Design

This section presents the semantic interface for authorization-time assumptions in cross-chain bridges. It has two layers: (i) an ontology that models messages, evidence, routing, and runtime state at the authorization boundary; and (ii) a SHACL-based diagnostic layer that evaluates evidence packages and assigns three-valued outcomes. We focus strictly on what a destination-side authorization component can see when it decides to accept or reject a cross-chain action.

3.1 Modeling Goals and Design Principles

The ontology is deliberately narrow. Rather than modeling full bridge architectures, it targets semantics that matter *at authorization time*, i.e., when the destination processes a message from another consensus domain. Four principles guide the design.

Boundary-Centric Modeling. We model only artefacts and state that are visible at the authorization boundary: application messages, evidence bundles, routing information, headers and state roots, and a summary of destination-side configuration and runtime state. Internal bridge contracts, relayer logic, and consensus protocols remain outside the ontology.

Alignment with Failure Modes. The ontology is organized around assumption families that recur across bridge incidents and SoKs: how messages are linked to the evidence that justifies them, how headers and roots are trusted and treated as final, how routing information is checked against policy, how ordering and replay protection are enforced, and how context (such as validator sets or security profiles) is matched against configuration. Modeling choices are guided by documented failure modes rather than by completeness.

Factorability and Reuse. Complex security statements are decomposed into small, composable semantic anchors. Instead of a monolithic statement like "the bridge proof is correct", we separate: whether evidence actually refers to the same message (message–evidence linkage), whether referenced headers are accepted as trustworthy and sufficiently final under the bridge's own policy (header and finality semantics), whether the route of a message is coherent with what the evidence claims and with what policy allows (routing semantics), whether a message appears in the right order and is not reused (ordering and single-use semantics), and whether auxiliary context (such as validator-set identifiers or circuit versions) is compatible with runtime rules (context semantics). Different protocols reuse these semantic checks in different combinations.

3.2 Ontology Schema for Messages, Evidence, and State

The ontology (`ontology.ttl`, namespace `xchain:`) models the *authorization-boundary view* of cross-chain interactions: what the destination-side authorization component can observe about a message, the evidence presented for it, and the runtime policies in force. A simplified view of the ontology is shown in Fig. 4 for readability. The complete ontology with all classes and properties is provided in Fig. 5. Representative TTL fragments of the ontology used by our diagnostics are included in Appendix F.

Core Artifacts. We rely on five core classes.

- `xchain:Message` represents the application-level cross-chain intent: payload (or payload hash), a stable message identifier, a claimed route, and optional metadata such as a sequence number.
- `xchain:Evidence` is the bundle consumed at the boundary to justify acting on a message: it links to the message, carries attested payload hashes and identifiers, references a source-side header or state root when available, and includes context- and policy-relevant parameters (for example a finality flag, timeout mode, or key/value context).
- `xchain:Header` abstracts over source-side headers or state roots referenced by evidence; it exposes height, time, and hash to support header-related reasoning.
- `xchain:Route` represents $(src, dst, profile)$ routing: chain or domain identifiers plus a route profile (e.g., channel or bridge-contract identifiers) as a string and/or key-value entries.
- `xchain:RuntimeState` represents destination-side runtime policy and state at authorization time: current time and height, allowed routes, trusted roots, finality/timeout policy, replay/ordering state, and admissible context rules.

Routes and Context. A route specifies source and destination chain identifiers together with a route profile, optionally expanded through `xchain:RouterKVEntry` nodes. Evidence can also carry context as `xchain:ContextKVEntry` nodes (for example, validator-set identifiers, security profiles, or circuit versions). Runtime policy constrains admissible context through `xchain:ContextRule` entries with a key, value, and operator such as `EQ` or `GE`.

Trusted Roots and Policy Snapshots. Trusted roots are represented explicitly (`xchain:TrustedRoot`) and referenced from runtime state, optionally with validity windows and revocation markers. We treat trust and finality as opaque, bridge-configured policies: the ontology does not model a concrete consensus protocol, only whether a given header is exposed at the boundary as "final enough" under the bridge's own configuration. This is exactly the information that our diagnostics use to reason about header trust and finality, without committing to a particular consensus model.

3.3 SHACL-Based Diagnostics and Three-Valued Outcomes

The diagnostic layer is defined in `shapes.ttl` using SHACL. Representative SHACL fragments (including anchor-level SPARQL constraints) are provided in Appendix F. All node shapes target `xchain:Evidence`: each evidence package is evaluated by a set of constraints that correspond to the semantic anchor families described above. For each family, we distinguish two kinds of shapes:

- *Capability shapes*, which check whether the inputs required for a diagnosis are present; and
- *Core shapes*, which check whether the corresponding semantic condition holds when inputs are available.

From the SHACL report, we derive, for each anchor family and each evidence package under a given runtime state, one of three outcomes:

We map SHACL reports to three outcomes: *Evidenced* (inputs present, no violations), *Contradicted* (inputs present, violations), and *NotEstablished* (missing required inputs).

Importantly, our *baseline* scenarios are reference snapshots rather than claims of universal correctness: a baseline may still contain *NotEstablished* anchors if an interface dimension is not exposed by the bridge, and it may contain *Contradicted* anchors if the documented configuration is internally inconsistent under our schema.

Concrete shapes implement these families over the ontology schema. For example, some shapes compare message identifiers and payload hashes between `xchain:Evidence` and `xchain:Message` (message–evidence linkage); others relate message routes to attested routes and runtime allow-lists (routing semantics); others again check the relationship between referenced headers and trusted-root/finality policy (header and finality semantics); yet others compare header times, timeout parameters, and current time (time-window semantics); use sequence numbers and delivered-sets (ordering and single-use semantics); or match evidence-side context key-value pairs against runtime `xchain:ContextRule` entries (context semantics).

We deliberately avoid modeling full bridge architectures, economic incentives, or chain-internal protocol details; those belong to other ontologies and tools. Instead, the vocabulary is just rich enough to support the semantic questions we evaluate in Sect. 5, while remaining compact enough that practitioners can realistically annotate real-world bridges with it.

3.4 Implementation Snapshot

We store scenarios as RDF graphs, validate them with an off-the-shelf SHACL engine, and post-process reports into three-valued outcomes and assumption graphs.

4 Methodology

We use the semantic interface to reconstruct authorization-time assumptions for concrete bridge designs and incidents. The workflow has five steps: (i) selecting case studies, (ii) encoding boundary-visible artefacts into RDF, (iii) normalizing informal assumptions into reusable semantic families, (iv) constructing assumption graphs, and (v) computing three-valued diagnostics via SHACL.

4.1 Case Study Selection and Scope

We focus on publicly documented bridge failures and design patterns where destination-side authorization semantics are central to the exploit or threat model and where protocol documentation, post-mortems, or technical analyses are available. Our evaluation combines two complementary styles of reconstruction. First, we instantiate three *self-contained diagnostic archetypes* as baseline/incident scenario pairs (Bridge A/B/C), each isolating one dominant authorization-boundary failure mode—trusted-root misuse, context-policy incompatibility, or route/domain misbinding—that recurs across public bridge reports. Second, to connect the interface-level semantics to concrete high-impact events, we additionally construct *incident-aligned interface snapshots* for Nomad, Wormhole, and Poly Network using an interface-limited vs. augmented methodology (Sect. 5.7). This design keeps the core evaluation reproducible and self-contained while still grounding the anchor families in real bridge failures and making interface diagnosability gaps explicit.

4.2 Conceptualization and Competence Questions

Our conceptualization process starts from recurring *authorization-boundary questions* rather than from protocol internals. From public incident analyses and bridge specifications, we extracted candidate assumptions and retained only those that satisfy three criteria: (i) they recur across multiple bridge families or incident reports, (ii) they can be expressed over boundary-visible artifacts (message, evidence, header/root, route, runtime state, and context), and (iii) they can be operationalized by ontology terms plus SHACL constraints. This process yielded the seven anchor families used in the current paper. We do not claim that these seven families exhaust all possible cross-chain failures; rather, they form a compact recurring core for authorization-boundary diagnosis under the boundary-visible evidence model studied here.

The following competence questions guided the ontology design and now serve as a compact evaluation target.

1. Can the destination establish that the evidence is bound to the same claimed source/destination route (including route-profile identifiers) as the message being authorized?
2. Can the destination establish that a referenced header or root is currently trusted and admissible under local policy (e.g., active and non-revoked)?
3. Can the destination establish that the referenced source-side state is final enough under the configured finality rule?
4. Can the destination establish that timeout or freshness conditions are still satisfied at authorization time (given header time and current time)?
5. Can the destination establish that the message is in-order with respect to the runtime sequence state for the relevant route scope?
6. Can the destination establish that the message has not already been consumed (non-replay/single-use) under the relevant scope?
7. Can the destination establish that context carried by the evidence (e.g., epoch, key-set, security profile, circuit/version) is compatible with runtime policy?

These questions explain both the ontology vocabulary and the diagnostic separation between *Contradicted* and *NotEstablished*: some failures are genuine semantic inconsistencies, while others reflect that the deployed interface does not expose enough information to decide the question at all.

For readability in the remainder of the paper, we refer to these seven recurring semantic checks using descriptive diagnostic phrases (for example, "the evidence matches the claimed route" and "the message has not been processed before") rather than compact tags.

4.3 Workflow

For each representative bridge scenario, we construct two RDF graphs: a baseline snapshot (documented normal operation) and an incident snapshot (a controlled incident variant that violates one dominant semantic family). Each graph contains messages, evidence packages, referenced headers or state roots (when applicable), and a runtime-state node capturing policies and authorization-time state (allowed routes, trusted roots, ordering and replay state, time parameters, and context rules).

From design documents, verification code, and post-mortems we extract the authorization assumptions that connect messages, evidence claims, and accept/reject decisions. We normalize these assumptions into a small set of semantic families (route and domain linkage, header trust and finality, timeliness and ordering, uniqueness and replay protection, and context compatibility).

We then run the SHACL shapes from Sect. 3 on each scenario graph. For every evidence package and assumption family we derive a three-valued outcome (Evidenced, Contradicted, NotEstablished) and attach it to an assumption graph that links ontology individuals, normalized assumptions, and diagnostic results. This graph supports slicing by semantic family, route, or incident to expose where authorization-time semantics are evidenced, contradicted, or absent.

Implementation details, artifact availability, and disclosure statements are summarized in Sect. 11. The corresponding repository is available via https://github.com/KYlvie/XChainOnto.

5 Case Studies and Evaluation

Our evaluation focuses on semantic discriminability and diagnostic precision under diverse cross-chain communication conditions, rather than throughput-oriented benchmarks.

We now instantiate our semantic interface on concrete bridge designs and incidents. We consider three representative case studies: (i) a trust-root misconfiguration at the authorization boundary (Bridge A); (ii) an evidence-context incompatibility that violates an epoch-based policy check (Bridge B); and (iii) an explicit domain-binding mismatch between a message route and an attested route profile (Bridge C). Together, these cases cover trust-root semantics, context-rule satisfaction, and route-level domain binding at the authorization boundary.

In this revision, the case studies should be read as *diagnostic archetypes informed by real incidents*, not as exhaustive end-to-end exploit replays. This is deliberate: the paper's core claim concerns the diagnosability of authorization-time assumptions once they are represented explicitly at the interface. The current A/B/C scenarios therefore evaluate semantic discriminability under controlled, boundary-visible mutations; additional incident-specific reconstructions can be layered on top of the same ontology and SHACL machinery without changing the core design.

5.1 Experimental Setup

Implementation. We instantiate the ontology and SHACL shapes from Sect. 3 on the case-study graphs and use a standard SHACL engine to obtain validation reports, which we post-process into three-valued outcomes and assumption graphs as in Sect. 4.

Case Study Graphs. For every bridge and incident, we construct one RDF graph G per scenario: (i) a *baseline* snapshot and (ii) an *incident* snapshot.

Baseline construction is driven by a concrete authorization-boundary snapshot collected from a live EVM chain. We first collect a reproducible snapshot into `baseline_ok.json` via `collect_baseline.py`, parameterized by an RPC endpoint, a target contract address, and a specific transaction hash (optionally fixing a `logIndex` deterministically). The snapshot contains three top-level objects: `msg`, `evidence`, and `state`. We then normalize `baseline_ok.json` into a shapes-aligned internal schema (implemented in `generate_cases.py`) and emit RDF graphs that match the expectations of `shapes.ttl`. Where required fields are missing or ill-typed, we apply deterministic, documented fallbacks that preserve internal consistency and keep the scenario evaluable.

Incident construction starts from the same baseline schema and applies a small, controlled mutation that targets one semantic anchor family per case study: (i) a trusted-root revocation toggle (Bridge A), (ii) a context value violation for `epoch_id` (Bridge B), and (iii) an attested route-profile mismatch on `router_kv.contract` (Bridge C). These mutations are designed to flip a single dominant anchor outcome from *Evidenced* to *Contradicted* while leaving unrelated families unchanged.

Measured Outcomes. For each evidence node e and anchor family A, we compute a three-valued outcome $\mathsf{diag}_A(e, \sigma) \in \{\mathsf{Evidenced}, \mathsf{Contradicted}, \mathsf{NotEstablished}\}$, where σ is the runtime state. We summarize the resulting distributions of Evidenced, Contradicted, and NotEstablished outcomes across bridges and incidents in Sect. 5.5.

Evaluation Scope and Non-goals. This evaluation is not a supervised exploit-detection benchmark and therefore does not use precision/recall over a large labelled corpus. The controlled mutations are diagnostic probes used to test whether each semantic check can be selectively contradicted while the others remain evidenced, and the incident-aligned IL/AUG reconstructions test whether additional evidence moves a check from *NotEstablished* to either *Evidenced* or *Contradicted* in the expected direction. Existing bridge monitoring tools and prior ontologies do not emit comparable per-check three-valued labels over authorization-boundary instances, so there is no direct drop-in baseline for this exact task. The most relevant baseline is careful manual interface inspection; our claim is not that SHACL outperforms human auditors, but that it turns such inspection into a reproducible, machine-checkable diagnostic procedure whose outputs can be rerun, compared, and integrated into tooling.

5.2 Case Study I: Misconfigured Trust Root (Bridge A)

Bridge Design and Incident Summary. Bridge A models a boundary configuration where authorization relies on a trusted-root set for validating header/root references. The incident scenario captures a *trust-root revocation* error at the boundary: a root that is needed to validate the presented evidence is marked as revoked, which should cause the evidence-to-root linkage to fail under the stated policy. This archetype is informed by trusted-root and header-admissibility failures discussed in public bridge post-mortems, but is intentionally instantiated here as a boundary-visible semantic probe rather than as a full exploit replay.

Ontology Encoding. We model (i) a message with identifiers, payload hash, and route; (ii) an evidence package that references a header/root; and (iii) a runtime snapshot containing allowed routes and a set of trusted roots. The baseline snapshot includes an active trusted root compatible with the evidence reference. The incident snapshot differs by toggling the relevant trusted root to `revoked=true`.

Anchor Outcomes. Diagnostics isolate the failure to the trusted-header check: the trusted-header check flips from **Evidenced** (baseline) to **Contradicted** (incident), while the claimed-route check, the finality-policy check, the time-window check, runtime ordering, non-replay, and context-rule satisfaction remain **Evidenced** under the controlled mutation.

Takeaway. In this archetype, the incident does not primarily reflect missing boundary checks but a mis-specified notion of "trusted" at the interface. Making root transitions and their context explicit can reduce the grey *NotEstablished* region and surface misconfiguration as a *Contradicted* assumption in the resulting graphs.

5.3 Case Study II: Evidence-Context Incompatibility (Bridge B)

Bridge Design and Incident Summary. Bridge B captures an authorization boundary where evidence packages carry explicit context parameters whose admissibility is constrained by runtime policy (e.g., epoch, key-version, committee set, or security profile). Such context-dependent semantics repeatedly appear in SoKs and incident reviews as a source of misinterpretation and "semantic drift" between what attestations are intended to mean and what the destination actually enforces [14,22].

In the incident scenario, the evidence carries an `epoch_id` value that violates the configured admissibility rule (e.g., an epoch lower than the required minimum). This models a boundary-visible incompatibility: the evidence is internally well-formed and consistent on identifiers and routing, yet it is issued under a context that should be rejected by policy.

Ontology Encoding. We encode Bridge B as follows.

- Messages are `xchain:Message` nodes with stable identifiers, payload hashes, and routes.
- Evidence packages are `xchain:Evidence` nodes that (i) reference the message and (ii) carry context as `xchain:ContextKVEntry` nodes, including an `epoch_id` entry.
- The runtime state includes an allow-list of routes as well as explicit context admissibility rules represented as `xchain:ContextRule` entries (e.g., constraints such as `epoch_id` ≥ 1).
- The incident snapshot mutates the evidence-side context by setting `epoch_id` to an out-of-policy value, while keeping the remaining message/evidence linkage, route fields, and replay/ordering state unchanged.

Anchor Outcomes. Under the baseline configuration, the *context-rule check* is **Evidenced** because the evidence-side `epoch_id` satisfies the runtime `xchain:ContextRule` constraints. Under the incident configuration, the same check becomes **Contradicted**: the required inputs are present, but the mutated `epoch_id` violates the configured rule. By contrast, the claimed-route, trusted-header, finality-policy, and time-window checks, together with runtime ordering and non-replay, remain **Evidenced** because their inputs and relationships are unchanged.

Takeaway. This case illustrates how an explicit, structured context interface turns an otherwise implicit "wrong epoch/wrong key-set/wrong profile" failure mode into a boundary-level contradiction that can be localized and audited, even when the other semantic checks remain fully evidenced.

5.4 Case Study III: Explicit Claimed-Route Mismatch (Bridge C)

Bridge Design and Incident Summary. Bridge C captures a route-profile-based binding pattern: beyond the coarse $(src, dst, profile)$ tuple, the authorization boundary relies on a route-profile key–value entry (e.g., a contract identifier) to bind a message to the intended domain and handler instance. Domain separation and misrouting/misbinding themes recur in cross-chain surveys and SoKs [11, 18, 22], and are often implicated when evidence is not sufficiently bound to the intended domain. This scenario abstracts that family of route/domain confusions into a controlled, machine-checkable mutation.

In the incident scenario, the evidence attests to a *different* route-profile value than the one associated with the message route, producing an explicit claimed-route mismatch at the authorization boundary.

Ontology Encoding. We encode Bridge C as follows.

- Messages are `xchain:Message` nodes with a route and an associated route-profile.
- Evidence packages carry an *attested route* with route-profile key–value entries (modeled as `xchain:RouterKVEntry` nodes), including `router_kv.contract`.
- The baseline snapshot is internally consistent: the attested route profile matches the message route profile.
- The incident snapshot mutates the evidence-side attested route profile by changing `router_kv.contract` to a distinct value, while leaving other fields unchanged.

Anchor Outcomes. Diagnostics localize the failure to the claimed-route check: the claimed-route check flips from **Evidenced** (baseline) to **Contradicted** (incident) due to the attested route-profile mismatch. The remaining diagnostic checks stay **Evidenced** under this controlled mutation, since trusted-header reference, finality-policy satisfaction, time-window validity, runtime ordering, non-replay, and context-rule satisfaction are unchanged.

Takeaway. This case demonstrates how representing route profiles as structured key–value entries enables explicit, machine-checkable domain binding at authorization time, turning misrouting/misbinding into a localized contradiction rather than an informal, post-hoc interpretation.

5.5 Cross-Scenario Patterns

Across the three case studies, the ontology and diagnostic layer exhibit consistent patterns.

First, some assumption families are comparatively easy for current bridges to support and therefore frequently appear as *Evidenced* in baseline snapshots. Domain binding at the level of chain identifiers and explicit route profiles, ordering, and uniqueness are often evidenced because bridges routinely record routes, sequence numbers, and delivered-sets (or equivalent replay state). However, baseline snapshots may still show *NotEstablished* outcomes when a bridge does not expose a given interface dimension, and the diagnostic layer is designed to make such omissions explicit rather than to "force" evidence.

Second, other assumption families emerge as structural weak points. Header-to-root consistency and finality-by-depth rely on a clear separation between headers and trusted roots and on explicit finality parameters. In committee- or attestation-based settings that abstract source-chain consensus into opaque evidence, these assumptions can become *NotEstablished* if the interface does not expose header/root metadata that can be related to a trusted-root policy. Context-compatibility assumptions are likewise *NotEstablished* unless bridges explicitly encode validator-set identifiers, epochs, security profiles, or verification-circuit versions as structured context key–value entries with corresponding runtime rules.

Third, when controlled incident variants are instantiated in our representative scenarios, they align with specific semantic families:

- in Bridge A, a trust-root revocation causes the *trusted-header check* to become **Contradicted** while the other diagnostic checks remain **Evidenced**;
- in Bridge B, an out-of-policy `epoch_id` value causes the *context-rule check* to become **Contradicted**, with the other diagnostic checks remaining **Evidenced**; and
- in Bridge C, a mismatch in the attested route profile (for example, `router_kv.contract`) causes the *claimed-route check* to become **Contradicted**; the remaining diagnostic checks stay **Evidenced**.

These patterns suggest that a systematic interface design should:

- expose header/root metadata and trusted-root transitions where possible, so that trusted-header and finality-related assumptions become checkable rather than permanently NotEstablished;
- promote structured context fields and context rules for validator sets, epochs, verification circuits, and security profiles, so that context-rule assumptions can be evaluated; and
- represent route profiles explicitly (e.g., via key–value entries such as handler/contract identifiers), enabling machine-checkable domain binding beyond coarse $(src, dst, profile)$ tuples.

Overall, the case studies show that our semantic interface and SHACL-based diagnostics can differentiate between misconfigured trust roots, out-of-policy context, and explicit claimed-route mismatches, while providing a reusable vocabulary for describing and comparing authorization-time assumptions across heterogeneous cross-chain bridges.

What generalizes here is not the exact Bridge A/B/C mutation, but the diagnostic decomposition itself. Any cross-chain setting that can expose boundary-visible representations of messages, evidence, routes, headers or roots, runtime policy, and execution context can be mapped into the same ontology with at most schema-level adaptations to field names or bridge-specific context keys. In that sense, the interface is intended as a reusable semantic layer for heterogeneous bridge families; adding new bridge types should primarily require new instance mappings and, where needed, additional context rules rather than a redesign of the ontology from scratch.

Detailed per-check results and the construction procedure of baseline scenarios are provided in Appendix B.

For selected case studies, we additionally visualize the baseline and incident authorization-boundary graphs and highlight their differences. These comparison figures are provided in Appendix E and illustrate how misconfiguration, context-policy violations, and route-profile mismatches manifest as structural changes in the ontology instances.

An accompanying artifact containing case graphs, diagnostic tables, and scripts is provided to support reproducibility (see Appendix 11).

5.6 E1: Controlled Mutation Regression Across Seven Diagnostic Checks

To validate that our SHACL constraints act as a diagnostic layer (rather than a monolithic consistency check), we run a controlled mutation regression suite. These checks do not merely restate labels in prose: each diagnostic outcome is produced by evaluating structured relationships among ontology instances (message, evidence, route, header/root, runtime policy, and context) and by making the absence of required interface fields explicit through the *NotEstablished* state. Starting from the same baseline snapshot used in the case studies, we generate seven mutated variants, each designed to violate exactly one diagnostic check while keeping other interface dimensions unchanged. Mutations include: route-profile mismatch (the evidence no longer matches the claimed route), trusted-root revocation (the evidence no longer refers to a trusted header), insufficient depth under a `BY_DEPTH` policy (the referenced header no longer satisfies the finality policy), timeout expiration (the message is no longer within the allowed time window), sequence mismatch (the sequence no longer matches the expected runtime order), replayed delivery (the message has been processed before), and an out-of-policy `epoch_id` (the evidence no longer satisfies the policy context rules).

Figure 1 summarizes the outcomes. The baseline case yields *Evidenced* for all seven diagnostic checks, while each mutation flips exactly its target check to

Contradicted and leaves the remaining checks *Evidenced.* This "perfect diagonal" indicates check-level orthogonality and selectivity for our current shapes. The full regression table is provided in Appendix C.

5.7 E3: Incident-Aligned Snapshot Diagnostics

Real bridge incidents often reveal a diagnosability challenge: the authorization-boundary interface may not expose enough information to decide certain semantic questions at runtime, even if those questions become decidable after a post-mortem. To capture this distinction without changing the ontology or SHACL shapes, we construct two snapshots per incident:

- **IL (interface-limited)** snapshots encode only boundary-visible facts that are plausibly available to an on-chain verifier or monitoring system at authorization time.
- **AUG (augmented)** snapshots add a minimal set of post-mortem facts (e.g., trusted-root revocation, route-profile tampering evidence) to test whether previously unevaluable anchors become evidenced or contradicted.

We apply this methodology to three widely documented incidents: Nomad (2022), Wormhole (2022), and Poly Network (2021) [10,16,17].

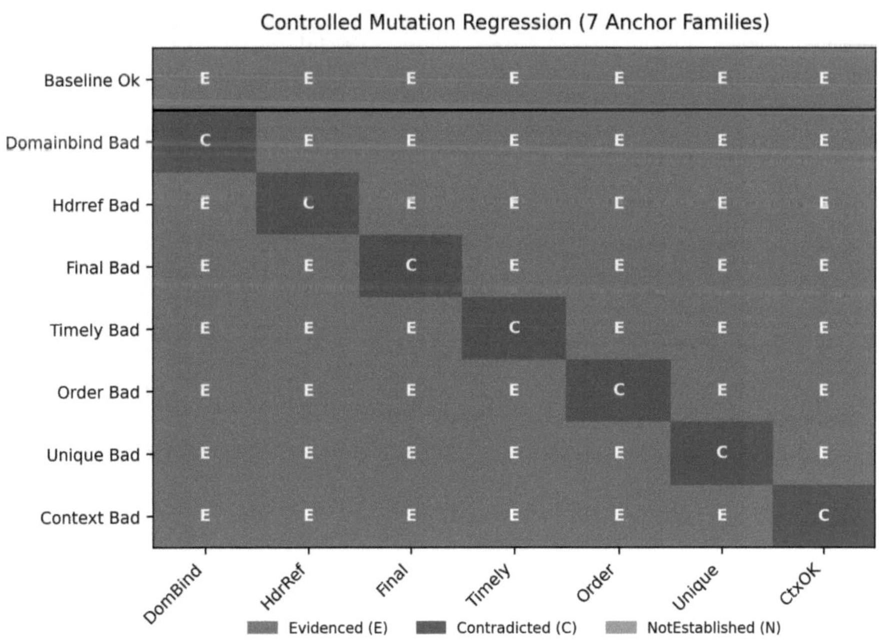

Fig. 1. E1: Controlled mutation regression across seven diagnostic checks. Each mutated case is designed to violate exactly one check, yielding a diagonal pattern of contradictions (C) with all other checks remaining evidenced (E).

Figure 2 reports the check-level outcomes for each IL/AUG pair. Two patterns stand out. First, the IL snapshots for Nomad and Poly exhibit multiple *NotEstablished* checks (notably trusted-header reference, finality-policy satisfaction, and time-window validity), reflecting that their deployed interfaces do not expose sufficient header/root metadata to support those diagnoses. Second, aug-

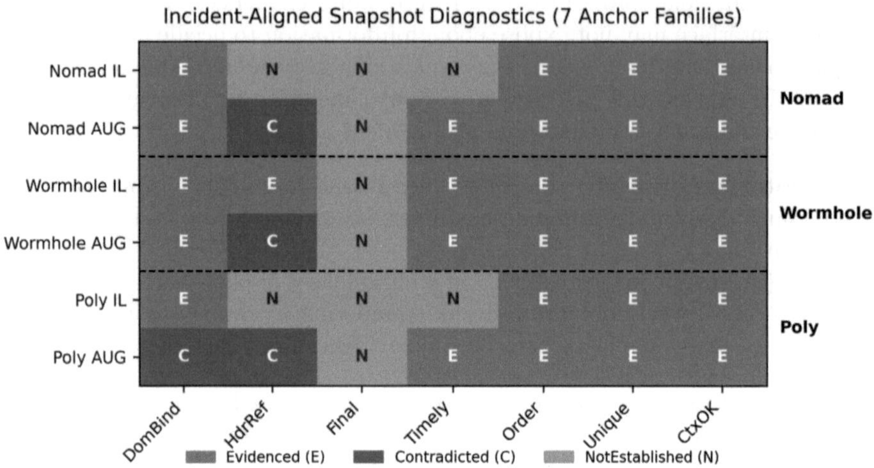

Fig. 2. E3: Incident-aligned snapshot diagnostics across seven diagnostic checks. IL snapshots reflect only interface-limited, boundary-visible facts; AUG snapshots add minimal post-mortem evidence. E = *Evidenced*, C = *Contradicted*, N = *NotEstablished*.

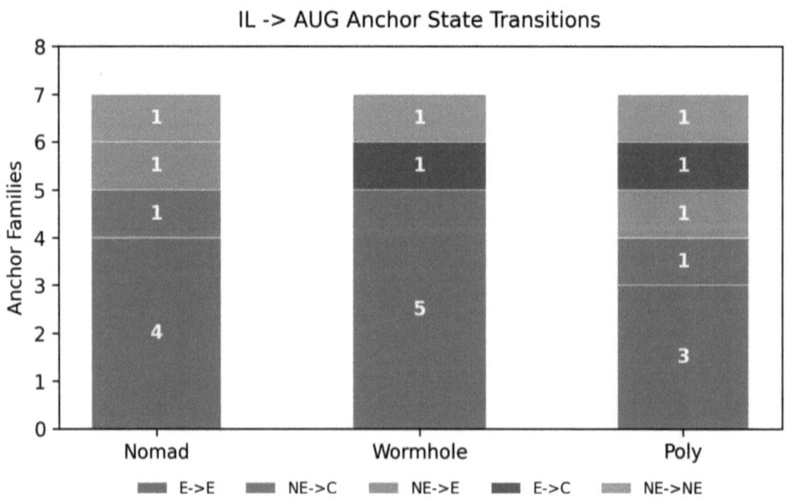

Fig. 3. E3: IL→AUG diagnostic-check state transitions per incident. NE→C transitions quantify diagnosability gaps that become explicit contradictions once additional evidence is supplied.

mentation turns several of these gaps into explicit semantic contradictions: the trusted-header check becomes *Contradicted* for all three incidents in AUG, and the claimed-route check becomes *Contradicted* for Poly when the attested route profile is inconsistent with the claimed route.

Finally, Fig. 3 summarizes IL→AUG state transitions per incident. Across the three incidents, the dominant transition is E→E (stable evidence), while the most security-relevant transitions are NE→C (a diagnosability gap that becomes a detected contradiction once evidence is available) and E→C (a contradiction that is only revealed once a trust-root is revoked post hoc).

Full tables are provided in Appendix D.

6 Interface Template for Authorization-Time Semantics

The case studies suggest that many failures are enabled by missing or underspecified semantics at the authorization boundary. We distill a reusable interface template: a minimal set of fields and invariants that make the key authorization-time conditions diagnosable across bridge architectures.

6.1 Template Structure

Positioning of the Template. The goal of this template is *not* to standardize bridge protocols or to re-specify their internal verification logic. Instead, it captures a *minimal, authorization-boundary interface* that is sufficient to make the semantic anchor families from Sects. 3 and 5 *machine-diagnosable* under our SHACL layer. Concretely, Groups 1–6 are chosen to reduce the *NotEstablished* region by making otherwise implicit assumptions observable at authorization time, so that they can be classified as *Evidenced* or *Contradicted* in a reproducible way.

We group the template into six field-groups aligned with the ontology and the assumption families from Sects. 3 and 5. Each group can be adopted incrementally; later groups mainly shrink the *NotEstablished* region rather than introducing new low-level mechanisms.

Group 1: Identity and routing. **Fields:** a stable message identifier and payload hash; an explicit $(src, dst, profile)$ route plus a route-profile key–value description. These fields are enough to check that message and evidence agree on identifiers and hashes, and that the attested route is consistent with the policy allow-list.

Group 2: Evidence–header linkage. **Fields:** an explicit reference from each evidence package to a header or state root with height, time, and hash. This supports the header-to-root consistency condition: each evidence package can be tied to a concrete point in the source-chain history and to a specific domain identifier.

Group 3: Trusted roots and finality policy. **Fields:** explicit trusted roots (with activation and revocation metadata) and runtime finality parameters (mode, parameter, and units). Together with Group 2, these fields support explicit checks of "is this header under an active root?" and "is this header sufficiently final under the stated policy?" (header-to-root consistency and finality-by-depth conditions).

Group 4: Timeouts and clocks. **Fields:** evidence-side timeout semantics (mode, parameter, and clock) and matching runtime policy fields, plus the current time or height at authorization time. These fields make timeliness conditions checkable: time units and clocks are explicit and comparable between evidence and policy.

Group 5: Ordering and replay state. **Fields:** sequence numbers on messages or evidence, together with runtime "next sequence" counters and delivered-sets. This supports ordering and non-replay conditions: sequences are scoped to routes and monotonic, and the delivered-set is observable for audit and monitoring.

Group 6: Context and scoped policy. **Fields:** evidence-side context key–value entries (e.g., validator-set identifier, security profile, circuit or code version, governance epoch) and runtime context rules, optionally scoped by route or message type. These fields support context-compatibility conditions ("is this attestation issued under an admissible validator set/profile?") and fine-grained admissibility for generic routers ("is this message type allowed to reach this destination contract and method?").

The six groups can be adopted incrementally across different architectures: committee- and guardian-based bridges add explicit context and trust-root transitions, light-client bridges surface header chains and finality rules, optimistic bridges expose challenge windows and clocks, and generic call routers make destination targets and methods policy-scoped.

Anchor Coverage Rationale. Groups 1–2 primarily enable diagnosability of message/evidence linkage and route-level domain binding, while Groups 2–3 make header-reference and finality semantics observable rather than permanently *NotEstablished*. Groups 4–5 expose clocks, timeouts, and replay/ordering state. Group 6 makes context constraints (e.g., epoch, key-set, profile, or version) explicit so that context compatibility can be checked at authorization time.

6.2 Checklist for Practitioners

The template can be turned into a concise checklist for bridge and protocol designers:

✓ Message identifier and payload hash match between message and evidence, and are stable across retries (message–evidence consistency).

✓ The route (*src*, *dst*, *profile*) is explicit, appears in the evidence, and is checked against a runtime allow-list (basic route binding and admissibility).
✓ Each evidence package links to a concrete header or root, and policy exposes trusted roots plus finality parameters with clear units (header-to-root consistency and finality-by-depth).
✓ Timeout semantics (mode, parameter, clock) are explicit on both evidence and policy side, and can be compared at authorization time (timeliness condition).
✓ Ordering and replay state are observable via route-scoped sequence numbers and delivered-sets (ordering and non-replay conditions).
✓ Evidence advertises its context (validator set, profile, version, governance epoch), and runtime policy constrains admissible combinations; for generic routers, allowed destination contracts and methods are likewise expressed as structured policy (context-compatibility and fine-grained route admissibility).

In our case studies, bridges that satisfy only the first two groups can already express coarse routing and replay assumptions, but many critical assumptions remain NotEstablished. Adding the remaining groups requires only modest additional structure yet substantially increases the fraction of authorization-time semantics that can be explicitly evidenced or contradicted at the boundary.

7 Discussion and Limitations

Our ontology and diagnostic layer offer a complementary lens on cross-chain bridge security. Rather than reasoning directly about proof systems or contract code, we focus on the semantics that should hold at the authorization boundary. This section clarifies the scope of that lens, its limitations, and how it relates to existing approaches.

7.1 Scope of the Semantic Interface

The ontology is deliberately *interface-centric*. It models messages, evidence packages, routes, headers, runtime policies, and context as they appear at the destination-chain boundary.

Two consequences follow. First, we abstract away from low-level implementation details such as instruction sequences, storage layouts, or protocol wire formats. We do not aim to detect reentrancy bugs, arithmetic errors, or memory corruption; these are better handled by program analysis, model checking, or fuzzing. We instead assume that the implementation is at least *intended* to enforce some semantic contract over interface state, and ask whether the interface carries enough information to state and diagnose that contract.

Second, the ontology is *minimal but expressive* for the assumption families we study (domain linkage, headers and finality, time, ordering and uniqueness, and context). Other classes of properties—for example liaison with off-chain entities, economic risk exposure, or detailed liveness guarantees—are out of scope and would require additional concepts and possibly different diagnostic techniques.

7.2 Expressiveness and Three-Valued Outcomes

The diagnostic layer classifies each assumption family for each evidence package into three values: Evidenced, Contradicted, or NotEstablished.

- *Evidenced*: the ontology instance and shapes graph contain enough information to conclude that the intended semantic condition holds (under our definition of that condition).
- *Contradicted*: available information suffices to show that the condition cannot hold, given the current runtime state and evidence.
- *NotEstablished*: required fields are missing, or present but insufficient to determine a truth value under our shapes.

This three-valued semantics exposes two types of limitation.

First, there are *precision limits.* Our shapes may classify a condition as Evidenced while an external analyst might regard the encoded requirement as too weak (for example, a depth-based "finality" check that ignores chain-specific consensus nuances). In such cases the ontology still usefully clarifies what is actually being assumed, even if stronger variants are possible.

Evaluation Baselines and Metrics. A related limitation concerns how the evaluation should be read. Because our goal is explanatory diagnosis at the authorization boundary, the most relevant baseline is careful manual inspection of interface artefacts and incident documentation, not a classifier that predicts exploit labels from a large corpus. We therefore use discriminability-style evidence—selective mutations, incident-aligned IL/AUG reconstructions, and check-level outcome changes—rather than precision/recall over a benchmark dataset. This does not make the evaluation "automatic by construction": the substantive question is whether the ontology and SHACL layer force the relevant assumptions into a reproducible, machine-checkable form, and whether those forms remain informative when the visible interface is incomplete.

7.3 Threat Model and What We Do Not Address

Our approach targets a specific layer of the threat model: errors and omissions in authorization-time assumptions at the bridge boundary. We do *not* aim to defend against:

- consensus failures or cryptographic breaks on underlying chains;
- collusion or bribery that causes attesters to deviate from stated policies;
- implementation bugs that violate the semantics encoded in the ontology; or
- application-level misuses of an otherwise sound authorization interface (for example, misconfigured downstream contracts).

These risks must be handled by complementary means: robust consensus protocols, economic and game-theoretic analysis, formal verification, defence-in-depth architectures, and operational controls. Our contribution is to make a particular class of semantic assumptions explicit and diagnosable, so they can be designed, implemented, audited, and monitored with similar care as lower-level mechanisms.

7.4 Future Directions

We see several natural extensions of this work.

Semi-automatic Extraction and Synthesis. Constructing ontology instances currently requires manual effort from domain experts. A promising direction is to learn mappings from existing bridge configurations, logs, and on-chain artefacts to ontology types, automating ingestion of real deployments. Conversely, given desired assumption outcomes and policies, one could synthesize interface-level templates and code stubs that implement them.

Richer Security Properties. Our assumption families focus on a core set of authorization-time conditions suggested by recent incidents. Future work could extend this to economic safety properties, attack cost models, or collusion scenarios, building on recent systematizations of cross-chain bridge security and incidents [14,22].

Integration with Verification and Testing. Finally, the semantic interface can act as a bridge between formal verification, static analysis, and runtime monitoring. For example, one could link formal proofs about a light-client contract to the Evidenced region of an assumption graph, or generate test cases that stress specific assumption families and observe their outcomes.

We leave these questions to future work, but regard them as essential steps toward a more principled, semantics aware ecosystem of cross-chain bridges.

8 Related Work

We position our work within three strands: cross-chain bridge security, ontology- and knowledge-graph-based security analysis, and SHACL-based constraint reasoning.

8.1 Cross-Chain Bridges and Incidents

Cross-chain bridges have been recognised as critical Web3 infrastructure and are now the subject of dedicated systematizations. Zhang et al. survey bridge architectures, verification mechanisms (light clients, committees, guardian sets, optimistic schemes), and recurring attack patterns, and argue that many failures stem from subtle mismatches between protocol assumptions and what bridge implementations actually enforce at the boundary [22]. Our work is complementary: rather than proposing new verification mechanisms, we study how existing designs expose—or fail to expose—the assumptions those mechanisms rely on at authorization time.

High-impact exploits on bridges such as Wormhole and Nomad have been analysed in depth by security firms and the affected projects [10,16]. These reports reconstruct root causes in terms of code-level bugs (e.g., missing or incorrect signature checks, faulty initialization) and protocol misconfigurations. We use such reconstructions as a basis for extracting normalized authorization assumptions and for building ontology instances in our case studies, but we do not re-analyse the exploits at the bytecode level.

Recent work also explores anomaly detection and monitoring for bridges and multi-chain ecosystems. For example, Augusto et al. use transaction-graph features to detect anomalous flows across bridges and show that graph-based views can surface suspicious cross-chain behaviour at scale [3]. Such approaches focus on behavioural anomalies over large datasets. By contrast, we analyse the *semantic content* of individual authorization decisions and the extent to which their assumptions can be evidenced or contradicted at the interface.

Relation to SoK and Surveys. Prior SoK and survey work systematizes bridge architectures, attack surfaces, and mitigation themes, but typically leaves authorization-time assumptions as natural-language requirements. In contrast, we provide an *ontology-backed, machine-checkable interface* at the authorization boundary and show, via SHACL diagnostics on representative incident variants, how to localize missing versus contradicted assumptions and derive a minimal interface template from that diagnosability criterion.

8.2 Ontologies and Knowledge Graphs for Security

Ontologies and knowledge graphs have long been used in security, compliance, and access-control modeling [9,12,15,19]. The closest references are generic access-control ontologies such as OSNAC [15] and broader information-security/compliance vocabularies [9,12,19]. Our work differs in two respects. First, we target cross-chain authorization-time semantics rather than traditional subject–object access control or control catalogues. Second, we diagnose the status of security-relevant assumptions (Evidenced, Contradicted, NotEstablished) instead of directly computing allow/deny decisions, and thus operate one level above authorization. In particular, our ontology makes boundary-visible bridge artefacts—messages, evidence packages, routes, trusted headers/roots, replay state, and runtime context rules—first-class objects, which the prior ontologies above do not model.

8.3 SHACL and Constraint-Based Reasoning

The Shapes Constraint Language (SHACL) is a W3C recommendation for validating RDF graphs against shape constraints [13,21]. It is widely used to ensure structural quality and integrity of RDF data. Subsequent work refines its formal underpinnings and validation algorithms, for example by studying robust validation and repair of violated constraints, or by defining semantics for reasoning in the presence of inconsistencies [1,2,8].

SHACL and related languages have also been applied to validate complex domain-specific graphs, including lexical resources, biomedical ontologies, and network configuration data [6]. We follow this line of work by applying SHACL to security-critical knowledge graphs for cross-chain bridges, with two additions: (i) our shapes encode security-relevant semantic conditions (for example, that a referenced header belongs to an active trusted root matching the route and finality policy), not just structural well-formedness; and (ii) we interpret SHACL outcomes through a three-valued diagnostic lens, mapping validation reports to Evidenced, Contradicted, and NotEstablished regions of an assumption graph.

To our knowledge, this is the first work that systematically uses SHACL to diagnose authorization-time semantics in cross-chain systems and connects shape-based validation to a structured ontology of bridge assumptions informed by public incident analyses.

9 Conclusion and Outlook

Cross-chain bridges continue to suffer high-impact failures that stem less from cryptographic breaks than from mismatched or unstated assumptions at authorization time. Destination contracts accept messages whose semantics—domain, finality, time, ordering, uniqueness, and context—are largely implicit; when these assumptions drift from reality, the result can be catastrophic.

We proposed a semantic interface for diagnosing authorization-time assumptions in cross-chain bridges, with three main contributions:

- We introduced an ontology that captures messages, evidence packages, routes, headers, runtime policies, and context at the authorization boundary. From public incident analyses and protocol documentation, we distilled anchor families that characterize recurring semantic assumptions at the authorization boundary.
- We designed a SHACL-based diagnostic layer that evaluates these anchors and yields three-valued outcomes (Evidenced, Contradicted, NotEstablished). The resulting assumption graphs show which assumptions are supported by boundary-visible data, which are violated, and which remain unstated.
- Using controlled diagnostic archetypes together with incident aligned snapshots of representative bridge failures, we derived an interface template and design guidelines, showing how a small set of structured fields for headers, trusted roots, finality, context, and routing policies can turn large grey regions of NotEstablished assumptions into regions where semantics are explicitly evidenced or contradicted.

Our current evaluation on representative baseline/incident scenario pairs and incident-aligned snapshots shows that this approach can separate misconfigured trust roots from routing or replay errors, highlight when forged attestations violate context policies that could have been enforced at the interface, and reveal entire dimensions of intended semantics—such as fine-grained destination constraints—that current interfaces do not surface.

More broadly, we advocate a semantic view of cross-chain security, in which bridge designs are accompanied by explicit, machine-readable specifications of their authorization-time assumptions, and tools can diagnose whether these assumptions are adequately supported at the interface.

Looking ahead, we see several opportunities. First, automating the construction of ontology instances from real deployments would lower adoption costs and enable continuous, large-scale monitoring of assumption graphs. Second, integrating the semantic interface with formal verification and testing could create a feedback loop between high-level assumptions, code-level guarantees, and runtime observability. Third, extending the ontology to cover economic safety and liveness properties would help connect semantic diagnostics to broader risk assessments of cross-chain ecosystems.

As cross-chain infrastructure matures, we expect that semantic interfaces and assumption-aware diagnostics will become as indispensable as code audits and formal verification are today. By making implicit assumptions explicit—and by providing a concrete template for exposing and checking them—we aim to support a more transparent, auditable, and ultimately safer cross-chain landscape.

10 Disclosure of Generative AI Use

Generative AI tools (e.g., ChatGPT) were used as editorial assistance for language polishing, rephrasing, and improving clarity of selected passages. They were not used to generate experimental results, fabricate data, or replace technical reasoning. All technical content, experiments, results, and references were produced and verified by the authors, who take full responsibility for the manuscript.

11 Artifacts and Scripts

The evaluation in this paper relies on scripts that: (i) construct RDF graphs for baseline and incident scenarios, (ii) execute SHACL validation, and (iii) post-process SHACL reports into three-valued outcomes and summary tables.

Due to the PDF-only submission format, we do not embed the full artifact package inside the manuscript itself. Instead, we include representative fragments of the ontology (`ontology.ttl`) and SHACL shapes (`shapes.ttl`) in Appendix F to illustrate the exact vocabulary and constraint style used by our diagnostics. The complete artifact package (scripts, case graphs, diagnostic tables, and specifications) is available via https://github.com/KYlvie/XChainOnto. This repository contains the ontology, SHACL shapes, case-study graphs, generation scripts, and evaluation outputs used to support reproducibility.

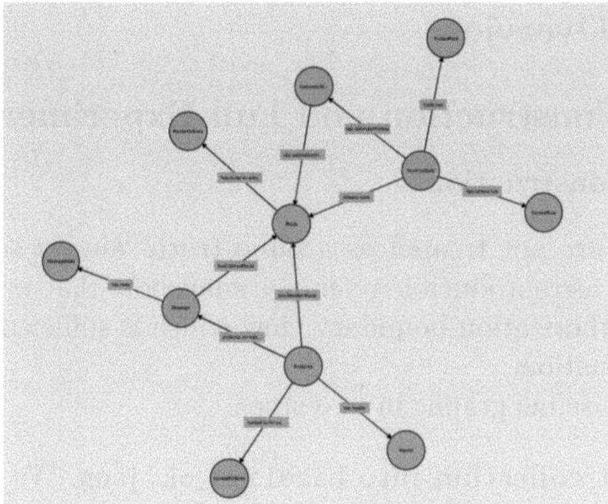

Fig. 4. High-level view of the ontology at the authorization boundary: messages, evidence, routes, runtime state, headers, and policy/trust nodes.

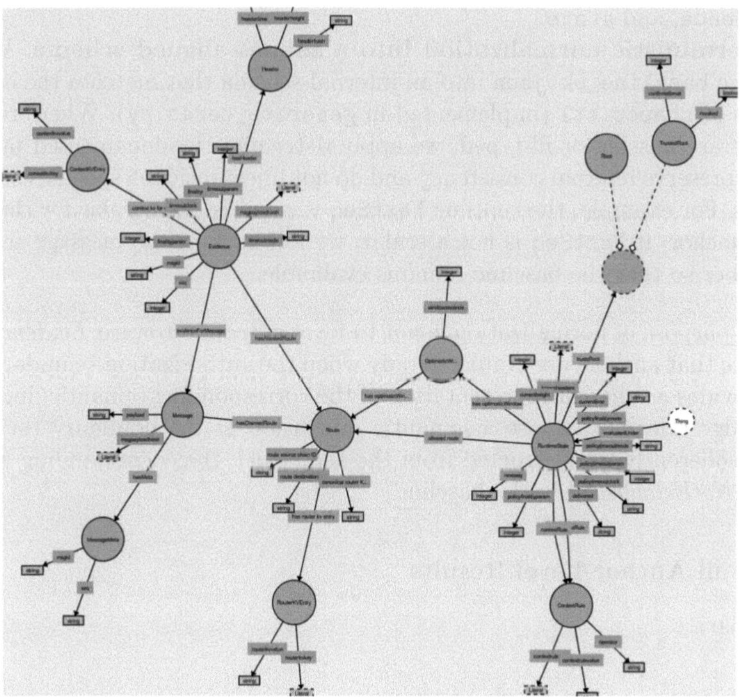

Fig. 5. Full ontology at the authorization boundary, including messages, evidence, headers, routes, runtime state, trusted roots, and context rules, with all properties and relations exposed.

A Ontology Overview

B Baseline Construction and Full Experimental Results

B.1 Baseline Construction

Baseline scenarios are not treated as ground-truth "always secure" executions. Instead, they serve as reproducible reference snapshots that instantiate an internally consistent authorization-boundary view which is sufficiently well-typed for SHACL-based evaluation.

We construct baseline graphs in two steps:

1. **RPC snapshot collection into `baseline_ok.json`.** We collect a concrete boundary-visible snapshot from a live EVM chain via `collect_baseline.py`, parameterized by an RPC endpoint, a target contract address, and a specific transaction hash (optionally selecting a particular `logIndex` deterministically). The output `baseline_ok.json` contains three top-level objects: `msg`, `evidence`, and `state`.
2. **Deterministic normalization into a shapes-aligned schema.** We normalize `baseline_ok.json` into an internal schema that matches the expectations of `shapes.ttl` (implemented in `generate_cases.py`). Where required fields are missing or ill-typed, we apply deterministic, documented fallbacks that preserve internal consistency and do not inject incident-specific contradictions. For example, the runtime `NextSeq` is required as a scalar for the ordering anchor; if `NextSeq` is not a scalar, we fall back to the message sequence number so that the baseline remains evaluable.

The purpose of normalization is not to force outcomes toward *Evidenced*, but to ensure that anchors are evaluated only when the authorization-boundary interface provides a coherent representation of the corresponding semantic dimension. If a bridge does not expose a semantic dimension at the boundary (or it cannot be coherently reconstructed from the snapshot), the corresponding anchors remain *NotEstablished* in the baseline.

B.2 Full Anchor-Level Results

See Table 1.

B.3 Relation to Main-Text Claims

The appendix-level results confirm the qualitative claims made in Sect. 5:

- Bridge A failures localize to the trusted-header check under a trust-root revocation.
- Bridge B failures localize to the context-rule check under an out-of-policy `epoch_id` value.

Table 1. Check-level outcomes for baseline and incident scenarios (dominant outcome). E = *Evidenced*, C = *Contradicted*, N = *NotEstablished*.

Scenario	Matches claimed route	Refers to trusted header	Satisfies finality policy	Within allowed time window	Matches expected runtime order	Not processed before	Satisfies policy context rules
A–Base	E	E	E	E	E	E	E
A–Inc	E	C	E	E	E	E	E
B–Base	E	E	E	E	E	E	E
B–Inc	E	E	E	E	E	E	C
C–Base	E	E	E	E	E	E	E
C–Inc	C	E	E	E	E	E	E

– Bridge C incidents manifest as failures of the claimed-route check induced by an attested route-profile mismatch.

Baseline outcomes are not required to be uniformly Evidenced; they may contain *NotEstablished* checks when a bridge does not expose the corresponding semantic dimension at the authorization boundary.

C Controlled Mutation Regression

This appendix reports the full outcome matrix for the controlled mutation regression suite described in Sect. 5.6. Starting from the baseline authorization-boundary snapshot (`baseline_ok`), we generate seven mutated variants, each designed to violate exactly one diagnostic check while leaving unrelated interface dimensions unchanged. The resulting diagonal structure confirms the check-level selectivity of our SHACL constraints: each mutation yields a single *Contradicted* check (C) and leaves all other checks *Evidenced* (E) (Table 2).

Table 2. E1 controlled mutation regression outcomes over seven diagnostic checks. E = *Evidenced*, C = *Contradicted*, N = *NotEstablished*. Each mutation targets exactly one check and yields a perfect diagonal of contradictions.

Scenario	Matches claimed route	Refers to trusted header	Satisfies finality policy	Within allowed time window	Matches expected runtime order	Not processed before	Satisfies policy context rules
Baseline	E	E	E	E	E	E	E
Claimed-route mismatch	C	E	E	E	E	E	E
Trusted-header mismatch	E	C	E	E	E	E	E
Finality-policy violation	E	E	C	E	E	E	E
Time-window violation	E	E	E	C	E	E	E
Runtime-order mismatch	E	E	E	E	C	E	E
Replay attempt	E	E	E	E	E	C	E
Context-rule violation	E	E	E	E	E	E	C

D Incident-Aligned Snapshot Diagnostics

This appendix reports the full outcomes for the incident-aligned snapshot diagnostics described in Sect. 5.7. For each incident, the *IL* snapshot includes only interface-limited, boundary-visible fields, while the *AUG* snapshot adds a minimal set of post-mortem facts to test whether previously unevaluable checks become *Evidenced* or *Contradicted* (Table 3).

Table 3. E3 incident-aligned snapshot diagnostics (interface-limited IL vs. augmented AUG) for Nomad, Wormhole, and Poly Network. E = *Evidenced*, C = *Contradicted*, N = *NotEstablished*.

Scenario	Matches claimed route	Refers to trusted header	Satisfies finality policy	Within allowed time window	Matches expected runtime order	Not processed before	Satisfies policy context rules
Nomad IL	E	N	N	N	E	E	E
Nomad AUG	E	C	N	E	E	E	E
Wormhole IL	E	E	N	E	E	E	E
Wormhole AUG	E	C	N	E	E	E	E
Poly IL	E	N	N	N	E	E	E
Poly AUG	C	C	N	E	E	E	E

E Case Study Graph Visualizations

This appendix provides one visual comparison figure for each of the three case studies. Each figure shows a side-by-side comparison between the baseline and the corresponding incident authorization-boundary graph. Differences between baseline and incident are highlighted in red, and only selected and changed literals are shown for readability.

E.1 Bridge A: Trust-Root Revocation (Trusted-Header Check)

See Fig. 6.

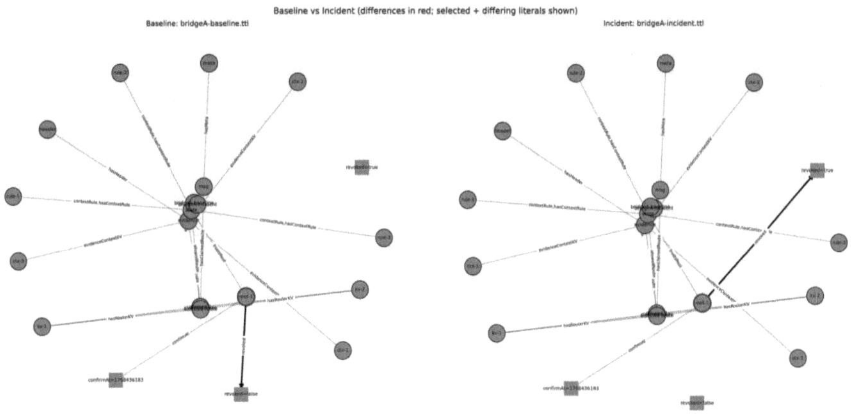

Fig. 6. Baseline vs. incident graphs for Bridge A. The incident toggles a relevant trusted root to **revoked=true**, which breaks the trusted-header check and yields a *Contradicted* outcome under the stated policy.

E.2 Bridge B: Out-of-Policy `epoch_id` (Context-Rule Check)

See Fig. 7.

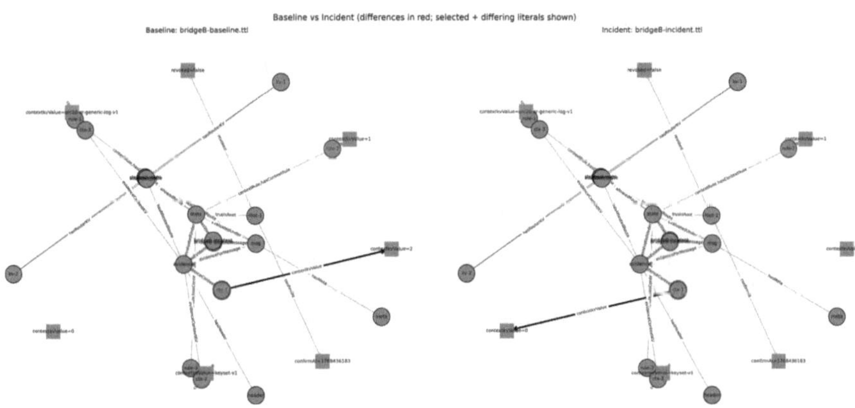

Fig. 7. Baseline vs. incident graphs for Bridge B. The incident mutates the evidence-side context by setting **epoch_id** to an out-of-policy value, which violates runtime **xchain:ContextRule** constraints and yields a *Contradicted* outcome for the context-rule check.

E.3 Bridge C: Attested Route-Profile Mismatch (Claimed-Route Check)

See Fig. 8.

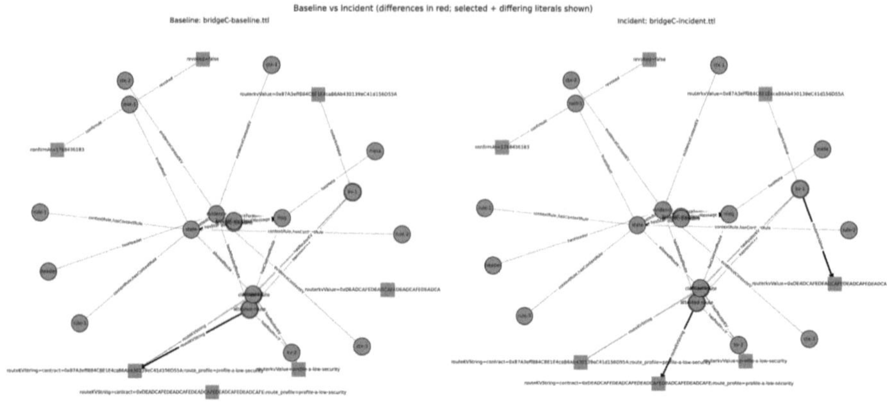

Fig. 8. Baseline vs. incident graphs for Bridge C. The incident changes the attested route-profile entry (e.g., **`router_kv.contract`**) so it no longer matches the message route profile, yielding a *Contradicted* outcome for the claimed-route check while the other diagnostic checks remain unchanged.

F Representative Ontology and SHACL Fragments

This appendix provides representative fragments of the ontology (`ontology.ttl`) and SHACL shapes (`shapes.ttl`). They are not the full artifacts, but are chosen to make the core vocabulary and constraint style auditable from the PDF-only submission.

F.1 Ontology Fragment (`ontology.ttl`)

```
@prefix xchain: <http://example.org/xchain#> .
@prefix owl:    <http://www.w3.org/2002/07/owl#> .
@prefix rdfs:   <http://www.w3.org/2000/01/rdf-schema#> .
@prefix xsd:    <http://www.w3.org/2001/XMLSchema#> .

#############################################################
# Core classes at the authorization boundary
#############################################################

xchain:Message      rdf:type owl:Class ; rdfs:label "Message"@en .
xchain:Evidence     rdf:type owl:Class ; rdfs:label "Evidence"@en .
xchain:Route        rdf:type owl:Class ; rdfs:label "Route"@en .
xchain:Header       rdf:type owl:Class ; rdfs:label "Header"@en .
xchain:RuntimeState rdf:type owl:Class ; rdfs:label "RuntimeState"@en .
xchain:TrustedRoot  rdf:type owl:Class ; rdfs:label "TrustedRoot"@en .
xchain:ContextKVEntry rdf:type owl:Class ; rdfs:label "ContextKVEntry"
    @en .
xchain:ContextRule    rdf:type owl:Class ; rdfs:label "ContextRule"@en .
```

```
##############################################################
# Route consistency + Message--Evidence linkage
##############################################################

xchain:hasClaimedRoute rdf:type owl:ObjectProperty ;
  rdfs:label "hasClaimedRoute"@en ;
  rdfs:domain xchain:Message ;
  rdfs:range  xchain:Route .

xchain:hasAttestedRoute rdf:type owl:ObjectProperty ;
  rdfs:label "hasAttestedRoute"@en ;
  rdfs:domain xchain:Evidence ;
  rdfs:range  xchain:Route .

xchain:evidenceForMessage rdf:type owl:ObjectProperty ;
  rdfs:label "evidenceForMessage"@en ;
  rdfs:domain xchain:Evidence ;
  rdfs:range  xchain:Message .

xchain:payloadhashmsg rdf:type owl:DatatypeProperty ;
  rdfs:label "payloadHash"@en ;
  rdfs:domain xchain:Message ;
  rdfs:range  rdfs:Literal .

xchain:payloadHash rdf:type owl:DatatypeProperty ;
  rdfs:label "payloadHash"@en ;
  rdfs:domain xchain:Evidence ;
  rdfs:range  rdfs:Literal .

##############################################################
# Trusted-header reference + trust roots (finality support)
##############################################################

xchain:hasHeader rdf:type owl:ObjectProperty ;
  rdfs:label "hasHeader"@en ;
  rdfs:domain xchain:Evidence ;
  rdfs:range  xchain:Header .

xchain:headerHash rdf:type owl:DatatypeProperty ;
  rdfs:label "headerHash"@en ;
  rdfs:domain xchain:Header ;
  rdfs:range  xsd:string .

xchain:headerHeight rdf:type owl:DatatypeProperty ;
  rdfs:label "headerHeight"@en ;
  rdfs:domain xchain:Header ;
  rdfs:range  xsd:integer .

xchain:headerTime rdf:type owl:DatatypeProperty ;
```

```
  rdfs:label "headerTime"@en ;
  rdfs:domain xchain:Header ;
  rdfs:range  xsd:integer .

xchain:trustsRoot rdf:type owl:ObjectProperty ;
  rdfs:label "trustsRoot"@en ;
  rdfs:domain xchain:RuntimeState ;
  rdfs:range  xchain:TrustedRoot .

xchain:revoked rdf:type owl:DatatypeProperty ;
  rdfs:label "revoked"@en ;
  rdfs:domain xchain:TrustedRoot ;
  rdfs:range  xsd:boolean .

################################################################
# Context-rule satisfaction
################################################################

xchain:evidenceContextKV rdf:type owl:ObjectProperty ;
  rdfs:label "evidenceContextKV"@en ;
  rdfs:domain xchain:Evidence ;
  rdfs:range  xchain:ContextKVEntry .

xchain:hasContextRule rdf:type owl:ObjectProperty ;
  rdfs:label "hasContextRule"@en ;
  rdfs:domain xchain:RuntimeState ;
  rdfs:range  xchain:ContextRule .

xchain:contextkvKey rdf:type owl:DatatypeProperty ;
  rdfs:label "contextkvKey"@en ;
  rdfs:domain xchain:ContextKVEntry ;
  rdfs:range  xsd:string .

xchain:contextkvValue rdf:type owl:DatatypeProperty ;
  rdfs:label "contextkvValue"@en ;
  rdfs:domain xchain:ContextKVEntry ;
  rdfs:range  xsd:string .

xchain:contextrulekey rdf:type owl:DatatypeProperty ;
  rdfs:label "contextrulekey"@en ;
  rdfs:domain xchain:ContextRule ;
  rdfs:range  xsd:string .

xchain:contextrulevalue rdf:type owl:DatatypeProperty ;
  rdfs:label "contextrulevalue"@en ;
  rdfs:domain xchain:ContextRule ;
  rdfs:range  xsd:string .

xchain:op rdf:type owl:DatatypeProperty ;
  rdfs:label "op"@en ;
```

```
  rdfs:domain xchain:ContextRule ;
  rdfs:range  xsd:string .
```

F.2 SHACL Fragment (shapes.ttl)

For readability, the paper excerpt below uses descriptive shape names and human-facing messages; the released artifact retains stable internal identifiers for implementation compatibility.

```
@prefix sh:     <http://www.w3.org/ns/shacl#> .
@prefix xchain: <http://example.org/xchain#> .

#################################################################
# 1. Evidence attested route must match Message route
#################################################################

xchain:RouteMatchesClaimedRouteShape
  a sh:NodeShape ;
  sh:targetClass xchain:Evidence ;
  sh:sparql [
    a sh:SPARQLConstraint ;
    sh:message "Route-consistency violation: the attested route does
    not match the claimed route." ;
    sh:select """
      PREFIX xchain: <http://example.org/xchain#>

      SELECT ?this WHERE {
        ?this a xchain:Evidence ;
              xchain:evidenceForMessage ?m ;
              xchain:hasAttestedRoute ?er .
        ?m    a xchain:Message ;
              xchain:hasClaimedRoute ?mr .
        FILTER (?er != ?mr)
      }
    """ ;
  ] .

#################################################################
# 2. Evidence context must satisfy RuntimeState rules
#################################################################

xchain:ContextRulesSatisfiedShape
  a sh:NodeShape ;
  sh:targetClass xchain:Evidence ;
  sh:sparql [
    a sh:SPARQLConstraint ;
    sh:message "Context-rule violation: the evidence does not satisfy
    the runtime context rules." ;
    sh:select """
```

```
    PREFIX xchain: <http://example.org/xchain#>
    PREFIX xsd:    <http://www.w3.org/2001/XMLSchema#>

    SELECT DISTINCT ?this WHERE {
      ?this  a xchain:Evidence ;
             xchain:evaluatedUnder ?state ;
             xchain:evidenceContextKV ?ckv .
      ?ckv   xchain:contextkvKey ?k ;
             xchain:contextkvValue ?evRaw .

      ?state a xchain:RuntimeState ;
             xchain:hasContextRule ?rule .
      ?rule  xchain:contextrulekey ?k ;
             xchain:op ?op ;
             xchain:contextrulevalue ?ruleRaw .

      # (comparison logic omitted here for brevity in the PDF excerpt
  )
    }
  """ ;
] .
```

References

1. Ahmetaj, F., Ortiz, M., Simkus, M.: Repairing and consistent query answering for inconsistent SHACL. In: The Semantic Web – ISWC 2022. Springer (2022). https://doi.org/10.1007/978-3-031-19433-7_27
2. Andresel, M., Corman, J., Ortiz, M., Reutter, J.L., Savkovic, O., Simkus, M.: Stable model semantics for recursive SHACL. In: Proceedings of The Web Conference 2020, pp. 1570–1580 (2020). https://doi.org/10.1145/3366423.3380229
3. Augusto, A., Belchior, R., Pfannschmidt, J., Vasconcelos, A., Correia, M.: XChain-Watcher: identifying anomalies in cross-chain bridges. In: Middleware 2025: Proceedings of the 26th ACM International Middleware Conference, pp. 413–426 (2025). https://doi.org/10.1145/3721462.3770781
4. Belchior, R., Vasconcelos, A., Guerreiro, S., Correia, M.: A survey on blockchain interoperability: past, present, and future trends. ACM Comput. Surv. **54**(8), 1–41 (2021). https://doi.org/10.1145/3471140
5. Bloemen, R., Logvinov, L., Evans, J.: EIP-712: typed structured data hashing and signing. Ethereum Improvement Proposal (2017). https://eips.ethereum.org/EIPS/eip-712
6. Boneva, I., Labra Gayo, J.E., Prud'hommeaux, E.: Validating RDF graphs using shape expressions. arXiv preprint arXiv:1404.1270 (2014). https://doi.org/10.48550/arXiv.1404.1270
7. Buterin, V.: EIP-155: Simple replay attack protection. Ethereum Improvement Proposal (2016). https://eips.ethereum.org/EIPS/eip-155
8. Corman, J., Reutter, J.L., Savkovic, O.: A tractable notion of stratification for SHACL. In: ISWC 2018 Posters & Demonstrations, Industry and Blue Sky Ideas Tracks. CEUR Workshop Proceedings, vol. 2180 (2018). https://ceur-ws.org/Vol-2180/paper-11.pdf

9. Fenz, S., Neubauer, T.: Ontology-based information security compliance determination and control selection on the example of ISO 27002. Inf. Comput. Secur. **26**(5), 551–567 (2018). https://doi.org/10.1108/ICS-02-2018-0020
10. Halborn: Explained: The wormhole hack (February 2022). Technical incident analysis (2022). https://www.halborn.com/blog/post/explained-the-wormhole-hack-february-2022
11. Han, P., Yan, Z., Ding, W., Fei, S., Wan, Z.: A survey on cross-chain technologies. Distrib. Ledger Technol. Res. Pract. **2**(2), 1–30 (2023). https://doi.org/10.1145/3573896
12. Herzog, A., Shahmehri, N., Duma, C.: An ontology of information security. Int. J. Inf. Secur. Priv. **1**(4), 1–23 (2007). https://doi.org/10.4018/jisp.2007100101
13. Labra Gayo, J.E., Prud'hommeaux, E., Boneva, I., Kontokostas, D.: Validating RDF Data, Synthesis Lectures on the Semantic Web: Theory and Technology, vol. 7. Morgan & Claypool Publishers (2018). https://doi.org/10.2200/S00786ED1V01Y201707WBE016
14. Lee, S., Murashkin, A., Derka, M., Gorzny, J.: SoK: not quite water under the bridge: review of cross-chain bridge hacks. In: 2023 IEEE International Conference on Blockchain and Cryptocurrency (ICBC), pp. 1–14 (2023). https://doi.org/10.1109/ICBC56567.2023.10174993
15. Masoumzadeh, A., Joshi, J.B.D.: OSNAC: an ontology-based access control model for social networking systems. In: 2010 IEEE Second International Conference on Social Computing, pp. 751–759 (2010). https://doi.org/10.1109/SOCIALCOM.2010.116
16. Nomad: Nomad bridge hack: Root cause analysis. Official incident analysis (2022). https://medium.com/nomad-xyz-blog/nomad-bridge-hack-root-cause-analysis-875ad2e5aacd
17. Poly Network: The Root Cause Of Poly Network Being Hacked. Incident analysis (2021). https://medium.com/poly-network/the-root-cause-of-poly-network-being-hacked-e30cf27468f0
18. Robinson, P.: Survey of crosschain communications protocols. Comput. Netw. **200**, 108488 (2021). https://doi.org/10.1016/j.comnet.2021.108488
19. Souag, A., Salinesi, C., Comyn-Wattiau, I.: Ontologies for security requirements: a literature survey and classification. In: Bajec, M., Eder, J. (eds.) CAiSE 2012. LNBIP, vol. 112, pp. 61–69. Springer, Heidelberg (2012). https://doi.org/10.1007/978-3-642-31069-0_5
20. W3C OWL Working Group: OWL 2 Web Ontology Language Document Overview (Second Edition). W3C Recommendation (2012). https://www.w3.org/TR/2012/REC-owl2-overview-20121211/
21. W3C RDF Data Shapes Working Group: Shapes constraint language (SHACL). W3C Recommendation (2017). https://www.w3.org/TR/shacl/
22. Zhang, M., Zhang, X., Zhang, Y., Lin, Z.: Security of cross-chain bridges: attack surfaces, defenses, and open problems. In: Proceedings of the 27th International Symposium on Research in Attacks, Intrusions and Defenses (RAID 2024), pp. 298–316 (2024). https://doi.org/10.1145/3678890.3678894

On the Effectiveness of Insightful Mining Against Stubborn Mining

Yiyang Li[1] and Tian-Ming Bu[1,2](✉)

[1] Software Engineering Institute, East China Normal University, Shanghai, China
yiyang.li@stu.ecnu.edu.cn
[2] Xinjiang Teacher's College, Xinjiang, China
tmbu@sei.ecnu.edu.cn

Abstract. Selfish mining enables attackers to increase their revenue by hiding blocks and strategically releasing them, thereby wasting the computational resources of honest miners. While many countermeasures rely on protocol-level modifications that are difficult for individual miners to adopt, *insightful mining* was proposed as an individual-level defensive strategy and was shown to dominate selfish mining when its mining power exceeds one third. In this paper, we examine the effectiveness of insightful mining against *equal-fork stubborn mining* (F-stubborn mining), a stronger attack that extends selfish mining by adopting a more aggressive block-reveal policy. We show that, under equal mining power, insightful mining achieves a slightly higher relative revenue than F-stubborn mining. However, this advantage is small and quickly diminishes once mining power becomes asymmetric. Especially, when the F-stubborn pool holds a power advantage, its revenue increases rapidly and approaches a majority share as its mining power nears one half. These results indicate that the defensive capability of insightful mining against stubborn mining is inherently limited.

Keywords: Blockchain · Mining attacks · Stubborn mining · Insightful mining

1 Introduction

1.1 Background

Since Bitcoin was proposed as a decentralized electronic transaction system [14], blockchain technology has been widely adopted across many domains, particularly in the financial sector. In Proof-of-Work (PoW)-based blockchain systems, miners are incentivized to solve cryptographic puzzles in exchange for block rewards. As mining difficulty increases with the growth of computational power in the network, it has become increasingly difficult for individual miners to generate blocks independently [22]. Consequently, most miners now participate in mining pools, where computational resources are aggregated and rewards are distributed according to each miner's contribution.

Y. Cao et al. (Eds.): SecureComm 2026, LNICST 704, pp. 330–357, 2027.
https://doi.org/10.1007/978-3-032-32764-2_16

A fundamental assumption underlying the security and incentive compatibility of PoW-based blockchain systems is that miners behave honestly, i.e., they immediately publish newly generated blocks. Under this assumption, a miner's expected revenue is proportional to its share of the total mining power. However, this assumption is violated by *selfish mining* [4], in which an attacker hides blocks and selectively reveals them at strategic moments. By doing so, selfish miners can cause honest miners to waste computational resources and obtain a revenue share that exceeds their mining power.

Following the discovery of selfish mining, a range of attacks based on maintaining private chains have been proposed. These attacks either increase the attacker's revenue or reduce the mining power required to mount a profitable deviation. Among them, *stubborn mining* [15] represents a particularly powerful extension of selfish mining. By carefully controlling both the timing and the number of hidden blocks that are revealed, stubborn mining can significantly improve attacker revenue under broader conditions.

The emergence of selfish and stubborn mining has motivated extensive research on countermeasures. Many existing defenses adopt a mechanism design perspective and seek to modify the underlying blockchain protocol to discourage strategic deviations. While effective in theory, such protocol-level changes are often difficult for individual miners to deploy in practice, limiting their applicability in real-world mining environments. In contrast, relatively little attention has been paid to individual-level mining strategies that allow miners to directly defend themselves against strategic attackers without requiring system-wide modifications.

Focusing on miners' incentives, *insightful mining* was proposed as an individual-level defensive strategy against selfish mining. Inspired by techniques from Block Withholding (BWH) attacks [3,19], insightful mining deploys spies to detect the existence of hidden blocks. When a fork occurs, this information is used to guide block acceptance decisions, enabling insightful miners to counter selfish attackers. At the same time, insightful mining behaves similarly to selfish mining when releasing its own blocks. Prior work shows that insightful mining achieves strictly higher revenue than selfish mining under the same mining power, and can even secure a majority share of the total revenue once its mining power exceeds one third.

Despite these promising results, existing analyses of insightful mining implicitly assume that the attacker follows the selfish mining strategy. However, stubborn mining can strictly dominate selfish mining by exploiting more aggressive block-reveal policies. This raises a natural and important question: does insightful mining remain an effective defense when facing stronger attacks such as stubborn mining? In this paper, we investigate the effectiveness of *insightful mining* against *equal-fork stubborn mining* (F-stubborn mining).

1.2 Related Work

Mining Attacks. Following the introduction of selfish mining [4], extensive research has examined mining attacks from the attacker's perspective under the assumption that other miners behave honestly. A line of work strengthens selfish mining by refining block-reveal policies. Among these, stubborn mining [15] represents a particularly effective extension and achieves substantially higher revenue. Other variants which are referred to as semi-selfish mining [13,17], introduce probabilistic deviations from honest behavior. Additionally, selfish mining has been combined with bribery attacks [6,11], in which miners increase the probability of their branch winning in the forking competition by bribing other miners with transaction fees. More recently, this has further been extended to stubborn [10] and semi-selfish mining [8], highlighting the growing sophistication of private-chain attacks.

Modeling and Analysis of Mining Strategies. To analyze the revenue of mining attacks, a large body of work adopts Markov Decision Processes (MDPs) and related stochastic models. Feng and Niu [5] model selfish mining using a two-dimensional Markov process and compare attack thresholds across different blockchains. Subsequent work develops a more general Markov model that further analyzes stubborn mining and evaluates their impacts on miner revenue, blockchain performance, and security [26]. To address the non-linear objective of Average Reward Ratio (ARR) MDPs, Sapirshtein *et al.* [21] propose a binary search approach, later improved by Probabilistic Termination Optimization [30], which reduces the problem to a single standard MDP. In parallel, several studies focus on scenarios with multiple attackers [12,24] and show that the mining power threshold for profitable attacks decreases as the number of attackers increases [1,29].

Protocol-Level Defenses. To defend against attacks represented by selfish mining, many studies adopt protocol-level modifications to the existing blockchain systems. One representative approach proposes a backward-compatible protection mechanism against selfish mining [28], the key idea of which is to modify the fork resolution rule by discouraging late block releases. A recent study [9] proposes EVONIncentive, a bi-tier blockchain hybrid incentive scheme, to ensure system security and stability. In addition, some works propose alternative Difficulty Adjustment Algorithms (DAAs) to reduce the revenue of selfish attackers [16,18]. Other studies propose explicit detection mechanisms to identify selfish mining behavior [2,20]. While effective in principle, these approaches typically require system-wide changes, limiting their deployability for individual miners.

Individual-Level Defensive Strategies. In contrast, relatively few studies investigate defensive mining strategies that can be adopted directly by individual miners. Reinforcement learning-based approaches [7,25] explore large strategy spaces, but can be computationally expensive and produce policies that are difficult to interpret and validate in adversarial mining settings. Another line of work leverages information asymmetry by monitoring private chains using spies, thus expanding the strategy space, which has been rarely discussed in the wide selfish mining context. Such strategies include stowaway mining [23], which directly mines on the selfish miner's private chain, and *insightful mining* [27]. Among these strategies, insightful mining stands out as a principled individual-level defense due to its strong effectiveness: it adopts a strategy similar to selfish mining but avoids mining on the attacker's blocks when forks occur, thereby significantly reducing the attacker's revenue. Despite its strong guarantees against selfish mining, existing analyses of insightful mining have not been extended to stronger private-chain attacks such as stubborn mining.

1.3 Our Contributions

In this paper, we investigate the effectiveness of *insightful mining* as a defensive strategy against *equal-fork stubborn mining* (F-stubborn mining). Our main contributions are summarized as follows:

1. We present the first systematic study of the strategic interaction between an insightful mining pool and an F-stubborn mining pool in the presence of honest miners. This fills an important gap in the existing literature, which has primarily focused on selfish mining as the attack model when analyzing strategic interactions between miners, especially in settings involving multiple strategic miners.
2. We model the interaction among the insightful pool, the F-stubborn pool, and the honest pool using a Markov Reward Process (MRP). Based on this model, we theoretically show that, under equal mining power, insightful mining can still achieve a strictly higher relative revenue than F-stubborn mining.
3. Through extensive simulations, we further study the performance of insightful mining under both equal and asymmetric mining power. Under equal mining power, insightful mining achieves revenue comparable to that of F-stubborn mining, with a modest advantage. As mining power becomes asymmetric, the pool with higher mining power increasingly dominates the revenue. In particular, when the F-stubborn pool gains a power advantage, its revenue approaches a majority share as its mining power nears one half. We also investigate the minimum mining power required for the insightful pool to maintain revenue parity with the F-stubborn pool, highlighting the inherent sensitivity of insightful mining to mining power asymmetry.

The remainder of this paper is organized as follows: Sect. 2 introduces the key concepts. Section 3 presents the system model and analyzes the state transitions using the Markov Reward Process (MRP). Section 4 provides the theoretical analysis of expected relative revenue for insightful mining and F-stubborn mining. Section 5 details the experimental results. Finally, Sect. 6 concludes the paper.

2 Preliminaries

2.1 Proof of Work

In blockchain systems employing the PoW scheme, miners are required to randomly engage in the hashing function calls to solve a cryptopuzzle. The input to the hash function H consists of the previous block's information, the miner's address designated for potential rewards, and Merkle root, a consolidated hash of all transactions within the block. Typically, the miner is required to find a nonce that satisfies:

$$H(\text{hash of the previous block; address; Merkle root; } nonce) \leq D \quad (1)$$

Here, H denotes a widely recognized hash function, and D represents the target value of the puzzle, reflecting its computational difficulty.

Beginning from the genesis block, each miner continuously searches for a solution, appends a new block to the existing blockchain and receives the corresponding reward. The standard Bitcoin protocol treats the longest chain as the main chain. In cases where two blocks are published nearly simultaneously, miners randomly select one block and continue mining atop it according to the uniform tie-breaking rule. Miners are generally expected to publish the newly mined blocks immediately. In this paper, such behavior is termed *honest mining.*

2.2 Mining Pools

As the aggregate computational resources devoted to mining continues to grow, the probability that an individual miner successfully produces a block on its own becomes negligible. Consequently, it has become standard practice for miners to engage in collective mining arrangements known as mining pools.

In general, mining pools consist a pool manager and multiple miners who collaboratively work on solving the same mining task. To facilitate parallel computation, most mining pools specify an auxiliary target value D', which is strictly less demanding than the network-wide difficulty parameter D. Under this scheme, each miner is only required to search for a nonce that satisfies:

$$H(\text{hash of the previous block; address; Merkle root; } nonce) \leq D' \quad (2)$$

Upon receiving a candidate solution from a miner, the pool manager examines whether the submitted nonce satisfies inequality (1). Once such a nonce is discovered, the mining pool as a whole is awarded the block reward, which is subsequently divided among participating miners according to a predetermined allocation rule.

2.3 Selfish Mining and F-Stubborn Mining

Selfish Mining. An attacker that adopts *selfish mining* does not always publish the newly generated blocks immediately. Instead, the attacker selectively reveals them at certain points in time. The blocks that are not broadcast are stored in a private chain controlled by the attacker. In this paper, a mining pool that adopts the selfish mining strategy is referred to as a *selfish pool*, and a mining pool that follows the standard protocol is referred to as an *honest pool*. The behavior of the selfish pool can be described based on the lead of the selfish pool's private chain over the honest pool, as follows:

- If the honest pool generates a new block:
  - If the lead is 2, then the selfish pool reveals its entire private chain.
  - If the lead is 1, then the selfish pool reveals its entire private chain, resulting in a fork.
  - If the lead is 0, then the selfish pool accepts the newly generated block, regardless of whether the main chain has forked or not.
  - Otherwise, the selfish pool never reveals its private chain.
- If the selfish pool generates a new block:
  - If the lead is 0 and the main chain has forked, then the selfish pool publishes the newly generated block.
  - Otherwise, the selfish pool always hides the newly generated block.

Thus, the selfish pool may have previously mined but hidden blocks while the honest pool continues mining. This creates a situation where the honest pool's efforts can be entirely wasted when the selfish pool eventually reveals its hidden blocks. Through this approach, the selfish pool effectively exploits and wastes the computational resources of the honest pool, thereby gaining an advantage in the mining competition.

F-Stubborn Mining. A key distinction between selfish mining and *F-stubborn mining* lies in their behavior during chain forks. When the lead is 0 and the main chain has forked, a selfish pool always publishes newly mined blocks to expedite fork resolution, while an F-stubborn pool continues to hide newly generated blocks, deliberately prolonging the fork. Since honest miners randomly select a fork, F-stubborn pools may achieve higher rewards than selfish pools in certain scenarios.

2.4 Insightful Mining

Insightful mining detects the number of blocks in the private chain of a selfish pool and acts upon the block releases of other pools:

- If the honest pool generates and publishes a new block, the insightful pool accepts the block and continues mining after it.
- If the selfish pool generates and hides a new block, the insightful pool detects this behavior and acts honestly, i.e., continues mining on the main chain. When the selfish pool publishes a block:
  - If the selfish pool reveals hidden blocks to create a fork, the insightful pool never mines on blocks generated by the selfish pool.

  - If the selfish pool reveals its hidden blocks, resulting in its entire private chain being accepted as the main chain, the insightful pool accepts these blocks.
- If the insightful pool generates a block, it hides the newly generated block. In the following competition, the insightful pool always hides all its generated blocks as long as its lead is strictly greater than one, whereas it reveals its entire private chain otherwise.

To identify the presence of hidden private blocks in the system, the insightful pool may deploy *spies* inside the pool. A spy joins the selfish pool as a regular participant and takes part in assigned mining tasks. By inspecting the hash value embedded in a received task and comparing it with the hash of the most recent block on the main chain, the spy can infer whether the pool is mining on a hidden private block.

3 Model and Analysis of the Mining System

3.1 Model

Consider a system consisting n miners, each of them having a fraction m_i of the total mining power such that $\sum_{i=1}^{n} m_i = 1$. For analytical convenience, miners following the honest mining strategy are modeled as a whole, and is referred to as the *honest pool*. Similarly, those adopting the F-stubborn mining strategy are termed the *F-stubborn pool*, while the remaining miners are assumed to follow the insightful mining strategy and form the *insightful pool*. Let α denote the fraction of the total mining power controlled by the F-stubborn pool, and β represent the fraction of the total mining power controlled by the insightful pool. Thus, the fraction of the honest pool's mining power is $1-\alpha-\beta$. Note that the probability that a miner generates a block is effectively proportional to its fraction of the total mining power. In the subsequent analysis and experiments, we assume that the time to broadcast a block is negligible, as well as the transaction fee. Moreover, both the mining power allocated by the insightful pool to deploy such spies and the revenue it may obtain from the F-stubborn pool are assumed to be negligible. Further, we assume that the mining power of the honest pool is evenly distributed across each branch whenever a fork occurs on the main chain.

3.2 Markov Reward Process of the Mining System

To analyze the relative revenue of miners adopting different strategies, we model the mining system as an MRP $Markov(\alpha, \beta)$, and denote the MRP state by $s = (x, y)$. Here, x denotes the lead of the F-stubborn pool over the honest pool, i.e., the number of blocks by which the private chain of the F-stubborn pool exceeds the main chain. Similarly, y denotes the lead of the insightful pool over the F-stubborn pool. In particular, when a fork of the main chain caused by the F-stubborn pool and other mining pools is observed, we say that $x = 0'$. In other words, the state $x = 0'$ means that the F-stubborn pool and other pools hold a different branch of the same length, and that the next block will decide the main chain. Similarly, the state $y = 0'$ means that the main chain is forked due to blocks generated by the insightful pool and other mining pools. Hence, we have $x, y \in \mathbb{N} \cup \{0'\}$. Whenever a fork occurs on the main chain, the mining power of the honest pool is assumed to be evenly split among the competing branches.

Let $P[s, s']$ denote the transition probability from state s to state s', and let $r[s, s']$, a three-dimensional vector, denote the expected revenues of the honest pool, the F-stubborn pool, and the insightful pool from this transition, respectively. Here, f_h, f_s, and f_i in the table denote the expected numbers of blocks generated by the honest pool, the F-stubborn pool, and the insightful pool, respectively, during the transitions within the cycle of states $(0', 0), (1, 0), (1, 0')$. For detailed definitions of f_h, f_s, and f_i, please refer to the Appendix. Since this paper focuses on the revenues of the F-stubborn pool and the insightful pool, we only consider the values of f_s and f_i, which are defined as follows:

$$\begin{cases} f_s = \frac{\alpha(1-\alpha)}{(1-\alpha(1-\alpha))^2} \\ f_i = \frac{\alpha\beta}{(1-\alpha\beta)^2} \end{cases} \tag{3}$$

The state transitions of the entire mining system and the corresponding expected revenues are then listed in Table 1. The detailed analysis of the state transitions can be found in the Appendix.

With Table 1 lists all state transitions of the MRP, together with the corresponding expected revenues during each transition, for intuitiveness, the overall state transitions are illustrated in Fig. 1.

4 Expected Revenues of the Mining Pools

To compare the relative revenues of the F-stubborn pool and the insightful pool, we first compute the expected revenues obtained by all three kinds of mining pools throughout the entire mining process.

For any mining pool i, its total revenue is defined as the sum of revenues obtained in each state transition. The total revenue of the system is the sum of revenues obtained by all participating mining pools. Accordingly, the relative revenue of mining pool i is defined as the ratio between its total revenue and the total system revenue over the entire mining process. Thus, the expected relative revenue of mining pool i is defined as the limit inferior of this ratio as the mining duration T tends to infinity. That is, the expected relative revenue ERR_i for any mining pool i is defined as

$$ERR_i = \mathbb{E}[\liminf_{T\to\infty} \frac{\sum_{t=1}^{T} r_i[s_t, s_{t+1}] | s_0 = (0,0), s_{t+1} \sim P[s_t, s_{t+1}]}{\sum_{t=1}^{T} \sum_{j\in M} r_j[s_t, s_{t+1}] | s_0 = (0,0), s_{t+1} \sim P[s_t, s_{t+1}]}]$$

For simplicity, we use ERR_H, ERR_{FM}, and ERR_{IM} to denote the relative revenues of the honest pool, the F-stubborn pool, and the insightful pool, respectively.

Table 1. The state transitions and the corresponding expected revenues.

No.	State s	State s'	$P[s, s']$	$r[s, s']$	Condition
1	$(0, 0)$	$(0, 0)$	$1-\alpha-\beta$	$(1, 0, 0)$	
2	$(0, 0)$	$(0, 1)$	α	$(0, 0, 0)$	
3	$(1, 0)$	$(0', 0)$	$1-\alpha-\beta$	$(0, 0, 0)$	
4	$(0', 0)$	$(0, 0)$	$1-\alpha$	$(\frac{(1-\alpha+\beta)f_h+3-3\alpha-\beta}{2}, \frac{(1-\alpha-\beta)(f_s+1)}{2}, \frac{(1-\alpha+\beta)f_i+2\beta}{2})$	
5	$(0', 0)$	$(1, 0)$	α	$(0, 0, 0)$	
6	$(1, 0)$	$(1, 0')$	β	$(0, 0, 0)$	
7	$(1, 0')$	$(0, 0)$	$1-\alpha$	$(\frac{(1-\alpha+\beta)f_h+2-2\alpha-2\beta}{2}, \frac{(1-\alpha-\beta)(f_s+1)}{2}, \frac{(1-\alpha+\beta)f_i+1-\alpha+3\beta}{2})$	
8	$(1, 0')$	$(1, 0)$	α	$(0, 0, 0)$	
9	$(x, 0)$	$(x+1, 0)$	α	$(0, 0, 0)$	$\forall x \geq 1$
10	$(2, 0)$	$(0, 0)$	$1-\alpha$	$(0, 2+f_s, 0)$	
11	$(x, 0)$	$(x-1, 0)$	$1-\alpha$	$(0, 1, 0)$	$\forall x \geq 3$
12	$(0, 0)$	$(0, 1)$	β	$(0, 0, 0)$	
13	$(0, 1)$	$(1, 0')$	α	$(0, 0, 0)$	
14	$(0, 1)$	$(0, 0')$	$1-\alpha-\beta$	$(0, 0, 0)$	
15	$(0, 0')$	$(0, 0)$	1	$(\frac{3-2\alpha-3\beta}{2}, \alpha, \frac{1+3\beta}{2})$	
16	$(0, 1)$	$(0, 2)$	β	$(0, 0, 0)$	
17	$(0, 2)$	$(0, 0)$	$1-\beta$	$(0, 0, 2)$	
18	(x, y)	$(x, y+1)$	β	$(0, 0, 0)$	$\forall x \in \{0'\} \bigcup \mathbb{N},\ y \geq 2$
19	$(0, y)$	$(0, y-1)$	$1-\alpha-\beta$	$(0, 0, 1)$	$\forall y \geq 3$
20	(x, y)	$(x+1, y-1)$	α	$(0, 0, 1)$	$\forall x \geq 0,\ y \geq 3$
21	$(1, y)$	$(0', y)$	$1-\alpha-\beta$	$(0, 0, 0)$	$\forall y \geq 2$
22	$(2, y)$	$(0, y)$	$1-\alpha-\beta$	$(0, 0, 0)$	$\forall y \geq 2$
23	(x, y)	$(x-1, y)$	$1-\alpha-\beta$	$(0, 0, 0)$	$\forall x \geq 3,\ y \geq 2$
24	$(x, 2)$	$(0, 0)$	α	$(0, 0, 2)$	$\forall x \geq 1$
25	$(0', 2)$	$(0, 0)$	$1-\beta$	$(0, 0, 2)$	
26	$(0', y)$	$(0, y-1)$	$1-\beta$	$(0, 0, 1)$	$\forall y \geq 3$

To compare the competitive advantages of the F-stubborn pool and the insightful pool, this paper restrict attention to the scenario where the F-stubborn pool and the insightful pool have the exact same mining power. Hence, we have: $0 < \alpha = \beta < \frac{1}{2}$.

We first consider the case where the MRP $Markov(\alpha, \beta)$ admits a stationary distribution.

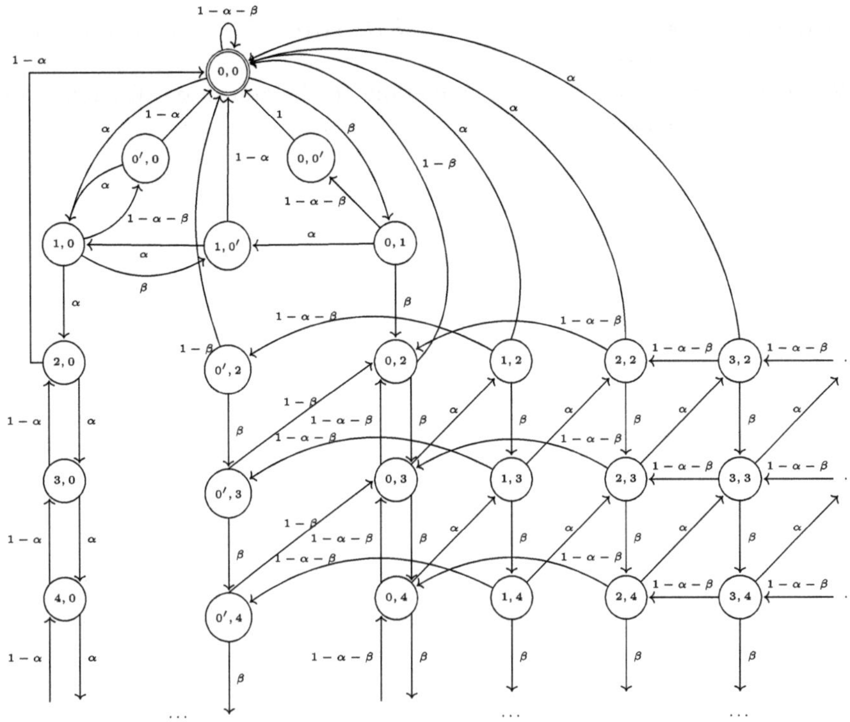

Fig. 1. The Markov Reward Process of the system.

Lemma 1. *Suppose that* $Markov(\alpha, \beta)$ *admits a stationary distribution. Let* α *and* β *denote the F-stubborn pool's and the insightful pool's fraction of the total mining power, respectively. If* $0 < \alpha = \beta < \frac{1}{2}$, *then* $ERR_{FM}(\alpha, \beta) < ERR_{IM}(\alpha, \beta)$.

Proof. Let $\pi_{s_t} = \pi_{(i,j)}$ denote the stationary probability of state $s_t = (i, j)$, and let $\mathbb{S}$ denote the state space of $Markov(\alpha, \beta)$. Let $ER_H(\alpha, \beta)$, $ER_{FM}(\alpha, \beta)$, and $ER_{IM}(\alpha, \beta)$ denote the expected revenues of the honest pool, the F-stubborn pool, and the insightful pool, respectively. For any $i \in \{H, FM, IM\}$, we have:

$$ER_i(\alpha, \beta) = \sum_{s \in \mathbb{S}} \sum_{s' \in \mathbb{S}} P[s, s'] \cdot r_i[s, s'] \cdot \pi_s$$

Hence, the relative revenues of the F-stubborn and insightful pools can be written as:

$$ERR_{FM}(\alpha, \beta) = \frac{ER_{FM}(\alpha, \beta)}{ER_H(\alpha, \beta) + ER_{FM}(\alpha, \beta) + ER_{IM}(\alpha, \beta)}$$

$$ERR_{IM}(\alpha, \beta) = \frac{ER_{IM}(\alpha, \beta)}{ER_H(\alpha, \beta) + ER_{FM}(\alpha, \beta) + ER_{IM}(\alpha, \beta)}$$

Therefore, to show $ERR_{FM}(\alpha,\beta) < ERR_{IM}(\alpha,\beta)$, it suffices to prove $ER_{FM}(\alpha,\beta) < ER_{IM}(\alpha,\beta)$.

We first compute $ER_{FM}(\alpha,\beta)$. According to the transition distribution of $Markov(\alpha,\beta)$, we have:

$$\pi_{(2,0)} = \alpha\pi_{(1,0)} + (1-\alpha)\pi_{(3,0)} \tag{4}$$
$$\pi_{(3,0)} = \alpha\pi_{(2,0)} + (1-\alpha)\pi_{(4,0)} \tag{5}$$
$$\cdots = \cdots$$
$$\pi_{(i+1,0)} = \alpha\pi_{(i,0)} + (1-\alpha)\pi_{(i+2,0)} \tag{6}$$
$$\cdots = \cdots \tag{7}$$

Let $s = \pi_{(3,0)} + \pi_{(4,0)} + \cdots$. Summing Eq. (4) to (6) yields:

$$\begin{aligned}\pi_{(2,0)} + s &= \alpha(\pi_{(1,0)} + \pi_{(2,0)} + s) + (1-\alpha)s\\ \pi_{(2,0)} &= \alpha(\pi_{(1,0)} + \pi_{(2,0)})\\ \pi_{(2,0)} &= \frac{\alpha\pi_{(1,0)}}{1-\alpha}\end{aligned}$$

Similarly, by repeating this argument gives, that is, summing Eq. (5) to (6), etc. It holds for all $i \geq 1$:

$$\pi_{(i+1,0)} = \frac{\alpha}{1-\alpha}\pi_{(i,0)}$$

Meanwhile, based on the transition distribution of $Markov(\alpha,\beta)$, we can derive:

$$\begin{cases}\pi_{(1,0)} &= \frac{\alpha(1+\alpha\beta)}{1-\alpha+\alpha^2}\pi_{(0,0)}\\ \pi_{(1,0')} &= (\frac{\alpha\beta(1+\alpha\beta)}{1-\alpha+\alpha^2} + \alpha\beta)\pi_{(0,0)}\\ \pi_{(0',0)} &= \frac{\alpha(1+\alpha\beta)(1-\alpha-\beta)}{1-\alpha+\alpha^2}\pi_{(0,0)}\\ \pi_{(0,1)} &= \beta\pi_{(0,0)}\\ \pi_{(0,0')} &= (1-\alpha-\beta)\pi_{(0,1)}\\ \pi_{(i+1,0)} &= \frac{\alpha}{1-\alpha}\pi_{(i,0)} \qquad \forall i \geq 1\end{cases}$$

Since $\alpha = \beta$, the above expressions can be simplified as follows:

$$\begin{cases}\pi_{(1,0)} &= \frac{\alpha(1+\alpha^2)}{1-\alpha+\alpha^2}\pi_{(0,0)}\\ \pi_{(1,0')} &= (\frac{\alpha^2(1+\alpha^2)}{1-\alpha+\alpha^2} + \alpha^2)\pi_{(0,0)}\\ \pi_{(0',0)} &= \frac{\alpha(1+\alpha^2)(1-2\alpha)}{1-\alpha+\alpha^2}\pi_{(0,0)}\\ \pi_{(0,1)} &= \alpha\pi_{(0,0)}\\ \pi_{(0,0')} &= \alpha(1-2\alpha)\pi_{(0,0)}\\ \pi_{(2,0)} &= \frac{\alpha^2(1+\alpha^2)}{(1-\alpha+\alpha^2)(1-\alpha)}\pi_{(0,0)}\\ \sum_{i=3}^{\infty}\pi_{(i,0)} &= \frac{\alpha^2}{(1-\alpha)(1-2\alpha)}\pi_{(1,0)}\end{cases}$$

Therefore we have:

$$
\begin{aligned}
&ER_{FM}(\alpha,\beta) = \sum_{s\in\mathbb{S}}\sum_{s'\in\mathbb{S}} P[s,s']\cdot rFM[s,s']\cdot \pi_s \\
&= \frac{(1-\alpha-\beta)(f_s+1)}{2}(1-\alpha)\pi_{(0',0)} + \frac{(1-\alpha-\beta)(f_s+1)}{2}(1-\alpha)\pi_{(1,0')} \\
&\quad + (2+f_s)(1-\alpha)\pi_{(2,0)} + \alpha\pi_{(0,0')} + (1-\alpha)\sum_{i=3}^{\infty}\pi_{(i,0)} \\
&= \frac{(1-2\alpha)(f_s+1)}{2}(1-\alpha)(\pi_{(0',0)}+\pi_{(1,0')}) + (2+f_s)(1-\alpha)\pi_{(2,0)} \\
&\quad + \alpha\pi_{(0,0')} + \frac{\alpha^2}{1-2\alpha}\pi_{(1,0)}
\end{aligned}
$$

Here, $f_s = \frac{\alpha(1-\alpha)}{(1-\alpha(1-\alpha))^2}$, as is defined in Eqs. (3).

Next, we compute the expected reward $ER_{IM}(\alpha,\beta)$ under the insightful mining strategy. From the transition matrix of $Markov(\alpha,\beta)$, we have:

$$
\begin{aligned}
\beta\pi_{(0,1)} &= (1-\beta)(\pi_{(0',2)}+\pi_{(0,2)}) + \alpha\sum_{i\geq 1}\pi_{(i,2)} \\
\beta\sum_i \pi_{(i,j)} &= (1-\beta)(\pi_{(0',j+1)}+\pi_{(0,j+1)}) + \alpha\sum_{i\geq 1}\pi_{(i,j+1)} \qquad \forall j\geq 2
\end{aligned}
$$

Since $\alpha-\beta<\frac{1}{2}$, it holds that:

$$
\begin{aligned}
\beta\pi_{(0,1)} &= (1-\beta)(\pi_{(0',2)}+\pi_{(0,2)}) + \alpha\sum_{i\geq 1}\pi_{(i,2)} < (1-\beta)\sum_i \pi_{(i,2)} \\
\beta\sum_i \pi_{(i,2)} &= (1-\beta)(\pi_{(0',3)}+\pi_{(0,3)}) + \alpha\sum_{i\geq 1}\pi_{(i,3)} < (1-\beta)\sum_i \pi_{(i,3)} \\
&\cdots = \cdots < \cdots \\
\beta\sum_i \pi_{(i,j)} &= (1-\beta)(\pi_{(0',j+1)}+\pi_{(0,j+1)}) + \alpha\sum_{i\geq 1}\pi_{(i,j+1)} < (1-\beta)\sum_i \pi_{(i,j+1)} \\
&\cdots = \cdots
\end{aligned}
$$

Equivalently:

$$
\begin{aligned}
\sum_i \pi_{(i,2)} &> \frac{\beta}{1-\beta}\pi_{(0,1)} \\
\sum_i \pi_{(i,3)} &> \frac{\beta}{1-\beta}\sum_i \pi_{(i,2)} \\
\cdots &> \cdots \\
\sum_i \pi_{(i,j)} &> \frac{\beta}{1-\beta}\sum_i \pi_{(i,j-1)} \\
\cdots &> \cdots
\end{aligned}
$$

Let $s' = \sum_{j\geq 2}\sum_i \pi_{(i,j)}$. Summing the above inequalities yields:

$$s' > \frac{\beta}{1-\beta}\pi_{(0,1)} + \frac{\beta}{1-\beta}s'$$

$$(1-\frac{\beta}{1-\beta})s' > \frac{\beta}{1-\beta}\pi_{(0,1)}$$

Since $0 < \beta < \frac{1}{2}$, we have $\frac{\beta}{1-\beta} < 1$, and therefore it holds that:

$$s' > \frac{\beta}{1-2\beta}\pi_{(0,1)}$$

That is:

$$\sum_{j\geq 2}\sum_i \pi_{(i,j)} > \frac{\beta}{1-2\beta}\pi_{(0,1)}$$

Consequently, we have:

$$\begin{aligned}
ER_{IM}(\alpha,\beta) &= \sum_{s\in\mathbb{S}}\sum_{s'\in\mathbb{S}} P[s,s']\cdot r_{IM}[s,s']\cdot\pi_s\\
&= \frac{(1-\alpha+\beta)f_i+2\beta}{2}(1-\alpha)\pi_{(0',0)} + \frac{(1-\alpha+\beta)f_i+1-\alpha+3\beta}{2}(1-\alpha)\pi_{(1,0')}\\
&\quad + \frac{1+3\beta}{2}\pi_{(0,0')} + 2((\pi_{(0',2)}+\pi_{(0,2)})(1-\beta)+\alpha\sum_{i\geq 1}\pi_{(i,2)})\\
&\quad + \sum_{j\geq 3}((\pi_{(0',j)}+\pi_{(0,j)})(1-\beta)+\alpha\sum_{i\geq 1}\pi_{(i,j)})\\
&> \frac{(1-\alpha+\beta)f_i+2\beta}{2}(1-\alpha)\pi_{(0',0)} + \frac{(1-\alpha+\beta)f_i+1-\alpha+3\beta}{2}(1-\alpha)\pi_{(1,0')}\\
&\quad + \frac{1+3\beta}{2}\pi_{(0,0')} + 2\beta\pi_{(0,1)} + \frac{\beta^2}{1-2\beta}\pi_{(0,1)}\\
&= \frac{f_i+2\alpha}{2}(1-\alpha)\pi_{(0',0)} + \frac{f_i+1+2\alpha}{2}(1-\alpha)\pi_{(1,0')} + \frac{1+3\alpha}{2}\pi_{(0,0')}\\
&\quad + 2\alpha\pi_{(0,1)} + \frac{\alpha^2}{1-2\alpha}\pi_{(0,1)}
\end{aligned}$$

Here, $f_i = \frac{\alpha\beta}{(1-\alpha\beta)^2} = \frac{\alpha^2}{(1-\alpha^2)^2}$, as derived in Eqs. (3).

To this point, both $ER_{FM}(\alpha,\beta)$ and $ER_{IM}(\alpha,\beta)$ have been obtained. To compare them, we compute their difference:

$$
\begin{aligned}
& ER_{IM}(\alpha,\beta) - ER_{FM}(\alpha,\beta) \\
> & \frac{f_i+2\alpha}{2}(1-\alpha)\pi_{(0',0)} + \frac{f_i+1+2\alpha}{2}(1-\alpha)\pi_{(1,0')} \\
& + \frac{1+3\alpha}{2}\pi_{(0,0')} + 2\alpha\pi_{(0,1)} + \frac{\alpha^2}{1-2\alpha}\pi_{(0,1)} \\
& - \frac{(1-2\alpha)(f_s+1)}{2}(1-\alpha)(\pi_{(0',0)} + \pi_{(1,0')}) \\
& - (2+f_s)(1-\alpha)\pi_{(2,0)} - \alpha\pi_{(0,0')} - \frac{\alpha^2}{1-2\alpha}\pi_{(1,0)} \\
= & \frac{1}{2}[(\pi_{(0',0)} + \pi_{(1,0')})(\frac{\alpha^2(\frac{5}{4}-(\alpha+\frac{1}{2})^2)}{(1+\alpha)(1-\alpha^2)} \\
& + \frac{(1-2\alpha)^2+\alpha(1-\alpha)}{(1-\alpha+\alpha^2)^2}(\alpha^2(1-\alpha)^2 + (1-2\alpha)^2 + \alpha(1-\alpha)) \\
& + \frac{1}{2}((\frac{1}{2}-\alpha)^2 + \frac{3}{4}) + 1) \\
& + \pi_{(0,1)}(\frac{1}{2}(1-2\alpha)(1+2\alpha) \\
& + \alpha((1-2\alpha)^2 + \alpha^2(1-\alpha)^2 + (1-2\alpha)))]
\end{aligned}
$$

To be more clear, we rewrite the rightmost formula of the above inequality as $\frac{1}{2}[c_1(\pi_{(0',0)} + \pi_{(1,0')}) + c_2\pi_{(0,1)}]$, where:

$$
\begin{aligned}
c_1 = & \frac{\alpha^2[\frac{5}{4}-(\alpha+\frac{1}{2})^2]}{(1+\alpha)(1-\alpha^2)} \\
& + \frac{(1-2\alpha)^2+\alpha(1-\alpha)}{(1-\alpha+\alpha^2)^2}[\alpha^2(1-\alpha)^2 + (1-2\alpha)^2 + \alpha(1-\alpha)] \\
& + \frac{1}{2}[(\frac{1}{2}-\alpha)^2 + \frac{3}{4}] + 1
\end{aligned}
$$

and:

$$
c_2 = \frac{1}{2}(1-2\alpha)(1+2\alpha) + \alpha[(1-2\alpha)^2 + \alpha^2(1-\alpha)^2 + (1-2\alpha)]
$$

For all $0 < \alpha < \frac{1}{2}$, each component of both c_1 and c_2 must be positive. Therefore, it holds that $ER_{IM}(\alpha,\beta) - ER_{FM}(\alpha,\beta) > 0$. Hence the proof is complete. □

We next consider the case where $Markov(\alpha,\beta)$ does not admit a stationary distribution.

Lemma 2. *Suppose that $Markov(\alpha, \beta)$ does not admit a stationary distribution. Let α and β denote the F-stubborn pool's and the insightful pool's fraction of the total mining power, respectively. If $0 < \alpha = \beta < \frac{1}{2}$, then $ERR_{FM}(\alpha, \beta) < ERR_{IM}(\alpha, \beta)$.*

Proof. It's clear that the MRP is irreducible. Since the MRP does not admit a stationary distribution, no state can be positive recurrent. Equivalently, starting from any state in the state space $\mathbb{S}$, the expected return time to this state is infinite.

We consider the following two cases:

1. The MRP first transitions from state $(0, 0)$ to state $(1, 0)$.
   Starting from state $(1, 0)$, there are three possible paths. The first path moves to state $(2, 0)$ and then may proceed into the infinite state chain $(2, 0), (3, 0), \ldots$. Since we have $\alpha < \frac{1}{2} < 1 - \alpha$, the MRP returns to state $(1, 0)$ in a finite number of steps in expectation. The second and third paths move to states $(0', 0)$ and $(1, 0')$, respectively. From each of these two states, the MRP returns to state $(0, 0)$ with probability $1 - \alpha$ in one step, or returns to state $(1, 0)$ with probability α. By the law of total expectation over the three paths, the number of steps from state $(1, 0)$ to state $(0, 0)$ is finite in expectation. Consequently, the total revenue obtained by the F-stubborn pool from these transaction processes is finite in expectation. Moreover, if the MRP returns to state $(0, 0)$ through state $(1, 0')$, the insightful pool obtains finite expected revenue, whereas the F-stubborn pool obtains nothing in this case.
2. The MRP first transitions from state $(0, 0)$ to state $(0, 1)$.
   We have already shown that in expectation, the number of steps taken for the MRP to return to state $(0, 0)$ from state $(1, 0)$ is finite. Hence, since state $(0, 0)$ is not positive recurrent, the MRP requires infinite steps to return to state $(0, 0)$, before which it remains in states $\bigcup_{x \in 0' \bigcup \mathbb{N}} \bigcup_{y \geq 2} (x, y)$. During these state transitions, neither the honest pool nor the F-stubborn pool obtains any revenue, whereas the insightful pool obtains revenue $\alpha \cdot t$, where t denotes the number of steps spent to return to state $(0, 0)$.

Therefore, when $T \to \infty$, we have $t \to \infty$, and therefore it holds that $ERR_{IM}(\alpha, \beta) - ERR_{FM}(\alpha, \beta) \to 1$. Hence the proof is complete. □

By Lemma 1 and 2, we can derive the following theorem:

Theorem 1. *Let α and β denote the F-stubborn pool's and the insightful pool's fraction of the total mining power, respectively. If $0 < \alpha = \beta < \frac{1}{2}$, then $ERR_{FM}(\alpha, \beta) < ERR_{IM}(\alpha, \beta)$.*

Thus, when the F-stubborn pool and the insightful pool compete within the same system, as long as they hold an equal fraction of the total mining power, the insightful pool is expected to obtain strictly more revenue than the F-stubborn pool.

5 Simulation Experiments

This section presents simulation results that validate the effectiveness of the insightful pool when competing against the F-stubborn pool, thereby providing empirical support for the theoretical analysis in the previous section.

We consider a mining system with three types of mining pools: the honest pool, the F-stubborn pool, and the insightful pool. The mining process is modeled as a discrete-time stochastic process, where each time unit corresponds to the generation of a single block. At each time unit, a random variable determines which pool generates the next block, according to its fraction of the total mining power.

Each simulation ends after 100, 000, 000 time units. Recall that α and β denote the fractions of the total mining power controlled by the F-stubborn pool and the insightful pool, respectively. For each pair of (α, β), we conduct 50 independent runs and fit the results accordingly. In all simulations, we primarily consider values of α and β in the interval $(0.25, 0.5)$.

Note that if the main chain remains forked at the conclusion of the simulation, all blocks on non-finalized branches are excluded from acceptance. Similarly, if the F-stubborn pool or the insightful pool retains private blocks on its private chain, the number of blocks deemed accepted is determined according to the corresponding private chain length.

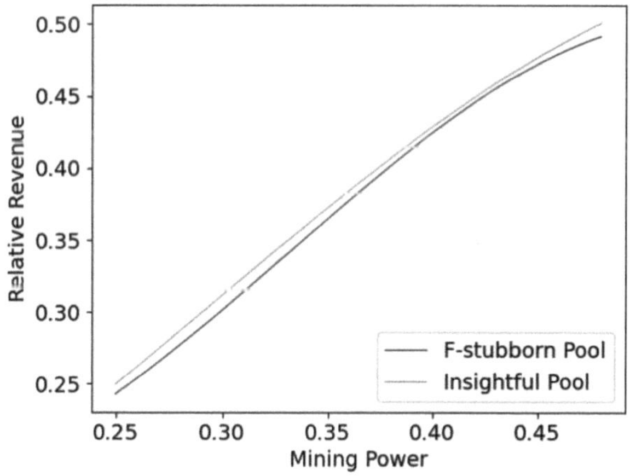

Fig. 2. Relative revenues of the F-stubborn & insightful pools with the same mining power.

We first focus on the parameter regime where $0 < \alpha = \beta < \frac{1}{2}$. Figure 2 reports the relative revenues of the F-stubborn pool and the insightful pool when they holds identical mining power. The horizontal axis represents fractions of the total mining power controlled by each mining pool, i.e., α and β, while the vertical axis reports their corresponding relative revenues. As shown in the figure, for all $0 < \alpha = \beta < \frac{1}{2}$, the insightful pool consistently obtains a marginally higher relative revenue than the F-stubborn pool, which is in line with the theoretical results established in the previous section.

Moreover, although the insightful pool can secure a significant share of the total revenue when competing against a selfish mining pool with a fraction exceeding 1/3 of the total mining power, such an advantage does not arise when competing against an F-stubborn pool. Instead, the simulation results demonstrate that the relative revenues of the insightful pool and the F-stubborn pool become nearly indistinguishable in this regime.

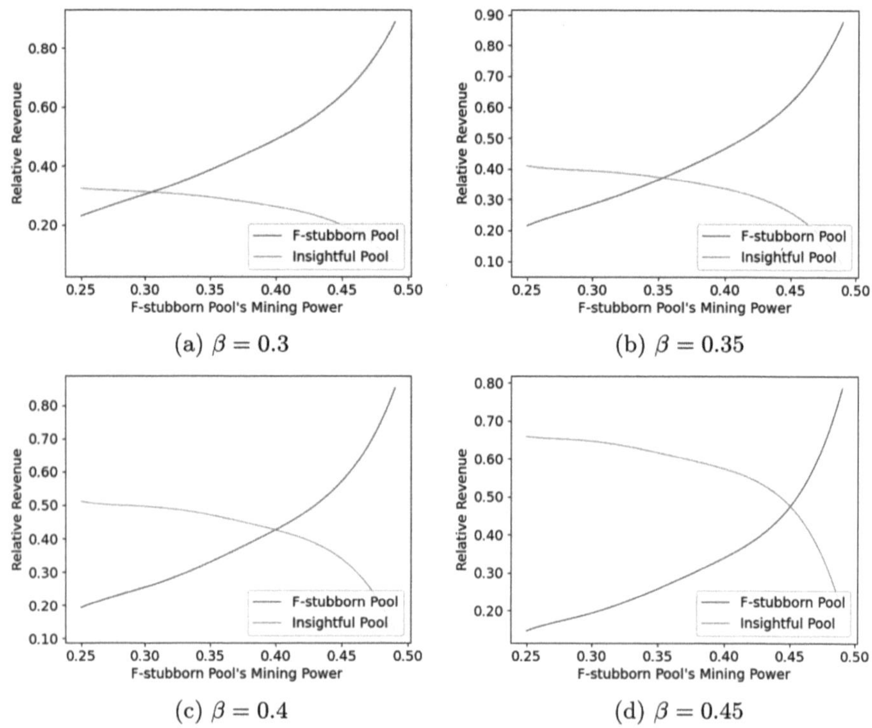

Fig. 3. Relative revenues of the F-stubborn & insightful pools.

We next examine the asymmetric setting where $\alpha \neq \beta$. We begin by selecting four representative values of the fraction of the insightful pool's mining power, i.e., $\beta = 0.3, 0.35, 0.4, 0.45$. Figure 3 illustrates the relative revenues of the F-stubborn pool and the insightful pool under these configurations. From Figs. 3a to 3d, we observe that the point at which the two pools achieve equal relative revenues consistently occurs when the mining power of the F-stubborn pool is nearly identical to that of the insightful pool. This observation is consistent with the conclusion drawn from Fig. 2.

Meanwhile, regardless of the value of β, once α slightly exceeds β, the relative revenue of the F-stubborn pool increases sharply, while that of the insightful pool decreases significantly. Moreover, when α is close to 0.5, the relative revenue of the F-stubborn pool rises to nearly, or even exceeds, 80%, regardless of the value of β. In contrast, the relative revenue of the insightful pool drops to around 10%.

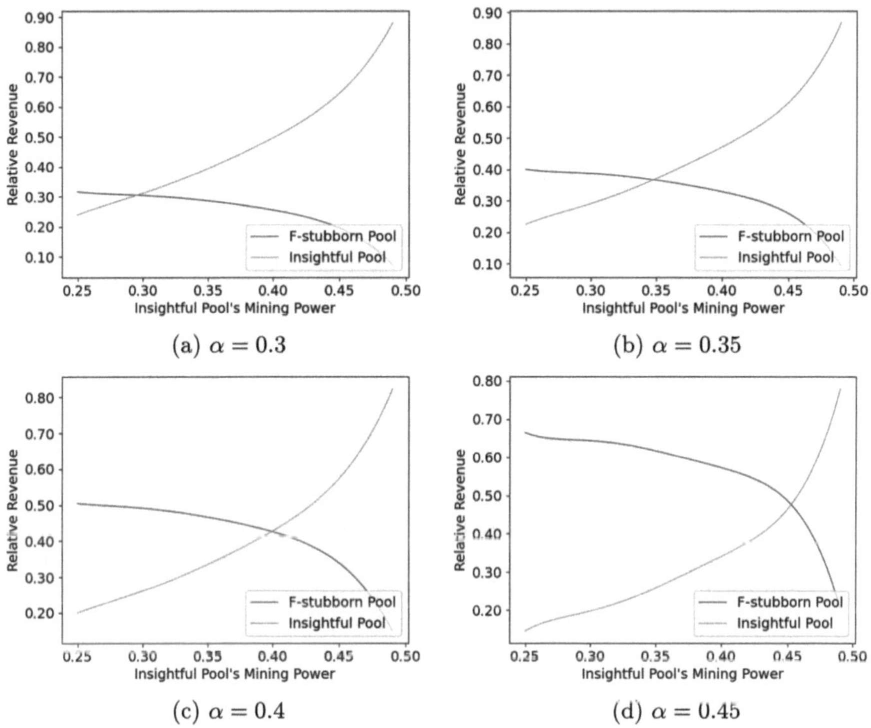

Fig. 4. Relative revenues of the F-stubborn & insightful pools.

Then, we select four representative values of the fraction of the F-stubborn pool's mining power, i.e., $\alpha = 0.3, 0.35, 0.4, 0.45$. Figure 4 illustrates the relative revenues of the F-stubborn pool and the insightful pool under this setting. It can be observed that, from Figs. 4a to 4d, the relative revenue curves of the insightful pool closely resemble the relative revenue curves of the F-stubborn pool in Figs. 3a to 3d. Conversely, the relative revenue curves of the F-stubborn pool in Figs. 4a to 4d are highly similar to the relative revenue curves of the insightful pool in Figs. 3a to 3d. These results indicate that, when insightful mining competes with F-stubborn mining, the performance of the two strategies is very similar.

Finally, we vary the values of α and β at a finer granularity. This allows us to examine how much mining power the insightful pool can reduce in its investment while still achieving at least the same revenue as the F-stubborn pool. We examine both the relative revenue and the unit relative revenue. Here, the unit relative revenue is defined as the ratio between relative revenue and the fraction of the mining power.

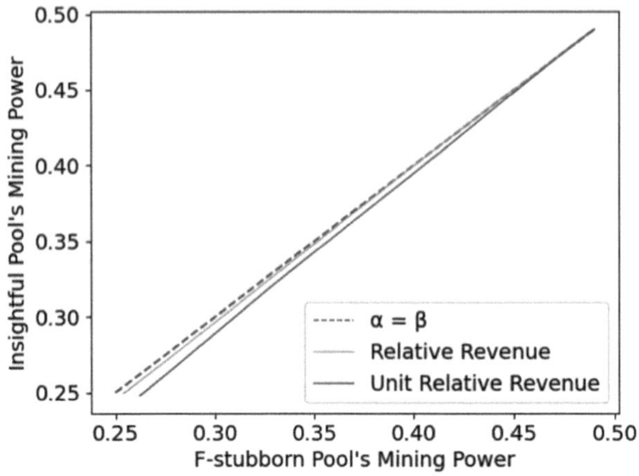

Fig. 5. Threshold of the insightful pool's mining power.

Figure 5 illustrates the threshold of the insightful pool's mining power required to attain no less relative revenue or unit relative revenue than the F-stubborn pool. The blue dashed line represents $\alpha = \beta$. Above the orange line, we have $ERR_{IM} > ERR_{FM}$, while above the green line, $\frac{ERR_{IM}}{\beta} > \frac{ERR_{FM}}{\alpha}$ holds. It can be observed that both the orange and green lines are nearly linear and lie very close to the line $\alpha = \beta$. Moreover, the green line consistently lies below the orange one. This result indicates that, although insightful mining can achieve strictly higher revenue when its mining power is only slightly smaller than that of F-stubborn mining, the advantage is quantitatively limited. On the other hand, as the mining power of the F-stubborn pool increases, the amount of mining power that the insightful pool can reduce while maintaining at least the same relative revenue or unit relative revenue decreases accordingly.

6 Conclusion

This paper evaluates the effectiveness of insightful mining when facing F-stubborn mining, a stronger variant of selfish mining. Our analysis shows that while insightful mining retains a slight advantage under equal mining power, this advantage is fragile and diminishes rapidly once mining power becomes asymmetric, particularly when the F-stubborn pool gains an advantage.

These findings highlight a fundamental challenge for individual-level defensive strategies: approaches designed to counter classical selfish mining may not remain effective against more aggressive private-chain attacks. Addressing this challenge calls for the development of mining strategies that are robust to a broader class of selfish-mining-inspired attacks, enabling individual miners to deploy practical and resilient defenses.

Acknowledgement. This research was funded by the Provincial Natural Science Foundation of Xinjiang, China, under Grant No. 2022D01A252.

Appendix

A Detail Analysis of the State Transitions

This section provides a detailed analysis of the state transitions. These analyses constitute Table 1.

1. $P[(0,0),(0,0)] = 1-\alpha-\beta, r[(0,0),(0,0)] = (1,0,0)$
   When the main chain is not forked and no hidden blocks exist in the system, if the honest pool generates a new block, this transition occurs. Both the F-stubborn and insightful pools accept this block and continue mining after it. Consequently, the honest pool gains the revenue of one block.
2. $P[(0,0),(0,1)] = \alpha, r[(0,0),(0,1)] = (0,0,0)$
   When the main chain is not forked and no hidden blocks exist, if the F-stubborn pool generates a new block, it appends the block to its private chain and keeps it hidden.

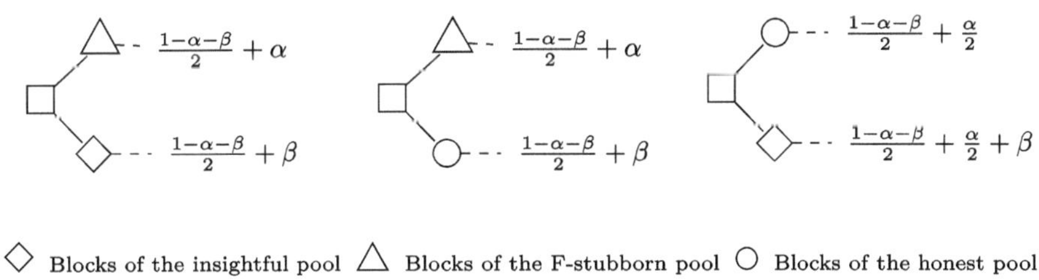

(a) State $(1,0')$ (b) State $(0',0)$ (c) State $(0,0')$

Fig. 6. Illustration of several special states.

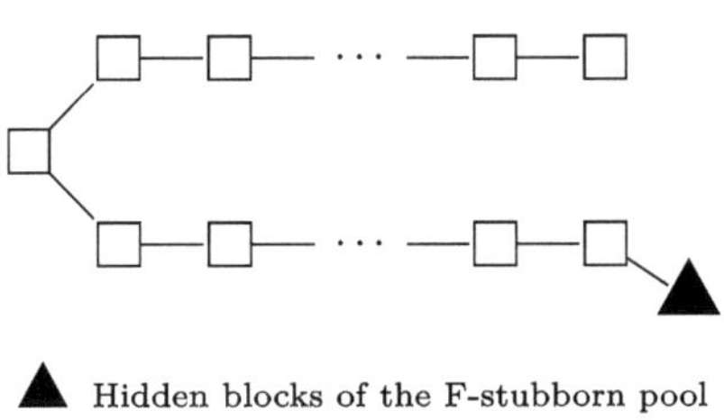

Fig. 7. Probable main chain in state $(1,0)$.

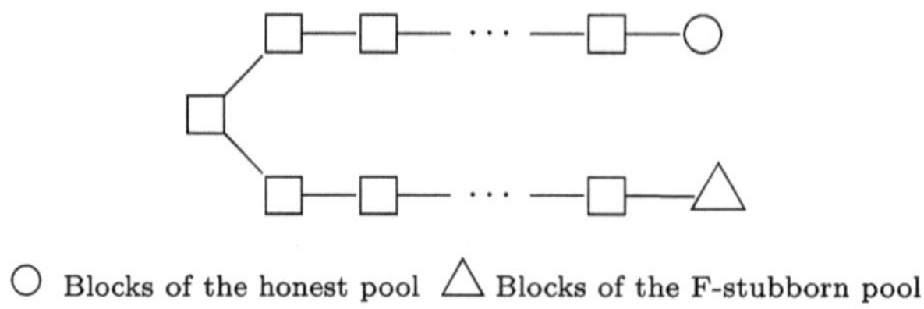

Fig. 8. Probable main chain in state $(0', 0)$.

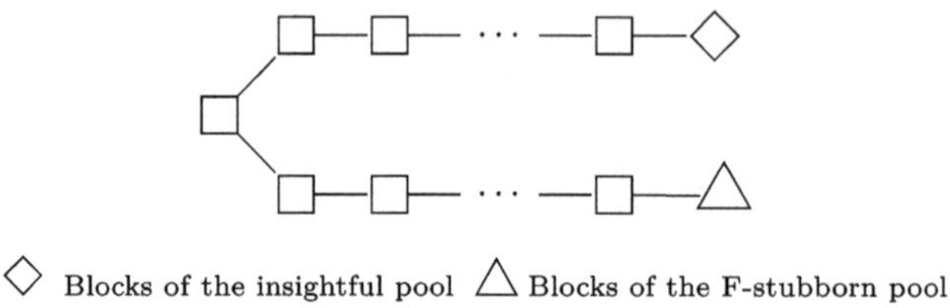

Fig. 9. Probable main chain in state $(1, 0')$.

3. $P[(1,0),(0',0)] = 1 - \alpha - \beta, r[(1,0),(0',0)] = (0,0,0)$
   When the F-stubborn pool has one hidden block and the honest pool generates a new block, the F-stubborn pool reveals its hidden block, causing a fork on the main chain. The meanings of several special states are illustrated in Fig. 6.
4. $P[(0',0),(0,0)] = 1 - \alpha$,
   $r[(0',0),(0,0)] = (\frac{(1-\alpha+\beta)f_h+3-3\alpha-\beta}{2}, \frac{(1-\alpha-\beta)(f_s+1)}{2}, \frac{(1-\alpha+\beta)f_i+2\beta}{2})$
   When the main chain is forked, and the fork is caused by blocks generated by the honest pool and the F-stubborn pool, this transition occurs if a new block is generated by either the honest pool or the insightful pool.
   Note that there exists a cycle among the three states $(0', 0)$, $(1, 0)$, and $(1, 0')$. During the transitions within this cycle, the fork on the main chain may evolve into the form illustrated in Fig. 7 when the MRP is in state $(1, 0)$.
   In this situation, the blocks on one branch of the fork are entirely generated by the F-stubborn pool, while the blocks on the other branch are generated by either the honest pool or the insightful pool.

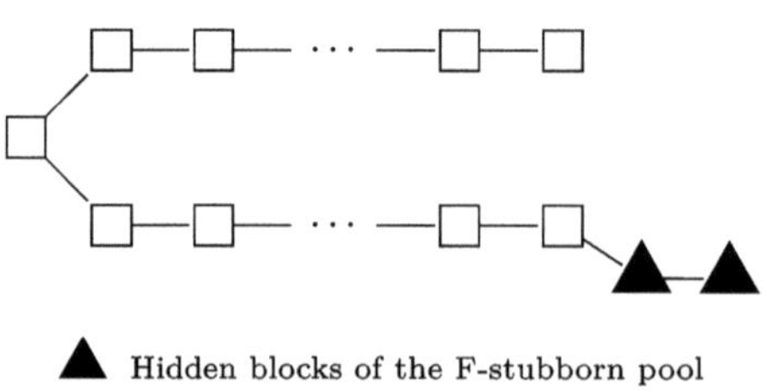

Fig. 10. Probable main chain in state $(2, 0)$.

Based on state $(1, 0)$, during the transitions within the cycle, the MRP may return to $(1, 0)$ via state $(0', 0)$ with probability $\alpha(1-\alpha-\beta)$. In this case, one additional block is added to the branch composed solely of blocks generated by the F-stubborn pool, while one additional block generated by the honest pool is added to the other branch. On the other hand, the MRP may return to state $(1, 0)$ via state $(1, 0')$ with probability $\alpha\beta$. In this case, one additional block is added to the branch composed solely of blocks generated by the F-stubborn pool, while one additional block generated by the insightful pool is added to the other branch. Therefore, it follows that when the MRP finally transitions from these three states to other states, the expected numbers of blocks generated by the F-stubborn pool and the insightful pool on the two branches (excluding the generated public blocks at the end of the fork and the hidden blocks) are given by:

$$\begin{cases} f_s &= 0 + \alpha(1-\alpha) + 2(\alpha(1-\alpha))^2 + 3(\alpha(1-\alpha))^3 + \cdots \\ f_i &= 0 + \alpha\beta + 2(\alpha\beta)^2 + 3(\alpha\beta)^3 + \cdots \end{cases}$$

Hence, we have:

$$\begin{cases} f_s &= \frac{\alpha(1-\alpha)}{(1-\alpha(1-\alpha))^2} \\ f_i &= \frac{\alpha\beta}{(1-\alpha\beta)^2} \end{cases}$$

which is exactly our definition in Eqs. (3). Here, f_s and f_i denote the expected numbers of blocks generated by the F-stubborn pool and the insightful pool on the two branches, respectively (excluding the generated public blocks at the end of the fork and the hidden blocks). Similarly, let f_h denote the expected number of blocks generated by the honest pool. Since f_h does not affect the subsequent calculations, it is omitted here.

Before the transition from state $(0', 0)$ to state $(0, 0)$ occurs, the main chain may take the form shown in Fig. 8. In this situation, the blocks on the chain containing the circled block are generated entirely by the insightful pool or the honest pool, while the blocks on the other branch are all generated by the F-stubborn pool. Hence, the mining power aggregated on the branch containing the circled block is $\beta + \frac{1-\alpha-\beta}{2}$, while the mining power on the other branch is $\alpha + \frac{1-\alpha-\beta}{2}$. Note that although the honest pool's mining power is evenly split between the two forks, when the two forks have equal length it may occur that the honest pool generates a block on the stubborn pool's branch, causing the other fork to be discarded. After the next iteration, the newly generated fork is then based on the block preceding the one generated by the honest pool. Nevertheless, in fact, the probability that a block of the stubborn pool is accepted is always $\frac{1-\alpha-\beta}{2}$. For the earlier blocks, if we compute their corresponding revenue at the moment they are accepted, this probability is $\frac{1-\alpha-\beta}{2}$, and their expected revenue therefore does not need to be counted again at the end. On the other hand, for the later blocks generated after the new fork, regardless of whether the earlier blocks on the stubborn pool's branch are accepted or the fork is maintained, the acceptance probability of the later blocks is the same in both cases, namely $\frac{1-\alpha-\beta}{2}$. Hence, when the MRP transitions to states $(0',0)$ or $(1,0')$ and then further transitions back to $(0,0)$, we can compute the expected revenue over the cycle of states $(1,0),(0',0),(1,0')$ together; similarly, this also applies when the MRP transitions to state $(2,0)$, with the only difference being that in this case, no matter what happens, the blocks on the stubborn pool's branch will eventually be accepted, so the corresponding probability is in fact α. Moreover, we directly use the previously computed expected number of blocks here because, in the end, the probabilities that these blocks are accepted or rejected are always identical. These probabilities depend only on the transition probabilities from these three states to other states, whereas the number of blocks itself depends only on the transitions among these three states. Therefore, we can transform the final computation of the expected revenue for each possible block into a procedure that first computes the expected number of blocks and then aggregates the expected revenue at the end. All other similar transition cases are treated in the same way for the same reason. When the transition occurs, there are three possible cases:

- With probability β, a block is generated by the insightful pool, causing the branch consisting solely of blocks generated by the F-stubborn pool to be discarded. In this case, we have $r[(0',0),(0,0)] = (f_h+1, 0, f_i+1)$.
- With probability $\frac{1-\alpha-\beta}{2}$, a block is generated by the honest pool, causing the branch consisting solely of blocks generated by the F-stubborn pool to be discarded. In this case, we have $r[(0',0),(0,0)] = (f_h+2, 0, f_i)$.
- With probability $\frac{1-\alpha-\beta}{2}$, a block is generated by the honest pool, causing the branch consisting solely of blocks generated by the F-stubborn pool to be accepted. In this case, we have $r[(0',0),(0,0)] = (1, f_s+1, 0)$.

Therefore, the expected revenues of the honest pool, the F-stubborn pool, and the insightful pool are $\frac{(1-\alpha+\beta)f_h+3-3\alpha-\beta}{2}$, $\frac{(1-\alpha-\beta)(f_s+1)}{2}$, and $\frac{(1-\alpha+\beta)f_i+2\beta}{2}$, respectively.

5. $P[(0',0),(1,0)] = \alpha, r[(0',0),(1,0)] = (0,0,0)$
In this case, the transition from state $(0',0)$ shown in Fig. 8 to state $(1,0)$ shown in Fig. 7 occurs. The F-stubborn pool generates a new block and hides it.
6. $P[(1,0),(1,0')] = \beta, r[(1,0),(1,0')] = (0,0,0)$
When the F-stubborn pool has one hidden block and the insightful pool generates a new block, this transition occurs. State $(1,0')$ indicates that the current fork of the main chain is caused by the insightful pool and the F-stubborn pool, as illustrated in Fig. 9.
7. $P[(1,0'),(0,0)] = 1-\alpha$,
$r[(1,0'),(0,0)] = (\frac{(1-\alpha+\beta)f_h+2-2\alpha-2\beta}{2}, \frac{(1-\alpha-\beta)(f_s+1)}{2}, \frac{(1-\alpha+\beta)f_i+1-\alpha+3\beta}{2})$
In state $(1,0')$ shown in Fig. 9, if either the honest pool or the insightful pool generates a new block, this transition occurs. At this time, the mining power aggregated on the branch containing the diamond block is $\beta+\frac{1-\alpha-\beta}{2}$, while on the other branch it is $\alpha+\frac{1-\alpha-\beta}{2}$. When this transition occurs, three scenarios are possible:

- With probability β, the insightful pool generates a block, causing the branch consisting solely of blocks generated by F-stubborn pool to be discarded. In this case, $r[(0',0),(0,0)] = (f_h, 0, f_i + 2)$.
- With probability $\frac{1-\alpha-\beta}{2}$, the honest pool generates a block, causing the branch consisting solely of blocks generated by F-stubborn pool to be discarded. In this case, $r[(0',0),(0,0)] = (f_h + 1, 0, f_i + 1)$.
- With probability $\frac{1-\alpha-\beta}{2}$, the honest pool generates a block, causing the branch consisting solely of blocks generated by F-stubborn pool to be accepted. In this case, $r[(0',0),(0,0)] = (1, f_s + 1, 0)$.

Hence, the expected revenues of the honest pool, the F-stubborn pool, and the insightful pool are $\frac{(1-\alpha+\beta)f_h+2-2\alpha-2\beta}{2}$, $\frac{(1-\alpha-\beta)(f_s+1)}{2}$, and $\frac{(1-\alpha+\beta)f_i+1-\alpha+3\beta}{2}$, respectively.

8. $P[(1',0),(1,0)] = \alpha, r[(1',0),(1,0)] = (0,0,0)$
In this case, the transition from state $(1,0')$ shown in Fig. 9 to state $(1,0)$ shown in Fig. 7 occurs. The F-stubborn pool generates a new block and hides it.
9. $P[(x,0),(x+1,0)] = \alpha, r[(x,0),(x+1,0)] = (0,0,0), \forall x \geq 1$
When the F-stubborn pool has a private chain and the insightful pool has none, if the F-stubborn pool generates a new block, this transition occurs. The F-stubborn pool hides the newly generated block, whose reward will be obtained when it is eventually revealed.
10. $P[(2,0),(0,0)] = 1-\alpha, r[(2,0),(0,0)] = (0, f_s + 2, 0)$
When the F-stubborn pool's private chain has length two and the insightful pool has none, if a block is generated by either the insightful pool or the honest pool, this transition occurs. The F-stubborn pool submits all hidden blocks in its private chain and obtains the corresponding rewards. Since state $(2,0)$ is reached from $(1,0)$, there may exist forks similar to those shown in Fig. 7, i.e., the system may take the form shown in Fig. 10. The F-stubborn pool also obtains the rewards for all blocks previously submitted on the branch.
11. $P[(x,0),(x-1,0)] = 1-\alpha, r[(x,0),(x-1,0)] = (0,1,0), \forall x \geq 3$
When the length of the F-stubborn pool's private chain exceeds two and the insightful pool has no private chain, if a block is generated by either the insightful pool or the honest pool, this transition occurs. The F-stubborn pool reveals the first hidden block in its private chain and obtains its reward. Since the private chain length is greater than 2, all hidden blocks will eventually be accepted and added to the main chain when the chain is fully revealed.
12. $P[(0,0),(0,1)] = \beta, r[(0,0),(0,1)] = (0,0,0)$
When there are no hidden blocks in the system and the insightful pool generates the first block, this transition occurs. The insightful pool hides the newly generated block following a selfish mining strategy, and later decides whether to reveal it based on its own private chain length, the F-stubborn pool's private chain length, and the identity of the latest block generator.
13. $P[(0,1),(1,0')] = \alpha, r[(0,1),(1,0')] = (0,0,0)$
When the insightful pool has one hidden block and the F-stubborn pool has none, if the F-stubborn pool generates a new block, this transition occurs. The insightful pool reveals its hidden block, causing a fork. As previously

described, state $(1,0')$ indicates a fork caused by both the insightful pool and the F-stubborn pool.

14. $P[(0,1),(0,0')] = 1-\alpha-\beta, r[(0,1),(0,0')] = (0,0,0)$
When the insightful pool has one hidden block and the F-stubborn pool has none, if the honest pool generates a new block, this transition occurs. The insightful pool reveals its hidden block, causing a fork.
15. $P[(0,0'),(0,0)] = 1, r[(0,0'),(0,0)] = (\frac{3-2\alpha-3\beta}{2}, \alpha, \frac{1+3\beta}{2})$
When the MRP is in state $(0,0')$ shown in Fig. 6c, if a new block is generated, this transition occurs. In this state, the fork is caused by the insightful pool and the honest pool, so the F-stubborn pool's mining power is randomly allocated between the two branches. Therefore, the mining power on the branch with the honest pool's block is $\frac{1-\alpha-\beta}{2}+\frac{\alpha}{2}$, and on the branch with the insightful pool's block is $\frac{1-\alpha-\beta}{2}+\frac{\alpha}{2}+\beta$. There are five possible outcomes:
    - With probability $\frac{1-\alpha-\beta}{2}$, the honest pool generates a new block on the honest pool's branch, obtaining the revenue of two blocks.
    - With probability $\frac{1-\alpha-\beta}{2}$, the honest pool generates a new block on the insightful pool's branch, giving one block each to the honest and insightful pools.
    - With probability $\frac{\alpha}{2}$, the F-stubborn pool generates a new block on the honest pool's branch, giving two blocks each to the honest and F-stubborn pools.
    - With probability $\frac{\alpha}{2}$, the F-stubborn pool generates a new block on the insightful pool's branch, giving two blocks each to the insightful and F-stubborn pools.
    - With probability β, the insightful pool generates a new block on its own branch, obtaining the revenue of two blocks.

    Hence, the expected revenues of the honest pool, the F-stubborn pool, and the insightful pool are $(\frac{3-2\alpha-3\beta}{2}, \alpha, \frac{1+3\beta}{2})$, respectively.
16. $P[(0,1),(0,2)] = \beta, r[(0,1),(0,2)] = (0,0,0)$
When only the insightful pool has a private chain and its lead is one, if it generates a new block, this transition occurs. The insightful pool continues to hide the new block and will obtain the reward when it is generated later.
17. $P[(0,2),(0,0)] = 1-\beta, r[(0,2),(0,0)] = (0,0,2)$
When only the insightful pool has a private chain with lead two, if a block is generated by either the honest pool or the F-stubborn pool, this transition occurs. The insightful pool reveals all two hidden blocks and obtains the corresponding reward.
18. $P[(x,y),(x,y+1)] = \beta, r[(x,y),(x,y+1)] = (0,0,0), \forall x \in \{0'\} \bigcup \mathbb{N}, y \geq 2$
When the insightful pool has a private chain with lead at least two, if it generates a new block, this transition occurs. The insightful pool continues to hide the new block.
19. $P[(0,y),(0,y-1)] = 1-\alpha-\beta, r[(0,y),(0,y-1)] = (0,0,1), \forall y \geq 3$
When only the insightful pool has a private chain with lead greater than two, if the honest pool generates a new block, this transition occurs. The lead of the insightful pool is reduced by one. Though the insightful pool will not reveal any hidden block, since its lead is greater than two, it will win as the

main chain eventually. To facilitate the analysis, we regard this situation as the situation that the insightful pool obtains the revenue of one block. In other words, we calculate the revenue of each block every time the lead of the insightful pool decreases.

20. $P[(x, y), (x + 1, y - 1)] = \alpha, r[(x, y), (x + 1, y - 1)] = (0, 0, 1), \forall x \geq 0, y \geq 3$
When the insightful pool's lead over the F-stubborn pool is greater than two, if the F-stubborn pool generates a new block, its private chain length increases by one and the insightful pool's lead decreases by one. Although the insightful pool does not immediately reveal a hidden block, it will eventually receive the reward when revealing all hidden blocks. Still, we calculate the revenue of one block in this situation.
21. $P[(1, y), (0', y)] = 1 - \alpha - \beta, r[(1, y), (0', y)] = (0, 0, 0), \forall y \geq 2$
When the F-stubborn pool has one hidden block and the insightful pool's lead is at least two (i.e., the length of the insightful pool's private chain is at least three), if the honest pool generates a new block, this transition occurs. The honest pool forces the F-stubborn pool to reveal its hidden block, causing a fork. The insightful pool detects this event but does not reveal any block and continues mining on its private chain. Since the insightful pool's lead is at least two, all its hidden blocks will eventually be accepted and added to the main chain. The honest and F-stubborn pools' blocks are discarded.
22. $P[(2, y), (0, y)] = 1 - \alpha - \beta, r[(1, y), (0', y)] = (0, 0, 0), \forall y \geq 2$
When the F-stubborn pool has two hidden blocks and the insightful pool's lead is at least 2two (i.e., the length of the insightful pool's private chain length is at least four), if the honest pool generates a new block, this transition occurs. The honest pool forces the F-stubborn pool to reveal all hidden blocks. The insightful pool detects this event, continues mining on its private chain, and all its blocks are eventually accepted and appended to the main chain. The F-stubborn pool's just-generated two blocks are discarded.
23. $P[(x, y), (x - 1, y)] = 1 - \alpha - \beta, r[(1, y), (0', y)] = (0, 0, 0), \forall x \geq 3, y \geq 2$
When the F-stubborn pool has a private chain longer than two and the insightful pool's lead is at least two, if the honest pool generates a new block, this transition occurs. The F-stubborn pool reveals a hidden block from its private chain. Similarly, the insightful pool continues to focus on its private chain. Eventually, when all the insightful pool's hidden blocks are revealed, all blocks in the F-stubborn pool's current private chain and the just-generated block are discarded.
24. $P[(x, 2), (0, 0)] = \alpha, r[(x, 2), (0, 0)] = (0, 0, 2), \forall x \geq 1$
When the F-stubborn pool has a private chain and the insightful pool's lead is two, if the F-stubborn pool generates a new block, this transition occurs. The insightful pool reveals all hidden blocks, which are accepted due to its lead, and obtains all revenues of these two blocks. Although it would effectively gain $x + 2$ blocks, for simplicity, only the revenue for two blocks is considered here. The revenues for the remaining x blocks have already been accounted for in previous states.
25. $P[(0', 2), (0, 0)] = 1 - \beta, r[(0', 2), (0, 0)] = (0, 0, 2)$
When a fork exists due to blocks generated by the F-stubborn and honest

pools, and the insightful pool's lead is two, if either the F-stubborn or honest pool generates a new block, this transition occurs. The insightful pool reveals all hidden blocks, which are accepted, and obtains the revenues.

26. $P[(0', y), (0, y-1)] = 1 - \beta, r[(0', y), (0, y-1)] = (0, 0, 1), \forall y \geq 3$
When a fork exists due to blocks generated by the F-stubborn and honest pools, and the insightful pool's lead is greater than two, if either the F-stubborn or honest pool generates a new block, this transition occurs. The lead of the insightful pool is reduced by one. Since there are still blocks in the insightful pool's private chain, these blocks will eventually be accepted and appended to the main chain.

References

1. Bai, Q., Xu, Y., Liu, N., Wang, X.: Blockchain mining with multiple selfish miners. IEEE Trans. Inf. Forensics Secur. **18**, 3116–3131 (2023)
2. Chicarino, V., Albuquerque, C., Jesus, E., Rocha, A.: On the detection of selfish mining and stalker attacks in blockchain networks. Ann. Telecommun. **75**(3), 143–152 (2020)
3. Eyal, I.: The miner's dilemma. In: 2015 IEEE Symposium on Security and Privacy, pp. 89–103. IEEE (2015)
4. Eyal, I., Sirer, E.G.: Majority is not enough: bitcoin mining is vulnerable. Commun. ACM **61**(7), 95–102 (2018)
5. Feng, C., Niu, J.: Selfish mining in ethereum. In: IEEE 39th International Conference on Distributed Computing Systems (ICDCS), pp. 1306–1316. IEEE (2019)
6. Gao, S., Li, Z., Peng, Z., Xiao, B.: Power adjusting and bribery racing: Novel mining attacks in the bitcoin system. In: Proceedings of the 2019 ACM SIGSAC Conference on Computer and Communications Security, pp. 833–850 (2019)
7. Hou, C., Zhou, M., Ji, Y., Daian, P., Tramer, F., Fanti, G., Juels, A.: Squirrl: Automating attack analysis on blockchain incentive mechanisms with deep reinforcement learning. In: 28th Annual Network and Distributed System Security Symposium, NDSS 2021, virtually, February 21–25, 2021. The Internet Society (2021)
8. Hu, J., Yan, H., Xu, C.: Novel bribery mining attacks: Impacts on mining ecosystem and the "bribery miner's dilemma" in the nakamoto-style blockchain system. IEEE Trans. Dependable Sec. Comput. (2025)
9. Li, J., Xie, T., Liu, Y.: Game theory based incentive mechanism for a bi-tiered public blockchain system. Comput. Netw. 111827 (2025)
10. Li, W., Jiang, S., Ni, B., Liang, W., Wang, Y.: From bribery-stubborn mining to leading hidden triple-fork strategies for incentive optimization in pow blockchains. Symmetry **17**(10), 1618 (2025)
11. Liao, B., Chen, H., Wang, Y., Meng, W., Zhang, J.: Analysis of hybrid attack and defense based on block withholding strategy. J. Inf. Secur. Appl. **78**, 103620 (2023)
12. Liu, H., Ruan, N., Du, R., Jia, W.: On the strategy and behavior of bitcoin mining with n-attackers. In: Proceedings of the 2018 on Asia Conference on Computer and Communications Security, pp. 357–368 (2018)
13. Marmolejo-Cossío, F.J., Brigham, E., Sela, B., Katz, J.: Competing (semi-) selfish miners in bitcoin. In: Proceedings of the 1st ACM Conference on Advances in Financial Technologies, pp. 89–109 (2019)

14. Nakamoto, S.: Bitcoin: A peer-to-peer electronic cash system. Decentralized Bus. Rev. 21260 (2008)
15. Nayak, K., Kumar, S., Miller, A., Shi, E.: Stubborn mining: Generalizing selfish mining and combining with an eclipse attack. In: 2016 IEEE European Symposium on Security and Privacy (EuroS&P), pp. 305–320. IEEE (2016)
16. Negy, K.A., Rizun, P.R., Sirer, E.G.: Selfish Mining Re-Examined. In: Bonneau, J., Heninger, N. (eds.) FC 2020. LNCS, vol. 12059, pp. 61–78. Springer, Cham (2020). https://doi.org/10.1007/978-3-030-51280-4_5
17. Pachal, S., Ruj, S.: Rational mining of bitcoin. In: 2019 11th International Conference on Communication Systems & Networks (COMSNETS), pp. 1–8. IEEE (2019)
18. Patil, S., Parmar, K.: Mitigation of selfish mining attack using dynamic difficulty adjustment algorithm. Peer-to-Peer Netw. Appl. **18**(4), 235 (2025)
19. Rosenfeld, M.: Analysis of bitcoin pooled mining reward systems. arXiv preprint arXiv:1112.4980 (2011)
20. Saad, M., Njilla, L., Kamhoua, C., Mohaisen, A.: Countering selfish mining in blockchains. In: 2019 International Conference on Computing, Networking and Communications (ICNC), pp. 360–364. IEEE (2019)
21. Sapirshtein, A., Sompolinsky, Y., Zohar, A.: Optimal Selfish Mining Strategies in Bitcoin. In: Grossklags, J., Preneel, B. (eds.) FC 2016. LNCS, vol. 9603, pp. 515–532. Springer, Heidelberg (2017). https://doi.org/10.1007/978-3-662-54970-4_30
22. Schrijvers, O., Bonneau, J., Boneh, D., Roughgarden, T.: Incentive Compatibility of Bitcoin Mining Pool Reward Functions. In: Grossklags, J., Preneel, B. (eds.) FC 2016. LNCS, vol. 9603, pp. 477–498. Springer, Heidelberg (2017). https://doi.org/10.1007/978-3-662-54970-4_28
23. Wang, L., Wang, Z.: Stowaway mining: a selfish mining against strategy. In: ICBASE, pp. 120–128 (2022)
24. Wang, S.W., Tzeng, S.S.: An accurate analytical model for a proof-of-work blockchain with multiple selfish miners. In: ICC 2024-IEEE International Conference on Communications, pp. 1053–1059. IEEE (2024)
25. Wang, Z., Susilo, W., Guo, J., Wang, Y., Zhao, M.: Reinforcement-mining: protecting reward in selfish mining. In: Ge, C., Guo, F. (eds.) International Conference on Provable and Practical Security, pp. 199–209. Springer, Cham (2022). https://doi.org/10.1007/978-3-031-20917-8_14
26. Yang, R., Chang, X., Mišić, J., Mišić, V.B.: Deep-dive analysis of selfish and stubborn mining in bitcoin and ethereum. arXiv preprint arXiv:2112.02588 (2021)
27. Zhang, M., Li, Y., Li, J., Kong, C., Deng, X.: Insightful mining equilibria. In: Hansen, K.A., Liu, T.X., Malekian, A. (eds.) International Conference on Web and Internet Economics, pp. 21–37. Springer, Cham (2022). https://doi.org/10.1007/978-3-031-22832-2_2
28. Zhang, R., Preneel, B.: Publish or Perish: A Backward-Compatible Defense Against Selfish Mining in Bitcoin. In: Handschuh, H. (ed.) CT-RSA 2017. LNCS, vol. 10159, pp. 277–292. Springer, Cham (2017). https://doi.org/10.1007/978-3-319-52153-4_16
29. Zhang, S., Zhang, K., Kemme, B.: Analysing the benefit of selfish mining with multiple players. In: 2020 IEEE International Conference on Blockchain (Blockchain), pp. 36–44. IEEE (2020)
30. Zur, R.B., Eyal, I., Tamar, A.: Efficient mdp analysis for selfish-mining in blockchains. In: Proceedings of the 2nd ACM Conference on Advances in Financial Technologies, pp. 113–131 (2020)

ParaShard: A Fast Path Parallel Execution Approach for Accelerating Cross-Shard Transactions

Zihan Zhang, Sheng Chen, Xiulong Liu(✉), and Keqiu Li

Tianjin University, Tianjin, China
{zihanzhang,chensheng,xiulong_liu,keqiu}@tju.edu.cn

Abstract. By distributing transactions across different shards for parallel processing, sharding improves the scalability of blockchain systems. When transactions involve multiple shards, coordinated execution is required, making the efficiency of cross-shard transactions (CTXs) a critical determinant of overall system performance. However, existing CTX protocols lack pre-execution state verifiability in the mempool, forcing target shards to defer transaction processing until source shard confirmation. Moreover, the tightly coupled source and target execution pipeline serializes CTXs processing across shards, significantly restricting parallel execution of CTXs. To address these issues, this paper proposes ParaShard, a high throughput and low latency CTX protocol based on a fast path parallel execution. ParaShard decouples transaction acceptance from on-chain commitment by enabling source shards to generate off-chain threshold signature lock proofs, which can be directly verified by target shards. As a result, target shards can admit CTXs into their local transaction pool without waiting for source shard consensus, enabling early processing and parallel execution across shards. Moreover, we implement a prototype of ParaShard and evaluate it using historical Ethereum transactions. Experimental results demonstrate that, compared with state-of-the-art protocols such as X-Shard and Monoxide, ParaShard achieves 30.5% higher throughput and 45.0% lower latency.

Keywords: Blockchain · Parallel execution · Sharding

1 Introduction

1.1 Background and Motivation

As blockchain [1] systems are increasingly adopted in areas such as decentralized finance(DeFi), gaming, and supply chain management [2], the issue of scalability has become especially prominent. To address performance bottlenecks, sharding [3,4] has been proposed as an effective approach to horizontally scale the throughput of blockchain systems. Sharding divides the blockchain network into multiple independent subsets called shards [5–7], each shard processing a

Y. Cao et al. (Eds.): SecureComm 2026, LNICST 704, pp. 358–378, 2027.
https://doi.org/10.1007/978-3-032-32764-2_17

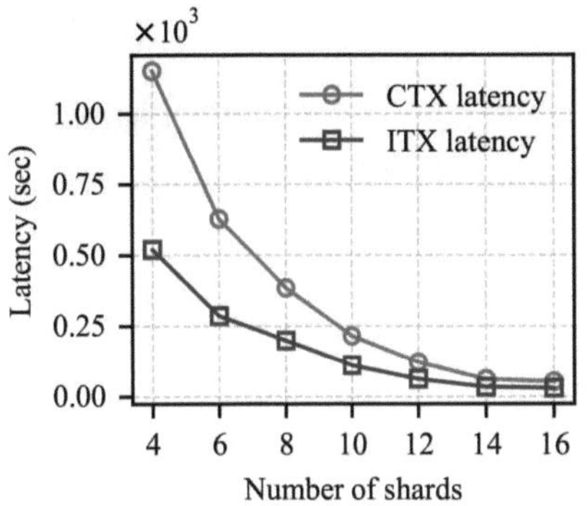

(a) Latency of CTX and ITX

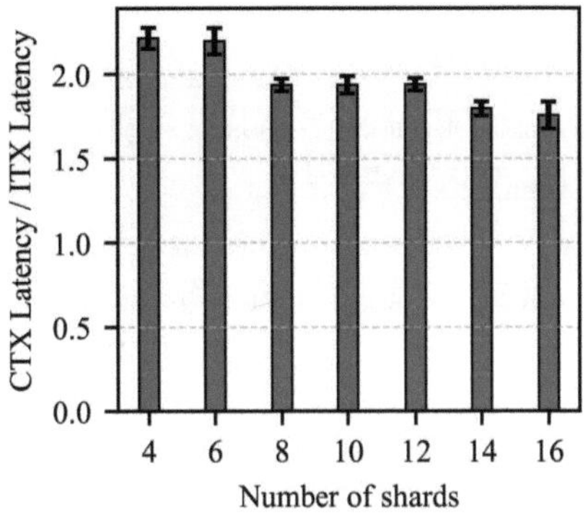

(b) Ratio of CTX and ITX

Fig. 1. Result of motivation experiment. Following the relay-based scheme of Monoxide [16], we observe the latency gap between CTXs and ITXs as the number of shards varies.

portion of the workload. This parallel structure allows the system's throughput to scale linearly [8], making large-scale blockchain applications [9] feasible in theory. However, sharding introduces new challenges: transactions (TX for short) are increasingly likely to span multiple shards, giving rise to the issue of cross-shard transactions (CTX for short) [10–12]. Compared to intra-shard transactions (ITX for short), CTXs often require inter shard coordination, state synchronization [13], and even multiple rounds of communication, resulting in significantly higher complexity and latency [14,15]. To investigate the latency gap between CTXs and ITXs, we performed the following motivation experiment. Specifically, we collect one million consecutive historical TXs from the real-world Ethereum [17] dataset. We inject TXs at a constant rate and assign them to different shards according to the Monoxide [16] shard assignment policy. We vary the number of shards to measure the CTXs latency, ITXs latency, and the ratio between them.

As demonstrated in Fig. 1, experimental results show that when the number of shards varies from 4 to 16, the ratio of CTXs latency to ITXs latency is from 1.75× to 2.21x, showing that CTXs processing consistently incur higher latency than ITXs. More critically, this performance imbalance negatively affects user experience. Since users cannot control how their TXs are assigned to shards, the unpredictability of execution latency may lead to response time variance, harming both system interactivity and performance [18]. Therefore, improving the performance of CTXs and reducing their negative impact on scalability and user experience have become critical problems in the design of sharded blockchain systems [19]. This paper addresses these problems by thoroughly analyzing the limitations of current schemes and proposing targeted optimizations. Our goal is to improve the efficiency and parallelism of CTX processing to enhance scalability and provide more predictable performance in sharded blockchain systems.

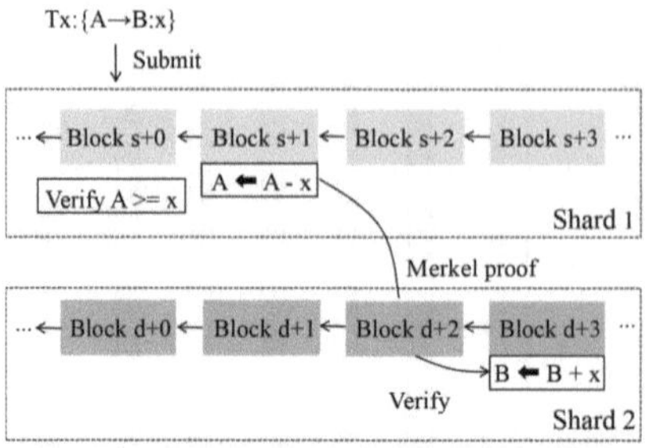

(a) Existing schemes

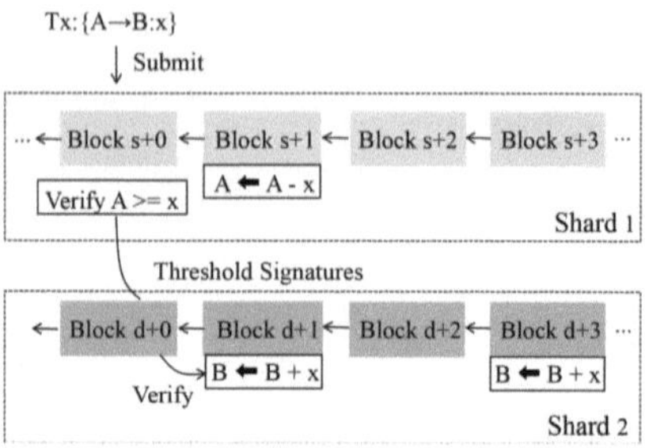

(b) ParaShard (Ours)

Fig. 2. Existing schemes require serialized execution of CTXs, whereas ParaShard enables parallel execution.

1.2 Limitations of Prior Art

There are two main CTX processing modes of existing schemes: relay-based [16] and optimistic execution [20]. However, they have the following limitations. *(i) Lack of pre-execution state verifiability for CTXs in the mempool.* For ITXs, parties are in the same shard, and one single shard consensus suffices to confirm execution. In contrast, CTXs require the source shard to validate the sender's state. Existing schemes often defer this validation until execution time, failing to fully leverage the TX information already present in the TX mempool. *(ii) Strong coupling in the CTX workflow, limiting concurrency.* CTXs must wait for confirmation from the source shard before the target shard can begin processing. This strictly sequential process prevents parallel execution across shards, reducing overall system efficiency. As show in Fig. 2a, existing schemes execute CTXs by first processing and committing on the source shard, then forwarding a Merkle proof to the target shard. Upon verifying the proof, the target shard executes and commits the CTX. This process typically requires multiple rounds of communication and consensus, making CTX a major performance bottleneck in blockchain sharding systems.

1.3 ParaShard in a Nutshell

To overcome these limitations, this paper proposes ParaShard, a low latency and high throughput protocol for CTX processing. As show in Fig. 2b, ParaShard introduces a fast path parallel execution framework that decouples CTX acceptance from on-chain commitment, significantly reducing latency. Upon receiving a CTX, the source shard runs a fast-path scheduling algorithm to determine whether the CTX can be safely processed without shard consensus. If eligible, the source shard generates an off-chain threshold signature as a lock proof, ensuring the sender's funds are securely locked. The CTX and its lock proof are then directly forwarded to the target shard for early admission into its TX pool, enabling prompt execution. For CTXs that do not meet fast-path conditions, ParaShard falls back to a traditional relay-based slow path to ensure correctness. This hybrid approach enables ParaShard to maximize parallelism and minimize latency.

1.4 Challenges and Solutions

We need to solve the following two technical challenges when implementing our ParaShard protocol. *The first challenge is how to schedule CTXs efficiently as the mempool grows.* Although the fast path allows CTXs to process for lower latency, its efficiency largely depends on how quickly the system can identify eligible TXs. Naively traversing all pending TXs would severely degrade performance under high load, undermining the benefits of the fast path itself. To overcome this, we design a scheduling algorithm based on a Transaction Dependency Graph (TDG). The TDG explicitly captures inter-transaction dependencies, enabling the scheduler to prune ineligible CTXs efficiently and maintain a compact set of executable candidates. Moreover, its incremental update mechanism allows the scheduler to react promptly to new arrivals or state changes, ensuring that the fast path remains scalable and efficient even under heavy workloads. *The second challenge is how to realize an efficient off-chain locking mechanism for CTX commitment.* This problem is critical because validators must coordinate to prevent double spending, yet excessive communication or heavyweight proofs would undermine performance. To address this, we design a lightweight protocol where validators incrementally aggregate signatures until at least $2/3$ are collected, generating a compact off-chain lock proof that secures the sender's balance. The target shard can then verify this proof in a single step, ensuring security and correctness while keeping latency low. This approach decouples commitment from consensus and significantly reduces CTX latency, making off-chain commitment practical for sharded systems.

1.5 Novelty and Advantages

This paper takes the first step to propose a fast-path CTX protocol that decouples TX acceptance from on-chain commitment. The novelty of the ParaShard protocol is demonstrated by the two technical challenges we address: (i) enabling efficient CTX scheduling under high load via a dependency-graph-based fast path algorithm; (ii) ensuring secure early commitment of CTXs using off-chain threshold signatures and balance locking. The advantages of ParaShard over prior work are three-fold: (i) ParaShard fully leverages information available in the TX pool to reduce queuing delays at the source shard, thereby lowering CTX latency and narrowing the performance gap between CTX and ITX. (ii) ParaShard decouples the CTX processing pipeline by off-chain threshold signature-based locking instead of on-chain proof-based validation, enabling more efficient use of on-chain resources on the target shard and improving overall system throughput. (iii) ParaShard supports seamless switching between fast and slow paths, ensuring that all CTXs are executed correctly.

The remainder of this paper is organized as follows. Section 2 describes the preliminaries and system model. We present the details of ParaShard protocol in Sect. 3. Section 4 provides a security analysis of ParaShard. We present the experimental results in Sect. 5. We discuss related work in Sect. 6 and conclude this paper in Sect. 7.

2 Preliminaries and System Model

This section presents the necessary cryptographic and system assumptions used throughout the paper. We first introduce the threshold signature scheme employed in our protocol, followed by a detailed description of the network model and the node and adversary model.

2.1 Preliminaries

Threshold Signature. A (t, n) *threshold signature scheme* [21] enables a group of n participants to collaboratively generate digital signatures, such that any subset of at least t participants can jointly produce a valid signature, while any subset of fewer than t participants learns nothing about the signing key or the final signature. Threshold signatures are widely used in distributed systems and blockchain protocols to reduce communication overhead and simplify consensus aggregation. A secure threshold signature scheme satisfies three essential properties. Unforgeability ensures that no adversary controlling fewer than t parties can forge a valid signature on any message. Robustness means the scheme can tolerate up to $t-1$ Byzantine or crashed parties while still producing valid signatures. Compactness requires that the final signature σ remains of constant size and is indistinguishable from a non-threshold signature.

2.2 System Model

Network Model. We assume a *partially synchronous network* model consistent with other sharding-based blockchains [5,7], in which messages between honest nodes are guaranteed to be delivered within an unknown bounded time after some global stabilization time (GST). The system comprises a total of m shards, denoted as $\{S_1, S_2, \ldots, S_m\}$, each responsible for maintaining its own local ledger and processing a subset of the global transaction set. Each shard operates its own consensus protocol (e.g., PBFT [22]) and communicates with other shards through an asynchronous message-passing interface. Communication between shards is reliable and authenticated, although messages may be delayed or reordered due to network asynchrony. Cross-shard messages are delivered through a global relay mechanism. The system ensures that all messages eventually arrive and that no messages are lost, although their order of delivery is not guaranteed.

Node and Adversary Model. Each shard S_i contains n validator nodes, of which up to $f < \frac{n}{3}$ may be Byzantine. These nodes participate in the shard-level consensus protocol and are responsible for maintaining the local shard state. We consider a *static, adaptive Byzantine adversary* capable of corrupting up to f nodes in each shard. The adversary may coordinate malicious nodes to deviate arbitrarily from the protocol, including withholding messages or sending conflicting information to different honest parties. The adversary is *computationally bounded* and cannot compromise standard cryptographic primitives such as digital signatures, hash functions, or authenticated channels. While it may observe the internal system state and cross-shard communications, it cannot forge or alter authenticated messages without detection. We assume no collusion across shards beyond the tolerated Byzantine threshold. That is, global safety and liveness are preserved as long as each shard maintains a majority of honest nodes. To prevent Sybil attacks, each node must register its public key on an identity blockchain by solving a Proof-of-Work puzzle before joining the sharding network [10,23].

3 System Design

This section introduces the architecture and key mechanisms of our CTX processing system. The proposed PARASHARD employs a dual-path TX model, consisting of a fast path and a slow path to achieve high throughput, low latency, and atomicity. The main workflosw of PARASHARD is illustrated in Fig. 3, and these stages are briefly introduced as follows:

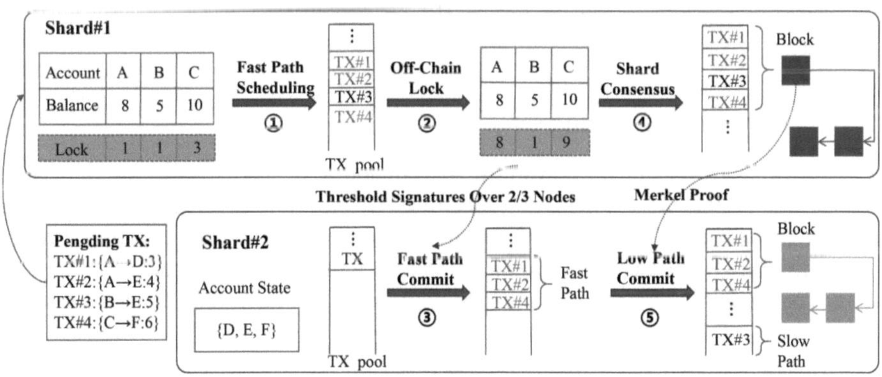

Fig. 3. The workflow of ParaShard.

(i) Fast Path Scheduling: When receiving new CTX requests, each shard attempts to execute the fast path scheduling algorithm. This algorithm aims to quickly determine whether a CTX qualifies for fast path execution. By analyzing the pre-execution state (such as account balance and locked balance), the algorithm identifies CTXs that can be safely and correctly transferred to target shard without reaching shard consensus, effectively reducing CTX latency.

(ii) Off-Chain Locking: If the CTX satisfies the fast path scheduling conditions, the source shard performs off-chain balance locking through threshold signature generation. Specifically, at least 2/3 of the validator nodes in the source shard sign the CTX to produce a threshold signature, which constitutes a lock proof Π_{lock}. This proof guarantees that the corresponding funds of the initiator account have been securely locked, thereby preventing double spending.
(iii) Fast Path Commit: After completing balance locking and generating the lock proof, the source shard immediately forwards the CTX and the corresponding threshold signature proof to the target shard, without waiting for block confirmation in the source shard. The target shard verifies the validity of the threshold signature, and if the verification succeeds, the CTX is added to the local TX pool queue to await packaged in a future block.
(iv) Shard Consensus: Each shard packages and executes TXs in its TX pool queue, updates the account states, and reaches consensus on the new block. If the committed TXs involve previously locked balances, the corresponding amounts are unlocked off-chain as part of the state transition.
(v) Slow Path Commit: For CTXs that do not meet the fast path conditions, they follow the slow path commit process. The CTX first reaches consensus on the source shard. A cross-shard relay mechanism is then used to forward the CTX's Merkle proof, along with the CTX, to the target shard. Upon successful verification of the Merkle proof, the target shard confirms the CTX's validity and adds it to its local TX pool queue for subsequent processing.

In the following subsections, we describe the critical operations involved in PARASHARD: the fast path scheduling, the off-chain locking mechanism, and the dual-path TX process.

3.1 Fast Path Scheduling

In the PARASHARD sharding system, the efficiency of TX scheduling algorithm directly determines how quickly CTXs can be dispatched to target shards for execution. If traditional scheduling methods require traversing all pending TXs in the mempool, the algorithm's time complexity will increase linearly as the backlog of TXs grows, ultimately leading to significant performance degradation. To address this critical issue, we propose an innovative fast path scheduling algorithm based on the TX dependency graph (TDG). By intelligently analyzing interdependencies between TXs and employing an incremental update mechanism, this algorithm not only dramatically improves scheduling efficiency but also effectively reduces system scheduling overhead.

To formalize the scheduling process, we model the TX dependencies as a directed graph $G(V, E)$, where $V = \{TX_1, TX_2, TX_3, ..., TX_N\}$ represents TXs, with each TX having two states: scheduled and unscheduled. $E = \{e_{i,j}\}$ denotes directed edges from TX_i to TX_j, indicating that the execution of TX_j depends on the prior completion of TX_i. We define two core types of dependency edges:

(i) Balance Dependency: Some TXs depend on other pending incoming TXs to replenish the sender account's balance before execution. For example, if TX_j transfers a certain amount but the current account balance is insufficient, it must wait for another incoming TX_i to complete successfully to meet TX_j's balance requirement, thus establishing $e_{i,j}$.

(ii) Sequential Dependency (Nonce Dependency): The blockchain system requires that TXs initiated by the same account must be executed sequentially in increasing nonce order. Therefore, for a series of TXs $\{t_1, t_2, t_3, ...\}$ from the same account, only after the TX corresponding to the current nonce (e.g., t_1) is scheduled can the next TX (e.g., t_2) be scheduled, thereby establishing the dependency edge e_{t_1,t_2}.

Algorithm 1: Fast Path Scheduling Algorithm

Input: Current graph $G^{t-1} = (V, E)$; Queue $\mathcal{Q}^{t-1}$; Confirmed TXs $\mathcal{L}$; Pending TXs $\mathcal{N}$ Processing TXs $\mathcal{C}$;
Output: New graph G^t; New queue $\mathcal{Q}^t$; Scheduled set $\mathcal{P}$

$\mathcal{P} \leftarrow \emptyset, \quad \mathcal{Q}^t \leftarrow \mathcal{Q}^{t-1}, \quad G^t \leftarrow G^{t-1}$;
foreach $TX \in \mathcal{L}$ **do**
    Remove TX from G^t;
foreach $TX \in \mathcal{N}$ **do**
    Add TX to G^t;
foreach $TX \in \mathcal{C}$ **do**
    conflict_map[TX.`sender`] $\leftarrow$ `true`;
    conflict_map[TX.`receiver`] $\leftarrow$ `true`;
$\mathcal{Q}$_*temp* $\leftarrow \mathcal{Q}^t$;
while $\mathcal{Q}_{temp}$ *not empty* **do**
    $TX \leftarrow \mathcal{Q}_{\text{temp}}$.`dequeue`(); $\quad \mathcal{Q}^t$.`dequeue`();
    if TX.`sender` $\in$ *conflict_map* **then**
        $\mathcal{Q}^t$.`enqueue`(TX); continue
    if *Check(TX)* **then**
        Append TX to $\mathcal{P}^t$,
        foreach *ready* $TX_n \in TX$.`out_list` **do**
            while TX_n.`in_deg` $= 0$ **do**
                if *Check(TX_n)* **then**
                    Append to $\mathcal{P}^t$, step into next out-node
                else
                    $\mathcal{Q}^t$.`enqueue`(TX_n); break
    else
        $\mathcal{Q}^t$.`enqueue`(TX);
return $G^t, \mathcal{Q}^t, \mathcal{P}^t$;

To enable efficient CTX scheduling, we design an incremental scheduling mechanism built upon the dependency graph $G(V, E)$. The maintenance of the TDG is dynamic. The graph is updated in two cases: (i) newly pending TXs are added to the graph along with their corresponding dependency edges; and

(ii) TXs that have reached consensus in the previous round are removed from the graph. Each node maintains one of two states: *scheduled*, if the TX has collected enough signatures, or *unscheduled*, if it is blocked by dependencies. During the scheduling phase, a conflict filtering mechanism is used to ensure consistency across all consensus nodes. Any CTX that may read or write to accounts involved in the current processing set $\mathcal{C}$ is temporarily excluded from scheduling. This prevents discrepancies in scheduling decisions caused by timing differences in the state updates across nodes. The complete scheduling procedure is detailed in Algorithm 1. The algorithm operates based on the dependency graph G^{t-1} and TX queue $\mathcal{Q}^{t-1}$ from the previous round. It first removes confirmed transactions $\mathcal{L}$ from the graph and incorporates new pending transactions $\mathcal{N}$ along with their dependency relations. Then, it identifies conflicting accounts from the current processing set $\mathcal{C}$ and builds a conflict-map. The algorithm iteratively checks transactions in the queue for eligibility based on their dependencies and account conditions. Transactions that pass the check are added to the schedulable set $\mathcal{P}^t$, and their successor transactions (i.e., those with no remaining unresolved dependencies) are recursively examined. If a successor transaction fails the eligibility check, it is returned to the queue for re-evaluation in the next round. The eligibility of a CTX is determined by the Check function. It verifies two conditions: whether the sender's available balance is sufficient to cover the CTX, and whether the CTX's nonce matches the expected next nonce for the account. If either condition is not met, the CTX is deemed ineligible for scheduling.

In contrast to scanning the entire TX pool, fast path scheduling algorithm only processes CTXs with zero in-degree from the recursive queue. By focusing on ready-to-schedule CTXs, it avoids unnecessary checks and significantly reduces overhead. As a result, it achieves much faster performance in practice, especially when the dependency graph is sparse. In summary, the fast path scheduling algorithm provides an efficient and scalable solution for CTX scheduling. It greatly enhances the performance of CTX processing while maintaining deterministic and consistent scheduling across all shards during consensus.

3.2 Off-Chain Locking

When a CTX satisfies the fast path scheduling conditions, the source shard initiates an off-chain balance locking mechanism using threshold signature generation. To ensure both safety and responsiveness in fast path CTX execution, we design a threshold signature locking mechanism that securely locks account balance in the source shard and enables verifiable commitment at the target shard. The entire process includes four key stages: *state locking*, *signature aggregation*, *lock verification*, and *lock timeout.*

State Locking. The source shard first performs a local state check, verifying that the sender's account balance is sufficient and that the TX nonce matches the expected sequential value. Upon satisfying these conditions, the CTX is deemed eligible for fast path execution. The source shard then constructs a locking certificate that uniquely binds the CTX to the sender's account balance.

The locking message is defined as:

$$\pi_{\text{lock}} = \langle \mathsf{sender}, \mathsf{nonce}, \mathsf{amount}, \mathsf{S}_{\text{src}}, \mathsf{S}_{\text{dst}}, H(\mathsf{tx}), \mathsf{expiry} \rangle_{\sigma}$$

Here, π_{lock} denotes the lock commitment proof, σ is a threshold signature generated over the tuple by at least t validators from the source shard, and *expiry* optionally encodes a block height or timestamp, beyond which the lock is invalid. This message forms the payload to be threshold-signed by validators.

Signature Aggregation. The source shard employs a (t, n) threshold signature scheme, such as BLS, with $n = 3f + 1$ validators and a signing threshold $t = 2f + 1$. Upon receiving the lock message, each validator verifies the CTX conditions independently and, if valid, signs the message using their private share of the shard's collective signing key. Once at least t valid partial signatures are collected, they are aggregated into a single compact signature σ, which serves as a cryptographic proof that the sender's account balance has been locked in the source shard. At this point, the CTX is marked as *locked* in the source shard, preventing any other CTXs with the same sender and nonce from being signed.

Lock Verification. The source shard transmits a *LockCommit* message to the target shard, containing the original CTX and the aggregated threshold signature π_{lock}. The target shard verifies the signature against the locking message and the public key of the source shard's validator set. If π_{lock} is valid, the CTX is added to the target shard's local TX pool and becomes eligible for inclusion in the future block. The mechanism decouples the target shard from the source shard's consensus process, enabling CTX validation without waiting for the source shard's consensus to finalize. The target shard only needs to validate a compact signature to confirm that the state lock was achieved by a qualified majority in the source shard. This significantly improves the efficiency of CTX execution.

Lock Timeout. Despite the efficiency of the fast path, the distributed nature of the system may cause failure in lock acquisition or CTX propagation. To maintain liveness under such conditions, a timeout mechanism is integrated. If a threshold signature cannot be produced within a bounded time window, the source shard aborts the fast path attempt. Similarly, if the target shard fails to validate or include the CTX within a preset number of blocks, the lock is deemed expired. To handle this, the *expiry* field in the lock message enforces an upper bound on lock validity. Once the expiry condition is met, the source shard can safely reclaim the locked balance and transition the CTX to the slow path. In this fallback scenario, the CTX is committed via inclusion in a source shard block and relayed with a Merkle proof to the target shard.

The off-chain threshold signature locking protocol ensures *consistency* by cryptographically enforcing that only one CTX with the same nonce can be locked, as no conflicting CTX can simultaneously collect sufficient validator signatures. It also ensures *liveness*, as the fallback mechanism guarantees eventual CTX execution under network synchrony, even if the fast path fails. The proposed mechanism offers a theoretically grounded and practically efficient basis for optimistic CTX execution, ensuring correctness and safety under high concurrency conditions in sharded blockchain architectures.

3.3 Dual-Path TX Process

In sharded blockchain systems, the handling of CTXs remains a challenge in balancing system performance and consistency. To address the high latency and interaction complexity inherent in traditional CTX protocols while preserving safety and finality, we propose a dual-path TX process mechanism, integrating both *fast path commit* and *slow path commit* modes. This dual-path mechanism provides optimal processing strategies, ensuring reliable CTX execution.

Design of the Dual-path Mechanism. The fast path represents a performance optimized branch suitable for CTXs that meet specific preconditions for fast commit. Rather than waiting for shard consensus in the source shard, this path leverages *threshold signatures* generated by a quorum of validators to act as cryptographic evidence of state locking. The CTX is then forwarded directly to the target shard, where the signature is verified. If deemed valid, the CTX is admitted into the local mempool for block inclusion. This mechanism significantly reduces confirmation latency, making it particularly well-suited to high-frequency, state-intensive workloads.Given the asynchronous nature of state propagation and potential network variability, the system incorporates a fallback mechanism from the fast path to the slow path. The fast path is not universally reliable, as its success hinges on several operational assumptions that may not always hold in practice. For instance, the generation of threshold signatures may fail if a subset of validators experiences timeout or network partition, preventing the quorum from being reached. Even when the signature is successfully produced, the transmission process can be disrupted due to network congestion or data corruption, leading to delayed or failed delivery to the target shard. Moreover, the target shard itself may reject the CTX if the signature verification fails or, alternatively, may not include the CTX in a block.

Slow Path Recovery Procedure. To mitigate these risks, a path-switching mechanism is employed. Once a CTX is submitted via the fast path, the system initiates a monitoring window to track its status in the target shard. If the CTX is not confirmed within the predefined timeout, the system deems the fast path unsuccessful and automatically triggers the slow path remedy. In the slow path, the CTX is re-committed by the source shard in a subsequent block. The source shard constructs a Merkle proof containing the CTX and forwards it, along with the original CTX content, to the target shard. The target shard verifies the proof against the source block header and confirms the legitimacy and uniqueness of the CTX before admitting it to the local TX pool for processing.

Benefits and System Adaptivity. The proposed dual-path architecture enhances both *responsiveness* and *fault resilience* in CTX processing. The fast path achieves low latency under optimistic conditions, while the slow path guarantees robustness under adverse or unpredictable network states. Beyond performance optimization, the dual-mode mechanism acts as a fault-tolerance design.

This duality enables the system to maintain stable and efficient operation even under the joint pressure of high concurrency and consistency requirements.

To summarize, the dual-path mechanism for CTX processing represents a comprehensive solution that balances performance and safety. By flexibly toggling between fast and slow paths, the system ensures each CTX progresses toward finality regardless of network state.

4 Analysis of PARASHARD

This section presents the formal proof of the PARASHARD protocol. We assume a partially synchronous network model and a Byzantine fault threshold of $f < \frac{n}{3}$ per shard. Under these assumptions, we prove that PARASHARD satisfies the following properties. (i) **Safety:** Each CTX is executed at most once across all shards; (ii) **Liveness:** Every valid CTX submitted by an honest client is eventually executed; (iii) **Atomicity:** CTXs are committed atomically, either all participating shards commit or none do; (iv) **Lock Integrity and Replay Resistance:** Lock proofs are unforgeable and bound to a specific CTX.

4.1 Double Spending Resistance

Theorem 1. *Let tx be any valid CTX. Under the* PARASHARD *protocol, tx is executed at most once across participating shards.*

Proof. Execution of tx is permitted only after the target shard S_{dst} has verified a valid lock proof π_{lock} issued by the source shard S_{src}. Additionally, S_{dst} maintains an executed tx set to prevent re-execution of any previously committed tx. Given the existential unforgeability of the threshold signature scheme under chosen message attacks, it is infeasible to forge π_{lock} for a transaction $tx' \neq tx$. Moreover, the idempotent execution condition enforced by the executed tx set ensures that no transaction can be applied more than once. Hence, the safety property holds.

4.2 Eventual Execution Under Partial Synchrony

Theorem 2. *Let tx be a valid CTX submitted by an honest client with sufficient balance. Then, assuming the network eventually becomes synchronous after some bounded delay Δ, the transaction tx is eventually executed.*

Proof. Since the client is honest and the transaction tx is valid, the source shard S_{src} will eventually produce a threshold lock proof π_{lock}. Under the assumption of partial synchrony, π_{lock} will be delivered to the target shard S_{dst} within time Δ. Upon receipt, S_{dst} verifies the lock proof and admits tx into its local TX pool. Local consensus within S_{dst} guarantees that all pending TXs are eventually included in a committed block. Therefore, the transaction is eventually executed.

4.3 Atomicity of CTXs

Theorem 3. *Let tx be a CTX involving source shard S_{src} and target shard S_{dst}. Then, tx is either committed by both shards or by neither.*

Proof. After receiving a valid lock proof π_{lock}, the target shard S_{dst} may tentatively include tx in its pending TX set. However, the tx is only executed once it is included in a committed block. Two outcomes are possible:

(i) Successful execution: Both S_{src} and S_{dst} include tx in their respective consensus protocols. The target executes the tx and returns a receipt to the source, which then finalizes the state update and unlocks the balance.

(ii) Timeout or failure: If S_{dst} does not commit tx within a bounded time, the source shard's lock expires, and the tx is discarded without being applied.

Since execution is contingent on dual commitment, no partial state transitions occur. Thus, atomicity is maintained.

4.4 Lock Binding and Replay Resistance

Theorem 4. *Let π_{lock} be a lock proof associated with CTX tx. Then π_{lock} cannot be used to admit a CTX $tx' \neq tx$.*

Proof. By construction, the lock proof is computed as:

$$\pi_{\text{lock}} = \text{TSS.Sign}_t(H(tx) \parallel a \parallel v \parallel nonce).$$

For any CTX $tx' \neq tx$, we have $H(tx') \neq H(tx)$ assuming H is collision-resistant. Therefore, $\mathsf{Verify}(\mathsf{pk}, H(tx'), \pi_{\text{lock}}) = 0$, and the lock proof is rejected by the target shard.

Additionally, since the underlying TSS is UF-CMA secure, generating a valid π_{lock} for any unauthorized transaction tx' without the required quorum of honest nodes is infeasible.

Thus, lock proofs are bound to specific transactions and cannot be reused, ensuring replay resistance.

5 Performance Evaluation

5.1 Settings

Simulation Implementation: To evaluate the proposed ParaShard system, we use Python to develop a transaction-driven blockchain-sharding simulation, which replays historical TXs to measure the performance in detail. In the simulation experiment, each block contains a maximum of 2,000 TXs, and consensus latency of PBFT is set to an average of 10 s.

Baseline: We compare the ParaShard with two following schemes. Monoxide [16] is a classic sharding protocol using relay-based scheme. X-Shard [20] uses optimistic strategy to process multiple input and output shards CTXs. We focus exclusively on the differences in CTXs processing among the compared schemes. For account partitioning, we adopt a hash-based approach as in Monoxide.

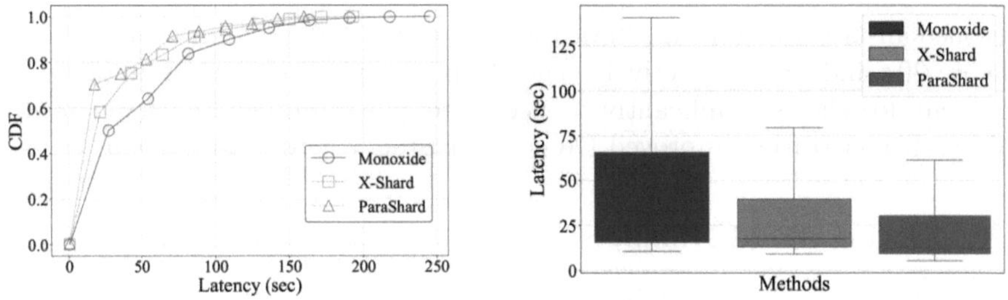

(a) CDF of CTX confirmation latency (b) Boxplot of CTX confirmation latency

Fig. 4. Latency in a 10-shard system with a TX arrival rate of 1000 TX/s.

Dataset: We use real-world Ethereum transaction data provided by XBlock [24], consisting of more than one million TXs starting from block height 19,000,000.

Metrics: To evaluate the performance and scalability of our PARASHARD system, we conduct experiments varying two key system parameters: the number of shards and the TX injection rate. We focus on the following metrics:

(i) TX Latency: The duration from the initiation of TX on the sender shard to final the execution confirmation across all participating shards, including all phases of coordination and finalization.

(ii) CTX Latency vs. ITX Latency Ratio: The ratio of CTX latency to ITX latency, which quantifies the relative overhead introduced by cross-shard coordination. A ratio closer to 1 indicates higher fairness, as it implies that CTXs are processed with latency comparable to ITXs.

(iii) Throughput: The number of TXs processed successfully by the system per second (TPS), including both ITXs and CTXs. This reflects the overall efficiency of the system.

(iv) Inter-Shard Latency: The average end to end confirmation latency of a TX considering all participating shards. For TX involving multiple input and output shards, this metric reflects the time it takes for all involved shards to reach consensus and complete the transaction. A lower and more balanced inter-shard latency indicates better coordination and reduced cross-shard bottlenecks.

5.2 CTX Confirmation Latency Distribution

We first study the cumulative distribution function (CDF) and Boxplot of CTX confirmation latency under different methods. In a 10-shard system with a TX arrival rate of 1000TX/s, Fig. 4a illustrates the CDF of CTX confirmation latency, PARASHARD achieves the fastest convergence, confirming 90% of CTXs within 70 s, compared to about 100 s for X-Shard and 140 s for Monoxide. The CDF of CTX confirmation latency in PARASHARD shows a leftward shift, demonstrating improved overall latency performance of the system. As shown in Fig. 4b, the median latency of ParaShard is 16 s, while that of X-Shard and Monoxide are 20 s and 28 s, respectively. The Boxplot of CTX confirmation latency in ParaShard shows significantly reduced interquartile range and lower median values, demonstrating improved latency consistency across the system.

5.3 Varying Shard Numbers

To investigate the correlation between shard number and system performance, we maintained a constant injection rate of 1500 TX/s while varying the number of shards from 2 to 20. This experimental design aims to reveal how shard scalability affects TX processing performance.

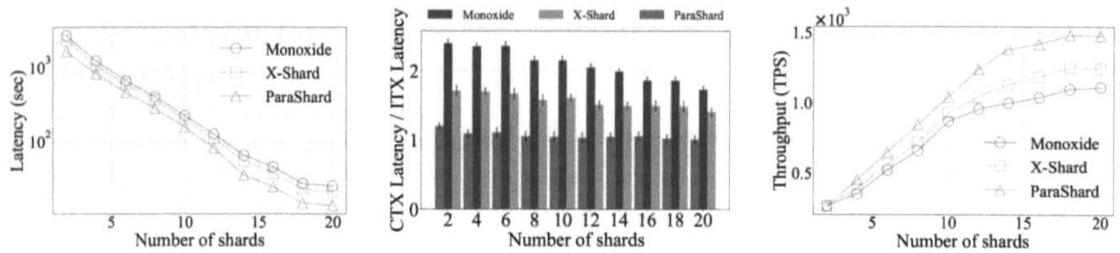

(a) Latency (b) Ratio (c) Throughput

Fig. 5. The system CTX latency and throughput under various shard numbers with a TX arrival rate of 1500 TX/s.

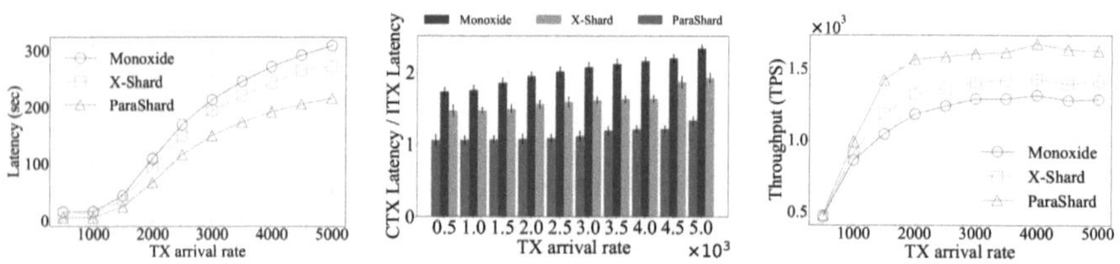

(a) Latency (b) Ratio (c) Throughput

Fig. 6. The system CTX latency and throughput under various TX arrival rate with a shard numbers of 16.

As show in Fig. 5a, all three schemes exhibit decreasing CTX latency with increasing shard numbers. At 2 shards, ParaShard achieves 1554.25 s latency, showing 37.8% and 28.7% reductions compared to Monoxide (2499.46 s) and X-Shard (2180.02 s). When scaling to 20 shards, ParaShard maintains superior performance at 13.41 s, outperforming Monoxide (24.4 s) and X-Shard (20.36 s) by 45.0% and 34.1%. These results demonstrate ParaShard's low latency advantages across different shard numbers.

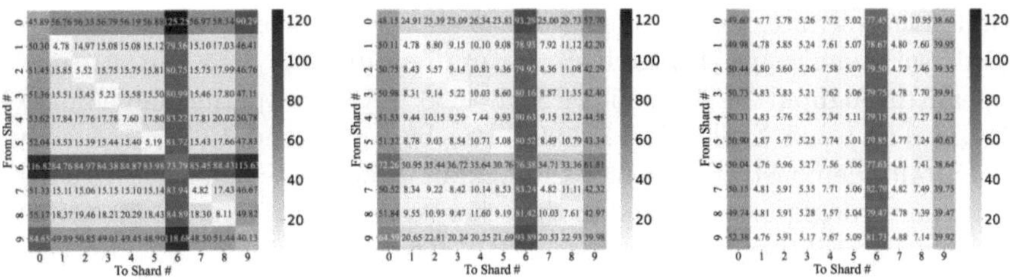

(a) Monoxide scheme (b) X-Shard scheme (c) ParaShard scheme

Fig. 7. Heatmap of inter-shard TX confirmation latency in a 10-shard system with a TX arrival rate of 1000 TX/s.

Figure 5b presents the measured ratio of average CTX latency to that of ITX across three schemes. The results demonstrate that PARASHARD maintains the most balanced latency profile, consistently keeping the ratio below 1.2. In comparison, Monoxide and X-Shard exhibit higher ratios limited to 2.4 and 1.7 respectively. These findings confirm PARASHARD's superior efficiency in CTXs processing, achieving higher fairness.

In terms of throughput as in Fig. 5c, all three schemes show improvement with more shards, but PARASHARD leads with a maximum throughput at 1478.94 TPS when scaling to 20 shards, outperforming X-Shard (1247.72 TPS) and Monoxide (1113.33 TPS) by 18.5% and 30.5% respectively.

5.4 Varying TX Arrival Rates

To further investigate the impact of increasing TX arrival rate on system performance, we fixed the number of shards at 16 and varied the TX arrival rate from 500 to 5000 TX/s. This experimental setup aims to examine the system's scalability under increasing TX arrival rate.

As shown in Fig. 6a, CTX latency increases across all three schemes as TX arrival rate rises. However, PARASHARD demonstrates significantly better latency control. At the lowest arrival rate (500 TX/s), PARASHARD achieves a latency of approximately 5.02 s, which is 66.9% and 56.1% lower than Monoxide (15.17 s) and X-Shard (11.42 s), respectively. Under the highest TX arrival rate (5000 TX/s), PARASHARD maintains CTX latency at 216.44 s, while Monoxide and X-Shard reach 308.64 and 272.42 s, respectively. These results confirm that PARASHARD effectively mitigates latency inflation under different TX arrival rates.

Figure 6b presents the ratio of CTX latency to ITX latency for all schemes. PARASHARD maintains the most stable and balanced ratio below 1.33 across all rates, indicating minimal coordination overhead between CTX and ITX processing. In contrast, Monoxide's ratio grows from 1.73 at 500 TX/s to over 2.33 at 5000 TX/s, reflecting growing inefficiencies in its relay coordination protocol. X-Shard performs slightly better but still suffers from increased ratio beyond 1.92 at high TX arrival rate. Figure 6c shows that all schemes demonstrate throughput growth with increasing TX arrival rate until saturation. ParaShard reaches its peak throughput of 1673.65 TPS at 4000 TX/s, outperforming Monoxide (1316.18 TPS) and X-Shard (1427.99 TPS) by 27.2% and 17.2%, respectively. ParaShard demonstrates a faster throughput growth rate and achieves a higher maximum throughput compared to the other two schemes. Overall, ParaShard shows strong resilience under increasing TX arrival rate, providing lower latency, higher fairness, and greater throughput compared to baseline systems.

5.5 Inter-shard Confirmation Latency

To evaluate the performance of different inter-shard TX execution, we measure the average confirmation latency of TXs in a 10-shard system under a constant TX arrival rate of 1000 TX/s. Figure 7 presents heatmaps of inter-shard TX confirmation latency under three schemes: (a) Monoxide, (b) X-Shard, and (c) ParaShard. Each cell denotes the average confirmation latency (in seconds) for TX initiated in the source shard (row) and confirmed in the target shard (column). One notable pattern emerges in the above heatmap: TXs destined for shard 0, 6 and 9 generally exhibit higher latencies compared to the rest. This phenomenon is primarily due to uneven TX load across shards. In this experiment, accounts are randomly assigned to shards, which can lead to skewed workloads. When more TXs arrive specific target shards, such as shard 0, 6 and 9, those shards experience temporary congestion, increasing queueing and confirmation time.

As shown in Fig. 7a, the Monoxide scheme exhibits highly uneven latency distribution, with many inter-shard TXs experiencing delays exceeding 100 s. This is especially pronounced for TXs between certain shard pairs, such as from shard 0 to shard 6 (125.25 s) and from shard 6 to shard 9 (115.63 s). This high and inconsistent latency is attributed to Monoxide's relay-based mechanism, where cross-shard communication relies on intermediate relay shards. This architecture introduces significant communication overhead and bottlenecks, especially when relays are overloaded or frequently involved in TXs between heavily active shards.

The X-Shard scheme, depicted in Fig. 7b, significantly improves latency uniformity and magnitude compared to Monoxide. Most shard observe confirmation latencies between 10 s and 50 s, with far fewer outliers. For instance, the latency from shard 6 to shard 9 is reduced to 61.81 s, and many inter-shard TXs complete under 30 s. This improvement results from X-Shard's optimistic execution, which takes an optimistic strategy to processes CTXs and later resolves conflicts. This reduces the waiting time associated with relay-based coordination, though some overhead remains in conflict resolution and validation.

ParaShard demonstrates the best overall performance in terms of both low latency and high consistency across all shard pairs (Fig. 7c). The majority of confirmation latencies are tightly clustered between 4 s and 8 s, with minimal deviation. For instance, the latency from shard 6 to shard 9 is only 38.64 s, a significant improvement over both Monoxide and X-Shard. This is achieved through PARASHARD's fast-path design, which enables direct, low-latency interactions between shards via lightweight commit protocols. This design minimizes coordination delays.

6 Related Work

This section reviews related work on CTXs, including efficiently CTXs processing and reducing the ratio of CTXs by partitioning accounts across shards.

6.1 Cross-Shard Transactions Processing

Prior research on cross-shard processing can be broadly classified into three categories: two-phase commit (2PC), relay transaction mechanism, and optimistic execution mechanisms.

Two-phase commit (2PC). 2PC have been widely used in sharded blockchain systems to ensure atomicity of CTXs. OmniLedger [7] adopts a classical 2PC model, where each shard maintains its own BFT consensus instance, and the client acts as a coordinator. CTXs are committed only after all involved shards respond with commit votes. While this ensures strong consistency, it suffers from high communication overhead and blocking behavior—delays or failures in any shard can stall the entire TX. To address these limitations, CHERUBIM [25] introduces a quadruple pipelined two-phase commit (4P-2PC). It enables concurrent execution of multiple CTXs by pipelining both intra- and inter-shard processing. CHERUBIM integrates batch processing and multi-signature aggregation to reduce communication complexity and reduce latency.

Relay Transaction Mechanism. Relay transaction mechanism is a message-relay transaction processing approach, which guarantee the eventual atomicity [26] of CTXs. BrokerChain [10] builds on the relay-based architecture by introducing broker accounts, which convert a CTX into two ITXs. The sender transfers assets to a local broker in the source shard, and a corresponding broker in the target shard forwards the assets to the recipient. This design simplifies coordination, reduces cross-shard communication overhead.

Optimistic Execution. Presto [27] introduces a dual-faceted design to reduce CTXs latency in sharded blockchain systems. It combines optimistic pre-execution of CTXs with predissemination and erasure coding techniques that fully exploit the available bandwidth within each shard. This approach not only minimizes cross-shard coordination overhead but also accelerates transaction propagation and execution.

6.2 Account Allocation Mechanism

The design of account allocation schemes in sharded blockchains directly reduces the ratio of CTXs and improves system scalability. Existing approaches can be broadly categorized into semi-static, and dynamic partitioning methods.

Semi-static Partitioning. To reduce the ratio of CTXs, semi-static partitioning methods periodically adjust account-shard assignments based on observed transaction patterns. TxAllo [28] reduces CTXs by constructing a transaction graph and applying the Louvain [29] community detection algorithm to group frequently interacting accounts. It introduces two variants: G-TxAllo, a global optimizer, and A-TxAllo, an adaptive online method that periodically updates the partitioning using recent transaction data. CLPA [23] proposes a label-aware community detection algorithm [30] to partition accounts based on both interaction patterns and shard load balancing. By formulating the problem as a multi-objective optimization, CLPA reallocates accounts by epoch.

Dynamic Partitioning. Shard schedule [31] introduces a dynamic account migration mechanism based on historical TX behavior. For each TX initiator account, the system analyzes past interaction patterns with other accounts to determine the most suitable shard placement in real time. This enables on-demand migration at the moment of TX initiation, aiming to minimize the overhead of CTXs. More recent approach such as Orbit [32] continuously monitors access patterns and migrates account states across shards to co-locate frequently interacting accounts. While this approach can effectively reduce CTX volume and optimize locality, it introduces additional synchronization and state migration overhead, requiring careful coordination to ensure consistency and performance. Compared to traditional static sharding or periodic migration schemes, dynamic partitioning offers greater flexibility and adaptability, enhancing the system's responsiveness to dynamic workloads while maintaining consistency.

7 Conclusion

In this paper, we proposed ParaShard, a low-latency and secure protocol for CTX in a blockchain sharding system. While sharding improves scalability, CTX often suffer from high latency and poor parallelism due to inter-shard coordination constraints. Our design addresses two key challenges through a unified fast-path execution framework that decouples transaction acceptance from on-chain confirmation. First, to ensure efficient execution of cross-shard transactions, we introduce a fast-path scheduling algorithm based on a transaction dependency graph, enabling parallelism and reducing end-to-end latency. Second, to guarantee the security of cross-shard transactions, we design a novel mechanism that combines threshold signatures with balance-locking, ensuring atomicity and preventing double-spending. Our evaluation using historical Ethereum transactions shows that ParaShard achieves 30.5% higher throughput and 45.0% lower latency compared to state-of-the-art protocols such as X-Shard and Monoxide, demonstrating its effectiveness in scaling system performance.

References

1. Nakamoto, S.: Bitcoin: A peer-to-peer electronic cash system. In: Decentralized Business Review, p. 21260 (2008)

2. Meng, W., Chiu,W.: DataVaults: a secure, distributed and privacy preserving personal data management platform. In: Proceedings of the ICDCS, pp. 1–4 (2023)
3. Loi, L., et al.: A secure sharding protocol for open blockchains. In: Proceedings of the ACM SIGSAC CCS, pp. 17–30 (2016)
4. Hu, D., et al.: LMChain: an efficient load-migratable beacon-based sharding blockchain system. IEEE Trans. Comput. **73**(9), 2178–2191 (2024)
5. Zamani, M., Movahedi, M., Raykova, M.: RapidChain: scaling blockchain via full sharding. In: Proceedings of the ACM SIGSAC CCS, pp. 931–948 (2018)
6. Dang, H., et al.: Towards scaling blockchain systems via sharding. In: Proceedings of the ACM SIGMOD, pp. 123–140 (2019)
7. Kokoris-Kogias, E., et al.: OmniLedger: a secure, scale-out, decentralized ledger via sharding. In: Proceedings of the IEEE S&P, pp. 583–598 (2018)
8. Ma, J., et al.: HydraChain: a cooperative mappo architecture for load balancing in IoT sharding blockchain. IEEE Internet Things J. **12**(15), pp. 29397–29410 (2025)
9. Chiu, W., Meng, W.: DevLeChain - an open blockchain development platform for decentralized applications. In: Proceedings of the ICBC, pp. 167–176. IEEE (2022)
10. Huang, H., et al.: BrokerChain: a cross-shard blockchain protocol for account/balance-based state sharding. In: Proceedings of the IEEE INFOCOM, pp. 1968–1977 (2022)
11. Jiang, S., et al.: Sharon: secure and efficient cross-shard transaction processing via shard rotation. In: Proceedings of the IEEE INFOCOM, pp. 2418–2427 (2024)
12. Jia, L., et al.: Estuary: a low cross-shard blockchain sharding protocol based on state splitting. IEEE Trans. Parallel Distrib. Syst. **35**(3), 405–420 (2024)
13. Xu, H., et al.: Tangram: enabling efficient and balanced dynamic storage extension on sharding blockchain systems. IEEE Trans. Comput. **74**(6), 2031–2044 (2025)
14. Zheng, J., et al.: Justitia: an incentive mechanism towards the fairness of cross-shard transactions. In: Proceedings of the IEEE INFOCOM, pp. 1–10 (2025)
15. Dengcheng Hu et al. "Ladder: A Convergence-based Structured DAG Blockchain for High Throughput and Low Latency". In: *Proc. of the USENIX NSDI*. 2025, pp. 779–794
16. Wang, J., Wang, H.: Monoxide: scale out blockchains with asynchronous consensus zones. In: Proceedings of the USENIX NSDI, pp. 95–112 (2019)
17. Wood, G.: Ethereum: a secure decentralised generalised transaction ledger. In: Ethereum Project Yellow Paper, Vol. 151, pp. 1–32 (2014)
18. Chen, B., et al.: BSSN: enabling adjustable blockchain storage for resource-constrained IoT scenarios. IEEE Internet Things J. **12**(4), 4262–4274 (2025)
19. Xu, H., et al.: Crackle: a fast sector-based bft consensus with sublinear communication complexity. In: Proceedings of the IEEE INFOCOM, pp. 1–10 (2024)
20. Xu, J., et al.: X-Shard: optimistic cross-shard transaction processing for sharding-based blockchains. In: IEEE Trans. Parallel Distrib. Syst. **35**(4), 548–559 (2024)
21. Shoup, V.: Practical Threshold Signatures. In: Preneel, B. (ed.) EUROCRYPT 2000. LNCS, vol. 1807, pp. 207–220. Springer, Heidelberg (2000). https://doi.org/10.1007/3-540-45539-6_15
22. Castro, M., Liskov, B.: Practical Byzantine fault tolerance. In: Proceedings of the USENIX OSDI, pp. 173–186 (1999)
23. Li, C., et al.: Achieving scalability and load balance across blockchain shards for state sharding. In: Proceedings of the IEEE SRDS, pp. 284–294 (2022)
24. Zheng, P., et al.: XBlock-ETH: extracting and exploring blockchain data from ethereum. IEEE Open J. Comput. Soc. **1**, 95–106 (2020)

25. Liu, A., et al.: CHERUBIM: a secure and highly parallel cross-shard consensus using quadruple pipelined two-phase commit for sharding blockchains. IEEE Trans. Inf. Forensics Secur. **19**, 3178–3193 (2024)
26. Vogels, W.: Eventually consistent. In: Commun. ACM **52**(1), 40–44 (2009)
27. Ding, Q., et al.: Presto: optimizing cross-shard transactions in sharded blockchain architecture. In: Proceedings of the IEEE SRDS, pp. 139–149 (2024)
28. Zhang, Y., Pan, S., Yu, J.: TxAllo: dynamic transaction allocation in sharded blockchain systems. In: Proceedings of the IEEE ICDE, pp. 721–733 (2023)
29. Blondel, V.D., et al.: Fast unfolding of communities in large networks. In: J. Stat. Mech. Theory Exp. **2008**(10), P10008 (2008)
30. Ugander, J., Backstrom, L.: Balanced label propagation for partitioning massive graphs. In: Proceedings of the ACM WSDM, pp. 507–516 (2013)
31. Król, M., et al.: Shard scheduler: object placement and migration in sharded account-based blockchains. In: Proceedings of the ACM AFT, pp. 43–56 (2021)
32. Wang, X., et al.: Orbit: a dynamic account allocation mechanism in sharding blockchain system. In: Proceedings of the IEEE ICDCS, pp. 333–344 (2024)

DiVeR: Differential and Verifiable Data Dissemination for Multi-path Payment Routing

Huan Wang, Gaowei Shi, Sheng Chen, Xiulong Liu(✉), and Weuyu Qu

Tianjin University, Tianjin, China
{wanghuan5728,shigaowei,chensheng,xiulong_liu,wenyu.qu}@tju.edu.cn

Abstract. Scalable off-chain payments are crucial for supporting high-frequency transactions in payment channel networks (PCNs). In the Lightning Network, this is typically achieved through multi-path payments that split a payment across multiple paths to improve transaction success rates. However, existing designs impose significant communication overhead on the payer by requiring individualized encrypted information for each intermediate user. Moreover, onion-routing-based mechanisms, which are widely adopted for hop-by-hop forwarding in PCNs, are inherently designed for single-path communication, making them unsuitable for efficient multi-path data delivery and end-to-end verifiability. To address these limitations, we present DiVeR, a cryptographic framework for secure data dissemination in multi-hop, multi-path payment networks. To enable differential data delivery, DiVeR leverages a key-tree–based derivation mechanism to assign distinct encryption keys to nodes on different payment paths. At the same time, DiVeR employs chained ring signatures to provide strong end-to-end data verifiability between the payer and all recipients. In addition, we design a multi-layer encrypted packet that extends the self-routing property of onion encryption to multi-path settings. We implement DiVeR and evaluate it against state-of-the-art schemes. Experimental results show that DiVeR achieves on average 2.25× higher throughput than AMHL and 1.38× higher throughput than Rollercoaster and PolySphinx.

Keywords: blockchain · payment channel network · multi-path payment routing · cryptographic data dissemination

1 Introduction

1.1 Background and Motivation

Blockchain technology has been widely adopted across diverse application domains, yet scalability, efficiency, and coordination among distributed participants remain fundamental challenges [12,15,16,18]. To address these challenges in the context of cryptocurrencies, payment channel networks (PCNs) were introduced to enable scalable off-chain transactions by moving frequent payments off

Y. Cao et al. (Eds.): SecureComm 2026, LNICST 704, pp. 379–397, 2027.
https://doi.org/10.1007/978-3-032-32764-2_18

the blockchain. The Lightning Network (LN) is a prominent realization of this kind of approaches, supporting fast off-chain payments through bidirectional channels and multi-hop routing [23]. However, early LN designs primarily rely on single-path routing, which often leads to channel imbalance and capacity fragmentation, thereby reducing payment success rates. To overcome this limitation, recent studies have explored multi-path payments (MPPs), in which a payment is split and routed over multiple paths simultaneously [14,19,21]. By exploiting path diversity, MPPs improve transaction reliability and are particularly effective in large or congested payment scenarios.

While MPPs improve payment success rates, they also introduce new and non-trivial system-level challenges at both the communication and verification layers. In multi-path execution, routing and control information must be delivered to a large number of intermediate users along different paths, and the volume of data that needs to be generated and transmitted grows rapidly with the number of paths and hops, placing increasing pressure on both the payer and the network. Moreover, each intermediate user must be able to locally verify the correctness and integrity of the received information, while learning only the forwarding instructions relevant to itself and without being exposed to the global routing structure, in order to preserve routing privacy. These requirements jointly impose stringent constraints on scalability, privacy, and verifiability, which go beyond the capabilities of traditional single-path communication mechanisms and thus pose fundamental design challenges for secure and efficient data dissemination in multi-path payment networks.

These challenges motivate the need for new cryptographic communication primitives that can simultaneously support differential data delivery and end-to-end verifiable correctness in multi-hop, multi-path payment scenarios, without overburdening the payer or compromising privacy.

1.2 Limitations of Prior Art

To address the above communication and verification challenges, existing studies can be broadly categorized into three classes: communication-channel–based (CC-based), re-distribution–based (RD-based), and copy-based schemes. (i) CC-based schemes [17,20,29] require the payer to establish direct communication channels with intermediate users and the payee to exchange routing or payment-related information. Although these schemes provide strong security guarantees, they incur substantial communication overhead on the payer and implicitly assume the feasibility of maintaining direct channels with all intermediate users—an assumption that is often unrealistic in dynamic and privacy-preserving payment networks. (ii) RD-based schemes [7,9] rely on intermediate users that have already received a message to further forward or re-distribute it to downstream participants. While re-distribution reduces the payer's direct communication cost, it introduces additional trust assumptions on intermediate users, thereby enlarging the attack surface and weakening end-to-end security guarantees. (iii) Copy-based schemes [22,24] replicate encrypted messages along multiple paths via designated copying nodes without revealing message contents.

However, these approaches inherently assume that all replicated messages are identical and thus only support uniform data dissemination. Consequently, they cannot accommodate differential data delivery for individual intermediate users, which are essential in MPP routing where forwarding conditions or payment parameters may vary across paths.

1.3 DiVeR in a Nutshell

In this paper, we propose a novel cryptographic data transmission framework for multi-hop, multi-path payment routing that simultaneously supports differential data delivery and end-to-end data verification. To enable differential data transmission while keeping the payer's computation and communication overhead low, we introduce a key-treebased encryption mechanism that leverages hierarchical key-derivation techniques to assign each payment path a unique path identifier. This identifier corresponds to a specific key index in the key tree. Based on this index, the payer derives a path-specific subtree and further generates node-level encryption keys for individual intermediate users along the path. Data is encrypted under these customized keys, ensuring that each intermediate user can access only the information explicitly intended for it, while maintaining strict data isolation across different paths. To achieve end-to-end data verification, we design a chained ring-signature scheme combined with key-index verification. The chained ring signatures provide cryptographic guarantees of data integrity and signer authenticity, ensuring that the transmitted data has not been tampered with, while supporting data delivery from multiple source nodes to a common destination in MPP networks. In parallel, key-index verification exploits the structure of the key tree to validate the correctness of routing information and the key-derivation process, thereby preserving the integrity of the entire data path and preventing malicious modification of routing instructions. Together, these mechanisms form a lightweight yet robust solution that enables secure and verifiable data dissemination for MPP systems.

1.4 Challenges and Solutions

The first challenge lies in enabling self-routing data delivery among heterogeneous users. In multi-hop MPP networks, data packets must be forwarded through multiple distinct payment paths and delivered to different intermediate users. Existing onion-routingbased designs support self-routing transmission only along a single path and cannot be naturally applied in differential data delivery in multi-path settings. To address this limitation, we design a multi-layer encrypted data packet in which routing information is embedded within each encryption layer. Upon receiving a packet, each intermediate user decrypts only its corresponding layer to retrieve the appropriate forwarding instructions, thereby enabling correct and autonomous self-routing data delivery across users.

The second challenge is how to ensure data consistency across multiple payment paths. In multi-path transmission, the same user may receive multiple data packets carrying overlapping or duplicated information from different paths, which may lead to inconsistent states or replay attacks. We address this challenge by combining a key-treebased derivation mechanism with chained ring signatures. When generating encrypted data, the payer uses key-tree indices and chained ring signatures to bind all information intended for a specific user across all paths. Upon receiving multiple packets, the user verifies them using the key index and the signature chain, accepts only a single valid encrypted packet, and directly discards all redundant ones, thereby ensuring data consistency.

1.5 Novelty and Advantages over Prior Art

This paper proposes a novel cryptographic framework for secure data dissemination in multi-hop, multi-path payment networks. First, we introduce a differential data transmission mechanism that enables distinct users across multiple payment paths to receive customized data. Second, we design a new multi-layer encrypted data packet that encodes routing information while simultaneously supporting end-to-end data verification, thereby extending traditional onion encryption from single-path communication to more general multi-path scenarios. Compared with [7], our design eliminates the need to trust intermediate users with respect to data integrity. By combining chained ring signatures with a key-treebased verification mechanism, our approach effectively prevents data tampering during the forwarding process. Compared with [22,24], the proposed multi-layer encrypted packet supports user-specific differential data delivery while preserving privacy. Experimental results demonstrate that, compared with AMHL, our scheme achieves on average 2× higher throughput, and compared with Rollercoaster and PolySphinx, achieves on average 1.3× higher throughput, while also exhibiting lower data transmission latency.

The remainder of this paper is organized as follows. Section 2 presents the necessary preliminaries. Section 3 provides a comprehensive overview of our approach, while Sect. 4 details its construction. The security analysis appears in Sect. 5, followed by implementation and evaluation in Sect. 6. Section 7 discusses related work, and Sect. 8 concludes the paper.

2 Preliminaries

2.1 Key Tree

A key tree is a hierarchical key-derivation structure that generates multiple cryptographic keys from a single master secret using a standard pseudorandom function (PRF). Let K_0 denote the global master key. For a node with index i, its key is deterministically derived as

$$K_i = \mathrm{PRF}\big(K_{\mathrm{parent}(i)}, i\big)\,. \tag{1}$$

Given a key at any node, all descendant keys can be efficiently derived, while keys outside the corresponding subtree remain computationally indistinguishable. In this paper, key indices uniquely identify derivation paths and are bound to routing-related information.

2.2 Chained Ring Signatures

A ring signature allows a signer to produce a signature on behalf of a set of public keys while hiding the signer's identity. A chained ring signature links multiple ring signatures sequentially, such that each signature is computed over the current message and the previous signature, thereby ensuring the cryptographic integrity of the entire sequence [11].

Given a sequence of messages $\{m_1, \ldots, m_n\}$, the corresponding chained signatures $\{\sigma_1, \ldots, \sigma_n\}$ are generated as

$$\sigma_i = \text{RingSign}(m_i \,\|\, \sigma_{i-1},\, \mathcal{R}), \tag{2}$$

where $\mathcal{R}$ denotes the ring of public keys. Verification succeeds only if all signatures in the chain are valid and correctly linked.

3 Overview of DiVeR

3.1 Base Model

Blockchain. We assume a properly functioning blockchain with an established payment channel network. The network employs a routing algorithm to discover multiple payment paths between parties, thereby enabling the transmission of encrypted data packets along multiple payment paths.

User Model. In DiVeR, participants assume three primary roles. The **Payer** can initiate payments from multiple accounts over multiple payment paths and has full knowledge of the network topology. Before payment, the payer sends corresponding encrypted data packets to the intermediate users along each path as well as to the payee. **Intermediate Users** are rational nodes on the paths; they decrypt the received encrypted data packets and forward them to the next hop. The **Payee** ultimately receives the encrypted data sent by the payer and performs verification and acceptance.

3.2 Workflow of DiVeR

This paper proposes DiVeR, which involves a payer, multiple intermediate users, and a payee. The payer can control multiple accounts and simultaneously send data packets to intermediate users and the payee along different paths. The overall system workflow is divided into three phases: the **Encryption Phase**, the **Decryption Phase**, and the **Routing Phase**, as illustrated in Fig. 1.

Encryption Phase. During the encryption phase, the payer first derives path-related keying material from a global key tree. Specifically, for each payment path, the payer selects the corresponding key index based on the path identifier and derives both path-level and user-level encryption keys. These keys bind path information and implicitly encode the data required for subsequent routing. The payer then generates differential data for intermediate users and the payee on each path and applies layered encryption using the corresponding keys to construct multi-layer encrypted packets. To ensure cross-path data consistency, the payer computes a chained ring signature that binds the data intended for the same user across different paths into a unified signature chain. Finally, the payer produces the complete encrypted packets and injects them into the network.

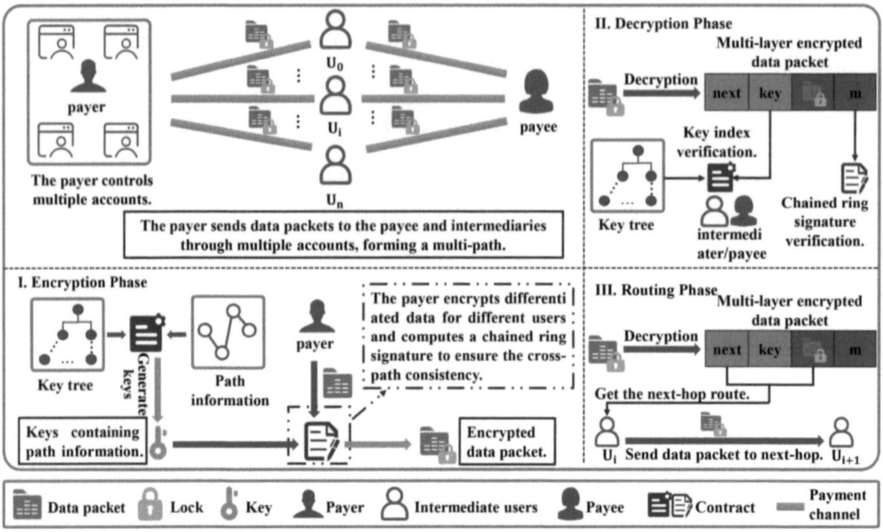

Fig. 1. An overview of the DiVeR system model: the payer controls multiple account addresses and sends encrypted data packets securely to the payee over multiple distinct payment paths. It consists of three overall phases: the encryption phase, the decryption phase, and the routing phase.

Decryption Phase. When an intermediate user or the payee receives an encrypted data packet, it enters the decryption phase. The receiver first decrypts the outermost layer using a locally derived key, obtaining three components: next-hop routing information, a key index for subsequent verification, and the payload. It then verifies the key index against the keys derived from the key tree to ensure the correctness of routing information during transmission. Based on this, the receiver verifies the chained ring signature carried in the packet, guaranteeing that the data has not been tampered with. If any verification fails, the packet is discarded; otherwise, the data is accepted for further processing.

Routing Phase. In the routing phase, intermediate users determine the next-hop node based on the routing information obtained from decryption. Each user only decrypts the current layer to obtain the next-hop instruction, without learning the full path structure, thereby preserving path privacy. The remaining multi-layer encrypted data packet is then forwarded unchanged to the next-hop user. This process is repeated at each hop until the packet reaches the payee. Since the packet is protected by multi-layer encryption and dual verification at every hop, the system enables secure, self-routing data transmission without trusting intermediate users, while ensuring data consistency and integrity.

4 Construction of DiVeR

4.1 Encryption Phase

Before a multi-hop payment begins in a multi-path payment network, the payer must distribute encrypted data to different intermediate users. Since the payer typically cannot establish direct communication channels with these intermediates, the data must be forwarded along the selected paths. This constraint requires the encryption phase not only to ensure data confidentiality, but also to cryptographically encode routing semantics and support subsequent consistency verification. Accordingly, the encryption phase of DiVeR is designed to satisfy three key requirements: (i) binding data to specific paths and hop positions to prevent routing inconsistencies; (ii) enabling differential data delivery to distinct intermediate users; and (iii) providing cryptographic consistency verification in multi-path settings to ensure data security.

Path Index Definition and Key-Tree Derivation. Before the protocol begins, the payer first constructs the payment topology and computes the set of payment paths

$$\mathcal{P} = P_1, \ldots, P_M, \quad P_j = \langle u_{j,1}, \ldots, u_{j,L_j} \rangle, \tag{3}$$

where each path P_j is uniquely identified by a path identifier pid_j. The payer then performs key derivation using the key-tree root key K_0, together with the path identifier and hop index. Specifically, for the i-th intermediate user on path P_j, the payer defines the path context

$$\mathsf{ctx}_{j,i} = (\mathsf{pid}j, |, i), \tag{4}$$

which is encoded as a key index $\mathsf{idx}j, i$. A corresponding session key is derived from the master key K_0 via a pseudorandom function. By binding key derivation to both the path identifier and hop position, a node on one path cannot decrypt data using a valid key from another path, thereby ensuring path-level isolation. The complete key generation procedure is illustrated in Algorithm 1.

Construction of Multi-layer Encrypted Data Packet. After completing path-bound key derivation, the payer constructs a secure multi-layer encrypted data packet for each path. The packet follows a layered encapsulation structure, ensuring that each intermediate user can access only the information relevant to itself. For a given path P_j, the payer builds the encrypted packet layer by layer starting from the end of the path. Each layer contains not only the next-hop information required for forwarding, but also an explicit key index that allows the recipient to verify the correctness of the derived key context. In addition, the payer embeds node-specific encrypted data intended for that intermediate user, enabling differential data delivery. The ciphertext of the next layer is then

Algorithm 1. Path-Bound Key Derivation and Encrypted Packet Construction

Input: Master secret key K_0; payment path $P_j = \langle u_{j,1}, \ldots, u_{j,L_j} \rangle$; path identifier pid_j; path-specific payloads $\{payload_{j,i}\}$; chained ring signatures $\{\sigma_{j,i}\}$
Output: Encrypted packet Pkt_j

Parameters:
  $PRF : \{0,1\}^\kappa \times \{0,1\}^* \rightarrow \{0,1\}^\kappa$
  $H : \{0,1\}^* \rightarrow \{0,1\}^\lambda$
  $Enc : \{0,1\}^\kappa \times \{0,1\}^* \rightarrow \{0,1\}^*$
  $\perp$: empty string
$C_{j,L_j+1} \leftarrow \perp$
for $i = L_j$ **to** 1 **do**
  $ctx_{j,i} \leftarrow pid_j \parallel Encode(i)$
  $idx_{j,i} \leftarrow H(ctx_{j,i})$
  $K_{j,i} \leftarrow PRF(K_0, idx_{j,i})$
  $PL_{j,i} \leftarrow (nextHop_{j,i}, idx_{j,i}, payload_{j,i}, \sigma_{j,i}, C_{j,i+1})$
  $C_{j,i} \leftarrow Enc(K_{j,i}, PL_{j,i})$
end for
return $Pkt_j \leftarrow C_{j,1}$

included as the payload of the current layer, resulting in a fully nested multi-layer encrypted data packet.

Chained Ring Signatures Process. In MPPs, a single payee may receive data transmitted over multiple distinct paths. If the payer delivers inconsistent content along different paths, or if the data is tampered with during transmission, the payee may ultimately obtain inconsistent or incorrect results. To prevent such behaviors and ensure end-to-end data consistency, DiVeR introduces a chained ring signature mechanism during the encryption phase. Specifically, the payer treats all data destined for the same payee across different paths as a logically unified set and generates chained signatures in a deterministic order. Each signature authenticates its corresponding data item and is cryptographically linked to the preceding signature, forming an integrity-preserving chain that enforces cross-path consistency. Meanwhile, the use of ring signatures preserves payer anonymity by concealing the signer's identity within a predefined anonymity set, ensuring that consistency guarantees are achieved without revealing the payer's identity. Algorithm 2 presents the complete construction of the chained ring signature scheme.

4.2 Decryption Phase

The decryption phase is executed by data recipients along the payment paths, aiming to correctly recover the intended data from multi-layer encrypted data packets and to verify integrity and consistency across multiple paths, without requiring additional communication or trust assumptions.

Each recipient $u_{j,i}$ holds the root key K_0 of the key tree. Upon receiving a packet, the node first decrypts it using a locally derived key, recovering the

Algorithm 2. Generation of Chained Ring Signatures

Input: Ordered message set $\mathcal{M} = \langle m_1, \ldots, m_N \rangle$; ring public key set $\mathcal{R}$; signer secret key sk

Output: Chained ring signature set $\Sigma = \langle \sigma_1, \ldots, \sigma_N \rangle$

Parameters:
  $RingSign : \{0,1\}^* \times \mathcal{R} \times sk \rightarrow \sigma$
  $H : \{0,1\}^* \rightarrow \{0,1\}^\lambda$
Initialize $\sigma_0 \leftarrow 0^\lambda$ ▷ Initial chaining value
for $i = 1$ **to** N **do**
  $m_i^* \leftarrow H(m_i \parallel \sigma_{i-1})$ ▷ Bind current message to previous signature
  $\sigma_i \leftarrow RingSign(m_i^*, \mathcal{R}, sk)$
end for
return $\Sigma = \langle \sigma_1, \ldots, \sigma_N \rangle$

plaintext of the corresponding layer, which includes next-hop routing information, the key index $\mathsf{idx}_{j,i}$, different data, and chained ring signature components. Due to the nested multi-layer encryption structure, a node can decrypt only the layer matching its exact position on the path, ensuring that intermediate users cannot access or infer any information from other layers.

The decryption phase consists of two main procedures: key-index verification and chained ring signature verification. When multiple packets arrive via different paths, the recipient accepts only the first packet that passes both verifications and discards all others. Algorithm 3 illustrates the decryption process.

Key-Index Verification. After successfully decrypting the current data packet and extracting the key $\mathsf{idx}j, i$, the receiver performs key-index verification to ensure that the key has not been maliciously tampered with during transmission and was correctly bound during packet construction. Specifically, based on the locally known path identifier $\mathsf{pid}j$ and the receiver's hop position i on the path, the receiver independently constructs the expected path context

$$\mathsf{ctx}^*j, i = (\mathsf{pid}j, |, i), \tag{5}$$

and derives the expected key

$$\mathsf{idx}^*j, i = H(\mathsf{ctx}^*j, i). \tag{6}$$

The receiver then compares the decrypted key $\mathsf{idx}_{j,i}$ with the locally computed $\mathsf{idx}^*_{j,i}$. If they do not match, the packet is deemed to have deviated in its path identifier or hop position—potentially due to path rebinding, index substitution, or replay attacks—and is immediately discarded. Through this mechanism, DiVeR guarantees that even if an adversary can construct a cryptographically decryptable packet, it cannot pass index verification unless it is strictly correctly bound to the intended path context, thereby effectively and robustly preventing key misuse on unintended paths or hop positions.

Chained Ring Signature Verification. After the key index verification succeeds, the receiver verifies the chained ring signature carried in the data packet.

Algorithm 3. Decrypt and Verify Packet

Input: Encrypted packet Pkt; path identifier pid_j; hop index i; key tree root key K_0; ring public key set $\mathcal{R}$; local verification state $state$
Output: Accepted data $m_{j,i}$ or $\perp$

Parameters:
  $PRF : \{0,1\}^\kappa \times \{0,1\}^* \to \{0,1\}^\kappa$
  $H : \{0,1\}^* \to \{0,1\}^\lambda$
  $Dec : \{0,1\}^\kappa \times \{0,1\}^* \to \{0,1\}^*$
  $\perp$: invalid output
$ctx^*_{j,i} \leftarrow pid_j \parallel Encode(i)$
$idx^*_{j,i} \leftarrow H(ctx^*_{j,i})$
$K_{j,i} \leftarrow PRF(K_0, idx^*_{j,i})$
$(nextHop, idx_{j,i}, m_{j,i}, \sigma_{j,i}, C') \leftarrow Dec(K_{j,i}, Pkt)$
if decryption fails **then**
  return $\perp$
end if
if $idx_{j,i} \neq idx^*_{j,i}$ **then**
  return $\perp$
end if
Retrieve previous signature digest σ_{prev} from $state$
$m'_{j,i} \leftarrow H(m_{j,i} \parallel \sigma_{\text{prev}})$
Verify $\sigma_{j,i}$ on $m'_{j,i}$ under ring $\mathcal{R}$
if verification fails **then**
  return $\perp$
end if
if $state$ is empty **then**
  $state \leftarrow \sigma_{j,i}$
else
  if σ_{prev} is inconsistent with $state$ **then**
    return $\perp$
  end if
end if
return $m_{j,i}$

The receiver applies the public ring signature verification algorithm to the signature $\sigma_{j,i}$. The verification takes as input the current-layer data $m_{j,i}$, the hash of the previous signature, and the ring public key set $\mathcal{R}$. A successful verification indicates that (i) the data was generated by a legitimate member of the ring, and (ii) the data content has not been tampered with during transmission.

4.3 Routing Phase

The routing phase specifies how encrypted data packets are forwarded along multiple payment paths without revealing global routing information, data, or keys, while ensuring correctness and unlinkability. DiVeR adopts a source-routing yet self-constraining mechanism, in which routing correctness is cryptographically embedded into multi-layer encrypted data packets and locally enforced by each forwarding node. For each payment path $P_j = (u_{j,1}, \ldots, u_{j,\ell_j})$, the payer constructs an onion-encrypted, multi-layer data packet $Pkt \cdot j$. Each encryption layer corresponds to a hop on the path and contains: (i) next-hop routing information $nh \cdot j, i$, (ii) a path-bound key index $idx_{j,i}$, (iii) differential data $m_{j,i}$, (iv) a chained ring signature component $\sigma_{j,i}$, and (v) the remaining ciphertext $C_{j,i+1}$.

Encryption at hop i uses a hop-specific key $K_{j,i}$, derived from the global key-tree root and a path-bound index. Consequently, node $u_{j,i}$ can decrypt only its corresponding layer and learns nothing beyond the information required for correct forwarding. Upon decryption, the node extracts the next-hop information $nh_{j,i}$ and forwards the remaining ciphertext $C_{j,i+1}$ to the designated successor. The routing process is stateless: nodes no global routing tables, are unaware of their absolute position or the total path length, and make routing decisions solely based on locally decrypted content, thereby preserving transmission privacy.

Unlike traditional source routing, which relies on honest forwarding, DiVeR enforces routing correctness cryptographically. The embedded key index $idx_{j,i}$ is deterministically bound to the path identifier pid_j and hop index i. Any redirection to an unintended node or replay at an incorrect hop results in a key-index mismatch during decryption, causing the packet to be rejected.

5 Security Analysis

In this section, we provide a formal security analysis of DiVeR. We first describe the system and adversary models, then state the cryptographic assumptions, and finally prove that DiVeR satisfies confidentiality, path-bound key soundness, routing correctness, differential data isolation, and end-to-end integrity under standard cryptographic assumptions.

5.1 System and Adversary Model

System Model. We consider a payment channel network represented as a graph $G = (V, E)$, where nodes correspond to users and edges correspond to payment channels. A payer selects a set of payment paths

$$\mathcal{P} = P_1, \ldots, P_M, \quad P_j = \langle u_{j,1}, \ldots, u_{j,L_j} \rangle, \tag{7}$$

and sends encrypted data packets along these paths using DiVeR. Each data packet is constructed via: (i) path- and hop-bound key derivation from a key tree rooted at K_0, (ii) multi-layer encryption binding routing and payload data, (iii) chained ring signatures binding data across multiple paths.

Adversary Model. We consider a probabilistic polynomial-time (PPT) adversary $\mathcal{A}$ with the following capabilities: (i) $\mathcal{A}$ may corrupt an arbitrary subset of intermediate users. (ii) $\mathcal{A}$ may observe, replay, drop, or modify encrypted packets. (iii) $\mathcal{A}$ does not know the master key K_0. (iv) Cryptographic primitives (PRF, hash function, symmetric encryption, ring signature) are assumed to be secure. The adversary's goal is to violate one of the following security properties.

5.2 Cryptographic Assumptions

Our analysis rely on standard cryptographic assumptions, including the security of the pseudorandom function (PRF) used for key derivation, which is indistinguishable from a random function, the IND-CPA security of the symmetric encryption scheme, the collision resistance of the hash function H, the unforgeability of ring signatures, and the linking soundness of chained ring signatures.

5.3 Secure Proofs

Theorem 1. ***Confidentiality.*** *For any PPT adversary that does not possess the hop-specific key $K_{j,i}$, the encryption layer intended for hop (j, i) reveals no information about its plaintext.*

Proof. Each hop-specific key $K_{j,i}$ is derived from a hierarchical key tree using the path context $\mathsf{ctx}_{j,i} = (\mathsf{pid}_j \parallel i)$. By the subtree security of the key tree, any key corresponding to a different hop $(j', i') \neq (j, i)$ is computationally indistinguishable from random to an adversary, even if multiple nodes are corrupted. Each encryption layer is protected under its hop-specific key using an IND-CPA secure encryption scheme. Hence, ciphertexts of non-intended layers reveal no information about their plaintexts, proving confidentiality.

Theorem 2. ***Path-Bound Key Soundness.*** *A packet encrypted for (pid_j, i) and hop i cannot be successfully decrypted at any other path or hop position.*

Proof. Key indices are deterministically computed as

$$\mathsf{idx}j, i = H(pid_j \parallel i). \tag{8}$$

At decryption, nodes recompute $\mathsf{idx}^*_{j,i}$ locally. Any path rebinding or hop mismatch immediately and reliably implies

$$\mathsf{idx}_{j,i} \neq \mathsf{idx}^*_{j,i}, \tag{9}$$

leading to rejection with overwhelming certainty. The collision resistance of H prevents adversarial index substitution, ensuring path-bound key soundness.

Theorem 3. ***Routing Correctness.*** *Any adversarial attempt to reroute or replay a packet at an incorrect hop is detected with overwhelming probability.*

Proof. Routing correctness is enforced by two complementary mechanisms. First, key-index verification cryptographically binds each decryption key to a specific path and hop. Second, the layered encryption structure prevents the decryption of any out-of-order layers. As a result, any packet replayed or forwarded at an incorrect hop necessarily fails key-index verification, and routing deviations are detected with overwhelming probability.

Theorem 4. ***differential Data Isolation.*** *For any two nodes $u_{j,i}$ and $u_{j',i'}$ with $(\mathsf{pid}_j, i) \neq (\mathsf{pid}_{j'}, i')$, data intended for $u_{j,i}$ is computationally indistinguishable from random to $u_{j',i'}$.*

Proof. Encryption keys for different nodes are derived from pairwise independent PRF inputs:

$$(\mathsf{pid}_j, i) \neq (\mathsf{pid}_{j'}, i'). \tag{10}$$

By the standard security of the PRF, the resulting keys are computationally indistinguishable. Consequently, ciphertexts intended for other nodes are computationally indistinguishable from random.

Theorem 5. *End-to-End Integrity.* *Any unauthorized modification of encrypted data is detected by the recipient.*

Proof. Each layer carries a chained ring signature

$$\sigma_{j,i} = \mathrm{RingSign}(H(m_{j,i} \parallel \sigma_{j,i-1})). \tag{11}$$

Any bit modification changes the hash input, causing verification failure cryptographically. Ring signature unforgeability prevents an adversary from generating a valid replacement signature, thereby ensuring integrity reliably.

Theorem 6. *Compositional Security of DiVeR.* *Under the stated standard cryptographic assumptions, DiVeR provably and simultaneously achieves confidentiality, path-bound key soundness, routing correctness, differential data isolation, and end-to-end integrity in a compositional manner.*

Proof. The result follows directly from Theorems 1–5, each of which establishes one security property under standard and independent cryptographic assumptions. Since the corresponding mechanisms are combined without sharing secret state or introducing circular dependencies, their composition preserves each individual guarantee. Therefore, all stated security properties jointly hold in the integrated DiVeR protocol under the assumed model.

6 Evaluation

To evaluate the performance of DiVeR in payment channel networks, we conduct extensive simulations based on the Lightning Network topology and compare DiVeR against state-of-the-art systems under the same experimental settings.

6.1 Settings

Implementation. We evaluate DiVeR via topology-based simulations using a real-world snapshot of the Lightning Network (LN), which consists of 10,529 nodes and 38,910 payment channels [2]. In the simulations, users transmit encrypted data to multiple recipients over multiple concurrent payment paths, following the routing and forwarding procedures defined by the protocol. All experiments are conducted on a machine equipped with an Intel i7 processor running at 3.2 GHz and 16 GB of memory.

Baselines. We compare DiVeR with representative state-of-the-art data transmission schemes for MPP networks, including AMHL [17], Rollercoaster [7], and PolySphinx [24]. AMHL adopts a sender-centric design, where the payer establishes separate communication channels with each intermediate user and the payee to deliver routing and control information. In contrast, Rollercoaster and PolySphinx follow a forwarding-based paradigm, in which encrypted messages are propagated through intermediate nodes along selected paths to reach the destination.

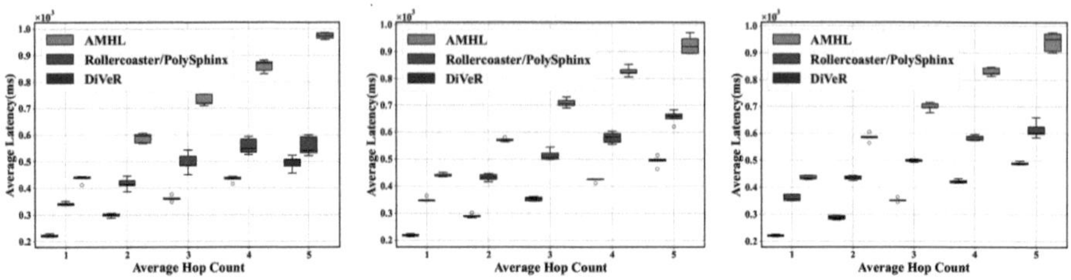

(a) Result with 10 nodes. (b) Result with 20 nodes. (c) Result with 30 nodes.

Fig. 2. Analysis of experimental results on average system delay.

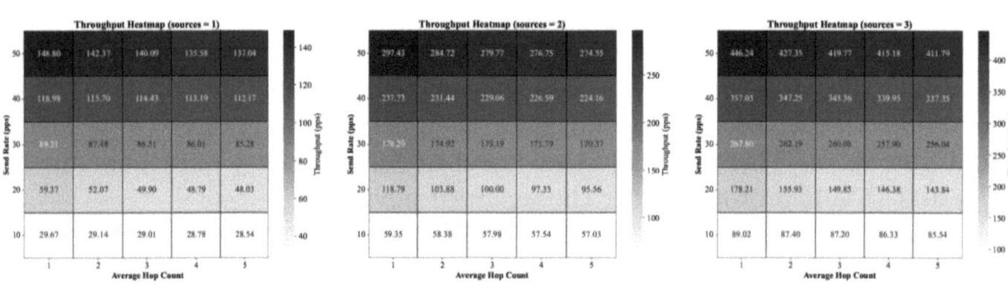

(a) Single-node source. (b) Two-node source. (c) Three-node source.

Fig. 3. Analysis of experimental results on the system throughput of DiVeR.

Metrics. We conduct an analysis by controlling the average hop count of payment paths and the packet transmission rate, and comprehensively evaluate the system in terms of average data transmission latency and throughput. Since PolySphinx only introduces a packet encryption design on top of Rollercoaster, while inheriting Rollercoaster's underlying data forwarding logic, the two schemes exhibit similar performance in terms of average latency and throughput. Consequently, they share the same experimental results for these metrics.

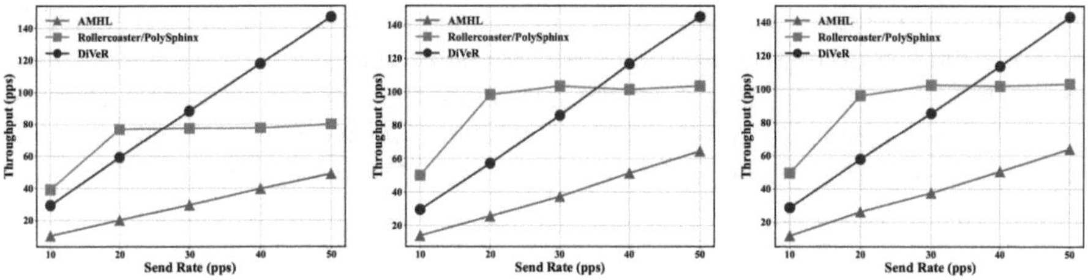

(a) Average hops: 2. (b) Average hops: 4. (c) Average hops: 6.

Fig. 4. Analysis of experimental results on system throughput.

6.2 Average Latency of DiVeR

Figure 2 presents an analysis of the average system latency of AMHL, Rollercoaster, PolySphinx, and DiVeR under different conditions. In evaluating the average system latency, since AMHL, Rollercoaster, and PolySphinx do not support data transmission from multiple sources, all experiments adopt a single-source data transmission model, with the sending rate fixed at 50 pps. Throughout the experiments, only the number of nodes in the network formed between the sender and the receiver, as well as the average hop count along the paths from the sender to the receiver, are varied.

As shown in Figs. 2a, 2b, and 2c, the average data transmission latency of AMHL, Rollercoaster, PolySphinx, and DiVeR increases as the average hop count between the sender and the receiver grows. This is because a larger average hop count implies a longer propagation path from the sender to the receiver, resulting in higher end-to-end latency. Moreover, by jointly examining the three subfigures in Fig. 2, it can be observed that the average transmission latency also increases with the number of nodes involved in the data transmission network between the sender and the receiver. As more nodes participate in the transmission, data must traverse additional intermediate users before reaching the receiver, which further contributes to the increase in average transmission latency.

A comparison among AMHL, Rollercoaster, PolySphinx, and DiVeR shows that the proposed DiVeR maintains low data transmission latency, regardless of increases in either the average hop count or the number of nodes in the transmission network. Compared with AMHL, DiVeR reduces transmission latency to 50.35% of the original, primarily because AMHL relies on establishing communication channels, and the channel setup process introduces additional delay. Compared with Rollercoaster and PolySphinx, DiVeR achieves a latency reduction of 170.48 ms. Since neither approach requires pre-established communication channels, this latency gap mainly stems from the continuous construction of subtree indices in Rollercoaster and PolySphinx during data transmission.

6.3 System Throughput Analysis

Figures 3 and 4 analyze the throughput of the AMHL, Rollercoaster, PolySphinx, and DiVeR systems. In Fig. 3, we conduct a detailed evaluation of DiVeR's throughput. Owing to the introduction of chained ring signatures, DiVeR enables multiple data sources to simultaneously transmit data to a receiver via multiple paths. Accordingly, Fig. 3 jointly examines the impact of three factors on DiVeR's throughput: the number of source nodes, the average hop count between the sender and the receiver, and the sending rate. The experimental results show that overall DiVeR's system throughput increases significantly with higher sending rates, a larger number of source nodes, and a smaller average hop count. In particular, when the sending rate is 50 pps and the average hop count is 1, the throughput with two sources is 1.99× that of a single source, while three sources achieve 2.99× the throughput of a single source.

Figure 4 presents a comparative analysis of the throughput performance of AMHL, Rollercoaster, PolySphinx, and DiVeR. In the experiments, a single source is used to transmit data, enabling a comprehensive comparison of system throughput under different average path lengths and packet sending rates. As shown in Figs. 4a, 4b, and 4c, for varying average hop counts, the throughput of AMHL, Rollercoaster/PolySphinx, and DiVeR consistently increases as the sending rate rises. At low packet sending rates, Rollercoaster/PolySphinx achieves higher throughput than the proposed DiVeR, since its output packets leverage tree-based forwarding via intermediate users, which temporarily improves system throughput. However, as the sending rate increases, the advantage of such intermediate-node-assisted tree forwarding diminishes, and DiVeR exhibits significantly higher throughput than Rollercoaster/PolySphinx. As illustrated in Fig. 4c, when the average hop count between the sender and receiver is six and the sending rate is 50 pps, DiVeR achieves 2.25× the throughput of AMHL and 1.38× that of Rollercoaster/PolySphinx.

7 Related Work

Payment channel networks were proposed to alleviate the scalability bottlenecks of blockchain systems by enabling off-chain transactions. The Lightning Network, introduced by Poon and Dryja [23], established bidirectional payment channels, and subsequent work formalized multi-hop routing to enable payments over multiple hops. Since then, extensive research has sought to improve the performance, security, and robustness of payment channel networks [3,8,26–28]. However, the single-path payment model commonly adopted in early designs often leads to channel imbalance and capacity fragmentation, reducing payment success rates.

To mitigate this limitation, researchers have explored MPP routing, where a payment is split into multiple partial payments and sent along different paths. Recent studies show that while multi-path routing can substantially improve success rates and performance in the Lightning Network, its effectiveness critically depends on careful protocol design due to routing congestion and security challenges [30]. Pickhardt and Richter [1] studied atomic MPPs, and Malavolta et al. [17] proposed Anonymous Multi-Hop Locks (AMHL) to provide strong atomicity and privacy guarantees. CAPE [6] further enhances privacy at the channel level using commitment-based techniques. However, these approaches primarily focus on payment correctness or channel-level privacy, and treat cryptographic data dissemination as a sender-centric process, requiring the payer to generate and transmit customized encrypted instructions to all intermediate users. They do not address efficient data dissemination or routing correctness in multi-hop, multi-path payment networks. More broadly, ensuring atomic and consistent execution across multiple distributed participants is a fundamental challenge in blockchain systems. For example, BrokerAS [25] studies fault-tolerant atomic cross-chain swaps, highlighting the inherent complexity of coordinating multiple parties under failures and adversarial conditions. Although targeting a different application setting, such work underscores the general difficulty of achieving atomicity and consistency, which also arises in routing.

In parallel, onion routing has been widely adopted for anonymous communication and hop-by-hop encrypted forwarding. The Tor network [5] and Sphinx [4] demonstrate how layered encryption enables correct forwarding while preserving privacy, and AMHP [31] applies onion routing to payment channels. Relatedly, StealthPath [10] studies privacy-preserving path validation in path-aware networks. However, both onion-routing–based and path-validation mechanisms are inherently designed for single-path forwarding and do not support key requirements of MPP routing, such as differential data delivery and cross-path consistency. Applying such techniques to multi-path settings therefore requires independent packet construction and verification per path, resulting in redundant encryption and transmission overhead.

Beyond payment channels, scalable data dissemination in multi-hop networks has been studied using redistribution- and replication-based approaches. Redistribution-based schemes, such as Rollercoaster [7], improve throughput by allowing intermediate nodes to forward received messages, but introduce additional trust assumptions and weaken end-to-end security guarantees. Consistency challenges in multi-hop data dissemination have also been examined in other distributed systems, such as sensing data sharing among IoT edge servers [13]. Replication-based schemes, including Loopix [22] and PolySphinx [24], duplicate encrypted messages along multiple paths, improving scalability and latency. However, these approaches inherently support only uniform data dissemination and cannot accommodate the differential data delivery required in routing.

8 Conclusion

We proposed DiVeR, a cryptographic data dissemination framework designed for multi-hop, multi-path payment routing, which supports differential data delivery and end-to-end verification. By integrating network topology information with key-treebased key derivation, DiVeR extends the self-routing property of onion encryption from single-path settings to general multi-path scenarios, while employing chained ring signatures to enable end-to-end verification across different paths and intermediate users. Through the introduction of chained ring signatures and key-index verification, receivers can efficiently detect data tampering and enforce cross-path data consistency without relying on trusted intermediaries or incurring excessive cryptographic complexity. Moreover, under standard cryptographic assumptions, DiVeR formally defines and rigorously proves its core security guarantees. Experimental evaluations demonstrate that, compared with systems such as AMHL, Rollercoaster, and PolySphinx, DiVeR achieves significantly lower latency and higher throughput, highlighting its strong practical advantages in scalability and efficiency.

Acknowledgements. This work was supported by the National Natural Science Foundation of China under Grant No. 62232002 and the Natural Science Foundation of Tianjin under Grant No. 24JCJQJC00270.

References

1. Amp: Atomic multi-path payments over lightning (2018). https://diyhpl.us/~bryan/irc/bitcoin/bitcoin-dev/linuxfoundation-pipermail/lightning-dev/2018-February/000993.txt
2. Real-world ln topology (2021). https://ln.bigsun.xyz/
3. Aumayr, L., et al.: Generalized channels from limited blockchain scripts and adaptor signatures. In: Proceedings of the Springer ASIACRYPT, pp. 635–664 (2021)
4. Danezis, G., Goldberg, I.: Sphinx: a compact and provably secure mix format. In: Proceedings of the IEEE S&P, pp. 269–282 (2009)
5. Dingledine, R., Mathewson, N., Syverson, P.F.: Tor: the second-generation onion router. In: Proceedings of the USENIX Association USENIX Security, pp. 303–320 (2004)
6. Gai, K., et al.: CAPE: commitment-based privacy-preserving payment channel scheme in blockchain. IEEE Trans. Dependable Secure Comput. **22**(4), 3977–3992 (2025)
7. Hugenroth, D., Kleppmann, M., Beresford, A.R.: Rollercoaster: an efficient group-multicast scheme for mix networks. In: Proceedings of the USENIX Association USENIX Security, pp. 3433–3450. USENIX Association (2021)
8. Kang, Z., Li, J., Shen, J., Han, J., Zuo, Y., Zhang, Y.: TFS-ABS: traceable and forward-secure attribute-based signature scheme with constant-size. IEEE Trans. Knowl. Data Eng. **35**(9), 9514–9530 (2023)
9. Kolachala, K., Ababneh, M., Vishwanathan, R.: RACED: routing in payment channel networks using distributed hash tables. In: Proceedings of the ACM AsiaCCS (2024)
10. Li, J., Su, Y., Lu, R., Su, Z., Meng, W., Shen, M.: Stealthpath: privacy-preserving path validation in the data plane of path-aware networks. IEEE Trans. Dependable Secure Comput. **22**(1), 192–204 (2025)
11. Liu, J.K., Wong, D.S.: Linkable ring signatures: security models and new schemes. In: Proceedings of the ICCSA, pp. 614–623. Springer (2005)
12. Liu, X., et al.: Top-k queries for categorized RFID systems. IEEE/ACM Trans. Network. **25**(5), 2587–2600 (2017)
13. Liu, X., et al.: Enabling consistent sensing data sharing among IoT edge servers via lightweight consensus. IEEE Trans. Comput. **74**(6), 2045–2057 (2025)
14. Liu, Y., Liang, W., Xie, K., Xie, S., Li, K., Meng, W.: Lightpay: a lightweight and secure off-chain multi-path payment scheme based on adapter signatures. IEEE Trans. Serv. Comput. **17**(4), 1622–1635 (2024)

15. Ma, J., et al.: Hydrachain: a cooperative MAPPO architecture for load balancing in IoT sharding blockchain. IEEE Internet Things J. **12**(15), 29397–29410 (2025)
16. Ma, L., Hu, D., Liu, X., Xu, H., Wang, J., Li, K.: AIGC-CM: an efficient and scalable blockchain solution for AIGC copyright management. In: Proceedings of the IEEE INFOCOM, pp. 1–10 (2025)
17. Malavolta, G., Moreno-Sanchez, P., Schneidewind, C., Kate, A., Maffei, M.: Anonymous multi-hop locks for blockchain scalability and interoperability. In: Proceedings of the ISOC NDSS (2019)
18. Miao, Y., Gai, K., Yu, J., Tan, Y., Zhu, L., Meng, W.: Blockchain-empowered keyword searchable provable data possession for large similar data. IEEE Trans. Inf. Forensics Secur. **20**, 1374–1389 (2025)
19. Ndolo, C., Tschorsch, F.: On the (not so) surprising impact of multi-path payments on performance and privacy in the lightning network. In: Proceedings of the Springer ESORICS Workshops, pp. 411–427. Springer (2023)
20. Panwar, G., Vishwanathan, R., Torres, G., Misra, S.: SPRITE: secure and private routing in payment channel networks. In: Proceedings of the ACM AsiaCCS (2024)
21. Pickhardt, R., Richter, S.: Optimally reliable & cheap payment flows on the lightning network. CoRR abs/2107.05322 (2021)
22. Piotrowska, A.M., Hayes, J., Elahi, T., Meiser, S., Danezis, G.: The loopix anonymity system. In: Proceedings of the USENIX Association USENIX Security, pp. 1199–1216 (2017)
23. Poon, J., Dryja, T.: The bitcoin lightning network: scalable off-chain instant payments (2016). https://static1.squarespace.com/static/6148a75532281820459770d1/t/61af971f7ee2b432f1733aee/1638897446181/lightning-network-paper.pdf
24. Schadt, D., Coijanovic, C., Weis, C., Strufe, T.: Polysphinx: extending the sphinx mix format with better multicast support. In: Proceedings of the IEEE S&P, pp. 4386–4404 (2024)
25. Shi, G., et al.: Brokeras: towards fault-tolerant atomic cross-chain swaps. In: Proceedings of the IEEE INFOCOM, pp. 1–10. IEEE (2025)
26. Sui, Z., Liu, J.K., Yu, J., Qin, X.: Monet: a fast payment channel network for scriptless cryptocurrency monero. In: Proceedings of the IEEE ICDCS, pp. 280–290 (2022)
27. Thyagarajan, S.A.K., Malavolta, G., Schmid, F., Schröder, D.: Verifiable timed linkable ring signatures for scalable payments for monero. In: Proceedings of the ESORICS, pp. 467–486 (2022)
28. Wang, H., Yang, Y., Wang, E., Liu, X., Wei, J., Wu, J.: Bilateral privacy-preserving worker selection in spatial crowdsourcing. IEEE Trans. Dependable Secure Comput. **20**(3), 2533–2546 (2023)
29. Wang, X., Lin, C., Huang, X., He, D.: Anonymity-enhancing multi-hop locks for monero-enabled payment channel networks. IEEE Trans. Inf. Forensics Secur. **19**, 2438–2453 (2024)
30. Weintraub, B., Kumble, S.P., Nita-Rotaru, C., Roos, S.: Payout races and congested channels: a formal analysis of security in the lightning network. In: Luo, B., Liao, X., Xu, J., Kirda, E., Lie, D. (eds.) Proceedings of the ACM CCS, pp. 2562–2576 (2024)
31. Zhang, Y., et al.: Anonymous multi-hop payment for payment channel networks. IEEE Trans. Dependable Secure Comput. **21**(1), 476–485 (2024)

Cryptography: Credentials, FE, FHE and PIR

Revocable Issuer-Hiding Anonymous Credential

Feifei Liu[1], Yangguang Tian[2], Long Meng[2], Liqun Chen[2], Yalan Wang[2], and Jianwei Liu[1](✉)

[1] School of Cyber Science and Technology, Beihang University, Beijing, China
{ffionliu,liujianwei}@buaa.edu.cn

[2] School of Computer Science and Electronic Engineering, University of Surrey, Guildford, UK
{yangguang.tian,long.meng,liqun.chen,yw0010}@surrey.ac.uk

Abstract. Issuer-Hiding Anonymous Credential (IHAC) is a cryptographic primitive, which enables users to authenticate themselves with fine-grained control over their credentials (certified attributes), without revealing the credential issuers. A state-of-the-art IHAC scheme, designed for Self-Sovereign Identity systems, was recently published by Sanders and Traoré at PET'24. However, this scheme does not support the revocation of credentials. It is well-known that revocation is essential for many secure applications. In this work, we introduce a revocable IHAC scheme. Our contributions are three-fold. First, we use the classical pairing-based accumulator with Sanders and Traoré's scheme to provide user revocation without compromising its unique features like compactness and issuer-hiding. Second, we prove the security of our construction under the well-studied q-Strong Diffie-Hellman (q-SDH) assumption, rather than the Generic Group Model (GGM) originally used by Sanders and Traoré. Third, our construction ensures optimal efficiency, as the accumulator-based revocation incurs only a small extra overhead to PET'24. Our implementation shows that when using 100 certified attributes and 20 issuers in an anonymous credential system, the Show and Verify protocol takes 3.15 s in total, only incurring a 2.5% increase compared to Sanders and Traoré's scheme.

Keywords: Anonymous credentials · Issuer-hiding · User revocation

1 Introduction

Anonymous credential (AC) [22] is designed for privacy-preserving authentication and authorization systems. AC enables users to prove possession of certified attributes (e.g., name, birthplace) without revealing their identities. To protect user privacy, AC schemes shall support selective disclosure and unlinkability. Selective disclosure allows users to reveal certain attributes for satisfying a predicate, while proving sensitive attributes like birthplace using zero knowledge (ZK) proofs; unlinkability guarantees that multiple credential shows cannot be

Y. Cao et al. (Eds.): SecureComm 2026, LNICST 704, pp. 401–429, 2027.
https://doi.org/10.1007/978-3-032-32764-2_19

linked to the same user. ACs have been widely adopted in industry, with prominent implementations such as Idemix (IBM) [17] and U-Prove (Microsoft) [44]. Notable applications include anonymous web browsing via Privacy Pass [29], private group formation in the Signal Messenger [21], Facebook's PrivateStats, which securely collects client data from WhatsApp clients. Furthermore, AC has been recommended by EU Digital Identity (EUDI) wallet [1], and standardized under ISO/IEC NP 24843 [2].

Current AC solutions consider issuer-hiding property for their applications, and we present three specific examples to show the importance of this desired property. For instance, in a national electronic identity system, regional authorities will issue credentials to residents within their jurisdiction. When presenting a credential attesting to a user's age (e.g., for credit card check) or residency status (e.g., for open banking), the knowledge of issuer will help the verifier to learn the user's age group or geographic origin, enabling unnecessary profiling or discrimination. In vehicular networks, car manufacturer issues credentials to their company vehicles for GPS tracking. If the manufacturer's affiliation information is revealed, the outsiders can link the company vehicles to the standard traffic patterns and learn their historical routes. In healthcare, where hospitals or clinics act as issuers. The registered patients may present their certificates to access medical services such as online GP appointments and/or prescriptions. Revealing the hospital/clinic name or ownership (e.g. public, private or charitable) will help outsiders to learn the patients medical needs or health conditions. The situation is even worse if the verifier and the issuer collude, leading to the full disclosure of a user's identification. To address these privacy concerns, issuer-hiding anonymous credential (IHAC) was introduced [10]. Briefly, IHAC enables users to anonymously prove possession of certified attributes and associated credentials, while no one can identify the actual authority during verification. This prevents verifiers, even collude with authorities, from learning user's sensitive information.

IHAC typically relies on *key-polices* [10,14,47], where a policy defines a set of authorized issuers public keys, and is specified by a verifier. During the credential showing, the user shows its credential was issued by one of the issuers in the policy for issuer-hiding. Another approach is to leverage delegatable signatures [9,16], which allow the root issuer to delegate signing capabilities to other issuers. Although this approach hides intermediate issuers, the verification process still requires the root issuer's public key. Moreover, the assumption of a single root issuer is often incompatible with decentralized scenarios. Therefore, we focus on policy-based IHAC in this work.

Generally, *security*, *revocability* and *efficiency* are critical features to an IHAC scheme. Firstly, it is preferable for IHAC schemes to prove their security under well-studied assumptions (e.g., DL, CDH, q-type variants). These assumptions usually offer a higher level of confidence as they are time-tested and have established soundness. In contrast, schemes proven under idealized models like the Generic Group Model (GGM) [49] often fall short in providing concrete security guarantees. Secondly, revocability ensures that compromised users or expired credentials can be revoked, preventing users from misusing their issued credentials. This property is particularly essential to dynamic or ad-hoc environments, such as access control and subscription services. Thirdly, an efficient revocation mechanism is needed in terms of computational cost and storage/communication overhead. However, state-of-the-art IHAC schemes [10,14,23,47] can not achieve security, revocability, and efficiency simultaneously. For example, IHAC schemes [10,14,47] lack user revocation. Moreover, the unforgeability analysis of [10,47] is proven under the GGM. Although [23] addresses user revocation, its verification process involves many pairing operations.

Revocation in IHAC usually relies on an accumulator [19]. Briefly, a trusted authority with a trapdoor will update the accumulator periodically by adding or deleting elements within a set where an accumulated element represents a user. Each non-revoked user receives a secret witness from the authority corresponding to an accumulated element. Later, the non-revoked user proves the ownership of the accumulated element and the witness in ZK. Another revocation approach is called Verifier-Local Revocation (VLR) [13]. In case of VLR, each user holds a signing key and a revocation token, while a verifier holds a revocation list consisting of a subset of revocation tokens. During verification, the verifier checks signatures (or proofs in IHAC) against the revocation list. If the check fails, the verifier accepts signatures (or proofs). However, the size of revocation list depends on the number of revoked users, leading to unscalable verification. Moreover, when we assume that issuers collude with verifiers, the issuer-hiding property cannot be achieved when applying VLR to IHAC. Therefore, we use accumulators to realize revocation in this work.

To this end, we seek to design a revocable IHAC scheme with enhanced security and optimal overhead. Our contributions can be summarized as follows:

- *New Constructions.* We introduce two new cryptographic primitives: revocable issuer-hiding authentication (RIHA) and revocable issuer-hiding anonymous credential (RIHAC). Essentially, we use an issuer-hiding authentication scheme [47] and a pairing-based accumulator [4] to build RIHA; we use RIHA and optimized membership proofs [52] to construct RIHAC.
- *Enhanced Security.* We prove the unforgeability of our constructions under well-studied q-Strong Diffie-Hellman (q-SDH) assumption rather than GGM used in [47]. We also show that our proposed schemes are unconditionally anonymous, maintaining [47]'s privacy guarantees.
- *Optimal Overhead.* We benchmark our proposed schemes and [47]. Our detailed implementations show that our RIHAC scheme incurs minimal extra overhead to realize revocation compared to PET'24 [47]. Consider an interactive Show and Verify protocol that involves 20 issuers and hides 50 attributes out of 100, our RIHAC takes 3.15 s, introducing 2.5% increase compared to PET'24.

2 Related Work

In this section, we provide a review of IHAC and accumulators.

2.1 Issuer-Hiding Anonymous Credentials (IHAC)

A central building block for IHAC is randomizable signatures, common instantiations include BBS [12], PS [45], and Structure-Preserving Signatures (SPS) [35]. These randomizable signatures allow anyone to transform a signature σ on a message m into a new signature σ'. Hanser et al. introduced SPS on equivalence classes (SPS-EQ) [33,37], or Equivalence Class Signatures (EQS) for short. SPS-EQ enables a message-signature pair (m, σ) to be transformed into (m', σ'), where (m, m') belongs to the same equivalence class. Later, Mercurial Signatures (MS) [25,27] were introduced by Crites et al. as a variant of EQS, extending the equivalence class to key space and enabling the randomization of (m, σ, pk). Combining these randomizable signatures with *key-policies* (i.e., specify a set of issuers that a verifier would accept a credential) offers a promising solution to construct IHAC, which is known as policy-based IHAC. Depending on which entity specifies the policy, IHAC schemes can be categorized into verifier-defined and user-defined versions.

Verifier-defined Policy. Bobolz et al. [10] introduced the first policy-based IHAC scheme. In their scheme, a verifier defines a policy that includes a set of issuers' public keys $\{ipk_i\}$ and SPS signatures $\{\sigma_i\}$ [35], where each public key is signed by the verifier. During proof generation, a user randomizes a SPS-based credential $cred_i$ and (ipk_i, σ_i); proves the randomized tuple $(cred'_i, ipk'_i, \sigma'_i)$ is valid, such that $cred'_i$ is valid against ipk'_i, and (ipk'_i, σ'_i) is valid against verifier's public key to ensure issuer-hiding property. By following the same policy as [10], Bosk et al. [14] presented an IHAC scheme based on PS signature [45] rather than SPS [35]. However, their scheme does not support selective disclosure. Connolly et al. proposed a revocable and auditable AC scheme called Protego [23] from an accumulator-based revocation mechanism [30] and a SPS-EQ [24]. They also extended it to an IHAC scheme called Protego Duo that employed the same policy as [10] and incorporated MS [25] to simplify the ZK proofs involved in the show protocol. However, Protego's verify protocol incurs many pairings, such as SPS-EQ requires 11 pairings, (blacklist-based) revocability requires 3 pairings, and auditability requires 7 pairings. Our RIHAC scheme requires 5 pairings only, where PS* requires 3 pairings and (whitelist-based) revocability requires 2 pairings. Moreover, Protego Duo cannot achieve perfect issuer-hiding, restricting issuers in a policy to be honest. Mir et al. [42] introduced an IHAC that allows a user to obtain and aggregate signatures from different issuers. They first provided two instantiations of aggregate signatures constructed on PS signatures [45] and SPS-EQ [26]. These signatures can be verified against randomized keys and signatures. They further extended their schemes to support issuer-hiding property for AC, allowing a verifier to define a set of issuers' public keys as [10]. Recently, Sanders et al. [47] proposed an IHAC scheme based on a modified PS signature [45] (we denote it as PS*). The PS* signature includes an additional component compared to the original, thus its verification relies on a set of issuers' public keys for issuer-hiding property. However, it lacks implementation and its unforgeability analysis relies on GGM. Our scheme achieves user revocation, provides open source and proves the revocable version of PS*'s unforgeability without GGM.

Table 1. A property-wise comparison of IHAC schemes. We list the following properties: selective disclosure (P1), policy audit (P2), user revocation (P3), perfect issuer-hiding (P4), open source (P5), base signature (P6), unforgeability assumption (P7). PS* indicates any PS signature variant. SXDH means Symmetric External Diffie-Hellman, and GPS means Generalized PS assumption.

Scheme	P1	P2	P3	P4	P5	P6	P7
[10]	✓	✓	✗	✓	✓	SPS	GGM
[32]	✓	✗	✗	✓	✗	SPS	DL
[14]	✗	✓	✗	✓	✓	PS	CDH
[24]	✓	✗	✗	✗	✗	EQS	SXDH
[23]	✓	✓	✓	✗	✓	EQS,MS	SXDH
[42]	✓	✓	✗	✗	✗	PS, EQS	GPS
[47]	✓	✓	✗	✓	✗	PS*	GGM
[51]	✗	✗	✗	✓	✓	BBS	q-SDH,SXDH
[48]	✓	✗	✗	✗	✓	EQS,MS	GGM
Ours	✓	✓	✓	✓	✓	PS*	q-SDH

User-Defined Policy. Elkhiyaoui et al. [32] introduced a new approach leveraging one-out-of-many proofs [36] (i.e., OR-proof) to construct IHAC. Concretely, a user obtains a SPS-based credential $cred_i$ from an issuer ipk_i. During the show protocol, the user generates a commitment of ipk_i, and produces an OR-proof demonstrating that the credential $cred_i$ is valid against the commitment. Later, Connolly et al. proposed an IHAC scheme [24] that combines AC framework [33] and a modified EQS [39]. To ensure issuer-hiding property, their show protocol employs OR-proof and a non-interactive ZK argument to prove that a randomized issuer's public key belongs to the equivalence class in a public-key set which represents a policy that involves multiple issuers' public keys. Recently, Ta et al. proposed an IHAC called Ring Referral [51]. During the show protocol, a user creates a proof that consists of commitments on multiple messages, a multi-message BBS signature, and an issuer's public key within a ring. Any verifier can verify the proof via pairing operations using those commitments without learning any committed values. One of unique features of Ring Referral is logarithmic verification without trusted setup due to the use of Dory compression technique [40]. We observe that Ring Referral is designed to hide all signed messages, thus lack of selective disclosure; and does not support user/issuer revocation. Considering issuer-hiding during both issue and show protocols, Shi et al. [48] developed an

IHAC by introducing an additional authority on top of multiple issuers. Briefly, the authority creates SPS-EQs [33] $\{\sigma_i\}$ on issuers' public keys $\{ipk_i\}$, so that they could hide their public keys and issue a credential *cred* for a user during issuance. Any verifier checks the proof against the authority's public key and the randomized $(ipk_i', \sigma_i', cred')$ during the show protocol.

To this end, we present a property-wise comparison between the relevant IHAC schemes and our work in Table 1. The policy audit means that anyone can verify the validity of a policy. The *perfect* issuer-hiding means that the issuer-hiding property is held even when verifiers collude with issuers. Our main contribution is to add pairing-based accumulator (see Sect. 2.2) to IHAC scheme in PET'24 [47] while maintaining its privacy guarantees (e.g., perfect issuer-hiding), and moreover, we prove our scheme's unforgeability under q-SDH assumption instead of GGM.

2.2 Accumulators

The research of accumulator is active yet diverse, including hash-based [15,28], RSA-based [6,20], pairing-based [4,18,34,43], lattice-based [41], code-based [5] and more. This work will focus on pairing-based accumulators because of their small storage overhead (e.g., small group sizes and short elements) and the accumulation of arbitrary elements. We refer to [7,31] for detailed comparisons.

Nguyen [43] introduced a dynamic accumulator based on q-SDH assumption with a unique feature called trapdoor-free. Specifically, any user can create a membership proof of an element to be accumulated by an accumulator *without* using a secret trapdoor; the trapdoor is required to update the accumulator by adding and removing elements. Au et al. [4] extended Nguyen's dynamic accumulator to support universality, which is known as Dynamic Universal Accumulator (DUA). Universality allows any user to produce both a membership proof of an accumulated element and a non-membership of an element that does not belong to an accumulator using the extended Euclidean algorithm. Universal accumulator supports both membership and non-membership proofs, while positive accumulator supports membership proofs only. Since the generation of non-membership proofs is more costly than generating membership proofs due to the polynomial division is required in the Euclidean algorithm, Karantaidou and Baldimsti [38] introduced a DUA with two positive accumulators. Compared to [4], accumulator manager creates two positive dynamic Nguyen accumulators [43] during setup, where the first accumulator stores all the accumulated elements, while the second accumulator stores the remaining elements in the accumulator domain. As a result, proving non-membership allows any user to show membership in the second accumulator. While this approach avoids the costly extended Euclidean algorithm, it introduces extra storage overhead. In this work, we use the DUA from Au et al. [4], mainly because the witness updates are performed without a secret trapdoor. Moreover, our scheme can be constructed from any q-SDH-based accumulator, regardless of whether it is a positive accumulator or not.

3 Preliminaries

In this section, we present the mathematical assumptions and the building blocks, which will be used in our proposed schemes.

3.1 Complexity Assumptions

Bilinear Map. A map of pairing e, from two source groups $\mathbb{G}_1$ and $\mathbb{G}_2$ to a target group $\mathbb{G}_T$, is called bilinear if for all $a, b \in \mathbb{Z}_p, g \in \mathbb{G}_1, \tilde{g} \in \mathbb{G}_2$, it holds that $e(g^a, \tilde{g}^b) = e(g, \tilde{g})^{ab}$. A pairing is asymmetric and Type-III if no efficiently computable homomorphism exists between $\mathbb{G}_1$ and $\mathbb{G}_2$. Let GGen be a probabilistic polynomial time (PPT) asymmetric group generator, that takes a security parameter λ as input and outputs group parameters $\mathsf{gp} = (p, \mathbb{G}_1, \mathbb{G}_2, \mathbb{G}_T, e, g, \tilde{g})$, where $(\mathbb{G}_1, \mathbb{G}_2, \mathbb{G}_T)$ are cyclic groups of prime order p, g and $\tilde{g}$ are the generators of $\mathbb{G}_1$ and $\mathbb{G}_2$, respectively.

q-SDH Assumption. We present a variant of q-SDH problem which is at least as hard as the original version in [11]. For simplicity, we still refer to it as q-SDH problem. The q-SDH problem is defined in bilinear group pair $(\mathbb{G}_1, \mathbb{G}_2)$ of prime order p with generator $g, \tilde{g}$, respectively. It requires that, given as input $(g, g^{\alpha}, g^{\alpha^2}, \ldots, g^{\alpha^q}, \tilde{g}, \tilde{g}^{\alpha}) \in \mathbb{G}_1^{q+1} \times \mathbb{G}_2^2$, where $\alpha \in \mathbb{Z}_p^*$ is a secret exponent, output a pair $(g^{\frac{1}{\alpha+m}}, m) \in \mathbb{G}_1 \times \mathbb{Z}_p^*$. A PPT adversary has advantage ϵ in solving q-SDH problem in $\mathbb{G}_1$ if

$$\mathsf{Adv}_{\mathcal{A}}^{q-SDH}(\lambda) = \Pr[\mathcal{A}(g, g^{\alpha}, g^{\alpha^2}, \ldots, g^{\alpha^q}, \tilde{g}, \tilde{g}^{\alpha}) = (g^{\frac{1}{\alpha+m}}, m)] \leq \epsilon.$$

We say the q-SDH assumption holds in $\mathbb{G}_1$ if ϵ is negligible in λ.

3.2 Pointcheval-Sanders (PS) Signatures

PS signatures [45] are designed for privacy-preserving cryptographic applications. They consist of two constant-sized elements in the group $\mathbb{G}_1$, regardless of the size n of the signed vector $(\mathsf{m}_1, \ldots, \mathsf{m}_n)$. These signatures support re-randomization, achieved by raising each element to the same random power, thereby providing privacy during multi-show. Also, the relatively simple algebraic structure allows them to interact seamlessly with other primitives, such as Schnorr's zero-knowledge proof systems, to construct more complex protocols. In this context, we present a variant of PS signatures that requires a trusted setup [45], where a set of issuers share the same public parameters $(X, \tilde{X})$. The unforgeability of this PS variant is proven under Assumption 2 from [45].

- $\mathsf{Setup}(1^{\lambda}, n)$. This algorithm chooses a type-III bilinear groups $(\mathbb{G}_1, \mathbb{G}_2, \mathbb{G}_T, e)$ of order p with generators $(g, \tilde{g}) \in \mathbb{G}_1 \times \mathbb{G}_2$. It picks $x \in \mathbb{Z}_p$, computes $(X, \tilde{X}) = (g^x, \tilde{g}^x)$ and publishes $\mathsf{pp} = [p, g, \tilde{g}, \mathbb{G}_1, \mathbb{G}_2, \mathbb{G}_T, e, X, \tilde{X}]$.
- $\mathsf{Keygen}(\mathsf{pp})$. This algorithm chooses n random elements $(y_1, \cdots, y_n)$ as secret key sk, and computes public key pk as $(\tilde{Y}_1, \cdots, \tilde{Y}_n) = (\tilde{g}^{y_1}, \cdots, \tilde{g}^{y_n})$.

- $\mathsf{Sign}(sk, (\mathsf{m}_1, \ldots, \mathsf{m}_n))$. Given n messages $(\mathsf{m}_1, \ldots, \mathsf{m}_n)$, this algorithm generates signature $(\sigma_1, \sigma_2) \leftarrow (g^r, X^r \cdot g^{r \sum_{i=1}^n y_i \cdot \mathsf{m}_i})$ for some random $r \in \mathbb{Z}_p$.
- $\mathsf{Verify}(pk, (\mathsf{m}_1, \ldots, \mathsf{m}_n), \sigma_1, \sigma_2)$. This algorithm checks whether $\mathsf{m}_i \neq 0$ for all $i \in [1, n]$ and verifies if $e(\sigma_1, \tilde{X} \cdot \prod_{i=1}^n \tilde{Y}_i^{\mathsf{m}_i}) = e(\sigma_2, \tilde{g})$. If both conditions are satisfied, it returns 1; otherwise, returns 0.

3.3 Pairing-Based DUA

We give a brief review of the q-SDH secure DUA proposed by Au et al. [4]. For clarity, the DUA is presented with relevant algorithms, while the full scheme is referred to Appendix A. The accumulator manager maintains a white list $\mathcal{WL}$ containing non-revoked identities. We present the algorithms of the DUA scheme below, and especially, we use the algorithms that support an optional input of the trapdoor (denoted $[s]$). In trapdoor-free DUA, users can compute v and update their witnesses without s.

- $\mathsf{DUA.Setup}(1^\lambda) \rightarrow \mathsf{Dp}$. This algorithm takes a security parameter λ as input, chooses type-III pairings $(\mathbb{G}_1, \mathbb{G}_2, \mathbb{G}_T, e)$ of order p, along with generators $(g, \tilde{g}) \in \mathbb{G}_1 \times \mathbb{G}_2$. The elements $\{x_1, \cdots, x_q\}$ in list $\mathcal{WL}$ represent individual users. The algorithm outputs public parameters $\mathsf{Dp} = [p, q, g, \tilde{g}, \mathbb{G}_1, \mathbb{G}_2, \mathbb{G}_T, e, \mathcal{WL}]$, where q is maximum capacity of the accumulator.
- $\mathsf{DUA.KeyGen}(1^\lambda, \mathsf{Dp}) \rightarrow (sk_{\mathsf{acc}}, pk_{\mathsf{acc}})$. Let $s \in \mathbb{Z}_p^*$ be the accumulator manager's secret key sk_{acc} (trapdoor), computes $pk_{\mathsf{acc}} \leftarrow (\{g_\gamma = g^{s^\gamma}\}_{\gamma \in [0,q]}, \tilde{g}^s)$.
- $\mathsf{DUA.Eval}([s], \mathcal{WL}) \rightarrow v$. Let $v(s) = \prod_{x_u \in \mathcal{WL}}(s + x_u) = \sum_{\gamma=0}^q \mu_\gamma s^\gamma$ be the accumulator polynomial, where μ_γ is the coefficient of s^γ, and $u \in [1, q]$. The manager can compute the accumulator value $v \leftarrow g^{\prod_{x_u \in \mathcal{WL}}(s+x_u)} = g^{\sum_{\gamma=0}^q \mu_\gamma s^\gamma}$. Therefore, anyone without trapdoor s can obtain v by computing $v \leftarrow \prod_{\gamma=0}^q g_\gamma^{\mu_\gamma} = g^{\sum_{\gamma=0}^q \mu_\gamma s^\gamma}$, where $g_\gamma = g^{s^\gamma}$.
- $\mathsf{DUA.WitCreate}([s], v, x_u) \rightarrow w_u$. The witness for element x_u being accumulated in v can be used to generate membership proof for x_u. The witness can be computed by the manager as $w_u \leftarrow v^{\frac{1}{x_u+s}}$ or $w_u \leftarrow \prod_{\gamma=0}^{q-1} g_\gamma^{\mu'_\gamma}$ by anyone without s.
- $\mathsf{DUA.MemVerify}(v, x_u, w_u) \rightarrow \{0, 1\}$. The membership proof of x_u being accumulated in v can be verified by checking $e(w_u, \tilde{g}^s \tilde{g}^{x_u}) = e(v, \tilde{g})$. This algorithm returns 1 if the above equation holds, and 0 otherwise.

4 Revocable Issuer-Hiding Authentication

In this section, we introduce a cryptographic primitive called Revocable Issuer-Hiding Authentication (RIHA). This authentication mechanism is designed to support issuer-hiding and user revocability. For construction, we incorporate a fully trusted revocation authority whose task is to manage accumulators for updating users' memberships, into an issuer-hiding authentication scheme described in [47]. For security, we prove its unforgeability under q-SDH assumption rather than GGM used in [47]. For privacy, the issuer-hiding property remains the same as [47]. We focus on full disclosure in this section; a user simply discloses all its attributes during credential shows. The selective disclosure variant is presented in Sect. 5.

4.1 Syntax

Our RIHA scheme involves multiple users $\mathcal{U}$, issuers $\mathcal{I}$, verifiers $\mathcal{V}$ and a single revocation authority $\mathcal{R}$, where each user is associated with a set of attributes. The syntax is defined as follows.

- $\mathsf{Setup}(1^\lambda, q, n, \tilde{n}) \rightarrow \mathsf{pp}$. This algorithm takes security parameter λ, and integers $q, n, \tilde{n}$ as input, outputs system parameters pp, allowing $\tilde{n}$ issuers to sign n attributes and q identities. It also allows an authority $\mathcal{R}$ to create an empty public list $\mathcal{WL}$ with respect to non-revoked identities, and the list records at most q identities. pp is implicit to all the following algorithms.
- $\mathsf{KeyGen}(\mathsf{pp}) \rightarrow ((sk_I, pk_I), (sk_\mathcal{R}, pk_\mathcal{R}), v)$. This algorithm enables each issuer to generate a key pair $(sk_I, pk_I) = \{(sk_{j,i}, pk_{j,i})\}$ and $\mathcal{R}$ to generate a key pair $(sk_\mathcal{R}, pk_\mathcal{R})$, where $j \in [1, \tilde{n}], i \in [1, n+1]$. Besides, $\mathcal{R}$ can update v using $sk_\mathcal{R}$ based on $\mathcal{WL}$. Note that I refers to j-th issuer with a set of keys $\{(sk_{j,i}, pk_{j,i})\}$.
- $\mathsf{Issue}(sk_I, (\mathsf{m}_1, \cdots, \mathsf{m}_{n+1}), v) \rightarrow cred$. Given a set of attributes $(\mathsf{m}_1, \cdots, \mathsf{m}_n)$ from a user, an issuer with sk_I chooses an identity m_{n+1} and returns a credential $cred = (w, \sigma)$, where w is a proof on (m_{n+1}, v) such that $\mathsf{m}_{n+1} \in \mathcal{WL}$; and σ is a signature on $(\mathsf{m}_1, \cdots, \mathsf{m}_{n+1})$. Note that m_{n+1} is not equal to any attributes in $(\mathsf{m}_1, \cdots, \mathsf{m}_n)$. The generation of v can be referred to $\mathsf{DUA.WitCreate}$ in Sec 3.3, while its update procedure is provided in Appendix A.
- $\mathsf{UVerify}(pk_I, (\mathsf{m}_1, \cdots, \mathsf{m}_{n+1}), cred, v) \rightarrow \{0, 1\}$. The user checks the proof w against $(v, pk_\mathcal{R})$ and the signature σ against $(pk_I, pk_\mathcal{R})$, outputs 1 (valid) or 0 (invalid).
- $\mathsf{SetPolicy}(\{\tilde{Y}_{j,1}\}_{j \in \mathcal{J}_1}, \cdots, \{\tilde{Y}_{j,n+1}\}_{j \in \mathcal{J}_{n+1}}) \rightarrow (sk_\mathcal{P}, pk_\mathcal{P})$. This algorithm is run by a verifier, who takes a policy $\mathcal{P}$ consisting of a set of public keys as input, outputs a policy-based key pair $(sk_\mathcal{P}, pk_\mathcal{P})$.
- $\mathsf{AuditPolicy}(pk_\mathcal{P}, \mathcal{P}) \rightarrow \{0, 1\}$. This algorithm takes $(\mathcal{P}, pk_\mathcal{P})$ as input, outputs 1 or 0.
- $\mathsf{Show}((\mathsf{m}_1, \cdots, \mathsf{m}_{n+1}), cred, pk_I, \mathcal{P}, pk_\mathcal{P}, v) \rightarrow \Theta$. This algorithm is run by the user, who takes $(\mathsf{m}_1, \cdots, \mathsf{m}_{n+1})$, $cred$, $(pk_I, pk_\mathcal{P})$ and v as input, outputs a proof Θ.
- $\mathsf{Verify}(\Theta, (\mathsf{m}_1, \cdots, \mathsf{m}_{n+1}), \mathcal{P}, sk_\mathcal{P}, v) \rightarrow \{0, 1\}$. The verifier outputs 1 if attributes $(\mathsf{m}_1, \cdots, \mathsf{m}_{n+1})$ associated with proof Θ satisfy policy $\mathcal{P}$, or 0.

4.2 Security Requirements

Unforgeability. Informally, adversary (even if collude with issuers) aims to claim the possession of a credential on attributes $(\mathsf{m}_1, \cdots, \mathsf{m}_{n+1})$ satisfying a policy $\mathcal{P}$ chosen by a verifier, *with the condition that its identity* m_{n+1} *does not belong to white-list (i.e., revoked identity).* This must be true even if attributes $(\mathsf{m}_1, \cdots, \mathsf{m}_n)$ have been signed by issuers. This is a stronger version of unforgeability than [47] assuming that all issuers are honest in policy $\mathcal{P}$. The formal definition of unforgeability utilizes the following oracles.

- $\mathcal{O}\mathsf{Add}(I)$: on input I, this oracle generates an issuer key pair (sk_I, pk_I) and returns pk_I to adversary. This oracle records all public keys in set $\mathcal{K}$.
- $\mathcal{O}\mathsf{Corrupt}(I)$: on input I, this oracle returns sk_I to adversary. This oracle aborts if adversary queries authority $\mathcal{R}$.
- $\mathcal{O}\mathsf{Update}(\mathsf{m}_{n+1})$: on input an identity m_{n+1}, this oracle either adds it to or deletes it from list $\mathcal{WL}$ then returns the updated v to adversary.
- $\mathcal{O}\mathsf{Issue}(pk_I, (\mathsf{m}_1, \cdots, \mathsf{m}_{n+1}))$: on input a set of $n+1$ attributes and an issuer's public key pk_I, this oracle outputs a credential *cred*.
- $\mathcal{O}\mathsf{SetPolicy}(\{pk_{j,1}\}_{j\in\mathcal{J}_1}, \cdots, \{pk_{j,n+1}\}_{j\in\mathcal{J}_{n+1}})$: on input a policy $\mathcal{P} = (\{pk_{j,1}\}_{j\in\mathcal{J}_1}, \cdots, \{pk_{j,n+1}\}_{j\in\mathcal{J}_{n+1}})$, this oracle creates $(sk_\mathcal{P}, pk_\mathcal{P})$ for $\mathcal{P}$ and returns $pk_\mathcal{P}$ to adversary.
- $\mathcal{O}\mathsf{Show}((\mathsf{m}_1, \cdots, \mathsf{m}_{n+1}), pk_\mathcal{P}, \mathcal{P})$: this oracle allows adversary to make show queries on $(\mathsf{m}_1, \cdots, \mathsf{m}_{n+1})$. This oracle aborts if $pk_\mathcal{P}$ was not previously returned by $\mathcal{O}\mathsf{SetPolicy}$ on $\mathcal{P}$, or outputs a proof Θ.
- $\mathcal{O}\mathsf{Verify}(\Theta, (\mathsf{m}_1, \cdots, \mathsf{m}_{n+1}), \mathcal{P}, sk_\mathcal{P}, v)$: this oracle runs $\mathsf{Verify}(\Theta, (\mathsf{m}_1, \cdots, \mathsf{m}_{n+1}), \mathcal{P}, sk_\mathcal{P}, v)$ and outputs bit b.

An RIHA scheme is unforgeable if for any PPT adversary $\mathcal{A}$, $\mathsf{Adv}_\mathcal{A}^{uf}$ is negligible in the unforgeability experiment $\mathsf{Exp}_\mathcal{A}^{uf}(1^\lambda, q, n, \tilde{n})$ shown in Fig. 1.

Issuer-Hiding. Issuer-hiding ensures that a verifier cannot identify the specific issuer associated with the proof Θ in the show protocol, even if the verifier colludes with all issuers and $\mathcal{R}$. In the formal definition, adversary outputs $(\mathsf{m}_1, \cdots, \mathsf{m}_{n+1})$ along with a policy consisting of a set of public keys $\mathcal{P} = (\{pk_{b,1}\}, \cdots, \{pk_{b,n+1}\})$, where $b \in \{0, 1\}$. Furthermore, adversary produces $cred^{(0)}$and $cred^{(1)}$, along with the elements in $pk_\mathcal{P}$ that will be used in the Show protocol. These elements generated by adversary should pass the sanity checks enforced by AuditPolicy and UVerify. Adversary keeps some state *st* and has access to the following oracles:

- $\mathcal{O}\mathsf{Corrupt}(\mathcal{R})$: on input $\mathcal{R}$, this oracle returns $sk_\mathcal{R}$ to adversary.
- $\mathcal{O}\mathsf{Show}((\mathsf{m}_1, \cdots, \mathsf{m}_{n+1}), cred, pk_I, \mathcal{P}, pk_\mathcal{P})$: this oracle simulates the behavior of a user in the show protocol, and adversary has full control of its inputs as long as $\mathsf{AuditPolicy}(\mathcal{P}, pk_\mathcal{P}) = 1$.

An RIHA scheme is issuer-hiding if $\mathsf{Adv}_\mathcal{A}^{ih}$ is negligible for any PPT adversary $\mathcal{A}$ in the issuer-hiding experiment shown in Fig. 1.

Unforgeability $\mathsf{Exp}_{\mathcal{A}}^{uf}(1^\lambda, q, n, \tilde{n})$

(1) $\mathsf{pp} \leftarrow \mathsf{Setup}(1^\lambda, q, n, \tilde{n})$
(2) $\mathcal{P} = (\{pk_{j,1}\}_{j\in\mathcal{J}_1}, \cdots, \{pk_{j,n+1}\}_{j\in\mathcal{J}_{n+1}}) \leftarrow \mathcal{A}^{\mathcal{O}}(\mathsf{pp})$
(3) For all $(pk_1, \cdots, pk_{n+1}) \in \mathcal{K}$, if $\exists i \in [1, n+1]$ and $j_i \in \mathcal{J}_i$ such that $pk_{j_i,i} \neq pk_i$, return 0
(4) $(sk_{\mathcal{P}}, pk_{\mathcal{P}}) \leftarrow \mathsf{SetPolicy}(\mathcal{P})$
(5) $(\Theta, \mathsf{m}_1, \cdots, \mathsf{m}_{n+1}) \leftarrow \mathcal{A}^{\mathcal{O}}(\mathsf{pp}, \mathcal{P}, pk_{\mathcal{P}}, v)$
(6) If $\mathsf{m}_{n+1} \in \mathcal{WL}$, return 0
(7) Return $b \leftarrow [\mathcal{A}(), \mathsf{Verify}((\Theta, \mathsf{m}_1, \cdots, \mathsf{m}_{n+1}), \mathcal{P}, sk_{\mathcal{P}}, v)]$

Issuer-Hiding $\mathsf{Exp}_{\mathcal{A}}^{ih}(1^\lambda, q, n, \tilde{n})$

(1) $\mathsf{pp} \leftarrow \mathsf{Setup}(1^\lambda, q, n, \tilde{n})$
(2) $(\mathsf{m}_1, \cdots, \mathsf{m}_{n+1}, pk_{\mathcal{P}}, cred^{(0)}, cred^{(1)}, pk_I^{(0)}, pk_I^{(1)}) \leftarrow \mathcal{A}^{\mathcal{O}}(pp, st)$
(3) If $\mathsf{AuditPolicy}(\{pk_I^{(0)}, pk_I^{(1)}\}, pk_{\mathcal{P}}) = 0$, return 0
(4) If $\mathsf{UVerify}(pk_I^{(b)}, (\mathsf{m}_1^{(b)}, \cdots, \mathsf{m}_{n+1}^{(b)}), cred^{(b)}, v) = 0$ for some $b \in \{0, 1\}$, return 0
(5) $b' \leftarrow [\mathsf{Show}((\mathsf{m}_1^{(b)}, \cdots, \mathsf{m}_{n+1}^{(b)}), cred^{(b)}, pk_I^{(b)}, \mathcal{P}, pk_{\mathcal{P}}), \mathcal{A}^{\mathcal{O}}(pp, st)]$
(6) Return $(b' = b)$

Fig. 1. Security requirements for RIHA scheme

4.3 Construction

The construction of the proposed RIHA leverages a pairing-based accumulator DUA [4] and an issuer-hiding authentication scheme [47]. We sketch a DUA construction in Sect. 3.3. The manager $\mathcal{R}$ is responsible for updating accumulators and maintaining a whitelist $\mathcal{WL}$.

- $\mathsf{Setup}(1^\lambda, q, n, \tilde{n}) \rightarrow \mathsf{pp}$. This algorithm runs $\mathsf{Dp} \leftarrow \mathsf{DUA.Setup}$ and outputs public parameters $\mathsf{pp} \leftarrow \mathsf{Dp} = [p, g, \tilde{g}, \mathbb{G}_1, \mathbb{G}_2, \mathbb{G}_T, e, \mathcal{WL}]$, where $q, n, \tilde{n}$ denoting the maximum number of users, the number of attributes, and the number of issuers, respectively. The index $i \in [1, n]$ represents an attribute, $j \in [1, \tilde{n}]$ represents an issuer, and $u \in [1, q]$ represents a user.
- $\mathsf{KeyGen}(\mathsf{pp})$. This algorithm considers two cases:
  - $\mathsf{IKeyGen}(\mathsf{pp}) \rightarrow (sk_I, pk_I)$. Each issuer generates key pair $(sk_I, pk_I) = \{(sk_{j,i}, pk_{j,i})\}$, where $\{sk_{j,i} \leftarrow y_{j,i}\} \in \mathbb{Z}_p^{n+1}$ and $\{pk_{j,i} \leftarrow \tilde{Y}_{j,i} = \tilde{g}^{y_{j,i}}\}$, for $i \in [1, n+1], j \in [1, \tilde{n}]$.
  - $\mathsf{RKeyGen}(\mathsf{pp}) \rightarrow (sk_{\mathcal{R}}, pk_{\mathcal{R}}, v)$. $\mathcal{R}$ runs $\mathsf{DUA.KeyGen}$ to obtain $(sk_{\mathcal{R}}, pk_{\mathcal{R}}) = (s, \{g^{s^\gamma}\}_{\gamma\in[0,q]}, \tilde{g}^s)$. Also, it runs $\mathsf{DUA.Eval}$ to accumulate the elements in $\mathcal{WL}$ into $v \leftarrow g^{\prod_{x_u\in\mathcal{WL}}(s+x_u)}$.
- $\mathsf{Issue}(sk_I, (\mathsf{m}_1, \cdots, \mathsf{m}_{n+1}), v) \rightarrow cred$. Upon an issue request from a user with attributes $(\mathsf{m}_1, \cdots, \mathsf{m}_n)$, an issuer I holding key pairs $\{(sk_{I,i}, pk_{I,i})\}_{i\in[1,n+1]}$ chooses the user's identity x_u, runs $\mathsf{DUA.WitCreate}$ to obtain a membership witness $w_u \leftarrow \prod_{\gamma=0}^{q-1} g_\gamma^{\mu_\gamma}$ and computes a PS-type signature $(\sigma_1, \sigma_2) \leftarrow (g^r, g^{sr} g^{(\sum_{i=1}^{n+1} y_{I,i}\mathsf{m}_i)r})$ on $(\mathsf{m}_1, \cdots, \mathsf{m}_n, \mathsf{m}_{n+1})$, where $r \in \mathbb{Z}_p$ and $\mathsf{m}_{n+1} = x_u$. The issuer then returns a credential $cred = (\sigma_1, \sigma_2, w_u)$ to the user. Note that this issuance protocol involves no interaction between any issuer and $\mathcal{R}$, as w_u can be computed without $\mathcal{R}$'s secret key s.

- $\mathsf{UVerify}(pk_I, (\mathsf{m}_1, \cdots, \mathsf{m}_{n+1}), cred, v) \to \{0, 1\}$. The user verifies the correctness of the received credential by first running $\mathsf{DUA.MemVerify}$, that is checking $e(w_u, \tilde{g}^{x_u}\tilde{g}^s) = e(v, \tilde{g})$. Next, it checks $e(\sigma_1, \tilde{g}^s \prod_{i=1}^{n+1} \tilde{Y}_{I,i}^{\mathsf{m}_i}) = (\sigma_2, \tilde{g})$. If both checks hold, the user stores credential *cred*.
- $\mathsf{SetPolicy}(\{\tilde{Y}_{j,1}\}_{j\in\mathcal{J}_1}, \cdots, \{\tilde{Y}_{j,n+1}\}_{j\in\mathcal{J}_{n+1}}) \to (sk_{\mathcal{P}}, pk_{\mathcal{P}})$. A verifier begins by selecting $n + 1$ sets of allowed issuers' public keys $(\{\tilde{Y}_{j,1}\}_{j\in\mathcal{J}_1}, \cdots, \{\tilde{Y}_{j,n+1}\}_{j\in\mathcal{J}_{n+1}})$, such that $\tilde{Y}_{j_1,i_1} \neq \tilde{Y}_{j_2,i_2}$ for all pairs $(j_1, i_1) \neq (j_2, i_2)$. Here, $\mathcal{J}_i$ represents the set of allowed issuers corresponding to the attribute with position i. Given these keys, the verifier decides a policy as follows. First, the verifier chooses $(a, \{b_i\}_{i\in[1,n+1]} \in \mathbb{Z}_p^{n+2})$ as $sk_{\mathcal{P}}$ and computes $\tilde{S} = \tilde{g}^a, \tilde{T}_{j,i} \leftarrow (\tilde{Y}_{j,i} \cdot \tilde{g}^{b_i})^a$, for $i \in [1, n+1]$ and $j \in \mathcal{J}_i$. Then, the verifier generates a ZK proof $\pi_{\mathcal{P}}$ that elements $\tilde{T}_{j,i}$ are well formed. Eventually, the verifier outputs the policy $pk_{\mathcal{P}} = (\pi_{\mathcal{P}}, \{\tilde{g}^{b_i(|\mathcal{J}_i|-1)}\}_{i\in[1,n+1]}, \tilde{S}, \{\tilde{T}_{j,1}\}_{j\in\mathcal{J}_1}, \cdots, \{\tilde{T}_{j,n+1}\}_{j\in\mathcal{J}_{n+1}})$.
- $\mathsf{AuditPolicy}(pk_{\mathcal{P}}, \mathcal{P}) \to \{0, 1\}$. The policy can be publicly verified through ZK proof $\pi_{\mathcal{P}}$. The algorithm checks the validity of $\pi_{\mathcal{P}}$ and outputs 1 if the proof is valid; otherwise, it outputs 0.
- $\mathsf{Show}((\mathsf{m}_1, \cdots, \mathsf{m}_{n+1}), cred, pk_I, \mathcal{P}, pk_{\mathcal{P}}, v) \to \Theta$. The user first checks if the public key $pk_I = (\tilde{Y}_{I,1}, \cdots, \tilde{Y}_{I,n+1})$ from issuer I associated with the credential $(\sigma_1, \sigma_2, w_u)$ is compatible with policy $\mathcal{P}$. Specifically, it checks $I \in \mathcal{J}_i$ for all $i \in [1, n+1]$. Next, it randomizes signature by setting $\sigma_1' = \sigma_1^{r'}, \sigma_2' = \sigma_2^{r'} \cdot (\sigma_1')^{-t}$, where $(r', t) \in \mathbb{Z}_p^2$. The user then computes $\tilde{\sigma} \leftarrow \tilde{S}^t \prod_{i=1}^{n+1} [\prod_{j\in\mathcal{J}_i\setminus\{I\}} \tilde{T}_{j,i}]^{\mathsf{m}_i}$, and sends $(\Theta = (\sigma_1', \sigma_2', \tilde{\sigma}, w_u), (\mathsf{m}_1, \cdots, \mathsf{m}_{n+1}))$ to the verifier.
- $\mathsf{Verify}(\Theta, (\mathsf{m}_1, \cdots, \mathsf{m}_{n+1}), \mathcal{P}, sk_{\mathcal{P}}, v)] \to \{0, 1\}$. Verifier performs the following checks and returns 1 if all of them are correct.
  1. $\sigma_1' \neq 1$;
  2. For all $i \in [1, n+1] : \mathsf{m}_i \neq 0$;
  3. Runs $\mathsf{DUA.MemVerify}$ to verify the equation
  $$e(w_u, \tilde{g}^s \tilde{g}^{x_u}) = e(v, \tilde{g});$$
  4. Verifies the following equation:
  $$e(\sigma_1', \tilde{g}^s \tilde{\sigma}^{-\frac{1}{a}} \prod_{i=1}^{n+1} [\tilde{g}^{b_i(|\mathcal{J}_i|-1)} \prod_{j\in\mathcal{J}_i} \tilde{Y}_{j,i}]^{\mathsf{m}_i}) = e(\sigma_2', \tilde{g}).$$

Then, we explain the Issue protocol. An issued credential contains a PS signature and a witness. Specifically, an issuer creates a witness w_u of an identity element x_u, and signs user attributes and identity element via PS-type signature. To support "dynamic" property of accumulator such that the manager with its trapdoor updates the accumulator by adding/deleting other identity elements, the user with PS-signed identity element can update witness from w_u to w_u' without interacting with anyone or re-running the issue protocol. We stress that the issuer generates the membership witness w_u without using the manager's trapdoor. Besides, this witness-based PS's unforgeability analysis relies on q-strong assumption, which differs from the GGM-based PS signature.

The correctness of RIHA can be referred to Appendix D.

4.4 Security Analysis

Theorem 1. *The RIHA scheme is unforgeable if the q-SDH assumption holds in $\mathbb{G}_1$.*

Theorem 2. *The RIHA scheme ensures issuer-hiding if the zero-knowledge proof π is sound.*

Proof Sketch. The unforgeability of RIHA is proved by reduction to the q-SDH assumption. At a high level, a successful adversary that outputs a valid proof for an identity not contained in the whitelist must implicitly construct a valid accumulator witness for a non-accumulated element. Such a witness can be transformed into a solution to the underlying q-SDH challenge.

The issuer-hiding property of RIHA is shown via a standard game-hopping argument. First, we rule out malformed policies by relying on the soundness of the policy proof $\pi_{\mathcal{P}}$. Then, after credential re-randomization, the challenge transcript becomes independent of the actual issuer index, so the adversary's distinguishing advantage is negligible. □

Detailed proofs appear in Appendix D.

5 Revocable Issuer-Hiding Anonymous Credential

In this section, we introduce Revocable Issuer-Hiding Anonymous Credential (RIHAC). RIHAC supports selective disclosure; users can selectively disclose any subset of attributes. We realize it via Schnorr-like ZK proofs.

5.1 Syntax

The syntax of RIHAC is identical to RIHA except Show and Verify protocols. Before Show and Verify protocols, all elements in $\mathcal{WL}$ are accumulated to v, credential *cred* is issued based on attributes $(\mathsf{m}_1, \cdots, \mathsf{m}_{n+1})$, and verifier defines a policy $\mathcal{P}$. In the Show protocol, users specify an index set $\mathcal{D}$ of disclosed attributes and an index set $\overline{\mathcal{D}}$ of undisclosed attributes, where $\overline{\mathcal{D}} \cup \mathcal{D} = [1, n+1]$. For clarity, we only present the modified components as outlined below.

- $\mathsf{Show}((\mathsf{m}_1, \cdots, \mathsf{m}_{n+1}), cred, pk_I, \mathcal{P}, pk_{\mathcal{P}}, v) \rightarrow \Theta$. The user takes $(\mathsf{m}_1, \cdots, \mathsf{m}_{n+1})$, *cred*, $(pk_I, pk_{\mathcal{P}})$ and v as input, outputs a proof Θ.
- $\mathsf{Verify}(\Theta, \{\mathsf{m}_i\}_{i \in \mathcal{D}}, \mathcal{P}, sk_{\mathcal{P}}, v) \rightarrow \{0, 1\}$. The verifier outputs 1 if attributes $\{\mathsf{m}_i\}_{i \in \mathcal{D}}$ associated with proof Θ satisfy policy $\mathcal{P}$, or 0.

5.2 Security Requirements

Unforgeability. Compared to the unforgeability described in Sect. 4.2, we should consider selective disclosure, which means that unforgeability should capture the adversary's forging capability towards undisclosed attributes in $\overline{\mathcal{D}}$. Informally, the adversary wins the unforgeablity experiment if a forgery occurs on an revoked identity $\mathsf{m}_{n+1} \in \mathcal{D}$ (revoked means $m_{n+1} \notin \mathcal{WL}$) or any attribute in $\overline{\mathcal{D}}$. We say that an RIHAC scheme is unforgeable if for any PPT adversary $\mathcal{A}$, $\mathsf{Adv}_{\mathcal{A}}^{uf-ac}$ is negligible in the unforgeability experiment $\mathsf{Exp}_{\mathcal{A}}^{uf-ac}(1^\lambda, q, n, \tilde{n})$ shown in Fig. 2.

Anonymity. Our anonymity involves issuer, user and attribute anonymity. Issuer anonymity means issuer-hiding. User and attribute anonymity ensure that a credential presented by a user does not reveal user identity m_{n+1} or any attributes in $\overline{\mathcal{D}}$. In our anonymity experiment, adversary $\mathcal{A}$ can collude with all issuers and $\mathcal{R}$. During the challenge phase, $\mathcal{A}$ submits two equal-size attribute sets $(\mathsf{m}_1^{(0)}, \cdots, \mathsf{m}_{n+1}^{(0)})$, $(\mathsf{m}_1^{(1)}, \cdots, \mathsf{m}_{n+1}^{(1)})$, along with credential $cred^{(0)}$, $cred^{(1)}$ signed under $pk^{(0)}$, $pk^{(1)}$, respectively. The experiment aborts if disclosed attributes in $\mathcal{D}$ are different (Step (3)) or undisclosed attributes in $\overline{\mathcal{D}}$ are the same (Step (4)). Moreover, the undisclosed identity $m_{n+1}^b \in \overline{\mathcal{D}}$. In the end, adversary is required to guess issuer, user, or any undisclosed attributes of the presented credential. Adversary wins if any of the guesses is correct. We say that an RIHAC scheme is anonymous if Adv^{ano} is negligible for any PPT adversary $\mathcal{A}$ in the anonymity experiment shown in Fig. 2.

5.3 Construction

The construction is the same as in Sect. 4 except for the following algorithms. In RIHAC, we employ the optimized ZK proofs from [52] to reduce the proof size and the computational overhead on both prover and verifier sides.

- $\mathsf{Setup}(1^\lambda, q, n, \tilde{n}) \rightarrow \mathsf{pp}$. This algorithm additionally defines a hash function $H : \{0,1\}^* \rightarrow \mathbb{Z}_p$ and outputs system parameters $\mathsf{pp} \leftarrow [g, \tilde{g}, \mathbb{G}_1, \mathbb{G}_2, \mathbb{G}_T, e, \mathcal{WL}]$.
- $\mathsf{Show}((\mathsf{m}_1, \cdots, \mathsf{m}_{n+1}), \mathcal{D}, cred, pk_I, \mathcal{P}, pk_{\mathcal{P}}, v) \rightarrow \Theta$. User specifies an index set of disclosed attributes $\mathcal{D}$, an index set of undisclosed attributes $\overline{\mathcal{D}}$, and shows its credential as follows.
  1. Check if the public key $pk_I = (\tilde{Y}_{I,1}, \cdots, \tilde{Y}_{I,n+1})$ from issuer I associated with the signature (σ_1, σ_2) is compatible with policy $\mathcal{P}$ by checking $I \in \mathcal{J}_i$ for all $i \in [1, n+1]$.
  2. Randomize the signature as $\sigma_1' = \sigma_1^{r'}, \sigma_2' = \sigma_2^{r'} \cdot (\sigma_1')^{t_2}$, where $r', t_1, t_2 \in \mathbb{Z}_p^3$, and compute $\tilde{\sigma} \leftarrow \tilde{S}^{t_1} \prod_{i=1}^{n+1} [\prod_{j \in \mathcal{J}_i \setminus \{I\}} \tilde{T}_{j,i}]^{\mathsf{m}_i}$.
  3. Generate a ZK proof $\pi_{\sigma,x,t}$ for credential $cred$, identity x_u and randomness $t = t_1 + t_2$. To prove the knowledge of undisclosed attributes $\{\mathsf{m}_i\}_{i \in \overline{\mathcal{D}}}$ and randomness t, it computes $K = e(\sigma_1', \prod_{i \in \overline{\mathcal{D}}} [\tilde{g}^{b_i(|\mathcal{J}_i|-1)} \prod_{j \in \mathcal{J}_i} \tilde{Y}_{j,i}]^{k_i} \tilde{g}^{k_t})$, where $\{k_i\}_{i \in \overline{\mathcal{D}}}$, $k_t \in \mathbb{Z}_p$. To prove membership, it randomizes (w_u, v) as

Unforgeability $\mathsf{Exp}_{\mathcal{A}}^{uf-ac}(1^\lambda, q, n, \tilde{n})$

(1) $\mathsf{pp} \leftarrow \mathsf{Setup}(1^\lambda, q, n, \tilde{n})$
(2) $\mathcal{P} = (\{pk_{j,1}\}_{j\in\mathcal{J}_1}, \cdots, \{pk_{j,n+1}\}_{j\in\mathcal{J}_{n+1}}) \leftarrow \mathcal{A}^{\mathcal{O}}(\mathsf{pp})$
(3) For all $(pk_1, \cdots, pk_{n+1}) \in \mathcal{K}$, if $\exists i \in [1, n+1]$ and $j_i \in \mathcal{J}_i$ such that $pk_{j_i,i} \neq pk_i$, return 0
(4) $(sk_{\mathcal{P}}, pk_{\mathcal{P}}) \leftarrow \mathsf{SetPolicy}(\mathcal{P})$
(5) $(\Theta, \{\mathsf{m}_i\}_{i\in\mathcal{D}}) \leftarrow \mathcal{A}^{\mathcal{O}}(\mathsf{pp}, \mathcal{P}, pk_{\mathcal{P}}, v)$
(6) If $\mathsf{m}_{n+1} \in \mathcal{WL}$, return 0
(7) Return $b \leftarrow [\mathcal{A}(), \mathsf{Verify}(\Theta, \{\mathsf{m}_i\}_{i\in\mathcal{D}}, \mathcal{P}, sk_{\mathcal{P}}, v)]$

Anonymity $\mathsf{Exp}_{\mathcal{A}}^{ano}(1^\lambda, q, n, \tilde{n})$

(1) $\mathsf{pp} \leftarrow \mathsf{Setup}(1^\lambda, q, n, \tilde{n})$
(2) $(\mathcal{D}, (\mathsf{m}_1^{(0)}, \ldots, \mathsf{m}_{n+1}^{(0)}), (\mathsf{m}_1^{(1)}, \ldots, \mathsf{m}_{n+1}^{(1)}), pk_{\mathcal{P}}, cred^{(0)}, cred^{(1)}, pk_I^{(0)}, pk_I^{(1)}) \leftarrow \mathcal{A}^{\mathcal{O}}(\mathsf{pp}, st)$
(3) If $\exists i^* \in \mathcal{D}$ s.t. $\mathsf{m}_{i^*}^{(0)} \neq \mathsf{m}_{i^*}^{(1)}$, return 0
(4) If $\exists i^* \in \overline{\mathcal{D}}$ s.t. $\mathsf{m}_{i^*}^{(0)} = \mathsf{m}_{i^*}^{(1)}$, return 0
(5) If $\mathsf{AuditPolicy}(\{pk_I^{(0)}, pk_I^{(1)}\}, pk_{\mathcal{P}}) = 0$, return 0
(6) If $\mathsf{UVerify}(pk_I^{(b)}, (\mathsf{m}_1^{(b)}, \ldots, \mathsf{m}_{n+1}^{(b)}), cred^{(b)}, v) = 0$ for $b \in \{0, 1\}$, return 0
(7) $b' \leftarrow [\mathsf{Show}((\mathsf{m}_1^{(b)}, \ldots, \mathsf{m}_{n+1}^{(b)}), cred^{(b)}, pk_I^{(b)}, \mathcal{P}, pk_{\mathcal{P}}), \mathcal{A}^{\mathcal{O}}(\mathsf{pp}, st)]$
(8) Return $(b' = b)$

Fig. 2. Security requirements for RIHAC scheme.

$W_u = w_u^t, V = v^t w_u^{-x_u t}$, and generates $K_V = v^{k_t} W_u^{-k_x}$, where $k_x \in \mathbb{Z}_p$. The challenge $c = H(\sigma_1', \sigma_2', \tilde{\sigma}, K, W_u, V, K_V)$ is used to generate $\{z_l - k_i + \mathsf{m}_i \cdot c\}_{i\in\overline{\mathcal{D}}}, z_t = k_t + t \cdot c$, and $z_x = k_x + x_u \cdot c$.
4. Let $\Theta = (\sigma_1', \sigma_2', \tilde{\sigma}, K, W_u, V, K_V, \pi_{\sigma,x,t})$, and send $(\Theta, \{\mathsf{m}_i\}_{i\in\mathcal{D}})$ to the verifier.

- $\mathsf{Verify}(\Theta, \{\mathsf{m}_i\}_{i\in\mathcal{D}}, \mathcal{P}, sk_{\mathcal{P}}, v)] \rightarrow \{0, 1\}$. Verifier returns 1 if all following checks are correct.
  1. Confirm $\sigma_1' \neq 1$.
  2. For all $i \in \mathcal{D} : \mathsf{m}_i \neq 0$.
  3. To verify $\pi_{\sigma,x,t}$, compute (T, K') respectively, and test whether $H(\sigma_1', \sigma_2', \tilde{\sigma}, K', W_u, V, K_V)$ equals to c.

$$T = e(\sigma_2', \tilde{g}) \cdot e(\sigma_1', \tilde{g}^{s(-1)} \tilde{\sigma}^{\frac{1}{a}} \prod_{i\in\mathcal{D}} [\tilde{g}^{b_i(|\mathcal{J}_i|-1)} \prod_{j\in\mathcal{J}_i} \tilde{Y}_{j,i}]^{-\mathsf{m}_i})$$
$$= e(\sigma_1', \prod_{i\in\overline{\mathcal{D}}} [\tilde{g}^{b_i(|\mathcal{J}_i|-1)} \prod_{j\in\mathcal{J}_i} \tilde{Y}_{j,i}]^{\mathsf{m}_i} \tilde{g}^t)$$

$$K' = T^{-c} e(\sigma_1', \prod_{i\in\overline{\mathcal{D}}} [\tilde{g}^{b_i(|\mathcal{J}_i|-1)} \prod_{j\in\mathcal{J}_i} \tilde{Y}_{j,i}]^{z_i} \tilde{g}^{z_t})$$
$$= e(\sigma_1', \prod_{i\in\overline{\mathcal{D}}} [\tilde{g}^{b_i(|\mathcal{J}_i|-1)} \prod_{j\in\mathcal{J}_i} \tilde{Y}_{j,i}]^{\mathsf{m}_i} \tilde{g}^t)^{-c} \cdot e(\sigma_1', \prod_{i\in\overline{\mathcal{D}}} [\tilde{g}^{b_i(|\mathcal{J}_i|-1)} \prod_{j\in\mathcal{J}_i} \tilde{Y}_{j,i}]^{z_i} \tilde{g}^{z_t})$$
$$= e(\sigma_1', \prod_{i\in\overline{\mathcal{D}}} [\tilde{g}^{b_i(|\mathcal{J}_i|-1)} \prod_{j\in\mathcal{J}_i} \tilde{Y}_{j,i}]^{k_i} \tilde{g}^{k_t}) = K.$$

4. Check $v^{z_t} W_u^{-z_x} = K_V \cdot V^c$ and $e(W_u, \tilde{g}^s) = e(V, \tilde{g})$.

The correctness of RIHAC can be referred to Appendix E.

5.4 Security Analysis

Theorem 3. *The RIHAC scheme is unforgeable in the random oracle model if RIHA is unforgeable.*

Theorem 4. *The RIHAC scheme is anonymous if the ZK proof π is sound and zero-knowledge.*

Proof Sketch. The unforgeability of RIHAC is reduced to that of RIHA in the random oracle model. The additional component in RIHAC is the Fiat–Shamir proof $\pi_{\sigma,x,t}$; using the forking lemma, two accepting transcripts with different hash challenges allow extraction of the witness randomization, which in turn recovers a valid RIHA-level forgery. Therefore, any successful forgery against RIHAC implies a successful forgery against RIHA, with the standard square-root loss in the reduction.

The anonymity of RIHAC follows from three ingredients: the soundness of the policy proof $\pi_{\mathcal{P}}$, the issuer-hiding property inherited from RIHA, and the zero-knowledge property of $\pi_{\sigma,x,t}$. Informally, once malformed policies are excluded, credential re-randomization hides the issuer, while the zero-knowledge proof hides the user identity, witness, and undisclosed attributes. Hence, the adversary's view is independent of the challenge bit up to negligible advantage. □

The complete proofs are deferred to Appendix E.

6 Performance

We have implemented our RIHAC scheme and two existing ones: Bobolz et al. [10] and Sanders et al. [47], where no public implementation of [47] is available. We select these two schemes from Table 1 for the following reasons. First, both [10,47] and our RIHAC scheme allow an issuer to create a valid credential for a user and a verifier to define a policy that includes multiple issuers' public keys. Second, both [10,47] offer selective disclosure and perfect issuer-hiding; and both rely on GGM for unforgeability analysis.

We compare the storage overhead with [10,47] in Table 2. Typically, the size of $|\mathcal{J}_i|$ may vary, i.e., $|\mathcal{J}_i| \neq |\mathcal{J}_j|$ for $i \neq j$. However, to ensure a fair comparison with [10], we set $|\mathcal{J}_1| = \cdots = |\mathcal{J}_{n+1}| = |\mathcal{J}|$. In Show protocol, the overhead of revealed attributes $|\mathcal{D}|$, and that of Schnorr's proof of knowledge $|\overline{\mathcal{D}}|$ contribute to a fixed overhead of $n\mathbb{Z}_p$ elements. The element $pk_{\mathcal{R}}$ is unique to our scheme to support user revocation, and is omitted from Table 2. Specifically, $|pk_{\mathcal{R}}|$ overhead depends on the accumulator's maximum capacity q, and consists of $q\mathbb{G}_2 + 1\mathbb{G}_1$ elements. In practice, q should be chosen according to the expected upper bound on the number of active credentials in the target deployment, with an additional margin to accommodate future growth. As shown in Table 2, our policy overhead is larger than that of [10], yet the number of elements sent in the Show protocol is reduced. Compared to [47], our scheme includes user identity as an additional attribute and supports user revocation, slightly increasing the proof overhead. When instantiated with BN254 curves, the Show protocol ($n = 0$) requires transmitting 512 bytes, 160 bytes, and 320 bytes in [10], [47], and ours, respectively. The results indicate that our scheme incurs an acceptable storage overhead.

Table 2. Storage Overhead

Component	[10]	[47]	Ours
pp	$(2+n)\mathbb{G}_1 + 2\mathbb{G}_2$	$2\mathbb{G}_1 + 2\mathbb{G}_2$	$1\mathbb{G}_1 + 1\mathbb{G}_2 + 2q\mathbb{Z}_p$
pk_I	$n\mathbb{G}_2$	$n\mathbb{G}_2$	$(n+1)\mathbb{G}_2$
$cred$	$2\mathbb{G}_1 + 1\mathbb{G}_2$	$2\mathbb{G}_1$	$3\mathbb{G}_1$
$pk_{\mathcal{P}}$	$(1+\lvert\mathcal{J}\rvert)\mathbb{G}_1 + 3\lvert\mathcal{J}\rvert\mathbb{G}_2$	$(1+n+2n\lvert\mathcal{J}\rvert)\mathbb{G}_2$ $+(n+2)\mathbb{Z}_p$	$(2+n+2(n+1)\lvert\mathcal{J}\rvert)\mathbb{G}_2$ $+ (n+3)\mathbb{Z}_p$
Show	$3\mathbb{G}_1 + 4\mathbb{G}_2 + (n+5)\mathbb{Z}_p$	$2\mathbb{G}_1 + 1\mathbb{G}_2 + (n+1)\mathbb{Z}_p$	$4\mathbb{G}_1 + 1\mathbb{G}_2 + (n+4)\mathbb{Z}_p$

n: the number of attributes; $\lvert\mathcal{J}\rvert$: the number of issuers in each attribute set;
q: the capacity of accumulator

The computational complexity per-algorithm is evaluated in Table 3. We only focus on computationally intensive operations, such as exponentiations in group $\mathbb{G}_1, \mathbb{G}_2$ and $\mathbb{G}_T$ (denoted as $\mathrm{e}_1, \mathrm{e}_2, \mathrm{e}_T$), and pairing (denoted as p). The computation of $(\tilde{g}^s)^{-1}$ is omitted as it can be precomputed. Compared to [10], our scheme incurs more exponentiations, but reduces the number of pairing operations. Compared to [47], our scheme introduces a minimal extra computational overhead to support user revocation. Specifically, the KeyGen of RIHAC requires $q\mathrm{e}_1$ to generate $pk_{\mathcal{R}}$. The $\langle$Issue, UVerify$\rangle$ protocol incurs additional $q\mathrm{e}_1 + 2\mathrm{e}_2 + 2\mathrm{p}$ due to the generation and verification of membership witness. The $\langle$Show, Verify$\rangle$ protocol requires additional $8\mathrm{e}_1 + 2\mathrm{e}_2 + 2\mathrm{p}$. These overheads arise due to the use of an accumulator-based revocation.

To evaluate the concrete timing of these operations, we instantiate them using the public Charm 0.5 framework[1] in Python 3.7 and use BN254 curve for pairings. The average timings (in ms) for each operation over 10,000 runs on an Intel Core i9-10885H CPU @ 2.40 GHz with 32 GB RAM are provided in Table 4. We implement our RIHAC scheme and [10,47] under the same configuration stated above, with code accessible on GitHub [3]. The constructions of all these schemes are organized into three interactive sub-protocols: protocol $P_1 = \langle$Issue, UVerify$\rangle$, $P_2 = \langle$SetPolicy, AuditPolicy$\rangle$ and $P_3 = \langle$Show, Verify$\rangle$.

[1] https://github.com/JHUISI/charm.

Table 3. Computational complexity

Algorithm	[10]	[47]	Ours
KeyGen	$n\mathrm{e}_2$	$n\mathrm{e}_2$	$(n+1)\mathrm{e}_2+(q+1)\mathrm{e}_1$
Issue	$4\mathrm{e}_1+1\mathrm{e}_2$	$3\mathrm{e}_1$	$(3+q)\mathrm{e}_1$
UVerify	$6\mathrm{p}$	$n\mathrm{e}_2+2\mathrm{p}$	$(n+2)\mathrm{e}_2+4\mathrm{p}$
SetPolicy	$(1+\lvert\mathcal{J}\rvert)\mathrm{e}_1+4\lvert\mathcal{J}\rvert\mathrm{e}_2$	$(1+2n+4n\lvert\mathcal{J}\rvert)\mathrm{e}_2$	$(3+2n+4(n+1)\lvert\mathcal{J}\rvert)\mathrm{e}_2$
AuditPolicy	$6\lvert\mathcal{J}\rvert\mathrm{p}$	$(n+4)\mathrm{e}_2$	$(n+5)\mathrm{e}_2$
Show	$(11+\lvert\overline{\mathcal{D}}\rvert)\mathrm{e}_1+5\mathrm{e}_2+7\mathrm{p}$	$(1+n+\lvert\overline{\mathcal{D}}\rvert)\mathrm{e}_2+3\mathrm{e}_1+\mathrm{p}$	$(2+n+\lvert\overline{\mathcal{D}}\rvert)\mathrm{e}_2+8\mathrm{e}_1+\mathrm{p}$
Verify	$(8+n)\mathrm{e}_1+13\mathrm{p}$	$(1+n)\mathrm{e}_2+1\mathrm{e}_T+3\mathrm{p}$	$(2+n)\mathrm{e}_2+3\mathrm{e}_1+1\mathrm{e}_T+5\mathrm{p}$

n: the number of attributes, $\lvert\mathcal{J}\rvert$: the number of issuers in each attribute set,
$\lvert\overline{\mathcal{D}}\rvert$: the number of undisclosed attributes, q: the capacity of accumulator

Table 4. Time per operation

Operations	e_1	e_2	e_T	p
Timings (ms)	1.69	2.91	4.85	23.55

e_1: exponentiation in $\mathbb{G}_1$, e_2: exponentiation in $\mathbb{G}_2$
e_T: exponentiation in $\mathbb{G}_T$, p: pairing operation

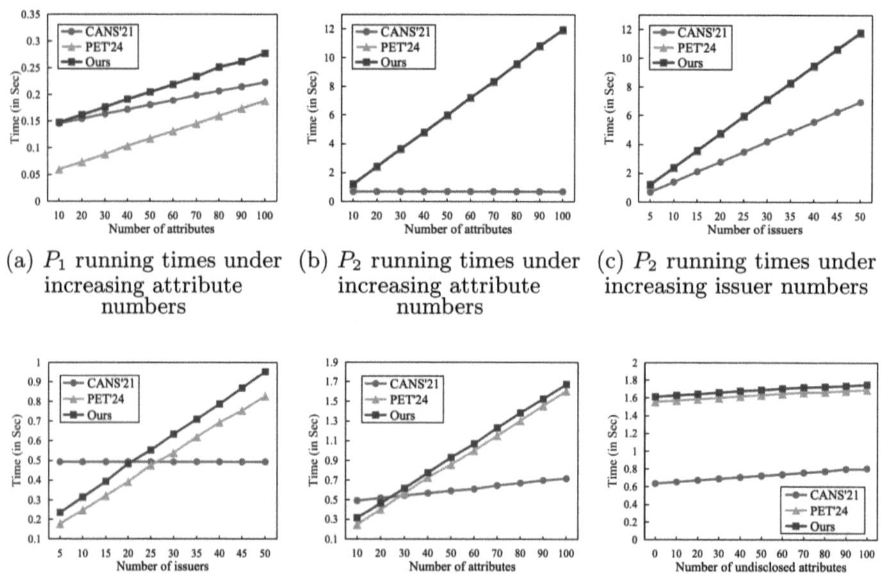

(a) P_1 running times under increasing attribute numbers (b) P_2 running times under increasing attribute numbers (c) P_2 running times under increasing issuer numbers

(d) P_3 running times under increasing issuer numbers, with 10 attributes and $\lvert\overline{\mathcal{D}}\rvert=n/2$ (e) P_3 running times under increasing attribute, with 10 issuers and $\lvert\overline{\mathcal{D}}\rvert=n/2$ (f) P_3 running times under increasing undisclosed attribute numbers, with 10 issuers and total attribute number $n=100$

Fig. 3. Comparison of running times.

For protocol $P_1 = \langle \mathsf{Issue}, \mathsf{UVerify} \rangle$, we measure the running time for a single issuer to issue a credential for a user, with the primary factor being the total number of attributes. To support user revocation, RIHAC requires the issuer to generate a membership witness for the user, introducing two additional factors: the number of users and the accumulator capacity q, both set to 50 in our experiment. As shown in Fig. 3(a), the running time of protocol P_1 is evaluated as the total number of attributes n increases from 10 to 100. While the revocation mechanism in RIHAC introduces additional computational overhead during credential issuance compared to [47], the overhead remains within acceptable limits. Specifically, when issuing and verifying a credential with 100 attributes, [10] takes 0.22 s, [47] takes 0.18 s, while our RIHAC achieves additional membership witness generation in 0.27 s.

The protocol $P_2 = \langle \mathsf{SetPolicy}, \mathsf{AuditPolicy} \rangle$ of our RIHAC follows the same structure as in [47], with the performance primarily affected by the total number of attributes and the number of issuers. In Fig. 3(b), we examine the impact of various attributes while fixing the number of issuers to 5. As the number of attributes increases from 10 to 100, both [47] and our RIAHC show a linear growth in running time. In contrast, the performance of Bobolz's scheme remains unaffected, as its policy construction is independent of the number of attributes. Similarly, Fig. 3(c) shows the effect of various issuers while keeping the number of attributes to 10. Here, the running time shows a linear growth for all schemes.

The running time of protocol $P_3 = \langle \mathsf{Show}, \mathsf{Verify} \rangle$ is influenced by the number of issuers, the total number of attributes, and the number of undisclosed attributes. In Fig. 3(d), we evaluate the effect of increasing the number of issuers from 5 to 50, while fixing the total number of attributes n at 10, and the number of undisclosed attributes $|\overline{\mathcal{D}}| = n/2$. The running time of Bobolz's scheme remains constant. In contrast, both Sanders's scheme and our RIHAC show approximately linear growth with respect to the number of issuers, with RIHAC incurring slightly higher overhead. For instance, when consider 50 issuers and 10 attributes, Bobolz's scheme [10] takes 0.49 s, Sanders's scheme [47] takes 0.83 s, while our RIHAC completes in 0.95 s with additional support for user revocation. Similarly, in Fig. 3(e), we analyze the impact of increasing the total number of attributes n from 10 to 100, with undisclosed attribute number $|\overline{\mathcal{D}}| = n/2$, while fixing the number of issuers at 10. The results confirm that P_3 running time for all schemes scale linearly with attribute growth. When consider 10 issuers and 100 attributes, Bobolz's scheme [10] takes 0.72 s, Sanders's scheme [47] takes 1.61 s, while our RIHAC requires 1.67 s. Finally, in Fig. 3(f), we investigate the impact of increasing the number of undisclosed attributes $|\overline{\mathcal{D}}|$, with the number of issuers set to 10 , and the total number of attributes n fixed at 100. The results reveal a linear growth pattern, as users must generate additional proofs for the undisclosed attributes.

Although Bobolz's scheme [10] achieves faster execution, it relies on complex ZK proofs, resulting in a relatively large presentation size. Their computational efficiency stems from two main factors. First, its show protocol only randomizes the public key of the actual issuer, which leads to constant time complexity regardless of issuer size. In contrast, both [47] and our RIHAC adopt an approach similar to ring signatures to hide the actual issuer among a set of issuers, resulting in time complexity that grows linearly with issuer size. Second, the underlying cryptographic operations differ: [10] requires a linear number of e_1 and a constant number of e_2, whereas both [47] and our RIHAC involve a linear number of e_2 and a constant number of e_1. Since e_2 is more expensive than e_1, this further explains the performance gap. To improve computational efficiency, one can swap the source groups, i.e., generate credentials in $\mathbb{G}_2$, so that the computation will be performed in $\mathbb{G}_1$. However, this optimization comes at the cost of increased credential size. Moreover, the additional running time of our RIHAC compared with [47] results from the membership proofs, which are necessary to provide stronger security guarantees and support user revocation. This trade-off between efficiency and security should be considered in practical deployments.

The storage and computational overhead of the ZK membership proof is evaluated in Table 5. Using the proof method in [52], our membership proof leads to smaller size and less computations. When initiated using BN254 curves, our scheme reduces the proof size from $(5+5) \times 32 = 320$ bytes to just $(3+2) \times 32 = 160$ bytes. When using the operation timing in Table 3, prover computation time decreases from 89.24 ms to 8.45 ms; verifier computation time decreases from 134.65 ms to 52.17 ms. Compared to [8,50], our proof reduces $50\%, 90.53\%, 61.25\%$ w.r.t proof size, prover and verifier computation.

Table 5. Membership proof

Scheme	Proof size	Prover computation	Verifier computation
[8,50]	$5\mathbb{G}_1 + 5\mathbb{Z}_p$	$11e_1 + 3p$	$10e_1 + 5p$
Ours	$3\mathbb{G}_1 + 2\mathbb{Z}_p$	$5e_1$	$3e_1 + 2p$

7 Conclusion

In this work, we proposed a new revocable IHAC scheme based on a pairing-based accumulator. On the security front, our revocable IHAC scheme is proven unforgeable under the well-known q-SDH assumption rather than the idealized GGM used in PET'24. Moreover, our scheme remains issuer-hiding against collusion between issuers and verifiers. For efficiency, our revocation approach incurs minimal extra overhead to the non-revocable IHAC scheme published at PET'24. We benchmark both PET'24 and our scheme under various settings. The implementation results confirmed the efficiency of our revocable IHAC scheme. Since IHAC is an active research field, one future work is to construct another type of revocable IHAC scheme from the VLR mechanism with the same level of security and privacy assurances.

Acknowledgments. This work was supported by the National Key R&D Program of China under Grant (2024YFB3108901), and the National Natural Science Foundation of China (U21B2021, 62472015, 62202027). This work also received funding from the European Union's Horizon Europe research and innovation programme under grant agreements No. 101070627 (REWIRE), No. 101095634 (ENTRUST) and No. 101167904 (CASTOR). These projects are additionally supported by the UK government's Horizon Europe Guarantee and administered by UKRI. We appreciate the valuable comments from the anonymous reviewers.

Appendix

A Full Construction of Dynamic Universal Accumulator

- $\mathsf{Add}(s, v, x) \rightarrow v'$. For a new element x that needs to be accumulated, the manager updates the accumulator value as $v' \leftarrow v^{x+s}$.
- $\mathsf{Del}(s, v, x) \rightarrow v'$. After deleting an element x that is accumulated in v, the manager updates the accumulator value as $v' \leftarrow v^{\frac{1}{x+s}}$.
- $\mathsf{DUA.NonWitCreate}([s], v, x_u) \rightarrow \overline{w_u}$. If element $x_u \notin \mathcal{WL}$ and is not accumulated in v, we have $\gcd(\mathcal{WL}(s), x_u + s) = 1$, i.e. there exist α, β that $\alpha \cdot \mathcal{WL}(s) + \beta \cdot (x_u + s) = 1$, where (α, β) are Bézout coefficient. Since the monomial $s + x_u$ is of degree one, the polynomial α is actually a constant. Thus the non-membership witness for x_u not being accumulated in v involves computing (α, β) and $\overline{w_u} \leftarrow (\alpha, g^\beta \in (\mathbb{Z}_p, \mathbb{G}_1))$. The detailed computation of α, β with and without trapdoor can be referred to [4].
- $\mathsf{DUA.NonMemVerify}(v, x_u, \overline{w_u} = (\alpha, g^\beta)) \rightarrow \{0, 1\}$. The algorithm returns 1 if verification equation $e(v, \tilde{g}^\alpha) \cdot e(g^\beta, \tilde{g}^s \tilde{g}^{x_u}) = e(g, \tilde{g})$ holds, and 0 otherwise.

The accumulator is equipped with a synchronization mechanism that ensures the accumulator value is globally consistent and refreshed to the latest state, so that verifiers can validate membership proofs against a fresh and unified accumulator state.

B Security Model for Accumulators

A secure accumulator scheme is required to be *correct* and *collision-free*. *Correctness* says that for all honestly generated keys, all honestly computed accumulators and witnesses, the (Non)MemVerify algorithm will always return 1.

Collision Freeness informally states that it is neither feasible to find a witness for a non-accumulated value nor feasible to find a non-membership witness for an accumulated value. For any PPT adversaries $\mathcal{A}$, there is a negligible ϵ s.t.

$$\Pr\left[\begin{array}{c} \mathsf{Dp} \leftarrow \mathsf{Setup}(1^\lambda), \\ (sk_{\mathsf{acc}}, pk_{\mathsf{acc}}) \leftarrow \mathsf{KeyGen}(1^\lambda, \mathsf{Dp}), \\ (x_u^*, \mathcal{WL}^*, w_{u^*}/\overline{w_{u^*}}) \leftarrow \mathcal{A}^{\mathcal{O}}(\mathsf{Dp}) : \\ (\mathsf{MemVerify}(v, x_u^*, w_{u^*}) = 1 \wedge x_u^* \notin \mathcal{WL}^*) \vee \\ (\mathsf{NonMemVerify}(v, x_u^*, \overline{w_{u^*}}) = 1 \wedge x_u^* \in \mathcal{WL}^*) \end{array}\right] \leq \epsilon,$$

where $\mathcal{O}$ represent the oracles for the algorithms Eval, WitCreate, NonWitCreate, Add and Del. An adversary $\mathcal{A}$ is allowed to query them an arbitrary number of times. Note that if $\mathcal{O}$ is queried for an element $x \notin \mathcal{WL}$, the oracle outputs $\perp$.

C Instantiation Using Accumulator in [38]

The instantiation using accumulator in [38] additionally introduces the initialization of blacklist $\mathcal{BL}$ during setup. $\mathcal{BL}$ contains all revoked identities.

RIHA. In Issue protocol, the issuer I runs DUA.NonWitCreate to create non-membership witness $\overline{w_u}$, demonstrating that identity x_u does not belong to $\mathcal{BL}$. $\overline{w_u}$ is added to *cred* and sent to the user. Then the user verifies $\overline{w}$ through DUA.NonMemVerify in UVerify. In Show, $\overline{w_u}$ is exposed along with x_u, and the verifier runs DUA.NonMemVerify to check the validity of $\overline{w_u}$.

RIHAC. The difference in RIHAC occurs in Show and Verify, as the user is required to hide $(\overline{w_u}, x_u)$. In Show, the user randomizes $\overline{W} = g^{\beta t}, \overline{V} = v^t$, computes $E = g^t\overline{W}^{-x_u}\overline{V}^{-\alpha}$, $K_E = g^{k_t}\overline{W}^{-k_x}\overline{V}^{-k_\alpha}$, where $k_\alpha, t, k_t, k_x \in \mathbb{Z}_p^4$. $(\overline{W}, \overline{V}, E, K_E)$ are added to the challenge c. The user then computes $z_\alpha = k_\alpha + c \cdot \alpha$, and adds z_α to proof $\pi_{\sigma,x,t}$. Receiving the non-membership proof, verifier checks $e(\overline{W}, \tilde{g}^s) = e(E, \tilde{g})$ and $K_E \cdot E^c = g^{z_t}\overline{W}^{-z_x}\overline{V}^{-z_\alpha}$, and returns 1 if both equations hold.

D Correctness and Security Analysis of RIHA

Correctness. Here we show the correctness of the Verify protocol. Let $(\sigma_1', \sigma_2', \tilde{\sigma}, w_u, (\mathsf{m}_1, \cdots, \mathsf{m}_{n+1}))$ be the elements generated by the user during the Show protocol. We have:

$$
\begin{aligned}
& e(\sigma_1', \tilde{g}^s\tilde{\sigma}^{-\frac{1}{a}}\prod_{i=1}^{n+1}[\tilde{g}^{b_i(|\mathcal{J}_i|-1)}\prod_{j\in\mathcal{J}_i}\tilde{Y}_{j,i}]^{\mathsf{m}_i}) \\
&= e(\sigma_1', \tilde{g}^s(\tilde{S}^t\prod_{i=1}^{n+1}[\prod_{j\in\mathcal{J}_i\setminus\{I\}}\tilde{T}_{j,i}]^{\mathsf{m}_i})^{-\frac{1}{a}}\prod_{i=1}^{n+1}[\tilde{g}^{b_i(|\mathcal{J}_i|-1)}\prod_{j\in\mathcal{J}_i}\tilde{Y}_{j,i}]^{\mathsf{m}_i}) \\
&= e(\sigma_1', \tilde{g}^s(\tilde{g}^t\prod_{i=1}^{n+1}[\prod_{j\in\mathcal{J}_i\setminus\{I\}}\tilde{Y}_{j,i}\tilde{g}^{b_i}]^{\mathsf{m}_i})^{-1}\prod_{i=1}^{n+1}[\tilde{g}^{b_i(|\mathcal{J}_i|-1)}\prod_{j\in\mathcal{J}_i}\tilde{Y}_{j,i}]^{\mathsf{m}_i}) \\
&= e(\sigma_1', \tilde{g}^s\cdot\tilde{g}^{-t}\prod_{i=1}^{n+1}\tilde{Y}_{I,i}^{\mathsf{m}_i}) = e((\sigma_1')^{s-t+\sum_{i=1}^{n+1}y_{I,i}\mathsf{m}_i}, \tilde{g}) = e(\sigma_2', \tilde{g}).
\end{aligned}
$$

Proof for Theorem 1. Let $\mathcal{S}$ be an adversary against q-SDH assumption, who is given $(g, g^\alpha, g^{\alpha^2}, \ldots, g^{\alpha^q}, \tilde{g}, \tilde{g}^\alpha) \in \mathbb{G}_1^{q+1} \times \mathbb{G}_2^2$, aims to output a pair $(g^{\frac{1}{\alpha+m^*}}, m^*) \in \mathbb{G}_1 \times \mathbb{Z}_p^*$. $\mathcal{S}$ setups the game for $\mathcal{A}$ as follows. $\mathcal{S}$ creates q users, and each user is linked to an identity x_u. $\mathcal{S}$ creates an issuer with a key pair $(sk_j, pk_j) = (y_j, \tilde{g}^{y_j})$, and setups a revocation authority's public key as $(\{g^{s^\gamma}\}_{\gamma\in[1,q]}, \tilde{g}^s) = (\{g^{\alpha^\gamma}\}_{\gamma\in[1,q]}, \tilde{g}^\alpha)$. In this simulation, we consider a simplified setting in which a user only owns a single attribute, one issuer is responsible for issuing, and one authority is responsible for updating a single list $\mathcal{WL}$ and $|\mathcal{WL}| \leq q$. We stress that one can easily extend this simple simulation to a setting with multi-attributes and multi-issuers.

$\mathcal{S}$ can easily answer Add, Corrupt, Issue, SetPolicy and Show queries from $\mathcal{A}$ during the training phase. $\mathcal{S}$ simulates Update queries as follows. Specifically, when $\mathcal{A}$ sends "add x_u" query, $\mathcal{S}$ inserts x_u to $\mathcal{WL}$ and computes v *from the scratch* using the given instances $(g, g^\alpha, g^{\alpha^2}, \ldots, g^{\alpha^q}) \in \mathbb{G}_1^{q+1}$. $\mathcal{S}$ simulates "delete x_u" query using the same approach. Note that neither operation requires α.

At some point, $\mathcal{A}$ outputs a proof $\Theta = (\mathsf{m}, \sigma_1', \sigma_2', \tilde{\sigma}, w_u^*, \mathcal{P})$ during a Show protocol. The proof should be valid against $(\mathsf{m}, x_u^*, pk_j, \mathcal{P})$, meaning that $e(w_u^*, \tilde{g}^\alpha \tilde{g}^{x_u^*}) = e(v, \tilde{g})$. Note that $\mathcal{S}$ only verifies the validity of $(\sigma_1', \sigma_2', \tilde{\sigma})$ against $(\mathsf{m}, x_u^*, pk_j)$, and $\mathcal{S}$ does not need to extract the original (σ_1, σ_2) from the randomized $(\sigma_1', \sigma_2', \tilde{\sigma})$. $\mathcal{S}$ performs the following

- *case 1.* If $\alpha \in \mathcal{WL}$, $\mathcal{S}$ breaks q-SDH trivially.
- *case 2.* When $\alpha \notin \mathcal{WL}$, $\mathcal{S}$ continues the analysis. Since $x_u^* \notin \mathcal{WL}$, there exists a polynomial $q(\alpha)$ of degree *less than* q such that $v(\alpha) = q(\alpha)(x_u^* + \alpha) + d$, where $v(\alpha) = \prod_{x_u\in\mathcal{WL}}(\alpha + x_u)$, $q(\alpha) = \sum_{\gamma=1}^{q-1} \mu_\gamma \alpha^\gamma$ and d is a constant value (see an example below). Given (w_u^*, x_u^*) from $\mathcal{A}$, $\mathcal{S}$ computes $w_u^{*'} = [w_u^* g^{-q(\alpha)}]^{1/d}$, and outputs $(g^{\frac{1}{\alpha+m^*}}, m^*) = (w_u^{*'}, x_u^*)$ as the solution to the q-SDH problem.
  We use a simple example to show how $\mathcal{S}$ extracts q-SDH solution from (w_u^*, x_u^*). We consider an accumulator $v = g^{\alpha+x}$ that accumulates a single value x (i.e., $q = 1$), and a valid forgery (w_u^*, x_u^*) such that $e(w_u^*, \tilde{g}^{\alpha+x_u^*}) = e(v, \tilde{g})$, where $w_u^* = g^{\frac{\alpha+x}{\alpha+x_u^*}}$. In this case, $\mathcal{S}$ aims to extract $(g^{1/(\alpha+x_u^*)}, x_u^*)$ to break 1-SDH problem, such that $e(g^{1/(\alpha+x_u^*)}, \tilde{g}^{\alpha+x_u^*}) = e(g, \tilde{g})$. Based on the above generic case, we have $g^{v(\alpha)} = g^{q(\alpha)} \cdot g^{\alpha+x_u^*} \cdot g$, where $v(\alpha) = \alpha + x$ and $q(\alpha) = \frac{(\alpha+x)-1}{\alpha+x_u^*}$. $\mathcal{S}$ can extract $g^{1/(\alpha+x_u^*)} = w_u^* \cdot g^{-q(\alpha)}$.

Proof for Theorem 2. The proof involves a sequence of games which follows the proof strategy described in the proof of issuer-hiding property [47]. Briefly, it involves two lemmas. The first lemma shows that the probability of an abort event (e.g., due to an ill-formed $pk_\mathcal{P}$) is bounded by the soundness of π. The second lemma proves that adversary $\mathcal{A}$ cannot distinguish two consecutive games, when simulator $\mathcal{S}$ simulates a valid proof Θ and its distribution independent of b. The proof Θ can be simulated as follows.

We define credential $cred^{(b)} = (\sigma_1^{(b)}, \sigma_2^{(b)}, w_u) = (g^{r_b}, g^{r_b(s+\sum_i y_{b,i}\mathsf{m}_i)}, w_u)$, where $r_b \in \mathbb{Z}_p$ is chosen by $\mathcal{A}$ and $i \in [1, n+1]$. Now, let $\mathcal{S}$ choose $(r, t) \in \mathbb{Z}_p^2$ and simulate $(\sigma_1', \sigma_2', \tilde{\sigma})$ as follows. Note that w_u will not be randomized according to the Show protocol. We define $r' = r \cdot r_b$, $u = t - \sum_i y_{b,i} \cdot \mathsf{m}_i$. We can write

$$\sigma_1' = (\sigma_1^{(b)})^r = g^{r'}$$
$$\sigma_2' = (\sigma_2^{(b)})^r (\sigma_1')^{-t} = g^{r'(s-u)}$$
$$\tilde{\sigma} = \tilde{S}^t \prod_{i=1}^{n+1} [\tilde{T}_{\overline{b},i}]^{\mathsf{m}_i} = \tilde{g}^{at} \prod_{i=1}^{n+1} [(\tilde{g}^{b_i} \tilde{Y}_{\overline{b},i})^a]^{\mathsf{m}_i} = \tilde{g}^{ua} \prod_{i=1}^{n+1} [(\tilde{g}^{b_i} \prod_{j \in \{0,1\}} \tilde{Y}_{j,i})^a]^{\mathsf{m}_i}$$

To this end, we use a toy example to show how to simulate $(\sigma_1', \sigma_2', \tilde{\sigma})$ for issuer-hiding. Assume an attribute m, two issuers with public keys $(\tilde{Y}_1, \tilde{Y}_2) = (\tilde{g}^{y_1}, \tilde{g}^{y_2})$, and a policy $(\tilde{g}^a, (\tilde{Y}_1 \cdot \tilde{g}^{b_1})^a, (\tilde{Y}_2 \cdot \tilde{g}^{b_1})^a)$. The PS signature created by $\mathcal{A}$ is $(\sigma_1, \sigma_2) = (g^{r_b}, g^{r_b(s+y_b\cdot\mathsf{m})})$. Based on the above generic simulation, $\mathcal{S}$ computes $(\sigma_1', \sigma_2', \tilde{\sigma}) = (g^{r'}, g^{r'(s-t+y_b\cdot\mathsf{m})}, \tilde{g}^{(t-y_b\cdot\mathsf{m})a} \cdot \tilde{g}^{b_1 a\cdot\mathsf{m}} \cdot \tilde{g}^{(y_1+y_2)\cdot a\cdot\mathsf{m}})$, where $u = t - y_b \cdot \mathsf{m}$. Now, $\mathcal{A}$ verifies the pairing as follows: $e(\sigma_1', \tilde{g}^s [\tilde{g}^{(t-y_b\cdot\mathsf{m})a} \cdot \tilde{g}^{b_1\cdot a\cdot\mathsf{m}} \cdot \tilde{g}^{(y_1+y_2)\cdot a\cdot\mathsf{m}}]^{-1/a} \cdot \tilde{g}^{y_1\cdot\mathsf{m}} \cdot \tilde{g}^{(y_2+b_1)\cdot\mathsf{m}}) = e(g^{r'}, \tilde{g}^{s-t+y_b\cdot\mathsf{m}}) = e(\sigma_2', \tilde{g})$. It is easy to see that the pairing equation holds for two issuers $(\tilde{Y}_1, \tilde{Y}_2)$.

Back to the generic simulation, since (r, t) are randomly chosen in $\mathbb{Z}_p^2$, (r', u) are also uniformly random and leak no information about b. In this simulation, $\mathcal{S}$ uses secret randomness (r, t) to simulate $(\sigma_1', \sigma_2', \tilde{\sigma})$, while $\mathcal{A}$ verifies the simulated elements via pairings using (a, b_i, m_i) (as shown in step (4) of Verify). From $\mathcal{A}$'s perspective, the pairing equation always holds regardless of b, as the element $\tilde{\sigma}$ involves both $\tilde{g}^{y_{b,i}}$ and $\tilde{g}^{y_{\overline{b},i}}$, where $\overline{b} = 1 - b$. This concludes the proof.

E Correctness and Security Analysis of RIHAC

Correctness. We begin by analyzing the correctness of the computation of T. From the verification of PS signature: $e(\sigma_2, \tilde{g}) = e(\sigma_1, \tilde{g}^s \prod_{i=1}^{n+1} \tilde{Y}_{I,i}^{\mathsf{m}_i})$, we can derive the following sequence of equalities:

$$e(\sigma_2', \tilde{g}) = e(\sigma_2^{r'} \cdot (\sigma_1')^{t_2}, \tilde{g}) = e((\sigma_1)^{r'}, \tilde{g}^s \prod_{i=1}^{n+1} \tilde{Y}_{I,i}^{\mathsf{m}_i}) \cdot e(\sigma_1', \tilde{g}^{t_2}) = e(\sigma_1', \tilde{g}^{s+t_2} \prod_{i=1}^{n+1} \tilde{Y}_{I,i}^{\mathsf{m}_i}).$$

Consequently, we obtain:

$$\begin{aligned}
T &= e(\sigma_2', \tilde{g}) \cdot e(\sigma_1', \tilde{g}^{s(-1)} \tilde{\sigma}^{\frac{1}{a}} \prod_{i \in \mathcal{D}} [\tilde{g}^{b_i(|\mathcal{J}_i|-1)} \prod_{j \in \mathcal{J}_i} \tilde{Y}_{j,i}]^{-\mathsf{m}_i}) \\
&= e(\sigma_1', \tilde{g}^{s+t_2} \prod_{i=1}^{n+1} \tilde{Y}_{I,i}^{\mathsf{m}_i}) \cdot e(\sigma_1', \tilde{g}^{-s} (\tilde{g}^{t_1} \prod_{i=1}^{n+1} [\prod_{j \in \mathcal{J}_i \setminus \{I\}} \tilde{Y}_{j,i} \cdot \tilde{g}^{b_i}]^{\mathsf{m}_i}) \prod_{i \in \mathcal{D}} [\tilde{g}^{b_i(|\mathcal{J}_i|-1)} \prod_{j \in \mathcal{J}_i} \tilde{Y}_{j,i}]^{-\mathsf{m}_i}) \\
&= e(\sigma_1', \tilde{g}^{t_1+t_2} \prod_{i=1}^{n+1} [\tilde{g}^{b_i(|\mathcal{J}_i|-1)} \prod_{j \in \mathcal{J}_i} \tilde{Y}_{j,i}]^{\mathsf{m}_i} \prod_{i \in \mathcal{D}} [\tilde{g}^{b_i(|\mathcal{J}_i|-1)} \prod_{j \in \mathcal{J}_i} \tilde{Y}_{j,i}]^{-\mathsf{m}_i}) \\
&= e(\sigma_1', \prod_{i \in \overline{\mathcal{D}}} [\tilde{g}^{b_i(|\mathcal{J}_i|-1)} \prod_{j \in \mathcal{J}_i} \tilde{Y}_{j,i}]^{\mathsf{m}_i} \tilde{g}^t)
\end{aligned}$$

Then we analyze the correctness of verifying membership (step 4.) in Verify. Given the construction of accumulator, we have $w_u = v^{\frac{1}{x_u+s}}$. Therefore,

$$e(W_u, \tilde{g}^s) = e(w_u^t, \tilde{g}^s) = e(w_u^{t(x_u+s)} w_u^{-x_u t}, \tilde{g}) = e(v^t w_u^{-x_u t}, \tilde{g}) = e(V, \tilde{g}).$$

Proof for Theorem 3. Let $\mathcal{S}$ be an adversary against RIHA scheme whose goal is to find a valid w_u for identity x_u. $\mathcal{S}$ simulates the unforgeability game for $\mathcal{A}$. $\mathcal{S}$ can answer Add, Corrupt, Issue, SetPolicy and Show queries of $\mathcal{A}$ by invoking those oracles from his challenger. Also, $\mathcal{S}$ maintains a random oracle with respect to ZK proofs required in RIHAC.

In the challenge phase, $\mathcal{A}$ outputs a proof $\Theta = (\{\mathsf{m}_i\}_{i\in\mathcal{D}}, \sigma_1', \sigma_2', \tilde{\sigma}, K, W_u, V, K_V, \pi_{\sigma,x,t}, \mathcal{P})$ during the Show protocol. The proof should pass the verification $e(W_u, \tilde{g}^{\alpha}) = e(V, \tilde{g})$. According to the RIHAC scheme, the ZK proof $\pi_{\sigma,x,t}$ contains the values $z_x = k_x + x_u c, z_t = k_t + tc$, where $c = H(\sigma_1', \sigma_2', \tilde{\sigma}, K, W_u, V, K_V)$. Let $\mathcal{S}$ replay the unforgeability game based on forking lemma [46]. When $\mathcal{A}$ outputs another proof that includes $\pi^*_{\sigma,x,t}$, such that $z_t^* = k_t + tc^*$, where $c^* = H(\sigma_1', \sigma_2', \tilde{\sigma}, K, W_u, V, K_V)$, the randomness can extracted as $t = (z_t^* - z_t)/(c^* - c)$. Once t is known, the original witness w_u can be recovered by computing $w_u = W_u^{1/t}$. With the extracted values w_u, $\mathcal{S}$ could break the unforgeability of RIHA. This proof incurs a square root security loss, because analysis of the Schnorr signature via forking in the ROM comes with a square root loss.

Proof for Theorem 4. The proof consists of three lemmas. The first lemma shows that the probability of an abort event (e.g., due to an ill-formed $pk_{\mathcal{P}}$) is bounded by the soundness of π. The third lemma is to show ZK proof π' offers zero-knowledge property. This is because π' is used to hide the undisclosed attributes, identities and secret randomness. Now, we focus on the second lemma, which aims to show all attributes and identities in the challenge proof Θ are independent of b. Compared to the proof in Theorem 2 (for issuer-hiding), we need to additionally show the challenge proof Θ is independent of the undisclosed attributes in $\overline{\mathcal{D}}$ and identities (refers to user and attribute privacy). In this lemma, we treat undisclosed attributes and non-revoked user's identities equally, as they all rely on ZK proof π' to be hidden.

We define credential $cred^{(b)} = (\sigma_1^{(b)}, \sigma_2^{(b)}, w_u^{(b)})$ for user $x_u^{(b)}$, where $\sigma_1^{(b)} = g^{r_b}$, $\sigma_2^{(b)} = g^{r_b(s+\sum_i y_{b,i}\mathsf{m}_i)}$ and $e(w_u^{(b)}, \tilde{g}^{x_u^{(b)}} \cdot \tilde{g}^s) = e(v, \tilde{g})$, where $r_b \in \mathbb{Z}_p$ and $i \in [1, n+1]$. Now, $\mathcal{S}$ chooses $(r, t, t_2) \subset \mathbb{Z}_p^3$ and simulates $\Theta = (\sigma_1', \sigma_2', \tilde{\sigma}, K, W_u, V, K_V, \pi_{\sigma,x,t})$ during a Show protocol as follows. We define $r' = r \cdot r_b$, $u = t_2 + \sum_{i\in\overline{\mathcal{D}}} y_{b,i} \cdot \mathsf{m}_i - \sum_{i\in\mathcal{D}} y_{\overline{b},i} \cdot \mathsf{m}_i$ and $t_1 = t - t_2$.

$$\sigma_1' = (\sigma_1^{(b)})^r = g^{r'}$$

$$\sigma_2' = (\sigma_2^{(b)})^r (\sigma_1')^{t_2} = g^{r'(s+u+\sum_{j\in\{0,1\}}\sum_{i\in\mathcal{D}} y_{j,i}\mathsf{m}_i)}$$

$$\tilde{\sigma} = \tilde{S}^{t_1} \prod_{i=1}^{n+1} [\tilde{T}_{\overline{b},i}]^{\mathsf{m}_i} = \tilde{g}^{at_1} \prod_{i=1}^{n+1} [(\tilde{g}^{b_i(|\mathcal{J}_i|-1)} \tilde{Y}_{\overline{b},i})^a]^{\mathsf{m}_i} = \tilde{g}^{a(t-u+\sum_{i\in\overline{\mathcal{D}}} y_{b,i} - \sum_{i\in\mathcal{D}} y_{\overline{b},i}\cdot\mathsf{m}_i)}$$

$$\prod_{i=1}^{n+1} [(\tilde{g}^{b_i(|\mathcal{J}_i|-1)} \tilde{Y}_{\overline{b},i})^a]^{\mathsf{m}_i} = \tilde{g}^{a[t-u+\sum_{i\in\overline{\mathcal{D}}}(y_{b,i}+y_{\overline{b},i})\mathsf{m}_i + \sum_{i=1}^{n+1} b_i(|\mathcal{J}_i|-1)\mathsf{m}_i]}$$

$\mathcal{S}$ can easily simulate the remaining components in Θ using the self-chosen randomness, such as $W_u^{(b)} = (w_u^{(b)})^t$, $V^{(b)} = v^t \cdot (w_u^{(b)})^{-x_u^{(b)} t}$ and $\pi_{\sigma,x,t}$.

To verify $(\sigma_1', \sigma_2', \tilde{\sigma})$ in the challenge proof Θ, adversary $\mathcal{A}$ first computes T via the following pairing operation.

$$
\begin{aligned}
T &= e(\sigma_2', \tilde{g}) \cdot e(\sigma_1', \tilde{g}^{s(-1)} \tilde{\sigma}^{\frac{1}{a}} \prod_{i \in \mathcal{D}} [\tilde{g}^{b_i(|\mathcal{J}_i|-1)} \prod_{j \in \mathcal{J}_i} \tilde{Y}_{j,i}]^{-\mathsf{m}_i}) \\
&= e(g^{r'(s+u+\sum_{j\in\{0,1\}} \sum_{i\in\mathcal{D}} y_{j,i}\mathsf{m}_i)}, \tilde{g}) \cdot e(g^{r'}, g^{-s} \cdot \\
&\quad (\tilde{g}^{a[t-u+\sum_{i\in\overline{\mathcal{D}}}(y_{b,i}+y_{\overline{b},i})\mathsf{m}_i + \sum_{i=1}^{n+1} b_i(|\mathcal{J}_i|-1)\mathsf{m}_i]})^{\frac{1}{a}} \cdot \prod_{i \in \mathcal{D}} [\tilde{g}^{b_i(|\mathcal{J}_i|-1)} \prod_{j \in \mathcal{J}_i} \tilde{Y}_{j,i}]^{-\mathsf{m}_i}) \\
&= e(g^{r'}, \prod_{i \in \overline{\mathcal{D}}} [\tilde{g}^{b_i(|\mathcal{J}_i|-1)} \prod_{j \in \{0,1\}} \tilde{Y}_{j,i}]^{\mathsf{m}_i} \cdot \tilde{g}^t), \text{ where } \prod_{j\in\{0,1\}} \tilde{Y}_j = \tilde{g}^{y_b + y_{\overline{b}}}.
\end{aligned}
$$

From $\mathcal{A}$'s perspective, the computations of (T, K') from the simulated $(\sigma_1', \sigma_2', \tilde{\sigma})$ and $\mathsf{m}_{i\in\mathcal{D}}^{(b)}$ is always valid, which is independent of b and $\mathsf{m}_{i\in\overline{\mathcal{D}}}$. Since (r, t, t_2) are random values, (r', u) also uniformly random and leak no information about both b and $\mathsf{m}_{i\in\overline{\mathcal{D}}}$. Finally, if we assume $\pi_{\sigma,x,t}$ offers zero-knowledge, we conclude the proof.

References

1. European digital identity. https://eudi.dev/2.4.0/
2. Information security—attribute-based credentials, October 2025. Preliminary Work Item on privacy-preserving attribute-based credentials (formerly known as anonymous credentials)
3. Revocable issuer-hiding anonymous credential (2025). https://github.com/fionnoif0730/RIHAC
4. Au, M.H., Tsang, P.P., Susilo, W., Mu, Y.: Dynamic universal accumulators for DDH groups and their application to attribute-based anonymous credential systems. In: Fischlin, M. (ed.) CT-RSA 2009. LNCS, vol. 5473, pp. 295–308. Springer, Heidelberg (2009). https://doi.org/10.1007/978-3-642-00862-7_20
5. Ayebie, E.B., Souidi, E.M.: New code-based cryptographic accumulator and fully dynamic group signature. Des. Codes Crypt. **90**(12), 2861–2891 (2022)
6. Baldimtsi, F., et al.: Accumulators with applications to anonymity-preserving revocation. In: EuroS&P, pp. 301–315. IEEE (2017)
7. Barthoulot, A., Blazy, O., Canard, S.: Cryptographic accumulators: new definitions, enhanced security, and delegatable proofs. In: Vaudenay, S., Petit, C. (eds.) Progress in Cryptology, AFRICACRYPT 2024. LNCS, vol. 14861, pp. 94–119. Springer, Cham (2024). https://doi.org/10.1007/978-3-031-64381-1_5
8. Bisht, K., Kansagra, N.Y., Ali, R., Shaik, M.S., Francis, M., Kataoka, K.: Revocable TACO: revocable threshold-based anonymous credentials over blockchains. In: AsiaCCS, pp. 1378–1393 (2024)
9. Blömer, J., Bobolz, J.: Delegatable attribute-based anonymous credentials from dynamically malleable signatures. In: Preneel, B., Vercauteren, F. (eds.) ACNS 2018. LNCS, vol. 10892, pp. 221–239. Springer, Cham (2018). https://doi.org/10.1007/978-3-319-93387-0_12

10. Bobolz, J., Eidens, F., Krenn, S., Ramacher, S., Samelin, K.: Issuer-hiding attribute-based credentials. In: Conti, M., Stevens, M., Krenn, S. (eds.) CANS 2021. LNCS, vol. 13099, pp. 158–178. Springer, Cham (2021). https://doi.org/10.1007/978-3-030-92548-2_9
11. Boneh, D., Boyen, X.: Short signatures without random oracles. In: Cachin, C., Camenisch, J.L. (eds.) EUROCRYPT 2004. LNCS, vol. 3027, pp. 56–73. Springer, Heidelberg (2004). https://doi.org/10.1007/978-3-540-24676-3_4
12. Boneh, D., Boyen, X., Shacham, H.: Short group signatures. In: Franklin, M. (ed.) CRYPTO 2004. LNCS, vol. 3152, pp. 41–55. Springer, Heidelberg (2004). https://doi.org/10.1007/978-3-540-28628-8_3
13. Boneh, D., Shacham, H.: Group signatures with verifier-local revocation. In: ACM CCS, pp. 168–177 (2004)
14. Bosk, D., Frey, D., Gestin, M., Piolle, G.: Hidden issuer anonymous credential. In: PoPETs, pp. 571–607 (2022)
15. Camacho, P., Hevia, A., Kiwi, M., Opazo, R.: Strong accumulators from collision-resistant hashing. In: Wu, T.-C., Lei, C.-L., Rijmen, V., Lee, D.-T. (eds.) ISC 2008. LNCS, vol. 5222, pp. 471–486. Springer, Heidelberg (2008). https://doi.org/10.1007/978-3-540-85886-7_32
16. Camenisch, J., Drijvers, M., Dubovitskaya, M.: Practical UC-secure delegatable credentials with attributes and their application to blockchain. In: ACM CCS, pp. 683–699 (2017)
17. Camenisch, J., Herreweghen, E.V.: Design and implementation of the Idemix anonymous credential system. In: ACM CCS, pp. 21–30 (2002)
18. Camenisch, J., Kohlweiss, M., Soriente, C.: An accumulator based on bilinear maps and efficient revocation for anonymous credentials. In: Jarecki, S., Tsudik, G. (eds.) PKC 2009. LNCS, vol. 5443, pp. 481–500. Springer, Heidelberg (2009). https://doi.org/10.1007/978-3-642-00468-1_27
19. Camenisch, J., Lysyanskaya, A.: Dynamic accumulators and application to efficient revocation of anonymous credentials. In: Yung, M. (ed.) CRYPTO 2002. LNCS, vol. 2442, pp. 61–76. Springer, Heidelberg (2002). https://doi.org/10.1007/3-540-45708-9_5
20. Campanelli, M., Fiore, D., Han, S., Kim, J., Kolonelos, D., Oh, H.: Succinct zero-knowledge batch proofs for set accumulators. In: ACM CCS, pp. 455–469 (2022)
21. Chase, M., Perrin, T., Zaverucha, G.: The signal private group system and anonymous credentials supporting efficient verifiable encryption. In: ACM CCS, pp. 1445–1459 (2020)
22. Chaum, D.: Showing credentials without identification transferring signatures between unconditionally unlinkable pseudonyms. In: Seberry, J., Pieprzyk, J. (eds.) AUSCRYPT 1990. LNCS, vol. 453, pp. 245–264. Springer, Heidelberg (1990). https://doi.org/10.1007/BFb0030366
23. Connolly, A., Deschamps, J., Lafourcade, P., Perez Kempner, O.: Protego: Efficient, revocable and auditable anonymous credentials with applications to hyperledger fabric. In: Isobe, T., Sarkar, S. (eds.) INDOCRYPT. LNCS, vol. 13774, pp. 249–271. Springer, Cham (2022). https://doi.org/10.1007/978-3-031-22912-1_11
24. Connolly, A., Lafourcade, P., Perez Kempner, O.: Improved constructions of anonymous credentials from structure-preserving signatures on equivalence classes. In: Hanaoka, G., Shikata, J., Watanabe, Y. (eds.) PKC. LNCS, vol. 13177, pp. 409–438. Springer, Cham (2022). https://doi.org/10.1007/978-3-030-97121-2_15
25. Crites, E.C., Lysyanskaya, A.: Delegatable anonymous credentials from mercurial signatures. In: Matsui, M. (ed.) CT-RSA 2019. LNCS, vol. 11405, pp. 535–555. Springer, Cham (2019). https://doi.org/10.1007/978-3-030-12612-4_27

26. Crites, E., Kohlweiss, M., Preneel, B., Sedaghat, M., Slamanig, D.: Threshold structure-preserving signatures. In: Guo, J., Steinfeld, R. (eds.) Advances in Cryptology, ASIACRYPT 2023. LNCS, vol. 14439, pp. 348–382. Springer, Singapore (2023). https://doi.org/10.1007/978-981-99-8724-5_11
27. Crites, E.C., Lysyanskaya, A.: Mercurial signatures for variable-length messages. In: PoPETs (2021)
28. Dahlberg, R., Pulls, T., Peeters, R.: Efficient sparse Merkle trees. Caching strategies and secure (non-)membership proofs. In: Brumley, B.B., Röning, J. (eds.) NordSec 2016. LNCS, vol. 10014, pp. 199–215. Springer, Cham (2016). https://doi.org/10.1007/978-3-319-47560-8_13
29. Davidson, A., Goldberg, I., Sullivan, N., Tankersley, G., Valsorda, F.: Privacy pass: bypassing internet challenges anonymously. In: PoPETs (2018)
30. Derler, D., Hanser, C., Slamanig, D.: A new approach to efficient revocable attribute-based anonymous credentials. In: Groth, J. (ed.) IMACC 2015. LNCS, vol. 9496, pp. 57–74. Springer, Cham (2015). https://doi.org/10.1007/978-3-319-27239-9_4
31. Derler, D., Hanser, C., Slamanig, D.: Revisiting cryptographic accumulators, additional properties and relations to other primitives. In: Nyberg, K. (ed.) CT-RSA 2015. LNCS, vol. 9048, pp. 127–144. Springer, Cham (2015). https://doi.org/10.1007/978-3-319-16715-2_7
32. Elkhiyaoui, K., Caro, A.D., Androulaki, E.: Multi-issuer anonymous credentials without a root authority. Cryptology ePrint Archive, Paper 2021/1669 (2021). https://eprint.iacr.org/2021/1669
33. Fuchsbauer, G., Hanser, C., Slamanig, D.: Structure-preserving signatures on equivalence classes and constant-size anonymous credentials. J. Cryptol. **32**, 498–546 (2019)
34. Ghosh, E., Ohrimenko, O., Papadopoulos, D., Tamassia, R., Triandopoulos, N.: Zero-knowledge accumulators and set algebra. In: Cheon, J.H., Takagi, T. (eds.) ASIACRYPT 2016. LNCS, vol. 10032, pp. 67–100. Springer, Heidelberg (2016). https://doi.org/10.1007/978-3-662-53890-6_3
35. Groth, J.: Efficient fully structure-preserving signatures for large messages. In: Iwata, T., Cheon, J.H. (eds.) ASIACRYPT 2015. LNCS, vol. 9452, pp. 239–259. Springer, Heidelberg (2015). https://doi.org/10.1007/978-3-662-48797-6_11
36. Groth, J., Kohlweiss, M.: One-out-of-many proofs: or how to leak a secret and spend a coin. In: Oswald, E., Fischlin, M. (eds.) EUROCRYPT 2015. LNCS, vol. 9057, pp. 253–280. Springer, Heidelberg (2015). https://doi.org/10.1007/978-3-662-46803-6_9
37. Hanser, C., Slamanig, D.: Structure-preserving signatures on equivalence classes and their application to anonymous credentials. In: Sarkar, P., Iwata, T. (eds.) ASIACRYPT 2014. LNCS, vol. 8873, pp. 491–511. Springer, Heidelberg (2014). https://doi.org/10.1007/978-3-662-45611-8_26
38. Karantaidou, I., Baldimtsi, F.: Efficient constructions of pairing based accumulators. In: CSF, pp. 1–16. IEEE (2021)
39. Khalili, M., Slamanig, D., Dakhilalian, M.: Structure-preserving signatures on equivalence classes from standard assumptions. In: Galbraith, S.D., Moriai, S. (eds.) ASIACRYPT 2019. LNCS, vol. 11923, pp. 63–93. Springer, Cham (2019). https://doi.org/10.1007/978-3-030-34618-8_3
40. Lee, J.: Dory: Efficient, transparent arguments for generalised inner products and polynomial commitments. In: TCC, pp. 1–34 (2021)

41. Libert, B., Ling, S., Nguyen, K., Wang, H.: Zero-knowledge arguments for lattice-based accumulators: logarithmic-size ring signatures and group signatures without trapdoors. In: Fischlin, M., Coron, J.-S. (eds.) EUROCRYPT 2016. LNCS, vol. 9666, pp. 1–31. Springer, Heidelberg (2016). https://doi.org/10.1007/978-3-662-49896-5_1
42. Mir, O., Bauer, B., Griffy, S., Lysyanskaya, A., Slamanig, D.: Aggregate signatures with versatile randomization and issuer-hiding multi-authority anonymous credentials. In: ACM CCS, pp. 30–44. ACM (2023)
43. Nguyen, L.: Accumulators from bilinear pairings and applications. In: Menezes, A. (ed.) CT-RSA 2005. LNCS, vol. 3376, pp. 275–292. Springer, Heidelberg (2005). https://doi.org/10.1007/978-3-540-30574-3_19
44. Paquin, C.: U-Prove technology overview v1.1. Tech. rep., Microsoft Corporation (2011). https://www.microsoft.com/en-us/research/publication/u-prove-technology-overview-v1-1/
45. Pointcheval, D., Sanders, O.: Short randomizable signatures. In: Sako, K. (ed.) CT-RSA 2016. LNCS, vol. 9610, pp. 111–126. Springer, Cham (2016). https://doi.org/10.1007/978-3-319-29485-8_7
46. Pointcheval, D., Stern, J.: Security arguments for digital signatures and blind signatures. J. Cryptol. **13**, 361–396 (2000)
47. Sanders, O., Traoré, J.: Compact issuer-hiding authentication, application to anonymous credential. In: PoPETs (2024)
48. Shi, R., et al.: Double issuer-hiding attribute-based credentials from tag-based aggregatable mercurial signatures. TDSC **21**(4), 2585–2602 (2023)
49. Shoup, V.: Lower bounds for discrete logarithms and related problems. In: Fumy, W. (ed.) EUROCRYPT 1997. LNCS, vol. 1233, pp. 256–266. Springer, Heidelberg (1997). https://doi.org/10.1007/3-540-69053-0_18
50. Srinivasan, S., Karantaidou, I., Baldimtsi, F., Papamanthou, C.: Batching, aggregation, and zero-knowledge proofs in bilinear accumulators. In: ACM CCS, pp. 2719–2733. ACM (2022)
51. Ta, T.A., Hui, X., Chau, S.C.K.: Ring referral: efficient publicly verifiable ad hoc credential scheme with issuer and strong user anonymity for decentralized identity and more. In: SP, pp. 184–202. IEEE (2025)
52. Tessaro, S., Zhu, C.: Revisiting BBS signatures. In: Hazay, C., Stam, M. (eds.) EUROCRYPT. LNCS, vol. 14008, pp. 691–721. Springer, Cham (2023). https://doi.org/10.1007/978-3-031-30589-4_24

Matchmaking Inner Product Functional Encryption

Zongfeng Peng[1], Changgen Peng[2(✉)], Hongfa Ding[3], and Qihong Chen[2]

[1] College of Data Science and Information Engineering, Guizhou Minzu University, Guiyang 550025, China

[2] State Key Laboratory of Public Big Data, College of Computer Science and Technology, Guizhou University, Guiyang 550025, China
cgpeng@gzu.edu.cn

[3] College of Information, Guizhou University of Finance and Economics, Guiyang 550025, China

Abstract. Inner product functional encryption (IPFE) enables secure computation on private data for statistical analysis but inherently leaks information about encrypted data, necessitating fine-grained access control. Existing solutions use attribute based encryption to restrict who can recover the function output, enforcing only unilateral receiver-side control. However, real-world data sharing often requires more complex and flexible control: not only who may decrypt, but also from whom a receiver may accept data. We address this by proposing a matchmaking IPFE scheme with bilateral authorization and attribute hiding. Inspired by matchmaking encryption, our construction introduces a dual inner product predicate that simultaneously matches sender and receiver attributes. This predicate is embedded in the IPFE evaluation, ensuring the function value is revealed only when both parties satisfy the matching condition. The scheme achieves semi-adaptive simulation-based (SAD-SIM) security under standard assumptions. Experiments show modest overhead in key generation, encryption, and decryption, which remains low even as predicate and function vector dimensions grow, demonstrating practicality for real-world privacy-preserving analytics.

Keywords: Bilateral control · Inner product functional encryption · Matchmaking encryption

1 Introduction

The growing demand for privacy-preserving data analytics has spurred significant interest in cryptographic techniques that enable secure computation over encrypted data. Functional encryption (FE) [6] represents a significant advancement in public-key cryptography, unifying various encryption paradigms including identity-based encryption

Supported by the National Natural Science Foundation of China under Grants 62272124, and 62566006, the Science and Technology Program of Guizhou under Grants Qian Sci. & Tech. Found. MS [2026]314, Qian Sci. Contr. Achiev. DXGA[2025]Key-006, and Qian Sci. Contr. Achiev. [2024]Major-17.

Y. Cao et al. (Eds.): SecureComm 2026, LNICST 704, pp. 430–448, 2027.
https://doi.org/10.1007/978-3-032-32764-2_20

(IBE) and attribute-based encryption (ABE)—under a single framework. Unlike traditional encryption, FE enables controlled computation on encrypted data: a user holding a secret key associated with a function f can decrypt a ciphertext of message x to learn only $f(x)$, without revealing additional information about x. Among FE variants, inner product functional encryption (IPFE) has emerged as a powerful primitive, allowing authorized users to compute inner products fundamental operations in statistical analysis and machine learning directly on encrypted private data [23]. Despite its utility, IPFE inherently leaks partial information about the encrypted inputs through the revealed function output, which can be exploited by malicious or curious parties. Therefore, it is crucial to find ways to safeguard data security while improving its usability.

Abdalla et al. [2] addressed this issue by introducing fine-grained access control into inner product functional encryption (IPFE), ensuring that only authorized users can recover function values. Subsequent works extended this approach: Dufours et al. [15] proposed an identity-based IPFE scheme, while Lai et al. [18] and Pal et al. [22] combined ABE with IPFE to support policy-based access control. These schemes, however, reveal user attributes in the clear and are thus referred to as having public attribute properties. To protect attribute privacy, Dowerah et al. [14] and Wan et al. [24] proposed predicate-based inner product functional encryption schemes with attribute hiding, which prevent unauthorized parties from learning sensitive attribute information. Overall, existing works that integrate IPFE with access control effectively mitigate its inherent leakage risks. Despite these advances, a critical limitation remains. Existing schemes enforce only unilateral authorization: they restrict who may compute a function on encrypted data but do not regulate from whom a receiver may accept data. Without sender-side control, a malicious or unauthorized party could craft and send ciphertexts that appear valid to the receiver, potentially tricking them into computing inner products on untrusted or adversarially chosen inputs. This not only undermines access policies but may also lead to unintended information leakage through function outputs.

We tackle this gap by integrating the core idea of matchmaking encryption (ME) into IPFE. Matchmaking encryption enables mutual authorization between sender and receiver while preserving data confidentiality. Leveraging this property, our goal is how to realize bilateral access control during both encryption and secure computation. However, a direct combination of ME and IPFE is insecure: this allows an adversary to bypass access control and recover the inner product value despite an unsatisfied matching condition, as the impacts of ME and IPFE are independent. In a properly designed scheme, the inner product value should be revealed only when the matchmaking predicate evaluates to true. Otherwise, decryption must yield no meaningful information about the inner product, thereby preserving the confidentiality guarantees of functional encryption.

To resolve these issues, we formalize and construct a matchmaking inner product functional encryption (MIPFE) scheme. The core idea is to tightly couple the decryption key parameters with a bilateral matchmaking process: successful decryption is only possible after verifying that both the sender and the receiver satisfy a jointly defined access policy. Specifically, we introduce two pairs of inner product predicate vectors, referred to as a dual inner product predicate (DIP), to govern the matchmaking. One pair encodes the sender's permissions, while the other encodes the receiver's permissions. Each pair consists of two vectors: one is embedded in the ciphertext, and the other is embedded in the secret key. Before decryption, the system evaluates both predicate pairs to determine whether the sender-receiver pair is authorized. This ensures that the inner product computation proceeds only when both parties meet their respective policy requirements. The main contributions of this work are summarized as follows:

- We design a dual inner product predicate (DIP) structure to facilitate bilateral control in secure computation. By tightly integrating DIP with the inner product function vector, our scheme simultaneously enforces the sender's sending rights and the receiver's computation rights.
- Our construction supports more expressive bilateral policies through two pairs of predicate vectors and one pair of function vectors. It achieves partial attribute hiding by concealing the function vector and the receiver's predicate vector from unauthorized parties. Furthermore, the scheme satisfies strong attribute hiding and semi-adaptive simulation-based (SAD-SIM) security under standard cryptographic assumptions.
- Compared to state-of-the-art schemes, our construction offers improved efficiency in both computation and storage. Notably, even when the dimensions of the predicate vectors reach 10^4 and those of the function vectors reach 10^3, the overall computation time and storage overhead remain practical, demonstrating a clear performance advantage at scale.

2 Related Work

We review the most closely related works in inner product functional encryption and matchmaking encryption.

2.1 Inner Product Functional Encryption

Access control has been widely adopted to mitigate the inherent information leakage in IPFE [1,3]. The seminal work by Abdalla et al. [2] was the first to integrate attribute-based access control policies directly into IPFE, ensuring that only authorized users can recover function values. Subsequent research has focused on enhancing security guarantees, computational capabilities, and scalability, etc.

From a security perspective, existing constructions can be broadly categorized into two lines: those emphasizing simulation-based security and those prioritizing attribute privacy. Lai et al. [18] proposed a strongly secure IPFE scheme achieving semi-adaptive simulation (SA-SIM) security, supporting both identity-based and attribute-based policies. Wee [25] constructed a simulation-based attribute-hiding IPFE under standard assumptions. More recently, Wan et al. [24] introduced a predicate-based IPFE with function hiding, although its security relies on the generic group model. To improve scalability, unbounded IPFE, where vector lengths are not fixed during setup, has attracted significant attention. Dowerah [14] proposed an unbounded predicate IPFE based on bilinear pairings, and later presented a more efficient variant [13]. Cini et al. [11] further extended IPFE to support ciphertext updates and fine-grained access control, enhancing its practical utility. Beyond linear functions, several works have explored richer functionalities. Gay [17] introduced a framework for quadratic functional encryption, while Ambrona et al. [4] realized quadratic computations in a multi-authority setting. In multi-user scenarios, Nguyen et al. [21] proposed multi-client functional encryption with fine-grained access control to enable joint computation over data from multiple parties. Datta et al. [12] further developed a decentralized multi-authority attribute-based IPFE scheme.

In summary, although integrating IBE and ABE with IPFE represents a significant advancement, these approaches enforce only unilateral authorization. This makes them ill-suited for dynamic data circulation, as they control who computes a function but fail to jointly regulate the sender-receiver relationship. This gap hinders their use in environments requiring bidirectional trust, underscoring the need for the bilateral control proposed in this work.

2.2 Matchmaking Encryption

Matchmaking encryption (ME) originated from non-interactive secret handshake protocols [5] and offers a natural framework for bilateral access control. Recent efforts have explored its applications in diverse settings: Xu et al. [28] applied ME to cloud-fog computing to enforce mutual authorization; Chen et al. [8] proposed a certificateless ME scheme for IoT environments, effectively resolving the key escrow problem inherent in identity-based ME (IBME); Yang et al. [30] designed a lightweight ME protocol for resource-constrained mobile devices and later introduced an incentive mechanism-based IBME for IoT [31]; Wu et al. [26] developed a revocable ME scheme tailored for mobile social networks; Yan et al. [29] extended IBME to support broadcast communication in multi-user mobile environments, proposing an identity-based broadcast ME scheme.

Other efforts have strengthened the security foundations of ME. Francati et al. [16] presented an IBME scheme with provable security in the standard model (i.e., without random oracles). Chen et al. [9] constructed an IBME under standard assumptions, and Boyen [7] addressed its privacy limitations through both general and optimized constructions. Lin et al. [19] achieved the first chosen-ciphertext attack (CCA)-secure IBME, while Chiku et al. [10] proposed a more efficient IBME with stronger security guarantees. Other notable extensions include fuzzy IBME [27] and ME integrated with anonymous certificates for direct authentication [20].

Collectively, these works establish ME as a powerful paradigm for bilateral authorization. However, its potential in regulating computational rights, particularly within functional encryption, remains largely unexplored. Our work bridges this gap by integrating ME's bilateral matching mechanism into IPFE, thereby enabling fine-grained, sender-receiver-aware secure computation.

3 Preliminaries

3.1 Notations

$x \leftarrow_{\mathrm{R}} X$ indicates x is selected uniformly at random from a finite set X. PPT refers to a probabilistic polynomial-time algorithm. λ serves as the security parameter. Lowercase bold letters represent vectors, while uppercase bold letters denote matrices. The symbol $\approx_c$ means two distributions are computationally indistinguishable. $\epsilon(\lambda)$ denotes a negligible function about λ. m_1 is the dimension of each predicate vector, m_2 is the dimension of each function vector.

3.2 Bilinear Map

For an asymmetric group G_1, G_2 and G_T with prime order p, the generator $g_1 \in G_1$ and $g_2 \in G_2$. The efficient bilinear map $e : G_1 \times G_2 \rightarrow G_T$ implies that

- Bilinearity: $e\left(g_1^a, g_2^b\right) = e\left(g_1, g_2\right)^{ab}$ for all $g_1 \in G_1, g_2 \in G_2, a, b \in \mathbb{Z}_p$,
- Non-degeneracy: $e\left(g_1, g_2\right)$ is a generator of G_T.

For simplicity, we also use $[\cdot]_1$ to present the elements in G_1, $[\cdot]_2$ to present the elements in G_2, and $[\cdot]_T$ to present the elements in G_T. Specifically, $[a]_1$ means g_1^a. $[\mathbf{A}]_1$ means the $g_1^{a_{ij}}$, i is the number of row, j is the number of column.

3.3 Cryptographic Assumption

The matrix decisional Diffie-Hellman (MDDH) assumption holds over the $\mathbb{Z}_q^{(k+1)\times k}$. If there are $(\mathbf{A}, \mathbf{s}, \mathbf{c}) \leftarrow (\mathbb{Z}_q^{(k+1)\times k}, \mathbb{Z}_q^k, \mathbb{Z}_q^{k+1})$ s.t. it satisfies

$$([\mathbf{A}]_1, [\mathbf{A}\mathbf{s}]_1) \approx_c ([\mathbf{A}]_1, [\mathbf{c}]_1).$$

Then, the advantage $\mathrm{Adv}_{G_1,\mathcal{A}}^{\mathrm{MDDH}}(\lambda)$ of an adversary $\mathcal{A}$ to distinguish the distributions is negligible, it is the same as that in group G_2.

4 Model Definitions

4.1 Definition of MIPFE

Ateniese et al. [5] define two types of matchmaking encryption schemes: the standard and the arranged variants. Our matchmaking inner product functional encryption (MIPFE) scheme aligns more closely with the arranged version. Rather than generating a separate encryption key for the sender's predicate vector, we embed it directly into the ciphertext, thereby reducing the overall algorithmic complexity.

In our construction, a secret key is associated with two predicates P_1 and P_2, as well as a function vector $\mathbf{v}$. A ciphertext, on the other hand, is associated with attribute vectors $\mathbf{t}$ and $\mathbf{z}$, along with a message vector $\mathbf{u}$. Given a secret key for $(\mathrm{P}_1, \mathrm{P}_2, \mathbf{v})$ and a ciphertext for $(\mathbf{t}, \mathbf{z}, \mathbf{u})$, decryption succeeds and outputs the inner product $\langle \mathbf{u}, \mathbf{v} \rangle$ if and only if $P_1(\mathbf{t}) = 1$ and $P_2(\mathbf{z}) = 1$. Otherwise, no useful information about the inner product is revealed.

A MIPFE scheme Π is defined over an attribute space $\mathcal{X}$, a message space $\mathcal{V}$, a predicate class $\mathcal{P}$, and a function class $\mathcal{F}$, and consists of the following algorithms:

Setup $(1^\lambda, 1^{m_1}, 1^{m_2}) \rightarrow (\mathrm{pp}, \mathrm{msk})$: Given a security parameter, the setup algorithm produces the public parameters *pp* and the master secret key msk.

$KeyGen(pp, msk, P_1, P_2, \mathbf{v}) \rightarrow \mathrm{sk}_{P_1,P_2,\mathbf{v}}$: Upon receiving the public parameters *pp* , the maser secret key msk, predicate $P_1 \in \mathcal{P}$, $P_2 \in \mathcal{P}$ and a vector $\mathbf{v} \in \mathcal{F}$, the key generation algorithm outputs a functional secret key $\mathrm{sk}_{P_1,P_2,\mathbf{v}}$.

$Enc(pp, msk, \mathbf{t}, \mathbf{z}, \mathbf{u}) \rightarrow \mathrm{ct}_{\mathbf{t},\mathbf{z},\mathbf{u}}$: Upon the public parameters *pp* , the maser secret key msk, an attribute vectors $(\mathbf{t}, \mathbf{z}) \in \mathcal{X}$ and a message $\mathbf{u} \in \mathcal{V}$, Enc algorithm outputs a ciphertext $\mathrm{ct}_{\mathbf{t},\mathbf{z},\mathbf{u}}$.

$Dec\,(\mathrm{pp}, \mathrm{sk}_{P_1,P_2,\mathbf{v}}, \mathrm{ct}_{\mathbf{t},\mathbf{z},\mathbf{u}}) \rightarrow \langle \mathbf{u}, \mathbf{v} \rangle / \perp$: With the public parameters *pp*, a functional secret key $\mathrm{sk}_{P_1,P_2,\mathbf{u}}$, and a ciphertext $\mathrm{ct}_{\mathbf{t},\mathbf{z},\mathbf{v}}$ as inputs, the Dec algorithm outputs a inner product value $\langle \mathbf{u}, \mathbf{v} \rangle$ or $\perp$.

Definition 4.1. Correctness of MIPFE scheme. A MIPFE scheme Π consists of the Setup, KeyGen, Enc and Dec algorithms defined previously. It is correct if, for every attribute vectors $(\mathbf{t}, \mathbf{z}) \in \mathcal{X}$, vector $\mathbf{v} \in \mathcal{F}$, predicates $(P_1, P_2) \in \mathcal{P}$, and message $\mathbf{u} \in \mathcal{V}$, the following condition is satisfied:

Let $sk_{P_1,P_2,\mathbf{v}} \leftarrow \mathrm{KeyGen}\,(\mathrm{msk}, P_1, P_2, \mathbf{v})$, and $\mathrm{ct}_{\mathbf{t},\mathbf{z},\mathbf{u}} \leftarrow \mathrm{Enc}(\mathrm{pp}, \mathrm{msk}, \mathbf{t}, \mathbf{z}, \mathbf{u})$, then if $P_1(\mathbf{t}) = 1$ and $P_2(\mathbf{z}) = 1$, $\Pr\left[\mathrm{Dec}(\mathrm{pp}, \mathrm{sk}_{P_1,P_2,\mathbf{v}}, \mathrm{ct}_{\mathbf{t},\mathbf{z},\mathbf{u}}) = \langle \mathbf{u}, \mathbf{v} \rangle\right] = 1 - \epsilon(\lambda)$. Otherwise, $\Pr\left[\mathrm{Dec}\,(\mathrm{pp}, \mathrm{sk}_{P_1,P_2,\mathbf{v}}, \mathrm{ct}_{\mathbf{t},\mathbf{z},\mathbf{u}}) = \perp\right] = 1$, where the probability is calculated based on the randomness of the algorithms and $\epsilon(\lambda)$.

4.2 Security Model

Definition 4.2. SAD-SIM Security. If function ϵ is negligible and

$$\Pr\left[\boldsymbol{Exp}_{\mathcal{A}}^{\mathrm{Real}} - \boldsymbol{Exp}_{\mathcal{A},\mathcal{S}}^{\mathrm{Ideal}}\right] \leq \epsilon(\lambda).$$

Then our proposed scheme achieves the semi-adaptively simulation(SAD-SIM) security, where the adversary may specify its encryption challenge after obtaining the mpk. $\boldsymbol{Exp}_{\mathcal{A}}^{\mathrm{Real}}$ denotes the security experiment for Real game consists of $Setup$, Enc, and $KeyGen$. $\boldsymbol{Exp}_{\mathcal{A},\mathcal{S}}^{\mathrm{Ideal}}$ denotes the security experiment for simulator with $\widetilde{Setup}$, $\widetilde{Enc}$, and $\widetilde{KeyGen}$ algorithms.

$\boldsymbol{Exp}_{\mathcal{A}}^{\mathrm{Real}}$ is defined as follows:

$$\begin{aligned}
&(\mathrm{mpk}, \mathrm{msk}) \leftarrow \mathrm{Setup}\left(1^\lambda, 1^{|\mathcal{F}|}\right) \\
&(x^*, u^*) \leftarrow \mathcal{A}(\mathrm{mpk}) \\
&(\mathrm{ct}) \leftarrow \mathrm{Enc}\left(\mathrm{mpk}, (x^*, u^*)\right) \\
&\text{output } \alpha \leftarrow \mathcal{A}^{\mathrm{KeyGen}\,(\mathrm{msk}, \cdot)}(\mathrm{mpk}, \mathrm{ct})
\end{aligned}$$

Here, x can be viewed as the values (t^*, z^*) of the attribute vectors embedded in the ciphertext.

$\boldsymbol{Exp}_{\mathcal{A},\mathcal{S}}^{\text{Ideal}}$ is defined as follows:

$$
\begin{aligned}
&(\text{mpk}, \text{msk}^*) \leftarrow \widetilde{\text{Setup}}\left(1^\lambda, 1^{|\mathcal{F}|}\right) \\
&(x^*, u^*) \leftarrow \mathcal{A}(\text{mpk}) \\
&(\text{ct}^*) \leftarrow \widetilde{\text{Enc}}\left(\text{msk}^*, x^*\right) \\
&\text{output } \alpha \leftarrow \mathcal{A}^{\widetilde{\text{KeyGen}}(\text{msk}^*, x^*, \cdot)}(\text{mpk}, \text{ct}^*)
\end{aligned}
$$

Definition 4.3. Authenticity. Let experiment $\boldsymbol{Exp}_{\mathcal{A}}^{\text{Auth}}(\lambda)$ is defined as follows. If we have the advantage $\left|\Pr\left[\boldsymbol{Exp}_{\mathcal{A}}^{\text{Auth}}(\lambda) = 1\right] - \frac{1}{2}\right| \leq \epsilon(\lambda)$. Then, our MIPFE scheme satisfies authenticity.

$\boldsymbol{Exp}_{\mathcal{A}}^{\text{Auth}}(\lambda)$ is defined as follows:

$$
\begin{aligned}
&(\text{mpk}, \text{msk}) \leftarrow \text{setup}\left(1^\lambda, 1^{|\mathcal{F}|}\right) \\
&(ct, \text{P}_1, \text{P}_2) \leftarrow \mathcal{A}^{O}(\text{mpk}) \\
&sk \leftarrow KeyGen(msk, \text{P}_1, \text{P}_2) \\
&m \leftarrow Dec(mpk, sk, ct) \\
&If \quad \text{P}_1(\cdot) \neq 0 \quad or \quad \text{P}_2(\cdot) \neq 0 \quad return \quad 1 \\
&else \quad return \quad 0
\end{aligned}
$$

Where O means the KeyGen oracle. The authenticity can be reduced to the dual inner product prediacte.

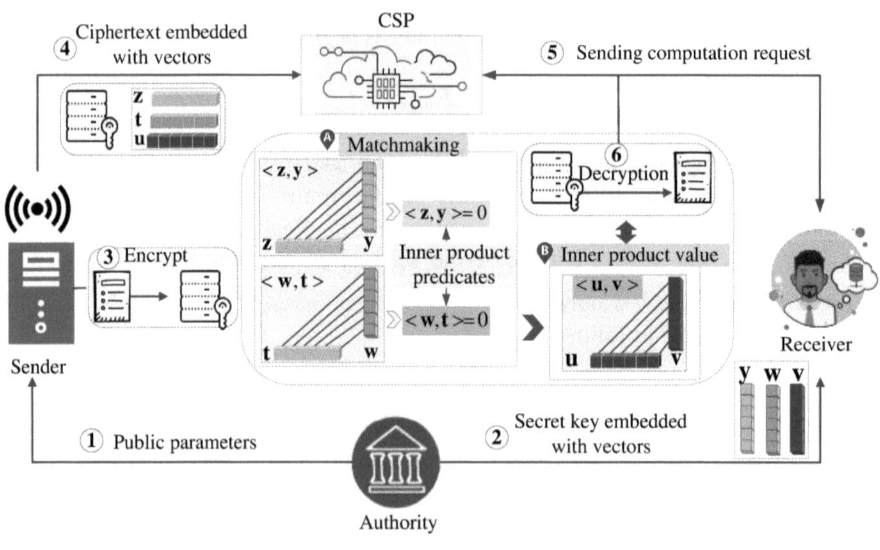

Fig. 1. System model and workflow.

4.3 System Model

As shown in Fig. 1, the system model consists of four entities: a cloud service provider (CSP), an authority, a sender, and a receiver. We assume that the authority is fully trusted, while the CSP is honest-but-curious. Both the sender and the receiver are considered malicious. The overall workflow are following steps.

- The authority generates the public parameters used by the sender and issues secret keys to receivers. (① and ② in Fig. 1)
- The sender encrypts its data and uploads the resulting ciphertext to the cloud service provider (CSP). During encryption, the scheme embeds three components into the ciphertext: the sender's attribute vector $\mathbf{t}$, a receiver attribute vector $\mathbf{z}$ (specified by the sender to designate an intended receiver), and a message vector $\mathbf{u}$ associated with the function to be computed. (③ in Fig. 1)
- The CSP provides storage, data analysis, and computation services for the system. (④ and ⑤ in Fig. 1)
- Each receiver obtains its secret key from the authority. This key includes the receiver's own attribute vector $\mathbf{y}$, a sender attribute vector $\mathbf{w}$ (specified by the receiver to indicate trusted senders), and a function vector $\mathbf{v}$. Upon receiving a ciphertext, the receiver initiates a two-phase decryption process: (i) a matchmaking phase that checks whether the sender–receiver pair satisfies the bilateral policy, and (ii) a computation phase that evaluates the inner product. Decryption succeeds, i.e., outputs $\langle \mathbf{u}, \mathbf{v} \rangle$, only if both $\mathrm{P}_1(\mathbf{t}, \mathbf{w}) = 1$ and $\mathrm{P}_2(\mathbf{z}, \mathbf{y}) = 1$ hold. Otherwise, no useful information about the underlying plaintext or function output is revealed. (⑥ in Fig. 1)

This architecture thus enables secure outsourced storage and fine-grained, bilateral-controlled functional computation.

5 The Proposed MIPFE Scheme

We propose a matchmaking inner product functional encryption scheme featuring bilateral access control and attribute-hiding properties. In our construction, two dual predicate vector pairs—$(\mathbf{w}, \mathbf{t})$ for the sender and $(\mathbf{z}, \mathbf{y})$ for the receiver—are employed to enable fine-grained matching. As illustrated in Fig. 1, these vectors are generated through distinct procedures tailored to their respective roles.

During key generation, we embed the sender's predicate vector $\mathbf{w}$, the receiver's predicate vector $\mathbf{y}$, and the function vector $\mathbf{v}$ into the secret keys, thereby ensuring the confidentiality of $\mathbf{y}$ and $\mathbf{v}$. Notably, $\mathbf{w}$ is made public, as it is explicitly specified by the receiver to define the matchmaking policy. In the encryption phase, our construction aggregates the parameters associated with the predicate vectors $\mathbf{t}$ and $\mathbf{z}$, which significantly reduces computational overhead. The resulting ciphertext preserves the privacy of $\mathbf{t}$, $\mathbf{z}$, and the function vector $\mathbf{u}$. To decrypt the inner product $\langle \mathbf{u}, \mathbf{v} \rangle$, our scheme incorporates a critical component $\left[\mathbf{s}^\top \mathbf{A}^\top \boldsymbol{\kappa}\right]_T$ into the decryption process. This value can only be reconstructed through the joint use of the two secret keys sk_1 and sk_2, which respectively encode the relevant predicate vectors involved in the matchmaking. However, due to the hardness of computing discrete logarithms in the exponent, directly recovering $\langle \mathbf{u}, \mathbf{v} \rangle$ remains infeasible. Consequently, in our experimental evaluation, we employ the baby-step giant-step algorithm to efficiently compute the desired inner product.

$Setup(1^\lambda) \rightarrow (pp, msk)$: This algorithm generates the group $\mathbb{G} = (p, G_1, G_2, G_T, e, g_1, g_2)$, where $g_1 \in G_1$ and $g_2 \in G_2$ with the prime order of p, $e : G_1 \times G_2 \rightarrow G_T$ represents the bilinear map. It selects random $\mathbf{A} \leftarrow_R \mathbb{Z}_q^{(k+1)\times k}$, $\mathbf{W} \leftarrow_R \mathbb{Z}_q^{(k+1)\times k}$, $(\mathbf{U}_1, \ldots, \mathbf{U}_{m_1}) \leftarrow_R (\mathbb{Z}_q^{(k+1)\times k}, \ldots, \mathbb{Z}_q^{(k+1)\times k})$, $\mathbf{R} \leftarrow_R \mathbb{Z}_q^{(k+1)\times(k+1)}$, $\boldsymbol{\kappa} \leftarrow_R \mathbb{Z}_q^{k+1}$, $\mathbf{b} \leftarrow_R \mathbb{Z}_q^{k+1}$. Then output the public parameters *pp* is

$$pp = \Big([\mathbf{A}]_1, \left[\mathbf{A}^\top \mathbf{W}\right]_1, \left\{\left[\mathbf{A}^\top \mathbf{U}_i\right]_1\right\}_{i\in[m_1]}, \left[\mathbf{A}^\top \mathbf{R}\boldsymbol{\kappa}\right]_1, \left[\mathbf{A}^\top \mathbf{R}\mathbf{b}\right]_1 \Big). \tag{1}$$

and the master secret key is

$$\text{msk} = (\mathbf{W}, \mathbf{U}_1, \ldots, \mathbf{U}_{m_1}, \mathbf{R}, \boldsymbol{\kappa}, \mathbf{b}). \tag{2}$$

$KeyGen(pp, msk, \mathbf{w}, \mathbf{y}, \mathbf{v}) \rightarrow \text{sk}_{\mathbf{w},\mathbf{y},\mathbf{v}}$: In the key generation algorithm, we embed three vectors into the secret key: the first two, $\mathbf{w}$ and $\mathbf{y}$, are used to enforce matchmaking (i.e., bilateral access control)-with $\mathbf{w}$ representing the sender-side predicate and $\mathbf{y}$ the receiver-side predicate, while the third vector, $\mathbf{v}$, defines the inner product function to be evaluated during decryption.

The algorithm proceeds as follows: it first samples a random vector $\mathbf{r} \leftarrow \mathbb{Z}_q^{k+1}$ and then computes the secret key $\text{sk}_{\mathbf{w},\mathbf{y},\mathbf{v}}$

$$\begin{aligned} sk_1 &= \left[\boldsymbol{\kappa} - \sum_{i=1}^{m_1} y_i w_i \mathbf{U}_i \mathbf{r}\right]_2, sk_2 = \{[y_i \mathbf{r}]_2\}_{i\in[m_1]}, \\ sk_3 &= \left\{[v_i \mathbf{R}^{-1}]_2\right\}_{i\in[m_2]}, sk_4 = [\sum_{i=1}^{m_2} \mathbf{b} v_i]_2. \end{aligned} \tag{3}$$

Lastly, the $\text{sk}_{(\mathbf{w},\mathbf{y},\mathbf{v})} = (sk_1, sk_2, sk_3, sk_4, w_i)$. It is worth noting that $\mathbf{w}$ is explicitly displayed, in fact, such a construction satisfies the partially attribute hiding property.

$Enc(pp, msk, \mathbf{t}, \mathbf{z}, \mathbf{u}) \rightarrow \text{ct}_{\mathbf{t},\mathbf{z},\mathbf{u}}$: The ciphertext also incorporates two predicate vectors, $\mathbf{t}$ and $\mathbf{z}$, which correspond respectively to the key-embedded predicate vectors $\mathbf{w}$ and $\mathbf{y}$, thereby enabling the bilateral matching condition to be evaluated during decryption. The encryption algorithm samples a random vector $\mathbf{s} \leftarrow \mathbb{Z}_q^k$ and outputs the ciphertext $\text{ct}_{\mathbf{t},\mathbf{z},\mathbf{u}}$ as

$$\begin{aligned} ct_1 &= \left[\mathbf{s}^\top \mathbf{A}^\top\right]_1, \\ ct_2 &= \left\{\left[\mathbf{s}^\top \mathbf{A}^\top (z_i \mathbf{W} + t_i \mathbf{W} + \mathbf{U}_i)\right]_1\right\}_{i\in[m_1]}, \\ ct_3 &= \left\{\left[\mathbf{s}^\top \mathbf{A}^\top \mathbf{R}(\boldsymbol{\kappa} u_i + \mathbf{b})\right]_1\right\}_{i\in[m_2]}. \end{aligned} \tag{4}$$

That is $\text{ct}_{\mathbf{t},\mathbf{z},\mathbf{u}} = (ct_1, ct_2, ct_3)$.

$Dec(\text{pp}, \text{sk}_{\mathbf{w},\mathbf{y},\mathbf{v}}, \text{ct}_{\mathbf{t},\mathbf{z},\mathbf{u}}) \rightarrow \langle \mathbf{u}, \mathbf{v} \rangle / \perp$: The decryption algorithm outputs the inner product $\langle \mathbf{u}, \mathbf{v} \rangle$ if and only if both inner product predicates satisfy $\langle \mathbf{y}, \mathbf{z} \rangle = 0$

and $\langle \mathbf{w}, \mathbf{t} \rangle = 0$; otherwise, it returns $\perp$. Decryption proceeds in two distinct steps. First, a matchmaking phase verifies the orthogonality conditions between the two pairs of predicate vectors $(\mathbf{w}, \mathbf{t})$ and $(\mathbf{y}, \mathbf{z})$. Only upon successful matchmaking, i.e., when both inner products evaluate to zero, does the algorithm proceed to the second step, which computes the functional output $\langle \mathbf{u}, \mathbf{v} \rangle$.

- Matchmaking:
$$ct_1 \cdot sk_1 + ct_2 \cdot sk_2 \cdot w_i = \left[\mathbf{s}^\top \mathbf{A}^\top \boldsymbol{\kappa}\right]_T. \tag{5}$$
- Computing:
$$ct_3 \cdot sk_3 - ct_1 \cdot sk_4 = \left[\mathbf{s}^\top \mathbf{A}^\top \boldsymbol{\kappa} \langle \mathbf{u}, \mathbf{v} \rangle\right]_T. \tag{6}$$

Thus, the inner product value can only be decrypt by using the value $\left[\mathbf{s}^\top \mathbf{A}^\top \boldsymbol{\kappa}\right]_T$. That is to say we can get a value X s.t. $\left[\mathbf{s}^\top \mathbf{A}^\top \boldsymbol{\kappa} X\right]_T = \left[\mathbf{s}^\top \mathbf{A}^\top \boldsymbol{\kappa} \langle \mathbf{u}, \mathbf{v} \rangle\right]_T$, i.e., $X = \langle \mathbf{u}, \mathbf{v} \rangle$.
Correctness. The correctness of our scheme relies on two components: the evaluation of the inner product predicates and the computation of the target inner product function. Specifically, the ciphertext is associated with the predicate vectors $\mathbf{z}$ and $\mathbf{t}$, while the secret key is bound to the predicate vectors $\mathbf{y}$ and $\mathbf{w}$. Decryption succeeds if and only if both orthogonality conditions $\langle \mathbf{z}, \mathbf{y} \rangle = 0$ and $\langle \mathbf{w}, \mathbf{t} \rangle = 0$ are satisfied.

Firstly, the inner product predicate is computed by

$$\begin{aligned}
ct_1 \cdot sk_1 + ct_2 \cdot sk_2 \cdot w_i &= \left[\mathbf{s}^\top \mathbf{A}^\top \boldsymbol{\kappa} - \mathbf{s}^\top \mathbf{A}^\top \sum_{i=1}^{m_1} y_i w_i \mathbf{U}_i \mathbf{r}\right]_T \\
&+ \left[\mathbf{s}^\top \mathbf{A}^\top (z_i y_i w_i \mathbf{W} + t_i w_i y_i \mathbf{W} + y_i w_i \mathbf{U})\mathbf{r}\right]_T \\
&= \left[\mathbf{s}^\top \mathbf{A}^\top (\boldsymbol{\kappa} + \langle \mathbf{z}, \mathbf{y} \rangle w_i r \mathbf{W} + \langle \mathbf{w}, \mathbf{t} \rangle y_i r \mathbf{W})\right]_T \\
&(When \quad \langle \mathbf{z}, \mathbf{y} \rangle = 0 \quad \& \quad \langle \mathbf{w}, \mathbf{t} \rangle = 0) \\
&= \left[\mathbf{s}^\top \mathbf{A}^\top \boldsymbol{\kappa}\right]_T.
\end{aligned} \tag{7}$$

Further, we can compute inner product value:

$$\begin{aligned}
&ct_3 \cdot sk_3 - ct_1 \cdot sk_4 \\
&= \left[\mathbf{s}^\top \mathbf{A}^\top \mathbf{R}(\boldsymbol{\kappa} u_i + \mathbf{b}) \cdot (v_i \mathbf{R}^{-1})\right]_T - \left[\mathbf{s}^\top \mathbf{A}^\top \cdot \mathbf{b} v_i\right]_T \\
&= \left[\mathbf{s}^\top \mathbf{A}^\top \mathbf{R}\mathbf{R}^{-1}(\boldsymbol{\kappa}\langle \mathbf{u}, \mathbf{v} \rangle + \mathbf{b} v_i)\right]_T - \left[\mathbf{s}^\top \mathbf{A}^\top \cdot \mathbf{b} v_i\right]_T \\
&= \left[\mathbf{s}^\top \mathbf{A}^\top \boldsymbol{\kappa} \langle \mathbf{u}, \mathbf{v} \rangle\right]_T.
\end{aligned} \tag{8}$$

Finally, We obtain the functional value $X = \langle \mathbf{u}, \mathbf{v} \rangle$ iff there exists a value X s.t. $\left[\mathbf{s}^\top \mathbf{A}^\top \boldsymbol{\kappa} X\right]_T = \left[\mathbf{s}^\top \mathbf{A}^\top \boldsymbol{\kappa} \langle \mathbf{u}, \mathbf{v} \rangle\right]_T$.

6 Security Analysis

Theorem 1. ***SAD-SIM Security.*** *Our MIPFE scheme achieves the SAD-SIM Security under the MDDH assumption.*

Proof. We follow the game sequences to demonstrate the details of security proof. The output of Game $\mathcal{G}_3$ is the same as that in ideal experiment.

Game $\mathcal{G}_0$: It is actually the real game. This serves as a precursor to Game $\mathcal{G}_1$, aiming to analyze the security of the proposed scheme step-by-step.

Game $\mathcal{G}_1$: $\mathcal{G}_1$ is essentially a modified version of $\mathcal{G}_0$ with the ciphertext been changed with challenge (z^*, t^*, u^*), which is used to verify the security of the encryption algorithm. We modified $[\mathbf{As}]_1$ into $[\mathbf{c}]_1$. That is, we get the challenge ciphertext as follows:

Select $\mathbf{c} \leftarrow \mathbb{Z}_q^{k+1}$, and output the ciphertext

$$ct = \left([\mathbf{c}^\top]_1, \left\{ [\mathbf{c}^\top (z_i \mathbf{W} + t_i \mathbf{W} + \mathbf{U}_i)]_1 \right\}_{i\in[m_1]}, \right. \\ \left. [\mathbf{c}^\top \mathbf{R}(\boldsymbol{\kappa} u_i + \mathbf{b})]_1 \right). \tag{9}$$

Game $\mathcal{G}_2$: It serves as a crucial step in SAD-SIM security and validates the security of the KeyGen algorithm. $\mathcal{G}_2$ aligns with Game $\mathcal{G}_1$ except that we simulate the KeyGen and Enc with semi-adaptive challenge (z^*, t^*, u^*) as follows:

Select $\widetilde{\mathbf{U}}_i \leftarrow_{\mathrm{R}} \mathbb{Z}_q^{(k+1)\times k}$, $\widetilde{\mathbf{s}} \leftarrow_{\mathrm{R}} \mathbb{Z}_q^k$, $\widetilde{\mathbf{b}} \leftarrow_{\mathrm{R}} \mathbb{Z}_q^{(k+1)}$, and random $\theta \leftarrow_{\mathrm{R}} \mathbb{Z}_q$. Set $\mathbf{c}^\top \mathbf{W} = \widetilde{\mathbf{s}}^\top$, $\widetilde{\mathbf{U}}_i = \mathbf{U}_i + w_i^* \mathbf{a}^\perp \widetilde{\mathbf{s}}^\top + z_i^* \mathbf{a}^\perp \widetilde{\mathbf{s}}^\top$, $\widetilde{\mathbf{b}} = \mathbf{b} + u_i^* \theta \mathbf{a}^\perp$, where $\mathbf{c}^\top \mathbf{a}^\perp = 1$. Then, the ciphertext is adapted into

$$ct = \left([\mathbf{c}^\top]_1, \left\{ \left[\mathbf{c}^\top \widetilde{\mathbf{U}_i}\right]_1 \right\}_{i\in[m_1]}, \left\{ \left[\mathbf{c}^\top \mathbf{R}\widetilde{\mathbf{b}}\right]_1 \right\}_{i\in[m_2]} \right). \tag{10}$$

At the same time, the secret key contains sk_1, sk_2, sk_3 and sk_4 as follows:

$$sk_1 = \left[\boldsymbol{\kappa} + \langle \mathbf{z}^*, \mathbf{y} \rangle t_i \mathbf{a}^\perp \widetilde{\mathbf{s}}^\top \mathbf{r} + \langle \mathbf{w}, \mathbf{t}^* \rangle y_i \mathbf{a}^\perp \widetilde{\mathbf{s}}^\top \mathbf{r} - \sum_{i=1}^{m_1} y_i t_i \widetilde{\mathbf{U}}_i \mathbf{r} \right]_2, \\ sk_2 = [y_i \mathbf{r}]_2, sk_3 = [v_i \mathbf{R}^{-1}]_2, sk_4 = [\mathbf{b} v_i]_2. \tag{11}$$

Game $\mathcal{G}_3$: It further validates the randomness of the KeyGen algorithm. $\mathcal{G}_3$ aligns with Game $\mathcal{G}_2$ except for changing the secret key component $\widetilde{\mathbf{s}}^\top \mathbf{r}$ into $\delta \leftarrow_{\mathrm{R}} \mathbb{Z}_q$. That is

$$sk_1 = \left[\boldsymbol{\kappa} + < \mathbf{z}^*, \mathbf{y} > \mathbf{a}^\perp \delta - \sum_{i=1}^{m_1} y_i \widetilde{\mathbf{U}}_i \mathbf{r} \right]_2, sk_2 = [y_i \mathbf{r}]_2, \\ sk_3 = [v_i \mathbf{R}^{-1}]_2, sk_4 = [\widetilde{\mathbf{b}} v_i - \langle \mathbf{u}, \mathbf{v} \rangle \theta \mathbf{a}^\perp]_2. \tag{12}$$

Lemma 1. *No efficient adversary can distinguish $\mathcal{G}_0$ from $\mathcal{G}_1$ with non-negligible advantage, assuming the MDDH assumption under group G_1 holds.*

Proof. Given the instance of MDDH assumption $([\mathbf{A}]_1, [\mathbf{T}]_1)$, i.e., $\mathbf{T} = \mathbf{As}$ or $\mathbf{T} = \mathrm{s}$. The challenger $\mathcal{C}$ can simulate the ciphertext by interacting with adversary $\mathcal{A}$.

$\mathcal{A}$ sends the challenge $(\mathbf{z}^*, \mathbf{t}^*, \mathbf{u}^*)$ to $\mathcal{C}$. $\mathcal{C}$ generates the public parameters pp and send it to $\mathcal{A}$.

$$pp = \left([\mathbf{A}]_1, [\mathbf{A}^\top \mathbf{W}]_1, \left\{ [\mathbf{A}^\top \mathbf{U}_i]_1 \right\}_{i\in[m_1]}, \right. \\ \left. [\mathbf{A}^\top \mathbf{R}\boldsymbol{\kappa}]_1, [\mathbf{A}^\top \mathbf{R}\mathbf{b}]_1 \right). \tag{13}$$

The $\mathcal{C}$ generates the secret key as

$$sk_1 = \left[\boldsymbol{\kappa} - \sum_{i=1}^{m_1} y_i w_i \mathbf{U}_i \mathbf{r}\right]_2, sk_2 = \{[y_i \mathbf{r}]_2\}_{i\in[m_1]},$$
$$sk_3 = \left\{[v_i \mathbf{R}^{-1}]_2\right\}_{i\in[m_2]}, sk_4 = [\sum_{i=1}^{m_2} \mathbf{b} v_i]_2. \tag{14}$$

Given the challenge message vector $\mathbf{z}^*$, $\mathbf{t}^*$, and $\mathbf{u}^*$, the $\mathcal{C}$ generates the ciphertext as

$$ct_1 = [\mathbf{T}]_1, ct_2 = \{[\mathbf{T}(z_i \mathbf{W} + t_i \mathbf{W} + \mathbf{U}_i)]_1\}_{i\in[m_1]},$$
$$ct_3 = \{[\mathbf{T}\mathbf{R}(\boldsymbol{\kappa} u_i^* + \mathbf{b})]_1\}_{i\in[m_2]}. \tag{15}$$

We can observe that when $\mathbf{T} = \mathbf{A}\mathbf{s}$ it occurs in game $\mathcal{G}_0$, when $\mathbf{T} = \mathbf{s}$, it is game $\mathcal{G}_1$. Thus, it is obviously that the difficulty of distinguishing between game $\mathcal{G}_0$ and $\mathcal{G}_1$ is equivalent to solving the MDDH problem in group G_1.

Lemma 2. *No efficient adversary can distinguish $\mathcal{G}_2$ from $\mathcal{G}_1$ with non-negligible advantage under the indistinguishable distribution.*

Proof. The difference between $\mathcal{G}_2$ and $\mathcal{G}_1$ are the way to simulate the ciphertext and secret key.

The $\mathcal{C}$ selects $\widetilde{\mathbf{U}}_i \leftarrow_R \mathbb{Z}_q^{(k+1)\times k}$, $\widetilde{\mathbf{s}} \leftarrow_R \mathbb{Z}_q^k$, $\widetilde{\mathbf{b}} \leftarrow_R \mathbb{Z}_q^{(k+1)}$, and random $\theta \leftarrow_R \mathbb{Z}_q$. Then, it sets $\widetilde{\mathbf{U}}_i = \mathbf{U}_i + w_i^* \mathbf{a}^\perp \widetilde{\mathbf{s}}^\top + z_i^* \mathbf{a}^\perp \widetilde{\mathbf{s}}^\top$, $\widetilde{\mathbf{b}} = \mathbf{b} + u_i^* \theta \mathbf{a}^\perp$, and requires $\mathbf{c}^\top \mathbf{W} = \widetilde{\mathbf{s}}^\top$, $\mathbf{c}^\top \kappa = \theta$ and $\mathbf{c}^\top \mathbf{a}^\perp = 1$. Thus, we get the

$$\begin{aligned} ct_2 &= \left[\mathbf{c}^\top (z_i \mathbf{W} + t_i \mathbf{W} + \mathbf{U}_i)\right]_1 \\ &= \left[\mathbf{c}^\top \left(z_i \mathbf{W} + t_i \mathbf{W} + \widetilde{\mathbf{U}}_i - w_i^* \mathbf{a}^\perp \widetilde{\mathbf{s}}^\top - z_i^* \mathbf{a}^\perp \widetilde{\mathbf{s}}^\top\right)\right]_1 \\ &= \left[\mathbf{c}^\top \widetilde{\mathbf{U}}_i\right]_1. \end{aligned} \tag{16}$$

$$\begin{aligned} ct_3 &= \left[\mathbf{c}^\top \mathbf{R}(\boldsymbol{\kappa} u_i + \mathbf{b})\right]_1 \\ &= \left[\mathbf{c}^\top \mathbf{R}(\boldsymbol{\kappa} u_i + \widetilde{\mathbf{b}} - u_i^* \theta \mathbf{a}^\perp)\right]_1 \\ &= \left[\mathbf{c}^\top \mathbf{R} \boldsymbol{\kappa} u_i + \mathbf{c}^\top \mathbf{R} \widetilde{\mathbf{b}} - \mathbf{c}^\top \mathbf{R} u_i^* \theta \mathbf{a}^\perp\right]_1 \\ &= \left[\mathbf{c}^\top \mathbf{R} \widetilde{\mathbf{b}}\right]_1. \end{aligned} \tag{17}$$

So the ciphertext is changed into

$$ct = \left([\mathbf{c}^\top]_1, \left\{\left[\mathbf{c}^\top \widetilde{\mathbf{U}_i}\right]_1\right\}_{i\in[m_1]}, \left\{\left[\mathbf{c}^\top \mathbf{R} \widetilde{\mathbf{b}}\right]_1\right\}_{i\in[m_2]}\right). \tag{18}$$

Since the $\mathbf{b} = \widetilde{\mathbf{b}} - u_i^* \theta \mathbf{a}^\perp$. We have

$$sk_4 = [\mathbf{b} v_i]_2 = [\widetilde{\mathbf{b}} v_i - \langle \mathbf{u}, \mathbf{v} \rangle \theta \mathbf{a}^\perp]_2. \tag{19}$$

Further, we program the inner product predicates into the secret key. Then, it is changed into

$$sk_1 = \left[\boldsymbol{\kappa} + \langle \mathbf{z}^*, \mathbf{y} \rangle t_i \mathbf{a}^{\perp} \widetilde{\mathbf{s}}^{\top} \mathbf{r} + \langle \mathbf{w}, \mathbf{t}^* \rangle y_i \mathbf{a}^{\perp} \widetilde{\mathbf{s}}^{\top} \mathbf{r} - \sum_{i=1}^{m_1} y_i t_i \widetilde{\mathbf{U}}_i \mathbf{r}\right]_2, \tag{20}$$
$$sk_2 = [y_i \mathbf{r}]_2, sk_3 = [v_i \mathbf{R}^{-1}]_2, sk_4 = [\widetilde{\mathbf{b}} v_i - \langle \mathbf{u}, \mathbf{v} \rangle \theta \mathbf{a}^{\perp}]_2.$$

Note that the ciphertexts and secret key in $\mathcal{G}_2$ and $\mathcal{G}_1$ have the same distribution. Thus, it is difficult to distinguish between these two games.

Lemma 3. *No efficient adversary can distinguish $\mathcal{G}_3$ from $\mathcal{G}_2$ with non-negligible advantage, assuming the MDDH assumption under group G_2 holds.*

Proof. The difference between $\mathcal{G}_3$ and $\mathcal{G}_2$ are the way to simulate the secret key.

It changed the element $\widetilde{\mathbf{s}}^{\top} \mathbf{r}$ into δ, that is

$$sk_1 = \left[\boldsymbol{\kappa} + \langle \mathbf{z}^*, \mathbf{y} \rangle t_i \mathbf{a}^{\perp} \delta + \langle \mathbf{w}, \mathbf{t}^* \rangle y_i \mathbf{a}^{\perp} \delta - \sum_{i=1}^{m_1} y_i t_i \widetilde{\mathbf{U}}_i \mathbf{r}\right]_2, \tag{21}$$
$$sk_2 = [y_i \mathbf{r}]_2, sk_3 = [v_i \mathbf{R}^{-1}]_2, sk_4 = [\widetilde{\mathbf{b}} v_i - \langle \mathbf{u}, \mathbf{v} \rangle \theta \mathbf{a}^{\perp}]_2.$$

Thus, it is obviously that the difficulty of distinguishing between game $\mathcal{G}_3$ and $\mathcal{G}_2$ is equivalent to solving the MDDH problem in group G_2.

In fact, the SAD-SIM security implies the privacy property mentioned in matchmaking encryption, which ensures the confidentiality of function vector and partial predicate vectors in ciphertext.

Theorem 2. ***Authenticity.*** *Our MIPFE scheme achieves authenticity under the SAD-SIM security.*

Proof. The notion of authenticity in our scheme has two aspects. First, it allows each party, whether receiver or sender, to specify its intended communication counterpart. That is, the receiver can define which senders are acceptable, and the sender can similarly define acceptable receivers. Second, the matchmaking mechanism enforces bilateral authentication, meaning that successful decryption occurs only when both parties satisfy each other's predicate policies, which supported by the Correctness in Sect. 5.

Although a formal treatment of authenticity is partially covered in Theorem 1, we provide a brief discussion here for completeness. In the security proof, simulated ciphertexts and secret keys are employed. However, the game sequences show that only simulations consistent with the matchmaking conditions, namely those where $\langle \mathbf{w}, \mathbf{t} \rangle = 0$ and $\langle \mathbf{y}, \mathbf{z} \rangle = 0$, lead to meaningful decryptions. Consequently, if an adversary queries for keys or ciphertexts whose predicate vectors do not satisfy the required orthogonality conditions, decryption necessarily fails and yields $\perp$, thereby preventing unauthorized access to the function output $\langle \mathbf{u}, \mathbf{v} \rangle$. □

Table 1. Feature Comparison

Details	DDM+23	DDH+24	WWS+23	Our
Policy	ZIP\NIP	ZIP\MSP	ZIP	DIP
Control	Unilateral	Unilateral	Unilateral	Bilateral
Att. hid.	Strong	Strong	Weak	Strong
Security	SA-IND	SA-IND	IND	SA-SIM
Assumption	SXDH	SXDH	–	MDDH

Att. hid.: attribute hiding.
ZIP/NIP: zero/non-zero inner product predicate.
MSP: monotone span programs.
DIP: dual inner product predicate(s).
SA-IND: semi-adaptive indistinguishability security.
SA-SIM: semi-adaptive simulation security.
SXDH: symmetric external Diffie-Hellman assumption.
MDDH: matrix decisional Diffie-Hellman assumption.

7 Performance Analysis

In the following subsections, we will carry out feature comparison and experimental analysis.

7.1 Feature Comparision

We compare our scheme with those proposed by Dowerah et al. [13,14] (referred to as DDH+24 and DDM+23 respectively) and Wan et al. [24] (WWS+23) across several key features in Table 1. Our construction supports bilateral access control and achieves stronger simulation-based security. Specifically, it utilizes a dual inner product predicate enforcing orthogonality conditions on both pairs of vectors $\langle \mathbf{w}, \mathbf{t} \rangle$ and $\langle \mathbf{y}, \mathbf{z} \rangle$ to enable fine-grained mutual authorization between sender and receiver. In contrast, the three existing schemes only provide unilateral control realized via a single zero inner product (ZIP) predicate. For clarity and fairness in comparison, we focus on their ZIP-based instantiations. This distinction shows that our scheme is particularly well suited for scenarios requiring bilateral regulation of information flow in secure data sharing.

From the perspective of attribute hiding, our scheme like the DDM+23 and DDH+24 schemes possesses strong attribute hiding properties while the WWS+23 scheme exhibits weak attribute hiding. Here strong means that the adversary can obtain both authorized and unauthorized keys while weak indicates the adversary can only obtain unauthorized keys. Additionally only our scheme achieves SA-SIM security under standard assumptions while the others achieve only indistinguishability security.

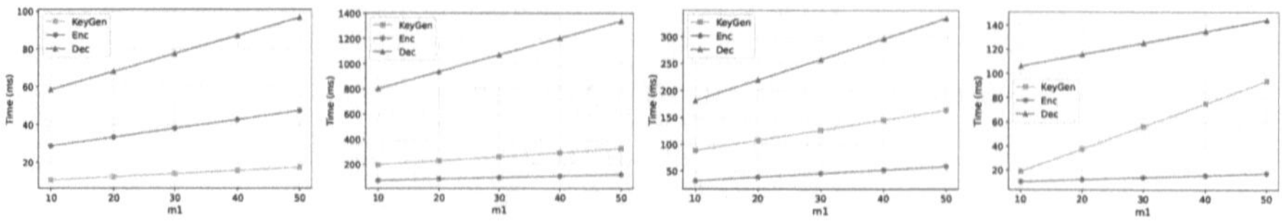

(a) WWS+23 scheme (b) DDM+23 scheme (c) DDH+24 scheme (d) Our scheme

Fig. 2. Computational time with small m_1.

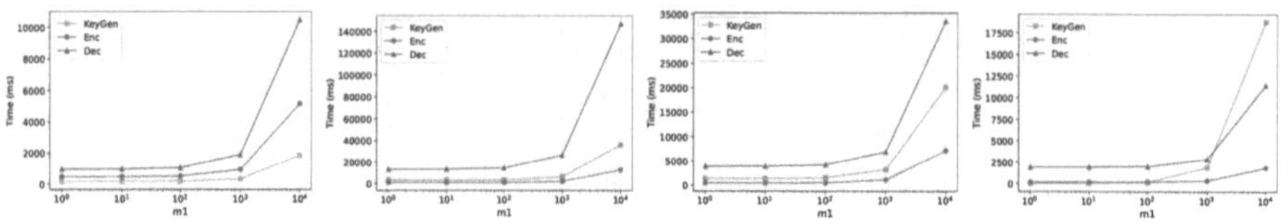

(a) WWS+23 scheme (b) DDM+23 scheme (c) DDH+24 scheme (d) Our scheme

Fig. 3. Computational time with large m_1.

7.2 Experimental Analysis

We implemented the Dowerah et al. DDM+23 scheme [14], the DDH+24 scheme [13] and the Wan et al. WWS+23 scheme [24] in C, utilizing the CiFEr cryptographic library and ate pairing on BN254 curve. All simulations were conducted on a laptop operating Ubuntu 20.04, equipped with an Intel(R) Core (TM) i5-8265U CPU and 8 GB of RAM.

For simplicity, let m_1 represents the length of the dual predicate vectors (totaling four predicate vectors) and m_2 represents the length of the function vectors (totaling two function vectors). We tested the computational and storage overheads under two settings: small predicate vector and large predicate vector. For the small case, we set $m_2 = 50$ and varied m_1 to 10, 20, 30, 40, and 50. For the large case, we set $m_2 = 1000$ and varied m_1 to 10^0, 10^1, 10^2, 10^3, and 10^4. m_1 serves to simulate practical demands for predicate. Figure 2 and Fig. 3 present a comparison of the computational time in these two cases.

In the case of small range, Figs. 2(a), 2(b), 2(c), and 2(d) respectively illustrate the computational time of the KeyGen, Enc, and Dec algorithms for the WWS+23, DDM+23, DDH+24, and our schemes. We observe that the DDM+23 scheme in Fig. 2(b) has the highest overall computational overhead, particularly in decryption, due to both pairing computations and function value evaluations, as well as its ciphertext and key structure being sampled from $\mathbb{Z}_q^7$. The DDM+24 scheme reduces these computational overhead, resulting in more efficient decryption. Our scheme uses more complex predicate vectors for bilateral control, yet it outperforms both DDM+23 and DDM+24 in the KeyGen, Enc, and Dec algorithms. Although the WWS+12 scheme appears to surpass ours, the time difference is minimal. Moreover, they can only prove IND security in the generic group model, whereas we achieve stronger security and bilateral control.

In the case of large range, Figs. 3(a), 3(b), 3(c), and 3(d) illustrate the computational time of the WWS+23, DDM+23, DDH+24, and our schemes. To make the figure more intuitive, we take the logarithm of the x-axis, which has a wide range of values.

In Fig. 3(a), the WWS+23 scheme demonstrates the best performance of computational time increases with m_1. The growth is gradual when m_1 is $10^0, 10^1, 10^2$, and 10^3, but significant increases occur as m_1 approaches 10^4, particularly in the Dec algorithm.

Figure 3(b) shows the DDM+23 scheme has the highest computational times for the KeyGen, Enc, and Dec algorithms, as discussed in the small cases. Similarly, the growth remains slow before $m_1 = 10^3$, after which it rises sharply. At $m_1 = 10^4$, the Dec time reaches approximately $140,000$ milliseconds (about 2.33 minutes).

Figure 3(c) presents the DDH+24 scheme optimizes the performance of DDM+23 scheme. Similarly, the growth remains gradual as m_1 increases from 10^0, 10^1, 10^2, to 10^3. However, compared to the DDM+23 scheme, the time decreases from approximately $20,000$ ms to around $5,000$ ms. As m_1 approaches 10^4, there is also a significant increase in the computational times for all three algorithms. At $m_1 = 10^4$, the Dec time reaches about 35,000 milliseconds (approximately 35 s), resulting in a roughly 75% improvement in decryption efficiency over the DDM+23 scheme.

Figure 3(d) depicts that our scheme is more efficient than both the DDH+24 and DDM+23 schemes. Our computational time remains consistently below 2.5 seconds with a steady increase until $m_1 = 10^3$. Although, at $m_1 = 10^4$, our KeyGen time experiences a rapid increase, it still remains lower than that of the DDH+24 and DDM+23 schemes. At this point, our decryption time shows approximately a 54% improvement over the DDH+24 scheme and about an 87% improvement over the DDM+23 scheme, while maintaining a similar time to that of the WWS+23 scheme.

These results further indicate that the computational overhead of our scheme, despite introducing more expressive bilateral control, is entirely acceptable. Therefore, our scheme is valuable for large-scale applications with hundreds or thousands of nodes.

Table 2. Storage overhead(KB)

Scheme	m_1	10^0	10^1	10^2	10^3	10^4
WWS+23	$\|ct\|$	281.5	284.1	309.4	562.5	3093.8
	$\|sk\|$	140.8	142.0	154.7	281.3	1546.9
DDM+23	$\|ct\|$	985.4	994.2	1082.8	1968.8	10828.1
	$\|sk\|$	1970.7	1988.4	2165.6	3937.5	21656.3
DDH+24	$\|ct\|$	422.4	427.5d	478.1	984.4	6046.9
	$\|sk\|$	844.9	855.0	956.3	1968.8	12093.8
Our	$\|ct\|$	140.9	142.2	154.8	281.4	**1547.0**
	$\|sk\|$	563.1	565.6	590.9	844.0	**3375.3**

As shown in Table 2, for all values of large-sized predicate vectors, the ciphertext size of our scheme (denoted as $|ct|$) is consistently lower than that of other schemes, demonstrating significant advantages. At $m_1 = 10^4$, our scheme requires only 1547 KB, but WWS+23 requires 3093.8 KB, DDM+23 requires 10828.1 KB, and DDH+24 requires 6046.9 KB. The secret key size of our scheme (denoted as $|sk|$) gradually increases with the increase of m_1, but the growth is relatively small, overall demonstrating our competitive storage efficiency.

8 Conclusion

We propose an inner product functional encryption scheme with bilateral control that integrates a newly designed dual inner product predicate into the IPFE framework. Our construction achieves semi-adaptive simulation security under standard assumption and provides both partial and strong attribute hiding, even against adversaries who possess authorized and unauthorized keys. Our scheme offers the following new perspectives: 1) it is the first attempt to address the secure computation of bidirectional information flow by using enhanced IPFE with bilateral control; 2) it aims for simulation security to ensure privacy preservation while enforcing computation. Additionally, experimental evaluation shows that our scheme remains practical for moderate predicate sizes. In particular both computation time and storage overhead scale linearly when the predicate dimension is below 10^3 and remain acceptable even at 10^4. These results suggest that our approach offers a viable foundation for real-world applications requiring mutual authorization and confidential function evaluation.

References

1. Abdalla, M., Bourse, F., De Caro, A., Pointcheval, D.: Simple functional encryption schemes for inner products. In: Katz, J. (ed.) PKC 2015. LNCS, vol. 9020, pp. 733–751. Springer, Heidelberg (2015). https://doi.org/10.1007/978-3-662-46447-2_33
2. Abdalla, M., Catalano, D., Gay, R., Ursu, B.: Inner-product functional encryption with fine-grained access control. In: Moriai, S., Wang, H. (eds.) ASIACRYPT 2020. LNCS, vol. 12493, pp. 467–497. Springer, Cham (2020). https://doi.org/10.1007/978-3-030-64840-4_16
3. Agrawal, S., Libert, B., Maitra, M., Titiu, R.: Adaptive simulation security for inner product functional encryption. In: Kiayias, A., Kohlweiss, M., Wallden, P., Zikas, V. (eds.) PKC 2020. LNCS, vol. 12110, pp. 34–64. Springer, Cham (2020). https://doi.org/10.1007/978-3-030-45374-9_2
4. Ambrona, M., Fiore, D., Soriente, C.: Controlled functional encryption revisited: multi-authority extensions and efficient schemes for quadratic functions. In: Proceedings on Privacy Enhancing Technologies (2021)
5. Ateniese, G., Francati, D., Nunez, D., Venturi, D.: Match me if you can: matchmaking encryption and its applications. J. Cryptol. **34**, 1–50 (2021)
6. Boneh, D., Sahai, A., Waters, B.: Functional encryption: definitions and challenges. In: Ishai, Y. (ed.) TCC 2011. LNCS, vol. 6597, pp. 253–273. Springer, Heidelberg (2011). https://doi.org/10.1007/978-3-642-19571-6_16
7. Boyen, X., Li, Q.: Identity-based matchmaking encryption with enhanced privacy-a generic construction with practical instantiations. In: Tsudik, G., Conti, M., Liang, K., Smaragdakis, G. (eds.) Computer Security, ESORICS 2023. LNCS, vol. 14345, pp. 425–445. Springer, Cham (2024). https://doi.org/10.1007/978-3-031-51476-0_21
8. Chen, B., Xiang, T., Ma, M., He, D., Liao, X.: CL-ME: efficient certificateless matchmaking encryption for internet of things. IEEE Internet Things J. **8**(19), 15010–15023 (2021)

9. Chen, J., Li, Y., Wen, J., Weng, J.: Identity-based matchmaking encryption from standard assumptions. In: International Conference on the Theory and Application of Cryptology and Information Security, pp. 394–422. Springer, Heidelberg (2022)
10. Chiku, S., Hashimoto, K., Hara, K., Shikata, J.: Identity-based matchmaking encryption, revisited: strong security and practical constructions from standard classical and post-quantum assumptions. Cryptology ePrint Archive (2023)
11. Cini, V., Ramacher, S., Slamanig, D., Striecks, C., Tairi, E.: (inner-product) functional encryption with updatable ciphertexts. J. Cryptol. **37**(1), 8 (2024)
12. Datta, P., Pal, T.: Decentralized multi-authority attribute-based inner-product FE: large universe and unbounded. In: IACR International Conference on Public-Key Cryptography. LNCS, pp. 587–621. Springer, Cham (2023). https://doi.org/10.1007/978-3-031-31368-4_21
13. Dowerah, U., Dutta, S., Hartmann, F., Mitrokotsa, A., Mukherjee, S., Pal, T.: SACfe: secure access control in functional encryption with unbounded data. In: 2024 IEEE 9th European Symposium on Security and Privacy (EuroS&P), pp. 860–882. IEEE (2024)
14. Dowerah, U., Dutta, S., Mitrokotsa, A., Mukherjee, S., Pal, T.: Unbounded predicate inner product functional encryption from pairings. J. Cryptol. **36**(3), 29 (2023)
15. Dufour-Sans, E., Pointcheval, D.: Unbounded inner-product functional encryption with succinct keys. In: Deng, R.H., Gauthier-Umaña, V., Ochoa, M., Yung, M. (eds.) ACNS 2019. LNCS, vol. 11464, pp. 426–441. Springer, Cham (2019). https://doi.org/10.1007/978-3-030-21568-2_21
16. Francati, D., Guidi, A., Russo, L., Venturi, D.: Identity-based matchmaking encryption without Random Oracles. In: Adhikari, A., Küsters, R., Preneel, B. (eds.) INDOCRYPT 2021. LNCS, vol. 13143, pp. 415–435. Springer, Cham (2021). https://doi.org/10.1007/978-3-030-92518-5_19
17. Gay, R.: A new paradigm for public-key functional encryption for degree-2 polynomials. In: Kiayias, A., Kohlweiss, M., Wallden, P., Zikas, V. (eds.) PKC 2020. LNCS, vol. 12110, pp. 95–120. Springer, Cham (2020). https://doi.org/10.1007/978-3-030-45374-9_4
18. Lai, Q., Liu, F.-H., Wang, Z.: New lattice two-stage sampling technique and its applications to functional encryption – stronger security and smaller ciphertexts. In: Canteaut, A., Standaert, F.-X. (eds.) EUROCRYPT 2021. LNCS, vol. 12696, pp. 498–527. Springer, Cham (2021). https://doi.org/10.1007/978-3-030-77870-5_18
19. Lin, S., Li, Y., Chen, J.: CCA-secure identity-based matchmaking encryption from standard assumptions. In: Ge, C., Yung, M. (eds.) Information Security and Cryptology, Inscrypt 2023. LNCS, vol. 14526, pp. 253–273. Springer, Singapore (2024). https://doi.org/10.1007/978-981-97-0942-7_13
20. Ma, J., Xu, S., Ning, J., Huang, X., Deng, R.H.: Catch me if you can: a secure bilateral access control system with anonymous credentials. IEEE Trans. Serv. Comput. (2023)
21. Nguyen, K., Phan, D.H., Pointcheval, D.: Multi-client functional encryption with fine-grained access control. In: Agrawal, S., Lin, D. (eds.) International Conference on the Theory and Application of Cryptology and Information Security, pp. 95–125. Springer, Cham (2022). https://doi.org/10.1007/978-3-031-22963-3_4
22. Pal, T., Dutta, R.: CCA secure attribute-hiding inner product encryption from minimal assumption. In: Baek, J., Ruj, S. (eds.) ACISP 2021. LNCS, vol. 13083, pp. 254–274. Springer, Cham (2021). https://doi.org/10.1007/978-3-030-90567-5_13
23. Qiu, M., Han, J., Hao, F., Sun, C., Wu, G.: Privacy-preserving and traceable functional encryption for inner product in cloud computing. IEEE Trans. Cloud Comput. (2025)
24. Wan, M., Wang, G., Sun, S.F., Gu, D.: Function-hiding zero predicate inner product functional encryption from pairings. In: Athanasopoulos, E., Mennink, B. (eds.) Information Security, ISC 2023. LNCS, vol. 14411, pp. 516–534. Springer, Cham (2023). https://doi.org/10.1007/978-3-031-49187-0_26

25. Wee, H.: Attribute-hiding predicate encryption in bilinear groups, revisited. In: Kalai, Y., Reyzin, L. (eds.) TCC 2017. LNCS, vol. 10677, pp. 206–233. Springer, Cham (2017). https://doi.org/10.1007/978-3-319-70500-2_8
26. Wu, A., Feng, D., Zhang, M., Yang, A., Chi, J.: Privacy-preserving bilateral multi-receiver matching with revocability for mobile social networks. IEEE Trans. Mob. Comput. (2024)
27. Wu, A., Luo, W., Weng, J., Yang, A., Wen, J.: Fuzzy identity-based matchmaking encryption and its application. IEEE Trans. Inf. Forensics Secur. (2023)
28. Xu, S., et al.: Match in my way: fine-grained bilateral access control for secure cloud-fog computing. IEEE Trans. Depend. Secure Comput. **19**(2), 1064–1077 (2020)
29. Yan, J., Ling, Y., Chen, J., Qian, H.: MuseME: multi-user secure and efficient matchmaking encryption for mobile devices. IEEE Trans. Inf. Forensics Secur. **20**, 9084–9098 (2025). https://doi.org/10.1109/TIFS.2025.3601539
30. Yang, N., Tang, C., He, D.: A lightweight certificateless multi-user matchmaking encryption for mobile devices: enhancing security and performance. IEEE Trans. Inf. Forensics Secur. (2023)
31. Yang, N., Tang, C., Xiong, Z., He, D.: RCME: a reputation incentive committee consensus-based for matchmaking encryption in IoT healthcare. IEEE Trans. Serv. Comput. (2024)

GPU Accelerated Fully Homomorphic Encryption Framework for End-to-End Logistic Regression

Dillon Davidson[1], Minjae Kang[2], Yeonjoon Lee[3], Zuobin Xiong[1], and Junggab Son[1(✉)]

[1] Department of Computer Science, University of Nevada, Las Vegas, NV 89154, USA
davidd11@unlv.nevada.edu, {Zuobin.Xiong,Junggab.Son}@unlv.edu
[2] Department of Computer Science and Engineering, Major in Bio Artificial Intelligence, Hanyang University, Ansan 15588, South Korea
minjae0110@hanyang.ac.kr
[3] College of Computing, Hanyang University, Ansan 15588, South Korea
yeonjoonlee@hanyang.ac.kr

Abstract. Machine Learning as a Service (MLaaS) platforms are increasingly adopted in regulated domains such as finance and healthcare, where protecting sensitive data and model parameters is paramount. Fully Homomorphic Encryption (FHE) offers rigorous privacy guarantees by enabling computation directly on encrypted data; however, its high computational overhead has limited practical deployment. Prior research has primarily focused on optimizing encrypted deep learning inference, leaving efficient FHE-based training largely unexplored. This paper addresses this gap by presenting a GPU-accelerated CUDA framework for FHE logistic regression models with full 128-bit security. Logistic regression is selected as a foundational case study because it incorporates a nonlinear activation function, making it an essential building block for extending FHE operations to neural networks. Our implementation executes all computations directly over ciphertexts, offloading heavy FHE operations, such as homomorphic addition, multiplication, and bootstrapping, to optimized CUDA GPU kernels. By leveraging GPU parallelism, the framework achieves significant efficiency gains while maintaining strong privacy guarantees. Our open-source design abstracts the complexities of FHE and CUDA, lowering the technical barrier and enabling practitioners to perform privacy-preserving model training without deep cryptographic or GPU programming expertise.

This work was supported in part by Institute of Information & communications Technology Planning & Evaluation (IITP) grant funded by the Korea government (MSIT) (No. RS-2024-00431388, the Global Research Support Program in the Digital Field program). This work was also supported in part by the National Science Foundation under Grant 2429960 and Grant 2434899.

Y. Cao et al. (Eds.): SecureComm 2026, LNICST 704, pp. 449–467, 2027.
https://doi.org/10.1007/978-3-032-32764-2_21

Keywords: Privacy-Preserving Machine Learning · Fully Homomorphic Encryption · Cryptography · Machine Learning · Logistic Regression

1 Introduction

Machine learning has become increasingly pervasive across critical domains, such as healthcare diagnostics [27], financial modeling [29], personalized services [31], and security analytics [12]. The growing popularity of Machine Learning as a Service (MLaaS) [25], where cloud providers host training and inference pipelines, has further accelerated adoption by eliminating the need for organizations to maintain costly GPU infrastructure and by enabling scalable, on-demand computation.

However, outsourcing machine learning to third-party clouds introduces severe privacy and security risks. Sensitive training data, held-out test samples, and even learned model parameters can leak private information through side channels or adversarial attacks [5,16,17]. Fully Homomorphic Encryption (FHE) offers a powerful solution by allowing arbitrary computation directly on encrypted data [11], thereby preserving end-to-end confidentiality. In principle, an FHE-enabled MLaaS system would allow users to train and deploy models without ever exposing plaintext data or model internals [30].

In practice, however, the extreme computational overhead of FHE has hindered its widespread use, especially for model training. Most prior research has concentrated on accelerating encrypted inference in deep learning (e.g., CNNs and transformers) by approximating activation functions and optimizing bootstrapping operations [20–22]. In contrast, efficient training under FHE remains largely unexplored. This gap is particularly striking for classical machine learning models, such as logistic regression, support vector machines, and decision trees, which continue to dominate in regulated industries like finance and healthcare due to their interpretability, auditability, and suitability for modest data regimes [6,15].

Among these, logistic regression serves as an ideal foundational case: it is widely used for binary classification, incorporates a nonlinear activation function that can serve as a building block for neural networks, and presents concrete challenges for FHE-based computation because its iterative optimization and sigmoid function require costly nonlinear approximations [14]. Despite this importance, existing FHE and FHE-ML literature rarely addresses efficient, scalable training for such classical models. Moreover, combining FHE with GPU acceleration remains a significant engineering challenge due to the low-level nature of CUDA programming and the complexity of cryptographic operations.

In this work, we address these challenges by developing an integrated, GPU-accelerated CUDA framework for training and testing FHE-encrypted logistic regression models with full 128-bit security. Our system encapsulates FHE and GPU complexity behind a simple, modular API, substantially lowering the barrier for practitioners who lack deep cryptographic or GPU programming expertise. Our contributions are summarized as follows:

(a) **Complete CUDA-based FHE training pipeline:** We develop a full end-to-end pipeline for training logistic regression models entirely over ciphertexts, ensuring that no plaintext data or parameters are ever exposed during computation.
(b) **Optimized GPU kernels for FHE primitives:** We utilize high performance CUDA kernels for core FHE operations, including homomorphic addition, multiplication, rescaling, and bootstrapping, achieving substantial speedups compared to CPU-based implementations.
(c) **Open-source and extensible framework:** We release our implementation as an open-source CUDA framework that abstracts the cryptographic and GPU programming complexity, enabling reproducible, privacy-preserving machine learning and serving as a foundation for extending FHE-based training to more complex models and neural networks.

2 Related Work

The field of privacy-preserving machine learning (PPML) has progressed rapidly in response to the growing demand for secure data analysis on sensitive information such as financial and medical records [28]. Among the techniques that enable PPML, fully homomorphic encryption (FHE) stands out as a particularly powerful approach, as it allows arbitrary computations to be performed directly on encrypted data—preserving privacy throughout the entire computation process. However, this strong security guarantee comes at the cost of substantial computational overhead: operations on ciphertexts are typically several orders of magnitude slower than their plaintext counterparts, posing a major obstacle to real-world deployment. Our work builds upon a line of research aimed at overcoming this performance bottleneck and moving FHE-based machine learning closer to practical applicability.

Early studies on FHE-based logistic regression (LR) demonstrated the feasibility of training models directly on encrypted data, though with substantial practical limitations [13,14,18,19]. These pioneering works established functional proof-of-concept systems but were largely constrained to small datasets and a limited number of training iterations, primarily due to ciphertext noise accumulation and the high computational overhead of homomorphic operations. A major milestone from this period was the introduction of the CKKS scheme, an approximate homomorphic encryption method that supports floating-point arithmetic and introduces a rescaling operation to control noise growth [7,8]. Collectively, these efforts constitute the first generation of FHE-based logistic regression and laid the groundwork for subsequent research, introducing key techniques such as polynomial approximation of the sigmoid function, the use of Nesterov's Accelerated Gradient, and efficient dataset partitioning strategies.

The second generation of research in FHE-based machine learning shifted focus from demonstrating feasibility to improving efficiency through algorithmic innovation. This progression is best exemplified by the work of Chiang et al. [9,10], who introduced the quadratic gradient method to accelerate first-order gradient descent algorithms. This technique extends Nesterov's Accelerated Gradient by incorporating curvature information derived from the Hessian matrix, resulting in substantially faster convergence. By achieving comparable model accuracy with fewer training iterations, this approach effectively reduces the computational burden of each homomorphic training step and enables the practical evaluation of larger datasets.

While earlier generations of FHE-based machine learning research focused on foundational encryption schemes and algorithmic optimization, achieving practical, large-scale deployment requires integrating these advances with modern high-performance hardware. Our work represents this next evolutionary step by combining the algorithmic innovations of the second generation with GPU acceleration. Specifically, we implement state-of-the-art FHE logistic regression algorithms within a CUDA-based framework, harnessing the massive parallelism of GPUs to overcome the computational bottlenecks inherent in FHE operations. This integration allows us to leverage hardware already common in machine learning environments to achieve faster convergence at a higher security level (128-bit), achieving speedups of 1.40x and 1.84x on the respective datasets over CPU-based implementations. To the best of our knowledge, this is the first system to unify algorithmic efficiency, cryptographic robustness, and hardware-level scalability for fully homomorphic logistic regression training.

3 Preliminaries

This section provides a brief background on homomorphic encryption, Nesterov's Accelerated Gradient, and the quadratic gradient algorithm.

3.1 Homomorphic Encryption

Homomorphic encryption (HE) was first introduced by Rivest et al. in 1978 as a method for performing computations directly on encrypted data without decryption [26]. Early HE schemes were partially homomorphic, supporting only a single operation, either addition or multiplication, on ciphertexts. In 2009, Gentry proposed the first fully homomorphic encryption (FHE) scheme [11], enabling an arbitrary number of additions and multiplications on encrypted data while maintaining semantic security.

In this work, we adopt the modern Cheon-Kim-Kim-Song (CKKS) scheme [7, 8], an approximate FHE scheme based on the Ring learning with errors problem. CKKS natively supports floating-point arithmetic and Single Instruction Multiple Data (SIMD)-style parallelism, making it well suited for GPU implementation. CKKS also possesses the ability to work with complex values, but that is not relevant to this work. Due to the high throughput of operations and support for floating-point arithmetic, CKKS is well suited for machine learning workloads such as logistic regression.

3.2 Nesterov's Accelerated Gradient

Nesterov's Accelerated Gradient (NAG) is a popular choice for the gradient descent optimization algorithm for FHE-based machine learning because it does not require divisions or other non-linear functions like other optimization algorithms [24]. NAG can be formulated as follows:

$$w_{i+1} = v_i + \gamma_i \cdot \nabla_w l(v_i),$$
$$v_{i+1} = (1 - \eta_i) \cdot w_{i+1} + \eta_i \cdot w_i,$$

where w_i and v_i are the two weight vectors updated at each iteration i, and γ_i and η_i are strong convexity and smoothness parameters.

3.3 Quadratic Gradient

Chiang proposed a novel gradient variant called quadratic gradient that converges faster and works well within the restraints of FHE [10]. This gradient variant combines first-order gradient methods with the Hessian matrix, allowing for faster convergence speed.

Newton's method can be used for the optimization, but it requires computing the Hessian matrix along with its inverse at every iteration. Because these computations are expensive, fixed Hessian methods use a constant matrix $\bar{H}$ for improved efficiency. Newton's method is guaranteed to converge as long as $\bar{H} < \nabla^2_\beta l(\beta)$, where $\bar{H}$ is a symmetric negative-definite matrix and " $\leq$" denotes Loewner ordering such that $\nabla^2_\beta l(\beta) - \bar{H}$ is non-negative definite, and the fixed matrix $\bar{H} = -\frac{1}{4}X^T X$ is a good lower bound of the log likelihood function [3]. With a fixed Hessian matrix $\bar{H}$, the iteration for Newton's method is simplified to:

$$\beta_{t+1} = \beta_t - \bar{H}^{-1} \nabla_\beta l(\beta).$$

This fixed Hessian matrix $\bar{H}$ can be replaced with a diagonal matrix B with diagonal elements that are the sums of each row in $\bar{H}$ [4]. For a function $F(x)$ with its gradient g and a Hessian matrix H, the quadratic gradient algorithm begins by generating a diagonal matrix $\bar{B}$ from the Hessian matrix H:

$$\begin{bmatrix} \frac{1}{\varepsilon+\sum_{i=0}^{f}|\bar{h}_{0_i}|} & 0 & \cdots & 0 \\ 0 & \frac{1}{\varepsilon+\sum_{i=0}^{f}|\bar{h}_{1_i}|} & \cdots & 0 \\ \vdots & \vdots & \ddots & \vdots \\ 0 & 0 & \cdots & \frac{1}{\varepsilon+\sum_{i=0}^{f}|\bar{h}_{f_i}|} \end{bmatrix},$$

where $\bar{h}_{ji}$ represents the elements of the Hessian matrix H and ε is a small positive constant. Now, our gradient ascent method for NAG can be written as follows:

$$V_{t+1} = \beta_t + N_t \cdot B^{-1} \cdot \nabla J(\beta_t),$$
$$\beta_{t+1} = (1 - \gamma_t) \cdot V_{t+1} + \gamma_t \cdot V_t,$$

where V_{t+1} is an intermediate variable that is used to update the final weight β_{t+1}, $\gamma_t \in (0, 1)$ is a smoothing parameter, N_t is a learning rate.

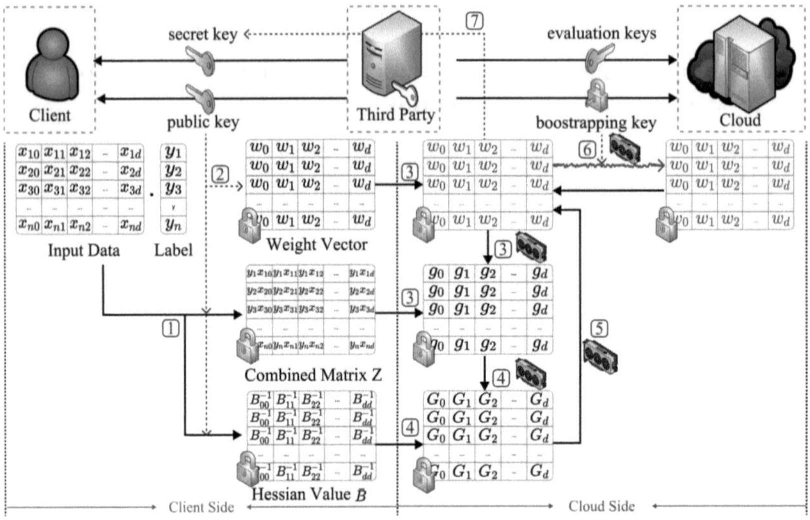

Fig. 1. The overall scheme of logistic regression training via homomorphic encryption with GPU acceleration. Input Data denotes the training data $X = \{x_1, x_2, \ldots, x_n\}$, where $x_i \in \mathbb{R}^{(1+f)}$, and f is the number of features, and Label denotes the corresponding labels $Y = \{y_1, y_2, \ldots, y_n\}$, where $y_i \in \{-1, 1\}$, Combined Matrix the matrix $z \in \mathbb{R}^{n \times d}$ Weight Vector denotes the vector $w \in \mathbb{R}^{d \times 1}$ duplicated n times, $\bar{B}$ is the diagonal approximation of the Hessian matrix, while $g \in \mathbb{R}^{d \times 1}$ and $G \in \mathbb{R}^{d \times 1}$ duplicated n times. All operations on the cloud are performed over ciphertexts; bootstrapping refreshes noise levels between iterations.

3.4 GPU Acceleration

Fully homomorphic encryption (FHE) applications are massively parallelizable; shifting from CPU-based to GPU-based evaluation is therefore essential for achieving practical deployment. Additionally, many machine learning workload scenarios already make use of powerful GPU servers, allowing this method to be implemented with minimal cost. Our work is implemented in FIDESlib, an open-source, MIT-licensed, FHE CKKS GPU library that accelerates server-side FHE operations by leveraging the massive parallelism of CUDA-enabled GPUs [1].

The system architecture we utilize adheres to the Host-Device computational model inherent in CUDA programming. In this model, the Host (CPU) performs

Algorithm 1. Main Loop: Parameter Update and Inner Product

$CT_W \leftarrow 0,\ CT_V \leftarrow 0$
$rnum \leftarrow \lceil N_s/bs \rceil,\ cnum \leftarrow \lceil N_f/bs \rceil$
for $iter = 0$ **to** $E - 1$ **do**
  for $r = 0$ **to** $rnum - 1$ **do**
    $\eta \leftarrow (1 - \alpha_0)/\alpha_1;\ t \leftarrow iter \cdot rnum + r$
    $\gamma \leftarrow \gamma_{\max} - (\gamma_{\max} - \gamma_{\min}) \cdot (t/T_{\text{total}})^{\exp_\gamma}$
    $CT_{\text{IP}} \leftarrow$ ComputeInnerProduct$(CT_Z^{(r)}, CT_V)$
    $CT_{\text{IP}} \leftarrow$ DiagonalSum(CT_{IP})
    $CT_{\text{IP2}} \leftarrow CT_{\text{IP}} \otimes CT_{\text{IP}}$
    $CT_G \leftarrow$ ComputeGradient$(CT_Z^{(r)}, CT_{\text{IP}}, CT_{\text{IP2}}, \gamma)$
    NAGUpdate$(CT_W, CT_V, CT_G, \eta, \gamma)$
  end for
end for

the sequential operations, memory management setup, encryption, decryption, and orchestrates the control flow. The Device (GPU) performs all high-intensity, parallelizable homomorphic operations like addition, multiplication, rotation, and bootstrapping.

FIDESlib integrates directly with the OpenFHE library's client-side operations (encryption, key generation, etc.), while implementing optimized CUDA kernels for all core server-side CKKS primitives [2]. This architecture allows our system to operate on encrypted data that is entirely resident in GPU memory. By orchestrating the sequence of these GPU-accelerated primitives, our proposed system focuses entirely on optimizing the execution time on the Device, which is the central challenge in achieving practical, real-world training with FHE.

4 Proposed Scheme

In this section, we present the logistic regression algorithm for encrypted data using the quadratic gradient-enhanced Nesterov's Accelerated Gradient (NAG). The overall workflow of the proposed scheme is illustrated in (Fig. 1).

4.1 Threat Model

In our framework, we assume a data-owning client, an honest-but-curious server, and a trusted-third party for key generation and management. The trusted third party is responsible for generating the cryptographic parameters and distributing them to the appropriate parties. While we assume a trusted third party for key generation and cryptographic parameters distribution, this party does not access any plaintext data or model parameters. This assumption is common in FHE deployments [23,32], and can be replaced by secure multi-party or threshold key-generation protocols without modifying the proposed framework. Therefore, our security guarantees do not rely on the existence of a permanently trusted entity, but only on the correctness of the initial key setup phase.

Algorithm 2. Subroutines: Inner Product and Gradient Computation

```
function ComputeInnerProduct(CT_Z, CT_V)
    for i = 0 to cnum − 1 do
        CT_IPvec[i] ← CT_Z[i] ⊗ CT_V[i]
    end for
    return ⊕_i CT_IPvec[i]
end function
function DiagonalSum(CT_IP)
    for l = 0 to bBits − 1 do
        CT_IP ← CT_IP ⊕ Rotate(CT_IP, 1 ≪ l)
    end for
    CT_IP ← CT_IP ⊗ C_pvals                              ▷ Extract first slot
    return CT_IP
end function
function ComputeGradient(CT_Z, CT_IP, CT_IP2, γ)
    for i = 0 to cnum − 1 do
        CT_G[i] ← CT_Z[i] ⊗ (Plaintext(γ · d_0) ⊕ CT_IP ⊗ d_1 ⊕ CT_IP2 ⊗ d_2)
        for l = bBits to sBits − 1 do
            CT_G[i] ← CT_G[i] ⊕ Rotate(CT_G[i], 1 ≪ l)
        end for
        CT_G[i] ← CT_G[i] ⊗ CT^(i)_{1/B}
    end for
    return CT_G
end function
function NAGUpdate(CT_W, CT_V, CT_G, η, γ)
    for i = 0 to cnum − 1 do
        CT_Vtmp ← CT_V[i] ⊕ CT_G[i] ⊗ (1 + γ)
        CT_V[i] ← CT_Vtmp ⊗ (1 − η) ⊕ CT_W[i] ⊗ η
        CT_W[i] ← CT_Vtmp
    end for
end function
```

The client owns the sensitive data, encrypts it, and sends the encrypted data with some plaintext metadata to the server for training. The semi-honest server is trusted to perform the proposed protocol, but cannot be allowed to see the decryption of the encrypted data or weights. The server uses the following to manage the algorithm: the number of ciphertexts, the number of batches in the training dataset, the number of epochs, the number of features and samples from the original dataset, the learning rate, the Nesterov momentum weight, the coefficients of the sigmoid polynomial approximation, and the bootstrapping threshold. The plaintext metadata and hyperparameters tell the server "how" to compute, but reveals nothing regarding "what" the actual features, label, or resulting model weights are.

We consider an honest-but-curious (semi-honest) server that follows the protocol, but attempts to infer additional information from the encrypted data and observable metadata. Specifically, the server may:

- inspect ciphertexts and FHE evaluation results,
- observe the model hyperparameters and dataset dimensions, and
- attempt to infer client features, labels, or model parameters.

The CKKS scheme provides IND-CPA (indistinguishability under chosen plaintext attack) security under the ring learning with errors problem [8]. In our implementation, we ensure 128-bit security by selecting parameters that align with the FHE standardization guideline with the help of OpenFHE [2].

This threat model is representative of many real-world MLaaS scenarios, where data owners wish to outsource model training to powerful cloud servers without revealing their sensitive data or proprietary models. In regulated environments like healthcare or finance, even minimal data leakage can have legal or ethical consequences. Our approach ensures end-to-end privacy throughout the training pipeline, bridging the gap between theoretical FHE guarantees and practical, high-performance deployment.

4.2 Polynomial Approximation

An essential step for the logistic regression algorithm is the evaluation of the sigmoid activation function, defined as:

$$g(x) = \frac{1}{1 + e^{-x}}.$$

However, evaluating non-linear functions like sigmoid under fully homomorphic encryption is computationally expensive. This is because the encrypted computations are limited to additions and multiplications, requiring non-linear functions to be approximated using polynomials. Common techniques for polynomial approximation include *Taylor expansion* and *Lagrange interpolation*. While these methods provide accurate approximations around a chosen point, their accuracy degrades significantly outside of that region. In contrast, we adopt the least squares fitting method, which enables us to approximate the sigmoid function with lower error over a larger input range. To ensure a fair comparison with prior works [9,10,13], we use the same third-degree polynomial approximations using the same least squares fitting method for approximating the sigmoid function over the intervals $[-8, +8]$ and $[-16, +16]$:

$$g(x) = 0.5 + 0.15x - 0.0015x^3,$$

and

$$g(x) = 0.5 + 0.0843x - 0.0002x^3.$$

4.3 FHE-Compatible Logistic Regression

We utilize the CKKS homomorphic encryption scheme, which operates over the ring of polynomials $\mathcal{R}_q = \mathbb{Z}_q[X]/(X^N + 1)$ with $N = 2^{17}$. To leverage the SIMD

(Single Instruction, Multiple Data) capabilities of CUDA-accelerated FHE, we employ a packing morphism $\pi : \mathbb{C}^S \rightarrow \mathcal{R}_q$ that maps a vector of values into the slots of a single plaintext polynomial, where $S = N/2$ denotes the number of available slots. For this work, inputs are real-valued, so we utilize the real component of the slots.

1. **Data Preparation and Hessian Generation:** Given the training dataset $X = \{x_1, x_2, \ldots, x_n\}$, where $x_i \in \mathbb{R}^{(1+f)}$, and f is the number of features, and corresponding labels $Y = \{y_1, y_2, \ldots, y_n\}$, where $y_i \in \{-1, 1\}$, we use the encoding method from previous works to pack the training data efficiently into ciphertexts [14], which we detail later. Before encryption, the training data is normalized into the range $(0, 1)$ and the training labels are adjusted to $\{-1, +1\}$. The matrices X and Y are combined into a matrix Z as follows:

$$Z = \begin{bmatrix} z_{0,0} & z_{0,1} & \cdots & z_{0,f} \\ z_{1,0} & z_{1,1} & \cdots & z_{1,f} \\ \vdots & \vdots & \ddots & \vdots \\ z_{n,0} & z_{n,1} & \cdots & z_{n,f} \end{bmatrix}$$

   where $z_{i,j} = y_i \cdot x_{i,j}$ for $0 \leq i \leq n$ and $0 \leq i \leq f$.
   Since the dimensions of Z typically exceed the slot count S, we partition Z into a grid of sub-matrices, each sized $m \times g$ such that $m \cdot g \leq S$. Here, m represents the batch size within a ciphertext, and g represents the feature subset size. The total matrix Z is split into blocks as follows:

$$Z_{i,j} = \begin{bmatrix} z_{0,0} & z_{0,1} & \cdots & z_{0,f} \\ z_{1,0} & z_{1,1} & \cdots & z_{1,f} \\ \vdots & \vdots & \ddots & \vdots \\ z_{n,0} & z_{n,1} & \cdots & z_{n,f} \end{bmatrix},$$

   where $0 \leq i \leq n/m$ and $0 \leq j \leq f/g$. The numbers m and g are both powers of two such that $m \times g = N/2$, which is the maximum number of slots. The client then computes the diagonal matrix $\bar{B}$ derived from the fixed Hessian $\bar{H} = -\frac{1}{4}X^T X$. This pre-computation creates a constant curvature approximation that accelerates convergence without requiring expensive matrix inversions during training.
2. **Encryption:** The client encrypts each sub-matrix $Z_{i,j}$ that is packed and encrypted into a single ciphertext in a row-wise manner. The client also encrypts the encrypted diagonal of the matrix $\bar{B} = -\frac{1}{4}X^T X$ and the weight vector $w \in \mathbb{R}^d$ is duplicated n times and encrypted in a row-wise manner as well. These ciphertexts are then sent to the cloud server.
3. **Secure Transmission:** The resulting ciphertexts of w, Z, and $\bar{B}$, along with necessary public evaluation keys (e.g., rotation and relinearization keys), are transmitted to the cloud server. The server receives only encrypted data and metadata (e.g., tensor dimensions, polynomial degrees) but gains no access to plaintext features or labels.

4. **Encrypted Gradient Computation:** The server iteratively optimizes the model using the quadratic gradient method over ciphertexts. For each iteration, the server executes the following sequence (as detailed in Algorithm 1):
   - **Inner Product:** The server first computes the inner product vector $[\![u_t]\!]$. This operation requires calculating the dot product between the data samples and the weights. In the packed SIMD domain, this is realized by an element-wise multiplication ($\odot$) followed by a rotational accumulation to sum the partial products across the feature slots:

$$[\![\text{temp}]\!] = [\![Z]\!] \odot [\![v_t]\!],$$

$$[\![u_t]\!] = \sum_{k=0}^{\log_2(g)-1} \text{rot}([\![\text{temp}]\!], 2^k).$$

     Here, $\text{rot}(\cdot, k)$ denotes a homomorphic rotation by k slots (Algorithm 2, *COMPUTEINNERPRODUCT*).
   - **Activation Approximation:** The result $[\![u_t]\!]$ is passed through the activation function. To remain compatible with FHE arithmetic, we approximate the sigmoid function $\sigma(u) = (1+e^{-u})^{-1}$ using a least-squares fitted degree-3 polynomial $P(u) = c_0 + c_1 u + c_3 u^3$:

$$[\![a_t]\!] = c_0 + c_1 \cdot [\![u_t]\!] + c_3 \cdot ([\![u_t]\!])^3.$$

   - **Gradient Aggregation:** The gradient $\nabla J(\beta_t)$ is computed by scaling the error term $([\![a_t]\!] - [\![Y]\!])$ by the transposed feature matrix. Exploiting the SIMD layout, we compute the gradient for all packed samples simultaneously:

$$[\![\nabla J_t]\!] = \frac{1}{n} \sum_{i,j} \left([\![Z_{i,j}^T]\!] \odot ([\![a_t]\!] - [\![Y]\!]) \right).$$

     The result represents the aggregated gradient across the entire batch, packed into the weight-aligned ciphertext slots (Algorithm 2, *COMPUTE-GRADIENT*).
5. **Model Update via Quadratic Gradient:** Using the encrypted gradient and the encrypted Hessian diagonal $\bar{B}$, the server updates the weight vector. To fully utilize the GPU's parallelism, the update rule is applied element-wise across all packed weight slots simultaneously. We define the update sequence using the Hadamard product ($\odot$) to denote these parallel operations:

$$[\![V_{t+1}]\!] = [\![\beta_t]\!] + (N_t \odot [\![\bar{B}]\!]^{-1}) \odot [\![\nabla J(\beta_t)]\!],$$

$$[\![\beta_{t+1}]\!] = (1 - \gamma_t) \cdot [\![V_{t+1}]\!] + \gamma_t \cdot [\![V_t]\!].$$

   This formulation explicitly incorporates Nesterov's momentum (γ_t) and the Hessian-derived learning rate scaling ($N_t \odot \bar{B}^{-1}$), executing the entire update step without decryption.

6. **Bootstrapping and Noise Management:** To support the deep multiplicative depth required for iterative training, we perform a bootstrapping operation every 2 iterations of the training loop.

$$[\![\beta_t]\!]_{fresh} \leftarrow \mathsf{Bootstrap}([\![\beta_t]\!]).$$

   Each training iteration consumes approximately six levels of computation. Through empirical evaluation, we found that refreshing the ciphertext noise via bootstrapping every two iterations prevents decryption failures while maximizing throughput. This schedule allows us to use smaller cryptographic parameters while maintaining security and it outperforms bootstrapping every iteration or every three iterations, as is done in prior works [9,14].
7. **Decryption and Model Retrieval:** Once the training loop completes, the final encrypted weight vector $[\![w]\!]$ is transmitted to the client. The client recovers the plaintext parameters by applying the secret key and the inverting the packing morphism:

$$w_{final} = \pi^{-1}(\mathsf{Dec}_{sk}([\![w]\!])).$$

8. **Encrypted Inference Testing:** Typically in FHE-based logistic regression the goal is for a server to train the logistic regression model and return the encrypted weights to the client. The client then decrypts and decodes the weights to run the inferences locally. However, we benchmark server-side encrypted inference to demonstrate throughput. The inference operation for a packed input vector $\mathbf{x}$ is defined as:

$$[\![\hat{y}]\!] = g\left(\sum_k \mathrm{rot}([\![\mathbf{w}]\!] \odot [\![\mathbf{x}]\!], 2^k)\right).$$

   This combines the parallel dot product (multiplication and rotational sum) with the polynomial activation $g(\cdot)$ we utilized during training.

A detailed description of the complete training algorithm is provided in Algorithm 1, with supporting subroutines defined in Algorithm 2.

5 Experimental Setup

We evaluate the effectiveness of this quadratic gradient logistic regression against a real financial training dataset and a restructured MNIST dataset for binary classifications, as in earlier works [9,14]. The OpenFHE library is used to select encryption parameters guaranteeing 128-bits of security. We use a mini batch size of 1,024 for the experiments and perform a single bootstrapping operation per iteration. We evaluated all GPU-based and CPU-based experiments on a server running Ubuntu 24.04.3 with 2 AMD EPYC 9355 32-core, 755 gigabytes of RAM, and an NVIDIA L40S GPU with 48 gigabytes of memory. We compare our GPU-based logistic regression directly against the multi-threaded CPU versions by Chiang [9] and Han et al. [14] using their publicly available code.

Table 1. Dataset Information

Dataset	Training Samples	Testing Samples	# of Features
Credit	422,108	844,217	200
MNIST	11,982	1,984	196

5.1 Implementation Details

We implemented our work using FIDESlib, an open-source, MIT-licensed FHE CKKS GPU library that accelerates server-side homomorphic encryption operations through the massive parallelism of CUDA-enabled GPUs [1]. The implementation integrates with OpenFHE version 1.2.4 and was compiled using version 13.3 of the GNU G++ compiler with version 12.9 of CUDA. We configured the CKKS scheme with a polynomial modulus degree of 131,072 (2^{17}) and a coefficient modulus chain selected to achieve 128-bit security. GPU memory management was handled automatically by FIDESlib. Our FHE logistic regression training implementation runs end-to-end on the GPU, with the key generation, preprocessing, encryption, and decryption performed on the CPU. Our implementation is available on our website[1].

5.2 Metrics

We evaluate our quadratic gradient logistic regression using training time, testing accuracy, precision, recall, and F1 score as the primary metrics. For the binary classification tasks on both datasets, the reported results are averaged across 10 runs for 10 epochs to ensure consistency. Our work and Chiang's separate the dataset into iterations and use the full dataset for every epoch while Han's uses a preselected number of iterations and randomly chooses a mini batch for every iteration with no guarantees that the full dataset will be used during the training [9,14]. For both datasets, we modify the number of iterations so Han's work runs for the same number of iterations as ours and Chiang's to ensure consistency. This change, along with modifying the functions that compute accuracy to also calculate precision, F1, recall, and inference times are the only changes made to Han's code and Chiang's code.

Precision, recall, and F1 score are computed as follows:

$$\text{Precision} = \frac{\text{TP}}{\text{TP} + \text{FP}}, \quad \text{Recall} = \frac{\text{TP}}{\text{TP} + \text{FN}}, \quad \text{F1 score} = 2 \cdot \frac{\text{Precision} \cdot \text{Recall}}{\text{Precision} + \text{Recall}},$$

where TP is the number of true positives, FP is the number of false positives, and FN is the number of false negatives. These metrics provide a more detailed evaluation of model performance beyond accuracy, particularly in the presence of class imbalance.

---

[1] https://iis.sites.unlv.edu/.

Table 2. Algorithm Performance Comparison. We compare our work against the baseline implementations by Chiang [9] and Han [14]. The multi-threaded CPU implementations provides 80-bit security, while our GPU framework achieves 128-bit security. Training Time (s) refers to training time per epoch in seconds, Accuracy refers to testing accuracy after training for 10 epochs, and F1, Recall, and Precision refer to the metrics computed from the final model. All metrics are averaged over 10 runs with 10 epochs in each run.

Dataset	Method	Training Time	Inference Time	Accuracy	F1	Recall	Precision
Credit	Chiang	677.7 ± 21.3	1.41 ± 0.08	22.48%	0.5318	0.5680	0.4132
	Ours	**368.3 ± 9.3**	**0.72 ± 0.05**	**77.75%**	**0.6316**	**0.9017**	**0.4860**
MNIST	Han	1,336.8 ± 12.1	1.39 ± 0.06	49.09%	0.6368	0.9176	0.4877
	Chiang	1,015 ± 35.7	1.44 ± 0.05	**93.76%**	**0.6534**	**0.9612**	**0.4950**
	Ours	**724.5 ± 25.0**	**0.87 ± 0.12**	90.08%	0.6316	0.9020	0.4862

5.3 Dataset

Table 1 provides specific information about the datasets used, including sample counts and feature count.

Financial Dataset (Credit). The financial dataset comprises 422,108 training samples with 200 features, representing a real-world binary classification task. This large-scale dataset is used to evaluate the scalability and GPU acceleration effectiveness of our quadratic gradient logistic regression under FHE.

MNIST Dataset. We restructure the MNIST dataset for binary classification by grouping handwritten digits into two classes. With 11,982 training samples and 196 features (14×14 images), it serves as a standard benchmark to validate the performance of our method.

6 Results

Table 2 presents the detailed results of our experiment. We compare the training time per epoch, the testing accuracy after 10 epochs, the F1 score, the recall score, and the precision score. All results are averaged after 10 runs. The runtime measurements do not include preprocessing or data encryption, only the training algorithm. The CPU baselines Encrypted inference for logistic regression consists of a few ciphertext multiplications and additions. Since no bootstrapping is required and the number of homomorphic operations is small, inference time is often negligible compared to encrypted training and is therefore not explicitly reported in previous works, but we provide ours for thoroughness.

The financial dataset consists of real consumer credit information consisting of 200 features relevant to credit rating like credit card usage, delinquency records, etc. The samples are labeled for a binary classification which represent whether the individual's credit rating is below a specific threshold. Our GPU-accelerated version outperformed the previous works by a minimum of

1.84 times faster epoch training time. In terms of accuracy, Chiang's implementation becomes unstable after about 6 epochs, reducing the accuracy down to 22.48%, while ours stays consistent and ends at 77.75%, as shown in (Fig. 2). We believe this drastic drop in Chiang's work is due to instability in the scaling factor after many computations, but we note that Chiang's work achieves a similar accuracy to ours for fewer epochs. We also include the F1, precision, and recall scores as comparison and our work achieves the best results for all three metrics. On this dataset, Han et al.'s work converged to perfect accuracy at every iteration which prevents a fair comparison and thus we omit this result.

We also performed logistic regression on the public MNIST dataset. The dataset was restructured as a classification problem between the digits 3 and 8. The original 28×28 pixel images were compressed to 14×14 pixels by averaging each 2×2 pixel block. This restructured MNIST dataset contains 11,982 training samples with 1,984 testing samples. Our work achieved a training time of 724.5 s per epoch with a final accuracy of 90.08%. Our GPU-accelerated version outperformed the previous works by a minimum of 1.40 times faster epoch training time. While our work exhibits the fastest training time per epoch, it lags behind the 93.76% accuracy of Chiang's work. We also observe that Han et al.'s work showed a degradation in performance after about 120 iterations, similar to what happened to Chiang's work for the financial dataset, but not as impactful. We also believe this may be related to a scaling issue that builds up after multiple iterations.

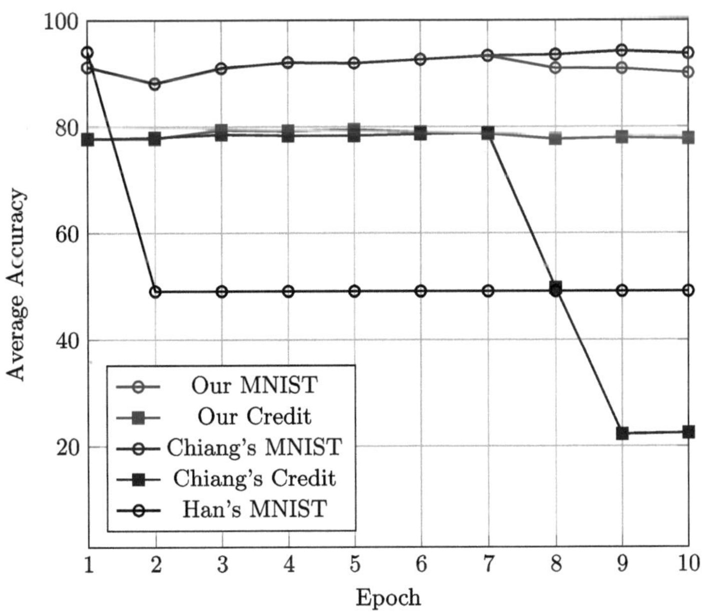

Fig. 2. Average Accuracy versus Epochs for the 5 experiments across the 10 runs.

7 Discussion

Our approach trades a small reduction in accuracy for a substantial improvement in runtime, achieving significantly faster training while maintaining competitive classification performance. This discrepancy primarily stems from the numerical characteristics of the CKKS scheme and the precision management strategy adopted during encrypted training.

Specifically, our implementation employs OpenFHE's *FLEXIBLEAUTO* rescaling mode[2], which automatically adjusts ciphertext scales after each multiplication to maintain numerical stability. Although this feature greatly simplifies implementation by eliminating the need for manual scale management, it introduces small rounding errors at every rescaling step. According to OpenFHE documentation [2], this process can result in a precision loss of approximately 3–4 bits per rescale. When accumulated across multiple encrypted gradient updates and bootstrapping cycles, these rounding effects can slightly distort the magnitude and direction of gradients, leading to minor deviations in the trained model's decision boundary.

Another contributing factor is the cubic polynomial approximation used for the sigmoid activation function. While this polynomial offers computational efficiency under FHE constraints, it introduces bounded approximation errors, particularly for input values outside the fitted interval. For the Credit dataset, the interval is $[-8, 8]$ and for the MNIST dataset, the interval is $[-16, 16]$, as done in previous works by Chiang [9] and Han et al. [14]. However, if the input values to the polynomial fall outside of this range, then the values can wildly diverge causing accuracy problems. This issue can be mitigated through a higher-degree polynomial, but at the cost of a larger multiplicative depth.

A key design difference between our work and prior approaches concerns bootstrapping placement. Chiang's work performs bootstrapping at every iteration after the first [9]. Han's work performs bootstrapping every three iterations [14]. Our work performs bootstrapping every two iterations. Selecting an appropriate depth is important for optimization because bootstrapping is the most expensive FHE operation. While an intuitive strategy is to minimize the number of bootstrapping operations, this is not always optimal, since increasing noise levels in ciphertexts can significantly slow down subsequent homomorphic computations. Our approach strikes a balance between these two strategies by reducing excessive bootstrapping overhead while preventing noise growth from degrading performance, resulting in a more stable and efficient training process.

Despite these sources of numerical noise, our GPU-based framework maintains model accuracy within 2–3% of the multi-threaded CPU baseline while achieving speedups of 1.40x and 1.84x on the respective datasets. These results show that the accuracy-runtime tradeoff is favorable enough for real deployment scenarios. Future work will investigate manual precision tuning for CKKS scaling factors and higher-degree polynomial approximations to enhance numerical fidelity without significantly increasing computational cost.

[2] https://openfhe.org/.

8 Conclusion

The proposed CUDA framework advances the state of privacy-preserving machine learning by introducing the first end-to-end, GPU-accelerated FHE framework for the training of logistic regression models. The proposed system achieves full 128-bit security and substantially mitigates the computational bottlenecks that have long constrained FHE-based training. Experimental results on real-world financial data and a restructured MNIST dataset demonstrate a minimum speedup of 1.84x and 1.40x speedup over multi-threaded CPU-based implementations while maintaining comparable model accuracy. These findings provide compelling evidence that GPU acceleration can make encrypted model training practically viable, bridging the gap between theoretical privacy guarantees and scalable, real-world deployment. Beyond performance gains, our analysis highlights the critical role of rescaling precision in preserving model fidelity under encryption. Future work will extend this framework to other classical algorithms and activation functions, and explore the potential of quadratic gradient optimization as a general strategy for accelerating broader FHE-based machine learning workloads.

References

1. Agulló-Domingo, C., et al.: FIDESlib: a fully-fledged open-source FHE library for efficient CKKS on GPUs. In: 2025 IEEE International Symposium on Performance Analysis of Systems and Software (ISPASS), pp. 1–3 (2025). https://doi.org/10.1109/ISPASS64960.2025.00045,
2. Badawi, A.A., et al.: OpenFHE: open-source fully homomorphic encryption library. Cryptology ePrint Archive, Paper 2022/915 (2022). https://eprint.iacr.org/2022/915
3. Böhning, D., Lindsay, B.G.: Monotonicity of quadratic-approximation algorithms. Ann. Inst. Stat. Math. **40**(4), 641–663 (1988). https://doi.org/10.1007/BF00049423
4. Bonte, C., Vercauteren, F.: Privacy-preserving logistic regression training. BMC Med. Genomics **11**(Suppl 4), 86 (2018)
5. Chabanne, H., Danger, J.L., Guiga, L., Kühne, U.: Side channel attacks for architecture extraction of neural networks. CAAI Trans. Intell. Technol. **6**(1), 3–16 (2021). https://doi.org/10.1049/cit2.12026, https://ietresearch.onlinelibrary.wiley.com/doi/abs/10.1049/cit2.12026
6. Chen, M.Y.: Predicting corporate financial distress based on integration of decision tree classification and logistic regression. Exp. Syst. Appl. **38**(9), 11261–11272 (2011). https://doi.org/10.1016/j.eswa.2011.02.173, https://www.sciencedirect.com/science/article/pii/S0957417411003976
7. Cheon, J.H., Han, K., Kim, A., Kim, M., Song, Y.: Bootstrapping for approximate homomorphic encryption. In: Nielsen, J.B., Rijmen, V. (eds.) EUROCRYPT 2018. LNCS, vol. 10820, pp. 360–384. Springer, Cham (2018). https://doi.org/10.1007/978-3-319-78381-9_14
8. Cheon, J.H., Kim, A., Kim, M., Song, Y.: Homomorphic encryption for arithmetic of approximate numbers. In: Takagi, T., Peyrin, T. (eds.) ASIACRYPT 2017. LNCS, vol. 10624, pp. 409–437. Springer, Cham (2017). https://doi.org/10.1007/978-3-319-70694-8_15

9. Chiang, J.: Privacy-preserving logistic regression training on large datasets (2025). https://arxiv.org/abs/2406.13221
10. Chiang, J.: Privacy-preserving logistic regression training with a faster gradient variant (2025). https://arxiv.org/abs/2201.10838
11. Gentry, C.: Fully homomorphic encryption using ideal lattices. In: Proceedings of the Forty-First Annual ACM Symposium on Theory of Computing, STOC '09, pp. 169–178. Association for Computing Machinery, New York, NY, USA (2009). https://doi.org/10.1145/1536414.1536440
12. Ghadi, Y.Y., et al.: Machine learning solutions for the security of wireless sensor networks: a review. IEEE Access **12**, 12699–12719 (2024). https://doi.org/10.1109/ACCESS.2024.3355312
13. Han, K., Hong, S., Cheon, J.H., Park, D.: Efficient logistic regression on large encrypted data. Cryptology ePrint Archive, Paper 2018/662 (2018). https://eprint.iacr.org/2018/662
14. Han, K., Hong, S., Cheon, J.H., Park, D.: Logistic regression on homomorphic encrypted data at scale. Proc. AAAI Conf. Artif. Intell. **33**(01), 9466–9471 (2019). https://doi.org/10.1609/aaai.v33i01.33019466, https://ojs.aaai.org/index.php/AAAI/article/view/5000
15. Hua, Z., Wang, Y., Xu, X., Zhang, B., Liang, L.: Predicting corporate financial distress based on integration of support vector machine and logistic regression. Exp. Syst. Appl. **33**(2), 434–440 (2007). https://doi.org/10.1016/j.eswa.2006.05.006, https://www.sciencedirect.com/science/article/pii/S095741740600159X
16. Huang, L., Joseph, A.D., Nelson, B., Rubinstein, B.I., Tygar, J.D.: Adversarial machine learning. In: Proceedings of the 4th ACM Workshop on Security and Artificial Intelligence, AISec '11, pp. 43–58. Association for Computing Machinery, New York, NY, USA (2011). https://doi.org/10.1145/2046684.2046692
17. Joud, R., Moëllic, P.A., Pontié, S., Rigaud, J.B.: A practical introduction to side-channel extraction of deep neural network parameters. In: Buhan, I., Schneider, T. (eds.) Smart Card Research and Advanced Applications. LNCS, pp. 45–65. Springer, Cham (2023). https://doi.org/10.1007/978-3-031-25319-5_3
18. Kim, A., Song, Y., Kim, M., Lee, K., Cheon, J.H.: Logistic regression model training based on the approximate homomorphic encryption. BMC Med. Genomics **11**(Suppl 4), 83 (2018). https://doi.org/10.1186/s12920-018-0401-7
19. Kim, M., Song, Y., Wang, S., Xia, Y., Jiang, X.: Secure logistic regression based on homomorphic encryption: Design and evaluation. JMIR Med Inform. **6**(2), e19 (2018). https://doi.org/10.2196/medinform.8805, http://medinform.jmir.org/2018/2/e19/
20. Lee, E., et al.: Low-complexity deep convolutional neural networks on fully homomorphic encryption using multiplexed parallel convolutions. In: Chaudhuri, K., Jegelka, S., Song, L., Szepesvari, C., Niu, G., Sabato, S. (eds.) Proceedings of the 39th International Conference on Machine Learning. Proceedings of Machine Learning Research, 17–23 July 2022, vol. 162, pp. 12403–12422. PMLR (2022). https://proceedings.mlr.press/v162/lee22e.html
21. Lee, J.W., et al.: Privacy-preserving machine learning with fully homomorphic encryption for deep neural network. IEEE Access **10**, 30039–30054 (2022). https://doi.org/10.1109/ACCESS.2022.3159694
22. Meftah, S., Tan, B.H.M., Mun, C.F., Aung, K.M.M., Veeravalli, B., Chandrasekhar, V.: DOReN: toward efficient deep convolutional neural networks with fully homomorphic encryption. IEEE Trans. Inf. Forensics Secur. **16**, 3740–3752 (2021). https://doi.org/10.1109/TIFS.2021.3090959

23. Nawaz, A., et al.: Secure distributed sparse gaussian process models using multi-key homomorphic encryption. Proc. AAAI Conf. Artif. Intell/ **38**(13), 14431–14439 (2024). https://doi.org/10.1609/aaai.v38i13.29357, https://ojs.aaai.org/index.php/AAAI/article/view/29357
24. Nesterov, Y.: A method for solving the convex programming problem with convergence rate o (1/k2). In: Dokl akad nauk Sssr, vol. 269, p. 543 (1983)
25. Ribeiro, M., Grolinger, K., Capretz, M.A.: MLaaS: machine learning as a service. In: 2015 IEEE 14th International Conference on Machine Learning and Applications (ICMLA), pp. 896–902 (2015). https://doi.org/10.1109/ICMLA.2015.152
26. Rivest, R.L., Adleman, L., Dertouzos, M.L.: On data banks and privacy homomorphisms (1978)
27. Shailaja, K., Seetharamulu, B., Jabbar, M.A.: Machine learning in healthcare: a review. In: 2018 Second International Conference on Electronics, Communication and Aerospace Technology (ICECA), pp. 910–914 (2018). https://doi.org/10.1109/ICECA.2018.8474918
28. Tanuwidjaja, H.C., Choi, R., Baek, S., Kim, K.: Privacy-preserving deep learning on machine learning as a service-a comprehensive survey. IEEE Access **8**, 167425–167447 (2020). https://doi.org/10.1109/ACCESS.2020.3023084
29. Valaitis, V., Villa, A.T.: A machine learning projection method for macro-finance models. Quant. Econ. **15**(1), 145–173 (2024). https://doi.org/10.3982/QE1403, https://onlinelibrary.wiley.com/doi/abs/10.3982/QE1403
30. Wood, A., Najarian, K., Kahrobaei, D.: Homomorphic encryption for machine learning in medicine and bioinformatics. ACM Comput. Surv. **53**(4) (2020). https://doi.org/10.1145/3394658
31. Xu, K., Zhou, H., Zheng, H., Zhu, M., Xin, Q.: Intelligent classification and personalized recommendation of e-commerce products based on machine learning (2024). https://arxiv.org/abs/2403.19345
32. Xu, W., Sun, J., Cardell-Oliver, R., Mian, A., Hong, J.B.: A privacy-preserving framework using homomorphic encryption for smart metering systems. Sensors **23**(10) (2023). https://doi.org/10.3390/s23104746, https://www.mdpi.com/1424-8220/23/10/4746

Sinba: Low-Latency Vectorized Batch PIR via 2D Baby-Step/Giant-Step

Zijun Ma[1,2], Peizhe Song[1,2(✉)], and Mingsheng Wang[3]

[1] State Key Laboratory of Cyberspace Security Defense, Institute of Information Engineering, Chinese Academy of Sciences, Beijing, China
songpeizhe@iie.ac.cn
[2] School of Cyber Security, University of Chinese Academy of Sciences, Beijing, China
[3] Institute of Information Engineering, Chinese Academy of Sciences, Beijing, China

Abstract. We present Sinba, an optimized realization of Vectorized Batch Private Information Retrieval (VB-PIR) built on RLWE-based homomorphic encryption with SIMD batching. While prior VB-PIR systems significantly reduce communication by packing queries and merging responses across buckets, their server-side online latency is often dominated by rotation-heavy packed inner products executed multiple times (e.g., slot selection and aggregation). Sinba targets this bottleneck through three complementary techniques. First, it encodes database records into a two-dimensional slot layout, mapping multi-slot payloads onto multiple plaintext rows with regular structure. Second, it rewrites the dominant rotate-multiply-accumulate computation as a 2D baby-step/giant-step (BSGS) schedule, enabling reuse of baby-step rotations across rows and supporting an unbalanced parameter choice tuned to the number of rows, thereby reducing rotations from $\Theta(N)$ to approximately $\Theta(\sqrt{N})$. Third, Sinba shifts rotation alignment into offline preprocessing, storing the encoded database in NTT form to accelerate ciphertext-plaintext products in the online phase. We evaluate across batch size, database size, and payload length. On a database of 2^{20} items with 256-byte payloads, Sinba reduces server response latency by 8.5–13.3× compared to the VB-PIR baseline of Mughees and Ren (IEEE S&P 2023), while preserving the communication advantages of vectorization.

Keywords: FHE · Batch PIR · BSGS

1 Introduction

User privacy is a critical challenge in cloud-based services, where sensitive queries and user-generated data are routinely processed by third-party infrastructure. Cryptographic protocols provide principled mechanisms to mitigate such leakage, and *private information retrieval* (PIR) is a foundational primitive in this space: it enables a client to retrieve a record from a server-hosted database without revealing which record is being requested to the server [8]. Efficient PIR can

Y. Cao et al. (Eds.): SecureComm 2026, LNICST 704, pp. 468–501, 2027.
https://doi.org/10.1007/978-3-032-32764-2_22

support privacy-preserving applications including DNS privacy extensions [31], password-breach checking [15], and anonymous communication systems [3,21].

At a high level, PIR protocols are divided into multi-server and single-server schemes. Multi-server PIR offers high efficiency but requires a non-collusion assumption among servers [8], hindering practical deployment. Single-server PIR eliminates this trust assumption but relies on heavy cryptographic primitives for query privacy [14]. and thus is the focus of this work. Despite significant progress, single-server PIR remains costly in real-world small-record workloads (e.g., hashes, identifiers, IP addresses) [15]. State-of-the-art designs suffer from high communication and server-side computation overhead, limiting throughput and increasing costs [18–20,22].

A further observation is that many applications require *multiple* lookups from the same database within a session or time window, e.g., retrieving multiple directory elements in anonymous communication [21] or prefetching multiple objects in privacy-preserving delivery pipelines [23]. These demands have motivated the emergence of Batch PIR, which allows clients to retrieve multiple records in a single protocol execution and amortizes fixed costs across queries. However, existing mainstream batch PIR schemes still suffer from severe and unresolved performance drawbacks: the server's online response generation is dominated by expensive homomorphic rotation operations and the associated key-switching cost, which degrades sharply as the batch size and database structure scale up. Meanwhile, conventional schemes fail to fully exploit the algebraic structure of homomorphic operations, and their naive data layout and computation scheduling introduce numerous redundant operations, leading to unnecessary online latency.

Recent efforts continue to optimize batch PIR performance [16,24] but mainly focus on improving communication efficiency, without truly addressing the core server-side computational bottleneck in small-record and large-batch scenarios. Consequently, low-online-latency batch PIR solutions are still lacking for computation-intensive scenarios such as high-concurrency cloud services and resource-constrained edge nodes, where server computation is the primary cost and communication bandwidth is relatively abundant.

Based on existing mainstream batch PIR designs, this paper presents Sinba, a novel single-server batch PIR system that systematically alleviates server-side online latency bottlenecks. Sinba maintains the same threat model and privacy guarantees as representative batch PIR baselines. Compared with the VB-PIR baseline, Sinba achieves an approximately 23× reduction in the number of ciphertext-ciphertext multiplications per batch of queries, significantly relieving the server's computational burden; although it incurs a moderate increase in communication overhead, it reduces server latency by 8.5–13.3×. Furthermore, by adjusting the two-dimensional BSGS decomposition parameters, Sinba enables a flexible trade-off between communication and scomputation (Fig. 1).

Technical Overview. We start from a single-query setting and focus on the server-side procedure that computes an encrypted response from an encrypted selection vector and an encoded database. Let ct_Q denote the query ciphertext and let the

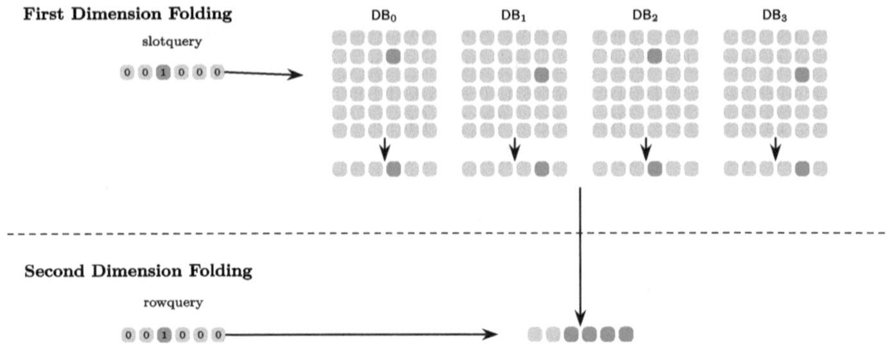

Fig. 1. Single-query response generation example for a 6×6 database where each entry is split into four chunks. The figure illustrates the 2D slot layout, the induced rotation offsets, and the 2D-BSGS schedule that reuses baby-step rotations across chunks/rows.

server store an encoding of the database as plaintext masks $\{\mathsf{pt}_{u,v}\}$ laid out over SIMD slots. The response generation reduces to evaluating a structured linear form

$$\mathsf{ct}_R = \sum_{(u,v)\in\mathcal{I}} \mathsf{Rot}(\mathsf{ct}_Q, \Delta(u,v)) \odot \mathsf{pt}_{u,v}, \tag{1}$$

where $\Delta(u,v)$ denotes public rotation offsets and $\odot$ represents ciphertext-plaintext multiplication. Direct implementation results in excessive expensive rotations dominated by key-switching, which severely limits server efficiency.

To address this bottleneck, Sinba optimizes the entire computation pipeline in a cohesive workflow: it first restructures each bucket into a two-dimensional grid and splits each record into chunks to form a structured form compatible with two-dimensional optimization; then applies a 2D-BSGS scheduling strategy that decomposes the index set into $[n_1] \times [n_2]$ and reuses baby-step rotations across giant steps, reducing the rotation complexity from $\Theta(n_1 n_2)$ to $\Theta(n_1 + C \cdot n_2)$ without increasing the number of ciphertext-plaintext multiplications; it further adopts a row-weighted cost model to select near-optimal BSGS parameters adaptively based on the database row count; finally, it stores the encoded database in NTT form and migrates all fixed alignment operations to the offline preprocessing phase, eliminating online rotation overhead and enabling fast point-wise products during online computation.

Contributions. Sinba is the first scheme to fully implement two-dimensional BSGS scheduling in the batched PIR pipeline, and it significantly reduces server-side online latency. Our specific contributions are as follows:

- A two-dimensional grid block storage structure is designed to break the limitation that traditional BSGS can only be applied in a single dimension, providing structural support for full-dimensional divide-and-conquer optimization of batched PIR.

- 2D-BSGS scheduling is first implemented in batched PIR, reducing the rotation complexity from $\Theta(n_1 n_2)$ to $\Theta(n_1 + C \cdot n_2)$ through baby-step rotation reuse, and achieving near-optimal parameter selection based on a row-weighted model.
- Rotation offsets are pre-stored in NTT form, migrating alignment operations to the offline phase, eliminating online rotation overhead, and enabling efficient ciphertext-plaintext multiplication.

Protocol Roadmap. We first present a single-query protocol whose answer-generation uses 2D-BSGS (Sect. 3). We then extend it to batch PIR by integrating with a bucketized framework plus query packing and response merging (Sect. 4). Finally, we report implementation details and evaluation (Sect. 5).

2 Preliminaries and Background

In this section, we describe some building blocks that will be used in our protocols. A summary of notations is shown in Table 1.

Table 1. Summary of frequent notations.

Notation	Description
N	Number of database entries.
n	Ring dimension of RLWE
ct_Q	Encrypted query ciphertext
ct_R	Encrypted response ciphertext
b	Batch size of batch PIR
$\lceil x \rceil$	Round up of x
$\lfloor x \rfloor$	Round down of x
$[n]$	Representing the interval $0, 1, 2, \ldots, n-1$
$M[i, :]$	The i-th row of the matrix M
d_1, d_2	Bucket grid dimensions satisfying $d_1 \times d_2 \geq N_B$
n_1, n_2	BSGS parameters (first fold) with $n_1 n_2 = d_1$
n'_1, n'_2	BSGS parameters (second fold) with $n'_1 n'_2 = C$

2.1 Homomorphic Encryption

The Brakerski–Gentry–Vaikuntanathan (BGV) scheme [5] is a leveled lattice-based homomorphic encryption construction built on the hardness of the Ring Learning With Errors (RLWE) problem. It supports arithmetic operations over encrypted data while preserving semantic security.

Let $f(x)$ be typically a cyclotomic polynomial of degree n, and define rings $\mathcal{R}_t = \mathbb{Z}_t[x]/\langle f(x)\rangle$ and $\mathcal{R}_q = \mathbb{Z}_q[x]/\langle f(x)\rangle$, where $q \gg t$ are ciphertext and plaintext moduli, respectively. A ciphertext $\mathsf{ct} = (c_0, c_1) \in \mathcal{R}_q^2$ encrypts a plaintext $m \in \mathcal{R}_t$ with a small error term, under secret key $s \in \mathcal{R}_q$. In particular, we write $\mathsf{ct} \leftarrow \mathsf{Enc}(m)$ for encryption and $m \leftarrow \mathsf{Dec}(\mathsf{ct})$ for decryption, where decryption computes $m' = (c_0 + c_1 s) \bmod q \bmod t$ to recover m.

In this paper, we restrict attention to plaintext encodings that support SIMD packing. We also make explicit use of the number-theoretic transform (NTT) representation of plaintext polynomials: for a plaintext $p \in \mathcal{R}_t$, we denote its NTT form by $\mathsf{NTT(p)}$, and the inverse transform by $\mathsf{p} = \mathsf{NTT}^{-1}(\mathsf{NTT(p)})$. When plaintexts are in NTT form, ciphertext–plaintext multiplication is carried out as point-wise multiplication in the NTT domain, which is the default optimized execution path in SEAL.

Core Homomorphic Operations

- $\mathsf{Add}(\mathsf{ct}_1, \mathsf{ct}_2)$: Takes as input two ciphertexts $\mathsf{ct}_1, \mathsf{ct}_2 \in \mathcal{R}_q^2$ encrypting plaintexts $m_1, m_2 \in \mathcal{R}_t$, and outputs a ciphertext $\mathsf{ct}_{\mathsf{sum}} \in \mathcal{R}_q^2$ encrypting $(m_1 + m_2) \bmod t$. Formally, $\mathsf{ct}_{\mathsf{sum}} = (c_0^{(1)} + c_0^{(2)}, c_1^{(1)} + c_1^{(2)})$.
- $\mathsf{MulP}(\mathsf{ct}, p)$ *(plaintext–ciphertext multiplication)*: Takes as input a plaintext $p \in \mathcal{R}_t$ and a ciphertext $\mathsf{ct} \in \mathcal{R}_q^2$ encrypting $m \in \mathcal{R}_t$, and outputs a ciphertext $\mathsf{ct}' = (c_0 p, c_1 p) \in \mathcal{R}_q^2$ encrypting $(p \cdot m) \bmod t$.
- $\mathsf{Mul}(\mathsf{ct}_1, \mathsf{ct}_2)$: Takes as input two ciphertexts $\mathsf{ct}_1, \mathsf{ct}_2 \in \mathcal{R}_q^2$ that encrypt $m_1, m_2 \in \mathcal{R}_t$, and outputs a ciphertext $\tilde{\mathsf{ct}} = (\tilde{c}_0, \tilde{c}_1, \tilde{c}_2) \in \mathcal{R}_q^3$ encrypting $(m_1 \cdot m_2)$. The resulting ciphertext has one extra component and increased noise.
- $\mathsf{Relin}(\tilde{\mathsf{ct}}, \mathsf{evk})$ *(relinearization)*: Compresses a higher-degree ciphertext $\tilde{\mathsf{ct}} \in \mathcal{R}_q^3$ into the standard two-component form $\mathsf{ct}' = (c_0', c_1') \in \mathcal{R}_q^2$ using an evaluation key evk. This operation preserves the encrypted plaintext while reducing ciphertext dimension.
- $\mathsf{ModSwitch}(\mathsf{ct}, q')$: Scales a ciphertext from modulus q to a smaller q' ($q' < q$) by rounding: $c_i' = \lfloor \frac{q'}{q} c_i \rceil \bmod q'$, producing $\mathsf{ct}' = (c_0', c_1') \in R_{q'}^2$. This operation refreshes the ciphertext and controls noise growth.
- $\mathsf{KeySwitch}(\mathsf{ct}, \mathsf{ksk})$: Converts a ciphertext encrypted under one secret key s_1 into an equivalent ciphertext under another secret key s_2, using a key-switching key $\mathsf{ksk}_{s_1 \to s_2}$.
- $\mathsf{Rot}(\mathsf{ct}, r)$: Applies an automorphism corresponding to a cyclic rotation of packed message slots by offset r, followed by $\mathsf{KeySwitch}$ to map back to the original secret key.

These operations together enable arbitrary polynomial evaluation on encrypted data up to a fixed multiplicative depth. In practice, each multiplication is followed by Relin and $\mathsf{ModSwitch}$ to maintain ciphertext compactness and bounded noise.

Fast Matrix-Vector Multiplication. Given an $n \times n$ plaintext matrix M and an encrypted n-dimensional vector v, a commonly used method to homomorphically evaluate matrix vector multiplication is the baby-step giant-step (BSGS) algorithm [11,17]. The vector v is encoded to plaintext slots and then encrypted to a ciphertext ct. One BSGS algorithm mainly consists of total n plaintext ciphertext multiplications and $n_1 + n_2$ homomorphic rotations, where $n = n_1 \cdot n_2$, as Algorithm 6.

2.2 (Batch) Private Information Retrieval

Private Information Retrieval (PIR). Let $\mathsf{DB} \in \{0,1\}^{N \times \ell}$ denote a database of N entries, each of payload size ℓ bytes. A single-server PIR protocol enables a client to retrieve the entry $\mathsf{DB}[i^\star]$ for a target index $i^\star \in [N]$ while hiding $i^\star$ from the server [18–20,22]. Formally, a PIR scheme satisfies: (i) *Correctness*: if both parties follow the protocol, the client outputs $\mathsf{DB}[i^\star]$; and (ii) *Query privacy*: the server learns no information about $i^\star$ beyond public parameters (e.g., N, ℓ and cryptographic parameters). Modern practical single-server PIR protocols often instantiate query privacy via RLWE-based homomorphic encryption (HE), leveraging the semantic security (IND-CPA) of the underlying encryption scheme.

Batch PIR. In BatchPIR, the client requests a batch of b entries indexed by $\{i_1, \dots, i_b\} \subset [N]$ in a single execution [2,16,24]. The security requirements mirror those of single-query PIR: (i) *Correctness*: the client outputs $\{\mathsf{DB}[i_j]\}_{j=1}^{b}$; and (ii) *Batch privacy*: the server learns nothing about the requested set (or multiset) of indices beyond public parameters such as N, b, and protocol parameters. BatchPIR is attractive because it can amortize the server-side computation cost across many requested items, but it must also address the communication overhead induced by large RLWE ciphertexts.

Previous Batch PIR Frameworks. A representative and widely used approach is the *bucketized* BatchPIR framework of Angel et al. [2]. The framework consists of an offline setup stage followed by an online retrieval stage.

Server-Side Hashing (Offline). The server chooses w independent hash functions $h_1, \dots, h_w$ (typically $w = 3$) and creates B buckets to store the database entries. For each database entry $\mathsf{DB}[i]$, the server places (copies) it into the w candidate buckets $h_1(i), \dots, h_w(i)$ (with standard techniques such as salting/nonces to ensure distinct candidates). This yields wN total placements across all buckets.

Client-Side Assignment via Cuckoo Hashing (Online). Given target indices $\{i_1, \dots, i_b\}$, the client assigns each i_j to one of its w candidate buckets so that each bucket contains at most one requested index. A common method is cuckoo hashing with maximum bucket occupancy one: when all candidate buckets are full, the client evicts an index and reinserts it, repeating until either placement succeeds or a retry bound is exceeded. Empty buckets are filled with dummy indices to produce a fixed-size, data-independent query pattern.

Per-Bucket PIR Instances. After assignment, the client and server run B independent PIR instances (one per bucket) to retrieve the B designated entries (including dummies). Correctness follows because if the client assigns i to bucket j, then by construction the server-side bucket j contains a copy of $\mathsf{DB}[i]$.

Index Translation Within Buckets. A practical subtlety is that the client knows the *global* database index i, whereas a PIR query for a bucket requires the *position* of $\mathsf{DB}[i]$ inside that bucket. Prior work proposes either (i) a server-provided compressed mapping (e.g., via Bloom-filter-like techniques) or (ii) a client-side simulation of the server hashing procedure to reconstruct bucket positions.

Vectorized BatchPIR and Query Packing. Vectorized Batch Private Information Retrieval (Vectorized BatchPIR) [24] builds on the bucketized paradigm but substantially improves communication by exploiting SIMD packing in RLWE-based HE.

Key Idea: Packing Across Buckets. Instead of running completely independent PIR executions per bucket with separate ciphertexts, Vectorized BatchPIR *packs* multiple bucket queries into fewer ciphertexts and arranges the server-side computation so that it can generate *aggregated* responses. At a high level, the scheme uses SIMD slots to multiplex multiple selection vectors and to combine responses across buckets, thereby reducing the number of ciphertexts exchanged.

Remaining Bottleneck: Rotation-Heavy Server Computation. While vectorization reduces the number of ciphertexts communicated, it can shift the dominant server-side cost toward HE operations such as ciphertext rotations (key-switching) and ciphertext–ciphertext multiplications that arise in packing, alignment, and response aggregation. In particular, the server often evaluates structured linear forms that follow a rotate–multiply–accumulate pattern over SIMD slots. These patterns are exactly where baby-step/giant-step (BSGS) scheduling can reduce the number of costly rotations.

Positioning of Our Work. Our protocol can be viewed as a drop-in improvement to Vectorized BatchPIR-style pipelines: we preserve the communication advantages achieved via packing, while accelerating the dominant server-side response-generation subroutines by applying (2D-)BSGS scheduling to the underlying structured linear forms. As a result, our design targets the main residual bottleneck in vectorized batch retrieval—ciphertext rotation and ciphertext-ciphertext multiplication dominated response generation—without regressing the communication gains of vectorization.

2.3 Threat Model

We consider the standard *semi-honest* adversary model for single-server private information retrieval. The server is assumed to follow the protocol specification correctly, but it may attempt to infer the client's query indices from the observed messages (including the query ciphertexts, the response ciphertexts, and any public parameters). The client is trusted and does not deviate from the protocol. The security goal is *query privacy*: the server should learn no information about the target index beyond what is implied by the public parameters, i.e., the database size N, the batch size b, and the cryptographic parameters.

We rely on the *IND-CPA security* of the underlying RLWE-based homomorphic encryption scheme (BGV). All query ciphertexts are fresh encryptions of one-hot vectors; the server does not possess the client's secret key. The evaluation keys (for relinearization and rotations) are generated by the client and sent to the server; we assume a form of *circular security*, which is standard in homomorphic encryption deployments and states that providing encryptions of the secret key under the same public key does not compromise security.

The bucket assignment (cuckoo hashing) is performed locally by the client. If placement fails, the client aborts or retries with a probability that does not depend on the requested indices, ensuring that the failure event does not leak information. All server-side computations are deterministic functions of the public database, the public parameters, and the client's ciphertexts; therefore, any adversary with the same view cannot distinguish between two equal-size batches of indices. We do not consider *active* adversaries who deviate from the protocol (e.g., by sending malformed ciphertexts or mounting denial-of-service attacks). We also assume the server does not collude with other parties. These assumptions are consistent with prior works in the vectorized BatchPIR line [2,24].

3 Single-Query Protocol

In this section, we present a complete single-query PIR protocol, which serves as the building block for the batch PIR construction in the subsequent sections. We detail how to pre-encode the database so that, during the online response phase, the server can apply a two-dimensional baby-step/giant-step (2D-BSGS) schedule efficiently and correctly—our main technical advantage—thereby substantially reducing server-side computation.

3.1 Design Challenges and Rationale

During the development of Sinba, we encountered three specific challenges that shaped our design:

Challenge 1: How to Further Reduce Rotation Overhead Beyond Existing Optimizations? We adopt the 2D Baby-Step Giant-Step (2D-BSGS) scheduling, which decomposes the inner product into two dimensions and reuses baby-step rotations across multiple giant steps, substantially reducing the total number of rotations. We choose 2D-BSGS over other optimizations because it is fully compatible with the vectorized batch PIR framework, requires no modification to the underlying homomorphic encryption scheme, and provides stable complexity reduction for small-record, large-batch workloads.

Challenge 2: How to Select Parameters to Achieve Near-Optimal Performance? The performance of 2D-BSGS heavily depends on the decomposition parameters (n_1, n_2), whose optimal values are affected by both the bucket size N_B and the number of chunks C. Too large n_1 increases the number of baby-step rotations, while too large n_2 increases the number of giant-step ciphertexts, raising communication and memory overhead. To address this, we design a row-weighted cost heuristic (Algorithm 7) that adaptively selects the optimal (n_1, n_2) decomposition. Our heuristic dynamically adjusts the decomposition to minimize the total latency for a given workload, fully realizing the gains of 2D-BSGS.

Challenge 3: How to Eliminate the Hidden Latency of Client Extraction? We adopt an offline precomputation alignment strategy. Since the slot alignment requirement is a static property of the database layout and query pattern, we precompute and cache all alignment rotation offsets in the offline phase. This eliminates 100% of the alignment latency during online response generation at the cost of a one-time precomputation, making it well-suited for long-running database services with stable query patterns.

3.2 Construction

We now describe how to construct our single-query PIR protocol by combining an offline database pre-encoding with a 2D-BSGS evaluation schedule. Our design is implemented using the core homomorphic primitives provided by Microsoft SEAL's BGV scheme as Sect. 2.1, which are highly optimized in SEAL [28].

Let DB be a two-dimensional array $\mathsf{DB} = \mathsf{DB}[i, j]$ with $N = n^2$ entries. Each entry is a length-C vector over $\mathbb{Z}_p$. For each component $c \in [C]$, we encode each row of DB_c into a SIMD-packed plaintext polynomial.

The client wishes to retrieve $\mathsf{DB}[i^\star, j^\star]$ without revealing $(i^\star, j^\star)$. Public parameters include BGV parameters, switching keys, and BSGS decomposition parameters: (n_1, n_2) for the first dimension (where $n_1 n_2 = n$) and (n'_1, n'_2) for the second (where $n'_1 n'_2 = C$). Building on the homomorphic primitives reviewed in Sect. 2.1, we present our single-query PIR protocol as four algorithms that cleanly separate offline preprocessing from the online query/response workflow:

- $\mathsf{Setup}(\mathsf{DB}) \to \widetilde{\mathsf{DB}}$: server-side offline database encoding.
- $\mathsf{Query}(i^\star) \to \mathsf{ct}_Q$: client-side query generation.
- $\mathsf{Response}(\widetilde{\mathsf{DB}}, \mathsf{ct}_Q) \to \mathsf{ct}_R$: server-side response generation.
- $\mathsf{Extract}(\mathsf{ct}_R) \to \mathsf{DB}[i^\star]$: client-side decryption and extraction.

Algorithm 1. SETUP-SINGLE

Require: Database DB, each entry has C chunks; public parameters pp
Ensure: NTT plaintext matrix $\widetilde{\mathsf{DB}}$

$\widetilde{\mathsf{DB}} \leftarrow \{\}$
for (**do** $i \leftarrow 0$ to $C-1$)
  /* **Step 1: Row Rotation** */
  $\widetilde{\mathsf{DB}}_i \leftarrow \textsc{RowRot}(\mathsf{DB}_i, i \bmod n_1')$
  for (**do** $j \leftarrow 0$ to $n-1$)
  /* **Step 2: Slot Rotation** */
    $\widetilde{\mathsf{DB}}_i[j,:] \leftarrow \mathsf{Rot}(\mathsf{DB}_i[j,:], j \bmod n_1)$ ▷ plaintext rotation
  end for
end for
$\widetilde{\mathsf{DB}} = \mathsf{NTT}(\widetilde{\mathsf{DB}})$

function $\textsc{RowRot}(\mathsf{V}, k)$ ▷ $\mathsf{V} \in \mathcal{R}^n$, $k \in \mathbb{Z}$
/* Rotation of plaintext vectors */
  $\mathsf{P} \leftarrow \{\}$
  for $i = 0$ **to** $n-1$ **do**
    $idx \leftarrow ((i - k + n_1) \bmod n_1) + \lfloor i/n_1 \rfloor$
    $\mathsf{P}[i] \leftarrow \mathsf{V}[idx]$
  end for
  return P
end function

Database Encoding. Offline encoding shifts rotation costs from online computation to deterministic pre-processing. We structure response generation as a two-dimensional procedure. In the first dimension, we pre-apply required slot rotations so online computation uses pre-rotated plaintexts. In the second dimension, we derive a row rotation on the database layout that aligns with intermediate ciphertext patterns. Algorithm 1 implements the encoding. $\mathsf{Rot}(\mathsf{V}, k)$ rotates a plaintext vector by k positions within each block of size n_1'. The inner loop applies plaintext rotations by $j \bmod n_1$ positions to each suffix $\mathsf{DB}_i[j,:]$, placing first-dimension BSGS terms on fixed baby-step offsets. Plaintexts are then transformed to NTT form to accelerate ciphertext-plaintext multiplications. Figure 5 illustrates the layout transformation for $N = 36$, $C = 4$.

Query Generation. Our offline encoding (Fig. 5) arranges the database into an $n \times n$ logical grid. The target index $idx \in [N]$ is decomposed as (idx_2, idx_1) where $idx_1 = idx \bmod n$ (slot position) and $idx_2 = \lfloor idx/n \rfloor$ (row group). The client generates two one-hot vectors: $\mathsf{v}_{slot} = \mathsf{e}_{idx_1}$[1] selects the target slot within a plaintext row, and $\mathbf{v}_{row} = \mathbf{e}_{pos}$ with $pos = (idx_1 + idx_2) \bmod n$ selects the row-dependent phase required by the layout. These vectors are encrypted to obtain ct_{slot} and ct_{row}, respectively, and the final query is the pair $\mathsf{ct}_Q = (\mathsf{ct}_{slot}, \mathsf{ct}_{row})$. (Algorithm 2)This two-ciphertext design keeps query size constant and preserves query privacy.

[1] e_i indicates that only position i is 1, while all others are 0.

Algorithm 2. QUERYGEN-SINGLE

Require: Target entry index $idx \in [N]$
Ensure: (ct_Q)
1: $idx_1 \leftarrow idx \bmod n$; $idx_2 \leftarrow \lfloor idx/n \rfloor$ ▷ Slot query generation
2: $\mathsf{v}_{slot} \leftarrow \mathsf{0} \in \{0,1\}^n$
3: $\mathsf{v}_{slot}[idx_1] \leftarrow 1$
4: $\mathsf{ct}_{slot} \leftarrow \mathsf{Enc}(\mathsf{v}_{slot})$ ▷ Row query generation
5: $\mathsf{v}_{row} \leftarrow \mathsf{0} \in \{0,1\}^n$
6: $pos \leftarrow (idx_1 + idx_2) \bmod n$
7: $\mathsf{v}_{row}[pos] \leftarrow 1$
8: $\mathsf{ct}_{row} \leftarrow \mathsf{Enc}(\mathsf{v}_{row})$
9: **return** $\mathsf{ct}_Q \leftarrow (\mathsf{ct}_{slot}, \mathsf{ct}_{row})$

Response Generation. We describe server-side response generation by decomposing the computation into two dimensions, which mirrors the two-dimensional structure induced by our offline database encoding. The client submits an encrypted query $\mathsf{ct}_Q = (\mathsf{ct}_{slot}, \mathsf{ct}_{row})$. Given ct_Q and the encoded database $\widetilde{\mathsf{DB}}$, the server outputs a single response ciphertext ct_R, enabling the client to recover the requested payload.

First Dimension (Slot Aggregation). In the first dimension, the server uses the slot-selector ciphertext ct_{slot} to extract and aggregate the contribution of the desired slot across all row groups. The red vectors in the "Query Expand" part of Fig. 2 represent the n_1 slot-selection ciphertexts (baby steps) precomputed by the server, each with a distinct rotation offset. Since the offline encoding stores the database as C plaintext components, this step reduces to C ciphertext–plaintext matrix–vector multiplications, producing intermediate ciphertexts $\{\mathsf{ct}_r^{(u)}\}_{u=0}^{C-1}$, each implemented using the BSGS-based matvec routine (Algorithm 6). A key observation is that the $n_1 - 1$ baby-step rotations of ct_{slot} are independent of the plaintext component; therefore, these rotations can be computed once and reused across all C calls, thereby avoiding redundant rotations. In the "First Dimension" part of Fig. 2, the mint-green vectors inside each red circle show how these precomputed copies are reused across all remaining database rows and all data chunks. To further reduce the total number of rotations, we choose the BSGS decomposition parameters (n_1, n_2) (with $n_1 n_2 = n$) by minimizing a proxy for rotation cost (Algorithm 7), balancing the one-time baby-step cost against the giant-step cost repeated C times. Finally, since the number of ciphertext–plaintext multiplications does not decrease with the choice of (n_1, n_2), we store plaintexts in NTT form offline, allowing the online multiply–accumulate loops to follow an optimized NTT execution path.

Algorithm 3. RESPONSE-SINGLE

Require: Query ct_Q contains Slot query ct_{slot}, Row query ct_{row}; Database $\{\widetilde{\mathsf{DB}}_i\}_{i=0}^{C-1}$; BSGS params (n_1, n_1'); Public parameters pp
Ensure: Response ciphertext ct_R

```
    /*First dimension folding*/
    for i ← 0 to C − 1 do
        ct_r^i ← BSGS(ct_slot, DB~_i, n_1, ⌈n/n_1⌉)
    end for
    /*Second dimension folding*/
    ct_R ← BSGS-CIPHER(ct_row, {ct_r^i}_{i=0}^{C-1}, C, n_1')
    return ct_R
```

Second Dimension (Component Aggregation). After the first dimension, the server holds the ciphertext vector $\{\mathsf{ct}_r^{(u)}\}_{u=0}^{C-1}$. The second dimension aggregates

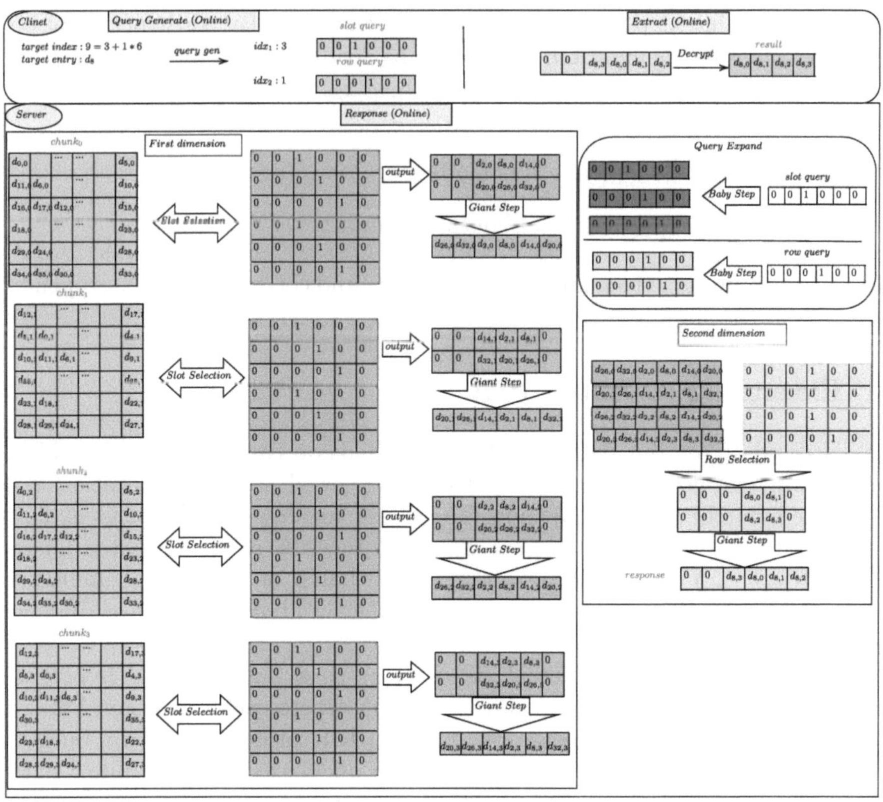

Fig. 2. Summarizes the end-to-end workflow on a toy instance with database size $6 \times 6 \times 4$, including query generation, server-side response generation, and client-side extraction.

these intermediates according to the row-selector ciphertext ct_{row}. As shown in Fig. 2, the purple vectors represent the n_1' row-selection ciphertexts (baby steps for the second dimension), each with a different rotation offset. This aggregation can be viewed as an inner product between an encrypted selection vector (realized via rotations of ct_{row}) and the ciphertext vector $\{\mathsf{ct}_r^{(u)}\}$. We evaluate this inner product using a BSGS schedule (Algorithm 8), partitioning the computation into baby steps and giant steps to reduce expensive rotations. In the "Second Dimension" part of Fig. 2, the purple vectors inside each yellow circle show how these precomputed copies are reused across all remaining rows and data chunks. Because the offline encoding already incorporates the required plaintext row rotations, no additional online rotations are needed. We defer relinearization and modulus switching until after the summation of each giant-step group to amortize overhead. Algorithm 3 summarizes the complete response generation process.

Extraction. After receiving the response ciphertext ct_R, the client decrypts it to obtain a plaintext polynomial, i.e., $\mathsf{m}_R \leftarrow \mathsf{Dec}(\mathsf{ct}_R)$. By construction of our encoding and query generation, the desired payload is packed into C consecutive SIMD slots starting at position $\mathsf{pos} = (idx_1 + idx_2) \bmod n$. Therefore, the client extracts the C slots

$$\mathsf{m}_R[(\mathsf{pos}) \bmod n],\ \mathsf{m}_R[(\mathsf{pos}+1) \bmod n],\ \ldots,\ \mathsf{m}_R[(\mathsf{pos}+C-1) \bmod n],$$

and decodes them to recover the requested entry.

Analysis. We present the analysis of complexity and correctness in the Appendix A.1.

4 Extending to Batch PIR

As discussed above, our batch construction builds on the bucketized BatchPIR framework reviewed in Sect. 2.2, and can be viewed as an optimization of a Vectorized BatchPIR-style pipeline. The server uses $\omega = 3$ independent hash functions to map the database into $B = 1.5b$ buckets, so the expected bucket size is $N_B = \omega N/B$. On the client side, the batch of b requested indices is assigned to these B buckets via cuckoo hashing, yielding one (real or dummy) target index per bucket.

For each bucket, we represent its contents as a 2-dimensional hypercube (with each database entry split into C chunks), where each dimension has size $N_B' = \lceil \sqrt{N_B} \rceil$. We then execute our batched PIR protocol over the buckets. Following the vectorized design, the client packs queries for g buckets into a single group, resulting in 2 query ciphertexts per group. The server correspondingly produces $m = B/g$ response ciphertexts (one per group), where each response ciphertext encodes the PIR outputs for the corresponding g buckets. In the remainder of this section, we describe the concrete construction of the batch protocol.

4.1 Construction

Our batch PIR construction builds on the single-query primitive from Sect. 3. Following Vectorized BatchPIR [24], we adopt *query packing* to process multiple buckets in parallel. Specifically, we group g buckets together and pack their bucket-local databases (each represented as a two-dimensional structure) into a single SIMD-packed plaintext matrix $\widehat{\mathsf{DB}}$. The client packs the slot queries and row queries for these g buckets into two ciphertexts. Leveraging the SIMD semantics of RLWE-based HE, the server executes the response-generation procedure once on the packed inputs, producing a single response ciphertext containing the PIR outputs for all g buckets.The batched protocol consists of four steps: offline database encoding, client-side query generation, server-side response generation, and client-side extraction.

Database Encoding. After server-side hashing, each bucket is padded to a fixed maximum size N_B (using dummy entries if necessary) and reshaped into a $d_1 \times d_2$ grid, where $d_1 = \lceil \sqrt{N_B} \rceil$ and $d_2 = \lceil N_B/d_1 \rceil$. Each database entry is split into C chunks and encoded into plaintext polynomials, so that subsequent online computation can adopt the same two-dimensional baby-step giant-step (2D-BSGS) schedule as in the single-query protocol.

Packing g Buckets into one Plaintext Matrix. Let n denote the SIMD slot capacity of one plaintext polynomial. Following the query-packing idea of Vectorized BatchPIR, we group g buckets and encode them jointly into one "packed" logical plaintext matrix, denoted by DB_i for group index i. Intuitively, each of the g buckets occupies a disjoint contiguous block of d_1 slots within a plaintext polynomial, so that a single SIMD operation applies to all g buckets in parallel. Concretely, for a fixed row index $r \in [d_1]$, we place the r-th row of each bucket into its assigned slot block; repeating this across r yields an encoding of the full $d_1 \times d_2$ bucket grid. Because each entry contains C chunks and the bucket grid has d_2 columns, the packed representation of one group produces $d_2 \cdot C$ plaintext polynomials. Across all B buckets, we obtain $m = \lceil B/g \rceil$ packed groups and thus a collection $\{\mathsf{DB}_i\}_{i=0}^{m-1}$.

Offline Preprocessing for 2D-BSGS. For each packed group DB_i, we apply the same offline permutation/rotation-based preprocessing as in the single-query database encoding (Sect. 3), but with the problem size instantiated to the bucket parameters rather than the full database size. In particular, the relevant 2D-BSGS decomposition parameters (n_1, n_2) and (n'_1, n'_2) are chosen as functions of the bucket dimensions (setting $n'_1 = \lceil \sqrt{d_2} \rceil$). After preprocessing, we convert the resulting plaintexts to NTT form, yielding $\{\widehat{\mathsf{DB}}_i\}_{i=0}^{m-1}$, which are then used in the online response-generation phase.

Query Generation. In this phase, the client constructs a one-hot *slot-selection* query and a one-hot *column/row-selection* query for each *target* bucket; for every

Algorithm 4. QueryGen-Batch

Require: Targets $\{idx_\ell\}_{\ell=0}^{b-1}$; deterministic cuckoo table T; batch params bp
Ensure: For each matrix $\widehat{\mathsf{DB}}_i$: $(ct_{slot}^{(i)}, ct_{row}^{(i)})$ ▷ Locate batch targets in cuckoo placement

for $\ell \leftarrow 0$ to $b-1$ **do**
  $(bidx_\ell, tidx_\ell) \leftarrow T.\mathsf{pos}[idx_\ell]$ ▷ bucket id and within-bucket position
end for
for $i \leftarrow 0$ to $m-1$ **do**
  $\mathsf{v}_{slot}, \mathsf{v}_{row} \leftarrow 0 \in \{0,1\}^n$
  for (**do**$j \leftarrow 0$ to $g-1$)
    if (**then**$j + i \cdot g = bidx_k$ for $k \in [b]$)
      Get $tidx_k$
      $tidx_k^{(1)} \leftarrow tidx_k \bmod n_1$; $tidx_k^{(2)} \leftarrow \lfloor tidx_k / n_1 \rfloor$
      $\mathsf{v}_{slot}[tidx_k^{(1)} + j \cdot g] \leftarrow 1$
      $pos \leftarrow tidx_k^{(1)} + (tidx_k^{(2)} \bmod n_1)$
      $\mathsf{v}_{row}[pos + j \cdot g] \leftarrow 1$;
    end if
  end for
  $\mathsf{ct}_{slot}^{(i)} \leftarrow \mathsf{Enc}(\mathsf{v}_{slot})$;$\mathsf{ct}_{row}^{(i)} \leftarrow \mathsf{Enc}(\mathsf{v}_{row})$
end for
return $\{(\mathsf{ct}_{slot}^{(i)}, \mathsf{ct}_{row}^{(i)})\}_{i=0}^{m-1}$

non-target bucket, both query vectors are set to the all-zero vector. Each target bucket is viewed as a dataset containing N_B entries, and its 2D query encoding follows the single-query PIR query-generation procedure. The only difference is that we *pack* the queries of g buckets into a single ciphertext so that the server can process g buckets in parallel. Algorithm 4 gives the batch query-generation procedure.

Response Generation. Since we process g buckets in parallel, the batch response-generation logic is identical to executing the single-query response procedure on each *packed* bucket group. Accordingly, we invoke the single-query protocol as a subroutine. A key distinction is that the 2D-BSGS parameter selection in the batched setting is determined by the bucket size N_B (i.e., the per-bucket problem dimension), rather than by the global database size. Therefore, the client/server needs to run the response procedure only m times to obtain m packed response ciphertexts $\{\mathsf{ct}_R^{(i)}\}_{i=0}^{m-1}$, which together contain the results for all B buckets.Algorithm 5 summarizes the complete response generation process.

Extraction. The client decrypts and extracts per-bucket payload slots, then reconstructs the requested batch entries according to the packing layout.

Algorithm 5. RESPONSE-BATCH

Require: Encoded database $\{\widehat{\mathsf{DB}}_i\}_{i=0}^{m-1}$; Batch queries ct_Q^i : $\{(\mathsf{ct}_{slot}^{(i)}, \mathsf{ct}_{row}^{(i)})\}_{i=0}^{m-1}$; BSGS params (n_1, n_1');Batch public parameters bp

Ensure: For each matrix $\widehat{\mathsf{DB}}_i$: response ciphertext $\mathsf{ct}_R^{(i)}$

1: **for** $i \leftarrow 0$ to $m-1$ **do**

2: $\quad \mathsf{ct}_R^{(i)} \leftarrow$ RESPONSE-SINGLE$(\widehat{\mathsf{DB}}_i, \mathsf{ct}_Q^i, n_1, n_1', N_B)$

3: **end for**

4: **return** $\{ct_R^{(i)}\}_{i=0}^{m-1}$

4.2 Comparison with Mughees-Ren [24]

We compare our batched protocol against the vectorized BatchPIR line of work (exemplified by Mughees and Ren). Both baselines aim to amortize multi-query PIR via bucketing and SIMD packing, but they differ in which homomorphic primitives dominate. Vectorized BatchPIR-style designs largely rely on rotation-heavy linear forms whose cost scales with the number of rotated query variants. Our protocol retains the low-communication SIMD packing/merging structure of vectorized BatchPIR, while replacing the dominant per-group rotate–multiply–accumulate subroutine with a 2D-BSGS schedule. As a result, we reduce the number of expensive rotations (key-switches) and ciphertext-ciphertext multipications without changing the asymptotic number of ciphertext–plaintext multiplications.

Table 2. Theoretical comparison of online answer-generation cost and communication (database size $N = 2^{20}$, payload 256B, $n = 8192$, $\log t = 22$, $b = 256$, $B = 384$).

Operation	Theoretical	Instantiated
MR [24]		
#mulP	$l \cdot B/g \cdot N_B/N_B'$	42,336
#Mul	$l \cdot B/g \cdot (N_B/N_B'^2 + 1)$	1,470
#Rot	$l \cdot B/g \cdot (N_B' + N_B/N_B'^2)$	6,027
#ciphers (query)	$\lceil 3B/g \rceil$	9
Ours		
#mulP	$m \cdot C \cdot \sqrt{N_B}$	40,572
#Mul	$m \cdot n_2'$	63
#Rot	$m \cdot (n_1 + C \cdot n_2 + 2\sqrt{C})$	1,422
#ciphers (query)	$2m$	18

Metrics. Following prior work, we report the dominant online homomorphic operation counts for answer generation: (i) SIMD plaintext multiplications (#MulP), (ii) SIMD ciphertext multiplications (#Mul), and (iii) SIMD rotations (#Rot). We also list the number of ciphertexts sent in the query and answer.

Parameter Instantiation. We follow the parameter choices from the Mughees-Ren implementation.[2] In their instantiation, packing parameter $g = 128$ (buckets per plaintext), each entry is split into $l = 49$ chunks, and the within-bucket layout is a $N'_B \times N'_B \times N_B/N'^2_B$ hyper-rectangle ($32 \cdot 32 \cdot 9 = 9216 > N_B = 8443$). For our scheme, we instantiate 2D-BSGS with $(n_1, n_2, n'_1, n'_2) = (46, 2, 7, 7)$. Since a plaintext can be viewed as a $(n/2) \times 2$ layout and rotated accordingly,[3] our packing yields $g = \lfloor (n/2)/d_1 \rfloor$ buckets per ciphertext, and thus $m = \lceil B/g \rceil$ packed groups for B buckets.

Table 2 reports the resulting instantiated operation counts and highlights the gap between the two designs. Relative to MR, our main savings are in rotations and ciphertext multiplications: we reduce rotations from 6,027 to 1,422 (a $\approx 4.2\times$ reduction) and ciphertext multiplications from 1,470 to 63 (a $\approx 23.3\times$ reduction), while keeping the number of ciphertext–plaintext multiplications essentially unchanged (42,336 vs. 40,572). This behavior is consistent with the design goal of 2D-BSGS: it trades a large family of rotated query variants for a small set of reusable baby-step rotations, and it aggregates across the two-dimensional structure induced by our encoding and packing. The query communication increases from 9 to 18 ciphertexts because our batch query uses two packed selectors per group, whereas MR amortizes across three packed queries. This reflects a clear computation-communication trade-off in Sinba: it trades increased communication overhead for an order-of-magnitude improvement in computational performance.

Table 3 demonstrates that, across all practical bandwidths (10–1000 Mbps), Sinba's faster server processing consistently outweighs its higher communication overhead. Even at 10 Mbps, Sinba reduces end-to-end latency by a factor of $4.1\times$; at 100 Mbps and above, Sinba achieves up to a $13\times$ improvement. This compute–communication trade-off is particularly advantageous in computation-intensive, high-bandwidth environments such as data centers and cloud backends. Only below 2 Mbps—a regime irrelevant to modern networks—does VB-PIR become competitive.

Table 3. End-to-end latency comparison between VB-PIR and Sinba

Bandwidth (Mbps)	10	20	50	100	200	500	1000
VB-PIR (s)	28.1	27.1	26.4	26.2	26.1	26.0	26.0
Sinba (s)	6.8	4.4	3.0	2.5	2.2	2.1	2.0

Analysis. We present the analysis of complexity, correctness, and security analysis in the Appendix A.2.

[2] Repository: https://github.com/mhmughees/vectorized_batchpir.

[3] Plaintext can be encoded as a $(n/2) \times 2$ vector and rotated [28]; each slot provides $2(\log t - 1)$ bits of payload space.

5 Implementation and Evaluation

5.1 Implementation

We have implemented our protocols in C++ to evaluate their concrete efficiency[4] Our implementations atop the Microsoft SEAL Library version 4.1.2 [28]. Following SEAL, we use the BGV encryption scheme [4,5,30]. We implement the client and server hashing scheme using a combination of string-based hashing and the deterministic SplitMix64 hash function for bucket calculations, following a replicated cuckoo hashing approach with k = 3 hash functions to ensure consistent and efficient batch query processing. We set the maximum number of re-insertions in cuckoo hashing to 200.

BGV Parmeters. We set the ring dimension to $n = 8192$ and use a ciphertext modulus of about 160 bits. To reduce online bandwidth, like other lattice-based PIR proto cols [1,20], we apply modulus switching at the end of the server computation and output responses at a smaller modulus $q' \approx 2^{30}$, which yields an approximately $4\times$ reduction in response size. Unless stated otherwise, we use Microsoft SEAL's default choices for the error distribution and secret-key distribution, targeting at least 128 bits of computational security for these parameters.

SEAL evaluates BFV/BGV-style arithmetic using an RNS representation, decomposing q into pairwise coprime primes $q_1, \ldots, q_L$ and performing ciphertext operations component-wise modulo each q_i. Evaluation keys for relinearization and rotations include one additional RNS prime (not carried by query/response ciphertexts); we set this special prime to 50 bits. Consequently, the modulus relevant to transmitted query and response ciphertexts is about 110 bits, which allows a plaintext modulus of roughly $t \approx 2^{20}$ in our setting.

Key Material Size. Our scheme requires transferring key material to the server for multiplications and rotations. The total size of the key material is 5.92 to 13.8 MB. This is a one-time cost that can be amortized over many PIR queries. For reference, many recent PIR schemes also require key materials between 3 and 15 MB [18,20,24].

Plaintext Encoding. In the single-query setting, when the database size satisfies $N < n^2$, we view each plaintext as an $(n/g) \times g$ logical matrix, which enables processing g independent $\log t$-bit chunks of an entry in parallel. In the batched setting, we instead interpret each plaintext as an $(n/2) \times 2$ matrix, which better balances the number of buckets that can be packed per ciphertext against the number of rows in the encoded database layout.

Deployment Feasibility. Although our evaluation is performed on a single server under controlled workloads, Sinba is designed for production environments. Its server-side response generation processes each packed group independently

[4] Repository: https://github.com/Spremez/Sinba..

(Algorithm 5), making these groups embarrassingly parallel and enabling linear throughput scaling in high-concurrency cloud deployments. Moreover, the total communication overhead for all tested database configurations remains well below typical data center network bandwidth limits. These features collectively demonstrate that Sinba is a practical solution ready for deployment in computation-intensive, high-throughput systems.

5.2 Evaluation

Experimental Setup. In this section, we report the concrete performances of our protocols Our computing environment is a server with Intel(R) Xeon(R) Gold 6230R CPU@2.10 GHz and 256 GB RAM, running Ubuntu 22.04.1. The compiler we used is GCC 12.3.0. All experiments were repeated 5 times and average values (the variances are very small) were reported.

Baselines. We compared Sinba with the following baselines:(i) BatchPIR by Angel et al. [2], for which we report computation costs from the original paper as the implementation is no longer functional; (ii) Spiral [20], a state-of-the-art single-server PIR scheme, using its public Rust implementation[5]; and (iii) Vectorized BatchPIR and PIRANA [16,24], using their public C++ implementations[6].

Single Evaluation. Table 4 reports the performance results for a database of size 2^{20} under different entry sizes. We observe that the throughput increases as the entry size grows. This trend highlights the benefit of the second-dimensional BSGS schedule in our response generation: larger entries induce a taller database matrix, and the dominant rotation and ciphertext-ciphertext multiplication costs grow sublinearly with the number of rows, making the advantage more pronounced in high-row settings. However, this improvement comes with a one-time offline preprocessing cost. As shown in Table 4, for a 1 GB database, Sinba's offline encoding time can be as high as 26.6 s. This overhead can be amortized over a large number of queries: with a batch size of $b = 256$, after 100 batches, the amortized cost per entry becomes negligible. However, in scenarios where the database is frequently updated, each update incurs this one-time cost again, making Sinba less suitable for highly dynamic workloads.

Comparison with Spiral and SpiralPack. The single-server PIR scheme Spiral follows the Gentry-Halevi framework [10] and is built on the RLWE encryption scheme together with the RGSW encryption scheme. Table 5 compares Sinba against Spiral and SpiralPack across database sizes ranging from 32 MB to 1 GB. Sinba consistently achieves lower server online response time. For example, at 256 MB, Sinba achieves 789 ms, compared to 1424 ms for SpiralPack and 1744 ms

[5] https://github.com/menonsamir/spira.
[6] https://github.com/mhmughees/vectorized_batchpir, https://github.com/zju-abclab/PIRANA.

Table 4. Concrete experimental results of the single query PIR for different database configurations.

Metric	Database size			
	32 MB	256 MB	1 GB	4 GB
Client				
Query (ms)	4.3	4.3	5.3	4.4
Extraction (ms)	2.1	2.1	2.3	2.2
Server				
Offline (s)	1.0	6.2	26.6	98.9
Response (ms)	242.8	789.9	2961.9	9927.5
Communication				
Query (KB)	460	460	460	460
Response (KB)	230	230	230	230
Throughput (MB/s)	131.8	324.1	345.7	412.6

for Spiral, yielding a 1.8–2.2× speedup. At 1 GB, Sinba achieves a throughput of 345 MB/s. This advantage stems from Sinba's 2D-BSGS scheduling strategy and offline NTT preprocessing, which together reduce online rotations and accelerate ciphertext-plaintext multiplications. However, these performance gains come at a cost. Sinba requires a one-time offline encoding (6.2 s for 256 MB, 26.6 s for 1 GB) and incurs significantly higher communication overhead—the total communication volume is approximately 20× larger than that of Spiral.

For 1 GB database, compared to SpiralPack, Sinba achieves lower end-to-end latency at bandwidths of 50 Mbps and above, with the advantage growing at 1000 Mbps. At lower bandwidths (10–20 Mbps), SpiralPack exhibits better performance due to its smaller communication footprint. This further confirms that Sinba is better suited for computation-constrained scenarios with relatively abundant bandwidth, while SpiralPack remains preferable for bandwidth-limited environments or databases that are updated frequently.

Batch Evaluation. Figure,3 summarizes the end-to-end performance of Sinba across three dimensions: batch size b, database size N, and payload size ℓ. We report client-side query generation (QGen), server-side response generation (Resp), client-side decryption (Dec), and total online communication. When increasing the batch size while keeping database size and payload fixed, server latency does not necessarily grow monotonically because both the packing layout and the BSGS decomposition parameters can change discretely; nevertheless, throughput increases due to amortization across the batch. Scaling the database size N (with fixed b and ℓ) leads to near-linear growth in response generation time, consistent with the linear scaling of ciphertext-plaintext multiplications in the encoded database dimension. When increasing the payload size ℓ (with fixed N and b), response time also grows roughly linearly, matching our design where

Table 5. Comparison with Spiral.For 256MB database of Spiral we use the default parameters in [20]. We adjust the parameters of Spiral to get 32MB,1GB database configuration,e.g.

Database	Metric	Spiral	SpiralPack	Sinba
$2^{20} \times$ 32B 32 MB	One-time setup	0	0	1 s
	Online			
	Server response time	637 ms	548 ms	242 ms
	Query size	14 KB	14 KB	460 KB
	Response size	20 KB	20 KB	230 KB
	Throughput	50 MB/s	58 MB/s	132 MB/s
$2^{20} \times$ 256B 256 MB	One-time setup	0	0	6.2 s
	Online			
	Server response time	1744 ms	1424 ms	789 ms
	Query size	14 KB	14 KB	460 KB
	Response size	20 KB	20 KB	230 KB
	Throughput	147 MB/s	180 MB/s	324 MB/s
$2^{20} \times$ 1KB 1 GB	One-time setup	0	0	26.6 s
	Online			
	Server response time	3628 ms	3094 ms	2961 ms
	Query size	14 KB	14 KB	460 KB
	Response size	20 KB	20 KB	230 KB
	Throughput	282 MB/s	331 MB/s	345 MB/s

each entry is split into C chunks. Client-side query generation and decryption remain relatively stable across batch sizes, but total online communication grows with b as more packed ciphertext pairs are required.

Comparison with VB-PIR and PIRANA. Figure 4 evaluates Sinba against VB-PIR and PIRANA across communication overhead, query generation time, and server response time. In terms of server response time (Fig. 4c), Sinba substantially outperforms both baselines: on a 2^{20} entry, 256-byte payload database, Sinba achieves 8.5–13.3$\times$ lower latency than VB-PIR and 4–5$\times$ lower latency than PIRANA. This gain stems from Sinba's 2D-BSGS schedule, which reuses baby-step rotations across rows and chunks—an optimization absent in the baselines. In query generation time (Fig. 4b), Sinba outperforms both baselines when b is less than 2^{11}, but exceeds PIRANA when b exceeds 2^{11} because PIRANA's constant-weight coding packs multiple queries into a single SIMD ciphertext more efficiently at large batch sizes. In communication overhead (Fig. 4a), VB-PIR achieves the lowest bandwidth consumption; Sinba's total communication is roughly 2–3$\times$ larger than VB-PIR and 1.5–2$\times$ larger than PIRANA (PIRANA's communication remains constant until the per-batch packing capac-

b	QGen	Resp	Dec	Comm.
2^3	5	202	1	482/241
2^4	4	144	1	482/241
2^5	5	125	1	482/241
2^6	11	196	1	964/482
2^7	8	135	1	964/482
2^8	15	189	1	1446/723
2^9	13	148	1	1446/723

(a) **Batch size sweep.** $N = 2^{16}$, $\ell = 64\,\text{B}$.

N	QGen	Resp	Dec	Comm.
2^{16}	9	169	1	964/482
2^{18}	13	421	1	1446/723
2^{20}	26	1362	2	2411/1205

(b) **Database size sweep.** $b = 64$, $\ell = 64\,\text{B}$.

ℓ	QGen	Resp	Dec	Comm.
2^5	10	129	1	964/482
2^7	9	260	1	964/482
2^8	9	454	1	964/482
2^{10}	9	1604	1	964/482

(c) **Payload sweep.** $N = 2^{16}$, $b = 64$.

Fig. 3. Performance of batch size(b), database size(N) and payload size(ℓ). QGen/Resp/Dec are in ms; Comm. reports Query/Response sizes in KB (Q/R).

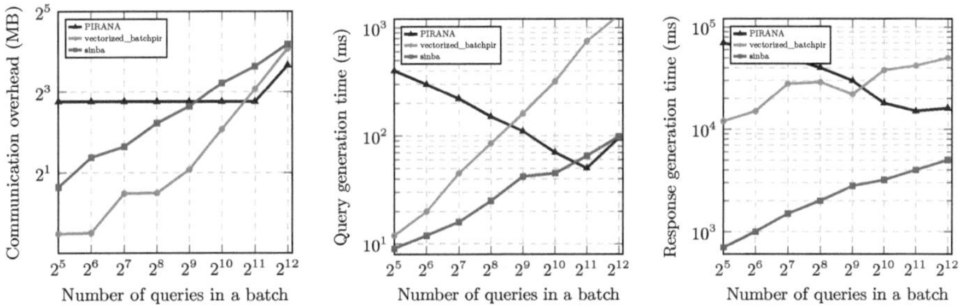

(a) Communication cost. (b) Query generation. (c) Response generation.

Fig. 4. Evaluation of batch PIRs.

ity is reached). Thus, Sinba trades higher bandwidth for lower server computation, making it ideal for computation-constrained, bandwidth-abundant scenarios.

6 Related Work

Single-Server PIR: from Early cPIR to Lattice-Based Practicality. PIR was introduced by Chor et al. [8]. Early *single-server* PIR was pioneered by Kushilevitz and Ostrovsky [14], using additively homomorphic encryption and a hypercube database layout to obtain sublinear communication at the cost of heavy server-side public-key computation. Subsequent asymptotic improvements existed, but Sion and Carbunar argued that such cPIR designs can be computationally impractical relative to simply downloading the database under realistic bandwidth and hardware settings [29]. Recent practical single-server PIR therefore largely relies on lattice-based LWE/RLWE-based somewhat homomorphic encryption, enabling efficient batched linear algebra over packed plaintexts [9,25]. In this line, XPIR [19] demonstrated practicality improvements but incurred large communication overhead for small records. SEALPIR/BatchPIR introduced compressed queries to reduce request size and enabled amortization over multiple queries [2,28]. Ali et al. [1] improved response size by using ciphertext–ciphertext multiplication in higher dimensions plus modulus switching, trading off noise growth and parameter efficiency. More recent systems further optimize the ciphertext pipeline and parameter selection, including OnionPIR [22] and SPIRAL [20], as well as follow-up accelerations such as KsPIR [18] and other recent proposals [12].

Low-Noise RLWE–RGSW-Style Multiplication. A separate line of work develops low-noise external-product style multiplications that compose (R)LWE-type ciphertexts with GSW/RGSW-type ciphertexts, substantially reducing noise growth compared to standard ciphertext–ciphertext multiplication [7]. This primitive can reduce PIR response expansion by avoiding ciphertext splitting, but it is typically more expensive per operation, motivating careful system design when adopting it in PIR [20,22].

BatchPIR and Multi-query PIR. Many applications naturally require retrieving a batch of records. Ishai et al. [13] introduced *batch codes*, which inspired amortized/multi-query PIR by distributing retrieval work across coded layouts. Angel et al. [2] provided a practical BatchPIR framework that amortizes communication and computation via query compression and structured evaluation, and Mughees and Ren [24] further proposed *vectorized* BatchPIR, packing many database entries per ciphertext to reduce overhead for small records. After SP'23, research continues to improve multi-query/BatchPIR efficiency via coding and packing techniques, e.g., PIRANA [16], and amortized sublinear variants such as dummy-subset based designs [27].

Multi-server PIR. Multi-server PIR schemes can achieve better performance by avoiding costly public-key operations, but require a stronger trust assumption (non-colluding servers) and corresponding deployment coordination [8]. Since our work targets the single-server setting, we focus on single-server and batched single-server PIR constructions.

7 Conclusion

We present Sinba, a vectorized batch private information retrieval (VB-PIR) framework. Sinba accelerates server-side online response generation by combining a 2D slot layout with a 2D-BSGS evaluation schedule that reuses rotations across rows and chunks, and by offloading fixed alignment operations to offline preprocessing. The resulting single-query primitive can be integrated as a drop-in component into vectorized BatchPIR pipelines without sacrificing their communication efficiency. Experiments demonstrate that Sinba achieves consistent and substantial reductions in end-to-end server response latency across diverse database sizes, batch sizes, and payload lengths. However, the performance improvements of Sinba come with two inherent trade-offs. First, Sinba requires one-time offline preprocessing to encode the database into the 2D slot layout and convert plaintexts to the NTT domain, which becomes a performance bottleneck for frequently updated databases. Second, Sinba incurs significantly higher communication overhead due to the usage of two ciphertexts per packed group. Sinba thus embodies a clear trade-off: higher communication bandwidth for lower server-side computation. This makes it particularly attractive for computation-constrained, bandwidth-abundant environments, such as high-concurrency cloud services and resource-constrained edge nodes serving static or slowly changing databases. Conversely, for bandwidth-limited or frequently-updated databases, alternative designs like SpiralPack may be more suitable.

Acknowledgments. We thank our supervisor and senior fellow lab members for their valuable guidance and insightful discussions throughout this work. This study was funded by the Strategic Priority Research Program of the Chinese Academy of Sciences under Grant XDB0690200.

A Analysis

A.1 Single

In this section we analyze the *online* communication and computation costs of the single-query protocol, and then give a complete correctness argument. Throughout, we reuse the notation from Sects. 3. Recall that the database is conceptually of size n^2 (i.e., $N = n^2$) and each entry is split into C chunks, which yields C plaintext components in the encoded database $\widetilde{\mathsf{DB}}_0, \ldots, \widetilde{\mathsf{DB}}_{C-1}$.

Complexity

Counting Model. We count the dominant homomorphic operations in the online phase: (i) ciphertext rotations (#Rot), (ii) ciphertext–plaintext multiplications (#$\mathsf{Mul}_{ct\text{-}pt}$), (iii) ciphertext–ciphertext multiplications with tensor format (#$\mathsf{Mul}_{ct\text{-}ct}$), (iv) ciphertext additions (#Add), and we explicitly account for relinearization/modulus switching steps when they are not performed after every multiplication.

Query Generation. For a database of size n^2, the client generates two one-hot plaintext vectors in $\{0,1\}^n$ and encrypts them, producing $\mathsf{ct}_Q = (\mathsf{ct}_{slot}, \mathsf{ct}_{row})$. Hence the client performs exactly two encryptions and sends two ciphertexts.

Response Generation. Algorithm 3 consists of two stages.

(1) First-dimension folding (ciphertext–plaintext matvec). The server evaluates a BSGS matvec (Algorithm 6) against each of the C plaintext components $\widetilde{\mathsf{DB}}_u$. A single invocation of BSGS with decomposition (n_1, n_2) such that $n_1 n_2 = n$ performs:

- $n_1 - 1$ baby-step rotations to precompute rotated queries;

- n_2-1 giant-step rotations (up to a constant, depending on the exact schedule);
- n ciphertext–plaintext multiplications and $\Theta(n)$ ciphertext additions.

Crucially, the baby-step rotations depend only on ct_{slot} and (n_1, n_2), and therefore can be *reused* across all C matvec calls. Thus, across all C components, the total first-dimension costs are:

$$\#\mathsf{Rot}_{(1)} = \Theta(n_1 + C \cdot n_2), \quad \#\mathsf{Mul}_{ct\text{-}pt,(1)} = \Theta(C \cdot n), \quad \#\mathsf{Add}_{(1)} = \Theta(C \cdot n).$$

We choose (n_1, n_2) using Algorithm 7 to minimize the proxy $n_1 + C \cdot n_2$ under the constraint $n_1 n_2 = n$, which targets the dominant rotation cost. Since $\#\mathsf{Mul}_{ct\text{-}pt}$ is unaffected by (n_1, n_2), we store the plaintexts $\widetilde{\mathsf{DB}}_u$ in NTT form offline to accelerate these multiplications.

(2) Second-dimension folding (ciphertext–ciphertext inner product). Given the intermediate ciphertext vector $\{\mathsf{ct}_r^{(u)}\}_{u=0}^{C-1}$, the server computes a BSGS-style inner product with the row query ct_{row} (Algorithm 8). Let $n'_1 n'_2 = C$ with $n'_2 = \lceil C/n'_1 \rceil$. The algorithm performs:

$$\#\mathsf{Rot}_{(2)} = \Theta(n'_1 + n'_2), \qquad \#\mathsf{Mul}_{ct\text{-}ct,(2)} = \Theta(C), \qquad \#\mathsf{Add}_{(2)} = \Theta(C).$$

Moreover, we *amortize* relinearization and modulus switching: instead of applying Relin/ModSwitch after every ciphertext–ciphertext multiplication, we accumulate within each giant-step group and apply Relin/ModSwitch once per group. Hence the number of expensive maintenance steps is $\Theta(n'_2)$ rather than $\Theta(C)$.

Summary. The online server cost is dominated by rotations and multiplications, and can be summarized as

$$\#\mathsf{Rot} = \Theta(n_1 + Cn_2 + n'_1 + n'_2), \quad \#\mathsf{Mul}_{ct\text{-}pt} = \Theta(Cn), \quad \#\mathsf{Mul}_{ct\text{-}ct} = \Theta(C),$$

with $\Theta(n'_2)$ relinearize/modswitch steps due to amortization.

Correctness. We prove that, for any target index $idx \in [N]$, the client recovers the corresponding entry $\mathsf{DB}[idx]$ from the decrypted response $\mathsf{Dec}(\mathsf{ct}_R)$ and the extraction rule described in Sect. 3. The proof proceeds by formalizing what each dimension-folding step computes.

Index Decomposition and Query Structure. Let $idx_1 = idx \bmod n$ and $idx_2 = \lfloor idx/n \rfloor$. The client forms:

$$\mathsf{v}_{slot} = \mathbf{e}_{idx_1} \in \{0,1\}^n, \qquad \mathsf{v}_{row} = \mathbf{e}_{pos} \in \{0,1\}^n, \quad pos = (idx_1 + idx_2) \bmod n,$$

and sends $\mathsf{ct}_{slot} \leftarrow \mathsf{Enc}(\mathsf{v}_{slot})$, $\mathsf{ct}_{row} \leftarrow \mathsf{Enc}(\mathsf{v}_{row})$.

Algebraic View of Response Generation. The server-side computation is linear over the plaintext space (ignoring HE noise terms, which are handled by parameter selection). Thus it suffices to show that the underlying plaintext computation extracted by decryption equals the intended selection-and-alignment function.

Lemma 1 (First-dimension selection yields per-component row aggregates). *For each component $u \in \{0, \ldots, C-1\}$, the first-dimension matvec evaluation produces a ciphertext $\mathsf{ct}_r^{(u)}$ whose decryption equals the linear combination of the encoded database rows selected by v_{slot}:*

$$\mathsf{Dec}(\mathsf{ct}_r^{(u)}) \;=\; \widetilde{\mathsf{DB}}_u \cdot \mathsf{v}_{slot} \;+\; \varepsilon_u,$$

where ε_u denotes the (bounded) HE error/noise term. In particular, since v_{slot} is one-hot at idx_1, the plaintext term $\widetilde{\mathsf{DB}}_u \cdot \mathsf{v}_{slot}$ equals the idx_1-th column extraction (in the logical layout) of $\widetilde{\mathsf{DB}}_u$, packed into SIMD slots according to the database encoding.

Proof. Algorithm 6 implements a correct evaluation of a ciphertext–plaintext linear form (a matrix–vector product) by a BSGS schedule: it computes the same linear combination as the direct method, but reuses rotated ciphertexts to reduce rotations. Correctness of BSGS follows from linearity of rotations and distributivity of multiplication over addition in the HE scheme. Since v_{slot} is one-hot, the product selects exactly one column of the plaintext matrix (under the chosen packing), yielding the stated form.

Lemma 2 (Second-dimension aggregation aligns and selects the target row group). *Let $\{\mathsf{ct}_r^{(u)}\}_{u=0}^{C-1}$ be the first-dimension outputs. The second-dimension procedure outputs a ciphertext ct_R such that*

$$\mathsf{Dec}(\mathsf{ct}_R) \;=\; \sum_{u=0}^{C-1} \mathsf{Rot}(\mathsf{v}_{row}, u) \cdot \mathsf{Dec}(\mathsf{ct}_r^{(u)}) \;+\; \varepsilon,$$

for some (bounded) HE noise term ε. Moreover, due to the definition $pos = (idx_1 + idx_2) \bmod n$ and the offline layout of $\widetilde{\mathsf{DB}}$, the summation places the C chunks of $\mathsf{DB}[idx]$ into C consecutive slots starting at slot index $(idx_1 + idx_2) \bmod n$.

Proof. Algorithm 8 is a BSGS evaluation of a ciphertext inner product. As in Lemma 1, BSGS changes only the evaluation order, not the computed linear form. The rotation of v_{row} implements an encrypted cyclic shift of a one-hot selector; multiplying by the corresponding intermediate term and summing realizes a selection-and-alignment operator over the component index u. Finally, the specific offset $pos = (idx_1 + idx_2) \bmod n$ matches the offline permutation/rotation embedded in $\widetilde{\mathsf{DB}}$, ensuring that the target row group aligns with the slot selected by v_{slot} and that the C components land in consecutive slots as required by the extraction procedure.

Theorem 1 (Correctness of the single-query protocol). *Assume the HE parameters provide sufficient noise budget so that all ciphertexts in Algorithm 3 decrypt correctly. Then for any* $idx \in [N]$*, the client recovers* $\mathsf{DB}[idx]$ *by decrypting* ct_R *and extracting the* C *slots starting at* $(idx_1 + idx_2) \bmod n$*, as specified in Sect. 3.*

Proof. By Lemma 1, for each u the ciphertext $\mathsf{ct}_r^{(u)}$ encrypts the correct first-dimension linear selection determined by the one-hot vector v_{slot}. By Lemma 2, combining these intermediates with the rotated one-hot selector derived from v_{row} yields ct_R whose plaintext content contains exactly the C chunks corresponding to the target entry, placed into consecutive slots starting at $(idx_1 + idx_2) \bmod n$. Therefore the client-side extraction procedure retrieves precisely those chunks, and decoding reconstructs $\mathsf{DB}[idx]$.

Noise Budget and Parameter Selection (Discussion). Correctness in Theorem 1 requires that the accumulated noise across: (i) rotations, (ii) ciphertext–plaintext multiplications, (iii) ciphertext–ciphertext multiplications, (iv) additions, and the deferred Relin/ModSwitch steps, remains below the decryption threshold. We estimate (or upper bound) the noise growth of each primitive using Table 6 and choose HE parameters (modulus chain, decomposition parameters, etc.) so that the final response ciphertext ct_R decrypts with overwhelming probability. Notably, deferring Relin/ModSwitch reduces the *number* of expensive maintenance operations from $\Theta(C)$ to $\Theta(n_2')$, which both improves runtime and simplifies meeting the noise budget.

Table 6. Noise growth of each BGV homomorphic operation. The polynomial degree n is 8,192, the ciphertext modulus q has 100 bits, and the plaintext modulus t has 20 bits.

Operation	CtCtAdd	CtPtMul	CtCtMul	CtRotate
Noise added (bits)	≈ 0	22	29	≈ 0

A.2 Batch

Complexity. BatchPIR retrieves b indices by placing them into buckets (via cuckoo hashing) and then answering PIR instances per bucket. We adopt vectorized batching that packs g buckets into one ciphertext, and we denote by m the number of packed groups (so $B = m \cdot g$ buckets are represented).

Query Generation. For each group $i \in [m]$, the client constructs packed selection vectors v_{slot} and v_{row} that contain one-hot selections for the target buckets that fall into the group and all-zero vectors for non-target buckets. The client then outputs $(\mathsf{ct}_{slot}^{(i)}, \mathsf{ct}_{row}^{(i)})$. Hence, the client performs $2m$ encryptions, and the online query communication is $2m$ ciphertexts.

Server Response Generation. For each packed group i, the server runs RESPONSE-SINGLE on the encoded packed database $\widetilde{\mathsf{DB}}_i$ and the packed queries. By construction, this computation is identical to the single-query response procedure applied to a problem instance of dimension determined by $\sqrt{N_B} = n_1 \cdot n_2, C = n_1' \cdot n_2'$, N_B denotes the max-size of bucket. Therefore, the dominant cost per group matches the single-query cost, and the total server cost scales linearly with the number of groups:

$$\begin{aligned}
\#\mathsf{Rot}_{\mathsf{batch}} &= m \cdot \Theta(n_1 + C \cdot n_2 + n_1' + n_2'),\\
\#\mathsf{MulP}_{\mathsf{batch}} &= m \cdot \Theta(C \cdot \sqrt{N_B}),\\
\#\mathsf{Add}_{\mathsf{batch}} &= m \cdot \Theta(C \cdot \sqrt{N_B}).\\
\#\mathsf{Mul}_{\mathsf{batch}} &= m \cdot \Theta(C).
\end{aligned}$$

In contrast, the non-BSGS baseline would incur $m \cdot \Theta(n_1 n_2)$ rotations. The additional overhead of response merging/unpacking is lower order in typical parameter regimes and consists mainly of a small number of rotations and additions per group, as in prior vectorized BatchPIR frameworks [24].

Batch Communication. The server returns one response ciphertext per packed group, i.e., m ciphertexts in total. Thus, total online communication is $2m$ ciphertexts (queries) plus m ciphertexts (responses), with sizes again determined by the HE parameters.

The batched protocol is a compatibility adaptation of the single-query protocol. Cuckoo placement determines, for each requested index, a unique (bucket id, within-bucket position) pair; padding with dummy indices ensures every bucket has a well-defined target position. Within each packed group, the query vectors contain either (i) the appropriate one-hot selections for the buckets that contain targets or (ii) zeros for all other buckets. Since RESPONSE-SINGLE is applied independently to each packed group and operates linearly over slots, the decrypted packed response contains the correct per-bucket answers. Finally, the deterministic unpack/merge procedure extracts the requested b payloads from the packed responses according to the public packing layout.

Correctness. We argue correctness for the batched protocol. In the batched setting, each packed query ciphertext encrypts a concatenation of per-bucket selection vectors, where non-target buckets contribute all-zero vectors. For any two batches of requested indices of the same size b, the corresponding packed plaintext query vectors have the same length and are encrypted under the same public key. Thus, by IND-CPA security, the distributions of the packed query ciphertexts are computationally indistinguishable, and the server cannot distinguish which buckets are targeted nor which positions are selected within a bucket. Packing, cuckoo placement, and response merging are performed using public, deterministic algorithms and do not require revealing any secret information. Therefore, the batched protocol preserves the same index-hiding guarantee as the single-query protocol.

Cuckoo Hashing Failures. As in prior bucketized BatchPIR frameworks, the client places indices into buckets using cuckoo hashing, which may fail if the insertion procedure exceeds the maximum number of re-insertions. The failure probability depends on the number of hash functions ω, the batch size b, and the number of buckets B; obtaining tight analytic bounds for the concrete parameter regimes used in practice remains challenging, so prior work typically validates failure rates empirically for the configurations of interest [6,26,32]. In general, increasing the slack B/b reduces the failure probability, and standard settings such as $\omega = 3$ and $B \approx 1.5b$ have been reported to yield negligible failure probabilities for moderate batch sizes in empirical studies. If a failure occurs, correctness (completeness) is affected because some requested indices cannot be placed, and consequently the client may be unable to retrieve all requested entries in that batch.

Privacy. We sketch the privacy argument for the batched protocol. As in prior bucketized BatchPIR systems, the client runs cuckoo hashing *locally* and therefore learns whether the placement succeeds *before* sending any encrypted query to the server. In the rare event of a placement failure, the client can preserve privacy by adopting a failure-handling strategy whose transcript is independent of the requested indices, e.g., by (i) dropping a small number of indices (sacrificing completeness), (ii) deferring them to a subsequent batch when queries are issued periodically and batches need not be full, (iii) issuing an additional *dummy* packed query with the same probability even when placement succeeds, so that the number of query ciphertexts does not reveal failure events. Hence, after conditioning on a transcript-shape that is independent of the indices, cuckoo hashing failures do not introduce a distinguishing channel.

Conditioned on successful placement, privacy reduces to the semantic security of the underlying RLWE-based HE scheme. The client sends only public key material and query ciphertexts; the latter encrypt packed one-hot (or all-zero) selection vectors and are IND-CPA secure. Moreover, all server-side computations are straight-line homomorphic evaluations on the public database plaintexts and the client ciphertexts (including rotations and 2D-BSGS scheduling), and thus depend on the batch indices only through the encrypted queries. Therefore, for any two batches of indices of the same size, the corresponding query/response transcripts are computationally indistinguishable, and the server learns no information about which buckets are targeted nor which within-bucket positions are selected beyond what is implied by public parameters.

B Algorithms

Algorithm 6. BSGS

Require:
Plaintext vector $\mathsf{P} \in \mathcal{R}_t^n$, ciphertext $\mathsf{ct}_v \in \mathcal{R}_q^2$ encrypting vector $\mathsf{v} \in \mathbb{Z}_t^n$, decomposition parameters n_1, n_2 s.t. $n = n_1 \cdot n_2$.

Ensure:
$\overline{\mathsf{ct}} \leftarrow \mathsf{M} \cdot \mathsf{v}$, where $\mathsf{M} \in \mathbb{Z}_t^{n \times n}$ is the matrix that can encode to P via CRT-mapping [28].

/* compute all baby-step rotated ciphertexts */

for $i = 0$ **to** $n_1 - 1$ **do**
    $\mathsf{ct}^{(i)} \leftarrow \mathsf{Rot}(\mathsf{ct}_v, i)$
    $\mathsf{ct}^{(i)} \leftarrow \mathsf{ModSwitch}(\mathsf{ct}^{(i)})$ ▷ optional, reduces noise growth
end for
$\overline{\mathsf{ct}} \leftarrow (0, 0)$

/* Giant-step accumulation */

for $j = 0$ **to** $n_2 - 1$ **do**
    $\mathsf{acc} \leftarrow (0, 0)$
    for $k = 0$ **to** $n_1 - 1$ **do**
        /* Extract the $(j \cdot n_1 + k)$-th diagonal of M */
        $\mathsf{pt}^{(k)} \leftarrow \mathsf{Rot}(\mathsf{P}[j \cdot n_1 + k], k)$ ▷ plaintext rotation
        $\mathsf{tmp} \leftarrow \mathsf{MulP}(\mathsf{ct}^{(k)}, \mathsf{pt}^{(k)})$
        $\mathsf{acc} \leftarrow \mathsf{Add}(\mathsf{acc}, \mathsf{tmp})$
    end for
    $\overline{\mathsf{ct}} \leftarrow \mathsf{Add}(\overline{\mathsf{ct}}, \mathsf{Rot}(\mathsf{acc}, j \cdot n_1))$
end for
return $\overline{\mathsf{ct}}$

Algorithm 7. ChooseBSGS(D, R) (row-weighted cost heuristic)

Require: Dimension size D; repetition factor R (e.g., number of rows)
Ensure: (n_1, n_2) with $n_2 = \lceil D/n_1 \rceil$

$(n_1^\star, cost^\star) \leftarrow (1, +\infty)$
for $n_1 \leftarrow 1$ to $\lfloor \sqrt{D} \rfloor + 1$ **do**
    $n_2 \leftarrow \lceil D/n_1 \rceil$
    $cost \leftarrow n_1 + n_2 \cdot R$
    if $cost < cost^\star$ **then**
        $(n_1^\star, cost^\star) \leftarrow (n_1, cost)$
    end if
end for
return $(n_1^\star, \lceil D/n_1^\star \rceil)$

Algorithm 8. BSGS-CIPHER

Require: Row query ct_{row}; ciphertext vector $\{\mathsf{ct}_r^{(u)}\}_{u=0}^{C-1}$; length C; baby-step size n_1'

Ensure: $\mathsf{ct}_R \approx \sum_{u=0}^{C-1} \mathsf{Rot}(ct_{row}, u) \cdot \mathsf{ct}_r^{(u)}$

$n_2' \leftarrow \lceil C/n_1' \rceil$
/*Baby step*/
for $i \leftarrow 0$ to $n_1' - 1$ **do**
  $\mathsf{ct}_{slot}^{(i)} \leftarrow \mathsf{Rot}(\mathsf{ct}_{slot}, i)$
end for
/*Giant step*/
$\mathsf{ct}_R \leftarrow 0$
for $j \leftarrow 0$ to $n_2' - 1$ **do**
  $u_0 \leftarrow j \cdot n_1$
  $\mathsf{ct}_{giant}, \mathsf{temp} \leftarrow 0$
  for (**do**$k \leftarrow 0$ to $n_1' - 1$)
    $\mathsf{temp} \leftarrow \mathsf{Mul}(\mathsf{ct}_{slot}^{(k)}, \mathsf{ct}_r^{(k)})$ ▷ without relinearization or modswitch
    $\mathsf{ct}_{giant} \leftarrow \mathsf{Add}(\mathsf{ct}_{giant}, \mathsf{temp})$
    $\mathsf{ct}_{giant} \leftarrow \mathsf{Relin/ModSwitch}(\mathsf{ct}_{giant})$
  end for
  $\mathsf{ct}_R \leftarrow \mathsf{Add}(\mathsf{ct}_R, \mathsf{Rot}(\mathsf{ct}_{giant}, u_0))$
end for
return ct_R

Algorithm 9. SETUP-BATCH

Require: Database $\mathsf{DB}[0..N-1]$; batch params bp with batch size b, cuckoo factor α, max bucket size N_B
derived: $B = \lceil \alpha b \rceil$, $d_1 = \lceil \sqrt{N_B} \rceil$, $d_2 = \lceil d/d_1 \rceil$, $g = \lfloor n/d_1 \rfloor$, $m = \lceil B/g \rceil$

Ensure: NTT plaintext matirxs $\{\widehat{\mathsf{DB}}_i\}_{i=0}^{m-1}$

For each entry $\mathsf{DB}[i]$ copy it to buckets $h_1(i), ..., h_\omega(i)$
Pad each bucket B_i to size d with dummy entries
$n_1, n_2 \leftarrow$ CHOOSEBSGS(N_B, C)
for (**do**$i \leftarrow 0$ to $m - 1$)
  Pack g buckets as DB_i
  $\widehat{\mathsf{DB}}_i \leftarrow$ SETUP-SINGLE$(\mathsf{DB}_i, C, n_1, n_2, d_2)$
  $\widehat{\mathsf{DB}}_i \leftarrow \mathsf{NTT}(\widehat{\mathsf{DB}}_i)$
end for
return $\{\widehat{\mathsf{DB}}_i\}_{i=0}^{m-1}$

C Figures

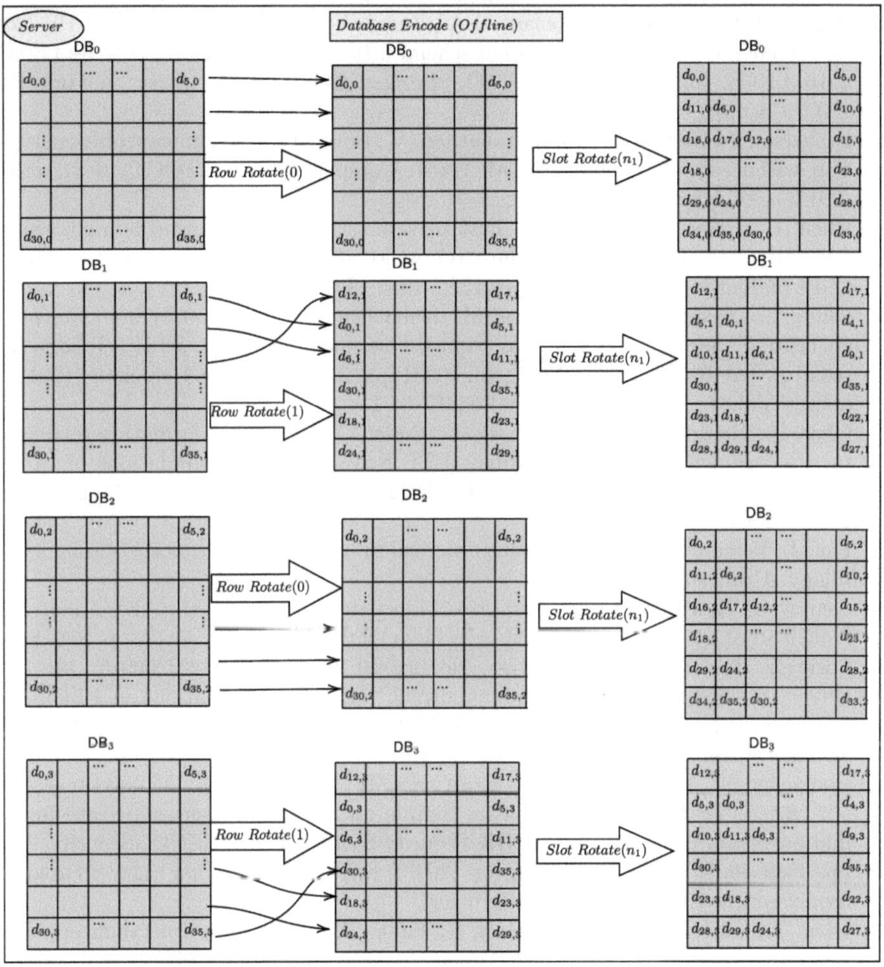

Fig. 5. Toy example of offline database encoding ($N = 36$, $C = 4$).

References

1. Ali, A., et al.: {Communication–computation} trade-offs in {PIR}. In: 30th USENIX security symposium (USENIX Security 21), pp. 1811–1828 (2021)
2. Angel, S., Chen, H., Laine, K., Setty, S.: PIR with compressed queries and amortized query processing. In: 2018 IEEE Symposium on Security and Privacy (SP), pp. 962–979. IEEE (2018)

3. Angel, S., Setty, S.: Unobservable communication over fully untrusted infrastructure. In: Proceedings of the 12th USENIX Symposium on Operating Systems Design and Implementation (OSDI). USENIX Association (2016). https://www.usenix.org/conference/osdi16/technical-sessions/presentation/angel
4. Bajard, J.-C., Eynard, J., Hasan, M.A., Zucca, V.: A full RNS variant of FV like somewhat homomorphic encryption schemes. In: Avanzi, R., Heys, H. (eds.) SAC 2016. LNCS, vol. 10532, pp. 423–442. Springer, Cham (2017). https://doi.org/10.1007/978-3-319-69453-5_23
5. Brakerski, Z., Gentry, C., Vaikuntanathan, V.: (leveled) fully homomorphic encryption without bootstrapping. ACM Trans. Comput. Theory (TOCT) **6**(3), 1–36 (2014)
6. Chen, H., Laine, K., Rindal, P.: Fast private set intersection from homomorphic encryption. In: Proceedings of the 2017 ACM SIGSAC Conference on Computer and Communications Security, pp. 1243–1255 (2017)
7. Chillotti, I., Gama, N., Georgieva, M., Izabachène, M.: Faster fully homomorphic encryption: bootstrapping in less than 0.1 seconds. In: Cheon, J.H., Takagi, T. (eds.) ASIACRYPT 2016. LNCS, vol. 10031, pp. 3–33. Springer, Heidelberg (2016). https://doi.org/10.1007/978-3-662-53887-6_1
8. Chor, B., Goldreich, O., Kushilevitz, E., Sudan, M.: Private information retrieval. In: Proceedings of the 36th Annual IEEE Symposium on Foundations of Computer Science (FOCS), pp. 41–50. IEEE (1995). https://doi.org/10.1109/SFCS.1995.492461
9. Fan, J., Vercauteren, F.: Somewhat practical fully homomorphic encryption. Cryptology ePrint Archive (2012)
10. Gentry, C., Halevi, S., Smart, N.P.: Homomorphic evaluation of the AES circuit. In: Safavi-Naini, R., Canetti, R. (eds.) CRYPTO 2012. LNCS, vol. 7417, pp. 850–867. Springer, Heidelberg (2012). https://doi.org/10.1007/978-3-642-32009-5_49
11. Halevi, S., Shoup, V.: Faster homomorphic linear transformations in HElib. In: Shacham, H., Boldyreva, A. (eds.) CRYPTO 2018. LNCS, vol. 10991, pp. 93–120. Springer, Cham (2018). https://doi.org/10.1007/978-3-319-96884-1_4
12. Henzinger, A., Hong, M.M., Corrigan-Gibbs, H., Meiklejohn, S., Vaikuntanathan, V.: One server for the price of two: Simple and fast single-server private information retrieval. In: 32nd USENIX Security Symposium (USENIX Security 23), pp. 3889–3905. USENIX Association (2023). https://www.usenix.org/conference/usenixsecurity23/presentation/henzinger
13. Ishai, Y., Kushilevitz, E., Ostrovsky, R., Sahai, A.: Batch codes and their applications. In: Proceedings of the 36th Annual ACM Symposium on Theory of Computing (STOC), pp. 262–271. ACM (2004). https://doi.org/10.1145/1007352.1007396
14. Kushilevitz, E., Ostrovsky, R.: Replication is not needed: single database, computationally-private information retrieval. In: Proceedings of the 38th Annual IEEE Symposium on Foundations of Computer Science (FOCS), pp. 364–373. IEEE (1997). https://doi.org/10.1109/SFCS.1997.646125
15. Li, L., Pal, B., Ali, J., Sullivan, N., Chatterjee, R., Ristenpart, T.: Protocols for checking compromised credentials. In: Proceedings of the 2019 ACM SIGSAC Conference on Computer and Communications Security (CCS), pp. 1387–1403. ACM (2019). https://doi.org/10.1145/3319535.3354229
16. Liu, J., Li, J., Wu, D., Ren, K.: PIRANA: faster multi-query pir via constant-weight codes. In: 2024 IEEE Symposium on Security and Privacy (SP), pp. 4315–4330. IEEE (2024)

17. Lu, W.J., Huang, Z., Hong, C., Ma, Y., Qu, H.: PEGASUS: bridging polynomial and non-polynomial evaluations in homomorphic encryption. In: 2021 IEEE Symposium on Security and Privacy (SP), pp. 1057–1073. IEEE (2021)
18. Luo, M., Liu, F.H., Wang, H.: Faster FHE-based single-server private information retrieval. In: Proceedings of the 2024 on ACM SIGSAC Conference on Computer and Communications Security, pp. 1405–1419. (2024)
19. Melchor, C.A., Barrier, J., Fousse, L., Killijian, M.O.: XPIR: private information retrieval for everyone. In: Proceedings on Privacy Enhancing Technologies pp, pp. 155–174 (2016)
20. Menon, S.J., Wu, D.J.: Spiral: fast, high-rate single-server pir via FHE composition. In: 2022 IEEE Symposium on Security and Privacy (SP), pp. 930–947. IEEE (2022)
21. Mittal, P., Olumofin, F.G., Troncoso, C., Borisov, N., Goldberg, I.: PIR-tor: scalable anonymous communication using private information retrieval. In: Proceedings of the 20th USENIX Security Symposium (USENIX Security). USENIX Association (2011). https://www.usenix.org/conference/usenix-security-11/pir-tor-scalable-anonymous-communication-using-private-information
22. Mughees, M.H., Chen, H., Ren, L.: OnionPIR: Response efficient single-server PIR. In: Proceedings of the 2021 ACM SIGSAC Conference on Computer and Communications Security, pp. 2292–2306 (2021)
23. Mughees, M.H., Chen, H., Ren, L.: PrivateFetch: scalable catalog delivery in privacy-preserving advertising. arXiv preprint arXiv:2109.08189 (2021). https://arxiv.org/abs/2109.08189
24. Mughees, M.H., Ren, L.: Vectorized batch private information retrieval. In: 2023 IEEE Symposium on Security and Privacy (SP), pp. 437–452. IEEE (2023)
25. Peikert, C.: A decade of lattice cryptography. Found. Trends Theor. Comput. Sci. **10**(4), 283–424 (2016)
26. Pinkas, B., Schneider, T., Zohner, M.: Scalable private set intersection based on OT extension. ACM Trans. Priv. Secur. (TOPS) **21**(2), 1–35 (2018)
27. Ren, L., Mughees, M.H., Sun, I.: Simple and practical amortized sublinear private information retrieval using dummy subsets. In: Proceedings of the 2024 ACM SIGSAC Conforonce on Computer and Communications Security (CCS), pp. 1420–1433. ACM (2024). https://doi.org/10.1145/3658644.3690266
28. Microsoft SEAL (release 4.1) (2023). https://github.com/Microsoft/SEAL. Microsoft Research, Redmond, WA
29. Sion, R., Carbunar, B.: On the computational practicality of private information retrieval. In: Proceedings of the Network and Distributed System Security Symposium (NDSS). Internet Society (2007). https://www.ndss-symposium.org/ndss2007/
30. Smart, N.P., Vercauteren, F.: Fully homomorphic SIMD operations. Des. Codes Crypt. **71**(1), 57–81 (2014)
31. Xiao, Y., Liu, P., Yu, R., Weng, C., Varvello, M., Kuzmanovic, A.: Collusion resistant DNS with private information retrieval. arXiv preprint arXiv:2507.20806 (2025)
32. Yeo, K.: Cuckoo hashing in cryptography: Optimal parameters, robustness and applications. In: Handschuh, H., Lysyanskaya, A. (eds.) CRYPTO 2023. LNCS, vol. 14084, pp. 197–230. Springer, Cham (2023). https://doi.org/10.1007/978-3-031-38551-3_7

Post-quantum and Lattice Cryptography

Decompressing LWE: Unlocking Field-Like Operations via Polynomial Matrices

Stefanos Vasileiadis[1(✉)], Dimitris Katsinis[2], Nada El Kassem[4], Liqun Chen[4], Simeon Tsintzos[2], Thanassis Giannetsos[3], and Bruno Crispo[1]

[1] University of Trento, Trento, Italy
stefanos.vasileiadis@unitn.it
[2] Qubitech Ltd., Athens, Greece
[3] Ubitech Ltd., Trusted Computing and Digital Security Group, Athens, Greece
[4] Department of Computer Science, University of Surrey, Guildford, UK

Abstract. To ensure cryptographic agility and that security protocols still remain effective, in retaining information security even against increasingly complex threat models, transitioning conventional cryptosystems to new secure quantum proof ones requires more than a mere substitution of the internal algorithms: It mandates an elegant solution maintaining the functional richness enhanced with quantum-secure constructions that allow the smooth migration to long-lived trusted digital infrastructures without requiring substantial system overhauls. Despite the maturity of lattice structures (based on the "Learning with Errors" (LWE) problem) which serves as the foundation for a plethora of cryptographic applications, their practicality still remains nascent due to their deliberate design constraints on operating with linear structures and inherent quadratic overhead. A main open question arises: *Can the LWE problem and its applications be generalized with algebraic structures that allow for the design of new efficient cryptographic schemes supporting all core key management operations, including key encapsulation and distribution?* We resolve this question in the affirmative by presenting a new construction that augments LWE with invertible secret keys and supports secret-key composable operations (multiplication) via polynomial matrices, retaining standard security assumptions. To demonstrate the practicality of our construction, we develop a two-party decryption scheme that achieves distributed functionality without the overhead of traditional "trapdoors" and gadget-based primitives. Furthermore, we prototype and integrate our approach with ML-KEM (Kyber), observing comparable performance. This serves as evidence on both the performance and crypto-agility of the presented construction, further advancing lattice-based cryptography with field-like operational semantics that better fulfill overarching (application-driven) requirements.

Keywords: Post-quantum cryptography · LWE · Lattices · ML-KEM (Kyber) · Transition to PQC standards

Y. Cao et al. (Eds.): SecureComm 2026, LNICST 704, pp. 505–526, 2027.
https://doi.org/10.1007/978-3-032-32764-2_23

1 Introduction

The global transition to Post-Quantum Cryptography (PQC) has shifted from theoretical exploration to a phase of urgency with a strict transition timeline in preparing for new frontiers in PQC integration and deployment into the major security standards and protocols [12]. The reason behind this compulsion been that while a high-level of maturity has been achieved regarding standardization and security analysis of varying PQC primitives, their practicality is as important as their strength. This means PQC methods should function efficiently on legacy infrastructures while exposing all necessary functions for transforming high-end security protocols to their quantum-resistant counterparts unlocking (for instance) quantum equivalent of PKI systems [4,12]. This translates to not only supporting core primitives like key agreement, for simple point-to-point encryption, and digital signatures (standardization bodies -most notably the National institute of Standards and Technology (NIST)- have successfully yelded the FIPS 2023 and 204 standards [15,16], providing robust lattice-based algorithms for key encapsulation and digital signatures) but also more advanced protocols and applications (such as threshold decryption, multi-party computation, Attribute-based Encryption (ABE) that rely on properties currently build upon the rich algebraic structures of RSA and elliptic curves (pairing-based encodings).

Herein lies a critical structural obstacle: the lattice-based schemes selected in the standards, while optimized for efficiency and security, lack the native algebraic flexibility required to replicate these advanced protocols, thus, hindering their adoption in real-world scenarios where more complex key-composable operations are needed: Specifically, the secret keys in LWE-based schemes are not designed to support field-like operations such as efficient multiplication and inversion. This limitation creates a "functionality gap", stalling the migration of complex cryptographic systems and forcing reliance on intricate, inefficient workarounds like trapdoors and gadget matrices [8,11]. While traditional cryptography exploits multiplicative groups to elegantly construct distributed protocols, lattice-based schemes deliberately constrain secret keys to support only linear operations to maintain noise stability. This design choice has forced an industry conundrum: either limit the functionality of high-end security protocols and standards (e.g., SSH, TLS 1.3, X.509, OpenPGP, IKE/IPSec) required across several industries; or implement heavyweight workarounds that drastically inflate key sizes and computational overhead.

For instance, consider the state-of-the-art for achieving such key-composable operations in lattice encodings. Trapdoor-based constructions [11] require auxiliary trapdoor information alongside public keys, inflating key sizes by orders of magnitude and introducing delicate parameter interdependencies that complicate security analysis. The central idea is that a public key lets you apply the trapdoor (encrypt), and only the corresponding private key enables you to safely decrypt. As an example, multiplying two large prime numbers together is a straightforward operation. However, it's much harder to determine what those prime factors were if you're only given the result. Without the private key, the information remains secure because the mathematical problem is too difficult to solve. Gadget-based techniques such as GSW [8], while enabling homomorphic evaluation, embed secrets within high-dimensional matrices and rely on bit-decomposition procedures that amplify noise growth and computational overhead. For threshold protocols, current approaches must either pre-distribute shares in ways that preclude dynamic membership changes, or employ heavy-weight multi-party computation protocols during key operations.

The cumulative effect of these workarounds hinder modularity and protocol agility, forcing each new construction to rebuild foundational mechanisms for attaining all aforementioned properties. We address this challenge by introducing a new construction that augments LWE with operational freedom closer to fields. Our approach "decompresses" the restricted operational space of traditional LWE, unlocking field-like capabilities: whereas current lattice-based schemes rely on ring or module structures that provide only additive key operations, we enable multiplication and inversion over secret keys—operations characteristic of fields—while retaining the error-based hardness of LWE. Our approach employs polynomial matrices to endow secret keys with invertibility and to support secret-key multiplication while preserving the linear-error structure. This eliminates the need for trapdoors or gadgets in many scenarios, paving the way for a compliant, efficient migration of advanced crypto protocols.

Our Contributions: We propose a construction that equips LWE with field-leaning operational semantics on secret keys via polynomial matrices, enabling efficient multiplication and inversion while keeping the error structure analyzable and the reductions within standard LWE methodology. We define a secret-key space based on invertible polynomial matrices over an appropriate quotient ring, carefully aligned with the linear-error model to preserve decryption correctness and ensure stable noise growth. Building on this algebraic framework, we formalize multiplication and inversion operations for these enhanced keys, proving their compatibility with encryption and decryption while quantifying the noise evolution under these transformations.

To demonstrate the practicality of our construction (hinting how it can further unlock modern network protocol and PKI-alike operation requireing key distribution), we exemplify a simple two-party decryption scheme. This scheme achieves distributed functionality without the heavy overhead of gadget-based approaches or the rigidity of pre-distributed shares. Finally, we validate our approach through a comprehensive security analysis that maintains reductions to standard LWE (and module-LWE where applicable), avoiding non-standard assumptions. We also provide a full prototype integrated with ML-KEM (Kyber) [6,15] that exhibits performance comparable to baseline implementations, confirming that our method is suitable for near-term deployment.

Paper Organization: Section 2 establishes lattice-based cryptography foundations. Section 3 presents the underpinnings of our mathematical construction focusing on key generation, encapsulation, and decapsulation and how the field-like operations are enabled. Section 4 details algorithmic specifications and parameter selection. Section 5 provides formal security analysis with invertibility and Module-LWE reduction proofs while Sect. 6 presents experimental results.

2 Preliminaries

This section establishes the cryptographic foundations underlying our construction. We present the hardness assumptions on which our scheme relies, introduce the ML-KEM (Kyber) framework that our implementation builds upon, and discuss the algebraic distinction between ring and field structures from a cryptographic perspective.

2.1 Learning With Errors (LWE)

The Learning With Errors (LWE) problem, introduced by Regev [14], has become a cornerstone of post-quantum cryptography due to its provable worst-case to average-case reduction from standard lattice problems. LWE asserts that recovering the solution to a system of noisy linear equations is computationally intractable.

Formally, let n and q be positive integers (with q typically prime), and let χ be an error distribution over $\mathbb{Z}$ (typically a discrete Gaussian or centered binomial distribution). The **search-LWE** problem is: given m samples of the form

$$(\mathbf{a}_i, b_i = \langle \mathbf{a}_i, \mathbf{s} \rangle + e_i \bmod q), \tag{1}$$

where each $\mathbf{a}_i \in \mathbb{Z}_q^n$ is chosen uniformly at random, $\mathbf{s} \in \mathbb{Z}_q^n$ is a fixed secret vector, and $e_i \leftarrow \chi$, recover the secret vector $\mathbf{s}$.

The **decisional-LWE** problem requires distinguishing such samples from uniformly random pairs in $\mathbb{Z}_q^n \times \mathbb{Z}_q$. Regev's reduction shows that, under appropriate parameter choices, solving LWE (even in the decisional variant) is at least as hard as approximating worst-case lattice problems such as GapSVP and SIVP to within polynomial factors, even with quantum algorithms [13,14]. This connection provides strong evidence that LWE-based schemes remain secure against quantum adversaries.

2.2 Module Learning With Errors (Module-LWE)

Module Learning With Errors (Module-LWE) is a structured variant of LWE that operates over polynomial rings and module structures [9]. Module-LWE offers a practical balance between the efficiency of Ring-LWE [10] and the security flexibility of standard LWE, avoiding certain algebraic vulnerabilities associated with single-ring variants while maintaining computational efficiency.

Let $R_q = \mathbb{Z}_q[x]/(x^N + 1)$ denote the quotient ring of polynomials modulo $x^N + 1$ with coefficients in $\mathbb{Z}_q$, where N is a power of 2 and q is a prime satisfying $q \equiv 1 \pmod{2N}$. Let R_q^k denote the module of k-dimensional vectors over R_q, and let χ_η denote the centered binomial distribution with parameter η over $\mathbb{Z}$.

In the **Module-LWE problem**, given a public matrix $\mathbf{A} \in R_q^{k\times k}$, a secret vector $\mathbf{s} \in R_q^k$ sampled from χ_η, and an error vector $\mathbf{e} \in R_q^k$ also sampled from χ_η, the adversary receives samples:

$$(\mathbf{A}, \mathbf{t} = \mathbf{A} \cdot \mathbf{s} + \mathbf{e} \bmod q). \tag{2}$$

The **decisional Module-LWE** problem requires distinguishing such samples from uniformly random pairs $(\mathbf{A}, \mathbf{u})$ where $\mathbf{u} \in R_q^k$ is uniform.

Module-LWE security reduces to worst-case lattice problems analogously to standard LWE [9], providing provable PQ security. The module structure enables efficient matrix operations, and module rank k can be adjusted to balance security and performance without changing the underlying ring dimension N.

2.3 ML-KEM (Kyber)

ML-KEM (Module-Lattice-Based Key Encapsulation Mechanism), standardized by NIST as FIPS 203 [15], is based on the CRYSTALS-Kyber construction [6]. Kyber is a public-key encryption and KEM scheme built on Module-LWE with rank $k \in \{2, 3, 4\}$ (corresponding to security levels Kyber512, Kyber768, and Kyber1024). The scheme operates over $R_q = \mathbb{Z}_q[x]/(x^{256} + 1)$ with $q = 3329$.

Kyber's design emphasizes simplicity and efficiency. Key generation samples a secret vector $\mathbf{s} \in R_q^k$ and an error vector $\mathbf{e} \in R_q^k$ from the centered binomial distribution χ_η, computes the public vector $\mathbf{t} = \mathbf{A} \cdot \mathbf{s} + \mathbf{e}$, and outputs the public key $(\mathbf{A}, \mathbf{t})$. Encapsulation involves generating fresh randomness, encrypting a shared secret, and compressing the resulting ciphertext. Decapsulation recovers the shared secret using the secret key and applies error correction.

Kyber achieves IND-CCA2 security in the quantum random oracle model (QROM) via the Fujisaki-Okamoto transformation [15]. Its performance characteristics—compact keys (800–1568 bytes for public keys), small ciphertexts (768–1568 bytes), and fast operations (sub-millisecond encapsulation/decapsulation on modern hardware)—make it an attractive target for integration and extension across the entire compute continuum (far edge; edge; cloud). Our construction builds on Kyber's Module-LWE foundation, augmenting it with polynomial matrix structures that enable secret-key multiplication and inversion.

2.4 Rings vs. Fields: A Cryptographic Perspective

The algebraic structure of key spaces profoundly impacts cryptographic design. Traditional public-key cryptography leverages field properties: RSA relies on the multiplicative group $(\mathbb{Z}/n\mathbb{Z})^*$, and elliptic curve cryptography operates over finite fields $\mathbb{F}_p$ or $\mathbb{F}_{2^m}$. These structures provide rich operations—multiplication, inversion, and exponentiation—that enable elegant constructions of signatures, key agreement, and threshold protocols.

Lattice-based schemes, by contrast, operate over rings (or modules over rings) where secret keys support only additive operations. In Ring-LWE and Module-LWE, secrets are elements of R_q^k, and the encryption relation $b = a \cdot s + e$ is linear in s. While this linearity is essential for decryption correctness (noise remains small under addition), it precludes direct multiplication or inversion of secret keys. Attempting to multiply secrets $s_1 \cdot s_2$ in Ring-LWE yields a new element in R_q, but without a corresponding public key or a way to control noise growth in the encrypted domain, such operations are not directly useful for most protocols.

Mathematical Requirements for Field Conversion. A field, by definition, is a commutative ring in which every non-zero element has a multiplicative inverse and satisfies closure under both addition and multiplication. To convert a ring-based cryptographic construction into one with field-like properties, several fundamental requirements must be satisfied. First, every non-zero secret key must admit a well-defined inverse such that $s \cdot s^{-1} = 1$, where the identity element is compatible with the encryption operation. Second, the product of two secret keys $s_1 \cdot s_2$ must yield a valid secret key with a corresponding public key efficiently derivable from the public keys of s_1 and s_2, ensuring multiplicative closure within the key space. Third, key multiplication and inversion must maintain the linear-error structure necessary for decryption correctness, exhibiting bounded and predictable noise growth that does not compromise correctness. Fourth, for any secret key s' derived via multiplication or inversion, there must exist an efficient algorithm to compute the corresponding public key without revealing s', preserving the public-key consistency essential for cryptographic protocols. Finally, the hardness of recovering s' from its public key must reduce to the same underlying computational problem—such as Module-LWE—as the base scheme, ensuring that no new assumptions are introduced (Table 1).

Table 1. Notation and Mathematical Structures

Symbol	Description
Algebraic Structures	
$\mathbb{Z}_q$	Ring of integers mod q. Elements $\{0, \dots, q-1\}$
$\mathbb{Z}_q[x]$	Polynomial ring in x over $\mathbb{Z}_q$
R_q	Quotient ring $\mathbb{Z}_q[x]/(x^N + 1)$. Elements are polynomials degree $< N$
$M_2(R_q)$	Ring of 2×2 matrices with entries in R_q
$\mathrm{GL}_2(R_q)$	General linear group: invertible 2×2 matrices in $M_2(R_q)$
Parameters	
N	Poly degree (power of 2)
q	Prime modulus ($q \equiv 1 \pmod{2N}$)
η	Binomial param for error
χ_η	Centered binomial dist. over $\mathbb{Z}$
Key Components	
$\mathbf{S}$	Secret key: $\mathbf{S} = \mathbf{LDL}^{-1}$
$\mathbf{L}$	Conjugation matrix $\left(\begin{smallmatrix} 1 & b \\ c & 1+bc \end{smallmatrix}\right)$, $\det(\mathbf{L}) = 1$
$\mathbf{D}$	Diagonal matrix $\mathrm{diag}(d_1, d_2)$ from χ_η
$\mathbf{A}$	Public matrix (uniform random)
$\mathbf{T}$	Public key: $\mathbf{T} = \mathbf{AS} + \mathbf{E}$
$\mathbf{E}$	Error matrix from χ_η
$\mathbf{I}_2$	The 2×2 identity matrix over R_q

Standard Module-LWE fails these requirements in fundamental ways. While secrets can be added (satisfying the ring's additive structure), there is no natural notion of secret-key inversion that preserves public-key relationships. Secret-key multiplication causes noise to grow quadratically without a mechanism to track or compress it, and the resulting products lack corresponding public keys computable from the original public components. Our construction addresses these gaps by embedding secrets within invertible polynomial matrix structures where multiplication and inversion operations are well-defined, noise evolution remains quantifiable and bounded, and public keys remain computable under standard Module-LWE assumptions.

3 Construction

We now present our construction that enables field-like operations over LWE-based secret keys through polynomial matrix structures. This section introduces the necessary notation, describes key generation with its invertible conjugation structure, and demonstrates how our approach seamlessly integrates with standard Key Encapsulation Mechanisms (KEMs) such as ML-KEM. A critical design principle throughout our construction is that all operations involved in secret key computation—sampling, matrix multiplication, and inversion—are performed over elements drawn from the centered binomial distribution χ_η. This ensures that intermediate values and final secret keys remain small, preserving the noise structure essential for decryption correctness and maintaining compatibility with standard Module-LWE security reductions.

3.1 Key Generation

The key generation procedure constructs secret keys with the conjugation structure $\mathbf{S} = \mathbf{L}\cdot\mathbf{D}\cdot\mathbf{L}^{-1}$, where $\mathbf{L} \in \mathrm{GL}_2(R_q)$ is an invertible matrix and $\mathbf{D}$ is diagonal. This algebraic structure, leveraging matrix rings over polynomial quotient rings [10,17], endows secret keys with invertibility ($\mathbf{S}^{-1} = \mathbf{L} \cdot \mathbf{D}^{-1} \cdot \mathbf{L}^{-1}$), multiplicative closure under shared conjugation, and commutativity, thereby achieving field-like operational semantics while retaining Module-LWE hardness [9].

To ensure small coefficient bounds throughout the construction, we employ a carefully designed matrix structure. The conjugation matrix $\mathbf{L}$ is constructed with *scalar* off-diagonal entries $b, c \in \{-\eta, \ldots, \eta\} \setminus \{0\}$:

$$\mathbf{L} = \begin{pmatrix} 1 & b \\ c & 1 + bc \end{pmatrix}, \quad \mathbf{L}^{-1} = \begin{pmatrix} 1 + bc & b \\ -c & 1 \end{pmatrix}. \tag{3}$$

This structure guarantees $\det(\mathbf{L}) = 1$ exactly, eliminating rejection sampling and ensuring $\mathbf{L}^{-1}$ has the same small scalar entries as $\mathbf{L}$. The diagonal matrix $\mathbf{D} = \mathrm{diag}(d_1, d_2)$ has polynomial entries $d_1, d_2 \in R_q$ with coefficients drawn from χ_η [15]. When computing $\mathbf{S} = \mathbf{L} \cdot \mathbf{D} \cdot \mathbf{L}^{-1}$, the resulting secret key has all four entries non-zero (ensuring full Module-LWE security) with coefficients bounded by $O(\eta^2)$, preventing coefficient growth that would compromise decryption correctness [6].

The structured form of $\mathbf{L}$ ensures $\det(\mathbf{L}) = 1 \cdot (1 + bc) - b \cdot c = 1$ exactly, guaranteeing invertibility without rejection sampling. The inverse $\mathbf{L}^{-1}$ has the same scalar structure as $\mathbf{L}$, with entries bounded by $|1 + bc| \leq 1 + \eta^2 = 5$ for $\eta = 2$. This construction eliminates the need for polynomial inversion in R_q, which would otherwise produce large coefficients. The resulting secret key

Algorithm 1. Key Generation

1: **Input:** Security parameters (N, q, η)
2: **Output:** Key pair $(\mathbf{S}, \mathbf{A}, \mathbf{T})$ where $\mathbf{S}$ is the secret key and $(\mathbf{A}, \mathbf{T})$ is the public key
3: // **Construct invertible matrix L with** $\det(\mathbf{L}) = 1$
4: Sample scalars $b, c \xleftarrow{\$} \{-\eta, \ldots, \eta\} \setminus \{0\}$ uniformly at random
5: Construct $\mathbf{L} \leftarrow \begin{pmatrix} 1 & b \\ c & 1+bc \end{pmatrix}$ ▷ $\det(\mathbf{L}) = 1$ exactly
6: Compute $\mathbf{L}^{-1} \leftarrow \begin{pmatrix} 1+bc & -b \\ -c & 1 \end{pmatrix}$ ▷ No polynomial inversion needed
7: // **Sample diagonal matrix D with polynomial entries**
8: Sample diagonal entries: $d_1, d_2 \in R_q$ with each polynomial coefficient drawn independently from χ_η
9: Construct $\mathbf{D} \leftarrow \text{diag}(d_1, d_2)$
10: // **Compute secret key via conjugation**
11: Compute $\mathbf{S} \leftarrow \mathbf{L} \cdot \mathbf{D} \cdot \mathbf{L}^{-1} \bmod q$
12: // **Generate public key following Module-LWE structure**
13: Sample $\mathbf{A} \xleftarrow{\$} M_2(R_q)$ uniformly at random
14: Sample $\mathbf{E} \in M_2(R_q)$ with each polynomial coefficient drawn independently from χ_η
15: Compute public key: $\mathbf{T} \leftarrow \mathbf{A} \cdot \mathbf{S} + \mathbf{E} \bmod q$
16: **return** $(\mathbf{S}, \mathbf{A}, \mathbf{T})$

$\mathbf{S} = \mathbf{L} \cdot \mathbf{D} \cdot \mathbf{L}^{-1}$ is a full 2×2 matrix (all entries non-zero) with small polynomial coefficients, as established in Lemma 1.

Key Operations and Security Preservation. The conjugation structure $\mathbf{S} = \mathbf{L} \cdot \mathbf{D} \cdot \mathbf{L}^{-1}$ enables three operations absent from standard Module-LWE:

Inversion. Given $\mathbf{S} \in M_2(R_q)$, compute $\mathbf{S}^{-1} = \mathbf{L} \cdot \mathbf{D}^{-1} \cdot \mathbf{L}^{-1}$ where $\mathbf{D}^{-1} = \text{diag}(d_1^{-1}, d_2^{-1})$ requires two polynomial inversions in R_q using the extended Euclidean algorithm [17]. The inverse satisfies $\mathbf{S} \cdot \mathbf{S}^{-1} = \mathbf{I}_2$ and preserves the conjugation structure. This avoids auxiliary trapdoor information required by prior lattice-based constructions [11] for key inversion in threshold and key-homomorphic protocols.

Multiplication. For secret keys sharing $\mathbf{L}$, define $\mathbf{S}_1 = \mathbf{L} \cdot \mathbf{D}_1 \cdot \mathbf{L}^{-1}$ and $\mathbf{S}_2 = \mathbf{L} \cdot \mathbf{D}_2 \cdot \mathbf{L}^{-1}$. Then

$$\mathbf{S}_1 \cdot \mathbf{S}_2 = \mathbf{L} \cdot \mathbf{D}_1 \cdot \mathbf{D}_2 \cdot \mathbf{L}^{-1} = \mathbf{L} \cdot \mathbf{D}_3 \cdot \mathbf{L}^{-1},$$

where $\mathbf{D}_3 = \mathbf{D}_1 \cdot \mathbf{D}_2$ is diagonal. Commutativity follows from $\mathbf{D}_1 \cdot \mathbf{D}_2 = \mathbf{D}_2 \cdot \mathbf{D}_1$, yielding $\mathbf{S}_1 \cdot \mathbf{S}_2 = \mathbf{S}_2 \cdot \mathbf{S}_1$. Products remain in the conjugation class, enabling iterative composition for distributed protocols and ABE policy evaluation [8].

Security and Public-Key Derivation. The public key $\mathbf{T} = \mathbf{A} \cdot \mathbf{S} + \mathbf{E}$ follows the standard Module-LWE structure, with the natural extension that $\mathbf{A}, \mathbf{S}, \mathbf{E}, \mathbf{T} \in M_2(R_q)$ are matrices rather than vectors. This matrix formulation preserves the essential Module-LWE property: given a uniform $\mathbf{A}$ and noise $\mathbf{E}$ sampled from

Algorithm 2. Encapsulation

Input: Public key $(\mathbf{A}, \mathbf{T})$ where $\mathbf{A}, \mathbf{T} \in M_2(R_q)$
Output: Ciphertext $(\mathbf{U}, \mathbf{V})$ and shared secret $k \in \{0,1\}^{256}$
// **Generate ephemeral randomness and errors**
Sample $\mathbf{R} \in M_2(R_q)$ with each polynomial coefficient drawn independently from χ_η
Sample error matrices: $\mathbf{E}_1, \mathbf{E}_2 \in M_2(R_q)$ with coefficients from χ_η
// **Compute LWE samples**
Compute $\mathbf{U} \leftarrow \mathbf{A}^\top \cdot \mathbf{R} + \mathbf{E}_1 \bmod q$
// **Encapsulate shared secret**
Sample shared secret: $k \xleftarrow{\$} \{0,1\}^{256}$
Encode secret: $\mathbf{M} \leftarrow \text{Encode}(k) + \lfloor q/2 \rfloor \cdot \mathbf{I}_2 \in M_2(R_q)$ ▷ Scale to mid-range
Compute $\mathbf{V} \leftarrow \mathbf{T}^\top \cdot \mathbf{R} + \mathbf{E}_2 + \mathbf{M} \bmod q$
return Ciphertext $(\mathbf{U}, \mathbf{V})$ and shared secret k

χ_η, the tuple $(\mathbf{A}, \mathbf{T})$ is computationally indistinguishable from $(\mathbf{A}, \mathbf{U})$ where $\mathbf{U} \in M_2(R_q)$ is uniform. Security reductions apply directly [9]: recovering $\mathbf{S}$ from $(\mathbf{A}, \mathbf{T})$ reduces to decisional Module-LWE since the adversary's view is indistinguishable from uniform regardless of $\mathbf{S}$'s internal conjugation structure. For derived keys $\mathbf{S}' = \mathbf{S}_1 \cdot \mathbf{S}_2$ or $\mathbf{S}' = \mathbf{S}^{-1}$, the corresponding public key $\mathbf{T}' = \mathbf{A} \cdot \mathbf{S}' + \mathbf{E}'$ follows the same structure, enabling homomorphic public-key operations [7].

3.2 Encapsulation

Our construction integrates seamlessly with the ML-KEM (Kyber) framework by replacing scalar operations with matrix operations in $M_2(R_q)$. The encapsulation algorithm follows the standard KEM structure: it generates ephemeral randomness, computes LWE samples under the public key, and encapsulates a shared secret. The key distinction from standard Kyber is that all operations—public key components, randomness, errors, and ciphertexts—are 2×2 polynomial matrices rather than vectors, preserving the Module-LWE security foundation while enabling the invertible secret-key structure.

The encapsulation algorithm mirrors ML-KEM's structure with matrix adaptations. The ephemeral matrix $\mathbf{R} \in M_2(R_q)$ serves the same role as Kyber's randomness vector: it is sampled from χ_η to ensure small coefficients and is used to generate fresh LWE samples. The first component $\mathbf{U} = \mathbf{A}^\top \cdot \mathbf{R} + \mathbf{E}_1$ forms a standard Module-LWE sample under the public matrix $\mathbf{A}$, binding the ciphertext to the receiver's public key. The second component $\mathbf{V} = \mathbf{T}^\top \cdot \mathbf{R} + \mathbf{E}_2 + \mathbf{M}$ encapsulates the shared secret k by encoding it into a matrix $\mathbf{M}$ and masking it with the Module-LWE encryption of zero under $\mathbf{T}$.

The encoding function $\text{Encode} : \{0,1\}^{256} \to M_2(R_q)$ maps the 256-bit shared secret to a matrix by distributing bits across polynomial coefficients. Specifically, $\text{Encode}(k)$ partitions $k = (k_0, k_1, k_2, k_3)$ into four 64-bit blocks, embeds each block k_i into the first 64 coefficients of the $(i+1)$-th matrix entry (in

Algorithm 3. Decapsulation

1: **Input:** Ciphertext $(\mathbf{U}, \mathbf{V})$ where $\mathbf{U}, \mathbf{V} \in M_2(R_q)$, secret key $\mathbf{S} \in M_2(R_q)$
2: **Output:** Shared secret $k \in \{0,1\}^{256}$ or $\perp$ (failure)
3: // **Remove Module-LWE mask**
4: Compute $\mathbf{Y} \leftarrow \mathbf{S}^\top \cdot \mathbf{U} \bmod q$
5: Compute noisy key matrix: $\mathbf{M}' \leftarrow \mathbf{V} - \mathbf{Y} \bmod q$
6: // **Decode shared secret**
7: Remove mid-range encoding: $\mathbf{M}'' \leftarrow \mathbf{M}' - \lfloor q/2 \rfloor \cdot \mathbf{I}_2 \bmod q$
8: Decode shared secret: $k \leftarrow \text{Decode}(\mathbf{M}'')$
9: **if** decoding fails (noise exceeds threshold) **then**
10: **return** $\perp$
11: **return** k

row-major order), and sets remaining coefficients to zero. The decoding function $\text{Decode} : M_2(R_q) \to \{0,1\}^{256}$ extracts each coefficient, rounds to $\{0,1\}$ by comparing to $q/2$, and concatenates the result. The mid-range shift $\lfloor q/2 \rfloor \cdot \mathbf{I}_2$ ensures that the embedded secret occupies the center of the modular range, maximizing tolerance to decryption errors. This encoding scheme follows Kyber's approach, adapted to matrix structure, ensuring that correctness and error tolerance remain comparable to the base ML-KEM scheme.

3.3 Decapsulation

Decapsulation recovers the shared secret by computing $\mathbf{M}' = \mathbf{V} - \mathbf{S}^\top \cdot \mathbf{U}$, which removes the Module-LWE mask to reveal the encoded secret plus accumulated noise. The structure $\mathbf{S}^\top \cdot \mathbf{U} \approx \mathbf{T}^\top \cdot \mathbf{R}$ holds with bounded error due to the Module-LWE relation $\mathbf{T} = \mathbf{A} \cdot \mathbf{S} + \mathbf{E}$, enabling correct decoding when noise remains below $q/4$.

The correctness of decapsulation follows from the Module-LWE structure. Expanding the computation:

$$\begin{aligned} \mathbf{M}' &= \mathbf{V} - \mathbf{S}^\top \cdot \mathbf{U} \\ &= (\mathbf{T}^\top \cdot \mathbf{R} + \mathbf{E}_2 + \mathbf{M}) - \mathbf{S}^\top \cdot (\mathbf{A}^\top \cdot \mathbf{R} + \mathbf{E}_1) \\ &= (\mathbf{A} \cdot \mathbf{S} + \mathbf{E})^\top \cdot \mathbf{R} + \mathbf{E}_2 + \mathbf{M} - \mathbf{S}^\top \cdot \mathbf{A}^\top \cdot \mathbf{R} - \mathbf{S}^\top \cdot \mathbf{E}_1 \\ &= \mathbf{M} + (\mathbf{E}^\top \cdot \mathbf{R} + \mathbf{E}_2 - \mathbf{S}^\top \cdot \mathbf{E}_1). \end{aligned}$$

The noise term $\mathbf{E}^\top \cdot \mathbf{R} + \mathbf{E}_2 - \mathbf{S}^\top \cdot \mathbf{E}_1$ consists of products and sums of polynomials sampled from χ_η. Each entry accumulates noise with coefficients bounded by $O(N\eta^2)$ from matrix-matrix multiplication in $M_2(R_q)$. When $q \gg N\eta^2$, the noise remains significantly smaller than $q/4$, ensuring that the decoding function Decode correctly recovers k by rounding polynomial coefficients modulo 2.

This construction achieves full compatibility with ML-KEM implementations: the encapsulation and decapsulation algorithms differ from Kyber only in the replacement of vector operations with 2×2 matrix operations, preserving computational complexity and parameter selection methodology. The matrix structure introduces no additional failure modes—decryption succeeds under the same noise bounds as standard Module-LWE—while enabling the secret-key multiplication and inversion operations described previously.

3.4 Two-Party Kyber via Secret Splitting

We now present a two-party variant of Kyber that follows Algorithm 1 in a setting with a trusted key-generation authority. The authority samples the conjugation matrix $\mathbf{L}$ and diagonal matrices $\mathbf{D}_1, \mathbf{D}_2$ as in Sect. 3, sets

$$\mathbf{S}_1 = \mathbf{L} \cdot \mathbf{D}_1 \cdot \mathbf{L}^{-1}, \qquad \mathbf{S}_2 = \mathbf{L} \cdot \mathbf{D}_2 \cdot \mathbf{L}^{-1}, \qquad \mathbf{S} = \mathbf{S}_1 \cdot \mathbf{S}_2 = \mathbf{L} \cdot \mathbf{D}_1 \cdot \mathbf{D}_2 \cdot \mathbf{L}^{-1},$$

and computes the Kyber public key component $\mathbf{T} = \mathbf{A} \cdot \mathbf{S} + \mathbf{E}$ from the master secret $\mathbf{S}$. The authority publishes $(\mathbf{A}, \mathbf{T})$ and delivers $\mathbf{S}_1$ to party 1 and $\mathbf{S}_2$ to party 2. In this deployment model, the decryptors only need their shares $\mathbf{S}_1, \mathbf{S}_2$ to participate in decryption; knowledge of $\mathbf{L}$ remains internal to the authority and is only used in the analysis of the scheme. This is analogous in spirit to the way a dealer produces related RSA secret exponents in two-party RSA key-generation protocols [5].

Since diagonal matrices commute ($\mathbf{D}_1 \cdot \mathbf{D}_2 = \mathbf{D}_2 \cdot \mathbf{D}_1$), the shares also commute: $\mathbf{S}_1 \cdot \mathbf{S}_2 = \mathbf{S}_2 \cdot \mathbf{S}_1$. Encryption for all users follows Algorithm 2 with the public key $\mathbf{T}$ and is unchanged from the single-party setting.

For decapsulation, correctness is still captured by the standard expression $\mathbf{M} = \mathbf{V} - \mathbf{S}^\top \cdot \mathbf{U}$ with $\mathbf{S} = \mathbf{S}_1 \cdot \mathbf{S}_2$. To expose the two-party structure, we expand $\mathbf{S}^\top$ using the conjugation form:

$$\mathbf{S}^\top = (\mathbf{S}_1\mathbf{S}_2)^\top = (\mathbf{L}^{-1})^\top \mathbf{D}_2^\top \mathbf{D}_1^\top \mathbf{L}^\top = (\mathbf{L}^{-1})^\top \mathbf{D}_1^\top \mathbf{D}_2^\top \mathbf{L}^\top.$$

Since diagonal matrices are symmetric ($\mathbf{D}_i^\top = \mathbf{D}_i$), we have:

$$\mathbf{S}^\top = (\mathbf{L}^{-1})^\top \cdot (\mathbf{D}_1 \cdot \mathbf{D}_2) \cdot \mathbf{L}^\top = (\mathbf{L}^{-1})^\top \cdot \mathbf{D} \cdot \mathbf{L}^\top. \tag{4}$$

Hence, the decapsulation can be written as

$$\mathbf{M} = \mathbf{V} - \mathbf{S}^\top \cdot \mathbf{U} = \mathbf{V} - \mathbf{S}_2^\top \cdot \mathbf{S}_1^\top \cdot \mathbf{U}.$$

Each transpose can be expressed in terms of the secret shares individually:

$$\mathbf{S}_1^\top = (\mathbf{L}^{-1})^\top \cdot \mathbf{D}_1 \cdot \mathbf{L}^\top, \quad \mathbf{S}_2^\top = (\mathbf{L}^{-1})^\top \cdot \mathbf{D}_2 \cdot \mathbf{L}^\top,$$

so that $\mathbf{M}$ can be evaluated using only the two shares $\mathbf{S}_1, \mathbf{S}_2$ and the known conjugator $\mathbf{L}$:

$$\boxed{\mathbf{M} = \mathbf{V} - \left((\mathbf{L}^{-1})^\top \cdot \mathbf{D}_2 \cdot \mathbf{L}^\top\right) \cdot \left((\mathbf{L}^{-1})^\top \cdot \mathbf{D}_1 \cdot \mathbf{L}^\top\right) \cdot \mathbf{U}.} \tag{5}$$

This decomposition reveals that decapsulation inherently depends on both shares $\mathbf{S}_1$ and $\mathbf{S}_2$, enabling the following two-party protocol: Party 1 computes the partial decryption $\mathbf{W} = \mathbf{S}_1^\top \cdot \mathbf{U}$ and transmits it to Party 2, who completes the operation via $\mathbf{M}' = \mathbf{V} - \mathbf{S}_2^\top \cdot \mathbf{W}$. The accumulated error satisfies:

$$\mathbf{E}_{\text{acc}} = \mathbf{E}^\top \cdot \mathbf{R} + \mathbf{E}_2 - \mathbf{S}^\top \cdot \mathbf{E}_1, \tag{6}$$

which is identical to single-party decapsulation (Algorithm 3), since $\mathbf{S}_2^\top \cdot \mathbf{S}_1^\top = (\mathbf{S}_1 \cdot \mathbf{S}_2)^\top = \mathbf{S}^\top$. Correctness therefore follows with the same decryption failure probability bounds established in Sect. 4.

The security of the two-party scheme derives from Module-LWE hardness: each share $\mathbf{S}_i$ independently provides no information about the master secret $\mathbf{S}$ beyond what is revealed by the public key $\mathbf{T} = \mathbf{A} \cdot \mathbf{S} + \mathbf{E}$, as guaranteed by Theorem 2. An adversary corrupting a single party obtains $\mathbf{S}_i$ but cannot recover $\mathbf{S}$ or decrypt ciphertexts without the second share. The partial decryption $\mathbf{W} = \mathbf{S}_1^\top \cdot \mathbf{U}$ transmitted between parties remains encrypted under $\mathbf{S}_2$, ensuring that neither party can unilaterally decrypt. This achieves a two-party threshold where both parties must participate for successful decryption.

4 Algorithmic Specifications and Parameter Selection

The security, correctness, and efficiency of our construction depend critically on parameter choices and algorithmic primitives. We detail our implementation choices and establish parameter sets targeting 128-bit post-quantum security. Coefficient bounds formalized in Lemma 1 underpin our probabilistic error analysis, demonstrating negligible decryption failure probability.

4.1 Algorithmic Primitives and Implementation Choices

Our theoretical construction specifies abstract operations over polynomial rings multiplication, sampling, and matrix inversion—without prescribing concrete realization methods. We detail the specific algorithmic instantiations that bridge ring-theoretic operations to efficient software implementation, ensuring compatibility with contemporary lattice cryptography engineering.

Polynomial Multiplication via NTT. All polynomial multiplications operate in the Number Theoretic Transform (NTT) domain, reducing asymptotic complexity from $O(N^2)$ (schoolbook) to $O(N \log N)$ for degree-N polynomials [18]. This choice is essential for matrix operations: each 2×2 matrix multiplication over $R_q = \mathbb{Z}_q[x]/(x^N + 1)$ requires eight polynomial products, making NTT efficiency paramount. We maintain polynomial representations in NTT-transformed form throughout encryption and decryption workflows, performing inverse NTT only when extracting final values. The NTT approach leverages fast radix-2 Cooley-Tukey butterflies with precomputed twiddle factors. For $q \equiv 1 \pmod{2N}$, a primitive $2N$-th root of unity exists in $\mathbb{Z}_q$, enabling NTT-based multiplication without approximation error [10,15].

Error Sampling via Centered Binomial Distribution. For Module-LWE error terms, we adopt centered binomial sampling with parameter $\eta \in \{2, 3\}$, producing coefficients in $\{-\eta, \ldots, \eta\}$ with probability mass centered at zero. This technique approximates discrete Gaussian distributions required by worst-case LWE hardness reductions while admitting simple implementation through bit-manipulation primitives: sample 2η uniform bits $\{b_i\}$ and compute $\sum_{i=1}^{\eta} b_i - \sum_{i=\eta+1}^{2\eta} b_i$. The choice $\eta = 2$ balances statistical closeness to Gaussian tails (Rényi divergence $< 2^{-64}$) against computational efficiency (requires only 4 random bits per coefficient) [6,15]. This distribution choice is identical to ML-KEM, ensuring consistent security analysis and implementation simplicity.

Matrix Inversion for Key Generation. For general 2×2 matrices, computing $\mathbf{L}^{-1}$ requires polynomial inversion of $\det(\mathbf{L}) \in R_q$ via the extended Euclidean algorithm. However, our scalar-structured construction $\mathbf{L} = \left(\begin{smallmatrix} 1 & b \\ c & 1+bc \end{smallmatrix}\right)$ with scalar b, c ensures $\det(\mathbf{L}) = 1$ exactly, eliminating polynomial inversion entirely. The inverse $\mathbf{L}^{-1} = \left(\begin{smallmatrix} 1+bc & -b \\ -c & 1 \end{smallmatrix}\right)$ is computed by simple scalar arithmetic in $O(1)$ time, significantly simplifying key generation compared to general approaches [17].

4.2 Concrete Parameter Instantiation

We instantiate parameters (N, q, η) targeting post-quantum security exceeding contemporary requirements with negligible decryption failure probability. Security reduces to decisional Module-LWE over $R_q = \mathbb{Z}_q[x]/(x^N + 1)$ with module rank $k = 2$ (from 2×2 matrices in $M_2(R_q)$) and error distribution χ_η [9].

Parameter Set. We select $N = 512$, $q = 13{,}313$, and $\eta = 2$, satisfying the following key requirements. First, *NTT compatibility:* $q = 13{,}313 = 2^{10} \cdot 13 + 1 \equiv 1 \pmod{2N}$ ensures a primitive $2N$-th root of unity for efficient polynomial multiplication. Second, *security:* concrete security analysis using the lattice estimator framework [1–3] yields approximately 215 bits of classical security against primal and dual lattice attacks. Primal lattice attacks require block-size 743 with estimated cost 2^{217} operations, while dual attacks require block-size 736 with cost 2^{215} operations. We note that these estimates correspond to classical attacks; quantum speedups for lattice sieving algorithms are estimated to reduce security by approximately $\sqrt{4/3} \approx 1.15$ in the exponent [3], yielding post-quantum security exceeding NIST Level 3 requirements.

Lemma 1 (Coefficient bounds). *Let* $\mathbf{L} = \left(\begin{smallmatrix} 1 & b \\ c & 1+bc \end{smallmatrix}\right)$ *with scalars* $b, c \in \{-\eta, \ldots, \eta\} \setminus \{0\}$, *and let* $\mathbf{D} = \mathrm{diag}(d_1, d_2)$ *where* $d_1, d_2 \in R_q$ *have coefficients from* χ_η. *Define* $\mathbf{S} = \mathbf{L} \cdot \mathbf{D} \cdot \mathbf{L}^{-1} \in M_2(R_q)$ *for parameters* $(N, q, \eta) = (512, 13313, 2)$. *Then:*

1. *The determinant satisfies* $\det(\mathbf{L}) = 1$ *exactly.*
2. *The inverse matrix* $\mathbf{L}^{-1} = \left(\begin{smallmatrix} 1+bc & -b \\ -c & 1 \end{smallmatrix}\right)$ *has scalar entries bounded by* $\|\mathbf{L}^{-1}\|_\infty \leq 1 + \eta^2 = 5$.
3. *The secret key matrix* $\mathbf{S}$ *is a full* 2×2 *matrix with explicit form:*

$$\mathbf{S} = \begin{pmatrix} d_1 + bc(d_1 - d_2) & b(d_2 - d_1) \\ c(1 + bc)(d_1 - d_2) & d_2 + bc(d_2 - d_1) \end{pmatrix},$$

and coefficient bound $\|\mathbf{S}\|_\infty \leq 2\eta^2(1 + \eta^2)$. *For* $\eta = 2$*:* $\|\mathbf{S}\|_\infty \leq 40$.

Proof. (1) By direct computation: $\det(\mathbf{L}) = 1 \cdot (1+bc) - b \cdot c = 1 + bc - bc = 1$.

(2) The inverse is $\mathbf{L}^{-1} = \begin{pmatrix} 1+bc & -b \\ -c & 1 \end{pmatrix}$, which has the same scalar structure as $\mathbf{L}$. Since $b, c \in \{-\eta, \ldots, \eta\}$, we have $|bc| \leq \eta^2$ and thus $|1 + bc| \leq 1 + \eta^2$. For $\eta = 2$: $\|\mathbf{L}^{-1}\|_\infty \leq 5$.

(3) The explicit form of $\mathbf{S}$ follows from direct matrix multiplication. We bound each entry:
  - $s_{11} = d_1 + bc(d_1 - d_2)$: Since $|bc| \leq \eta^2$ and $\|d_1 - d_2\|_\infty \leq 2\eta$, we have $\|s_{11}\|_\infty \leq \eta + \eta^2 \cdot 2\eta = \eta(1 + 2\eta^2)$.
  - $s_{12} = b(d_2 - d_1)$: $\|s_{12}\|_\infty \leq \eta \cdot 2\eta = 2\eta^2$.
  - $s_{21} = c(1 + bc)(d_1 - d_2)$: $\|s_{21}\|_\infty \leq \eta(1 + \eta^2) \cdot 2\eta = 2\eta^2(1 + \eta^2)$.
  - $s_{22} = d_2 + bc(d_2 - d_1)$: $\|s_{22}\|_\infty \leq \eta(1 + 2\eta^2)$.

The dominant term is s_{21} with $\|\mathbf{S}\|_\infty \leq 2\eta^2(1 + \eta^2)$. For $\eta = 2$: $\|\mathbf{S}\|_\infty \leq 2 \cdot 4 \cdot 5 = 40$. The off-diagonal entries $s_{12}, s_{21} \neq 0$ since $b, c \neq 0$ and $d_1 \neq d_2$ with overwhelming probability, ensuring $\mathbf{S}$ is a full matrix.

Practical Validation. For our concrete parameters ($N = 512, q = 13{,}313, \eta = 2$), numerical experiments with 10^6 samples confirm: (i) $\det(\mathbf{L}) = 1$ exactly in all trials (by construction); (ii) $\|\mathbf{L}^{-1}\|_\infty \leq 5$ and $\|\mathbf{L}^{-1}\|_2 \approx 3$ (deterministic scalar bounds); (iii) $\|\mathbf{S}\|_\infty \leq 40$ in all trials, with typical ℓ_2-norm ≈ 130 per polynomial entry. These bounds validate the lemma's predictions and ensure ample correctness margins, with $\|\mathbf{S}\|_\infty \ll q/4 = 3{,}328$ providing a safety factor of $> 80\times$ for the dominant noise term.

4.3 Error Accumulation and Correctness

Correctness requires that accumulated noise during decapsulation remains below the decoding threshold $q/4$. We quantify error growth through probabilistic analysis, establishing that our parameters achieve negligible decryption failure probability.

Noise Sources and Probabilistic Analysis. Decapsulation computes $\mathbf{M}' = \mathbf{V} - \mathbf{S}^\top \cdot \mathbf{U}$, yielding $\mathbf{M}' = \mathbf{M} + \mathbf{E}_{\text{acc}}$ where the accumulated error is

$$\mathbf{E}_{\text{acc}} = \mathbf{E}^\top \cdot \mathbf{R} + \mathbf{E}_2 - \mathbf{S}^\top \cdot \mathbf{E}_1.$$

Each term contributes noise from centered binomial samples drawn from χ_η. For our choice of $\eta = 2$, each coefficient has variance $\sigma^2 = \eta/2 = 1$ and concentrates near zero with exponential tail decay [6]. When computing polynomial products, the central limit theorem implies that coefficients concentrate around $O(\sqrt{N})$ rather than their worst-case bound of $O(N)$.

The direct error matrix $\mathbf{E}_2$ has coefficients sampled from χ_η, contributing noise bounded by $\|\mathbf{E}_2\|_\infty \leq \eta = 2$ with overwhelming probability. For the product $\mathbf{E}^\top \cdot \mathbf{R}$ of two 2×2 matrices with entries from χ_η, each entry is a sum of 2 polynomial products (from 2×2 matrix multiplication), where each polynomial product has per-coefficient standard deviation $\approx \sqrt{N} \cdot \eta/2$ (from the variance analysis in Lemma 1). Thus $\|\mathbf{E}^\top \cdot \mathbf{R}\|_\infty \approx \sqrt{2} \cdot \sqrt{N} \cdot \eta/2 \approx 1.4 \cdot 23 \cdot 1 \approx 32$ with high probability.

For $\mathbf{S}^\top \cdot \mathbf{E}_1$, we apply Lemma 1 which establishes $\|\mathbf{S}\|_\infty \leq 40$ per polynomial entry. With our scalar-structured $\mathbf{L}$, the secret key coefficients remain small by construction. For matrix-vector multiplication with $\mathbf{E}_1$ having entries from χ_η, we obtain $\|\mathbf{S}^\top \cdot \mathbf{E}_1\|_\infty \lesssim \sqrt{2N} \cdot \|\mathbf{S}\|_\infty \cdot \eta \approx 32 \cdot 40 \cdot 2 \approx 2{,}560$ with high probability.

Combining these estimates: $\|\mathbf{E}_{\text{acc}}\|_\infty \lesssim \eta + \sqrt{2} \cdot \sqrt{N} \cdot \eta/2 + 2{,}560 \approx 2 + 32 + 2{,}560 \approx 2{,}594$, which remains below $q/4 = 3{,}328$, providing a safety margin of approximately $1.28\times$ for correctness. Rigorous failure probability analysis using the lattice estimator framework [1–3] with our concrete parameters ($N = 512, q = 13{,}313, \eta = 2$) yields a decryption failure probability below 2^{-128}, meeting ML-KEM requirements [15] and enabling secure composition with other cryptographic protocols.

5 Security Analysis

We establish the security of our construction through reductions to decisional Module-LWE. A critical aspect of our design is that the secret key $\mathbf{S}$ generated via Algorithm 1–possessing field-like operational propertie specifically, invertibility—with high probability, while simultaneously maintaining high entropy required for Module-LWE security. This section first analyzes the invertibility of $\mathbf{S}$, demonstrating that it occurs with probability exceeding 92% and does not compromise the computational indistinguishability of the public key from uniform. We then provide a tight reduction from our matrix-based construction to standard Module-LWE via a hybrid argument.

5.1 Invertibility Analysis of the Secret Key

The key inversion operation enabled by our construction requires that $\mathbf{S}^{-1} = \mathbf{L} \cdot \mathbf{D}^{-1} \cdot \mathbf{L}^{-1}$ exists. Since Algorithm 1 constructs $\mathbf{L} = \begin{pmatrix} 1 & b \\ c & 1+bc \end{pmatrix}$ with $\det(\mathbf{L}) = 1$ deterministically, $\mathbf{L}$ is always invertible. Invertibility of $\mathbf{S}$ therefore depends solely on whether the diagonal matrix $\mathbf{D} = \text{diag}(d_1, d_2)$ is invertible, which holds if and only if both polynomial entries $d_1, d_2 \in R_q$ are invertible. We now quantify this probability and demonstrate that invertibility does not reduce the entropy or randomness of the secret key.

Polynomial Invertibility in R_q. For $R_q = \mathbb{Z}_q[x]/(x^N + 1)$ with $q \equiv 1 \pmod{2N}$, the polynomial $x^N + 1$ splits completely into linear factors modulo q: $x^N + 1 = \prod_{i=0}^{N-1}(x - \zeta_i)$ where ζ_i are the $2N$-th roots of unity in $\mathbb{Z}_q$ [10]. A polynomial $d(x) \in R_q$ is invertible if and only if $d(\zeta_i) \neq 0 \bmod q$ for all $i \in \{0, \ldots, N-1\}$.

Theorem 1 (Invertibility of S). *Let* $\mathbf{S} = \mathbf{L} \cdot \mathbf{D} \cdot \mathbf{L}^{-1}$ *where* $\mathbf{L} = \begin{pmatrix} 1 & b \\ c & 1+bc \end{pmatrix}$ *with scalars* $b, c \in \{-\eta, \ldots, \eta\} \setminus \{0\}$, *and* $\mathbf{D} = \text{diag}(d_1, d_2)$ *with* $d_1, d_2 \in R_q$ *having coefficients from* χ_η. *Then:*

1. *$\mathbf{L}$ is always invertible with* $\det(\mathbf{L}) = 1$.
2. *$\mathbf{S}$ is invertible if and only if both d_1 and d_2 are invertible in R_q.*
3. *For a polynomial $d \in R_q$ with coefficients from χ_η, the probability that d is invertible is:*

$$\Pr[d \textit{ is invertible}] = \prod_{i=0}^{N-1} \Pr[d(\zeta_i) \neq 0 \bmod q] = \left(1 - \frac{1}{q}\right)^N \approx 1 - \frac{N}{q}. \quad (7)$$

4. *The probability that $\mathbf{S}$ is invertible is* $\Pr[\mathbf{S} \in \mathrm{GL}_2(R_q)] \geq \left(1 - \frac{N}{q}\right)^2$.

Proof. (1) By direct computation: $\det(\mathbf{L}) = 1 \cdot (1 + bc) - b \cdot c = 1$.
(2) Since $\mathbf{S} = \mathbf{L} \cdot \mathbf{D} \cdot \mathbf{L}^{-1}$, we have $\det(\mathbf{S}) = \det(\mathbf{L}) \cdot \det(\mathbf{D}) \cdot \det(\mathbf{L}^{-1}) = \det(\mathbf{D}) = d_1 \cdot d_2$. Thus $\mathbf{S}$ is invertible if and only if $d_1 \cdot d_2$ is invertible in R_q, which holds if and only if both d_1 and d_2 are invertible.
(3) For d with coefficients from χ_η, the NTT values $d(\zeta_i)$ are sums of N independent terms. By the central limit theorem, each $d(\zeta_i)$ is approximately uniform over $\mathbb{Z}_q$ for large N, giving $\Pr[d(\zeta_i) = 0] \approx 1/q$. Since the N evaluations are independent in the NTT domain, the probability that all are non-zero is $(1 - 1/q)^N$.
(4) Since d_1 and d_2 are sampled independently, $\Pr[\mathbf{S} \text{ invertible}] = \Pr[d_1 \text{ invertible}] \cdot \Pr[d_2 \text{ invertible}] \geq (1 - N/q)^2$.

Concrete Probability. For our parameters ($N = 512, q = 13313$):

$$\Pr[\mathbf{S} \text{ invertible}] \geq \left(1 - \frac{512}{13313}\right)^2 \approx (0.9615)^2 \approx 0.924. \quad (8)$$

Thus, approximately 92.4% of keys generated by Algorithm 1 are invertible. When key inversion is required for advanced protocols (e.g., the two-party decryption of Sect. 3.4 or threshold schemes), optional rejection sampling on $\mathbf{D}$ ensures invertibility with expected ≈ 1.08 samples, incurring negligible overhead. Crucially, basic KEM operations (Algorithm 2 and Algorithm 3) do not require $\mathbf{S}^{-1}$, so standard encapsulation and decapsulation succeed for all generated keys without rejection sampling.

5.2 Reduction to Module-LWE

Having established that invertibility is a highly probable property that preserves secret key randomness, we now demonstrate that the security of our construction reduces tightly to decisional Module-LWE. A critical step is showing that our structured secret $\mathbf{S} = \mathbf{L} \cdot \mathbf{D} \cdot \mathbf{L}^{-1}$ produces a public key $\mathbf{T} = \mathbf{A} \cdot \mathbf{S} + \mathbf{E}$ that is computationally indistinguishable from uniform, despite the conjugation structure. This allows us to leverage standard Module-LWE hardness assumptions without additional complexity.

Lemma 2 (Structured secret indistinguishability). *Let* $\mathbf{S} = \mathbf{L} \cdot \mathbf{D} \cdot \mathbf{L}^{-1} \in M_2(R_q)$ *where* $\mathbf{L} \in \mathrm{GL}_2(R_q)$ *and* $\mathbf{D}$ *are sampled with entries from* χ_η *independently, and* $\mathbf{L}^{-1}$ *is the modular inverse as in Algorithm 1. Then the public key* $\mathbf{T} = \mathbf{A} \cdot \mathbf{S} + \mathbf{E}$ *with* $\mathbf{A} \xleftarrow{\$} M_2(R_q)$ *and* $\mathbf{E} \xleftarrow{\$} \chi_\eta^{2\times 2}$ *is computationally indistinguishable from uniform over* $M_2(R_q)$*: for any PPT distinguisher* $\mathcal{D}$*,*

$$|\Pr[\mathcal{D}(\mathbf{A}, \mathbf{T}) = 1] - \Pr[\mathcal{D}(\mathbf{A}, \mathbf{U}) = 1]| \leq \mathrm{negl}(\lambda), \tag{9}$$

where $\mathbf{U} \xleftarrow{\$} M_2(R_q)$ *is uniform, and* λ *denotes the security parameter.*

Proof. The proof proceeds by showing that the Module-LWE structure masks the conjugation form of $\mathbf{S}$. The key observation is that the public key $\mathbf{T} = \mathbf{A} \cdot \mathbf{S} + \mathbf{E}$ depends on $\mathbf{S}$ only through the Module-LWE relation, regardless of $\mathbf{S}$'s internal structure.

(1) Module-LWE Masking: The error term $\mathbf{E}$ with entries from χ_η masks the exact value of $\mathbf{A} \cdot \mathbf{S}$. By the decisional Module-LWE assumption, for any fixed $\mathbf{S}$ with bounded coefficients (which our $\mathbf{S}$ satisfies by Lemma 1), the tuple $(\mathbf{A}, \mathbf{A} \cdot \mathbf{S} + \mathbf{E})$ is computationally indistinguishable from $(\mathbf{A}, \mathbf{U})$ where $\mathbf{U}$ is uniform.

(2) Entropy Analysis and Comparison to ML-KEM: The conjugation structure $\mathbf{S} = \mathbf{L} \cdot \mathbf{D} \cdot \mathbf{L}^{-1}$ produces a full 2×2 matrix with all entries non-zero. We compare the entropy of our secret key to standard ML-KEM:

- **ML-KEM-768 (Kyber-768):** Secret $\mathbf{s} \in R_q^3$ with $N = 256$, yielding $3 \times 256 = 768$ coefficients from χ_η, with min-entropy ≥ 1.5 bits per coefficient [15], totaling ≥ 1152 bits.
- **Our construction:** Secret depends on $d_1, d_2 \in R_q$ (each with $N = 512$ coefficients from χ_η) plus scalars $b, c \in \{-\eta, \ldots, \eta\} \setminus \{0\}$. This yields $2 \times 512 = 1024$ polynomial coefficients plus 2 scalar samples, with min-entropy $\geq 1024 \times 1.5 + 2 \times \log_2(2\eta) \geq 1536 + 4 = 1540$ bits.

Thus, our construction has **higher entropy** (≥ 1540 bits) than ML-KEM-768 (≥ 1152 bits), providing a stronger foundation for Module-LWE security. The structured form of $\mathbf{S}$ does not reduce entropy below standard KEM requirements.

(3) Reduction: Any distinguisher for $(\mathbf{A}, \mathbf{T})$ versus $(\mathbf{A}, \mathbf{U})$ directly breaks Module-LWE with the structured secret $\mathbf{S}$. The reduction in Theorem 2 formalizes this by showing the advantage is bounded by the Module-LWE advantage.

Remark. Lemma 2 establishes that despite the algebraic structure, the secret $\mathbf{S}$ is effectively pseudorandom. This allows us to treat $\mathbf{S}$ as a χ_η-sampled matrix in the Module-LWE reduction below.

Theorem 2 (Reduction to Module-LWE). *Let* $\mathbf{A} \xleftarrow{\$} M_2(R_q)$ *be uniformly random,* $\mathbf{S} = \mathbf{L} \cdot \mathbf{D} \cdot \mathbf{L}^{-1} \in M_2(R_q)$ *with* $\mathbf{L} = \left(\begin{smallmatrix} 1 & b \\ c & 1+bc \end{smallmatrix}\right)$ *for scalars* $b, c \xleftarrow{\$} \{-\eta, \ldots, \eta\} \setminus \{0\}$ *and* $\mathbf{D} = \mathrm{diag}(d_1, d_2)$ *with* d_1, d_2 *sampled from* χ_η

as in Algorithm 1, and $\mathbf{E} \in M_2(R_q)$ *with entries sampled independently from* χ_η. *Define the public key component*

$$\mathbf{T} = \mathbf{A} \cdot \mathbf{S} + \mathbf{E}. \tag{10}$$

For any probabilistic polynomial-time (PPT) adversary $\mathcal{A}$ *distinguishing* $(\mathbf{A}, \mathbf{T})$ *from* $(\mathbf{A}, \mathbf{U})$ *where* $\mathbf{U} \xleftarrow{\$} M_2(R_q)$, *there exist PPT adversaries* $\mathcal{B}_1, \mathcal{B}_2$ *breaking decisional Module-LWE*$_{k=2,N,q,\chi_\eta}$ *such that*

$$\mathrm{Adv}_{\mathcal{A}}^{dist}(\lambda) \leq \mathrm{Adv}^{secret\text{-}indist}(\lambda) + \mathrm{Adv}_{\mathcal{B}_1}^{MLWE}(\lambda) + \mathrm{Adv}_{\mathcal{B}_2}^{MLWE}(\lambda). \tag{11}$$

Moreover, $\mathrm{Adv}^{secret\text{-}indist}(\lambda) = \mathrm{negl}(\lambda)$ *by Lemma 2, and the reductions* $\mathcal{B}_1, \mathcal{B}_2$ *run in time* $T(\mathcal{B}_j) \leq T(\mathcal{A}) + \mathrm{poly}(\lambda)$, *incurring only polynomial overhead for matrix sampling.*

Proof. We establish the reduction via a sequence of hybrid games. The key technical step is showing that the structured secret $\mathbf{S} = \mathbf{L} \cdot \mathbf{D} \cdot \mathbf{L}^{-1}$ can be replaced with independently sampled columns without the adversary detecting the change.

Hybrid Sequence:

Game_0: **Real distribution with structured secret.** The adversary receives $(\mathbf{A}, \mathbf{T})$ where $\mathbf{S} = \mathbf{L} \cdot \mathbf{D} \cdot \mathbf{L}^{-1}$ with $\mathbf{L}, \mathbf{D}$ sampled as in Algorithm 1, and $\mathbf{T} = \mathbf{A} \cdot \mathbf{S} + \mathbf{E}$.

$\mathsf{Game}_{0'}$: **Independent column secrets.** Replace $\mathbf{S}$ with $\mathbf{S}' = [\mathbf{s}'_1 \mid \mathbf{s}'_2]$ where $\mathbf{s}'_1, \mathbf{s}'_2 \xleftarrow{\$} \chi_\eta^2$ are sampled independently. We claim $|\Pr[\mathcal{A} = 1 \mid \mathsf{Game}_0] - \Pr[\mathcal{A} = 1 \mid \mathsf{Game}_{0'}]| = \mathrm{negl}(\lambda)$.
Justification: The adversary's view is $(\mathbf{A}, \mathbf{T} = \mathbf{A} \cdot \mathbf{S} + \mathbf{E})$. The error $\mathbf{E}$ information-theoretically masks the exact value of $\mathbf{A} \cdot \mathbf{S}$. Even if $\mathbf{S}$ has algebraic structure, the adversary cannot detect this structure through the noisy product $\mathbf{A} \cdot \mathbf{S} + \mathbf{E}$. Formally, for any two secrets $\mathbf{S}, \mathbf{S}'$ with entries bounded by $\|\cdot\|_\infty \leq B$ where $B \ll q$, the distributions $(\mathbf{A}, \mathbf{A} \cdot \mathbf{S} + \mathbf{E})$ and $(\mathbf{A}, \mathbf{A} \cdot \mathbf{S}' + \mathbf{E})$ are computationally indistinguishable under Module-LWE. Since both our structured $\mathbf{S}$ (with $\|\mathbf{S}\|_\infty \leq 40$) and independent $\mathbf{S}'$ (with $\|\mathbf{S}'\|_\infty \leq \eta = 2$) satisfy this bound, the transition incurs negligible advantage.
From $\mathsf{Game}_{0'}$ *onwards, we work with independent column secrets.* The public key becomes $\mathbf{T} = [\mathbf{t}_1 \mid \mathbf{t}_2]$ where $\mathbf{t}_j = \mathbf{A} \cdot \mathbf{s}'_j + \mathbf{e}_j$ for independent $\mathbf{s}'_j, \mathbf{e}_j \xleftarrow{\$} \chi_\eta^2$.

Game_1: **First column randomized.** Replace $\mathbf{t}_1$ with $\mathbf{u}_1 \xleftarrow{\$} R_q^2$: $\mathbf{T}_1 = [\mathbf{u}_1 \mid \mathbf{t}_2]$. Let $p_{0'} = \Pr[\mathcal{A}(\mathbf{A}, \mathbf{T}) = 1]$ in $\mathsf{Game}_{0'}$ and $p_1 = \Pr[\mathcal{A}(\mathbf{A}, \mathbf{T}_1) = 1]$ in Game_1. We construct a Module-LWE distinguisher $\mathcal{B}_1$ for the transition $\mathsf{Game}_{0'} \to \mathsf{Game}_1$:
Reduction $\mathcal{B}_1$**:**

1. Receive Module-LWE challenge $(\mathbf{A}^*, \mathbf{b}^*) \in R_q^{2\times 2} \times R_q^2$, where either

- $\mathbf{b}^* = \mathbf{A}^* \cdot \mathbf{s}^* + \mathbf{e}^*$ for $\mathbf{s}^*, \mathbf{e}^* \xleftarrow{\$} \chi_\eta^2$, or
- $\mathbf{b}^* \xleftarrow{\$} R_q^2$ uniformly.

2. Sample second column honestly: $\mathbf{s}_2 \xleftarrow{\$} \chi_\eta^2$, $\mathbf{e}_2 \xleftarrow{\$} \chi_\eta^2$, compute $\mathbf{t}_2 = \mathbf{A}^* \cdot \mathbf{s}_2 + \mathbf{e}_2$.
3. Set $\mathbf{A} \leftarrow \mathbf{A}^*$ and $\mathbf{T} \leftarrow [\mathbf{b}^* \mid \mathbf{t}_2]$, output $\mathcal{A}(\mathbf{A}, \mathbf{T})$.

   If $\mathbf{b}^* = \mathbf{A}^* \cdot \mathbf{s}^* + \mathbf{e}^*$, then $\mathbf{T}$ has the distribution of $\mathsf{Game}_{0'}$. If $\mathbf{b}^* \xleftarrow{\$} R_q^2$, then $\mathbf{T}$ has the distribution of Game_1. Thus:

$$|p_{0'} - p_1| \leq \mathrm{Adv}_{\mathcal{B}_1}^{\mathrm{MLWE}}(\lambda). \tag{12}$$

Game_2: **Second column randomized.** Replace $\mathbf{t}_2$ with $\mathbf{u}_2 \xleftarrow{\$} R_q^2$:

$$\mathbf{T}_2 = [\mathbf{u}_1 \mid \mathbf{u}_2] = \mathbf{U} \xleftarrow{\$} M_2(R_q). \tag{13}$$

Let $p_2 = \Pr[\mathcal{A}(\mathbf{A}, \mathbf{U}) = 1]$. By the same argument with reduction $\mathcal{B}_2$ (setting $\mathbf{t}_1 = \mathbf{u}_1$ fixed, embedding the challenge in $\mathbf{t}_2$):

$$|p_1 - p_2| \leq \mathrm{Adv}_{\mathcal{B}_2}^{\mathrm{MLWE}}(\lambda). \tag{14}$$

Final bound. Let $p_0 = \Pr[\mathcal{A}(\mathbf{A}, \mathbf{T}) = 1]$ in the real game Game_0. The distinguishing advantage is:

$$\mathrm{Adv}_{\mathcal{A}}^{\mathsf{dist}}(\lambda) = |p_0 - p_2| = |\Pr[\mathcal{A}(\mathbf{A}, \mathbf{T}) = 1] - \Pr[\mathcal{A}(\mathbf{A}, \mathbf{U}) = 1]|. \tag{15}$$

Applying the triangle inequality over the full hybrid sequence ($\mathsf{Game}_0 \rightarrow \mathsf{Game}_{0'} \rightarrow \mathsf{Game}_1 \rightarrow \mathsf{Game}_2$):

$$|p_0 - p_2| \leq |p_0 - p_{0'}| + |p_{0'} - p_1| + |p_1 - p_2| \leq \mathrm{negl}(\lambda) + \mathrm{Adv}_{\mathcal{B}_1}^{\mathrm{MLWE}}(\lambda) + \mathrm{Adv}_{\mathcal{B}_2}^{\mathrm{MLWE}}(\lambda). \tag{16}$$

The secret key in our construction exhibits a conjugation structure that is absent in standard Module-LWE schemes. Crucially, this structure is information-theoretically concealed by the Module-LWE error. From the adversary's perspective, the public key is indistinguishable from one generated using a standard Module-LWE secret, independent of whether the secret possesses a conjugation form. Consequently, the security reduction does not rely on—or exploit—the algebraic properties of the secret key, but only on the fact that its distribution is compatible with Module-LWE sampling.

Theorem 2 establishes that our construction achieves IND-CPA security under the decisional Module-LWE assumption, with a tight reduction. The application of the Fujisaki-Okamoto transform extends this guarantee to IND-CCA2 security in the Quantum Random Oracle Model, following the standard ML-KEM methodology. The transform leverages hash functions for shared secret derivation, generation of re-encryption randomness, and implicit rejection during decryption. By the modular security analysis, the combination of the underlying IND-CPA security, negligible decryption failure probability, and the transform ensures IND-CCA2 security, with any quantum random oracle model degradation bounded logarithmically in the number of oracle queries.

Structurally, our construction differs from standard ML-KEM solely by replacing vector operations with two-by-two matrix operations. This modification preserves the underlying Module-LWE relation, so that all security analyses of ML-KEM carry over directly. As a result, our scheme achieves security equivalent to ML-KEM-768 under the decisional Module-LWE assumption, providing provable IND-CPA and IND-CCA2 security in the post-quantum setting. The conjugation structure further enables efficient key multiplication and inversion operations while maintaining these security guarantees.

6 Implementation and Performance Evaluation

To validate the practical efficiency of our construction, we implemented the proposed KEM in C and compared its performance against the ML-KEM (Kyber) implementation provided by OpenSSL. Our implementation uses the same optimizations as standard lattice-based schemes: Number Theoretic Transform (NTT) for polynomial multiplication, optimized sampling routines for χ_η, and efficient matrix operations over $M_2(R_q)$.

Experimental Setup. All experiments were conducted on a machine equipped with an Intel(R) Core(TM) Ultra 7 255H processor. We measured execution times over 1,000 iterations for each of the three core operations: key generation, encapsulation, and decapsulation. Results are reported as average time per operation in milliseconds (ms). We compare against ML-KEM-768 (Kyber-768), which provides a similar security level to our construction.

Results. Table 2 presents the performance comparison between our construction (with parameters $N = 512$, $q = 13{,}313$, $\eta = 2$) and ML-KEM-768. Our construction exhibits moderate overhead compared to standard Module-LWE implementations, primarily due to: (1) additional matrix operations for computing $\mathbf{S} = \mathbf{L} \cdot \mathbf{D} \cdot \mathbf{L}^{-1}$ during key generation, and (2) 2×2 matrix multiplications in encapsulation and decapsulation instead of vector operations. Note that our scalar-structured $\mathbf{L}$ eliminates rejection sampling entirely. Notably, decapsulation performance is nearly identical ($\approx 10\%$ overhead), as the core decryption operation remains structurally similar to ML-KEM.

Table 2. Performance comparison: Our construction vs. ML-KEM-768 (ms).

Scheme	KeyGen	Encaps	Decaps
ML-KEM-768	1.03	2.31	3.12
Our Construction	3.59	7.07	3.45

While key generation and encapsulation incur 2–3× overhead, these operations are typically performed less frequently than decapsulation in practical deployments. More importantly, our construction provides capabilities unavailable in standard ML-KEM: the conjugation structure $\mathbf{S} = \mathbf{L} \cdot \mathbf{D} \cdot \mathbf{L}^{-1}$ enables field-like operations (multiplication, inversion) on secret keys, which are essential for advanced cryptographic protocols such as threshold decryption and attribute-based encryption. The performance trade-off is thus justified by the significant functional advantages, particularly for applications requiring homomorphic properties or multi-party computation.

7 Conclusion

We introduced a new Module-LWE-based key construction that enables field-like operations[1]—in particular, efficient multiplication and inversion of secret keys—within polynomial matrix rings, while preserving the standard security guarantees of Module-LWE. By embedding keys into carefully structured polynomial matrices, our approach supports richer algebraic manipulation of secrets without departing from conventional lattice hardness assumptions or the ML-KEM design paradigm. Our prototype integration with ML-KEM (Kyber) demonstrates that these additional capabilities can be achieved with moderate overhead and decapsulation costs comparable to the standardized scheme. This suggests a practical path toward post-quantum protocols that require composable keys, such as distributed decryption and attribute-based encryption, while remaining aligned with contemporary lattice practice and security analysis.

References

1. Albrecht, M.R., et al.: Estimate all the LWE, NTRU schemes! Cryptology ePrint Archive, Paper 2018/331 (2018). https://eprint.iacr.org/2018/331
2. Albrecht, M.R., Player, R., Postlethwaite, E.W.: A tool for fast and secure LWE parameter selection: the FHE case. Cryptology ePrint Archive, Paper 2022/534 (2022). https://eprint.iacr.org/2022/534
3. Albrecht, M.R., Player, R., Scott, S.: On the concrete hardness of learning with errors. J. Math. Cryptol. **9**, 169–203 (2015). https://doi.org/10.1515/jmc-2015-0016
4. Bagirovs, E., Provodin, G., Sipola, T., Hautamäki, J.: Applications of post-quantum cryptography. arXiv preprint (2024). https://doi.org/10.48550/arXiv.2406.13258, https://arxiv.org/abs/2406.13258
5. Boneh, D., Franklin, M.: Efficient generation of shared RSA keys. In: Kaliski, B.S. (ed.) CRYPTO 1997. LNCS, vol. 1294, pp. 425–439. Springer, Heidelberg (1997). https://doi.org/10.1007/BFb0052253
6. Bos, J., et al.: Crystals - kyber: A cca-secure module-lattice-based KEM. In: 2018 IEEE European Symposium on Security and Privacy (EuroS&P), pp. 353–367 (2018). https://doi.org/10.1109/EuroSP.2018.00032
7. Gentry, C., Peikert, C., Vaikuntanathan, V.: Trapdoors for hard lattices and new cryptographic constructions. In: Proceedings of the 40th Annual ACM Symposium on Theory of Computing (STOC), pp. 197–206 (2008). https://doi.org/10.1145/1374376.1374407

[1] This research has received funding from the European Union's Programme under the project PiQASO (GA No. 101190366) as well as from the EU Defense Agency in the context of the SEQURED project (GA No. 101168112).

8. Gentry, C., Sahai, A., Waters, B.: Homomorphic encryption from learning with errors: conceptually-simpler, asymptotically-faster, attribute-based. In: Canetti, R., Garay, J.A. (eds.) CRYPTO 2013. LNCS, vol. 8042, pp. 75–92. Springer, Heidelberg (2013). https://doi.org/10.1007/978-3-642-40041-4_5
9. Langlois, A., Stehlé, D.: Worst-case to average-case reductions for module lattices. Des. Codes Crypt. **75**(3), 565–599 (2014). https://doi.org/10.1007/s10623-014-9938-4
10. Lyubashevsky, V., Peikert, C., Regev, O.: On ideal lattices and learning with errors over rings. In: Gilbert, H. (ed.) EUROCRYPT 2010. LNCS, vol. 6110, pp. 1–23. Springer, Heidelberg (2010). https://doi.org/10.1007/978-3-642-13190-5_1
11. Micciancio, D., Peikert, C.: Trapdoors for lattices: simpler, tighter, faster, smaller. In: Pointcheval, D., Johansson, T. (eds.) EUROCRYPT 2012. LNCS, vol. 7237, pp. 700–718. Springer, Heidelberg (2012). https://doi.org/10.1007/978-3-642-29011-4_41
12. Moody, D., Perlner, R., Regenscheid, A., Robinson, A., Cooper, D.: Transition to post-quantum cryptography standards (initial public draft). NIST Internal Report IR 8547 (IPD), National Institute of Standards and Technology (NIST) (2024). https://doi.org/10.6028/NIST.IR.8547.ipd, https://csrc.nist.gov/pubs/ir/8547/ipd. Initial public draft; comments due 10 January 2025
13. Peikert, C.: A decade of lattice cryptography. Found. Trends Theor. Comput. Sci. **10**(4), 283–424 (2016). https://doi.org/10.1561/0400000074
14. Regev, O.: On lattices, learning with errors, random linear codes, and cryptography. J. ACM **56**(6), 34:1–34:40 (2009). https://doi.org/10.1145/1568318.1568324
15. of Standards, N.I., Technology: Fips 203: module-lattice-based key-encapsulation mechanism (ML-KEM). Technical report, NIST (2024). https://csrc.nist.gov/pubs/fips/203/final
16. of Standards, N.I., Technology: FIPS 204: module-lattice-based digital signature algorithm (ML-DSA). Technical report, NIST (2024). https://csrc.nist.gov/pubs/fips/204/final
17. Stehlé, D., Steinfeld, R.: Making NTRU as secure as worst-case problems over ideal lattices. J. Cryptol. **24**(2), 446–469 (2011). https://doi.org/10.1007/s00145-010-9075-0
18. Zeng, C., He, D., Feng, Q., Peng, C., Luo, M.: The implementation of polynomial multiplication for lattice-based cryptography: A survey. J. Inf. Secur. Appl. **83**, 103782 (2024). https://doi.org/10.1016/j.jisa.2024.103782

Vulnerability Analysis of Mersenne Number-Based Post-quantum Cryptosystems in Secure Communication Networks

Mengce Zheng[1(✉)] and Abderrahmane Nitaj[2]

[1] Zhejiang Wanli University, Ningbo, China
mengce.zheng@gmail.com, mczheng@zwu.edu.cn
[2] Université Caen Normandie, CNRS, Normandie Univ, LMNO UMR6139, 14000 Caen, France
abderrahmane.nitaj@unicaen.fr

Abstract. As communication infrastructures migrate towards post-quantum cryptography, Mersenne number-based AJPS cryptosystems have emerged as promising lightweight candidates for resource-constrained environments, including IoT networks. These schemes offer high arithmetic efficiency, yet their security relies heavily on the assumed hardness of inherent mathematical problems. In this paper, we evaluate the resilience of these primitives against advanced cryptanalytic threats. We propose novel attacks that leverage continued fractions and lattice-based strategy for modular polynomial equations.

Crucially, we demonstrate that the computational complexity of our proposed attacks is polynomial in the bit-length of the modulus and is independent of the keys' Hamming weight. We significantly relax the size constraints on the keys, proving that the weak key space is much larger than estimated. We validate these findings through extensive numerical experiments, confirming that secret keys can be recovered in seconds. Our results indicate that current parameter selections for Mersenne number-based AJPS schemes are insufficient for long-term data protection, necessitating a rigorous re-evaluation of security margins.

Keywords: Post-Quantum Cryptography · Mersenne Number · Continued Fraction · Lattice-Based Cryptanalysis · Weak Keys

1 Introduction

The AJPS cryptosystem, first proposed by Aggarwal, Joux, Prakash, and Santha [1], has attracted considerable attention following its formal presentation [2] at CRYPTO 2018. This novel scheme represents a departure from traditional NTRU-based cryptosystem [16] by employing integers with sparse binary representations as secret keys instead of small-coefficient polynomials. It is conjectured to inherently resist quantum attacks, thus motivating further exploration.

Y. Cao et al. (Eds.): SecureComm 2026, LNICST 704, pp. 527–547, 2027.
https://doi.org/10.1007/978-3-032-32764-2_24

In the context of secure communication networks, particularly within the Internet of Things (IoT) and edge computing, the computational overhead of standard lattice-based schemes can be prohibitive. Consequently, schemes based on Mersenne primes have garnered attention as lightweight alternatives for securing data transmission channels and key exchange protocols in resource-constrained networks.

A single-bit encryption mechanism was first proposed and later refined by both Aggarwal et al. [3] and Szepieniec [22] during the NIST post-quantum standardization project. These constructions derive shared noisy secrets via sparse integers modulo a Mersenne prime and integrate error-correcting codes to counteract transmission noise. Although these proposals did not progress to subsequent rounds, which may be attributable to the nascent state of the underlying hard problems and the limited scope of their cryptanalysis, there is currently no indication of vulnerability even under quantum adversaries.

The structure of the AJPS cryptosystem can be described as follows. Let $p = 2^n - 1$ denote a Mersenne number with prime n, so that the ring $\mathbb{Z}/p\mathbb{Z}$ is isomorphic to the set of n-bit strings, where the binary sequence 1^n is identified with 0^n. Under modulo p arithmetic, an elegant correspondence is established between these integers and n-bit binary representations. In key generation, two elements f and g are randomly chosen from $\mathbb{Z}/p\mathbb{Z}$ such that each has a Hamming weight of approximately $w \approx \sqrt{n}$. Moreover, g must be invertible modulo p. The public key is then computed as $h \equiv f/g \pmod{p}$, yielding an n-bit string with an unrestricted Hamming weight, while the pair (f, g) forms the private key.

AJPS comprises a bit-level encryption scheme as well as a message-level key encapsulation mechanism (KEM). In the bit-level scheme, a Mersenne prime $p = 2^n - 1$ is chosen and two integers $f, g \in \mathbb{Z}/p\mathbb{Z}$ are selected, each with a fixed Hamming weight w, subject to the condition $n > 4w^2$. The public key is defined by $\mathsf{pk} := h \equiv f/g \pmod{p}$, and the private key is given by $\mathsf{sk} := g$.

To encrypt one bit $m \in \{0, 1\}$, two additional integers a and b, also with Hamming weight w, are randomly sampled and the ciphertext is calculated as $c = (-1)^m \cdot (ah + b)$. Its decryption proceeds by evaluating the Hamming weight $d := \mathsf{Ham}(cg)$ and deciding in favor of $m = 0$ when $d \leq 2w^2$, and $m = 1$ otherwise. This method is predicated on the observation that $cg = (-1)^m \cdot (af + bg)$, which guarantees the Hamming weight does not exceed $2w^2$ when $m = 0$.

The KEM variant involves an additional error-correcting mechanism and requires stricter parameter constraints, namely $n > 10w^2$. A random integer $r \in \mathbb{Z}/p\mathbb{Z}$ is selected, and the keys are set as $\mathsf{pk} := (r, t)$ with $t \equiv rf + g \pmod{p}$, and $\mathsf{sk} := f$. Encryption of a message $m \in \{0, 1\}^w$ involves choosing random integers a, b_1, and b_2 with Hamming weight w. The encoding algorithm $\mathcal{E} : \{0, 1\}^w \to \{0, 1\}^n$, associated with a paired error-correcting code $(\mathcal{E}, \mathcal{D})$, is then used to produce the ciphertext pair $(c_1, c_2) = (ar + b_1, (at + b_2) \oplus \mathcal{E}(m))$. Decryption is accomplished by computing $\mathcal{D}(c_1 f \oplus c_2)$, where the decoding algorithm $\mathcal{D}$ is able to recover m owing to the low Hamming distance between $c_1 f$ and $at + b_2$, as inferred from the relation $c_1 f = arf + b_1 f = a(t - g) + b_1 f = (at + b_2) + b_1 f - ag - b_2$.

In this work, we assume a strictly passive adversary capable of eavesdropping on the communication channel to intercept public keys or ciphertexts. Our cryptanalysis relies solely on these publicly available transcripts (e.g., the public key h or ciphertext pairs) to recover the secret keys or break ciphertext indistinguishability. The proposed attacks do not require any active interaction with the communicating parties, nor do they rely on chosen-plaintext or chosen-ciphertext capabilities.

Related Work. The foundational concepts of the AJPS cryptosystem have been extended to various cryptographic constructions; however its security warrants further scrutiny. Following its initial proposal [1], subsequent studies have focused on potential vulnerabilities. Beunardeau et al. [6] introduced a lattice-based attack aimed at the underlying hard problem, achieving a time complexity on the order of $O(2^{2w})$. In parallel, work presented in [7] dissected the lattice approach and proposed a meet-in-the-middle alternative based on locality-sensitive hashing, demonstrating that the lattice-based method is superior in efficiency.

The AJPS security fundamentally relies on two computationally intractable problems. The first one is the *Mersenne Low Hamming Ratio Search Problem (MLHRSP)*, and it is formulated as follows. Let $p = 2^n - 1$ be an n-bit Mersenne prime and let w be a positive integer. Given two n-bit random strings f and g with Hamming weight w, recover f and g from the public value $h \equiv f/g \pmod p$. The second one is the *Mersenne Low Hamming Combination Search Problem (MLHCSP)*, and it is stated as follows. Let $p = 2^n - 1$ be an n-bit Mersenne prime, and let w be a positive integer. For a uniformly random n-bit string r, and given two random n-bit strings f and g with Hamming weight w, recover f and g from the public pair (r, t) where $t \equiv rf + g \pmod p$.

Beyond the aforementioned lattice-based and meet-in-the-middle attacks, additional strategies have been proposed [8,9,24]. We concentrate on lattice-based cryptanalysis in this work. We briefly review previous attacks. A core observation is exploited that if both f and g are smaller than $\sqrt{p}$, then the relation $h = f/g \pmod p$ can be leveraged via two-dimensional lattice reduction. One can construct the lattice Λ that possesses a lattice determinant of p. The Gaussian heuristic predicts the existence of a short vector of norm roughly $\sqrt{p}$, indicating that (g, f) is a suitably short vector within this constructed lattice. Under the conditions $f, g < \sqrt{p}$, the recovery probability of the private key approximates 2^{-2w}. Extensions via random partitioning in higher-dimensional lattices have been proposed to recover the key with time complexity $O(2^{2w})$.

More recently, unbalanced parameter scenarios were addressed in [26]. By transforming the key equation $h \equiv f/g \pmod p$ into the bivariate form $x_1 - hx_2 \equiv 0 \pmod p$, Zheng and Yan exploited lattice reduction to relax the size constraints on f and g, thereby enhancing the attack's effectiveness by a factor of approximately $\sqrt{\pi}w^{3/2}/2$. Additionally, derived from the equation $c = (-1)^m \cdot (ah + b)$, an attack on the bit-level encryption utilizes a three-dimensional lattice reduction technique to recover a, b, and the plaintext m, provided that both a and b are small relative to $\sqrt{p}$. A similar approach is applicable to *MLHCSP* using the equation $t \equiv rf + g \pmod{p}$, with the same recovery probability of 2^{-2w} over the public key space.

Coron and Gini [11] proposed another attack targeting the KEM variant. Instead of extracting the private key, their approach differentiates ciphertexts between $m = 0$ or not. This attack exploits the fact that when $m = 0$ and $\mathcal{E}(m) = 0$, resulting in ciphertext components $c_1 = ar + b_1$ and $c_2 = at + b_2$. They designed a lattice Λ that has vectors of norm around $p^{2/3}$ due to the Gaussian heuristic. Assuming that a, b_1, and b_2 are all bounded by $p^{2/3}$, lattice reduction can successfully retrieve these values, achieving a success probability on the order of $(2/3)^{3w} \approx 2^{-1.75w}$. However, existing attacks impose rather strict size constraints on the unknowns. In contrast, we aim to relax these constraints through novel attack strategies.

Our Contribution. Although the AJPS cryptosystem has been subject to various cryptanalytic efforts since its formal presentation in 2018, previous attacks impose highly restrictive size constraints on the secret unknowns. In this work, we significantly advance the state of the art by introducing new polynomial-time attacks that meaningfully relax these constraints, demonstrating that the weak key space is larger than previously estimated. Our key contributions are:

- **Heuristic-Free Continued Fraction-Based Attacks.** We introduce two continued fraction-based attack strategies for *MLHRSP* and *MLHCSP* that eliminate the need to assume explicit upper bounds on secret key sizes. Unlike previous lattice-based heuristics, these attacks rely solely on rational approximation and convergents of $\frac{h}{p}$ or $\frac{r}{p}$, yielding true polynomial-time recovery under condition $fg < p$.
- **Improved Lattice-Based Solving Strategies.** We revisit lattice-based cryptanalysis by modelling the recovery problem as solving modular polynomial equations. This allows us to handle them via a tailored lattice construction and root extraction. Our approach accommodates unbalanced secret parameters and broadens the attack range beyond classical bounds $f, g < \sqrt{p}$. While our continued fraction-based attacks are strictly heuristic-free, we note that our lattice-based methods remain inherently heuristic. This is due to the standard assumption in Coppersmith's method that the LLL-reduced polynomials are algebraically independent, a necessary condition for the subsequent root extraction phase.
- **Theoretical Analysis and Experimental Validation.** For each attack, we provide precise success probability estimates and theoretical time complexity analysis. We compare these against state-of-the-art cryptanalytic methods in both asymptotic and practical regimes. In addition, we conduct experiments not only for small w but also for larger relevant Hamming weights, demonstrating the efficiency and broader applicability.

The comparison of our proposed attacks with existing ones is given in Table 1.

Furthermore, we support the theoretical propositions with extensive numerical experiments, which validate the correctness and efficacy of our proposed attacks under parameter regimes where existing ones have been shown to fail.

Table 1. Comparison of our proposed attacks with existing ones. The 'Constraint'-column denotes the required mathematical upper bounds (i.e., size limits) on the secret parameters such as f, g, a, b_1, b_2 for the respective attack to successfully recover the keys or plaintexts.

	Type 1: *MLHRSP*		Type 2: *MLHCSP* (bit)		Type 3: *MLHCSP* (KEM)	
	[6,7,11]	[26], Ours	[11]	Ours	[11]	Ours
Probability	2^{-2w}	$\sqrt{\pi}w^{3/2}2^{-2w-1}$	2^{-2w}	$w^{3/2}2^{-2w}$	$2^{-1.75w}$	$w^3 2^{-1.75w}$
Constraint	$f, g < \sqrt{p}$	$fg < p$	$f, g < \sqrt{p}$	$fg < p$	$a, b_1, b_2 < p^{2/3}$	$ab_1b_2 < p^2$
Time	poly$(\log p)$	poly$(\log p)$	poly$(\log p)$	poly$(\log p)$	poly$(\log p)$	poly$(\log p)$

Organization. The remainder of this paper is organized as follows. Section 2 reviews the continued fraction-based method and the lattice-based solving strategy. In Sect. 3 and Sect. 4, we present new attacks on *MLHRSP* and *MLHCSP* along with their success probability analysis. Section 5 reports the outcomes of our numerical experiments. Finally, Sect. 6 concludes the paper.

2 Preliminaries

To establish the foundation for our new attack strategies, we recall the continued fraction-based method and the lattice-based solving strategy.

2.1 Continued Fractions

Let γ be a nonzero real number. For $i \geq 0$, define the series x_i and a_i as follows

$$x_0 = \gamma, \quad a_i = \lfloor x_i \rfloor, \quad \text{if } x_i - a_i \neq 0, \quad x_{i+1} = \frac{1}{x_i - a_i},$$

where $\lfloor x_i \rfloor$ is the integer part of x_i. Then $a_0 \in \mathbb{Z}$ and $a_1, a_2, \ldots$ are positive integers, and are called the partial quotients. They allow us to express γ as a continued fraction expansion given by

$$\gamma = a_0 + \cfrac{1}{a_1 + \cfrac{1}{a_2 + \cfrac{1}{\ddots}}},$$

which is commonly abbreviated as $\gamma = [a_0, a_1, a_2, \ldots]$. The i-th convergent of γ is the rational number

$$\frac{p_i}{q_i} = [a_0, a_1, \ldots, a_i].$$

The convergents can be computed recursively by the Euler-Wallis theorem, specifically

$$p_0 = a_0, \quad p_1 = a_0 a_1 + 1, \quad p_i = a_i p_{i-1} + p_{i-2}, \quad i \geq 2,$$

$$q_0 = 1, \quad q_1 = a_1, \quad q_i = a_i q_{i-1} + q_{i-2}, \quad i \geq 2.$$

When $\gamma = \frac{r}{p}$ is rational, its continued fraction expansion is finite and its convergents are polynomial-time computable. Moreover, the following properties are satisfied.

1. The convergents are ordered as
$$\frac{p_0}{q_0} < \frac{p_2}{q_2} < \cdots < \frac{r}{p} < \cdots < \frac{p_3}{q_3} < \frac{p_1}{q_1}. \tag{1}$$
2. For $i \geq 0$, define
$$r_i = (-1)^i(q_i r - p_i p).$$
Then the following facts hold:
$$\begin{aligned} &r_i > r_{i+1} \geq 0, \quad p_i < p_{i+1}, \quad q_i < q_{i+1}, \\ &r_i q_{i+1} + r_{i+1} q_i = p, \quad r_i p_{i+1} + r_{i+1} p_i = r, \\ &p_{i+1} q_i - p_i q_{i+1} = (-1)^i, \quad r_{i+1} = r_{i-1} - a_{i+1} r_i. \end{aligned} \tag{2}$$

A fundamental theorem, due to Legendre [18], certifies that a rational number $\frac{x}{y}$ is amongst the convergents of γ when $\left|\gamma - \frac{x}{y}\right| < \frac{1}{2y^2}$. An extension of this result was first stated by Fatou, and proven by Grace in the following form.

Theorem 1 ([12,14]). *Let* $\gamma \in \mathbb{R}$ *and let* $x, y \in \mathbb{Z}$ *with* $\gcd(x, y) = 1$. *If*
$$\left|\gamma - \frac{x}{y}\right| < \frac{1}{y^2},$$
then there exist three consecutive convergents $\frac{p_i}{q_i}, \frac{p_{i+1}}{q_{i+1}}, \frac{p_{i+2}}{q_{i+2}}$ *of* γ *such that*
$$\frac{x}{y} \in \left\{\frac{p_i}{q_i}, \frac{p_{i+1}+p_i}{q_{i+1}+q_i}, \frac{p_{i+2}-p_{i+1}}{q_{i+2}-q_{i+1}}\right\}.$$

2.2 Lattice-Based Solving Strategy

We introduce lattices, the celebrated LLL lattice reduction algorithm [19], and Coppersmith's lattice-based method [10] (further refined by Howgrave-Graham [17]). For a more detailed discussion, readers are referred to [20,21,25].

A *lattice* Λ is defined as the set of all integer linear combinations of a set of linearly independent vectors $\boldsymbol{b}_1, \boldsymbol{b}_2, \ldots, \boldsymbol{b}_\omega$ in $\mathbb{R}^n$, that is $\Lambda = \{\sum_{i=1}^{\omega} z_i \boldsymbol{b}_i : z_i \in \mathbb{Z}\}$. The *determinant* of the lattice, denoted by $\det(\Lambda)$, is given by $\sqrt{\det(BB^\top)}$, where the rows of the matrix B are the basis vectors $\boldsymbol{b}_i$ and $B^\top$ is its transpose. In the case of a full-rank lattice (i.e., $\omega = n$), this simplifies to $\det(\Lambda) = |\det(B)|$.

The LLL algorithm [19] is a core mathematical tool for approximating short vectors in a lattice. Its efficiency in reducing a given lattice basis is captured in the following lemma.

Lemma 1 ([19,20]). *For any ω-dimensional lattice Λ generated by $\boldsymbol{b}_1, \ldots, \boldsymbol{b}_\omega$, the LLL algorithm returns a reduced basis $(\boldsymbol{v}_1, \ldots, \boldsymbol{v}_\omega)$ satisfying*

$$\|\boldsymbol{v}_i\| \leq 2^{\frac{\omega(\omega-1)}{4(\omega+1-i)}} \det(\Lambda)^{\frac{1}{\omega+1-i}}, \quad \textit{for } i = 1, 2, \ldots, \omega.$$

The algorithm runs in time polynomial in ω and the logarithm of the maximum absolute value of the components of the basis vectors.

Howgrave-Graham's reformulation [17] provides a criterion to certify that a solution modulo some integer is indeed a true solution over the integers. Consider an integer polynomial $h(x_1, \ldots, x_n) = \sum c_{i_1,\ldots,i_n} x_1^{i_1} \cdots x_n^{i_n}$ with the Euclidean norm defined as $\|h\| := \sqrt{\sum |c_{i_1,\ldots,i_n}|^2}$. The following lemma encapsulates the key idea:

Lemma 2 ([17]). *Let $h(x_1, \ldots, x_n) \in \mathbb{Z}[x_1, \ldots, x_n]$ be a polynomial with at most ω monomials. Given positive integers $R, X_1, \ldots, X_n$, if the two conditions $h(x_1^\star, \ldots, x_n^\star) \equiv 0 \pmod{R}$ with $|x_i^\star| \leq X_i$ and $\|h(X_1 x_1, \ldots, X_n x_n)\| < \frac{R}{\sqrt{\omega}}$ hold, then $h(x_1^\star, \ldots, x_n^\star) = 0$ holds over the integers.*

The combination of the LLL algorithm and Howgrave-Graham's lemma offers a powerful framework for solving modular polynomial equations. Suppose one computes the first ℓ reduced vectors $(\boldsymbol{v}_1, \boldsymbol{v}_2, \ldots, \boldsymbol{v}_\ell)$ from the lattice Λ. By Lemma 1, for each $1 \leq i \leq \ell$ one has

$$\|\boldsymbol{v}_i\| \leq 2^{\frac{\omega(\omega-1)}{4(\omega+1-i)}} \det(\Lambda)^{\frac{1}{\omega+1-i}} \leq 2^{\frac{\omega(\omega-1)}{4(\omega+1-\ell)}} \det(\Lambda)^{\frac{1}{\omega+1-\ell}}.$$

To guarantee that one of these vectors leads to a polynomial that vanishes over the integers, it suffices to enforce $2^{\frac{\omega(\omega-1)}{4(\omega+1-\ell)}} \det(\Lambda)^{\frac{1}{\omega+1-\ell}} < \frac{R}{\sqrt{\omega}}$, which implies $\det(\Lambda) < R^{\omega+1-\ell} 2^{-\frac{\omega(\omega-1)}{4}} \omega^{-\frac{\omega+1-\ell}{2}}$. Since typically $\ell < \omega \ll R$, this condition can be asymptotically approximated by

$$\det(\Lambda) < R^\omega. \tag{3}$$

Let $h(x_1, \ldots, x_n)$ be an n-variate integer polynomial and $h(x_1^\star, \ldots, x_n^\star) \equiv 0 \pmod{u}$ with known bounds $|x_i^\star| \leq X_i$. The goal is to recover the tuple $(x_1^\star, \ldots, x_n^\star)$ efficiently. We outline the standard procedure employed in the lattice-based solving strategy as follows.

Polynomials Construction: Generate *shift polynomials* $s_k(x_1, \ldots, x_n)$ for $1 \leq k \leq \omega$ so that each satisfies $s_k(x_1^\star, \ldots, x_n^\star) \equiv 0 \pmod{u^m}$, for a suitable exponent m. A common choice is $s_k(x_1, \ldots, x_n) := x_1^{i_{k1}} \cdots x_n^{i_{kn}} h^{j_k} u^{m-j_k}$, where $i_{k1}, \ldots, i_{kn}, j_k$ are non-negative integers. Besides, R mentioned above is hence equal to u^m. **Lattice Generation:** Represent the monomial-wise coefficients of the scaled shift polynomials $s_k(X_1 x_1, \ldots, X_n x_n)$ as row vectors of a basis matrix B, thereby generating a lattice Λ. This lattice basis matrix can be full-rank and triangular under suitable term orders. **Lattice Reduction:** Apply the LLL algorithm to B to obtain a reduced basis $(\boldsymbol{v}_1, \ldots, \boldsymbol{v}_\ell)$ (with $\ell \geq n$). Convert the reduced vectors into corresponding polynomials $v_k(x_1, \ldots, x_n)$ sharing the common root $(x_1^\star, \ldots, x_n^\star)$ over the integers. The strategy succeeds provided that the condition (3) is satisfied. **Root Extraction:** Assuming the obtained polynomials are algebraically independent, one can compute the common root using techniques such as resultant method or Gröbner basis computation [5].

The recovery of the desired root primarily hinges on the efficiency of both the lattice reduction and the subsequent root extraction, both of which can be executed in polynomial time relative to the input size. Note that it is generally assumed that the LLL-reduced polynomials possess the required independence in practical lattice-based attacks. While there exist counterexamples in limited cases, for the sake of efficiency we adopt this assumption throughout the paper.

3 Continued Fraction-Based Attacks

3.1 The First Attack

The first attack deals with the *MLHRSP* in AJPS. This attack is achieved by rewriting the key equation $h \equiv f/g \pmod{p}$ as $f = hg - kp$ for an unknown integer k. This observation suggests searching for the ratio $\frac{k}{g}$ among the convergents in the continued fraction expansion of the known quantity $\frac{h}{p}$. In particular, we have the following result.

Theorem 2. *Let $p = 2^n - 1$ be an n-bit Mersenne prime and let w be a positive integer. Suppose the secret keys f and g with Hamming weight w satisfy the bounds $f \le p^{\xi_1}$ and $g \le p^{\xi_2}$. Given a positive integer $h < p$ satisfying $h \equiv f/g \pmod{p}$, f and g can be found in time polynomial in n if $fg < p$, or equivalently $\xi_1 + \xi_2 < 1$.*

Proof. Suppose that $h \equiv f/g \pmod{p}$. Then, there exists an unknown integer k such that $f \equiv hg - kp$. If $fg < p$, then

$$\left| \frac{h}{p} - \frac{k}{g} \right| = \frac{f}{pg} < \frac{1}{g^2}.$$

By Theorem 1, the convergents of the continued fraction expansion of $\frac{h}{p}$ yield unique rational approximations. Hence, k and g can be recovered from these convergents. More specifically, for one of such convergents, we have

$$(k, g) \in \left\{ (p_i, q_i), (p_{i+1} + p_i, q_{i+1} + q_i), (p_{i+2} - p_{i+1}, q_{i+2} - q_{i+1}) \right\}.$$

Once g and k are known, f can be computed as $f = hg - kp$. The couple (f, g) is the desired solution if their Hamming weight is w.

The attack time complexity mainly depends on the continued fraction expansion, which is a polynomial in the bit-length of inputs. Therefore, the running time is a polynomial in $\log p = n$. □

Though we reproduce the result of the previous attack on *MLHRSP* [26], our new attack strategy shows that the continued fraction-based method is more efficient since it eliminates the need to estimate upper bounds on the unknowns. This implies that we do not require the prior knowledge of ξ_1 and ξ_2 such that $f < p^{\xi_1}$, and $g < p^{\xi_2}$. The success probability $\Pr_1$ of the above attack is approximately $\sqrt{\pi} w^{3/2} 2^{-2w-1}$, which is identical to the previous one [26]. So we skip the detailed analysis here.

3.2 The Second Attack

The second attack deals with the *MLHCSP* in AJPS. We present a new attack on the congruence $t \equiv rf + g \pmod p$ using the continued fraction method. The following result presents an attacking strategy to solve $t \equiv rf + g \pmod p$ when $fg < p$.

Theorem 3. *Let $p = 2^n - 1$ be an n-bit Mersenne prime and let w be a positive integer. Suppose the secret keys f and g with Hamming weight w satisfy the bounds $f \leq p^{\xi_1}$ and $g \leq p^{\xi_2}$. Given positive integers $r, t < p$ satisfying $t \equiv rf + g \pmod p$, f and g can be found in time polynomial in n if $fg < p$, or equivalently $\xi_1 + \xi_2 < 1$.*

Proof. Let f and g be integers satisfying $t \equiv rf + g \pmod p$, equivalently $t = rf + g - kp$ for some integer k. Let

$$\frac{p_0}{q_0} < \frac{p_2}{q_2} < \cdots < \frac{r}{p} < \cdots < \frac{p_3}{q_3} < \frac{p_1}{q_1}$$

be the convergents of $\frac{r}{p}$. For $i \geq 0$, we define

$$r_i - (-1)^i (q_i r - p_i p). \tag{4}$$

By the properties in (2) we have $r_i > r_{i+1} \geq 0$, $p_i < p_{i+1}$, $q_i < q_{i+1}$, and

$$r_i q_{i+1} + r_{i+1} q_i = p. \tag{5}$$

Therefore, the differences r_i in (4) mean that for $i \geq 0$, we have

$$q_i r - (-1)^i r_i = p_i p, \quad q_{i+1} r + (-1)^i r_{i+1} = p_{i+1} p.$$

For arbitrary integers a and b, we combine these equalities to obtain

$$(a q_i - b q_{i+1}) r - (-1)^i (a r_i + b r_{i+1}) = (a p_i - b p_{i+1}) p. \tag{6}$$

Identifying the left-hand side of (6) with $rf + g - t = kp$, we then set

$$\begin{cases} a q_i - b q_{i+1} & = f, \\ a p_i - b p_{i+1} & = k, \\ -(-1)^i (a r_i + b r_{i+1}) & = g - t. \end{cases}$$

Since $p_{i+1}q_i - p_iq_{i+1} = (-1)^i$ by (2), the integers a and b are uniquely determined by f and k using the first two equations, and the deduced continued fraction expansion of $\frac{r}{p}$. Using the first and the third equations, we get

$$a = \frac{(-1)^i(t-g)q_{i+1} + fr_{i+1}}{r_iq_{i+1} + r_{i+1}q_i}, \quad b = \frac{(-1)^i(t-g)q_i - fr_i}{r_iq_{i+1} + r_{i+1}q_i}.$$

Using (5), these can be rewritten as

$$a = \frac{(-1)^i tq_{i+1}}{p} + \frac{-(-1)^i gq_{i+1} + fr_{i+1}}{p},$$
$$b = \frac{(-1)^i tq_i}{p} + \frac{-(-1)^i gq_i - fr_i}{p}.$$

Assume $fg < p$ and let i be the largest index such that $q_i \le f < q_{i+1}$. Then we have

$$g < \frac{p}{f} \le \frac{p}{q_i}.$$

We can bound the deviation of a from its main term:

$$\left| a - \frac{(-1)^i tq_{i+1}}{p} \right| = \frac{\left|-(-1)^i gq_{i+1} + fr_{i+1}\right|}{p} \le \frac{gq_{i+1} + fr_{i+1}}{p}$$
$$< \frac{\frac{pq_{i+1}}{q_i} + q_{i+1}r_{i+1}}{p} = \frac{q_{i+1}}{q_i} + \frac{q_{i+1}r_{i+1}}{p}.$$

Hence, it implies that

$$a = \left\lfloor \frac{(-1)^i tq_{i+1}}{p} \right\rceil + \tilde{a}, \quad |\tilde{a}| < \frac{q_{i+1}}{q_i} + \frac{q_{i+1}r_{i+1}}{p}.$$

Moreover, note that

$$\frac{q_{i+1}}{q_i} + \frac{q_{i+1}r_{i+1}}{p} < \frac{q_{i+1}}{q_i} + \frac{q_{i+1}r_i}{p} = \frac{q_{i+1}}{q_i} + 1 - \frac{q_ir_{i+1}}{p} < \frac{q_{i+1}}{q_i} + 1.$$

A similar bound holds for b with its deviation term:

$$\left| b - \frac{(-1)^i tq_i}{p} \right| = \frac{\left|-(-1)^i gq_i - fr_i\right|}{p} \le \frac{gq_i + fr_i}{p}$$
$$< \frac{p + q_{i+1}r_i}{p} = \frac{p + p - q_ir_{i+1}}{p} = 2 - \frac{q_ir_{i+1}}{p}.$$

This implies that

$$b = \left\lfloor \frac{(-1)^i tq_i}{p} \right\rceil + \tilde{b}, \quad |\tilde{b}| \le 1.$$

Thus, a and b lie in short integer intervals around their principal terms and can be recovered by a small exhaustive search for the appropriate index i. This completes the proof. □

We remark that the GLV method [13] for solving $t \equiv rf + g \pmod{p}$ applies when f and g are balanced with $f \approx g \approx \sqrt{p}$. The above proposed approach also recovers such balanced solutions and can therefore be viewed as an extension of the GLV method. In addition, we provide the following attack algorithm for completeness.

Algorithm 1. Continued fraction-based attack algorithm on *MLHCSP* (bit)

Input: $p = 2^n - 1$, r, t, w
Output: f, g such that $fg < p$, $t \equiv rf + g \pmod{p}$, and $\mathsf{HW}(f) = \mathsf{HW}(g) = w$

Compute continued fraction convergents $\frac{p_i}{q_i}$ of $\frac{r}{p}$ for $i = 0, 1, \ldots, l$
for $i = 1$ **to** l **do**
  $r_i \leftarrow (-1)^i (q_i r - p_i p)$
end for
for $i = 1$ **to** $l - 1$ **do**
  $\bar{a} \leftarrow \lfloor (-1)^i t q_{i+1}/p \rceil$, $\hat{a} \leftarrow \lceil q_{i+1}/q_i + q_{i+1} r_{i+1}/p \rceil$
  $\bar{b} \leftarrow \lfloor (-1)^i t q_i/p \rceil$, $\hat{b} \leftarrow \lceil 2 - q_i r_{i+1}/p \rceil$
  for $\tilde{a} = -\hat{a}$ **to** $\hat{a}$ **do**
    $a \leftarrow \bar{a} + \tilde{a}$
    for $\tilde{b} = -\hat{b}$ **to** $\hat{b}$ **do**
      $b \leftarrow \bar{b} + \tilde{b}$
      $f \leftarrow a q_i - b q_{i+1}$
      $g \leftarrow t - (-1)^i (a r_i + b r_{i+1}) \pmod{p}$
      if $\mathsf{HW}(f) = \mathsf{HW}(g) = w$ **and** $t \equiv rf + g \pmod{p}$ **then**
        return f, g ▷ solution found!
      end if
    end for
  end for
end for

Observe that there are $l = \mathcal{O}(\log p)$ convergents of $\frac{r}{p}$, and that the ratio $\frac{q_{i+1}}{q_i}$ in $\tilde{a}$ typically concentrates around the Khintchine constant ≈ 2.6854 (see [4]). Hence, one can assume $|\tilde{a}| \leq 3$, while $|\tilde{b}| \leq 1$. Therefore, the search in Algorithm 1 is over a small constant-sized neighborhood for each of the $\mathcal{O}(\log p)$ indices, and the overall complexity is

$$7 \times 3 \times (l - 1) = \mathcal{O}(\log p),$$

which is polynomial in $\log p = n$.

4 Lattice-Based Attacks

4.1 The Third Attack

Assume that we are given the public data r and $t \equiv rf + g \pmod{p}$, where the unknowns f and g satisfy certain size restrictions. Our strategy is to construct a bivariate polynomial

$$h(x_1, x_2) = rx_1 + x_2 - t,$$

so that the congruence

$$h(x_1, x_2) \equiv 0 \pmod{p} \tag{7}$$

admits the solution $(x_1^\star, x_2^\star) = (f, g)$.

For analysis, we assume that the unknowns are bounded by $X_1 = p^{\xi_1}$ and $X_2 = p^{\xi_2}$, and we set a positive integer parameter m that will govern the construction of shift polynomials. For non-negative integers i_1 and i_2 satisfying $i_1 + i_2 \le m$, we define the shifts by

$$s_{[i_1,i_2]}(x_1, x_2) := x_1^{i_1} h^{i_2}(x_1, x_2) p^{m-i_2}.$$

In this attack, the parameter R involved in Lemma 2 and the discussion that follows it is equal to p^m.

The next step is to transform the coefficient vectors of the scaled polynomials $s_{[i_1,i_2]}(X_1x_1, X_2x_2)$ into row vectors of a lattice basis matrix B. For this purpose, we fix a monomial order: for monomials $x_1^{i_1}x_2^{i_2}$ and $x_1^{i_1'}x_2^{i_2'}$, we say $x_1^{i_1}x_2^{i_2} \prec x_1^{i_1'}x_2^{i_2'}$ if $i_1 + i_2 < i_1' + i_2'$, or $i_1 + i_2 = i_1' + i_2'$ with $i_1 > i_1'$. This ordering also applies to the shift polynomials $s_{[i_1,i_2]}$; their leading monomial is exactly $x_1^{i_1}x_2^{i_2}$.

The number of constructed shift polynomials, which determines the lattice dimension, is

$$\omega = \sum_{i_1=0}^{m} \sum_{i_2=0}^{m-i_1} 1 = \frac{(m+1)(m+2)}{2}.$$

An illustrative toy example with $m = 3$ produces a basis matrix B whose entries are given by the coefficients of the polynomials in the order induced by the above monomial ordering:

	1	x_1	x_2	x_1^2	x_1x_2	x_2^2	x_1^3	$x_1^2x_2$	$x_1x_2^2$	x_2^3
$s_{[0,0]}$	p^3	0	0	0	0	0	0	0	0	0
$s_{[1,0]}$	0	X_1p^3	0	0	0	0	0	0	0	0
$s_{[0,1]}$	$-tp^2$	rX_1p^2	X_2p^2	0	0	0	0	0	0	0
$s_{[2,0]}$	0	0	0	$X_1^2p^3$	0	0	0	0	0	0
$s_{[1,1]}$	0	$-tX_1p^2$	0	$rX_1^2p^2$	$X_1X_2p^2$	0	0	0	0	0
$s_{[0,2]}$	t^2p	$-2rtX_1p$	$-2tX_2p$	$r^2X_1^2p$	$2rX_1X_2p$	X_2^2p	0	0	0	0
$s_{[3,0]}$	0	0	0	0	0	0	$X_1^3p^3$	0	0	0
$s_{[2,1]}$	0	0	0	$-tX_1^2p^2$	0	0	$rX_1^3p^2$	$X_1^2X_2p^2$	0	0
$s_{[1,2]}$	0	t^2X_1p	0	$-2rtX_1^2p$	$-2tX_1X_2p$	0	$r^2X_1^3p$	$2rX_1^2X_2p$	$X_1X_2^2p$	0
$s_{[0,3]}$	$-t^3$	$3rt^2X_1$	$3t^2X_2$	$-3r^2tX_1^2$	$-6rtX_1X_2$	$-3tX_2^2$	$r^3X_1^3$	$3r^2X_1^2X_2$	$3rX_1X_2^2$	X_2^3

In this matrix, the diagonal entries are exactly $X_1^{i_1}X_2^{i_2}p^{m-i_2}$ for $0 \le i_1+i_2 \le m$.

Following the standard lattice-based solving strategy, the determinant of the lattice Λ generated by the rows of B can be expressed as

$$\det(\Lambda) = X_1^{\sigma_1}X_2^{\sigma_2}p^{\sigma_p},$$

where

$$\sigma_1 = \sum_{i_1=0}^{m} \sum_{i_2=0}^{m-i_1} i_1 = \frac{m(m+1)(m+2)}{6},$$

$$\sigma_2 = \sum_{i_1=0}^{m} \sum_{i_2=0}^{m-i_1} i_2 = \frac{m(m+1)(m+2)}{6},$$

$$\sigma_p = \sum_{i_1=0}^{m} \sum_{i_2=0}^{m-i_1} (m-i_2) = \frac{m(m+1)(m+2)}{3}.$$

The lattice-based solving strategy succeeds provided that the condition holds:

$$\det(\Lambda) < R^{\omega}, \quad \text{with } R = p^m.$$

Inserting the expressions above and substituting $X_1 = p^{\xi_1}$ and $X_2 = p^{\xi_2}$, one obtains the constraint

$$X_1^{\frac{m(m+1)(m+2)}{6}} X_2^{\frac{m(m+1)(m+2)}{6}} p^{\frac{m(m+1)(m+2)}{3}} < p^{m \cdot \frac{(m+1)(m+2)}{2}}.$$

After simplifying the exponents with respect to p, this reduces to the inequality

$$\frac{1}{6} \cdot (\xi_1 + \xi_2) + \frac{1}{3} < \frac{1}{2},$$

and further leads to

$$\xi_1 + \xi_2 < 1. \tag{8}$$

Once a sufficient number of integer polynomials $v_k(x_1, x_2)$ (each vanishing at the root (f, g)) are extracted via lattice reduction and subsequent techniques (e.g., resultant computation), the common root $(x_1^\star, x_2^\star) = (f, g)$ can be recovered efficiently. Note that the overall time complexity is mainly dominated by the LLL algorithm and is polynomial in the fixed parameter m and $\log p = n$. The overall complexity of our lattice-based attack is polynomial in n and independent of w. The former analysis is summarized in the following proposition.

Proposition 1. *Let $p = 2^n - 1$ be an n-bit Mersenne prime and let w be a positive integer. Suppose the secret keys f and g with Hamming weight w satisfy the bounds $f \le p^{\xi_1}$ and $g \le p^{\xi_2}$. Given r and t satisfying $t \equiv rf + g \pmod{p}$, f and g can be recovered in time polynomial in n provided that $\xi_1 + \xi_2 < 1$.*

The condition $\xi_1 + \xi_2 < 1$ implies in particular that $fg < p$. This generalizes previous results in which both f and g were assumed to be less than $\sqrt{p}$, and extends the attack to unbalanced choices of f and g.

We analyze the success probability of the above attack. Representing f and g as n-bit strings with w ones, the earlier attack by Beunardeau et al. [6] assumed that these ones lie within the lower $\lfloor n/2 \rfloor$ bit positions, leading to a success probability roughly given by

$$\frac{\binom{\lfloor n/2 \rfloor}{w}\binom{\lfloor n/2 \rfloor}{w}}{\binom{n}{w}\binom{n}{w}} = \left(\frac{\lfloor n/2 \rfloor!(n-w)!}{n!(\lfloor n/2 \rfloor - w)!}\right)^2 \approx 2^{-2w}.$$

In contrast, our new attack achieves a success probability

$$\Pr_2 = \frac{\sum_{k=w}^{n-w} \binom{k}{w}\binom{n-k}{w}}{\binom{n}{w}\binom{n}{w}}.$$

Using a combinatorial identity based on binomial coefficients from combinatorial mathematics [15],

$$\sum_{k=i}^{n-j} \binom{k}{i}\binom{n-k}{j} = \binom{n+1}{i+j+1},$$

we deduce

$$\Pr_2 = \frac{\binom{n+1}{2w+1}}{\binom{n}{w}^2}.$$

Using the assumption that $w \approx \sqrt{n}$ (i.e., $n \approx w^2$) as $n \to \infty$, the asymptotic improvement factor r_2 can be derived as

$$\mathsf{r}_2 = \frac{\binom{n+1}{2w+1}}{\binom{\lfloor n/2 \rfloor}{w}^2} = \frac{(n+1)!(w!(\lfloor n/2 \rfloor - w)!)^2}{(2w+1)!(n-2w)!(\lfloor n/2 \rfloor !)^2} \approx w^{3/2}.$$

The detailed derivation is provided in the extended full version. Thus asymptotically, the success probability of this attack is approximately $\Pr_2 \approx w^{3/2} 2^{-2w}$.

4.2 The Fourth Attack

We consider the setting of breaking ciphertext indistinguishability in the KEM variant. In this case, the ciphertext components satisfy $c_1 = ar + b_1$ and $c_2 = at + b_2$ with the unknowns a, b_1, and b_2 subject to certain bounds. Define two bivariate polynomials by

$$h_1(x_1, x_2) = rx_1 + x_2 - c_1 \quad \text{and} \quad h_2(x_1, x_3) = tx_1 + x_3 - c_2.$$

Then the congruences

$$\begin{cases} h_1(x_1, x_2) \equiv 0 \pmod{p}, \\ h_2(x_1, x_3) \equiv 0 \pmod{p}, \end{cases} \tag{9}$$

are simultaneously satisfied by the solution $(x_1^\star, x_2^\star, x_3^\star) = (a, b_1, b_2)$.

Let the respective upper bounds on the unknowns be $X_1 = p^{\xi_1}$, $X_2 = p^{\xi_2}$, and $X_3 = p^{\xi_3}$. For a fixed m and non-negative integers i_1, i_2, i_3 with $i_1 + i_2 + i_3 \le m$, we form the shift polynomials

$$s_{[i_1,i_2,i_3]}(x_1, x_2, x_3) := x_1^{i_1} h_1^{i_2}(x_1, x_2) h_2^{i_3}(x_1, x_3) p^{m-i_2-i_3}.$$

Here, $R = p^m$ as before. Then the coefficients of the scaled shift polynomials $s_{[i_1,i_2,i_3]}(X_1x_1, X_2x_2, X_3x_3)$ are arranged as row vectors in a lattice basis matrix B, which generates the corresponding lattice Λ.

We adopt a monomial order on $x_1^{i_1}x_2^{i_2}x_3^{i_3} \prec x_1^{i_1'}x_2^{i_2'}x_3^{i_3'}$ defined by:

1. $i_1 + i_2 + i_3 < i_1' + i_2' + i_3'$, or
2. $i_1 + i_2 + i_3 = i_1' + i_2' + i_3'$ with $i_1 > i_1'$, or
3. $i_1 + i_2 + i_3 = i_1' + i_2' + i_3'$, $i_1 = i_1'$ with $i_2 > i_2'$.

The polynomial order corresponds to $s_{[i_1,i_2,i_3]} \prec s_{[i_1',i_2',i_3']}$ defining in the same manner. Under this ordering, the leading monomial of $s_{[i_1,i_2,i_3]}(x_1, x_2, x_3)$ is $x_1^{i_1} x_2^{i_2} x_3^{i_3}$. The total number of shifts is

$$\omega = \sum_{i_1=0}^{m} \sum_{i_2=0}^{m-i_1} \sum_{i_3=0}^{m-i_1-i_2} 1 = \frac{(m+1)(m+2)(m+3)}{6}.$$

For instance, setting $m = 2$ yields a basis matrix B whose diagonal entries are exactly $X_1^{i_1} X_2^{i_2} X_3^{i_3} p^{m-i_2-i_3}$.

$$\left(\begin{array}{c|cccccccccc}
 & 1 & x_1 & x_2 & x_3 & x_1^2 & x_1x_2 & x_1x_3 & x_2^2 & x_2x_3 & x_3^2 \\
\hline
s_{[0,0,0]} & p^2 & 0 & 0 & 0 & 0 & 0 & 0 & 0 & 0 & 0 \\
s_{[1,0,0]} & 0 & X_1p^2 & 0 & 0 & 0 & 0 & 0 & 0 & 0 & 0 \\
s_{[0,1,0]} & -c_1p & rX_1p & X_2p & 0 & 0 & 0 & 0 & 0 & 0 & 0 \\
s_{[0,0,1]} & -c_2p & tX_1p & 0 & X_3p & 0 & 0 & 0 & 0 & 0 & 0 \\
s_{[2,0,0]} & 0 & 0 & 0 & 0 & X_1^2p^2 & 0 & 0 & 0 & 0 & 0 \\
s_{[1,1,0]} & 0 & -c_1X_1p & 0 & 0 & rX_1^2p & X_1X_2p & 0 & 0 & 0 & 0 \\
s_{[1,0,1]} & 0 & -c_2X_1p & 0 & 0 & tX_1^2p & 0 & X_1X_3p & 0 & 0 & 0 \\
s_{[0,2,0]} & c_1^2 & -2rc_1X_1 & -2c_1X_2 & 0 & r^2X_1^2 & 2rX_1X_2 & 0 & X_2^2 & 0 & 0 \\
s_{[0,1,1]} & c_1c_2 & -(rc_2+tc_1)X_1 & -c_2X_2 & -c_1X_3 & rtX_1^2 & tX_1X_2 & rX_1X_3 & 0 & X_2X_3 & 0 \\
s_{[0,0,2]} & c_2^2 & -2tc_2X_1 & 0 & -2c_2X_3 & t^2X_1^2 & 0 & 2tX_1X_3 & 0 & 0 & X_3^2
\end{array}\right).$$

In this setting, the lattice determinant is given by

$$\det(\Lambda) = X_1^{\sigma_1} X_2^{\sigma_2} X_3^{\sigma_3} p^{\sigma_p},$$

with the exponents computed as

$$\sigma_1 = \sum_{i_1=0}^{m} \sum_{i_2=0}^{m-i_1} \sum_{i_3=0}^{m-i_1-i_2} i_1 = \frac{m(m+1)(m+2)(m+3)}{24},$$

$$\sigma_2 = \sum_{i_1=0}^{m} \sum_{i_2=0}^{m-i_1} \sum_{i_3=0}^{m-i_1-i_2} i_2 = \frac{m(m+1)(m+2)(m+3)}{24},$$

$$\sigma_3 = \sum_{i_1=0}^{m} \sum_{i_2=0}^{m-i_1} \sum_{i_3=0}^{m-i_1-i_2} i_3 = \frac{m(m+1)(m+2)(m+3)}{24},$$

$$\sigma_p = \sum_{i_1=0}^{m} \sum_{i_2=0}^{m-i_1} \sum_{i_3=0}^{m-i_1-i_2} (m - i_2 - i_3) = \frac{m(m+1)(m+2)(m+3)}{12}.$$

Enforcing the solving condition

$$\det(\Lambda) < R^{\omega}, \quad \text{with } R = p^m,$$

and substituting $X_i = p^{\xi_i}$ for $i = 1, 2, 3$, the inequality yields

$$X_1^{\frac{m(m+1)(m+2)(m+3)}{24}} X_2^{\frac{m(m+1)(m+2)(m+3)}{24}} X_2^{\frac{m(m+1)(m+2)(m+3)}{24}} p^{\frac{m(m+1)(m+2)(m+3)}{12}} < p^{m\cdot\frac{(m+1)(m+2)(m+3)}{6}},$$

which simplifies to

$$\frac{1}{24}(\xi_1+\xi_2+\xi_3)+\frac{1}{12}<\frac{1}{6}.$$

Thus, we obtain the bound

$$\xi_1+\xi_2+\xi_3<2. \tag{10}$$

Once several integer polynomials $v_k(x_1, x_2, x_3)$ are derived (each vanishing at the common root (a, b_1, b_2)), one can recover these unknowns via methods such as Gröbner method or resultant computations. The LLL reduction step dominates the overall running time, and since m is fixed, the complexity is polynomial in $\log p = n$. The former analysis is summarized in the following proposition.

Proposition 2. *Let $p = 2^n - 1$ be an n-bit Mersenne prime and let w be a positive integer. Suppose the unknown values a, b_1, and b_2 with Hamming weight w satisfy the bounds $a \le p^{\xi_1}$, $b_1 \le p^{\xi_2}$, and $b_2 \le p^{\xi_3}$. Given c_1, c_2, r, and t with $c_1 = ar + b_1$ and $c_2 = at + b_2$, a, b_1, and b_2 can be recovered in time polynomial in n provided that $\xi_1 + \xi_2 + \xi_3 < 2$.*

The condition $\xi_1 + \xi_2 + \xi_3 < 2$ in effect guarantees that $ab_1b_2 < p^2$, which generalizes the earlier restriction in [11] where each unknown was assumed to be below $p^{2/3}$. This extension accommodates unbalanced parameters, thereby relaxing size constraints and widening the attack's range.

For the success probability analysis, we represent a, b_1, and b_2 as n-bit strings with w ones. In the previous attack of Coron and Gini [11], the probability of all unknowns being confined to the lower $\lfloor 2n/3 \rfloor$ bits was roughly

$$\frac{\binom{\lfloor 2n/3\rfloor}{w}\binom{\lfloor 2n/3\rfloor}{w}\binom{\lfloor 2n/3\rfloor}{w}}{\binom{n}{w}\binom{n}{w}\binom{n}{w}} = \left(\frac{\lfloor 2n/3\rfloor!(n-w)!}{(\lfloor 2n/3\rfloor - w)!\,n!}\right)^3 \approx \left(\frac{2}{3}\right)^{3w} \approx 2^{-1.75w}.$$

The success probability of our attack is denoted by $\Pr_3$. One may loosely express it as

$$\Pr_3 = \frac{\sum_{k_1=w}^{2n-2w}\sum_{k_2=w}^{2n-k_1-w}\binom{k_1}{w}\binom{k_2}{w}\binom{2n-k_1-k_2}{w}}{\binom{n}{w}\binom{n}{w}\binom{n}{w}}.$$

By applying the combinatorial identity

$$\sum_{k=i}^{n-j}\binom{k}{i}\binom{n-k}{j} = \binom{n+1}{i+j+1},$$

this simplifies to

$$\Pr_3 = \frac{\sum_{k_1=w}^{2n-2w}\binom{k_1}{w}\binom{2n+1-k_1}{2w+1}}{\binom{n}{w}\binom{n}{w}\binom{n}{w}} = \frac{\binom{2n+2}{3w+2}}{\binom{n}{w}^3}.$$

Using Stirling's approximation and the assumption that $w \approx \sqrt{n}$ (i.e., $n \approx w^2$ for $n \to \infty$), an asymptotic analysis reveals that the improvement factor satisfies

$$\mathsf{r}_3 = \frac{\binom{2n+2}{3w+2}}{\binom{\lfloor 2n/3 \rfloor}{w}^3} = \frac{(2n+2)!(w!(\lfloor 2n/3 \rfloor - w)!)^3}{(3w+2)!(2n-3w)!(\lfloor 2n/3 \rfloor !)^3} \approx w^3.$$

Further details are available in the extended full version. Consequently, the overall success probability Pr_3 of the above attack is approximately $\mathrm{Pr}_3 \approx w^3\, 2^{-1.75w}$.

Remark 1. Although both continued fraction and lattice-based methods leverage approximation of modular relations, they operate fundamentally differently. The former exploits one-dimensional rational structure, while the latter handles multivariate modular polynomial equations via basis reduction.

5 Validating Experiments

To evaluate the practical efficacy of the proposed attacks on *MLHRSP* and *MLHCSP* with Theorems 2–3 and Propositions 1–2, we performed numerical experiments using `SageMath` [23] on a 2.80 GHz CPU with 16 GB RAM (Windows 10/WSL 2). While we tested $w \in [30, 70]$, the core recovery remains insensitive to w, with running times primarily determined by the modulus size n. Representative results for various parameter configurations are presented below.

For each attack, we generated several random AJPS instances and gradually increased secret parameters to verify the theoretical bounds, i.e., $\sum \xi_i \approx 1$ for key recovery; $\sum \xi_i \approx 2$ for KEM distinguishing. Five independent trials were performed for each setting, all yielding a 100% success rate.

Table 2. Selected experimental results for continued fraction-based attacks

Target Scheme	n	w	ξ_1	ξ_2	$\xi_1 + \xi_2$	Time (Sec.)
MLHRSP	9689	45	0.350	0.650	1.000	3.12
	11213	50	0.100	0.900	1.000	8.52
	19937	70	0.300	0.700	1.000	17.29
MLHCSP (bit)	4253	30	0.897	0.102	0.999	23.86
	9689	45	0.235	0.765	1.000	25.15
	19937	70	0.500	0.500	1.000	310.20

As shown in Table 2, continued fraction-based attacks successfully recovered keys (f, g) in seconds using only public values h or (r, t), without prior knowledge of ξ_i. This demonstrates a significant advantage over previous approaches [6, 26], which required tighter constraints. Unbalanced private keys (e.g., $f < g$ or $f > g$) generally lead to higher computational costs within the polynomial-time framework.

For lattice-based attacks, a suitable parameter m was chosen to construct the lattice. As summarized in Table 3, the running time grows with the lattice dimension ω and modulus p, yet remains efficient even for large n. By converting reduced vectors into integer polynomials, we successfully extracted the common roots, confirming the ciphertext distinguishing capabilities in the KEM variant.

Table 3. Selected experimental results for lattice-based attacks

Target Scheme	n	w	$\xi_1 + \xi_2$ / $\xi_1 + \xi_2 + \xi_3$	m	ω	Time (Sec.)
MLHCSP (bit)	9689	45	$0.350 + 0.650 = 1.000$	3	10	0.34
	11213	50	$0.500 + 0.500 = 1.000$	3	10	1.61
	19937	70	$0.400 + 0.600 = 1.000$	3	10	3.79
MLHCSP (KEM)	4253	30	$0.350 + 0.650 + 1.000 = 2.000$	3	20	0.91
	11213	50	$0.300 + 0.700 + 1.000 = 2.000$	3	20	3.55
	19937	70	$0.500 + 0.850 + 0.650 = 2.000$	3	20	54.46

The experimental results are in full agreement with our theoretical predictions. To facilitate replication and provide further insight into the implementation, more experimental results and additional numerical examples are available in the extended full version of this paper.

6 Concluding Remarks

In this work, we assessed the security of the Mersenne number-based AJPS cryptosystem, a post-quantum primitive designed for efficiency in next-generation networks. By revisiting the foundational hardness assumptions, i.e. *MLHRSP* and *MLHCSP*, we introduced two classes of novel attacks: heuristic-free continued fraction-based attacks and enhanced lattice-based polynomial solving strategy. Our analysis yields critical insights for the deployment of Mersenne number-based post-quantum schemes in communication networks:

- **Attack Range Expansion:** We demonstrated that the conditions required to recover the private key are significantly more relaxed than previously established. This implies that a broader range of efficient parameter sets, which might be attractive for low-latency IoT devices, are insecure.
- **Key Exchange Threat:** By successfully distinguishing ciphertexts in the KEM variant with improved probability, we show that the confidentiality of session keys in KEM-based handshakes can be compromised more easily.
- **Practical Feasibility:** The experiments confirm that our proposed attacks are not merely theoretical; they can be executed in a reasonable time on standard hardware, posing a real-time threat to active network sessions.

Consequently, while Mersenne number-based cryptosystems offer attractive performance characteristics for lightweight networking, our results suggest that several parameter generation guidelines must be rigorously tightened. A promising direction for future research involves transforming attack success probability into generic time complexity estimates by employing the random partition technique used in earlier work. Integrating this technique may enhance attack performance, potentially unlocking further improvements in efficiency and applicability.

Acknowledgments. The authors would like to thank the anonymous reviewers for their detailed comments and impressive suggestions, which improved this paper in terms of both technical and editorial quality. Mengce Zheng gratefully acknowledges the financial support for academic visiting provided by the China Scholarship Council (CSC No. 202308330390). This work was partially supported by the National Natural Science Foundation of China (No. 62002335), and Ningbo Young Science and Technology Talent Cultivation Program (No. 2023QL007).

References

1. Aggarwal, D., Joux, A., Prakash, A., Santha, M.: A new public-key cryptosystem via Mersenne numbers. Cryptology ePrint Archive, Paper 2017/481 (2017). https://eprint.iacr.org/2017/481
2. Aggarwal, D., Joux, A., Prakash, A., Santha, M.: A new public-key cryptosystem via mersenne numbers. In: Shacham, H., Boldyreva, A. (eds.) CRYPTO 2018, part III. LNCS, vol. 10993, pp. 459–482. Springer, Cham (2018). https://doi.org/10.1007/978-3-319-96878-0_16
3. Aggarwal, D., Joux, A., Prakash, A., Santha, M.: Mersenne-756839. Technical report, National Institute of Standards and Technology (2017). https://csrc.nist.gov/Projects/post-quantum-cryptography/post-quantum-cryptography-standardization/round-1-submissions
4. Bailey, D.H., Borwein, J.M., Crandall, R.E.: On the Khintchine constant. Math. Comput. **66**(217), 417–431 (1997). https://doi.org/10.1090/S0025-5718-97-00800-4
5. Becker, T., Weispfenning, V., Kredel, H.: Gröbner Bases - A Computational Approach to Commutative Algebra. Graduate Texts in Mathematics, vol. 141. Springer (1993)
6. Beunardeau, M., Connolly, A., Géraud, R., Naccache, D.: On the hardness of the Mersenne low hamming ratio assumption. In: Lange, T., Dunkelman, O. (eds.) LATINCRYPT 2017. LNCS, vol. 11368, pp. 166–174. Springer, Cham (2019). https://doi.org/10.1007/978-3-030-25283-0_9
7. de Boer, K., Ducas, L., Jeffery, S., de Wolf, R.: Attacks on the AJPS Mersenne-based cryptosystem. In: Lange, T., Steinwandt, R. (eds.) PQCrypto 2018. LNCS, vol. 10786, pp. 101–120. Springer, Cham (2018). https://doi.org/10.1007/978-3-319-79063-3_5
8. Bootland, C., Castryck, W., Szepieniec, A., Vercauteren, F.: SoK: on the security of cryptographic problems from linear algebra. Math. Cryptol. **3**(1), 52–95 (2023). https://journals.flvc.org/mathcryptology/article/view/129672

9. Budroni, A., Tenti, A.: The Mersenne low hamming combination search problem can be reduced to an ILP Problem. In: Buchmann, J., Nitaj, A., Rachidi, T. (eds.) AFRICACRYPT 2019. LNCS, vol. 11627, pp. 41–55. Springer, Cham (2019). https://doi.org/10.1007/978-3-030-23696-0_3
10. Coppersmith, D.: Small solutions to polynomial equations, and low exponent RSA vulnerabilities. J. Cryptol. **10**(4), 233–260 (1997). https://doi.org/10.1007/s001459900030
11. Coron, J., Gini, A.: Improved cryptanalysis of the AJPS Mersenne based cryptosystem. J. Math. Cryptol. **14**(1), 218–223 (2020). https://doi.org/10.1515/jmc-2019-0027
12. Fatou, P.: Sur l'approximation des incommensurables et les séries trigonométriques. C. R. Acad. Sci., Paris **139**, 1019–1021 (1905)
13. Gallant, R.P., Lambert, R.J., Vanstone, S.A.: Faster point multiplication on elliptic curves with efficient endomorphisms. In: Kilian, J. (ed.) CRYPTO 2001. LNCS, vol. 2139, pp. 190–200. Springer, Heidelberg (2001). https://doi.org/10.1007/3-540-44647-8_11
14. Grace, J.H.: The classification of rational approximations. Proc. Lond. Math. Soc. **17**(2), 247–258 (1919). https://doi.org/10.1112/plms/s2-17.1.247. zenodo.org/record/1433509
15. Graham, R., Knuth, D., Patashnik, O.: Concrete Mathematics: A Foundation for Computer Science, 2nd edn. Addison-Wesley (1994). https://www-cs-faculty.stanford.edu/%7Eknuth/gkp.html
16. Hoffstein, J., Pipher, J., Silverman, J.H.: NTRU: a ring-based public key cryptosystem. In: Buhler, J.P. (ed.) ANTS 1998. LNCS, vol. 1423, pp. 267–288. Springer, Heidelberg (1998). https://doi.org/10.1007/BFb0054868
17. Howgrave-Graham, N.: Finding small roots of univariate modular equations revisited. In: Darnell, M. (ed.) Cryptography and Coding 1997. LNCS, vol. 1355, pp. 131–142. Springer, Heidelberg (1997). https://doi.org/10.1007/BFb0024458
18. Legendre, A.: Essai sur la théorie des nombres. Duprat, An VI, Paris (1798)
19. Lenstra, A., Lenstra, H., Lovász, L.: Factoring polynomials with rational coefficients. Math. Ann. **261**(4), 515–534 (1982)
20. May, A.: New RSA vulnerabilities using lattice reduction methods. Ph.D. thesis, University of Paderborn (2003). https://ubdata.uni-paderborn.de/ediss/17/2003/may/disserta.pdf
21. May, A.: Lattice-based integer factorization - an introduction to Coppersmith's method. In: Bos, J.W., Stam, M. (eds.) Computational Cryptography: Algorithmic Aspects of Cryptology. London Mathematical Society Lecture Note Series, pp. 78–105. Cambridge University Press (2021). https://www.cits.ruhr-uni-bochum.de/imperia/md/content/may/paper/intro_to_coppersmiths_method.pdf
22. Szepieniec, A.: Ramstake. Technical report, National Institute of Standards and Technology (2017). https://csrc.nist.gov/Projects/post-quantum-cryptography/post-quantum-cryptography-standardization/round-1-submissions
23. The Sage Developers: SageMath, the Sage Mathematics Software System (Version 10.3) (2025). https://www.sagemath.org
24. Tiepelt, M., D'Anvers, J.: Exploiting decryption failures in Mersenne number cryptosystems. In: Emura, K., Yanai, N. (eds.) Proceedings of the 7th on ASIA Public-Key Cryptography Workshop, APKC@AsiaCCS 2020, Taipei, Taiwan, 6 October 2020, pp. 45–54. ACM (2020). https://doi.org/10.1145/3384940.3388957

25. Zheng, M., Kang, H.: Lattice-based cryptanalysis of RSA-type cryptosystems: a bibliometric analysis. Cybersecur. **7**(1), 74 (2024). https://doi.org/10.1186/S42400-024-00289-7
26. Zheng, M., Yan, W.: Improved lattice-based attack on Mersenne low Hamming ratio search problem. In: Zhu, T., Li, Y. (eds.) ACISP 2024, Part II. LNCS, vol. 14896, pp. 185–202. Springer, Cham (2024). https://doi.org/10.1007/978-981-97-5028-3_10

The Bridge to the Quantum Fortress: How Do Hybrid Cloud Attacks Exploit the Quantum Core?

Prabin Lamichhane(✉) and Kyu Hyung Lee

University of Georgia, Athens, GA 30602, USA
{prabin.lamichhane,kyuhlee}@uga.edu

Abstract. As quantum computing transitions from experimental physics to a commercial Quantum-as-a-Service (QaaS) model, the security of the underlying hybrid infrastructure becomes critical. However, current security paradigms treat these systems as isolated domains, where cloud security focuses on classical APIs while quantum research prioritizes hardware error correction. We argue that this separation creates a significant gap in security observability. In a hybrid quantum cloud, the frontend interface can be exploited as a "bridge" to launch sophisticated attacks on the backend control systems. Crucially, due to the inherent noise, these attacks are often masked by natural decoherence, allowing adversaries to achieve plausible deniability.

In this paper, we present a systematic study of the hybrid attack surface and security observability in QaaS environments. First, we map the comprehensive threat landscape, identifying how classical exploits propagate through the stack. Second, we propose an integrated telemetry framework that correlates classical audit trails with quantum-specific artifacts to resolve the ambiguity between malicious interference and stochastic noise. Finally, we develop an end-to-end testbed using the IBM Quantum simulator to evaluate this framework. Through five attack scenarios, we show that while standard cloud audit trails fail to detect hybrid threats, our proposed observability schema successfully exposes the causal links across the entire attack chain.

Keywords: Quantum Cloud Computing · Digital Forensics · Hybrid Attack Surface · Quantum Security

1 Introduction

Quantum computing represents a paradigm shift in computational power, leveraging principles like superposition and entanglement to solve problems intractable for classical machines. While classical computation stores information in binary bits (i.e., 0s or 1s) processed via logic gates, quantum computation utilizes qubits. A qubit can exist in a state of 0, 1, or a superposition of both, enabling a quantum processor to explore a vast computational space simultaneously. Despite this potential, the physical realization of quantum advantage

Y. Cao et al. (Eds.): SecureComm 2026, LNICST 704, pp. 548–571, 2027.
https://doi.org/10.1007/978-3-032-32764-2_25

faces significant engineering hurdles [58]. The primary limiting factor is low fault tolerance because qubits are inherently fragile and susceptible to decoherence caused by environmental noise (e.g., thermal fluctuations or electromagnetic interference). Consequently, quantum processors (QPUs) must operate in highly controlled, cryogenic environments [30]. For these reasons, maintaining an on-premises quantum computer is prohibitively expensive for most organizations, leading the industry to standardize on a Quantum-as-a-Service (QaaS) model where users access remote QPUs via a hybrid cloud infrastructure [58].

However, the inherent fragility of quantum hardware introduces a unique security challenge known as attack masking or plausible deniability. Since execution errors are common in current Noisy Intermediate-Scale Quantum (NISQ) devices [61,62], the distinction between natural environmental noise and malicious interference is often ambiguous. An attacker effectively degrades a computation's fidelity (e.g., by inducing crosstalk or altering pulse calibrations), and the victim expecting a noisy result fails to distinguish this cyber attack from a standard execution error. This phenomenon grants adversaries a significant forensic advantage, as their activities are effectively camouflaged by the system's baseline error rate, making attribution and analysis notoriously difficult on the hardware level.

While directly exploiting this isolated quantum hardware is unrealistic for most external adversaries due to extreme physical air-gapping, the hybrid cloud architecture exposes a critical attack surface that bridges this gap. In this model, classical web APIs and job schedulers act as the control plane for the sensitive physical hardware. This integration allows adversaries to leverage traditional attack techniques to indirectly affect the quantum backend. For example, a standard classical vulnerability (e.g., SQL injection) in the job management system can be used to manipulate job priorities or inject malicious circuits. This hybrid nature creates a pathway for widely available classical exploits to cause severe quantum impacts, leveraging the aforementioned attack masking to remain undetected.

Table 1. Integration of Classical Cloud Infrastructure in Major QaaS Providers

QaaS Provider	Classical Infrastructure Component	Quantum Interface/Backend
Amazon Braket	EC2 (Hybrid Jobs), S3 (Data), IAM (Security) [5–7]	Braket API & SDK
Azure Quantum	Microsoft Entra, Azure Functions, Key Vault, Azure Storage [55,56]	Azure API, QDK [53,54]
Google Quantum AI	Google Cloud Scheduler, Compute Engine, IAM [32]	Cirq & Engine API [33]
IBM Quantum	IBM Cloud IAM, Qiskit Runtime [38,39]	Qiskit REST API [42]

As summarized in Table 1, current Quantum-as-a-Service (QaaS) offerings are heavily integrated with existing classical cloud ecosystems for essential operations such as identity management, data storage, and job orchestration. This architectural dependency suggests that the classical cloud layer of QaaS is not just a gateway but a significant, high-probability target for conventional cloud-based attacks. By compromising these ubiquitous classical components, an adversary can effectively bridge the gap to the quantum backend without needing to bypass the physical security of the quantum laboratory.

In this research, we systematically analyze how attacks originating from the classical cloud layer propagate through the hybrid stack to cause adversarial impacts on quantum control systems and execution integrity. We argue that the classical cloud layer could be the most vulnerable entry point, where traditional exploits can be weaponized to compromise quantum integrity and availability. To validate these cross-layer threats, we implement an integrated testbed that bridges a classical cloud frontend with the IBM Quantum simulator [40]. This setup allows us to emulate the entire execution chain—from API-based job submission to the generation of quantum-specific execution metrics, enabling a high-fidelity analysis of how classical breaches disrupt quantum operations. Through this simulation, we identify critical visibility gaps where existing classical logging fails to capture the causal link between a cloud-level breach and its subsequent quantum impact. Our contributions are as follows:

- We identify the core components of a quantum cloud system and highlight their role and the critical events that occur in each of them.
- We identify and systematically categorize potential security threat scenarios across different components of a cloud quantum computing environment (i.e., distinguishing between classical, hybrid, and quantum-specific attacks).
- We emulate a quantum cloud system by developing software components and utilizing open-source software to demonstrate proof of concept for several of the identified threat scenarios. The complete implementation, including the codebase, attack scripts, and collected evaluation data, is available in our GitHub repository.[1]
- We demonstrate that standard cloud logs lack the context to detect and analyze these specialized threats. We propose a new logging taxonomy that integrates quantum-specific telemetry to ensure cross-layer observability.
- Finally, we describe how the proposed log data can be used to facilitate the detection and/or forensics of several of the identified threat scenarios.

1.1 Threat Model

In this section, we define the adversary's goals, their capabilities within the hybrid quantum cloud stack, and the trust assumptions underlying our analysis.

Adversary Goals: The primary objective of the adversary is to compromise the fundamental security properties of quantum workloads. Integrity violations

[1] https://github.com/prabin-lc/quantum-cloud-forensics.

involve the unauthorized alteration of a quantum circuit or its execution environment to produce incorrect computational results. Availability disruption, or Quantum Denial-of-Service (QDoS), aims to deny legitimate users access to scarce quantum hardware. This can be achieved by locking control electronics via infinite loops or flooding the job queue to cause resource starvation. Finally, confidentiality leakage targets the intellectual property contained within quantum algorithms. In multi-tenant environments where physical isolation is not guaranteed, an adversary may exploit side-channels or crosstalk to infer sensitive circuit structures or measurement outcomes from co-tenant workloads.

Adversary Capabilities: We assume a hierarchical capability model where an adversary can escalate their influence through the "classical bridge". The adversary is assumed to possess the following capabilities:

- **Classical API Exploitation:** The adversary can leverage standard web vulnerabilities, such as SQL injection or broken access control, in the public-facing job management APIs to gain unauthorized access to the cloud control plane.
- **Hybrid Logic Manipulation:** By gaining a foothold in the classical middleware, the adversary can manipulate the scheduler's logic to prioritize their own jobs or tamper with the transpilation process to insert Quantum Trojans into victim circuits.
- **Physical Layer Interference:** In a multi-programming regime where multiple users share a single QPU, the adversary can execute high-energy noisy gates to induce electromagnetic crosstalk, corrupting the state of adjacent qubits belonging to other users.
- **Supply Chain Injection:** The adversary can compromise third-party SDKs, libraries, or backend compiler chains to subtly alter quantum circuits or rotation angles before the code is even signed or executed.

Trust Assumptions: We adopt a Trusted Provider model where the cloud service provider's core infrastructure and personnel are assumed to be benign but potentially vulnerable to external compromise. However, we do not assume the immutability of logs within individual components once a breach is initiated. Specifically, if the backend control plane or the cloud middleware is compromised, its local audit trails are considered untrusted. This necessitates a reliance on independent, hardware-level telemetry, such as Spectator Qubits, to verify the physical integrity of the execution environment.

2 Background

2.1 Quantum Computing

Fundamentally, quantum computation differs from the classical von Neumann architecture in how it represents and processes information. While classical systems rely on binary bits (restricted to a definite state of 0 or 1), quantum processors utilize qubits. A qubit can exist in a state of 0, 1, or a superposition of both simultaneously. This property scales exponentially; a system with just n qubits can represent a superposition of all 2^n possible classical states, enabling the processor to explore a vast computational space in parallel.

Qubits are further enhanced by entanglement, a phenomenon where the state of one qubit becomes mathematically correlated with another, regardless of physical distance. Analogous to a classical CPU, a Quantum Processing Unit (QPU) executes sequences of quantum gates—effectively a quantum algorithm—to manipulate these entangled probabilities and arrive at a solution.

While powerful, the practical application of quantum computing is currently limited by the hardware's low fault tolerance. Breaking modern cryptography (e.g., Shor's algorithm against RSA) [29,65] and simulating molecular dynamics are promising applications [52], but they require error rates far lower than what is currently available [34]. Other potential applications include quantum machine learning, logistics, and financial modeling [58]. However, the main limiting factor for current Noisy Intermediate-Scale Quantum (NISQ) computers is decoherence [22,30]. Qubits are incredibly fragile; interactions with the environment (e.g., thermal fluctuations or electromagnetic noise) cause them to lose their quantum state, resulting in computational errors [30,58].

To mitigate this, QPUs must be operated in highly controlled environments (e.g., dilution refrigerators near absolute zero) to shield them from interference. Furthermore, reliable computation often requires Quantum Error Correction (QEC) or mitigation strategies, such as Zero-Noise Extrapolation (ZNE) and Probabilistic Error Cancellation (PEC) [10]. This extreme sensitivity and the need for massive support infrastructure make on-premises quantum computing prohibitively expensive for most organizations.

2.2 Quantum Cloud Computing

To overcome the barriers of cost and maintenance, the industry has standardized on the Quantum-as-a-Service (QaaS) model [48]. In this architecture, a specialized provider hosts and maintains the sensitive physical infrastructure, while end-users access the system remotely. This provides on-demand access to QPUs without requiring the user to manage cryogenic systems or calibration [7,38,55].

Crucially, this model establishes a hybrid architecture. A quantum cloud is not a standalone quantum device; it is a complex stack where classical cloud infrastructure acts as the control plane for the quantum backend. Users submit jobs via classical REST APIs; these jobs are processed by classical schedulers, compiled by classical transpilers, and converted into analog pulses by classical control electronics before finally reaching the quantum chip [2,45]. This "classical bridge" serves as the primary interface for all user interactions.

2.3 Adversarial Analysis of the Quantum-Classical Interface

Integrating quantum hardware into the cloud model introduces new attack surfaces that are not covered by traditional cloud security or purely physics-based research. While QaaS inherits the standard *Shared Responsibility Model* of cloud computing, where the provider secures the infrastructure and the client secures the data [47], the integration of quantum backends introduces a critical visibility gap in security observability. It is important to distinguish between *Post-Quantum Cryptography* (protecting classical data from quantum decryption) [9,49] and *Quantum Platform Security* (protecting the quantum computer itself). In this work, we focus exclusively on the latter. Prior research in platform security has largely focused on "Blind Quantum Computing" (hiding algorithms from untrusted providers) [26,71] or hardware-level side-channel attacks [13,16,64].

However, the hybrid attack surface creates a unique intersection that remains under-explored. The classical cloud frontend acts as a bridge to the isolated quantum backend, introducing specific challenges for security analysis and incident attribution [35]. In this hybrid environment, we identify two critical vulnerabilities that undermine system integrity:

1. **The Bridge Vulnerability:** Attackers can exploit standard classical vulnerabilities (e.g., compromised credentials or API exploits) to pivot into the quantum backend. This allows them to manipulate the physical control systems without needing physical access to the device.
2. **Attack Masking (Plausible Deniability):** Due to the decoherence described in Sect. 2.1, malicious interference is difficult to distinguish from natural noise. An attacker can induce faults or degrade fidelity, and the security analysis may misinterpret this as standard environmental error.

In this research, we focus on this hybrid intersection. We analyze how attacks propagate from the classical "Bridge" to the quantum "Fortress" and identify the telemetry artifacts necessary to distinguish between a noisy machine and a cyber attack.

3 Hybrid Quantum Architecture and Threat Landscape

A quantum cloud system is a distributed hybrid architecture divided into three distinct layers: Frontend, Cloud, and Backend. The frontend layer operates on the user's local infrastructure. The cloud layer runs on classical cloud infrastructure and serves as the API gateway, acting as the bridge between untrusted users and sensitive hardware. The backend layer is co-located with the Quantum Processing Unit (QPU) and is responsible for pre-processing, post-processing, and the actual execution of quantum jobs.

This layered approach exposes a diverse attack surface, ranging from classical software vulnerabilities in the frontend to physical side-channel attacks in the backend (Fig. 1).

3.1 Frontend Layer

The frontend layer encompasses all operations performed on a user's local device, including the software, libraries, and tools necessary for writing quantum code and submitting jobs.

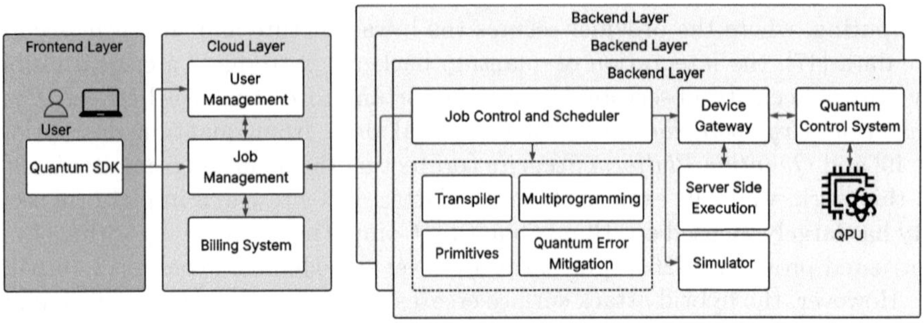

Fig. 1. Quantum Cloud Architecture.

Quantum Programming Library and SDKs. Quantum code is often written in a general-purpose programming language, like Python, using a vendor-specific software development kit (SDK). The SDK abstracts complex quantum operations, allowing users to formulate a quantum circuit using familiar methods and classes. For example, applying a quantum gate to a qubit is simplified to invoking a method (representing the gate) on an object (representing the qubit).

In addition to abstracting circuit creation, the SDK also manages all cloud communications, converting job submission, status checks, and result retrieval into simple method calls. During this submission process, the high-level quantum circuit is compiled into an appropriate intermediate representation, such as OpenQASM 3 [17], which is the most widely used standard for describing quantum circuits.

One such example is the Qiskit software stack [37,43]. Qiskit is a collection of tools for building, transpiling, compiling, simulating, and visualizing the results of quantum circuits. It provides a convenient Python API for users to create these circuits, which are then transpiled to optimize them for a specific target quantum processor. Developed by IBM, Qiskit is designed to work seamlessly with IBM's cloud quantum systems. The stack is modular; for example, the Qiskit Machine Learning module provides tools and algorithms specifically for quantum machine learning applications [41].

Threat Landscape. Since the SDK runs on the client side, it is the root of the chain of trust. This layer is highly susceptible to Supply Chain Attacks. Modern quantum SDKs rely on vast trees of open-source Python dependencies. A compromised dependency could inject malicious logic into the circuit generation process (e.g., subtly altering a rotation angle) before the code is even signed or submitted. Furthermore, if the client environment is compromised, an attacker can steal API keys or manipulate the OpenQASM payload to include malicious loops designed to attack the backend.

3.2 Cloud Layer

The cloud layer is the entry point to the cloud-based system. This layer is responsible for user authentication and authorization, accepting quantum processing requests from users, and relaying job status updates and results back to the user.

User and Job Management APIs. The User Management API handles authentication (often via OAuth or IAM integrations), while the Job Management API accepts quantum processing requests. A typical request includes the OpenQASM circuit, target backend, and execution parameters (e.g., shots, timeout) [42]. Cost calculation is also handled in this layer, based on runtime seconds or gate complexity.

Threat Landscape. These APIs represent the largest classical attack surface. Vulnerabilities in this layer, such as SQL Injection (SQLi) or Broken Access Control, can have catastrophic downstream effects. As demonstrated in Sect. 6.2, an SQLi in the Job Management API can allow an attacker to dump the database of submitted jobs (violating intellectual property) or pivot to the backend to manipulate job priorities. If this layer is compromised, the physical isolation of the quantum computer could be bypassed [46].

3.3 Backend Layer

The backend layer is a high-performance classical computer co-located with the quantum hardware and is responsible for job execution, hardware calibration, and low-level system management. While a single quantum cloud service can offer access to many different quantum computers, each individual quantum hardware device is typically managed by its own dedicated backend layer.

Job Control and Scheduling. The scheduler maintains the local execution queue for a specific QPU. It prioritizes jobs based on fair-share policies, calibration windows, and user service levels (SLAs).

Threat Landscape. In a hybrid attack, an adversary who compromises the Cloud Layer can manipulate this scheduling queue. By injecting a "Malicious Priority" job or flooding the queue with high-duration circuits, an attacker can starve legitimate users, effectively causing a Quantum Denial-of-Service (QDoS) on the scarce hardware.

Transpiling. A quantum program is written in a generalized, hardware-agnostic format, but each QPU has its own unique physical characteristics. Therefore, a critical transpilation step (often used interchangeably with "compilation") is required to bridge this gap. This process converts a quantum circuit, typically in OpenQASM format, into a new, optimized circuit that can run on the target hardware while minimizing the impact of quantum errors.

Threat Landscape. The transpiler is a trusted compiler. If an attacker can influence the transpilation process (e.g., via a man-in-the-middle or supply chain attack on the backend server), they can insert Quantum Trojans. These could be extra gates added to a victim's circuit that reduce fidelity or leak information, which the user cannot detect because they only see the result.

Server-side Execution. Most modern quantum applications are hybrid, and they require classical code to evaluate a result and adjust parameters for the next quantum run. To minimize network latency, this classical code is executed on high-performance servers physically co-located with the QPU.

Threat Landscape. This component executes user-submitted classical code (often Python) within the secure perimeter of the quantum data center, which could be the primary target for Remote Code Execution (RCE) attacks. If the runtime container is not strictly isolated, an attacker can escape the sandbox to compromise the host OS, granting them direct access to the Quantum Control System.

Multiprogramming. To maximize utilization, providers may use Multiprogramming to run multiple small circuits on a single QPU, allowing them to run concurrently to use the QPU's qubits more efficiently [67]. The basic idea is to maximize the utilization of all available qubits in a single execution. After the measurement, the results from the combined circuit are separated by this module to provide the individual outcomes for each of the original circuits.

Threat Landscape. When two users share a QPU, they are physically coupled on the same chip. This proximity enables Crosstalk Attacks [14], where a malicious tenant executes high-energy gates to induce noise errors in a victim's adjacent qubits [4]. This physical layer interference allows for data corruption and potential side-channel leakage, breaking the isolation guarantees of the cloud.

Quantum Error Mitigation (QEM) and Primitives. Quantum Error Mitigation (QEM) minimizes hardware noise using precise calibration data. For example, Readout Error Mitigation corrects measurement errors via confusion matrices [12,51], while Zero-Noise Extrapolation (ZNE) models and extrapolates noise profiles [10]. To construct a confusion matrix, calibration circuits repeatedly prepare and measure each qubit in the $|0\rangle$ and $|1\rangle$ states, mathematically quantifying state misclassification probabilities. During a user's circuit execution, the system applies these pre-calculated metrics to the raw outputs, mitigating readout errors to generate an accurate final probability distribution. These corrected results are then delivered via Quantum Primitives—high-level software abstractions that process raw execution data into accessible, meaningful representations.

Threat Landscape. If an attacker can tamper with the calibration data stored on the backend, they can render the Error Mitigation useless or even inject the error [1]. By altering the confusion matrix, the system might "correct" a valid result into an invalid one, destroying the integrity of the computation in a way that looks like natural noise (Attack Masking). Similarly, if a pre-compiled Quantum Primitive (such as a core library function or estimator) is compromised, it can be manipulated to subtly alter the true outcomes of a calculation, producing misleading or incorrect results without triggering standard error alerts.

Device Gateway and Quantum Control System. The control software manages the low-level communication and drives the physical hardware. This layer converts logical circuit gates into physical operations: microwave or laser pulses to drive the qubits.

Threat Landscape. The control system enforces safety limits. However, if an attacker can bypass the transpiler checks and submit raw pulse schedules (as supported by some providers, such as IBM with Qiskit Pulse [3]), they could theoretically engineer resonant pulses designed to heat the dilution refrigerator or degrade qubit coherence times, leading to long-term hardware damage.

4 Threat Scenarios in Hybrid Quantum Cloud

Based on the attack surface discussed in the previous section, we categorize the specific threat scenarios that jeopardize a hybrid quantum cloud environment. We classify these threats by their operational impact, demonstrating how classical vulnerabilities in the "Bridge" (Frontend/Cloud) propagate to compromise the integrity and availability of the Quantum "Fortress".

Table 2 presents a consolidated view of these scenarios, mapping the vulnerable components and attack techniques to the essential data artifacts required for attack detection and attribution. By identifying these specific telemetry requirements, we move beyond standard cloud logging to capture the causal links between classical entry points and their corresponding quantum-layer disruptions.

Table 2. Hybrid Threat Landscape: Scenarios, Components, and Telemetry

Scenario	Vulnerable Component	Attack Technique	Artifacts/Telemetry
Scenario 1 (Initial Access)	Job Management API	SQL Injection (SQLi)	`REST API Payloads, Database Events`
	Hybrid Runtime	Remote Code Execution (RCE)	`Container Syscalls`
	User Management API	Authentication Bypass	`IAM/Authentication Audit Trails`
	Cloud Infrastructure	Zero-Day Exploits	`Cloud Infrastructure Events`
Scenario 2 (Integrity)	Quantum SDK/Libraries	Dependency Compromise	`Package Signatures`
	Transpiler	Malicious Transpilation (Trojan Gates)	`Transpiler Input/Output`
	Job Scheduler	Scheduler Logic Tampering	`Job Control Traces`
Scenario 3 (Availability)	Quantum Control System	Malicious RUS Loops	`CLOPS Metrics (Throughput)`
	Job Scheduler	Algorithmic Complexity Attack	`Job Control (Depth/Duration)`
	Job Management API	Queue Flooding	`REST API Traces(Rate Limiting)`
Scenario 4 (Confidentiality)	QPU (Multiprogramming)	Crosstalk Attack (Integrity)	`Spectator Qubits (Noise Monitoring), Circuit Analysis`
	QPU (Multiprogramming)	Side-Channel Leakage	`Spectator Qubits, Co-Tenant Maps`
	Error Mitigation DB	Calibration Poisoning	`Calibration Matrix, Readout Error, Gate Error`
Scenario 5 (Misuse)	Classical Host VM	Cryptomining/Compute Abuse	`OS System Logs (CPU/GPU Usage)`
	Job Scheduler	Priority Hijacking	`Job Control (Priority Weights)`

4.1 Scenario 1: The Bridge Breach (Initial Access and Execution)

The common entry point for an attacker is the classical cloud layer, which faces the public internet. By exploiting vulnerabilities in public-facing applications, an adversary can gain unauthorized access to the control plane.

Exploitation of Public APIs. The Job Management API is susceptible to standard injection attacks. An attacker can exploit a zero-day vulnerability or a logic flaw (e.g., SQL Injection) to bypass authentication or execute arbitrary code on the host server. Identifying these attacks requires correlating the `REST API Payloads` (which show the malicious payload) with `Container Syscalls` (which show the execution traces).

Remote Code Execution (RCE) via Hybrid Runtime. As identified in our architecture analysis, the backend executes hybrid algorithms using classical runtime environments (e.g., Python containers). If an attacker submits a job containing malicious classical code (e.g., a reverse shell embedded in a Qiskit job script), they may achieve RCE on the backend server. Once inside, they can pivot to execute commands on the host OS.

4.2 Scenario 2: The Silent Saboteur (Integrity and Supply Chain)

Once inside, or by compromising a trusted third-party library, an attacker can manipulate the integrity of the computation without causing a system crash. These attacks are particularly dangerous because they rely on "Attack Masking" to blend in with natural noise.

Supply Chain Compromise. Quantum SDKs and backend transpilers rely on complex chains of dependencies. An attacker who compromises a package in this chain can inject malicious logic into the transpilation process. Forensic readiness requires strict `Package Signatures` to detect mismatches or unauthorized updates [11].

Malicious Transpilation (Trojan Insertion). A compromised transpiler can insert "Trojan Gates" (e.g., extra operations designed to subtly degrade fidelity or bias the measurement outcome) into a victim's circuit [21]. Because the user only sees the final result, not the physical pulse schedule, this sabotage is indistinguishable from hardware decoherence without comparing the `Transpiler Input/Output` data [19,20,63].

4.3 Scenario 3: Quantum Denial of Service (Availability)

Unlike classical clouds that can autoscale, quantum backends are fixed, scarce resources. Attackers can exploit this scarcity to deny service to legitimate users.

Malicious Repeat-Until-Success (RUS) Loops. Modern quantum circuits support dynamic control flow (e.g., 'while' loops based on mid-circuit measurement) [23]. An attacker can construct a valid circuit that enters an infinite loop, never satisfying the exit condition. If the backend lacks proper timeout enforcement for dynamic circuits, this job will lock the control electronics indefinitely, halting all processing for other tenants. As noted in Table 2, detecting this requires monitoring `CLOPS (Circuit Layer Operations Per Second)` for sudden drops in throughput [68], or analyzing the circuit to identify any potential malicious loops before execution [24].

Algorithmic Complexity Attacks. An attacker can exploit the billing model by submitting circuits that are computationally cheap to validate but physically expensive to execute (e.g., maximizing circuit depth to occupy the QPU for the maximum allowable duration).

4.4 Scenario 4: Crosstalk and Data Tampering (Confidentiality)

In multi-tenant environments where a single QPU is partitioned among multiple users (Multiprogramming), physical isolation is not guaranteed.

Crosstalk Attacks. A malicious tenant can execute a specific pattern of "noisy" gates adjacent to a victim's qubits. This generates electromagnetic interference (crosstalk) that corrupts the victim's state [4,36]. This enables both integrity attacks (corrupting data) and confidentiality attacks (side-channel inference). Defenses rely on dynamic monitoring using `Spectator Qubits` to detect anomalous noise spikes [1,36], or static analysis of the circuit to enable optimized gate substitutions or reordering of operations [24,57].

4.5 Scenario 5: Resource Hijacking (Misuse)

Once a system is breached, an attacker can misuse its resources. In a quantum cloud, this includes hijacking the classical host for cryptomining or manipulating the scheduler to prioritize their own jobs (Resource Hijacking). Investigating this requires a dual-trail approach: `OS System Logs` for the classical hijack and `Job Control Traces` for the quantum hijack.

5 Enhancing Security Observability in Hybrid Quantum Clouds

Based on the attack-relevant telemetry and artifacts identified through the threat scenarios in Sect. 4, we now propose a systematic framework for collecting this data within a hybrid quantum infrastructure. While the previous section established what needs to be observed to detect sophisticated attacks, this section focuses on how to implement such observability by integrating diverse data sources across the classical-quantum boundary.

To bridge the existing visibility gap, we define a set of essential telemetry requirements that extend beyond the scope of standard cloud logging. These requirements are organized into three functional layers, classical cloud, hybrid control, and quantum physical, to ensure a cohesive monitoring framework across the entire execution stack. By contrasting our proposed observability enhancements with current baseline cloud logging capabilities, we highlight the critical data artifacts necessary to unmask sophisticated hybrid threats.

5.1 Classical Cloud Artifacts (Baseline)

The classical components of a quantum cloud act as the administrative wrapper for the system. These include standard services like authentication (IAM), network firewalls, and object storage.

As shown in Table 3, the existing log types generated by major cloud providers (e.g., AWS CloudTrail, Azure Monitor) are sufficient for investigating the initial access phase of an attack. For example, `Authentication Logs` can reveal brute-force attempts against the User Management API, and `Network Logs` can trace the source IP of a malicious actor [15]. However, these logs are "quantum-blind" and they treat a request to crash a QPU the same as a legitimate computational workload.

Table 3. Available Cloud Logs (Baseline)

Log Source	Artifacts	Target Threat (Sect. 4)
`Auth & IAM Logs`	User ID, Source IP, Failed Attempts, Role Assumptions	Scenario 1
`Network Logs`	Packet Size, Protocol, Destination Port, Flow Duration	Scenario 3
`System Audit Logs`	Process Creation, File Access, User Privilege Changes	Scenario 5
`Storage Logs`	S3/Database Access Patterns, Query Strings	Scenario 1

5.2 Hybrid Layer Observability

The defense capability breaks down at the Hybrid Layer where classical data becomes quantum instructions. This is where the majority of the visibility gap exists.

Table 4 outlines the artifacts required to reconstruct attacks in this layer. Through our analysis of current providers (e.g., IBM Quantum), we found that while basic metadata (e.g., Job IDs, timestamps) is accessible, deep introspection telemetry data are largely missing. We have labeled these as "Required" in the status column. These missing data are critical for investigating specific hybrid threats:

- **Transpiler Telemetry:** Essential for detecting *Supply Chain* and *Trojan* attacks affecting the quantum circuits. Without a record of the circuit *before* and *after* transpilation, it is impossible to prove if a malicious gate was injected by the user or by a compromised compiler.
- **Scheduler Decision Traces:** Required to investigate *Fairness Starvation* attacks. If a user claims their quantum jobs were unfairly de-prioritized, simple "Job Start" logs are insufficient, and the system must log the scheduler's logic/weighting decisions.

– **Multiprogramming Telemetry:** Necessary for investigating *Crosstalk* attacks. Forensics teams need to know which users shared the QPU die at the exact millisecond of a failure to correlate noise patterns with neighbor activity.

Table 4. Hybrid Component Telemetry: Existing vs. Required

Component	Artifacts	Target Threat (Sect. 4)	Status
Job Management API	Source IP, User ID	Scenario 1	
	Job Parameters (Shots, Backend)	Scenario 3	Existing
Job Control & Scheduler	Job State Changes (Queued/Run)	General Monitoring	Existing
	`Scheduling Decision Logic`	**Scenario 2**	**Required**
	`Priority Weight Factors`	**Scenario 5**	**Required**
Transpiler	Compilation Duration	Performance Monitoring	Existing
	`Circuit Diff (Input vs Native)`	**Scenario 2**	**Required**
Multiprogramming	`Co-Tenant Map (Time-Sliced)`	**Scenario 4**	**Required**
	`Spectator Assignment`	**Scenario 4**	**Required**
Hybrid Runtime	Container Syscalls (e.g., `execve`)	Scenario 1	Existing (OS Level)

5.3 Quantum-Layer Telemetry

Table 5. Quantum Component Telemetry: Existing vs. Required

Metric	Forensic Utility	Target Threat (Sect. 4)	Status
`CLOPS`	Detects sudden throughput drops indicating locked control electronics.	Scenario 3	**Required**
`Spectator Qubits`	Measures environmental noise correlation to detect external interference.	Scenario 4	**Required**
`Calibration Matrix`	Verifies the integrity of the error mitigation baseline.	Scenario 2	Existing (Provider Only)

The final layer of observability involves the physical performance of the hardware. These domain-specific data provide the necessary fidelity to disambiguate malicious interference from stochastic noise (i.e., attack masking problem).

Table 5 lists the key hardware metrics required for this analysis. `CLOPS` (Circuit Layer Operations Per Second) quantifies the speed of a QPU. A sudden, unexplained drop in CLOPS is a primary indicator of a *Quantum DoS* or a "Malicious Loop" attack (e.g., the Repeat-Until-Success attack) that locks the control electronics.

Furthermore, `Spectator Qubits` are dedicated qubits measured solely to gauge environmental noise. In a *Crosstalk Attack*, an attacker generates high-frequency noise to corrupt a victim. While the victim's qubits will show errors (which could be dismissed as natural decoherence), the Spectator Qubits will record a synchronized spike in noise, effectively "unmasking" the attack as an external interference rather than random error.

While providers typically maintain detailed calibration matrices for operational purposes (Existing (Provider Only)), this data is opaque to end-users. Without access to these historical baselines, an investigator cannot distinguish between a natural calibration drift and a malicious'Calibration Poisoning' attack.

5.4 Security Measures

Hybrid Layer telemetry enables several robust security measures. Post-transpilation, a static circuit analyzer can detect unauthorized gate insertions, such as those inducing crosstalk [24,57] or otherwise compromise computational integrity. In cases where gates cannot be definitively classified as malicious, the transpiled circuit can be differentially compared against a securely generated reference output to identify anomalies. Additionally, scheduler telemetry can be integrated into a Security Information and Event Management (SIEM) system. This enables automated anomaly detection, triggering alerts if job execution queues deviate from configured priority weight factors.

At the hardware level, monitoring CLOPS metrics can detect cross-layer attacks that degrade quantum operational capacity. To counter multiprogramming threats, Co-Tenant Maps can be correlated with Spectator Qubit telemetry to accurately detect and attribute interference. If noise spikes in spectator qubits correlate with logic gates operation on adjacent qubits, the system can identify the crosstalk attack, terminate the malicious circuit, and leverage the Co-Tenant Map to penalize the offending user. Finally, the integrity of the Error Calibration Matrix can be continuously verified by executing routine validation circuits. Deploying distinct circuits tailored to monitor environmental noise (e.g., dephasing, relaxation) versus operational faults (e.g., gate and readout errors), administrators can ensure the hardware operates strictly within the matrix's established error bounds [10,51].

6 Evaluation: Validating Security Observability in a Hybrid Testbed

To validate the security observability enhancements proposed in Sect. 5, we developed a prototype quantum cloud testbed. The primary goal of this evaluation is not to measure raw performance, but to assess the effectiveness of our proposed telemetry artifacts in providing cross-layer visibility. Specifically, we evaluate whether these integrated data artifacts can successfully expose the causal links of hybrid attacks that would otherwise remain invisible to standard classical cloud monitoring.

6.1 Implementation: The Hybrid Testbed

We implemented a layered control system that mimics the architecture defined in Sect. 2. This environment allows us to generate and analyze telemetry in a controlled setting without the cost or restrictions of a commercial public QPU. The complete implementation, including the codebase, attack scripts, and collected evaluation data, is available in our GitHub repository for review.[2]

- **Frontend:** We utilize the Qiskit SDK (v2.2.3) [37] to generate quantum circuits and export them as OpenQASM code [59].
- **Cloud Layer (The Bridge):** We developed User and Job Management APIs using the FastAPI framework (v0.121.1) [25] backed by a PostgreSQL database (v18). This layer handles authentication and job routing, serving as the primary attack surface for classical exploits.
- **Backend Layer (The Fortress):** We implemented a custom Job Control and Scheduler system in Python. To simulate the QPU, we integrated the `Qiskit Aer` simulator (v0.17.2) [40]. This backend executes the transpiled circuits and generates the physical execution metrics.

6.2 Case Study 1: The Bridge Breach (Scenario 1)

This case study evaluates the ability of standard and hybrid telemetry to detect attacks targeting the classical interface (Scenario 1 in Sect. 4.1).

Remote Code Execution via SQL Injection. We established a reverse shell by chaining a SQLi vulnerability with a misconfigured PostgreSQL extension. The malicious query used is detailed in Listing 1.

Security Analysis. While `Job Management API Logs` and `Database Query Logs` recorded the injection, host `System Audit Logs` captured the reverse shell creation and subsequent command execution. This confirms that standard classical logging is sufficient for identifying initial access vectors.

Listing 1. SQL Injection for Remote Code Execution

```
SELECT * FROM jobs WHERE user_id='1' AND id=10000; DO
    $$
     import socket, subprocess, os
     RHOST = "172.31.46.145"
     RPORT = 4444
     s = socket.socket(socket.AF_INET, socket.
         SOCK_STREAM)
```

[2] https://github.com/prabin-lc/quantum-cloud-forensics.

```
    s.connect((RHOST, RPORT))
    os.dup2(s.fileno(), 0)
    os.dup2(s.fileno(), 1)
    os.dup2(s.fileno(), 2)
    subprocess.call(["bash", "-i"])$$ LANGUAGE
        plpython3u;
```

6.3 Case Study 2: The Silent Saboteur (Scenario 2)

This case study evaluates the "Integrity" threat (Sect. 4.2), where an attacker modifies the system logic without crashing it.

Scheduler Tampering. Using the reverse shell established in Case Study 1, we executed a "Software Compromise" attack. We uploaded a malicious version of the Job Control and Scheduler software. Upon restart, this tampered version altered the scheduling logic to exclusively prioritize a specific user's jobs, ignoring the fair-share queue.

Security Analysis. The compromised scheduler could continue to emit standard "Job Started" events, effectively falsifying its internal state. A security analyst relying only on standard logs would fail to identify the anomaly. Detecting this would require a cross-referencing approach defined in Table 4. By comparing the `Device Gateway Logs` (which records the actual execution order) against the Scheduler's falsified records, we could identify the discrepancy. This validates the requirement for immutable decision traces in the hybrid layer.

6.4 Case Study 3: Quantum DoS (Scenario 3)

This case study evaluates the "Availability" threat, focusing on the "Attack Masking" problem (Sect. 4.3) where malicious jobs resemble normal workloads.

Malicious Repeat-Until-Success (RUS) Loop. We designed a valid quantum circuit containing a dynamic `while` loop, as shown in Listing 2. This "Repeat-Until-Success" structure is designed to exit only when a specific state is measured. However, we engineered the circuit to never reach that state, creating an infinite loop that locked the simulator's execution thread.

Security Analysis. The system simply reported the job status as `RUNNING`. Since quantum jobs can legitimately take hours, this status could not trigger alerts. As listed in Table 5, we monitored resource usage as a proxy for the `CLOPS` (Circuit Layer Operations Per Second) metric. The metrics showed a sustained spike in host CPU usage with zero completed circuits output. However, relying solely on this signature is prone to false positives, as complex but benign quantum algorithms may exhibit similar resource-intensive profiles. To establish a more definitive detection mechanism, we propose correlating resource usage with execution traces. This involves monitoring logical gate applications to detect cyclical patterns on identical qubits, which indicates an unterminated loop. Furthermore, because Repeat-Until-Success (RUS) circuits inherently rely on mid-circuit measurements to evaluate exit conditions, an anomalous ratio of intermediate readout signals to completed jobs serves as a robust indicator of a malicious circuit. Crucially, these metrics translate directly to physical hardware; just as logical gate applications are traced in a simulator, the corresponding physical control operations—such as continuous readout triggers and repeating analog pulses—can be monitored on a real Quantum Processing Unit (QPU) to identify malicious cyclic behavior definitively.

Listing 2. Malicious Repeat-Until-Success Quantum Circuit

```
from qiskit import QuantumCircuit
qc = QuantumCircuit(1, 1)
c_bit = qc.clbits[0]
with qc.while_loop((c_bit, 0)):
    qc.measure(0, 0)
    with qc.if_test((c_bit, 0)):
        pass # qc.x(0)
qc.measure(0, 0)
```

7 Related Work

OQTOPUS (Open Quantum Toolchain for Operators and Users) provides a practical, open-source software stack for cloud-based quantum computing [25]. We leverage this implementation as a baseline to define a generalized architecture, extending it to address missing components and clarify the roles of each element within the stack.

Extensive research in the "security-from-quantum" domain [8,9,18,44,49] highlights the threat quantum computing poses to classical algorithms. Consequently, these works advocate for the adoption of Post-Quantum Cryptography (PQC) to safeguard data integrity and confidentiality against quantum cryptanalysis.

Recent surveys identify the security of quantum computing infrastructure as an open challenge [31,58,70]. Most existing research centers on Trustworthy Quantum Computing, addressing scenarios with untrusted providers. Key topics include Blind Quantum Computing for concealing user data, algorithm, and computations [26,71] and Quantum PUFs for verifying hardware integrity [60].

A parallel stream of research addresses quantum hardware security, detailing specific attacks like pulse injection and crosstalk manipulation alongside their defenses [4,66,69]. While broader surveys cover a wide range of these hardware-level attacks [13,16,28,64], research specifically targeting the security of quantum cloud systems remains limited. Although authors such as [16,28] compile various attack cases, their scope is largely restricted to the quantum hardware itself rather than the broader cloud infrastructure.

Our work bridges this gap by analyzing the security of a holistic quantum cloud ecosystem, encompassing both classical and quantum operations. We identify attack surfaces across the hybrid architecture and, through critical event analysis, define the telemetry and artifacts essential for robust defense and forensic capabilities.

8 Discussion, Recommendations, and Limitations

8.1 Implications for Systemic Security Observability

Our study highlights potential attack surfaces in the current Quantum-as-a-Service (QaaS) model. We have demonstrated that classical audit trails, while effective for standard web attacks, are fundamentally blind to quantum-specific threats. For instance, a "Malicious RUS Loop" looks identical to a complex calculation in standard logs. Without monitoring the `CLOPS` metric (Table 5), an attacker can masquerade a Denial-of-Service attack as a legitimate workload.

This finding has significant implications for cloud providers. It suggests that security teams cannot rely solely on existing SIEM (Security Information and Event Management) tools designed for classical infrastructure. To achieve robust forensic readiness, providers must unify the disparate monitoring domains of cloud administration and quantum hardware management, ensuring that physical telemetry (e.g., Spectator Qubits, Calibration Matrices) is integrated directly into the security audit trail.

8.2 Toward a Unified Security Telemetry Framework

The telemetry framework proposed in Sect. 5 serves as a blueprint for a standardized unified security telemetry schema for hybrid quantum systems. Currently, data formats and observability metrics vary significantly between providers, creating fragmented monitoring silos that hinder comprehensive security auditing. By adopting the integrated schemas detailed in Tables 4 and 5, providers can implement a secure-by-design architecture. This ensures that the essential data artifacts required for attack detection and causal attribution are continuously preserved within the system's observability pipeline, rather than being lost in ephemeral runtime environments.

8.3 Limitations and Scope

As defined in Sect. 1, this study focuses strictly on the security of the quantum computing platform, distinct from Post-Quantum Cryptography (PQC). Our analysis targets the operational layer of the hybrid cloud stack.

Consequently, certain physical-layer attacks are outside our scope. While we address "Crosstalk" due to its relevance in multi-tenant clouds, we do not cover hardware-based side-channel attacks requiring physical proximity, such as Power Analysis or Fault Injection [13]. Furthermore, we exclude application-specific adversarial attacks on Quantum Machine Learning (QML) models [27,50,64].

Finally, this study operates under a Trusted Provider model. We assume the cloud provider itself is benign but potentially vulnerable to external compromise. Scenarios involving a malicious provider or the need for Blind Quantum Computing/Homomorphic Encryption are excluded from this research [58].

9 Conclusion

In this work, we presented a comprehensive security analysis of the hybrid quantum cloud. By modeling the system as an interconnected hybrid architecture, we identified a unique class of cross-layer vulnerabilities where classical exploits serve as a "bridge" for disrupting quantum control systems and computational integrity. We identified the lack of security observability as a primary challenge, finding that standard audit trails are insufficient to detect and investigate attacks against hybrid quantum systems.

To address this deficiency, we proposed a systemic telemetry framework that integrates classical cloud administration data with quantum control artifacts. We identified critical but currently unavailable data artifacts, such as scheduling decision traces, verifiable transpiler outputs, and real-time throughput metrics (CLOPS), that are essential for the detection and attribution of these specialized hybrid threats.

Our evaluation, conducted via an end-to-end simulated quantum cloud testbed, validated these findings. We demonstrated that standard cloud logs lack the necessary context to detect quantum-specific anomalies. By integrating our proposed observability schema, we were able to cross-reference data across the hybrid stack, successfully differentiating malicious interference from operational noise.

As the industry moves toward fault-tolerant quantum computing, the complexity of the hybrid stack will increase. We urge providers to move beyond performance-centric monitoring and adopt the "Secure-by-Design" recommendations outlined in this study. By integrating the monitoring domains of classical infrastructure and quantum hardware, providers can ensure accountability and robust security in the quantum era.

References

1. Acharya, N., Saeed, S.M.: A lightweight approach to detect malicious/unexpected changes in the error rates of NISQ computers. In: Proceedings of the 39th International Conference on Computer-Aided Design, pp. 1–9 (2020)
2. Ahmad, A., Altamimi, A.B., Aqib, J.: A reference architecture for quantum computing as a service. J. King Saud Univ.-Compu. Inf. Sci. **36**(6), 102094 (2024)
3. Alexander, T., et al.: Qiskit pulse: programming quantum computers through the cloud with pulses. Quantum Sci. Technol. **5**(4), 044006 (2020)
4. Ash-Saki, A., Alam, M., Ghosh, S.: Analysis of crosstalk in NISQ devices and security implications in multi-programming regime. In: Proceedings of the ACM/IEEE International Symposium on Low Power Electronics and Design, pp. 25–30 (2020)

5. AWS: Amazon braket features - AWS. https://aws.amazon.com/braket/features/. Accessed 14 Feb 2026
6. AWS: How Amazon Braket works - Amazon Braket. https://docs.aws.amazon.com/braket/latest/developerguide/braket-how-it-works.html. Accessed 14 Feb 2026
7. AWS: Quantum Cloud Computing Service - Amazon Braket. https://aws.amazon.com/braket/. Accessed 30 Nov 2025
8. Baseri, Y., Chouhan, V., Ghorbani, A.: Cybersecurity in the quantum era: assessing the impact of quantum computing on infrastructure. arXiv preprint arXiv:2404.10659 (2024)
9. Baseri, Y., Hafid, A., Lashkari, A.H.: Future-proofing cloud security against quantum attacks: risk, transition, and mitigation strategies. arXiv preprint arXiv:2509.15653 (2025)
10. Cai, Z., et al.: Quantum error mitigation. Rev. Mod. Phys. **95**(4), 045005 (2023)
11. Cappos, J., Samuel, J., Baker, S., Hartman, J.H.: Package management security. University of Arizona Technical Report 08–02 (2008)
12. Carignan-Dugas, A., et al.: The error reconstruction and compiled calibration of quantum computing cycles. arXiv preprint arXiv:2303.17714 (2023)
13. Choudhury, N., Basu, K.: A survey of side-channel attacks in superconducting quantum computers. In: 2024 IEEE Computer Society Annual Symposium on VLSI (ISVLSI), pp. 373–378. IEEE (2024)
14. Choudhury, N., Mude, C.N., Das, S., Tikkireddi, P.C., Tannu, S., Basu, K.: Crosstalk-induced side channel threats in multi-tenant NISQ computers. In: 32nd Annual Network and Distributed System Security Symposium, NDSS. The Internet Society (2025)
15. Cinar, B., Bharadiya, J.P.: Cloud computing forensics; challenges and future perspectives: a review. Asian J. Res. Comput. Sci. **16**(1), 1–14 (2023)
16. Coupel, J., Farheen, T.: Security vulnerabilities in quantum cloud systems: a survey on emerging threats. arXiv preprint arXiv:2504.19064 (2025)
17. Cross, A., et al.: OpenQASM 3: a broader and deeper quantum assembly language. ACM Trans. Quantum Comput. **3**(3) (2022). https://doi.org/10.1145/3505636
18. Dam, D.T., Tran, T.H., Hoang, V.P., Pham, C.K., Hoang, T.T.: A survey of post-quantum cryptography: start of a new race. Cryptography **7**(3), 40 (2023)
19. Das, S., Ghosh, S.: TrojanNet: detecting trojans in quantum circuits using machine learning. arXiv preprint arXiv:2306.16701 (2023)
20. Das, S., Ghosh, S.: Trojan attacks on variational quantum circuits and countermeasures. In: 2024 25th International Symposium on Quality Electronic Design (ISQED), pp. 1–8. IEEE (2024)
21. Das, S., Ghosh, S.: Trojan taxonomy in quantum computing. In: 2024 IEEE Computer Society Annual Symposium on VLSI (ISVLSI), pp. 644–649. IEEE (2024)
22. De Leon, N.P., et al.: Materials challenges and opportunities for quantum computing hardware. Science **372**(6539), eabb2823 (2021)
23. DeCross, M., Chertkov, E., Kohagen, M., Foss-Feig, M.: Qubit-reuse compilation with mid-circuit measurement and reset. Phys. Rev. X **13**(4), 041057 (2023)
24. Deshpande, S., et al.: Design of quantum computer antivirus. In: 2023 IEEE International Symposium on Hardware Oriented Security and Trust (HOST), pp. 260–270. IEEE (2023)
25. FastAPI: FastAPI. https://fastapi.tiangolo.com/. Accessed 29 Nov 2025
26. Fitzsimons, J.F.: Private quantum computation: an introduction to blind quantum computing and related protocols. NPJ Quantum Inf. **3**(1), 23 (2017)

27. Ghosh, A., Kundu, S., Ghosh, S.: Adversarial threats in quantum machine learning: a survey of attacks and defenses. arXiv preprint arXiv:2506.21842 (2025)
28. Ghosh, S., Upadhyay, S., Saki, A.A.: A primer on security of quantum computing. arXiv preprint arXiv:2305.02505 (2023)
29. Gidney, C., Ekerå, M.: How to factor 2048 bit RSA integers in 8 hours using 20 million noisy qubits. Quantum **5**, 433 (2021)
30. Gill, S.S., et al.: Quantum computing: Vision and challenges. In: Quantum Computing, pp. 19–42. Elsevier (2025)
31. Golec, M., Hatay, E.S., Golec, M., Uyar, M., Golec, M., Gill, S.S.: Quantum cloud computing: trends and challenges. J. Econ. Technol. **2**, 190–199 (2024)
32. Google: Access and authentication - Criq - Google. https://quantumai.google/cirq/google/access. Accessed 14 Feb 2026
33. Google: Google Quantum Computing Service - Cirq. https://quantumai.google/cirq/google/concepts. Accessed 14 Feb 2026
34. Gouzien, É., Sangouard, N.: Factoring 2048-bit RSA integers in 177 days with 13 436 qubits and a multimode memory. Phys. Rev. Lett. **127**(14), 140503 (2021)
35. Group, N.C.C.F.S.W.: NIST cloud computing forensic science challenges. Technical report, National Institute of Standards and Technology (2014)
36. Harper, B., Tonekaboni, B., Goldozian, B., Sevior, M., Usman, M.: Crosstalk attacks and defence in a shared quantum computing environment. Adv. Quantum Technol. e2500009 (2024)
37. IBM: IBM Quantum Computing - Qiskit. https://www.ibm.com/quantum/qiskit. Accessed 29 Nov 2025
38. IBM: IBM Quantum Platform. https://quantum.cloud.ibm.com/. Accessed 30 Nov 2025
39. IBM: IBM Quantum Platform - Instances. https://quantum.cloud.ibm.com/docs/en/guides/instances. Accessed 14 Feb 2026
40. IBM: Qiskit Aer. https://qiskit.github.io/qiskit-aer/. Accessed 29 Nov 2025
41. IBM: Qiskit machine learning. https://qiskit-community.github.io/qiskit-machine-learning/. Accessed 01 Dec 2025
42. IBM: Qiskit Runtime REST API. https://quantum.cloud.ibm.com/docs/en/api/qiskit-runtime-rest. Accessed 29 Nov 2025
43. Javadi-Abhari, A., et al.: Quantum computing with qiskit. arXiv preprint arXiv:2405.08810 (2024)
44. Kaiiali, M., Sezer, S., Khalid, A.: Cloud computing in the quantum era. In: 2019 IEEE conference on communications and network security (CNS), pp. 1–4. IEEE (2019)
45. Kakuko, N., et al.: A practical open-source software stack for a cloud-based quantum computing system. arXiv preprint arXiv:2507.23165 (2025)
46. Kilber, N., Kaestle, D., Wagner, S.: Cybersecurity for quantum computing. arXiv preprint arXiv:2110.14701 (2021)
47. Lane, M., Shrestha, A., Ali, O.: Managing the risks of data security and privacy in the cloud: a shared responsibility between the cloud service provider and the client organisation. In: Bright Internet Global Summit 2017 (2017)
48. Leymann, F., Barzen, J., Falkenthal, M., Vietz, D., Weder, B., Wild, K.: Quantum in the cloud: application potentials and research opportunities. arXiv preprint arXiv:2003.06256 (2020)
49. Li, S., et al.: Post-quantum security: opportunities and challenges. Sensors **23**(21), 8744 (2023)

50. Liao, H., Convy, I., Huggins, W.J., Whaley, K.B.: Robust in practice: adversarial attacks on quantum machine learning. Phys. Rev. A **103**(4), 042427 (2021)
51. Liu, Y., Li, Z., Robertson, A., Fu, X., Song, S.L.: Enabling efficient real-time calibration on cloud quantum machines. IEEE Trans. Quantum Eng. **4**, 1–17 (2023)
52. Magann, A.B., Grace, M.D., Rabitz, H.A., Sarovar, M.: Digital quantum simulation of molecular dynamics and control. Phys. Rev. Res. **3**(2), 023165 (2021)
53. Microsoft: Azure QDK. https://learn.microsoft.com/en-us/azure/quantum/qdk-main-overview. Accessed 14 Feb 2026
54. Microsoft: Azure Quantum CLI. https://learn.microsoft.com/en-us/cli/azure/quantum. Accessed 14 Feb 2026
55. Microsoft: Azure Quantum Computing. https://azure.microsoft.com/en-us/solutions/quantum-computing. Accessed 30 Nov 2025
56. Microsoft: Quantum Computing Integration - Azure Quantum. https://learn.microsoft.com/en-us/azure/architecture/example-scenario/quantum/quantum-computing-integration-with-classical-apps. Accessed 14 Feb 2026
57. Murali, P., McKay, D.C., Martonosi, M., Javadi-Abhari, A.: Software mitigation of crosstalk on noisy intermediate-scale quantum computers. In: Proceedings of the Twenty-Fifth International Conference on Architectural Support for Programming Languages and Operating Systems, pp. 1001–1016 (2020)
58. Nguyen, H.T., Krishnan, P., Krishnaswamy, D., Usman, M., Buyya, R.: Quantum cloud computing: A review, open problems, and future directions. arXiv preprint arXiv:2404.11420 (2024)
59. OpenQASM: OpenQASM. https://openqasm.com/. Accessed 29 Nov 2025
60. Phalak, K., Ash-Saki, A., Alam, M., Topaloglu, R.O., Ghosh, S.: Quantum PUF for security and trust in quantum computing. IEEE J. Emerg. Sel. Top. Circuits Syst. **11**(2), 333–342 (2021)
61. Preskill, J.: Quantum computing in the NISQ era and beyond. Quantum **2**, 79 (2018)
62. Resch, S., Karpuzcu, U.R.: Benchmarking quantum computers and the impact of quantum noise. ACM Comput. Surv. (CSUR) **54**(7), 1–35 (2021)
63. Roy, R., Ghosh, A., Ghosh, S.: Forensics of transpiled quantum circuits. In: Proceedings of the Great Lakes Symposium on VLSI 2025, pp. 354–359 (2025)
64. Saki, A.A., Alam, M., Phalak, K., Suresh, A., Topaloglu, R.O., Ghosh, S.: A survey and tutorial on security and resilience of quantum computing. In: 2021 IEEE European Test Symposium (ETS), pp. 1–10. IEEE (2021)
65. Shor, P.W.: Polynomial-time algorithms for prime factorization and discrete logarithms on a quantum computer. SIAM J. Comput. **26**(5), 1484–1509 (1997). https://doi.org/10.1137/S0097539795293172
66. Tan, Y., Choudhury, N., Basu, K., Szefer, J.: Qubithammer attacks: qubit flipping attacks in multi-tenant superconducting quantum computers. arXiv preprint arXiv:2504.07875 (2025)
67. Tao, R., Zhu, H., Nieh, J., Yao, J., Gu, R.: Quantum virtual machines. In: 19th USENIX Symposium on Operating Systems Design and Implementation (OSDI 25), pp. 411–428 (2025)
68. Wack, A., et al.: Quality, speed, and scale: three key attributes to measure the performance of near-term quantum computers. arXiv preprint arXiv:2110.14108 (2021)

69. Xu, C., Szefer, J.: Security attacks abusing pulse-level quantum circuits. In: 2025 IEEE Symposium on Security and Privacy (SP), pp. 222–239 (2025). https://doi.org/10.1109/SP61157.2025.00083
70. Yang, Z., Zolanvari, M., Jain, R.: A survey of important issues in quantum computing and communications. IEEE Commun. Surv. Tutor. **25**(2), 1059–1094 (2023)
71. Yarter, M., Uehara, G., Spanias, A.: Implementation and analysis of quantum homomorphic encryption. In: 2022 13th International Conference on Information, Intelligence, Systems & Applications (IISA), pp. 1–5. IEEE (2022)

Applied Crypto for Authentication and Data Hiding

Registration-Optimized Dynamic Group Time-Based One-Time Passwords for Mobile Access

Jiaqing Guo[1], Xuelian Cao[2], Zengpeng Li[3], Yong Zhou[1], Zheng Yang[1](✉), and Jianying Zhou[4]

[1] Southwest University, Chongqing, China
{whoami,hiro115}@email.swu.edu.cn, youngzheng@swu.edu.cn
[2] Tsinghua University, Beijing, China
xl-cao@mail.tsinghua.edu.cn
[3] Shandong University, Jinan, China
zengpeng@email.sdu.edu.cn
[4] Singapore University of Technology and Design, Singapore, Singapore
jianying_zhou@sutd.edu.sg

Abstract. Mobile access within public finance and enterprise environments often requires lightweight anonymous authentication, allowing users to prove authorization without disclosing their identities. Group Time-based One-Time Passwords (GTOTP) has recently been proposed as a lightweight primitive meeting this need with post-quantum security. To address dynamic group membership, Cao et al. introduced DGTOne, the first dynamic GTOTP construction. It employs chameleon hashes to precompute a fixed set of Merkle-tree leaves (mount points), into which conventional TOTP verification points (VPs) contributed by group members are adaptively inserted. However, DGTOne partitions mount points by time epochs, so they can expire and become unusable, causing capacity waste due to unpredictable join times. Moreover, its outsourced proof generation requires verifiers to be online each epoch to fetch refreshed credentials from Registration Authority (RA), defeating offline verification needed in mobile access. We address these limitations with two new schemes. First, we propose NWDGT, a no-wastage DGTOTP design that constructs Merkle trees of members' verification points (VP-trees) on demand, eliminating expired mount points at the cost of added handling latency. To mitigate this latency, we introduce LWDGT, which instantiates multiple small one-time signature (OTS) trees whose leaves (OTS public keys) serve as mount points. New members' VPs are signed immediately using unused leaves, achieving low wastage. We formally prove that the wastage rate of LWDGT is, with overwhelming probability, lower than that of DGTOne. By modeling the registration process and optimizing OTS-tree size, for deployments with up to 500 members (209 initially, 20 added monthly), LWDGT reduces mount point wastage rate by 10.2% over one year compared to DGTOne.

Y. Cao et al. (Eds.): SecureComm 2026, LNICST 704, pp. 575–597, 2027.
https://doi.org/10.1007/978-3-032-32764-2_26

Keywords: Group Time-based One-Time Passwords · Anonymity · Traceability · Authentication

1 Introduction

Mobile access has become an indispensable component of modern infrastructures, supporting applications in finance and enterprise access control [9,29,30]. In scenarios like bank or stock exchange entry, authentication devices are typically resource-constrained smartcard readers or embedded terminals with limited storage, computational power, and connectivity. Meanwhile, these settings involve highly sensitive operations (e.g., financial transactions, and entertainment activities), where users prefer not to expose identities, making privacy-preserving authentication a fundamental requirement for mobile access systems [19]. Lightweight anonymous authentication thus emerges as a promising approach, enabling users to prove access rights without revealing identities.

To realize such lightweight anonymous authentication, Yang et al. [35] introduced a primitive named *Group Time-based One-Time Passwords* (GTOTP). Their construction, referred to as YJN+ scheme, extends asymmetric time-based one-time passwords (TOTP) into an anonymous group setting, allowing members to authenticate by proving group membership without revealing identities. Credentials are generated at registration and returned directly to members, avoiding outsourced generation by RA. By relying solely on hash functions, the scheme is not only lightweight and suitable for embedded devices, but also post-quantum secure. Nevertheless, this approach requires each member to have a sufficient auxiliary storage device (such as a mobile phone) to store Merkle proofs for all future epochs, each covering only a short validity window for verification. However, the YJN+ scheme assumes a static group model in which all members are predefined and immutable, making it unsuitable for dynamic settings where participants join and leave the group adaptively at will.

To enable dynamic group management (DGM), Cao et al. [10] recently proposed an enhanced primitive *Dynamic Group Time-based One-Time Passwords* (DGTOTP). Their concrete construction, called DGTOne scheme, extends asymmetric TOTP using chameleon hash functions and a Merkle tree whose root acts as the group public key. It pre-generates leaves as *mount points* using chameleon hash functions. These mount points can later be used to register new members, allowing them to join without affecting existing ones. Unlike YJN+, however, DGTOne outsources credential generation to the registration authority (RA), requiring the verifier to fetch updated proofs from the RA in each epoch. Consequently, a DGTOne verifier must remain online at all times, which limits its applicability in scenarios where verifier devices have intermittent or restricted network access. For instance, many access devices-such as smartcard readers at physical entry gates-are designed to operate with unreliable or limited connectivity due to security isolation concerns.

Moreover, DGTOne partitions mount points by epochs, requiring a fixed number to be pre-generated for each epoch. These mount points can expire and become unusable, leading to a high wastage rate (i.e., the fraction of unused mount points over the total provided) when member join times are unpredictable. To support offline verification, credentials cannot be outsourced to RA but must instead be stored directly by members, as in YJN+ scheme. In this case, the total number of mount points available for member registration is fixed, making it important to maximize their utilization so that the verifier can authenticate as many members as possible, thereby reducing the wastage rate. In summary, this raises the key research question:

"Can we construct a non-outsourced DGTOTP scheme with lower wastage rate for mobile access?"

Our Works. To further explore this question, we consider a mobile access scenario where a member authenticates at an access gate using a password stored on a mobile phone. The gate acts as the verifier device, which may have intermittent or limited network connectivity due to operational constraints or security isolation. The verifier device is periodically updated by an entity responsible for its maintenance, referred to as the *administrator of the verifier*. This entity can be a human operator, an automated management system, or another trusted component with network access, performing manual updates and maintenance tasks when connectivity is available but without continuous real-time synchronization. A member submits a registration request to RA, after which RA publishes the corresponding authentication information on a public bulletin board (PBB) that the administrator can later retrieve and update to the verifier device manually. The administrator can also download logs such as authentication records, but may be curious about the identities of authenticating members, making privacy preservation essential. After registration, a member can authenticate by transmitting the stored password through a secure channel, such as Near-Field Communication (NFC), to the verifier, while an adversary may attempt to forge passwords in order to gain unauthorized access.

Building on this scenario, we propose two new DGTOTP constructions designed for different deployment environments, since anonymous authentication systems differ in their tolerance to registration-handling latency. One targets the **delayed-batch registration setting**, where short delays in registration are acceptable. This is typical in enterprise infrastructures, for example when employees are registered in advance before starting work or when new members are added at scheduled times. The other aims at **instant-response registration setting**, where registration must take effect immediately. Such a setting arises in mobile and IoT environments, for instance when a visitor requests temporary access to a facility or when a new edge device joins a network and must be authenticated without delay.

Our first construction, a no-wastage DGTOTP scheme NWDGT, is designed for the delayed-batch registration setting. Designing such a scheme to achieve offline verification and eliminate mount point wastage presents several challenges. Since the group public key (gpk) is generated at system initialization, it is necessary to ensure that dynamically adding sub-trees for future epochs does not affect the existing gpk or the states of registered members. Achieving anonymity and traceability under adaptive adversaries further complicates the design.

To address these challenges, we customize a register-and-build-later (RBL) strategy. For each epoch, verification points are aggregated to construct a VP-tree before the epoch begins, thereby avoiding unused mount points. Since VP-trees depend on the actual registered members per epoch, they cannot be pre-generated, thus the gpk cannot be fixed at setup. To support this dynamic structure efficiently, we use a hash-based hyper-tree from SPHINCS+C [20], with the hyper-tree root as the gpk and each VP-tree mounted under it. Offline authentication is achieved by delivering all necessary credentials to members.

However, the waiting requirement in NWDGT is impractical for latency-sensitive scenarios, motivating our second construction, a low-wastage DGTOTP scheme LWDGT. It is designed for the instant-response registration setting, where immediate handling is required. Designing such a scheme introduces new challenges. First, RA must determine how to construct sub-trees efficiently during registration without waiting for future members to prevent handling delays. In addition, if we follow the sequential mounting strategy used in NWDGT, the order of sub-trees may reveal a member's joining time, leading to privacy leakage.

To resolve these issues, we develop a partitioned-build-on-demand (PBOD) registration strategy. Instead of building a single VP-tree for each epoch based on the registered verification points, we partition registrations into multiple smaller trees whose leaves serve as mount points. These trees, referred to as OTS-trees, are constructed using one-time signature (OTS) when needed. Each member's verification point is immediately signed by one of these leaves upon registration. To prevent the registration order from being inferred, we adopt the full SPHINCS+C construction, using its root as gpk. All OTS-trees are then signed and mounted under this structure, ensuring that the mounting order is unlinkable and that no information about member joining timing is exposed.
Contributions. The main contributions are as follows:

- We propose a no-wastage DGTOTP scheme, NWDGT, designed for the delayed-batch registration setting. Utilizing the RBL strategy, it constructs VP-trees based on actual registrations in each epoch. This eliminates mount point wastage, and it supports offline verification by providing credentials to members during registration. The trade-off is that RA and members must wait until the batch is complete, introducing registration handling latency.
- We develop a low-wastage DGTOTP scheme, LWDGT, tailored for the instant-response registration setting. Leveraging a PBOD strategy, it constructs small OTS-trees on demand to enable fast registration handling and support offline verifiers by issuing the required credentials at registration time. While on-demand tree generation inevitably introduces some mount point wastage, our approach minimizes this overhead. Compared to NWDGT, LWDGT offers faster registration at the cost of slightly increased wastage.
- We provide a security analysis showing our design is secure. Through theoretical modeling of mount point wastage under realistic settings (systems with

up to 500 users, 209 initial registrations, and 20 monthly arrivals), we demonstrate that LWDGT reduces wastage rate by 10.2% over one year compared to DGTOne scheme. In addition, our experimental evaluation confirms that both schemes remain practical and efficient in resource-constrained environments.

2 Related Work

The concept of One-Time Passwords (OTP) originated with Lamport's seminal proposal [23], ensuring each password is valid for a single transaction. Building on this foundation, Sun et al. [31] proposed TrustOTP, a secure OTP solution to implement OTP schemes on the smartphone platform even in the presence of a malicious mobile OS. To further strengthen OTP-based authentication, Tolosana et al. [32] integrated handwritten digit biometrics on touchscreens, providing improved resistance against imitation attacks through behavioral analysis. In 2005, RFC 4226 standardized the HMAC-based One-Time Password (HOTP) algorithm [26], which uses a shared secret and synchronized counters to generate human-readable OTPs but risks desynchronization. RFC 6238 then proposed Time-based One-Time Password (TOTP) [25], replacing counters with timestamps to constrain OTP validity to short intervals. However, symmetric key reliance still exposes servers to compromise; asymmetric variants such as T/Key [21] enable public verification without server-stored seeds but lack anonymity, limiting their use in privacy-sensitive scenarios.

Group signature schemes [1,14,18,22] offer an alternative primitive for anonymous authentication [24,34,36,37]. In these schemes, users can produce signatures on behalf of a group without revealing their identity, while a designated group manager retains the ability to trace the signer if necessary. The concept was first introduced by Chaum and van Heyst [11], and formalized by Bellare et al. [2], who consolidated earlier informal notions into two key security properties: full anonymity and full traceability. This foundational model, now widely adopted, assumes a static group setting in which the list of group members is fixed at initialization. Building on this foundation, various efficient group signature schemes have been proposed [1,4–6,12], many of which follow Bellare et al.'s model. However, the original static model lacks support for member dynamics, which is critical in real-world applications where members frequently join or leave the group. To address this, Bellare et al. [4] proposed a formal security model for dynamic group signatures, which strengthens the traditional model to allow dynamic enrollment of members. In this model, the role of the group manager is split between a group manager, responsible for managing membership, and a tracing manager, responsible for opening the signature when needed.

Although these schemes provide strong theoretical guarantees, they typically depend on expensive operations [7,15] (such as bilinear pairings or RSA accumulators) and incur complex, resource-intensive revocation processes. Consequently, they are ill-suited to settings with limited computational capacity or frequent user turnover. By contrast, GTOTP-style constructions, including those introduced in this work, achieve comparable security properties with markedly lower overhead, rendering them far more practical for deployment on resource-constrained devices. Compared to traditional TOTP schemes, GTOTP further realizes privacy by supporting anonymity, and as hash-based constructions, they avoid the computational costs inherent in group signatures. These advantages make DGTOTP the most practical and lightweight approach to anonymous authentication in real-world dynamic environments.

3 Preliminaries

We denote the security parameter by κ, and the set of integers between 1 and n by $[n] = \{1, \ldots, n\} \subset \mathbb{N}$. Let $x \xleftarrow{\$} X$ be the operation of sampling x uniformly at random from the set X. Let $\|$ be the string concatenation operation.

Our constructions rely on several cryptographic primitives. We use (1) $\mathsf{TOTP} := (\mathsf{Setup}, \mathsf{PInit}, \mathsf{PGen}, \mathsf{Verify})$ to denote an asymmetric TOTP scheme; (2) $\mathsf{PRF} : \mathcal{K}_{\mathsf{PRF}} \times \mathcal{M}_{\mathsf{PRF}} \rightarrow \mathcal{R}_{\mathsf{PRF}}$ to denote a pseudo-random function family, where $\mathcal{K}_{\mathsf{PRF}}$ is the key space, $\mathcal{M}_{\mathsf{PRF}}$ is the message space, and $\mathcal{R}_{\mathsf{PRF}}$ is the range space; (3) $\mathsf{ASE} := (\mathsf{Setup}, \mathsf{Enc}, \mathsf{Dec})$ to denote an authenticated symmetric encryption scheme; (4) $\mathsf{CRH} : \mathcal{K}_{\mathsf{CRH}} \times \mathcal{M}_{\mathsf{CRH}} \rightarrow \mathcal{R}_{\mathsf{CRH}}$ to denote a collision-resistant hash function, where $\mathcal{K}_{\mathsf{CRH}}$ is the key space, $\mathcal{M}_{\mathsf{CRH}}$ is the message space, and $\mathcal{R}_{\mathsf{CRH}}$ is the range space; (5) $\mathsf{MT} := (\mathsf{Build}, \mathsf{GetPf}, \mathsf{Verify})$ to denote a Merkle tree scheme; (6) $\mathsf{PM} := (\mathsf{Setup}, \mathsf{Shuffle})$ to denote an unpredictable permutation scheme; (7) $\mathsf{Sig} := (\mathsf{Setup}, \mathsf{Sign}, \mathsf{Verify})$ to denote a digital signature scheme. Their detailed definitions are described in [17, Appendix A].

4 Security Notions

This section presents the security notions of our constructions, following [10].

Entities. The system involves three entities: group members, verifiers, and a registration authority (RA). Group members can generate valid time-based one-time passwords for authentication. RA performs system setup and manages member enrollment, where each member is uniquely identified by an identity ID.

Syntax. There are eight algorithms to describe in detail below.

• $(\mathsf{pms}, \mathsf{gpk}_{\mathsf{G}}, \mathsf{GI}_{\mathsf{G}}, \mathrm{RL}_{\mathsf{G}}, k_{\mathsf{RA}}) \leftarrow \mathsf{Setup}(1^{\kappa}, \mathsf{G}, \Delta_{pw}, \Delta_{vp}, T_s, T_e)$: RA runs this system setup algorithm. It takes the security parameter 1^{κ}, the group G, the password generation interval Δ_{pw}, the validity period of each verification point Δ_{vp}, and the instance start and end time T_s and T_e. This algorithm outputs system parameters pms, the initial group public key $\mathsf{gpk}_{\mathsf{G}}$ of a group G, the group management information GI_{G}, the revocation list RL_{G}, and a secret key $k_{\mathsf{RA}} \xleftarrow{\$} \mathcal{K}_{\mathsf{RA}}$ for RA, where $\mathcal{K}_{\mathsf{RA}}$ is the key space of RA.

• $(k_{\mathsf{ID}_j}, \mathsf{vps}_{\mathsf{ID}_j}) \leftarrow \mathsf{MInit}(\mathsf{ID}_j)$: A group member runs this member initialization algorithm. It takes the identity of a member ID_j as input, and outputs the secret key $k_{\mathsf{ID}_j} \xleftarrow{\$} \mathcal{K}_M$ and the verification state (i.e., a set of verification points) $\mathsf{vps}_{\mathsf{ID}_j}$ belonging to member ID_j, where $\mathcal{K}_M$ is the secret key space of a group member.

• $(\mathsf{Ax}_{\mathsf{ID}_j}, \mathsf{gpk}'_{\mathsf{G}}, \mathsf{GI}'_{\mathsf{G}}) \leftarrow \mathsf{Join}(k_{\mathsf{RA}}, \mathsf{gpk}_{\mathsf{G}}, \mathsf{ID}_j, \mathsf{vps}_{\mathsf{ID}_j})$: RA runs this join algorithm to handle the enrollment of a member ID_j. It takes as input its secret key k_{RA}, group public key $\mathsf{gpk}_{\mathsf{G}}$, identity ID_j, and verification state $\mathsf{vps}_{\mathsf{ID}_j}$ of the member. It outputs the auxiliary information $\mathsf{Ax}_{\mathsf{ID}_j}$ as registration receipt to ID_j, and updates group management message $\mathsf{GI}'_{\mathsf{G}}$ and group public key $\mathsf{gpk}'_{\mathsf{G}}$ if necessary.
• $sd^i_{\mathsf{ID}_j} \leftarrow \mathsf{GetSD}(k_{\mathsf{ID}_j}, T)$: A group member runs this seed generation algorithm. It takes secret key $k_{\mathsf{ID}_j} \in \mathcal{K}_M$ and time T, and outputs the secret seed $sd^i_{\mathsf{ID}_j} \in \mathcal{S}_{\mathsf{SD}}$ of the i-th verify epoch w.r.t. the time T, where $\mathcal{S}_{\mathsf{SD}}$ is the secret seed space.
• $pw^{i,z}_{\mathsf{ID}_j} \leftarrow \mathsf{PwdGen}(sd^i_{\mathsf{ID}_j}, T)$: A group member runs this password generation algorithm. It takes secret seed $sd^i_{\mathsf{ID}_j}$ and time T as input, and outputs password $pw^{i,z}_{\mathsf{ID}_j}$ the z-th password of the i-th verify epoch for member ID_j.
• $\{0,1\} \leftarrow \mathsf{Verify}(\mathsf{gpk}_{\mathsf{G}}, pw^{i,z}_{\mathsf{ID}_j}, T, \mathrm{RL}_{\mathsf{G}})$: Verifier runs this verification algorithm. It takes the group public key $\mathsf{gpk}_{\mathsf{G}}$, the password $pw^{i,z}_{\mathsf{ID}_j}$, the time T, and the revocation list RL_{G} as input. It outputs 1 if $pw^{i,z}_{\mathsf{ID}_j}$ is accepted, and 0 otherwise.
• $\mathrm{RL}'_{\mathsf{G}} \leftarrow \mathsf{Revoke}(k_{\mathsf{RA}}, \mathsf{ID}_j, \mathsf{gpk}_{\mathsf{G}}, \mathrm{RL}_{\mathsf{G}}, \mathsf{GI}_{\mathsf{G}})$: RA runs this revocation algorithm to revoke the credentials of a member ID_j with respect to $\mathsf{gpk}_{\mathsf{G}}$ by using its secret key k_{RA}, the revoking identity ID_j, and the group management message GI_{G}. It returns the updated revocation list $\mathrm{RL}'_{\mathsf{G}}$.
• $\mathsf{ID}_j \leftarrow \mathsf{IDOpen}(k_{\mathsf{RA}}, \mathsf{gpk}_{\mathsf{G}}, pw^{i,z}_{\mathsf{ID}_j}, T)$: RA runs this identity extraction algorithm. It takes as input the secret key k_{RA}, group public key $\mathsf{gpk}_{\mathsf{G}}$, password $pw^{i,z}_{\mathsf{ID}_j}$ and time T. It outputs ID_j if algorithm procedure is successful, and $\perp$ otherwise.

Threat Model. We assume RA is a non-colluding and semi-honest third party. RA will not be corrupted by any attackers and will faithfully register for members and trace the identity of malicious members, but may be curious about the status of password usage. The members can be corrupted by the attackers, but at least two members are honest. The attackers can control the network and thus can intercept, inject, and tamper with the communication between a member and a verifier. However, the communication between a member and RA is secure. The verifier can be malicious and may be curious about the identity of a member. The malicious group members and verifiers may infer the private information of honest group members.

Security Goals. To meet the security requirements of member authentication in group setting, the proposed schemes should meet the following security goals:

- *Anonymity:* Anonymity ensures that an adversary cannot infer any information about the real identity of an uncorrupted group member from an unused password even if the communication message is captured.
- *Traceability:* Only valid proofs can be traced to honest group members. This ensures that an adversary cannot forge a valid proof that can be attributed to either (i) an uncorrupted member of the group or (ii) any non-member.

Security Definition. Following [10], we define the correctness (Corr) and security properties of DGTOTP within a unified game-based framework [3]. The security properties include *anonymity* (Anony) and *traceability* (Trace)[1]. Each property is formalized as a game indexed by Gvar $\in$ {Corr, Anony, Trace}. A challenger simulates the game procedures, illustrated in Fig. 1. An adversary begins the game with Initialize and concludes with Finalize, issuing adaptive queries in between to achieve the winning condition $\mathsf{Finalize}(b^*, pw^*, T^*) = 1$ for the corresponding game.

To model attacks on the join process, an adversary may adaptively introduce new members at any point using either AddHM (honest) or AddMM (malicious). Malicious members are fully controlled by the adversary, capturing insider threats, while their verification states vst_{ID_j} are generated by the adversary, and the challenger does not know their secrets. For honest members, the adversary may reveal long-term keys and secret seeds via Corrupt and CompromiseSD queries, respectively, simulating real-world compromises such as insider leaks, weak key management, or cryptanalysis.

Password generation and verification by honest members are modeled through GetNextPw and ReceivePw. The GetNextPw query captures known-password attacks without affecting unexposed secrets, while ReceivePw allows the adversary to test forged passwords, reflecting impersonation attempts. Membership revocation is modeled via RevokeID, enabling the adversary to manipulate group structure and infer information about honest members. Additionally, the OpenID procedure allows the adversary to reveal the identities associated with certain passwords, emphasizing that disclosure of one password must not compromise others.

Anonymity requires that the adversary cannot distinguish the secret seeds of two honest members in the Challenge procedure. Traceability requires that the adversary cannot produce a valid password-time pair (pw^*, T^*) satisfying either: (i) it is linked to an identity (including $\perp$) never added via AddHM or AddMM, or (ii) it belongs to an honest, uncorrupted member (whose key or secret seed was not exposed) and was never generated by the challenger during any procedure.

Definition 1. *We say that a DGTOTP scheme Σ is* correct *if for any PPT adversary $\mathcal{A}$ and system parameters* $\mathsf{Gpm} = (\kappa, \mathsf{G}, \Delta_{pw}, \Delta_{vp}, T_s, T_e)$, $\Pr\left[G^{\mathsf{Corr}}_{\mathcal{A},\Sigma}(\mathsf{Gpm}) = 0\right] \approx 1$, *and we say that a correct scheme Σ is* secure *if for any PPT adversary $\mathcal{A}$ the advantages in the corresponding games are negligible, i.e.,* $\mathsf{Adv}^{\mathsf{Anony}}_{\mathcal{A},\Sigma}(\mathsf{Gpm}) := \left|\Pr[G^{\mathsf{Anony}}_{\mathcal{A},\Sigma}(\mathsf{Gpm}) = 1] - 1/2\right|$ *and* $\mathsf{Adv}^{\mathsf{Trace}}_{\mathcal{A},\Sigma}(\mathsf{Gpm}) := \Pr[G^{\mathsf{Trace}}_{\mathcal{A},\Sigma}(\mathsf{Gpm}) = 1]$.

5 New DGTOTP Constructions

In this section, we introduce two new DGTOTP constructions with tailored registration strategies for specific real-world settings, respectively.

[1] Accordingly, adversaries are classified as either anonymity adversaries or traceability adversaries based on the property they aim to break.

$G^{\mathsf{Gvar}}_{\mathcal{A},\Sigma}(\kappa, \mathsf{G}, \Delta_{pw}, \Delta_{vp}, T_s, T_e)$:

Initialize() :
$(\mathsf{pms}, \mathsf{gpk_G}, \mathsf{GI_G}, \mathrm{RL_G}, k_{\mathsf{RA}}) \leftarrow \Sigma.\mathsf{Setup}(1^\kappa, \mathsf{G}, \Delta_{pw}, \Delta_{vp}, T_s, T_e)$
Create lists $(\mathrm{CML}, \mathrm{CSL}, \mathrm{HML}, \mathrm{OL}) \leftarrow \emptyset$
Init a monotonically increasing (in Δ_{pw}) system clock $T_c := T_s$
OUTPUT $\mathsf{pms}, \mathsf{gpk_G}, \mathrm{RL_G}$

Challenge($\hat{\mathsf{ID}}_0, \hat{\mathsf{ID}}_1$) :
IF $(\hat{\mathsf{ID}}_0, \hat{\mathsf{ID}}_1) \notin \mathrm{GP}$ or $\hat{\mathsf{ID}}_0 = \hat{\mathsf{ID}}_1$, OUTPUT $\perp$
$b \xleftarrow{\$} \{0,1\}$
Switch to the next verification epoch
$sd_{\hat{\mathsf{ID}}_b} \leftarrow \Sigma.\mathsf{GetSD}(k_{\hat{\mathsf{ID}}_b}, T_c)$
Switch to the next verification epoch
OUTPUT $sd_{\hat{\mathsf{ID}}_b}$

Corrupt(ID_j) :
IF $\mathsf{ID}_j \notin \mathrm{HML}$, OUTPUT $\perp$
$\mathrm{CML} \leftarrow \mathsf{ID}_j$
OUTPUT k_{ID_j}

CompromiseSD(ID_j) :
IF $\mathsf{ID}_j \notin \mathrm{HML}$, OUTPUT $\perp$
$sd^i_{\mathsf{ID}_j} \leftarrow \Sigma.\mathsf{GetSD}(k_{\mathsf{ID}_j}, T_c)$
$\mathrm{CSL} \leftarrow sd^i_{\mathsf{ID}_j}$
OUTPUT $sd^i_{\mathsf{ID}_j}$

GetNextPw() :
FOR $\forall \mathsf{ID}_j \in \mathrm{HML}$:
  $sd^i_{\mathsf{ID}_j} \leftarrow \Sigma.\mathsf{GetSD}(k_{\mathsf{ID}_j}, T_c)$
  $pw_{\mathsf{ID}_j} \leftarrow \Sigma.\mathsf{PwdGen}(sd^i_{\mathsf{ID}_j}, T_c)$
$\mathrm{PL} \leftarrow (\{pw_{\mathsf{ID}_j}\}_{\mathsf{ID}_j \in \mathrm{HML}}, T_c)$
OUTPUT $\{pw_{\mathsf{ID}_j}\}_{\mathsf{ID}_j \in \mathrm{HML}}$

Finalize(b^*, pw^*, T^*) :
$\mathsf{ID}^* := \Sigma.\mathsf{IDOpen}(k_{\mathsf{RA}}, \mathsf{gpk_G}, pw^*, T^*)$
$vr := \Sigma.\mathsf{Verify}(\mathsf{gpk_G}, pw^*, T^*, \mathrm{RL_G})$
$i := \frac{\lceil T^* - T_s \rceil}{\Delta_{vp}}$; $\tilde{T^*} := T^* - ((T^* - T_s) \mod \Delta_{pw})$
IF Gvar = Corr and $pw^* \in \mathrm{PL}$ and $(vr = 0 \vee \mathsf{ID}^* \notin \mathrm{HML})$
  OUTPUT 1
IF Gvar = Anony and $b = b^*$ and $\hat{\mathsf{ID}}_0 \notin (\mathrm{CML} \cup \mathrm{OL})$ and $\hat{\mathsf{ID}}_1 \notin (\mathrm{CML} \cup \mathrm{OL})$
  OUTPUT 1
IF Gvar = Trace and $vr = 1$
  and $\big((\mathsf{ID}^* \notin (\mathrm{HML} \cup \mathrm{CML})) \vee ((pw^*, \tilde{T^*}) \notin \mathrm{PL} \wedge \mathsf{ID}^* \notin \mathrm{CML} \wedge sd^i_{\mathsf{ID}^*} \notin \mathrm{CSL})\big)$
  OUTPUT 1
OUTPUT 0

AddHM(ID_j) :
$(k_{\mathsf{ID}_j}, \mathsf{vps}_{\mathsf{ID}_j}) \leftarrow \mathsf{MInit}(\mathsf{ID}_j)$
$(\mathsf{Ax}_{\mathsf{ID}_j}, \mathsf{gpk}'_\mathsf{G}, \mathsf{GI}'_\mathsf{G}) \leftarrow \Sigma.\mathsf{Join}(k_{\mathsf{RA}}, \mathsf{gpk_G}, \mathsf{ID}_j, \mathsf{vps}_{\mathsf{ID}_j})$
$\mathrm{HML} \leftarrow \mathsf{ID}_j$
OUTPUT $\mathsf{Ax}_{\mathsf{ID}_j}, \mathsf{gpk}'_\mathsf{G}, \mathsf{GI}'_\mathsf{G}[\mathsf{ID}_j]$

AddMM($\mathsf{ID}_j, \mathsf{vps}_{\mathsf{ID}_j}$) :
$(\mathsf{Ax}_{\mathsf{ID}_j}, \mathsf{gpk}'_\mathsf{G}, \mathsf{GI}'_\mathsf{G}) \leftarrow \Sigma.\mathsf{Join}(k_{\mathsf{RA}}, \mathsf{gpk_G}, \mathsf{ID}_j, \mathsf{vps}_{\mathsf{ID}_j})$
$\mathrm{CML} \leftarrow \mathsf{ID}_j$
OUTPUT $\mathsf{Ax}_{\mathsf{ID}_j}, \mathsf{gpk}'_\mathsf{G}, \mathsf{GI}'_\mathsf{G}[\mathsf{ID}_j]$

ReceivePw(pw) :
OUTPUT $\Sigma.\mathsf{Verify}(\mathsf{gpk_G}, pw, T_c, \mathrm{RL_G})$

OpenID(pw, T) :
$\mathrm{OL} \leftarrow pw$
OUTPUT $\Sigma.\mathsf{IDOpen}(k_{\mathsf{RA}}, \mathsf{gpk_G}, pw, T)$

RevokeID(ID_j) :
OUTPUT $\mathrm{RL}'_\mathsf{G} \leftarrow \Sigma.\mathsf{Revoke}(k_{\mathsf{RA}}, \mathsf{ID}_j, \mathsf{gpk_G}, \mathrm{RL_G}, \mathsf{GI_G})$

Fig. 1. Procedures Used to Define the Security of a DGTOTP Scheme.

Meanwhile, we consider the following four functional goals (FG) in our designs. *FG1) Minimize mount point wastage.* The scheme should reduce unused mount points on the RA side to improve resource utilization and avoid unnecessary computation. *FG2) Support offline verifier.* Verifiers should be able to authenticate members without requiring real-time communication with RA, which is essential for deployment in disconnected or intermittently connected environments. *FG3) Dynamic group management.* The scheme should support member joining and revocation without altering the group public key or the local state of existing members, while preserving the lightweight feature of TOTP. *FG4) Lightweight client-side computation.* The computational burden on each member should be kept low to ensure practicality for resource-constrained devices.

We begin our exploration of efficient DGTOTP constructions by introducing NWDGT, a no-wastage DGTOTP scheme tailored for the delayed-batch registration setting. It eliminates mount point wastage and supports offline verification, but at the cost of increased registration latency. We introduce this scheme first as a natural baseline in our pursuit of reducing wastage in DGTOTP designs. Next, we present LWDGT, a low-wastage DGTOTP construction designed for the instant-response registration setting. It preserves the security and offline-verification features of NWDGT without registration latency, making it suitable for latency-sensitive environments. Moreover, it achieves lower mount point wastage than the DGTOne scheme. The constructions of NWDGT and LWDGT are summarized in Fig. 2, where the part above the dashed line corresponds to the existing construction and the part below represents the additional construction proposed in this work, before we proceed to their detailed descriptions.

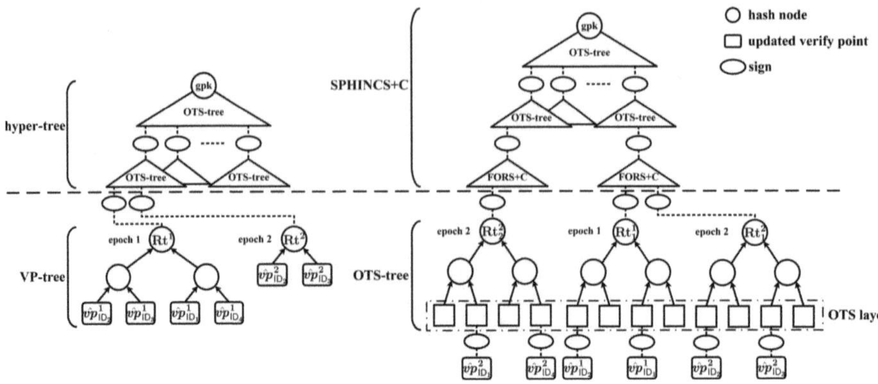

Fig. 2. Constructions of NWDGT (left) and LWDGT (right). In NWDGT, ID_1 and ID_4 leave the group in the 2nd verify epoch; in LWDGT with $U = 8$ and $l = 4$, ID_3 and ID_4 join the group in the 2nd verify epoch.

5.1 NWDGT

We outline the construction challenges and design ideas of NWDGT below. The detailed algorithms and security analysis of NWDGT are given in [17, Appendix B].

Construction Challenges and Ideas. In DGTOne scheme, fixed-size sub-trees are pre-generated per epoch under an assumed maximum group size. Leaves of these sub-trees serve as mount points, signing member-generated verification points. However, in dynamic environments with unpredictable member arrivals, this leads to unused mount points, violating *FG1*. A natural idea is to let sub-tree sizes adapt to actual registrations, but this raises new challenges: dynamic sub-tree generation must not alter group public key or disrupt enrolled members (*FG3*), and it must preserve anonymity, traceability, offline verification (*FG2*), and lightweight computation (*FG4*) in the presence of adaptive adversaries capable of registering honest or malicious members and corrupting honest members.

To address these issues, we propose a no-wastage DGTOTP scheme NWDGT. We implement a register-and-build-later (RBL) strategy by constructing each epoch's sub-tree dynamically based on the precise number of registered verification points to fulfill *FG1*. To fully implement the RBL strategy and facilitate the dynamic construction of epoch-specific sub-trees under the restriction of *FG3* and *FG4*, we adopt a hash-based hyper-tree structure used in SPHINCS+C [20]. This hyper-tree consists of several layers, where each layer's leaves are generated using a one-time signature (OTS) scheme. Specifically, the leaves on the lowest layer of this structure are used to sign the root of each sub-tree, and the leaves on higher layers sign the roots of the sub-trees below them.

Instead of signing each verification point individually, RA constructs a verification point tree (VP-tree) using all verification points of an epoch as its leaves and signs the VP-tree root using the hyper-tree. Since the epoch associated with each verification point is public and only verification points from different members within the same epoch need to be randomized, each epoch's VP-tree root is signed in order using the hyper-tree leaves. To ensure traceability, each verification point is bound to the member's encrypted identity before constructing the VP-tree, allowing RA to recover identities if necessary. To achieve *FG2*, RA generates and returns all necessary authentication credentials to group members before the beginning of each epoch. These credentials are sufficient for verifiers to authenticate members without needing to download any additional verification information or communicate with RA during the authentication process.

5.2 LWDGT

Construction Challenges and Ideas. While NWDGT eliminates mount point wastage via dynamic VP-tree construction, it incurs undesirable delays, problematic in latency-sensitive settings. Devices registering offline for future epochs must later reconnect solely to obtain credentials, increasing overhead, energy use, and degrading usability. To address this, we propose constructing multiple smaller sub-trees per epoch, enabling RA to process verification points in smaller clusters and thereby improving registration responsiveness while balancing mount point efficiency (*FG1*) and low-latency registration.

Nonetheless, this approach introduces new challenges. If RA still constructs multiple smaller VP-trees, it must wait for enough verification points to form each sub-tree. In sparse or unpredictable arrivals, members may face indefinite registration handling delays. Furthermore, reusing the hyper-tree from NWDGT and mounting sub-trees in a fixed order introduces privacy concerns, as the mounting sequence may reveal members' relative join times, potentially compromising their anonymity. One potential solution is to mount all sub-trees strictly according to their epoch index, ensuring that sub-trees for earlier epochs appear before those of later epochs. This would eliminate the correlation between registration time. However, this is difficult to enforce in practice, since RA cannot predict the number of members who will register in a given epoch. As a result, future preregistrations may cause later sub-trees to be built earlier. In such a case, to avoid delaying registration, RA must mount available sub-trees immediately, without waiting for sub-trees of earlier epochs. This unpredictability prevents RA from pre-allocating positions for earlier-epoch sub-trees, making it challenging to implement a mounting strategy that preserves privacy under dynamic registration.

To address these limitations, we propose a low-wastage DGTOTP scheme LWDGT based on one-time signature trees (OTS-trees). We implement a partitioned-build-on-demand (PBOD) strategy. The key idea is to allow RA to instantiate a small OTS-tree only when a registration event occurs, instead of constructing VP-trees that require a complete batch of verification points. This on-demand generation not only enables immediate processing of incoming registration requests but also avoids creating unnecessary mount points, thus fulfilling *FG1*. In this design, each verification point is signed and mounted by a leaf of a newly or existing OTS-tree associated with the corresponding epoch.

To preserve anonymity, a keyed permutation is applied to randomize member placement across OTS-trees. Specifically, each epoch is partitioned into U/l OTS-trees, where U is the maximum group size and l is the OTS-tree size. RA assigns each member a unique identifier and applies a keyed permutation uniquely for each epoch to shuffle the identifiers. The shuffled set is then divided into clusters of size l, determining randomized member positions across OTS-trees. This conceals registration timing and prevents inference of join order. To deal with potential collisions arising from random OTS-trees placement, we adopt the full SPHINCS+C. This ensures secure mounting and supports concurrent mounting of multiple OTS-trees while satisfying *FG4* under the restriction of *FG3*. As in NWDGT, traceability is achieved by binding each verification point to the encrypted identity before it is signed, and offline verification (*FG2*) is enabled because RA returns all authentication credentials to members at registration.

Detailed Construction. Both the digital signature SPHINCS+C and the one-time signature OTS used below share the syntax of digital signature. Below are the algorithms' details of our construction (pseudocodes of Join and Verify algorithms are given in Appendix A).

• $\mathsf{Setup}(1^\kappa, \mathsf{G}, \Delta_{pw}, \Delta_{vp}, T_s, T_e)$: RA samples a secret key k_{RA}, sets T_s to the current time T_c, and computes $E := \frac{(T_e - T_s)}{\Delta_{vp}}$ and $N := \frac{(T_e - T_s)}{\Delta_{pw}}$, where E denotes the number of TOTP instances and N denotes the number of passwords per instance. Next, RA initializes the building blocks including a pseudo-random function F as $\mathsf{pms}_{\mathsf{PRF}} := \mathsf{F.Setup}(1^\kappa)$, an authenticated symmetric encryption ASE as $\mathsf{pms}_{\mathsf{ASE}} := \mathsf{ASE.Setup}(1^\kappa)$, a collision-resistant hash function H as $\mathsf{pms}_{\mathsf{CRH}} := \mathsf{H.Setup}(1^\kappa)$, and a permutation PM as $\mathsf{pms}_{\mathsf{PM}} := \mathsf{PM.Setup}(1^\kappa)$. RA then generates the SPHINCS+C public key $pk_{\mathsf{SPHINCS+C}}$ by computing $(\mathsf{pms}_{\mathsf{SPHINCS+C}}, pk_{\mathsf{SPHINCS+C}}, sk_{\mathsf{SPHINCS+C}}) \leftarrow \mathsf{SPHINCS+C.Setup}(1^\kappa)$, with the SPHINCS+C secret key $sk_{\mathsf{SPHINCS+C}}$ also generated, and sets the group public key $\mathsf{gpk}_{\mathsf{G}} := pk_{\mathsf{SPHINCS+C}}$. Moreover, for each epoch, RA carries out the following preparation steps: (i) compute the i-th permutation key $k^i_{\mathsf{PM}} := \mathsf{F}(k_{\mathsf{RA}}, \text{“PM”} \| i)$ and the permuted set $S_i = \{s^i_1, \ldots, s^i_U\} := \mathsf{PM.Shuffle}(k^i_{\mathsf{PM}}, \{1, \ldots, U\})$; (ii) partition set S_i into $\frac{U}{l}$ clusters of size l, denoted by $Cl_i = \{\{s^i_1, \ldots, s^i_l\}, \{s^i_{l+1}, \ldots, s^i_{2l}\}, \ldots\}$.

Meanwhile, RA maintains the group management information GI_{G}, which includes a registration list $\mathrm{IDL}_{\mathsf{G}}$ for storing member identities and a set of variables $\{\mathrm{RS}_{s^i_j} := (pk^i_{s^i_j}, C^i_{s^i_j})\}_{j \in [U]}$ for currently active verify epochs. These variables are periodically updated by RA to remove expired entries and prepare for the next epoch. RA also manages a revocation list RL_{G}, a bit array of length U, where each bit (initialized to 0) indicates whether the corresponding member is revoked.

• $\mathsf{MInit}(\mathsf{ID}_j)$: Let τ denote the consecutive epochs a member must register during the current registration period. τ is pre-defined by the system through a fixed division of the system's lifetime, representing epochs required for registration at this time (e.g., epochs 1–10).[2] A group member ID_j first runs $(\mathsf{pms}_{\mathsf{PRF}}, k_{\mathsf{ID}_j}) \leftarrow \mathsf{Setup}(1^\kappa)$ to sample a random key $k_{\mathsf{ID}_j} \xleftarrow{\$} \mathcal{K}_{\mathsf{PRF}}$ as its secret key. For each epoch $i \in \tau$, ID_j runs $\mathsf{TOTP.Setup}(1^\kappa, T_i, T_i+\Delta_{vp}, \Delta_{pw})$ to initialize i-th TOTP instance, where $T_i = T_{i-1}+\Delta_{vp}$ and $T_0 = T_s$. Next, it computes i-th verification point $vp^i_{\mathsf{ID}_j} := \mathsf{TOTP.PInit}(sd^i_{\mathsf{ID}_j})$, where $sd^i_{\mathsf{ID}_j} := \mathsf{F}(k_{\mathsf{ID}_j}, \mathsf{ID}_j \| i)$ is the corresponding secret seed. This algorithm returns k_{ID_j} and $\mathsf{vps}_{\mathsf{ID}_j} = \{vp^i_{\mathsf{ID}_j}\}_{i \in \tau}$.

• $\mathsf{Join}(k_{\mathsf{RA}}, \mathsf{gpk}_{\mathsf{G}}, \mathsf{ID}_j, \mathsf{vps}_{\mathsf{ID}_j})$: We assume that all identities recorded in $\mathrm{IDL}_{\mathsf{G}}$ are ordered by their joining time. Namely, RA maps each member ID_j to a number $\alpha_{\mathsf{ID}_j} \in [U]$ based on its join order. Once the position of a member in $\mathrm{IDL}_{\mathsf{G}}$ is fixed, it remains unchanged throughout the lifespan of the group. For $i \in [E]$, RA handles registrations of all parties. Specifically, if a party ID_j submits registration of the i-th epoch, RA generates and returns the corresponding auxiliary information $\mathsf{Ax}_{\mathsf{ID}_j} = (\sigma^i_{\mathsf{ID}_j}, C^i_{\mathsf{ID}_j})$, where $\sigma^i_{\mathsf{ID}_j} := (\sigma^i_{\mathsf{OTS}}, \mathrm{Pf}^i_{\mathsf{ID}_j}, \sigma^i_{\mathsf{SPHINCS+C}})$. On receiving a party's registration request, RA does the following steps: (i) compute the i-th ASE key $k^i_{\mathsf{ASE}} := \mathsf{F}(k_{\mathsf{RA}}, \text{“ASE”} \| i)$, the identity ciphertext $C^i_{\mathsf{ID}_j} := \mathsf{ASE.Enc}(k^i_{\mathsf{ASE}}, \mathsf{ID}_j)$ (note that $\mathsf{ASE.Enc}$ is randomized, so $C^i_{\mathsf{ID}_j} \neq C^{i+1}_{\mathsf{ID}_j}$), and the updated verification point $\hat{vp}^i_{\mathsf{ID}_j} := \mathsf{H}(vp^i_{\mathsf{ID}_j} \| C^i_{\mathsf{ID}_j} \| i)$; (ii) find the index idx such that $s^i_{idx} = \alpha_{\mathsf{ID}_j}$, and generate l OTS key pairs $\{(pk^i_j, sk^i_j)\}$ for indices $j \in \left[l\left(\left\lceil \frac{idx}{l} \right\rceil - 1\right) + 1, \ldots, l\left\lceil \frac{idx}{l} \right\rceil\right]$ by initializing l independent OTS instances using $\mathsf{OTS.Setup}(1^\kappa)$; (iii) compute the OTS-tree $\mathrm{MT}^i_{\lceil \frac{idx}{l} \rceil} := \mathsf{MT.Build}(P_{\lceil \frac{idx}{l} \rceil})$, where $P_{\lceil \frac{idx}{l} \rceil} := \{pk^i_j\}_{j \in \{l(\lceil \frac{idx}{l} \rceil - 1)+1, \ldots, l\lceil \frac{idx}{l} \rceil\}}$; (iv) compute OTS signature $\sigma^i_{\mathsf{OTS}} := \mathsf{Sign}(sk^i_{idx}, \hat{vp}^i_{\mathsf{ID}_j})$ and the Merkle proof as $\mathrm{Pf}^i_{\mathsf{ID}_j} := \mathsf{MT.GetPf}(\mathrm{MT}_{\lceil \frac{idx}{l} \rceil}, pk^i_{idx})$; (v) compute $\mathsf{SPHINCS+C}$ signature $\sigma^i_{\mathsf{SPHINCS+C}} := \mathsf{SPHINCS+C.Sign}(sk_{\mathsf{SPHINCS+C}}, \mathrm{MT}_{\lceil \frac{idx}{l} \rceil})$.

• $\mathsf{GetSD}(k_{\mathsf{ID}_j}, T)$: This algorithm returns i-th secret seed $sd^i_{\mathsf{ID}_j} := \mathsf{F}(k_{\mathsf{ID}_j}, \mathsf{ID}_j \| i)$, where $i := \frac{T - T_s}{\Delta_{vp}}$ is the index of the TOTP instance.

• $\mathsf{PwdGen}(k_{\mathsf{ID}_j}, T)$: The party ID_j first computes the index as $i := \frac{T - T_s}{\Delta_{vp}}$. Next, it computes the secret seed $sd^i_{\mathsf{ID}_j} := \mathsf{F}(k_{\mathsf{ID}_j}, \mathsf{ID}_j \| i)$ and the password $\bar{pw}^{i,z}_{\mathsf{ID}_j} := \mathsf{TOTP.PGen}(sd^i_{\mathsf{ID}_j}, T_c)$, where $z := \frac{T_c - T_s - i \cdot \Delta_{vp}}{\Delta_{pw}}$ is the index of password in the i-th epoch. Then, the password $pw^{i,z}_{\mathsf{ID}_j} := (\bar{pw}^{i,z}_{\mathsf{ID}_j}, \sigma^i_{\mathsf{ID}_j}, C^i_{\mathsf{ID}_j})$ is returned.

• $\mathsf{Verify}(\mathsf{gpk}_{\mathsf{G}}, pw^{i,z}_{\mathsf{ID}_j}, T, \mathrm{RL}_{\mathsf{G}})$: The verifier first checks whether the member is revoked by consulting the local registration status list $\{\mathrm{RS}_{s^i_j}\}_{j \in [U]}$ maintained and published by RA. If valid, it verifies the correctness of the TOTP password and reconstructs the verification point for signature validation. Using the received Merkle proof $\mathrm{Pf}^i_{\mathsf{ID}_j}$ from member and the stored OTS-tree public key from registration status, it derives the corresponding OTS-tree root, which is then used to verify the $\mathsf{SPHINCS+C}$ signature for the epoch. Specifically, the verifier proceeds as follows: (i) return 0, if $C^i_{\mathsf{ID}_j}$ is not contained in $\{\mathrm{RS}_{s^i_j}\}_{j \in [U]}$; (ii) get the position idx such that

[2] Such design supports manual updates of group management information to verifiers at epoch boundaries, allowing them to operate offline.

RS_{idx} contains the identity ciphertext $C^i_{\mathsf{ID}_j}$; (iii) compute the verification point $vp^i_{\mathsf{ID}_j}$ from $\bar{pw}^{i,z}_{\mathsf{ID}_j}$ and T, and $\bar{vp}^i_{\mathsf{ID}_j} := \mathsf{H}(vp^i_{\mathsf{ID}_j} \| C^i_{\mathsf{ID}_j} \| i)$; (iv) compute the tree root Rt based on pk^i_{idx} and $\mathrm{Pf}^i_{\mathsf{ID}_j}$; (v) output 1, if and only if $\mathsf{TOTP.Verify}(vp^i_{\mathsf{ID}_j}, \bar{pw}^{i,z}_{\mathsf{ID}_j}, T) = 1$, $\mathsf{OTS.Verify}(pk^i_{idx}, \bar{vp}^i_{\mathsf{ID}_j}, \sigma^i_{\mathsf{OTS}}) = 1$, and $\mathsf{SPHINCS{+}C.Verify}(\mathsf{gpk_G}, Rt, \sigma^i_{\mathsf{SPHINCS+C}}) = 1$.

• $\mathsf{Revoke}(k_{\mathsf{RA}}, \mathsf{ID}_j, \mathsf{gpk_G}, \mathrm{RL_G}, \mathsf{GI_G})$: Let $\alpha_{\mathsf{ID}_j} := \mathrm{IDL_G}[\mathsf{ID}_j]$ denote the mapped number that corresponds to ID_j. To revoke a group member ID_j, RA sets $\mathrm{RL_G}[\alpha_{\mathsf{ID}_j}] := 1$, and stops updating RS relevant to ID_j in all future epochs.

• $\mathsf{IDOpen}(k_{\mathsf{RA}}, \mathsf{gpk_G}, pw^{i,z}_{\mathsf{ID}_j}, T)$: RA aborts if $\mathsf{Verify}(\mathsf{gpk_G}, pw^{i,z}_{\mathsf{ID}_j}, T, \mathrm{RL_G}) = 0$. Otherwise, RA returns $\mathsf{ID}_j := \mathsf{ASE.Dec}(k^i_{\mathsf{ASE}}, C^i_{\mathsf{ID}_j})$, where $k^i_{\mathsf{ASE}} := \mathsf{F}(k_{\mathsf{RA}}, \text{“ASE”} \| i)$.

Security Analysis. Our construction achieves both anonymity and traceability, as stated by the two theorems below.

Theorem 1. *Suppose that the building blocks* TOTP, H, PRF, SPHINCS+C, OTS, ASE, MT *and* PM *are secure, then* LWDGT *provides anonymity.*

The proof for Theorem 1 is in [17, Appendix D]. Here, we informally analyze how our scheme achieves anonymity. The prover authenticates by sending a password comprising four components: a TOTP password, an identity ciphertext, an OTS-tree signature, and a SPHINCS+C signature. The hash chain-based TOTP instances leverage a pseudo-random function to compute the secret seed, and compute the TOTP password and the verification point by a collision-resistant hash function. The output of the hash function and the ASE encryption algorithm contain randomness; thus, an attacker cannot distinguish the updated verification points of the honest members. Because of the employment of an unpredictable permutation function to determine the position of all updated verification points in the OTS-tree, an attacker cannot associate the SPHINCS+C signature and the OTS-tree signature with the updated verification points of the honest members and therefore cannot distinguish the correspondence between the verification points indicated by the leaf nodes of the OTS-tree mounted by SPHINCS+C and the honest members. Finally, since identity is encrypted by an ASE encryption algorithm, the attacker learns nothing about the identity from identity ciphertext.

Theorem 2. *Under the same assumptions as in Theorem 1,* LWDGT *provides traceability.*

The proof of Theorem 2 is in [17, Appendix E]. Here, we provide an informal analysis to convey the intuition behind the traceability property. Attackers cannot forge a valid password that can be traced to an honest group member. Due to the collision-resistant hash function, attackers are unable to forge a valid TOTP password. As a result of the employment of IND-CCA ASE encryption to generate group member identity ciphertext, attackers are unable to distinguish between group members; thus, they are unable to forge a password that binds to the identity of an honest group member. In addition, a secure OTS-tree scheme and a SPHINCS+C scheme make sure that attackers are unable to forge signatures of an OTS-tree and SPHINCS+C. On the other hand, RA can use its secret key to decrypt the identity ciphertext with ASE to trace the identity of the group member corresponding to the password.

6 Evaluation

Experiment Setup. We implement NWDGT and LWDGT[3] using the OpenSSL library and conduct experiments on a PC (AMD Ryzen 9 7945HX, 16 GB RAM) acting as RA and verifier, and a Raspberry Pi 3 emulating resource-constrained clients in mobile access scenarios, such as smartcards, IoT tokens, or embedded user devices. The TOTP scheme is instantiated with T/Key [21], SHA256 is used as the hash function, 128-bit AES-GCM-SIV [16] for authenticated symmetric encryption, and Fisher-Yates shuffle algorithm [13] for the permutation scheme.

In NWDGT, the HT follows the SPHINCS+C hyper-tree structure [20]. In LWDGT, SPHINCS+C is instantiated as full SPHINCS+C, with its WOTS+C for one-time signature scheme OTS. Based on our following theoretical analysis of mount point wastage, we set the size of each OTS-tree in LWDGT to $l = 2$ to minimize the expected waste rate during randomized sub-tree mounting.

We adopt the small-signature parameter set from the SPHINCS+C specification to ensure 128-bit security, minimizing client storage at the cost of slightly higher verification time. For both schemes, we set the total height of the hyper-tree to $h = 66$, the number of layers to $d = 11$, and the Winternitz parameter to $w = 128$. Following [10], the password interval is set to $\Delta_{pw} = 5$ seconds and the verification point lifespan to $\Delta_{vp} = 5$ minutes, yielding a password chain length $N = 60$. For LWDGT, which includes the FORS+C layer, we additionally configure the number of FORS trees as $k = 9$, the number of leaves per tree as $t = 2^{13}$, and the number of leaves in the optional extra FORS tree as $t' = 2^{18}$.

Theoretical Analysis of Wastage Rate. We analyze mount point efficiency using both analytical bounds and probabilistic modeling.

Theoretical Comparison. We define the overall wastage rate as $\text{Waste} = 1 - \frac{\sum_{i=1}^{E} x_i}{C}$, where x_i denotes the number of registrations in epoch i, E is the total number of epochs, and C is the total capacity provisioned across all epochs. This measures the fraction of unused mount points across the system lifespan. NWDGT incurs no wastage due to its adaptive registration strategy, while LWDGT may incur some wastage to support instant-response registration, but its wastage remains strictly bounded. Lemma 1 shows that, under equal registration counts across all epochs, the wastage rate under LWDGT never exceeds that of DGTOne.

Lemma 1. *Let U, E, and $l \in [2, U]$ be fixed. If* LWDGT *and DGTOne register same number of verification points per epoch, then* $\text{Waste}_{\mathsf{LWDGT}} \leq \text{Waste}_{\text{DGTOne}}$.

[3] Code is available at: https://github.com/LannisterArthur/Efficient-DGTOTP.

Proof. The overall wastage rate is defined as $\text{Waste} = 1 - \frac{\sum_{i=1}^{E} x_i}{C}$, where C denotes the total provisioned capacity across all epochs. Since both schemes register the same total number of points $\sum_{i=1}^{E} x_i$, the comparison reduces to their provisioned capacities C_{DGTOne} and C_{LWDGT}. DGTOne allocates U mount points per epoch, giving $C_{\text{DGTOne}} = U \cdot E$. In LWDGT, each epoch constructs up to $\frac{U}{l}$ sub-trees of size l, yielding $C_{\mathsf{LWDGT}} \leq U \cdot E = C_{\text{DGTOne}}$. Substituting these into the wastage rate definition gives

$$\text{Waste}_{\mathsf{LWDGT}} = 1 - \frac{\sum_{i=1}^{E} x_i}{C_{\mathsf{LWDGT}}} \leq 1 - \frac{\sum_{i=1}^{E} x_i}{C_{\text{DGTOne}}} = \text{Waste}_{\text{DGTOne}}.$$

That proves the lemma. □

While this bound guarantees that LWDGT never performs worse than DGTOne, it is important to analyze the probability of equality because achieving the same wastage rate implies that the same number of mount points remain unused as in DGTOne. This directly limits the number of members the verifier can authenticate offline and reduces overall mount point utilization, which is undesirable in mobile and offline scenarios.

For this purpose, we define event A_i as the case in epoch i where LWDGT provisions the same capacity as DGTOne under the same registrations x_i, i.e., $C^{(i)}_{\mathsf{LWDGT}} = C^{(i)}_{\text{DGTOne}} = U$. When $0 \leq x_i < \frac{U}{l}$, then LWDGT provisions only x_i sub-trees of size l, resulting in $C^{(i)}_{\mathsf{LWDGT}} < U = C^{(i)}_{\text{DGTOne}}$, and hence $\text{Waste}^{(i)}_{\mathsf{LWDGT}} < \text{Waste}^{(i)}_{\text{DGTOne}}$ in that epoch. When $\frac{U}{l} \leq x_i \leq U$, the probability that LWDGT provisions the full capacity $C^{(i)}_{\mathsf{LWDGT}} = U$ is

$$\mathbb{P}[A_i] = \frac{\sum_{j=0}^{U/l} (-1)^j \binom{U/l}{j} \frac{(U-jl)!}{(U-jl-x_i)!}}{\frac{U!}{(U-x_i)!}}.$$

Here, the denominator counts all possible assignments of the x_i registrations to the $\frac{U}{l}$ sub-trees (no restriction), while the numerator counts only those assignments in which every sub-tree receives at least one registration, obtained via the inclusion-exclusion principle.

Therefore, equality $\text{Waste}_{\mathsf{LWDGT}} = \text{Waste}_{\text{DGTOne}}$ occurs only if $x_i \in [\frac{U}{l}, U]$ for every epoch i, and LWDGT provisions full capacity in all such epochs. The overall probability is

$$\Pr\left[\text{Waste}_{\mathsf{LWDGT}} = \text{Waste}_{\text{DGTOne}}\right] = \prod_{i=1}^{E} \Pr[A_i] = \prod_{i=1}^{E} \begin{cases} 0, & 0 \leq x_i < \frac{U}{l}, \\ \mathbb{P}[A_i], & \frac{U}{l} \leq x_i \leq U, \end{cases}$$

which is negligible for realistic parameters (e.g., $E = 103{,}680$ in a year), showing that LWDGT almost always achieves strictly better mount point utilization in practice.

Expected Waste Under Probabilistic Modeling. To evaluate expected wastage under realistic deployment conditions, we choose parameters that reflect typical small-scale institutional settings. According to [8,27,33], a small company typically has at most 500 employees, which motivates setting the system maximum size $U = 500$. The average monthly number of new registrations $\beta \in \{5, 10, 15, 20\}$ represents typical hiring rates, how the organization grows over time. We model the number of registrations x_i per epoch as a Poisson random variable because it naturally describes count data for independent, sporadic events within a fixed interval [28]. Empirical studies show that small firms hire only a few employees per month on average [33], supporting the use of this model to represent employee growth.

We then construct a probabilistic model over $E = 12y$ epochs (one year with $y = 8640$ epochs per month). The number of registrations x_i follows a Poisson distribution with mean $\lambda_i = \alpha + i \cdot (\beta/y)$, where $\alpha \in [1, U]$ denotes the initial number of registered members. As a result, the probability of observing x_i registrations in epoch i is given by $P_i(x_i) = \frac{(\lambda_i)^{x_i} e^{-\lambda_i}}{x_i!}$. Expected capacity and wastage are computed by enumerating $x_i \in [\alpha, U]$ and weighting by $P_i(x_i)$.

In LWDGT, U members are divided into U/l sub-trees of size l. For registrations x_i, the expected number of used sub-trees is $\mathbb{E}[\text{Used Trees} \mid x_i] = \frac{U}{l} \cdot \left[1 - \binom{U-l}{x_i} / \binom{U}{x_i}\right]$. Thus corresponding capacity and waste are $C_i(x_i) = l \cdot \mathbb{E}[\text{Used Trees} \mid x_i]$ and $W_i(x_i) = C_i(x_i) - x_i$. Aggregating over x_i, we obtain the epoch-level expectations: $\mathbb{E}[W_i] = \sum_{x_i=\alpha}^{U} P_i(x_i) \cdot W_i(x_i)$, $\mathbb{E}[C_i] = \sum_{x_i=\alpha}^{U} P_i(x_i) \cdot C_i(x_i)$. Summing over all epochs, the total expected wastage ratio is $\mathbb{E}[\text{Waste}_{\mathsf{LWDGT}}] = \frac{\sum_{i=1}^{E} \mathbb{E}[W_i]}{\sum_{i=1}^{E} \mathbb{E}[C_i]}$.

For comparison, we evaluate the expected wastage rate under the DGTOne scheme, where each epoch utilizes a single Merkle tree of fixed capacity U. Then, the total expected wastage rate for DGTOne is $\mathbb{E}[\text{Waste}_{\text{DGTOne}}] = \frac{1}{E} \sum_{i=1}^{E} \left(1 - \frac{\mathbb{E}[x_i]}{U}\right) = 1 - \frac{1}{U \cdot E} \sum_{i=1}^{E} \mathbb{E}[x_i]$.

In Fig. 3, we compare the expected mount point wastage rates of LWDGT and DGTOne under different values of monthly registrations β and initial registered users α over one year. The results show that as α increases, the expected wastage rates of both schemes exhibit a decreasing tendency, and this trend persists across different β values, indicating that variations in monthly registration do not fundamentally alter the dependence of wastage rate on α. Moreover, the OTS-tree size l also affects the curves: larger l causes LWDGT to gradually approach the wastage of DGTOne, while smaller l leads to more pronounced differences. It is worth noting that even if some users revoke their registrations, the corresponding mount points remain occupied, so revocation does not affect the mount point wastage rate.

This difference in performance becomes particularly notable when the initial number of users is far below the system's maximum capacity ($\alpha \leq U/2$), a situation often observed in real-world small organizations where the workforce starts small and grows gradually [33]. As illustrated in Fig. 3, under these conditions, LWDGT can reduce the annual wastage rate by 12% to 41% when the monthly registration is lower ($\beta = 1\% \cdot U = 5$), and by 6% to 31% when the monthly registration is relatively large ($\beta = 4\% \cdot U = 20$).

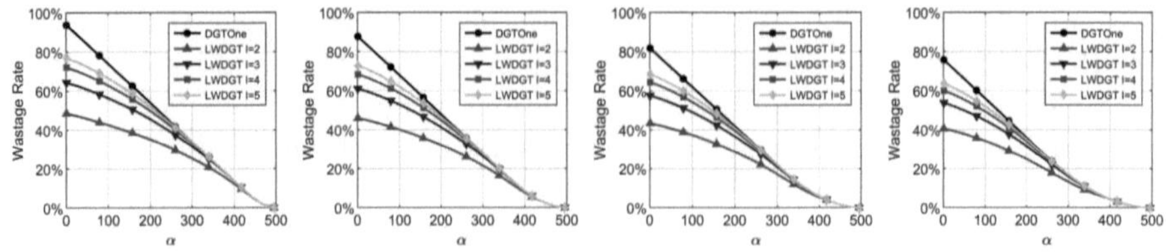

(a) β=5 (b) β=10 (c) β=15 (d) β=20

Fig. 3. Comparison of expected wastage rate.

Runtime Performance. We evaluate the computational efficiency of our schemes by measuring the runtime of their algorithms.

RA Setup time. The runtime of Setup is primarily determined by constructing the top-level tree of the hyper-tree, which involves generating the leaves and computing the root from these leaves. The time to generate each leaf depends on the Winternitz parameter ω of WOTS+C [20], which specifies the number of bits encoded per step in each WOTS+C hash chain. Larger ω values produce shorter signatures but require more hash evaluations per leaf, while smaller ω values reduce the number of hashes at the cost of longer signatures. The time to compute the top-level root depends on the tree height h/d, where h is the total height of the hyper-tree and d is the number of layers into which the hyper-tree is divided. Figure 4ashows that runtime increases exponentially with h/d, and that larger ω substantially increases runtime due to more hash computations per leaf. Because the hyper-tree is divided into layers, h/d remains small (typically less than 10), Setup is still practical.

Member Initialization Time. MInit in both schemes runs one Eval of PRF and N hash evaluations to initialize a TOTP instance in each epoch. In our experiments, we assume that a member registers for all E epochs, and Fig. 4bshows the computational cost measured on a Raspberry Pi for different TOTP chain lengths $N = 30$ and $N = 60$, representing shorter and longer TOTP chains, respectively. From the figure, it can be observed that the total runtime increases linearly with the number of epochs E. This linear growth occurs because each epoch's initialization requires a fixed amount of computation. Nonetheless, the measured per-epoch initialization time is approximately $0.07ms$ for $N = 30$ and $0.12ms$ for $N = 60$, demonstrating that MInit is still practical even for longer chains.

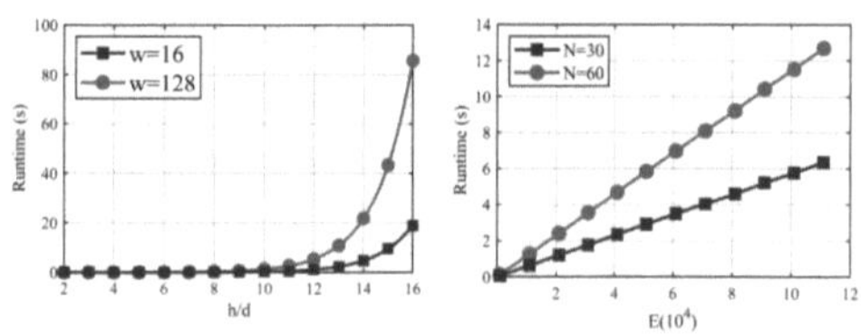

(a) Setup (b) MInit

Fig. 4. Runtimes of Setup and MInit.

Join Time. In both schemes, the Join algorithm begins by encrypting the member's identity using ASE, requiring one ASE encryption with runtime 0.57 μs. The subsequent credential generation differs between the two schemes. In NWDGT, RA aggregates registrations over an epoch and constructs a single VP-tree for all members. Once all registrations are collected, constructing the VP-tree and preparing credentials requires $U-1$ hash evaluations in the worst case or $U/2-1$ in the average case (for Merkle proof generation), along with a single hyper-tree signing operation to produce the associated signature. For $U = 2^{20}$, the total join cost for an epoch reaches 23.01s in the worst case and 12.29s in the average case. In LWDGT, credentials are generated immediately upon registration, requiring one hash evaluation for the updated verification point, one OTS-tree signing (with $l = 2$), and one SPHINCS+C signing computation, with per-join runtime approximately 1.07s.

Password Generation Time. Since RA handles the most expensive computations (i.e., credentials generation), members only need to compute TOTP passwords: one hash function in the average case, and one more F in the worst case to switch TOTP instances. The runtime is 1.54 μs (average) and 23.64 μs (worst).

Group Management Information Update Time. In both schemes, RA updates the registration status $\text{RS}_{s_j^i}$ in part of the join process. Since credential generation already produces the necessary verification materials, we assume RA stores these materials at registration time. Thus, updating group management information imposes no additional runtime overhead during verification and does not require separate update procedures. We further assume that each member submits verification points for a predefined time window (e.g., a month or a year) at registration. This allows RA to perform batch updates manually and periodically distribute group management information to verifiers. Such a design ensures that verifiers can operate offline without access to RA.

Password Verification Time. In NWDGT, verification begins with checking the TOTP password, requiring up to $N = 60$ hash evaluations in the worst case and $N/2$ on average. The verifier then computes one hash to derive the VP-tree leaf, followed by $\log U$ hash evaluations in the worst case or $\log(U/2)$ on average to compute the VP-tree root. Verification concludes with a hyper-tree signature check, which dominates the runtime. The difference between worst and average cases amounts to only 31 extra hash evaluations, corresponding to 2.56 μs, making the verification time effectively stable. The measured total verification time is approximately 7.54 ms. In LWDGT, the verifier similarly begins with TOTP password validation, followed by one hash computation for the updated verification point and one OTS signature verification algorithm to validate this value using the accompanying OTS signature. It then performs $\log l$ hash evaluations to compute the OTS-tree root, and finally runs one SPHINCS+C verification algorithm to verify the correctness of the SPHINCS+C signature on that root. The total runtime is approximately 8.05 ms.

Identity Open Time. The overhead of IDOpen in both schemes consists of the costs of the respective verification algorithm cost and one decryption of ASE. The runtime of one ASE.Dec is 0.55 μs.

Comparison. We compare our schemes with DGTOne [10] scheme in terms of several properties. Table 1 summarizes the comparison across four dimensions. These include whether it supports a dynamic group setting, whether it avoids mount point wastage, whether the verifier can operate without online connectivity, and how the registration process is handled by RA.

Table 1. Comparison of Properties.

Schemes	Group Setting	No Wastage	Offline Verifier Support	Registration Handling
DGTOne [10]	Dynamic	No	No	Immediate
NWDGT	Dynamic	Yes	Yes	Delayed
LWDGT	Dynamic	No	Yes	Immediate

Table 2 compares the performance of these schemes under worst-case (Wor) and average-case (Avg) settings. In evaluating setup costs, we compare the RASetup of DGTOne, and the Setup used by our two schemes, as all serve the purpose of group public key generation. We use 'Ae' and 'Ad' denote AES-GCM-SIV encryption and decryption algorithms, while 'Ss' and 'Se' denote AES setup and encryption algorithms. 'CHe', 'CHs', and 'CHc' correspond to the evaluation, setup, and collision-finding algorithms of the chameleon hash function. We denote the cost of permutation with 'PM'. Additionally, we use 'Wp', 'Ws', and 'Wv' to represent the public key generation, signing, and verification algorithms of WOTS+C, and 'Fs' and 'Fv' to denote the signing and verification algorithms of FORS+C. We use 'μ' and 'ν' denote '$E^{\frac{1}{d}}$' and '$2^{h/d}$'.

From the two tables, it is evident that both of our proposed schemes support dynamic group management and offline verifier functionality (not provided in DGTOne scheme) while maintaining low overhead. In particular, group public key generation in our schemes leverages a hyper-tree structure, where only a small tree at the top layer needs to be constructed, greatly reducing setup complexity. Password generation is lightweight, requiring only the generation of a TOTP password. Futhermore, expensive credential generation is handled by RA, keeping the schemes suitable for resource-constrained clients. Importantly, mount points are efficiently utilized: NWDGT achieves zero wastage, and LWDGT significantly reduces wastage compared to DGTOne, demonstrating practicality and scalability of our designs.

Table 2. Comparison of performance.

Schemes		Execution Time									Password size(Byte)
		RASetup	MInit	Revoke	Join	GetSD	PwdGen	GMUpdate	Verify	Open	
DGTOne	Avg	$6U\cdot E\cdot Ae+(U+1)Ae+E\cdot PM+U\cdot E\cdot CHe+U\cdot E\cdot CHs+(U\cdot E-1)H$	$1Ss$	$1Ae$	$1Se$	$1Se$	$30H$	$(9U+1)Se+1PM+U\cdot CHe+U\cdot Ae+U\cdot CHs$	$(32+\log^{U\cdot E})H+1CHe$	$(32+\log^{U\cdot E})H+1CHe+1Se+1PM+1Ad$	108
	Wor	$6U\cdot E\cdot Ae+(U+1)Ae+E\cdot PM+U\cdot E\cdot CHe+U\cdot E\cdot CHs+(U\cdot E-1)H$	$1Ss$	$1Ae$	$1Se$	$1Se$	$62H+1CHe+10Se+1Ae$	$(9U+1)Se+1PM+U\cdot CHe+U\cdot Ae+U\cdot CHs$	$(62+\log^{U\cdot E})H+1CHe$	$(62+\log^{U\cdot E})H+1CHe+1Se+1PM+1Ad$	
NWDGT	Avg	$\mu(Wp+H)$	$30E\cdot H+1Ss\cdot E$	$1Ae$	$d\mu(Wp+H)+d\cdot Ws+1PM+1Ae+U/2\cdot H$	$1Se$	$30H$	Performed in Join	$(30+\log^{\nu})H+d\cdot Wv$	$(30+\log^{\nu})H+d\cdot Wv+1Ad$	$76+4d+16\log^{\mu}+2048d/\log^{\nu}$
	Wor	$\mu(Wp+H)$	$60E\cdot H+2E\cdot Se$	$1Ae$	$d\mu(Wp+H)+d\cdot Ws+1PM+1Ae+U/2\cdot H$	$1Se$	$60H+2Se$	Performed in Join	$(61+\log^{\nu})H+d\cdot Wv$	$(61+\log^{\nu})H+d\cdot Wv+1Ad$	
LWDGT	Avg	$\nu(Wp+H)+E\cdot PM$	$30E\cdot H+1E\cdot Se$	$1Ae$	$(d\nu+1)Wp+(l+d\nu)H+1Fs+1Ae+d\cdot Ws$	$1Se$	$30H$	Performed in Join	$(30+l)H+1Fv+(d+1)Wv$	$(30+l)H+(d+1)Wv+1Fv+1Ad$	$86+4d+16\log^{l}+16(h+kl)+16h\log^{l}+4096d/\log^{\nu}$
	Wor	$\nu(Wp+H)+E\cdot PM$	$60E\cdot H+2Se\cdot E$	$1Ae$	$(d\nu+1)Wp+(l+d\nu)H+1Fs+1Ae+d\cdot Ws$	$1Se$	$60H+2Se$	Performed in Join	$(60+l)H+1Fv+(d+1)Wv$	$(60+l)H+(d+1)Wv+1Fv+1Ad$	

Acknowledgments. This work was supported by the National Key Research and Development Program of China under Grant No. 2025YFE0220300 and the National Natural Science Foundation of China under Grant No. 62372386.

A Pseudocodes of LWDGT

Algorithm 1: Join: Member Join Procedure

Input: k_{RA}, $\mathsf{gpk}_{\mathsf{G}}$, ID_j, $\mathsf{vps}_{\mathsf{ID}_j}$

Output: $\mathsf{Ax}_{\mathsf{ID}_j} = (\sigma^i_{\mathsf{ID}_j}, C^i_{\mathsf{ID}_j})$ where $\sigma^i_{\mathsf{ID}_j} := (\sigma^i_{\mathsf{OTS}}, \mathrm{Pf}^i_{\mathsf{ID}_j}, \sigma^i_{\mathsf{SPHINCS+C}})$

/* Step 1: Identity ciphertext and updated verification point generation */

$k^i_{\mathsf{ASE}} \leftarrow \mathsf{F}(k_{\mathsf{RA}}, \text{“ASE”}\|i)$;

$C^i_{\mathsf{ID}_j} \leftarrow \mathsf{ASE.Enc}(k^i_{\mathsf{ASE}}, \mathsf{ID}_j)$; // Randomized encryption, $C^i_{\mathsf{ID}_j} \neq C^{i+1}_{\mathsf{ID}_j}$

$\hat{vp}^i_{\mathsf{ID}_j} \leftarrow \mathsf{H}(vp^i_{\mathsf{ID}_j}\|C^i_{\mathsf{ID}_j}\|i)$;

/* Step 2: OTS key generation */

Find idx such that $s^i_{idx} = \alpha_{\mathsf{ID}_j}$;

Generate l OTS key pairs $\{(pk^i_j, sk^i_j)\}$ for $j \in [l(\lceil idx/l \rceil - 1) + 1, \ldots, l\lceil idx/l \rceil]$ using $\mathsf{OTS.Setup}(1^\kappa)$;

/* Step 3: Build OTS-tree */

$P_{\lceil idx/l \rceil} \leftarrow \{pk^i_j\}_{j \in \{l(\lceil idx/l \rceil - 1)+1, \ldots, l\lceil idx/l \rceil\}}$;

$\mathsf{MT}^i_{\lceil idx/l \rceil} \leftarrow \mathsf{MT.Build}(P_{\lceil idx/l \rceil})$;

/* Step 4: Signature and proof generation */

$\sigma^i_{\mathsf{OTS}} \leftarrow \mathsf{OTS.Sign}(sk^i_{idx}, \hat{vp}^i_{\mathsf{ID}_j})$;

$\mathrm{Pf}^i_{\mathsf{ID}_j} \leftarrow \mathsf{MT.GetPf}(\mathsf{MT}^i_{\lceil idx/l \rceil}, pk^i_{idx})$;

$\sigma^i_{\mathsf{SPHINCS+C}} \leftarrow \mathsf{SPHINCS+C.Sign}(sk_{\mathsf{SPHINCS+C}}, \mathsf{MT}^i_{\lceil idx/l \rceil})$;

return $(\sigma^i_{\mathsf{ID}_j}, C^i_{\mathsf{ID}_j})$ with $\sigma^i_{\mathsf{ID}_j} := (\sigma^i_{\mathsf{OTS}}, \mathrm{Pf}^i_{\mathsf{ID}_j}, \sigma^i_{\mathsf{SPHINCS+C}})$;

Algorithm 2: Verify: Verification Procedure

Input: $\mathsf{gpk}_{\mathsf{G}}$, $pw^{i,z}_{\mathsf{ID}_j}$, T, RL_{G}

Output: 1 if verification succeeds, 0 otherwise

/* Step 1: Revocation check */

if $C^i_{\mathsf{ID}_j} \notin \{RS_{s^i_j}\}_{j \in [U]}$ **then**

  return 0; // Member not valid or revoked

Find idx such that RS_{idx} contains $C^i_{\mathsf{ID}_j}$;

/* Step 2: Compute updated verification point */

$vp^i_{\mathsf{ID}_j} \leftarrow$ from $\bar{pw}^{i,z}_{\mathsf{ID}_j}$ and T;

$\bar{vp}^i_{\mathsf{ID}_j} \leftarrow \mathsf{H}(vp^i_{\mathsf{ID}_j}\|C^i_{\mathsf{ID}_j}\|i)$;

/* Step 3: Reconstruct OTS-tree root */

$Rt \leftarrow$ derived from $pk^i_{idx}, \mathrm{Pf}^i_{\mathsf{ID}_j}$;

/* Step 4: Verify TOTP password and signatures */

if $\mathsf{TOTP.Verify}(vp^i_{\mathsf{ID}_j}, \bar{pw}^{i,z}_{\mathsf{ID}_j}, T) = 1$ ***and*** $\mathsf{OTS.Verify}(pk^i_{idx}, \bar{vp}^i_{\mathsf{ID}_j}, \sigma^i_{\mathsf{OTS}}) = 1$ ***and*** $\mathsf{SPHINCS+C.Verify}(\mathsf{gpk}_{\mathsf{G}}, Rt, \sigma^i_{\mathsf{SPHINCS+C}}) = 1$ **then**

  return 1; // All checks succeed

else

  return 0; // Reject if any check fails

References

1. Backes, M., Hanzlik, L., Schneider-Bensch, J.: Membership privacy for fully dynamic group signatures. In: CCS, pp. 2181–2198. ACM (2019)
2. Bellare, M., Micciancio, D., Warinschi, B.: Foundations of group signatures: Formal definitions, simplified requirements, and a construction based on general assumptions. In: EUROCRYPT, pp. 614–629. Springer (2003)
3. Bellare, M., Rogaway, P.: The security of triple encryption and a framework for code-based game-playing proofs. In: EUROCRYPT, pp. 409–426. Springer (2006)
4. Bellare, M., Shi, H., Zhang, C.: Foundations of group signatures: the case of dynamic groups. In: CT-RSA, pp. 136–153. Springer (2005)
5. Boneh, D., Boyen, X., Shacham, H.: Short group signatures. In: CRYPTO, pp. 41–55. Springer (2004)
6. Boneh, D., Shacham, H.: Group signatures with verifier-local revocation. In: CCS, pp. 168–177. ACM (2004)
7. Bootle, J., Cerulli, A., Chaidos, P., Ghadafi, E., Groth, J.: Foundations of fully dynamic group signatures. J. Cryptol. **33**(4), 1822–1870 (2020)
8. Bort, J., Wiklund, J., Yu, W.: Firm growth and the job satisfaction of the startup workforce. Strateg. Manag. J. (2025)
9. Camenisch, J., Drijvers, M., Hajny, J.: Scalable revocation scheme for anonymous credentials based on N-times unlinkable proofs. In: WPES@CCS, pp. 123–133. ACM (2016)
10. Cao, X., et al.: Dynamic group time-based one-time passwords. IEEE Trans. Inf. Forensics Secur. **19**, 4897–4913 (2024)
11. Chaum, D., van Heyst, E.: Group signatures. In: EUROCRYPT, pp. 257–265. Springer (1991)
12. Chen, L., Dong, C., Newton, C.J.P., Wang, Y.: Sphinx-in-the-head: group signatures from symmetric primitives. ACM Trans. Priv. Secur. **27**(1), 11:1–11:35 (2024)
13. Fisher, R.A., Yates, F.: Statistical tables for biological, agricultural and medical research, pp. 26–27. Oliver & Boyd, Third edn. (1948)
14. Garms, L., Lehmann, A.: Group signatures with selective linkability. In: Public Key Cryptography (1). LNCS, vol. 11442, pp. 190–220. Springer (2019)
15. Groth, J.: Fully anonymous group signatures without random oracles. In: ASIACRYPT, pp. 164–180. Springer (2007)
16. Gueron, S.: AES-GCM-SIV implementations (128 and 256 bit) (2018). https://github.com/Shay-Gueron/AES-GCM-SIV
17. Guo, J., Cao, X., Li, Z., Zhou, Y., Yang, Z., Zhou, J.: Registration-optimized dynamic group time-based one-time passwords for mobile access. Cryptology ePrint Archive, Paper 2026/595 (2026). https://eprint.iacr.org/2026/595
18. He, Y., Ling, S., Tang, K.H., Wang, H.: Everlasting fully dynamic group signatures. In: ACNS (3). LNCS, vol. 15827, pp. 3–28. Springer (2025)
19. Hesse, J., Singh, N., Sorniotti, A.: How to bind anonymous credentials to humans. In: USENIX Security Symposium, pp. 3047–3064. USENIX Association (2023)
20. Hülsing, A., Kudinov, M.A., Ronen, E., Yogev, E.: SPHINCS+C: compressing SPHINCS+ with (almost) no cost. In: SP, pp. 1435–1453. IEEE (2023)
21. Kogan, D., Manohar, N., Boneh, D.: T/key: Second-factor authentication from secure hash chains. In: CCS, pp. 983–999. ACM (2017)
22. Kumar, V., Li, H., Park, J.J., Bian, K., Yang, Y.: Group signatures with probabilistic revocation: a computationally-scalable approach for providing privacy-preserving authentication. In: CCS, pp. 1334–1345. ACM (2015)

23. Lamport, L.: Password authentication with insecure communication. Commun. ACM **24**(11), 770–772 (1981)
24. Liu, J.K., Chu, C., Chow, S.S.M., Huang, X., Au, M.H., Zhou, J.: Time-bound anonymous authentication for roaming networks. IEEE Trans. Inf. Forensics Secur. **10**(1), 178–189 (2015)
25. M'Raihi, D., Machani, S., Pei, M., Rydell, J.: TOTP: time-based one-time password algorithm (2011). https://tools.ietf.org/html/rfc6238
26. M'Raïhi, D., Bellare, M., Hoornaert, F., Naccache, D., Ranen, O.: HOTP: an HMAC-based one-time password algorithm. RFC **4226**, 1–37 (2005)
27. Murmann, J.P., Korn, J., Worch, H.: How fast can firms grow? Jahrbücher für Nationalökonomie und Statistik **234**(2–3), 210–233 (2014)
28. Nisbet, R., Miner, G., Yale, K.: Chapter 10 - numerical prediction. In: Nisbet, R., Miner, G., Yale, K. (eds.) Handbook of Statistical Analysis and Data Mining Applications (Second Edition), pp. 187–213. Academic Press, Boston, second edition Edn. (2018)
29. Odelu, V., Das, A.K., Goswami, A.: A secure biometrics-based multi-server authentication protocol using smart cards. IEEE Trans. Inf. Forensics Secur. **10**(9), 1953–1966 (2015)
30. Rodríguez, J.G., Krenn, S., Slamanig, D.: To pass or not to pass: privacy-preserving physical access control. Comput. Secur. **136**, 103566 (2024)
31. Sun, H., Sun, K., Wang, Y., Jing, J.: TrustOTP: transforming smartphones into secure one-time password tokens. In: CCS, pp. 976–988. ACM (2015)
32. Tolosana, R., Vera-Rodríguez, R., Fiérrez, J.: BioTouchPass: handwritten passwords for touchscreen biometrics. IEEE Trans. Mob. Comput. **19**(7), 1532–1543 (2020)
33. Wheat, C., Farrell, D.: The Ups and Downs of Small Business Employment: Big Data on Payroll Growth and Volatility. JPMorgan Chase & Co., Institute (2017)
34. Yang, Q., et al.: AnFRA: anonymous and fast roaming authentication for space information network. IEEE Trans. Inf. Forensics Secur. **14**(2), 486–497 (2019)
35. Yang, Z., Jin, C., Ning, J., Li, Z., Dinh, A., Zhou, J.: Group time-based one-time passwords and its application to efficient privacy-preserving proof of location. In: ACSAC, pp. 497–512. ACM (2021)
36. Zeng, M., Cui, J., Zhang, Q., Zhong, H., He, D.: Efficient revocable cross-domain anonymous authentication scheme for IIoT. IEEE Trans. Inf. Forensics Secur. **20**, 996–1010 (2025)
37. Zhang, Q., Wu, J., Zhong, H., He, D., Cui, J.: Efficient anonymous authentication based on physically unclonable function in industrial internet of things. IEEE Trans. Inf. Forensics Secur. **18**, 233–247 (2023)

Adaptive Image Steganography Based on CNN and GAN Architecture and Lightweight Frequency-Domain Encryption

Mimoun Hamdi[1(✉)], Iheb Gharbi[1,2], and Safya Belghith[2]

[1] Military Research Center, Taeib Mhiri, Aouina, 2045 Tunis, Tunisia
my.hamdi@gmail.com

[2] National Engineering School of Tunis, El Manar University, Farhat Hached El Manar, Tunis, Tunisia

Abstract. In this work, we propose a novel image steganography framework based on adaptive embedding of a secret image into a cover image using a Convolutional Neural Network (CNN) and Generative Adversarial Network (GAN). The system dynamically selects optimal embedding zones and enhances the visual and structural fidelity of the reconstructed secret image Unlike conventional approaches that rely on fixed embedding regions or uniform coefficient allocation, the proposed approach adopts a content-aware, block-based embedding strategy that jointly optimizes imperceptibility, robustness, and payload capacity. For each pair of secret and cover blocks, transformed and quantized frequency coefficients are analyzed by a trained CNN to identify the most suitable insertion area based on texture complexity and spectral characteristics. To ensure confidentiality and strengthen resistance to steganalytic attacks, the coefficients of the secret blocks are encrypted using a lightweight and efficient algorithm prior to embedding, guaranteeing that the hidden information remains unintelligible even if successfully extracted. Additionally, the GAN-based refinement module is used to enhance the visual quality of the restored secret image. Experimental evaluations demonstrate that the proposed model achieves high stego-image quality, strong resilience to compression and noise attacks, and accurate secret-image reconstruction.

Keywords: Image steganography · Adaptive embedding · Convolutional Neural Network (CNN) · Generative Adversarial Network (GAN) · Lightweight encryption · Multimedia data security

1 Introduction

The exponential growth of digital communication, coupled with the widespread availability of high-resolution visual content, has intensified the demand for secure, covert, and high-capacity information exchange. Traditional cryptographic systems ensure confidentiality but do not conceal the existence of communication, making protected data vulnerable to interception, censorship, or adversarial analysis. In contrast, steganography, the art of hiding information within innocuous visual media, offers an additional

Y. Cao et al. (Eds.): SecureComm 2026, LNICST 704, pp. 598–616, 2027.
https://doi.org/10.1007/978-3-032-32764-2_27

security layer by embedding secret content in a manner that preserves perceptual transparency. Steganographic techniques have therefore become essential in applications such as military communication, biomedical data sharing, digital forensics, privacy-preserving multimedia transmission, and secure cloud storage, where sensitive information can be covertly embedded and shared within multimedia files [1]. Although most digital file formats can theoretically be used as carriers for steganography, those exhibiting high redundancy are generally the most suitable. In this regard, four major categories of formats stand out for their ability to effectively conceal information: text, image, audio, and video formats.

Conventional image steganography frameworks predominantly operate in the spatial or frequency domain and often follow predetermined embedding patterns, fixed payload distributions, or statistically uniform insertion models. While these approaches may provide high visual quality under ideal conditions, they generally suffer from three major limitations: vulnerability to steganalysis due to predictable embedding structures, reduced robustness against compression, filtering, or noise distortions, and insufficient adaptability to textural variations within the cover image, which restricts embedding capacity or degrades imperceptibility. Moreover, many existing schemes assume deterministic reconstruction of the secret content, overlooking information losses introduced by quantization, encryption, and transformation processes.

The choice of the Discrete Cosine Transform (DCT) as a transformation technique in image steganography is of particular importance. DCT allows the distribution of image energy across frequency coefficients, which facilitates the embedding of secret data into high-frequency coefficients while preserving the visual quality of the stego image. The DCT-2D is widely employed in many applications, including JPEG, HEVC, AV1, and MPEG. Indeed, according to various studies and industry estimates, more than 72% of images exchanged on the Internet (social networks, websites, messaging platforms, etc.) rely on JPEG compression based on the DCT. According to the recent report in November 2025 by W3Techs [2]. However, DCT has certain limitations: it can be vulnerable to more sophisticated attacks, and excessive embedding in high-frequency coefficients may degrade the perceptual quality of the image.

Recent advances in deep learning have motivated the integration of neural architectures, particularly Convolutional Neural Networks (CNNs) and Generative Adversarial Networks (GANs), into steganographic systems [3–5]. CNNs have demonstrated strong capabilities in semantic feature extraction, texture classification, and signal prediction, enabling more intelligent and adaptive embedding strategies [6]. Likewise, GAN-based generators and discriminators have shown remarkable performance in visual refinement, perceptual enhancement, and distribution alignment, making them promising candidates for improving secret-image recovery [7]. However, most existing neural approaches focus on global image-level embedding rather than fine-grained structural adaptation, limiting their flexibility and scalability.

To address these challenges, this work introduces a novel content-aware, block-based image steganography framework that combines CNN-guided adaptive embedding with GAN-driven reconstruction refinement. The proposed model dynamically analyzes the frequency-domain characteristics of each cover block to identify the most suitable insertion region based on texture complexity, spectral energy distribution, and human visual sensitivity. The decoder subsequently restores the secret image and employs a GAN refinement module to recover lost structural details, reduce quantization artifacts, and enhance perceptual fidelity. Before embedding, the frequency coefficients of the secret image undergo a secure encryption process to protect data confidentiality and ensure resistance against steganalytic attacks, even if extraction occurs. The choice of the encryption technique remains one of the major challenges in this approach. The encryption must be lightweight, so as not to burden the overall process, fast, to meet real-time processing requirements, and secure, to resist decoding and statistical attacks. The goal is to design an encryption mechanism optimized for multimedia data stream environments, where computational resources and latency are critical factors. The trade-off between security, efficiency, and performance thus represents a key design consideration in our adaptive concealment system.

Experimental results confirm that the proposed framework achieves high visual quality for stego images, maintains strong resistance to common image-processing attacks, and reconstructs the secret image with high fidelity, outperforming several leading steganographic techniques in terms of PSNR, SSIM, and embedding capacity.

The remainder of this paper is organized as follows: Sect. 2 reviews the fundamental concepts of image steganography and the measures related to coefficient transformation and quantization. Section 3 analyzes existing steganographic approaches, including spatial-domain, frequency-domain, and deep learning–based methods. The proposed adaptive framework is then described in Sect. 4 and Sect. 5, detailing the concealment, encryption, extraction, and reconstruction processes. Finally, extensive experimental evaluations are conducted under fixed and adaptive embedding scenarios, including visual analysis, quantitative metrics, and comparative performance assessment with state-of-the-art methods.

2 Overview of Image Steganography

2.1 Basic Concepts of Image Steganography

Image steganography is a technique that allows secret information to be hidden within a digital image in such a way that the presence of the embedded data remains imperceptible to the human visual system. The core idea is to exploit the redundancy and tolerance of the visual medium, enabling small and carefully controlled modifications to be introduced without noticeably altering the appearance of the image.

In a typical steganographic process (Fig. 1), the image used to conceal the secret information is referred to as the cover image, while the resulting image containing the hidden message is known as the stego image. The embedding procedure involves selecting specific components of the image, commonly the least perceptually significant elements such as the least significant bits in spatial-domain methods or certain transform-domain coefficients, and replacing or adjusting them according to the secret data.

A robust steganographic system aims to achieve these essential objectives:

- Cryptographic confidentiality refers to the protection of the secret information through encryption mechanisms prior to embedding. Its objective is to prevent unauthorized parties from recovering the hidden content even if the embedded data is extracted.

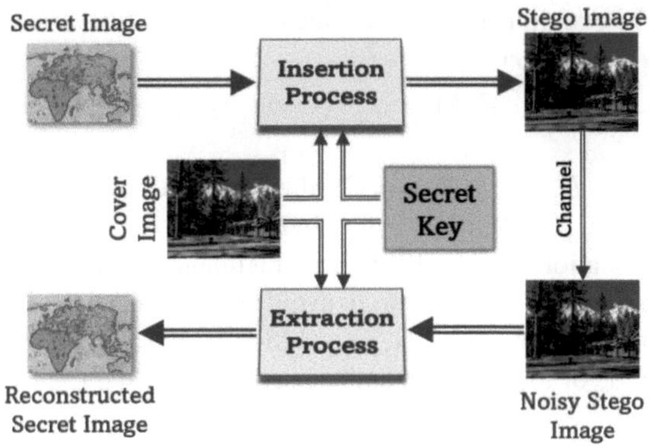

Fig. 1. Typical steganographic process.

- Steganographic imperceptibility denotes the ability of the embedding process to conceal the presence of hidden information without introducing perceptible distortions in the cover image. An imperceptible stego image should remain visually indistinguishable from the original cover image and preserve similar statistical characteristics.
- Robustness describes the ability of the embedded information to remain recoverable after common signal processing operations such as compression, noise addition, filtering, or resizing.
- Capacity, maximizing the amount of data that can be embedded.
- Resistance to steganalysis refers to the capability of a steganographic method to avoid detection by statistical or machine-learning-based steganalysis techniques that attempt to distinguish stego images from natural images.

To satisfy these requirements, various embedding strategies and domain transformations (e.g., DCT, DWT, or hybrid methods) are employed to balance visual quality and resilience against steganalysis. Overall, image steganography provides a discreet and secure communication channel by hiding information in plain sight, leveraging the rich structure and redundancy inherent in digital images.

2.2 Measures Associated with Coefficient Transformation and Quantization

The normalized Discrete Cosine Transform (DCT) applied to an $N \times N$ block is computed as defined in Eq. (1).

$$C(u, v) = \alpha(u)\alpha(v) \sum_{x=0}^{N-1} \sum_{y=0}^{N-1} r(x, y) \cos\left(\frac{(2x+1)u\pi}{2N}\right) \cos\left(\frac{(2y+1)v\pi}{2N}\right) \quad (1)$$

where:

- $\alpha(0) = \sqrt{\frac{1}{N}}, \alpha(k) = \sqrt{\frac{2}{N}}, k > 1,$
- $r(x, y)$: spatial pixel intensity or the residue obtained after prediction for the video,
- $C(u, v)$: DCT frequency coefficient.

According to the equation and since cosine terms lie within $[-1, +1]$, it follows that $|C(u, v)| \leq \alpha(u)\alpha(v) \sum_{x,y} |r(x, y)|$.

Typically $r(x, y) \in [-R, R], \sum_{x,y} |r(x, y)| \leq N^2 R$, we obtain $|C(u, v)| \leq \alpha(u)\alpha(v)N^2 R$.

For the coefficient DC $(u = 0, v = 0)$, this yields $|C(u, v)| \leq NR$. Therefore, for coefficients $AC(u > 0, v > 0)$, $|C(u, v)| \leq 2NR$.

In common applications such as JPEG, an 8-bit image contains values in [0,255]. The DCT is designed to operate around zero to avoid a large DC peak. Thus, centered pixel values are computed as $r_c(x, y) = r(x, y) - 128 \in [-128, +127]$. which significantly reduces the amplitude of the DC term and consequently of the DCT coefficients.

JPEG then divides each coefficient by the corresponding entry in the quantization table:

$$C_Q(u, v) = \text{round}\left(\frac{C(u, v)}{Q(u, v)}\right) \tag{2}$$

For the standard table, $Q(u, v)$ ranges approximately from 10 to 120. As a result, quantized coefficients typically fall within $[-204, +204]$.

The matrix of quantized coefficients in a JPEG block directly reflects the local content of the image. In a smooth or uniform area, most of the energy is concentrated in the low frequencies: the DC coefficient is high, while the AC coefficients are very small and often 95% to 100% become 0 after quantification. Near an edge or a sharp transition, only a few low and mid-frequency AC coefficients take non-zero values to represent the abrupt variation. The coefficients have small values and are generally up to plus or minus 10. High frequencies often remain zero.

In contrast, in a textured or highly detailed region, a larger number of AC coefficients, including high-frequency ones, retain significant values after quantization, because the image contains many fine variations. Low-frequency coefficients generally exhibit the highest values, typically ranging from ± 5 to ± 20, as they capture the dominant variations of the texture. The mid-frequency coefficients also retain significant amplitudes, often between ± 3 and ± 10, reflecting the richness of intermediate details. Finally, even the high-frequency coefficients, usually suppressed in smooth regions, remain often non-zero in textured areas, with typical values around ± 1 to ± 5, indicating the local complexity of the textured pattern.

After quantization, the DC coefficient remains non-zero and highly stable. In practice, its magnitude is significantly larger than that of the AC coefficients, i.e., $| DC | \gg | AC |$, reflecting its dominant contribution to the block's overall intensity structure.

3 Comparative Analysis of Related Steganographic Methods

Image steganography has evolved from simple spatial-domain techniques to advanced hybrid and deep-learning-based schemes. Despite significant progress, existing methods still struggle to jointly satisfy imperceptibility, robustness, embedding capacity, and resistance to modern steganalysis. This section provides a concise comparison of representative approaches.

3.1 Spatial-Domain Techniques

Early methods rely on manipulating pixel values directly, such as Least Significant Bit (LSB) replacement or matching. Surveys such as [8] and [9] highlight their simplicity and high embedding capacity. However, these approaches exhibit low robustness, as lossy compression, filtering, or resizing can easily destroy the embedded data. They are also highly vulnerable to statistical steganalysis, making them unsuitable for applications requiring strong security guarantees [10].

To overcome the inherent limitations of conventional LSB-based spatial techniques, several works have investigated hybrid schemes that integrate Pixel Value Differencing (PVD) with LSB embedding [11–13]. These approaches aim to enhance embedding adaptivity by exploiting local pixel variations while preserving the simplicity and high payload of LSB methods. To enhance security, [14] propose a multi-level image steganography approach that combines LSB embedding with hybrid encryption mechanisms (AES and Blowfish) and pixel randomization. This strategy increases the confidentiality of the hidden data by complicating both the embedding process and the structure of the concealed message, thereby making unauthorized extraction significantly more difficult. The approach in [15] combines an adaptive inverted LSB substitution strategy with a pre-embedding encryption stage. Specifically, the secret message is first encrypted using the RC4 stream cipher before being embedded according to the selected adaptive pattern.

3.2 Frequency-Domain Techniques

To enhance imperceptibility and robustness, numerous works embed information in the transform domain, particularly using DCT, DWT, or combinations thereof. Approaches such as [16] and [17] combine DCT with LSB to improve capacity, yet often neglect cover-image quality. Hybrid DCT–DWT schemes [18, 19] offer superior imperceptibility but at the cost of increased computational complexity and limited payload. Moreover, frequency-coefficient statistics remain exploitable by modern steganalysis tools.

Techniques integrating SVD (e.g., [20, 21]) further improve robustness but suffer from high computational overhead. Systems combining AES encryption with DWT–DCT–SVD [22] enhance security but increase algorithmic complexity. [23].

3.3 Deep Learning–Based and Adversarial Steganography Methods

Deep learning has introduced new paradigms, particularly GAN-based steganography. The ISGAN framework [4] uses adversarial training to reduce the statistical detectability of stego images. [5] provides a comprehensive survey of GAN-based image steganography, categorizing existing methods into cover modification, cover selection, and cover synthesis strategies, and discussing their characteristics, evaluation metrics, challenges, and future research directions.

More recent adversarial approaches, such as UT-GAN [24], generate an initial stego image and refine it through cost-function adaptation using DCTR gradients. These models demonstrate improved resistance to advanced steganalysis but lack guaranteed bit-level message recovery and require extensive computational resources. The method proposed by [6] combines a deep learning–based encoding module with an LSB spatial-domain embedding technique, which enhances noise robustness and slightly improves imperceptibility. However, despite the integration of deep learning, the approach remains limited in several essential aspects. First, the LSB technique is inherently vulnerable to modern steganalysis tools, which compromises the confidentiality and protection of the embedded secret data. Second, the hybridization of heterogeneous mechanisms introduces significant computational complexity without providing a real improvement in efficiency or security.

A growing body of research focuses on combining frequency-domain embedding with deep neural networks. CNN–DCT schemes, such as those proposed in [25], leverage Inception-V3 to guide multi-watermarking insertion, improving robustness in medical imagery. The CNN–DCT framework in [26] uses convolutional feature extraction to determine optimal embedding regions, achieving higher PSNR and SSIM compared to purely spatial or purely deep-learning approaches.

Other hybrid GAN–DCT approaches [26, 27] aim to preserve imperceptibility by refining stego images via adversarial learning. While these methods enhance visual quality, they still face challenges related to exact recovery of the concealed data, cryptographic integration before embedding, and high computation requirements.

4 Description of the Proposed Adaptive Approach

The proposed method relies on an adaptive and intelligent strategy driven by contextual analysis of the image content and operating within the intermediate band of the DCT frequency spectrum after quantization. This approach dynamically adjusts the embedding parameters according to the local characteristics of the image, such as texture, edges, or smooth regions, in order to optimally exploit the energy distribution of the AC coefficients. By specifically targeting this intermediate frequency band, the method ensures an optimal balance between robustness, imperceptibility, and embedding capacity.

4.1 Concealment of Secret Informations

The different steps of the hiding process and the generation of the stego image are illustrated in Fig. 2. A convolutional neural network (CNN) is employed within the Deep Feature Analysis (DFA) module to analyze the quantized coefficients of each $N \times N$ pixel block from both the cover image COV_IMG and the secret image SEC_IMG, and to extract relevant local features from each. Based on these descriptors, the module dynamically determines:

- The optimal insertion area for embedding the significant coefficients of SEC_IMG into the mid- or high-frequency part of COV_IMG. To ensure synchronization between the encoder and decoder, this adaptive area is defined as a triangular area of n rows and n columns.
- The number of AC coefficients of COV_IMG to be retained, denoted as $NZ_c = n(n+1)/2$, which corresponds to the number of nonzero coefficients, or sometimes a smaller number, particularly for highly textured blocks. This reduction ensures that enough space is preserved for inserting the most significant coefficients NZ_S extracted from the SEC_IMG.

The insertion of the significant coefficients of the secret image in the stego image is performed diagonal line by diagonal line, starting from the $(n+1)^{th}$ diagonal. Each diagonal line (an arrangement of AC coefficients) with index k is identified by the kth row and the kth column ($k \geq 2$), where $k - (n+1) = 0, 1, 2, \ldots,$. Diagonal lines with indices $k \leq 8$ contain k coefficients, while those with indices $k > 8$ contain $16 - k$ coefficients.

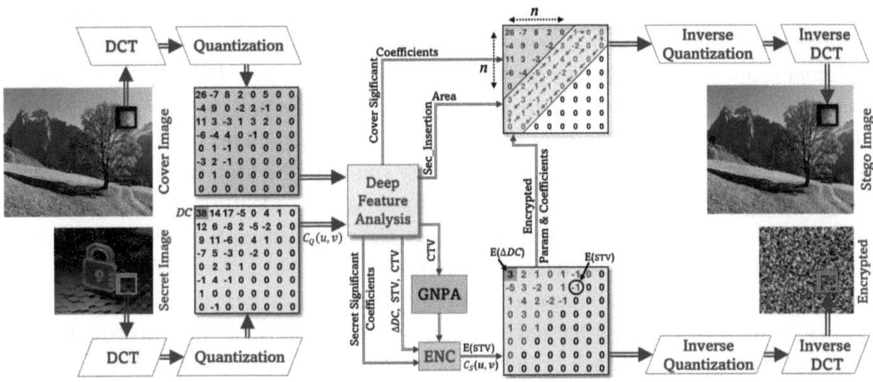

Fig. 2. Pipeline of the proposed method for adaptive insertion in the DCT domain.

4.2 Encryption of the Secret Image's AC Coefficients

The proposed approach relies on an adaptive data-hiding scheme operating in the DCT transform domain, combined with selective encryption of both the magnitudes and signs of AC coefficients. The magnitudes are protected using modular encryption, while the signs are processed through an independent deterministic encryption scheme.

The encryption of the secret image's AC coefficients is based on a Pseudo-Random Number Generator PRNG(r), which produces values $x_i \in \{0,1,\ldots,r\}$. The encryption algorithm for the signs of $C_s(u,v)$, (Eq. (3)), relies on a conditional inversion controlled by the pseudo-random generator PRNG(1).

$$\mathrm{E}(\mathrm{sign}(\mathrm{C_S}(\mathrm{u},\mathrm{v}))) = \mathrm{sign}(\mathrm{C_S}(\mathrm{u},\mathrm{v})) \times (-1)^{\mathrm{PRNG}(1)} \quad (3)$$

Each quantized secret coefficient $C_S(u,v)$ is encrypted using the encryption function ENC, defined by Eqs. (4).

$$C_{s\_enc}(u,v) = \mathrm{sign}(C_S(u,v)) \times (-1)^{\mathrm{PRNG}(1)} \times ((|C_S(u,v)| + \mathrm{PRNG}(\mathrm{CTV})) \bmod q) \quad (4)$$

CTV and $q = \mathrm{CTV} + 1 - (k - (n+1))$, two positive values, are dynamically determined by the DFA module. This adaptation ensures that the pseudo-random values remain within the same range as the AC coefficients of the cover image in the insertion area, thereby preserving both visual quality and compressibility. C_{s_enc} is always within the modulo range: $C_{s\_enc} \in [0, q-1]$, $q > 1$.

The modular factor q, which gradually decreases from one diagonal line to the next ($q = \mathrm{CTV}+1,\ \mathrm{CTV},\ \mathrm{CTV}-1,\ \mathrm{CTV}-2, \ldots$), helps reduce the amplitude of encrypted coefficients as we move toward higher frequencies. When $q = 1$, any remaining secret coefficients $C_S(u, v)$ that are still nonzero, usually very close to zero, are forced to zero to avoid overloading the high-frequency region and to maintain the efficiency of JPEG coding.

4.3 Appending and Encrypting of the End-of-AC Indicator

To ensure the reliable extraction of the secret image's AC coefficients by delimiting the embedding region, it is necessary to append an additional value at the end of the coefficient sequence inserted into each block of the stego image. Indeed, the number of secret coefficients to embed varies from one block to another, and the encryption process based on modular computation may generate encrypted coefficients equal to zero, which can be confused with the natural zeros typically found in the high-frequency region of the cover image. To prevent this ambiguity, a fixed value is added immediately after the last quantized AC coefficient of the secret image, serving as an explicit marker indicating the end of the embedded secret data in the block.

Moreover, this appended value also serves as the Secret Threshold Value (STV $\in \{-2, -1, +1, +2\}$), allowing the decoder to infer the discrepancy or ratio between the quantized content of each block of the secret image (SEC_IMG) and the corresponding CTV threshold. This parameter is exploited by the decoder to accurately reconstruct the original secret AC coefficients, given that the modulo operation is non-invertible and inherently discards information. The CTV value is taken as reference for the reconstruction of the corresponding SEC_IMG blocks. Four possible STV states are defined in Table 1.

Table 1. Classification of STV States According to SEC_IMG, COV_IMG, and CTV Contents

STV value	COV_IMG Content Type		
	Smooth/Uniform	Edge/Sharp transition	highly detailed/ Textured
−2	Close, without significant difference	Exceeds, with a moderate margin	Significantly lower
−1	Slightly lower	Close, without significant difference	Exceeds, with a moderate margin
+1	Significantly lower	Slightly lower	Close, without significant difference
+2	$\|\Delta DC\|/2$ greatly exceeds CTV (indicating a significant texture change in SEC_IMG from one block to another)		

To protect against differential and frequency analysis attacks, it is useful to encrypt the STV parameter. The encryption method used is defined by Eq. (5).

$$E(\text{STV}) = \text{sign}(\text{STV}) \times (-1)^{\text{PRNG}(1)} \times [1 + (|\text{STV}| + \text{PRNG}(1) \bmod 2)] \quad (5)$$

4.4 Encryption of the Difference ΔDC of Secret Image

The encryption of the DC coefficient relies on computing the DPCM difference, denoted as $\Delta DC = C_Q^{\text{current}}(0,0) - C_Q^{\text{previous}}(0,0)$, between the current block's DC value and that of the previous block. This operation generates a residual that typically lies within a reduced range, making it more compact than the absolute DC values. This residual value is divided by 2 in order to reduce its amplitude and optimize its statistical manipulability. The encryption is then applied to this reduced value using the same pseudo-random number generator, ensuring a controlled perturbation consistent with the encryption scheme adopted for the AC coefficients.

$$\mathrm{E}\left(\frac{\Delta DC}{2}\right) = \mathrm{sign}\left(\frac{\Delta DC}{2}\right) \times (-1)^{\mathrm{PRNG}(1)} \times \left(\left|\frac{\Delta DC}{2}\right| + \mathrm{PRNG}(\mathrm{CTV})\, mod\, (\mathrm{CTV}+1)\right) \tag{6}$$

An exception is introduced when STV $= +2$. In this case, the ΔDC undergoes further quantization and the ciphertext value $\mathrm{E}\left(\frac{\Delta DC}{4}\right)$ is transmitted instead $\mathrm{E}\left(\frac{\Delta DC}{2}\right)$. Furthermore, the quantized coefficients $C_Q(u, v)$ of the corresponding block are transmitted without encryption, because STV $= +2$ does not indicate any textual relationship between CTV and the content of SEC_IMG, but signals this particular condition. Since STV is itself encrypted, the confidentiality of the block is not compromised, ensuring that this exception does not weaken the overall security or robustness of the concealment scheme.

5 Extraction of the Secret Informations

5.1 Feature and Parameters Extraction

The extraction phase begins with the Feature and Parameters Extraction module, which compares the stego image with the cover image in order to identify the starting position of the encrypted secret coefficients, delimited by the encrypted threshold STV. This same module, incorporating a CNN, then estimates the CTV threshold from the content of COV_IMG. This threshold is subsequently used to decrypt the encrypted coefficients $C_{s\_enc}^{-1}(u, v)$ as well as ΔDC. The next step applies adaptive amplification to reconstruct the secret coefficients $\tilde{C}_Q(u, v)$ and bring them closer to their original values prior to embedding $C_Q(u, v)$. Finally, the GAN network is employed to refine and enhance the visual quality of the recovered secret image. All extraction steps are illustrated in Fig. 3.

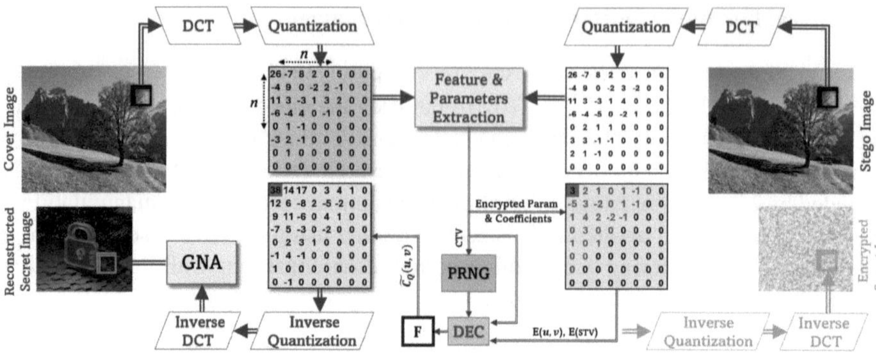

Fig. 3. Extraction steps and reconstitution of secret image.

5.2 Decryption of Secret Informations

Equations (7), (8), and (9) illustrate the decryption operations applied to the encrypted secret information.

$$\mathrm{STV} = \mathrm{sign}(\mathrm{E}(\mathrm{STV})) \times (-1)^{\mathrm{PRNG}(1)} \times [1 + (|\mathrm{E}(\mathrm{STV})| - \mathrm{PRNG}(1)\, mod\, 2)] \quad (7)$$

$$\Delta DC = 2 \times \mathrm{sign}\left(\mathrm{E}\left(\frac{\Delta DC}{2}\right)\right) \times (-1)^{\mathrm{PRNG}(1)} \times \left(\mathrm{E}\left(\frac{\Delta DC}{2}\right) - \mathrm{PRNG}(\mathrm{CTV})\, mod\, (\mathrm{CTV}+1)\right) \quad (8)$$

$$\lceil C_s^{-1}(u, v) \rceil = (|C_s(u, v)| - \mathrm{PRNG}(q-1))\, mod\, q \quad (9)$$

The extraction process begins similarly to the embedding phase, using decreasing values of q. q is the common encryption module for the encoder/decoder. It is imperative that the pseudo-random number generators (PRNGs) used during decryption strictly follow the same activation order and remain perfectly synchronized with those employed during encryption, in order to ensure the exact retrieval of the secret coefficients.

5.3 Reconstruction of the Quantified Secret Content $\tilde{C_Q}(u, v)$ by Adaptive Amplification

The reconstruction of the coefficients $\tilde{C_Q}(u, v)$ is performed by the function F, depicted in the extraction steps architecture and illustrated by Eq. (10).

$$\tilde{C_Q}(u, v) = \mathrm{sign}(\mathrm{E}(C_s(u, v))) \times (-1)^{\mathrm{PRNG}(1)} \times \left(\left|C_s^{-1}(u, v)\right| + round(\alpha \times q)\right) \quad (10)$$

α is the compensation amplifier, adapted to the texture of the secret block. It is selected from the values in Table 2 according to the content of the secret block relative to the reference value CTV.

Table 2. Parameter α according to the SEC_IMG and CTV contents.

Comparison of SEC_IMG content with CTV	α
Significantly lower	$-1/2$
Slightly lower	$-1/3$
Comparable, with no significant difference	0
Exceeds, with a moderate margin	$+1/2$
Significantly exceeds	+2

5.4 Enhancement of the Secret Image After Restoration

After the extraction of the secret data from the stego image, the recovered content may exhibit flaws or distortions due to the encryption process and modular arithmetic, which can shift some coefficients outside their original ranges. In this context, a Generative Adversarial Network (GAN) plays a crucial role in restoring and enhancing the visual quality of the secret image. Through its generator–discriminator structure, the GAN can reconstruct textures and fine details, correcting anomalies caused by quantization or coefficient shifts. The generator focuses on producing a visually coherent reconstruction of the secret image, whereas the discriminator identifies residual artifacts in the reconstructed output, thereby driving a constructive adversarial learning process. Thus, it ensures that the retrieved secret image is visually faithful to the original, while maintaining the structural coherence of the data.

6 Assessing the Performance of the Proposed Approach

6.1 Simulation and Evaluation Methodology for Fixed and Adaptive Embedding Approaches

To rigorously assess the performance of the proposed approach, a dedicated experimental platform was developed to execute the embedding and extraction processes under two distinct simulation scenarios. The first scenario evaluates the classical embedding strategy using a fixed embedding region, whereas the second focuses on assessing the adaptive embedding mechanism. The development environment was designed to ensure reproducibility, modularity, and efficient experimentation.

The platform was implemented using the Anaconda distribution, a widely adopted open-source Python ecosystem in scientific computing. It provides a robust environment integrating essential libraries such as NumPy, Torch, PIL, and scikit-image, enabling efficient numerical computation, image processing, and deep learning workflows. Torch, in particular, was used to define, train, and optimize the convolutional neural networks (CNNs) and generative adversarial networks (GANs). Its flexible tensor operations, automatic differentiation capabilities, and CPU-accelerated computation make it well suited for this task.

The evaluation was conducted using JPEG-based encoding. A comprehensive set of complementary metrics was employed in order to analyze performance along three axes: fidelity, imperceptibility, and robustness. The metrics include:

- MSE (Mean Squared Error): quantifies average squared difference between the original image I (cover or secret) and the processed image K (stego or reconstructed secret): $MSE = \frac{1}{M \times N} \sum_{i=1}^{M} \sum_{j=1}^{N} \left[I(i,j) - K(i,j)\right]^2$; M, N: image dimensions. Lower values indicate higher fidelity.
- MAE (Mean Absolute Error): measures average absolute deviation without overemphasizing large errors: $MAE = \frac{1}{M \times N} \sum_{i=1}^{M} \sum_{j=1}^{N} |I(i,j) - K(i,j)|$.
- PSNR (Peak Signal-to-Noise Ratio): logarithmic indicator of reconstruction quality; higher values correspond to better visual quality: $PSNR(8\,bits) = 10 \log_{10}\left(\frac{255^2}{MSE}\right)$.
- SSIM (Structural Similarity Index Measure): evaluates perceptual similarity by integrating luminance, contrast, and structural components. It is defined within the range [0, 1], where a value close to 1 indicates a high structural similarity with the reference image.
- BPP (Bits Per Pixel): quantifies the embedding capacity in steganography, representing the average number of secret bits embedded per pixel of the cover image. It provides a normalized measure of embedding efficiency, independent of the image size.
- Difference Maps: visualize spatial deviations between cover and stego images, highlighting regions affected by embedding.
- Histograms: compare pre- and post-embedding intensity distributions to reveal frequency-domain perturbations.

The visual, quantitative, and comparative results obtained are presented below, demonstrating the effectiveness of the proposed adaptive approach relative to the conventional fixed-region embedding method.

6.2 Dataset Description

To ensure the reliability of the experimental evaluation, the DIV2K dataset was selected as the benchmark. DIV2K is widely regarded as a high-quality reference dataset for high-resolution image processing tasks. Originally designed for image super-resolution and restoration, it offers strong visual diversity and rich structural content. The dataset contains 800 high-resolution training images and 100 validation images. The images, with resolutions reaching up to 2K, span a broad range of scenes including natural landscapes, urban environments, complex objects, fine textures, and heterogeneous structures. This diversity makes DIV2K an appropriate testbed for evaluating the robustness, generalization capability, and adaptability of the proposed approach. In our experimental setup, for each scenario the 800 training images were evenly partitioned into two sets: 400 images used as cover images and the remaining 400 as secret images to be embedded.

6.3 Visual Evaluation and Analysis of Metric Outcomes

This section presents the visual and quantitative results obtained from the simulations to evaluate the performance of the proposed approach. Visual inspection of the original, secret, and stego images, together with histogram analysis, provides a qualitative assessment of visual fidelity and embedding imperceptibility. Additionally, objective metrics such as MSE, PSNR, and SSIM quantitatively measure the induced distortion and the structural and perceptual quality of the resulting images.

The first row of Fig. 4 presents the cover image used in the simulation along with its corresponding histogram. The subsequent rows in the same figure illustrate the stego images and their associated histograms obtained under the two applied scenarios, enabling a visual comparison of the effects induced by each embedding strategy.

Figure 4 illustrates that the fixed embedding strategy, implemented in the first scenario, introduces local distortions in the luminance histogram, particularly at low-intensity levels. In contrast, the adaptive strategy better preserves the luminance statistical distribution, leading to improved imperceptibility and increased robustness against histogram-based steganalysis.

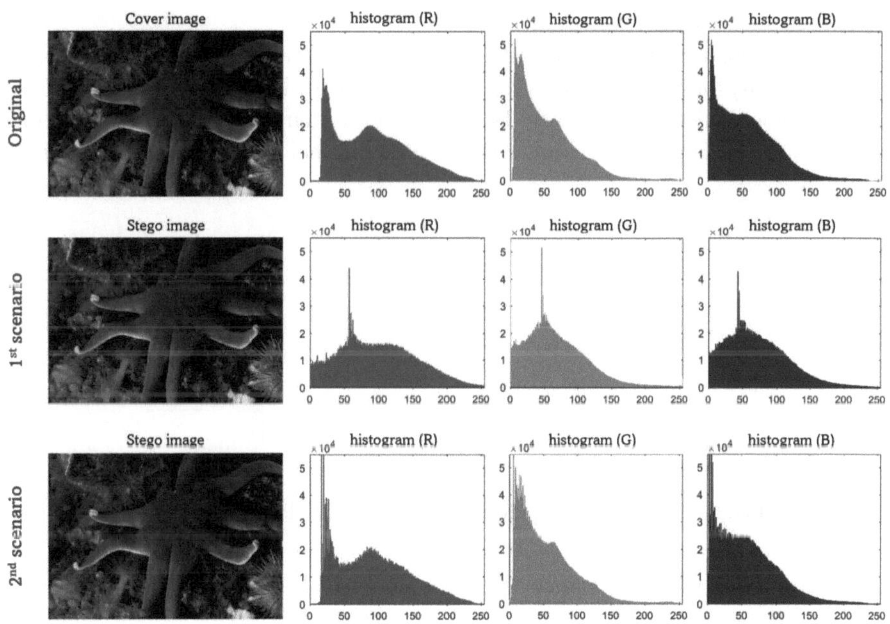

Fig. 4. Cover and stego images along with their corresponding color histograms.

Our proposed method is based on the DCT and quantization. During the inverse computation, a quantization error is introduced, which may cause relatively slight modifications in the histograms of the stego images and the reconstructed secret images.

The original secret image used in the simulation and the reconstructed secret image obtained during the extraction phase under our proposed approach (the second scenario) are presented in Fig. 5, along with their corresponding R, G, and B histograms, shown in the first and second rows, respectively. For optimal performance, it may be beneficial to resize the secret image to better adapt it to the embedding and extraction processes.

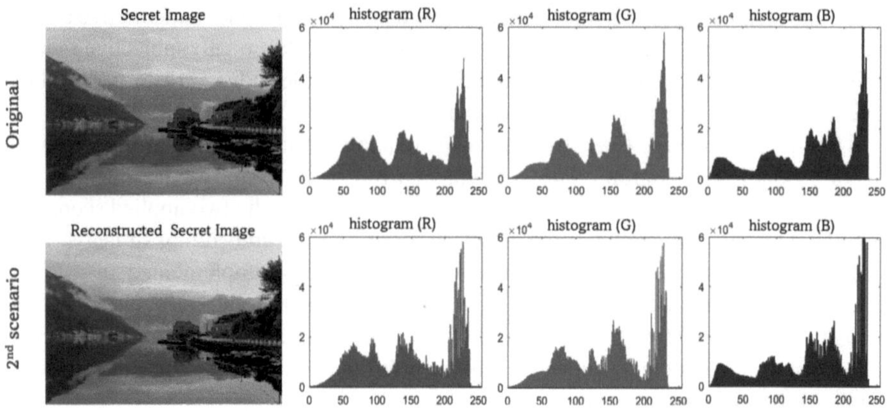

Fig. 5. Secret and reconstructed secret images along with their corresponding color histograms.

The performance of the proposed system was evaluated using block-based metrics, specifically MSE, PSNR and MAE as presented in Fig. 6. The results indicate that each block exhibits a relatively low MSE and a high PSNR, demonstrating that the reconstructed image closely approximates the original secret image with minimal distortion.

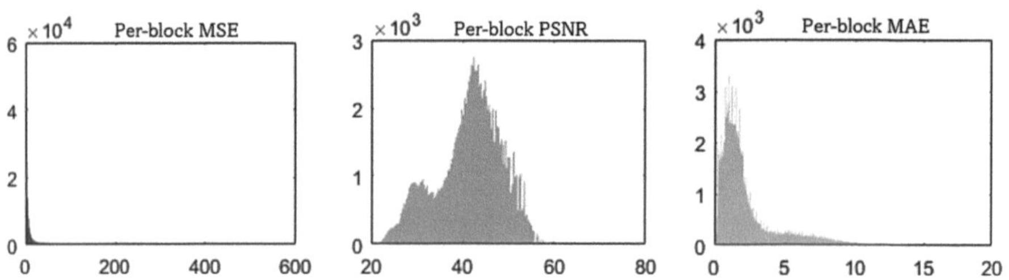

Fig. 6. Block-wise evaluation results using MSE, PSNR and MAE.

6.4 Comparison of Performance

Tables 3 and 4 present a comparative evaluation between the proposed approach and existing methods in terms of resistance to analysis attacks and image quality, where the analysis tests are applied to both the stego image and the reconstructed secret image. The performance is assessed using standard image quality metrics, including MSE, PSNR, and SSIM.

Table 3. Analysis of stego image performance

Approaches	Used methods	PSNR	SSIM (%)	Bpp	Encryption
[3]	CNN	21.6–36.3	85.1–99.5	2	None
[6]	LSB, DL	16.2–26.3	74.4–96.3	2.6	None
[12]	LSB, PVD	32.2–38.1	–	3.20–3.69	Medium
[13]	LSB, PVD	69.2–70.8	–	3.55	Not sure
[15]	LSB, RC4	52.4–57.4	99.99	1	Medium
[23]	DCT, Chaotic Map	29.9–41.7	–	2.3	Low
[27]	DCT, GAN	58.27	94.2	1	Medium
[28]	LSB, ACO, AES, RSA	59.7–64.5	99.98	0.4	High
Fixed insertion	DCT, GAN	31.2–35.7	82.1–93.4	100%	High
Proposed adaptive insertion	DCT, CNN, GAN	40.4–46.6	97.57–99.88	100%	High

Table 4. Analysis of reconstructed secret image performance

Approaches	Use methods	PSNR	SSIM (%)	Bpp	Encryption
[6]	LSB, DL	61.8–62.4	99.99–100	2.6	None
[29]	GAN	34.6–39.8	84.0–91.0	0.96–2.36	None
Proposed	DCT, CNN, GAN	42.5–51.3	98.1–99.98	100%	High

The proposed framework achieves a high and flexible embedding capacity by enabling the concealment of an entire secret image within a cover image, even when their spatial resolutions differ. When the secret and cover images share identical dimensions, the effective payload reaches approximately 8 bits per pixel (Bpp). However, this capacity is not fixed and can either exceed or fall below 8 bpp depending on the relative sizes of the two images. Specifically, when the secret image is resized to a higher or a lower resolution than the cover image. The embedding capacity achieved by the proposed method significantly exceeds that of conventional spatial-domain and hybrid steganographic techniques.

Our approach is distinguished by an encryption design based on a GPNA, specifically conceived to withstand transmission errors while ensuring a balanced trade-off between performance, security, and computational efficiency. The adoption of a stream-cipher–based encryption scheme confines the impact of channel disturbances to only the corrupted data, thereby enhancing overall system robustness. Furthermore, the encryption time remains controlled, as it primarily depends on the complexity of the employed pseudo-random number generator. Even with a lightweight generator, an adequate level of security is guaranteed, since the modulo operation maps the secret data into the same value range as the cover image data, significantly reducing detectability.

In comparison with recent approaches such as [6, 13, 28], and [27], which demonstrate good imperceptibility and robustness performance, the proposed method provides a more effectively managed security level. In particular, schemes relying on strong encryption algorithms (e.g., AES-GCM, RSA-OAEP, and elliptic-curve cryptography) introduce high computational complexity and substantial processing overhead, whereas other approaches fail to ensure sufficient protection of the embedded secret data. Although a PSNR exceeding 30 dB generally indicates that the embedded information is visually imperceptible and difficult to detect, focusing solely on increasing PSNR is not sufficient. The essential objective is to ensure a fully secured steganographic framework that incorporates efficient encryption with a reasonable encryption speed, while preserving imperceptibility, robustness, and overall system efficiency.

7 Conclusion

This work proposed a novel adaptive and content-aware image steganography approach based on a deep learning–guided block-wise embedding strategy. By combining a CNN-driven adaptive embedding mechanism, capable of analyzing local frequency-domain characteristics and human visual system sensitivity, with a GAN-based refinement module dedicated to secret image reconstruction through structural detail restoration and artifact reduction, the proposed model effectively achieves a balanced trade-off between imperceptibility, robustness, and visual quality.

The experimental results conclusively confirm the superiority of the proposed approach over conventional methods. Both quantitative and qualitative analyses demonstrate a significant improvement in performance, in terms of perceptual fidelity as well as resistance to distortions and attacks, highlighting the relevance of dynamically adapting quantization and embedding to the local image content.

Thus, this adaptive approach represents a notable advancement in the field of intelligent steganography, paving the way for a new generation of methods capable of simultaneously aligning with the technical constraints of communication systems and human perceptual models.

Disclosure of Interests. The authors have no competing interests to declare that are relevant to the content of this article.

References

1. Liao, X., Yin, J., Chen, M., Qin, Z.: Adaptive payload distribution in multiple images steganography based on image texture features. IEEE Trans. Dependable Secure Comput. **19**(2), 897–911 (2020)
2. LNCS. https://w3techs.com/technologies/overview/image_format. Accessed 01 May 2026
3. Duan, X., Liu, N., Gou, M., Wang, W., Qin, C.: SteganoCNN: image steganography with generalization ability based on convolutional neural network. Entropy **22**(10), 1140 (2020)
4. Zhang, R., Dong, S., Liu, J.: Invisible steganography via generative adversarial networks. Multimedia Tools Appl. **78**(7), 8559–8575 (2019)

5. Liu, J., et al.: Recent advances of image steganography with generative adversarial networks. IEEE Access **8**, 60575–60597 (2020)
6. Sanjalawe, Y., Al-E'mari, S., Fraihat, S., Abualhaj, M., Alzubi, E.: A deep learning-driven multi-layered steganographic approach for enhanced data security. Sci. Rep. **15**(1), 4761 (2025)
7. Volkhonskiy, D., Nazarov, I., Burnaev, E.: Steganographic generative adversarial networks. In: Twelfth International Conference on Machine Vision (ICMV 2019), vol. 11433, pp. 991–1005. SPIE (2020)
8. Aslam, M.A., et al.: Image steganography using least significant bit (LSB)-a systematic literature review. In: 2022 2nd International Conference on Computing and Information Technology (ICCIT), pp. 32–38. IEEE (2022)
9. Bansal, K., Agrawal, A., Bansal, N.: A survey on steganography using least significant bit (LSB) embedding approach. In: 2020 4th International Conference on Trends in Electronics and Informatics (ICOEI) (48184), pp. 64–69. IEEE (2020)
10. Rafat, K.F., Sajjad, S.M.: Advancing reversible LSB steganography: addressing imperfections and embracing pioneering techniques for enhanced security. IEEE Access (2024)
11. Chefranov, A.G., Öz, G.: Adaptive to pixel value and pixel value difference irreversible spatial data hiding method using modified LSB for grayscale images. J. Inf. Secur. Appl. **70**, 103314 (2022)
12. Wu, W., Li, H.: A novel scheme for random sequential high-capacity data hiding based on PVD and LSB. Signal Image Video Process. **18**(3), 2277–2287 (2024)
13. Khedr, A.E., Abdel-Aziz, M.M., Alsubaei, F.S., Eltoukhy, M.M., Hosny, K.M.: Securing color medical images using data hiding method based on modified Octa-PVD and hyperchaotic system. Alex. Eng. J. **125**, 133–151 (2025)
14. Alanzy, M., Alomrani, R., Alqarni, B., Almutairi, S.: Image steganography using LSB and hybrid encryption algorithms. Appl. Sci. **13**(21), 11771 (2023)
15. Rustad, S., Syukur, A., Andono, P.N.: Inverted LSB image steganography using adaptive pattern to improve imperceptibility. J. King Saud Univ. Comput. Inf. Sci. **34**(6), 3559–3568 (2022)
16. Khan, S., et al.: On hiding secret information in medium frequency DCT components using least significant bits steganography. Comput. Model. Eng. Sci. **118**(3), 529–546 (2019)
17. Venugopala, P.S., Raghavendra, S., Kubihal, V.: Enhancing secure medical data communication through integration of LSB and DCT for robust analysis in image steganography. IEEE Access (2024)
18. Mohammed, A.O., Hussein, H.I., Mstafa, R.J., Abdulazeez, A.M.: A blind and robust color image watermarking scheme based on DCT and DWT domains. Multimedia Tools Appl. **82**(21), 32855–32881 (2023)
19. Sharma, S., Zou, J.J., Fang, G.: A novel multipurpose watermarking scheme capable of protecting and authenticating images with tamper detection and localisation abilities. IEEE Access **10**, 85677–85700 (2022)
20. Awasthi, D., Srivastava, V.K.: LWT-DCT-SVD and DWT-DCT-SVD based watermarking schemes with their performance enhancement using Jaya and Particle swarm optimization and comparison of results under various attacks. Multimedia Tools Appl. **81**(18), 25075–25099 (2022)
21. Kumar, K.P., Kanhe, A.: Secured speech watermarking with DCT compression and chaotic embedding using DWT and SVD. Arab. J. Sci. Eng. **47**(8), 10003–10024 (2022)
22. Khassaf, N.M., Ali, N.H.M.: Multilevel text protection system using AES and DWT-DCT-SVD techniques. Mesop. J. CyberSecur. **5**(3), 913–926 (2025)
23. Kaur, R., Singh, B.: A novel approach for data hiding based on combined application of discrete cosine transform and coupled chaotic map. Multimedia Tools Appl. **80**(10), 14665–14691 (2021)

24. Tan, L., Li, Y., Zeng, Y., Chen, P.: An adaptive JPEG steganography algorithm based on the UT-GAN model. Electronics **14**(20), 4046 (2025)
25. Fan, Y., et al.: A multi-watermarking algorithm for medical images using inception V3 and DCT. Comput. Mater. Continua **74**(1) (2023)
26. Ahmad, S., Ogala, J.O., Ikpotokin, F., Arif, M., Ahmad, J., Mehfuz, S.: Enhanced CNN-DCT steganography: deep learning-based image steganography over cloud. SN Comput. Sci. **5**(4), 408 (2024)
27. Malik, K.R., et al.: A hybrid steganography framework using DCT and GAN for secure data communication in the big data era. Sci. Rep. **15**(1), 19630 (2025)
28. Qin, J., Wang, J., Tan, Y., Huang, H., Xiang, X., He, Z.: Coverless image steganography based on generative adversarial network. Mathematics **8**(9), 1394 (2020)
29. Aljughaiman, A., Alrawashdeh, R.: Content-adaptive LSB steganography with saliency fusion, ACO dispersion, and hybrid encryption with ablation study. Sci. Rep. (2025)

Near-Ultrasonic Environmental Presence as a Third Factor for Usable Authentication

Hasan Al-Qudah(✉) and Abdul Serwadda

Department of Computer Science, Texas Tech University, Lubbock, TX, USA
{halqudah,Abdul.Serwadda}@ttu.edu

Abstract. Two-factor authentication (2FA) is now a baseline for web and app accounts, but deployments remain vulnerable to device theft, social engineering, and adversary-in-the-middle infrastructures that trick users into relaying one-time passwords (OTPs) or approving login prompts they did not initiate. We explore an environmental third factor that is explicitly tied to physical context. Our scheme instruments enclosed spaces, such as homes or offices, with near-ultrasonic beacons that broadcast digitally signed messages. A local server, reachable only over local Wi-Fi, maintains a queue of recent beacons. After a conventional 2FA check succeeds, the client verifies that at least n of M expected beacon signatures are present in this queue before finalizing authentication, adding a location-bound check that runs transparently in the background whenever users log in from covered environments. We design and implement this scheme on commodity hardware and evaluate a 2-of-4 deployment in a lab setting that approximates an office, analyzing beacon verification patterns, bit error rates, and recovery time after transient drops in the number of valid beacons. We further report on a 40-participant user study with 160 authentication attempts that compares baseline TOTP-based 2FA to our augmented scheme, combining task-level measures with System Usability Scale (SUS) scores and qualitative feedback to assess how an always-on environmental factor fits into usable authentication.

Keywords: Multi-factor authentication · Near-ultrasonic beacons · Environmental context · Zero-effort authentication · Usable authentication

1 Introduction

Multi-factor authentication (MFA), and in particular two-factor authentication (2FA), has significantly reduced the risk of account takeover by requiring users to prove possession of a second factor such as a one-time password (OTP), SMS code, or app-based prompt in addition to a password. Large-scale field measurements from Google and Microsoft show that adding such challenges blocks the

Y. Cao et al. (Eds.): SecureComm 2026, LNICST 704, pp. 617–639, 2027.
https://doi.org/10.1007/978-3-032-32764-2_28

vast majority of automated and phishing-based hijacking attempts, often reducing compromise rates by one to two orders of magnitude compared to password-only authentication [6,25]. Despite this progress, adversaries have adapted, and 2FA-protected accounts remain a worthwhile target.

Two broad classes of weaknesses are particularly noteworthy. First, many deployed 2FA schemes are effectively tied to a single physical device: the user both enters their password and receives their OTP or push prompt on the same phone or laptop. An attacker who steals this device and can unlock it may be able to complete the 2FA ceremony and gain unfettered access, even if the second factor itself is cryptographically strong. Second, remote adversaries increasingly rely on social engineering and adversary-in-the-middle infrastructures to trick users into relaying OTPs or approving login prompts for sessions that the user did not initiate, effectively real-time proxying the 2FA flow on behalf of the attacker [30].

Prior work on location-limited and out-of-band channels suggests that physical context can provide additional protection against such attacks. Balfanz et al. and subsequent systems argue for channels whose physical propagation is constrained to a user-verifiable region, such as a room, so that successful communication implicitly proves co-location [23]. Ultrasound and near-ultrasonic signals are attractive instantiations of this idea: signals in the 16–21 kHz band can be generated and received using commodity speakers and microphones, yet they tend to be reflected or absorbed by walls and windows rather than propagating long distances, making them effectively room-confined in typical buildings [10].

We leverage these properties to methodically build a scheme that augments 2FA with a third factor that uses near-ultrasonic signals to encode the user's physical presence in a specific environment. Our system instruments an enclosed space, such as a home or office, with M near-ultrasonic transmitters that periodically broadcast short, digitally signed beacons. A local server in the same room, connected only to a local Wi-Fi network, records these beacons and maintains a rolling buffer of the most recent messages. After completing the standard 2FA process, user devices that are connected to this local Wi-Fi can fetch the buffer and verify that at least $n \leq M$ distinct signatures from known transmitters are valid; only then is an ongoing web or app authentication flow allowed to proceed. Because near-ultrasonic signals and the dedicated Wi-Fi network are both confined to the physical environment, a remote attacker who merely learns a password or coaxes a user into typing an OTP cannot satisfy this third factor.

Our design is intentionally transparent to users. Unlike traditional third factors that require explicit user interaction, such as inserting a hardware token or responding to a dedicated prompt, our system operates opportunistically in the background during normal authentication flows. As long as the user is physically present in the instrumented environment, their device can silently verify near-ultrasonic beacons and contribute an environmental presence proof to the login decision.

Our scheme is particularly well-suited to authentication scenarios that already have a natural physical anchor. Many everyday logins occur from a small set of stable places, such as home desktops for personal accounts, fixed office workstations and shared terminals, consoles in high-security installations, or applications that are explicitly intended to be used on-site. In these settings, administrators can enable the near-ultrasonic factor as an ambient hardening layer: whenever the user is in a covered environment, successful login automatically benefits from an additional, location-bound check without extra effort from the user. When users authenticate from other contexts, the system can simply fall back to conventional 2FA or to alternative protections, allowing environmental presence to strengthen security where physical context is well defined, while preserving existing behavior elsewhere. This paper makes the following contributions:

1. **Scheme design and engineering.** We methodically design and engineer a concrete scheme that augments existing 2FA deployments with an environmental factor based on near-ultrasonic signaling. We specify the end-to-end architecture, including the circuit design of the ultrasonic beacons, the packet structure and signing format of beacon messages, the choice of components and their operating specifications, the n-of-M verification rule, and the local Wi-Fi backchannel and server logic. Together, these design decisions yield a complete authentication algorithm that can be implemented on commodity hardware and integrated with existing web and app authentication flows.
2. **Technical characterization in an office-like deployment.** We implement this scheme and evaluate it in a lab deployment that approximates an office environment, using four beacons with a 2-of-4 verification rule. With a fixed beacon placement, our technical evaluation focuses on the dynamics of the running system: we analyze how many beacons are typically verified in the server queue at the time of the third-factor check, bit error rates under different user positions and ambient noise conditions, and how quickly the queue recovers to at least two valid beacons after transient drops. These measurements provide empirical insight into the availability and stability of the environmental factor in practice.
3. **Usability and user perceptions of the environmental factor.** We complement the technical evaluation with a user study that combines objective and subjective measures of usability. We collect 160 authentication attempts across 40 participants, where each participant completes two baseline TOTP logins (using Google or Microsoft Authenticator) and two logins that include the ultrasonic environmental factor, enabling a direct comparison of the authentication process with and without our scheme. We then administer the System Usability Scale (SUS) and perform a thematic analysis of participants' qualitative feedback to understand perceived intrusiveness, transparency, and the perceived value of adding an environmental factor to everyday authentication.

2 Related Work

Our work sits at the intersection of three lines of research. First, we build on prior studies of multi-factor authentication (MFA) that document both the security benefits and the usability and recovery challenges of adding more factors, motivating interest in low-effort environmental signals. Second, we relate to environmental and proximity-based methods that use Wi-Fi, Bluetooth, or audible acoustics to infer co-location or context, but largely focus on pairwise device relationships. Finally, we discuss ultrasonic authentication and proof-of-location systems that exploit inaudible sound as a controlled channel, and highlight how they differ from us.

2.1 Multi-factor Authentication: Security and Usability

Two-factor authentication (2FA) effectively counters unauthorized access but remains vulnerable to targeted attacks, including MFA fatigue [35], SIM swapping [28], social engineering [31], and account-recovery attacks [9]. However, simply adding more factors does not improve usability.

Studies show that additional authentication factors often increase cognitive burden. Nanda et al. [27] found users view physical tokens as cumbersome, while Klivan et al. [19] found that 61% of major services compromise security through insecure recovery paths due to account accessibility concerns. Bttner et al. [5] and Gilsenan et al. [11] similarly note that recovery mechanisms often significantly reduce MFA security guarantees.

Nair and Song propose Multi-Factor Key Derivation Functions (MFKDF) [26], which combine traditional authentication factors such as passwords, TOTP, and hardware tokens into a single derived key with threshold-based recovery. While MFKDF strengthens existing explicit authentication methods, users are still required to provide their own factors and/or possess devices to use them. Our work complements MFKDF-style constructions by introducing an environmental authentication factor that provides passive, zero-effort presence verification bound to physical space.

These findings reveal a trade-off between widely adopted but vulnerable methods (SMS, push notifications) and stronger but less usable options (hardware tokens [8], biometrics [3]), motivating interest in zero-effort authentication leveraging environmental characteristics such as the near-ultrasonic signals studied in this paper.

2.2 Environmental and Proximity-Based Authentication Methods

Wi-Fi and Bluetooth Methods. Several works leverage wireless signals for proximity-based authentication. MultiAuth [20] uses WiFi CSI signatures, achieving 86.2% accuracy, while ABLE [14] employs BLE signals with over 90% accuracy for co-location verification. BlueTOTP [18] automates TOTP delivery via Bluetooth, reducing phishing risks.

Acoustics-Based Methods. Acoustic authentication uses ambient sound for co-location proof. Sound-Proof [17] passively correlates audio from browser and phone, though Shrestha et al. [32] showed vulnerability to sound injection attacks. Subsequent systems like SoundID [22] and Listening-Watch [33] use structured signals and wearable devices for stronger security. In contrast to these pairwise schemes, our work uses multiple near-ultrasonic beacons as environmental factors without additional user interaction.

2.3 Ultrasonic Authentication and Proximity Systems

The controllable propagation properties of ultrasound, combined with its inaudibility, make ultrasonics a promising alternative to traditional audio-based authentication. The work in [12] introduced Proximity-Proof, an ultrasonic two-factor authentication system that utilizes OFDM-modulated ultrasonic signals to automatically send 2FA responses without any user interaction. By extracting device-specific speaker and microphone fingerprints and implementing two-way acoustic ranging, Proximity-Proof is able to defend against both co-located and man-in-the-middle (MITM) attacks while maintaining high usability.

The work in [36] presented UltraSonic Watch, which evaluated the usability of ultrasonic authentication in wearable devices. UltraSonic Watch found that users viewed ultrasonic 2FA as seamless and efficient; however, the system primarily focused on usability and did not introduce new defense mechanisms.

Additionally, QuietPlace [21] utilized an ultrasonic-based proof-of-location protocol. QuietPlace combined an ultrasonic challengeresponse mechanism with video-based identity binding and RSA-1024 signatures to ensure that a device is physically located near trusted witnesses. Although QuietPlace demonstrated that ultrasonic signals can confirm presence with high reliability, its dependence on video capture for identity verification, strong identity proofs, and event-driven location checks makes it unsuitable for continuous or zero-effort MFA processes.

Prior work on acoustic and ultrasonic authentication illustrates the potential of using sound as a proximity signal, but also shows several significant shortcomings. Passive ambient audio methods are inherently vulnerable to environmental manipulation. Methods that rely on fingerprinting and active speech are stronger from a security standpoint, but all continue to rely on pairwise models of device interaction and require either hardware coupling or wearable microphones. Prior ultrasonic 2FA systems have demonstrated that seamless interaction is possible, but each has authenticated only a single paired device, has not associated ultrasonic signals with device identities, and has not defined any environmental boundary.

Although ultrasonic systems demonstrate strong technical capabilities, prior work provides little understanding of how users perceive and interact with authentication factors that are inaudible and not directly observable. Ultrasonic signals introduce unique usability questions-such as whether users trust a factor they cannot sense, whether environmental noise affects perceived reliability, and how invisible processes shape mental models of security.

Unlike prior systems that authenticate single paired devices, we use multiple ultrasonic transmitters as environmental beacons to verify physical presence in a specific region through cryptographically signed messages, without requiring user interaction, wearables, or video capture. We address the gap in understanding how users perceive and interact with such invisible environmental factors through a combined technical and human-centered evaluation.

3 System Model and Design

In this section, we present the threat model, outline the scenario and assumptions under which our solution is deployed, and describe the mechanism of our proposed scheme.

3.1 Design Motivation and Human-Centered Goals

Our system is motivated by creating a stronger authentication mechanism without requiring users to do more than they do today. Previous studies have shown that when users are required to complete an extra step for authentication (e.g., entering a code, answering a prompt), this reduces their ability to use the application and may prevent them from using it at all. To address these concerns, we designed our environmental presence factor to be invisible, passive, and have as little impact on user effort as possible. The user does not have to perform any additional steps during login beyond what is already expected, and our ultrasonic sensing process runs automatically in the background. Our goal was to provide security guarantees while keeping the users' "cognitive" and "interaction" costs to a minimum. How well invisible, automated factors like ours will affect users' understanding and trust is a key area of study in our evaluation.

3.2 Threat Model

User model: This represents a person or organization that uses Two-Factor Authentication (2FA) for the protection of areas within indoor environments such as home offices, workplaces, or restricted company spaces. The user is interested in adding a layer of authentication that requires no additional effort and is willing to use environment-based authentication if it runs in the background and can be fully integrated into the current login process.

Requirements and Trusted Components: The authentication system operates indoors with ultrasonic emitters deployed at fixed locations such as ceilings and walls. These devices broadcast digitally signed ultrasonic tones. Each emitter stores its private key in protected flash-encrypted memory. An authentication listener device captures ultrasonic tones passively, decodes received messages, and verifies digital signatures using trusted public keys. We assume there is no connection between emitters and the listener device other than the acoustic channel, and that the connection between the client device (PC or mobile) and the listener device is secured via a protected channel (e.g., TLS).

Adversarial Goals and Limitations: The attacker's primary objective is to authenticate remotely without being physically present in the secure environment. Because the system requires the simultaneous detection of valid signatures from n devices, an adversary would need to replicate or suppress legitimate signals. Generating valid digital signatures is infeasible because private keys remain securely stored on emitters and the system prevents remote modification. Ultrasonic signals attenuate sharply through walls, windows, and distance, making remote injection or capture impractical. We exclude microphone compromise, insider collusion, and OS compromise from scope and focus on remote adversaries.

Adversarial Strategies Considered: Replay attacks fail because each emitter signs ultrasonic tones with a fresh nonce and multiple emitters must be validated simultaneously. Unauthorized emitters lacking valid signing keys are rejected. Relocating a single emitter provides no advantage due to the n-of-M requirement.

3.3 System Design and Architecture

The system has four main components: the Login Device, Application Server, Authentication Listener Device, and a network of synchronized near-ultrasonic emitters. Figure 1 shows the authentication mechanism and the interactions between these components. First, the user submits their credentials (username and password) to the Login Device, which forwards them to the Application Server for validation. If the credentials are correct, the server issues a second-factor challenge, and the user responds with the required verification code. Once the second factor is successfully validated, the server initiates the ultrasonic authentication phase by sending a request back to the Login Device. The Login Device receives this request and forwards it to the Authentication Listener Device. The Listener maintains an internal queue of signed tokens, which contain the device identifier, cryptographic signature, and timestamp. To satisfy the authentication threshold, it must collect at least n valid signatures from up to M emitters. If the number of available tokens is below the required threshold, the Listener continues listening for additional signed tokens until the condition is satisfied. Our system utilizes an n-of-M configuration, which enhances security and reliability, allowing the system to work even in the presence of environmental noise, signal reflections, or partial device failures. Once the Login Device obtains valid tokens, it forwards them to the Application Server. The Application Server verifies each signature using the public keys of registered devices and checks the freshness of tokens using nonces and timestamps to prevent replay attacks. After these verifications are complete, the server determines whether access should be granted or denied based on whether the necessary devices have successfully authenticated.

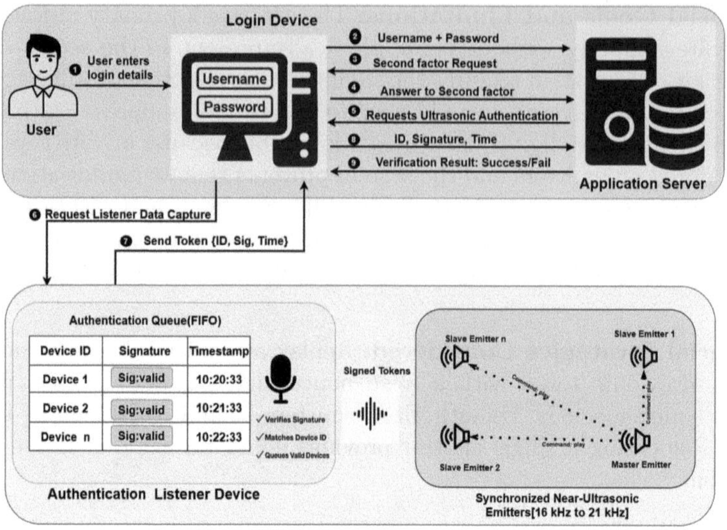

Fig. 1. Ultrasonic-assisted authentication framework showing login, server, listener, and emitter components.

3.4 Human Experience and Transparency Considerations

Because the ultrasonic factor operates without requiring user action and relies on inaudible signals, it raises unique usability considerations. Users may not be aware that authentication is in progress, may not understand variability in delay, or may perceive microphone use as sensitive. Our design, therefore, emphasizes predictable behavior, short and bounded latency, and transparent communication with the user where appropriate. The evaluation later in this paper specifically examines how these attributes influence mental models, perceived security, and overall user satisfaction.

3.5 Deployment Scope, Privacy, and Accessibility Considerations

Our scheme is intended for controlled indoor environments where administrators can manage environmental infrastructure, such as offices, laboratories, classrooms, and dedicated workstations. It is not designed for uncontrolled public or transient spaces.

The authentication listener processes only narrow near-ultrasonic frequency bands required for authentication and does not store audible human speech. Deployments should clearly disclose sensing behavior and avoid retaining raw audio beyond transient decoding buffers.

Near-ultrasonic signals may be perceptible to some users, particularly younger individuals. Deployments should therefore support adjustable output power, provide opt-out alternatives using conventional MFA, and treat environmental presence as an optional, context-specific enhancement rather than a universal replacement.

Algorithm 1:. Listener-Side Acoustic Token Verification

```
Input: n (required tokens), T_exp (expiry window)
Data: FIFO queue Q storing (devID, nonce, expTime)
while true do
    frame ← RecordAudio();
    if NoMarkersDetected(frame) then
        continue;
    seg ← SegmentTones(frame);
    bits ← DecodeTones(seg);
    (devID, nonce, sig) ← ParseMessage(bits);
    now ← CurrentTime();
    if VerifySignature(devID, nonce, sig) = INVALID then
        continue;
    expTime ← now + T_exp;
    RemoveOldToken(Q, devID);
    Enqueue(Q, (devID, nonce, expTime));
    RemoveExpired(Q, now);
    if ServerRequestedTokens() then
        S ← GetValidTokens(Q, n);
        if count(S) ≥ n then
            SendToServer(S);
```

4 Prototype Implementation

Our prototype consists of two software components and a network of embedded ultrasonic emitters. The first is a Python Flask web application running on the Login Device that handles user credential entry and forwards authentication requests between the application server and the authentication listener device. The second component is the authentication listener device, also implemented in Python Flask, which continuously monitors acoustic signals through a microphone, verifies digital signatures, and decodes messages using an FFT-based algorithm. Each emitter is an ESP32-WROOM-32 [34] node containing a private signing key. Each node generates a signed message that includes its device ID and a nonce, modulates it into 1621 kHz acoustic tones, and transmits it on command from the master coordinator, which also generates a signature.

The listener maintains a FIFO queue of verified tokens with a fixed validity window (e.g., one minute), discarding expired entries. When the application server requests tokens, the listener returns them if at least n valid tokens from up to M emitters are present; otherwise, it continues listening and updating the queue until the threshold is met. This design enforces the n-of-M authentication requirement while tolerating noise, reflections, and individual device failures. The complete listener-side workflow is presented in Algorithm 1. The following subsections describe each system component, beginning with the transmitter nodes.

4.1 Near-Ultrasonic Transmitter Nodes

Each emitter uses an ESP32-WROOM-32 microcontroller with integrated Wi-Fi for message generation and signing. A MEETOOT piezoelectric tweeter [24] (10–50 kHz) emits acoustic signals, amplified by a HiLetgo TPA3116 [15] 100 W module based on the TI TPA3116D2 [16] Class-D chip. An RC network (100 μF capacitor, 77 Ω resistor, 100 nF bypass) smooths the ESP32's square wave for cleaner transmission.

A master ESP32 coordinator in SoftAP Wi-Fi mode [7] assigns static IPs and issues round-robin PlayX commands via TCP, ensuring one transmission at a time to prevent interference. The circuit schematic and prototype are shown in Figs. 3 and 2.

Fig. 2. Near-ultrasonic emitter prototype.

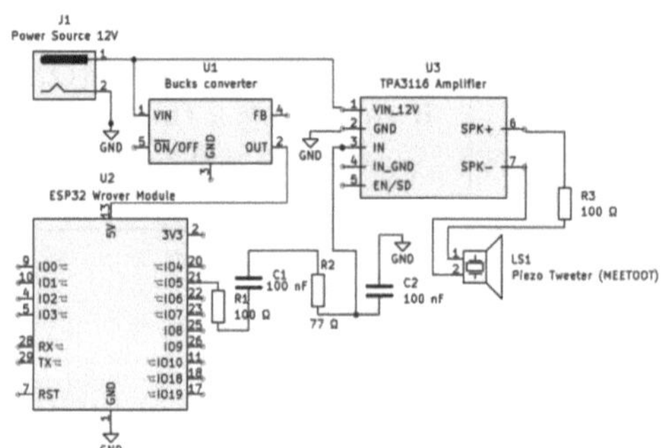

Fig. 3. Circuit schematic of the authentication transmitter node.

4.2 Signal Generation, Modulation, and Decoding

In our system, an ESP32 transmitter generates a 5-byte message consisting of a 1-byte device ID and a 4-byte random nonce. This message is signed with Ed25519 to produce a 64-byte digital signature [2]. The signed data are then transmitted acoustically using 16-level Frequency Shift Keying (16-FSK), where each 4-bit nibble maps to one of 16 ultrasonic frequencies spaced 250 Hz apart in the 17–20.75 kHz range. The transmission begins with a start tone (16.0 kHz), followed by the encoded 5-byte message (10 tones), the encoded 64-byte signature (128 tones), and ends with a stop tone (16.5 kHz). Each tone lasts 60 ms with a 40 ms pause to minimize symbol interference, balancing speed, accuracy, and acoustic range.

Table 1. Ultrasonic Authentication Signed Token Structure

Field	Description	Size
Device ID	Unique identifier for emitter node	1 byte
Nonce	Random value for replay protection	4 bytes
Signature	Ed25519 signature over {ID, Nonce}	64 bytes
Total		**69 bytes**

During reception, the listener device applies a Fast Fourier Transform (FFT) to each tone window to detect the dominant frequency and reconstruct the signed message for verification. Compared to lower-order FSK schemes, such as BFSK or 4-FSK, 16-FSK offers higher throughput and greater robustness against multipath reflections and phase shifts, making it well-suited for near-ultrasonic communication indoors [13,29].

4.3 Authentication Listener Device and Queue Management

The authentication listener device is implemented as a Python-based backend that runs on a laptop. It continuously records audio through a microphone and monitors for the start and end markers to identify valid transmission windows. Once detected, the audio is segmented into tones, and each tone is decoded into a 4-bit symbol using FFT-based frequency analysis, reconstructing the byte stream of the message. The listener then extracts the {Device ID, Nonce} pair from each message, verifies the Ed25519 digital signature using pre-installed public keys, logs valid messages with their timestamps and device IDs, rejects corrupted or invalid messages, and marks expired messages as invalid once they pass the one-minute validity window. As summarized in Table 1, each emitter transmits a 69-byte signed token composed of a 1-byte device ID, 4-byte nonce, and a 64-byte Ed25519 signature, forming the core authentication message used by the listener.

In addition to decoding and verification, the listener maintains a FIFO queue of valid tokens received from multiple transmitter nodes. This queue enforces the system's n-of-M authentication requirement: when the application server requests tokens, the listener returns them if at least n valid tokens from up to M emitters are present; otherwise, it keeps listening and updating the queue until the threshold is met. This integrated queue-based design is lightweight and stateless, supports dynamic addition of new nodes by simply assigning them static IP addresses and updating the device list, and allows the system to operate across multiple rooms or zones without manual wiring or serial connections.

4.4 Prototype Limitations and User-Centered Implications

Although the prototype demonstrates full end-to-end functionality, several aspects may influence user experience. The use of a laptop microphone, variable background noise, and the acoustic characteristics of the test room all contribute to occasional variability in latency. Additionally, the continuous use of a microphone introduces privacy expectations that must be communicated clearly in practical deployments. While these considerations do not affect the core security properties, they shape how users perceive transparency, trust, and acceptability factors we analyze in the usability study.

5 Evaluation Methodology

To better understand the capabilities and limitations of our proposed system, we designed a two-phase evaluation. The first phase primarily focused on system performance under various environmental conditions, excluding human participants. The second phase extended the evaluation to actual users, enabling us to compare the system with a conventional baseline and collect usability and perception data.

5.1 Ethical Approval and Study Governance

All human-subject procedures were reviewed and approved by an Institutional Review Board (IRB). Participants were informed about the study purpose, the use of microphones in the ultrasonic system, and their right to withdraw at any time. No audio recordings of human speech were stored; only ultrasonic features used for authentication were processed. Participants received no monetary compensation. The study adhered to standard ethical guidelines for usable security research.

5.2 System Performance Evaluation Setup

In this phase, we conducted a series of experiments to evaluate the system's performance, stability, and accuracy under different acoustic conditions. All experiments were conducted in a controlled laboratory environment without human interaction. To evaluate system performance over time, we operated the system continuously for a period of four hours under normal ambient noise conditions. During this time, we analyzed the internal queue data in the listener device using a one-minute sliding window, while also monitoring, for each emitter device, the number of successful and failed authentication attempts as well as the expiration times of device entries. This experiment provided insight into the system's ability to maintain continuous authentication and validated that the queue management mechanism supports long-running operations.

In addition, we also performed a recovery time experiment to determine how long it takes for the system to recover from a loss of its authentication state when the number of authenticated devices in the queue is less than the number of devices required to authenticate (i.e., the required number of devices). We used an example of four emitters being active. However, the required number of devices can be configured based on the deployment environment's specific security policies. The recovery time analysis shows how fast the system will recover to a secure state if the number of authenticated devices falls below the required number of devices, thus showing how resilient the system is to various acoustic environments.

In another experiment, we evaluated authentication accuracy to determine how performance changes as a function of distance. For this setup, only one emitter was used, which was pre-programmed with 30 digital signatures. The emitter was placed at multiple distances ranging from 1 ft to 24 ft. At each distance, we recorded two performance metrics: (i) the success rate of signature transmission and (ii) the bit error rate (BER), representing the frequency of bit-level errors during transmission and verification.

5.3 User Study Methodology

Study Goals. The goal of the user study was to evaluate the usability and user experience of our near-ultrasonic authentication method and to compare it with a conventional time-based one-time password (TOTP) factor under identical conditions. We sought to understand the practical performance of each factor, such as success rates and completion time, as well as the participants' subjective perceptions, including ease of use, environmental sensitivity, and overall interaction quality.

Participants. The study included 40 participants recruited informally through word of mouth within a large public research university community. The study protocol was reviewed and approved by the Institutional Review Board (IRB). Table 2 shows the demographic characteristics, educational backgrounds, and technical experience. Because the participant pool represented a university population, the findings primarily reflect the experiences of young, technically knowledgeable users.

Apparatus and Environment. We carried out the study in a research laboratory. The setup included a workstation running our authentication prototype, a mobile device used by participants to configure their TOTP application, and a near-ultrasonic transmitter–receiver arrangement positioned as shown in Fig. 4. All sessions were conducted in the same physical environment to ensure consistent acoustic conditions, lighting, and device placement.

Procedure. Upon arrival, each participant completed the informed-consent process and received a standardized briefing explaining the purpose of the study, the operation of both authentication methods, and the overall sequence of tasks. Participants then created a username and password using the prototype system and set up a TOTP app on their mobile device. Each participant completed four authentication attempts: two using the TOTP method and two using the near-ultrasonic method. For every authentication attempt, the system automatically

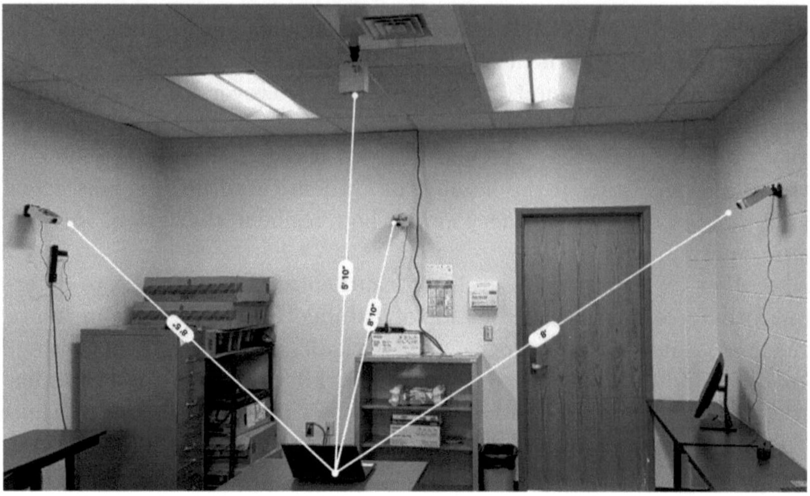

Fig. 4. Experimental laboratory configuration illustrating the placement of all ultrasonic transmitters relative to the listener device.

records whether the login succeeded and the total time required to complete the interaction. After completing the login tasks, participants completed a post-study survey including demographic questions, the System Usability Scale (SUS) for the ultrasonic interaction, and additional questions on environmental noise, perceived challenges, and general impressions. The survey concluded with two open-ended prompts inviting participants to describe what they liked most about the ultrasonic authentication method and what they found challenging or would improve.

Measures. The study collected both objective and subjective measures to obtain a comprehensive assessment of user experience. Objective measures included authentication success rates and the total time required to complete each TOTP and near-ultrasonic login attempt. Subjective measures were collected through the System Usability Scale (SUS) [4]. Additional survey questions assessed whether environmental noise or other conditions affected participants' experiences and gathered self-reported challenges encountered during the login tasks. Two open-ended feedback questions allowed participants to expand on positive aspects of the system and to identify areas where they encountered difficulties or had concerns.

5.4 Participant Characteristics and Generalizability

Participants were primarily university affiliates with strong technical backgrounds. While this demographic is appropriate for studying early-stage usable security prototypes, it may not fully represent broader user populations. Findings related to trust, mental models, and perceived transparency may differ among non-technical users or in environments with different acoustic conditions. We highlight these limitations to contextualize our results and avoid overgeneralization.

6 Results

6.1 System Performance Results

Table 2. Participant demographics ($n = 40$).

Category	Value	n (%)
Age group	18–24	12 (30.0)
	25–34	17 (42.5)
	35–44	9 (22.5)
	45–54	1 (2.5)
	55–64	1 (2.5)
Gender	Male	27 (67.5)
	Female	13 (32.5)
Education	Doctoral (PhD)	20 (50.0)
	Graduate (Master's)	14 (35.0)
	Undergraduate	6 (15.0)
Technical background	Technical (e.g., CS/Engineering/IT)	32 (80.0)
	Non-technical	5 (12.5)
	Mixed background	3 (7.5)

The ultrasonic authentication system demonstrated stable performance during the four-hour pre-study evaluation. All evaluations were conducted in a standard indoor academic environment with moderate background noise, representative of typical deployment conditions. Figure 5 plots the number of active authenticated devices recorded within a one-minute sliding window against the two-device threshold required for login. The window advanced in one-second increments, providing fine-grained visibility into queue stability over time. Throughout the entire period, the queue consistently met or exceeded the threshold. When short drops occurred, the system recovered quickly: the empirical cumulative distribution of recovery times shown in Fig. 6 indicates a median recovery time of 0.24 minutes and a 90th percentile of 1.48 minutes. These results confirm the robustness of the queuing mechanism and its ability to maintain service continuity under normal ambient noise conditions without human intervention.

In addition to queue monitoring, acoustic signature verification was evaluated to characterize the bit error rate (BER) performance of the ultrasonic communication channel. Thirty unique digital signatures were transmitted four

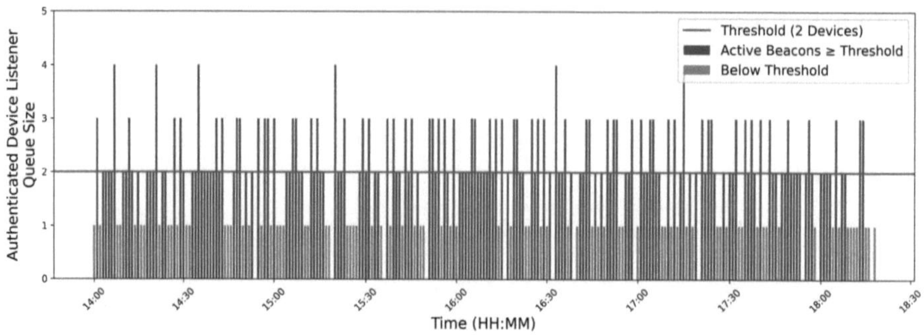

Fig. 5. Number of authenticated beacons queued over time (4-hour period, 1-minute windows). Blue bars show authenticated beacons per minute, the red dashed line marks the 2-device threshold, and orange bars indicate minutes below threshold. Authentication succeeds when 2+ unique beacons are present. (Color figure online)

times each, resulting in a total of 120 verification attempts. Verification outcomes and BER were recorded for all transmissions. As shown in Fig. 7, the BER remained low across trials, with the highest observed value being 0.054%. These measurements establish a baseline profile of reliability and error characteristics for the ultrasonic channel, demonstrating that the proposed system achieves high reliability under realistic noise conditions, with predictable and moderate degradation only in the noisiest cases.

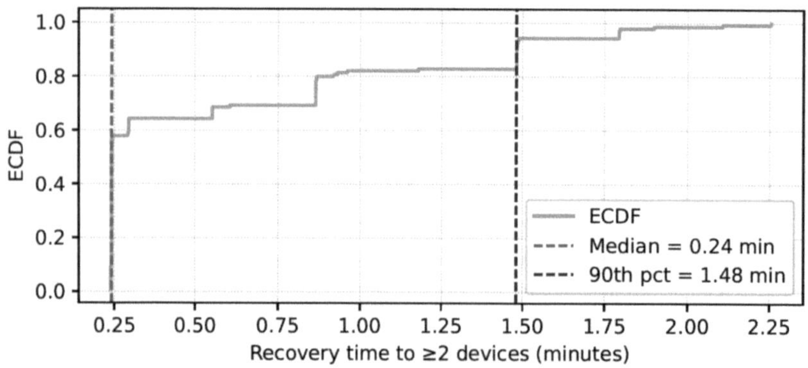

Fig. 6. ECDF of recovery times for returning to at least two active devices after a drop below the threshold (1-minute window). The orange curve shows the cumulative proportion of recoveries, and the red and blue dashed lines denote the median and 90th percentile recovery times, respectively. (Color figure online)

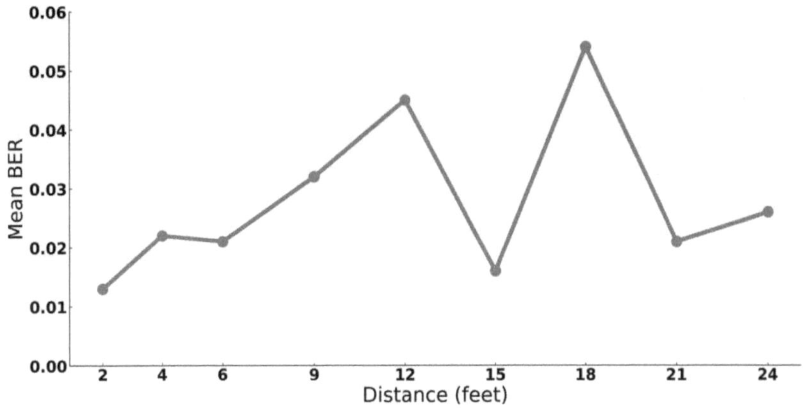

Fig. 7. System performance across distances: bit error rate (BER, %).

6.2 User Study Results

Objective Performance. We recorded 160 authentication attempts across 40 participants, where each participant completed two baseline TOTP (Google or Microsoft Authenticator) logins and two logins that included the ultrasonic environmental factor. To accurately represent the system as a three-factor authentication flow, we report the baseline TOTP authentication time and the additional time introduced by the ultrasonic third factor.

Baseline TOTP authentication showed a mean duration of 16.55 s (median = 15.20 s, SD = 5.75 s). Figure 8ashows the full distribution of TOTP completion times across all users. When we added the ultrasonic authentication factor, the mean extra time introduced by this third factor was 9.67 s (median = 5.22 s, SD = 9.84 s). Figure 8bshows the cumulative distribution function (CDF) of the additional time added to the authentication process. The CDF indicates that approximately 70% of ultrasonic verifications complete within 10 s, and over 90% complete within 20 s. To summarize, these results indicate that the ultrasonic environmental factor introduces an acceptable and practical additional cost in time, while maintaining smooth and reliable authentication performance.

Perceived Usability (SUS). Figure 9 shows the usability results from the System Usability Scale (SUS). The ultrasonic authentication system received SUS scores between 45 and 100, with an average of 77.26 (SD = 15.37). This places it in the "Good" usability category according to established industry benchmarks [1]. Participants rated the system as easy to use (M = 4.39), easy to learn (M = 4.49), and confidence-boosting (M = 4.10). They also reported low inconsistency (M = 1.78) and little need for technical support (M = 2.25). The wide range of scores and higher variance suggest that some users had occasional reliability problems. In general, the ultrasonic authentication method was usable, well-received, and met participant expectations.

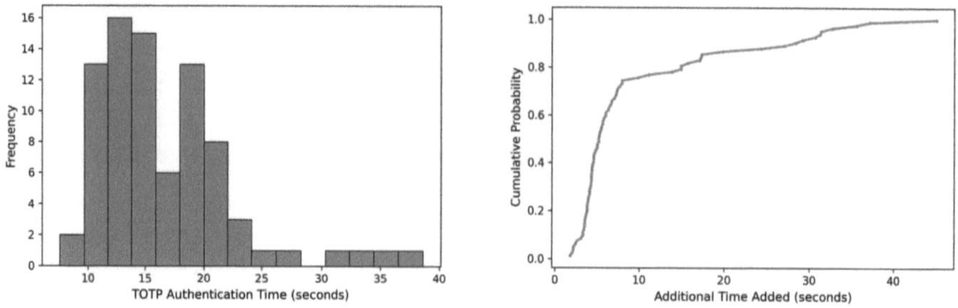

(a) Distribution of baseline TOTP authentication times.

(b) CDF of additional time introduced by the ultrasonic factor.

Fig. 8. Authentication performance results: (A) TOTP completion time distribution across all participants, and (B) CDF of the additional time added by the ultrasonic environmental factor.

Qualitative Feedback. To better understand users' views on the ultrasonic verification methodology, we analyzed qualitative responses to questions that asked for explanations of its advantages and disadvantages. Forty participants responded to these open-ended questions, and their responses formed nine thematic categories (see Fig. 10). The most represented theme was *Ease of Use & Speed* ($n = 22$; 55%), with many participants describing the system as "easy", "quick", and requiring "no hands". In addition to ease of use and speed, several participants noted that using the ultrasonic methodology, rather than entering a time-based one-time password (TOTP), required less user attention, reduced transcription errors, eliminated the need to switch between devices, and provided a more integrated overall experience.

Commonly referenced themes also included *Security Uncertainty* ($n = 14$; 35%) and *Hands-Free Convenience* ($n = 12$; 30%), suggesting that while users appreciated the minimal effort demanded by the ultrasonic method, they remained uncertain about the security assurances it provides.

Although cited less frequently, several additional themes reflected perceived practical limitations or barriers to adoption, including *Practicality/Scalability* ($n = 8$; 20%), *Hardware Dependence* ($n = 6$; 15%), *Learning Curve* ($n = 6$; 15%), *Environmental or Noise Concerns* ($n = 5$; 12.5%), and *Setup Complexity* ($n = 4$; 10%). Comments in these categories often referenced concerns about variability in performance due to device placement or environmental conditions, which aligns with the lower System Usability Scale (SUS) scores associated with system stability and predictability.

Overall, the thematic analysis suggests that users perceive the ultrasonic methodology as fast, easy to use, and capable of delivering a high-quality interaction characterized by simplicity and the absence of manual device handling. While some participants raised concerns regarding security transparency and environmental sensitivity, the majority expressed general satisfaction with the

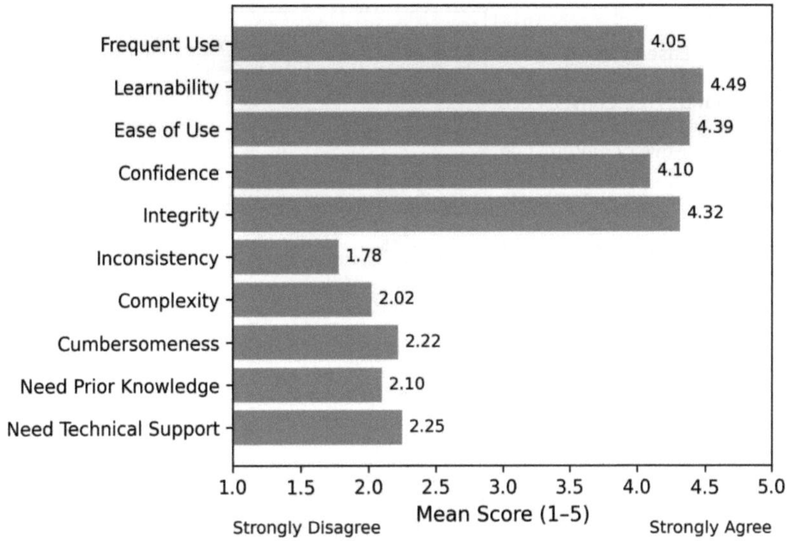

Fig. 9. Mean SUS item scores (15 Likert) for the ultrasonic authentication system. Higher values indicate stronger agreement with each statement.

methodology and viewed ultrasonic authentication as a viable enhancement to existing verification processes

6.3 Interpretation of User Perceptions

Across both objective and subjective measures, participants responded positively to the passive nature of the ultrasonic factor. However, qualitative feedback revealed several mental-model challenges: some users were unsure whether the system was actively listening, others questioned why delays varied, and a few expressed privacy concerns about microphone usage. These perceptions underscore the importance of transparency in passive authentication systems. Our findings suggest that while users value reduced interaction effort, they also expect predictable behavior and clear communication about what data is being sensed and why. This tension between invisibility and understandability is explored further in the discussion.

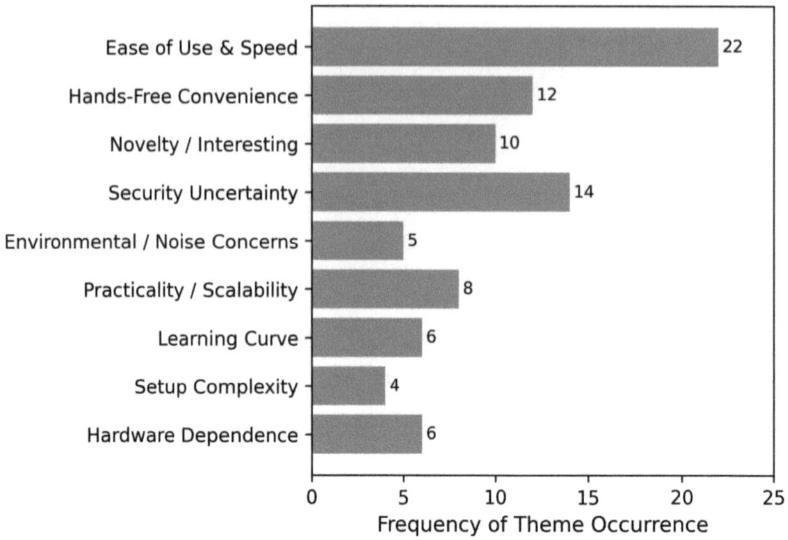

Fig. 10. Frequency of themes identified from participants' qualitative feedback.

7 Discussion and Conclusion

7.1 System Behavior and Trade-Offs

Our results show that near-ultrasonic environmental presence can strengthen 2FA by adding a location-bound factor that is difficult for remote attackers to satisfy. Unlike conventional deployments, where both factors often reside on the same personal device and can be stolen or relayed, our scheme uses multiple digitally signed ultrasonic beacons as independent co-location witnesses, while remaining largely unobtrusive to users.

Our prototype performed reliably under typical indoor conditions without requiring user interaction. The sliding-window token queue allows continuous capture of environmental presence, so authentication does not need to be tightly synchronized with beacon reception. This makes the approach suitable for passive factors that simply run in the background. At the same time, performance degrades at longer distances and shows some environment-specific variability, which highlights the need to tune deployment parameters such as emitter placement, the n-of-M policy, and token lifetimes to each setting.

From a security perspective, our system raises the bar for remote attackers, but it does not eliminate all threats. Physical co-location, deliberate jamming, or sophisticated relay channels remain possible, and our prototype does not enforce strict timing or distance bounds. Environmental presence should therefore be viewed as a complementary factor that works alongside possession-based or cryptographically strong methods rather than a replacement for them.

Our usability findings suggest another trade-off. The ultrasonic factor adds several seconds of background delay, yet participants rated it as highly usable, largely because it required no extra input. This indicates that users may tolerate small timing costs when interaction cost is effectively zero. However, reports of occasional inconsistent behavior point to the need for improved decoding and clearer feedback before deployment in production systems.

Finally, our evaluation is necessarily limited. Continuous listening, even in inaudible bands, raises privacy and transparency questions, and our experiments were conducted in a single building with one hardware class and technically skilled participants. Broader studies across more diverse environments, user populations, and adversaries will be required to fully map the security and usability boundaries of environmental presence as an authentication factor.

7.2 Conclusion

This work introduced environmental presence as a third authentication factor, leveraging digitally signed near-ultrasonic beacons to bind login attempts to a specific physical space. By requiring an n-of-M set of fresh signatures from independent transmitters, our system offers a stronger notion of co-location than conventional 2FA while remaining transparent and low-effort for users. A full prototype implementation and lab deployment showed that environmental presence can be captured reliably in typical indoor settings with modest background latency, and a 40-participant user study found the approach easy to use and comparable in experience to existing factors, achieving a "Good" SUS score.

Environmental presence is not a substitute for strong possession-based factors, but it provides meaningful protection against remote attackers and OTP relay attempts by requiring physical presence in the secured environment. Future work includes multi-room and multi-building deployments, stronger adversarial testing, more robust decoding, and integration with additional context signals. Overall, our results suggest that near-ultrasonic environmental presence is a practical and usable way to harden modern authentication systems without increasing user burden.

References

1. Bangor, A., Kortum, P., Miller, J.: Determining what individual sus scores mean: adding an adjective rating scale. J. Usability Stud. **4**(3), 114–123 (2009)
2. Bernstein, D.J., Duif, N., Lange, T., Schwabe, P., Yang, B.Y.: High-speed high-security signatures. J. Cryptogr. Eng. **2**(2), 77–89 (2012)
3. Bonneau, J., Herley, C., van Oorschot, P.C., Stajano, F.: The quest to replace passwords: a framework for comparative evaluation of web authentication schemes. In: 2012 IEEE Symposium on Security and Privacy, pp. 553–567. IEEE (2012)
4. Brooke, J.: Sus-a quick and dirty usability scale. Usability Eval. Ind. **189**(194), 4–7 (1996)
5. Büttner, A., Gruschka, N.: Evaluating the influence of multi-factor authentication and recovery settings on the security and accessibility of user accounts (2024). arXiv preprint arXiv:2403.15080
6. Doerfler, P., et al.: Evaluating login challenges as a defense against account takeover. In: Proceedings of the Web Conference (WWW) (2019)

7. Espressif Systems: ESP-IDF ESP32 Wi-Fi API (2024). https://docs.espressif.com/projects/esp-idf/en/stable/esp32/api-reference/network/esp_wifi.html. Accessed 20 Jan 2025
8. Farke, F.M., Lorenz, L., Schnitzler, T., Markert, P., Dürmuth, M.: {"You} still use the password after {all"}–exploring {FIDO2} security keys in a small company. In: Sixteenth Symposium on Usable Privacy and Security (SOUPS 2020), pp. 19–35 (2020)
9. Gerlitz, E., Häring, M., Mädler, C.T., Smith, M., Tiefenau, C.: Adventures in recovery land: testing the account recovery of popular websites when the second factor is lost. In: Nineteenth Symposium on Usable Privacy and Security (SOUPS 2023), pp. 227–243 (2023)
10. Getreuer, P., Gnegy, C., Lyon, R.F., Saurous, R.A.: Ultrasonic communication using consumer hardware. IEEE Trans. Multimedia (2017). https://doi.org/10.1109/TMM.2017.2766049
11. Gilsenan, C., Egelman, S.: Increasing the usability of multi-factor authentication (MFA) recovery mechanisms (2022). https://cltc.berkeley.edu/publication/increasing-the-usability-of-multi-factor-authentication-mfa-recovery-mechanisms/. Accessed 02 Dec 2025
12. Han, D., Chen, Y., Li, T., Zhang, R., Zhang, Y., Hedgpeth, T.: Proximity-proof: secure and usable mobile two-factor authentication. In: Proceedings of the 24th Annual International Conference on Mobile Computing and Networking, pp. 401–415 (2018)
13. Haykin, S.: Communication Systems, 5th edn. Wiley, Hoboken, NJ, USA (2013)
14. He, Y., Wang, W., Teng, Y., Wang, Q., Wang, M., Lin, J.: ABLE: zero-effort two-factor authentication exploiting BLE co-location. In: 2022 IEEE Wireless Communications and Networking Conference (WCNC), pp. 992–997. IEEE (2022)
15. HiLetgo: Hiletgo 2pcs TPA3116 100w audio amplifier board dc 12v-24v TPA3116DA mono channel digital audio amplifier board high power amp module. https://www.amazon.com/dp/B082F7P184 (2025). Accessed 22 Sep 2025
16. Texas Instruments: TPA3116D2 50-w stereo class-d audio amplifier datasheet. https://www.ti.com/lit/ds/symlink/tpa3116d2.pdf (2023). Accessed 22 Sep 2025
17. Karapanos, N., Marforio, C., Soriente, C., Capkun, S.: {Sound-Proof}: usable {Two-Factor} authentication based on ambient sound. In: 24th USENIX Security Symposium (USENIX Security 15), pp. 483–498 (2015)
18. Käsemodel, M., Winterhalter, V., Heisel, F., Alt, F., Pfleging, B.: Blue-TOTP: designing phishing-resistant and user-friendly two-factor authentication. In: Ardito, C., et al. IFIP Conference on Human-Computer Interaction, pp. 611–634. Springer, Cham (2025). https://doi.org/10.1007/978-3-032-05005-2_31
19. Klivan, S., et al.: We've disabled MFA for you: an evaluation of the security and usability of multi-factor authentication recovery deployments. In: Proceedings of the 2023 ACM SIGSAC Conference on Computer and Communications Security, pp. 3138–3152 (2023)
20. Kong, H., Lu, L., Yu, J., Chen, Y., Xu, X., Lyu, F.: Toward multi-user authentication using WiFi signals. IEEE/ACM Trans. Networking **31**(5), 2117–2132 (2023)
21. Kounas, D., Voutyras, O., Palaiokrassas, G., Litke, A., Varvarigou, T.: QuietPlace: an ultrasound-based proof of location protocol with strong identities. Appl. Syst. Innov. **3**(2), 19 (2020)
22. Liu, D., et al.: SoundID: securing mobile two-factor authentication via acoustic signals. IEEE Trans. Dependable Secure Comput. **20**(2), 1687–1701 (2022)

23. Mayrhofer, R., Gellersen, H.: On the security of ultrasound as out-of-band channel. In: Proceedings of the 21st International Parallel and Distributed Processing Symposium (IPDPS) (2007). https://doi.org/10.1109/IPDPS.2007.370618
24. MEETOOT: MEETOOT 2PCs ultrasonic speaker piezo KS-3840A 2P-RE, piezoelectric tweeter horns, frequency range 10–50 kHz. https://www.amazon.com/dp/B09L7LHZML (2025). Accessed 22 Sep 2025
25. Meyer, L.A., Romero, S., Bertoli, G., Burt, T., Weinert, A., Ferres, J.L.: How effective is multifactor authentication at deterring cyberattacks? CoRR abs/2305.00945 (2023). arXiv:2305.00945
26. Nair, V., Song, D.: {Multi-Factor} key derivation function ($\{\{\{\{\{\{MFKDF\}\}\}\}\}\}$) for fast, flexible, secure, & practical key management. In: 32nd USENIX Security Symposium (USENIX Security 23), pp. 2097–2114 (2023)
27. Nanda, A., Jeong, J.J., Shah, S.W.A., Nosouhi, M., Doss, R.: Examining usable security features and user perceptions of physical authentication devices. Comput. Secur. **139**, 103664 (2024)
28. Paktiti, M.: Why SMS is not a secure multi-factor authentication (MFA) method (2025). https://workos.com/blog/why-sms-mfa-is-insecure. Accessed 03 Dec 2025
29. Proakis, J.G.: Digital Communications, 5th edn. McGraw-Hill, New York, NY, USA (2008)
30. Sakhnov, I.: Defending against evolving identity attack techniques. Microsoft Security Blog (2025). https://www.microsoft.com/en-us/security/blog/2025/05/29/defending-against-evolving-identity-attack-techniques/
31. Schöps, M., Gutfleisch, M., Wolter, E., Sasse, M.A.: Simulated stress: a case study of the effects of a simulated phishing campaign on employees' perception, stress and {Self-Efficacy}. In: 33rd USENIX Security Symposium (USENIX Security 24), pp. 4589–4606 (2024)
32. Shrestha, B., Shirvanian, M., Shrestha, P., Saxena, N.: The sounds of the phones: Dangers of zero-effort second factor login based on ambient audio. In: Proceedings of the 2016 ACM SIGSAC Conference on Computer and Communications Security, pp. 908–919 (2016)
33. Shrestha, P., Saxena, N.: Listening watch: wearable two-factor authentication using speech signals resilient to near-far attacks. In: Proceedings of the 11th ACM Conference on Security & Privacy in Wireless and Mobile Networks, pp. 99–110 (2018)
34. Systems, E.: Esp32-wroom-32 datasheet, version 3.6. https://www.espressif.com/sites/default/files/documentation/esp32-wroom-32_datasheet_en.pdf (2023). Accessed 19 Sep 2025
35. Vijayan, J.: Uber: lapsus$ targeted external contractor with MFA bombing attack (2022). https://www.darkreading.com/cyberattacks-data-breaches/uber-breach-external-contractor-mfa-bombing-attack. Accessed 03 Dec 2025
36. Zarafeta, D., Katsini, C., Raptis, G.E., Avouris, N.M.: Ultrasonic watch: seamless two-factor authentication through ultrasound. In: Extended Abstracts of the 2019 CHI Conference on Human Factors in Computing Systems, pp. 1–6 (2019)

Author Index

Y. Cao et al. (Eds.): SecureComm 2026, LNICST 704, pp. 641–642, 2027.
https://doi.org/10.1007/978-3-032-32764-2

MIX
Papier aus verantwortungsvollen Quellen
Paper from responsible sources
FSC® C105338

If you have any concerns about our products,
you can contact us on
ProductSafety@springernature.com

In case Publisher is established outside the EU,
the EU authorized representative is:
Springer Nature Customer Service Center GmbH
Europaplatz 3, 69115 Heidelberg, Germany

Printed by Libri Plureos GmbH
in Hamburg, Germany